The Life Span

Human Development for Helping Professionals

Fifth Edition

The Life Span

Human Development for Helping Professionals

Patricia C. Broderick
Bennett Pierce Prevention Research Center at Penn State University

Pamela Blewitt
Villanova University

Director and Portfolio Manager: Kevin M. Davis
Content Producer: Janelle Rogers
Sr. Development Editor: Jeffrey Johnston
Media Producer: Lauren Carlson
Portfolio Management Assistant: Maria Feliberty
Executive Field Marketing Manager: Krista Clark
Executive Product Marketing Manager: Christopher Barry
Procurement Specialist: Carol Melville
Full Service Project Management: Pearson CSC, Kathy Smith
Cover Designer: Pearson CSC
Cover Image: Rich Iwasaki/gettyimages©
Composition: Pearson CSC
Printer/Binder: LSC Communications/Willard
Cover Printer: Phoenix Color/Hagerstown
Text Font: Palatino LT Pro

Credits and acknowledgments for material borrowed from other sources and reproduced, with permission, in this textbook appear on the appropriate page within the text.

Every effort has been made to provide accurate and current Internet information in this book. However, the Internet and information posted on it are constantly changing, so it is inevitable that some of the Internet addresses listed in this textbook will change.

Library of Congress Cataloging-in-Publication Data

Names: Broderick, Patricia C., author. | Blewitt, Pamela, author.
Title: The life span : human development for helping professionals / Patricia
    C. Broderick, Penn State Prevention Research Center, Pamela Blewitt,
    Villanova University.
Description: Fifth edition. | New York : Pearson, [2020] | Includes
    bibliographical references and index.
Identifiers: LCCN 2018044603| ISBN 9780135227763 | ISBN 0135227763
Subjects: LCSH: Developmental psychology.
Classification: LCC BF713 .B755 2020 | DDC 155—dc23
LC record available at https://lccn.loc.gov/2018044603

ISBN-13: 978-013-522776-3
ISBN-10:   0-13-522776-3

10 2021

Dedication

For Connor, Owen, Wesley, and Will.

Brief Contents

Contents

Preface

What's New in This Edition?

The first and most comprehensive developmental textbook written specifically for helping professionals, *The Life Span: Human Development for Helping Professionals* is now in its fifth edition. Major changes and new features include:

- New introductory vignettes in each chapter that help students to see the relevance of chapter content for their own lives and those of the people they serve.

- Clear and comprehensive coverage of emerging data on the biological and neuropsychological underpinnings of development.

- Revamped and extended explanations of the nature of stress, its role in development, and its effects on behavior at every life stage.

- New figures and tables throughout the text that summarize and organize large amounts of data and/or provide accessible information about programs and interventions. For example, Chapter 5 presents a table listing some skills taught in parent training programs, and a table in Chapter 9 gives students pointers on ways to communicate with transgender youth.

- Expanded coverage of the best empirical work on the implications for development of cultural, ethnic, and socioeconomic contexts.

- New topics with special importance to helping professionals in every chapter. Examples include the nature of translational research (Chapter 1), the consequences of bilingual child rearing (Chapter 3), the development of children's lying (Chapters 7), bullies and victims (Chapter 7), the differential development of self-esteem, self-efficacy, and narcissism (Chapter 7), the impact of praise on self-development (Chapter 7), gender nonconformity and ways of helping sexual minority youth (Chapters 8 and 9), parental monitoring of teens (Chapter 10), the "hook-up" culture (Chapter 12), a narrative approach to career counseling (Chapter 12), promoting well-being in adulthood (Chapter 14), and many others.

- Fully updated research and applications to practice in all chapters.

MyLab Education

One of the most visible changes in the fifth edition, also one of the most significant, is the expansion of the digital learning and assessment resources embedded in the eText and the inclusion of MyLab Education in the text. MyLab Education is an online homework, tutorial, and assessment program designed to work with the text to engage learners and improve learning. Learners see key concepts demonstrated through video footage, practice what they learn, test their understanding, and receive feedback to guide their learning and to ensure their mastery of key learning outcomes. Designed to help learners see the real and powerful impact of development concepts covered in this book, the online resources in My Lab Education with the Enhanced eText include:

- Video Examples. About four or five times per chapter, an embedded video provides an illustration of a child development principle or concept in action.

- Self-Checks. In each chapter, self-check quizzes help assess how well learners have mastered the content. The self-checks are made up of self-grading multiple-choice items that not only provide feedback on whether questions are answered correctly or incorrectly, but also provide rationales for both correct and incorrect answers.

- Application Exercises. These exercises give learners opportunities to practice applying the content and strategies from the chapters. The questions in these exercises are usually constructed-response. Once learners provide their own answers to the questions, they receive feedback in the form of model answers written by experts.

The Conceptual Framework of This Book

The study of human development over the life span reveals the fascinating story of human beings and how they change over time. The story is both universal and uniquely personal, because it speaks to us about ourselves and the people who are important in our lives. Besides being intrinsically interesting, knowledge about development has obvious relevance for professionals engaged in psychology, counseling, education, social work, and other helping and health-related fields. We believe that in order to understand the strengths and challenges of our clients or students, we must see them in context. One important context is developmental history. As helping professionals, we must take into account the threads of continuity and change in people's lives that bring them to their present point in development. This text provides the background and the tools to enable professionals to view their clients from a developmental perspective.

This text also reflects the contemporary view that life span development is a process deeply embedded within and inseparable from the context of family, social network, and culture. People do not progress through life in isolation; rather, their developmental course influences and is influenced by other people and systems. Some of these forces are related to the cultural differences that exist in a world of increasing diversity. We recognize the importance of these factors in understanding human development and emphasize cultural and systemic influences on human growth and change throughout the book.

We would also be remiss if we neglected to emphasize the rapidly growing body of knowledge from neuroscience that is refining our appreciation of how biology and context interact. The marriage of "nature and nurture" and our greater awareness of how they interrelate contribute significantly to a more fully informed understanding of how people change over the life course. This emphasis, which has been strengthened in this new edition, provides an overarching template for practitioners to use in understanding development and in applying developmental knowledge to their work.

Research and applications within the field of human development are becoming more and more interdisciplinary with expanding links to health, social processes, well-being, and so forth. This can make it exceptionally difficult to summarize this dynamic field. Presumably, every author of a book of this nature needs to make some choices about what to include. This particular text is configured to emphasize selected theories and research that have useful applications for helping professionals. A main purpose of this book is to provide students in the helping professions with information that can be translated into professional "best practice" applications. To this end, we have tried to use the most current research available to summarize domains of knowledge that remain, essentially, fields "under investigation." Science by its very nature continually evolves in its efforts to reveal the nature of human experience. Thus, one of the assumptions we continue to emphasize in this edition is the importance of reflective practice for helping professionals.

Reflective practice involves "active, persistent, and careful consideration of any belief or supposed form of knowledge in light of the grounds that support it and the further conclusions to which it leads" (Dewey, 1933/1998, p. 9). Our primary vehicle for accomplishing this goal is twofold: (1) encouraging the reader to reflect on personal experience and assumptions about development, and (2) communicating the value of research-based knowledge as a means of understanding human development. Our particular orientation intentionally emphasizes the significance of developmental research to the work of the professional helper. We attempt to integrate various lines of developmental research into a useful whole that has practical value for helpers in applied settings. This book bears witness to the enormous amount of work done by developmental researchers, particularly in the last several decades. Without their groundbreaking contributions, helping professionals' efforts to improve people's lives would be greatly impoverished. It has been a challenge and an honor to record their contributions in this book.

Coverage and Organization

The opening chapters establish the theme of the text and introduce broad issues in development. Chapter 1 begins with an examination of the role of developmental knowledge in reflective practice. Students are introduced to classic and contemporary theoretical models and to issues that appear and reappear throughout the text. They are encouraged to reflect on their own theoretical assumptions about development and on the impact those assumptions could have in practice. Students are introduced to developmental psychopathology in a focus feature, where they can learn about prevention science and its connection to developmental research.

Chapter 2 takes a close look at the coaction of genetic and environmental factors in the development of all aspects of the human organism. Students are introduced to genetic mechanisms in the context of epigenesis, the control of genetic expression by forces beyond the genes themselves. Sections on atypical early developments and on early brain development highlight the coaction of many genetic and environmental factors in prenatal and early postnatal development. Students are also introduced to the concept of development as adaptation and to the critical stress and adaptation system. Students emerge with an understanding of how biology and experience together craft this system and determine healthy and unhealthy outcomes.

The remaining chapters follow a chronological sequence, covering a full range of critical topics in physical, cognitive, social, and emotional development. In Chapters 3 through 5, the infancy and preschool periods are the focus. Among the topics covered are the many aspects of early cognitive growth, such as the development of representational thought and memory, executive functions, early "theory of mind" or naive psychology, the early understanding of symbols and of language, and more. Coverage of early social development includes the emergence of emotions, emotion regulation, attachment processes, early self-development, temperament, and the role of parental disciplinary style in the growth of self-regulation.

Chapters 6, 7, and 8 examine important developments in middle childhood and in the transition to adolescence, including the growth of logical thinking, the expanding capacity to process and remember information, perspective taking skills and friendship development, influences on cognitive functioning, such as teacher and school characteristics, influences on the developing self-concept, developments in moral thinking, influences on the emergence of prosocial and antisocial behavior, gender-role development, and peer relationships. The impact of culture and context for many of these developments, such as self-concept, are highlighted.

Adolescence is the subject of Chapters 9 and 10, covering pubertal change, advances in logical and metacognitive skill, changes to the brain and stress system, identity development, sexual orientation, risk taking, and the influences of biology, peers, parents, school, media, and culture on adolescent behavior. Chapters 11 and 12 describe the young adult period, or what has been called "emerging adulthood," and include a close look at the way thinking changes as adulthood looms and at the progress of work, career, and intimate relationships.

Chapters 13, 14, and 15 are concerned with developmental processes in middle and late adulthood. Chapter 13 focuses on changes in physical, cognitive, and social functioning during the middle adult years. Chapter 14 considers the questions that all middle adults face: What constitutes a well-lived life, and how do normally functioning adults cope with the enormous demands, progress, and setbacks that adult life brings? Finally, Chapter 15 reviews the challenges and developmental processes involved in late adulthood and end-of-life experiences. These chapters examine the many kinds of change that adults experience and the maintenance of well-being in the face of loss. Among the key developmental tasks discussed are marriage and its discontents, the experience of child rearing, spirituality, coping and health, the role of wisdom, stereotypes about aging, facing death and bereavement, and many more.

Features and Highlights

- **Depth of coverage:** Because the book is designed for graduate and advanced undergraduate students, most topics, especially those that have special relevance to helping professionals, are covered in greater depth than in a typical life span text. The expanded coverage of research in specific areas will enhance students' understanding of the scientific basis for applications.

- **Applications:** Blending empirically supported information about treatments with the issues covered in each chapter, these revised and expanded sections offer extensive discussion of how developmental science can inform practice. Applications sections include new and expanded topics such as preventing child maltreatment, prenatal and postnatal maternal depression, managing sibling rivalry and other common problems of early childhood, improving children's executive functions, advancing children's social-emotional learning, reducing hostile attributional bias, helping sexual minority youth, family therapy with adolescents, helping college students develop critical thinking skills, narrative approaches to career counseling, and fostering adult wellness, among many others.

- **Focus on Developmental Psychopathology:** In many chapters, sections on psychopathology trace the developmental roots of autism, attachment disorders, conduct problems, depression, eating disorders, and PTSD. These specific disorders were selected because each represents an example of how developmental processes interact to produce psychopathology. Linkages between normal and abnormal pathways of development are explained. A review of basic concepts of developmental psychopathology and prevention science is also included.

- **Boxed features:** In many chapters, boxes highlight special topics and provide opportunities for in-depth coverage of research. These may be the biographies of influential theorists or detailed examinations of issues such as how adversity alters child outcomes, children's credibility as eyewitnesses, issues facing children of immigrant families, the effects of divorce on children, the criminal culpability of juveniles, identity processes in multiracial individuals, gay and lesbian couples and their families, gender differences in STEM fields, leadership development in women and men, the burden of caring for elderly relatives, cross-cultural differences in funeral rituals, and many others.

- **Culture and gender:** In every chapter, cross-cultural and cross-gender issues are discussed wherever relevant developmental research is available. Many tables examine cultural differences, such as in parenting, in identity development, and in coping strategies.

- **Chapter summaries:** Every chapter ends with a summary of the major topics covered in that chapter, providing a study tool for students and a planning tool for instructors.

- **Case studies and case study discussion questions:** Case studies and questions at the end of each chapter are another set of pedagogical tools for helping students think about the clinical implications of the developmental facts and theories they have learned.

- **Journal questions:** Journal questions at the end of each chapter help students reflect on the issues they have read about, encouraging them to consider the relevance of these issues in their own development. They also provide instructors an additional resource for generating class discussion.

- **Key concepts:** Throughout the text, new or technical terms are printed in **bold** and defined. At the end of each chapter, a list of these key terms is provided as a study tool.

- **Glossary:** A glossary at the end of the text provides students with a handy reference for key terms.

- **Appendix:** An appendix helps students understand how developmental processes are studied scientifically and how scientifically established information can be useful in practice.

- **Writing style:** The writing style is conversational in tone and is aimed at making even complex material accessible. To avoid sexist language use and yet still have the luxury of using singular pronouns such as "she" and "he," we use feminine pronouns in odd-numbered chapters and masculine pronouns in even-numbered chapters.

Supplemental Materials

Two online supplements are available for instructors at www. pearsonhighered.com/educator. Simply enter the author, title, or ISBN and select this textbook. Click on the "Resources" tab to view and download the available supplements.

- Online Instructor's Manual and Test Bank: A new Online Instructor's Manual and Test Bank (ISBN: 0-13-520616-2) has been developed with an average of 30 multiple-choice test items and 3 to 5 essay-style questions per chapter. Carefully scrutinized for accuracy, the multiple-choice questions in the Test Bank include both lower-level and higher-level questions. The lower-level questions expect students to access content knowledge and comprehension; the higher-level questions assess students' ability to synthesize, compare and contrast, and apply their knowledge to problem solving.

- Online PowerPoint® Slides: The Online PowerPoint® slides (ISBN: 0-13-520613-8) include key concept summaries, outlines, and other graphic aids to enhance learning. These slides are designed to help students understand, organize, and remember concepts and developmental theories.

Acknowledgments

We are very grateful to Janette Herbers, Ph.D., for her expert contributions to Chapters 8 and 15. We want to express our deep appreciation to Kevin Davis, our publisher, who has nurtured this project with his expertise and encouragement since we proposed the first edition. We also thank Jeffrey Johnston, who did a careful reading and evaluation of each chapter, and who provided us with positive guidance and support throughout this revision process. We especially appreciate Kathy Smith, our expert copy editor. Kathy has made many improvements to the manuscript, always with a gentle hand! We also are grateful to those who developed the excellent supplementary materials that accompany this text. We also thank the following reviewers of the previous edition, who provided many useful suggestions: Vanessa Ewing, University of Northern Colorado; Harry Lehwald, The Ohio State University; Anne T. Lewis, California State University Fresno; Kara McGoey; Duquesne University. Finally, our deepest gratitude goes to our families for their love and ongoing support.

Chapter 1
Organizing Themes in Development

 ## Learning Objectives

After reading this chapter, you should be able to:

1.1 Explain the role of developmental science (research and theory) in the problem-solving processes of reflective practitioners.

1.2 Identify distinguishing characteristics and core issues of classic theoretical approaches in developmental science, particularly classic stage theories and incremental theories.

1.3 Explain how and why contemporary multidimensional developmental theories synthesize the extreme positions of classic theorists and assess advantages and disadvantages of using multidimensional approaches.

1.4 Identify three core developmental issues and contrast current research-based conclusions with classic assumptions on each core issue.

Mai is a 56-year-old woman who was born to a poor Vietnamese immigrant family in rural California. When Mai was 5, her parents moved the family to a large city where they eventually succeeded in building a stable business that provided an adequate income. Mai was typically quiet and shy, and she had difficulty making friends in elementary school, often feeling left out of her peers' activities. Her social life improved in adolescence, but she often felt the need to hide her outstanding academic skills in order to fit in. In college and medical school, Mai felt more accepted for her intellectual prowess and freer to be herself, but she still ruminated at times about what others thought of her, and was plagued by vague anxieties. By her mid-twenties, cyclical problems with depression and anxiety had become a part of her existence. Her marriage at 33 to a scholarly man provided a haven for her, and life seemed calmer and less frightening. After the birth of a son at age 38, Mai again felt overwhelmed by anxiety. The couple struggled to balance the complex needs of a fragile infant with their own careers, and Mai's husband found her heavy dependence on his attention and calming influence difficult to accommodate. As their son grew, however, the couple handled the balancing act more skillfully. Now, Mai's child is starting college. Mai is busy with her work and usually finds her anxiety manageable. She continues to view her husband as the steadying force in her life.

Mai's story raises a host of questions about the influences that have shaped her life. How important was Mai's early poverty, her cultural background, and her parents' immigrant status? What was the source of her early social inhibition? Would things have been different for her if her parents had not been able to eventually provide economic stability? Were Mai's early difficulties forming social relationships just a "stage," or were they foundational to her later problems with depression and anxiety? Did stereotype threat (expecting to be judged on the basis of ethnicity or gender) play a role? How unusual is it for a married couple to experience increased conflicts following the birth of a child? If Mai and her husband had divorced, would their child have suffered lasting emotional damage? Is Mai's intellectual ability likely to change as she continues to age? Are her emotional problems likely to increase or decrease? What factors enable any person to overcome early unfavorable experiences and become a successful, healthy adult? And conversely, why do some people who do well as children experience emotional or behavioral problems as adults? These intriguing questions represent a sampling of the kinds of topics that developmental scientists tackle. Their goal is to understand life span development: human behavioral change from conception to death. "Behavioral" change refers broadly to change in both observable activity (e.g., from crawling to walking) and mental activity (e.g., from disorganized to logical thinking). More specifically, developmental science seeks to

- describe people's behavioral characteristics at different ages,
- identify how people are likely to respond to life's experiences at different ages,
- formulate theories that explain how and why we see the typical characteristics and responses that we do,
- understand what factors contribute to developmental differences from one person to another, and
- understand how behavior is influenced by cultural context and by changes in culture across generations.

Using an array of scientific tools designed to obtain objective (unbiased) information, developmentalists make careful observations and measurements, and they test theoretical explanations empirically. The Appendix, *A Practitioner's Guide to the Methods of Developmental Science*, provides a guide to these techniques. An understanding of the processes that lead to objective knowledge will help you evaluate new information from any source as you move forward in your career as a practitioner.

Developmental science is not a remote or esoteric body of knowledge. Rather, it has much to offer helping professionals in both their careers and their personal lives. As you study developmental science, you will build a knowledge base of information about age-related behaviors and about causal theories that help organize and make sense of these behaviors. These tools will help you better understand client concerns that are rooted in shared human experience. And when you think about clients' problems from a developmental perspective, you will increase the range of problem-solving strategies that you can offer. Finally, studying development can facilitate personal growth by providing a foundation for reflecting on your own life.

Reflection and Action

1.1 Explain the role of developmental science (research and theory) in the problem-solving processes of reflective practitioners.

Despite strong support for a comprehensive academic grounding in scientific developmental knowledge for helping professionals (e.g., Van Hesteren & Ivey, 1990), there has been a somewhat uneasy alliance between practitioners, such as mental health professionals, and those with a more empirical bent, such as behavioral scientists. The clinical fields have depended on research from developmental psychology to inform their practice. Yet in the past, overreliance on traditional experimental methodologies sometimes resulted in researchers' neglect of important issues that could not be studied using these rigorous methods (Hetherington, 1998). Consequently, there was a tendency for clinicians to perceive some behavioral science literature as irrelevant to real-world concerns (Turner, 1986). Clearly, the gap between science and practice is not unique to the mental health professions. Medicine, education, and law have all struggled with the problems involved in preparing students to grapple with the complex demands of the workplace. Contemporary debate on this issue has led to the development of serious alternative paradigms for the training of practitioners.

One of the most promising of these alternatives for helping professionals is the concept of **reflective practice**. The idea of "reflectivity" derives from Dewey's (1933/1998) view of education, which emphasized careful consideration of one's beliefs and forms of knowledge as a precursor to practice. Donald Schon (1987), a pioneer in the field of reflective practice, describes the problem this way:

> In the varied topography of professional practice, there is a high, hard ground overlooking a swamp. On the high ground, manageable problems lend themselves to solution through the application of research-based theory and technique. In the swampy lowland, messy confusing problems defy technical solutions. The irony of this situation is that the problems of the high ground tend to be relatively unimportant to individuals or society at large, however great their technical interest may be, while in the swamp lie the problems of greatest human concern. (p. 3)

The Gap Between Science and Practice

Traditionally, the modern, university-based educational process has been driven by the belief that problems can be solved best by applying objective, technical, or scientific information amassed from laboratory investigations. Implicit in this assumption is that human nature operates according to universal principles that, if known and understood, will enable us to predict behavior. For example, if I understand the principles of conditioning and reinforcement, I can apply a contingency contract to modify my client's inappropriate behavior. Postmodern critics have pointed out the many difficulties associated with this approach. Sometimes a "problem" behavior is related to, or maintained by, neurological, systemic, or cultural conditions. Sometimes the very existence of a problem may be a cultural construction. Unless a problem is viewed within its larger context, a problem-solving strategy may prove ineffective.

Most of the situations helpers face are confusing, complex, ill defined, and often unresponsive to the application of a simple, specific set of scientific principles. Thus, the training of helping professionals often involves a "dual curriculum." The first is more formal and may be presented as a conglomeration of research-based facts, whereas the second, often learned in a practicum, field placement, or first job, covers the curriculum of "what is really done" when working with clients. Unfortunately, some practitioners lose sight of the value of research-based knowledge in this process. The antidote to this dichotomous pedagogy, Schon (1987) and his followers suggest, is reflective practice. This is a creative method of thinking about practice in which the helper masters the knowledge and skills base pertinent to the profession but is encouraged to go beyond rote technical applications to generate new kinds of understanding and strategies of action. Rather than relying solely on objective technical applications to determine ways of operating in a given situation, the reflective practitioner constructs solutions to problems by engaging in personal hypothesis generating and hypothesis testing. Reflective practices are now used across a wide range of helping professions, from counseling and psychology to education to medicine and nursing (Curtis, Elkins, Duran, & Venta, 2016).

How can you use the knowledge of developmental science in a meaningful and reflective way? What place does it have in the process of reflective construction?

A consideration of another important line of research, namely, that of characteristics of expert problem solvers, will help us answer this question. Research studies on expert–novice differences in many areas such as teaching, science, and athletics all support the contention that experts have a great store of knowledge and skill in a particular area. Expertise is domain-specific. When compared to novices in any given field, experts possess well-organized and integrated stores of information that they draw on, almost automatically, when faced with novel challenges. Because this knowledge is well practiced, truly a "working body" of information, retrieval is relatively easy (Lewandowsky & Thomas, 2009). Progress in problem solving is closely self-monitored. Problems are analyzed and broken down into smaller units, which can be handled more efficiently.

If we apply this information to the reflective practice model, you will see some connections. One core condition of reflective practice is that practitioners use theory as a "partial lens through which to consider a problem" (Nelson & Neufelt, 1998). Practitioners also use another partial lens: their professional and other life experience. In reflective practice, theory-driven hypotheses about client and system problems are generated and tested for goodness of fit. A rich supply of problem-solving strategies depends on a deep understanding of and thorough grounding in fundamental knowledge germane to the field. Notice that there is a sequence to reflective practice. Schon (1987), for example, argues against putting the cart before the horse. He states that true reflectivity depends on the ability to "recognize and apply standard rules, facts and operations; then to reason from general rules to problematic cases in ways characteristic of the profession; and only then to develop and test new forms of understanding and action where familiar categories and ways of thinking fail" (p. 40). In other words, background knowledge is important, but it is most useful in a dynamic interaction with contextual applications. The most effective helpers can shift flexibly between the "big picture" that their knowledge base provides and the unique problems and contexts that they confront in practice (Ferreira, Basseches, & Vasco, 2016). A working knowledge of human development supplies the helping professional with a firm base from which to proceed.

Given the relevance of background knowledge to expertise in helping and to reflective practice, we hope we have made a sufficiently convincing case for the study of developmental science. However, it is obvious that students approaching this study are not "blank slates." You already have many ideas and theories about the ways that people grow and change. These implicit theories have been constructed over time, partly from personal experience, observation, and your own cultural "take" on situations. Dweck and her colleagues have demonstrated that reliably different interpretations of situations can be predicted based on individual differences in people's implicit beliefs about certain human attributes, such as intelligence or personality (see Dweck, 2006, 2017). Take the case of intelligence. If you happen to hold the implicit belief that a person's intellectual capacity can change and improve over time, you might be more inclined to take a skill-building approach to some presenting problem involving knowledge or ability. However, if you espouse the belief that a person's intelligence is fixed and not amenable to incremental improvement, possibly because of genetic inheritance, you might be more likely to encourage a client to cope with and adjust to cognitive limitations. For helping professionals, the implicit theoretical lens that shapes their worldview can have important implications for their clients.

We are often reluctant to give up our personal theories even in the face of evidence that these theories are incorrect (Lewandowsky & Oberauer, 2016; Rousseau & Gunia, 2016). The critical thinking that reflective practice requires can be impaired for many reasons, especially if we are busy and feel overwhelmed by the demands of the moment. The best antidote to misapplication of our personal views is self-monitoring: being aware of what our theories are and recognizing that they are only one of a set of possibilities. (See Chapter 11 for a more extensive discussion of this issue.) Before we discuss some specific beliefs about the nature of development, take a few minutes to consider what you think about the questions posed in Box 1.1.

Box 1.1: Questionnaire

Examine Your Beliefs About Development

Rate yourself using the forced-choice format for each of the following items.

1. Physical characteristics such as eye color, height, and weight are primarily inherited through genes.

   ❑ Strongly Disagree ❑ Moderately Disagree ❑ Moderately Agree ❑ Strongly Agree

2. Intelligence is primarily inherited through genes.

   ❑ Strongly Disagree ❑ Moderately Disagree ❑ Moderately Agree ❑ Strongly Agree

3. Personality is primarily inherited through genes.

   ❑ Strongly Disagree ❑ Moderately Disagree ❑ Moderately Agree ❑ Strongly Agree

4. Events in the first 3 years of life have permanent effects on a person's psychological development.

   ❑ Strongly Disagree ❑ Moderately Disagree ❑ Moderately Agree ❑ Strongly Agree

5. People's personalities do not change very much over their lifetimes.

   ❑ Strongly Disagree ❑ Moderately Disagree ❑ Moderately Agree ❑ Strongly Agree

6. People all go through the same stages in their lives.

   ❑ Strongly Disagree ❑ Moderately Disagree ❑ Moderately Agree ❑ Strongly Agree

7. Parents' socialization practices are the primary determiners of their children's mental health.

   ❑ Strongly Disagree ❑ Moderately Disagree ❑ Moderately Agree ❑ Strongly Agree

8. The cultural context in which the individual lives profoundly affects the psychological development of that person.

   ❑ Strongly Disagree ❑ Moderately Disagree ❑ Moderately Agree ❑ Strongly Agree

9. Common sense is a better guide to child rearing than is scientific knowledge.

   ❑ Strongly Disagree ❑ Moderately Disagree ❑ Moderately Agree ❑ Strongly Agree

MyLab Education Self-Check 1.1

A Historical Perspective on Developmental Theories

1.2 Identify distinguishing characteristics and core issues of classic theoretical approaches in developmental science, particularly classic stage theories and incremental theories.

Now that you have examined some of your own developmental assumptions, let's consider the theoretical views that influence developmentalists, with special attention to how these views have evolved through the history of developmental science. Later, we will examine how different theoretical approaches might affect the helping process.

Like you, developmental scientists bring to their studies theoretical assumptions that help to structure their understanding of known facts. These assumptions also guide their research and shape how they interpret new findings. Scientists tend to develop theories that are consistent with their own cultural background and experience; no one operates in a vacuum. A core value of Western scientific method is a pursuit of objectivity, so that scientists are committed to continuously evaluating their theories in light of evidence. As a consequence, scientific theories change over time. Throughout this text, you will be introduced to many developmental theories. Some are broad and sweeping in their coverage of whole areas of development, such as Freud's theory of personality development (see Chapters 7 and 8) or Piaget's theory of cognitive development (see Chapters 3, 6, and 9); some are narrower in scope, focusing on a particular issue, such as Vygotsky's theory of the enculturation of knowledge (see Chapter 3) or Bowlby's attachment theory (see Chapters 4 and 12). You will see that newer theories usually incorporate empirically verified ideas from older theories. Scientific theories of human development began to emerge in Europe and America in the 19th century. They had their roots in philosophical inquiry, in the emergence of biological science, and in the growth of mass education that accompanied industrialization. Throughout medieval times in European societies, children and adults of all ages seem to have been viewed and treated in very similar ways (Aries, 1960). Only infants and preschoolers were free of adult responsibilities, although they were not always given the special protections and nurture that they are today. At age 6 or 7, children took on adult roles, doing farmwork or learning a trade, often leaving their families to become apprentices. As the Industrial Revolution advanced, children worked beside adults in mines and factories. People generally seemed "indifferent to children's special characteristics" (Crain, 2005, p. 2), and there was no real study of children or how they change.

The notion that children only gradually develop the cognitive and personality structures that will characterize them as adults first appeared in the writings of 17th- and 18th-century philosophers, such as John Locke in Great Britain and Jean-Jacques Rousseau in France. In the 19th century, Charles Darwin's theory of the evolution of species and the growth of biological science helped to foster scholarly interest in children. The assumption grew that a close examination of how children change might help advance our understanding of the human species. Darwin himself introduced an early approach to child study, the "baby biography," writing a richly detailed account of his young son's daily changes in language and behavior. By the 18th and 19th centuries, the Industrial Revolution led to the growth of "middle-class" occupations (e.g., merchandizing) that required an academic education: training in reading, writing, and math. The need to educate large numbers of children sharpened the public's interest in understanding how children change with age.

The first academic departments devoted to child study began to appear on American college campuses in the late 19th and early 20th centuries. The idea that development continues even in adulthood was a 20th-century concept and a natural outgrowth of the study of children. If children's mental and behavioral processes change over time, perhaps such processes continue to evolve beyond childhood. Interest in adult development was also piqued by dramatic increases in life expectancy in the 19th and 20th centuries, as well as cultural changes in how people live. Instead of single households combining three or four generations of family members, grandparents and other relatives began to live apart from "nuclear families," so that understanding the special needs and experiences of each age group took on greater importance. Most classic developmental theories emerged during the early and middle decades of the 20th century. Contemporary theories integrate ideas from many classic theories, as well as from other disciplines: modern genetics, neuroscience, cognitive science, psycholinguistics, anthropology, and social and cultural psychology. They acknowledge that human development is a complex synthesis of diverse processes at multiple levels of functioning. Because they embrace complexity, contemporary developmental theories can be especially useful to helping professionals (Melchert, 2016). See the timeline in Figure 1.1 for a graphic summary of some of the key theories and ideas in the history of developmental science.

You can expect that the most up-to-date theories you read about in this text will continue to change in the future, because theoretical ideas evolve as research testing

FIGURE 1.1 Timeline of selected influences on developmental science with dates of representative works.

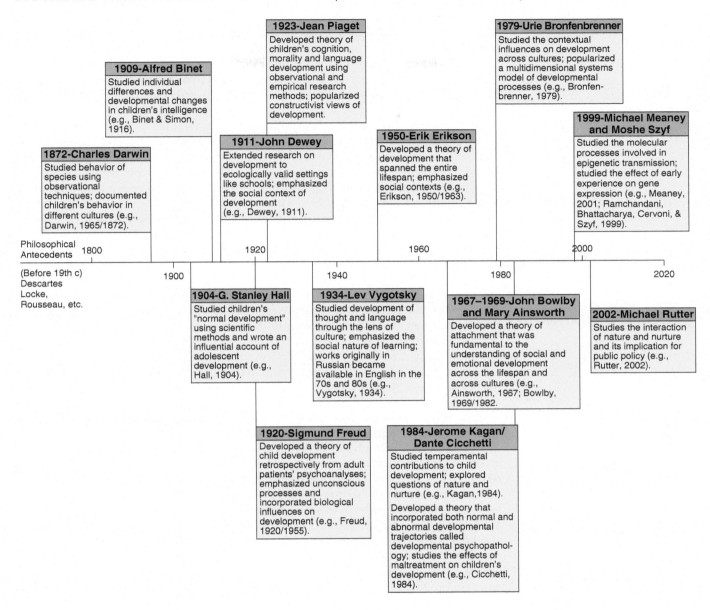

them either supports or does not support them. But theories are also likely to need adjusting because global shifts in immigration patterns, climate, and access to technology and information are likely to modify behavior and perhaps even some of the processes that govern the development of behavior. Developmental theories must accommodate such changes (Jensen, 2012).

Emphasizing Discontinuity: Classic Stage Theories

Some of the most influential early theories of development described human change as occurring in stages. Imagine a girl when she is 4 months old and then again when she is 4 years old. If your sense is that these two versions of the same child are fundamentally different in kind, with different intellectual capacities, different emotional structures, or different ways of perceiving others, you are thinking like a stage theorist. A **stage** is a period of time, perhaps several years, during which a person's activities (at least in one broad domain) have certain characteristics in common. For example, we could say that in language development, the 4-month-old girl is in a preverbal stage:

Among other things, her communications share in common the fact that they do not include talking. As a person moves to a different stage, the common characteristics of behavior change. In other words, a person's activities have similar qualities within stages but different qualities across stages. Also, after long periods of stability, qualitative shifts in behavior seem to happen relatively quickly. For example, the change from not talking to talking seems abrupt or discontinuous. It tends to happen between 12 and 18 months of age, and once it starts, language use seems to advance very rapidly. A 4-year-old is someone who communicates primarily by talking; she is clearly in a verbal stage.

The preverbal to verbal example illustrates two features of stage theories. First, they describe development as qualitative or transformational change, like the emergence of a tree from a seed. At each new stage, new forms of behavioral organization are both different from and more complex than the ones at previous stages. Increasing complexity suggests that development has "directionality." There is a kind of unfolding or emergence of behavioral organization.

Second, they imply periods of relative stability (within stages) and periods of rapid transition (between stages). Metaphorically, development is a staircase. Each new stage lifts a person to a new plateau for some period of time, and then there is another steep rise to another plateau. There seems to be discontinuity in these changes rather than change being a gradual, incremental process. One person might progress through a stage more quickly or slowly than another, but the sequence of stages is usually seen as the same across cultures and contexts, that is, universal. Also, despite the emphasis on qualitative discontinuities between stages, stage theorists argue for functional continuities across stages. That is, the same processes drive the shifts from stage to stage, such as brain maturation and social experience.

Sigmund Freud's theory of personality development began to influence developmental science in the early 1900s and was among the first to include a description of stages (e.g., Freud, 1905/1989, 1949/1969). Freud's theory no longer takes center stage in the interpretations favored by most helping professionals or by developmental scientists. First, there is little evidence for some of the specific proposals in Freud's theory (Loevinger, 1976). Second, his theory has been criticized for incorporating the gender biases of early 20th-century Austrian culture. Yet, some of Freud's broad insights are routinely accepted and incorporated into other theories, such as his emphasis on the importance of early family relationships to infants' emotional life, his notion that some behavior is unconsciously motivated, and his view that internal conflicts can play a primary role in social functioning. Currently influential theories, like those of Erik Erikson and John Bowlby, incorporated some aspects of Freud's theories or were developed to contrast with Freud's ideas. For these reasons, it is important to understand Freud's theory. Also, his ideas have permeated popular culture, and they influence many of our assumptions about the development of behavior. As you work to make explicit your own implicit assumptions about development, it will help to understand their origins and how well the theories that spawned them stand up in the light of scientific investigation.

FREUD'S PERSONALITY THEORY

Sigmund Freud's **psychoanalytic theory** both describes the complex functioning of the adult personality and offers an explanation of the processes and progress of its development throughout childhood. To understand any given stage it helps to understand Freud's view of the fully developed adult.

Id, Ego, and Superego. According to Freud, the adult personality functions as if there were actually three personalities, or aspects of personality, all potentially in conflict with one another. The first, the **id**, is the biological self, the source of all psychic energy. Babies are born with an id; the other two aspects of personality develop later. The id blindly pursues the fulfillment of physical needs or "instincts," such as the hunger drive and the sex drive. It is irrational, driven by the **pleasure principle**, that is, by the pursuit of gratification. Its function is to keep the individual, and the species, alive, although Freud also proposed that there are inborn aggressive, destructive instincts served by the id.

The **ego** begins to develop as cognitive and physical skills emerge. In Freud's view, some psychic energy is invested in these skills, and a rational, realistic self begins to take shape. The id still presses for fulfillment of bodily needs, but the rational ego seeks to meet these needs in sensible ways that take into account all aspects of a situation. For example, if you were hungry, and you saw a child with an ice cream cone, your id might press you to grab the cone away from the child—an instance of blind, immediate pleasure seeking. Of course, stealing ice cream from a child could have negative consequences if someone else saw you do it or if the child reported you to authorities. Unlike your id, your ego would operate on the **reality principle**, garnering your understanding of the world and of behavioral consequences to devise a more sensible and self-protective approach, such as waiting until you arrive at the ice cream store yourself and paying for an ice cream cone.

The **superego** is the last of the three aspects of personality to emerge. Psychic energy is invested in this "internalized parent" during the preschool period as children begin to feel guilty if they behave in ways that are inconsistent with parental restrictions. With the superego in place, the ego must now take account not only of instinctual pressures from the id, and of external realities, but also of the superego's constraints. It must meet the needs of the id without upsetting the superego to avoid the unpleasant anxiety of guilt. In this view, when you choose against stealing a child's ice cream cone to meet your immediate hunger, your ego is taking account not only of the realistic problems of getting caught but also of the unpleasant feelings that would be generated by the superego.

The Psychosexual Stages. In Freud's view, the complexities of the relationships and conflicts that arise among the id, the ego, and the superego are the result of the individual's experiences during five developmental stages. Freud called these **psychosexual stages** because he believed that changes in the id and its energy levels initiated each new stage. The term *sexual* here applies to all biological instincts or drives and their satisfaction, and it can be broadly defined as "sensual."

For each stage, Freud posited that a disproportionate amount of id energy is invested in drives satisfied through one part of the body. As a result, the pleasure experienced through that body part is especially great during that stage. Children's experiences satisfying the especially strong needs that emerge at a given stage can influence the development of personality characteristics throughout life. Freud also thought that parents typically play a pivotal role in helping children achieve the satisfaction they need. For example, in the **oral stage**, corresponding to the first year of life, Freud argued that the mouth is the body part that provides babies with the most pleasure. Eating, drinking, and even nonnutritive sucking are presumably more satisfying than at other times of life. A baby's experiences with feeding and other parenting behaviors are likely to affect her oral pleasure, and could influence how much energy she invests in seeking oral pleasure in the future. Suppose that a mother in the early 20th century believed the parenting advice of "experts" who claimed that nonnutritive sucking is bad for babies. To prevent her baby from sucking her thumb, the mother might tie the baby's hands to the sides of the crib at night—a practice recommended by the same experts! Freudian theory would predict that such extreme denial of oral pleasure could cause an **oral fixation**: The girl might grow up needing oral pleasures more than most adults, perhaps leading to overeating, to being especially talkative, or to being a chain smoker. The grown woman might also exhibit this fixation in more subtle ways, maintaining behaviors or feelings in adulthood that are particularly characteristic of babies, such as crying easily or experiencing overwhelming feelings of helplessness. According to Freud, fixations at any stage could be the result of either denial of a child's needs, as in this example, or overindulgence of those needs. Specific defense mechanisms, such as "reaction formation" or "repression," can also be associated with the conflicts that arise at a particular stage.

In Table 1.1, you will find a summary of the basic characteristics of Freud's five psychosexual stages. Some of these stages will be described in more detail in later chapters. Freud's stages have many of the properties of **critical (or sensitive) periods** for personality development. That is, they are time frames during which certain developments must occur or can most fully form. Freud's third stage, for example,

TABLE 1.1 Freud's Psychosexual Stages of Development

STAGE	APPROXIMATE AGE	DESCRIPTION
Oral	Birth to 1 year	Infants develop special relationships with caregivers. Mouth is the source of greatest pleasure. Too much or too little oral satisfaction can cause an "oral fixation," leading to traits that actively (smoking) or symbolically (overdependency) are oral or infantile.
Anal	1 to 3 years	Anal area is the source of greatest pleasure. Harsh or overly indulgent toilet training can cause an "anal fixation," leading to later adult traits that recall this stage, such as being greedy or messy.
Phallic	3 to 5 or 6 years	Genitalia are the source of greatest pleasure. Sexual desire directed toward the opposite-sex parent makes the same-sex parent a rival. Fear of angering the same-sex parent is resolved by identifying with that parent, which explains how children acquire both sex-typed behaviors and moral values. If a child has trouble resolving the emotional upheaval of this stage through identification, sex role development may be deviant or moral character may be weak.
Latency	6 years to puberty	Relatively quiescent period of personality development. Sexual desires are repressed after the turmoil of the last stage. Energy is directed into work and play. There is continued consolidation of traits laid down in the first three stages.
Genital	Puberty through adulthood	At puberty, adult sexual needs become the most important motivators of behavior. The individual seeks to fulfill needs and expend energy in socially acceptable activities, such as work, and through marriage with a partner who will substitute for the early object of desire, the opposite-sex parent.

provides an opportunity for sex typing and moral processes to emerge (see Table 1.1). Notice that Freud assumed that much of personality development occurs before age 5, during the first three stages. This is one of the many ideas from Freud's theory that has made its way into popular culture, even though modern research clearly does not support this position.

By the mid-1900s, two other major stage theories began to significantly impact the progress of developmental science. The first, by Erik Erikson, was focused on personality development, reshaping some of Freud's ideas. The second, by Jean Piaget, proposed that there are stagelike changes in cognitive processes during childhood and adolescence, especially in rational thinking and problem solving.

ERIKSON'S PERSONALITY THEORY

Erik Erikson studied psychoanalytic theory with Anna Freud, Sigmund's daughter, and later proposed his own theory of personality development (e.g., Erikson, 1950/1963). Like many "neo-Freudians," Erikson deemphasized the id as the driving force behind all behavior, and he emphasized the more rational processes of the ego. His theory is focused on explaining the psychosocial aspects of behavior: attitudes and feelings toward the self and toward others. Erikson described eight **psychosocial stages**. The first five correspond to the age periods laid out in Freud's psychosexual stages, but the last three are adult life stages, reflecting Erikson's view that personal identity and interpersonal attitudes are continually evolving from birth to death.

The "Eight Stages of Man." In each stage, the individual faces a different "crisis" or developmental task (see Chapter 9 for a detailed discussion of Erikson's concept of crisis). The crisis is initiated, on one hand, by changing characteristics of the person—biological maturation or decline, cognitive changes, advancing (or deteriorating) motor skills—and, on the other hand, by corresponding changes in others' attitudes, behaviors, and expectations. As in all stage theories, people qualitatively change from stage to stage, and so do the crises or tasks that they confront. In the first stage, infants must resolve the crisis of **trust versus mistrust** (see Chapter 4). Infants, in their relative helplessness, are "incorporative." They "take in" what is offered, including not only nourishment but also stimulation, information, affection, and attention. If infants' needs for such input are met by responsive caregivers, they will begin to trust others, to feel valued and valuable, and to view the world as a safe place. If caregivers are not consistently responsive, infants will fail to establish basic trust or to feel valuable, carrying mistrust with them into the next stage of development, when the 1- to 3-year-old toddler faces the crisis of **autonomy versus shame and doubt**. Mistrust in others and self will make it more difficult to successfully achieve a sense of autonomy.

The new stage is initiated by the child's maturing muscular control and emerging cognitive and language skills. Unlike helpless infants, toddlers can learn not only to control their elimination but also to feed and dress themselves, to express their desires with some precision, and to move around the environment without help. The new capacities bring a strong need to practice and perfect the skills that make children feel in control of their own destinies. Caregivers must be sensitive to the child's need for independence and yet must exercise enough control to keep the child safe and to help the child learn self-control. Failure to strike the right balance may rob children of feelings of autonomy—a sense that "I can do it myself"—and can promote instead either shame or self-doubt.

These first two stages illustrate features of all of Erikson's stages (see Table 1.2 for a description of all eight stages). First, others' sensitivity and responsiveness to the individual's needs create a context for positive psychosocial development. Second, attitudes toward self and toward others emerge together. For example, developing trust in others also means valuing (or trusting) the self. Third, every psychosocial crisis or task involves finding the right balance between positive and negative feelings, with the positive outweighing the negative. Finally, the successful resolution of a crisis at one stage helps smooth the way for successful resolutions of future crises. Unsuccessful resolution at an earlier stage may stall progress and make maladaptive behavior more likely.

Erikson's personality theory is often more appealing to helping professionals than Freud's theory. Erikson's emphasis on the psychosocial aspects of personality focuses attention on precisely the issues that helpers feel they are most often called on to address: feelings and attitudes about self and about others. Also, Erikson assumed

MyLab Education

Video Example 1.1

The children in this preschool classroom are preparing for their lunch. As you watch, note the ways that the children demonstrate a developed sense of autonomy and an emerging sense of initiative.

TABLE 1.2 Erikson's Psychosocial Stages of Development

STAGE OR PSYCHOSOCIAL "CRISIS"	APPROXIMATE AGE	SIGNIFICANT EVENTS	POSITIVE OUTCOME OR VIRTUE DEVELOPED	NEGATIVE OUTCOME
Trust vs. Mistrust	Birth to 1 year	Child develops a sense that the world is a safe and reliable place because of sensitive caregiving.	Hope	Fear and mistrust of others
Autonomy vs. Shame & Doubt	1 to 3 years	Child develops a sense of independence tied to use of new mental and motor skills.	Willpower	Self-doubt
Initiative vs. Guilt	3 to 5 or 6 years	Child tries to behave in ways that involve more "grown-up" responsibility and experiments with grown-up roles.	Purpose	Guilt over thought and action
Industry vs. Inferiority	6 to 12 years	Child needs to learn important academic skills and compare favorably with peers in school.	Competence	Lack of competence
Identity vs. Role Confusion	12 to 20 years	Adolescent must move toward adulthood by making choices about values, vocational goals, etc.	Identity and fidelity	Inability to establish sense of self
Intimacy vs. Isolation	Young adulthood	Adult becomes willing to share identity with others and to commit to affiliations and partnerships.	Love	Fear of intimacy, distancing
Generativity vs. Stagnation	Middle adulthood	Adult wishes to make a contribution to the next generation, to produce, mentor, create something of lasting value, as in the rearing of children or community services or expert work.	Care	Self-absorption
Ego Integrity vs. Despair	Late adulthood	Adult comes to terms with life's successes, failures, and missed opportunities and realizes the dignity of own life.	Wisdom	Regret

that the child or adult is an active, self-organizing individual who needs only the right social context to move in a positive direction. Further, Erikson was himself an optimistic therapist who believed that poorly resolved crises could be resolved more adequately in later stages if the right conditions prevailed. Erikson was sensitive to cultural differences in behavioral development. Finally, developmental researchers frequently find Eriksonian interpretations of behavior useful. Studies of attachment, self-concept, self-esteem, and adolescent identity, among other topics addressed in subsequent chapters, have produced results compatible with some of Erikson's ideas. (See Chapter 4, Box 4.2 for a biographical sketch of Erikson.)

PIAGET'S COGNITIVE DEVELOPMENT THEORY

In Jean Piaget's cognitive development theory, we see the influence of 18th-century philosopher Jean-Jacques Rousseau (e.g., 1762/1948), who argued that children's reasoning and understanding emerges naturally in stages and that parents and educators can help most by allowing children freedom to explore their environments and by giving them learning experiences that are consistent with their level of ability. Similarly, Piaget outlined stages in the development of cognition, especially logical thinking, which he called *operational thought* (e.g., Inhelder & Piaget, 1955/1958, 1964; Piaget, 1952, 1954). He assumed that normal adults are capable of thinking logically about both concrete and abstract contents but that this capacity evolves in four stages through childhood. Briefly, the first sensorimotor stage, lasting for about two years, is characterized by an absence of representational thought (see Chapter 3). Although babies are busy taking in the sensory world, organizing it on the basis of inborn reflexes or patterns, and then responding to their sensations, Piaget believed that they cannot yet symbolically represent their experiences, and so they cannot really reflect on them. This means that young infants do not form mental images or store memories symbolically, and they do not plan their behavior or intentionally act. These capacities emerge between 18 and 24 months, launching the next stage.

Piaget's second, third, and fourth stages roughly correspond to the preschool, elementary school, and the adolescent-adult years. These stages are named for the kinds of thinking that Piaget believed possible for these age groups. Table 1.3 summarizes each stage briefly, and we will describe the stages more fully in subsequent chapters.

Piaget's theory is another classic stage model. First, cognitive abilities are qualitatively similar within stages. If we know how a child approaches one kind of task, we should be able to predict her approaches to other kinds of tasks as well. Piaget acknowledged that children might be advanced in one cognitive domain or lag behind in another. For example, an adolescent might show more abstract reasoning about math than about interpersonal matters. He called these within-stage variations décalages. But generally, Piaget expected that a child's thinking would be organized in similar ways across most domains. Second, even though progress through

TABLE 1.3 Piaget's Cognitive Stages of Development

STAGE	APPROXIMATE AGE	DESCRIPTION
Sensorimotor	Birth to 2 years	Through six substages, the source of infants' organized actions gradually shifts. At first, all organized behavior is reflexive—automatically triggered by particular stimuli. By the end of this stage, behavior is guided more by representational thought.
Preoperational	2 to 6 or 7 years	Early representational thought tends to be slow. Thought is "centered," usually focused on one salient piece of information, or aspect of an event, at a time. As a result, thinking is usually not yet logical.
Concrete operational	7 to 11 or 12 years	Thinking has gradually become more rapid and efficient, allowing children to now "decenter," or think about more than one thing at a time. This also allows them to discover logical relationships between/among pieces of information. Their logical thinking is best about information that can be demonstrated in the concrete world.
Formal operational	12 years through adulthood	Logical thinking extends now to "formal" or abstract material. Young adolescents can think logically about hypothetical situations, for example.

the stages could move more or less quickly depending on many individual and contextual factors, the stages unfold in an invariant sequence, regardless of context or culture. The simpler patterns of physical or mental activity at one stage become integrated into more complex organizational systems at the next stage (**hierarchical integration**). Finally, despite the qualitative differences across stages, there are functional similarities or continuities from stage to stage in the ways in which children's cognitive development proceeds. According to Piaget, developmental progress depends on children's active engagement with the environment. This active process, which will be described in more detail in Chapter 3, suggests that children (and adults) build knowledge and understanding in a **self-organizing** way. They interpret new experiences and information to fit their current ways of understanding even as they make some adjustments to their understanding in the process. Children do not just passively receive information from without and store it "as is." And, knowledge does not just emerge from within as though preformed. Instead, children actively build their knowledge, using both existing knowledge and new information. This is a **constructivist** view of development.

Piaget's ideas about cognitive development were first translated into English in the 1960s, and they swept American developmental researchers off their feet. His theory filled the need for an explanation that acknowledged complex qualitative changes in children's abilities over time, and it launched an era of unprecedented research on all aspects of children's intellectual functioning that continues today. Although many of the specifics of Piaget's theory have been challenged by research findings, researchers, educators, and other helping professionals still find the broad outlines of this theory very useful for organizing their thinking about the kinds of understandings that children of different ages can bring to a problem or social situation. Piaget's theory also inspired some modern views of cognitive change in adulthood. As you will see in Chapter 11, post-Piagetians have proposed additional stages in the development of logical thinking, hypothesizing that the abstract thinking of the adolescent is transformed during adulthood into a more relativistic kind of logical thinking, partly as a function of adults' practical experience with the complexity of real-world problems.

MyLab Education
Video Example 1.2
Piaget proposed stagelike changes in cognitive processes as children develop. Compare preoperational thinking to concrete operational thinking as you observe two children's responses to Piagetian conservation tasks in this video.

Emphasizing Continuity: Incremental Change

Unlike stage theories, some theoretical approaches characterize development as a more continuous process. Change tends to be incremental, metaphorically resembling not a staircase but a steadily rising mountainside. Again, picture a 4-month-old girl, and the same girl when she is 4 years old. If you tend to "see" her evolving in small steps from a smiling, attentive infant to a smiling, eager toddler, to a smiling, mischievous preschooler, always noting in your observations threads of sameness as well as differences, your own theoretical assumptions about development may be more compatible with one of these **incremental models**. Like stage models, they can be very different in the types and breadth of behaviors they attempt to explain. They also differ in the kinds of processes they assume to underlie psychological change, such as the kinds of processes involved in learning. But they all agree that developmental change is not marked by major, sweeping reorganizations that affect many behaviors at once, as in stage theories. Rather, change is steady and specific to particular behaviors or behavioral domains. Incremental theorists, like stage theorists, tend to see "change for the better" as a key feature of development. So, adding words to your vocabulary over time would be a typical developmental change, but forgetting previously learned information might not. Social learning theory and most information processing theories are among the many incremental models available to explain development.

LEARNING THEORIES

Learning theories, in what is called the **behaviorist tradition**, have a distinguished history in American psychology. They were the most widely accepted class of theories through much of the 20th century, influenced by many thinkers from

John B. Watson (e.g., 1913) to B. F. Skinner (e.g., 1938) to Albert Bandura (e.g., 1974). These theories trace their philosophical roots from ancient Greece and the writings of Aristotle through John Locke and the British empiricists of the 17th and 18th centuries. In this philosophical tradition, knowledge and skill are thought to accumulate as the result of each person's individual experiences. The environment gradually leaves its imprint on one's behavior and mind, a mind that in infancy is like a blank slate. Locke described several simple processes—association, repetition, imitation, reward, and punishment—by which the environment can have an impact. Many of the processes Locke described were incorporated into behaviorist approaches to development.

Some learning theories explain behavioral change as a function of chains of specific environmental events, such as those that occur in **classical conditioning** and **operant conditioning**. In these processes, change in behavior takes place because environmental events (stimuli) are paired with certain behaviors. Let's begin with classical conditioning, also called **respondent conditioning** (Vargas, 2009). A **respondent** is an automatic response to a stimulus. For example, when you hear an unexpected loud noise you will automatically produce a startle response. This stimulus/response association is unconditioned, built-in to your biological system. But the response can be conditioned to a new, neutral stimulus. Suppose a child calmly watches a dog approach her. At first, sight of the dog is a neutral stimulus. But the dog suddenly barks loudly, causing the child to automatically startle and pull back. Suppose that the next time the child sees the dog, it does not bark. Even so, just the sight of the dog triggers the same response as loud barking would: The child automatically startles and pulls back. The child has learned a new response, because the formerly neutral event (sight of dog) has been paired with an event (loud barking) that automatically causes a startle. Perhaps the startle reaction is also accompanied by feelings of fear. If so, the child has learned to fear this dog and will likely generalize that fear to other, similar dogs. When a neutral event or stimulus is associated with a stimulus that causes an automatic response, the neutral stimulus can become a **conditioned stimulus**, meaning that it can cause the person to make the same automatic response in the future, called a **conditioned response**. This is classical conditioning.

Operant conditioning is different. First, a person performs some behavior. The behavior is an **operant**, any act with potential to lead to consequences in the environment (that is, to "operate" on the environment). Immediately after the operant occurs, there is a "reinforcing event," or **reinforcement**, something that is experienced by the person as pleasurable or rewarding. For example, suppose that a young child happens to babble "da" just as a dog appears in the child's line of sight, and the child's mother excitedly claps and kisses the child. (The mother has mistakenly assumed that the child has tried to say "dog.") The mother's reaction serves as a reinforcement for the child, who will repeat the "da" sound the next time a dog comes into view. In operant conditioning, the child learns to produce a spontaneous behavior or operant (e.g., "da") in response to a cue (e.g., the appearance of a dog) because the behavior was previously reinforced in that situation. A reinforcement is a consequence of the operant behavior that maintains or increases the likelihood of that behavior when the cue occurs again (Sparzo, 2011). The mother's approving reaction is an example of a **positive reinforcement**: Something pleasurable is presented after the operant occurs. There are also rewarding consequences that are called **negative reinforcements**: An aversive experience *stops* or is removed after the operant occurs. If your brother releases you from a painful hammer-hold when you yell "Uncle," you have been negatively reinforced for saying "Uncle" (the operant) in that situation.

Social learning theories, which have focused specifically on how children acquire personality characteristics and social skills, consider conditioning processes part of the story, but they also emphasize "observational learning," or **modeling**. In this kind of learning, one person (the learner) observes another (the model) performing some behavior, and just from close observation, learns to do it too. The observer may or may not imitate the modeled behavior, immediately or in the future, depending on many factors, such as whether the observer expects a reward for the behavior, whether the model is perceived as nurturing or competent, and even whether the observer believes that the performance will meet the observer's own performance standards. Current

MyLab Education
Video Example 1.3
Modeling is a particularly effective teaching strategy with young children, who can observe and replicate the behavior better than they can understand complicated instructions for how to do a task.

versions of social learning theory emphasize many similar cognitive, self-regulated determiners of performance and suggest that they too are often learned from models (e.g., Bandura, 1974, 1999).

Whatever the learning processes that are emphasized in a particular learning theory, the story of development is one in which behaviors or beliefs or feelings change in response to specific experiences, one experience at a time. Broader changes can occur by **generalization**. If new events are experienced that are very similar to events in the original learning context, the learned behaviors may be extended to these new events. For example, the child who learns to say "da" when a particular dog appears may do the same when other dogs appear, or even in the presence of other four-legged animals. Or a child who observes a model sharing candy with a friend may later share toys with a sibling. But these extensions of learned activities are narrow in scope compared to the sweeping changes hypothesized by stage theorists. While these processes explain changes in discrete behaviors or patterns of behavior, learning theories do not explain developmental reorganizations and adaptations in the ways classic stage theories do.

INFORMATION PROCESSING THEORIES

Since the introduction of computing technologies in the middle of the 20th century, some theorists have likened human cognitive functioning to computer processing of information. Not all **information processing theories** can be strictly classified as incremental theories, but many can. Like learning theories, these do not hypothesize broad stages, but emphasize incremental changes in narrow domains of behavior or thought. The mind works on information—attending to it, holding it in a temporary store or "working memory," putting it into long-term storage, using strategies to organize it or to draw conclusions from it, and so on. How the information is processed depends on general characteristics of the human computer, such as how much information can be accessed, or made available for our attention, at one time. These characteristics can change to some degree over time. For example, children's attentional capacity increases gradually with age. Yet most changes with age are quite specific to particular domains of knowledge, such as changes in the strategies children use to solve certain kinds of problems.

Furthermore, processing changes are not stagelike; they do not extend beyond the particular situation or problem space in which they occur. For example, Siegler and his colleagues (e.g., Siegler, 1996, 2007; Siegler & Svetina, 2006) describe changes in the ways that children do arithmetic, read, solve problems of various kinds, and perform many other tasks and skills. Siegler analyzes very particular changes in the kinds of strategies that children use when they attempt these tasks. Although there can be similarities across tasks in the ways that strategies change (e.g., they become more automatic with practice, they generalize to similar problems, etc.), usually the specific strategies used in one kind of task fail to apply to another, and changes are not coordinated across tasks. To illustrate, a kindergartner trying to solve an addition problem might use the strategy of "counting from one." "[T]his typically involves putting up fingers on one hand to represent the first addend, putting up fingers on the other hand to represent the second addend, and then counting the raised fingers on both hands" (Siegler, 1998, p. 93). This strategy is characteristic of early addition efforts, but would play no role in tasks such as reading or spelling. Overall, then, cognitive development in this kind of model is like social development in social learning theories: It results from the accrual of independent changes in many different domains of thought and skill. Development involves change for the better, but it does not lead to major organizational shifts across domains.

Classic Theories and the Major Issues They Raise

Classic theories of development have typically addressed a set of core issues. In our brief review, you have been introduced to just a few of them. Is developmental change qualitative (e.g., stagelike) or quantitative (e.g., incremental)? Are some developments restricted to certain critical periods in the life cycle or are changes in brain and behavior possible at any time given the appropriate opportunities? Are there important continuities across the life span (in characteristics or change processes) or is everything in flux? Are people actively influencing the course and nature of their own development (self-organizing), or are they passive products of other forces? Which is more important in causing developmental change, nature (heredity) or nurture (environment)? Are there universal developmental trajectories, processes, and changes that are the same in all cultures and historical periods, or is development more specific to place and time?

Classic theorists usually took a stand on one side or the other of these issues, framing them as "either-or" possibilities. However, taking an extreme position does not fit the data we now have available. Contemporary theorists propose that human development is best described by a synthesis of the extremes. The best answer to all of the questions just posed appears to be "Both."

MyLab Education Self-Check 1.2

Contemporary Multidimensional or Systems Theories: Embracing the Complexity of Development

1.3   Explain how and why contemporary multidimensional developmental theories synthesize the extreme positions of classic theorists and assess advantages and disadvantages of using multidimensional approaches.

Throughout this text you will find evidence that development is the result of the relationships among many causal components, interacting in complex ways. Modern developmental theories, which we refer to as multidimensional or systems theories, explain and describe the enormous complexity of interrelated causal processes in development. They generally assume that in all behavioral domains, from cognition to personality, there are layers, or levels, of interacting causes for change: physical/molecular, biological, psychological, social, and cultural. What happens at one level both causes and is caused by what happens at other levels. That is, the relationships among causes are reciprocal or bidirectional processes. For example, increased testosterone levels at puberty (biological change) might help influence a boy to pursue an aggressive sport, like wrestling. The boy's success at wrestling may cause his status and social dominance to rise among his male friends (social change), and this social change can reciprocally influence his biological functioning. Specifically, it can lead to additional increases in his testosterone levels (Cacioppo & Berntson, 1992).

These theories acknowledge and incorporate many kinds of change: qualitative, transforming changes, both great (stagelike) and small (such as strategy changes within a particular problem-solving domain), as well as continuous, incremental variations that can even be reversible, such as learning and then forgetting new information (e.g., Overton, 1990). This is one example of how contemporary theories integrate features of many classic theories of development.

Think again about a girl who is 4 months old, and then later 4 years old. Do you perceive so many changes that she is transformed into a different sort of creature, and yet, at the same time, do you see enduring qualities that characterize her at both ages? Does your sense of the forces that have changed her include influences such as her family, community, and culture? Do you also recognize that she has played a significant role in her own change and in modifying those other forces? If so, your implicit assumptions about development may be more consistent with multidimensional models than with either stage or incremental theories alone.

Multidimensional theories portray the developing person metaphorically as a vine growing through a thick forest (Kagan, 1994). In doing so, the vine is propelled by its own inner processes, but its path, even its form, is in part created by the forest it inhabits. There is continuous growth, but there are changes in structure too—in its form and direction—as the vine wends its way through the forest. Finally, its presence in the forest changes the forest itself, affecting the growth of the trees and other plants, which reciprocally influence the growth of the vine.

Many multidimensional theories have been proposed, but they are remarkably similar in their fundamental assumptions and characteristics. They are typically different in which aspects of development they provide most detail about. They include transactional theory (e.g., Sameroff & Chandler, 1975), relational theory (e.g., Lerner, 1998), dialectical theory (e.g., Sameroff, 2012), bioecological theory (e.g., Bronfenbrenner & Ceci, 1994), bio-social-ecological theory (e.g., Cole & Packer, 2011), epigenetic theory (e.g., Gottlieb, 1992), life course theory (Elder & Shanahan, 2006), life span developmental theory (e.g., Baltes, 1997; Baltes, Lindenberger, & Staudinger, 2006), dynamic systems theory (e.g., Thelen & Smith, 1998), and several others. (See Overton, 2015, for a deeper analysis of the similarities and differences among these theories.) Figure 1.2 provides one illustration of the multiple, interacting forces that these theories identify. Two examples of multidimensional models will help flesh out the typical characteristics of many of these theories.

MyLab Education
Video Example 1.4
As he describes what he does when he is not in school, this young boy discusses primarily proximal processes. What are some of the more distal processes that also have an effect on his development?

BRONFENBRENNER'S BIOECOLOGICAL THEORY

In his **bioecological theory**, Urie Bronfenbrenner and his colleagues (e.g., Bronfenbrenner & Ceci, 1994; Bronfenbrenner & Morris, 1998, 2006) described all developments—including personality and cognitive change—as a function of **proximal processes**. These are reciprocal interactions between an "active, evolving biopsychological human organism and the persons, objects and symbols in its immediate external environment" (Bronfenbrenner & Morris, 1998, p. 996). In other words, proximal processes refer to a person's immediate interactions with people or with the physical environment or with informational sources (such as books or movies). Proximal processes are truly interactive: The organism both influences and is influenced by the immediate environment. These proximal processes are modified by more **distal processes**. Some of these are within the organism—such as genes. Others are outside the immediate environment—such as features of the educational system or of the broader culture.

The quality and effectiveness of the immediate environment—its responsiveness to the individual's particular needs and characteristics and the opportunities it provides—depend on the larger context. For example, parental monitoring of children's homework benefits children's academic performance. But monitoring is more effective if parents are knowledgeable about the child's work. A parent who insists that his child do her algebra homework may have less effect if the parent cannot be a resource who guides and explains the work. Thus, the parent's own educational background affects the usefulness of the monitoring (Bronfenbrenner & Ceci, 1994).

An individual's characteristics also influence the effectiveness of the environment. For example, motivations affect the impact of learning opportunities in a given context. A man interested in gambling may learn to reason in very complex ways about horses and their relative probability of winning at the track, but he may not display such complex reasoning in other contexts (Ceci & Liker, 1986). Other important individual qualities include **demand characteristics**, behavioral tendencies that often either encourage or discourage certain kinds of reactions from others. A child who is shy and inhibited, a trait that appears to have some biological roots (Kagan & Fox, 2006), may often fail to elicit attention from others, and may receive less support when she needs it, than a child who is open and outgoing (Bell & Chapman, 1986; see also Chapters 4 and 5).

Changes in the organism can be emergent, stagelike, qualitative changes, such as a shift from preoperational to concrete operational thought (see Table 1.3), or they can be more continuous, graded changes, such as shifts in academic interest or involvement in athletics. Both kinds of change are the result of proximal processes, influenced by more distal internal and external causes. Once changes occur, the individual brings new resources to these proximal processes. For example, when a child begins to demonstrate concrete operational thought, she will be given different tasks to do at home or at school than before, and she will learn things from those experiences that she would not have learned earlier. This is a good example of the bidirectionality of

FIGURE 1.2 A multidimensional (systems) model of development.
This figure illustrates the external influences described in Bronfenbrenner's bioecological theory along with internal influences on the developing child over time. Two-way arrows show bidirectional causality between all adjacent levels and between different parts of the same level. Proximal processes occur at the interface between the child and her microsystems.

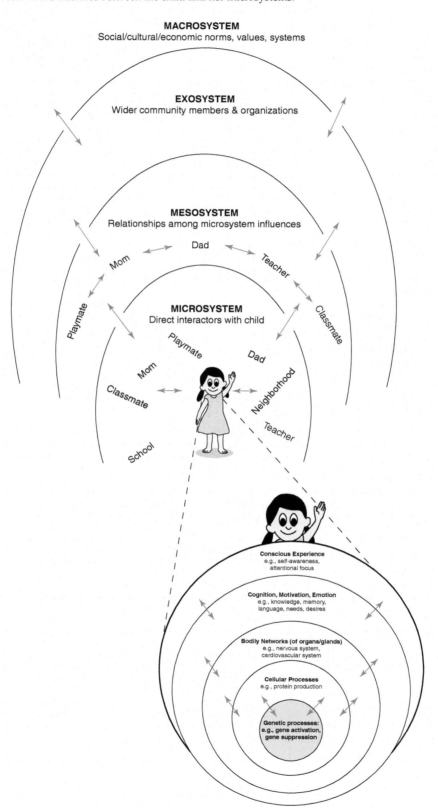

proximal processes: Change in the child fosters change in the environment, leading to more change in the child, and so on.

In earlier versions of his theory, Bronfenbrenner characterized in detail the many levels of environment that influence a person's development. He referred to the immediate environment, where proximal processes are played out, as the microsystem. Babies interact primarily with family members, but as children get older, other microsystems, such as the school, the neighborhood, or a local playground and its inhabitants, become part of their lives. The microsystems interact with and modify each other. For example, a discussion between a child's parent and a teacher might change how one or both of them interacts with the child. The full set of relationships among the microsystems is called the mesosystem. The next level of the environment, the exosystem, includes settings that children may not directly interact with but that influence the child nonetheless. For example, a teacher's family life will influence the teacher and thereby the child. Or a child's socioeconomic status influences where her family lives, affecting the school the child will attend, and thus affecting the kinds of experiences the child has with teachers. Finally, there is the macrosystem, including the customs and character of the larger culture that help shape the microsystems. For example, cultural attitudes and laws regarding the education of exceptional students influence the operation of a school and therefore a child's interactions with teachers.

The environment, then, is like "a set of nested structures, each inside the next, like a set of Russian dolls" (Bronfenbrenner, 1979). In newer versions of his theory, Bronfenbrenner gave equal attention to the nested internal levels of the organism. As we have seen, a person brings to proximal processes a set of dispositions, resources (preexisting abilities, experiences, knowledge, and skills), and demand characteristics. These, in turn, are influenced by biological and physical levels of functioning that include the genes. Bronfenbrenner also emphasized, as other multidimensional theorists do, the bidirectional effects of each level on the adjacent levels. For example, proximal psychological processes playing out in the immediate context are both influenced by, and influencing, physiological processes (Bronfenbrenner & Morris, 1998, 2006). Finally, these interactions continue and change across time.

LIFE SPAN DEVELOPMENTAL THEORY

In life span developmental theories, the same developmental processes that produce the transformation of infants into children, and children into adults, are thought to continue throughout adulthood until death. Developmental change is part of what it means to be alive. Adaptation continues from conception to death, with proximal interactions between the organism and the immediate context modified by more distal processes both within the individual and in the environment. Life span theorists like Paul Baltes (e.g., 1997; Baltes, Lindenberger, & Staudinger, 2006) refer to the interacting web of influences on development as the "architecture" of biological and cultural supports. Baltes proposed that successful adaptation is benefited more by biological supports in childhood than in adulthood. Cultural supports are important in childhood, but if not optimal, most children have biological supports (we could think of them as a complex of biological protective factors) that have evolved to optimize development in most environments. For adults, successful adaptation is more heavily dependent on cultural supports or protective factors. "The older individuals are, the more they are in need of culture-based resources (material, social, economic, psychological) to generate and maintain high levels of functioning" (Baltes, Lindenberger, & Staudinger, 1998, p. 1038). We will have more to say about life span developmental theories in Chapter 13.

Applying Theory to Practice

We have described both classic theoretical approaches to development and the more integrative and complex multidimensional theories that contemporary developmentalists favor. Preferring one of these paradigms can influence the way helping professionals assess and interpret client concerns. Let's consider how various theoretical orientations to development might apply to a counseling situation:

Juliana is a 26-year-old Latina female who was raised in an intact, middle-class family. Her father was a teacher and her mother a housewife who occasionally worked in a neighborhood preschool as a teacher's aide. Juliana was the second child in the family, which included an older brother and a younger sister. She attended parochial schools from kindergarten through 12th grade, where she worked very hard to achieve average and sometimes above-average grades. During her early years in school, Juliana had reading difficulties and received remedial instruction. At home, her parents stressed the value of education and kept a close watch on the children. The children were well behaved, respectful, and devoted to the family. Most of their spare time was spent with their close relatives, who lived nearby. Despite Juliana's interest in dating during high school, her parents did not permit her to spend time with boyfriends. They told her that she needed to concentrate on her schoolwork so that she could be a nurse when she grew up. After graduation, Juliana entered a small local college and enrolled in a program designed to prepare her for a career in nursing. She lived at home and commuted to school on a daily basis. Life proceeded as it had for most of her high school years. Her course work, however, became increasingly more difficult for her. She also felt isolated from most of her classmates, many of whom were working and living on their own. She tried to participate in some of the college's social events, but without much satisfaction or success. To pass her science courses, Juliana had to spend most of her time studying. By the middle of her academic program, it was clear that she was in danger of failing. She felt frustrated and angry. At this point, she became romantically involved with Bill, a young White man who worked at the college. She dropped out of school and moved in with him, hoping their relationship would lead to marriage. Her family was shocked and upset with her decision and put pressure on her to come home. Eventually, the relationship with Bill ended, and Juliana, unwilling to return home, moved in with a group of young students who were looking for someone to share the rent. She found a low-wage job, changed her style of dress to look more like the younger students, and quickly became involved in a series of other romantic relationships. Juliana grew increasingly despondent about her inability to maintain a relationship that would lead to marriage and a family. In addition, she felt some distress about not completing her college degree. She enrolled in a night-school program at a local community college to retake her science courses. Once again, she experienced confusion, problems fitting in, and academic difficulty. She went to the college counseling center to ask for help.

Take a minute to think about how you would respond to Juliana. Do any of your views about development enter into your appraisal of her situation? If you tend to be a stage theorist, you might consider Juliana's problems to be based on Erikson's crisis of intimacy in early adulthood (see Table 1.2). She does seem to have difficulties with intimacy, and she is just at the age when these issues are supposed to become central to psychosocial development. But a rigid assumption of age–stage correspondence could prevent you from considering other possibilities, such as an unresolved identity crisis.

If you tend to be an incremental theorist, perhaps favoring social learning explanations, you might perceive Juliana's situation quite differently. You may see Juliana as having problems in her intimate relationships that are similar to her difficulties with school. In both domains she is apparently "delayed," perhaps because she has had insufficient opportunities to learn social and academic skills or perhaps because she has been reinforced for behaviors that are ineffective in more challenging contexts. Although this may be a useful way of construing Juliana's dilemma, any stage issues contributing to her distress may be missed. Also, there could be factors in her social environment, such as cultural expectations, that might not be considered.

If you take a more multidimensional approach, as we do, you will try to remain alert to multiple influences, both proximal and distal, on Juliana's development. The roles of her biological status, her individual capabilities, her stage of development, her earlier experiences, her family, and her culture will all be considered as possible influences and points of intervention. One disadvantage could be that the complexity of the interacting factors is so great that you may find it difficult to sort out the most effective place to begin. Another disadvantage is that macrosystem influences, such as cultural expectations about appropriate roles for women, may be quite resistant to intervention. However, one of the advantages of a multidimensional view is that it *does* highlight many possible avenues of intervention, and if you can identify one or a few that are amenable to change, you may have a positive influence on Juliana's future.

Helping professionals with different developmental assumptions would be likely to choose different approaches and strategies in working with Juliana. In a sense, any set of theoretical biases is like a set of blinders. It will focus your attention on some aspects of the situation and reduce the visibility of other aspects. Taking a multidimensional or systems view has the advantage of minimizing the constraints of those blinders. In any case, knowing your own biases can help you avoid the pitfalls of overreliance on one way of viewing development.

MyLab Education Self-Check 1.3

A New Look at Three Developmental Issues

1.4   Identify three core developmental issues and contrast current research-based conclusions with classic assumptions on each core issue.

In the following sections, we examine three classic developmental issues that have garnered a great deal of attention in recent years. As you read about these issues from the viewpoint of contemporary research, you will begin to see why modern developmental theories take a multidimensional approach. Notice whether any of the new information causes you to reexamine your own assumptions about development.

Nature *and* Nurture

How did you respond to the first three items of the questionnaire in Box 1.1? Did you say that physical traits are primarily inherited? Did you say that intelligence or personality is inherited? Your opinions on these matters are likely to be influenced by your cultural background. Through most of the last century, North Americans viewed intelligence as mostly hereditary, but Chinese and Japanese tended to disregard the notion of "native ability" and to consider intellectual achievements more as a function of opportunity and hard work (e.g., Stevenson, Chen, & Lee, 1993). Partially influenced by psychological research, North Americans have begun to see intelligence as at least partially dependent on education and opportunity, but they still are likely to see some achievements, such as in mathematics, as mostly dependent on ability. Alternatively, North Americans have traditionally viewed social adjustment as a result of environmental experiences, especially parents' nurturance and socialization practices, but East Asians typically see these qualities as mostly inherent traits.

Developmental researchers acknowledge that both nature and nurture influence most behavioral outcomes, but in the past they have often focused primarily on one or the other, partly because a research enterprise that examines multiple causes at the same time tends to be a massive undertaking. So, based on personal interest, theoretical bias, and practical limitations, developmental researchers have often systematically investigated one kind of cause of behavior, setting aside examination of other causes. Interestingly, what these limited research approaches have accomplished is to establish impressive bodies of evidence, *both* for the importance of genes *and* for the importance of the environment!

What theorists and researchers face now is the difficult task of specifying how the two sets of causes work together: Do they have separate effects that "add up," for example, or do they qualitatively modify each other, creating together, in unique combinations, unique outcomes? Modern multidimensional theories make the latter assumption, and evidence is quickly accumulating to support this view. Heredity and environment are interdependent: The same genes operate differently in different environments, and the same environments are experienced differently by individuals with different genetic characteristics. Developmental outcomes are always a function of interplay between genes and environment, and the operation of one cannot even be described adequately without reference to the other. In Chapter 2 you will learn more about this complex interdependence.

Neuroplasticity *and* Critical (Sensitive) Periods

Neuroplasticity refers to changes in the brain that occur as a result of some practice or experience. Neurons, the basic cells of the nervous system, become reorganized as a result of such practice, resulting in new learning and memory. Neural changes were once thought to occur primarily in infancy and early childhood. Contemporary neuroscientists recognize that "there is no period when the brain and its functions are static; changes are continuous throughout the lifespan. The nature, extent and the rates of change vary by region and function assessed and are influenced by genetic as well as environmental factors" (Pascual-Leone & Taylor, 2011, p. 183). The realization that our brains continue to change throughout life has revolutionized the way scientists regard the brain. As we have seen, modern multidisciplinary theories incorporate descriptions of relative life-long plasticity.

The time-related "variation by region and function" noted previously is at the heart of the classic question about *critical (sensitive) periods*. Although the brain exhibits plasticity throughout life, do some changes, such as first language learning, occur more easily and more effectively at certain ages and stages? Or, is the organism able to develop or learn any new skill at any time with the right opportunities? There is little doubt that there are some behavioral developments that usually take place within a particular period. In many ways, language acquisition is nearly complete by the age of 5 or 6, for example. But is it possible to acquire a language at another point in the life cycle if this usual time is somehow "missed"? Pinker (1994) reviewed several findings that led him to conclude that although language can be learned at other times, it is never learned as well or as effortlessly as it would have been in the critical period from about 1 to 5 years. Consider deaf individuals learning American Sign Language (ASL). ASL is a "real" symbolic language, with a complex grammar. Sometimes, however, American deaf children are not given the opportunity to learn ASL in their early years, often because of a belief that deaf children should learn to read lips and speak English (the "oralist" tradition). As a result, many deaf children simply do not learn any language. When these individuals are introduced to ASL in late childhood or adolescence, they often fail to acquire the same degree of facility with the grammar that children who learn ASL as preschoolers achieve.

If findings like these mean that a sensitive period has been missed, what could be the cause of such time-dependent learning? It is usually assumed that the end of a sensitive period is due to brain changes that make learning more difficult after the change. The environmental conditions that are likely to support the new learning may also be less favorable at certain times. As we have seen, the explanation is likely to be complex. For example, total immersion in a language may be just the right arrangement for a preschooler who knows no other communicative system. Older learners, even deaf children or adults who have learned no formal language early in life, may always filter a new language through previously established communication methods, such as an idiosyncratic set of hand signals. If so, for an older child or adult, total immersion may be less effective than a learning environment that can make correspondences between the new language and the old one. In later chapters, we will examine this issue as it relates to several developments, such as the emergence of sexual identity (Chapter 8) and the formation of bonds between mothers and infants (Chapter 4). In each case, the evidence indicates that time-dependent, region-specific windows of opportunity for rapid neural reorganization exist alongside continuing plasticity.

Universality *and* Specificity: The Role of Culture

Developmental science is concerned with explaining the nature and characteristics of change. Are developmental changes universal, having the same qualities across ethnic, racial, or socioeconomic status groups, between genders, and from one historical period to another? Or does development depend entirely on the specific group or time within which it occurs? Many classic developmental theories have posited basic similarities in development across different groups and historical periods. Stage theories, like Freud's theory in particular, often specify invariant sequences in personality or cognitive outcomes that are thought to apply to everyone, regardless of culture, group, or historical time. Yet even classic stage theories incorporate sociocultural influences.

In Erikson's psychosocial stage theory, for example, all adolescents confront the task of formulating an adult identity. But the nature of that identity will certainly differ across groups. How complex and arduous a struggle the adolescent might face in forming an identity could vary dramatically depending on her context. Erikson's studies of identity development in two Native American groups, the Sioux in South Dakota and the Yurok on the Pacific coast, and of mainstream White culture revealed different struggles and different outcomes in each (Erikson, 1950/1963).

Some **sociocultural theories**, which trace their roots to the work of Lev Vygotsky (e.g., 1934, 1978; see Chapter 3), argue that cognitive developments may be qualitatively different in different cultures (e.g., Rogoff, 2003; Sternberg, 2014). For example, in Western cultures classifying objects by functional associations (birds with nests) is a trademark of preschoolers' sorting behavior. Hierarchically organized taxonomic classification (e.g., collies and dachshunds grouped as kinds of dogs, dogs and birds grouped as animals) is more typical of elementary-school-age children. Piaget regarded taxonomic sorting to be an indicator of the logical thinking that emerges in middle childhood. But in some ethnic groups, such as the African Kpelle tribe, even adults do not sort objects taxonomically. They use functionally based schemes, perhaps because these are more meaningful in their everyday lives, and they would probably consider such schemes more sophisticated than a taxonomic one (Cole, 1998).

Even sub-cultural groups within the same society may show differences in the development of cognitive skills. For example, in most societies, boys perform better than girls on certain spatial tasks. Yet in a study that included low-, middle-, and high-income children in Chicago, low-income girls performed as well on spatial tasks as low-income boys, even though the usual gender difference was found in the other income groups (Levine, Vasilyeva, Lourenco, Newcombe, & Huttenlocher, 2005). Differences in the typical experiences of children in different social classes are the likely reason for these cognitive variations. Bronfenbrenner (1979) explained how culture could influence behavior through proximal processes, the daily give and take with others in one's social networks that he considered the primary engines of development. Adults in particular are "cultural experts," and their interactions with children embody cultural expectations and ways of doing things (Oyserman, 2017).

The bulk of social science research has been done on a relatively narrow sample of WEIRD (Western, Educated, Industrialized, Rich, and Democratic) people (Henrich, Heine, & Norenzayan, 2010), and developmental research is no exception (Fernald, 2010). Researchers have become acutely aware of the need to discover how developmental processes play out among other groups both within and outside North America to answer questions about universal versus specific developmental trajectories. To this end, culture, race, and ethnicity now have greater prominence in research than in the past, even though these constructs have proven somewhat difficult to define (Corbie-Smith et al., 2008).

Formerly, differences among **racial groups**, like Blacks, Whites, and Asians, were considered to be due to heredity, identifiable primarily by skin color, but also by variations in hair, bone structure, or other physiological markers. The assumption was that these superficial markers were indicators of deeper biological differences. But the range of genetic differences within groups is actually equal to or greater than those between racial groups (Richeson & Sommers, 2016). Racial groupings are now usually seen as social constructions, founded on superficial characteristics that change across time and circumstance (Saperstein, Penner, & Light, 2013). For example, Arab Americans were considered White before the terrorist attacks of September 11, 2001, but now are often considered non-White (Perez & Hirschman, 2010). **Ethnicity** is sometimes used interchangeably with *race*, although this too is problematic. Shared ancestry, language, a common place of origin, and a sense of belonging to the group are elements commonly used to describe membership in an ethnic group.

Adding to the complexity, culture includes a community's shared values, rituals, psychological processes, behavioral norms, and practices (Fiske, Kitayama, Markus, & Nisbett, 1998). The concept clearly overlaps in meaning with "ethnicity." Early studies often represented culture as a kind of "social address" (Bronfenbrenner, 1979) with gender, race, religion, age, language, ethnic heritage, and socioeconomic status as labels signifying aspects of cultural group membership. Think of your own status in relation to the items on this list. Then consider the status of another person you know. How similar to or different from you is this other person? Is there one category that stands out for you when you try to describe her social/cultural address? For someone you consider to be culturally similar to you, do all the labels overlap? Just a little reflection gives you a taste of the dizzying complexity of such distinctions.

Some research demonstrates that shared values might not be the most reliable indicator of culture. For example, a study of values drawn from approximately 169,000 participants from six continents revealed broad agreement in values, contrary to what one might expect. Autonomy, relatedness, and competence were highly ranked across all cultures although some differences were observed for the value of conformity (Fischer & Schwartz, 2011). This finding questions the assumption that cultures are reliably different in their value systems. People in the same cultural group may be too diverse to justify painting with a broad brush. In addition, increasing global migration and trade, as well as worldwide media and information networks, mean that more and more individuals have multiple ethnic/cultural experiences and many may be polycultural in perspective and behavior (Jensen, 2012; Morris, Chiu, & Liu, 2015). Cultural identities can be difficult to pin down. Currently, there is a tendency to move away from static conceptualizations of what constitutes ethnic/cultural group membership and toward more dynamic, process-oriented definitions for these important variables (Brubaker, 2009).

In particular, researchers are concerned about disaggregating social class, or socioeconomic status (SES), from race and ethnic/cultural distinctions. *Socioeconomic status is based on social standing or power, and is defined by characteristics of the adults in a household, including educational background, income, and occupation.* Frequently, variables of race/ethnicity and SES are conflated in research, leading to questionable findings. This conflation comes in at least two forms. First, SES is a characteristic that can directly affect how people perceive an individual's racial identity. If someone is affluent or highly educated, others may assume that she is White; if she is on welfare, others might assume that she is a member of a minority (e.g., Penner & Saperstein, 2008).

Second, SES and race/ethnicity can be conflated when research findings are attributed to one factor without examining the other. A good example of why disaggregation is important comes from a study of preschool children's everyday activities in four cultural communities (Black and White in the United States, Luo in Kenya, and European descent in Porto Allegre, Brazil). Tudge and his colleagues (2006) observed everyday behaviors of preschool children, hypothesizing that each culture provides its young with the kinds of opportunities (e.g., school or work-related activities) deemed important for successful participation in their culture. Equal numbers of high and low SES children within each culture were included to study the intersection of culture and class. The Brazilian children engaged in fewer academic activities compared to White and Kenyan groups. Nonetheless, middle-class Brazilian children were involved in more academic lessons than their working-class counterparts. Kenyan children participated in significantly more work-related activities than all other groups. However, the working-class Kenyan children engaged in twice as much work as those from all other groups, including middle-class Kenyan children.

As complex as the identification of culture is, it is clear that cultural experience is important to development. But does culture have effects only at a superficial level (e.g., learning different behaviors, manners, customs), or are there effects on more fundamental processes, such as information processing and developing brain structures (Fiske, 2009; Kitayama & Park, 2010)? This is precisely the kind of question that experimenters in the field of cultural psychology have taken on (Sternberg, 2014; Wang, 2016).

Consider, for example, the often-cited distinction between the holistic (interdependent) modes of interacting in cultures of the Eastern hemisphere and the analytic (independent) modes in cultures of the Western hemisphere. A body of research now supports the existence of reliable differences beyond just superficial behavioral ones. First, differences have been identified in information processing (attention, understanding cause and effect, memory, and categorization) between people from Eastern and Western cultures (Nisbett & Masuda, 2003). Some analysts have speculated that the historical-cultural antecedents of these processing differences may be ancient ways of viewing the world common to Chinese and Greek societies respectively (Nisbett, Peng, Choi, & Norenzayan, 2001). In turn, each of these ways may have been shaped by the respective economies of those societies (large-scale farming vs. hunting and trading) along with their different physical environments (open plain vs. seaside mountains). Freed from the interdependence required for massive farming and irrigation projects, ancient Greeks, the forebears of Western societies, came to view the world by focusing on central objects. In other words, the ancient Greeks inhabited a world where objects were typically perceived as relatively unchanging and detached from their context. The objects' features (size, shape, color, etc.) were investigated so as to understand their operating rules and to predict and control their operations. Logic and scientific empiricism are related to this perspective on the world.

Needing to pay attention to the larger context in order to thrive, members of Eastern societies such as China focused more holistically on interrelationships, paying as much attention to the field wherein objects existed as to the objects themselves. Understanding the world from this perspective was more likely to incorporate figure-ground relationships and to hold the dialectic of opposing points of view in balance (Nisbett & Masuda, 2003). It could be that these fundamental differences in Greek and Chinese social organization and cognition, based upon geographical constraints and the exigencies of survival, continued to affect the development of people and societies that followed in their wake.

Any study of cultural differences embodies a fundamental wish to see the world as others do. Imagine that you could literally see what people pay attention to as a way of gaining knowledge about their perspective. Seeing the world through the eyes of people who live in the Eastern and Western regions of the globe could be a fruitful place to start because any differences that evolved from long histories of practice might be more obvious. Recent studies of attention and visual processing that compare these two cultural groups, made possible by the development of a variety of advanced technologies, have indeed proved fruitful.

Results of many studies have demonstrated a greater tendency among Eastern participants to attend to context when compared to Western participants who are more likely to attend to central objects (e.g., in photos of animals in complex environments; Boduroglu, Shah, & Nisbett, 2009; Kitayama, Duffy, Kawamura, & Larsen, 2003; Masuda & Nisbett, 2001, 2006). Eastern research subjects also process groups of items in relationship to each other rather than by category (e.g., linking a cow and grass instead of a cow and chicken; Chiu, 1972; Ji, Zhang, & Nisbett, 2004). They typically make judgments of contextual characteristics more quickly than Westerners, and they engage fewer areas of the brain in the process (Goh et al., 2013).The Eastern emphasis on field also extends to making causal attributions for events. When Westerners were asked to explain the reasons for outcomes in athletic competitions or the causes of criminal events, they emphasized internal traits as causal, whereas Easterners gave more contextualized explanations for outcomes (Choi, Nisbett, & Norenzayan, 1999).

In an ingenious study demonstrating the interrelated effects of culture, development, and neuroplasticity, Goh et al. (2007) show that what you pay attention to makes a subtle yet enduring difference in your brain over time. Repeated practice results in changes in the brain that become our preferred modes of thought and action. The cultural shaping of visual processing in the brain was explored in groups of young and old North Americans and East Asians from Singapore. Researchers studied the visual ventral cortex, a complex of brain structures responsible for identifying what is being processed visually (Farah, Rabinowitz, & Quinn, 2000). Some parts of this complex process object information and other parts process background information (see Park & Huang, 2010). The inclusion of older individuals in this study allowed researchers to analyze whether sustained cultural experience with analytic (central object) versus holistic (background/context) processing sculpted the brain in unique ways over time.

During experimental sessions utilizing an adapted functional magnetic resonance imaging (fMR-A) paradigm (see Chapter 2), which shows which parts of the brain are in use during different tasks, all participants viewed pictures of objects in scenes. As you can see in Figure 1.3, young Westerners' and Easterners' brains were similar in where and to what extent they processed objects versus backgrounds. Older participants from both cultures showed reduced processing of objects relative to backgrounds compared to younger participants. But there was an East/West difference in the older participants: The older Asian participants showed much more of a reduction than older Western participants in object processing. These older Asians did not lose their ability to focus on central objects, but they needed to be prompted to do so. For them, holistic processing had become the default mode, suggesting a lifetime cultural habit of attention to context.

FIGURE 1.3 East/West differences in visual processing of younger and older individuals.

Colored areas show brain areas that are active when processing central objects (blue) and background (orange) visual information. Younger Easterners and Westerners show brain activity for visual processing in both central object and background areas. Older Western participants show activity for visual processing of background and reduced processing for central objects. Older Eastern participants show activity in background processing areas but no activity in central object processing areas.

SOURCE: Goh, J. O., & Park, D. C., J. Y. Chiao (Ed.) (2009). Culture sculpts the perceptual brain. *Progress in Brain Research, 178,* 95–111. Elsevier Ltd . Reprinted by Permission of Elsevier Ltd.

MyLab Education Self-Check 1.4

Applications

In this chapter, we discussed the importance of studying human development and introduced you to some of the worldviews and issues central to the field. The value of developmental knowledge to helping professionals cannot be underestimated because it brings an important perspective to practice. This unique perspective includes several elements: a sensitivity to the fact that persons grow and change over time and that their capacities and concerns also shift over the life course; a recognition of the influence of culture and environment over time; an appreciation for scientific knowledge about development; and a commitment to applying this knowledge to improve the lives of people across the lifespan.

Use of research-based developmental knowledge as a kind of meta-theory helps practitioners clarify complex mechanisms underlying human growth and change and sets the stage for effective prevention and intervention of problems (Beauchaine, Neuhaus, Brenner, & Gatzke-Kopp, 2008). Developmentally sensitive research can identify periods within the life span and intra-individual variables that present opportunities for maximal receptivity to certain interventions (Brunswasser & Garber, 2016; Malti, Noam, Beelman, & Sommer, 2016).

A developmental approach to mental health treatment also leads to personalized care because it emphasizes both individual *and* cultural differences. Culturally competent practice is now considered the standard for performance across many helping professions. Early advocates pioneered a set of guidelines that addressed cultural awareness, knowledge, and skills (Arredondo & Perez, 2006; Sue, Arredondo, & McDavis, 1992), and now many helping fields, including medicine, psychology, social work, education, nursing, and others, have incorporated similar aspects within their professional practice guidelines. Table 1.4 shows standards from psychology, nursing, and social work (American Nurses Association, 2015; American Psychological Association, 2003; National Association of Social Workers, 2017). Notice the general level of agreement in what constitutes good practice. The newly developed Multicultural and Social Justice Counseling Standards (Ratts, Singh, Nassar-McMillan, Butler, & McCullough, 2016) represent an even more contextualized approach to professional practice. In addition to the core elements listed in the first column of Table 1.4, these standards advocate awareness of such issues as privilege, power, and oppression insofar as they affect treatment and highlight the increasing diversity of provider–client relationships. Some provider–client identities might be shared (e.g., sexual orientation) or non-shared (e.g., race or immigrant status), but these identities may not always reflect the dominant paradigm of privileged counselor and disadvantaged client. According to these new standards, counselor–client identities and statuses should be addressed directly within the counseling relationship so as to reduce potential barriers to progress.

Knowledge of developmental science helps clinicians in other ways, as well. The helper should be able to distinguish typical developmental perturbations from atypical deviations. A deep understanding of the field allows clinicians to avoid prescriptive solutions based on rigid stage theories of development. Skilled helpers should keep themselves well informed about current research findings while avoiding overgeneralizations from single studies. A simplistic approach to developmental issues typically will miss the mark by ignoring the complexities of interacting factors, including contextual, cultural, and historical influences. The kinds of direct causal connections between experiences and outcomes that would make prediction much easier for helpers are, unfortunately, almost impossible to obtain. We will try to present the best available information that applies to helpers in these chapters; however, it is important to recognize that the field of developmental science is itself continually developing. Helpers and others need to keep an open mind and continually work to accommodate new information as they practice reflection in action.

Full Spectrum Research: Reducing the Divide Between Science and Practice

The gap between research and practice that we discussed earlier in this chapter is important to revisit. You may have already recognized the explosion of "research-based" or "empirically supported" treatments in the world of practice. Perhaps you have become curious about how these terms came to be contemporary buzzwords, de rigueur for any preventive or intervention effort. Have you wondered if these interventions will actually work with clients in your setting? Have you worried that research-based treatment requirements might make you feel constrained or uninspired? The *reflective practitioner model* offers a way to think about this research–practice divide at a personal level, but there is currently a substantial effort among researchers and clinicians to forge a more substantive and practical partnership.

A robust research–practice relationship offers benefits to both parties. Researchers need the input of clinicians to help identify important questions, to provide access to research participants, and to learn what works in the real world to alleviate suffering. Helping professionals understand that they can benefit from scientific advances by improving the quality and delivery of the care they provide (Houck, Forcehimes, Davis, & Bogenschutz, 2016). Needless or ineffective treatments will not improve individual or public health, and may actually do harm. Furthermore, resources like time and money, especially when they are limited, need to be targeted in ways that promise maximum benefit.

However, the path from scientific discovery to adoption by practitioners is generally not a straight line. Students of science know that people were aware of the existence

TABLE 1.4 Standards for Cultural Competence Across Three Helping Professions

CATEGORY	PSYCHOLOGY (APA, 2003)	NURSING (ANA, 2015)	SOCIAL WORK (NASW, 2017)
Self-Awareness	Understand that one's beliefs and values might be different from those of clients, become aware of personal attitudes, and work to increase contacts with diverse groups.	Understand one's personal beliefs, values, and cultural heritage.	Develop an understanding of personal values and beliefs. Recognize how personal identities, power, and privilege affect professional practice.
Sensitivity to/Gaining Knowledge About Other Cultures	Increase knowledge about others' worldviews, including the effects of stigmatization. Become knowledgeable about social policies that affect other cultures.	Become a life-long learner about different cultural worldviews and diverse ways of perceiving and acting in the world. Demonstrate respect and equitable treatment for all consumers of healthcare.	Continue to develop knowledge about cultural differences in areas such as race, ethnicity, gender, immigrant and refugee status, tribal heritage, sexual identity, age, mental and emotional disability, etc.
Professional Training	Infuse multicultural information into professional training and include it in coursework in psychology in general.	Work toward a multicultural workforce through education, retention, and recruitment policies. Provide training and continuing education in culturally congruent care and global health issues.	Participate in training and continuing lifelong education that advances cultural competence.
Research	Conduct culturally sensitive, ethical research. Ethnic, racial, and linguistic differences should be considered in research design, analysis, interpretation, and assessment.		
Skills for Practice	Apply culturally appropriate clinical skills in practice by focusing on the client within his or her cultural context, using culturally appropriate assessment tools, and having a broad repertoire of interventions.	Engage in culturally competent practice. Recognize acculturation stage and attendant needs of healthcare consumers. Consider the impact of discrimination and oppression in vulnerable groups as they affect health outcomes. Respect consumer decisions based on cultural norms. Employ culturally relevant verbal and nonverbal communication skills and interventions with evidence to support effectiveness with diverse groups.	Utilize a broad array of culturally appropriate skills and techniques and understand what role culture plays in the helping process. Utilize resources and services as appropriate when serving diverse client groups.
Operations of Organizations and Systems; Social Justice Advocacy	Apply culturally informed organizational practices and expand professional role to change agent.	Advocate for culturally competent care through policies that promote health and reduce harm among diverse or under-represented groups. Advocate for equal access to care and inclusion of patient's cultural beliefs in all aspects of health care.	Be aware of the effect of social policies and programs on diverse client populations and advocate for them whenever appropriate. Demonstrate leadership in communicating information about diverse groups to others. When appropriate, engage in policy development that advocates for disadvantaged and underrepresented groups. Advocate for diversity within the profession and assume leadership for advocacy efforts in the broader community when appropriate.

of microbes in the 16th century but disregarded their role in disease transmission. Instead, diseases were believed to be caused by miasmas (i.e., malodorous, poisonous clouds or vapors). Before the paradigmatic shift that cast miasmas into disrepute, 19th-century physicians in English hospitals routinely transitioned from performing autopsies to delivering babies without any preliminary ablutions. Rates of puerperal fever were understandably high, and it took determined research and advocacy from scientists like Semmelweis and others to shift awareness (Nuland, 2004). Even though scientific evidence might be clear on a certain subject, changing actual helping behavior is quite a different matter. Currently, despite evidence of its importance, only 40% of hospital personnel actually comply with standard hand-washing guidelines according to a meta-analysis of 98 studies (Erasmus et al., 2010). Efforts to change and improve health as well as clinical practice must be responsive to real people in real environments and provide more than convincing data.

Young and Borland (2011) argue that the research–practice gap exists because each group sees the world a little differently and uses knowledge differently. Research often proceeds in a top-down fashion. Researchers generate questions to be studied and tend to generalize their findings to large groups (e.g.,"best practice"). In contrast, practitioners serve real people and tend to use interventions that work in individuals' real-world contexts. Fortunately, a general consensus supported by the National Institutes of Health (https://ncats.nih.gov/translation) has coalesced around the need to move basic science from the laboratory to sustainable, practical, effective implementation. Translational research, or research "from bench to bedside" (Woolf, 2008), is the term commonly used to describe the spectrum of steps involved in this process. Originating from within the field of medicine, translational research starts with basic questions about mechanisms of action and translates knowledge gleaned from laboratory studies, which sometimes use animal models, into interventions with humans. An example of basic research might be identifying biomarkers for diabetes, while clinical research might involve the development and testing of biomarker assessments in controlled clinical trials as well as in real-world public health settings. Throughout the process, knowledge is refined and reassessed to allow for accurate information about individual or group differences to emerge and reshape interventions. Ultimately,

dissemination and implementation of innovations are translated into policy for appropriate patient groups (Rubio et al., 2010).

The translational research approach has been applied to many fields, from medicine (Waxman, 2005; Woolf, 2008) to developmental psychopathology (Cicchetti & Toth, 2006) to prevention science (Fishbein, Ridenour, Stahl, & Sussman, 2016). Findings from each step in the spectrum generate new questions, and each step requires distinct kinds of research methods. Knowledge from other disciplines is integrated into this process if it pertains to the problem under investigation. The field of molecular biology and epigenetics (see Chapter 2), for example, can inform many questions about attachment in early childhood. A key feature of translational research, called *back translation*, describes the recursive process of applying research findings to real-world settings, making revisions based on evidence, and then reassessing.

One model of translational research applied to youth development (see Figure 1.4) illustrates the multidirectional nature of this work (Hamilton, 2015).

Consider a hypothetical example using this framework. Epidemiological survey data show a higher rate of school dropout for certain populations (Quadrant 1). Basic research suggests links among dropping out, drug abuse, and unsupportive adult relationships (Quadrant 2). Prevention and treatment programs are developed to reduce the risk factors for dropping out and to enhance the protective factors that engage students in schooling (see the Focus on Developmental Psychopathology section). These programs are studied in well-controlled implementations, and results are used to improve the efficacy, accessibility, and acceptability

FIGURE 1.4 A model of translational research on youth development.

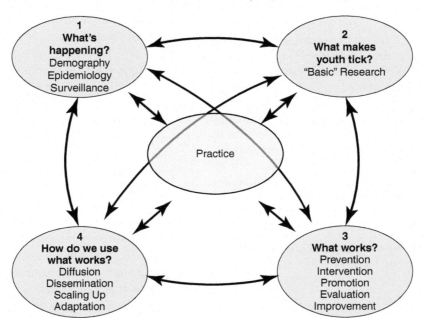

SOURCE: Hamilton, S. F. (2015). Translational research and youth development. *Applied Developmental Science, 19*, 60-73.

of interventions (Quadrant 3). Findings that programs are ineffective for certain groups of adolescents will send researchers back to the drawing board to make adaptations. For example, if an intervention is effective for males but less so for females, modifications are made and research trials continue. If epidemiological studies or basic research (Quadrants 1 and 2) provide new information about other variables that lead to dropping out, interventions (Quadrant 3) may also be revised to accommodate this knowledge. When support for the intervention reaches a significant level across many trials, the science of implementation research is applied to promote widespread adoption in real-world settings (Quadrant 4). Each quadrant influences and is influenced by the others, with the overall goal of making scientific knowledge practical, effective, and context sensitive.

What Helpers Should Know About Choosing Prevention or Intervention Programs: Some Rules of Thumb

Historically, clinicians interested in community-based mental health programs differentiated among primary, secondary, and tertiary prevention. **Primary prevention** is an attempt to forestall the development of problems by promoting health and wellness in the general population through group-oriented interventions. Requiring mandatory vaccinations for children or providing developmental guidance activities in schools might constitute primary prevention activities. **Secondary prevention** is an attempt to reduce the incidence of disorders among those who are at high risk or to provide treatment to forestall the development of more serious psychopathology in cases that are already established. Programs developed to identify students at risk for dropping out of school and to provide them with remedial programs might be examples of secondary-level prevention. In this case, a selected sample, rather than the general population, receives services. **Tertiary prevention** is directed toward rehabilitating persons with established disorders.

Because of the need to distinguish between the concepts of tertiary prevention and treatment, another way of categorizing types of prevention was suggested by the Institute of Medicine report (Institute of Medicine, 1994): universal, selective, and indicated. These three levels of prevention are clearly differentiated from treatment, which in this model is similar to tertiary prevention. **Universal prevention** is directed to the general population. **Selective prevention** targets individuals at some epidemiological risk, such as low-birth-weight babies. **Indicated prevention** addresses individuals who show subclinical symptoms of disorders, such as children whose behavioral problems are not yet serious enough to warrant a diagnosis of conduct disorder.

Some general points may be helpful to keep in mind when choosing which options to employ for prevention and treatment.

- *Understand why science is helpful to you:* Helping professionals base their decisions on scientific data derived from research in order to "do no harm." Science

has a formal way to investigate problems and draw conclusions about outcomes using statistical and other methods. Questions such as "Does this program or treatment work?" are subjected to a rigorous process so that conclusions can be as free from personal bias as possible. When evidence is aggregated, such as in meta-analyses that report results from multiple studies, the evidence can be particularly significant. As with any scientific endeavor, knowledge builds relatively slowly and is buttressed by repeated observations of similar results. Sometimes we have expectations that a practice or intervention works based on our own personal preferences or experience. However, this is not sufficient to justify program adoption from a scientific standpoint. There are a number of rigorous safeguards built into the research process that render its outcomes more likely to be correct than many other methods of proof. When consumers want to commit time and resources to programs or practices, it's ethical to consider the best evidence available.

The scientific research method also assumes that researchers will share their methods and ideas with others so that their work can be reviewed and improved. In essence, it is a collective process where many people are involved in furthering knowledge, reducing personal bias, and building an evidence base. The ultimate goal is that all findings become part of a public knowledge base for the good of the whole.

- *Be an informed consumer of information about the program or practice:* Be cautious about the sources of information you accept before adoption. A few conditions should be met to assure a basic standard of evidence. First, the intervention should be researched using established scientific methods. Then, a report of the study (called a paper or an article) should be reviewed by peers (other scientists familiar with the area). This process is called "peer review." Not all journals publish original research or utilize peer review, so it is important to differentiate a research journal from an "opinion" journal. Once the work has been reviewed by peers and has met professional standards, it can be readied for publication. Sometimes, reviews of interventions are published online but have not been given this kind of scrutiny. For example, program developers may hire private experts or consultants to do an evaluation of a program or a new treatment. In these cases, the reports are not subject to peer review in order to reduce bias. In addition, program evaluation results may include descriptive information, but not careful statistical analyses. Furthermore, some evaluation reports do not include any type of comparison group. Without any control or comparison group, consumers cannot tell if program effects were the result of the intervention or something else. This level of evidence does not meet the standard for empirical support.

Testimonials from satisfied clients certainly may be helpful, but they cannot be considered research evidence. Prospective program adopters may find personal anecdotes, recommendations, quotes, and other endorsements interesting and even compelling, but they are not sufficient. Remember that testimonials do not always include participants who fail to provide glowing reviews. There is no substitute for peer review if you are serious about scientific evidence.

- *Remember that ethics matter:* Scientific researchers are required to follow ethical guidelines in conducting and reporting research. Researchers are expected to describe in detail what their intervention involves. This makes it possible for others to replicate their research. Researchers should not overstate the outcomes of a study or draw conclusions that are not derived from the analyses. It is questionable to oversell program effectiveness if the results do not support such results directly, and if the evidence base is limited. This is an important caveat for potential consumers.

SOME FINAL TAKE-AWAY MESSAGES

- Contemporary practice guidelines advocate the use of empirically based prevention and treatment options that are appropriate to the individual or group.

- Although many programs and treatments are advertised as "empirically or research-based," these terms may be used loosely and inaccurately.

- Always look for supporting documentation that shows programs have been studied in a reputable way. The best way to see this evidence is through peer-reviewed publications. This guarantees that others, not just program developers, have reviewed the evidence objectively and without compensation. It also makes it possible to see if the program or intervention might be useful in your setting with your client population. You can also access online resources that provide evidence summaries relevant to interventions for practitioners in various fields (Rousseau & Gunea, 2016). Examples are the Cochrane Library, www.cochranelibrary.com for health care professionals, and the Campbell Library, www.campbellcollaboration.org for educators, social workers, and social scientists in general.

- The careful application of the scientific process to studying interventions provides a means of quality control that ultimately helps all professionals. It assures that claims are legitimate, have passed the test of scientific research, and will move the work of practice forward.

Focus on Developmental Psychopathology

In several chapters of this text, you will find sections titled *Focus on Developmental Psychopathology*, which highlight developmental approaches to specific behavioral disorders. These sections emphasize work in the field of developmental psychopathology, offering clinicians a unique perspective on dysfunctional behavior by integrating work from many disciplines, including developmental psychology, clinical psychology, abnormal psychology, biology, and genetics. This field takes a life span perspective on aberrant behavior by assuming that it is an outgrowth of complex but lawful developmental processes (e.g., Rutter & Sroufe, 2000). Unhealthy social, emotional, and behavioral processes, like depression or conduct disorder, emerge in the same way that healthy ones do: as a function of the individual's attempts to adapt to her environment in interaction with the environment's actions on the individual. Behaviors or coping strategies that are adaptive in one developmental circumstance can be maladaptive in other concurrent contexts, or they may establish a trajectory that can result in maladaptive outcomes later. "In contrast to the often dichotomous world of mental disorder/nondisorder depicted in psychiatry, a developmental psychopathology perspective recognizes that normality often fades into abnormality, adaptive and maladaptive may take on differing definitions depending on whether one's time referent is immediate circumstances or long-term development, and processes within the individual can be characterized as having shades or degrees of psychopathology" (Cicchetti & Toth, 2006, p. 498).

Developmental psychopathology is largely guided by multidimensional or systems theories of development (e.g., Cicchetti & Sroufe, 2000; Cicchetti & Toth, 2006; Rutter & Sroufe, 2000; Sameroff, 2000; Sameroff & MacKenzie, 2003). Every individual is seen as an active organism, influenced by multiple levels of internal processes, and continuously adapting to multiple embedded contexts. Increasingly, culture is also viewed as something that one "develops" over time through an intricate interplay of biology and environment. More than a fixed social group membership with only higher-order, macrosystem effects, culture should be viewed as a primary, proximal influence on development, affecting the course of beneficial and harmful outcomes as the person progresses through the life span (Causadias, 2013). Abnormality results from the same proximal processes that produce more normative patterns: As the individual transacts with the environment, she attempts to meet her needs and to adjust to environmental inputs and demands. She brings both strengths and vulnerabilities to these transactions, and the environment contributes both stressors and supports. Both the individual and the environment are somewhat altered by each transaction, reciprocally influencing each other. That is, the change processes are bidirectional. The individual's strengths and vulnerabilities as well as environmental stressors and supports are all variables or factors that impact the overall development of the individual. Both healthy and unhealthy outcomes are the result of the interplay of the individual's characteristics *and* her experiences across time. "Single factors can be potent in destroying systems . . . a gunshot can destroy a child. But single factors cannot *create* a child or any other living system" (Sameroff, 2000, p. 37).

The individual's strengths and the environment's supports are **protective factors**, helping to promote healthy outcomes; the individual's vulnerabilities and the environmental stressors she experiences are **risk factors** that can interfere with healthy development. Among the individual's characteristics that may matter are various genetic and other biological factors, temperamental traits, cognitive capacities, social skills, attitudes, beliefs, and so on. Among the environmental factors are socioeconomic status, safety of the neighborhood, quality of the schools, family history and culture, parental nurturing and monitoring, peer attitudes, friendships, marital and community supports, cultural dynamics including racial and ethnic processes, and so on.

You may recognize that many of these risks seem to fit together. As Garbarino (1999) points out, many children "fall victim to the unfortunate synchronicity between the demons inhabiting their own internal world and the corrupting influences of modern American culture" (p. 23). So, not only do risks gain power as they accumulate, but they also operate in clusters that serve as "correlated constraints" (Cairns & Cairns, 1994). In other words, they reinforce each other by their redundancy and work together to shape the developmental trajectory. As a result, although altering one or just a few risk factors *can* have a positive impact on behavior and outcomes, sometimes such limited changes have little effect because the other related risks maintain the status quo.

Certain risks, as well as certain protections, become more important at different points in development. For example, the protection offered by prosocial peers and the risks associated with exposure to deviant ones are particularly powerful as children approach adolescence but less so in early childhood (Bolger & Patterson, 2003). On the other hand, some protections, such as authoritative parenting, appear to retain their power throughout childhood and adolescence. Some risk factors (e.g., deficits in perspective taking or problems with peer relationships) may be related to the development of multiple disorders, such as conduct disorder or depression.

Work in developmental psychopathology has brought into focus the importance of both *mediating* and *moderating* relationships between variables or factors in development. Let's begin with **mediating variables**. Suppose that one factor appears to be a cause of some behavioral outcome. For example, when a child experiences early, pervasive poverty, she is at higher risk than other children for developing mental health problems and medical diseases

in adulthood, from depression to cardiovascular disease to some cancers (Chen, 2004). Even if children's economic circumstances improve in later childhood or adulthood, the increased risk of adult problems persists. One mediating variable that links early poverty to later health vulnerability is a compromised immune system. Specifically, poor children are more prone to inflammation. Changes in the functioning of certain genes cause this "pro-inflammatory profile," which lasts into adulthood and can contribute to poor health, including some mental health problems like depression (Chen, Miller, Kobor, & Cole, 2011).

Moderating variables are those that affect the strength of the relationship between other variables (Baron & Kenny, 1986). They interact with causal factors, altering and sometimes even eliminating their effects on outcome variables. For example, researchers have found that not all adults exposed to early poverty are characterized by a "pro-inflammatory profile" (Chen, Miller, Kobor, & Cole, 2011). Adults who suffered chronic early poverty but who report having a warm, supportive relationship with their mothers in childhood often have normal immune system functioning. Warm mothering appears to be a protective factor that *moderates* the impact of early poverty, a risk factor. See Figure 1.5 for a graphic illustration of both mediating and moderating factors related to early poverty's effects.

Recent research in psychopathology has focused on the role of **endophenotypes** as mediators and moderators. *Endophenotypes* are biobehavioral processes that can be traced to genes. These processes serve as intermediary links between the actual genes that contribute to disorders and their expressed behavioral manifestations. The "pro-inflammatory profile" that serves as a mediator between early childhood poverty and later mental and physical health problems is an example of an endophenotype, because it has been found to result from epigenetic processes (Chen et al., 2011; see Chapter 2). Lenroot and Giedd (2011) artfully describe endophenotypes as "bridges between molecules and behavior" (p. 429). Study of these intermediary links can help us better understand the processes by which genetic information exerts influence on observable behavior (Gottesman & Gould, 2003).

Because so many interacting factors are involved, there is no such thing as perfect prediction of who will have healthy outcomes, who will not, when problems may arise, and how they will evolve. A rough guideline for prediction is that the more risk factors and the fewer protective factors there are, the more likely an individual is to have adjustment problems. Developmental psychopathology also recognizes two axiomatic principles: *multifinality* and *equifinality* (e.g., Cicchetti & Rogosch, 1996). The **principle of multifinality** is that individual pathways of development may result in a wide range of possible outcomes. For example, children exhibiting conduct-disordered behavior in the elementary school years may, as adults, display one or more of several different disorders, including antisocial personality, depression, substance abuse, and so on. The complementary **principle of equifinality** specifies that different early developmental pathways can produce similar outcomes. For example, Sroufe (1989) has demonstrated two pathways,

FIGURE 1.5 Example of mediating and moderating variables.

The effects of chronic poverty on adult susceptibility to health problems are *mediated* by immune system changes and can be *moderated* by warm mother-child relationships.

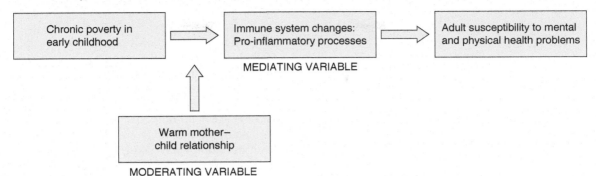

one primarily biological and one primarily related to parenting style, that lead to attention-deficit hyperactivity disorder (ADHD). Using these ideas from systems theory allows for the study of multiple subgroups and multiple pathways to disorders. Most important, it allows for a more realistic look at the problems people face (Cicchetti & Toth, 1994).

Here again, biobehavioral research is taking us a step closer to making better predictions about who will be affected by disorders and who will have more healthy outcomes. It may also help us unravel the mystery of multifinality. For example, why do some emotionally abused children become depressed as they age while others develop substance abuse disorders? Research on transdiagnostic risk factors (Nolen-Hoeksema & Watson, 2011), which are conceptually similar to endophenotypes, takes a close look at how risk factors other than the target one (e.g., history of emotional abuse) may moderate the effects of the target factor. Assessment of the moderating impact of different risk factors on each other is aimed at explaining "divergent trajectories": how different disorders evolve from the same target risk factors. Careful explication of these intervening sequences supports the fundamental goals of these new scientific fields.

Two primary goals of developmental psychopathology are to increase the probability of successfully predicting problematic outcomes and to find ways of preventing them. Developmental psychopathology is therefore closely linked to the field of prevention science, which aims at designing and testing prevention and intervention techniques for promoting healthy development in at-risk groups. Developmental psychopathologists also emphasize the value of studying individuals at the extremes of disordered behavior, for the purpose of enlightening us about how developmental processes work for everyone. Consider one example: Typically developing children eventually form a coherent and relatively realistic notion of self, so that they distinguish the self from others; they differentiate the real from the imagined; they form integrated memories of what they have done and experienced, and so on (see Chapters 5 and 7). Our understanding of when and how a coherent sense of self emerges in normal development has benefited from studies of maltreated children whose sense of self is often disorganized. In one study comparing maltreated with non-maltreated preschoolers, maltreated children showed substantially more dissociative behaviors, such as talking to imaginary playmates, being forgetful or confused about things the child should know, and lying to deny misbehavior even when the evidence is clear (Macfie, Cicchetti, & Toth, 2001). Note that all of these kinds of behaviors are typical of preschoolers *sometimes*. But finding that non-maltreated preschoolers are less likely to engage in these behaviors than maltreated youngsters helps substantiate two things: First, relationships with caregivers are important to the development of a coherent self-system, and second, typically developing preschoolers are beginning to form a cohesive self-system even though the process is not complete.

The field of developmental psychopathology has several practical implications for clinical practice. First, interventions and treatments need to be developmentally appropriate to be effective. One approach will not fit all situations or age groups. For example, maltreated preschoolers showing signs of excessive dissociative behavior can be helped to form a more coherent self-system if helpers intervene with primary caregivers to increase their positivity, sensitivity, and responsivity (see Chapters 4 and 5); interventions with adults who suffer from dissociative behaviors would require other approaches. Second, periods throughout the life span marked by disequilibrium or disorganization with resultant reorganization may be considered points at which individuals might be most receptive to change. Developmental psychopathologists suggest that at these sensitive periods, interventions may be most effective because the individual can incorporate treatment into newly emerging levels of cognitive, emotional, and behavioral organization. Thus, the issue of timing of interventions is one of great interest to this field. In addition, the wide variety of possible pathways and outcomes involved in the development of psychopathology is an argument for the use of multiple means of intervention and treatment. However, interventions should be carefully considered and based on a thoughtful assessment of a person's developmental level and quality of adaptation, the contexts that the person must function within, and the availability of external supports. This discipline's ideas and research findings hold out great promise for helpers.

Summary

Reflection and Action

1. The fields of counseling and human development have long been linked. Counselors are dedicated to the enhancement of human development, and researchers in human development provide counselors with theories and data that can contribute to therapeutic practice. In the approach to counseling called reflective practice, developmental research and theory are among the resources counselors use to generate hypotheses about appropriate problem solutions, which the counselor will then test and revise in practice. The more extensive and well organized the counselor's knowledge of basic developmental issues, the more able the counselor will be to retrieve developmental information that is useful to problem solving.

A Historical Perspective on Developmental Theories

2. Scientific theories of human development began to emerge in the 19th century, tracing their roots to the writings of 17th- and 18th-century philosophers, and were influenced by Darwin's theory of evolution and by the growth of universal education. Traditional theories of human development either emphasized discontinuity (stage theories) or continuity (incremental change theories). In stage theories, a person's activities share some common characteristics during the period called a stage; these characteristics change qualitatively as the person moves from one stage to another. Stages occur in a fixed sequence, though different individuals may progress through the stages at different rates.

3. In Freud's theory of psychosexual stages, personality develops in childhood through five periods: the oral, the anal, the phallic, the latency, and, finally, the genital stages. A child moves from one stage to another as the biological self, or id, changes. At each stage, the child's experiences of need fulfillment play a critical role in the formation and further development of the other aspects of personality—the ego and the superego. Although there is little evidence to support Freud's developmental theory, it has influenced other theories, and Freud's ideas are so widely known that they are a part of our culture.

4. In Erikson's eight psychosocial stages of development, personal identity and interpersonal attitudes are expanded and reworked throughout the life span. At each stage, changes in the individual's needs or abilities or changes in societal expectations create new challenges or crises. As each crisis is faced, a new aspect of self-concept emerges, along with feelings or attitudes toward others. If others are sensitive and responsive to the individual's needs during a given stage, positive feelings will result. If the individual's needs are not adequately met, predominantly negative feelings toward self or others may be the consequence. Erikson's emphasis on explaining the development of feelings about self and other has been appealing to helping professionals, and many of his ideas are compatible with findings from developmental research on issues such as attachment formation and the development of self-esteem.

5. Piaget's cognitive developmental theory describes changes in children's logical thinking skills through four stages. Infants in the sensorimotor stage do not yet have the capacity for representational thought. Children in the stage of preoperational thought, from 2 to 7 years of age, can think, but their thinking is not yet logical. In the concrete operational stage, 7- to 11-year-olds think logically, but they do so most effectively if what they are thinking about can be directly related to the concrete, real world. By the formal operational stage, however, young adolescents begin to be able to think logically about abstract concepts. Although many details of Piaget's theory are no longer considered correct, his general characterizations of children's abilities at different ages are widely seen as useful descriptions.

6. Incremental theories of development come in many different forms, but they all characterize behavioral change as a gradual, step-by-step process. Learning theories, for example, emphasize that behavior changes as children learn responses through the processes of classical and operant conditioning. Social learning theories stress one more learning process: modeling, or observational learning. All learning theories portray any change in behavior as a result of specific experiences, affecting specific behaviors. Development results from many independent changes in many different behaviors or mental processes.

7. Among incremental models are many information processing theories. As the mind attends to, analyzes, and stores information, there are gradual changes in the amount of information stored, in the availability of strategies to process information or solve problems, in the links established between or among pieces of information, and perhaps in the size of one's attentional capacity. Most of these changes are limited to whatever kind of information is being processed, so that, for example, acquiring a new strategy for adding or subtracting numbers does not affect the strategies a child might use in reading. Thus, development involves the accrual of small changes within specific domains of knowledge rather than broad, sweeping changes that affect many domains at once.

8. Classic theories have typically addressed a set of core issues in their attempts to characterize development, such as:

Are developmental changes qualitative or quantitative? Contemporary theories of development acknowledge that the answer to any such question is "Both."

Contemporary Multidimensional or Systems Theories: Embracing the Complexity of Development

9. Contemporary theories incorporate the complexity of interacting and divergent causal processes in development. There are many of these multidimensional or systems theories, but they are quite similar in the assumptions about and descriptions of developmental process. They are broad in scope, explaining both cognitive and social developments. Changes in behavior are the result of causes both within the organism and in the environment. These causes mutually influence one another as well as behavior. In Bronfenbrenner's bioecological model, for example, all developments are seen as the result of proximal processes—reciprocal interactions between an active organism and its immediate environment. More distal processes modify proximal processes and include aspects of the organism, such as genetic functioning, and aspects of the environment, such as family structure or cultural institutions. Proximal processes, such as a child's particular interactions with peers or adults, also influence distal processes, such as the child's internal physiological functioning or the dynamic structure of the child's family. In life span developmental theories, these same complex processes continue to influence change throughout adulthood.

10. Applying a particular developmental model to the assessment of a client's needs can assist helping professionals in organizing what they know about a client and gaining insight into how to intervene. But our theories also provide a set of blinders, focusing our attention on some aspects of a situation and reducing the visibility of other aspects. Maintaining an awareness of our own theoretical biases can help us avoid the problems of a narrowed perspective.

A New Look at Three Developmental Issues

11. Among the core issues that classic developmental theorists often addressed is whether nature (genes) or nurture (environment) is more important in development. Although specific theories often focus attention on the importance of just one type of cause, research has established that for most behavioral developments, genetic and environmental processes interact, mutually affecting each other and the behavior in question. Modern multidimensional theories take into account the complexity of this interdependency.

12. Another core issue addresses the question of whether some behaviors can develop only at certain crucial times in the life span (critical/sensitive periods) or whether the brain and behavior can change at any time (neuroplasticity). Some have argued, for example, that learning language is best accomplished in the preschool years. If critical periods for the development of behaviors like language exist, a further question (which may have different answers depending on the behavior) concerns whether developmental changes in the brain could be the source of time-limited opportunities for learning or whether favorable environmental conditions are simply more likely to exist in some developmental periods than in others.

13. A third core issue is whether some aspects of development (e.g., cognitive stages) are universal or whether some or all developments are specific to the individual's cultural context. In the past, much of developmental research focused on Western, middle-class samples, based on the assumption that fundamental developmental processes work the same way across all groups. But modern researchers more often investigate cultural, racial, ethnic, gender, and socioeconomic variations in developmental processes and outcomes. Multidimensional theories recognize the importance of context as causal in development, and current research supports the conclusion that the effects of factors such as culture are more than skin deep: They can change brain functioning over time.

Case Study

Anna is a 9-year-old third-grade student in a public school on the outskirts of a large industrial city. She is the oldest of three children who live in an apartment with their mother, a 29-year-old White woman recently diagnosed with rheumatoid arthritis. Despite her young age, Anna's past history is complicated. Anna's biological father, Walter, is a 37-year-old man who emigrated from Eastern Europe when he was in his early 20s. He married Anna's mother, Karen, when she was 19 years old. The couple married hastily and had a child, Anna, but Walter abandoned the

family shortly after Anna's birth. Walter and Karen had fought constantly about his problems with alcohol. Karen was particularly upset about Walter's behavior because her own father, now deceased, had suffered from alcoholism and left her mother without sufficient resources to care for herself.

Alone with a child to support and only a high school degree, Karen went to work in the office of a small family-owned business. There she met Frank, one of the drivers who worked sporadically for the company. They married within a few months of meeting and, within another year, had a son named John. Karen, with Frank's grudging consent, decided not to tell Anna about her biological father. She reasoned that Anna deserved to believe that Frank, who filled the role of father to both children, was her real parent. Anna was developing normally and seemed to be attached to Frank. But, unknown to Karen, Frank had some problems of his own. He had been incarcerated for theft as a young man and had an inconsistent employment history. The family struggled to stay together through many ups and downs. When Anna was 6, Karen became pregnant again. Frank wanted Karen to have an abortion because he didn't think the family's finances could support another child. Karen refused, saying that she would take on another job once the new baby was born. Ultimately, the marriage did not survive the many stresses the couple faced, and Karen and Frank were divorced when Anna was 7.

Karen's situation at work is tenuous because of her medical condition. Her employer balks at making accommodations for her, and she fears she might be let go. After the divorce, Karen filed for child support, and Frank was directed to pay a certain amount each month for the three children, but Frank was outraged that he should have to pay for Anna's care because she was not his biological child. During a particularly difficult conversation, Frank told Anna the "truth" that he was not her "real" father. Karen, still unable to deal with this issue, insisted to Anna that Frank

was her biological parent. Karen could not bring herself to mention Walter, whose existence had never been mentioned to the children before. Karen desperately needed the money for Anna's support, especially because she had amassed substantial credit card debt. She felt her only pleasure was watching shopping shows on TV and ordering items for her children.

In school, Anna is struggling to keep up with her peers. Her academic performance is a full grade level behind, and her teachers are concerned. The school Anna attends has high academic standards and pressures for achievement are intense. Anna behaves in immature ways with peers and adults, alternating between excessive shyness and overly affectionate behavior. She does not appear to have any friendships within the class.

Discussion Questions

1. Consider Anna's development with regard to the following issues or concepts: contributions of nature, contributions of nurture, interaction of nature and nurture, proximal processes, distal processes.
2. Can you predict outcomes? Consider issues of continuity and change.
3. What are the strengths and weaknesses of each of the family members?
4. What environmental modifications would be helpful to promote healthy developmental outcomes? Be specific about each family member.

Practice Using What You Have Learned

MyLab Education Application Exercise 1.1: Examining Bronfenbrenner's Multidimensional Model
MyLab Education Application Exercise 1.2: Case Study: Nature and Nurture in Beliefs About Teaching

Journal Questions

1. What do you hope to gain from this course? What are your specific learning goals?
2. The debate on the value of empirically based knowledge versus applied knowledge can be related to a course such as this. Empirically based knowledge is often explanatory, providing reasons that answer the question "Why does this happen?" Applied knowledge provides solutions and answers the question "What should I do about this?" As a helping professional, and as an educated person, what are your views on this debate?

3. Reflect on how the translational research model can be helpful to you as a clinician. What practical questions do you have that might be studied using the translational research process?
4. This chapter suggests that developmental knowledge could serve as a meta-theory that can organize your approach to helping clients. Describe a client or situation you have encountered or may encounter. Describe the problem situation and include some ways that developmental science can help you inform your approach to practice.

Key Concepts

life span development (p. 2)
reflective practice (p. 3)
stage (p. 7)
psychoanalytic theory (p. 8)
id (p. 8)
pleasure principle (p. 8)
ego (p. 9)
reality principle (p. 9)
superego (p. 9)
Freud's psychosexual stages (p. 9)
oral stage (p. 9)
oral fixation (p. 9)
critical (sensitive) period (p. 9)
anal stage (p. 10)
phallic stage (p. 10)
latency stage (p. 10)
genital stage (p. 10)
Erikson's psychosocial stages (p. 10)
trust versus mistrust (p. 10)
autonomy versus shame and doubt (p. 11)
Piaget's cognitive development theory (p. 12)
sensorimotor stage (p. 12)
preoperational stage (p. 12)
concrete operational stage (p. 12)
formal operational stage (p. 12)
décalages (p. 12)

hierarchical integration (p. 13)
self-organizing (p. 13)
constructivist (p. 13)
incremental models (p. 13)
behaviorist tradition (p. 13)
classical (respondent) conditioning (p. 14)
operant conditioning (p. 14)
respondent (p. 14)
conditioned stimulus (p. 14)
conditioned response (p. 14)
operant (p. 14)
reinforcement (p. 14)
positive reinforcement (p. 14)
negative reinforcement (p. 14)
social learning theories (p. 14)
modeling (p. 14)
generalization (p. 15)
information processing theories (p. 15)
multidimensional (systems) theories (p. 16)
bidirectional processes (p. 16)
Bronfenbrenner's bioecological theory (p. 17)
proximal processes (p. 17)
distal processes (p. 17)
demand characteristics (p. 17)
microsystem (p. 19)

mesosystem (p. 19)
exosystem (p. 19)
macrosystem (p. 19)
life span developmental theories (p. 19)
epigenetics (p. 29)
neuroplasticity (p. 22)
sociocultural theories (p. 23)
racial group (p. 23)
ethnicity (p. 23)
culture (p. 24)
socioeconomic status (SES) (p. 24)
translational research (p. 29)
primary prevention (p. 30)
secondary prevention (p. 30)
tertiary prevention (p. 30)
universal prevention (p. 30)
selective prevention (p. 30)
indicated prevention (p. 30)
developmental psychopathology (p. 31)
protective factors (p. 32)
risk factors (p. 32)
mediating variables (p. 32)
moderating variables (p. 32)
endophenotypes (p. 32)
principle of multifinality (p. 32)
principle of equifinality (p. 32)
prevention science (p. 33)

Chapter 2

Genetics, Epigenetics, and the Brain: The Fundamentals of Behavioral Development

 Learning Objectives

After reading this chapter, you should be able to:

2.1 Describe genetic and epigenetic processes in development and the coaction of heredity and the environment in mutually influencing development.

2.2 Identify cause-and-effect relationships between factors that influence atypical development and consequential outcomes.

2.3 Describe prenatal and early postnatal brain development including brain structures and neuron structures and functions.

2.4 Explain the central role of the brain in mediating stress-induced adaptations and recognize correlations between allostatic overload and the effects of subsequent epigenetic alterations.

Leo and George are identical twins. When they were born, George was a half-pound heavier than Leo, but otherwise they were so much alike that most people could not tell them apart. As they grew, friends and family used different tricks to distinguish them. If you were very observant, for instance, you might notice that George had a mole low on his left cheek, almost at the chin line. Leo also had a mole, but it was located just above his left cheekbone. Nonetheless, the boys were similar enough that they occasionally amused themselves by standing in for each other—fooling their third-grade teachers for a whole day of school or switching places with their junior prom dates. They had a shared passion for music and were gifted instrumentalists by their late teens. Yet, the boys also began to diverge more and more, both physically and psychologically. Leo's hair was somewhat lighter than George's by early adolescence; George was more agile on the soccer field. Leo began to excel in math and chose astronomy as his major in college. George became a theatre major and hoped for a career as a performer. Throughout their lives, George was more placid than Leo, who was more easily agitated. In early adulthood, Leo was diagnosed with schizophrenia. George suffered for his brother but never developed the disorder himself.

Identical twins will help us tell the story of heredity and environment. They are called "identical" because they carry the same biological inheritance. You may assume that twins' great similarity is due to their identical heredity—and that their differences must be somehow due to their environments. But what does that really mean? How can environments make a difference in traits such as the location of a mole or the shade of hair color? In fact, the similarities *and* the differences are the outcome of both heredity and environment. Neither can work alone.

The Nature–Nurture Illusion

2.1   **Describe genetic and epigenetic processes in development and the coaction of heredity and the environment in mutually influencing development.**

Look at the image in Figure 2.1. Do you see two faces or a vase? If the figure that you focus on is the vase, the other parts of the image fade into the background or become the "ground." If you change your focus, the two faces will become the "figure" and the rest background. It is virtually impossible to maintain both perspectives simultaneously.

Images like this one have been used by Gestalt psychologists to illustrate a perceptual phenomenon known as "figure-ground," but we introduce it here because it provides a useful model for understanding the nature–nurture debate. No one would dispute that both heredity and environment influence human development, but when we focus on information about one of these contributors, the other seems to fade into the background. Evidence from both sides is compelling, and the helper may be persuaded to attend to one side of the argument to the exclusion of the other. The challenge is to guard against taking such a one-sided perspective, which allows for consideration of only half of the story. The most effective way that we know to avoid this kind of oversimplification is to understand the fundamentals of how gene–environment interactions function. The "take away" message, as you will see, is that genes can do nothing without environmental input—and that environmental effects are shaped by genetic constraints. For helping professionals, learning about these intricate transactions makes clear that there is little value in placing "blame" for problematic outcomes (Fruzzetti, Shenk, & Hoffman, 2005). This knowledge also improves a helper's ability to fashion therapeutic interventions that are realistic and valid for clients, and to help both clients and the general public to understand the complex interplay of heredity and environment in physical and behavioral outcomes (Dick & Rose, 2002).

Epigenesis and Coaction

In this chapter, we consider the fundamental processes that determine who we are, both physically and psychologically. We begin by examining the earliest steps in the remarkable journey of human development. You will see that heredity and environment are intimate collaborators at every point along the way.

Conception and Early Growth

You probably know that the inheritance of traits begins with conception, when a man's sperm fertilizes a woman's egg, called an ovum. Fertile women usually release an ovum from one of their ovaries into a fallopian tube during every menstrual cycle. The human ovum is a giant cell with a nucleus containing 23 chromosomes, the physical structures that are the vehicles of inheritance from the mother. The sperm, in contrast, is a tiny cell, but it too carries 23 chromosomes: the father's contribution to inheritance. The ovum's nucleus is surrounded by a great deal of cellular material called cytoplasm; the cytoplasm is loaded with a vast array of chemicals. During fertilization, the tiny sperm penetrates the outer membrane of the ovum and makes the long journey through the

FIGURE 2.1 Head-to-head optical illusion.

SOURCE: *Ye Liew/Fotolia.*

FIGURE 2.2 Human karyotypes.

Female karyotype

Male karyotype

FIGURE 2.3 Cell dividing by mitosis. (Only 2 of the 23 pairs of chromosomes—pairs #3 and #20—are depicted for illustration.)

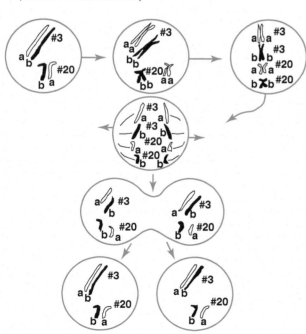

ovum's cytoplasm to finally penetrate the nucleus, where the sperm's outer structure disintegrates. The sperm's chromosomes become part of the nuclear material in the fertilized ovum, which is called a **zygote**.

The zygote contains 46 chromosomes, or more accurately, 23 pairs of chromosomes. One member of each pair comes from the mother (ovum) and one from the father (sperm). Twenty-two of these pairs are matched and are called **autosomes**. In autosome pairs, the two chromosomes look and function alike. The chromosomes of the 23rd pair are called **sex chromosomes**, because they have an important role to play in sex determination. In female zygotes, the 23rd pair consists of two matched chromosomes, called **X chromosomes**, but male zygotes have a mismatched pair. They have an X chromosome from their mothers but a much smaller **Y chromosome** from their fathers. Figure 2.2 presents two **karyotypes**, one from a male and one from a female. A *karyotype* displays the actual chromosomes from human body cells as seen under a microscope, arranged in matching pairs and then photographed. Notice the 23rd pair is matched in the female example but not in the male example. (See Chapter 8 for a fuller description of the role of sex chromosomes in human development.)

Chromosomes for a karyotype can be taken from cells anywhere in a person's body, such as the skin, the liver, or the brain. A duplicate copy of the original set of 46 chromosomes from the zygote exists in nearly every body cell. How did they get there? The chromosomes in a zygote begin to divide within hours after conception, replicating themselves. The duplicate chromosomes pull apart, to opposite sides of the nucleus. The nucleus then divides along with the rest of the cell, producing two new cells, which are essentially identical to the original zygote. This cell division process is called **mitosis** (see Figure 2.3). Most importantly, mitosis produces two new cells, each of which contains a duplicate set of chromosomes. The new cells quickly divide to produce four cells, the four cells divide to become eight cells, and so on. Each of the new cells also contains some of the cytoplasm of the original fertilized egg. The cell divisions continue in quick succession, and before long there is a cluster of cells, each containing a duplicate set of the original 46 chromosomes.

Over a period of about two weeks, the growing organism migrates down the mother's fallopian tube, into the uterus, and may succeed in implantation, attaching itself to the uterine lining, which makes further growth and development possible. Now it is called an embryo.

Defining Epigenesis and Coaction

If every new cell contains a duplicate set of the chromosomes from the zygote, and chromosomes are the carriers of heredity, then it would seem that every cell would develop in the same way. Yet cells differentiate during prenatal development and become specialized. They develop different structures and functions, depending on their surrounding environments. For example, cells located in the anterior portion of an embryo develop into parts of the head, whereas cells located in the embryo's lateral portion develop into parts of the back, and so on. Apparently, in different cells, different aspects of heredity are being expressed. The lesson is clear: Something in each cell's environment must interact with hereditary material to direct the cell's developmental outcome, making specialization possible.

Biologists have long recognized that cell specialization must mean that hereditary mechanisms are not unilaterally in charge of development. Biologists first used the term epigenesis just to describe the emergence of specialized cells and systems of cells (like the nervous system or the digestive system) from an undifferentiated zygote. It was a term to describe the emergence of different outcomes from the same hereditary material, which all seemed rather mysterious (Francis, 2011). The term has evolved as biology has advanced. Biologists now define *epigenesis* more specifically as the set of processes by which factors outside of hereditary material itself can influence how hereditary material functions (Charney, 2012). These "factors" are environmental. They include the chemicals in the cytoplasm of the cell (which constitute the immediate environment surrounding the chromosomes), factors in the cells and tissues adjacent to the cell, and factors beyond the body itself, such as heat, light, and even social interaction. The epigenome is the full set of factors, from the cell to the outside world, that controls the expression of hereditary material. "The activity of the genes can be affected through the cytoplasm of the cell by events originating at any other level in the system, including the external environment" (Gottlieb, 2003, p. 7).

But, as you will see, the chemicals in the cytoplasm of the cell are themselves partly determined by the hereditary material in the chromosomes. These chemicals can move beyond a cell to influence adjacent cells and ultimately to influence behavior in the outside environment. Heredity and environment are engaged from the very beginning in an intricate dance, a process called coaction, so that neither one ever causes any outcome on its own. Gottlieb (e.g., 1992, 2003) emphasizes coaction in his epigenetic model of development, a multidimensional theory. He expands the concept of epigenesis, describing it as the emergence of structural and functional properties and competencies as a function of the *coaction* of hereditary and environmental factors, with these factors having *reciprocal effects*, "meaning they can influence each other" (Gottlieb, 1992, p. 161). Figure 2.4 gives you a flavor of such reciprocal effects. It will be familiar to you from Chapter 1.

The Cell as the Scene of the Action

Understanding epigenesis starts with the cell. The chromosomes in the nucleus of the cell are made of a remarkable organic chemical called deoxyribonucleic acid or DNA. Long strands of DNA are combined with proteins called histones, wrapped and compacted to make up the chromosomes that we can see under a microscope. Chromosomes can reproduce themselves, because DNA has the extraordinary property of self-replication. Genes are functional units or sections of DNA, and they are often called "coded" sections of DNA. For each member of a pair of chromosomes, the number and location of genes are the same. So genes, like chromosomes, come in matched pairs, half from the mother (ovum) and half from the father (sperm).

FIGURE 2.4 An epigenetic model of gene/environment coaction.

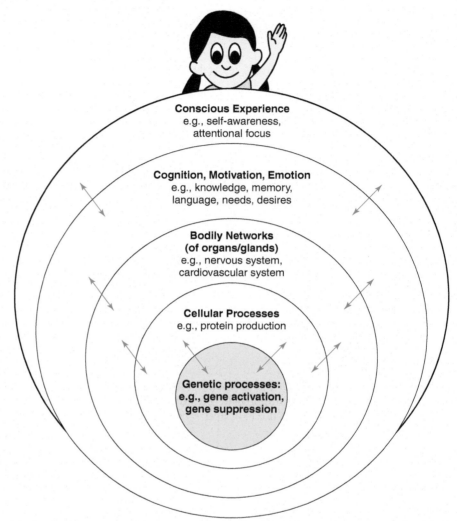

SOURCE: Gottlieb, G. (1992). *Individual development and evolution: The genesis of novel behavior*. p. 186. Used by permission of the Gottlieb Estate, Nora W. Gottlieb.

You may have read reports in the popular press of genetic "breakthroughs" suggesting that scientists have identified a gene for a trait or condition, such as depression or obesity. These reports are extremely misleading. Genes provide a code that a cell is capable of "reading" and using to help construct a protein, a complex organic chemical, made up of smaller molecules called amino acids. Proteins in many forms and combinations influence physical and psychological characteristics and processes by affecting cell processes.

First, let's consider the multistage process by which a gene's code affects protein production. The complexity of this process can be a bit overwhelming to those of us not schooled in biochemistry, so we will only examine it closely enough to get a sense of how genes and environment coact. The DNA code is a long sequence of molecules of four bases (that is, basic chemicals, not acids): adenine, cytosine, guanine, and thymine, identified as A, C, G, and T. In a process called transcription, intertwined strands of DNA separate, and one of the strands acts as a template for the synthesis of a new, single strand of messenger ribonucleic acid or mRNA. In effect, the sequence of bases (the "code") is replicated in the mRNA. Different sections of a gene's code can be combined in different ways in the mRNA it produces, so that a single gene can actually result in several different forms of mRNA. In a second step, called translation, the cell "reads" the mRNA code and produces a protoprotein, a substance that with a little tweaking (e.g., folding here, snipping there) can become a protein. Here again, the cell can produce several protein variations from the same protoprotein, a process called **alternative splicing** (Charney, 2017). Different cell climates (combinations of chemicals) can induce different protein outcomes. One example will help here. A gene labeled the "POMC" gene is eventually translated into a protoprotein called "proopiomelanocortin" (thus the POMC abbreviation). This protein can be broken up into several different types of proteins. Cells in different parts of the body, with their different chemical workforces, do just that. In one lobe of the pituitary gland (a small gland in the brain), POMC becomes adrenocorticotropic hormone (ACTH), an important substance in the stress reaction of the body, as you will see later in this chapter. In another lobe of the pituitary gland, the cells' chemical environments convert POMC into an opiate, called β-endorphin. In skin cells, POMC becomes a protein that promotes the production of melanin, a pigment (Francis, 2011; Mountjoy, 2015).

The moment of conception: Sperm and ovum unite to create a new organism.

You can see that the chemical environment of the cell affects the production of proteins at several points in the transcription and translation of coded genes. The entire transcription through translation process is referred to as **gene expression**. Whether or not genes will be expressed, and how often, is influenced by the environment of the cell. Most genes do not function full-time. Also, genes may be turned "on" in some cells and not in others. When a gene is on, transcription occurs and the cell manufactures the coded product or products. To understand how this works, let's begin by noting that coded genes make up only a small portion (2% to 3%) of the DNA in a human chromosome; the rest is called "intergenic" DNA. How and when a gene's code will be transcribed is partially regulated by sections of intergenic DNA, sometimes referred to as **noncoded genes** because they do not code for protein production. They function to either initiate or prevent the gene's transcription. This process is called **gene regulation**. All of a person's coded and noncoded DNA is referred to as his or her **genome**.

Gene Regulation: The Heart of Coaction

What provokes the gene regulation mechanisms to get the transcription process going? Some chemicals in the cells are **transcription factors**; they bind with the regulatory portions of the DNA, initiating the uncoiling of the strands of DNA at the gene location. This allows mRNA production to begin. Of course, it is more complicated than that. For example, transcription factors cannot bind to the regulatory DNA unless they first bind to another chemical called a **receptor**. Each kind of transcription factor binds to one or only a few receptors. Some receptors are found on the surface of a cell, binding with transcription factors coming from outside the cell. Other receptors are located inside the cell.

Let's follow the functioning of one transcription factor to illustrate how gene regulation works. Hormones, like testosterone and estrogen, are transcription factors. We'll focus on testosterone, produced in larger quantities by males than females. Testosterone is primarily produced in the testes, and then it circulates widely through the body via the blood. Only cells in some parts of the body, such as the skin, skeletal muscles, the testes themselves, and some parts of the brain, have receptors for testosterone. In each of these locations, testosterone binds with a different receptor. As a result, testosterone turns on different genes in different parts of the body. In a skeletal muscle, it triggers protein production that affects the growth of muscle fibers; in the testes, it turns on genes that influence sperm production.

Notice the bidirectionality of the processes we have been describing. Genes in the testes must be turned on by cellular chemicals (transcription factors and receptors) to initiate testosterone production. Then testosterone acts as a transcription factor turning on several different genes in different parts of the body where testosterone-friendly receptors are also produced. The cell's chemical makeup directs the activity of the genes, and the genes affect the chemical makeup of the cell. What makes all of this much more complex is that many influences beyond the cell moderate these bidirectional processes. For example, winning a competition tends to increase testosterone production in men, whereas losing a competition tends to decrease it. The effects of winning and losing on testosterone are found in athletes and spectators, voters in elections, even stock traders (Carre, Campbell, Lozoya, Goetz, & Welker, 2013). Coaction is everywhere.

How can factors outside of the cell, even outside the organism, influence gene regulation? Here again, the biochemistry of complex sequences of events can be daunting to follow, but let's consider a few fundamental mechanisms at the cellular level. One epigenetic change that can affect the expression of a gene is methylation, the addition of a methyl group (an organic molecule) to DNA, either to the coded gene or to regulatory DNA. Such methylation makes transcription of the gene more difficult. Heavy methylation may even turn off a gene for good. Methylation is persistent, and it is passed on when chromosomes duplicate during cell division, although some events can cause demethylation. That is, methyl groups may detach from DNA. In this case, gene transcription is likely to increase. Another class of epigenetic changes affects histones, the proteins that bind with DNA to make up the chromosomes. How tightly bound histones are to DNA affects how likely it is that a coded gene will be transcribed, with looser binding resulting in more transcription. A variety of biochemicals can attach to, or detach from, histones, such as methyl groups (methylation and demethylation) and acetyl groups (acetylation and deacetylation). Each of these can affect how tightly histones and DNA are bound together. Methylation causes tighter binding and reduces gene transcription; demethylation causes looser binding and more transcription. Acetylation loosens the binding, typically increasing gene transcription, and deacetylation tends to tighten the bonds again. Methylation, acetylation, and their reverse processes are common modifications of histones, but there are many others as well, each of them having some effect on the likelihood that a gene will be transcribed. In addition, other cellular components can shut down the impact of a gene, such as short sections of RNA called micro RNAs (miRNAs) that attach themselves to mRNAs and block their translation into proteins. These processes are all part of the cell's repertoire of DNA regulation devices (see Charney, 2012; Grigorenko, Kornilov, & Naumova, 2016).

When the environment outside the organism alters gene regulation, its effects on the body must eventually influence processes like methylation inside cells, so that certain genes in these cells become either more or less active. Let's consider one example that demonstrates the impact that the social environment can have on cellular processes in the development of rat pups. There is reason to suspect that somewhat analogous processes may occur in primates as well, including humans. Rat mothers differ in the care they give their pups, specifically, in how much licking and grooming (LG) they do. In a series of studies, Michael Meaney and his colleagues (see Kaffman & Meaney, 2007; Meaney, 2010, for summaries) discovered that variations in mothers' care during the first postnatal week alter the development of a rat pup's hippocampus. The hippocampus is a part of the brain with a central role to play in reactions to stress. The offspring of "high LG" mothers grow up to be more mellow—less reactive to stressful events—than the offspring of "low LG" mothers. Of course, these differences could simply indicate that the "high LG" mothers pass on to their offspring genes that influence low stress reactivity. But Meaney and colleagues were able to show that it is actually the mothers' care that makes the difference. They did a series of cross-fostering studies: They gave the offspring of high LG mothers to low LG mothers to rear, and they gave the offspring of low LG mothers to high LG mothers to rear. Rat pups reared by high LG foster mothers grew up to be more mellow than rat pups reared by low LG foster mothers. When Meaney and others studied the biochemistry of the rats' response to stress, they found that pups who receive extra maternal care respond to stress hormones (glucocorticoids) differently than other rats. (See later sections of this chapter for a description of the stress response in mammals, including humans.) Ordinarily, when glucocorticoids are produced, the body has been aroused for immediate action—fight or flight. But the body also launches a recovery from this arousal, reacting to reduce the further production of stress hormones. The hippocampus is the part of the brain that initiates the recovery. In rats that experience high LG as pups, just a tiny quantity of glucocorticoids is sufficient for the hippocampus to trigger a rapid reduction in the production of more stress hormones, resulting in a minimal behavioral response to stress.

Now you will see the importance of epigenesis. A mother rat's external stimulation of her pup causes changes in the regulatory DNA of the pup's hippocampus.

One of the changes is that the affected DNA is demethylated. Because of this demethylation, regulatory DNA turns on a gene that produces a stress hormone receptor in hippocampus cells. With larger amounts of the stress hormone receptor, the hippocampus becomes more sensitive, reacting quickly to small amounts of stress hormone, which makes the rat pup recover quickly from stressful events, which makes it a mellow rat. So maternal rearing, an environmental factor, changes the activity of the rat pup's DNA by demethylating it, which changes the pup's brain, affecting its behavioral response to stress. This change is permanent after the first week of life. What is truly remarkable is that this cascade of changes has consequences for the next generation of rat pups. Mellow female rats (who have experienced extra mothering as pups) grow up to be mothers who give *their* pups extra grooming and licking. And so their pups are also mellow—for life. Researchers are exploring how human infants' physiological responses to stress may be similarly calibrated by parental closeness and care (Gunnar & Sullivan, 2017; Tang, Reeb-Sutherland, Romeo, & McEwen, 2014; see Chapter 4). Epigenesis is one reason that identical twins can have the same genotype (type of gene or genes), but not have identical phenotypes (physical and behavioral traits). Their genotypes are exactly the same because they come from a single zygote. Usually after a zygote divides for the first time, the two new cells "stick together" and continue the cell division process, leading to a multi-celled organism. But in identical twinning, after one of the early cell divisions, one or more cells separate from the rest for unknown reasons. The detached cell or cells continue(s) the cell division process. Each of the new clusters of cells that form can develop into a complete organism, producing identical, or monozygotic twins. Yet, even though they have the same genotypes, their environments may diverge, even prenatally (e.g., Ollikainen et al., 2010). Different experiences throughout their lifetimes can affect the cellular environments of the twins, and these effects can cause differences in how, and how often, some genes are expressed. As a result, as they age twins tend to diverge more and more both physically and behaviorally (Kebir, Chaumette, & Krebs, 2018).

A large, longitudinal study of both monozygotic and dizygotic twins illustrates how variable epigenetic effects can be at the cellular level. *Dizygotic twins,* often called fraternal twins, are conceived when a mother releases two ova in the same menstrual cycle, and each ovum is fertilized by a separate sperm. Thus, these twins develop from two separate zygotes, and like any two siblings, they share about 50% of their genes on average. Wong, Caspi, and their colleagues (2010) studied a large number of both kinds of twins, taking cell samples when the children were 5 and 10 years old. For each child, the researchers measured the methylation of the regulatory DNA of three genes that affect brain function and behavior. You might expect a great deal of concordance (similarity between members of a pair of twins) in methylation, given that the members of each pair were exactly the same age and were growing up in the same families. Yet, the differences in the twins' experiences were enough to lead to substantial discordance (differences between members of a pair of twins) in methylation for both monozygotic and dizygotic twins. The investigators also found that gene methylation tended to change for individual children from age 5 to age 10. These changes sometimes involved increased methylation and sometimes involved decreased methylation. Differences between twins, and changes with age within each child, could partly be a result of random processes. But much of this variation is likely to be caused by the impact that differences in life experiences have on the functioning of each child's cells.

More About Genes

What significance is there to having matched pairs of genes, one from each parent? One important effect is that it increases hereditary diversity. The genes at matching locations on a pair of chromosomes often are identical, with exactly the same code, but they can also be slightly different forms of the same gene, providing somewhat different messages to the cell. These slightly different varieties of genes at the same location or locus on the chromosome are called alleles. For example, Tom has a "widow's peak," a distinct point in the hairline at the center of the forehead. He inherited from one parent an allele that would usually result in a widow's peak, but he inherited an

TABLE 2.1 Intergenerational Transmission of Recessive Traits (by parents who are carriers)

		MOTHER	FATHER	
	Genotype:	Ww	Ww	
	Phenotype:	Widow's peak	Widow's peak	
	CHILD$_1$	**CHILD$_2$**	**CHILD$_3$**	**CHILD$_4$**
Genotype:	WW	Ww	Ww	ww
Phenotype:	Widow's peak	Widow's peak	Widow's peak	Straight hairline*

*On average, one child in four will have the recessive trait if both parents are carriers.

NOTE: *W* stands for the dominant widow's peak allele; *w* stands for the recessive straight hairline allele.

allele that usually results in a straight hairline from the other parent. These two alleles represent Tom's *genotype* for hairline shape.

This example illustrates that two alleles of the same gene can have a **dominant-recessive relationship**, with only the first affecting the phenotype. In this case, the impact of the second gene allele is essentially overpowered by the impact of the first allele, so that the phenotype does not reflect all aspects of the genotype. Tom is a **carrier** of a recessive gene that could "surface" in the phenotype of one of his offspring. If a child receives two recessive alleles, one from each parent, the child will have the recessive trait. For instance, in Table 2.1, a mother and a father both have a widow's peak. Each of the parents has one dominant gene allele for a widow's peak and one recessive allele for a straight hairline, so they are both carriers of the straight hairline trait. On the average, three out of four children born to these parents will inherit at least one widow's peak allele. Even if they also inherit a straight hairline allele, they are likely to have a widow's peak. But one child out of four, on average, will inherit two straight hairline alleles, one from each parent. Without a widow's peak allele to suppress the effects of the straight hairline allele, such a child is likely to have a straight hairline, probably much to the surprise of the parents if they were unaware that they were carriers of the straight hairline trait!

Two different alleles will not necessarily have a dominant-recessive relationship. Sometimes alleles exhibit **codominance**, producing a blended or *additive* outcome. For example, Type A blood is the result of one gene allele; Type B blood is the result of a different allele. If a child inherits a Type A allele from one parent and a Type B allele from the other parent, the outcome will be a blend—Type AB blood.

Gene alleles at a single gene location can heavily influence some traits, as you have seen with hairline shape and blood type. But nearly all traits are influenced by the protein products of many different gene pairs. These genes may even be located on different chromosomes. Such **polygenic** effects make the prediction of traits from one generation to another very difficult and suggest that any one pair of gene alleles has a very modest influence on phenotypic outcomes. Height, skin color, and a host of other physical traits are polygenic, and most genetic influences on intelligence, personality, psychopathology, and behavior appear to be of this kind as well. One large study described 31 genes contributing to the onset of menstruation in girls, and more have been found (Tu et al., 2015). Polygenic determination on such a large scale is typical of gene influences on single traits. Do not lose sight of the importance of epigenesis in any of the gene effects we have been describing. Regulation of genes by the cellular environment, influenced by environments outside the cell, can trump dominance-recessive or codominance relationships between alleles. You will learn about some examples as we consider genetic sources of atypical development.

MyLab Education Self-Check 2.1

Atypical Development

2.2 **Identify cause-and-effect relationships between factors that influence atypical development and consequential outcomes.**

Typical prenatal development is an amazing story of orderly and continuous progress from a single fertilized cell to a highly differentiated organism with many interconnected and efficiently functioning systems. The 9-month gestational period spans the period of the zygote (about 2 weeks), from fertilization to implantation; the period of the embryo (from about the 3rd to 8th week), when most of the body's organ systems and structures are forming; and finally, the period of the fetus (from the 9th week until birth), when the reproductive system forms, gains in body weight occur, and the brain and nervous system continue to develop dramatically. (Figure 2.5 illustrates major developments during the periods of prenatal development.)

Typical development depends on the *genome* to code for the products that the body needs to grow and function normally; and it depends on the *environment* to provide a normal range of inputs, from nutrients to social interactions, in order for gene expression to be properly timed and regulated. The principle of coaction operates at every level of the developmental drama—with genes and environment in constant communication.

What role does the gene/environment dance play in atypical development? Deviations in *either* the genome *or* the environment can push the developing organism off course. In this section you will learn about genetic and chromosomal deviations as well as environmental distortions that can alter development as early as the period of the zygote. But remember: Neither ever works alone. The effects of the genome depend on the environment and vice versa. Watch for indicators of this coaction.

The Influence of Defective Gene Alleles

RECESSIVE, DEFECTIVE ALLELES

In sickle-cell anemia, the red blood cells are abnormally shaped, more like a half moon than the usual, round shape. The abnormal cells are not as efficient as normal cells in carrying oxygen to the tissues. Individuals with this disorder have breathing problems and a host of other difficulties that typically lead to organ malfunctions and, without treatment, to early death. Fortunately, modern treatments can substantially prolong life span. A recessive gene allele causes the malformed blood cells. If one normal gene allele is present, it will be dominant, and the individual will not have sickle-cell anemia. Many hereditary disorders are caused by such recessive, defective alleles, and it is estimated that most people are carriers of three to five such alleles. Yet, most of these illnesses are rare because to develop them an individual has to be unlucky enough to have both parents be carriers of the same defective allele and then to be the one in four (on average) offspring to get the recessive alleles from both parents. Table 2.2 lists some examples of these illnesses.

Some recessive, defective genes are more common in certain ethnic or geographic groups than in others. The sickle-cell anemia gene, for example, is most common among people of African descent. For some of these disorders, tests are available that can identify carriers. Prospective parents who have family members with the disorder or who come from groups with a higher than average incidence of the disorder may choose to be tested to help them determine the probable risk for their own offspring. Genetic counselors help screen candidates for such testing, as well as provide information and support to prospective parents, helping them to understand genetic processes and to cope with the choices that confront them—choices about testing, childbearing, and parenting (e.g., Madlensky et al., 2017).

DOMINANT, DEFECTIVE ALLELES

Some genetic disorders are caused by dominant gene alleles, so that only one defective gene need be present. Someone who has the defective gene will probably have the problem it causes, because the effects of a dominant gene allele overpower the effects

FIGURE 2.5 Fetal development.

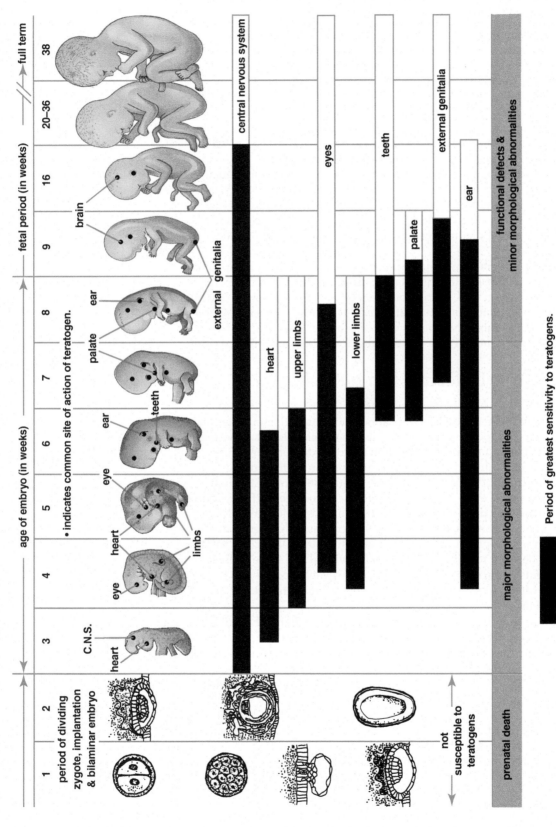

SOURCE: Moore, K. L., & Persaud, T. V. N. (1984). *Before we are born: Basic embryology and birth defects* (3rd ed.). Philadelphia, PA: Saunders. Copyright Elsevier. Reprinted with permission.

TABLE 2.2 Some Disorders Affected by Recessive, Defective Gene Alleles

DISORDER	DESCRIPTION
Cystic fibrosis	Inadequate mucus production; breathing and digestive problems; early death.
Phenylketonuria (PKU)	Metabolism of phenylalanines in food is insufficient; gradually compromises the nervous system, causing intellectual disability.
Sickle-cell anemia	Blood cells have an unusual "sickle" shape; causes heart and kidney problems.
Tay-Sachs disease	Enzyme disease; causes degeneration of the nervous system and death in the first few years of life.
Thalassemia	Blood cells abnormal; low energy, paleness, poor resistance to infection.
Hemophilia	Blood-clotting factor not produced; vulnerable to death by bleeding.
Duchenne's muscular dystrophy	Wasting of muscles produces gradual weakness, eventual death.

of a recessive allele. Suppose that such an illness causes an early death, before puberty. Then, the defective, dominant allele that causes the illness will die with the affected individual because no offspring are produced. When these alleles occur in some future generation, it must be through **mutation**, a change in the chemical structure of an existing gene. Sometimes mutations occur spontaneously, and sometimes they are due to environmental influences, like exposure to radiation or toxic chemicals (Strachan & Read, 2000). For example, **progeria** is a fatal disorder that causes rapid aging, so that by late childhood affected individuals are dying of "old age." Individuals with progeria usually do not survive long enough to reproduce. When the disease occurs, it is caused by a genetic mutation during the embryonic period of prenatal development, so that while it is precipitated by a genetic defect, it does not run in families.

Some disorders caused by dominant, defective alleles do not kill individuals affected by them in childhood, and thus can be passed on from one generation to another. When one parent has the disease, each child has a 50% chance of inheriting the dominant, defective gene from that parent. Some of these disorders are quite mild in their effects, such as farsightedness. Others unleash lethal effects late in life. Among the most famous is **Huntington's disease**, which causes the nervous system to deteriorate, usually beginning between 30 and 40 years of age. Symptoms include uncontrolled movements and increasingly disordered psychological functioning, eventually ending in death. In recent years the gene responsible for Huntington's disease has been identified, and a test is now available that will allow early detection, before symptoms appear. Unfortunately, there is no cure. The offspring of individuals with the disease face a difficult set of dilemmas, including whether to have the test and, if they choose to do so and find they have the gene, how to plan for the future. Again, genetic counselors may play a critical role in this process (Hines, McCarthy Veach, & LeRoy, 2010).

Often, having a dominant defective allele, or two recessive, defective alleles, seems like a bullet in the heart: If you have the defective gene or genes you will develop the associated disorder. Yet epigenetic effects can alter the course of events. The disorder may not develop if epigenetic processes prevent the transcription of defective alleles or the translation of mRNA to a protein. Consider another rodent example. A fat, diabetic yellow mouse, and a slim, healthy brown mouse can actually be identical genetically. Both mice carry a dominant "Agouti" gene allele that causes the problems of the yellow mouse. But in the brown mouse, that troublesome allele is heavily methylated. Dolinoy (2008) demonstrated that this epigenetic change can happen during fetal development if the mother mouse is fed a diet rich in folate, choline, and B12. Such a diet promotes methylation of the Agouti allele, shutting it down.

Research on the role of epigenesis in the expression of defective genes is in its infancy (Heijmans & Mill, 2012; Mazzio & Soliman, 2012). Yet it promises to help solve some medical mysteries, such as why occasionally one monozygotic twin develops a hereditary disease but the other does not, or why some people with the same genetic defect have milder forms of a disease than others (e.g., Ollikainen et al., 2010). Such outcomes illustrate that coaction is always in play. This is true for behavioral disorders as well. For example, Caspi and his colleagues (2002) studied people with a range of variations in the "MAOA" gene. This gene provides the cell with a template for production of the MAOA enzyme, a protein that metabolizes a number of important brain chemicals called neurotransmitters, like serotonin and dopamine. (You'll learn more about neurotransmitters later in this chapter.) Its effect is to inactivate these neurotransmitters, a normal process in neurological functioning. Apparently, while these neurotransmitters are critical to normal brain function, too much of them is a problem. Animals become extremely aggressive if the MAOA gene is deleted so that the enzyme cannot be produced. In humans, different alleles of the MAOA gene result in different amounts of MAOA enzyme production. Could alleles that cause low levels of production increase aggression and antisocial behavior in humans? Most research has suggested no such relationship. But Caspi and colleagues hypothesized that child rearing environment might affect how different gene alleles function. Specifically, they hypothesized that early abusive environments might make some MAOA alleles more likely to have negative effects on development. They studied a sample of New Zealand residents who had been followed from birth through age 26. They identified each person's MAOA alleles and looked at four indicators of antisocial, aggressive behavior, such as convictions for violent crimes in adulthood. Finally, they looked at each person's child-rearing history. Caspi and colleagues did find a link between gene alleles that result in low levels of MAOA enzyme production and aggression, but only when the individual carrying such an allele had experienced abuse as a child. For people with no history of abuse, variations in the MAOA gene were not related to adult aggressive behavior. This appears to be epigenesis in action. (See Ouellet-Morin et al., 2016 for related studies.)

POLYGENIC INFLUENCES

As with most normal characteristics, inherited disorders are usually related to more than one gene, such that some combination of defective alleles at many chromosomal sites predisposes the individual to the illness. Like all polygenic traits, these disorders run in families, but they cannot be predicted with the precision of disorders caused by genes at a single chromosomal location. Most forms of muscular dystrophy are disorders of this type. Polygenic influences have also been implicated in diabetes, clubfoot, some forms of Alzheimer's disease, and multiple sclerosis, to name just a few. As we noted earlier, genetic effects on behavioral traits are typically polygenic. This appears to be true for most mental illnesses and behavioral disorders, such as alcoholism, schizophrenia, and clinical depression (e.g., Halldorsdottir & Binder, 2017). For example, the MAOA gene is only one of several that are associated with antisocial behavior (Ouellet-Morin et al., 2016). Genes linked to serious behavioral problems and disorders affect brain function. It will not surprise you to learn that whether and when these genes or their normal variants are expressed also depend on epigenetic modifications that are associated with a person's experiences at different points in development, and researchers have begun to identify the biochemical processes involved (e.g., Matosin, Halldorsdottir, & Binder, 2018; Shorter & Miller, 2015).

The Influence of Chromosomal Abnormalities

Occasionally, a zygote will form that contains too many chromosomes, or too few, or a piece of a chromosome might be missing. Problems in the production of either the ovum or the sperm typically cause these variations. Such zygotes often do not survive. When they do, the individuals usually have multiple physical or behavioral problems. The causes of chromosomal abnormalities are not well understood. Either the mother or the father could be the source, and ordinarily, the older the parent, the more likely that an ovum or sperm will contain a chromosomal abnormality. Among the most common and well known of these disorders is Down syndrome (also called trisomy 21), caused by an extra copy of chromosome number 21. The extra chromosome in this syndrome usually comes from the ovum, but about 5% of the time it comes from the sperm. Children with Down syndrome experience some degree of intellectual impairment, although educational interventions can have a big impact on the severity of

MyLab Education
Video Example 2.1
Down syndrome is among the most common chromosomal abnormalities. Consider causal factors and resulting developmental variants.

TABLE 2.3 Some Chromosomal Abnormalities

SYNDROME	CHROMOSOMAL VARIATION	SOME FEATURES	HELPFUL WEBSITES
Cri du Chat	Missing portion of chromosome #5	High pitched cry (like a cat); severe intellectual disability and developmental delays; distinctive facial features (e.g., downward slant of eyes); small head; poor infant muscle tone; low birth weight; etc.	https://www.genome.gov/19517558/ https://ghr.nlm.nih.gov/condition/cri-du-chat-syndrome
Down (Trisomy 21)	Extra chromosome #21	Mild to severe intellectual disability and developmental delays; distinctive facial characteristics (e.g., flattening of features); poor infant muscle tone; increased risk of heart, digestive, hearing problems, Alzheimer's disease, etc.	http://www.ndss.org http://www.nads.org
Klinefelter	Extra X chromosome: XXY	Male; may have small testicles; low testosterone levels; delayed or incomplete puberty; breast growth; tall height; learning disability/speech delay; etc.	http://www.aaksis.org/ https://genetic.org/
Triple X	Extra X chromosome: XXX	Female; may have tall stature; learning problems; clinodactyly (curvature of fifth finger); seizures; kidney problems; etc.	https://genetic.org/ http://www.rarechromo.org/
Turner	Missing X chromosome: X	Female; short stature; webbed neck; infertility; some skeletal abnormalities; kidney or heart problems; etc.	https://genetic.org/ http://www.turnersyndrome.org/
XYY	Extra Y chromosome: XYY	Male; tall stature, low set ears; delayed motor development; delayed speech/language; etc.	https://genetic.org/ http://www.rarechromo.org/
Williams	Missing portion of chromosome #7	Mild to moderate intellectual disabilities; better language production than other cognitive skills; distinctive facial features (e.g., broad forehead, short nose, wide lips); overfriendliness, anxiety problems; etc.	https://williams-syndrome.org/ http://www.williams-syndrome.org.uk/ https://rarediseases.info.nih.gov/ (provides information about all syndromes listed)

cognitive deficits. In addition, these children are likely to have several distinctive characteristics, such as a flattening of facial features, poor muscle tone, small stature, and heart problems (Marchal et al., 2016). Table 2.3 provides some examples of disorders influenced by chromosomal abnormalities.

Teratogenic Influences

From conception, the environment is an equal partner with genes in human development. What constitutes the earliest environment beyond the cell? It is the mother's womb, of course, but it is also everything outside of the womb—every level of the physical and social and cultural context. For example, if a mother is stressed by marital conflict, her developing fetus is likely to be influenced by the impact that her distress has on the biochemical environment of the uterus. (For simplicity, we will use the term *fetus* to refer to the prenatal organism in this section, even though technically it might be a zygote or an embryo.) Even the ancient Greeks, like Hippocrates who wrote 2,500 years ago, recognized that ingestion of certain drugs, particularly during the early stages of pregnancy, could "weaken" the fetus and cause it to be misshapen. Environmental substances and agents that can harm the developing fetus are called teratogens. The name comes from the Greek and literally means "monstrosity making."

The fetus is surrounded by a placenta, an organ that develops from the zygote along with the embryo; it exchanges blood products with the baby through the umbilical cord. The placenta allows nutrients and oxygen from the mother's blood to pass into the baby's blood and allows carbon dioxide and waste to be removed by the mother's blood, but otherwise it usually keeps the two circulatory systems separate. Teratogens can cross the placental barrier from mother to fetus. They include some drugs and other chemicals, certain disease organisms, and radioactivity. The list of known teratogens is quite lengthy, so we have presented in Table 2.4 a summary of the main characteristics of a few of these agents.

Consider, for example, alcohol. Alcohol has been called "the most prominent behavioral teratogen in the world" (Warren & Murray, 2013) because its use is common across the globe. "Behavioral" here refers to the fact that the fetus's exposure is a result of the mother's behavior. Conservative estimates are that 2% to 5% of babies born in the United States suffer negative effects from prenatal exposure to alcohol. Worldwide, "it is the leading cause of preventable developmental disabilities" (Hoyme et al., 2016, p. 2).

Physicians have suspected the risks of drinking during pregnancy for centuries, but only in the last few decades has there been broad recognition of those risks (Warren, 2013). Identifying teratogens is difficult, because their effects are variable and unpredictable. Maternal drinking during pregnancy can cause no harm to the fetus, or it can result in one or more of a wide range of problems, called **fetal alcohol spectrum disorders (FASD)**. Most children on this spectrum experience some intellectual or behavioral problems. These can include specific learning disabilities, language delays, or memory problems, or more global and severe cognitive deficits, as well as difficulties with impulse control, hyperactivity, social understanding, and so on (Wilhoit, Scott, & Simecka, 2017). More severe intellectual and behavioral impairments are typically accompanied by gross structural brain anomalies. Prenatal development of the brain and the face are interrelated, so it is not surprising that alcohol exposure is also associated with facial abnormalities (del Campo & Jones, 2017). The most extreme of the disorders is **fetal alcohol syndrome (FAS)**, which is identified by a unique facial configuration with three especially likely characteristics: small eye openings so that the eyes look widely spaced, a smooth philtrum (the ridge between the nose and upper lip), and a thin upper lip. Other likely facial variations are a flattened nasal bridge, a small nose, and unusual ear ridges. Cognitive deficits are often accompanied by a small head and sometimes recurrent seizures. Children with FAS typically show growth retardation, either pre- or postnatally, both in weight and height. Many organ systems can be affected in addition to the central nervous system; problems with the heart, kidneys, and bones are common (see Table 2.4).

TABLE 2.4 Selected Teratogens

	COMMON EFFECTS ON FETUS	SAFE DOSAGE	REFERENCES
Legal and illegal drugs			
Alcohol	Brain abnormalities; distinct facial structure; cardiac, skeletal, and urogenital abnormalities; dental abnormalities; growth deficiencies; broad intellectual deficits and/or more specific attentional problems; social perception problems; language deficits; and other learning disorders.	No safe dosage during pregnancy	Hoyme et al., 2016; Wilhoit, Scott, & Simecka, 2017
Tobacco	Low birth weight due to constricted blood flow and reduced nutrition; prematurity; respiratory problems; cleft palate; learning problems; hyperactivity; disruptive behavior; chronic tic disorders.	No safe dosage during pregnancy	Leckman & Fernandez, 2016; Tong et al., 2013
Cocaine	Prematurity or stillbirth; low birth weight; drug withdrawal after birth including irritability, restlessness, tremors; medically and psychologically fragile; higher rates of later learning problems and ADHD; negative temperamental traits.	No safe dosage during pregnancy	Locke et al., 2016
Marijuana	Moderations in brain development and function that may make the child more vulnerable to postnatal stresses, enhancing potential for cognitive and emotional problems.	No safe dosage during pregnancy	Richardson Hester, & McLemore, 2016; Smith et al., 2016
Infections			
Rubella (German measles virus)	Cataracts and other vision abnormalities; heart malformations; brain abnormalities; genitourinary disorders.		Yazigi et al., 2017
Zika virus	Brain abnormalities; microcephaly (small brain and head).		Russo, Jungman, & Beltrão-Braga, 2017
Environmental hazards			
Lead	Prematurity; low birth weight; brain abnormalities; cognitive impairments.		Craft-Blachsheare, 2017; Nye et al., 2016
PCBs (Polychlorinated biphenyls)	Low birth weight; cognitive impairments.		Majidi, Bouchard, Gosselin, & Carrier, 2012

Teratogens impact fetal development by modifying both intracellular and intercellular activity in the placenta and in the fetus. Teratogens may sometimes actually cause mutations in coded DNA (Bishop, Witt, & Sloane, 1997). But more often they seem to operate by making epigenetic modifications to DNA and thereby altering gene expression. For example, changes in methylation patterns (both methylation of some genes and demethylation of others) have been found in children with FASD for clusters of genes that are important for neuro-development and behavior (e.g., Chater-Diehl, Laufer, & Singh, 2017).

The teratogenic effects of alcohol are so variable, ranging from none at all to FAS, because a whole set of other factors moderates any teratogen's impact. The unpredictability of teratogenic effects provides a good illustration of the multidimensionality of development. Damaging outcomes may be reduced or enhanced by the timing of prenatal exposure, the mother's and fetus's genomes (genetic susceptibility), the amount of exposure (dosage), and the presence or absence of other risks to the fetus.

TIMING OF EXPOSURE

The likelihood and the extent of teratogenic damage depends on when in development exposure occurs (refer again to Figure 2.5). In the first few months, the structure of major organ systems is formed. Brain structures could show unusual and/or insufficient development if a fetus is exposed to a teratogen like alcohol in the first trimester. If the exposure occurs in the last trimester, obvious structural anomalies are not as likely, but brain and other organ functions are still in jeopardy, so that processes such as learning and behavior regulation, vision, and hearing are still vulnerable. Whereas "there is no safe trimester to drink alcohol" (Hoyme et al., 2016, p. 2), some teratogens seem to be harmful primarily at certain times. For example, thalidomide is a sedative introduced in the 1950s and widely prescribed to pregnant women for morning sickness. When used in the first trimester, it caused serious limb deformities (Ito, Ando, & Handa, 2011). Before thalidomide was identified as the culprit, it had affected the lives of over 10,000 children around the world.

GENETIC SUSCEPTIBILITY

Not all fetuses are equally susceptible to a teratogen's effects. Both the mother's and the baby's genes play a role in sensitivity or resistance to a teratogen. For example, FASD is slightly more prevalent among boys than girls (May et al., 2014), and there is some indication from animal studies that maternal drinking affects males' social behavior more than females' (e.g., Rodriguez et al., 2016). For some teratogens, such as nicotine, researchers have identified specific genes, and gene alleles, that can increase or decrease the effects of prenatal exposure (e.g., Price, Grosser, Plomin, & Jaffee, 2010). This is, of course, an illustration of coaction.

DOSAGE

Larger amounts of a teratogenic agent and longer periods of exposure generally have greater effects than smaller doses and shorter periods. Alcohol's effects are dose dependent. Mothers who drink more days per week increase their babies' chances of FAS (Gupta, Gupta, & Shirisaka, 2016). Mothers' binge drinking seems to be especially harmful, although no "safe" dose has been found for alcohol (May et al., 2013). Note also that the effects of any amount of alcohol ingestion are always more potent for the fetus than they are for the mother. In other words, the fetus may have crossed a toxic threshold even if the mother experiences few or very mild alcohol-related effects. Consequently, the U.S. Department of Health and Human Services (2015) and the American Academy of Pediatrics (Williams & Smith, 2015) recommend that women refrain from drinking alcohol throughout a pregnancy. "No amount of alcohol intake during pregnancy can be considered safe" (Hoyme et al., 2016, p. 2).

NUMBER OF RISK FACTORS

As you learned in Chapter 1, risk factors are more likely to cause problems the more numerous they are. The developing organism can often correct for the impact of one risk factor, but the greater the number, the less likely it is that such a correction can be made. The negative effects of teratogens can be amplified when the fetus or infant is exposed to more than one. For example, poor maternal nutrition tends to increase the risk of FAS (Keen et al., 2010). Often, pregnant women who drink also smoke. They are also more likely to be poor, so it is fairly common that their babies have been exposed to multiple risks. The teratogenic effects of cocaine were once thought to include congenital malformations until researchers recognized that pregnant women who use cocaine frequently consume other drugs, such as alcohol, tobacco, marijuana, or heroin, and they often have poor nutrition as well. Cocaine users also tend to be poor and to experience more life stress during and after pregnancy than other women. Although prenatal cocaine exposure in the absence of other risk factors can have effects on some aspects of behavior, many of the outcomes once attributed to cocaine alone seem to result from combinations of risk factors (Terplan & Wright, 2011).

Nutritional Influences

Teratogens are problematic because they add something to the ordinary fetal environment, intruding on the developing system and driving it off course. But what happens when contextual factors that *belong* in the ordinary fetal environment are missing or in short supply? When food sources are lacking in protein or essential vitamins and minerals during prenatal and early postnatal development, an infant's physical, socioemotional, and intellectual development can be compromised (e.g., Aboud & Yousafzai, 2015), and epigenetic alterations seem to be at the root of these developmental problems (Champagne, 2016).

In a classic intervention study, Rush, Stein, and Susser (1980) provided nutritional supplements to pregnant women whose socioeconomic circumstances indicated that they were likely to experience inadequate diets. At age 1, the babies whose mothers received a protein supplement during pregnancy performed better on measures of play behavior and perceptual habituation (which is correlated with later intelligence) than those whose mothers received a high-calorie liquid or no supplement at all.

Are there longer-term behavioral consequences of inadequate prenatal nutrition? Some research does reveal enduring effects. When the fetus is unable to build adequate stores of iron, for example, the infant is likely to show signs of anemia by 4 to 6 months of age, and even if corrected, a history of anemia has been shown to affect later school performance. One large longitudinal study demonstrates the many long-term effects that famine can have on the developing fetus. During World War II, people in the western part of The Netherlands experienced a serious food shortage as a result of a food embargo imposed by Germany over the winter of 1944–45. At the end of the war, in 1945, scientists began studying the cohort of babies born to pregnant women who experienced the famine, comparing them either to siblings who were not born during the famine, or to another sample of Dutch people who were born in the same period, but who were not exposed to the famine (e.g., Lumey & van Poppel, 2013). Among the many long-term consequences of prenatal exposure to the famine are: higher rates of obesity by young adulthood; increased risk of schizophrenia and mood disorders, such as depression; more high blood pressure, coronary artery disease, and type II diabetes by age 50; and the list goes on (see Francis, 2011, for a summary). These long-term consequences appear to result from epigenetic changes at the cellular level. For example, one group of investigators found significant demethylation of a gene that codes for "insulin-like growth factor II" (IGF2) in individuals exposed to the famine very early in gestation, when methylation of this particular gene usually occurs (Heijmans et al., 2008). In another study, methylation and demethylation changes in six genes were identified. The kind of change depended on the gene, the gender of the individual, and the timing of fetal exposure to the famine (Tobi et al., 2009).

It is not surprising that prenatal nutrition has such effects, given what we have learned about the effects of postnatal nutrition on children's functioning. We have known for decades that children who experience severe protein and calorie shortages at any age may develop **kwashiorkor**, characterized by stunted growth, a protuberant belly, and extreme apathy (Roman, 2013). Therapeutic diets can eliminate the apathy of kwashiorkor, but cognitive impairments often persist. Some research indicates that even much less severe nutritional deficits may have impacts on children's cognitive functioning. An intriguing study of changes in the food supplied to New York City schools provides a strong illustration (Schoenthaler, Doraz, & Wakefield, 1986). In a three-stage process, from 1978 to 1983, many food additives and foods high in sugar (sucrose) were eliminated from school meals, so that children's consumption of "empty calories" was reduced, and, presumably, their intake of foods with a higher nutrient-to-calorie ratio increased. With each stage of this process, average achievement test scores increased in New York City schools, with improvements occurring primarily among the children who were performing worst academically.

Findings such as these suggest that children whose prenatal and postnatal environments are short on protein and other essential nutrients may not achieve the levels of behavioral functioning that they could have with adequate diets. But the long-range impact of early diet, like the effects of teratogens, is altered by the presence or absence of other risk and protective factors. Some studies have found, for example, that if children experience poor early nutrition because of extreme poverty or major events such as war, they are less likely to have cognitive impairments the more well educated their parents are (e.g., Boo, 2016). As with other risk factors, the effects of poor nutrition are lessened by other more benign influences. We note again that it is in combination that risk factors do the most harm. (See Box 2.2 for further discussion of this phenomenon.) One heartening consequence is that when we intervene to reduce one risk factor, such as malnutrition, we may actually reduce the impact of other negative influences on development as well.

MyLab Education Self-Check 2.2

The Developing Brain

2.3 **Describe prenatal and early postnatal brain development including brain structures and neuron structures and functions.**

Now that you have a sense of the genetic and epigenetic processes at work in development, we can begin to examine behavioral change over time. We will first focus on the physical system that underlies behavior: the central nervous system and, especially, the brain. Helping professionals can better understand how their clients think, feel, and learn if they give some attention to the workings of this marvelously complex system. We will guide you through the story of prenatal and immediate postnatal brain development. Then we will examine in depth a key process mediated by the brain: the stress and adaptation system. As you will see throughout this text, stress, and individual differences in the response to stress, are at the core of what helpers must understand about human development.

Early Prenatal Brain Development

When you were just a 2-week-old embryo, your very existence still unknown to your parents, cells from the embryo's upper surface began to form a sheet that rearranged itself by turning inward and curling into a neural tube. This phenomenon, called neurulation, signaled the beginning of your central nervous system's development. Once formed, this structure was covered over by another sheet of cells, to become your skin, and was moved inside you so that the rest of your body could develop around it. Around the 25th day of your gestational life, your neural tube began to take on a pronounced curved shape. At the top of your "C-shaped" embryonic self, three distinct bulges appeared, which eventually became your hindbrain, midbrain, and forebrain. (See Figure 2.6.)

FIGURE 2.6 Stages of brain development.

The developing human brain viewed from the side in a succession of embryonic and fetal stages.
The small figures beneath the first five embryonic stages are in proper relative proportion to the last
five figures.

Within the primitive neural tube, important events were occurring. Cells from
the interior surface of the neural tube reproduced to form **neurons**, or nerve cells, that
would become the building blocks of your brain. From about the 40th day, or 5th week,
of gestation, your neurons began to increase at a staggering rate—one quarter of a million per minute for 9 months—to create the 100 billion neurons that make up a baby's
brain at birth. At least half would be destroyed later either because they were unnecessary or were not used. We will have more to say about this loss of neurons later.

Your neurons began to migrate outward from their place of birth rather like filaments extending from the neural tube to various sites in your still incomplete brain.
Supporting cells called **glial cells**, stretching from the inside of the neural tube to its
outside, provided a type of scaffolding for your neurons, guiding them as they ven-
tured out on their way to their final destinations. Those neurons that developed first
migrated only a short distance from your neural tube and were destined to become the
hindbrain. Those that developed later traveled a little farther and ultimately formed
the **midbrain**. Those that developed last migrated the farthest to populate the **cerebral
cortex** of the **forebrain**. This development always progressed from the inside out, so
that cells traveling the farthest had to migrate through several other already formed
layers to reach their proper location. To build the six layers of your cortex, epigenetic
processes pushed each neuron toward its ultimate address, moving through the bottom layers that had been already built up before it could get to the outside layer. (See
Box 2.1 and Figures 2.7 and 2.8.)

Scientists have discovered that neurons sometimes need to find their destinations
(for example, on the part of the cortex specialized for vision) before that part of the

Box 2.1: The Major Structures of the Brain

Multidimensional models of mental health and psychopathology now incorporate genetics and brain processes into their conceptual frameworks. Thus, a working knowledge of the brain and its functioning should be part of a contemporary helper's toolkit. Consumers of research also need this background to understand studies that increasingly include brain-related measures. Here we present a very short introduction to some important brain areas and describe their related functions.

The complex human brain can be partitioned in various ways. One popular way identifies three main areas that track evolutionary history: hindbrain, midbrain, and forebrain. Bear in mind, however, that brain areas are highly interconnected by neural circuitry despite attempts to partition them by structure or function. In general, the more complex, higher-order cognitive functions are served by higher-level structures while lower-level structures control basic functions like respiration and circulation.

Beginning at the most ancient evolutionary level, the hindbrain structures of **medulla, pons, cerebellum**, and the **reticular formation** regulate **autonomic functions** that are outside our conscious control. The *medulla* contains nuclei that control basic survival functions, such as heart rate, blood pressure, and respiration. Damage to this area of the brain can be fatal. The *pons*, situated above the medulla, is involved in the regulation of the sleep–wake cycle. Individuals with sleep disturbances can sometimes have abnormal activity in this area. The medulla and the pons are also especially sensitive to an overdose of drugs or alcohol. Drug effects on these structures can cause suffocation and death. The pons transmits nerve impulses to the *cerebellum*, a structure that looks like a smaller version of the brain itself. The cerebellum is involved in the planning, coordination, and smoothness of complex motor activities such as hitting a tennis ball or dancing, in addition to other sensorimotor functions.

Within the core of the brainstem (medulla, pons, and midbrain) is a bundle of neural tissue called the reticular formation that runs up through the midbrain. This, together with smaller groups of neurons called **nuclei**, forms the **reticular activating system**, that part of the brain that alerts the higher structures to "pay attention" to incoming stimuli. This system also filters out the extraneous stimuli that we perceive at any point in time. For example, it is possible for workers who share an office to tune out the speech, music, or general background hum going on around them when they are involved in important telephone conversations. However, they can easily "perk up" and attend if a coworker calls their name.

The midbrain also consists of several small structures (**superior colliculi, inferior colliculi**, and **substantia nigra**) that are involved in vision, hearing, and consciousness. These parts of the brain receive sensory input from the eyes and ears and are instrumental in controlling eye movement.

The forebrain is the largest part of the brain and includes the **cerebrum, thalamus, hypothalamus**, and **limbic system** structures. The *thalamus* is a primary way station for handling neural communication, something like "information central." It receives information from the sensory and limbic areas and sends these messages to their appropriate destinations. For example, the thalamus projects visual information, received via the optic nerve, to the occipital lobe of the cortex (discussed later in this box). On both sides of the thalamus are structures called the **basal ganglia**. These structures, especially the **nucleus accumbens**, are involved in motivation and approach behavior.

The *hypothalamus*, situated below the thalamus, is a small but important area that regulates many key bodily functions, such as hunger, thirst, body temperature, and breathing rate. Lesions in areas of the hypothalamus have been found to produce eating abnormalities in animals, including obesity or starvation. It is also important in the regulation of emotional responses, including stress-related responses. The hypothalamus functions as an intermediary, translating the emotional messages received from the cortex and the amygdala into a command to the endocrine system to release stress hormones in preparation for fight or flight. We will discuss the hypothalamus in more detail in the section on the body's stress systems.

Limbic structures (**hippocampus, amygdala, septum**, and **cingulate cortex**) are connected by a system of nerve pathways (limbic system) to the cerebral cortex. Often referred to as the "emotional brain," the limbic system supports social and emotional functioning and works with the frontal lobes of the cortex to help us think and reason. The *amygdala* rapidly assesses the emotional significance of environmental events, assigns them a threat value, and conveys this information to parts of the brain that regulate neurochemical functions. The structures of the limbic system have direct connections with neurons from the olfactory bulb, which is responsible for our sense of smell. It has been noted that pheromones, a particular kind of hormonal substance secreted by animals and humans, can trigger particular reactions that affect emotional responsiveness below the level of conscious awareness. We will have more to say about the workings of the emotional brain and its ties to several emotional disorders in Chapter 4.

Other limbic structures, notably the *hippocampus*, are critical for learning and memory formation. The hippocampus is especially important in processing the emotional context of experience and sensitive to the effects of stress. Under prolonged stress, hippocampal neurons shrink and new neurons are not produced. The hippocampus and the amygdala are anatomically connected, and together they regulate the working of the HPA axis (described later in this chapter). In general, the amygdala activates this stress response system while the hippocampus inhibits it (McEwen & Gianaros, 2010).

The most recognizable aspect of the forebrain is the *cerebrum*, which comprises two thirds of the total mass. A crevice, or fissure, divides the cerebrum into two halves, like the halves of a walnut. Information is transferred between the two halves by a network of fibers comprising the **corpus callosum**. These halves are referred to as the left and right hemispheres. Research on **hemispheric specialization** (also called **lateralization**), pioneered by Sperry (1964), demonstrated that the left hemisphere controls functioning of the right side of

(continued)

the body and vice versa. Language functions such as vocabulary knowledge and speech are usually localized in the left hemisphere, and visual–spatial skills are localized on the right. Recently, this research was introduced to lay readers through a rash of popular books about left brain–right brain differences. Overall, many of these publications have distorted the facts and oversimplified the findings. Generally the hemispheres work together, sharing information via the corpus callosum and cooperating with each other in the execution of most tasks. There is no reliable evidence that underlying modes of thinking, personality traits, or cultural differences can be traced exclusively to hemispheric specialization.

Each hemisphere of the cerebral cortex can be further divided into lobes, or areas of functional specialization (see Figure 2.8). The **occipital lobe**, located at the back of the head, handles visual information. The **temporal lobe**, found on the sides of each hemisphere, is responsible for auditory processing. At the top of each hemisphere, behind a fissure called the **central sulcus**, is the **parietal lobe**. This area is responsible for the processing of somatosensory information such as touch, temperature, and pain. Finally, the **frontal lobe**, situated at the top front part of each hemisphere, controls voluntary muscle movements and higher-level cognitive functions.

The **prefrontal cortex (PFC)** is the part of the frontal lobe that occupies the front or anterior portion. This area is involved in processes like sustained attention, working memory, planning, decision making, and emotion regulation. Generally, the PFC plays a role in regulation and can moderate an overactive amygdala as well as the activity of the body's stress response system. Another important regulatory pathway involves the **anterior cingulate cortex (ACC)**, a structure in the middle of the brain above the corpus callosum. The ACC mediates cognition and affect. Impaired connections between the ACC and the amygdala are related to higher levels of anxiety and neuroticism, and lower ACC volume has been found in depressed patients (Kaiser, Andrews-Hanna, Wager, & Piagalli, 2015). The size of the various brain regions and the integrity of their circuitry play a role in individuals' cognition, affect, and behavior.

FIGURE 2.7 The major structures of the brain.

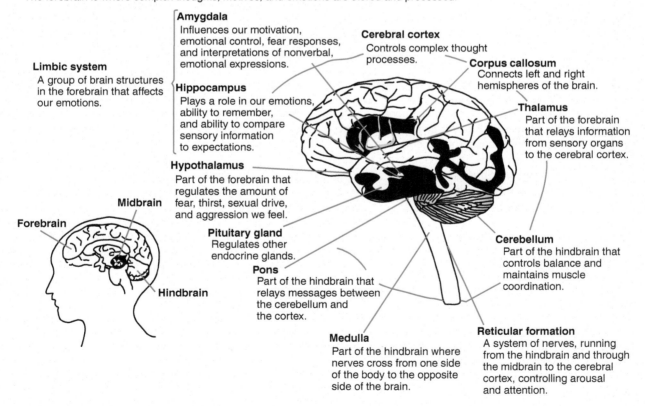

Hindbrain, Midbrain, and Forebrain
This is a picture of the brain from the left side. Beneath the cortex are three parts of the brain: the hindbrain, the midbrain, and the forebrain. The hindbrain controls some basic processes necessary for life. The midbrain is a relay station to the brain. The forebrain is where complex thoughts, motives, and emotions are stored and processed.

Amygdala
Influences our motivation, emotional control, fear responses, and interpretations of nonverbal, emotional expressions.

Cerebral cortex
Controls complex thought processes.

Corpus callosum
Connects left and right hemispheres of the brain.

Limbic system
A group of brain structures in the forebrain that affects our emotions.

Hippocampus
Plays a role in our emotions, ability to remember, and ability to compare sensory information to expectations.

Thalamus
Part of the forebrain that relays information from sensory organs to the cerebral cortex.

Hypothalamus
Part of the forebrain that regulates the amount of fear, thirst, sexual drive, and aggression we feel.

Midbrain

Forebrain

Pituitary gland
Regulates other endocrine glands.

Pons
Part of the hindbrain that relays messages between the cerebellum and the cortex.

Hindbrain

Cerebellum
Part of the hindbrain that controls balance and maintains muscle coordination.

Medulla
Part of the hindbrain where nerves cross from one side of the body to the opposite side of the brain.

Reticular formation
A system of nerves, running from the hindbrain and through the midbrain to the cerebral cortex, controlling arousal and attention.

SOURCE: Uba, L., & Huang, K. (1999). *Psychology*. Reprinted by permission of Laura Uba.

FIGURE 2.8 The cerebral cortex.

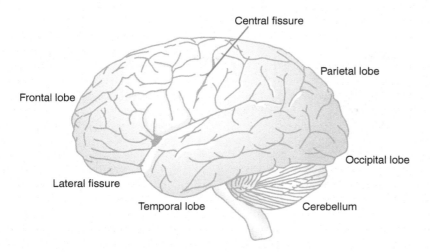

cortex develops. It's a little like traveling in outer space. Or as Davis (1997) has suggested, "It's a bit like an arrow reaching the space where the bull's-eye will be before anyone has even set up the target" (pp. 54–55). Certain cells behave like signposts, providing the traveling neurons with way stations as they progress on their journey. Neurons may also respond to the presence of certain chemicals that guide their movements in a particular direction.

About the fourth month of your prenatal life, your brain's basic structures were formed. Your neurons migrated in an orderly way and clustered with similar cells into distinct sections or regions in your brain, such as in the cerebral cortex or in the specific nuclei. The term **nucleus** here refers to a cluster of cells creating a structure, rather than to the kind of nucleus that is found in a single cell. An example is the nucleus accumbens, part of the basal ganglia in the brain's interior.

As we have seen, one important question concerns just how specialization of cells in different regions of the brain occurs and what directs it. This issue is complex and is the subject of intense investigation (Arlotta & Vanderhaeghen, 2017). However, most available evidence supports the view that cortical differentiation is an epigenetic process, primarily influenced by the kinds of environmental inputs the cortex receives. In other words, the geography of the cortex is not rigidly built in, but responds to activity and experiences by making changes in its structural organization (LaFrenier & MacDonald, 2013). This principle was demonstrated by researchers who transplanted part of the visual cortex of an animal to its parietal lobe (O'Leary & Stanfield, 1989). The transplanted neurons began to process somatosensory rather than visual information. Studies such as these show that the brain is amazingly malleable and demonstrates great **neuroplasticity**, particularly during early stages of development. In time, however, most cells become specialized for their activity, and it is harder to reverse their operation even though neuroplasticity continues to exist throughout life.

Structure and Function of Neurons

The neurons in your brain are among nature's most fantastic accomplishments. Although neurons come in various sizes and shapes, a typical neuron is composed of a cell body with a long extension, or **axon**, which is like a cable attached to a piece of electronic equipment. The axon itself can be quite long relative to the size of the cell's other structures because it needs to connect or "wire" various parts of the brain, such as the visual thalamus to the visual cortex. At the end of the axon are the **axon terminals**, which contain tiny sacs of chemical substances called **neurotransmitters**. Growing out from the cell body are smaller projections, called **dendrites**, resembling little branches, which receive messages or transmissions from other neurons. (See Figure 2.9.)

FIGURE 2.9 Structure of a neuron.

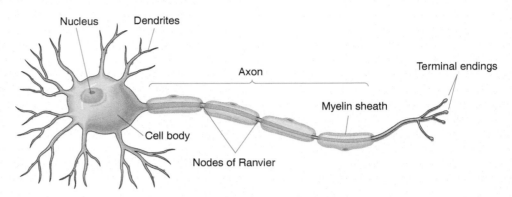

So how do brain cells "talk" to each other? Even though we speak of wiring or connecting, each neuron does not actually make physical contact with other neurons but remains separate. The points of near contact where communication occurs are called synapses. Communication is a process of sending and receiving electrochemical messages. Simply put, when a neuron responds to some excitation, or when it "fires," an electrical impulse, or message, travels down the axon to the axon terminals. The sacs in the axon terminals containing neurotransmitters burst and release their contents into the space between the neurons called the synaptic gap. Over a hundred different neurotransmitters have been identified, and many more are likely to be. Among those that have been widely studied are serotonin, acetylcholine, glutamate, gamma-amino butyric acid (GABA), epinephrine (adrenaline), norepinephrine (noradrenaline), and dopamine. Some of these are more common in specific parts of the brain than in others. They are literally chemical messengers that stimulate the dendrites, cell body, or axon of a neighboring neuron to either fire (excitation) or stop firing (inhibition). For example, glutamate is an excitatory transmitter that is important for transmission in the retina of the eye; GABA is an inhibitory transmitter that is found throughout the brain. Helpers should know that psychotropic drugs, such as anti-depressants and anti-psychotics, affect synaptic transmission. They change the availability of a neurotransmitter, either increasing or decreasing it, or they mimic or block a neurotransmitter's effects.

When neurons fire, the speed of the electrical impulse is greater if the axon is wrapped in glial cells forming a white, insulating sheath that facilitates conduction. This phenomenon, called myelination, begins prenatally for neurons in the sensorimotor areas of the brain but happens later in other areas. The term white matter mainly refers to bundles of myelinated axons, while grey matter refers to bundles of cell bodies, dendrites, and unmyelinated axons.

Myelination is a key aspect of brain maturation in childhood and adolescence, but it also continues into adulthood. Generally, the more myelination there is, the more efficient brain functions are. Changes in myelination accompany some kinds of learning and experience throughout life. Researchers have found white matter density changes in specific brain areas when people learn to juggle or they practice the piano intensively. Extended social isolation of either infant or adult mice leads to myelin deterioration accompanied by behavioral dysfunctions (see Klingseisen & Lyons, 2017).

Neurons are not "wired together" randomly. Rather, they are joined via their synaptic connections into groups called circuits. Circuits are part of larger organizations of neurons, called systems, such as the visual and olfactory systems. Two main types of neurons populate these systems, projection neurons, which have axons that extend far away from the cell body, and interneurons, which branch out closer to the local area. The intricate neural fireworks described earlier are going on all the time in your brain. Perhaps as you read this chapter, you are also listening to music and drinking a cup of coffee. Or you may be distracted by thoughts of a telephone conversation that you had earlier. The neuronal circuitry in your brain is processing all these stimuli, allowing your experiences to be perceived and comprehended.

Later Prenatal Brain Development

To return to your prenatal life story, your neurons began to fire spontaneously around the fourth month of gestation. This happened despite a lack of sensory input. Even though your eyes were not completely formed, the neurons that would later process visual information began firing as though they were preparing for the work they would do in a few months' time. By the end of the second and beginning of the third trimesters, your sense organs had developed sufficiently to respond to perceptual stimulation from outside your mother's womb. Sounds were heard by 15 weeks. Not only did you learn to recognize the sound of your mother's voice, but you also became familiar with the rhythms and patterns of your native language. In a classic study, DeCasper and colleagues conducted a project in which they directed pregnant women to recite a child's nursery rhyme out loud each day from the 33rd to the 37th week of pregnancy (DeCasper, Lecaneut, Busnel, Granier-Deferre, & Maugeais, 1994). During the 38th week, the women were asked to listen to a recording of either the familiar rhyme or an unfamiliar one while their fetuses' heart rates were being measured. The fetal heart rates dropped for the group who heard the familiar rhyme, signifying attention, but did not change for the group who heard the unfamiliar one. This result suggests that the fetus can attend to and discriminate the cadence of the rhyme. Studies such as this one should not be misinterpreted to mean that the fetus can "learn" as the term is commonly used. No one has suggested that the fetus can understand the poem. However, what this and other similar studies do indicate is an early responsivity to experience that begins to shape the contours of the brain by establishing patterns of neural or synaptic connections.

By your 25th week, you could open and close your eyes. You could see light then rather like the way you see things now when you turn toward a bright light with your eyes closed. At this point in development a fetus turns his head toward a light source, providing his visual system with light stimulation that probably promotes further brain development. Sensory experience has been found to be critical for healthy brain development after birth, and vision provides a good example of this principle. The interplay between neurons and visual experience was documented dramatically in another classic research project by Wiesel and Hubel (1965), who, in a series of experiments with kittens for which they won the Nobel Prize, showed that early visual deprivation has permanent deleterious effects. They sewed shut one of each kitten's eyes at birth so that only one eye was exposed to visual input. Several weeks later when the eyes were reopened, the kittens were found to be permanently blinded in the eye that had been deprived of stimulation. No amount of intervention or aggressive treatment could repair the damage. The neurons needed visual stimulation to make the proper connections for sight; in the absence of stimulation, the connections were never made, and blindness resulted. The existence of a critical or sensitive period for visual development was established. This research prompted surgeons to remove infant cataracts very shortly after birth instead of waiting several years, so that permanent damage to sight could be avoided.

Sensory systems, such as the auditory and visual systems, influence each other. Their eventual development is a function of their interrelationships (Murray, Lewkowicz, Amedi, & Wallace, 2016). The integration of these systems seems to serve the baby well in making sense of his world. So, for example, when a young infant sees an object he also has some sense of how it feels. Or when a 2-year-old watches lip movements, vocal sounds are easier to decipher.

Postnatal Brain Development

After your birth, your neurons continued to reproduce at a rapid pace, finally slowing down around 12 months of age. For many years it was assumed that neurons do not reproduce after early infancy. Newer research, however, has definitively documented the growth of new neurons throughout the life span in some parts of the brain (see Lux & van Ommen, 2016).These adult **neural stem cells** (NSCs) are generated in two principal brain areas, the **subventricular zone (SVZ)** located near the ventricles and in part of the hippocampus called the **dentate gyrus**. SVZ neurons migrate to the olfactory bulb where they appear to maintain its functioning by generating interneurons. New hippocampal neurons appear to integrate into existing networks that involve learning and memory. The location, migration patterns, and the ways adult neural stem cells integrate with existing neural networks are subjects of intense investigation. Available research indicates that increases and decreases in hippocampal neurogenesis during adulthood depend on environmental factors, including enriching stimulation, stress, and physical activity (Charney, 2012).

Brain growth after birth is also the result of the formation of new synapses. The growth spurt in synapses reflects the vast amount of learning that typically occurred for you and for most babies in the early months of postnatal life. Some areas of your developing brain experienced periods of rapid synaptic growth after birth, such as in the visual and auditory cortices, which increased dramatically between 3 and 4 months. In contrast, the synapses in your prefrontal cortex developed more slowly and reached their maximum density around 12 months. As you will see in the following sections, infants make rapid strides in cognitive development at the end of the first year, at about the time when prefrontal synapses have reached their peak density.

The growth of these connections was the product of both internal and external factors. Certain chemical substances within your brain, such as **nerve growth factor**, were absorbed by the neurons and aided in the production of synapses. Your own prenatal actions, such as turning, sucking your thumb, and kicking, as well as the other sensory stimulation you experienced, such as sound, light, and pressure, all contributed to synaptic development. However, as we noted earlier, the major work of **synaptogenesis**, the growth of new synapses, took place after birth, when much more sensory stimulation became available.

You arrived in the world with many more neurons than you would ever need. Over the next 12 years or so, through a process known as **neural pruning**, many neurons would die off and many synaptic connections would be selectively discarded. Some of these neurons migrated incorrectly and failed to make the proper connections, rendering them useless. Some of the synaptic connections were never established or were rarely used, so they ultimately disappeared as well. What counts most after birth is not the sheer number of neurons, but the number and strength of the interconnections. Those branching points of contact that remained to constitute your brain would be a unique reflection of your genetics and epigenetics, the conditions of your prenatal period, the nutrition you received, and your postnatal experience and environment. This rich network of connections is what makes your thinking, feeling brain, and its structure depends heavily upon what happens to you both before and after your birth.

You may be wondering how to account for the simultaneous processes of synaptogenesis and pruning, which seem to be acting at cross-purposes. What is the point of making new synaptic connections if many neurons and connections will just be culled eventually? In a classic analysis, Greenough and Black (1992) argued that **synaptic overproduction** occurs when it is highly likely that nature will provide the appropriate experience to structure the development of a particular system. For example, many animal species, as well as humans, go through a predictable sequence of activities designed to provide information for the brain to use in the development of vision. These include opening eyes, reaching for and grasping objects, and so on. This type of development depends upon environmental input that is **experience-expectant** because it is experience that is part of the evolutionary history of the organism and that occurs reliably in most situations. Hence, it is "expected." Lack of such experience results in developmental abnormalities, as we saw in the kitten experiments performed by Wiesel and Hubel. The timing of this particular kind of experience for nervous system growth is typically very important; that is, there is a critical period for such experience-expectant development. Nature may provide for an overabundance of synapses because it then can select only those that work best, pruning out the rest.

When human infants are neglected or deprived of typical parental caregiving, the cognitive consequences can be severe. One reason may be that ordinary caregiving behaviors—repeated vocalizations, facial expressions, touch—are necessary for experience-expectant development. McLaughlin and colleagues have argued that such caregiving helps direct infant's attention to relevant stimuli in the environment. This facilitates experience-expectant learning of basic associations between vocal sounds

TABLE 2.5 Studying the Developing Brain

TECHNIQUES	PROCEDURES AND PRODUCTS
Electroencephalography	Electrodes attached to the scalp can allow recording of the electrical (EEG) activity of the cerebral cortex. Recordings from the electrodes graph the frequency and amplitude of brain waves. Event related potentials (ERPs), which are specific brain wave changes in response to sights, sounds, or other experiences, can be recorded as well, helping to identify areas of cortex that process the type of input used.
Functional magnetic resonance imaging (fMRI)	A computerized system for recording activity anywhere in the brain by imaging responses to input. Stimulation causes the affected areas of the brain to increase blood flow and metabolism. A magnetic scanner detects these changes and sends the information to a computer, which produces an image that shows the differential activity of brain areas. fMRI is one of several MRI technologies, generally referred to, along with PET and fNIR techniques, as "brain imaging."
Positron emission tomography (PET)	Like the fMRI, a type of brain scan that detects changes in blood flow and metabolism in any part of the brain, and produces an image that shows the differential activity of brain areas. Requires either injection or inhalation of radioactive material.
Functional near-infrared spectroscopy (fNIRS)	Another technique that measures changes in cortical blood flow and metabolism in response to stimulation. It is especially useful with infants and young children, because it only requires wearing a cap that allows free head movements. Other imaging techniques require that the head remain motionless inside a machine that can produce loud sounds that may be startling. Disadvantages are more limited depth of measurement and less spatial resolution.

and situations, between actions and outcomes, and so on, that other learning depends upon (McLaughlin, Sheridan, & Nelson, 2017).

In contrast to overproducing synapses in anticipation of later experience, some synaptic growth occurs as a direct result of exposure to more individualized kinds of environmental events. This type of neural growth is called **experience-dependent**. The quality of the synaptic growth "depends" upon variations in environmental opportunities. Stimulating and complex environments promote such growth in rat pups and other mammals (e.g., Kolb, Gibb, & Robinson, 2003). It seems likely that the same is true for infants and children. Imagine what might be the differences in synaptic development between children raised by parents who speak two different languages in their home and children raised by those who speak only one, for example. Experience-dependent processes do not seem to be limited to sensitive periods but can occur throughout the life span. Connections that remain active become stabilized, whereas those that are not used die out. This type of experientially responsive synaptic growth and the concomitant changes in brain structure it induces have been linked to learning and the formation of some kinds of memory. This process fine-tunes the quality of brain structure and function and individualizes the brain to produce the best person–environment fit (Bialystock, 2017).

Clearly, your early experiences played a vital role in the functional and structural development of your brain. Your experiences helped stimulate the duplication of neurons in some parts of your brain, and they prompted synaptogenesis and pruning. These processes contribute to the plasticity of brain development, which can be quite remarkable. Suppose, for example, that you had suffered an injury to your left cerebral cortex during infancy. You can see in Box 2.1 that ordinarily, the left cerebral cortex serves language functions. Yet when the left hemisphere is damaged in infancy, the right hemisphere is very likely to take over language functions. Your language acquisition might have been delayed by an early left hemisphere injury, but by 5 or 6 years of age you would most likely have caught up with other children's language development. Adult brains also exhibit some plasticity after brain injury, but nothing as dramatic as we see in children (e.g., Gianotti, 2015; Stiles, 2001).

Understanding of postnatal brain development has improved dramatically over the last few decades, spurred by modern technologies. In Table 2.5, we describe several of the approaches that are recurrently mentioned in this and later chapters.

MyLab Education Self-Check 2.3

The Developing Stress and Adaptation System

2.4 **Explain the central role of the brain in mediating stress-induced adaptations and recognize correlations between allostatic overload and the effects of subsequent epigenetic alterations.**

Learning about early brain development can help you to understand how development proceeds more generally. You have seen that the intricate interplay of genes and the many layers of environment, from the cell to the outside world, produces an organized brain and nervous system. That system interacts with all other bodily systems and continuously re-organizes in response to experience. Development is a lifelong process of **adaptation**, which is adjustment to change: changing bodily needs as well as new and different opportunities and challenges from the environment. Some changes and the adaptations that we make to them are predictable and repetitious. For example, our bodies' needs for food and rest change predictably during the course of a day, and we respond by eating and sleeping on relatively consistent schedules. But much of our experience requires adjusting to less predictable events, which can alter our brains and behavior, sometimes temporarily and sometimes more permanently. Developmental science is particularly focused on understanding the process of **stress**, adaptation responses to challenges, and how stress helps to produce healthy and unhealthy life trajectories.

What Is Stress?

Stress is a word that most of us use often, usually to describe what we feel when life seems challenging or frightening or uncertain. We call our feelings "stress" when it looks like we will be late for class or work, or we discover that there is not enough money to cover the rent, or we find a skin lesion that might be cancerous. Scientists and practitioners also use the term to cover lots of situations, and as a result, it can sometimes be difficult to pin down its meaning. An early researcher, Hans Selye (e.g., 1956), first used the term *stress* and helped launch its worldwide popularity as well as the breadth of its use. It was Selye who characterized stress as a bodily response to any change or demand (i.e., an adaptation), and a **stressor** as an event that initiates such a response. Stressors can be noxious or positive; the key is that they induce adaptation.

Modern researchers often make more fine-grained distinctions among types of stress. McEwen and McEwen (2016) summarize these as **good stress**, **tolerable stress**, and **toxic stress**. *Good stress* is "the efficient, acute activation and efficient turning off of the normal physiological stress response when one faces a challenge" (p. 451)—a challenge such as giving a talk or managing the drive to work through heavy traffic. *Tolerable stress* is a more chronic physiological response, likely to be triggered by more serious and long-lasting threats such as losing a job, but the chronic response is turned off eventually as the individual finds ways to cope, relying on a range of strengths, such as self-esteem, supportive relationships, and so on. *Toxic stress* is the same kind of chronic response, but it fails to "turn off"—the individual is unable to cope effectively.

Determining whether an experience or event is a stressor is complicated by the fact that what is stressful is, to some degree, in the eye of the beholder. Although most people would agree that certain situations are more traumatic than others, individual differences in what people view as stressful are influenced by prior learning, memories, expectations, and perceptions about one's ability to cope. Also, whether a potential stressor triggers a stress reaction, and the strength and duration of that reaction, depend on many contextual factors, especially social context. A person's social standing matters; so does the presence of a loving, supportive caregiver or partner or friend (Rutter, 2016).

The concept of **allostasis** is helpful in understanding where stress fits into a person's overall physical and psychological development. *Allostasis* refers to the regulation of many interacting bodily processes affected by stressors, from the sleep–wake cycle to blood pressure to digestion, as the individual adjusts to experiences. Allostatic load is the accumulation of the effects of multiple stressors; and allostatic overload refers to pathological changes brought on by toxic stress (McEwen & McEwen, 2016).

Some general points about allostasis are important to keep in mind. Adaptations change our brains. The physiological events involved in the stress response alter gene expression and a variety of cellular and intercellular processes. We learn and change, sometimes in ways that are positive, sometimes not. Acute, mild to moderate stressors that are typically associated with good outcomes, such as exercise or giving a speech, are often brain-enhancing. The "good stress" they generate can promote synaptic or neuron growth. When stress is chronic and/or intensely negative, brain changes can make us less resilient (more cognitively rigid), reducing the capacity to learn in the future. Dendrites are lost, synaptic and neuron growth is suppressed, and processes that promote recovery from stress can be impaired. The costs of allostatic load mount up, leading to a host of mental and physical problems (McEwen et al., 2015).

Before we consider the pathological effects of toxic stress, let's review the typical response we call stress, or "good stress." It involves a complicated, multilevel set of physiological reactions, governed by many parts of the brain. Because what initiates stress is affected by an individual's cognitions and context, it is clear that cortical areas such as the prefrontal cortex play a role. Parts of the brain involved in emotional and social processing, especially the amygdala and basal ganglia, are pivotal, as are closely related areas, such as the hippocampus and hypothalamus.

The Architecture of the Stress Response

A stressor is first detected via an interconnected network of sensory areas in the cortex, thalamus, and amygdala, the brain's specialist in threat detection (LeDoux, 2012). The amygdala is involved in virtually all fear conditioning and works to jumpstart multiple stress-related networks peripheral to the central nervous system. Two major peripheral systems subject to this central control are the sympathetic nervous system (SNS) and the hypothalamic-pituitary-adrenal (HPA) axis. The *SNS* releases important chemicals such as epinephrine (adrenaline) and norepinephrine (noradrenalin) that send a burst of energy to those organs necessary for "fight or flight" (e.g., heart, lungs) while diverting energy from less necessary systems (e.g., growth, reproduction, digestion). Adrenaline is instrumental in causing the well-known effects of arousal, such as racing heart and sweaty palms. Once the threat has passed, the parasympathetic nervous system (PSNS) counteracts the sympathetic system's effects, down regulating its activity. The heart rate returns to base rate and ordinary bodily functions go back to normal functioning.

The *HPA axis* is activated when the amygdala stimulates the hypothalamus. The hypothalamus communicates the danger message to the pituitary gland by means of the chemical messenger corticotropin releasing factor (CRF). The message is read by the pituitary as a sign to release adrenocorticotropic hormone (ACTH) into the bloodstream. ACTH then makes its way to the adrenal glands, situated atop the kidneys, which receive the message to release cortisol. Cortisol is a key glucocorticoid hormone produced by humans. Glucocorticoid receptors (GRs) are located in organs and tissues throughout the body and brain. When cortisol and other glucocorticoids bind with these receptors, physiological responses to stressors are triggered. One of these, for example, is a reduction in inflammation, the body's normal response to a disease pathogen or irritant. Another is an increase in glucose production, increasing energy levels. Cortisol in the bloodstream also travels back to the brain, forming an important feedback loop. Cortisol binds to GRs in the amygdala and the hippocampus, efficiently shutting down the acute stress response and helping the body to return to a normal state (Spencer & Deak, 2016).

Toxic Stress and Allostatic Overload

You can see now that allostasis engages many regulatory systems, altering physiological functions temporarily as the body deals with an acute stressor. The typical "fight or flight" reaction rights itself quickly so that normal functions like digestion and fighting infection can proceed. It should not be surprising then, that chronic and intense stress can be toxic, creating allostatic load or overload with the potential to alter many physical and psychological functions, sometimes permanently. For example, cortisol secretion is part of many non–stress-related bodily processes (Spencer & Deak, 2016), and under normal circumstances, cortisol levels in the bloodstream (which can be measured in saliva samples) show a regular daily pattern of morning elevation and afternoon decline. This pattern is often disrupted in chronically stressed individuals. They might show elevated cortisol levels throughout the day or unusual daily variations (e.g., high afternoon levels). Allostatic overload also tends to make the stress response itself less efficient. It might remain activated even when a threat has ended or it may produce a blunted response to threat (Rutter, 2016).

Allostatic overload also affects the immune system. Chemical messengers of the immune system, called **cytokines**, are produced during the immune response. These proteins can be either pro-inflammatory or anti-inflammatory in nature. Inflammation, it should be noted, is the body's protective response to infection or injury. When appropriate, inflammation is adaptive; however, when inflammatory processes persist unremittingly, mental and physical diseases can result. During an acute stress response, as you have seen, cortisol reduces the body's immune response. But chronic activation of the stress-response system revamps the immune system, which becomes under-responsive to cortisol so that pro-inflammatory cytokines are then under-regulated. Persistent inflammation increases the risk of health problems over time, such as cardiovascular disease, type 2 diabetes, and rheumatoid arthritis. Along with other changes associated with toxic stress, it is also linked to an increased risk of psychopathology, such as depression and schizophrenia (Danese & Baldwin, 2017).

Toxic stress may do its damage largely by fostering epigenetic alterations that modify gene expression (e.g., Provencal & Binder, 2015; Tyrka, Ridout, & Parade, 2016). For example, children who are maltreated by their caregivers are victims of toxic stress. They experience many of the short- and long-term effects of allostatic overload that we have described. In a study of low income, school-aged children, researchers found substantial differences in methylation patterns for maltreated children as compared to nonmaltreated children. Especially noteworthy is that maltreated children showed methylation differences for genes that are linked to risk for many physical and psychiatric disorders (Cicchetti, Hetzel, Rogosch, Handley, & Toth, 2016).

The impact of stressors on the development of the stress response and all of the systems involved in that response begins in utero. In the prenatal period, stress experienced by the mother has teratogenic effects on the developing fetus. Maternal stress increases the risk of a wide range of negative outcomes, from miscarriage to low birth weight to postnatal neural and behavioral dysregulation, such as learning problems and increased anxiety levels. When glucocorticoids such as cortisol are present at typical, daily levels during pregnancy, they play a positive role in the development of a fetus's organs and tissues, especially in the third trimester. But human and animal studies have shown that when a fetus is overexposed prenatally to a mother's stress hormones, brain development can be altered, especially in the HPA axis (Provencal & Binder, 2015). Even mild prenatal maternal stress in later pregnancy has been shown in animal studies to increase DNA methylation levels in the frontal cortex and hippocampus; heavy doses of maternal stress dramatically decrease methylation in the same areas. In either case, epigenetic changes are induced in brain areas that are key to normal stress reactivity and to many cognitive functions as well (Bock, Wainstock, Braun, & Segal, 2015).

In humans and other mammals, the HPA axis is relatively immature at birth, and the environment can play a major role in its further development. You saw earlier in this chapter that early maternal caregiving can alter the reactivity of a rat pup's stress response for life. Rat pups who get lots of maternal licking and grooming produce more of the critical receptors in the hippocampus that bind with glucocorticoids, ending acute stress responses quickly. These pups mature into mellow adults (Meaney, 2010). With human babies, researchers have found that more sensitive maternal caregiving in infancy is linked to lower cortisol levels during and after exposure to stressors over the first three years of life (Laurent, Harold, Leve, Shelton & van Goozen, 2016). This suggests that just as in rats, the care babies receive early in life can alter the architecture of their stress response. In Box 2.2 and in the Applications section of this chapter, you will learn more about the long-term consequences of prenatal exposure to stressors and of chronic stress early in life. You will also learn how helpers might intervene to mitigate those consequences.

Box 2.2: Do Numbers Matter? Early Adverse Experiences Add Up

No doubt about it, early experience matters. In this chapter, we describe some of the processes that explain how adverse experiences exert harm. This knowledge raises serious concerns for practitioners. Which experiences pose risks for children's development? Is there a tolerable level of stress for children? Are there certain times during development when risks exert maximal influence? At first glance, these questions seem impossible to answer. Each individual possesses a unique blend of strengths and vulnerabilities, making exact prediction unlikely. Nonetheless, some large-scale epidemiological investigations of this question could provide useful guidance for clinicians and public health experts.

Several longitudinal investigations have looked at numbers of stressful experiences in children's lives and their subsequent relationship to health or adversity. A western Australian study (Robinson et al., 2011) followed a group of 2,868 pregnant women from 16 weeks gestation (updated at 34 weeks gestation) until their children were adolescents. During their pregnancies, mothers were asked about the number and types of stressors they experienced. Stressors included financial difficulties, job loss, deaths of relatives, residential moves, marital difficulties, separation, or divorce. The researchers controlled for maternal SES, age, ethnic status, smoking, drinking, education, and history of emotional problems. Child variables, including gestational age, birth weight, and histories of breastfeeding, were also controlled. Assessments of children's physical, emotional, and behavioral functions were made at ages 1, 2, 3, 5, 8, 10, and 14.

Results showed that offspring of mothers who reported zero to two stressors during pregnancy did not differ significantly on measures of **internalizing problems** (e.g., depression, low self-esteem) and **externalizing problems** (e.g., acting out, aggressive, disruptive behaviors). However, children whose mothers experienced three or more stressful events during their pregnancies exhibited significantly higher levels of internalizing and externalizing problems at every assessment period across the prospective study compared to the group with fewer stressors. Externalizing problems were more pronounced in children whose mothers experienced four events compared to children of mothers reporting no stress. If mothers experienced five or more events, higher rates of child internalizing disorders were observed even after controlling for many other possible contributions to depression and anxiety. Maternal stressors experienced at 16 weeks gestation were more strongly related to later problems than those experienced at 34 weeks. Overall, the results of this study support a **dose-response relationship** between numbers of prenatal stressors and later

maladaptive outcomes. This means that lower levels of stressors predicted lower symptom levels. Symptoms increased with each additional stressor exposure in a stepwise fashion. It's important to keep in mind, however, that the nature of some stressors (e.g., low SES, financial difficulty) can exert an ongoing influence on development in addition to having prenatal impact. Conditions of low SES can provide a context for ongoing development in which adverse consequences accumulate (Duncan & Brooks-Gunn, 1997).

Researchers from a large California health consortium took a similar epidemiological approach to the study of the effect of early life stress on subsequent illness. Chronic diseases like cancer, heart disease, and diabetes account for 70% of deaths in the United States (Centers for Disease Control [CDC], 2012). To a large degree, these diseases are related to unhealthy behaviors like smoking, overeating, drinking, lack of exercise, and so on. Because such behaviors are modifiable, efforts to understand the factors underlying unhealthy behaviors can improve public health, reduce mortality, and potentially decrease national health expenditures. Two waves of patient data from San Diego's Kaiser Permanente Medical System were collected for the Adverse Childhood Experiences (ACE) study (Felitti et al., 1998). Respondents (N = 17,421) reported their early experiences of adversity in the following 10 categories: emotional abuse, physical abuse, sexual abuse, physical neglect, emotional neglect, substance abuse in the home, mental illness of parent or household member, domestic violence, incarceration of a household member, parental divorce or separation. Close to two thirds of the sample reported having experienced at least one of these adverse childhood experiences (see Figure 2.10). Over 20% reported three or more ACEs, and rates of comorbidity were high. The most common adverse experience was substance abuse in the home. Findings showed a similar pattern to that observed in the Australian study. Mental and physical health consequences in adulthood increased in a stepwise fashion proportional to the number of early adverse experiences (Anda et al., 2006). To date, over 60 studies have supported the initial finding that early life experience of adversity confers risk. The higher the dose of early adversity, the greater the risk. Adversity's effects manifest in the following areas: alcoholism and alcohol abuse, behavioral problems and developmental delays in children, chronic obstructive pulmonary disease, depression, fetal death, financial stress, health-related quality of life, illicit drug use, ischemic heart disease, liver disease, obesity, poor work performance, risk for intimate partner violence, schizophrenia in males, multiple sexual partners,

(continued)

sexually transmitted diseases, smoking, suicide attempts, unintended pregnancies, early initiation of smoking and/or sexual activity, adolescent pregnancy, risk for sexual violence, use of prescription psychotropic medication, poor academic achievement and premature mortality (The Adverse Childhood Experience CDC website: www.cdc.gov/violenceprevention/acestudy/journal.html; Larkin, Shields, & Anda, 2012; Vallejos, Cesoni, Farinola, Bertone, & Prokopez, 2016).

Studies suggest that early adverse experiences contribute to the etiology of later illness by altering allostatic regulation and interfering with brain, immune, and endocrine system development (Danese & McEwen, 2012). If this is what is actually happening, you should expect that the effect would be present regardless of changing social attitudes about reporting mental illness, medication use, and so on. In other words, the biologically based changes attendant upon adversity would be fundamental. Analyses of ACEs in four patient cohorts from 1900 to 1978 provided supportive results (Dube, Felitti, Dong, Giles, & Anda, 2003). The strength of the dose-response association between ACEs and health outcomes was observed within each successive cohort, even though the prevalence of risk behaviors varied across decades. For example, changes in attitudes about smoking and variations in smoking behavior have occurred over the 78 years included in this analysis. Nevertheless, the relationship between ACE and smoking remained consistent. This evidence suggests that early adverse experiences contribute to multiple health problems by means of "inherent biological effects of traumatic stressors (ACEs) on the developing nervous systems of children" (Dube et al., 2003, p. 274).

The impact of ACE research has been profound because it connects some dots between the rich literature on early childhood maltreatment and that of adult health and productivity. Many states have begun to add ACE questions to their own assessments of statewide behavioral health (e.g., Austin & Herrick, 2014). However, the original work from Kaiser Permanente involved primarily White participants with college experience and health insurance. Recognition of racial disparities in both health and health care have prompted researchers to expand the list of conventional adversity categories to include experiences that may be more frequently observed in diverse groups. Since poverty has such a powerful impact on development (Evans & Kim, 2013), and because low SES children tend to report higher numbers of ACEs (Slopen et al., 2016), its inclusion in the list could improve ability to track outcomes and predict the needs of poor children as they age. In addition, factors outside the home such as community violence and racism have research support that indicates long-term adverse effects.

Using a racially and socioeconomically diverse sample in Philadelphia, Cronholm and his colleagues (2015) tested a "second-generation" measure of ACEs. This measure included the conventional categories but added five additional questions related to witnessing violence in one's community, having a

history of foster care, being bullied, experiencing racism, and living in an unsafe neighborhood. Survey results from a group of 1,784 predominantly African American respondents indicated higher incidences of conventional ACEs except for sexual abuse, physical neglect, and emotional neglect, which were more frequently reported in the original California sample. Notably, 50% of the Philadelphia sample experienced 1 to 2 expanded ACEs and 13% experienced 3 or more. Approximately one third reported no experience with expanded ACEs. As you might imagine, there was some overlap between conventional and expanded categories. Almost half of the Philadelphia sample had experienced both categories of early adverse events. About 14% experienced adversities only included in the expanded list. If not for these additional categories, researchers would have missed specific kinds of adversity faced by this lower income, urban group.

If we are to fully understand the developmental pathways to health and disease for everyone, it is crucial to understand the vulnerability profiles and specific stress exposure that may be related to culture, race, gender, disability, and socioeconomic status. This epidemiological approach provides a good example of early steps in the process of translational research. As the process moves forward, programs and policies can be developed, tested, and implemented to target common and specific risks, ultimately improving quality of life and reducing disease burden for all. With such clear evidence of risk factors and such potential for remediation, prevention and intervention may never have been more important than they are now.

FIGURE 2.10 Potential influences throughout the life span of adverse childhood experiences.
Adverse experiences in childhood add to the risk of physical, social, and emotional problems throughout the life span.

SOURCE: Republished with permission of Elsevier Ltd. from Relationship of childhood abuse and dysfunction to many of the leading causes of death in adults. *American Journal of Preventive Medicine*, by Felitti, V. J., Anda, R. F., Nordenberg, D., Williamson, D. F., Spitz, A. M., Edwards, V., Koss, M. P., & Marks, J. S. (1998); permission conveyed through Copyright Clearance Center, Inc.

MyLab Education Self-Check 2.4

Applications

In this chapter, we present some breakthroughs in research on nature and nurture and their complicated yet fascinating interdependence. It may be relatively intuitive to understand that different kinds and levels of exposure to environmental substances, like alcohol or toxins, in combination with different genetic combinations, interact to produce varying effects on a developing organism. For example, two hypothetical unrelated individuals, whose mothers were exposed to the same level of a toxin during pregnancy, might show greater or lesser effects depending upon genetic makeup, timing of exposure, and other contextual circumstances. This is just one possible scenario that illustrates gene–environment interactions. However, it's clearly more mystifying to contemplate how *other levels of environmental experience*, like caregiving, produce genetic differences. Caregiving is not a substance, like a drug, an x-ray, or a vitamin. Yet, as we have seen, nonrandom variations in caregiving have been shown to produce observable genetic modifications. The epigenome, which literally translates as "above the genome," has a way of exerting its influence via chemical changes to genetic material. Methylation, one major way of accomplishing the job, is like a signature that your environment writes on your DNA. These genetic signatures replicate throughout life and often across generations, although sometimes they can be reversed by environmental supports or chemical means. This is a striking discovery, and it brings us to a whole new level of discussion about nature and nurture. "From an epigenetic perspective, divisions between genes, brain, and behavior are artificial, as the environment becomes embodied in the genome. It is the epigenomic-modified DNA sequence that results in protein synthesis, which, in turn, canalizes development. In fact, to a large extent *nature is nurture*" (van Izjendoorn, Bakermans-Kranenburg, & Ebstein, 2011, p. 309).

Handle with Care

What is generally axiomatic to people everywhere has the backing of science and has come to be, perhaps, the singular developmental lesson: Children need loving care. While there are clearly individual differences in susceptibility to stress and risk, there is strong evidence that harm, substantial and often long-term, can be done to developing organisms when subjected to adversity. Breakthrough basic research is shedding light on the genetic and epigenetic mechanisms that translate early toxic experience into later illness. The old adage, "children will outgrow it," regardless of how difficult the situation might be, is not necessarily supported by the facts. More accurate is the message of Van der Kolk's (2014) compelling book on stress and trauma: *the body keeps the score*. For the helper, this knowledge can make practice decisions both clearer and more challenging. They are clearer because evidence is strong; they're more challenging because the need is so great and the stakes are so high.

The Baby Blues: Depression from Preconception Through Postpartum Periods

The health and well-being of mothers and fathers even before conception are important influences on children's development. So treatments, especially during the prenatal stage, can actually serve as prevention for infants. Given their exquisite sensitivity to experience, humans are most responsive to epigenetic programming from preconception to early childhood, that is, beginning before conception, while in utero, and continuing through childhood. During pregnancy high levels of maternal stress hormones can pass through the placenta, programming the settings like those of a thermostat to be more stress-reactive (DiPietro, 2004; Meaney, 2010). Studies report a variety of outcomes for infants exposed to maternal stress (both acute and chronic), depression, and anxiety. These include higher rates of anxiety, autism, schizophrenia, impaired insulin resistance, lower immune functioning, premature birth, low birth weight, attachment difficulties, and social and cognitive delays, to name a few (Entringer, Buss, & Wadhwa, 2015; Monk, Spicer, & Champagne, 2012). It does not appear that major stress is required to affect fetal development. Similar to the gradient of effects produced by alcohol during pregnancy, modest levels of maternal stress have been associated with subclinical symptoms (O'Connor, Monk, & Fitelson, 2014). Consequently, stress reduction information and support are critically important for all pregnant women, their partners, and families, not just for those with serious mental illness.

The knowledge that maternal stress and mental illness can impact the developing fetus in such consequential ways has thrown a spotlight on services for prenatal and postnatal depression. Several kinds of treatments can reduce postpartum depression in affected individuals (Dennis & Dowswell, 2013; Stuart & Koleva, 2014). Postpartum home visits from professionals, telephone support, Cognitive-Behavioral Therapy (CBT), Interpersonal Therapy (IP, see Chapter 11), and mindfulness meditation (see Chapter 14) are among those efforts that show the most promise. In general, CBT and IP therapies were most successful when they were manualized and adapted to women's specific concerns during the perinatal period.

Although many pregnant women prioritize non-pharmacological treatments for depression, use of medication may be warranted given the great risk posed by this illness. Research reviews show mixed results on the use of antidepressant medication during pregnancy (Berard et al., 2007; Grigoriadis et al., 2013; Yonkers, Blackwell, Glover, & Forray, 2014). There is a possible risk for spontaneous abortion and preterm birth with general **SSRI (selective serotonin reuptake inhibitor)** use and an increased risk of cardiac malformations with paroxetine use, especially during the first trimester (Knudsen, Hansen, Garne, & Andersen, 2014).

Neonatal behavioral difficulties such as irritability, excessive crying, feeding problems, difficulty breathing, seizure, vomiting, etc., which typically remit after the first two weeks, are also associated with SSRI use. Despite these effects, continued use of SSRIs during pregnancy is advised for women with a history of past or recurrent depression (American College of Obstetricians and Gynecologists [ACOG], 2006). Because no medication is completely free of side effects, women should carefully evaluate the benefits and risks of any drug in consultation with health care providers.

Pregnancy Anxiety

Emotions can run high when women and their partners decide to have a baby and try to conceive. Emotions can be even more voluble during pregnancy, when the reality of childbearing and future responsibility sets in. Many expectant parents experience episodes of joyful anticipation and even mild anxiety as they await the birth of their child. However, as may happen in times of stress, affective disorders can be triggered in vulnerable individuals. Depression and anxiety are highly comorbid, and it is difficult to disentangle them when we discuss emotional difficulties in the prenatal and postnatal periods. However, one clinical syndrome, pregnancy-related anxiety (PrA) (Blackmore, Gustafsson, Gilchrist, Wyman, & O'Connor, 2016), has generated interest. Efforts to isolate its specific features and determine its distinct clinical significance have grown.

While sharing some of the general characteristics of generalized anxiety, pregnancy-related anxiety reflects a specific constellation of concerns. These include worries about the health of the baby, ability to withstand the rigors of childbirth, fears about appearance, financial issues, and loss of control (Bayrampour et al., 2016). Some research suggests that pregnancy-related anxiety is a more sensitive predictor of infant birth weight, gestational age, and maternal postnatal mood than generalized anxiety alone (Blackmore et al., 2016; Blair, Glynn, Sandman, & Davis, 2011). More research needs to be done to determine which interventions might be most helpful; however, these specific concerns might well be important ones for helpers to address with pregnant women during counseling and in other supportive settings.

Healthy Baby Guidelines

As you have read in this chapter, certain practices really do promote healthy prenatal development and others put the fetus's well-being at substantial risk. Advice about diet, nutrition and weight gain, use of medications, avoidance of toxic substances and exposures, spacing pregnancies to give the body a chance to recover, etc. can be found on many reputable websites that report research-based evidence (e.g., March of Dimes, marchofdimes.org).

Table 2.6 (Zolotor & Carlough, 2014) provides a list of common issues facing pregnant women along with evidence-based advice for helpers.

TABLE 2.6 Counseling Topics in Pregnancy

TOPIC	COMMENTS
Air travel[6,10]	Air travel generally is safe for pregnant women up to four weeks before the due date; however, long flights are associated with an increased risk of venous thrombosi.
	Availability of medical resources at the destination should be considered.
	The Centers for Disease Control and Prevention provides information for pregnant travelers at http://wwwnc.cdc.gov/travel/yellowbook/2012/chapter-8-advising-travelers-with-specific-needs/pregnant-travelers.htm
Breastfeeding[9–11]	Breastfeeding should be recommended as the best feeding method for most infants.
	Breastfeeding contraindications include maternal human immunodeficiency virus infection, chemical dependency, and use of certain medications.
	Structured behavior counseling, one-on-one needs-based counseling, and breastfeeding education programs increase breastfeeding success.
Childbirth education[6,9–11]	Childbirth education is a common part of prenatal care in the United States.
	Although it may increase confidence, it does not change the experience of labor or birth outcomes.
Exercise[6,10]	At least 30 minutes of moderate exercise on most days of the week is a reasonable activity level for most pregnant women.
	Pregnant women should avoid activities that put them at risk of falls or abdominal injuries.
Fetal movement counts[6,9–11]	Routine counting of fetal movements should not be performed.
	This has been shown to increase the patient's anxiety and results in more triage evaluations, prenatal testing, and interventions without improving outcomes.
Hair treatments[10]	Although hair dyes and treatments have not been explicitly linked to fetal malformation, they should be avoided during early pregnancy.

TOPIC	COMMENTS
Heavy metals[9]	Exposure to heavy metals should be avoided during early pregnancy because of the potential for delayed fetal neurologic development.
Herbal therapies[6,9,10]	Pregnant women should avoid herbal therapies with known harmful effects to the fetus, such as ginkgo, ephedra, and ginseng, and should be cautious of substances with unknown effects.
Hot tubs and saunas[10,17]	Hot tubs and saunas should be avoided during the first trimester, because heat exposure during early pregnancy has been associated with neural tube defects and miscarriage.
Labor and delivery[9,10]	Pregnant women should be counseled about what to do when their membranes rupture, what to expect when labor begins, strategies to manage pain, and the value of having support during labor.
Medications (prescription and over-the-counter)[6,9,10]	Risks and benefits of individual medications should be reviewed.
	Few medications have been proven safe for use during pregnancy, particularly during the first trimester.
Radiation[9]	Pregnant women should avoid ionizing radiation, because it may affect fetal thyroid development.
	Adverse fetal effects are not associated with radiography that is in a normal diagnostic range (less than 50 mGy) and that avoids direct abdominal views; ultrasonography; or use of microwaves, computers, or cell phones.
Seat-belt use[6,9]	Pregnant women should use a three-point seat belt.
	Less than one-half of pregnant women use a seat belt, and less than one-third receive physician counseling about seat-belt use.
Sex[6,9,10]	Most women may continue to have sex during pregnancy; however, in certain situations (e.g., placenta previa), avoiding sex is generally recommended.
Solvents[9,11]	Pregnant women should avoid exposure to solvents, particularly in areas without adequate ventilation.
	Exposure to solvents has been associated with an increase in miscarriage rates.
Substance use	
Alcohol[6,9–11]	Pregnant women should be screened for alcohol use; no amount of alcohol consumption has been proven safe during pregnancy.
	Counseling is effective in decreasing alcohol consumption in pregnant women and associated infant morbidity.
Illicit drugs[6,9–11]	Pregnant women should be informed of the potential adverse effects of illicit drug use on the fetus.
	Pregnant women who use illicit drugs often require specialized interventions.
	Admission to a detoxification program may be indicated, as well as methadone therapy in women addicted to opiates.
Tobacco[6,9–11,18]	Pregnant women should be screened for tobacco use, and individualized, pregnancy-tailored counseling should be offered to smokers.
	Smoking cessation counseling and multicomponent strategies are effective in decreasing the incidence of low-birth-weight infants.
Workplace issues[6,10]	Although working in general is safe during pregnancy, some working conditions, such as prolonged standing and exposure to certain chemicals, are associated with pregnancy complications.

Helping the Most Vulnerable: Preterm and Low-Birth-Weight (LBW) Babies

Many variables are associated with the risk of delivering an infant preterm (less than 37 weeks gestation) or of low birth weight (less than 5 pounds, 8 ounces). There were unacceptably high increases in both categories through the 1990s and early 2000s, but rates have declined and have held steady in recent years. U.S. data from 2014 indicate 8% of live births were classified LBW and 9.5% of births were preterm births (Hamilton, Martin, Osterman, Curtin, & Matthews, 2015). Poverty, drug and alcohol use, smoking, chronically high blood pressure, diabetes, and insufficient weight gain during pregnancy all increase risk. The risk is also higher for women younger than 17 or older than 35. Preterm and LBW infants are much more likely to experience a number of chronic medical problems such as respiratory infections, delays in achievement of developmental milestones, behavioral problems, feeding difficulties, and related academic consequences (Conley & Bennett, 2002; Wallace & McCarton, 1997).

Field and her associates have applied the power of touch to enhance the development of preterm and LBW infants by developing a standard infant massage therapy protocol. Touch has long been recognized as one of the primary forms of human communication, bonding, and healing, and it appears to be the infant's best developed sense at birth (Hertenstein, 2002; Reisman, 1987). Outcome studies of this intervention demonstrate that massage is effective for increasing weight gain (Field et al., 1986; Scafidi, Field, & Schanberg, 1993); social responsiveness (Field, Scafidi, & Schanberg, 1987); bone growth and development (Moyer-Mileur, Brubstetter, McNaught, Gill, & Chan, 2000); and for decreasing cortisol levels, crying, and sleep disturbances

(Acolet et al., 1993). Improvements in weight gain and reductions in stress after massage therapy have also been found for infants exposed to cocaine and HIV (Field, Hernandez-Reif, & Freedman, 2004; Wheedon et al., 1993). Mothers suffering from postpartum depression who were trained to use massage therapy for one 15-minute period two times a week for 6 weeks were able to reduce infant crying and improve their infants' sleep. The mothers also reported less depression themselves (Field et al., 1996). Based on these findings, it appears that massage can be a useful skill to teach parents and grandparents because it helps reduce stress both for the one who gives and the one who receives.

Summary

The Nature–Nurture Illusion

1. Both heredity and environment influence human development, but when we focus our attention on one of these causes, the other seems to fade into the background. It is an especially important challenge for the helper to avoid taking a one-sided perspective.

Epigenesis and Coaction

2. Ova (eggs) in females and sperm in males contain only one member of each chromosome pair, or 23 chromosomes altogether. When a sperm fertilizes an ovum, the resulting zygote contains 46 chromosomes. Thus, mother's ovum and father's sperm each contribute one member of every chromosome pair to their offspring.

3. The 46 chromosomes in each body cell consist of 22 structurally and functionally matched pairs or autosomes, and one pair of sex chromosomes which are matched in females (2 X chromosomes), but mismatched in males (1 X and 1 Y chromosome). Growth is made possible by mitosis, or cell division, and each new cell contains a duplicate set of the original 46 from the zygote.

4. Epigenesis is the set of processes by which factors outside of the hereditary material itself can influence how hereditary material functions. For example, cells specialize (becoming liver or brain or skin cells) because chromosomal material is influenced by the environment surrounding the cell. Coaction describes the fact that all physical and behavioral developments are the result of environment acting on heredity and vice versa.

5. Chromosomes are made of DNA, and sections of DNA called genes are coded by the sequences of four basic chemicals that comprise them. The cellular processes of transcription and translation of genetic codes end with the production of proteins.

6. Because cellular environments vary in different parts of the body, transcription and translation of the same gene can produce different proteins in different cells. The environment of the cell is affected by genes and by the environment outside the cell, including the social environment.

7. A variety of epigenetic changes, such as methylation and acetylation, can affect whether, when, and how much a gene will be transcribed. For example, if rat mothers groom their newborn pups a great deal, a gene that affects development of the pups' stress response is permanently "demethylated," causing brain changes that make the pups quicker to recover from stressful events.

8. As a result of epigenesis, even monozygotic twins with identical heredity can show discordant physical and behavioral characteristics, because different experiences cause changes in cellular processes that affect gene expression.

9. Genes, like chromosomes, come in matched pairs, one from the mother, one from the father. Matching genes can come in slightly different forms, called alleles, presenting cells with slightly different blueprints to follow. Different alleles of the same gene can have a dominant-recessive relationship such that one has a larger influence on the phenotype. In this situation, a person is a carrier of an unexpressed trait, which can be passed on to the next generation. Sometimes two different alleles have a codominance relationship and together produce a blended trait.

Atypical Development

10. Hereditary diseases can occur either as a function of defective genes or because an ovum or a sperm contains the wrong number of chromosomes. Some disorders are caused by a single pair of genes. In this case,

defective gene alleles can be recessive, so that an individual must have two of them to have the disorder, or a defective allele can be dominant, causing the disorder in anyone who has one of the defective genes. Many hereditary diseases, including many mental illnesses and behavioral disorders, are polygenic. Finally, some hereditary disorders result when a zygote forms that contains too many chromosomes or too few. Genetic counselors can help parents and prospective parents who may be at risk of passing on hereditary diseases.

11. Teratogens are environmental agents, including many disease organisms and drugs, that can have negative effects on the developing fetus. Their effects depend on when they are introduced, the mother's and baby's genes, and the amount of exposure or dosage the fetus experiences. For example, the effects of prenatal exposure to alcohol can range from subtle learning and behavior problems to fetal alcohol syndrome, which includes physical abnormalities, mental retardation, and behavioral problems. The number of risk factors to which a child is exposed, both prenatally and postnatally, can also influence how severe the long-term effects of teratogens will be. Teratogens may sometimes produce their effects by causing genetic mutations in the fetus, but are most likely to alter gene expression through epigenetic processes.

12. Inadequate protein, vitamins, and minerals in the prenatal or early postnatal diet can have long-term consequences for children's physical, social, and cognitive development and health. Epigenetic changes at the cellular level seem to be a primary reason for the long-term effects of poor early nutrition. But like other risk factors, poor pre- or postnatal nutrition is more problematic the more other risks a child experiences. Social, educational, and medical advantages during childhood can moderate the impact of early food deprivation.

The Developing Brain

13. The embryo begins to form a neural tube at about 2 weeks of gestation. By birth there are 100 billion neurons. Until about 4 months of gestation much of brain development involves neuron migration. The first neurons produced at the interior surface of the neural tube migrate the shortest distance and form the hindbrain. Later developing neurons travel farther to form the midbrain, and the last neurons to be produced travel farthest and form the forebrain or cerebrum and its cortex. Neurons in different parts of the brain later specialize for certain functions. Specialization is influenced by the context or environment of the cell, that is, by epigenetic processes. Neurons from one part of the cortex will re-specialize if transplanted to another part of the cortex.

14. A neuron has one long extension called an axon, and may have many shorter extensions called dendrites. Electrical impulses begin when dendrites or cell bodies pick up a message from another cell. The impulse then passes through the axon to the axon terminals, where chemicals called neurotransmitters are released into the gap—or synapse—between neurons. The neurotransmitters carry the message to the next cell, causing it to fire or to stop firing. Myelination, formation of an insulating substance around axons, promotes efficient conduction of electrical impulses. Myelination occurs prenatally and throughout childhood and adolescence. It continues in adulthood, induced by learning. Neurons begin firing spontaneously at about 4 months of gestation. Before birth, sensory neurons are beginning to be functional. A fetus will turn toward a light source by 25 weeks of gestation, and she can begin to recognize some aspects of sounds, like her mother's voice, in the later weeks of pregnancy. Availability of appropriate stimulation appears to be critical in the late prenatal and early postnatal period for normal sensory functioning to develop. There is an optimal range of stimulation: Too much as well as too little may be problematic. Different sensory systems influence one another's development.

15. Rapid neuron reproduction continues after birth until the end of the first year. Although some neurons can reproduce even in adulthood, most nerve cell reproduction seems to end in infancy. The formation of synapses is ongoing throughout childhood and adolescence, and perhaps even into adulthood, and seems to be linked to cognitive advances. Many more synapses are formed than will be needed, and brain development postnatally involves synapse formation and neural pruning. Experience-expectant synapses are formed in anticipation of typical experiences. Experience shapes the pruning process: Synapses that are used remain, and those that are not may be discarded. Experience-dependent synapses are formed as a result of exposure to certain kinds of experience and may be pruned if they do not remain active.

The Developing Stress and Adaptation System

16. Stress is the body's adaptation response to any demand or challenge and can be categorized into three types. *Good stress* involves acute activation and efficient ending of a response; *tolerable stress* is more chronic but eventually ends; and *toxic stress* is chronic and fails to "turn off." Allostasis refers to the many interacting and balancing changes in bodily systems that take place as part of the stress response. Toxic stress may lead to allostatic overload, or pathological changes due to the cumulative cost of stress, including dysfunctions of the immune system.

17. The primary stress management apparatus is the hypothalamic-pituitary-adrenal (HPA) axis. The initial response to stressful challenges, executed through the sympathetic nervous system, releases epinephrine and norepinephrine, which activate some bodily systems preparing for "fight or flight." The heart beats faster, increasing activation in places like the heart and lungs,

but decreasing activation in less necessary parts, such as the reproductive system. When the threat is reduced, the parasympathetic nervous system reverses these effects.

18. Part of the stress response involves the release of glucocorticoids (primarily cortisol) by the adrenal glands. Receptors in the amygdala and hippocampus bind to the glucocorticoids, leading to an end to the stress response that originated in the HPA. In utero, stress experienced by the mother affects the developing fetus and is linked to increased risks of many sorts, from miscarriage to learning problems. Postnatally, environmental factors, such as quality of caregiving, shape the child's developing HPA axis for better or worse.

Case Study

Jennifer and Jianshe Li have been married for 10 years. Jennifer is a White, 37-year-old woman who is an associate in a law firm in a medium-sized, Midwestern city. Her husband, Jianshe, a 36-year-old Chinese American man, is a software developer employed by a large locally based company. The couple met while they were in graduate school and married shortly thereafter. They have no children. They own a home in one of the newly developed suburban areas just outside the city. Jennifer was adopted as an infant and maintains close ties with her adoptive parents. She is their only child. There has been no contact between Jennifer and her biological parents, and she has never attempted to learn their names or find out where they live. Jianshe's parents, two brothers, and one sister live on the U.S. West Coast, and all the family members try to get together for visits several times a year. Jennifer and Jianshe are active in a few local community organizations. They enjoy the company of many friends and often spend what leisure time they have hiking and camping.

The Lis have been unsuccessful in conceiving a child even though they have tried for the past four years. Both husband and wife have undergone testing. Jennifer has had infertility treatment for the past three years but without success. The treatments have been lengthy, expensive, and emotionally stressful. Approximately a year ago, Jennifer began to experience some mild symptoms of dizziness and dimmed vision. At first, she disregarded the symptoms, attributing them to overwork. However, they persisted for several weeks, and she consulted her physician. He thought that they might be a side effect of the medication she had been taking to increase fertility. Jennifer's treatment protocol was changed, and shortly afterward, much to the couple's delight, Jennifer became pregnant.

Unfortunately, the symptoms she had experienced earlier began to worsen, and she noticed some mild tremors in her arms and legs as well. Jennifer's physician referred her to a specialist, who tentatively diagnosed a progressive disease of the central nervous system that has a suspected genetic link and is marked by an unpredictable course. The Lis were devastated by the news. They were very concerned about the risks of the pregnancy to Jennifer's health. They also worried about the possible transmission of the disease to the new baby whom they had wanted for such a long time. In great distress, they sought counseling to help them deal with some of these concerns.

Discussion Questions

1. As a helper, what are some of the issues you would need to be prepared to discuss with this couple? What information or training do you think you would need to deal effectively with this family?
2. List the possible problems faced by this couple as well as the supports available to them. What are the options available to Jennifer and Jianshe?
3. As a genetic counselor, how would you help them in the decision-making process?

Practice Using What You Have Learned

MyLab Education Application Exercise 2.1: Case Study: Contrast Functional and Structural Brain Development in Two Toddlers
MyLab Education Application Exercise 2.2: Case Study: Stress Response to a Tornado Scare

Journal Questions

1. Consider one feature of your own development (a trait, talent, behavior). Discuss the development of this feature using the idea of nature–nurture coaction. How has this particular feature of your personality influenced and been influenced by other people?

2. Interview your mother or father, if possible, about your prenatal developmental period. What can you learn about this important period of your development?

3. How has increased knowledge about prenatal development changed the behaviors of pregnant women? Are there any beliefs specific to your particular cultural background that shaped the way your mother viewed her pregnancy or acted during her pregnancy? Ask a member of a different culture about the ways that culture views pregnancy.

4. Discuss the chronic stress in your life. How might it be affecting your health and well-being?

Key Concepts

ovum (p. 39)
chromosome (p. 39)
cytoplasm (p. 39)
zygote (p. 40)
autosomes (p. 40)
sex chromosomes (p. 40)
X chromosome (p. 40)
Y chromosome (p. 40)
karyotype (p. 40)
mitosis (p. 40)
implantation (p. 41)
embryo (p. 41)
epigenesis (p. 41)
epigenome (p. 41)
coaction (p. 41)
epigenetic model (p. 41)
deoxyribonucleic acid (DNA) (p. 41)
histones (p. 41)
gene (p. 41)
protein (p. 42)
transcription (p. 42)
messenger ribonucleic acid (mRNA) (p. 42)
translation (p. 42)
alternative splicing (p. 43)
gene expression (p. 43)
noncoded genes (p. 43)
gene regulation (p. 43)
genome (p. 43)
transcription factor (p. 43)
receptor (p. 43)
methylation (p. 44)
demethylation (p. 44)
acetylation (p. 44)
deacetylation (p. 44)
microRNA (miRNA) (p. 44)
cross-fostering study (p. 44)
genotype (p. 45)
phenotype (p. 45)
monozygotic (identical) twins (p. 45)

dizygotic (fraternal) twins (p. 45)
concordance (p. 45)
discordance (p. 45)
allele (p. 45)
dominant-recessive relationship (p. 46)
carrier (p. 46)
codominance (p. 46)
polygenic (p. 46)
period of the zygote (p. 47)
period of the embryo (p. 47)
period of the fetus (p. 47)
sickle-cell anemia (p. 47)
genetic counselor (p. 47)
mutation (p. 49)
progeria (p. 49)
Huntington's disease (p. 49)
Down syndrome (trisomy 21) (p. 50)
teratogen (p. 51)
placenta (p. 51)
fetal alcohol spectrum disorders (FASDs) (p. 52)
fetal alcohol syndrome (FAS) (p. 52)
kwashiorkor (p. 54)
neural tube (p. 55)
neurulation (p. 55)
neuron (p. 56)
glial cell (p. 56)
hindbrain (p. 56)
midbrain (p. 56)
cerebral cortex (p. 56)
forebrain (p. 56)
medulla (p. 57)
pons (p. 57)
cerebellum (p. 57)
reticular formation (p. 57)
autonomic functions (p. 57)
nuclei (p. 57)
reticular activating system (p. 57)
superior colliculi (p. 57)

inferior colliculi (p. 57)
substantia nigra (p. 57)
cerebrum (p. 57)
thalamus (p. 57)
hypothalamus (p. 57)
limbic system (p. 57)
basal ganglia (p. 57)
nucleus acumbens (p. 57)
hippocampus (p. 57)
amygdala (p. 57)
septum (p. 57)
cingulate cortex (p. 57)
corpus callosum (p. 57)
hemispheric specialization (lateralization) (p. 57)
occipital lobe (p. 58)
temporal lobe (p. 58)
central sulcus (p. 58)
parietal lobe (p. 58)
frontal lobe (p. 58)
prefrontal cortex (PFC) (p. 58)
anterior cingulate cortex (ACC) (p. 58)
nucleus (p. 59)
neuroplasticity (p. 59)
axon (p. 59)
axon terminals (p. 59)
neurotransmitters (p. 59)
dendrites (p. 59)
synapse (p. 60)
synaptic gap (p. 60)
serotonin (p. 60)
acetylcholine (p. 60)
glutamate (p. 60)
gamma-amino butyric acid (GABA) (p. 60)
epinephrine (adrenaline) (p. 60)
norepinephrine (noradrenaline) (p. 60)
dopamine (p. 60)
psychotropic drugs (p. 60)
myelination (p. 60)

white matter (p. 60)
grey matter (p. 60)
circuits (p. 60)
projection neurons (p. 60)
interneurons (p. 60)
neural stem cells (p. 61)
subventricular zone (SVZ) (p. 61)
dentate gyrus (p. 61)
nerve growth factor (p. 62)
synaptogenesis (p. 62)
neural pruning (p. 62)
synaptic overproduction (p. 62)
experience-expectant (p. 62)
experience-dependent (p. 63)

adaptation (p. 64)
stress (p. 64)
stressor (p. 64)
good stress (p. 64)
tolerable stress (p. 64)
toxic stress (p. 64)
allostasis (p. 64)
allostatic load (p. 65)
allostatic overload (p. 65)
sympathetic nervous system (SNS) (p. 65)
hypothalamic-pituitary-adrenal (HPA)
    axis (p. 65)
parasympathetic nervous system (PSNS)
    (p. 65)

pituitary gland (p. 65)
corticotropin releasing factor (CRF) (p. 65)
adrenocorticotropic hormone (ACTH)
    (p. 65)
adrenal glands (p. 65)
cortisol (p. 65)
glucocorticoid (p. 65)
glucocorticoid receptors (GRs) (p. 65)
cytokines (p. 66)
internalizing problems (p. 67)
externalizing problems (p. 67)
dose-response relationship (p. 67)
selective serotonin reuptake inhibitor
    (SSRI) (p. 69)

Chapter 3
Cognitive Development in the Early Years

 ## Learning Objectives

After reading this chapter, you should be able to:

3.1 Explain Piaget's constructivist theory of cognitive development and describe the value and limitations of his stages of development.

3.2 Describe Piaget's sensorimotor stage and current views of cognitive development in infants including development in the areas of object concept, representational thought, and intentional action.

3.3 Describe Piaget's preoperational stage and current views of cognitive development in preschool children including development in the areas of executive functions, numbers, theory of mind, and language.

3.4 Explain Vygotsky's sociocultural theory and its contribution to current views of cognitive development and compare his constructivist perspectives to those of Piaget.

Sayda is 3 years old. Her maternal grandparents immigrated to the United States from Honduras before her mother was born, and they spoke Spanish with their children. Now Sayda's mother is a high school English teacher and her father is an attorney. Sayda's parents value her mother's fluency in both English and Spanish, and they are raising Sayda to be bilingual. Since birth, Sayda has heard only English from her father and only Spanish from her mother. She also attends a child care program where teachers speak both languages. Her mother's family is delighted that Sayda is learning Spanish, but her paternal grandparents are not in favor of this bilingual strategy. They worry that Sayda will be confused and fall behind other children in her understanding of both languages and perhaps even develop learning problems. Recently, while taking care of Sayda over a weekend, her paternal grandparents had a conversation with her that alarmed them. On a walk through a city park, Sayda looked at a statue and said, "That's funny. Statues are not alive, but you can still see them." Her grandmother said, "What's funny about that?" and Sayda replied, "My abuelito (her maternal grandfather) is dead, and that's sad because we'll never see him again." Her grandmother tried to explain: "Things like statues and tables and chairs are never alive so they can't die," but Sayda was still confused. "Yeah," she said, "isn't that funny? Tables and chairs are not alive and we can still see them."

Sayda's grandparents were alarmed because her apparent understanding of "alive" and "dead" seemed so distorted, and they mistakenly attributed her confusion to her bilingual upbringing. Their worst fears seemed to be coming true! But they need not have worried. Sayda's odd thought process is typical of a 3-year-old. In fact, it is developmentally helpful that she is starting to notice the contradictions in her beliefs about life and death. She will soon make real progress in understanding what it means to be alive. Learning these concepts in two languages is not causing her misunderstanding, and she is likely to reap rich cognitive benefits from her bilingualism over time. (The conversation between Sayda and her grandparents is an adaptation of one between Susan Carey, a developmental scientist, and her own 3-year-old daughter [Carey, Zaitchik, & Bascandziev, 2015].)

Is there any value for helping professionals in learning the details of infants' and preschool children's cognitive development? The benefits are obvious if you work primarily with young children and their parents, but what if the majority of your clients are older children, adolescents, and adults? As you have already seen, developments at these later ages cannot be divorced from earlier events. Skills, abilities, and tendencies that develop in the early years of life establish trajectories that influence the progress and direction of later developments. To put it simply, who a person will become is at least partially channeled even before birth.

You might wonder why understanding early cognitive processes should be an important part of your concern. After all, helping professionals usually work with their clients on emotional and social issues. The fundamental reason is that cognitive, emotional, and social processes are so intimately interconnected that you can have little understanding of any one of these processes without some knowledge of all of them. Cognitive processes affect social functioning, and social experiences have important impacts on cognitive development, as you will readily see in this chapter. In fact, realms that seem discrete, like emotion and logic, are typically two different aspects of one global process. In the next chapter, where you will learn more about emotional development, you will find that logic without emotion turns out to be rather illogical!

In this chapter, we focus on the intellectual growth of infants and young children, looking first at how Jean Piaget described the many changes that occur in these early years. You will see that findings from modern research have led to revisions of many of his views. Especially influential in these re-interpretations are ideas from information processing theories. Finally, we take a look at another classic theory of cognitive development, that of Lev S. Vygotsky, a contemporary of Piaget's whose ideas and findings were compatible with his in many ways but who added a special emphasis on the importance of culture and social experience to the story of intellectual change in childhood.

Piaget's Constructivist Theory

3.1   Explain Piaget's constructivist theory of cognitive development and describe the value and limitations of his stages of development.

Debbie, age 10, and Mark, age 4, are overheard discussing their mother's pregnancy. Their parents have read them children's books about how babies are conceived and born, and the topic has been discussed openly in the family. The children have the following conversation:

Debbie:	Do you know how the baby got there?
Mark:	Sure. Mommy got a duck.
Debbie:	A duck?
Mark:	Yeah, they just get a duck or rabbit and it grows a little more and it turns into a baby.
Debbie:	A duck will turn into a baby?
Mark:	Sure. They give them some food, people food, and they grow into a baby.
Debbie:	Where did you get that idea?
Mark:	I saw it in a book and Mommy and Daddy told me.
Debbie:	They told you that ducks turn into babies?
Mark:	Yeah!

(Based on Cowan, P. A. (1978). *Piaget with feeling: Cognitive, social and emotional dimensions.* New York: Holt, Rinehart & Winston; and Bernstein, A. C. & Cowan, P. A. (1975). Children's concepts of how people get babies. *Child Development, 46,* 77–91.)

This anecdote illustrates a fundamental feature of learning, knowing, and understanding according to Piaget's theory: that the human mind constructs its knowledge. When infants and children are presented with new stimuli or pieces of information, what is learned or stored is not just a "true" reflection of what comes from the environment. That is, new information is not simply written on a blank slate, as John Locke and other empiricists assumed. Rather, children learn by a process of adaptation. You saw in Chapter 2 that *adaptation* is adjustment to change. Piaget used the term specifically to describe how children's knowledge adjusts to new stimulation from the environment. First, children interpret new stimulation in ways that fit with what they already know, sometimes distorting it as a result. This aspect of adaptation is called **assimilation**. As the new information is assimilated, the child's existing knowledge may be modified somewhat, providing a better match or fit to what is new. The latter process is called **accommodation**. Assimilation and accommodation are complementary activities involved in every interaction with the environment. To accommodate (learn), children must be able to assimilate. In other words, they cannot learn something that they cannot make some sense out of already. Assimilation often means that new information is distorted or changed so that sense can be made of it. A child's understandings are gradually changed as a result of interactions with the environment, although what a child will learn in any single step is always shaped by what the child already knows, and the new "understanding" may not be a completely accurate reflection of reality. In Mark's case, his parents' explanations, which apparently included comparing human reproduction to ducks laying eggs, far outstripped Mark's knowledge structures, and Mark's assimilation and accommodation of his parents' elaborate explanations produced a charmingly naive linear progression: Ducks turn into people.

Piaget spent a lifetime doing intensive research on the development of knowledge; he wrote dozens of books on his findings and hundreds of articles (see Box 3.1). His own ideas evolved and changed as new work was completed, discussed, and challenged by scientists around the world. Since his death, developmental researchers have followed up on his pioneering work, and, naturally, the field has moved on. Not all of his ideas have been corroborated, but in a remarkable number of areas, his research has been the starting point for more expanded, clarifying work, and his theoretical explanations have informed newer theories.

The idea that knowledge is constructed by the developing child (and adult) is a Piagetian view that has become an underlying assumption of much of the current research on cognitive development and educational practice (e.g., American Psychological Association, Coalition for Psychology in Schools and Education, 2015). This constructivist stance takes the child to be an active participant in the learning process, constantly seeking out and trying to make sense of new information. In other words, children are intrinsically motivated to learn—another idea that is now widely accepted by developmental scientists. Piaget also considered a child's active exploration to be organized and organizing. When children assimilate new information to what they already know, they are fitting the new information into an organized way of thinking—some sort of knowledge structure. When they accommodate their knowledge structures to fit what is new in the environment, the organization is changing. (We will have more to say about knowledge structures in later chapters.) The ideas that mental activity is organized and that the organization evolves in response to the environment are further Piagetian notions that seem to be taken for granted by modern researchers.

Thus, many widely accepted assumptions about cognitive development are derived from Piaget. But some of his fundamental ideas are particularly controversial. Among these is the idea that cognitive development can be characterized by stages (see Chapter 1). Although Piaget believed cognitive change was the result of small,

Piaget was one of the first theorists to propose that children actively construct their knowledge.

MyLab Education
Video Example 3.1
These children are observing tadpoles and learning something new about growth. They can assimilate the idea that the tadpole grows legs, but they need to accommodate their concept of growth to understand why the tadpole's tail gets smaller.

Box 3.1: Biographical Sketch: Jean Piaget

Jean Piaget (1896–1980) was remarkably precocious as a child, publishing his first scholarly paper at the age of 10. At 14, after producing a series of scientific reports, he was offered a position as curator of a museum of natural history—an offer promptly withdrawn when his age was discovered. Piaget completed a bachelor's degree by age 18 and a PhD by 22, despite spending a year away from school when he suffered a "nervous breakdown" (which he later attributed to his study of philosophy). His early education, research, and writing ranged widely from biological science (his first published article reported his observations of an albino sparrow) to mathematics and logic, to experimental psychology, to psychoanalysis, to psychopathology. He even wrote a philosophical novel! He found a way to integrate many of his interests when Henri Simon, an early developer of IQ tests, hired him to standardize an English test with French children. Piaget soon lost interest in the task he was assigned—asking children test questions, recording their responses, and specifying whether they were right or wrong for the purposes of quantifying intelligence. But he was intrigued by the qualitative features of the children's answers. Even children's wrong answers often seemed to reveal an underlying structure or pattern of thought. While studying psychopathology, Piaget had learned to conduct clinical interviews with mentally ill patients. He began to combine clinical interview techniques with the use of standardized questions in an effort to reveal the nature of children's knowledge and reasoning. After publishing several articles on his findings, Piaget was invited to become the director of studies in the Institute Jean-Jacques Rousseau in Geneva, a center for scientific child study and teacher training. At the age of 25, his life's work had begun. Until his death at 84, Piaget wrote prolifically on the development of children's knowledge, reporting an endless stream of studies and constructing a wide-ranging, coherent theory. His empirical methods combined observations of children's hands-on problem solving with the probing, clinical interview technique that he pioneered in Simon's laboratory. He originated a remarkable array of problem tasks that are easy for adults to solve, but not easy for children, revealing what appeared to be astonishing age changes in our reasoning about the world. As Piaget put it, "Just as the tadpole already breathes, though with different organs from those of the frog, so the child acts like the adult, but employing a mentality whose structure varies according to the stages of its development" (Piaget, 1970, p. 153).

It is rare today to find any subject in cognitive development, from perception to mathematical reasoning to memory to social perspective taking, for which Piaget did not pose key questions and design provocative, ingenious research tasks. Given the breadth, depth, and complexity of Piaget's work, it is not surprising that others often oversimplify it in their effort to understand. For example, Piaget has been described as a nativist by some and as an empiricist by others. In fact, Piaget was a true interactionist. He, like modern systems theorists, viewed development as taking place at the proximal interface between the organism and the environment. Biological and psychological systems affect how the knower acts on the environment, and the environment "feeds" the knower. What the environment provides is absorbed and changed by the organism, but the environment also shapes and changes the organism's knowledge.

Educators have been especially affected by Piaget's work, although again, they have sometimes misinterpreted its implications. Piaget saw schooling as an opportunity to provide children with food for their naturally occurring "mental digestion." He warned teachers, however, that children will either memorize new information by rote or ignore it if it is beyond their current level of understanding. But if information is at least partially comprehensible to them or moderately novel, children will actively and eagerly explore and absorb it. Unfortunately, educators have sometimes misinterpreted Piaget's emphasis on children's active exploration as a recommendation that children simply be provided with lots of interesting and fun "stuff" and then left on their own to learn. Instead, Piaget encouraged educators to plan the presentation of learning opportunities carefully, being especially sensitive to children's current level of functioning in introducing tasks and allowing children to actively explore and discover but recognizing that an orchestrated, if flexible, presentation of tasks aimed at the child's level of understanding can promote development (e.g., 1970).

Interestingly, although Piaget recognized the advantage of teachers' carefully crafting a program of learning opportunities to optimize a child's progress, he was somewhat exasperated by what he referred to as "the American question": "How can we speed up children's development?" He once remarked that kittens have been found to go through some developments in 3 months that take human babies 9 to 12 months to achieve. But "the kitten is not going to go much further. The child has taken longer, but he is capable of going further so it seems to me that the nine months were not for nothing" (as quoted in Elkind, 1968). His respect for and appreciation of children's cognitive pace as well as his enormous empathy may be what made Piaget so successful in uncovering the mysteries of cognitive development in general.

---

gradual reorganizations of knowledge structures, he described periods of time in which all of a child's mental structures can be expected to have some organizational properties in common. For example, the infancy and preschool periods covered in this chapter were divided by Piaget into two stages, the sensorimotor stage (from birth to about age 2) and the preoperational stage (between ages 2 and 7). Each of these stages was further divided into substages. The notion of stages implies that children's understandings within a stage (or a substage) about many different things will have some general similarities. So, for example, in the early preoperational stage, whether we are examining a child's understanding of number or causality, we should be able to detect some similarities in the ways in which children organize their thinking about these concepts.

Although Piaget did find many such similarities, more recent research, using different kinds of tasks, finds less support for the notion of overarching stages. In particular, infants and preschoolers sometimes show signs of understandings that Piaget believed to be possible only for much older children. And children's progress in understanding concepts from different domains of knowledge is not always organized or structured in the same ways at the same time. Rather, progress is often domain specific — development can proceed at different rates in different domains. Domains that have been studied in detail include number concepts, morality, biological versus physical realities, and so on. For example, if we want to learn about children's understanding of causality, we may need to look at it within particular domains of knowledge. Children's understanding of physical causality, such as how objects move, may progress differently from their understanding of human or animal agency, such as how animate organisms move. We should note that Piaget, in his later years, continued to revise his theory. Translations of his later work show that he put less emphasis on stages and more on the dynamic quality of repeated assimilation and accommodation in the context of feedback from the environment (e.g., Piaget, 1975/1985).

Nonetheless, most developmental scientists, clinicians, and educators still find Piaget's stage divisions to be useful for many purposes. On the whole, for example, infants' understandings of many different concepts are more similar to one another's than they are to those of a 5-year-old. For this reason, in this chapter and in other discussions of cognitive development in this book, we use Piaget's stage divisions as an aid in describing children's cognitive progress.

MyLab Education Self-Check 3.1

Infant Cognition:
The Sensorimotor Stage

3.2   Describe Piaget's sensorimotor stage and current views of cognitive development in infants including development in the areas of object concept, representational thought, and intentional action.

Infants' cognitive functioning seems more mysterious than that of older children and adults because infants do not talk. We cannot ask them to describe what they can see or how many objects are in front of them or to tell us their solutions to a problem. Most efforts to probe cognition at all other age levels depend on giving verbal instructions, and they usually require at least some verbal responses from study participants.

How then can we understand what a baby knows, thinks, or even feels? Piaget's research with infants, done primarily with his own three children, focused on detailed analyses of babies' motor interactions with the environment. A newborn's reflexive responses to sensory stimuli—like looking and following when a visual stimulus moves across the visual field, head turning in the direction of a sound, grasping at a touch to the palm, and sucking at a touch to the lips—were examined under many different stimulus conditions. Piaget carefully noted how these sensorimotor patterns functioned and, especially, how they changed with time and experience. From such observations, Piaget inferred what babies might actually understand or be capable of learning.

Careful observation of infants' reactions to environmental events is still at the heart of infant research, but today we have strategies that take advantage of technology to make these observations more precise. Among these strategies, for example, is the habituation paradigm, which takes advantage of a baby's tendency to orient to new stimulation and to habituate to repeated or old stimulation. Suppose, for example, that a baby is propped up in an infant seat in a darkened room in front of a large, blank video screen. Suddenly, a picture of a green circle flashes on the screen. The baby is likely to produce an orienting response to this new stimulus. She will look longer at the picture than she had at the blank screen. She will suck more vigorously on the pacifier in her mouth, and her blood pressure and her heart rate are likely to decrease from their previous base rate. If we repeatedly present the green circle, after a time the baby will seem to grow bored with the stimulus. Perhaps it now seems familiar, even "old." We call this response habituation, and it is indicated by shorter looking times, less vigorous sucking, and a return to base rate for heartbeat and blood pressure. With the help of video cameras and computers, all of these subtle response changes can be closely monitored. Now, suppose we flash a new picture on the screen, a picture of a yellow circle. We are looking for a dishabituation response, that is, a renewed orienting response, which we will take to mean that the baby has noticed the difference between the first circle and the second, and her interest is renewed. If the baby is a newborn, we will be disappointed. Newborns show no sign of being able to tell the difference between green and yellow: They do not dishabituate to yellow after becoming habituated to green. But if the baby is 3 months old, she probably will dishabituate to the yellow stimulus, indicating to us that she can discriminate between the two colors. Using this research strategy, we have learned that newborns cannot perceive differences between most colors, but that babies differentiate major color groups by 3 months old, and their color vision approximates that of an adult by 4 to 5 months old (Kellman & Arterberry, 2006). It is notable, however, that physiological measures such as electroencephalography show that color discrimination is not fully adult-like until the teen years (Boon & Dain, 2015).

Another strategy for studying infants' abilities is to determine what they prefer to look at or listen to or taste, and so on, using what are called preferential response paradigms, in which multiple stimuli are presented to the infant and we record which ones the baby seems to respond to most. In the *preferential looking paradigm*, for instance, we might present a baby with two visual stimuli, side by side, on a screen. Suppose one is a circle with black and white stripes, and the other is an entirely gray circle of the same size. Using video cameras focused on the baby's eyes, a computer can track the baby's looks to each circle. Babies tend to look more at patterns than at solid stimuli, and so our baby is likely to look more at the striped circle than the solid gray circle. Now we can use this preference to measure the baby's visual acuity, that is, to find the level of detail the baby can see. We can vary the stripe width for the striped circle, using finer and finer (narrower and narrower) stripes, until the baby shows no preference for the striped pattern. Because babies consistently prefer patterns, "no preference" suggests that the baby can no longer see the difference between the striped circle and the solid color circle. We have learned from such studies that newborns have substantially less visual acuity than adults (their vision is blurrier) but that by 8 months, babies' visual acuity is nearly adult-like (Cavallini, Fazzi, & Viviani, 2002; Huurneman & Boonstra, 2016). See Table 3.1 for more detailed information about infants' visual and auditory capacities and the kinds of motor abilities that correspond to these sensory developments.

Research using habituation and preferential response paradigms has provided us with much of what we know about infants' perceptual abilities, especially what they can see and hear. But researchers also use these methods to make inferences about what babies can understand and how they think, as you will see. Modern researchers do not always agree about what inferences to draw from such data, but their work has certainly stimulated a great deal of interest in looking more closely at infant development, and it has led to several challenges of Piaget's ideas. Let's consider now three interesting and important cognitive developments in infancy, combining data from both older and newer approaches.

TABLE 3.1 Major Milestones in Typically Developing Motor, Visual, and Auditory Processes

AGE	MOTOR DEVELOPMENT		VISUAL DEVELOPMENT	AUDITORY DEVELOPMENT
	GROSS MOTOR	**FINE MOTOR**		
1 Month	Holds head up without wobbling when held upright	Holds things placed in hands	Visual acuity: 20/600; scans edges of figures and visual objects	Alert to sounds; prefers human speech to nonspeech sounds, and prefers sound of mother's voice to other voices; distinguishes most speech sounds
2 Months	Rolls from side to back		Visual acuity: 20/300; shows preference for faces over objects; discriminates basic colors	
3 Months	On stomach, lifts chest with arms		Faces (especially mother's face) perceived as attractive; scans interiors of faces and objects	Locates where sounds come from
4 Months	Sits with support; rolls over from front to back	Visually guided reaching	Visual acuity: 20/160; smooth tracking of slowly moving objects; development of *stereopsis*, or ability to perceive depth based upon information from both left and right eyes	
5 Months	Rolls over from back to front			
6 Months	Sits without support	Transfers objects from hand to hand	Distinguishes faces, both human and animal	Coordination of vision and hearing; turns eyes to nearby sounds smoothly
7 Months	Stands with help	Plays with simple toys		Begins to show perceptual narrowing, e.g., sounds of native language more discriminable than sounds of other languages
8 Months	Pulls self to stand		Visual acuity: 20/20	
9 Months	Crawls	Pincer grasp (with thumb and forefinger)	Interprets others' facial expressions; shows perceptual narrowing, e.g., human faces easier to distinguish than animal faces	
10 Months	Stands holding on; drops and throws things			
11 Months	Stands alone			
12 Months	Walks holding on	Scribbles with crayon		
12–18 Months	Walks alone; begins to walk up stairs			
18–23 Months	Jumps in place	Draws lines; constructs simple tower; drinks from cup using one hand		
2–3 Years	Runs, jumps, climbs; balance improves; kicks ball forward; stands on one foot briefly	Pours milk; improves dressing and feeding skills; builds towers of 6 blocks; turns pages in book	Oldest age at which surgical correction of crossed eyes for depth perception can be successful	
3–4 Years	Walks up (and later down) stairs alternating feet; walks on tiptoes; hops on one foot; improves throwing skills; buttons clothing; eats with spoon and fork	Completes simple puzzles; uses art materials, scissors; is more careful in execution of art and drawing projects	Continued integration of visual-motor systems	
4–5 Years	Ties knots; dresses and undresses easily	More skillful with scissors		

Understanding Objects

You and I would understand very little about the physical or social world if we did not have a fundamental understanding that there are objects (including human objects) with substance and constancy, occupying locations in a spatial field. To become attached to a parent and to begin the process of healthy emotional development, a baby must have some conception of the parent as a permanent, substantive object in her world.

What must infants understand to "know" about objects—that is, to have an **object concept**? First, they need to know that objects have properties that can stimulate all of their senses: vision, hearing, taste, smell, and touch. What they feel in their mouths as they suck a pacifier is the same as what they see when Mom or Dad holds the pacifier up in front of them. When can they make such connections? It appears that they have some capacity to do so as early as the first month of life. In a classic study, Meltzoff and Borton (1979) gave 1-month-olds an opportunity to suck on either a smooth pacifier or a bumpy one, without letting the infants see the pacifiers. Then, the researchers used the preferential looking paradigm to explore whether the babies had learned anything about the visual characteristics of the pacifiers that they had sucked on but had never seen. The babies looked at a split video screen. On one side was a picture of the smooth pacifier, on the other side a picture of the bumpy pacifier. A camera recorded the infants' eye movements. The babies spent more time looking at whichever pacifier they had previously sucked—suggesting that they were capable of identifying the appearance of the pacifier from their tactile experience of it. Findings like this one indicate that when young babies perceive an object in one way, they can construct some notion of the object's other perceptual characteristics. This quality of **intersensory integration** (also referred to as cross-modal matching or **intermodal perception**) is not surprising given what we now know about prenatal brain development. The development of one sensory system is influenced by the development of other systems (e.g., Murray et al., 2016; see the discussion of the brain in Chapter 2). Piaget (1954), without the benefit of today's research methods, assumed that intersensory integration appeared later in infancy, after babies have learned to coordinate their reflexive responses to stimulation. For example, not until about 6 weeks do babies reach up to grasp an object that they are sucking; and not until 4 to 6 months do they smoothly coordinate grasping and looking, allowing easy exploration of objects through visually guided reaching. Surely, these motor coordinations enrich a baby's understanding of objects as "packages" of perceptual characteristics, but such understanding is facilitated by the brain's overlapping sensory processing earlier than Piaget realized.

What else must infants know to have an understanding of objects? Adults realize that objects have a separate existence from the perceiver. Think for a moment about something that is out of sight, like the sink in your bathroom. Despite your inability to see the sink at this moment, you realize that it still exists. Your perceptual processes or actions on the object are not necessary to its continuation. This quality is called **object permanence**: Objects exist apart from the perceiver.

To understand object permanence, a child must have at least a rudimentary capacity to keep an object in mind when it is not present. To put it another way, the child must have a mental representation of the object, like your mental image of the bathroom sink. The capacity to think about things or events that are not currently stimulating our senses is called **representational thought**. Thus, if we could find out when a baby understands object permanence, we would not only know something about her object concept, but we would also know that she was capable of representational thought. Piaget invented the **hidden object test** to assess object permanence. An interesting object, like a small toy, is placed in front of a baby, within her reach. As the baby watches, we cover the object with a cloth, so that it is out of sight. What we want to know is, will the baby search for the object under the cloth, or does the baby act as if the object's disappearance means that the object no longer exists? Studies using the hidden object test have consistently found that infants younger than 8 to 12 months fail to search for the object, even though they have the motor skills they need to succeed much earlier (e.g., they engage in visually guided reaching by about 4 months, and they can sit

MyLab Education
Video Example 3.2
Infants across cultures develop an understanding of object permanence at approximately the same age, beginning around the end of the first year of life.

without support by about 6 months). Piaget (1954) concluded that understanding object permanence has its rudimentary beginnings late in the first year of life and gradually improves thereafter. He also inferred that representational thought—the ability to form mental representations, such as images—is a skill that begins to develop only in the late months of the first year. Piaget's work demonstrated that representational ability improves through the second year of life, until, by the end of the sensorimotor period (18 to 24 months), children not only think about objects but can mentally plan their actions, solve simple problems "all in their heads," remember past experiences, and so on. In other words, they have developed a broad capacity for thinking.

Today, we know from studies using procedures such as the habituation paradigm that babies may have some understanding of object permanence, and therefore, perhaps, some representational thinking skills, much earlier in infancy. For example, Aguiar and Baillargeon (1999, 2002) showed infants a display with a doll standing to the left of one screen (see Figure 3.1). To the right of the screen was a space and then another screen. Babies watched as the doll moved toward the first screen and disappeared behind it. Even 2 1/2-month-olds acted surprised if the doll reappeared to the right of the second screen, without ever being visible in the space between the screens. You and I would be surprised as well, expecting the doll to follow a normal trajectory, emerging from behind the first screen, continuing to move to the right before disappearing again behind the second screen, and then emerging at the far right. If 2 1/2-month-olds expect hidden objects to follow that trajectory as well, perhaps young babies have some sense that objects continue to exist when they cannot be seen.

Studies by Baillargeon and her colleagues (see Baillargeon, 2008), as well as other infancy researchers, have created lively controversy about just when representational thinking begins, what the nature of early representations might be, and what aspects of objects young babies are likely to represent (see discussions by Allen & Bickhard, 2013; Bjorklund, 2015; Bremner, Slater, & Johnson, 2015; Carey, 2009; Haith, 2013; Schöner & Thelen, 2006). For Piaget, mental activity in early infancy is sensorimotor: It depends on sensory input and ends in motor output. Eventually these early organizational patterns are transformed into mental images and other products that support "true" representational thought. Many contemporary theorists have described somewhat similar ideas (e.g., Allen & Bickhard, 2013), but others argue that there is "something more" to infants' earliest mental activity. One view assumes there are innate, primitive concepts, say of objects, that infants can think about, perhaps very briefly, even when sensory input from objects is not there (e.g., Baillargeon, 2008). Nonetheless, there is general agreement that thinking and conceptual developments, such as object permanence that require thinking, gradually improve through the first and second years of life and beyond. In the next section, we will see that studies of infant memory and of babies' abilities to plan their actions indicate the same kind of gradual development.

MyLab Education
Video Example 3.3
The toddler in this video understands object permanence as he searches under the pillow for the toy. What is the connection between object permanence and representational thought?

FIGURE 3.1 Stimuli for a test of object permanence by Aguiar and Baillargeon.

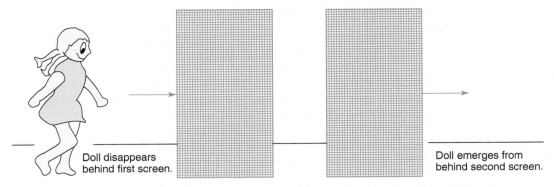

Doll disappears behind first screen.

Doll emerges from behind second screen.

SOURCE: Based on Aguiar, A., & Baillargeon, R. (1999). 2.5-month-old infants' reasoning about when objects should and should not be occluded. *Cognitive Psychology, 39,* 116–157.

Remembering

Developmental scientists use methods such as the habituation and preferential response paradigms as well as imaging techniques such as fMRI (see Chapter 2) to tap the mysteries of infant memory. Memory is a special interest of researchers who favor information processing theories of cognitive development (see Chapter 1). Learning and storage of information, duration of storage, retrieval of stored information—these are the centerpieces of cognitive functioning from the point of view of scientists who think about the human cognitive system as akin in some ways to a computer processor. What follows is only a sampling of what we are discovering about infant memory.

Remembering requires learning, storing, and then retrieving information. With preverbal babies, we look for behavioral signs of retrieval in order to understand what they are learning. **Recognition** and **recall** are two different types of retrieval. Suppose you see a person across the room, and you realize that you have seen that person before. The face is present—you are experiencing it—and you have a feeling that it is familiar, that this experience is not new. That feeling of familiarity is *recognition*.

Piaget (1952) guessed from the way babies use their reflexes that they are learning about the stimuli they experience right from the start, because they show early signs of recognition. Ordinarily, babies suck anything that touches their lips, but if they are hungry, they continue to suck only objects that have been associated with nourishment in the past, like nipples. Their preferential sucking demonstrates that babies have learned which stimuli are nutritive.

Today's researchers often use the habituation paradigm to assess infant recognition. When babies habituate to a stimulus that is repeatedly presented, they are showing us that the stimulus is becoming familiar. Because even newborns habituate to at least some repeatedly presented stimuli, we are now confident that newborns learn from some experiences and are capable of recognition. Operant conditioning has also demonstrated that recognition skills are present from birth. In a classic study, DeCasper and Fifer (1980) found that a 3-day-old infant will learn to suck harder for the reward of hearing its own mother's voice (rather than a stranger's voice), indicating that the baby recognizes the mother's voice. A host of additional studies have corroborated this finding, even with babies as young as 2 hours old (see Lee & Kisilevsky, 2012). A newborn's recognition of the mother's voice seems to be a result of many repeated opportunities to hear her voice before birth. Starting at about the 26th week of gestation, when the auditory system begins to function, every time a mother speaks she is likely to be stimulating the fetus's hearing. Sound pressure into the amniotic fluid causes fetal skull vibrations, leading to cochlear fluid vibrations. A newborn's familiarity with her mother's voice demonstrates that the capacity for recognition is already in place before birth, but many repetitions of the stimulus seem to be necessary. The fetus can also hear other sounds in the later weeks of pregnancy, such as the father's voice, but those sounds do not occur with the same frequency as the mother's voice, and newborns do not show recognition of them (Picciolini et al., 2014).

Recognition improves throughout infancy, demonstrating that infants become more efficient at learning and retrieving information. In the newborn period, signs of recognition usually fade after a few minutes or even seconds, but the duration of recognition increases with age, and the speed with which babies habituate increases as well. Younger babies need more exposures to a stimulus than older babies before they show signs of recognition. But there are also individual differences among babies of the same age. Interestingly, how quickly babies habituate to a new stimulus is one of the few measures of infant functioning that has been found to correlate with later intelligence and academic test performance. Recognition speed by 4 months old is an indicator of the efficiency with which a child may later process information (Bornstein, Hahn, & Wolke, 2013).

Recognition is a feeling of familiarity when an experience is repeated. Remembering an experience from the past when it is *not* being repeated is called *recall*. When you bring to mind the face of a friend who is not present, you are engaging in recall. To recall your friend's face, you must be able to form a mental representation, such as a mental image, that "stands for" the real face. In other words, thinking that involves the ability to form mental representations such as mental images is necessary for recall.

In contrast to the early and rapid development of recognition skills, the ability to recall seems to emerge later in infancy. One indicator of recall is deferred imitation: Children observe the actions of another person on one occasion, and then imitate those actions at a later time. To do that, children must be able to mentally represent the actions they previously observed. We should note that babies may imitate some *immediate* actions early in the first year. For example, if you stick out your tongue at a newborn, you may see the baby's tongue protrude as well (Meltzoff & Moore, 1977), although whether this response is really imitation has been vigorously debated (e.g., Oostenbroek et al., 2016). But babies do soon imitate some actions by others. If you clap your hands at a 4-month-old, she may clap her hands as well (Piaget, 1951). It seems that babies slowly work out the correspondences between their own and other people's body parts, and as they do, they extend their range of imitation. But immediate imitation does not indicate recall. Only if there is a time delay between the observed action and the baby's imitation of it can we say that the ability to form mental representations of previously experienced events was necessary for the imitation.

Based on observations of his own children's behavior, Piaget believed that deferred imitation begins rather late in the infancy period, around the middle of the baby's second year. At 16 months, for example, his daughter Jacqueline watched a visiting boy have a temper tantrum, screaming and stamping his feet in a playpen. The next day, Jacqueline did the same, only she was smiling and her foot stamping was gentle. She was not actually having a temper tantrum, but was imitating her little friend's fascinating performance (Piaget, 1962).

More precise testing methods show that infants from about 9 months of age will recall actions that they witnessed at a previous time. In another classic study, Meltzoff (1988) showed babies an interesting box, and then demonstrated that pushing a button on the box would produce a beep. The next day, the babies played with the box themselves for the first time. Nine-month-old babies who had watched the button pushing the previous day were much more likely to push the button than were babies who had not previously observed the action. As you might guess, there is some controversy about when recall begins, related to disagreements among researchers about when mental representation begins (e.g., Rovee-Collier & Cuevas, 2009), but on the whole, deferred imitation appears to begin in the last several months of the first year, consistent with Meltzoff's findings. It improves dramatically over the second year, both in duration and in the complexity of what can be recalled. For example, 11-month-old babies will imitate a simple action as long as 3 months later, but 20-month-olds can imitate more elaborate sequences as long as 12 months later (see Lukowski & Bauer, 2014).

Deferred imitation is, of course, what makes observational learning, or modeling, possible. Once children can mentally represent and thus recall the actions of others, they have gained a cognitive skill that is critical for social learning. A toddler who has watched his big sister painting pictures might on his own open a jar of paint, dip a paintbrush into it, and then sweep the paintbrush across some available surface. His proficiency at each of these actions will be limited, but the sequence will be executed more or less correctly because he recalls his big sister's past actions. The capacity to recall and repeat another's behavior helps infants learn actions from others, and it also supports language learning (Sundqvist, Nordqvist, Koch, & Heimann, 2016).

You have seen that babies usually begin searching for hidden objects at about 8 months of age, and that this is strong evidence that they believe objects are permanent. It also indicates that infants can recall hidden objects. A particularly important sign of such recall is the beginning of separation anxiety. When parents leave a young baby with another caregiver, the baby typically does not seem to miss the absent parents or to mourn their loss while they are gone. When they are out of sight, they seem to be out of mind. But in the second half of the first year, at about 8 months for most babies, leaving a child with another caregiver may be more difficult. The baby may continue for some time to watch for the missing parents, to cry or fuss, and to generally act distressed. Bouts of separation anxiety are usually of fairly short duration at first, but tend to increase in length, suggesting that the child's ability to recall the parents is increasing in duration. An 18- to 24-month-old left with a babysitter might show signs of anxiety repeatedly throughout the parents' absence. Of course, many factors contribute to separation anxiety: the familiarity of the alternate caregiver and of the surroundings, the quality of the infant's relationship to the parents, the infant's temperament (see Chapter 4), and so on. But the consistency with which babies around the world begin showing separation distress at about 8 months is attributable to advances in basic cognitive skills such as recall and object permanence (e.g., Super, Guldan, Ahmed, & Zeitlin, 2012).

Such related cognitive and social developments in the second half of the infant's first year also correspond to important brain developments. Rapid myelination of axons increases the efficiency of several brain areas, especially in the frontal lobes, which support thought processes like planning; in the corpus callosum, which enhances coordination of functions between the right and left sides of the brain; in the hippocampus, which is important for memory; and in the cerebellum, which helps control movement and balance (e.g., Deoni et al., 2016; Lee et al., 2017; O'Muircheartaigh, 2014). As a result, while representational processes like recall improve, so do motor skills, advancing the infant's capacity to explore the environment and to enrich her understanding of objects. Thus, biological, cognitive, motor, and social developments are intricately interdependent.

Having and Inferring Intentions

If we intentionally act, choosing to pick up a fork rather than a spoon, searching through a closet for just the right outfit to wear, or planning a presentation at work, we are thinking about what we do before we do it. Very little conscious effort may be involved in some intentional acts, but at least some thought is required. Like the other cognitive skills we have examined, the ability to intend to do something has important consequences not just for intellectual performance but for social interactions as well. A child who can choose whether to cry to call for attention, for example, is likely to be treated differently than one who can only reflexively cry in response to discomfort. Obviously, the development of intentional action is related to the development of self-control and decision making, which we will discuss at greater length later in this and other chapters.

HAVING INTENTIONS

When does intentional action begin? Piaget (1952) assumed that infants' earliest behaviors are entirely unintentional and are typically based on reflexive responses to incoming stimulation and on the need to act, that is, to repetitively exercise one's reflexes. By 4 to 8 months, infants' behaviors have expanded as a result of constant differentiation and integration of the original reflexes, according to Piaget, and now a baby has a large repertoire of behavioral responses to stimuli. If one of these behaviors accidentally produces an interesting event, a child is likely to notice the effect and repeat the action, as if she were hoping to repeat the effect. Piaget called this **making interesting sights last**. He did not consider it to be intentional behavior, but rather a precursor to intentional behavior. In fact, it appears to be simple operant conditioning. After a behavior occurs, there is a reinforcing event, and the behavior is likely to be repeated. But there is a twist. Piaget described infants as appearing somewhat reflective, as if they had noticed the connection between their action and the outcome, and they were trying to make it happen again. Modern researchers have observed similar sequences in infants as young as 3 months old (Rovee-Collier & Barr, 2001). When a mobile hanging over a baby's crib is tied to a baby's foot, the child will soon learn to shake her foot to make the mobile move. At some point, the baby appears to notice the connection, as if she were having an insight, and then she shakes her foot more vigorously afterward.

From these first inklings of intentional behavior, infants move to more clearly intentional action in that magical time, the last several months of the first year. By 8 to 12 months, Piaget reported that babies will engage in **means–end behavior**: They will divert their attention from a goal, such as grasping a toy, to produce another action that will help achieve the goal. For example, a baby might try to grasp a rattle that is behind a clear Plexiglas screen. When her hand touches the screen, the baby redirects her attention to the screen, perhaps pushing it aside, before focusing again on the rattle. Younger babies simply keep reaching for the rattle and failing. Their behavior seems more controlled by the stimulus of the rattle than by their own plans. Thus, again, it appears that a behavior that requires mental representation, planning, begins in the 8- to 12-month period. At this point, infants may do some fairly complex sizing up of such situations (e.g., Paulus & Sodian, 2015; Willatts, 1989). For example, 9-month-olds will put aside a barrier and then pull on a cloth to get an out-of-reach toy resting on the cloth. But when the toy is not on the cloth, they simply play with the barrier, as though they realize there is no point in pulling on the cloth.

More sophisticated intentional control of behavior emerges in the second year. Whereas a 10-month-old typically will use only previously practiced actions as means to an end, 12- to 18-month-olds begin to actively invent new variations on their actions to fit the situation, trying out one variation after another. By 24 months, toddlers' control of their mental representations is advanced enough that they will mentally invent new means to an end. Rather than trying this and trying that, sometimes they solve a problem by quietly studying the situation first, and producing a useful means to an end on the first try.

The beginning of intentional behavior by the end of the first year is evident in babies' communicative behaviors. When a younger baby repeats an action that has attracted attention in the past, such as patting Mommy's cheek, the child may be doing no more than "making interesting sights last." But by 8 to 12 months, most babies are using some of their behaviors, including some vocalizations, not just to attract attention but as a communicative means to an end. For example, a typical 12-month-old might make a wailing sound while intently looking at her father. When he looks in her direction, she extends her hand in an urgent reach in the direction of a particular toy, apparently indicating that she would like her father to retrieve it. These complex behavior sequences certainly look like intentional communication. Intentionally controlling our own behavior and thought—setting goals, determining what we will pay attention to, and choosing to make one response rather than another—are among a set of cognitive processes that researchers today refer to as **executive functions (EFs)**. These functions heavily engage areas of the prefrontal cortex, which, as we noted earlier, shows maturational gains late in the first year. You will learn more about executive functions later in this chapter.

INFERRING OTHERS' INTENTIONS

As babies are developing intentions of their own, what do they understand about the intentions of others? Researchers make a distinction between a child's understanding of human **agency** and of human **intention**. *Agency* refers to the ability to act without an external trigger (self-propulsion). People and animals have agency because they can act without being pushed or "launched" by some other force, whereas objects require launching. *Intention* is an internal mental state, such as a plan or a desire that is the source of an action. Infants begin to understand agency by the end of the first year. Just trying to get other people to do things for her, like the baby described in the last paragraph, suggests that the baby has some sense that others are agents. It is also likely that trying to maneuver her father into retrieving an object for her shows that she sees him as able to engage in goal-directed action, like herself. So, by the end of the first year, babies appear to view people both as agents and as intentional actors (see Baillargeon, Scott, & Bian, 2016). Knowing that others can act intentionally is just the start of understanding what other people's intentions, desires, feelings, beliefs, and knowledge might be. As you will see in the discussion of the preoperational stage, understanding intentions is part of developing a **theory of mind (ToM)**, and it is a complex and long-term process (e.g., Birch et al., 2017).

Yet, as with other cognitive skills, there appear to be preliminary developments in the understanding of intentions even early in the first year. Using a habituation task, Woodward (1998) found some apparent awareness of the goal-directedness (intentionality) of human action even in babies as young as 6 months. In her study, babies saw an actor's arm reach for one of two toys that were side by side on a platform. Say, for example, that the arm reached for the toy on the left. The sequence was repeated until the babies habituated. Then, the position of the toys was switched, so that the toy that had been on the left was now on the right. The babies now witnessed one of two events. In the first event, the actor reached for the same toy as before, but the actor's arm had to reach in a different direction (to the right in our example) because the toys had been switched. In other words, the actor's goal remained the same—to pick up the same toy. In the second event, the actor reached for a new toy that was now in the original location (on the left in our example). Babies dishabituated more to the second event, as though they were surprised by the change in goal. The change in the direction of movement in the first event did not seem to be experienced as particularly new or important. Rather, it was the change in goal that the babies noticed. The same study done with an inanimate rod "reaching" toward the toys did not produce the same results. The babies seemed to expect goal-directedness from humans, but they did not expect it from an inanimate rod. The results of Woodward's study suggest that although full understanding of human intentions may take a long time, babies appear to have a rudimentary sense that there are significant differences between humans and other objects as early as 6 months.

What helps a baby progress in understanding other people's intentions? There are many contributing factors. One is likely to be that as 1- to 2-year-olds more clearly experience their own actions, such as reaching for an object, as intentionally driven, seeing a similar action by another person helps them to view the other as "like me"—driven by similar intentions (Meltzoff, 2007). Interacting directly with other people seems to aid the process. Moll and Tomasello (2007) argued that "When the infant is truly jointly engaged with another, he or she has formed with that partner some kind of joint goal and joint plans of actions . . . In these interactions infants register . . . important aspects of what the partner is experiencing . . . "(p. 316). Joint attention and interaction may not be *necessary* for a baby to begin to access others' intentions—there are many cultures in which adults rarely interact in playful, "shared goal" kinds of interactions and yet children develop an understanding of others' intentions. But shared social experiences do seem to facilitate the process (Schneidman & Woodward, 2016).

> **MyLab Education** Self-Check 3.2

Preschoolers' Cognition: The Preoperational Stage

3.3   Describe Piaget's preoperational stage and current views of cognitive development in preschool children including development in the areas of executive functions, numbers, theory of mind, and language.

By the age of 2, children have moved beyond the limits of sensorimotor activity to become thinkers. They may begin life, as Piaget believed, responding to the world primarily by connecting sensation to action, constantly exercising and adapting reflexive patterns of behavior. But by age 2, children can engage the world on the plane of thought. They understand that objects exist apart from their own perceptions and actions. They can call to mind previously experienced events. They can plan and execute complex behaviors, even behaviors they have not tried before, and they know that humans, unlike objects, are agents of action whose behavior is goal directed. Whereas there are precursors to most or all of these skills even in early infancy, and scientists argue about when the earliest representations actually occur, the flowering of thinking in the second year of life is indisputable.

Among the abilities that toddlers' thinking permits is the use of **symbols** (Piaget, 1962). *Symbols* are stand-ins for other things. Words are symbols; so are the props used in pretend play when they stand for something else, the way a broom stands for a horse when a child gallops around "riding" the broom. To use and understand such symbols, children must be able to mentally represent the things being symbolized. As babies' representational skills grow, especially over the second year, language skill and pretend play begin to blossom. In this section, we will highlight some of the typical cognitive achievements of the preschool years. You will find that Piaget celebrated the growth of thinking skills in this period, but he also argued that young children are

MyLab Education
Video Example 3.4
When young children begin to understand that symbols such as words and pictures represent objects, their development of language and other cognitive processes expands.

"preoperational" or prelogical. He theorized that children's early thought tends to be slow and centered on one salient feature of an experience or event at a time, a tendency he called **centration**. They have trouble understanding the principles that govern events, the "underlying realities" (Flavell, Miller, & Miller, 1993). As children interact with the world and practice representing the events they observe, their thinking speeds up and becomes more efficient. Eventually they can "decenter." They consider multiple pieces of information simultaneously, a process referred to as **decentration**. As a result, important relationships among their observations can be discovered and represented, and their thinking becomes more logical and sensible from an adult's point of view.

Consider Sayda's confusion about what is alive and what is not at the beginning of this chapter. She conflates being "visible" with being "alive." Part of her confusion is that she has distorted the facts: Dead things are usually hidden away and eventually decay, but that does not mean they are invisible. In addition, Piaget would probably attribute Sayda's confusion to her inability to sufficiently decenter. She cannot reflect on all of the facts she has learned about life, death, and non-living things at one time in order to organize the information correctly; she is unable to sort out characteristics of the biological and physical world in order to construct more well-grounded concepts. She cannot yet identify the organizing principles that are "beneath the surface" of her observations.

Piaget's research on preschool children identified some of the limits of their logical thinking, as you will see. More recent data suggest that preschoolers possess greater skill than Piaget realized, and some of these findings have helped specify step-by-step changes in the abilities that Piaget first described.

You will also see that many significant changes in cognitive functioning through the preschool years are conceptualized by today's scientists as grounded in the development of *executive functions (EFs)*. The notion of executive functions emerged from information processing theories, which you will learn more about in Chapter 6. For now, let's consider what these EFs are, and how they develop in the preschool years.

Taking Control: The Mind in Charge

Suppose you see this word: *Green*. And suppose I ask you to tell me what the word *says*. Your response would be immediate: You would automatically read the word. Now suppose that I ask you to tell me the color of the ink the word is printed in. Your response on this "Stroop task" would probably be a little slower and would require more effort. Most people feel that they have to inhibit the automatic tendency to read the color named by the word in order to name the color of the ink. This kind of voluntary inhibition of a dominant response is an example of executive functions at work.

Executive functions are a set of general abilities needed to purposefully complete a task or reach a goal, especially in new situations. They have been called "the cognitive toolkit of success" (Hendry, Jones, & Charman, 2016, p. 2). The three fundamental tools in the toolkit are **working memory**, **self-regulation** (or inhibitory control), and **cognitive flexibility**. Together they allow us to control and regulate our attention and behavior, and they make it possible for us to do tasks that require conscious mental effort, such as planning and problem solving (e.g., Diamond, 2016; Zelazo, 2015).

Working memory holds information that we are thinking about at the moment. You might think of it as a "short-term memory" that also actively processes the information being "stored" (Cowan, 2014). Consider Piaget's claim that a preschooler's thinking is initially centered, tending to focus on one thought at a time. A modern version of this idea re-interprets centering as a working memory limitation (e.g., Case, 1985). A preschooler's working memory has a very small capacity compared to that of older children or adults. A simple way to test working memory capacity is to use a digit span test: Present a series of digits and ask a child to say the digits back in the correct order. Two-year-olds cannot always perform on this test, but typically they seem to be able to hold in mind only about 1 digit. Four-year-olds can generally recall 2 to 3 digits correctly, 12-year-olds about 6 digits, and average adults about 7 digits (e.g., Cowan, 2016). If we test working memory size with visual stimuli, children's capacity seems a bit greater, but on the whole young children are somewhat handicapped by the limitations of their working memories.

Self–regulation, or inhibitory control, is the ability to stay focused on what you want by suppressing your attention to other things. It also includes the ability to stop yourself from responding automatically and to make yourself perform a response that is not the dominant or automatic one (e.g., Diamond, 2016). Self-regulation is involved in much of what we consider to be "mature" behavior, such as ignoring distractions, waiting your turn, resisting temptations, sticking with a boring task until it's finished, and so on. The Stroop task presented at the beginning of this section is designed to test self-regulation. A child-friendly version (the *Silly Sounds Stroop*; Willoughby & Blair, 2016) asks children to bark like a dog when they see a picture of a cat and to meow like a cat when the picture shows a dog. Children's performance on this task gradually improves from 3 to 5 years.

When you purposefully shift your goals or attention back and forth as circumstances require you are showing *cognitive flexibility*. Imagine a set of cards with colored shapes on them. If we ask 3-year-olds to sort the cards by shape (squares in one pile, triangles in another, etc.), they will probably do that easily. But if we then ask them to take the same cards and sort them by color instead, they usually perseverate on the initial instruction and keep sorting by shape, even though they would have no trouble sorting the cards by color if we had started out with that request! Four- and 5-year-olds are much more likely to be able to make the switch, demonstrating cognitive flexibility (Zelazo et al., 2013).

The three aspects of executive functioning are difficult to separate. Taking charge of your own behavior in a goal-directed way seems to require all three at once. As a result, tasks that researchers use to test any one of these skills in children typically involve the others as well. For example, do you remember the game "Simon Says"? To play, one person acts as a guide, and everyone else is supposed to do what the guide says (e.g., "touch your elbow"), but ONLY if the instruction is preceded by "Simon says." More complex versions of this game are often used to assess self-regulation, but they also tap working memory and cognitive flexibility. In one version, "Head, Toes, Knees, Shoulders," children follow the directions of the guide as in Simon Says, but the rules require that children do the opposite of what the guide says. When the guide says "Touch your head," the rule is to touch your toes and vice versa. When the guide says "Touch your shoulders," the rule is to touch your knees and vice versa. For children to be successful at this game, their working memories must keep the rules available; children must inhibit their dominant responses (which is to do what the guide is saying to do) in order to follow the rules; and they must be cognitively flexible, shifting attention between the instruction and the rule (McClelland & Cameron, 2012).

Today's developmental scientists usually assume that advancing executive functions are necessary (if not sufficient) for children to reason carefully and to construct adequate understandings of the facts they learn. Self-regulation helps children maintain attention to a difficult mental task; working memory allows multiple facts to be kept in mind simultaneously; and cognitive flexibility helps children shift attention among possible interpretations of contradictory information. Three-year-old Sayda, who was beginning to keep in mind contradictory facts as she pondered life and death, would probably need more expanded working memory space and cognitive flexibility to begin to construct alternative explanations and assess their adequacy. "As Piaget insisted, (mental) construction is an *active* process, and the EFs are a seat of conceptual *activity*" (Carey et al., 2015, p. 51).

Infants and toddlers are clearly beginning to develop executive functions (Hendry, Jones, & Charman, 2016). Think of the 12-month-old who can shift her attention from the object she desires to her father in order to communicate her desire to him. Executive functions improve substantially from ages 2 to 5, and studies in several countries, including the United States, Taiwan, China, and South Korea, find that preschoolers' performance on tests of executive functioning predicts their later academic progress (e.g., Nelson et al., 2017). Even in preschool, children who score higher on EF tests are likely to become more engaged in learning activities, and they are less likely to be disruptive (Nesbitt, Fahran, & Fuhs, 2015).

Improvement of executive functions is a result of many factors, from the maturing prefrontal cortex to environmental variables, such as parents' caregiving and disciplinary strategies (see Chapters 4 and 5). And just as EFs support the development of many of the skills described in this chapter, such as theory of mind and language skills, these other skills also help improve executive functioning. For example, as children acquire language, their self-regulation skills also advance. As you will see, Vygotsky and others have argued that language in the form of private speech is especially important for the development of self-control (Alderson-Day & Fernyhough, 2015; Vygotsky & Luria, 1930).

Remember that influences on development are often bidirectional. Inter-relationships among causal processes make development very complex, but they can also provide a special benefit to helping professionals. It is often possible to make improvements in multiple skill areas by focusing on one or two areas that are intimately tied to all of the rest. For example, in the Applications section of this chapter, you will read about an intervention called "Tools of the Mind" that uses teacher-guided role play (focusing on theory of mind skills and language practice) to improve children's executive functions. This intervention helps children make gains in self-regulation, cognitive flexibility, and problem solving in general.

Understanding Numbers

Knowledge of numbers is central to cognitive development. Piaget (1952) launched the systematic study of children's number skills by inventing the number conservation task. A set of discrete items, let's say 5 candies, is laid out in a neatly spaced line. Below the first set is a second set, laid out the same way, with the candies in each row matched one to one. A child is asked if the two rows have the same number or whether one or the other has more candies. Typically, 3- and 4-year-olds recognize that the two rows have the same number of candies. But when the researcher then changes the appearance of the second row by spreading out the candies, preschoolers usually think that the number has changed along with the appearance of the row. Most frequently, they say that the longer row now has more candy. Even if they count the candies and report that each has 5, they believe that the longer row has more. Do they really believe that? They seem to. If you ask them which row they would rather have to eat, they will choose the longer row!

Much debate has swirled around the meaning of preschoolers' failure on this number conservation task. Piaget felt that children were revealing centered thinking, focusing on just one thing at a time. When they look at the rows of candies, preschoolers notice the differences in length, but they ignore the differences in density. If they thought about both, especially the transformations that occurred in both as the second row was reconfigured, they might recognize that as the length of the row increased, the density of the row decreased, so that the number of candies stayed the same despite the increased length. Because their thought is centered, Piaget argued, pre-operational children tend to link observations in serial order, rather than discovering and representing the more complex relationships among them. In the number conservation task, even when children notice both the change in length and the change in density of the second row, they observe these changes serially, and they cannot detect the reciprocal relationship between them. Piaget found that children's understanding of number conservation moves forward rapidly from ages 5 to 7. He attributed this achievement to decentering. With practice, children's thinking in situations like this speeds up, eventually allowing them to "see" beyond the superficial changes and realize that without adding or subtracting items the number must remain the same. Consistent with this idea, advances in executive functions, like working memory, are strongly related to preschoolers' progress in understanding numbers (Schmitt, Geldhof, Purpura, Duncan, & McClelland, 2017).

Newer research on number understanding emphasizes how much preschoolers do know, even though they still fail Piaget's number conservation task. Even newborns appear to discriminate differences between small numbers; they will habituate to displays of two items, but then dishabituate to a display of three items. Five-month-olds may even have some implicit understanding of simple addition and subtraction. If they see one doll placed behind a screen, and then a second doll placed behind the same screen, babies seem surprised if there is only one doll there when the screen is removed. They are not surprised if there are two dolls (see Siegler & Braithwaite, 2017).

In exploring the number skills of preschoolers, Gelman and her colleagues (e.g., Gelman & Gallistel, 1978; see also Gelman, 1982; Gelman & Williams, 1998) found that 2- to 3-year-olds have at least implicit understanding of many fundamental counting principles. For example, they know that counting requires the "one-to-one" principle: one number for one item. Such young children sometimes do mistakenly recount items, but they seem to realize that recounting is not really acceptable. Between 3 and 5 years, children can count the same set of items in versatile order, starting once with the item on the left, another time with the item on the right, and so forth. Gelman calls this the "order-irrelevance principle." She even found that children as young as 3 can sometimes remain focused on number despite changes in the length and density of rows.

In a classic series of studies using "magic number games," Gelman showed children two plates, each with a row of toy mice, two mice on one plate, and three mice on the other. For some children, the rows of mice were of equal length but of unequal density; for other children, the rows of mice were of unequal length but equal density. First, the children were trained to pick the "winner" plate (the one with three mice) by giving them lots of trials and telling them whether they were right or wrong. Once they had learned to pick the correct plate without error, the researcher surreptitiously changed the appearance of the plates. For example, if the rows of mice had been of equal length, they were changed to be of equal density. Children tended to register surprise when the changed plates were revealed, but they still correctly picked the winners. Thus, it was clear that they had learned to select the correct plate on the basis of number, not on the basis of length or density differences. It appears that under the right circumstances, young children can pay attention to "underlying realities," although their ability to do so is quite fragile and easily disrupted. The same children who succeeded in the magic number games still failed Piaget's classic number conservation tasks.

Gelman's magic number games are characteristic of many of the tasks that modern researchers have designed to explore the apparent limitations of preschoolers' thinking. They are different from Piaget's tasks in that they provide simple instructions, and they often do not require verbal responses or explanations. They also establish different criteria for granting children some knowledge or skill. Piaget's criteria were conservative. He wanted children to demonstrate that they had complete mastery of a skill or concept, such as the concept of number, so that it could not be disrupted by counter-suggestions or by superficial transformation, before he granted that the skill was present. He often required that children be able to give sensible explanations of their right answers before he credited them with true understanding. Today's researchers tend to make minimal demands on children and to grant them the presence of a skill even when children's success can be easily disrupted by increased demands. The data are not in dispute, but the interpretation of the data is (e.g., Geary, 2006).

One approach to resolving the dispute is to assume that children understand concepts such as number in ever-increasing depth and breadth. Today's researchers often focus on specifying what those levels of understanding are and determining what kinds of experiences help children to advance from one level to another (Bidell & Fischer, 1997; Blewitt, 1994; Jara-Ettinger, Piantadosi, Spelke, Levy, & Gibson, 2016).

Studies by Siegler (e.g., Laski & Siegler, 2014; Siegler & Ramani, 2009) are good examples of research that shows how experience can help preschoolers' number understanding. They began by noting that at the beginning of first grade, children vary greatly with regard to how much they know about numbers. For example, some children (especially higher SES children) can do a good job on "number line estimation." That just means that if we draw a line, and mark one end with a "1" and the other end with a "10," these children can figure out approximately where a 7 should go on the line. To do this right, a child has to have some implicit knowledge of the relative size of different numbers (e.g., 4 is twice as big as 2). It's an important understanding, one that is foundational for acquiring other math skills. Lower SES children are less likely than higher SES children to start school with this skill. Siegler and Ramani hypothesized that the difference is due to how often higher versus lower SES families play counting and number games with their children, including board games that involve numbers. They developed a number board game called *The Great Race*, somewhat like *Chutes and Ladders*, where the object of the game is to advance along a series of 10 squares, each marked by a number. If lower SES preschoolers played the number board game repeatedly over a 2-week period, the children's "number line estimation" skills improved dramatically in comparison to children who played a similar game that did not include numbers.

The effectiveness of *The Great Race* game highlights the value of play for cognitive development in early childhood. Toddlers and young preschoolers spontaneously engage in **exploratory play**. They manipulate objects, check out their properties, sort, and organize them. In so doing, children learn not only about the properties of objects, but also about spatial relations, numerical relations, categorical relations, and so on. For example, Mix, Moore, and Holcomb (2011) quite elegantly demonstrated the direct benefits of children's exploratory play for learning about number equivalence. First, they tested 3-year-olds for their ability to match one set of items (e.g., 3 turtles) with an equivalent set of other items (e.g., 3 flowers). Only children who failed the original test were included in the remainder of the study. The researchers gave the children sets of toys to take home and play with over the course of 6 weeks, with no instructions regarding what to do with the toys. Parents were asked to make sure the toys were continuously available and to keep a log of what children did with them. One group of children received "objects with slots" that made one-to-one correspondence play easy, such as six balls and a muffin tin—the balls fit just right into the six slots of the muffin tin. Another group of children received "objects with objects," such as six balls and six toy frogs (see Figure 3.2). Children who were given "objects with slots" engaged in much more one-to-one play as reported in parent logs, and when they were tested after 6 weeks, many of these children showed substantial improvement on the numerical equivalence matching test. Clearly, play is a medium for learning.

We have learned a great deal about children's number understanding since Piaget's early work, but many of Piaget's characterizations of the limitations of preoperational thought remain useful. Preschoolers do seem to make appearance-based conclusions, and they frequently miss the deeper significance of events. Also, their thinking often does seem especially affected by singular, salient dimensions of a situation. However, most researchers recognize that such limitations aptly describe young children's abilities sometimes, but not always, and that experience, especially the way adults interact with young children, can be an important factor in how early abilities develop.

Understanding the Mind

Piaget (1926; Piaget & Inhelder, 1956) pioneered the investigation of children's understanding of other people's mental processes by studying perspective-taking skills in preschoolers. In his "three mountains task," a three-dimensional model of three mountains was shown to children from several different angles. Children then had to select a picture of how the scene looked to them, as well as a picture of how it looked to another observer on a different side of the display. Until about age 7, children tended to select the same picture both times, suggesting that they believed that other observers shared their perspective. Piaget believed children's poor perspective-taking skills reflected **preoperational egocentrism**. Because preschoolers can think about only one thing at a time, they are centered on their own perspective and have no awareness of the possibility of a different perspective.

Young children often appear to be egocentric in their encounters with others. A young girl may suggest that

FIGURE 3.2 Examples of toys for one-to-one correspondence play from Mix, Moore, & Holcomb.

SOURCE: Mix, K. S., Moore, J. A., & Holcomb, E. (2011). One-to-one play promotes numerical equivalence concepts. *Journal of Cognition and Development, 12,* 468. Used with permission from Taylor & Francis.

Daddy would like a dollhouse for his birthday. She assumes that he wants what she wants. When parents eagerly ask for information about what happened in nursery school, their son fails to respond, as if he cannot fathom what it is the parents do not already know. If he knows what happened today, surely they do too. During a telephone conversation, when her grandmother asks a toddler what she's going to wear to her birthday party, the child responds "This!" and points to the dress she is wearing, as if her grandmother can see what she can see. These are all typical examples of a failure to take another person's perspective.

Today, researchers see perspective taking (or its failure) as an aspect of someone's *theory of mind* or "naive psychology," that is, the understanding that people's behavior is a function of their internal, subjective mental states—such as desires, emotions, and beliefs. Such understanding is critical for developing satisfactory relationships with others. You have already seen that in the first year of infancy children begin to have a sense that humans are agents of action and that others' (and perhaps their own) behaviors can be goal directed (intentional).

Around 18 months old, there are other signs that children are building skills that help them learn about minds. They often closely observe other people. From observations in simple situations, toddlers sometimes seem to gain an implicit sense of what another person "desires" or "knows," even if that is different from what the child wants or knows. In one early study, an adult offered 14- and 18-month olds something to eat: either crackers or broccoli. The children chose crackers; the adult then chose broccoli for herself. When the adult later asked children to give her something to eat, 14-month-olds gave her crackers—what *they* preferred. But 18-month-olds gave her broccoli. They had noted her choice and then repeated it for her (Repacholi & Gopnik, 1997; for other examples of early, implicit perspective taking, see Scott & Baillargeon, 2017).

Among the earliest signs that children have more explicit awareness of the existence of mental states is their use of "mental" words. Words for emotions or desires, such as *need*, *feel*, and *want*, tend to occur as early as age 2, and words such as *think*, *forget*, and *remember* that describe cognitive functions are often used by age 3 (Huttenlocher & Smiley, 1990; Lundy, 2016). What concepts underlie these words we do not really know. It is likely that they are not the same as those of an adult, but clearly the young preschooler is beginning to assign some meaning to these words.

Thus, in the early preschool years, children seem to believe that they and others have mental states, such as thoughts, desires, feelings, and plans. But when do they become overtly aware that their own mental states can be different from someone else's? And how does their ability to figure out alternate perspectives develop? Most research supports the idea that children very gradually build awareness and understanding of minds (e.g., Birch et al., 2017).

Let's consider visual perspective taking. As early as age 2, a child can understand that if she is looking at a picture of a cat and you are standing opposite her, looking at the back of the picture, you will not be able to see the cat. In other words, the child can figure out that even if she can see something, you may not be able to see it. This is sometimes called "Level 1 visual perspective taking," when a child knows whether an object can or cannot be seen from a particular perspective. However, suppose we place the picture of the cat on a table, face up, so that the child can see it right side up and you, sitting across from the child, see it upside down. At age 2, the child cannot understand that you have a different perspective on the cat, and she assumes that you also see it right side up. By age 4 to 5, in this simple situation, the child will be able to attribute a different visual perspective from her own to you. She still will not be able to compute any kind of complex perspective difference, such as Piaget's three mountains task requires, but she can understand that someone else might see the *same picture* differently from herself (e.g., Masangkay et al., 1974; Moll, Meltzoff, Merzsch, & Tomasello, 2013). This is sometimes called "Level 2 visual perspective taking."

When children start to pass tests of Level 2 visual perspective taking, they also begin to reason more accurately about what other people may *desire*, *believe*, or *know*, although here again, they seem to move along gradually, making progress from about age 3-1/2 to 5-1/2. Table 3.2 will give you a sense of the gradual progression of this

TABLE 3.2 Tasks in the Theory of Mind (ToM) Scale

TASK	WHAT UNDERSTANDING IS TESTED
Diverse desires	That two people can like and want different things
Diverse beliefs	That two people can have different beliefs about the same thing
Knowledge access	That people who see something happen will know about it, but if they don't see it happen they won't know about it
False belief	That people do things based on what they think, even if they are mistaken
Hidden emotion	That people can hide emotions using their facial expressions

SOURCES: Wellman, H. M., Fang, F. M., & Peterson, C. C. (2011). Sequential progressions in a theory of mind scale: Longitudinal perspectives. *Child Development, 82,* 783; Slaughter, V. & Perez-Zapata, D. (2014). Cultural variations in the development of mind reading. *Developmental Perspectives, 8,* 237–241.

kind of perspective taking during the preschool years. It provides a description of abilities as measured on the Theory of Mind scale, in the order that they emerge for typical American children. For example, children usually understand that people have *diverse desires* sooner than they understand that they have *diverse beliefs*. Comprehending that others may have *false beliefs* takes them even longer (Wellman, Fang, & Peterson, 2011).

Children's performance on false belief tasks illustrates how difficult they find it to escape their own perspective when it comes to what they know. In such tasks, one person has correct knowledge of a situation, but another person (or the same person at another time) has incorrect knowledge, or a "false belief." Suppose a child is aware that a box of candy has been removed from its original location and is now hidden in a cabinet. The child is asked where a second person, let's call him Sam, will look for the candy. Even though the child knows Sam was not present for the hiding, the child does not attribute a false belief to Sam but assumes that Sam will search in the appropriate hiding place, as if Sam also must know what the child knows to be true. In fact, until age 4 1/2 or 5 children have trouble realizing that they have not always known what they know now. If they open a candy box expecting to find candy and are surprised to find something else instead, say pencils, they will later say that they knew before they opened the box that the pencils were there (see Birch et al., 2017, for a review).

Overall, preschoolers are less egocentric than Piaget inferred based on his very complex visual perspective-taking task. But Piaget was on target in assuming that taking another's perspective and understanding the limits of your own perspective are difficult, and sometimes impossible, tasks for young children. The implications for children's social development are far-reaching. When toddlers want to grab a dog's tail or chase a ball into the street, they are not likely to understand that the adults who restrain them want something different. Disciplinary action by others is frustrating to a 2-year-old, not just because she does not get what she wants, but also because she does not understand the adult's thinking. Three-year-olds have better explicit awareness that others may not share their own desires. But when two people have different beliefs, even 3- and 4-year-olds are often mystified. For example, 3-year-olds found it difficult to comprehend that a girl in a story could think a toothbrush was hers when another child thought it was his (Flavell, Mumme, Green, & Flavell, 1992).

Finally, when children's own emotions are strongly involved, taking another's perspective seems especially difficult. Apparently the child's own perspective is so salient in an emotionally charged situation that it can undermine the child's fragile understanding of the differences between her own mental state and that of another person. One 6-year-old girl, who usually was quite capable of understanding that others have different feelings and motives than she, was furious whenever she lost a board game or any other competition, calling her competitor "mean." Her own desire to win was so overwhelmingly salient that she assumed that it was shared by others, and that any interference with her success was simply mean-spiritedness!

How do young children overcome their problems with perspective taking and build a more realistic theory of mind? Piaget credited two processes: first, the gradual improvement in a child's ability to hold in mind multiple ideas at the same time (decentering), and second, the continual give and take of social interaction in which a child repeatedly confronts feedback from other people, indicating that others do not always share the child's feelings, desires, or knowledge. Children find it difficult to assimilate such feedback, but gradually they accommodate their views of others until they can conceive of independent mental states.

Not surprisingly, there is now evidence that many factors contribute to theory of mind development. Improvements in executive functions play a role. Expanding working memory can help children mentally represent both their own and another person's experience at the same time. Improving self-regulation helps as well. For example, the ability to intentionally inhibit a dominant response in order to perform a less salient response might help children to respond correctly on false belief tasks. Children with poor inhibitory skills might find it very difficult to suppress saying what *they* know to be true in order to think about and report another person's false belief (e.g., Benson, Sabbagh, Carlson, & Zelazo, 2013; Shahaeian, Henry, Razmjoee, Teymoori, & Wang, 2015).

In line with Piaget, researchers have found children's experience in social interactions is important, especially if it involves conversation about different viewpoints. For example, children's theory of mind skills advance more quickly when mothers frequently engage them in turn-taking conversations and when they talk about mental states (e.g., "You were happy and excited when we decided to go to the party. But Sam was unhappy, because his Mom said he couldn't stay very long.") (e.g., Ensor & Hughes, 2008). Also, young children who have siblings, especially older siblings, make more rapid progress than other children (e.g., McAlister & Peterson, 2013), apparently because they often talk about who believes, knows, and wants what. Siblings may also be important because, like peers, they play together.

Many studies have found a link between social **pretend play** and theory of mind development. Pretend play, or make believe, generally begins at about age 2. It is a kind of "as if" behavior, where objects or people may be treated as symbols, "as if" they were something or someone else (Fein, 1981). In social pretend play, children enact roles, simulating the actions or characteristics of other people and interacting with other children playing other roles. As children's language skills improve, they may spend a good deal of time planning and negotiating who will do what and when. The more young children engage in social pretend play, the more rapidly they advance on theory of mind skills (see Weisberg, 2015; and the Applications in this chapter).

Further support for the importance of social interaction comes from cross-cultural research on how quickly, and in what order, children acquire theory of mind skills. In a series of studies, researchers found that middle-class children in China and Iran make somewhat slower progress on theory of mind tasks than children in Australia or the United States, even though, at least in China, children's executive functions progress a bit more quickly than in the United States. Despite their overall lag, however, Chinese and Iranian children make more rapid progress than American and Australian children on some tasks, particularly on understanding how knowledge is accessed (see Slaughter & Perez-Zepata, 2014, for a summary of these studies). In China and Iran, middle-class parents endorse collectivist child-rearing goals such as showing respect for elders; teaching that children should defer to parental authority, cherish traditional knowledge, and not express opposing views; and requiring that children curb their individual desires when they conflict with family needs. In the United States and Australia, middle-class parents tend to encourage more independence in their children and are more likely to endorse discussions and negotiations of family rules. "Middle class preschoolers growing up in Iran or China may well have less chance than those being reared in Australia or the United States to be exposed to opinion diversity during family conversations or disputes" (Shehaeian, Peterson, Slaughter, & Wellman, 2011, p. 1241), perhaps making it harder to learn about differences in beliefs, but supporting learning about where knowledge comes from.

Despite differences in timing or sequence, children in all cultures eventually achieve basic perspective-taking skills. You will see in Chapter 6 that expertise in perspective taking continues to develop throughout middle childhood and continues to depend on, and to influence, the quality of children's social interactions.

Understanding Language

Language development is a remarkable achievement of almost all young children, made even more notable by the fact that many aspects of language learning are nearly complete by the end of the preoperational stage. Volumes can, and have, been written summarizing the research on language acquisition. Here we will provide only a sampling of what infants and preschoolers must learn to master a language, including phonology, semantics, syntax, and pragmatics. We will then consider how children fare when they are exposed to more than one language. And finally we will look at some of the factors that facilitate language learning.

PHONOLOGY

When children learn a language they are learning its **phonology** or sound system: what sounds change meaning, how stress and intonation are used, and so on. The smallest units of sound that make a difference in meaning are called **phonemes** (like consonant and vowel sounds). If a phoneme in a word is changed, the word itself changes. So, for example, if we change the "d" sound in *dab* to a "t" sound, we have a different word, *tab*. Habituation and preferential listening studies show that when babies are born, they already can distinguish among many language phonemes; they prefer to listen to speech sounds over other kinds of sounds; and they even tend to favor listening to their native language over other languages (Valiante, Barr, Zelazo, Brant, & Young, 2013).

Every language employs only a subset of the phonemes that humans can use. Newborns are able to distinguish among most of these sounds. By 6 months old, babies show signs of sharpening their ability to discriminate phonemes that are important in their native language, and they begin to lose the ability to perceive sound distinctions that are not used in their language, a process called **perceptual narrowing**. They are becoming "specialists" in their native language. Japanese babies, for example, start to lose the ability to distinguish "l" sounds from "r" sounds by this time (Ferjan Ramirez & Kuhl, 2017; Kuhl et al., 2006).

Young infants make a wide range of vocal sounds, like cooing, but babies begin **babbling** at about 6 months, repeating consonant-vowel-consonant sequences such as *bababa* or *doodoodoo*. At first these babblings include most possible language sounds, but by 9 months babies are matching their babbling sounds to the phonemes of their native language, a process called **productive narrowing**. Soon they begin to use some of these sounds in ways that parents identify as meaningful, such as "mama" or "bye-bye," especially if caregivers react contingently to a baby's babbling with vocalizations, smiles, touch, and other reinforcements (e.g., Gros-Louis, West, & King, 2014). Even though phonological development begins before birth, the full sound system may not be mastered for many years. Most adults find it difficult to understand the speech of a 2-year-old, although doting parents, tuned in to the toddler's phonological errors, can usually translate. The problem often is that 2-year-olds have not learned how, where, or when to use some of the sound distinctions that are important for their native tongue. For example, in English, we take advantage of **voicing**, using our vocal cords to make some consonant sounds but not others. The difference between the "d" sound and the "t" sound is only that the "d" is voiced and the "t" is not. A toddler may perceive the distinction, but may not yet have caught its importance or figured out how to produce it, and when he means to say *toy* he may say *doy*. Children master most sound distinctions like these by age 3 but may struggle for much longer with other aspects of phonology, such as making the "th" sound the right way in the right places (e.g., consider the differences in the "th" sound in *then* vs. *teeth*). By age 3, most children can be understood by family members and others who are familiar with them. If a child's speech is still difficult for strangers to follow by age 4, evaluation by a

TABLE 3.3 From Birth to Five: Typical Changes in Communicative/Interactive Skills

AGE	SKILL
Newborn to 1 month	Reflexively signals needs through cries, facial expressions
1 to 3 months	Coos, grunts, makes some other vocal sounds Quiets or smiles when spoken to
3 to 5 months	Smiles and shows interest in favorite people Makes wider range of vocal sounds (e.g., vowel sounds, squeals)
6 to 7 months	Babbles (consonant-vowel-consonant repetitions); produces sounds of all languages
8 to 9 months	Productive narrowing: begins to limit babbling to sounds of native language
9 to 12 months	Shows, gives objects Reaches or points to indicate desired object Engages in simple interactive games, routines (e.g., peekaboo, patty-cake) Produces first meaningful gestures (e.g., nodding to mean "yes," waving "bye-bye") Responds to simple verbal requests (e.g., "Look at Daddy"); some vocabulary comprehension Produces one or two words (e.g., *bye-bye, mama*) Deaf child produces one or two signs
13 to 18 months	Increases expressive vocabulary slowly, acquiring up to 50 words for familiar actions, events, and objects (e.g., *bottle, all gone, no, kiss, shoe*) Engages in simple pretend play, using self-directed acts (e.g., eating, washing, phone to ear)
18 to 24 months	Vocabulary spurt: Increases expressive vocabulary rapidly (3 or more words per day) Uses short (2-word) sentences, using content words (e.g., "Baby ball?" "All gone Daddy.") Engages in pretend play involving some coordination with partners (e.g., exchanges parent–baby roles with adult)
2 to 3 years	Speaks clearly enough to be understood by family members Requests labels for objects Uses sentences of 3 or more words; uses some function words (e.g., prepositions, articles, word endings) Overuses some grammatical rules—over-regularization (e.g., "I *goed* to the store.") Takes turns in conversation
3 to 4 years	Speaks clearly enough to be understood by nonfamily members Uses some complex sentences (e.g., "I think I saw the truck.") Pretends in complex, reciprocal interactions with others, engages in interactive planning for play
4 to 5 years	Produces most speech sounds correctly (continued exceptions might be *l, s, r, v, z, ch, sh, th*) Tells stories that stick to the topic, have some structure (beginning, middle, end) Coordinates conversation with multiple partners

MyLab Education
Video Example 3.5
Children recognize that anything can be labeled, and they experience a vocabulary spurt. Consider the language skills already acquired and those yet to be acquired by the children in this video.

speech pathologist may be advisable. See Table 3.3 for these and other milestones to watch for in children's communicative development.

SEMANTICS

When children learn language they also are learning which words and word parts (prefixes and suffixes) express particular meanings. This is referred to as the **semantics** of a language. Progress in producing words begins by the end of the first year, as already noted, and moves slowly for a time. In the first 6 months of word use, many words are produced only in limited contexts, as though tied to particular cues. For example, a child might say *daw* only when she sees the family's cocker spaniel, and then only if the dog barks.

At about the time that children can produce about 50 words, they typically go into a new phase of vocabulary learning called the **vocabulary spurt**: At about 18 to 24 months, toddlers begin learning words very rapidly, expanding their productive vocabulary from 50 to about 500 words in just a few months. Their comprehension vocabulary appears to be even larger. The child behaves as though she has had a sudden insight into the fact that anything can be labeled and thus communicated through words. Some have suggested that the vocabulary spurt marks the end of the sensorimotor period and is made possible by a fully functioning representational capacity; words are now truly being used as symbols for concepts and ideas, rather than being triggered by contextual cues. By age 5, the typical child may understand 15,000 words, so that an average of 9 or 10 words have been added every day for 3 years! The rapidity with which young children add new words to functional vocabulary after only one or two exposures is described as **fast mapping**. Working out the full details of a word's meaning usually requires multiple exposures and is described as **slow mapping** (e.g., Blewitt, Rump, Shealy, & Cook, 2009).

SYNTAX

Learning language means learning to produce sentences that make sense. The aspect of language that specifies how to link words into meaningful sentences is called **syntax** or **grammar**. Words must be ordered in a sentence in just the right way to communicate what we mean to someone else. Linguists have found that proper ordering of words and word parts (such as prefixes and suffixes in English) is governed by a complex set of rules. One of the most baffling things about children's language acquisition is that they learn these rules with little difficulty, despite the fact that no one teaches them.

Beginning with two-word strings at about the time of the vocabulary spurt, children quickly progress, until by age 5 they can produce most sentence structures. To give you a sense of how complex the rules are that children implicitly know, consider the following "tag questions" in English:

> That boy kicked the dog, didn't he?
> The ceiling leaks all the time, doesn't it?
> You and I are getting along well, aren't we?

Making the right question tag at the end of the sentence requires knowledge of several rules, including how to add an auxiliary (such as *did* or *does*) to a verb and how to negate a verb, for starters. To make proper tag questions requires so many rules that children are slow to learn this particular sentence form (Brown & Hanlon, 1970). Nonetheless, most English-speaking children can produce tag questions effortlessly by age 5.

PRAGMATICS

The final area children must learn is the **pragmatics** of their language, that is, how people actually use the language to communicate effectively. Knowing how to put together a proper sentence, or knowing the labels for things, is not enough. You must be able to craft a **narrative**, a story or event description that conveys the full sense of an experience or gets at the point of an event while taking into account what the listener needs to hear to understand. Different listeners have different needs—say a little sister versus a grandfather—and there are different conventions of address that are acceptable in different situations. All of these kinds of language-use issues must be learned in addition to the mechanics of language. Preschoolers begin to construct narratives, usually with the help of others, by about 2 or 3 years old. Initially, their narratives are sketchy and largely uninformative. A child telling about an all-day trip to the zoo, for example, might mention only that "we went" and indicate one salient experience: "We saw a lion." A listener counting on the narrative to learn where, when, and what is likely to be quite disappointed. Some aspects of developing pragmatic skill are dependent on cognitive developments in perspective taking, which helps account for the inadequacy of children's early narratives (e.g., Uccelli, Hemphill, Pan, & Snow, 1999).

Pragmatic skill also requires making appropriate adjustments in speech depending on the listener. Most children gradually learn **code switching**, shifting from using, say, slang with friends to using more polite forms with teachers. They also learn, eventually, to distinguish between the literal meaning of people's words and what they *really* mean. Everyday expressions (idioms) such as "What do ya' know?" or "That's cool!" are not to be taken literally in most social exchanges. And many such expressions require similar idiomatic responses. For example, today a greeting like "What's happening?" is usually followed by "Nothing much!"

TWO LANGUAGES AT ONCE: THE BILINGUAL CHILD

Remember 3-year-old Sayda's grandparents, from the beginning of this chapter? Their worry about Sayda's bilingual upbringing is not unusual. Psychologists and educators in the early 1900s warned parents that bilingual childrearing could confuse their children or impair intellectual development (e.g., Goodenough, 1926), and many parents from immigrant families went to some lengths to avoid exposing children to their heritage language. Since the 1960s, though, researchers have been accumulating evidence that this early view was based on inadequate studies, and that, in fact, there can be many cognitive advantages to a bilingual upbringing (Bialystok & Werker, 2017). This is encouraging news, because the majority of people around the world are bilingual, as are approximately 20% of North Americans. In today's global climate, immigrant families are more likely to worry about making sure their children have adequate exposure to both their heritage language *and* the language of their new country.

Studying the effects of bilingualism is tricky. The timing and quantity of exposure to their languages vary greatly among bilingual children. They may have been immersed in two languages from birth, like Sayda, or they may begin learning their second language only after they head to preschool or elementary school. Their exposure to both languages might be equivalent, or it might be quite disproportionate. And of course, being bilingual, especially in the United States, is confounded with other factors: Immigrant children whose parents are poor are more likely to be bilingual than other children. Today's researchers are usually careful to take these complications into account. Here we will focus on children who are immersed in two languages from birth, like Sayda.

Do bilingual children learn either language as well as they would have learned just one? If exposure is relatively equivalent, the answer is "Yes." Whether we examine phonological, semantic, syntactic, or pragmatic language development, the progress of bilingual children seems to be comparable to that of monolingual children. In phonological development, monolingual babies quickly become "native language specialists," as you have learned (Ferjan Ramirez & Kuhl, 2017). Between 6 and 12 months, they get better at discriminating the sounds of their native language but worse at discriminating sounds used in foreign languages. During the same age range, infants in a bilingual environment make equally good progress in sound discrimination in *both* of the languages they hear, and at the same pace. A study of infant brain activity using MEG technology corroborated that bilingual 11-month-olds show similarly strong neural activity when hearing sounds in either of their languages, whereas monolingual babies show strong neural activity only when hearing the sounds of their native language (Ferjan Ramirez, Ramirez, Clarke, Taulu, & Kuhl, 2017).

In other aspects of language acquisition, the picture is more complex, but generally bilingual children do fine. Let's look at semantic development to illustrate. Bilingual babies produce their first words at about the same time as monolingual babies. They also learn words at about the same rate, so that early vocabulary size is equivalent or somewhat greater for bilinguals compared to monolinguals if you sum across both of the bilingual child's languages. But, because bilinguals are "splitting their time" between two languages, they do not usually know as many words in a single language as monolinguals do. However, they tend to "catch up" with monolinguals in each of their languages, usually by elementary school (Ferjan-Ramirez & Kuhl, 2017).

Despite the need to "split their time," bilingual children appear to have language-learning advantages that serve them well. For example, knowing a word in one of their languages can facilitate learning a word with the same meaning in their other language (e.g., Bilson, Yoshida, Tran, Woods, & Hills, 2015). They also have more "metalinguistic" understanding, meaning that they seem to know more about how language works at an earlier age. For example, young monolingual children behave as though objects and actions can only have one label, and so they assume that new words must apply to unfamiliar referents. This is called the "mutual exclusivity" assumption. But bilingual children are more likely to accept a novel word for something that already has a familiar label (such as accepting *automobile* when they already know *car*), as though they know a little more about how language works or as though they have an earlier sense of the relationships among words (Brown & Blewitt, 2014; DeAnda, Poulin-Dubois, Zesiger, & Friend, 2016).

One characteristic of both child and adult bilinguals is that they occasionally engage in "code mixing," substituting a word from one language into a sentence produced in the other language (Ferjan Ramirez & Kuhl, 2017). A child learning both Spanish and English might say, "La pulsera is beautiful" (*pulsera* is Spanish for *bracelet*). Parents sometimes worry that their bilingual children are confusing their languages, but the evidence suggests that it is a strategy for facilitating communication when a speaker knows a word better in one language than in the other. Just like adult bilinguals, children who code mix use the syntax that is appropriate to the particular language they are speaking.

Not only do bilingual children do fine with language learning, but also they gain some real benefits in other cognitive skills from the process of learning two languages. As early as 6 months old, bilingual children show attentional and memory advantages over monolingual children. For example, suppose we train an infant to look to the left to see a dancing monkey. Once she is habitually looking to the left, we make a switch: The dancing monkey starts appearing on the right. Monolingual infants continue looking in the original location, even though the reward is no longer there. Bilingual infants, however, much more quickly overcome the habitual response and begin looking to the new location (Kovács & Mehler, 2009).

Similarly, bilingual preschoolers outperform monolingual children on executive function tests, which require cognitive flexibility and self-regulation. For example, in a study of children participating in a Head Start program, Spanish/English bilinguals scored higher than English monolinguals from the same centers on tests like the "Silly Sounds" Stroop test, which you will recall requires children to inhibit their dominant response in order to follow rules like "Bark like a dog when you see a picture of a cat" (White & Greenfield, 2017). Regardless of the languages they are learning, bilingual children show more rapid executive function development when compared to monolinguals of similar SES and age (see Bialystok, 2017).

You have learned that experience shapes brain development, both structurally and functionally. It will be no surprise to you that the cognitive advantages of bilingualism are linked to underlying differences in brain development, suggesting that exposure to multiple languages is responsible. In a study of brain function, for example, 5-year-old bilinguals not only performed better than monolinguals on a test of response inhibition, but EEG recordings showed that their brains responded more quickly (Barac, Moreno, & Bialystok, 2016). A number of studies also show structural brain differences. For example, bilingual children show greater myelination of brain pathways important for word processing than monolingual children do (Mohades et al., 2015).

Overall, immersion in a bilingual environment appears to be a win-win situation for children. Infants and preschoolers learn two languages as effortlessly as they learn one. How do they do it? For young children, the key ingredients to learning two languages are the same as those for learning one. Let's consider those now.

HOW LANGUAGE IS LEARNED

Language consists of so many complex systems, and it is learned so early, that it is difficult to explain how children manage the task. Some psycholinguists have proposed that much of language is learned by special, genetically programmed procedures that are unique to language learning (e.g., Chomsky, 1968). In this view, children with language learning difficulties are likely to have impairments in the special brain mechanisms dedicated to language learning (e.g., Pinker, 1994). Others contend that the general analytic capacity of the human brain is such that even complex language rules can be worked out without any innate knowledge or special language acquisition procedures (e.g., D'Souza, D'Souza, & Karmiloff-Smith, 2017). In this view, both typical and atypical language development is determined by the general cognitive functioning of the child as she interacts with the environment. If a child shows atypical language development, she is likely to have other cognitive problems as well. This debate is still ongoing, although evidence is building for the latter view, that language learning depends on "domain general" cognitive processes (e.g., Kidd & Arciuli, 2016; Meylan, Frank, Roy, & Levy, 2017).

Regardless of which view is correct, a child's experience with language in social interactions must be critically important. Recognizing the importance of experience raises two questions: First, how much exposure to a language is necessary (quantity), and second, are there particular kinds of experiences that facilitate language learning (quality)?

Adults often speak differently to infants and young children than they do to each other. They spontaneously use what researchers call **infant-directed speech (IDS)**. IDS used to be called "motherese" and more often today **parentese** (the term we will use), but it is clear that most people, not just parents, use parentese with young children. Some of its special features, compared to adult-directed or standard speech, include slower speed, higher pitch, more exaggerated intonation, simpler and less varied vocabulary, shorter sentences, and exaggerated articulation of some vowel sounds, along with less clear articulation of some other phonemes (e.g., Eaves, Feldman, Griffiths, & Shafto, 2016). Parentese is usually accompanied by positive emotions—what some researchers call "happy talk" (e.g., Golinkoff, Can, Soderstrom, & Hirsh-Pasek, 2015). These qualities *in combination* seem to attract infants' attention—they prefer parentese to more typical adult speech. Parentese that is not accompanied by positive emotions, such as when depressed mothers speak to their infants, does not appeal to infants as much, however. The attention-getting quality of parentese helps babies focus on language, and some of its particular characteristics, like the slow delivery, appear to make it easier for young children to learn some phonemes and to identify words and some grammatical units.

The effect of parentese on infants and toddlers illustrates that the quality of the speech that children hear is important for language development. To give you a keener sense of how both the quantity and the quality of their experiences support children's learning, we will focus further on two aspects of language learning: semantic development (vocabulary growth) and pragmatic development (specifically, producing narratives).

Cross-cultural differences in vocabulary growth help demonstrate the importance of input for semantic development. Regardless of what language children learn, vocabulary milestones tend to be reached at similar ages. However, the types of words that children learn most readily differ across language environments. Children learning many languages, including English, seem to have a "noun bias": They learn concrete nouns, like *cat* and *chair*, earlier and apparently more easily than other types of words, like verbs. Yet children learning Mandarin Chinese, Korean, and a few other languages learn verbs at least as early and as readily as they learn nouns, suggesting that characteristics of individual languages and the way that adults speak to children may be extremely important in shaping a child's vocabulary. For example, when speaking to young children, English speakers tend to begin their sentences with verbs but end them with nouns, whereas Mandarin speakers more often both begin and end their sentences with verbs (Tardif, Shatz, & Nagles, 1997). Also, the verbs Mandarin speakers use with young children often are highly "image-able" or highly specific in meaning, qualities that make words easier for young children to learn (see Chan et al., 2011). Such differences in child-directed speech apparently make verbs at least as easy to learn as nouns for children acquiring Mandarin and similar languages.

Within a given culture, there are substantial individual differences among children in how rapidly they grow their vocabularies. Vocabulary differences are usually related to children's home and preschool environments (e.g., Rowe, Raudenbush, & Goldin-Meadow, 2012; Senechal & LeFevre, 2002; Tamis-LeMonda, Kuchirko, & Song, 2014). The amount and kind of language experience children have with adults in parent–child conversations, during mealtimes, play times, and activities like joint book reading, seem to be key. Fernald and colleagues have found that how much mothers speak to their 18-month-olds predicts not only how large their children's vocabularies will be but also how quickly the children can process familiar words at 24 months. These findings are the same whether children are reared in middle-class English-speaking families or low-income Spanish-speaking families (Hurtado, Marchman, & Fernald, 2008; Weisleder & Fernald, 2013). It seems that " . . . caregiver talk not only guides . . . vocabulary learning, but also sharpens the processing skills used during real-time language comprehension" (Hurtado et al., 2008, p. F31).

But again, quantity is not all that matters. Researchers have repeatedly demonstrated that quality is also key. Adults' **verbal responsiveness** to infants and preschoolers is especially important (e.g., Blewitt & Langan, 2016; Hirsh-Pasek et al., 2015;

MyLab Education

Video Example 3.6

Cross-cultural comparisons show both universals in language development and the diversity in the environmental input that young language learners hear. In general, children around the world show similar developmental trajectories overall, although substantial individual differences, especially in vocabulary development, are also apparent.

Tamis-LeMonda, Kuchirko, & Song, 2014). Tamis-LeMonda and her colleagues define adults' *verbal responsiveness* as making prompt, contingent, and appropriate (positive and meaningful) verbal responses to children's behaviors or vocalizations (e.g., when a baby points to a toy and a parent says, "Would you like your rattle?"). They find that children make more rapid progress in vocabulary acquisition (e.g., they reach the 50-word milestone earlier) when mothers are more verbally responsive in these early years, regardless of mothers' own productive vocabularies.

One of the most compelling demonstrations of the importance of input for children's vocabulary growth is a classic study in which researchers made monthly visits for over two years to the homes of children whose families were either poor and on welfare, lower middle class (mostly in blue-collar occupations), or upper middle class with at least one professional parent (Hart & Risley, 1995). All of the parents were actively involved with their children, playing with them, expressing affection, providing them with toys, and so on. But there were marked differences in how much the three groups of parents talked to their children right from the start. (Children were about 9 months old at the beginning of the study.) In a 100-hour week, a toddler in a professional family might hear 215,000 words on the average. In a lower middle-class family, children heard about 125,000 words, and in the poorest homes about 62,000 words. This discrepancy has come to be known as "the 30 million word gap": By age 4, children in the poorest families had heard 30 million fewer words addressed to them than children from professional families. All of the children learned to talk on schedule, but the differences in parental input were correlated with children's vocabulary measures by age 3. Children who heard the most language performed best. The content of parents' conversations with their youngsters also differed. Those who spoke with their children most tended to ask more questions and elaborated more on topics of conversation, using speech more to maintain a positive connection and to inform (features of verbal responsiveness) rather than to regulate children. Parents who spoke with their children the least tended to utter more prohibitions. Even when the researchers looked within a single socioeconomic group, so that social class was not a factor, children whose parents talked with them more had the most advanced vocabularies.

The quantity and quality of parent–child conversation is a significant factor in vocabulary expansion not just for monolingual children, but for bilingual children as well. Many fewer studies include bilingual children, but when they do, the findings are the same. For example, a study of Spanish/English bilingual families found that the amount of parentese in Spanish that their babies heard at ages 11 months and 14 months, in one-to-one interactions, predicted their Spanish vocabulary size at 24 months old. The same was true for the relationship between the amount of English parentese the babies heard and the size of their English vocabularies (Ramirez-Esparza, Garcia-Sierra, & Kuhl, 2017).

Children's narrative skills are also tied to the kinds of language opportunities that parents and other caregivers provide (see Box 3.2). Consider how different the narrative skills of two 5-year-olds in the same classroom proved to be. Both children were retelling a story they were told about a boy's trip to a grocery store. Both children were clearly familiar with all of the details of the story, having successfully acted it out with dolls and other props.

First child: John went to the grocery store. He got a cake for his grandmother's birthday party. And he paid the clerk and ran home.

Second Child: He got cake and he ran home. (Feagans & Farran, 1981, p. 723)

(*Source:* Feagans, L., & Farran, D. C. (1981). How demonstrated comprehension can get muddled in production. *Developmental Psychology, 17*, 718–727.)

Several studies have found that narrative skill differences like these are connected to the way that mothers converse with their children. If they use an elaborative style, engaging in lengthy discussions about children's past experiences, providing lots of details, asking questions, and encouraging children to provide details as well, their children's narratives tend to become more adequate and informative (e.g., Reese & Newcombe, 2007). Children's other language skills, such as phonological awareness and story comprehension, also benefit (see Salmon & Reese, 2016).

Box 3.2: Early Childhood Education: Helping All Children Succeed

Early experiences build the brain architecture and the behavioral foundations that support children's academic, emotional, and social futures. Throughout this text, you will find evidence that socioeconomic status in the United States is a key determiner of whether infants and young children will have the experiences they need to build a sturdy foundation for success. Children from low income or impoverished neighborhoods, whose family members are often undereducated and/or face significant adversity, are more likely than children from more advantaged circumstances to suffer a range of physical and mental health problems as adults. Their cognitive development is often so compromised by the end of the preschool period that they are less likely than other children to learn to read, are more likely to need special education placements, and are especially prone to dropping out of school (e.g., Burchinal, 2016; Magnuson & Duncan, 2006). Because school achievement is strongly linked to employability and income, poverty is passed on from one generation to another (e.g., Ramey, Sparling, & Ramey, 2012).

Can preschool education help provide low-income children with the experiences they need for positive development? Parents are the adults who have the most interaction with their young children and who have the most control over their early experiences. The more education and income parents have, the more likely they are to provide all of the experiences that support the cognitive, behavioral, and social developments that predict success in school and in life. Yet even for children from upper SES homes, time spent in a *quality* preschool can add value (e.g., Peisner-Feinberg et al., 2001). And for children from lower SES homes, high-quality preschool substantially improves school readiness, reduces a child's chances of a "special education" placement, increases chances of high school graduation, reduces crime and incarceration rates, and benefits later earnings (e.g., Anderson & Phillips, 2017; Campbell et al., 2012; Dodge, Bai, Ladd, & Muschkin, 2017; Ramey et al., 2012; Reynolds & Ou, 2016; Schweinhart et al., 2005). These benefits have been demonstrated in several long-term experiments that followed poor children well into adulthood (e.g., the Abecedarian Project—see Ramey et al., 2012; the High/Scope Perry Preschool Program—see Schweinhart et al., 2005; the Chicago Child-Parent Centers—see Reynolds & Ou, 2016). A number of larger longitudinal studies of public pre-kindergarten programs have looked at children's academic and social outcomes and found encouraging results as well (e.g., in Oklahoma—Anderson & Phillips, 2017; in North Carolina—Dodge et al., 2017).

Let's consider a bit of the history of preschool education in this country, how it is evolving, what its effects are, and how we can help parents from all income levels to assess its quality.

What Is Preschool Education?

Pre-K or preschool programs and their missions are quite diverse in the United States, and they fall roughly into four categories (Kagan & Kauerz, 2007). Child care (or day care) programs may serve children from infancy through school age; they are traditionally considered "custodial," meaning that they protect children's health and safety while their parents are working. Early education programs have a more academic purpose; they are intended to foster children's cognitive, social, and emotional development using "developmentally appropriate curricula" (Kostelnik, Soderman, & Whiren, 2014). They are usually open to children starting at age 3 and are the type that is likely to be offered by public schools. Special programs that can be considered early interventions, like the federally funded, state-administered Head Start and Early Head Start programs, are designed to enrich the social and educational experiences of infants and children who come from low-income families or who have disabilities. They combine classroom programs and family services for children who are at high risk of being unprepared for school, both cognitively and socially. Finally, there are nursery schools, which traditionally provide programs for a few hours a day, from 1 to 5 days per week. They give young children the opportunity to play with other children, to learn to get along with teachers, and to become accustomed to some classroom routines. Because programs have evolved for different purposes, there is very little systematicity in the preschool world. Different kinds of programs are often regulated and/or funded by different state and federal agencies. Child care programs in some states, for example, are governed by Departments of Public Welfare, whereas early education programs and nursery schools may be under the supervision of Departments of Education. As a result, regulations and quality control within the same state may differ quite substantially from one type of program to another.

A social and educational movement called "universal pre-K" aims to bring more uniformity of purpose and consistency of quality to preschool programs, and to use public funding to make good preschool programs accessible to all families. Advocates argue that the unifying goal for all programs, no matter what other purposes they might serve, should be to promote school readiness, that is, to make it possible for every child to be prepared to learn academic skills successfully by the time he or she enters first grade (see Zigler, Gilliam, & Barnett, 2011). The school readiness agenda is twofold. First, it is focused on maximizing each child's quality of life, both in early childhood and beyond. Early education is seen as a "powerful tool" for fostering positive development (Hyson, Copple, & Jones, 2006). Second, it is one approach to helping reduce the impediments to success faced by children in poverty and to addressing a range of social and economic problems (e.g., Davoudzeh, McTernan, & Grimm, 2015; Shonkoff, 2012). It seems to be more and more difficult for poor children to "bootstrap" their way to more middle-class status through access to public education after age 5. The failure of our schools to successfully educate substantial numbers of children has created widespread concern in the business community about America's ability to maintain a qualified workforce and to sustain economic growth (Committee for Economic Development, 2006; Cunha & Heckman, 2011). Social policy makers also emphasize the contribution of inadequate academic achievement to problems such as crime and homelessness, and to the soaring costs of crime management and social welfare programs (e.g., Schweinhart, 2007).

How Does Preschool Help?

A 5-year-old sits in front of a small computer screen. Beside the screen is a red button. Every two seconds a picture appears briefly on the screen. The pictures are familiar objects, like a butterfly or a flower. The child knows that her task is to push the red button, but *only* when a picture of a chair appears. The task continues for over 7 minutes, requiring the child to pay close attention, respond when the correct cue appears and, just as important, *not* respond to any of the wrong cues. This version of the "continuous performance task" is a test of sustained attention and inhibitory control (Rosvold, Mirsky, Sarason, Bransome, & Beck, 1956). You may recognize these now as among the cognitive skills called executive functions. Children's pre-kindergarten performance on tests of these skills is a good predictor of later academic achievement (e.g., Fuhs, Nesbitt, Farran, & Dong, 2014). So are measures of many other cognitive, behavioral, and social developments in the first 5 years, from the growth of vocabulary to the emergence of perspective taking. From this chapter on cognitive development in the early years, and the next two on social/emotional development, you will recognize that typical development in young children involves dramatic progress in learning language, understanding the self and the physical and social world, and controlling emotions and behavior. Much of this progress is foundational for later academic success. All of these developments are powerfully influenced by children's interpersonal experiences, especially with parents, but caring, well-trained teachers in preschool settings provide these experiences as well.

What, for example, makes a child ready to read? We learn to read and write by matching written forms to the spoken words they symbolize. Not surprisingly, many parents think that "learning your letters" in the preschool years is the quintessential pre-reading skill (e.g., Lewit & Baker, 1995). Some even drill their children on matching written letters to letter names. It *is* important, eventually, to learn the alphabet, but this is a task that is made more comprehensible and manageable if it builds on other pre-literacy skills, especially strong oral language abilities. Such abilities do not require memorization or drills; rather they mostly depend on conversational interactions between sensitive, responsive adults and young children. Here are some essentials:

- Growing a good vocabulary is important for reading. Pre-kindergarten vocabulary size is more predictive of reading skill by the end of third grade than knowing the alphabet before kindergarten. And, as you have seen in this chapter, vocabulary growth is grounded in adult–child conversation during play, at mealtimes, on outings both mundane (e.g., to the grocery store) and exotic (e.g., to the zoo), and so on.

- Narrative or story telling skill is also a building block for reading. Reading requires that children understand that language is symbolic and decontextualized. Telling and hearing stories about past experiences or fictional situations helps children to understand that language can function to represent events and experiences that are not part of the current context. Again, adult–child conversation about shared experiences, as in elaborative co-narration, is key to growing narrative skill.

- Extensive and positive early experience with books is another cornerstone of later literacy (e.g., Raikes et al., 2006; Senechal & LeFevre, 2002). When adults read to children (shared book reading), this helps children learn that books are a source of information and entertainment. Especially if enthusiastic adults engage children in conversation as they read, encouraging children to talk about the story, to discuss new words, and to make inferences that connect the story to the child's experience, language skills grow along with children's love of reading. Lots of experience with books also begins to teach children, quite naturally, about how print works: what letters look like, that print conveys meaning, that we (English readers anyway) read from left to right, that pages turn from right to left, and so on. As children become aware of what print looks like and what it conveys, they will notice it throughout their environment—on signs, on packaging, and so on. The prevalence of print creates "teachable moments," opportunities to point out the letters of the alphabet, for example.

- Phonological awareness, which means recognizing that words are composed of separable sounds or phonemes, is critical for beginning readers (e.g., Piasta, 2016). These phonemes eventually will be matched to printed letters or letter combinations. When adults engage children in play with language, "Let's find everything in the room that starts with the 'tuh' sound" or "What words do we know that rhyme with 'yes,'" they are directing children's attention to the smaller units of sound that make up words and therefore promoting phonological awareness. Many children's storybooks highlight phonology by having fun with alliteration (repeating the same beginning consonant sound over and over) or using rhyme (e.g., *The Cat in the Hat* by Dr. Seuss).

What Makes a Preschool Program "High Quality"?

As you can imagine, there are different "expert" views on this subject, but longitudinal studies analyzing preschool predictors of school readiness indicate that *quality of teacher–child interactions* is critical (e.g., Mashburn et al., 2008; Zaslow et al., 2016). Effective teacher–child interactions are marked by enthusiasm, respect, and mutual enjoyment, without displays of anger, aggression, or harshness. Teachers encourage and support child–child interactions that have the same high quality. Teachers are sensitive and responsive to children's emotional cues. Their conversation is elaborative, tuned in to children's level of understanding, with feedback that helps children to more fully develop their conceptual knowledge. Most teacher–child interactions are one-to-one or with small groups. Children's interests guide these interactions, and children are directly involved in planning daily activities and longer term projects. Activities foster practical opportunities for learning letters, phonemes, numbers, and facts about science, geography, and so on *without drilling or rote practice* (see Hamre & Pianta, 2007). Play, including exploratory, pretend, and physical (rough and tumble) play, is encouraged and supported. Play is encouraged as the medium through which children naturally learn. It is not treated simply as an occasional break from didactic teaching (Gopnik, 2016; Hirsh-Pasek, Golinkoff, Berk, & Singer, 2009).

(continued)

These kinds of proximal processes are very much like those that effective parents create with their young children. It is not always easy to evaluate these moment-to-moment features of quality, but there are some structural elements that parents and helpers can look for. The following suggestions are consistent with various guidelines offered by the National Association for the Education of Young Children (NAEYC) and the National Institute of Early Education Research (NIEER).

- *Teachers' education.* Look for teachers with bachelors' degrees and preparation in child development and early childhood education. They are more likely to engage children in the kinds of conversation and activities that promote positive development and appropriate curricular goals, such as phonological learning and vocabulary growth, than teachers with less education (e.g., Hamre, 2014; Kelley & Camilli, 2007). Unfortunately, many states do *not* require preschool teachers to have college degrees, particularly child care programs in which teachers have traditionally been construed to be babysitters rather than educators. Partly as a consequence, child care programs in the United States are *rarely* high quality; often they are poor to mediocre (see Brauner et al., 2004; Bassok, Fitzpatrick, Greenberg, & Loeb, 2016). All preschool programs should foster school readiness, whether they also serve parents' child care needs or provide additional services to families. In this regard, requiring the lead teacher in each classroom to have a college education and certification in early childhood education is an important standard to meet. Support staff should also have early childhood certification and all classroom personnel should have annual in-service training. Of course, high teacher standards require adequate pay. Salaries equivalent to those of kindergarten and first grade teachers are recommended.

- *Teacher–child ratios.* For 3-year-olds, maximum teacher–child ratios of 9:1 are recommended, with total class size not exceeding 18. For 4-year-olds, the recommended teacher–child maximum is 10:1, with no more than 20 children per group. (See Chapter 4 for infant/toddler recommendations.)

- *A variety of equipment and materials.* Material choices provide children with a range of opportunities to develop skills and knowledge, and they make it possible for children's interests and planning to play an important role in the curriculum. Children should have access to lots of books; art and writing supplies; opportunities to play with water, sand, and other media; and blocks and other building toys, as well as a range of toys and materials that support pretend play.

- *General characteristics.* Parents should be welcome to make an appointment to visit a classroom. Look for at least two teachers in each classroom. NIEER suggests looking for "safe spaces with children comfortable and engaged in what they are doing, not easily distracted or wandering aimlessly; children seem happy, not distressed, bored or crying; adults are caring, . . . responsive to children's needs and requests, and *involved* (emphasis added) in what children are doing" (Frede, 2008). Check the teacher turnover rate if possible. Teachers should be a "stable and reliable resource . . . Children recruit information and learn differently depending on who the person is and how they feel about them. Fundamental relationships of trust are more important than teaching strategies" (Gopnik, 2016, p. 146).

In a conversation about a recent haircut, 3-year-old Jesse's mother demonstrates an elaborative style:

Mother:	"What was the first thing he (the barber) did?"
Child:	"Bzzz." (running his hand over his head)
Mother:	"He used the clippers, and I think you liked the clippers. And you know how I know? Because you were smiling."
Child:	"Because they were tickling."
Mother:	"They were tickling, is that how they felt? Did they feel scratchy?"
Child:	"No."
Mother:	"And after the clippers, what did he use then?"
Child:	"The spray."
Mother:	"Yes. Why did he use the spray?"
Child:	(silent)
Mother:	"He used the spray to tidy your hair. And I noticed that you closed your eyes, and I thought 'Jesse's feeling a little bit scared,' but you didn't move or cry and I thought you were being very brave."

(*Source:* Salmon, K., & Reese, E. (2016). The benefits of reminiscing with young children. *Current Directions in Psychological Science, 25,* 233–238.)

An interesting twist is that mothers who engage their children in this kind of high-quality narrative practice also have children who remember past events in their own lives better. In one study, after 3-year-olds visited a museum with their mothers they could remember *only* what they had actually talked with their mothers about during the trip (Tessler & Nelson, 1994). Discussing an event with preschoolers before, during, or after it actually happens benefits children's later memory of it (McGuigan & Salmon, 2004). When mothers were trained to engage in this kind of "elaborative reminiscing" with their 2 1/2-year-olds, their children were better at remembering events even a year after their mothers were trained than children of untrained mothers (Reese & Newcombe, 2007).

Narrative practice is a key ingredient in the development of autobiographical memories (e.g., Fivush, 2011). We are all familiar with the phenomenon of infantile amnesia, the difficulty we have remembering events in our lives earlier than about our third or fourth year. There are probably many factors that contribute, but one is that our early experiences occur before we have much mastery of language. The mastery of narrative language appears to be particularly important (e.g., Bauer & Larkina, 2016). When we tell our own life experiences in conversation with others, we also learn to encode stories in language form, a form that is well suited for later recall. In a way, talking out loud about our experiences teaches us not just how to tell stories but how to remember them as well. As you will see in the next section, the importance of narrative skill in autobiographical memory is consistent with the ideas of a highly influential psychologist and educator, Lev Vygotsky, who was a contemporary of Piaget and who emphasized the importance of social experience in many aspects of cognitive development.

MyLab Education Self-Check 3.3

Vygotsky's Sociocultural Theory

3.4 **Explain Vygotsky's sociocultural theory and its contribution to current views of cognitive development and compare his constructivist perspectives to those of Piaget.**

It would be virtually impossible to consider the topic of cognitive development in children without considering Piaget's contributions. A contemporary of Piaget also lays claim to widespread influence on our current views of cognitive development. His name was Lev S. Vygotsky (see Box 3.3). Frequently, Vygotsky's ideas are presented as a counterpoint to Piaget's, as if the two theorists were in opposing camps. Although Vygotsky did criticize some of Piaget's ideas, the criticisms need to be understood in context. Both men understood that the advancement of science depends on the kind of dialectic that a mutual critique of ideas provides. Even though Piaget himself was slow to respond to Vygotsky's criticisms, he applauded the work of the young Russian scholar and actually came to agree with him in certain areas, such as the usefulness of egocentric speech (see below).

The celebrated differences between Vygotsky and Piaget reflect their differing *emphases*. Although Vygotsky acknowledged the constructive role of children in their own development, he did not focus as much attention on these internal processes as Piaget did (Raeff, 2014).

Vygotsky also did not identify a progression of stages that children traverse on their way to logical, abstract thought. His primary interest was the critical role that culture or society plays in the transmission of knowledge. As a result, his theory is called "sociocultural." It seems quite understandable that Vygotsky would take this point of view, embedded as he was in his own cultural context. He was a Marxist who had been powerfully influenced by the writings of Marx and Engels. He was accustomed to the concept of a dialectic, meaning that logical advancement comes from people mutually examining ideas, generating point and counterpoint and eventually a more adequate synthesis of ideas. He was grounded in the idea that society could be improved by the collective efforts of its members. Marxist philosophy also emphasized human mastery of the physical world by using and producing tools (Marx & Engels, 1846/1972).

Box 3.3: Biographical Sketch: Lev S. Vygotsky

Lev Semenovich Vygotsky was born in 1896 in the small Russian village of Orscha in the province of Belorussia. His parents were both well-educated, middle-class individuals of Jewish descent. Vygotsky's father, a manager for a local bank, actively supported educational causes such as the development of the local public library. Vygotsky's experience with the Russian school system began when he reached junior high school age. Prior to this time, his parents had paid for him to be educated by a private tutor.

Vygotsky was clearly an extraordinary student from a very early age. Like Piaget, he began to write while he was still a young man. His essay on *Hamlet* was written when he was 18 and was later published. He loved to study and had wide academic interests, which included the philosophy of history, literature, art, and poetry. When he entered the University of Moscow in 1913, he was a student in the medical school. During his first semester there, he decided to transfer to the law school. As if this were not challenging enough, Vygotsky simultaneously enrolled in Shaniavsky University to study history and philosophy with some of Russia's most brilliant professors of that time.

Upon graduation from Moscow University in 1917, he secured a position teaching literature in a secondary school in the province of Gomel, where his parents lived. He worked in this capacity from 1918 to early 1924, when he left the school to join the faculty of a nearby teachers' college. He also worked to complete the requirements for his doctoral degree, which was granted from Moscow University in 1925.

One of Vygotsky's responsibilities at the college was to give lectures in the area of psychology. While presenting a lecture to professionals at the Second Psychoneurological Congress in Leningrad in early 1924, he attracted the attention of a young man named Alexander Luria. Luria was the academic secretary at the Moscow Institute of Psychology and would go on to become quite famous in the area of neuropsychology. Luria was so impressed with Vygotsky that he prevailed upon his director to hire him. Toward the end of 1924, Vygotsky moved with his wife to Moscow to take this appointment.

During his career at the Institute, he studied the development of human mental functioning. Many of his ideas were not available to scientists and educators in the West until quite recently because of the general ban on dissemination of information during the Soviet era as well as problems involved in translation. Since the release of his ideas, Vygotsky has enjoyed great popularity in the West, particularly with those involved in education. During his lifetime, Vygotsky carried out many experiments on children using qualitative methods similar to those used by Piaget. His thinking was influenced by Piaget, and he actively tried to initiate a dialogue with him about certain points of disagreement. A full-fledged dialogue never developed, possibly because of the barriers of language and ideology. However, Piaget was aware of Vygotsky's ideas. In 1962, Piaget stated that he respected Vygotsky's position and noted their areas of agreement.

While at the Institute, Vygotsky wrote prodigiously and traveled extensively to oversee work in clinics with children and adults who had neurological disorders. Throughout much of his adult life, Vygotsky was in poor health. Toward the end of his life, colleagues such as Luria helped him conduct research projects because Vygotsky was too weak to leave Moscow. His promising life was cut short in 1934, when he succumbed to an attack of tuberculosis. In Vygotsky, we have another example of a truly great thinker whose ideas have inspired the work of many students of cognitive development.

Vygotsky took this concept and applied it to children's development, reasoning that cognitive growth also results from continuous expansion in the use and scope of **tools**. Tools, or **signs** as Vygotsky came to refer to them, meant anything that people used to help them think and learn, such as numbering or writing systems (see Deak, 2014). The most important tool for Vygotsky was language.

Let's consider the simple example of a vocabulary word, *television*. Vygotsky pointed out that the child does not independently construct a definition for such a word but rather learns the meaning that her culture has ascribed to it. Understanding this shared meaning enables the child to use the "tool" to communicate. But the word can be used not only in its literal sense. It can be transformed to create a new tool or sign, like "telemarketing," which incorporates part of the original idea but is qualitatively different. Such new signs are the products of cultural and historical **mediation**. That is, the signs are shaped and developed by others. Vygotsky claimed that a child's use of such tools or signs actually transforms thinking and shapes it into new kinds of thought. The idea of **mediated learning**, so central to Vygotsky's theory, is reminiscent of Piaget's concepts of assimilation and accommodation (van Geert, 1998), although Piaget tended to emphasize the development of thinking within the child, whereas Vygotsky's focus was squarely on the "child-in-context." In his view, because children acquire and use tools that are the products of others' thinking, "the mind is no longer to be located entirely inside the head" (Cole & Wertsch, 1996, p. 253) but is part of a collective experience. You have already learned that multidimensional models of development, such as Bronfenbrenner's bioecological model, recognize the powerful influence of the individual's environment on her development. Vygotsky went a step further. He believed that the individual's cognitive functions could never really be separated from her environment or culture.

To illustrate this point, recall that children's autobiographical memories improve when parents engage them in elaborative conversations about past experiences. This is a pattern of behavior that is fairly typical of middle-class Americans, perhaps because knowing our own stories is important for the development of self as an independent individual. But in cultures where self as an individual is not so highly valued, auto-biographical knowledge and the parenting strategies that support it may not be so important. If the culture emphasizes *inter*dependence and engaging in hierarchically defined roles, it may be more effective for parents to use non-elaborative styles with their children. Cross-cultural research is consistent with this view. In East Asian cultures, like those of China and Korea, middle-class parents do not typically engage in elaborative conversations with their children, and adults' autobiographical memories are less detailed than those of Americans (e.g., Leichtman, Wang, & Pillemer, 2003).

In one study comparing Taiwanese and U.S. middle-class families, when Taiwanese parents did engage in storytelling with young children, the content and orientation of their narratives were quite different from those of American parents. Taiwanese adults engaged in more didactic storytelling, often focusing on and explaining children's misdeeds (about one third of the narratives). They used the narrative frame to teach children about what they should and shouldn't do and why, emphasizing the effects on parents and family (parents will feel shame, sadness), and casting the child in the role of listener. American parents engaged in more co-narration, asking questions and elaborating on children's answers, and even when misbehavior was the topic (less than one tenth of the time) they tended to " . . . enact a child-affirming interpretive framework, erasing or downplaying children's misdeeds" (Miller, Fung, Lin, Chen, & Boldt, 2012, p. vii). It seems that not only the frequency of elaborative narration but also the content and process are very much in the service of enculturation, which affects how children cognitively process (e.g., remember) information. Vygotskian theorists suggest that parenting in more interdependently oriented societies is consistent with the goal of teaching children to see themselves as "a collection of roles in a social network" rather than, first and foremost, as individuals (Cole, 2006, p. 674).

Vygotsky's notion that cognitive development is largely socially mediated introduced developmentalists to the idea that there are likely to be cognitive differences among people reared in different cultures, and you have read about several examples of such differences. Recall from Chapter 1, for example, that people in Eastern cultures attend more to context than to focal objects in scenes, whereas Westerners focus more on focal objects. Even as early as 3 1/2 years old, Japanese and U.S. children begin to show differences in their attentional strategies, with Japanese children attending more to contextual characteristics than American children when processing information (Kuwabara, Son, & Smith, 2011).

Another theme in Vygotsky's work is that progress or improvement in thinking is both possible and desirable. The press toward more advanced levels of thinking not only pulls the individual forward but improves the society as well. Vygotsky placed great importance on the transmission of formal knowledge because he believed that learning culturally defined concepts, which he referred to as "scientific concepts," presented the learner with an internal organizational system for ideas and allowed the learner to utilize the ideas more efficiently (Vygotsky, 1934). But how do these cognitive advances occur? Vygotsky believed that more advanced thinkers or more capable members of a culture provide novice learners with **scaffolding** (a term coined by Wood & Middleton, 1975) that enables the novices to reach higher levels of thinking. Scaffolding serves as a temporary prop until the child has mastered a task. Interestingly, Vygotsky did not apply his ideas to specific kinds of educational practice despite the obvious parallels to teaching and the widespread popularity of his ideas among educators. He did discuss education in the broad sense of the term and highlighted the important role of society in providing the tools that form the basis for thinking.

In educational circles, the concept of scaffolding has been interpreted as guidance by a more cognitively advanced individual (a teacher or peer) with prompts, cues, and

MyLab Education
Video Example 3.7
Consider the role of adult prompting as the children in this video try to connect pieces of a puzzle and replicate a pattern. According to Vygotsky's theory, scaffolding by adults or others with advanced cognitive skills helps children reach higher levels of thinking.

other supports adjusted to the current skills of the learner, to help the learner show in actuality what had previously only been her potential (Pentimonti et al., 2017). The notion that children have a zone of proximal development is one of Vygotsky's most influential ideas. It describes the situation in which a learner is able to grasp a concept or perform some skill only with support or scaffolding from someone else. She would not yet be capable of the task on her own, but she can do it with assistance. Obviously, this does not mean simply telling a child an answer to a question! It means, instead, that a parent or teacher assesses the child's thinking, provides judicious support and appropriate cognitive tools, and in so doing, propels the child's development forward.

Suppose a teacher is trying to promote a preschooler's understanding of words and story content as she reads the child a story. Let's consider examples of scaffolding strategies that the teacher might use with children at different levels of language skill. For less advanced children, the teacher might try "high support strategies":

Co-participating—prompting by completing the task with the teacher: "Call out with me the word that can sit on a king's or a queen's head. Crown!"
Reducing choices—prompting by offering limited choices: "What is this tool called? A hammer or a wrench?"

For more advanced children, the teacher might offer less information and encourage the child to build on what she knows:

Reasoning—prompting an explanation: "The next day the snowman melted. Why do you think that happened?"
Predicting—prompting an hypothesis about next events: "Where do you think they will go next?"
(Strategy examples adapted from Pentimonti, J. M., Justice, L. M., Yeomans-Maldonado, G., McGinty, A. S., Slocum, L., & O'Connell, A. (2017). Teachers' use of high- and low-support scaffolding strategies to differentiate language instruction in high-risk/economically disadvantaged settings. *Journal of Early Intervention*, *39*, 125–146.)

By encouraging each child to consider questions designed for her level of skill, the teacher helps both to advance. The teacher involves each child in a joint effort made possible because both share information from the story and the teacher is aware of the likely level of each child's understanding. Teacher and child engage in a process that has been called intersubjectivity. From a Vygotskian point of view, the scaffolding occurs in the inter-mental space between adult and child.

Current research on young children's language learning, executive function development, problem solving, and planning support the importance of scaffolding, and you have read many examples already in this chapter. Parents and other adults often guide children's processing of new information in everyday social interactions, and doing so clearly helps children's cognitive progress (e.g., Blewitt et al., 2009; Mermelshtine, 2017).

Vygotsky's ideas have had a major impact on education in large measure because of their applicability to the teaching–learning process. Piaget was also sensitive to the role of outside influence on the developing learner. The frequent characterizations of Piaget as concerned only with individual cognitive development and of Vygotsky as concerned only with social influences on learning are both inaccurate. Piaget noted that the relationships between the individual and her social environment are essential to cognitive development (Piaget, 1977), as we have seen in his view of the development of perspective taking. Piaget's view of the role of teachers in cognitive development is also similar to that of Vygotsky (see Box 3.1). For his part, Vygotsky posited two kinds of "developmental lines" that accounted for cognitive development, one that was "sociohistorical" or cultural, and one that was "natural," coming from within the infant (Vygotsky, 1931/1981). Despite differences in their emphases, both Piaget and Vygotsky can be described as concerned with the interpenetration of the individual mind and society in the formation of thought.

One difference between Piaget's and Vygotsky's ideas concerns the role of egocentric or private speech in cognitive development. Piaget originally stated that the egocentric speech of the child (talking aloud to the self, with no apparent communicative function) serves no useful purpose and simply disappears with the growth of more mature language use. Vygotsky, who used the term "private speech," had a different idea. To him and his colleague Alexander Luria, private speech serves an eminently useful purpose in human development (Vygotsky & Luria, 1930). It is construed as the precursor to problem solving, planning ability, and self-regulation—what you will recognize as aspects of, or products of, executive functions. From this perspective, private speech eventually becomes internalized or transformed into inner speech, the kind of internal dialogue that facilitates thinking. If you happen to be someone who talks to yourself as you think something through, you can appreciate the organizing effect it can have.

Vygotsky identified three stages in the movement of private speech to inner speech. First, the child of about 3 years of age engages in running commentaries about his actions, intentions, objects of interest, and the like regardless of whether anyone is nearby to listen. Very often, young children manifest a kind of "parallel" conversation, playing side by side without really interacting. Children also talk themselves through problems such as "Where is my toy?" Despite the fact that they may pose the statement as a question, they act as though they do not really expect anyone to answer it. Vygotsky believed that this speech was actually directing their thoughts and keeping them focused on the task at hand. How do children come to use speech this way? Vygotsky argued that adults' verbal guidance (scaffolding) during joint activities such as problem solving, negotiating, and planning leads eventually to children using speech to guide their own actions.

As children reach about 6 years of age, this private speech becomes more subdued, abbreviated, and personally (rather than publicly) meaningful. Children may sub-vocalize the dialogue or only move their lips. Finally, around the age of 8, children truly internalize the dialogue, and it is no longer audible. Vygotsky claimed that private speech "went underground" and became inner speech, which was maintained for its self-regulatory properties, that is, directing and executing cognitive control over behavior and thought.

How have Vygotsky's ideas about the development of private speech fared in the light of modern research? First, the stages and ages that Vygotsky described have been largely corroborated by others (Winsler, 2009). However, private speech does not always "go underground" in the elementary school years; some people use it overtly even into adulthood (e.g., Duncan & Cheyne, 2002). Second, regarding the notion that adults' verbal guidance supports the development of self-regulation, parents' verbal scaffolding of children's behavior early in the preschool years does predict children's self-regulation later (e.g., Lengua, Honorado, & Bush, 2007). It appears that adult scaffolding affects children at least partially by fostering their private speech. Even within a single problem-solving session, when an adult uses verbal scaffolding successfully, children are more likely to use private speech to manage their problem solving (e.g., Winsler, Diaz, & Montero, 1997).

Finally, private speech seems to benefit executive functions more broadly. The use of private speech enhances children's attention and involvement when they face a challenging task, and it improves working memory (see Alderson-Day & Fernybough, 2015). Interestingly, the more prone children are to using private speech, the more detailed their autobiographical memories seem to be as well (Al-Namlah, Meins, & Fernybough, 2012). Overall, private speech is associated with a number of cognitive functions in children, including some executive functions.

Because of its potential role in what we refer to today as inhibitory control or self-regulation, Meichenbaum and Goodman (1971) pioneered the use of a self-talk intervention aimed at enhancing inner speech to facilitate impulse control in children. In fact, many schools of therapy, particularly cognitive-behavioral approaches, owe a debt to Vygotsky for his elucidation of the inner speech concept.

MyLab Education Self-Check 3.4

Applications

Some special skills are required of professionals who work with young children and their families. Children are not simply clients with limited vocabulary knowledge. Development brings about a series of qualitative reorganizations of competencies in cognitive, affective, behavioral, and social areas that need to be understood and respected. As you have seen, young children generally attend to things in their environment that grab their attention (centration) and react to salient perceptible features of the environment while ignoring its other more subtle aspects (concreteness). Helping professionals who take a "child's-eye view" are more successful in avoiding the unmodified application of adult helping models from therapy, education, or other fields to their work with young children. Perhaps the most important initial task for adult professionals, then, is to recognize their own cognitive egocentrism in the many ways it might present itself, from overreliance on verbal explanations to use of abstract language, to unfounded assumptions about young children's understanding of cause and effect, or to other age-inappropriate expectations. Young children's egocentrism often makes it impossible for them to consider other points of view, including those of their parents, siblings, and teachers. A helper may encounter parents who punish a 15-month-old for not being toilet trained. A preschool teacher might express concern that a 3-year-old is selfish because she won't share a special toy with her playmates. In these cases, the adults fail to recognize the nature of the young child's thinking, and they attribute to the child abilities that she may not be ready to master. Sometimes these expectations and biases also indicate deep frustration, high stress levels, or limited empathy on the part of the adults.

Professionals who work with children should also consider developmental processes as mediators of presenting problems. Very often, the shape of a symptom will change depending upon the cognitive and emotional resources available to the child. For example, sadness or depression in an adolescent subsequent to a family breakup may take the form of crying, ruminating, or writing long, self-absorbed diary entries. For a preschooler who lacks such verbal and introspective capacities, reaction to the same problem might be displayed in regressive behavior (wetting the bed, having tantrums) or pronounced social difficulties (biting, hitting).

Using Developmental Knowledge for Common Concerns of Early Childhood

Taking the child's point of view and her developmental level into consideration can be a useful approach to many common behavioral concerns. Consider sibling rivalry. Parents routinely fall in love with their babies. However, that doesn't necessarily mean that Baby Number One will feel the same way when Baby Number Two comes along. Sibling rivalry, or sibling jealousy, is a universal phenomenon, yet parents can be very disturbed when it arises in their own households. Because behaviors associated with sibling rivalry can range from mildly annoying to aggressive, this concern is understandable. Various theorists, from Freud to Bowlby, have sought to explain why young, innocent children might experience feelings of jealousy, envy, and competition (Volling, Kennedy, & Jackey, 2010). If we look at the situation through the child's eyes, a new baby is a tiny interloper, someone who can deplete the attention and affection of the most important people in the young child's world—parents! If we're honest with ourselves as adults, we probably can recall what it feels like to be deprived of what we think we deserve or to feel insecure when the people we depend upon are unavailable to us. Skillful management of sibling rivalry is warranted because research indicates that prolonged conflict can have deleterious effects on adolescent and adult emotional development (Buist, Deković, & Prinzie, 2013).

Some general facts and guidelines from developmental science may prove helpful to parents and others in managing this largely unavoidable problem during the early years.

- Remember that sibling conflict is quite common. Some research finds an incidence rate of 6.3 times per hour through toddler and preschool periods (Perlman & Ross, 1997), so overreacting to conflict is probably not helpful. Parents can model conflict resolution and mediation skills most effectively when they are aware of their own emotional reactivity and can manage it appropriately. The burgeoning literature on mindfulness suggests that mindfulness practice for parents can be quite helpful in this regard (see Chapter 14 for more about this).

- Manage conflicts as patiently and compassionately as possible. Modeling this behavior can teach children very important life lessons. Conflict is not pleasant, but it provides the opportunity to experience and learn about negative emotions, such as jealousy and disappointment, in a safe context. The sibling relationship can be an optimal context for learning about emotions and how to regulate them (Kramer, 2014).

- Consider episodes of conflict as opportunities to develop children's understanding of others (ToM skills). Parents of young children are familiar with "Why" questions, like "Why is he sad?" Wellman and Lagattuta (2004) note that "children evidence an early fascination with explanation, and central to this fascination is an extraordinary curiosity about how to explain the activities of human beings" (p. 482). Real-life conflicts provide fertile ground for expanding children's understanding of others by helping them learn about mental states.

- Be aware that children who are more aggressive before the birth of a sibling tend to be at greater risk for escalating sibling aggression later on (Song, Volling, Lane, & Wellman, 2016). These children may need more support in order to avoid developing a coercive inter-actional style (e.g., hitting, biting, demanding attention, etc.), especially when younger siblings are old enough to respond in kind. Aggressive children tend to have more difficulty with mentalizing and understanding the feelings of others as measured by ToM tasks. There-fore, parental scaffolding of social and emotional skills can be helpful in reducing this risk (Kramer, 2014).

- Manage expectations as a parent. It's not often help-ful to force sibling acceptance or to expect behavior or understanding that exceeds the capacities of the older child (e.g., "Big brothers love their baby sisters"). Invite older sibs to help and provide opportunities for play and mutual enjoyment with younger ones, but dial back expectations for perfection. Reinforce good behav-ior, but avoid connecting "good" or "bad" labels to the child herself.

Giving information to parents and caretakers about the normal fears of childhood can also reduce adults' misinter-pretations of child behavior. Most normal children exhibit mild to moderately intense fears over the course of child-hood (Murphy, 1985). In general, the younger the child, the more their fears result from what they *see* rather than from what they *hear* (Hayes & Birnbaum, 1980). Because preop-erational children do not necessarily distinguish playing from real life and because their understanding of the world is rather limited anyway, they tend to perceive what they see as reality. Therefore, younger children are more often frightened by fearful images, by ghosts, monsters, imagi-nary creatures, the dark, and being alone than are older, school-aged children whose fears are more often associ-ated with some real situation like school or personal safety. A sixth grader's intense test anxiety that is provoked by hearing about a particular teacher's reputation for giving impossible exams would be lost on a 3-year-old.

Before any clinical intervention is needed, helping profes-sionals should ask about the intensity and duration of the fears, because fears tend to wax and wane over childhood. Another very important question concerns the amount of distress the child is experiencing and the degree to which the fear is preventing the child from engaging in other activ-ities that are important for her development. Clinical inter-vention for severe, persistent fears and phobias of young children can involve a number of approaches, including systematic desensitization procedures, cognitive behavioral techniques, modeling, and operant conditioning (Burns, Hoagwood, & Mrazek, 1999). For more commonplace fears, adults should resist trying to explain to young children how their fears are irrational. Research indicates that "tell-ing yourself it's not real" is a largely ineffective interven-tion for young children (Cantor & Wilson, 1988). Concrete measures, such as crafting comforting rituals like bedtime routines, asking children to engage in an activity like hold-ing on to a favorite stuffed animal or doll, and decreasing the exposure to frightening images on TV and in movies are far more helpful.

Helping professionals, like parents, adjust the environment, including their own speech, to scaffold children's understanding.

When Play Is Learning and Learning Is Play

If you speak to primary grade teachers, they just might tell you that many students enter school lacking the skills necessary to learn. Clearly, they are not entirely referring to academic subjects like math or reading skills. Rather they might be referring to the capacities for paying atten-tion, taking turns, listening to others, staying on task, regulating behavior, and following classroom rules. These are the skills that provide the foundation for academic success.

As described in this chapter, such skills are called executive functions (EFs) and include working memory, self- regula-tion, and cognitive flexibility. EFs have been associated with better academic performance and are, in fact, better predic-tors of academic success than IQ (Blair, 2002; Duckworth & Seligman, 2006). How might these kinds of skills be culti-vated? One good example is a comprehensive preschool-K curriculum based on Vygotsky's principles called "Tools of the Mind" (Bodrova & Leong, 2007). The *Tools* curricu-lum focuses on the development of self-regulation, notably through the systematic scaffolding of mature play. Play is considered the "leading activity" of the preschool period and the means by which children learn foundational skills for later success in school. Vygotsky (1978) and his student (Elkonin, 2005) believed that play does not necessarily reach its most mature level, nor its potential to support EF, without social mediation provided by play partners (adults and peers). The *Tools* curriculum provides explicit support for play to strengthen imagination, cooperation, flexibility, imitation of adult roles, and enriched language use (Leong & Bodrova, 2012).

A useful assessment framework for play used in *Tools* cor-responds to the acronym PROPELS. The letters stand for

Plan, Roles, Props, Extended Time Frame, Language, and Scenario. A teacher can determine the level of a child's play by observing each of these elements. Doing so helps the teacher to scaffold her interactions, taking into account the child's level. For example, the teacher would know that the child is at the first or earliest stage of make-believe play if the following behaviors are observed:

1. The child does not plan during play (e.g., does not name actions prior to play) and does not demonstrate roles (e.g., teacher, policeman).
2. The child plays with objects as objects rather than as props or symbols as in creative play (e.g., a wooden block becomes a telephone).
3. The child does not appear to have a scenario in mind to enact (e.g., daddy fixing something in the garage while mommy works in the garden).
4. The child does not have an extended time frame for completing the scenario but engages instead in simple, repetitive actions. The child may explore objects but does not integrate objects into a scenario.
5. Relatively little language is used in play.

With these elements in mind, a teacher might first observe the level of children's play before scaffolding the interaction. Let's consider a teacher scaffolding play for a group of 4-year-olds who are at a more advanced stage of make-believe play. The children want to play "restaurant" in the kitchen area of their preschool playroom. A teacher might begin by asking them what role each of them wants to take. This provides an opportunity for the children to discuss the characteristics of the roles ("Restaurant servers don't cook the food") and the coordinated rules associated with the roles. Advance problem solving promotes conflict resolution, use of language, and cognitive flexibility. For example, what will the children do if there is only one stove and two children want to play chef? They may negotiate turn taking or create another stove from a box (or similar prop). Self-regulation is strengthened as a natural consequence of participating in social roles with peers for extended periods of time. Children at the most mature levels of play spend more time planning and coordinating play sequences than actually performing them. In the *Tools* curriculum, strategies to strengthen EFs are integrated into content areas, like reading and math, as well as play activities. Research by Adele Diamond and her colleagues (2007) demonstrated that the *Tools* curriculum improved urban, low-income preschoolers' EFs in areas of cognitive flexibility, working memory, and inhibitory control. Barnett and colleagues (2008) reported similar improvements in EFs and lower levels of problem behaviors in *Tools* classrooms.

In an age of increasing pressure on students and teachers to pass tests, it's important to note that these skills, once the focus of traditional preschool curricula, are still critical for success in life. Perhaps we should take another look at the value of learning to play. As one of Vygotsky's close colleagues noted, "Optimal educational opportunities for a young child to reach his or her potential and to develop in a harmonious fashion are not created by accelerated

ultra-early instruction aimed at shortening the childhood period—that would prematurely turn a toddler into a preschooler and a preschooler into a first-grader. What is needed is just the opposite—expansion and enrichment of the content in the activities that are uniquely "preschool": from play to painting to interactions with peers and adults" (Zaporozhets, 1986, p. 88).

Get Ready, Get Set . . .

Parents and guardians have an important role to play in supporting school readiness and later academic achievement. Unfortunately, a significant discrepancy in achievement exists among children from low-income families compared to their higher income counterparts. (See Figure 3.3.) Research from multiple intervention trials over many years provides strong evidence for what works to promote children's readiness. As you have seen, children with social-emotional competencies, interpersonal skills, good health, executive functions, and language skills are most ready for school and primed for success. However, social, cultural, and economic barriers often prevent many parents from taking advantage of the resources that could increase readiness skills for their children. Many opportunities exist for parent involvement in early childhood education, yet parent engagement programs aimed at preschool age children often fail to attract families living in poverty or who are low income (Hindman, Miller, Froyen, & Skibbe, 2012; McWayne, Melzi, Limligan, & Schick, 2016). Unless we can find ways that work to support these low-income families, we may fail to close this achievement gap. Intervention researchers have identified some of the best ways to promote engagement among socioeconomically disadvantaged families by making home visits, creating welcoming school environments, providing material support, and presenting culturally relevant information. Table 3.4 presents examples of three basic program types that have been rigorously tested and used successfully with low-income families.

Lessons from Piaget and Vygotsky

One of the most useful guidelines for helpers from Piaget's work is the idea that learning results from the dynamic interaction between assimilative and accommodative processes. Because much, if not all, of what transpires in any counseling or helping interaction comes under the broad rubric of learning and adaptation, these ideas can be readily translated into applications for therapeutic work with children and even adults. Piaget's ideas suggest that the helper should find ways to relate new information or insight to a client's current knowledge structures. In other words, if new knowledge, ideas, or information is too discrepant or if the individual lacks the context or experience to understand it, the new information will be ignored or discounted. On the other hand, if the new information is too similar to what the individual already knows, it will be assimilated into existing knowledge structures without any learning or cognitive change at all. To maximize learning, the helper needs to understand how clients are thinking and what

TABLE 3.4 Preschool Programs That Support Academic Readiness for Children from Low-Income Families*

PROGRAM FOCUS	PROGRAM OUTCOMES	PROGRAM EXAMPLES
Parenting Practices and Parent–Child Relationships	Less harsh punishment, increases in positive parenting behavior, reductions in behavior problems	***Parent Corps*** (Brotman et al., 2011) ***DARE To Be You*** (Miller-Heyl, MacPhee, & Fritz, 1998)
Parent–Teacher Partnerships	Teacher–home visits, increased collaboration, increased pre-reading and language skills	***Getting Ready Program*** (Sheridan, Knoche, Kupzyk, Edwards, & Marvin, 2011) ***Companion Curriculum*** (Mendez, 2010)
Child Physical Health	Increased parental knowledge about nutrition and exercise, reduced TV viewing in home, reduction in children's BMI	***Salud con la Familia*** (Barkin, Gesell, Po'e, Escarfuller, & Tempesti, 2012) ***Buffalo Healthy Tots*** (Quattrin, Roemmich, Paluch, Yu, Epstein, & Ecker, 2012)

SOURCE: Based on Bierman, K.L., Morris, P.A., & Abenavoli, R.M. (2017). *Parent engagement practices improve outcomes for preschool children*. Edna Bennett Pierce Prevention Research Center, Pennsylvania State University.

FIGURE 3.3 Readiness for school

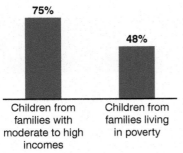

% of children prepared to enter kindergarten

75% — Children from families with moderate to high incomes

48% — Children from families living in poverty

SOURCE: Data from Bierman, K. L., Morris, P. A., & Abenavoli, R. M. (2017). *Parent engagement practices improve outcomes for preschool children*. Edna Bennett Pierce Prevention Research Center, Pennsylvania State University.

meanings they have already made. Interventions or examples that build on previous knowledge allow the client the best chance of incorporating the new information into useful working knowledge.

With young children, learning new things takes time. From studies of brain development we have seen that initial connections are somewhat fragile. The new connections involved in learning need to be reinforced regularly for them to be firmly established. Adults are sometimes dismayed by the number of times children need to hear an idea or message repeated before they can understand it. Yet, this is the essence of cognitive development. Mature thinking is constructed bit by bit, each part building on the previous one and helping to shape the next.

One of the particularly interesting legacies of Vygotskian theory for practice is his emphasis on culture in cognitive development. In this view, our ideas, including our ideas about children's development, are conditioned and shaped by our culture. It should be stressed, however, that culture is not monolithic. Within any kind of cultural group, be it ethnic, socioeconomic, gender-based, religious, or the culture of our family homes, individual differences still flourish. Indeed, some individuals may be more similar in

beliefs, values, and practices to members of another cultural group than they are to those with whom they share a similar cultural heritage (Greenfield & Suzuki, 1998). It has been frequently stated, for example, that Eurocentric cultures place more importance on the value of individualism than do Asian cultures, which hold more communitarian ideals. Certain assumptions, such as these about individualism and collectivism, need to be refined, clarified, and carefully evaluated to avoid dualistic overgeneralizations.

Nonetheless, members of distinct cultural groups can differ systematically in certain beliefs and values (Greenfield, 1994). Therefore, when the cultural orientation of a family is different from that of the helper, professionals need to recognize and appreciate that different developmental goals can and do exist. For example, Japanese parents generally place great value on the interdependence of family members and their mutual responsibilities toward each other. This value is expressed concretely in the sleeping arrangements parents make for their infants. Co-sleeping (or sharing a bed) is the most frequently used sleeping arrangement for children in many non-Western cultures worldwide (Konner & Worthman, 1980) even though it is less popular in the United States. A majority of U.S. mothers (65.5%) reported room sharing without bed sharing while only 20.7% reported co-sleeping (Smith et al, 2016). Unless practices are understood contextually, the risk of misinterpreting them as harmful is a real one. Helpers need to be able to separate culturally different child-rearing practices from those that are truly abusive or neglectful.

Whereas each cultural practice has its own costs and benefits, understanding the cultural underpinnings of different child-rearing approaches can provide us with helpful information that can reduce our own culture-bound ways of thinking.

Knowledge about the outcomes of cultural variations in practice may allow helpers to consider a fuller range of options for child care and to make sensible recommendations. Our communication with parents will be more helpful and compassionate if we understand, as Vygotsky pointed out, that our own ideas and values are mediated by the culture in which we live (see Table 3.5).

TABLE 3.5 Contrasting Cultural Models of Parent–Child Relations

	DEVELOPMENTAL GOALS	
	INDEPENDENCE	INTERDEPENDENCE
Developmental trajectory	From dependent to independent self	From asocial to socially responsible self
Children's relations to parents	Personal choice concerning relationship to parents	Obligations to parents
Communication	Verbal emphasis	Nonverbal emphasis (empathy, observation, participation)
	Autonomous self-expression by child	Child comprehension, mother speaks for child
	Frequent parental questions to child	Frequent parental directives to child
	Frequent praise	Infrequent praise
	Child negotiation	Harmony, respect, obedience
Parenting style	Authoritative: controlling, demanding, warm, rational	Rigorous and responsible teaching, high involvement, physical closeness
Parents helping children	A matter of personal choice except under extreme need	A moral obligation under all circumstances

SOURCES: Greenfield, P. M., & Suzuki, L. K. Cultural human development. In W. Damon et al. (1998). *Handbook of Child Psychology: Vol. 4* (5th ed. pp. 1059–1109). Hoboken: NJ. Copyright © 1998.This material is used by permission of John Wiley & Sons, Inc.

Focus On Developmental Psychopathology

Autism Spectrum Disorders

The number of diagnoses of **Autism Spectrum Disorders (ASDs)** are increasing throughout the world, leading to a surge of interest in etiology, diagnosis, and treatment. When autism was first identified (Kanner, 1943), it was considered to be very rare, with only 2–4 per 10,000 individuals affected. Incidence rates have increased dramatically since the last half of the 20th century to the current CDC estimate of 1 in 68 (Christensen et al., 2016). The latest revision of the psychiatric diagnostic manual (DSM-V) expanded diagnostic criteria, collapsing specific conditions without strong empirical distinctiveness into a spectrum of symptoms and conditions that map more reliably onto existing clinical and research evidence. Researchers now view ASDs as a complex, heterogeneous group of neurodevelopmental disorders at the severe endpoint of a continuously distributed range of human characteristics found in the general population. Our understanding of these spectrum disorders has come a long way since autism was first introduced.

Leo Kanner (1943), a psychiatrist at Johns Hopkins in the 1940s, identified *early infantile autism* and influenced psychiatric conceptualizations of the disorder that persisted for decades. Based upon his work with a small, overwhelmingly white, well-educated and relatively affluent sample of families, Kanner concluded that autism developed primarily as a result of cold and distant parenting, even though he believed that some inborn deficit was also present in children with autism. In line with the thinking of that age, mothers were primarily responsible for parenting. Kanner referred to the mothers of his patients with autism as "refrigerator mothers,"

because of their apparently aloof and intellectual tendencies. Austrian pediatrician Hans Asperger (1991/1944), a contemporary of Kanner's, also studied children with some autistic symptoms but whose overall functioning was more normal. In contrast to Kanner, Asperger viewed his patients as thinking "differently" from others, more eccentric than abnormal. Asperger presumed that the roots of the developmental problems he observed were essentially genetic. Unfortunately, Asperger's ideas were not to temper Kanner's until the late 1970s and 1980s when the former's works were translated from German. Some recent accounts suggest that Kanner probably knew of Asperger's work contemporaneously but failed to mention it in his own work (Silberman, 2016). Meanwhile, another famous psychologist, Bruno Bettleheim (1967), working at the University of Chicago, used his own considerable prestige to champion Kanner's ideas about toxic parenting as a cause of autism. Thus, an early historical emphasis on nurture, a possible suppression of divergent views, and a lack of technology to explore genetics combined to burden families of children with autism in the 1950s and 1960s with the guilt of having caused their children's disabilities through defective parenting.

Characteristics and Diagnostic Issues

In the DSM-IV-TR, five disorders constituted the spectrum: *Autism, Pervasive Developmental Disorder Not Otherwise Specified (PDD-NOS), Asperger's Disorder (AD, or Asperger Syndrome AS), Rett's Disorder,* and *Childhood Disintegrative Disorder.* The new DSM-V groups all categories into one because of highly overlapping symptoms and related etiology. Major behavioral features of ASDs include (1) deficits in social interaction and communication patterns and (2) behaviors or interests that are repetitive, stereotypical, or restrictive. A major advance in diagnosis involves not only counting the number of symptoms but also assessing the individual's level of impairment in adaptive functioning. Since "autistic" traits, like awkwardness in social situations, are normally distributed, it is possible for affected individuals to function quite well in certain contexts but show impairment in less accommodating circumstances. The level of adjustment to the current situation is an important consideration in deciding whether a diagnosis is warranted (Constantino & Charman, 2016).

Impairments in social engagement involve deficits in reciprocal interactions, understanding emotional cues, and expression of emotions. Communication disorders range from absence of non-verbal communication or meaningful language to having no language delays. Even when verbal communication is present, however, it is typically marked by deficits in the pragmatics of language, in highly literal interpretation of meaning, and in impairments in pitch, rhythm, or stress of speech (prosody). Behavioral symptoms such as "stimming" (non-sexual self-stimulating activity), self-injurious behavior (e.g., head-banging), hyperactivity, and disruptive behavior can be present in ASDs. Preoccupation with highly idiosyncratic interests (e.g., TV shows, trains, or weather), uncoordinated movement, and physical awkwardness are also characteristic symptoms. It is easy to see how pervasive the effects of these disorders can be over the course of development. Children with ASDs lack the foundation for many of the normal progressions expected to occur in development, especially those on which social relationships depend.

Well-validated instruments can be useful diagnostic tools for identifying ASDs since there is presently no definitive biological marker (see Charman & Gotham, 2013, for a review of assessments). Early identification efforts have shown reliability for very young children (age 2) and refinements in technology promise even earlier identification. A recent study of toddler video viewing found that neurotypically developing children were more likely to focus their gaze on the faces of the children in videotaped social scenes, whereas children with ASDs focused primarily on objects such as clothing (Constantino et al., 2017). This behavioral pattern does not appear to result from an aversion to eye contact, but rather to a failure to understand its social significance (Moriuchi, Klin, & Jones, 2016). The eye-tracking methods employed in such studies offer a potential means of early identification via social visual engagement patterns that appear to be highly heritable (Sarrett & Rommelfanger, 2015). In current clinical practice, identification of ASDs in young children is often done using a multidisciplinary team approach. Because ASD presentation can vary substantially, it can be helpful for experts in multiple areas to contribute to diagnostic and treatment planning (Volkmar, Paul, & Pelphrey, 2014).

Understanding the Roots

We do not yet have a definitive understanding of etiology, although the general consensus is that ASDs are neurobiological in nature and have high family concordance rates (Constantino et al., 2013; Folstein & Rutter, 1977). The search for causation is both aided and complicated by rapid advances in research methods and instrumentation. Presently, 300 to 500 identified and non-identified rare and common genetic variations may be implicated in etiology (Neale et al., 2012). Just as there is significant heterogeneity in causation, some of the rare genetic variants that are associated with ASDs can also cause syndromes such as ADHD, schizophrenia, epilepsy, language delays, and intellectual disabilities (Kim & State, 2014). This latter phenomenon is known as **pleiotropy**, whereby the same gene can contribute to multiple phenotypic traits that appear unrelated.

Brain growth abnormalities in young children with autism related to abnormal growth and pruning of synapses results in neuron "overgrowth." This may account for larger than normal cerebral volume in toddlers with autism and may be mediated by neurochemicals in the brain that support cell survival and disrupt pruning. Paradoxically, other neurochemicals present in the brains of individuals with autism appear to reduce neural growth in the cerebellum, which is reportedly smaller in this population. Reduced conductivity in those areas of the brain involved with social-emotional functions has also been observed across many studies (see Park et al., 2016).

Preferential looking or eye contact, which is strongly genetically influenced, appears to be an early marker. While infants later diagnosed with ASD did not differ in early looking behavior from normally developing peers at birth, declining interest in eyes has been observed using sophisticated eye tracking devices from 2 months through 6 months (Jones, Warren, Klin & Ami, 2013). This suggests a point in development where typical maturational processes go awry and may reveal an early window of opportunity for intervention.

Environmental factors that interact with genetics can also place vulnerable individuals at risk. The CHARGE study (Childhood Autism Risks from Genetics and the Environment), a long-term epidemiological study at University of California-Davis, illustrates an important lesson for students of developmental psychopathology (Hertz-Picciotto et al., 2006). Its strategy is to examine the interaction of genetic and plausible environmental factors, such as viruses, medications, toxins, social influences, and so on, that might be associated with ASDs, reflecting the contemporary understanding of gene–environment interactions.

Some recent controversy has centered on the association between autism and pediatric vaccines containing thimerosal, a preservative containing mercury. The evidence does not support a causal relationship between the two (Hornig et al., 2008; Lancet, 2010; Thompson et al., 2007). Both public health and professional associations have come out strongly against the notion that vaccines, like the MMR vaccine, cause autism (CDC, 2009; Maglione et al., 2014) and recommend a standard vaccination schedule for all children (CDC, 2018).

In the CHARGE study, other factors under investigation include pesticides, metals, flame retardants found in fabric, viruses, and bacteria. Evidence from CHARGE showed a 10% rise in rates of autism for children whose families lived closer to freeways in Los Angeles (within 1/4 mile) around the time of birth (Volk, Hertz-Delwiche, Lurmann, & McConnell, 2011). Other large-scale studies have found similar effects (Becerra, Wilhelm, Olsen, Cockburn, & Ritz, 2013), although researchers have not yet pinpointed the exact toxin or particulate that affects development. Nor do researchers yet understand how the environmental substance precisely affects genetic expression. Some associations have been found between autism and maternal lifestyle factors like smoking and use of alcohol and SSRIs, as well as preterm birth, but these are not conclusive and require further study (Harringon, Lee, Crum, Zimmerman, & Hertz-Piciotto, 2014; Lyall, Schmidt, & Hertz-Piciotto, 2014). A large prospective study of over 114,000 children from Norway found that mothers who experienced fevers, especially during their second trimester, showed an increased risk of ASDs in their offspring in a dose-dependent relationship. The more fevers, the higher the risk of ASDs. This suggests that immune-related disturbances, particularly inflammatory responses in mothers, may be related to ASDs.

Researchers have explored how this occurs by studying the role of biochemical reactions in the mitochondria, small organelles within cells that produce energy for the cell's metabolism and overall function. Some children with ASDs show signs of metabolic dysfunction (see Weissman et al., 2008). Mitochondrial dysfunction might have a genetic basis, but clearly interacts with environmental influences like infection and fever. Although more research is needed in this developing area, it appears that inflammatory processes are involved in mitochondrial dysfunction and play an etiological role in at least some cases of autism (Haas, 2010). More study is warranted to examine the safety of commonly used anti-inflammatory medication for fevers and infections during pregnancy.

Treatment Approaches

Efforts to diagnose ASDs very early in development support the conventional wisdom that the earlier the intervention, the better the outcomes. The high degree of neuroplasticity present in early childhood justifies this approach. However, we just do not have enough high-quality research to pinpoint the exact optimal timing for intervention initiation, especially because the progression of symptoms can be variable. Intervention can be effective regardless of when it begins during the preschool period, especially when children with ASD are being raised in family contexts that provide ongoing stimulation. This knowledge may help to relieve parental anxiety about treatments that might take time to access.

Behavioral treatments for ASD, when started early and sustained over time, have shown some success (Tanguay, 2000). Ole Ivar Lovaas, a pioneer in autism treatment, developed a technique called "Applied Behavior Analysis" (ABA). This approach applies learning theory principles to facilitate communicative, social, and academic performance and has been demonstrated to be effective for significant numbers of children with autism (Lovaas, 1987; McEachin, Smith, & Lovaas, 1993). More recently, non-behavioral interventions have been introduced that target those skills we know to be developing normally in most children, like social communication. In the UK, the PACT program (Parent-Mediated Communication Focused Treatment; Green et al., 2010) has proven quite successful in utilizing parents in treatment. Based on the premise that impaired social communication is the basis for a cascade of subsequent problems, efforts are directed toward strengthening typically emerging social communicative skills. Therapists videotape parents with their children and then help parents learn the signals sent by children that may be difficult to notice initially. Parents are taught to recognize bids for interaction, adapt their communications to suit the child, and increase communication synchrony. Results from a large trial showed increased parent–child synchrony in communication and increased child-initiated interactions after the intervention. However, generalization of these skills to people other than parents was not found, leading researchers to agree on the need for even more effective interventions.

The "Denver Model" (Rogers, Hayden, Hepburn, Charlifue-Smith, Hall, & Hayes, 2006; Rogers & Lewis, 1989) is a comprehensive, interdisciplinary program that utilizes parents, preschool teachers, and program coordinators to provide an intensive curriculum for 2- to 5-year-old children with autism. Several hours per day of one-to-one teaching makes such programs labor-intensive but necessary for severely affected children. Other structured learning experiences are embedded within the routine activities of school and home to supplement the intensive one-to-one exercises. The structured interventions in the Denver Model are targeted to improve cognitive and communication skills, social interactions, play quality, motor skills, and adaptive behaviors that promote independence and participation in family routines.

An adapted version of this program, the "Early Start Denver Model" (Smith, Rogers, & Dawson, 2008), is designed for children from 14 months to 3 years of age. Assuming the importance of early intervention, this program is designed to take advantage of the sensitive period for developing social networks in the brain by fostering parent–child synchronistic and contingent communication and, in particular, by stimulating the parts of the brain implicated in reinforcement of social interaction through intensive practice. The principles of coaction are clearly evident in the foundations of this program. Smith and colleagues assert that "because the expression and effects of many genes are influenced by environmental factors, it is possible that early treatment can alter genetic expression, brain development, and behavioral outcome in ASD, especially if intervention can begin early during the infant period before the symptoms of autism are fully manifest" (2008, p. 781). The results of a recent randomized control trial of this two-year intervention showed significant improvements for participating children in adaptive behavior, IQ, communication, and motor skills compared to a group who received traditional community-based interventions (Dawson et al., 2010).

Some general guidelines for intervention programs for children with ASDs from the Council for Children with

Disabilities (Myers, Johnson, & Council on Children With Disabilities, 2007), which was reaffirmed in 2010, include:

- Early entry into intervention program
- Intensive, year-round, developmentally appropriate treatment (25 hours per week minimum) with clearly identified objectives and active child participation
- Small group teacher–student ratio that allows for individual attention
- Parent training and support
- Appropriate opportunities to interact with typically developing peers
- Ongoing assessment of progress
- Incorporation of structure and lessons that address communication, social, adaptive, and school readiness skills and decrease disruptive behavior.

Embedded within these guidelines is the understanding that education and therapeutic programs should work toward generalization of skills in naturalistic settings.

Combining structured sessions with real-world instruction can help maintain educational gains and is actually more effective than structured sessions alone. This combination also makes it easier for parents to work with their children in the home (Levy, Mandell, & Schultz, 2009). Families of children on the autism spectrum experience strong emotions such as loss and sadness, worries about ability to cope, and frustration and isolation in settings that appear unresponsive to their needs. In some cases, they can be overwhelmed with the responsibilities of keeping their children safe. They experience much more stress than families with typically developing children; they need the help and support of informed, compassionate professionals. Comprehensive programs that facilitate social engagement and promote independence should not only help mitigate the effects of disorders among individuals on this spectrum, but also provide hope and support for parents, who are their children's most important teachers.

Summary

Piaget's Constructivist Theory

1. Piaget saw children as active learners, intrinsically motivated to seek out and understand new information. At any age their knowledge is organized or structured, and that organization changes over time as adaptation occurs. Adaptation is adjustment to change, and the cognitive level is the combination of assimilation (fitting new information to existing knowledge structures) and accommodation (changing knowledge structures to fit what is new). Children's understandings change only a little at a time, and the child may distort new information as she tries to assimilate it to her current knowledge structures. The idea that knowledge is constructed is now foundational both in developmental science and in educational practice.

2. According to Piaget, children progress through a series of cognitive stages. Within a stage, children organize their thinking across a variety of concepts in similar ways. Modern research indicates that cognitive development is often domain specific, so that understandings in different domains of knowledge are not always organized in similar ways. Although the idea of cognitive stages may not be strictly accurate, Piaget's stage divisions are broadly useful for organizing our thinking about children, their understandings, and their limitations at different ages.

Infant Cognition: The Sensorimotor Stage

3. Piaget studied infants' cognition in the sensorimotor stage (ages birth to 2) by making inferences from babies' motor interactions with the environment. Today's researchers use additional tools, such as the habituation and preferential response paradigms. Modern research techniques produce findings that challenge some of Piaget's ideas about infants.

4. The object concept requires knowing that objects can stimulate multiple senses and that objects are permanent. Piaget assumed that infants develop the first understanding at about 2 to 4 months, as they coordinate their reflexive motor responses to stimulation. The second understanding requires representational thought, and Piaget assumed it began between 8 and 12 months, when babies will search for a hidden object. Newer research indicates earlier understandings of both aspects of the object concept. Intersensory integration is apparently possible in the first weeks of life, and some early signs of object permanence have been observed in 4-month-olds.

5. Despite these findings, most memory research indicates that representational thought in infants begins in earnest in the last part of the first year. Recognition ability, which requires only that a stimulus can be identified as familiar, is present by birth. However, the earliest indicator of recall, which requires representational thought, occurs at about 8 or 9 months. Two indicators of recall are deferred imitation and separation anxiety.

6. Intentional or planful action has precursors in early infancy, but means–end behavior, which seems to require some degree of representational thought, begins in the last part of the first year, when babies' communicative behaviors also begin to appear. At the same time, intentional infants begin to attribute agency to others and to understand that other people have

intentions. These emerging skills mark the beginning of a child's "theory of mind" (ToM): an understanding of the mental underpinnings of human behavior.

Preschoolers' Cognition: The Preoperational Stage

7. By age 2, children are in Piaget's stage of preoperational (meaning prelogical) thought. By studying early cognitive abilities, such as number understanding and perspective-taking skill, Piaget identified apparent limitations on children's early representational thought. Preoperational thought tends to be centered in Piaget's terminology, focused on one salient experience or event at a time. Because they cannot keep in mind all the relevant facts in a situation at one time, young children have trouble identifying the underlying logical relationships among such facts.

8. Developmental scientists have reframed some of Piaget's ideas in information processing terms, emphasizing the importance of executive functions (EFs). During the preschool years, working memory grows (more and more information can be held in mind at one time), comparable to Piaget's notion of decentration, children's self-regulatory skills improve, and they become more cognitively flexible.

9. Improvements in EFs support the development of logical thinking, ToM, language, and other skills, but these skills in turn contribute reciprocally to better EFs.

10. Preschoolers tend to fail Piaget's number conservation task. Modern researchers use simpler tasks and have identified some early number skills that children do have. For example, they can adhere to the one-to-one principle and to the order-irrelevance principle in counting, and in very simple situations they can even recognize that a number stays the same when objects are rearranged. Modern theorists tend to view skills like number understanding as emerging gradually, with increasing breadth and depth. Researchers seek to identify the sequence of skill levels and the experiences that facilitate acquisition. Practice through play is clearly an important kind of experience.

11. Piaget pioneered the study of preschoolers' theory of mind with his perspective-taking tasks. Young children often assume that others have the same perspective that they do. Piaget argued that young children are egocentric, centered on their own perspective and therefore unaware of the possibility of another perspective. Newer work supports this idea, but identifies a gradual progression of perspective-taking skill in early childhood, such that even 2-year-olds realize that others do not always see what they can see. By age 3, children can sometimes attribute a different visual perspective on the same object to another viewer. Between ages 4 and 5, children begin to realize that others sometimes know or believe different things. These understandings are fragile, and when a situation is emotionally charged, even older children often fall back on the assumption that another's perspective must be like their own. Advances in perspective taking depend in part on experience with social interaction.

12. Children begin to learn the phonology of their native language even before birth. By 6 months, babies demonstrate perceptual narrowing: They have begun to lose the ability to discriminate sounds that are not important in their native language. By 9 months, they show productive narrowing: Their babbling is limited to only the sounds of their native language. Learning how, when, and where to use those sounds can take several years.

13. The semantic system includes the words and word parts that carry meaning. First words appear by the end of the first year, and a vocabulary spurt begins by 18 to 24 months. Typically, preschoolers learn new words at a rapid pace, fast mapping 9 or 10 new words a day. Working out a detailed understanding of word meanings is a slow mapping process.

14. Learning the syntactic system of a language requires learning the rules for creating meaningful sentences. Children begin to produce two-word utterances about the time of the vocabulary spurt, and can produce most sentence structures by the time they are 5.

15. Pragmatics involves using language effectively to communicate: learning to construct well-organized, clear narratives; code switching; and learning to distinguish actual meaning from literal meaning.

16. Bilingual upbringing does not impede children's language learning in either language. Because of "splitting their time," bilingual preschoolers may know fewer words in each language, but they learn as many words as monolingual children if we sum across languages. They also tend to catch up to monolinguals in each language by middle childhood, and they show some cognitive advantages, such as greater cognitive flexibility.

17. Because of the complexity of language learning, some theorists argue language is learned by special innate procedures unique to language. Others claim that general analytic and learning skills explain language learning without special procedures. But no one denies the importance of language experience for learning. For example, both the quantity and quality of adults' speech to children are related to children's vocabulary growth and narrative skill. Cross-cultural differences in adults' language and language use affect progress of language acquisition, such as the types of words (e.g., nouns vs. verbs) children learn first.

Vygotsky's Sociocultural Theory

18. Vygotsky's theory of cognitive development is focused on the role of culture and society in children's intellectual growth. One theme is that novice learners grasp a concept or perform a skill only when others provide scaffolding. When understanding or performance requires scaffolding, it is said to be in the child's zone of proximal development.

19. Vygotsky especially emphasized language as a tool through which others convey formal knowledge, that is, scientific concepts. Language mediates learning in

children and is one of the primary means by which culture and society help children's thinking to advance. Preschool children eventually come to use language as a way to mediate their own thinking. The private speech of 3-year-olds eventually becomes the inner speech of 8-year-olds. Internalization of speech is linked to the development of attentional and behavioral control, working memory, and autobiographical memory.

Case Study

Shady Grove Preschool is located in an old suburban neighborhood adjacent to a large metropolitan area. It serves infants, toddlers, and preschoolers from families with diverse cultural and ethnic backgrounds who have lower- to upper-middle-class income levels. The director of the facility, Mrs. Anthony, has decided to implement a new component, monthly group discussion sessions for parents. She has employed a counselor to facilitate the discussions and to field questions about child development from the parents who come to the sessions.

At the first meeting, the participants, primarily a group of mothers, begin with introductions and questions of a general nature. "How do I know when my toddler is ready for toilet training?" "How can I get my 6-month-old to sleep through the night?" Then the discussion becomes more animated. One mother, Mrs. Winger, a White woman, starts to raise concerns about the educational program at the school. Her son Brad, who is 4 1/2, is a precocious child who enjoys learning. "I can't understand why they don't teach the children how to use computers in this school," she says. "These children need to get a head start on technological education because they will be competing with so many other students in schools for good colleges and, eventually, good jobs. We need to give them every advantage that we can."

Mrs. Winger is quick to add that she does not believe the children should be stressed. However, she clearly feels the days when children spend their time in preschool playing in a sandbox, drawing, and building with blocks should be over. She mentions that she has been reading some new information in parenting magazines about children's brain development, and she cautions the group against letting opportunities for the children's brain development pass them by.

Mrs. Ramirez, a Latina, has a different concern. Her daughter Tina is 2 1/2 and her 8-month-old son Nicky is in the infant program. "Tina is so jealous of her baby brother," says Mrs. Ramirez, "that she can't stand when I pay attention to him. She whines and cries when I play with him, even if I let her watch TV when I'm doing it. She won't let him touch anything that is hers. Her father gets very upset with her behavior, too. We've talked to her about being a big girl and about sharing with her brother. We can't believe that she is so selfish." After a pause she notes, sadly, "My sister's children are the same ages and they seem to get along much better. We're too embarrassed to take her to family gatherings now, because she doesn't know how to behave and only draws attention to herself. My parents insist that we are spoiling her."

Discussion Questions

1. What are the underlying assumptions about child development in Mrs. Winger's comments? What is your assessment of her concerns based on what you know? How would you respond to her concerns?
2. Consider Mrs. Ramirez's statements. What are her beliefs about child development? How would you go about helping her resolve her problem? How have her assumptions about development affected her family relationships?
3. If you were the counselor in this situation, how would you plan a series of parent discussion sessions? What topics would you consider most important to cover? How could you present this information?
4. What is your position on accelerating development? Do you think that children can learn more than they are typically expected to? Should they be encouraged to do so?

Practice Using What You Have Learned

MyLab Education Application Exercise 3.1: Piaget's Preoperational Stage
MyLab Education Application Exercise 3.2: Case Study: Group Counseling with Parents of Preschoolers

MyLab Education Application Exercise 3.3: Preschoolers and the Zone of Proximal Development

Journal Questions

1. *Culture* is a broad concept. Identify an idea, belief, or value that you learned as a child that came from the culture of your family, one that came from the culture of your community or neighborhood, one that came from your broader cultural or ethnic background, and one that came from your religious culture.

2. Discuss why it might be easier to talk to people of your own culture(s) from the perspective of Vygotsky's notion of intersubjectivity. Give an example from your experience.

3. Visit a preschool program (or recall one you are familiar with) and describe your impressions of its quality. What things stood out as strengths? What were the weaknesses?

4. Design your own preschool program curriculum based on developmental science. What would you emphasize? What kinds of activities would you include? What innovations or changes might you introduce? How would you encourage parental participation, especially from low-income families?

Key Concepts

assimilation (p. 79)
accommodation (p. 79)
domain specific (p. 81)
habituation paradigm (p. 82)
orienting response (p. 82)
habituation (p. 82)
dishabituation (p. 82)
preferential response paradigms (p. 82)
visual acuity (p. 82)
object concept (p. 84)
intersensory integration (intermodal perception) (p. 84)
object permanence (p. 84)
representational thought (p. 84)
hidden object test (p. 84)
recognition (p. 86)
recall (p. 86)
deferred imitation (p. 87)
separation anxiety (p. 87)
making interesting sights last (p. 88)
means–end behavior (p. 88)
executive functions (EFs) (p. 89)

agency (p. 89)
intention (p. 89)
theory of mind (ToM) (p. 89)
symbols (p. 90)
centration (p. 91)
decentration (p. 91)
working memory (p. 91)
self-regulation (p. 91)
cognitive flexibility (p. 91)
number conservation task (p. 93)
exploratory play (p. 95)
preoperational egocentrism (p. 95)
false belief tasks (p. 97)
pretend play (p. 98)
phonology (p. 99)
phonemes (p. 99)
perceptual narrowing (p. 99)
babbling (p. 99)
productive narrowing (p. 99)
voicing (p. 99)
semantics (p. 100)
vocabulary spurt (p. 100)

fast mapping (p. 101)
slow mapping (p. 101)
syntax (grammar) (p. 101)
pragmatics (p. 101)
narrative (p. 101)
code switching (p. 101)
infant-directed speech (IDS) (p. 104)
parentese (p. 104)
verbal responsiveness (p. 104)
elaborative style (p. 105)
infantile amnesia (p. 109)
tools (signs) (p. 110)
mediation (p. 110)
mediated learning (p. 110)
scaffolding (p. 111)
zone of proximal development (p. 112)
intersubjectivity (p. 112)
egocentric or private speech (p. 112)
inner speech (p. 113)
autism spectrum disorder (ASD) (p. 118)
pleiotropy (p. 119)
mitochondria (p. 120)

Chapter 4
Emotional and Social Development in the Early Years

 Learning Objectives

After reading this chapter, you should be able to:

4.1 Develop working knowledge of emotions (what they are, how they are processed, their functions, development, and regulation) and make applications to clinical situations.

4.2 Examine factors that influence the quality of attachments in early social relationships and, recognizing the importance of early attachment quality on later socioemotional development, suggest parent skills to improve insensitive caregiving.

4.3 Identify risk factors (including exposure to adversity, abuse, or trauma) in the overlapping contexts of an infant's life that threaten attachment security and produce long-term negative effects on emotional functioning.

Alex was a full-term baby, but his mother, Marian, suffered complications after the delivery, and she had to have emergency surgery. Alex "roomed in" with her in the hospital while she recovered. His father, Stan, stayed with them much of each day, helping with Alex's care so that Marian could rest. Both parents were intrigued by everything about Alex—his noises, his sweet odor, his big eyes and tiny fingers. When Alex and Marian were finally released, both parents were greatly relieved to be able to bring their baby home. Yet they were soon exhausted by the demands of caring for a newborn—especially the repeated feedings during the night. And they were scared—Alex seemed so fragile, and they often felt unsure of whether they really were doing everything "right." Stan returned to work after a two-week leave; Marian stretched her own leave to six months to be sure she would be fully recuperated. Once Stan was back at work, things became more difficult. Stan was worn out from poor sleep, worries about missed income, and the challenges of getting home from a long day at work to a wife still recovering from surgery and a sometimes cranky infant. Sometimes Stan's frustration made him respond angrily to Marian's requests; sometimes Marian felt hurt and angry in turn. Although they were more irritable with each other than usual, an experienced visiting nurse helped them recognize that the heavy emotional and physical demands of this time in their lives were the real problem, and they usually recovered from their arguments quickly, often with humor and mutual expressions of affection. For both parents, their first priority was to be responsive to Alex's needs, especially when he seemed distressed. When Alex was in a quiet, alert state, both parents enjoyed holding him in their laps, talking to him and exchanging smiles and coos. They found their lives stressful, but they were consistent in their care throughout Alex's infancy and they each felt strongly bonded to him.

Care of an infant, especially for first-time parents, is one of the most challenging of adult experiences. Marian and Stan are fortunate that they are able to recognize the nature of their own emotional responses, and that they have good relationship skills, managing their conflicts with self-awareness, good perspective taking, and trust in each other. Alex is fortunate that his parents are able to manage their reactions as well as they do, and that they are unequivocally committed to being responsive to him and his needs. The nature of this early care will help Alex to begin managing his own emotional responses, to feel valued and safe, and to have positive expectations about others that will serve him well in his future relationships.

In the course of their daily work, most professional helpers, from teachers to nurses to counselors, encounter an array of human problems. Despite their differences, all concerns—Marian and Stan's increased conflicts after Alex's birth, a young child's difficulty adjusting to school, a teenager's uncertainty about the future, an aged widow's failure to keep up with her blood pressure medications—have a common aspect. They all, to a greater or lesser degree, involve human emotion. You can probably identify the most likely emotional responses of these hypothetical individuals. Marian and Stan are sometimes frustrated and angry; the child might feel lonely; the teenager, anxious, and the widow, sad.

Depending upon your particular theoretical orientation, you could probably suggest ways to help any of these folks. Yet, simply identifying the emotions and proposing techniques, as good a starting point as that may be, reveals nothing about the person's emotional development, nor does it provide you any insight as to whether your techniques might work. Are these individuals' reactions appropriate or even adaptive in light of their situations? How concerned should you be about their symptoms? What were the precursors that led to their particular level of emotional adjustment or maladjustment? What coping styles have they developed over time, and how useful are they? Unless we understand the process of emotional development in its normative context, we may view our clients' emotions only clinically, as if we were looking at their snapshots, detached from context and earlier experience. Their problems might be seen as manifestations of individual differences (for example, depressed versus anxious) rather than as reflections of their development, and their diagnoses might imply only possession of a set of clinical criteria. Overall, our understanding of clients would be impoverished.

The study of emotional development is critical for understanding emotional problems whenever they appear during the life span. Sroufe (1996) argued that "emotional development is the foundation for the study of individual adaptation and psychopathology. Pursuing these fields without being fully grounded in emotional development is analogous to trying to do research in genetics without being grounded in biology" (p. xii). Helpers aiming to increase emotional awareness in others and to forge affective change also need a fundamental working knowledge of emotional development. In this chapter, we review the beginnings of emotional development, the processes involved in early bonding, and the implications of these events for later well-being.

Emotions: Functions, Nature and Development

4.1 Develop working knowledge of emotions (what they are, how they are processed, their functions, development, and regulation) and make applications to clinical situations.

Before we can address the topic of emotional development, we need to concern ourselves briefly with the questions of what emotions are and what they do for us. These fundamental questions have occupied the time, attention, and brainpower of generations of gifted thinkers in many disciplines, from philosophy to biology, psychology, psychiatry, and the neurosciences. However, there are still many unanswered questions and some major controversies in this area. The scientific debate about the nature of emotions has even been called "The Hundred-Year Emotion War" (Lindquist et al., 2013). Yet, despite disagreements of interpretation, a great deal of useful information has been gathered, aided by scientific tools for measuring emotional expression, for tracking emotional development and regulation, and for identifying the neural underpinnings of emotion.

Functions of Emotions

Researchers generally agree that emotions serve many purposes for human beings. It would be hard to disagree that they provide us with a trusty arsenal of survival skills. The fear response that alerts us to a dangerous situation signals us to fight back or escape to protect ourselves. The urge to engage in sexual relations propagates the species. The disgust we experience when we encounter decaying material protects us from exposure to potentially toxic bacteria. The affection elicited by a baby's smiling face promotes the caregiving needed to ensure his continued survival. Emotional responses have ancient, evolutionary significance.

Examples of the role emotions play in survival demonstrate how powerful emotions are as motivators of behavior. Consider the force of conscience. Conscience is like a thermostat that is ordinarily set at the "feel good" level. If we do something we consider morally or ethically wrong, our emotional temperature changes and we may experience shame or guilt. These feelings prod us to make restitution or to change our errant ways so that we can regain the "feel good" setting (see Chapter 5). Reaching that guilt- or shame-free state can be a powerful reinforcer of behavior.

Emotions also serve as a major means of communication. An infant's distressed facial expression and piercing cry after receiving an inoculation serve as preemptory commands to the caretaker: "Help me! I'm in pain." When helpers speak of nonverbal communication, an essential component is always the emotional message conveyed through the face, posture, and gestures (e.g., Ekman, 2003). The view of emotion-as-communication underscores the basic social significance of emotions and captures an essential quality of the attachment relationship, to be discussed later in this chapter. Emotions are the stepping-stones that infants use to develop reciprocity with caregivers, ultimately leading to the capacity for emotion management.

Emotions are important for cognitive functions as well. Contrary to that age-old warning to keep your feelings out of your logical decision making, Damasio (1994) found compelling evidence that the absence of emotion clearly impairs rather than enhances cognition. He observed patients with damage to the frontal lobe region and noted that they shared a syndrome that he called the **Phineas Gage matrix**. This syndrome consists of cognitive dysfunctions such as poor planning, inadequate decision making, inability to take another's perspective, and problems in sustaining employment. These cognitive limitations went hand in hand with emotional problems such as shallow affect, lack of an enriched emotional life, lack of passion and initiative, and a diminished sense of pleasure and pain. Far from enabling us to be more "rational," the absence of emotion in our intellectual functioning leaves us sadly lacking in resourcefulness. Contemporary views of emotion emphasize the organizing role emotions play in higher-order cognitive functions like memory, decision making, and planful behavior (see Izard, 2009).

Last, but certainly not least, emotions have a role to play in overall mental health and wellness. Affective disturbances characterize a major category of mental illness and are strongly related to many other psychopathological conditions. On the positive side, research originally done by Salovey and Mayer (1990) and popularized by Goleman (1995) has emphasized the value of so-called **emotional intelligence** (or emotional IQ), defined as the ability to perceive emotions (our own and others'), to identify and differentiate the nuances among them, to integrate them with other kinds of cognition, and to manage them. For example, an adult with a "high" emotional IQ is likely to be able to specify his reaction to a violent tragedy: "My first reaction was terrible sadness . . . But the second reaction was . . . anger . . ." Whereas, someone else might not be able to identify specific feelings: "I felt a bunch of things I couldn't put my finger on . . . I just felt bad . . . Really bad" (Kashdan, Barrett, & McKnight, 2015, p. 10). It will not surprise you that greater emotional intelligence is correlated with greater self-regulation and increased psychological and social well-being (e.g., Extremera & Rey, 2016; Kashdan et al., 2015).

What Are Emotions?

The "Hundred-Year Emotion War" is mostly about defining what emotions are and determining the nature and sequence of neurological events that create our emotional experience. Old and new theories tend to agree that our emotional experiences usually have both physiological (changes in heart rate) and interpretative (rational, cognitive) components. For example, the old James-Lange theory (James, 1890) stated that a stimulus (some kind of threat) leads directly to a physical reaction (racing heart). When we become aware of that physical reaction, we "feel" the emotion (fear).

A problem with this description is that our physical reactions are often very similar from one emotion to another. For example, our hearts might race whether we are feeling fear, anger, or happy excitement, but we can usually tell the difference among these emotions. The Cannon-Bard theory (Cannon, 1927) argued that our rational interpretation of an emotional stimulus must be what comes first, or at least must be simultaneous with our bodily reaction, determining the emotion that we "feel."

Modern theorists have the advantage of decades of research on how the brain functions during emotional experiences, but they still debate what constitutes an emotion. How different are our physiological responses for different emotions (Lench, Flores, & Bench, 2011; Lindquist et al., 2013)? Do you have to have a "conscious" or "rational" interpretation to feel an emotion (LeDoux & Brown, 2017; Panksepp, Lane, Solms, & Smith, 2017)? Regardless of these fairly esoteric debates, there is a great deal of foundational knowledge that helpers can draw on to understand the development of emotions, emotional understanding, and emotion regulation.

Are There Basic Emotions?

There is some evidence that all humans experience a set of basic emotions that we share with other species and that serve important evolutionary functions (Al-Shawaf, Conroy-Beam, Asao, & Buss, 2016; Ekman, 2016). Charles Darwin (1872) proposed that certain emotions are innate and universal among humans and primates, rather like primitive instincts. He believed that facial expressions communicate underlying emotions and that these emotions are present because they are necessary for survival. Researchers have found that people across a wide variety of cultures, including societies without exposure to Western ideas, fundamentally agree on what constitute expressions of basic emotions (e.g., Ekman & Cardoro, 2011). The standard methodology used in cross-cultural research involves asking participants from different cultures to view pictures of facial expressions and then to identify the emotions depicted in the photographs. In reviewing studies conducted during the previous 50 years, Ekman (1992) concluded that certain facial expressions are interpreted as the same emotions regardless of cultural context. From American cities to the highlands of New Guinea, both industrialized and non-industrialized peoples appear to derive the same meanings from certain characteristic facial expressions.

Drawing on this Darwinian tradition, Izard (1992) focused his attention on babies and their ways of communicating emotional messages. He reasoned that infants have little time to learn social conventions and therefore will exhibit only those emotional responses that are inborn. Izard developed coding schemes that enable researchers and clinicians to identify different emotions based upon the position of the facial musculature (Izard, 1979; Izard, Dougherty, & Hembree, 1983). Infants display predictable facial expressions in certain circumstances, implying, according to Izard, the underlying presence of a comparable feeling. For example, when an infant is presented with a new and interesting picture, he will show the facial response of interest. When

FIGURE 4.1 Babies' faces express emotions.

SOURCE: Sullivan, M. W. Expressions. 5-month-olds during reward learning and its frustration NIMT Study #061778. Rutgers School of Nursing. Used by permission of Margaret Sullivan, PhD.

interacting pleasantly with a beloved caretaker, the infant's face conveys happiness or joy. (See Figure 4.1.)

Izard (1991, 2004) concluded that infant expressive behaviors reveal *basic emotions*, discrete feelings, each with its own unique pattern of underlying neural processes. His list of basic emotions includes joy/happiness, interest, sadness, anger, disgust, and fear. Other theorists who espouse the concept of basic emotions have closely related lists (see Ekman, 2016). From this perspective, a sad expression implies the operation of the neural circuitry associated with sadness. If a baby looks sad, he *is* sad because babies' faces are mirrors of their felt emotions.

According to Izard (e.g., 2011), basic emotions do not depend upon learning and do not require cognitive components, such as analysis or intent or memory for us to experience them. They only require the perception of a stimulus that triggers a set of physiological reactions; an expressive component (like a smile or frown); and a feeling component. All of these happen automatically. These emotions can occur without "reportable awareness," especially in infants. Although basic emotions may be experienced throughout life, Izard argues that older children and adults are more likely to experience **emotion schemas**. These are the products of experience and culture. Emotion schemas may include memories, thoughts, images, and non-cognitive elements like hormonal shifts that interact with and may amplify basic emotional experiences. Think of Stan from the beginning of this chapter. His experience of anger (a basic emotion) is likely to have become more complex over the course of his life. It might now be accompanied by memories of earlier frustrations, appraisals of certain cues as frustrating, self-statements that reinforce anger (e.g., "I deserve to have some time to myself"), and even changes in testosterone production in the presence of certain cues, such as when his wife Marian acts impatiently. Such emotion schemas can become quite durable and begin to reflect a person's typical response style. Izard has argued that interest and interest schemas hold a position of primacy in emotion and cognitive operations. Over time, the basic emotion of interest is profoundly connected to more overtly cognitive capacities like attention, intelligence, persistence, and goal-directed behavior (Izard, 2007). Interest drives selective attention, from which all processing of information occurs as well as subsequent positive and negative emotions. In Chapter 14 we discuss the foundational role of interest in adult flourishing.

Some theorists disagree that discrete, basic emotions are present from the start of development. Another view is that all emotional reactions are combinations of the same dimensions. For example, any felt emotion has both a valence (from pleasant to unpleasant) and a degree of arousal (from low to high) (e.g., Lindquist et al., 2013). These dimensional qualities constitute all emotions, and some kind of "meaning making" is necessary to make sense of the felt experiences—that is, to experience feelings as discrete emotions. Sroufe (1996) offers a view of emotional development that reflects this more constructivist analysis of the nature of emotions. He takes the position that emotions are not fully formed at birth but that they develop from undifferentiated negative (general distress) or positive (general contentment) responses into more differentiated ones and finally into an integrated emotional repertoire. This developmental change is an example of what is called the orthogenetic principle: As behavior becomes differentiated or elaborated, it also becomes hierarchically organized or controlled by higher levels of functioning. Early infant emotional expressions are considered to be precursors or forerunners of more mature emotions. Emotions start in this fashion, Sroufe reasons, because infants lack the cognitive ability needed to ascribe meaning to emotional experiences. For example, young infants certainly feel distress. At roughly 6 months, this distress can be differentiated into either fear or anger because the infant has learned the difference between threats and frustrating events. At this later time, the infant's facial expressions can be interpreted more reliably as communicating fear or anger, respectively.

The View from Neuroscience

For a long time, researchers have tried to identify brain-based correlates of emotion. Several influential contributions came from James Papez (1937), who identified the structures of the limbic circuit, and Paul MacLean (1952, 1970), who proposed that the limbic system was the *visceral brain*, or the site of emotions. Many early studies of anatomy supported the ties between limbic structures, especially the amygdala, and emotional responses, so that the limbic system as the processor and repository of emotions was dogma for many years. In Chapter 2 you learned about the importance of the amygdala in initiating the "fight or flight" stress response to a threat.

Newer research has suggested a much more complex picture. Some parts of the limbic system do not deal with emotions at all, whereas several parts of the cerebral cortex do. Structures from the brain stem to the prefrontal cortex participate in the coordinated production of emotions (Damasio & Carvalho, 2013). Conventional wisdom used to be that the cerebral cortex receives sensory input first before conveying such input to the limbic structures for an emotional "reading" (Schacter & Singer, 1962). But Joseph LeDoux (2012; LeDoux & Brown, 2017) identified a neural "back alley" through which information about fearful stimuli travels directly from the sensory systems through the thalamus to the amygdala, bypassing the cortex altogether and initiating the stress response. Information traveling via this "low road" pathway leads to quicker, more powerful, and longer lasting—but also less rational—responses than information processed first via the cortex.

Imagine that one sunny summer afternoon you are swimming alone in the ocean, off the coast of your beach resort. Out of the corner of your eye, you spot a gray triangular shape rising above the water not too far away. Your body responds in characteristically defensive ways, as you learned in Chapter 2. Your stomach tightens, your heart races, your eyes strain to see the object, and so on. The threat is transmitted to your brain's emotional centers almost instantaneously so that your body can ready itself against the danger. Now, suppose the putative shark fin turns out to be only a piece of debris. Upon closer observation, your cortex distinguishes the difference and allows you to adjust your response to one that is more appropriate. Your initial physiological reaction is only a split second ahead of your rational response. Nature has apparently given us an early warning emotional system to provide us with a survival advantage. It is the cortex's job to decide whether the response is warranted or not. Thus, high-road and low-road processing, involving both reason and emotion, work in concert.

The glitch is that low-road emotional processing could be responsible for persistent emotional responses that we don't understand. This can happen through *conditioning*, or the pairing of emotional responses to stimuli that were once neutral. If you happen to experience marked shortness of breath, heart palpitations, and tightness in your chest while riding an elevator, you may develop a strong aversion to this form of transportation, an example of fear conditioning. LeDoux has argued that phobias, panic, posttraumatic stress disorder, and anxiety all arise from the operation of the brain's fear system. As helpers know, these problems and reactions can persist despite the absence of real threat. Another tricky part is that these fears do not extinguish by themselves; probably active new learning or extinction training is needed for their control. They appear to lie in wait until, under stressful conditions, they rear their ugly heads again and affect our responses. Conscious awareness of the stimuli that trigger the response also helps. People with more myelinated pathways between the prefrontal cortex (mediating conscious awareness) and the amygdala (mediating physiological responses) are better able to regulate the strength of their reactions to fearful cues (e.g., Lapate et al., 2016).

A great deal of research on the neural processes underlying emotions has focused on one emotion: fear (LeDoux & Brown, 2017). Studying fear in humans overlaps with studying the stress response (Gunnar, 2017). And, as you have seen, we have learned a great deal about how our bodies respond to stressors, many of which are threat stimuli associated with fear. What about other emotions? Different emotional experiences, especially emotions with different valences (positive vs. negative), are at least partially mediated by different neural networks (J. A. Gray, 1990). A positive affect system (sometimes called the Behavioral Approach System or BAS) supports appetitive, approach-related behavior while the negative affect system (also called the Behavior Inhibition System or BIS) mediates withdrawal, especially under conditions of perceived threat. As you might expect, these systems also influence motivation. Think of your desire to enjoy a delicious dinner in a four-star restaurant as an example of motivated approach behavior. When you turn up your nose in disgust after noticing something moldy in the back of your refrigerator, your BIS has kicked in. The affective quality of disgust motivates you to avoid eating lest you come down with food poisoning. The same kind of thing applies to other behaviors, such as joining an interesting social group or avoiding social contacts if they happen to make you anxious.

Positive versus negative affect systems are also related to laterality, or right- and left-sided differences in some parts of the brain, largely in certain cortical structures (e.g., Constanzo et al., 2015). Measures of cortical activity (e.g., EEGs) have found more left-sided activation when people experience approach-related positive affect and more right-sided activation when they experience avoidance-related negative affect (e.g., Beraha et al., 2012; Harmon-Jones, Gable, & Peterson, 2010). In depressed individuals, lower levels of left- compared to right-sided activation have been observed, reflecting, and possibly accounting for, the dominance of negative emotional states and negative cognitions (Davidson, 2000). In these individuals, it appears that the prefrontal cortex is unable to effectively down-regulate the amygdala's activity, which is naturally on guard against potential threats. Davidson and Fox (1989) reported that 10-month-old infants who displayed greater right-sided activation cried more when separated from their mothers. In toddlers with lower left-side activation, more inhibited behavior was observed. Over time, these particular patterns of emotional responding can develop into one's habitual emotional way of responding to the world, or one's affective style (Davidson, 2012).

The differences in cortical activation between emotions associated with approach versus avoidance do not mean that different emotions are produced by entirely separate neural circuits. Remember that emotional reactions fundamentally serve survival functions, and all of these functions are carried out by neurological systems that operate in highly coordinated ways. You learned in Chapter 2, for example, the complex coordination of systems involved in the stress response. The very fact that the stress response sometimes leads to avoidance (flight) and sometimes to approach (fight) suggests that emotions like fear and anger are not highly distinctive at the neural level (e.g., Barrett & Satpute, 2017). It may be useful for helpers to keep in mind LeDoux's (2012) suggestion that emotion, motivation, and arousal are all various aspects of survival circuits, and we should expect them to be interrelated in complex ways.

How Do Emotions Develop?

Let's focus now on some of the normative changes we find in the early development of emotions. We begin with the emotion states that infants and young children express. Then we examine what they understand about other people's emotions. Finally, we consider how children begin to regulate their emotions.

Infant facial expressions, body posture, gaze, and so on, seem to give us a window on early emotional experiences. At birth or close to it, infants display distress (crying), contentment (smiling), disgust (avoiding bitter tastes or unpleasant odors), and interest (staring at faces and objects) (e.g., Izard & Malatesta, 1987). Anger, surprise, fear, and sadness seem to be differentiated and expressed by approximately 6 months (Lewis, 2016a). Children begin to show signs of the so-called self-conscious emotions, such as pride, shame, embarrassment, empathy, and guilt, late in infancy, about 18 to 24 months old. For children to experience these feelings, they apparently need to be capable of self-recognition, which depends on levels of cognitive functioning that emerge late in infancy (Lewis, 2016b; see Chapter 5). By 36 months or so, most children are showing signs that they experience a full range of human emotions.

Learning to recognize and interpret other people's emotional expressions also begins in infancy. Even in the newborn period babies register higher amplitudes on EEG recordings to fearful sounds than to happy or neutral ones, suggesting that a neonate's brain is already differentially responsive to some emotionally relevant signals (Cheng et al., 2012). By about 4 months, babies can discriminate among some facial and vocal expressions of emotion (Walle, Reschke, Camras, & Campos, 2017). For example, habituation studies have found that 4-month-olds can tell the difference between expressions of fear and anger, if both face and voice cues are present, although they may not yet understand the meaning of that difference. This research suggests that emotion processing via auditory channels emerges very early in infancy.

By 6 months old, babies respond differently to positive versus negative emotional expressions. For example, if an adult shows positive emotion toward one object and negative emotion toward another, babies will prefer to touch the first object, suggesting that they are starting to attach meaning to other people's emotional signals. By 18 to 24 months, infants will sometimes make choices based on even more fine-grained differences in emotional expressions. For example, they will push away food if an adult looks at it with disgust, but not if the adult shows a sad expression when the food is presented. They are also more likely to show prosocial behavior (e.g., helping) when adults express sadness than when they show joy. Nonetheless, interpreting others' emotional expressions can be difficult even for older children. One study found that the ability to recognize expressions of disgust, sadness, anger, and surprise improved with age from 5 years old up to adulthood. Five-year-olds showed adult levels of recognition only for happiness and fear (Rodger, Vizioli, Ouyang, & Caldara, 2015).

The Early Development of Emotion Regulation

Emotion regulation is one of the cornerstones of emotional well-being and positive adjustment throughout the life span. It encompasses the strategies and behaviors we use to moderate our emotional experiences in order to meet the demands of different situations or to achieve our goals. For example, healthy people find ways to comfort themselves in difficult times, keeping their distress from overwhelming them. They modulate their excitement in happy times so that they can organize and plan satisfying experiences, and they rally their excitement to push onward when challenges block the way toward desirable goals. Social problems are often linked to difficulties with managing emotions. Think of Stan from the beginning of this chapter. His frustration with the neediness of his wife and baby sometimes made him irritable and angry, which led to conflict between him and his wife. Stan typically recovered quickly, suggesting that he has reasonably good emotional management skills. But if he tended to be overwhelmed by such feelings, the stability of his marriage might be seriously undermined.

How do we learn to understand, identify, and manage the power of our emotions? It is a process that begins in infancy. The emotions of the newborn are poorly regulated. Emotional states can range from contentment to intense distress within minutes. Typically, adult caregivers serve the critical function of helping to manage the newborn's affect or to modulate affective expression while scaffolding the infant's own developing emotion regulation. The specific, facilitative environmental circumstances needed for healthy emotional development to occur include supportive, responsive caregiving.

Even in the first hours after birth, mothers and other caregivers interact with infants in ways that are likely to heighten positive affect and attention or to soothe negative affect. Mothers gaze at a newborn's face, smile, affectionately touch the baby, and vocalize in a high-pitched voice. And human newborns tend to respond to such behaviors. For example, if mothers touch, talk, and coo to newborns who are alertly scanning, babies become more alert (Feldman & Eidelman, 2007). And newborns seem to have some slight biases to attend to stimuli that are socially relevant. They look more at face-like stimuli than at other visual stimuli; they show some preference for voices over other sounds; and they look more at biological motion than other kinds (Grossman, 2015).

Interactions between young infants and their mothers soon exhibit a repetitive-rhythmic organization, a temporal coordination of nonverbal behaviors, called **synchrony**. If baby looks at mom, mom gazes back; if baby smacks his lips, mom may smack or smile. Mothers take the lead in maintaining the synchrony by responding contingently to newborns' cues in these interactions. Babies become more responsive and contribute more to the synchrony as they grow older. Consider smiling, for example. Even though newborns sometimes smile, these seem to be reactions to physiological states. They do not yet respond to other people by smiling. By 2 to 3 months, however, a baby often smiles at human faces, especially his mother's face, and especially if she is smiling at him. A 3-month-old is more responsive than a newborn in other ways as well. When his mother gazes at him, the 3-month-old gazes back and is likely to vocalize, which encourages mom's vocalizing, and so on. When mother and baby behaviors are highly synchronized in face-to-face interactions, even the mother's heart rate tends to be responsive. If the infant's heart rate either accelerates or decelerates, the mother's heart rhythm is likely to change in the same direction within 1 second (see Feldman, 2007; Gordon, Zagoory-Sharon, Leckman, & Feldman, 2015).

It is important to note that normal caregiver–infant interactions are "messy" (Tronick & Beehgly, 2011). Only about 30% of face-to-face interactions during the first year are positive in the sense that the baby is calm and alert and able to respond to the mother in a synchronous way. Moment-to-moment observations of mothers and infants demonstrate that most mismatches are repaired in the next interactive step, and the caregiver usually instigates the repair (e.g., Chow, Haltigan, & Messinger, 2010). Thus, babies typically experience repeated interactive derailment followed by successful repair. Through this process, sensitive, responsive caregivers modify their infants' emotions, gently prodding their babies toward longer and longer periods of positive affect and interactive coordination.

The importance of caregivers' responsiveness for infants' emotion regulation is stunningly demonstrated in a procedure called the **still-face paradigm** (introduced by Tronick, Als, Adamson, Wise, & Brazelton, 1978). A baby is placed in an infant seat directly in front of his mother. Following instructions, the mother at first interacts in a normally pleasant and playful way with her child, which usually involves lots of gazing, smiling, vocalizing, and touching. (This is the *baseline episode*.) Then, in the *still-face episode*, the mother becomes unresponsive, as though she were looking at the baby but not seeing him. Finally, in the *reunion episode*, the mother resumes normal behavior. Even 2- to 3-month-olds can be heartbreakingly distressed by their mothers' unresponsiveness in the still-face episode. Their natural response is to intensify the behaviors that usually "work," especially gazing intently at the mother and vocalizing. When the mother fails to respond to these **other-directed coping behaviors**, the baby's distress heightens, and he will usually resort to **self-directed coping behaviors** that seem designed for self-comfort. Babies look away or may even self-stimulate by rocking, sucking, rubbing their hair,

MyLab Education
Video Example 4.1
In this still-face procedure, the caregiver becomes unresponsive to the infant's appeals for attention. Note the ways in which the child tries to re-engage the adult. What do you suppose happened after the video ended?

and so on. Interestingly, this effect is observed if the mother is unresponsive for only a few seconds. The baby's negative mood persists even when the mother resumes contact. Babies look at their mothers less for several minutes after this experience. And the importance of mothers' behavior for helping babies manage their negative emotions is especially clear. First, the more responsive and positive mothers are during the actual reunion episode, the less avoidance and distress babies show (see Mesman, van IJzendoorn, & Bakermas-Kranenburg, 2009). Second, babies recover most quickly during the reunion episode if they have consistently experienced such sensitive care from their mothers in the past (Braungart-Reiker et al., 2014; Coppola, Aureli, Grazia, & Ponzetti, 2016).

The still-face paradigm illustrates that even very young infants have some natural strategies for coping with their emotions. It also suggests that when adults promote interactive repair, they are scaffolding infants' use of other-directed coping strategies. As you will see in the next section, the ultimate effects seem to be that infants come to see others as reliable sources of support and to see themselves as effective social agents. Thus, sensitive, responsive caregiving promotes positive social development in many ways. Note that the caregiver provides the experience-dependent environment in which the baby's coping strategies are practiced and further developed. Once again, the interplay of native and environmental factors is required for a successful outcome.

Babies' emotion regulation typically improves with age. They react less strongly in the still-face paradigm by 6 months old than they did earlier (e.g., Melinder, Forbes, Tronick, Fikke, & Gredeback, 2010). They are less physiologically reactive (e.g., produce less cortisol) and recover more quickly (e.g., stop crying sooner) in other kinds of distressing situations as well, such as after painful inoculations. For example, 2-month-olds show large increases in cortisol production after an inoculation; 4- to 6-month-olds show much smaller increases; and by their second year, babies may show no increases at all even though they might still cry and fuss (Gunnar, 2017).

Caregivers play a key role in this developmental change. In one study, researchers assessed how responsive mothers were to infants' crying as their babies were being inoculated at 2 months and 6 months old (Jahromi & Stifter, 2007). Mothers' soothing responses included kissing, hugging, patting, stroking, holding, rocking, vocalizing, distracting, looking into the baby's face, and so on. The more responsive mothers were when their babies were 2 months old, the more quickly the babies stopped crying when they were 6 months old, suggesting that early sensitive care helped the babies to improve their emotion regulation capacity by 6 months.

Caregivers' emotional messages influence babies' willingness to crawl over the edge of the visual cliff.

Sensitive adults adjust their management efforts to the needs and abilities of the infant as he grows. For example, in another study of infants' reactions to inoculations, mothers used primarily touch to soothe 2-month-olds, holding and rocking them, but they used more vocalizing and distracting efforts when their infants were 6 months old, apparently appreciating their infants' changing abilities to respond to visual and auditory stimuli (Jahromi, Putnam, & Stifter, 2004).

With older infants, the caregiver's emotional expressions can teach the child how to make sense of the world when dealing with emotionally charged situations. Experiments by Campos and his colleagues demonstrate that 10-month-old infants who are able to crawl over a "visual cliff" (a glass-covered surface that looks like a sharp "drop-off") actively seek out their mothers' responses before proceeding to crawl over the cliff (Campos, Barrett, Lamb, Goldsmith, & Sternberg, 1983). Infants whose mothers respond with fearful facial or vocal expressions do not advance, whereas those whose mothers respond with smiles or encouragement proceed to cross the surface. As early as 7 months old, infants are more likely to smile or laugh at absurd events (e.g., someone wearing a book on his head) if a parent smiles and laughs first (Mirault et al., 2015). These early "in kind" responses to adults' emotional expressions may be largely imitative or "contagious" as they are sometimes called. But 10- to 12-month-olds can intentionally modify their own behavior (see Chapter 3). Now you will see them closely monitoring their caregivers' emotional reactions to help themselves interpret situations that are ambiguous to them, a process called **social referencing** (e.g., Stenberg, 2017).

As children get older, their ability to regulate their own emotional responses gradually improves. In the Applications section of this chapter, you will learn more about the kinds of management strategies that sensitive caregivers tend to use as they continue to scaffold these improvements in toddlerhood and beyond.

MyLab Education Self-Check 4.1

Attachment: Early Social Relationships

4.2 **Examine factors that influence the quality of attachments in early social relationships and, recognizing the importance of early attachment quality on later socioemotional development, suggest parent skills to improve insensitive caregiving.**

As you have seen, human infants are emotionally and behaviorally equipped to elicit responsive care and stimulation from adults. Adults, in turn, are prepared by nature to stimulate and nurture infants. The social interactions that result help an infant to expand his emotional repertoire, and they support the development of his capacity for emotion regulation. But early interpersonal interactions may have a much broader impact on the infant's development. Theorists such as John Bowlby (1969/1982, 1973, 1980) and Erik Erikson (1950/1963) have proposed that the relationships an infant has with one or a few caregivers during the first year of life provide him with a working model of himself and of others. (See Box 4.1 and Box 4.2.) These emerging models play an important role in determining how secure and optimistic a child will later feel about venturing forth to explore the broader world. Thus, early relationships are said to lay the groundwork for future interactions with others, for the child's self-concept, and even for his outlook on life.

For Erikson, the characteristics of early caregiving enable a child to form his first feelings about others. When care is timely, sensitive to the infant's needs, and consistently available, he begins to establish **basic trust**, seeing others as dependable and trustworthy. As his rudimentary view of others takes shape, it influences how he begins to see himself. If others can be trusted to provide for his needs, then his needs must be important and he must be a worthy recipient of care. Feeling trust and feeling worthy emerge together, two sides of the same coin. These early attitudes toward others and toward the self create a sense of hope or optimism that experiences beyond the caregiving relationship will also be positive and are therefore worth pursuing.

Box 4.1: Two Biographical Sketches: John Bowlby and Mary D. Salter Ainsworth

In the 1950s, 7-year-old Marianne was hospitalized for a tonsillectomy. The small-town hospital where the surgery was performed had very strict policies governing visitors to its child patients: 1 hour in the afternoon, maximum of two visitors. Marianne's experiences with doctors had generally been positive up until then. In addition, her mother was a nurse, so Marianne was warmly disposed to women dressed in white from head to foot and smelling wonderfully clean, and she was, blessedly, old enough to understand what was happening to her. The first afternoon and evening, preoperatively, were a pleasant adventure, and Marianne was able to sleep without distress despite the separation from her

family. But the next day, after the early morning surgery, the pain struck, and Marianne wanted her mother's cool hand and soothing voice. The hours until her mother's first visit were endless, and the end of the visit was agony. The release into her parents' care the next afternoon was a respite from hell.

Through the middle 1900s, restricted visitation to child hospital patients was standard policy, based on concerns about infection and about disruptions to medical routines. Today, parents not only are allowed complete access to their children in most hospitals but also are encouraged to stay with their children continuously and to be part of the healing and helping process. Many

(continued)

hospitals provide cots and even rooms for showering and changing to encourage parental involvement. It was John Bowlby's groundbreaking theorizing and research on the sometimes devastating emotional costs of mother–child separations, especially during hospitalizations, that initiated a major shift in thinking about the relative benefits of separating children from their families.

John Bowlby (1907–1990) and Mary D. Salter Ainsworth (1913–1999) were jointly responsible for a revolution in the way that parent–child relationships are perceived by researchers and clinicians. Bowlby began his professional life in England as a psychoanalyst who worked with children. In the 1930s, Bowlby's clinical work was supervised by Melanie Klein, who invented psychoanalytic play therapy. Bowlby was inclined to look for a relationship between his young patients' behavior and the kind of parenting they were receiving, but Klein discouraged his family-oriented approach, arguing that the child's "object" relations (internalized representations of relationships) were a function of fantasy, not experience in relationships. Bowlby, however, was convinced that early relationships play a large role in personality and behavioral development. He was familiar with Charles Darwin's notion that ". . . for with those animals which were benefited by living in close association, the individuals which took the greatest pleasure in society would best escape various dangers . . ." (1872, Vol. 1, p. 80). Bowlby discovered in the work of **ethologists**, biologists who do careful observations of animal behavior in natural environments, that animals such as ducks and geese are inclined to become devoted followers of whatever they first see moving—usually their mothers, but sometimes a different animal, such as a human researcher. Such bonding, when it works "the way nature intended," promotes the survival of ducklings and goslings by keeping them close to a protective adult.

Eventually, Bowlby integrated ideas from ethology, from systems theory, from cognitive development (including the work of Piaget), and from psychoanalysis into attachment theory, arguing that some human infant behaviors, for example clinging and sucking, help keep the mother close, whereas others, for example smiling, naturally elicit maternal caregiving. Such behaviors initiate the development of an attachment system that promotes the infant's survival and creates a feeling of security. That system changes and consolidates over time as the child's skills develop. Early clinging and sucking are later replaced by other attachment behaviors, such as protesting when mother leaves or joyfully greeting her when she returns, but the system's evolutionary function remains the same. The attachment system is enhanced and developed by the responses of the environment (i.e., of the caregiver) and helps the child develop a working model of the self

(e.g., I am valuable, worthy of care) and of others (e.g., others are reliable and caring).

Bowlby's theoretical work was enhanced and enriched by research into the importance of early relationships on children's behavior. For example, he and his colleagues studied the effects of hospitalization and institutionalization on 15- to 30-month-olds using the careful, detailed observational style of ethology. They documented a series of stages of distress and withdrawal that helped create the impetus for change in hospital visitation policies described earlier. But the research that captured the attention of both the scientific and the clinical community was done by Ainsworth on mothers and babies in their own homes.

Ainsworth, who earned a Ph.D. in psychology at the University of Toronto, relinquished her own career to follow her husband to London. There she answered Bowlby's newspaper ad seeking researchers. His views of the importance of early relationships were consistent with many of her own ideas, and Ainsworth became an eager student and associate. When her husband's career took her to Uganda, she launched a study of local mothers caring for their unweaned infants. She became convinced from her observations that Bowlby was right: Babies actively help create an attachment system that protects them and provides a foundation for later developments. She also believed that the 28 Ganda babies she studied were forming attachments of different qualities, and she looked for relationships between the infants' attachment quality and the mothers' sensitivity and responsiveness.

When her husband moved again, this time to Baltimore, Ainsworth took a position at Johns Hopkins University. Eventually, she launched a more detailed and intensive study of 26 mother–infant dyads. After 18 home visits over the course of each baby's first year, she invented the "strange situation test" to assess the infants' feelings of security when they were 1 year old. That test is now the preeminent means for assessing attachment quality and has been used in dozens of studies since, by researchers around the world eager to test the tenets of attachment theory and to explore the precursors and consequences of an infant's first attachments. Ainsworth's careful research both enhanced the credibility of Bowlby's views and demonstrated that interpersonal relationships, not just individual behaviors, could be meaningfully investigated using scientific techniques.

SOURCES: Karen, R. (1998). *Becoming attached: First relationships and how they shape our capacity to love.* New York, NY: Oxford University Press. Simpson, J. A., & Belsky, J. (2016). Attachment theory within a modern evolutionary framework. In J. Cassidy & P. R. Shaver (Eds.), *Handbook of attachment: Theory, research, and clinical applications* (3rd ed., pp. 91–116). New York, NY: Guilford Press.

Bowlby described the infant's connection with the primary caregiver (usually the mother) as his first attachment relationship. Bowlby's theory of how it changes and what it means for the child's psychosocial life is called **attachment theory**. In Bowlby's description, infant and caregiver participate in an attachment system that has evolved to serve the purpose of keeping the infant safe and assuring his survival. As we have already noted, both the infant and the adult bring to the system a set of biologically prepared behaviors. These behaviors change as the infant's repertoire of abilities changes, partly as a function of interactions with others. In early infancy, as we have seen, the infant's cries and clinging bring a caregiver. Later, instead of clinging, the toddler may keep an eye on one particular adult, often the mother, keeping track of

Box 4.2: A Biographical Sketch: Erik H. Erikson

The parents of a 4-year-old boy named Peter brought him to Erik Erikson for treatment of a frightening problem that appeared to be emotionally based. Peter retained his feces for up to a week at a time, and his colon had become enlarged. As he learned more about Peter, Erikson came to see his problem as a reaction to the way others had dealt with normal, stage-appropriate behavior. Before the problem began, Peter had entered what Erikson described as the developmental stage of initiative versus guilt, when it is common for children to intrude themselves on others in a rather aggressive way—such as trying to take over the conversation at the dinner table or, as in Peter's case, being physically aggressive and bossy with adults (see Table 1.2 in Chapter 1). Peter's aggressive style was tolerated amiably by his nanny, but his mother was disturbed by it and by the nanny's tolerance, so she fired the nanny. Peter's anal retention problem started soon afterward. Eventually, Erikson helped Peter to see that his problem was related to his distress at losing his beloved nanny. Peter, Erikson felt, was identifying with the nanny, who had told Peter that she was going to have a baby of her own, and he was trying to hold on to her by retaining his feces.

Erikson's work with Peter reflects the Freudian roots of his perspective. He saw Peter's 4-year-old aggressiveness with his nanny as having sexual overtones, a normal process for a child in Freud's phallic stage. When Peter's aggressiveness led to the painful loss of the beloved nanny, he regressed to using behaviors more typical of the anal stage: holding on to his feces. But Erikson's interpretation also reveals his innovative, psychosocial perspective, which went well beyond his Freudian training. Preschoolers need to express their bold new sense of initiative. Adults can be accepting of this need, even as they impose some constraints so that children will learn to behave in socially acceptable ways. In the process, children will learn to curb their own behavior, controlled by their own feelings of guilt. But when constraints are imposed in an abrupt, disapproving, unsupportive way, or when they are excessive, children's appropriate exuberance can be stifled, leading a child to be overly restrained and guilty about normal behavior. Just as in infancy,

when children must form basic trust, the warmth, sensitivity, and understanding of responsive adults are important ingredients in the development of positive feelings about self or others.

Erik H. Erikson (1902–1994) was the son of Danish parents; his mother was Jewish, his father, Protestant. His parents separated before he was born, and he was raised in Germany by his mother and stepfather. His undistinguished youth seems an unlikely beginning for a great developmental theorist. He was something of a misfit as a young boy. His ethnicity as a Jew coupled with his Gentile appearance caused him to experience social rejection from both his Jewish and his Gentile peers. As a young man, Erik, born Erik Homberger, changed his surname to Erikson—a clear attempt to construct his own identity. He was not much of a student, and after high school, uncertain of his goals or interests, he wandered through Europe rather than attend college. He studied art for a while, wandered again, and eventually accepted an offer to teach children at a school where Anna Freud, daughter of Sigmund, was a cofounder. Thus began his life's work as a child clinician. He studied psychoanalysis with Anna Freud, and when he and his wife, Joan, fled Europe in 1933 with the rise of Hitler, he became the first child analyst in Boston. In his career as a therapist and developmental theorist, he held faculty appointments at Yale, in the University of California system, and finally at Harvard, despite the fact that he had earned no degrees beyond high school. In his scholarly work, he not only contributed to research and theory on normal personality development, including the formerly uncharted area of adult life stages, but also pioneered exploration into cross-cultural variations in development, observing the life experiences of Sioux Indians in South Dakota and of Yurok Indians in California. Although Erikson extended his work to include adult developmental issues, he seems to have had a special concern for the vulnerability of children. In his writing on child rearing, he urged parents to recognize that the most fundamental requirement of good parenting is to provide a sense of security, to give children the benefit of calm, reliable care, starting in earliest infancy.

her whereabouts in case of need. Instead of crying, the toddler may call to the caregiver or communicate by reaching or pointing. When he does cry, the caregiver may respond differently to different cries, assessing the level and kind of need from variations in the sound, apparently recognizing that crying can serve multiple purposes for the older baby (see Thompson & Leger, 1999). Thus, the system broadens to include and accommodate the infant's more advanced physical and cognitive abilities, but it still serves the purpose of making the child secure.

Attachment is a system, not a particular set of behaviors. The system serves three purposes: It maintains proximity between infant and caregiver, nurturing the emotional bond (called **proximity maintenance**); it provides the potential for ongoing protection (called **secure base**); and it creates a haven for the infant when he is distressed (called **safe haven**). Behaviors as diverse as smiling and crying all serve attachment functions, and as already noted, the particular behaviors serving these functions can change over time and circumstance. When helpers reflect on problems faced by children and families, attachment theory indicates that the proper unit of analysis is at the level of relationships. That is, a behavior (e.g., crying or clinging) must be interpreted within its social context to understand its significance.

Let's consider the notion of safe haven more specifically, for it is here that attachments serve the important function of stress management. Think back, for a moment, to the earlier discussion of emotion regulation. The infant has limited ability to regulate his episodes of physiological distress. Threats such as hunger, pain, fatigue, loneliness, or overstimulation can produce periods of dysregulation or heightened arousal. Some infants are more easily aroused than others because of individual differences in autonomic reactivity. For all infants, and especially for these more sensitive and vulnerable ones, the stressfulness of physical or emotional discomfort activates the attachment system. By crying, clinging, or showing distress in some other way, the infant signals his need for his caregiver to step in to help manage stress. Distress, triggered from within the infant or from without, activates the attachment system. The helpless infant needs a caregiver to deactivate his escalating discomfort. With time, sensitive caregiving episodes become associated with relief and love for the caregiver. The caregiver who scaffolds the child's own developing capacity to regulate his emotions also helps him form a positive social bond. Bowlby, like Erikson, assumed that the quality of care that an infant receives will affect the nature and the eventual impact of his attachments. With responsive, sensitive care, infants come to see their primary attachment figure as a source of security, a secure base from which to explore the world. They correspondingly feel confidence in themselves and in their ability to negotiate that world. The infant learns that his signals of distress are heard by others—that they are adaptive in helping him get needs for care and attention met. He also learns that the very expression of these needs is legitimate in that others take them seriously.

More broadly, the nature or quality of infants' first attachments affect their expectations and behaviors in other relationships. "These expectations develop into broader representations of their attachment figures, interpretations of their relational experiences, guidelines about how to interact with others, and even beliefs about themselves as relational partners" (Thompson, 2016, p. 332). In sum, early experience with a primary caregiver helps the child form his first representations of the self, of others, and of relationships. Bowlby referred to these representations as **working models**—prototypes of social functioning that affect the child's expectations and behaviors in future relationships.

Bowlby's attachment theory prompted developmental researchers to explore babies' earliest relationships, seeking a better understanding of how the first attachments develop and how important they really are for psychosocial development. In the following sections, we take a look at what this research has revealed and what it might mean for the helping professions.

The Developing Bond Between Infant and Caregiver

As part of the attachment system, an affectional bond develops. Bowlby argued that as a result of cognitive and emotional changes in the infancy period, the baby's connection to the caregiver emerges in stages, with a full-fledged attachment likely by about 8 months. In a classic study, Schaffer and Emerson (1964) followed the development of a group of infants through their first 18 months and found a sequence of attachment stages consistent with those Bowlby described. In the first 2 months, infants signal their needs, producing behaviors such as clinging, smiling, and crying. Although we now know that even newborns have some ability to recognize their mothers' voices (see Chapter 3), they show little sign of discriminating among potential caregivers or of having a social preference, so that babies cannot yet be seen as attached to anyone. Next, between about 2 and 6 months, infants gradually show stronger and stronger preferences for particular caregivers, as when a baby smiles more brightly or is more readily soothed by Mom or Dad than by Grandma or Uncle Bill. By about 6 months, babies begin to behave in ways that signal a strong preference for one caregiver, most often the mother. If more than one adult is available, the infant may consistently reach for its mother when stressed, for example. The infant may protest being separated from the mother and will greet her happily when she returns. By 8 to 9 months, the baby may show full-fledged *separation anxiety*, acting distressed well after the mother has disappeared from view, a behavior that depends on the baby's ability to recall the mother when she is not present (see Chapter 3 for a full description). Along with separation anxiety may come **stranger anxiety**: an increased tendency to be wary of strangers and to seek the comfort and protection of the primary caregiver when a stranger is present. Note that infants can recognize familiar faces and voices much earlier than 6 to 9 months, and they may show some wariness with strangers, but a more intense reaction is common once other indicators of the first attachment emerge. Not all babies show stranger anxiety—it seems to depend in part on how reactive the infant is to new stimulation (see the section on infant temperament later in this chapter). Stranger anxiety is also greatly reduced among infants in some cultures, like the Nso in Cameroon, where friendliness toward strangers is a cultural practice (Keller & Otto, 2009). Finally, Schaffer and Emerson observed that soon after babies show signs of their first emotional attachment, many of them are forming other attachments as well, with their fathers, with regular babysitters, with older siblings, and with other family members. By 18 months, most of the babies in their study were attached to more than one person.

As Bowlby theorized, researchers have found that both infants and parents typically display expressive and behavioral characteristics that appear to foster the growth of attachment bonds. Parsons and colleagues have characterized these as the "orienting," "recognition," and "intuitive parenting" systems (Parsons, Young, Murray, Stein, & Kringelbach, 2010). These systems partly depend on adults' rapid neurological responses to babies' cues, such as a smile or cry. Some of the emotion regulation behaviors you learned about earlier are part of this emerging set of behaviors. Adults' and babies' responses in these systems have some automatic components, but they also change with experience: They grow and expand over the course of the relationship (Parsons, Young, Parsons, Stein, & Kringelbach, 2012). We summarize some of the elements of these behavioral systems in Table 4.1. You will probably recognize many of the behaviors involved if you have had opportunities to observe parents interacting with their infants.

MyLab Education
Video Example 4.2
Separation anxiety and wariness of strangers appear across cultures, although the behaviors that the children show to indicate anxiety vary across cultures. How are these behaviors necessary for the development of attachment relationships?

TABLE 4.1 Dyadic Systems That Foster Social Bonding

SYSTEMS	MOTHER (CAREGIVER) BEHAVIORS	INFANT BEHAVIORS
Orienting system *(present from birth)* *Enhances proximity between infant and caregiver.*	Stays in the middle of the infant's field of vision. Makes exaggerated facial gestures (like surprise, joy) and vocalizations. Sustains eye contact. Attends quickly to infant cues.	Shows preference for human over non-human faces. Shows preference for human speech sounds. Displays "cuteness" or attractiveness to adults (e.g., large eyes, odor, high-pitched vocal sounds).
Recognition system *(present within a few days after birth)* *Enhances special responsiveness to each other and encourages contact.*	Recognizes own infant from cry, touch, and smell. Prefers to look at own baby's face compared to other baby's face; viewing own infant's face induces positive mood.	Shows clear preference for caregiver's voice and smell. Prefers to look at caregiver's face compared to that of a stranger.
Intuitive parenting system *(present in early months of infant's life)* *Enhances the attunement of communication between parent and caregiver.*	Mirrors infant's behaviors. "Reads" the behavior of infant and ascribes meaning to infant behavior; responds to cues promptly and accurately. Encourages greater tolerance by allowing for time lags in between responses to infant demands. Alters speech patterns (slows down speech, exaggerates vocalizations, uses "parentese" to direct speech to infant). Soothes negative affect in infant. Builds on infants' improved motor and visual skills through object play and repetitive games.	Mirrors caregiver's behavior. Anticipates response but is more tolerant. Expects contingency in communication; reacts to non-communication (still-face) with distress. Experiences feelings of joy and relief; smiles more in context of caregiving relationship. Learns repetitive action sequences.
Attachment *(early indicators by 6 months; full-fledged by 8 to 10 months after birth)* *Development of a stable preference and way of relating to caregiver in order to maintain proximity, provide security in times of stress, and serve as a base for later independent exploration.*	Shows heightened responsiveness and emotional connection to infant. Predictably soothes and comforts infant when distressed; minimizes separation. Demonstrates predictable and sensitive caregiving related to basic needs. Exhibits capacity to consider the mental state and experiences of infant (mind-mindedness).	Demonstrates preference for caregiver. Responds with distress upon separation; shows protest behaviors (cries, clings, etc.) and seeks contact when stressed. Develops sense of confidence that care will be predictable.

SOURCES: Kringelbach, Stark, Alexander, Bornstein, & Stein, 2017; Parsons, Young, Parsons, Stein, & Kringelbach, 2012; Parsons, Young, Murray, Stein, & Kringelbach, (2010).

The Biology of Infant Attachment

Armed with modern technological tools, researchers are rapidly uncovering the very complex neurological underpinnings of the typical social bonding behaviors described in Table 4.1 that support attachment formation. Many of the brain structures that are important for emotional processing are also involved in social bonding, from the amygdala and hypothalamus to areas of the frontal cortex (Kringelbach et al., 2017). A full description of all aspects is beyond the scope of this textbook. However, let's look at a few of the key biological ingredients in the bonding process. Findings in this area are directly relevant to practitioners' interest in prevention of mental and physical disorders.

Neuroendocrine systems help with bonding. Oxytocin is a hormone that is synthesized in the hypothalamus and released by the pituitary gland. It plays a role in affiliative behaviors: social cooperation, sexual and reproductive activities (in men and women), empathy and forgiveness, and so on (see Hane & Fox, 2016). In mothers, its production increases during pregnancy, labor, delivery, and breastfeeding. In both mothers and fathers, it promotes involvement in caregiving activities, such as physical proximity, responsive caregiving, empathy, and affection (Feldman, 2012). For example, one study followed parents and their firstborn babies until the children were 6 months old (Gordon et al., 2015). The researchers tested oxytocin levels from blood samples and found that mothers' and fathers' levels did not differ. Both parents produced more oxytocin as their babies got older. The researchers also observed mother–infant and father–infant interactions. Higher levels of oxytocin were associated with more caregiving behaviors for both parents, but the types of behaviors differed. Mothers produced more affectionate touch and positive facial expressions, for example, whereas fathers increased their stimulating play behavior.

As you know, correlations do not necessarily indicate a causal connection, but experimental studies in which parents' oxytocin levels have been manipulated (by administering doses nasally) show that increases in oxytocin directly promote engagement with an infant. In one study, fathers who received oxytocin showed cardiac changes associated with reduced stress and they interacted more with their infants than fathers who received a placebo (Weisman, Zagoory-Sharon, & Feldman, 2012). It is interesting to note that in response, their infants showed a spontaneous increase in oxytocin levels in their blood samples, as well as cardiac changes similar to those of their fathers! It is also noteworthy that for most adults, whether biological parents or not, close contact with infants promotes increases in oxytocin levels (see Young et al., 2017).

Oxytocin works in part by reducing neuroendocrine stress responding, although how effective it is depends on a person's own stress history. Individual differences in maternal oxytocin levels have been associated with a mother's own early experiences, both in animals and humans. Women who report early emotional neglect have significantly lower levels of oxytocin and may be less likely to provide positive, responsive caregiving (e.g., Grimm et al., 2014).

Oxytocin actually engages in "cross talk" with a wide range of other hormones that are implicated in infant caregiving (Feldman, 2015; Swain et al., 2014). For example, the oxytocin and dopamine systems are connected. Infant behaviors (crying, smiling, vocalizing, etc.) stimulate the release of oxytocin in caregivers, and they also trigger increases in dopamine, a neurotransmitter associated with reward. The links between these hormones and the neural pathways they affect are complicated, but it appears that they work in concert to increase how rewarding parents' caregiving behaviors are for them (Atzil et al., 2017).

Recall from the discussion of epigenetics that the environment has a lot to do with how brain structures and functions develop both before and after birth. We reported in Chapter 2 that Laurent and colleagues (2016) found that sensitivity of mothers' typical caregiving was associated with their toddlers' cortisol reactivity when the children were frightened. More sensitive moms had children whose cortisol responses normalized more rapidly. In another study, researchers examined DNA methylation patterns in 1-year-olds whose mothers had a major depressive disorder (Cicchetti, Hetzel, Rogosch, Handley, & Toth, 2016). These infants showed significantly different methylation patterns compared to infants whose mothers did not have this diagnosis, perhaps indicating that the quality of care was responsible. (As you will see later in this chapter, depressed mothers are less likely to provide sensitive, responsive care to their infants than other mothers; see Thompson, 2015.) These data are suggestive of how caregiving might affect children's brains, but much more work is needed to identify the neural processes that link caregiving, attachment, and children's social and emotional development.

Attachment Quality: Not All Attachments Are Alike

In a famous study, Mary Ainsworth and her colleagues found that infants form different kinds of attachments to their primary caregivers (Ainsworth, Blehar, Waters, & Wall, 1978). To measure attachment, they invented the **strange situation test**. Twelve-month-olds and their mothers were brought to a room (the strange situation) where the child experienced a series of eight 3-minute episodes, each one introducing changes in the social situation, some of which were likely to be stressful to an infant. The stress component was important, given that attachment theory assumes that infants cannot handle stress on their own. At first the mother and baby were left alone in the room; in subsequent episodes, the mother and a stranger (one of the researchers) entered and left the room in various combinations. The baby's reactions to all of these events were carefully recorded, particularly his tendency to explore the room and the toys and his reactions to his mother and the stranger. The researchers paid special attention to the baby's response to his mother when she returned after an absence.

Ainsworth and her colleagues identified three patterns of infant response, now considered indicative of three different kinds of infant attachment to an adult caregiver. Other researchers subsequently identified a fourth category (Main & Soloman, 1990). It is important to note that all of these patterns do represent attachments, as all babies seem to have needs for proximity maintenance, a secure base, and safe haven. The style of the attachment, however, varies. The following paragraphs describe all four types of attachment patterns.

SECURELY ATTACHED

Most babies are found to be **securely attached** (originally described as the "B" category). They show distress when separated from the mother, often crying and trying to go after her, but they greet her happily on her return, usually reaching up to be held, sometimes molding their bodies to the mother as they seek comfort. Once reassured by her presence and her gestures, they tend to go off and explore the room. Ainsworth argued that babies in this category can use the mother as a secure base from which to explore the world; perhaps they are showing the beginnings of optimism or hope, as Erikson suggested. They may also have learned to tolerate more separation because they have confidence in the mother's availability if they need her. Sixty-five percent of the 1-year-olds in the Ainsworth et al. (1978) study showed this response pattern, and in most subsequent research the majority of babies fit this description.

ANXIOUS AMBIVALENT—INSECURELY ATTACHED

Babies in this and the remaining two categories are considered to be attached, in that they show signs of having a special pattern of behavior vis-à-vis their mothers, but their attachments seem insecure, often laced with high levels of anxiety, as though the infant cannot quite achieve a sense of security and ease even when mother is available. **Anxious ambivalent** babies (originally called "C" babies, comprising about 10% of many samples) often seem stressed even in the initial episode (e.g., sometimes failing to explore at all), and they are quite distressed when separated from their mothers, crying more than babies in other attachment categories (Hane & Fox, 2016). It is their reunion behavior, however, that distinguishes them as insecurely attached. They may act angry, alternately approaching and resisting the mother, or they may respond listlessly to her efforts to comfort. They seem preoccupied with their mothers and rarely return to exploration after a separation.

AVOIDANT—INSECURELY ATTACHED

Avoidant babies (originally called "A" babies and comprising about 20% of most samples), typically fail to cry when separated from their mothers. They actively avoid or ignore her when she returns, sometimes combining proximity seeking and moving away, but mostly turning away. In contrast to babies in other categories, these children often appear unemotional during the episodes of separation and reunion. However, other studies indicate that their heart rates are elevated as much as other babies' during separations from their mothers. Their heart rates remain elevated for long periods after mothers return (as do those of anxious-ambivalent babies), whereas secure babies' heart rates return to baseline quickly (see Gunnar, 2017).

DISORGANIZED-DISORIENTED—INSECURELY ATTACHED

The category **disorganized-disoriented** (referred to as "D" babies and constituting a very small percentage of most samples) was first described by Main and Soloman (1986, 1990), who examined strange situation videotapes from several studies, focusing on babies who had previously been difficult to classify. These infants produced contradictory behaviors, showing both an inclination to approach the mother when stressed and a tendency to avoid her when she approached! "D" babies are more fully described in the *Focus on Developmental Psychopathology* later in this chapter.

Linking Quality of Caregiving to Attachment Quality

Where do attachment types or styles originate? As we have indicated, attachment theory suggests that the quality of caregiving during the baby's first year is the key, and Ainsworth's early study strongly supported that claim (Ainsworth et al., 1978). All 26 babies and mothers in her study had been observed in their homes at regular intervals from the time of birth. The middle-class mothers were their infants' primary caregivers, and they did not work outside the home. Yet, they did not all provide the same quality of care. Infants who became securely attached had mothers who responded promptly and consistently to crying during the first year, who handled the infant with sensitivity, who held the baby tenderly and often, and whose face-to-face interactions were responsive to the baby's signals. In other words, they showed many of the features that both Bowlby and Erikson proposed to be important for infant care to create security or trust.

Babies who became insecurely attached had mothers who seemed insensitive to their infants in one way or another. The mothers of ambivalent babies were affectionate but were often awkward in holding. They were inconsistent in their responsiveness to crying. In face-to-face interactions, they often failed to respond to their babies' signals. For example, in a game of peek-a-boo, an infant might begin to seem overstimulated and turn away his gaze. A responsive mother would be likely to wait until the baby reengaged before saying or doing anything, whereas an unresponsive mother might behave more intrusively, trying to force the reengagement by vocalizing or jiggling the baby.

The mothers of avoidant babies seemed to actively avoid holding their babies. They were more often rejecting and angry, and they showed less warmth and affection than other mothers. Babies in the disorganized-disoriented category of attachment were not identified in Ainsworth's study, but in research where they have been identified, this pattern has been associated with frightening and/or abusive parental behavior, as you will see in this chapter's *Focus on Developmental Psychopathology*.

Ainsworth's initial research linking mother care to infant security excited the research community and attracted the attention of helping professionals, especially those interested in developmental psychopathology. Decades of research are now available, corroborating the importance of sensitive, responsive care during infancy for attachment quality and deepening our understanding of the nature of such care.

One thing we have learned is that maternal sensitivity is linked to infant security, whether we look at middle-class or low-income families, in the United States, in other Western countries or in non-Western cultural groups (Fearon & Belsky, 2016; Mesman et al., 2017; see the "Cross-Cultural Influences on Infant Attachment" section later in this chapter).

What are the key ingredients of "sensitivity"? In other words, what really matters to promote secure attachments? Consistent with Ainsworth's observations, many studies support the importance of prompt responsiveness to distress; interactional synchrony; affectional warmth and positivity (and *not* expressing hostility, boredom, frustration); and moderately stimulating but nonintrusive interactive involvement with the infant (being supportive without interfering). It also helps if caregivers support the "exploration side" of security, giving their infants freedom to use their developing skills in a safe environment (Bernier, Matte-Gagne, Belanger, & Whipple, 2014; Fearon & Belsky, 2016; Kim, Chow, Bray, & Teti, 2017).

Sensitive and Insensitive Parenting

We also have a more detailed picture now of what happens when early relationships go awry. It is often because maternal responsiveness is compromised, just as Ainsworth and her colleagues (1978) found. Barrett and Fleming (2011) describe it in this way: "The interaction between a mother and her infant can be like a dance. There are routines, standards and missteps, there is give and take, there is unparalleled intimacy, there are often vast differences in skill level and motivation, there is learning . . . This dance can be beautiful, it can be tender, it can be awkward, it can be difficult. And sometimes it just does not occur!" (p. 368). Adverse or insensitive "dance" styles often fit into two major caregiver categories: intrusive or neglectful, although both patterns can be present in alternation. Many (but not all) depressed mothers show high rates of these caregiving patterns (Beeghly & Tronick, 2011; Conradt et al., 2016).

Neglectful (withdrawn) caregivers typically show a pattern of under-stimulation marked by reduced eye contact, infrequent holding, nonresponsiveness, less positive and more negative affect. Intrusive (over-stimulating) caregivers display more anger, irritability, coerciveness, and poorly timed responses. They fail to take their cues from the baby and often interfere with infant exploration. A baby needs help regulating his emotions and learning the predictability that characterizes well-coordinated interactions that make him feel safe and loved. Unfortunately, the depressed caregiver is unable to provide the kind of help that is needed. Both patterns can thwart babies' efforts to establish predictable contact, leading to more negative emotional periods for the infant. Infants may develop increased levels of withdrawal or distress in an effort to regulate the lack of synchrony (see Field, Hernandez-Reif, & Diego, 2006).

Physiological studies have documented differences in the brain activity of infants of depressed (withdrawn) and nondepressed mothers (see Coan, 2016). For example, Field and her colleagues (1995) reported asymmetrical electrical activity in the right frontal area of 3- to 4-month-old infants of depressed (withdrawn) mothers. As discussed earlier, heightened right frontal activation and lowered left frontal activation is consistent with the patterns observed in extremely fearful and inhibited children and in chronically depressed adults, suggesting the felt experience of more negative than positive emotions. Interactions frequently go unrepaired, and the infant resorts to a style of affective coping marked by escaping and turning away. By 4 months, infants of depressed mothers are less active in face-to-face interactions with their mothers than infants of non-depressed mothers, and by 5 months they do less laughing and more fussing when their mothers interact with them (Field et al., 2007a, 2007b). By 18 months, these infants are also more likely to be insecurely attached to their mothers than infants of nondepressed mothers (Beeghly et al., 2017). Intrusive mothers show higher levels of activation in the amygdala and less inhibitory functioning compared to sensitive mothers (Atzil, Hendler, & Feldman, 2011). The infants of such mothers tend to show higher rates of unmodulated and anxious behavior. Overall, such physiological markers may be useful indicators of infants who are at risk for emotional problems and who might profit from early intervention.

Clearly, extreme or intense experiences of caregiver withdrawal and/or harsh, coercive parenting constitute serious abuse. Abundant evidence documents the devastating consequences of early exposure to severe abuse and neglect (see Chapter 2 and later sections of this chapter). A more recent but growing body of evidence provides support for the emergence of different social-emotional outcomes related to

TABLE 4.2 Normal Variations in U.S. Caregiving: Giving the Baby a Bath

SENSITIVE	INSENSITIVE
"A highly sensitive mother identifies the components of the bath that her infant finds aversive and attenuates their negative consequences. She prepares the bath in such a way that the water is warm and sufficiently covering the body. She removes clothing and applies soap gently, so the infant is not overly stimulated. She skillfully maneuvers the necessarily invasive washing of the face, particularly around the eyes. She prepares the clothing before application by readying the sleeves and opening the neck widely, to minimize pulling and tugging. This style of maternal caregiving may be 'optimal' simply because it prevents infant discomfort, eliminating the need for the infant to mount a defensive response while being cared for. Mother is protecting the infant's comfort in nuanced, subtle, and remarkably ordinary ways." (p. 150)	"Take, for instance, undressing the infant prior to preparing the bath. This is not what most might consider an egregious parenting error. It is not abusive or neglectful. Yet, we have observed that the impact on quality of MCB can be considerable: The freshly disrobed infant is held with one arm as mother fills the bath and gathers supplies. Across this task, mother's arm becomes strained by the infant, and she shifts him awkwardly and frequently. The exposed infant is challenged by the chill of room temperature, and he squirms and cries. Mother's arm is further taxed by the aroused infant; her holding becomes less accommodating. Placement in the bath is more abrupt as mother is eager to free her arm. The infant's response to the water is more dramatic than it might have been, because his own body temperature has cooled, increasing the saliency of the water's warmth." (p. 151)

SOURCE: Hane, A. A. & Philbrook, L. E. (2012). Beyond licking and grooming: Maternal regulation of infant stress in the context of routine care. *Parenting: Science and Practice, 12*, 144–153. Used with permission from Taylor & Francis.

MyLab Education

Video Example 4.3

The toddler in this video responds enthusiastically to his mother. Based on the verbal and nonverbal exchange between caregiver and toddler, what type of attachment exists in this example?

"normal" variations in parental responsivity. The key lesson here may be the exquisite sensitivity of infants' developing affective systems to emotional communication from caregivers.

A close look at one large, longitudinal study may help demonstrate. Hane and colleagues (Hane & Fox, 2006; Hane, Henderson, Reeb-Sutherland, & Fox, 2010) videotaped 185 9-month-old infants and their U.S. mothers at home during three periods of interaction: mother busy in the kitchen, snack time (spoon-feeding), and caregiving and changing (change of clothes and applying lotion). The mothers were middle class and represented a range of ethnicities. They had at least a high school education and were not considered high risk. Mothers were assessed on a set of sensitivity and intrusiveness measures, allowing researchers to identify two maternal caregiving behavior (MCB) groups based on high and low quality. (Table 4.2 provides detailed examples of high- and low-quality maternal caregiving behaviors from a different study using an infant bathing observation.) Infants were assessed on frontal EEG symmetry, temperament, affect, and interaction quality with their mothers. Note that both high- and low-quality MCB were considered to be within the "normal" range of behaviors and not abusive.

Results showed that infants in the low-quality MCB group showed more negative emotions. Specifically, they showed more fearfulness, less joint attention with mother, and elevated right frontal activity compared to infants in the high-quality group. These effects were not related to infant temperament but rather associated with consistent differences in the quality of "normal" caregiving behavior.

A follow-up of these infants at ages 2 and 3 revealed persistent differences. At age 2, children from the low-quality MCB group showed increased stress reactivity, social inhibition, and more difficult and aggressive interactions with peers. Differences between groups in right frontal EEG asymmetry were observed at age 3, with children from the low-quality MCB group showing more negative affect. Mothers in the low-quality MCB group identified higher levels of social and behavior problems and more internalizing and externalizing disorders in their children compared to mothers in the high-quality MCB group. Conversely, children in the high-quality MCB group were better able to cope with stress and showed good social behavior.

You can see from this study that the effects of sensitive caregiving extend to mundane tasks like putting on baby lotion and responding to infant fussiness when you are busy in the kitchen. Even though subtle emotional insensitivity is often invisible to outsiders, the cost may be considerable. Efforts to assist parents and caregivers who are at risk of providing insensitive care, such as depressed mothers, should be a high priority for helpers (Stoltenborgh, Bakermans-Kranenburg, & van IJzendoorn, 2013).

The Child's Role in Attachment: Infant Temperament

Clearly, quality caregiving matters for an infant's emotional development and attachment formation, directly influencing both physiology and behavior. But infants do not come into the world as blank slates. A visit to a newborn nursery provides convincing demonstrations that different babies have different emotional and behavioral characteristics, or **temperaments**, from the time they are born. Consider Ahmed and Joseph, born at the same hospital on the same day. Ahmed has been sleeping in fairly long stretches, averaging 3 hours, with about 40 minutes of wakefulness between naps. When he is awake, he is often quiet, although like any newborn he cries when he's hungry or uncomfortable. When the nurses pick him up he calms quickly, and his breastfeeding mother says he sucks on the nipple peacefully, with moderate force. Joseph sleeps more irregularly; at 1 day old he has had two sleep periods of about 3 hours each, and many others that have ranged from 10 to 30 minutes. When he awakens, he cries lustily and is not easy to soothe. He also seems to be in constant motion, and his mother finds him squirmy and erratic in his breastfeeding attempts.

Various researchers have identified somewhat different infant traits, but they often include **fearfulness or reactivity** (the infant's proneness to cry or pull away from new stimuli), **irritability or negative emotionality** (the infant's tendency to react with fussiness to negative or frustrating events), **activity level** (the intensity and quantity of movement), **positive affect** (smiling and laughing, especially to social stimuli), **attention-persistence** (duration of orienting or looking), and **rhythmicity** (predictability of sleep, feeding, elimination, and so on). (See reviews by Kagan & Fox, 2006; Rothbart, 2011; and Thompson, Winer, & Goodvin, 2011 for the many ways of conceptualizing such traits.) Certain individual traits tend to be correlated with each other, revealing several relatively uncorrelated dimensions or domains of temperament. Although researchers do not always agree (e.g., Dyson et al., 2015 vs. Saudino & Micalizzi, 2015) about what these dimensions are, they typically include *emotionality* (quality and intensity of mood), *control* or *self-regulatory tendencies* (such as attentional control/persistence), and *activity level* or *surgency* (see Thompson et al., 2011).

The cataloguing of infant temperament traits raises a number of intriguing questions. Are these traits stable over time, predicting personality characteristics of older children and adults? Where do temperament traits come from? How is infant temperament related to parents' caregiving? This question has several component parts: Do infant traits affect the sensitivity and responsiveness of parents' caregiving? Can caregiving affect temperament? Are babies with different temperamental traits affected differently by sensitive versus insensitive caregiving? Finally, does temperament play a role in the development of attachment security?

We will save the first question, whether infant temperament is continuous with later personality characteristics, for later chapters. For now, we will focus on characterizing infant temperament, identifying its relationship to parental caregiving, and understanding its role in attachment security.

WHERE DO TEMPERAMENT TRAITS COME FROM?

Temperament traits are assumed to be biologically based reactivity patterns, and evidence is accumulating for the importance of genetic and epigenetic contributions to the physiological processes involved. For example, Jerome Kagan and his colleagues have focused on children who as infants are "high reactive" or "low reactive" (see Kagan & Fox, 2006; Fox, Snidman, Haas, Degnan, & Kagan, 2015). High reactive 4-month-olds produce frequent vigorous limb activity, have high levels of muscle tension, and react irritably (e.g., crying) to sensory stimulation, such as new smells or sounds. Low reactive infants, of course, score unusually low on these kinds of measures. Early reactivity is related to later measures of **behavioral inhibition**, or shyness. For example, by 7 to 9 months, when stranger anxiety tends to peak, high reactive U.S. infants show more extreme avoidance or distress than most other infants. These infants also tend to have relatively high heart rates before birth and in some contexts after birth. Kagan has proposed that the behavioral and physiological characteristics of high reactive infants may indicate a lower than average threshold of excitability in parts of the brain—the amygdala and many of its associated structures—that mediate stress responses.

A number of genes appear to contribute to these differences in brain function. Some affect the production and metabolism of neurotransmitters such as dopamine and serotonin. And, as we saw in Chapter 2, nature and nurture coact to influence stress reactivity from the prenatal period onward, so that even the biological functions that underlie high and low reactivity are likely to be an outgrowth of epigenetic processes (Field & Diego, 2008; Montirosso et al., 2016). Montirosso and colleagues found that premature infants who had endured the sometimes painful and highly stimulating environment of a neonatal infant care unit (NICU) showed greater methylation of a gene involved in serotonin production than full term infants. (They did not show that methylation pattern at birth.) At 3 months old, the premies with the increased methylation pattern were more behaviorally inhibited on average than full term infants or premies without the increased methylation.

Even environmental factors such as the hours of daylight during prenatal development can have epigenetic effects that modify temperament. Like all people, pregnant mothers secrete high levels of melatonin when daylight hours are decreasing, and melatonin can affect fetal brain development in several ways, binding to receptors in many locations and suppressing the release of gene products such as dopamine. If infants are conceived in the early fall in the Northern Hemisphere when hours of daylight are decreasing (February to April in the Southern Hemisphere), they are more likely to be extremely shy than if they are conceived at other times (see Kagan et al., 2007).

The biological underpinnings of other infant temperament characteristics have not been examined as intensively as high reactivity. It is not clear whether physiological correlates exist for other traits, but it seems likely that babies are born with several natural biases to react to environmental conditions in somewhat different ways.

HOW IS INFANT TEMPERAMENT RELATED TO PARENTS' CAREGIVING?

In the landmark New York Longitudinal Study, psychiatrists Alexander Thomas and Stella Chess (1977) found that they could categorize 3-month-olds in their large sample into four "temperament types" (using a set of nine temperament traits; see Table 4.3). Difficult babies (about 10%), compared to the others, were more fearful, more irritable, and more active, displayed less positive affect, were more irregular, and so on—a mix of traits that made them difficult and challenging to parents. Joseph, in the above example, might fit this category. The highly reactive babies described by Kagan and his colleagues would also be likely to be categorized as difficult. Easy babies (about 40%) were more

TABLE 4.3 The New York Longitudinal Study: Behavioral Traits Assessed in Infancy and Their Characteristic Levels in Babies with Easy and Difficult Temperaments

TRAIT	DESCRIPTION	LEVEL OF TRAIT IN TWO TEMPERAMENT STYLES
1. Activity level	Frequency and speed of movement	*Easy:* Low *Difficult:* High
2. Rhythmicity	Biological regularity, as in sleep–wake cycles and frequency of hunger	*Easy:* High regularity *Difficult:* Low regularity
3. Approach/withdrawal	Child's immediate reaction to new experience: acceptance or rejection	*Easy:* Approaches, acceptance *Difficult:* Withdraws, rejection
4. Adaptability	When child does withdraw, does adaptation take a short, moderate, or long time?	*Easy:* Short period of adaptation *Difficult:* Long period of adaptation
5. Threshold	Minimum strength of stimulus required for child to attend or react	*Easy:* High *Difficult:* Low
6. Intensity	Energy the child expends in expressing mood	*Easy:* Low *Difficult:* High
7. Mood	Predominance of positive vs. neutral or negative mood expression	*Easy:* More positive *Difficult:* More negative
8. Distractibility	Ease with which child's attention is drawn away from an ongoing activity by a new stimulus	*Easy:* Low *Difficult:* High
9. Attention span and persistence	Length of uninterrupted attention to a single activity, and spontaneous return to a task after interruption	*Easy:* Long *Difficult:* Short

SOURCES: Chess, S. & Hassibi, M. (1978). *Principles and practice of child psychiatry.* New York, NY; Plenum Press; Chess, S., & Thomas, A. (1987). *Origins and evolution of behavior.* Cambridge, MA: Harvard University Press.

placid, less active, more positive, and more regular in their rhythms than most, and thus easier to care for. Ahmed seems to fit this description. **Slow-to-warm-up babies** (about 15%) were like difficult babies in their fearfulness, showing more wariness in new situations than most other babies, but their reactions in general were less intense and negative than those of difficult babies. Babies in the last category (about 35%) were more variable in their traits and did not fit well into any of the more extreme groups.

In time, some of the children showed signs of socioemotional problems. The majority of these had displayed a difficult temperament in infancy. In fact, 70% of the difficult babies eventually had some adjustment problems, ranging from learning difficulties to stealing to phobias. What differentiated the 70% with later problems from the 30% who seemed well adjusted, however, was the "goodness of fit" that the parents were able to achieve between their caregiving and the child's needs. If the parents were consistent and patient, difficult babies often became less irritable and more adaptable in time, and they were less likely to have adjustment problems as they got older.

Not many easy babies were in the group with later adjustment problems. Even when their parents had trouble accepting their characteristics, they usually were able to cope effectively. But when they did have later problems, caregiving seemed to be a critical ingredient—there was usually a poor fit between parental demands and the child's temperament.

The picture that emerges from the Thomas and Chess study is complex. First, it suggests that infant temperament may show some persistence into childhood and beyond. Second, it provides some indication that infant temperament affects caregiving. For example, infant temperament can make it easier or harder for a parent to be a responsive, sensitive caregiver. Third, it indicates that caregiving can change or at least moderate temperamental qualities. A parent's care influences the impact of early temperament on later adjustment. A child with difficult temperamental traits appears to be at risk for later adjustment problems, but the right caregiving can make that child much less vulnerable. Finally, it suggests that some children, especially those with easy temperaments, can tolerate a wider range of caregiving responsiveness without developing emotional or behavioral problems later. These complex relationships between temperament and parenting factors in determining child outcomes have been corroborated by many subsequent studies (see Vaughn & Bost, 2016).

Children with difficult temperaments may be exhibiting **genetic vulnerability** (also referred to as **diathesis-stress**), meaning that their physiological makeup (diathesis) makes them more prone to the negative effects of unsupportive parenting or other negative environmental influences (stress) than other children. It may be, however, that difficult temperamental qualities, such as high reactivity, actually make infants more susceptible to environmental influences in general (**differential susceptibility**). What that means is that they would experience *both* more benefit from positive parenting *and* more harm from negative parenting than other children (e.g., Belsky & Pluess, 2013; Vaughn & Bost, 2016; see Chapter 5).

DOES TEMPERAMENT PLAY A ROLE IN THE DEVELOPMENT OF ATTACHMENT RELATIONSHIPS?

Thomas and Chess did not look at children's attachment security, but the **goodness of fit model** suggests that temperament and caregiving should interact in determining the quality of a child's attachment relationships. The relationship of temperament to attachment was once a contentious issue for both researchers and clinicians. Some argued strongly that what appears to be attachment security or insecurity could be nothing but a manifestation of infant temperament. Others argued that what appear to be biologically based temperamental differences among infants could be nothing but a reflection of the sensitivity of care the infant has experienced. For example, mothers who are inconsistent and unresponsive to infant cues may create babies who find social interactions stressful and frustrating. Soon their infants begin to look more irritable and negative than other babies (Groh et al., 2017).

Neither of these extreme views accounts for the full complement of research findings, however. A multidimensional view, such as Thomas and Chess's goodness of fit model, seems to best explain the available evidence: Temperament *and* sensitivity

MyLab Education
Video Example 4.4
Researchers Thomas and Chess (1977) identified three consistent temperamental patterns based on a set of typical behavioral traits shown in infants. How might the effectiveness of caregiving behaviors be different for children with each temperament?

of care (both also influenced by other variables) interact at several levels to produce attachment security.

Let's consider what some of these complex interactive processes are. First, as we have seen, infants whose mothers are more sensitive and responsive in early infancy are likely to make better progress on emotion regulation. For infants who are highly reactive, developing emotion regulation skills is especially important and can mitigate the effects of their reactivity, helping them to be calmer overall. This in turn may help caregivers to continue to be more responsive (see Ursache, Blair, Stifter, & Voegtline, 2013).

Second, however, highly reactive infants tax caregivers more. It is simply more difficult to provide sensitive, responsive care to an infant who has these temperamental traits. Caregivers of difficult infants may themselves become more distressed and unsupportive over time. Without adequate caregiver support, these infants are less likely than others to show strong development in emotion regulation, making them increasingly more challenging to care for as they grow. Imagine caring for a newborn who cries more than others, or trying to manage a toddler who cannot moderate his reaction to any frustration (see Gudmundson & Leerkes, 2012). In one study, researchers looked at families with two children. The sensitivity of parents' caregiving from infancy onward was not necessarily the same with each child. The researchers concluded that the children's own characteristics had an important impact on the parents' sensitivity (Hallers-Haalboom et al., 2017).

Third, some mothers are more likely than others to be able to respond sensitively to difficult infants. These include mothers with few other stressors to deal with, mothers with lots of external supports, mothers who are secure and adaptable, and mothers who are "mind minded," meaning that they see an infant as having a perspective (his own mental and emotional states and concerns) rather than as a bundle of needs (e.g., Jones, Cassidy, & Shaver, 2015; Meins et al., 2012). Overall then, temperament traits are linked to the formation of secure versus insecure attachments by the end of the first year, but their effects are largely the result of their influence on the quality of caregiving that infants are likely to experience (Vaughn & Bost, 2016).

Fourth, specific temperamental characteristics seem to affect the kind of *insecure* attachment that forms. In a classic study, Kochanska (1998) measured infants' fearfulness (comparable to Kagan's behavioral inhibition) and mothers' responsiveness when babies were 8 to 10 months and when they were 13 to 15 months. She measured attachment security with the strange situation test at the later time as well. Maternal responsiveness predicted whether babies would be securely or insecurely attached. But for insecurely attached infants, fearfulness predicted the *type* of insecurity. More fearful infants tended to be ambivalent; less fearful babies were more often avoidant. Even the tone of secure attachment behavior was related to the babies' fearfulness, with more fearful babies more highly aroused in the separation and reunion episodes.

Finally, temperamental traits seem to make infants differentially susceptible to both optimal and nonoptimal care in the formation of attachments. Reactive, irritable infants seem to be both more vulnerable to low-quality care and more benefitted by supportive care than babies with easier temperaments.

Two studies designed to improve infants' chances of forming a secure attachment illustrate many of the interactive processes at play between temperament and caregiving. Van den Boom (1994) was able to demonstrate that caregiving actually plays a causal role in attachment security, especially with children at the more difficult temperamental extreme. In a U.S. sample of low-income families, van den Boom identified a group of one hundred 1- to 2-week-olds who were assessed as highly "irritable." The author assigned half of the infants to a treatment condition in which their mothers were trained to be sensitive and responsive. The remaining infant–mother pairs simply had to fend for themselves. The mothers in both groups tended to be frustrated by their fussy babies, and, without intervention, their caregiving was often insensitive and unresponsive. By 12 months, 72% of the infants whose mothers had received no training were insecurely attached. But after being given caregiving support and training, the mothers in the intervention group treated their babies more sensitively and were more responsive to their needs. Sixty-eight percent of their infants were securely attached by 12 months! This study demonstrates experimentally that sensitive caregiving does make a difference in security of attachment.

In the second study, Cassidy and her colleagues (2011) identified both very irritable and less irritable infants in a low-income sample of families. As in the van den Boom study, half of the mothers were trained to be more accepting of their infants' temperaments and to provide more sensitive care, and half were part of a control condition where no such training was given. Infants whose mothers received the training were more securely attached by the end of their first year. However, there was clear evidence of differential susceptibility: Only the more irritable infants in the treatment group seemed to benefit from the more sensitive parenting; less irritable infants showed few effects. Also, the mothers' personality characteristics mattered. Only mothers who were more secure (rather than more fearful) in the treatment condition seemed to be able to profit from the training, and it was their infants who were most likely to benefit. It appears that helpers who aim to improve the trajectory of infants' early socioemotional development would be wise to be mindful of a broad range of caregiver characteristics and needs in devising family interventions. (See the Applications section for more information about interventions.)

Mothers and Fathers

Mother is usually the primary caregiver, and so infant–mother attachments tend to be the first to form and are certainly the most often studied. But we have already noted that soon babies become attached to their fathers and other significant caregivers in their lives. The existence of multiple attachments raises several questions.

First, is attachment quality uniform across caregivers? In other words, once attached to the primary caregiver, do babies extend the same kind of attachment to others? There does tend to be consistency among an infant's attachments. Fox, Kimmerly, and Schafer (1991) compared attachment quality for mothers and fathers in 11 studies and found substantial similarities. If an infant were securely attached to one parent, he was likely to be securely attached to the other, although many exceptions were found. Also, babies with secure attachments to their mothers are generally more cooperative even with strangers than babies with insecure attachments, establishing a positive interactive trajectory (see Lamb & Lewis, 2011). These findings are consistent with Bowlby's notion that an infant forms a working model of self and other from his primary attachment relationship and then extends that model to other attachments.

But does that mean that the infant's attachment is unaffected by the sensitivity of the particular caregiver? Not necessarily. Mothers' and fathers' responsiveness and sensitivity tend to be similar, which could be an explanation for the consistency of an infant's attachments to his parents (e.g., Belsky & Volling, 1987; Hallers-Haalboom et al., 2017). Also, the fact that not all mother and father attachments are alike suggests that the father's caregiving does matter. Some studies have also found discordance (inconsistency) between infants' maternal attachments and their attachments to nonfamily caregivers (see Fearon & Belsky, 2016), which could mean that the quality of caregiving in each relationship does make a difference. (See Box 4.3.) A review of 16 studies found that fathers' sensitivity of care predicts the security of babies' attachments to them, although the association is much weaker for fathers and babies than for mothers and babies (Lucassen et al., 2011).

It will not surprise you that how much a father is involved in his infant's care is important. The more involved he is, the more his own sensitivity seems to affect the quality of the infant's attachment to him (Brown, Mangelsdorf, & Neff, 2012). Some researchers have speculated that mothers' sensitivity has a stronger effect than fathers' on infants' attachment simply because mothers typically spend substantially more time caring for infants than fathers do (Hallers-Haalboom et al., 2017).

Overall, there appear to be multiple processes at work. If mother is the primary caregiver, the infant's attachment to the mother may serve as a working model, influencing the infant's reaction to the father, which may in turn influence how the father

MyLab Education
Video Example 4.5
Both fathers and mothers help to foster infants' coping strategies and emotion regulation skills and develop strong attachment relationships with their children. Notice how Madison's father adjusts his behavior in developmentally appropriate ways in response to Madison's needs.

MyLab Education
Video Example 4.6
Infants in nonmaternal care situations can develop secure attachments to caregivers who are responsive. In high-quality centers with a low infant–caregiver ratio, such as the one shown here, caregivers can serve as a secure base for many children at once.

Box 4.3: Does Day Care Pose a Risk to Infants?

John Bowlby (e.g., 1973) brought attention to the damage that could be done to young children's relationships if they were separated from attachment figures for long periods of time. For example, when hospitalized children are denied regular access to their mothers, their emotional distress is intense and it progresses through a worrisome series of stages. It begins with typical separation protest such as crying and searching for the lost parent, followed by "despair," which is marked by listlessness, loss of appetite, and reduced emotional vitality. Finally, after many days or weeks, the child seems to become detached, treating the mother with indifference when she visits, or attending only to the "treats" that mother brings (e.g., Fraley & Shaver, 2016).

Extrapolating from the effects of long-term separations, Bowlby also expressed concern about shorter-term separations. He worried about the daily breaks in maternal care that babies experience when their mothers are employed and leave their children with relatives or nonfamilial caregivers. Given that attachment quality is significantly related to sensitive, responsive caregiving, could regular interruptions of that caregiving impede the development of secure attachments? When there is a change in child care arrangements—when beloved nannies or day care teachers leave—does the disruption of the child's attachment to that caregiver also disrupt the child's sense of security? Bowlby felt that although there might not be definitive answers to these questions, the potential risks associated with forming insecure attachments were great enough that parents should be encouraged to avoid regular substitute care for children under age 3.

Research over several decades has examined the issues Bowlby raised, and a sense of the scope and nature of the risks in infant day care has emerged. We begin by summarizing the current status of findings on the relationship between substitute care and infant–mother attachments. Then we examine other long-term effects that researchers either have identified or are currently assessing. Over the last several decades, large longitudinal studies have been conducted in a number of different countries. One study sponsored by the National Institute of Child Health and Human Development (NICHD, 1997, 2006) included more than 1,100 U.S. babies, many of whom have been followed through age 18 (Vandell, Burchinal, & Pierce, 2016). Another included many thousands of Israeli mother–infant pairs in the babies' first few months and continued to follow 758 pairs (Sagi et al., 2002). Other major studies have been done in Canada (e.g., Côté, Borge, Geoffroy, Rutter, & Tremblay, 2008), Australia (Harrison & Ungerer, 2002), Norway (Dearing, Zachrisson, & Nærde, 2015) and several other countries. This report is based on findings from these and many smaller or shorter-term studies (for relevant reviews see Burchinal, Magnuson, Powell, & Hong, 2015; Friedman & Boyle, 2008; Lamb & Ahnert, 2006).

Mother–Infant Attachment

It appears that the majority of infants who experience nonmaternal care on a regular basis still form secure attachments to their mothers; there is little disagreement among studies or their authors on this point. There is, nonetheless, an increase in the risk of insecure attachments for infants in day care as compared to infants in full-time maternal care.

In the NICHD study, day care alone did not create an attachment risk. But there did appear to be a "dual risk" effect. Infants in poorer quality day care or in longer periods of substitute care were more likely to develop insecure attachments to their mothers, but only when these infants were also exposed to low levels of maternal sensitivity and responsiveness. In other words, when mothers were providing insensitive care themselves, infants in day care were even more likely than infants in full-time home care to develop insecure attachments. When mothers were sensitive and responsive to their infants, even low quality substitute care did not interfere with the formation of a secure infant–mother attachment.

However, in other studies, such as the Haifa study of Israeli infants, poor-quality center care *alone* predicted increased mother–infant attachment problems, even when maternal care was sensitive and responsive (Koren-Karie, Sagi-Schwartz, & Egoz-Mizrachi, 2005; Sagi et al., 2002). Researchers who have combined data from multiple studies conclude that the quality of center care has an impact on mother–infant attachment independent of the sensitivity of mothers' care or of the amount of time infants spend in care (Ahnert, Pinquart, & Lamb, 2006; Love et al., 2003).

The best supported inference overall is that mothers and babies can, and usually do, form secure attachments, even if mothers work outside the home during the first year, as long as the mother provides her infant with quality care when she is with the baby *and* as long as the substitute care is also of high quality. Substitute care becomes a significant risk to mother–infant attachment when the quality of alternative care arrangements is not adequate. The dual risk of insensitive maternal care combined with less than high-quality substitute care is particularly problematic.

Fortunately, employed mothers are about as likely as unemployed mothers to be attentive to their babies and to provide sensitive care, despite the stresses of balancing family responsibilities and work. In the NICHD study, mothers of infants who were in child care 30 hours a week interacted with their infants only 12 hours less per week than mothers whose infants spent no time in child care (Booth, Clarke-Stewart, Vandell, McCartney, & Owen, 2002). Also, the quality of maternal care in these two groups of mothers did not differ. Some research even indicates that employed mothers might be more positive in their caregiving (e.g., see Augustine, 2014). However, at least one study suggests that very early return to work (before the baby is 12 weeks old) might put a mother at risk of being a less sensitive caregiver than she might otherwise have been (Clark, Hyde, Essex, & Klein, 1997). Mothers who returned to work at 6 weeks postpartum were less sensitive to their 4-month-old babies than mothers who returned to work at 12 weeks, especially if the mothers were exposed to other risk factors, such as depressive symptoms or a baby with a difficult temperament. Very early return to work may make it more difficult for a mother to learn to read her baby's cues (Brazelton, 1986). It may also be harder to feel effective and competent as a caregiver when a mother begins work in her infant's first weeks because the baby has not yet become very socially responsive. Sensitive caregiving appears to be easier when mothers feel competent (Teti & Gelfand, 1991).

One of the outcomes of child care is that infants can form attachments to substitute caregivers. As you have seen, a secure attachment to a caregiver other than the mother can be a protective factor for an infant, but an insecure attachment can be a risk factor, diminishing to some extent the benefits of other secure attachments. As you might expect, the greater a nonmaternal caregiver's sensitivity, the more likely babies are to become securely attached. For infants, the specific care that the individual child experiences seems to be the key. General quality indicators, such as infant–caregiver ratio, may be cues to the likelihood of sensitive caregiving, but the child's individual experience is most important (Ahnert, Pinquart, & Lamb, 2006; Fearon & Belsky, 2016).

On the whole, mothers' use of substitute caregivers does not put the mother–infant attachment relationship in jeopardy. But clearly, parents are well advised to proceed cautiously in making decisions about alternative care arrangements for their infants. Substitute care is a risk when it combines with poor maternal care, and other risk factors, such as poor-quality day care, make the danger greater.

Longer Term Effects of Early Substitute Care

Parents should also recognize that attachment risk is not the only issue of concern for infants in alternative care arrangements. Development of social and cognitive skills is also related to the quality, quantity, and timing of substitute care. Recent analyses of the NICHD data indicate, for example, that although quality of maternal caregiving in the infancy period is a stronger predictor of children's later cognitive competence than measures of substitute care, amount and kind of substitute care still matter. If mothers were employed full time (30 hours per week or more) by the time their babies were 9 months old, their children were not scoring as well on general cognitive tests at 3 years old as children whose mothers returned to the workforce later or for fewer hours per week.

The quality of child care moderates cognitive effects. In the NICHD study, the more sensitive the mother was, the better the home care environment, and the better the alternative care environment, the less likely it was that early maternal employment would have negative effects on children's cognitive functioning (Brooks-Gunn, Han, & Waldfogel, 2002). By the end of high school, adolescents' academic performance was still related to the quality of their early child care experience, with poorer quality and more hours in care predicting poorer performance (Vandell, Burchinal, & Pierce, 2016).

Family income also moderates these cognitive effects. For children in the NICHD study who were living in poverty, infant child care was associated with significantly *better* cognitive and language outcomes by age 3 than full-time maternal care (McCartney, Dearing, Taylor, & Bub, 2007). (Note that for preschoolers, ages 3 to 5, quality child care and preschool experiences are generally beneficial to cognitive development and later academic performance regardless of the family's socioeconomic status; see Box 3.2 in Chapter 3.)

The NICHD study also found that the more time young children spend in nonmaternal care, especially center-based care, the more aggressive and oppositional they tend to be by kindergarten age, although the effects are small (e.g., Huston, Bobbitt, & Bentley, 2015). *Both the quantity and the quality of child care moderated these results*: They were most likely to occur with low quality substitute care and when children spent a great deal of time in large groups of peers. (Not all studies have found such effects, but when they have, quantity of care often appears to play a role; see Dearing & Zachrisson, 2017.) *Infant temperament also mattered*. Children were differentially susceptible based on the quality of child care (Pluess & Belsky, 2009). Children with more difficult temperaments (higher negative emotionality) were more likely than other children to show increased behavior problems over time when day care quality was low; but they had fewer behavior problems than other children when day care quality was high. More time in care tended to have negative effects regardless of infant temperament.

Whether infant nonmaternal care increases the likelihood of later behavior problems also depends on family risk factors (Côté et al., 2008). In a large Canadian study, infant day care was associated with fewer externalizing and internalizing problems and more social competence for children who came from high-risk families. Children from low-risk families showed the opposite pattern, although the effects of early nonmaternal care were small. Higher risk families were characterized by one or more of the following factors: poverty, poor education, high stress, conflict, single parenthood, young and inexperienced mothers, or parental psychopathology.

One of the most troubling effects of early substitute care concerns its apparent impact on stress regulation mechanisms. Gunnar and colleagues have found that many children in center-based or family day care show increases in stress levels in the course of a day as indicated by elevations in cortisol (a hormone produced in response to stress; see Chapter 2), especially if they have difficult or fearful temperaments (see Phillips, Fox, & Gunnar, 2011; Gunnar, 2017). What is striking is that when the same children have been tested at home with their families, their cortisol levels typically declined gradually over the course of a day. This is the normal diurnal pattern for individuals not exposed to acute stress. Cortisol increases in the child care setting have been found in about 35% of infants studied and in about 70% to 80% of older preschoolers. Toddlers (about 1 to 3 years), especially younger toddlers, show the steepest rise, suggesting that child care may be especially stressful for this age group (e.g., Ahnert, Gunnar, Lamb, & Barthel, 2004). It is worth noting that school age children, 5 and older, do not typically show these altered cortisol patterns on school days (Gunnar, 2017).

Children's experience of stress in child care programs is linked, not surprisingly, to the quality of the program. In one study of family-based child care, for example, stress-related increases in cortisol were unlikely if preschoolers were in high-quality

(continued)

programs where caregivers gave them focused attention and stimulation (Dettling, Parker, Lane, Sebanc, & Gunnar, 2000). In another study, young children's cortisol levels tended to rise during the day if they had teachers who were intrusive and over-controlling but not if their teachers were highly supportive (Gunnar, Kryzer, van Ryzin, & Phillips, 2010). And for children who had fearful, inhibited temperaments, cortisol rises at one test time were associated with increased internalizing problems and more anxious, vigilant behavior 6 months later, whereas for other children there was no increased risk of these kinds of problems (Gunnar, Kryzer, van Ryzin, & Phillips, 2011). Preschoolers who form secure attachments to their teachers are not as likely to show rising cortisol levels during a child care day, and secure attachments with mothers also appear to have a protective effect (Badanes, Dmitrieva, & Watamura, 2012), although not for toddlers (Ahnert et al., 2004).

Researchers speculate that child care environments challenge toddlers to manage peer relations when they are just beginning to develop skills for doing so. This challenge may be particularly stressful for children with fearful, inhibited temperaments. For children in high-quality child care, teachers may help children manage this stress and advance their skills, but in lesser quality care situations, temperamentally vulnerable and/or insecure children may flounder (Phillips et al., 2011).

One consequence of elevated stress levels during day care may be a reduced immune response. Watamura and her colleagues examined levels of immunoglobin A, an antibody that is present in saliva, as an indicator of children's immune functioning (Watamura, Coe, Laudenslager, & Robertson, 2010). They found that preschoolers whose cortisol rose during weekdays at day care had lower antibody levels at home on the weekends, and their parents reported more frequent child illness, especially upper respiratory symptoms, than children in day care who did not show the daily cortisol rise. Generally, children in day care do experience more infectious illnesses than those in full time maternal care, probably because of greater exposure to disease organisms. However, in the Watamura study, children whose stress levels were affected by day care were even more likely than other children in care to get sick.

Cortisol levels were not assessed in the early years of the NICHD study, but they were measured when the study participants reached 15 years old (Roisman et al., 2009). Both maternal insensitivity in infancy and longer hours in child care during the first 3 years were associated with atypical daily cortisol levels at age 15. Specifically, individuals with one or both of these risk factors in their histories showed lower awakening cortisol levels than average. The effects were quite small, but they do suggest that quality of early care, whether maternal or substitute, can have enduring effects on the stress reactivity of the individual.

It is obviously critical for parents to understand what constitutes quality in substitute care and to be able to weigh the risks and benefits of different care arrangements for specific children. In the Applications section of this chapter, we discuss considerations for helping parents make good infant care decisions.

cares for the infant. But the father's own caregiving proclivities are important as well, also affecting the quality of the infant's attachment to him.

What is clear is that infants become attached to their fathers. When babies are stressed they engage in the same kinds of attachment behaviors with their fathers as they do with their mothers. Whether they are stressed by fatigue or hunger or by some perceived threat such as a stranger approaching, they seek comfort and security from whichever parent is present. When both parents are present, infants are somewhat more likely to turn to the primary caregiver, who is usually the mother (Lamb & Lewis, 2011).

Cultural Influences on Infant Attachment

The broader culture is also a factor in understanding how attachment relationships evolve. Across cultures, the majority of infants studied have been categorized as securely attached to their mothers (Mesman, van IJzendoorn, & Sagi-Schwartz, 2016). In the strange situation test, they use their mothers as a secure base for exploration and they become distressed when separated from her, but they are comforted and return to exploration when she returns. In some studies the distribution of attachment patterns varies from one country to another. For example, infants in China (Archer et al., 2015), Korea (Jin, Jacobvitz, Hazen, & Jung, 2012), and Israel (Sagi et al., 2002) are less likely to form avoidant attachments and more likely to form ambivalent attachments than infants in the United States, whereas German infants show a higher rate of avoidant attachments (e.g., Grossmann, Grossmann, Huber, & Wartner, 1981). These differences may partly reflect how stressful the strange situation test is for infants with differing amounts of separation experience. The test was designed to be moderately stressful, and it appears to be that way for most infants in the United States. For Chinese or Korean infants, who are rarely parted from their mothers, it may be extremely stressful, whereas for many German infants who are strongly encouraged to be independent, it may not be stressful enough.

Some theorists argue that attachment theory describes only the development of relationship quality in Western cultures (e.g., Lancy, 2015; Weisner, 2015). They say that in many non-Western, rural, or isolated cultural communities, caregivers may be responsive only to their infants' distress cues, they show few obvious signs of warmth (smiling and talking enthusiastically with infants) or gentle handling, and they rarely engage in face-to-face interactions. But Mesman and colleagues (2017) point out that responsiveness to distress is the centerpiece of sensitive caregiving (e.g., Ainsworth et al., 1978). They also demonstrate that in cross-cultural research, knowing what to look for in assessing responsiveness is critical. For example, many cultures take a community approach to infant care. Mothers, fathers, aunts, grandparents, older siblings, and others may all be involved. It can look as though the mother is not particularly responsive, but in these communities, whoever happens to be nearest typically responds quickly and appropriately. Caregiver responses may also be of a different sort from the types typically shown by Western mothers. Consider the following example from an isolated forager community in the Philippines:

> An infant is sitting on her aunt's lap and next to her mother. The infant turns her head (apparently to look at some children who are passing by). Aunt, without speaking or looking at the infant, moves the infant's position so that she is now facing the children. The infant stretches her hand towards the children walking past. The aunt looks at the infant, waves her arm and says 'bye bye' in the direction of the children. Infant turns her head to face her aunt. Aunt changes her hold of the infant so that she is now facing her. Infant moves head to look at the children again. Aunt changes her hold of the infant so that she is now facing the children again. (Mesman et al., 2017, p. 7)

And so on. In the course of a 10-minute observation, the infant was handed back and forth between aunt and mother many times, each time following closely the infant's signals as she looked or reached to one or the other caregiver. "[T]hey were sensitively responsive but without showing the typical Western pattern of responding to infants that is far more extraverted and verbal" (p. 7).

Overall, the relationship between caregiver sensitivity and attachment security has been replicated across cultures in most studies (e.g., Broesch, Rochat, Olah, Broesch, & Henrich, 2016). Not only do the specifics of what constitutes sensitive care vary from culture to culture as you have just seen, but the ways in which maternal insensitivity is expressed can also differ across cultures.

Consider the Korean concept of *maternal dew*, a belief that mothers have an invisible, powerful bond with their infants, a kind of oneness that even confers "special healing powers" (Jin et al., 2012, p. 35). For example, a mother's touch to her infant's belly is expected to help stomachaches go away. Mothers keep their babies close and their attention is constantly on the baby. Sensitive caregiving seems very likely in this context, but when problems arise Korean mothers may be ". . . likely to err on the side of showing enmeshed over-involvement . . . ," demonstrating the intrusive behavior that is associated with ambivalent attachment (Jin et al., 2012, p. 36). What seems unlikely is that mothers will be rejecting and distancing, behavior that is associated with infants' avoidant attachment.

It appears from the available research that the tenets of attachment theory apply universally. Yet differences in cultural context contribute in meaningful ways to the kinds of attachments that are likely to develop. If different degrees of dependency are valued (or devalued) in different ways in different cultures, perhaps the working models of self and other spawned by attachment relationships have different meanings and consequences in different cultures as well. For example, an ambivalent attachment pattern in Korea may be more adaptive and have more positive impact on a child's future development than it would in North America.

The Importance of Early Attachments

Secure early attachments are said to pave the way for later psychosocial developments. Erikson and Bowlby portrayed the trusting, secure infant as one who is fortified with positive attitudes toward self and others. He enters new relationships with an expectation that his needs will be respected and with a willingness to respect the needs of others. His security helps him face new challenges; he trusts in the future.

Yet, neither Erikson nor Bowlby saw the positive outlook of the secure child as immutable. Whereas secure children play a role in making their positive expectations come true by their choice of partners and through their own responses to others (Sroufe, Egeland, Carlson, & Collins, 2005), they are not all powerful. If later experiences, especially with caregivers, violate their expectations, their burgeoning ideas about self and others can be modified, incorporating more negative expectations. In sum, early attachment is said to launch processes that can have long-term consequences, but the quality of care that the child continues to receive can either strengthen or redirect those processes (Thompson, 2016).

Does early attachment quality predict later psychosocial functioning? In a classic study, Sroufe and his colleagues followed a large sample of Minneapolis children longitudinally, beginning with two assessments of infant–mother attachment status in the strange situation at 12 and 18 months (Vaughn, Egeland, Sroufe, & Waters, 1979; Sroufe et al., 2005). Even though attachment security was usually stable after 12 months, it did change for about one third of the dyads. Most of the change was from insecure to secure, as inexperienced mothers gained confidence and skill. Mothers whose babies shifted from secure to insecure were more likely than other mothers to report significant increases in their life stresses during the intervening 6 months. Apparently, the attachment relationship can be vulnerable to events that may distract, depress, or preoccupy the mother or otherwise upset family life (see also Belsky & Fearon, 2002).

Children whose attachment status was stable from the first to the second assessment were later evaluated on a variety of interpersonal and cognitive dimensions, and differences were found between the insecurely and securely attached children on many measures. For example, when the children were 4 years old, 40 of them participated in a summer nursery school program at the University of Minnesota (Sroufe, Fox, & Pancake, 1983). Teachers who knew nothing about the earlier attachment ratings ranked the children each day on characteristics related to autonomy, such as attention seeking, extreme reliance on the teacher, involvement with teachers at the expense of peers, and so on. The children who had been securely attached as toddlers were more often viewed by teachers as direct and appropriate in their dependency behaviors, seeking help when they realistically needed it but functioning independently in other situations. Insecurely attached children were more likely to act helpless, to act out for attention, or in some cases to passively avoid seeking help when they genuinely needed it.

In assessments at later ages, the children in the Minneapolis project showed other continuities as well. In a summer camp at age 10, for example, securely attached children tended to be more self-confident, to have more friends, to have better social skills, and so on (Sroufe et al., 2005). By age 16, securely attached children were more likely to trust a best friend, and by age 20 to 21, they were better able to resolve conflicts with a romantic partner (Simpson, Collins, & Salvatore, 2011). Many longitudinal studies, though not all, have found similar continuities. As one research team put it ". . . infant insecurity appears to amplify detrimental cascades, whereas infant security appears to defuse such risks" (Boldt, Kochanska, & Jonas, 2017, p. 584; see also Groh et al., 2017; Madigan, Brumariu, Vallani, Atkinson, & Lyons-Ruth, 2016).

If infant–mother attachments predict later developments, what about infant–father attachments? When infants are securely attached to both parents they seem to have the best outcomes. If they are securely attached to one parent, but not the other, their outcomes are as good or nearly so as if they were securely attached to both. Children are most likely to develop behavior problems (either internalizing or externalizing) if they are "double-insecure"—insecurely attached to both parents (Kochanska & Kim, 2013). Thus, for a child with an insecure attachment to one parent, a secure attachment relationship with a second parent is a protective factor.

Several investigators have also suggested that because fathers and mothers tend to interact differently with their infants, the attachment relationship with each parent may affect different aspects of the child's psychosocial development. For example, in North American families, mothers spend more time with infants in quiet, ritualized routines such as peekaboo games, where synchrony of eye contact, vocalizations, and facial expressions are key factors. Fathers tend to engage in more energetic, stimulating games (such as whirling the baby through the air). They are more unpredictable and exciting (MacDonald & Parke, 1986; Pecheux & Labrell, 1994). Of course, mothers and fathers also often interact with their infants in similar ways, especially when fathers are highly involved in routine infant care. Whether infant attachments to mothers versus fathers affect different aspects of later social functioning is yet to be determined. It is important to note, however, that such differences in parental effects may be highly dependent on culture. Although North American fathers spend substantial proportions of their time with infants in active play, fathers in many other cultures do not. In some cultures (e.g., in Sweden and in Israeli kibbutz families), there is little difference between fathers' and mothers' interactions with infants (see Parke, 2002).

Overall, there is little doubt that infant attachments are predictive of some later behaviors. But does the early attachment actually have long-term effects, or could more recent and current caregiving environments be responsible for the apparent continuities? In the Minneapolis study, for example, some children who had been securely attached as infants were having behavior problems by age 4. The quality of parenting during the preschool period helped account for this change. Mothers of these children were less supportive when engaging their children in educational tasks at age 3. They provided less encouragement and were less effective teachers than mothers whose children did not develop later behavior problems. Also, children who had been insecurely attached as infants but who were well adjusted at 4 years tended to have mothers who were supportive and effective in their interactions with their preschoolers (Erickson, Sroufe, & Egeland, 1985). It seems that the role of early attachments in later development can be diminished when parental acceptance, support, and responsiveness changes substantially, either rising to the challenges of the child's new developmental stage or failing to do so. Other longitudinal studies have found quite similar patterns (e.g., Beijersbergen, Juffer, Bakers-Kranenberg, & van IJzendoorn, 2012). The importance of ongoing quality parenting for children's socioemotional development will be taken up again in Chapter 5.

What, then, is the value of getting a "good start" with a secure infant attachment? First, a primary influence of infant attachments is their tendency to perpetuate themselves. Once a relationship pattern between parent and child is established, it tends to be repeated. When it is, the older child's behavior is consistent with predictions from the early attachment. As Erikson and Bowlby proposed, in his first relationships a baby may form an incipient "working model" of what to expect from interactions. That model affects his expectations about and his physiological and behavioral reactions to social experiences in the future. But the model is in progress and will be reworked in the context of new interactions. Some findings suggest, however, that even if experiences after infancy modify a child's attachment pattern and working model, there may be lasting sequelae of the original pattern (Thompson, 2016).

Working Models of Attachment

As we have just seen, infant attachments appear to influence the internal working model of relationships that children begin to construct. Researchers studying adult romantic relationships describe the concept of the internal working model of attachment as providing a template for adult social relationships. Investigators now study the nature and development of these models, or representations. We will examine some of this work in later chapters, as we discuss the development of self-concept and relationship capacity beyond the infancy period, but one aspect of this research bears directly on the formation of infant attachments, and we will touch on this work here.

Main and her colleagues (Main et al., 1985) evaluated mothers' and fathers' own models of attachment using a structured interview procedure called the **Adult Attachment Interview (AAI)** (see Chapter 12 for a full discussion; Hesse, 2008). Parents described their memories of the parenting they had received and their beliefs about whether that parenting influenced their own personalities. The "security" of their attachment representations (categorized using a procedure devised by Main & Goldwyn, 1985–1994) was related to the quality of attachment these parents had established with their own infants.

"Secure-autonomous" parents valued relationships and believed that their own personalities had been influenced by them. They could talk openly and objectively about their early experiences, good or bad. Their ideas were coherent and showed signs of previous reflection. Not all of these adults recalled their early experiences as positive; some had even been abused. But by whatever means, these adults had apparently come to terms with their early experiences and had faith in the power of relationships. These parents tended to have secure attachments with their own infants.

"Insecure" parents showed several patterns. In one, attachment relationships were not readily recalled, not valued, and not seen as influential. Infants tended to have avoidant attachments with parents who showed this "dismissive" pattern. Another group of parents ("preoccupied-entangled") were preoccupied with their own parents, often still struggling to please, and they seemed confused, angry, or especially passive. Their infants' attachments to them were typically ambivalent. Finally, an "unresolved-disorganized" pattern characterized parents who made irrational and inconsistent comments, especially when discussing traumatic experiences. For example, they might talk about a dead parent as if he were alive. Infants whose parents showed this pattern tended to be disorganized-disoriented in the strange situation test.

A substantial correspondence between parents' and infants' attachment classifications has been found in many other studies as well (see Verhage et al., 2016, 2017). This correspondence could be affected by many factors, including similarities in temperament between parent and infant. But the match in parent–infant security measures may indicate that parents' working models of attachment can influence their infant caregiving, thereby affecting their babies' attachment security. Substantial evidence supports this suggestion. Verhage and her colleagues analyzed data from a large number of studies, all of which had measures of parents' attachment style, the sensitivity of their caregiving, and their infants' attachment security. Secure-autonomous parents were more likely to respond sensitively to their infants than parents with insecure patterns.

Parenting Practices Versus Relationship Quality in Infant Development

It should be clear from this overview of theory and research on infant attachments that focusing attention on relationship quality in infant–caregiver interactions has proven to be a highly productive enterprise. As Mary Ainsworth noted in her earliest observations of mother–infant dyads, the specifics of parenting practices may not be very important in the long run. For example, breastfeeding versus bottle-feeding does not seem to be critical for later emotional adjustment. Rather, it is the relationship context within which such practices occur that is significant. Some parenting practices may be more conducive to, or consistent with, responsive caregiving. Breastfeeding, for example, requires that a mother hold her baby close during feeding, providing the "contact comfort" infants find soothing. When babies are bottle-fed, they can be held and soothed just as effectively, but it is also possible to "prop" a bottle or to hold a baby away from the caregiver's body when feeding, thus failing to provide contact comfort. So, both breast- and bottle-feeding can be practiced in a way that provides close, comforting interactions, but breastfeeding is more conducive to such interactions. In addition, breastfeeding affects the mother's production of hormones related to caregiving (Jansen, de Weerth, & Riksen-Walraven, 2011). For example, a baby's sucking stimulates the release of oxytocin in the mother, supporting milk production. As we have seen, increased levels of oxytocin tend to increase infant caregiving and its rewarding effects for the caregiver. Breastfeeding mother–infant pairs tend to show physiological signs of being more relaxed overall than non-breastfeeding pairs (Quigley, Moore, Propper, Goldman, & Cox, 2017). A large study of maternal breastfeeding and attachment found that mothers were likely to be more sensitive in their caregiving at 3 months postpartum if they breastfed their infants, suggesting that there is some likelihood that breastfeeding mothers will be more sensitive caregivers. But infants' attachment was not correlated with breastfeeding specifically; only the mother's sensitivity mattered (Britton, Britton, & Gronwaldt, 2006). That's good news for fathers, adoptive parents, and other non-breastfeeding caregivers.

You should note that although both breastfeeding and bottle-feeding can be done sensitively and responsively, breastfeeding has substantial advantages for healthy physical and cognitive development that bottle-feeding does not (American Academy of Pediatrics, 2012). In comparison to baby formulas, breast milk is more digestible and more adequately balanced for infant nutrition. It contains antibodies that the mother carries, and it is sterile, a particularly important benefit in countries where water may contain disease organisms. Breast milk even carries growth hormones and other substances that may affect long-term development. The World Health Organization recommends exclusive breastfeeding for the first 6 months and breastfeeding with solid food supplements through the second year.

Ainsworth's observations of a Ugandan baby and his mother (as described in Karen, 1998) help illustrate that feeding by breast is not the critical factor in the formation of secure attachments. Muhamidi's mother kept him close most of the time, as is the custom in Ugandan families. She slept with him and breastfed him on demand. Yet by 8 months, Muhamidi seemed insecure. Not yet having invented the strange situation test, Ainsworth depended on a variety of observations to make this classification, most notably that over time he seemed to lose his vitality, to become sadder and duller. Unlike other babies whose mothers used similar infant care practices, he did not tolerate his mother's absence even when left with an older sibling. Muhamidi's mother seemed anxious and overtaxed by the demands of her large family, and Ainsworth observed that despite her nearly constant availability, the mother's caregiving responses were somewhat brusque and did not necessarily match Muhamidi's needs. For example, on one visit, she responded to Muhamidi's crying by putting him "immediately to breast, without stopping to wipe his nose, which was streaming, or to wipe his face, which was muddy" (Ainsworth, 1967, p. 144).

A student of social and personality development in the mid-1900s would probably have read extensive discussions about the relative importance of particular child-rearing practices such as breastfeeding versus bottle-feeding. The current trend, spawned by attachment theory, is to emphasize the overall quality of infant–caregiver relationships instead. This approach seems to be bringing us much closer to an understanding of the role of infancy in later socioemotional development.

MyLab Education Self-Check 4.2

Attachment in Context

4.3 **Identify risk factors (including exposure to adversity, abuse, or trauma) in the overlapping contexts of an infant's life that threaten attachment security and produce long-term negative effects on emotional functioning.**

The attachments that develop between infants and their caregivers are embedded in a system of overlapping contexts: the parents' relationship, sibling interactions, extended family processes, parents' work, extra-familial child care, the neighborhood, and the larger community. All of these contexts can affect infants' emotional well-being and their attachment security. Sometimes contextual influences are *indirect*, and their effects are filtered through parents' caregiving. For example, a father is not as likely to be a responsive caregiver, and therefore is less likely to foster a secure attachment with his infant, if he and his wife are often in conflict (whereas a mother's care is less affected by marital disharmony) (Lamb & Lewis, 2004). But factors beyond caregiving can also have *direct* effects on infant emotional functioning. When the parents' marriage is characterized by lots of arguing, infants have more negative emotional reactions to novelty and can be less well-regulated emotionally. The quality of parent caregiving is also an influence but it may not eliminate the effects that witnessing conflict can have on an infant (e.g., Crockenberg, Leerkes, & Lekka, 2007). One problem may be that even parents who provide sensitive caregiving in ordinary circumstances can be less able to comfort their infants during frightening periods of parental conflict. The parents are then unreliable, inconsistent caregivers from a baby's perspective (Gustafsson, Brown, Mills-Koonce, & Cox, 2017; Zhou, Cao, & Leerkes, 2017).

Unfortunately, infants and children under age 5 are more likely than any other age group to be exposed to negative experiences that can reduce their emotional well-being and feelings of security (Lieberman, Chu, Van Horn, & Harris, 2011). These experiences include traumatizing events such as maltreatment, accidents, marital conflict, and family violence. Poor and minority children are especially likely to have such experiences, along with exposure to community violence and many types of deprivation, such as homelessness (Herbers, Cutuli, Supkoff, Narayan, & Masten, 2014). Many studies document the problematic effects of childhood adversity on long-term physical and mental health, even when a child's circumstances improve after the early years, as you saw in Chapter 2. These effects appear to be a function of cumulative risk: The more risk factors (e.g., adverse events) to which infants and young children are exposed, the more likely they will experience negative health and behavioral consequences into adulthood. Child maltreatment is discussed in more detail in the Applications section.

Infants' attachment security is one of the most important protective factors for moderating the long-term impact of adversity. Infants who are securely attached have more capacity to regulate their stress reactions than those who are insecurely attached (Gunnar, 2017). They are also less likely to suffer long-term negative physical and behavioral health problems (Erlich, Miller, Jones, & Cassidy, 2016). For example, one study focused on adults who had experienced poor socioeconomic environments early in life. If they had warm early relationships with their mothers, they were less likely than those who did not have the benefit of such relationships to suffer from the chronic inflammatory processes that typically plague adults from similar early life environments (Chen, Miller, Kobor, & Cole, 2011).

As we noted earlier, infants' attachment status can be affected by exposure to contextual adversity in both direct and indirect ways. Here again, the balance of risk and protective factors is important. Infants from poor families and/or who have been victims of trauma are more likely to develop insecure attachments than infants in better circumstances. One reason is that many adverse events (e.g., family violence, inadequate material resources) simultaneously affect both infants and their parents, making it likely that infants are more difficult to manage and comfort at the same time that parents are themselves stressed and depleted of emotional energy. Sensitive and responsive caregiving that would foster secure attachments often seem to be a casualty of this mixture.

Some adverse events, such as violence against the mother, seem to be especially traumatizing and disorganizing for infants and much more difficult to redress with quality caregiving. The long-term behavioral and emotional consequences seem to be more severe than for most other traumatic experiences (Scheeringa, Wright, Hunt, & Zeanah, 2006). Yet, even under these highly stressful circumstances, early sensitive caregiving from mothers can be a buffer. In one large-scale study of low-income families, mothers reported on the levels of partner violence in their homes. Mothers' caregiving was observed at 7 months, and infants' emotional reactivity (cortisol levels) in frustrating or frightening tasks was measured at three ages (Hibel, Granger, Blair, Cox, & The Family Life Project Key Investigators, 2011). Infants from violent homes showed much higher emotional reactivity than other infants, and their reactivity showed increases with age instead of the usual declines with age. Yet if mothers in violent homes were able to remain highly sensitive in their early caregiving, their babies were less likely to show this increased reactivity.

Perhaps the most problematic traumatic experiences for young children are perpetrated by caregivers who abuse the children who are counting on them to be their safe havens. As we have already seen, infants are highly likely to form insecure attachments with abusing parents, especially disorganized attachments. Indeed, across many laboratories, 80% to 90% of abused infants have been found to form disorganized attachments (see Cyr, Euser, Bakersmans-Kranenburg, & van IJzendoorn, 2010). Neither the child's temperamental characteristics nor the genetic markers that sometimes accompany them appear to have much influence when caregiving is so completely untrustworthy (Cicchetti, Rogosch, & Toth, 2011). Why do some parents abrogate the most fundamental of their parenting obligations in such ways?

Most often, abusing parents are themselves the victims of adversity and a variety of mental health problems. Many abusive parents are repeating with their children the patterns of trauma, rejection, and maltreatment that shaped their own lives. This is the phenomenon of intergenerational transmission: When maltreated children become maltreating parents, they pass on their insecure attachment status. When parents' own early attachments are disorganized, they often seem unable to ". . . access, process, and resolve painful affect associated with past experience" (Lieberman et al., 2011, p. 401). Thus, they tend to experience high levels of dissociation, that is, a detachment from their own emotional reality. Attachment theorists have argued that victims of unresolved childhood trauma may have particular difficulty helping their infants regulate their emotions, ". . . because they curtail their conscious attention to the child's signals of need in an effort to protect themselves from re-experiencing their early trauma" (Lieberman et al., 2011, p. 401). One mother who suffered early sexual abuse, and who was participating in a therapeutic intervention so that she could avoid hurting her own child, describes her struggle against this dissociative tendency: "I couldn't identify my own emotions, much less help him identify his . . . I was definitely needing to help myself grow up in a sense and learn about myself while trying to do that for my child . . ." (Wright, Fopma-Loy, & Oberle, 2012, p. 545). A second mother in the same intervention described how difficult it was for her to empathize with her child's pain: "Or, if they get hurt somewhere, I'll go outside to see how she is but I think it's just, it's like an act for me . . . It feels like I'm standing back and watching them . . ." (Wright et al., 2012, p. 544).

Adults whose caregiving history is marked by neglect and abuse may also have had little direct experience with effective parenting, so that they have not learned strategies for managing children's emotions or behavior from competent models. The second mother quoted above provided a poignant description of her ignorance of parenting strategies: "When my daughter first went to preschool, her very first day I took her into preschool and I just left her. I didn't know . . . you kiss them and say have a good day—I didn't know you did that stuff" (Wright et al., 2012, p. 544).

Not all parents with a history of abuse go on to abuse their offspring, and not all abusive parents have a history of being abused themselves. Clearly, there are multiple interacting processes at work. Not surprisingly, many contextual factors matter. It is worth reiterating that the more contextual risk factors and the fewer protective factors there are, the more likely there will be a problematic outcome such as infant/child maltreatment. Parents, like children, are more likely to behave in dysfunctional ways the more adversity accumulates: poverty with its deprivations and displacements, violence in the home and community, minority status, and so on (see Feeney & Woodhouse, 2016). Relationship variables are important contextual factors as well. For example, intergenerational transmission is more likely if mothers feel socially isolated, that is, if they do not feel they have other adults they can turn to for support (Berlin, Appleyard, & Dodge, 2011). Intergenerational transmission is also more likely for mothers with strong dissociative tendencies. But many mothers who suffered abuse themselves do not have such tendencies (e.g., Egeland, Bosquet, & Chung, 2002). When they do not, they often have had experiences of quality caregiving after infancy and/or in the context of adult relationships. A good marital relationship, for example, can modify an adult's attachment status and help him or her to integrate early negative experiences into a coherent self view (see Chapter 12).

Applications

No one has demonstrated that relatively infrequent incidents of caretaker unavailability will harm a child for life, nor are chronic interactive failures the single pathway to developmental disturbances. However, it would be incorrect to assume that early interactive patterns have no influence at all on later emotional and social development. As Tronick (1989) observed:

> The pathways leading to the varieties of normalcy and psychopathology derive from the divergent experiences infants have with success, reparation of failure, and the transformation of negative emotions to positive emotions. Typically, there is no single traumatic juncture or special moment separating these pathways, only the slowly accumulating interactive and affective experiences with different people and events in different contexts that shape the regulatory processes and representations of the infant over time. (p. 117)

If we conceptualize the infant as constructing a framework for interacting with the world, using both the tools provided by nature and the materials available in daily experience, it is difficult to imagine that this early experience-dependent affective learning would not be important for brain development, emotion regulation, and social relationships. Social attachments are rarely the result of only one early relationship. Although mothers are most often primary caretakers, fathers, siblings, grandparents, and others are significant influences. While future outcomes involve co-occurring experiences with multiple people in the baby's social world, research suggests that the infant's primary caregiver does appear to have a particularly important role to play in shaping subsequent development.

Infant Mental Health

Because the primary caregiver's behavior and mental representations are so important to attachment quality, how can we help parents with troubled attachment histories do better for their own children? What can be done for less troubled but stressed-out families to support security of attachment? Researchers and practitioners in the field of infant mental health (Zeanah & Zeanah, 2001) hold that interventions must take into account the needs of the parent as well as the child because such interventions are more effective than those that focus on the child alone (Letourneau, Tryphonopoulos, Giesbrecht, Dennis, Bhogal, & Watson, 2015). Thus, the parent–child dyad or the family becomes the target of intervention with the goal of repairing or improving a *relationship*, not just one member's behavior. Lieberman and Van Horn (2008) identify several key areas of knowledge that provide a foundation for clinicians' work in infant mental health: developmental psychology and psychopathology, trauma theory, issues of culture and diversity, and reflective practice skills.

Providing parents with basic knowledge about child development is an important contribution. We believe that this knowledge should not just be descriptive of ages and stages, but should also emphasize the needs of infants, particularly in the affective area. Sometimes parents feel that babies will be spoiled if they are picked up and held or that they should be spanked for some perceived misbehavior. Parents may view their babies as "not listening" to them or as disrespectful. Or they may believe that infants need lots of exposure to groups of children to develop good social skills, a developmental goal that is inappropriate at this age.

These misperceptions and flawed attributions are often the basis for insensitive caregiving. Therefore, the mother of an angry 14-month-old who does not want to share his toy can be helped to understand that the child is not selfish but is asserting his will and acting as most normal toddlers do. The mother of a difficult infant might benefit from an understanding of the concept of temperament. With the professional's support, she can be given ways to understand her baby's communication and respond to it sensitively. Her baby's fussiness might signal his feeling overstimulated, or his clinging behavior might mean that he needs more "laptime" from her. Tomlin and Viehweg (2003) suggest that clinicians take a nonjudgmental, coaching approach when "speaking for the baby" (p. 621). The helper might ask, for example, "I wonder why Devon is fussing so much. Do you think she might want to be held for a while?"

Recognizing the baby's bids for attention will be useful only if the parent also recognizes that these needs are normal and, if sufficiently met, will foster emotional security in the long run. These shifts in knowledge and attitude, as well as new skills, can bolster parents' confidence. Active listening skills, well known to helpers, could be used to communicate a nonjudgmental and supportive attitude toward parents. Parents have reasons for the ways they behave toward their children. Sometimes their parenting reflects their own painful history of emotional neglect or abuse. Often they are preoccupied and may not be paying attention due to stress, depression, illness, or overwork.

Teaching parents new skills within a counseling or coaching framework is helpful. However, just "talking about" the way parenting practices should be done may be less effective than actually allowing the parent to engage with the child in session. Interventions that include a treatment manual also show greater effectiveness than non-manualized treatments, presumably due to improved implementation fidelity. Videotaped parent–child interactions allow both parent and clinician the opportunity to discuss observations and recognize opportunities for more sensitive parenting (Juffer, Bakermans-Kranenburg, & van IJzendoorn, 2007). A classic technique developed by Greenspan (Greenspan & Weider, 1999), called "floor time," is a good example. This approach is designed to improve parents' observational skills, to assist them in sharing experiences and meanings with a child, to teach them to communicate in a respectful give and take with the child taking the lead, and to ultimately teach recognition of emotions. Parents literally get down on the floor for approximately 30 minutes and tune into the child's world. The goal is to let the child take the lead rather than allow parents to dominate or turn the session into a "teachable moment." The tasks vary depending upon the age of the child. Parents of infants are helped to recognize their babies' signals and temperamental styles. They are asked to notice, for example, when the baby smiles, what kind of touch the baby likes or dislikes, when the child makes eye contact, and are required to respond fully to his bids for attention. At about 4 months of age, babies show more interest in the outside world. Parents are helped to notice what the baby is attending to, such as a kitten sleeping nearby, and to enjoy the sight together. When maternal interaction is intrusive, teaching mothers to slow down and be silent when the baby is quiet can be a useful way to restore synchrony (Field et al., 2006). Parents of older, more mobile infants, about 8 months and beyond, can learn to join in their child's play or movement while not trying to control the activity. Essentially, the parent is taught to notice the child's intention, to mirror and expand on the child's activity, and to respond to the child's words and gestures.

Helpers can also teach games or routines that practice turn-taking and sharing. Even something as simple as passing a toy back and forth, "Now it's Brandon's turn," teaches the basics of social interaction. Also important are family routines or rituals, such as bedtime and mealtime patterns. Clinicians can help busy parents identify routines that work for them and encourage parents to adopt simple ones. Predictable routines provide security for children and opportunities for parents and children to relate to each other in a calm, attentive, and loving way.

The Day Care Dilemma

Helping professionals may also be called upon to help parents make important decisions about caretaking arrangements for their infants. Even though child care has been the subject of research interest for years, there are questions that await further investigation. Addressing these questions is a pressing concern because so many infants and toddlers in this country are cared for in some form of nonmaternal arrangement. In the NICHD longitudinal studies, 72% of the infants in the sample experienced regular, nonparental child care during their first 12 months. Most of these babies entered day care before they were 4 months old. Many parents have few choices available to them as they struggle to care for families and maintain jobs. The high cost of infant and toddler care, the limited availability of caregiving options in some areas, the pressures of the workplace on dual-career couples, and the poor quality of too many facilities increase the stresses on families with young children. It is impossible to draw easy solutions to this problem. However, researchers in general no longer accept the argument that all nonmaternal child care initiated in the first year of life is completely risk-free.

Because this is a complex area to investigate, research results are often conflicting, and methodologies may not realistically reflect the actual child care arrangements families use. For example, studies often compare part-time with full-time care categorically, despite the wide time variation in nonmaternal care that occurs in real-world families. In addition, most of the available studies have come from the United States (Dearing & Zachrisson, 2017). Additional ecologically valid and more diverse investigations into the questions of age of entry, quantity of time spent in nonparental care, and so on could improve our understanding and allow for more conclusive suggestions for clinicians. With these caveats in mind, some general points may be helpful.

1. *Consider the combination of age of entry and the amount of time spent in day care.* Although there are no absolutes, some studies suggest a dose–response relationship between early (before 4 months), more extensive (full or almost full time), and cumulative (across many years) care that is associated with greater noncompliance, aggression, and neediness at school age (Huston, Bobbit, & Bentley, 2015). These findings should be interpreted with care because other studies have found weaker or even contradictory results (Dearing & Zachrisson, 2017). Perhaps future studies will take a more fine-grained approach to this question in order to provide more definitive information. One such study analyzed convergent evidence from two unrelated samples of 7- to 8-month-olds to identify a maximum threshold of time in care that reliably predicted risk of disorganization (Hazen, Allen, Christopher, Umemura, & Jacobvitz, 2015). Results demonstrated that over 60 hours per week in nonmaternal care independently predicted the risk of disorganized attachment for infants at this age.

2. *Consider the quality of the day care providers.* Infants and toddlers need the experience of felt security that comes from sensitive caregiving. Do the caregivers respond quickly and sensitively to the needs of the children? Are they warm, affectionate, and patient, or do they ignore the children or become easily irritated by their needs? Do they hold the children and provide physical comfort? Are they educated in child development so that their expectations for children are reasonable and age appropriate? Do they tend to remain in the facility or is there rapid staff changeover?

3. *Consider the quality of the center.* Unfortunately, reports indicate that the quality of 85% to 90% of out-of-home child care in the United States is less than high quality (Brauner et al., 2004). Before making decisions about care, parents should consider the stability and child–caregiver ratios in the facility. Is the staff stable or is there a frequent turnover of employees? Stability of caregivers, perhaps even allowing caregivers to remain with a group of babies over several years (Greenspan, 2003), is important for children in the construction of

attachments. Is the caregiver–child ratio small enough to ensure enough attention and promote nurturant interactions? The optimal ratio is *up to* 3 infants to 1 adult (American Academy of Pediatrics, American Public Health Association, and National Resources Center for Health and Safety in Child Care, 2002). Greenspan (2003) suggests only 2 babies per caregiver. In the large-scale Israeli study mentioned earlier, the infant–adult ratio was the major factor in determining security of attachment between infants in center care and those cared for by home-based providers (Sagi et al., 2002).

4. *Consider the uniqueness of the child.* Not every child responds to child care in the same way. Both temperament and gender appear to be related to differential outcomes. Greenspan (2003) notes that children with underreactive or overreactive sensory system thresholds (sensitivity to sounds, touch, movement, etc.) may find the experience of group care more challenging than other children. Overreactive, difficult-to-soothe children may have trouble modulating arousal and regulating emotions in a context that is noisy, possibly crowded, and filled with children whose needs compete with their own. Underreactive children risk becoming more disengaged without adults to scaffold nurturant interactions. The higher risk of insecure attachment due to low quality care is greater for boys than for girls, and increases in internalizing behavior, which sometimes result from long hours in care, have been found more often for boys than for girls (Tout, deHann, Campbell, & Gunnar, 1998; Howes & Olenick, 1986). Out-of-home care insofar as it involves coping with the demands of a group situation can be somewhat stressful for all young children, let alone those with temperamental sensitivities (Watamura et al., 2003).

5. *Consider the family.* Parental sensitivity is of the utmost importance to the baby's well-being. Parent training or counseling, as we have discussed, can benefit the baby by increasing caregiver sensitivity. The NICHD studies stress the importance of the "dual risk" interaction between low quality day care and maternal insensitivity. In some cases, high quality out-of-home care can have a positive impact on children's cognitive and social development, particularly when families are stressed or when caregivers are insensitive. Yet it is also possible that exposure to low quality care on a regular basis may stress infants to the point that they challenge their primary caregivers' capacity for sensitive care, thus giving rise to insecure attachments (Cassidy & Berlin, 1994). Biringen and colleagues report on a program for child care workers that supports their emotional availability. Young children who spend much of their day in care can benefit from enhanced emotional relationships with staff, so this concept has the potential to facilitate secure bonds and to reduce risks (Biringen et al., 2012).

6. *Consider advocating for child care.* Various governmental policies related to taxes, subsidies, welfare, and so on can be shaped to help families better provide for their young children. Employers can offer more flexible schedules and alternative work assignments that allow parents more time to care for children, especially during the critical first year. Professional day care providers should be afforded adequate wages, education, supervision, and respect for the important contribution they make to our children's future.

Preventing Maltreatment

Decades of research on the effects of physical, sexual, and emotional abuse and neglect have delivered an unequivocal message: Child maltreatment is one of the most harmful experiences a child can face. Early maltreatment affects individuals in every socioeconomic, racial, and ethnic group, and the problem is widespread. In 2015, 30.1 per every 1,000 children in the United States were "screened-in" to the child welfare system (i.e., received a report because of the severity of the referral). As you learned, our youngest children, infants under 12 months of age, are most likely to be victimized (24.2 per 1,000). Neglect is the most common form of maltreatment, and parents are the most likely perpetrators (U.S. Department of Health and Human Services, 2017). Clearly, the potential for unimaginable consequences, the death of a child, is the most serious outcome of maltreatment. However, maltreatment also leaves hidden scars that can persist throughout life to rob individuals of health and well-being. In this section, we use the terms *maltreatment*, *trauma*, and *abuse* somewhat interchangeably, although each may have specific legal and scientific connotations in other contexts.

The new field of **developmental traumatology** is dedicated to the study of biological and psychological processes related to trauma experience across the life span. We have learned a great deal about the effects of trauma on the developing brain, and this knowledge contributes to the burgeoning interest in trauma-focused interventions. Other related advances in neurobiology, including **neuro-immunology** or the relationship between the nervous and immune systems, add to our knowledge base. Knowing how exposure to trauma, including early maltreatment, affects physiological and psychological development can equip helpers to make informed clinical choices.

Not very long ago, scientists believed that the nervous system and the immune system didn't communicate extensively with each other. As you learned in Chapter 2, we now know that these systems do, in fact, engage in cross talk largely because immune cells, such as cytokines, can penetrate the blood-brain barrier. Chronic inflammation, which can be a consequence of early harsh treatment, is now seen as a potential causal factor in some types of depression and is implicated in a host of adult disease processes (Baumeister, Akhtar, Ciufolini, Pariante, & Mondelli, 2016). Table 4.4 reviews some of the main neurobiological consequences of early maltreatment.

Generally, trauma-focused interventions for adults include psycho-education about the effects of trauma, skill building

TABLE 4.4 Neurobiological Consequences of Early Maltreatment: Gene, Brain, and Immune System Effects

NEUROBIOLOGICAL CONSEQUENCES OF MALTREATMENT (COMPARED TO NON-MALTREATED GROUPS)	MECHANISMS	POSSIBLE BEHAVIORAL RESULTS
Impaired neuronal development.	Smaller hippocampal volume, impaired attentional and prefrontal networks.	Impairments in cognition, memory, and attention.
Impaired reward circuitry (Anterior cingulate cortex, basal ganglia and ventral striatum).	Reduced responses to reward anticipation and reduced ability to learn from positive experiences.	Relationship to depression and addiction.
Greater amygdala activation.	Insensitive parenting increases threat perception; HPA axis and other physiological systems repeatedly activated; normal period of amygdala-prefrontal cortex connection development is interrupted.	Relationship to various disorders including depression and anxiety; bias toward negative cognitions; preoccupations about safety and perception of threats may alter relationships and impair functioning in many areas.
Chronic HPA and cortisol dysregulation.	Cortisol abnormalities include (1) heightened cortisol with inability to down-regulate; (2) cortisol suppression or blunted cortisol patterns.	Potential damage to brain and other organs; greater perceived stress; higher reactivity for new stress. Although there are inconsistencies in research regarding which kind of maltreatment results in which cortisol pattern, elevated cortisol profiles have been related to affective disorders and blunted profiles to antisocial disorders in general.
Epigenetic modification of glucocorticoid receptors.	Reduced gene expression; fewer glucocorticoid receptors; impairments in cortisol reuptake and reduced ability to "turn-off" stress system.	Hyper-vigilance, anxiety, and depression.
Immune system activation; excessive cell production.	Immune cells programmed to become more reactive and produce higher levels of proinflammatory cytokines.	Imbalance in immune responses; chronic inflammation can result because of insufficient signals from immune system to reduce inflammation; chronic inflammation is related to physical illnesses, anxiety and depression.

SOURCES: Danese & Baldwin, 2017; McCrory, De Brito, & Viding, 2010; Thijssen, Muetzel, Bakermans-Kranenburg, Jaddoe, Tiemeier, Verhulst, White, & Van Ijzendoorn, 2017.

for greater emotion regulation, and cognitive integration of the trauma (see Marzillier, 2014). Many of these approaches are not appropriate for young children, and the general consensus is that early maltreatment programs should target the mother–child relationship as the context for intervention. Improvements in quality of attachment and maternal sensitivity are well-recognized indicators of therapeutic success. However, we may also consider shifts in biobehavioral regulation as important reflections of relational improvement.

You have seen that for a small child, whose emotion regulation capacities are limited, the parent serves to temper distress and, through soothing and proximity, helps the child regulate. From the attachment perspective, the parent is a co-regulator of emotions, the child's ally on the road to self-regulation (see Chapter 5 for further discussion). Cooperation and synchrony in relationship builds biological regulation of neuroendocrine systems and greater emotional control, so it makes sense to include the parents/guardians in any intervention for traumatized/maltreated children. The ABC Program (Attachment and Biobehavioral Catch Up; Bernard, Dozier, Bick, & Gordon, 2015) is a 10-week intervention designed to reduce the incidence of child maltreatment in high-risk families by working with caregivers directly. Goals include (1) reduction of frightening parental behavior (e.g., harsh discipline, threatening

looks, and verbal threats), (2) increasing parental insight about the effects of their own childhood experiences on current parenting, and (3) providing support and guidance for more sensitive interactions. Caregivers' behaviors are scaffolded by parent-coaches and videotaped in caregivers' own homes while they interact with their young (6 months to 2 years) children. Although the program is manualized, the parent-coach's role is to respond to interaction "in the moment" in order to support a parent's awareness of child signals and to encourage sensitive responding. Videotaped sequences are viewed and discussed by the parent and coach.

Intervention developers make the assumption that reductions in neglectful and/or harsh interactions would be manifested in lower child stress and more typical neuroendocrine (e.g., cortisol) functioning. Post-intervention assessments do show more normal cortisol profiles for high-risk infants and toddlers compared to controls (Bernard et al., 2015; Yarger, Hoye, & Dozier, 2016). Lower rates of disorganized attachment and higher rates of secure attachments were also demonstrated after intervention. Similarly, improved cortisol profiles were observed for young children living in foster homes after the ABC intervention (Dozier, Peloso, Lewis, Laurenceau, & Levine, 2008).

As infants move into toddlerhood, the regulation of behavior and emotion is more internalized (see Chapter 5).

Still, the toddler is far from mature when it comes to managing his stress, his feelings, and his actions. In secure attachment relationships, caregivers model and support emergent regulatory competencies and fill in the gaps when the child's own skills are insufficient. A 2-year-old who has a "melt-down" on the playground because he wants a toy that is being used by a peer may be soothed by the caregiver, have his desires and distress labeled and recognized by the caregiver, and may engage in a way to work out the problem—or to wait his turn—with understanding and sensitivity. Note how this approach differs from more behavioral approaches like time out or ignoring misbehavior that are more top-down and parent directed. In addition to affecting cortisol functioning in research samples, the ABC program also improved executive functions in fostered toddlers compared to a control group. Following the intervention, ABC toddlers showed levels of attention and cognitive flexibility that were similar to those of low-risk toddlers (Lind, Raby, Caron, Roben, & Dozier, 2017), possibly an indication of changes to neural networks that subserve these skills.

There is a need for more rigorous outcome research to point clinicians in the right direction when working with children and families at high risk. Although existing findings are promising, overall evidence is often inconclusive because it is derived from small studies and may lack methodological rigor. This does not mean that there are no benefits to intervention or that all interventions are equally effective. Rather, the work of elucidating attachment-related mechanisms of action in various contexts still needs to be done. Roisman and Cichetti (2017) stress the need for collaborative, large-scale studies that compare attachment interventions to active controls. We still have much to learn about what works best in the prevention and treatment of these pressing social concerns, and clinicians should be good consumers of evidence as this work unfolds.

Summing Up

Attachment theory provides many useful ideas for clinicians as they assess the socioemotional needs of parents and children. First, the concept of attachment as a constellation of behaviors in a goal-corrected partnership is particularly significant in helping us understand problems and motivations for behavior. This perspective emphasizes the fundamentally social nature of human development. It reminds us that all human growth and human problems occur in some relational context. Second, attachment theory provides clinicians with a new way to view behavior that might, at first glance, seem puzzling. Because the principal goal of attachment is to maintain proximity, either physical or psychological, seemingly contradictory behaviors can be interpreted as means to this end. Even avoidant behaviors, for example, can help maintain some distant relationship while minimizing psychological threat to the self. As Greenberg and Speltz (1988) have pointed out, noncompliant child behaviors can be interpreted as bids for more attention (or closer attachment).

Presumably, all behaviors are functional in that they help individuals adapt to present circumstances. Their adaptiveness may be more or less well suited to any given situation or context. For the infant who needs to reduce the risk of rejection, avoidant behaviors or withdrawal may be an effective method for adapting to negative circumstances. However, this pattern of withdrawal from close relationships, particularly when under stress, can be counterproductive in the context of close adult relationships. Even though the behavior is not suited to the new context, it certainly can be understood. Finally, for distressed mother–child dyads, intervention should include both a focus on improving maternal sensitivity to her child, and, equally, on provision of emotional and material support for the maltreating parent who may be suffering from trauma as well (Thompson, 2015).

Focus on Developmental Psychopathology

Insecure and Disorganized Attachment and Attachment Disorders

Security of attachment is a robust protective factor in development, and abnormalities of attachment place children at risk for social and emotional problems throughout the life span. Despite this straightforward claim, empirically validated assessments, diagnoses, and treatments for attachment-related problems in infancy and childhood remain murky, misunderstood, and even controversial. Attachment-related problems (such as insecure or disorganized attachments) need to be distinguished from attachment disorders. The first category describes disturbed patterns in relationships to specific caregivers. It is possible that a person could display an insecure attachment to a caregiver but show secure attachment to another adult. Insecure and disorganized patterns of attachment are clearly risk factors for disorders, but they are distinct from attachment disorders. Attachment disorders are maladjusted patterns of interpersonal connections that pervade social relationships in general. Insecure attachments are not that uncommon, but attachment disorders are quite rare. In fact, Regier and colleagues report that extensive research on attachment disorders was unavailable when the DSM-V revision was being written because there were too few cases to examine (Regier et al., 2013).

Both insecure/disorganized attachment patterns and attachment disorders are viewed as having roots in early caregiving that is inadequate, neglectful, or maltreating/abusive (Zeanah & Gleason, 2015). Despite some interest in genetic predispositions for attachment disorders, research in this area is still in its infancy (Roisman, Booth-Laforce, Belsky, Burt, & Groh, 2013). One promising lead involves considering the potential genetic contribution of callous-unemotional (CE) traits as a potential risk factor for attachment disorders. These are a constellation of genetically influenced qualities that include lack of empathy, manipulative relationships with others, and lack of guilt. This approach may be a promising area of investigation in the future (Mayes, Calhoun, Waschbusch, Breaux, & Baweja, 2017).

Disorganized Attachment

Disorganized (D) attachment was first described by Main and Solomon in 1986. These attachment researchers added this category based on their study of 200 cases that were not classifiable within existing A (avoidant), B (secure), and C (ambivalent) designations. The primary behavioral manifestations of disorganized attachment, noted during Strange Situation assessments, are sequential or simultaneous displays of contradictory, conflicted behaviors (approach and avoidance), misdirected movements, disorientation, "freezing in place" for a significant length of time, and fearfulness or apprehension of the parent (Main & Solomon, 1990).

Recall that the strange situation is essentially an infant stress management assessment. Under normal circumstances, securely attached infants (B) will generally seek out and welcome the comfort provided by their attachment figures upon reunion. Infants classified in nonsecure categories also reflect an organized or coherent, albeit insecure, way of managing the stress of separation, either through avoidant (A) or clinging/angry (C) behavior patterns. The bizarre behavior of D infants is considered to be a reflection of stress that goes unmanaged. It demonstrates the absence of an organized pattern of emotion regulation, hence, the term *disorganized*. The relatively high incidence of disorganized attachment in nonclinical, middle-class U.S. samples (15%) and nonclinical, lower-class U.S. samples (25% to 34%) is surprising (van IJzendoorn, Schuengel, & Bakermans-Kranenburg, 1999).

There is a strong association between disorganization and child maltreatment and institutionalization. Studies have reported that 32% (Valenzuela, 1990) to 86% (Barnett, Ganiban, & Cicchetti, 1997) of maltreated children fall into the D category. Overall, approximately 48% of maltreated children compared to 17% of non-maltreated children show disorganized attachment (van IJzendoorn, 1999). This makes some intuitive sense given that the threatening parent, who is also the presumable source of security, presents the child with an unsolvable problem. The attachment figure is both threat and safe haven, constituting a paradox that Hesse and Main (1999a) call "fright without solution." The rates for disorganized attachment are higher in children who have spent time in institutional settings compared to home-reared peers (Zeanah, Smyke, Koga, & Carlson, 2005). A meta-analysis of 10 studies revealed this breakdown for institutionally reared children: 18% secure, 28% insecure, and 54% disorganized/cannot classify (Lionettia, Pastore, & Barone, 2015).

The lack of an organized way to handle stress seems understandable in the face of serious abuse and neglect that can overwhelm the child's resources. However, what can account for the development of disorganization in 15% to 33% of non-maltreating, low-risk samples (Abrams, Rifkin, & Hesse, 2006)? A good deal of interest has focused on disordered parental behavior that does not meet standards for abuse but which constitutes a risk factor for D classification. In their early conceptualizations of disorganization, Main and Hesse (1992) theorized that frightened or frightening (called FR) behavior by the parent could lead to infant disorganization in much the same way that maltreatment appears to do.

In fact, studies do suggest that FR parental behavior is significantly correlated with infant disorganized attachment (Schuengal, Bakermans-Kranenburg, & van IJzendoorn, 1999). FR behavior is more likely among low-risk non-maltreating mothers who themselves are classified as U/d on the Adult Attachment Interview. It appears that parents who struggle with the ongoing and unresolved loss of their attachment figures are more likely to relate in ways that can cause significant disruption to their own children's attachments to them (Jacobvits, Leon, & Hazen, 2006; van IJzendoorn, 1995).

Hesse and Main (1998) identified six primary subtypes of FR behavior. They include parental behaviors that are (1) threatening, as in suddenly looming or abruptly coming up close to the infant's field of vision; (2) frightened, as in showing a fearful face with wide eyes and facial grimaces; (3) timid or deferential, as in acting as if the infant were in control; (4) spousal or romantic, as in sexualized or overly intimate behavior toward the infant; and (5) disorganized, as in asymmetrical and mistimed movements. A final behavioral category is (6) dissociative, which is exemplified by the parent's freezing all movements as if in a trance while the infant is actively trying to gain parental attention or speaking in a ghostly or "haunted" voice (i.e., speaking while pulling in on the diaphragm). Of all six subtypes, threatening and dissociative behaviors are most highly associated with D infant attachment in low-risk, non-maltreating samples (Abrams et al., 2006). This makes sense if we consider that threatening and dissociative behaviors can be intensely frightening and can overwhelm a child's meager capacity to regulate emotions independently. With regard to parents themselves, dissociative behavior was most likely to occur among those with a history of unresolved trauma, mourning, or loss (Abrams et al., 2006). Some have suggested that parental marital discord is also related to disorganization in children, but further study is needed to support this claim (Owen & Cox, 1997).

The previously mentioned study by Hazen and colleagues (2015) suggests another possible route to disorganized attachment. Using convergent evidence from a sample in Texas and data from the NICHD study, the authors found that more than 60 hours per week spent in child care placed infants at risk of disorganized attachments independent of other risk factors. The authors hypothesize that mothers who work long hours (and who need extensive child care) may come home more tired and unresponsive than those under less work stress. Prolonged separations, including overnight parental visitations in divorce situations, may provide an alternate pathway to disorganized attachment because the baby may not have been given sufficient time and experience with the primary caregiver to establish a reliable sense of security.

What Is Reactive Attachment Disorder?

Although the term "attachment disorder" is often used to describe children with poor social relatedness and frustratingly high levels of disruptive behavior, there is actually no real "attachment disorder" diagnosis. The term **Reactive Attachment Disorder** or **RAD** (APA, 2000) was introduced into the DSM in 1980. This disorder was characterized by highly disturbed and inappropriate social relatedness in early childhood (beginning before age 5) that was not due to other mental disorders (e.g., ADHD, ODD, or CD) or to developmental delay (e.g., MR or PDD). The disorder was presumed to result from grossly pathological early caregiving, which might include extreme child abuse, severe neglect of physical and emotional needs, or frequent changes in caregivers that disrupt attachment formation. Although attachment theory is related to RAD because of the important effects of early maltreatment, RAD has been primarily a within-person diagnosis that manifests across settings while attachment status always refers to a relationship.

In earlier versions of the DSM, two types of RAD were recognized (see Gleason et al., 2011). One type was characterized by a high degree of resistance and non-responsiveness to social interaction (*emotionally withdrawn/inhibited type*) such that children fail to show attachment behaviors, either organized or disorganized. They do not seek comfort from selected adults when distressed nor do they respond to it when present. When placed in nurturing settings, emotionally withdrawn characteristics may diminish. Another subtype (*indiscriminantly social/disinhibited type*) showed indiscriminant familiarity and attention seeking directed toward relative strangers, frequently in combination with lack of selective attachments to primary caregivers. The length of time that children spent in institutions or in foster care is related to severity and persistence of indiscriminant social behavior (Rutter et al., 2007). These children may or may not form attachments to adults, but indiscriminant social behavior tends to persist regardless of circumstances.

Currently, there is evidence that both RAD subtypes are separate disorders due to their distinct symptom sets and divergent outcomes (Zeanah & Smyke, 2008). A validation study of children from the Bucharest Early Intervention Project (BEIP) (Gleason et al., 2011) sought to differentiate both subtypes from related conditions (e.g., depression and ADHD). The children in this project had spent much of their lives in Romanian institutional care before being moved to foster homes. Results supported the conclusion that both RAD subtypes were distinct from each other and, despite some overlaps, from other related disorders. This strengthened the proposal that each subtype be considered a distinct diagnosis, which is the approach taken in the DSM-V. Presently, there are two diagnoses instead of one: Reactive Attachment Disorder and Disinhibited Social Engagement Disorder.

Despite the significant contribution of the research just described, there are still many questions that warrant further research. A report by the American Professional Society on the Abuse of Children (APSAC) summed up the problem by saying that RAD was "one of the least researched and most poorly understood disorders in the DSM" (Chaffin et al., 2006, p. 80). This may be due, at least in part, to limited longitudinal research on the course of the disorder and to clinicians' failure to distinguish among diagnoses with precision (Boris & Renk, 2017). Much of our previous knowledge of RAD came from case study reports, but well-validated diagnostic tools that involve structured interviews or videotaping interactions are now being developed. One clinical interviewing tool, the Disturbances of Attachment Interview (Smyke, Dumitrescu, & Zeanah, 2002), is an example.

Treatment Concerns

Frequently RAD, DSED, or both are ascribed to children in foster care or adoption systems, often because of disturbed behavior and adjustment and relationship difficulties. Caregivers and adoptive parents, for example, can be understandably frustrated when problems seen intractable. The generic term "attachment disorder" may also be given to older children and adolescents whose behavioral and social problems are presumed to derive from attachment failures. Despite the fact that new empirical work provides guidelines for therapy (see the Applications section), a variety of controversial techniques have been popularized.

Among the controversial and non-empirically based subset of attachment therapies are approaches variously termed rage-reduction, holding therapy, or rebirthing therapy (e.g., Cline, 1991). Several basic assumptions provide these approaches with a theoretical framework for understanding attachment problems that contradicts the more established framework we have presented in this chapter. For example, proponents of controversial attachment therapies hold that children must release or express underlying, primal rage before healthy attachments can be formed and that any defiance or protest by children signals resistance and attempted manipulation of adults. It is assumed that defiant or resistant behavior can lead to the development of sociopathy, so relatively minor infractions are perceived as ominous. "Putting off chores, incompletely executing chores, or arguing, is interpreted as a sign of an attachment disorder that must be forcibly eradicated. From this perspective, parenting a child with an attachment disorder is a battle, and winning the battle by defeating the child is paramount" (Chaffin et al., 2006, p. 79). Other parenting techniques in this category can involve physical restraint and coercion, withholding food or water, or prolonged social isolation, and have, on occasion, resulted in the deaths of several children who were being treated with "attachment therapy" (Mercer, Sarner, & Rosa, 2003).

Authors of the aforementioned APSAC report recommend that all treatments be based on empirically supported and extant behavioral principles, which have shown effectiveness for conduct problems (see Buckner, Lopez, Dunkel, & Joiner, 2008). Empirically based parent training components are also useful. Core principles of attachment development, such as provision of safety and security, patience, stability, sensitivity, and nurturance should be paramount in any intervention protocol. Coercive and potentially abusive techniques should never be used to treat children. It is important to note that behavioral problems in children and adolescents can often result from acute stress, such as that experienced in residential transitions. Treatments that view children as deliberately manipulative and deceitful and that attempt to break down their defenses so as to avert impending psychopathy do not make therapeutic sense, fail to support healthy attachments, and can compound stress and maltreatment in already traumatized children.

Summary

Emotions: Functions, Nature and Development

1. Theorists do not all agree about how to define or characterize emotions. For example, they disagree about how different the physiological aspects of different emotions are, or whether you have to have a "conscious" interpretation to feel an emotion. They do agree that emotions have survival value. Emotions are powerful motivators of behavior, and spontaneous emotional expressions help us to communicate with one another. For infants, this communicative function helps initiate reciprocal interaction with a caregiver. Emotions enhance cognitive functioning such as planning and social perspective taking, and they play a role in mental health and wellness. More positive life outcomes are associated with higher levels of emotional intelligence.

2. Researchers agree that basic emotions are similar across cultures. Izard argues that even infants' expressive behaviors reveal these emotions (happiness, interest, sadness, anger, disgust, and fear), that they are innate, and that each has its own neural circuitry, although more elaborate emotion schemas emerge as a function of experience. A more constructivist approach argues that all emotional reactions are combinations of two dimensions, valence (pleasant to unpleasant) and arousal (low to high). In Sroufe's orthogenetic theory of emotional development, newborns begin by displaying general distress or general contentment. These early emotional expressions are precursors of more mature emotions, and the later emotions depend on cognitive developments that give children the ability to ascribe meaning to emotional experience. Emotions are differentiated over time and come under the control of higher levels of functioning.

3. Many lower and higher order brain systems, including the limbic system and the cerebral cortex (which tends to assign meaning), are typically involved in emotion processing. LeDoux found that there is an "early warning emotional system." Some sensory information bypasses the cortex, causing fear and allowing a rapid response to stimuli that may pose a threat. Rational processing by the cortex is a split second behind, and sometimes determines that there is no threat, allowing fear to subside. If rapid emotional responses are paired with formerly neutral stimuli, we may be conditioned to automatically respond with fear to stimuli that are not threatening, perhaps explaining phobias, panic reactions, and posttraumatic stress disorder.

4. There appear to be two major, partially separate networks related to positive and negative affect. Left brain activation is more closely associated with approach-related positive reactions and right brain activation is more associated with avoidance-related negative reactions. Depressed individuals show lower levels of left-sided activation compared to right-sided activation.

5. Although not all theorists agree about how emotions develop, generally it appears that soon after birth babies show distress, contentment, disgust, and interest through body posture, gaze, and facial expressions. Anger, surprise, fear, and sadness seem to be differentiated and expressed by about 6 months old. And self-conscious emotions such as pride and embarrassment emerge at about 18 to 24 months. Newborns show different brain activity to fearful versus happy or neutral sounds, and by 6 months babies respond differently to positive versus negative facial and vocal expressions. By 18 months, infants are making more fine-grained distinctions, such as between expressions of disgust versus sadness.

6. Emotion regulation is a cornerstone of emotional well-being and positive adjustment. Mothers and other caregivers interact with infants in ways that scaffold the development of emotion regulation. Interactions

between mothers and infants often exhibit a repetitive-rhythmic organization called synchrony. When synchrony breaks down, infants tend to show distress and mothers tend to initiate repairs that regulate the infants' emotions, encouraging longer periods of positive affect. The still-face paradigm is used to study synchrony, along with its breakdown and repair. Sensitive adults adjust their emotion management behaviors to the needs and abilities of infants as they grow. And as infants get older, they engage in social referencing, basing their own emotional reactions to ambiguous situations on their caregivers' behaviors.

Attachment: Early Social Relationships

7. Theorists such as Bowlby and Erikson have proposed that the infant's first relationships with caregivers provide him with working models of the self, of others, and of relationships. Erikson argued that consistent, sensitive care helps the infant establish basic trust in others and feelings of worthiness, both of which contribute to optimism about future relationships. In Bowlby's attachment theory, biologically prepared behaviors bring infant and mother into a close relationship, or attachment system, that emerges in stages such that by about 8 months the infant has a strong affectional bond to the primary caregiver, which leads to both separation anxiety and stranger anxiety. The attachment system serves the purpose of proximity maintenance and provides a secure base and safe haven.

8. Research demonstrates that both infants and parents typically display expressive and behavioral characteristics that foster attachment, from orienting behaviors (e.g., caregiver stays in infant's field of vision), to recognition (e.g., infant's early recognition of mother's voice), to intuitive parenting (e.g., caregiver ascribes meaning to infant behavior). Researchers have identified some of the neurological processes and structures involved in this bonding system. For example, oxytocin is associated with more caregiving behavior in both mothers and fathers, and for most adults close contact with infants promotes increases in oxytocin levels.

9. Using the strange situation test to measure the quality of infant–mother attachments, Ainsworth and her colleagues identified three different types of attachment quality. Securely attached infants explore a new situation when mother is present, are distressed if she leaves, and are comforted and happy when she returns. They appear to use their mothers as a secure base. Anxious ambivalent babies are insecurely attached. They are most clearly different from other babies in their response to their mothers' return from an absence. They may alternately approach and resist the mother, or may respond listlessly to her, rather than taking ready comfort. Avoidant babies are also insecurely attached. They actually avoid or ignore their mothers when they return after an absence, although their heart rates reveal that they are stressed in her absence. Main and others have identified a fourth attachment category,

another insecurely attached group called disorganized-disoriented. These babies react to their mothers in contradictory ways, engaging in an odd array of behaviors.

10. Maternal caregiving through the first year of life is correlated with infants' attachment quality at 12 months. The mothers of securely attached babies provide consistent, sensitive care to their infants. Mothers of insecurely attached babies are more likely to be insensitive in one way or another, and the mothers of disorganized-disoriented babies can be abusive.

11. As early work by Ainsworth suggested, even "normal" variations in maternal responsivity and sensitivity are linked to differences in infant attachment security and emotion regulation. Adverse or insensitive maternal care tends to fit into two major categories: intrusive or neglectful. Depressed mothers show high rates of these kinds of patterns, and their infants tend to show heightened right brain activation and lower left brain activation, suggesting more negative than positive emotional experiences.

12. Infant temperament may be one influence on attachment quality. Babies have different emotional and behavioral characteristics. Such traits make up infant temperament, and for at least one of these traits, reactivity, physiological correlates have been identified, such as high heart rates before birth. Some babies have difficult temperaments: They are highly reactive and irritable and have a number of other traits that make them more difficult than average babies to care for. Easy babies have a combination of traits that make them easy to care for. A longitudinal study by Thomas and Chess included babies with different temperaments and indicates that temperament can persist beyond infancy and that it can affect caregiving, making it easier or harder for a parent to be responsive and sensitive. But this study also found that parents who adjust to their infants' temperament, creating goodness of fit between their caregiving and the needs of a particular infant, can moderate their child's temperament and influence the impact of early temperament on later adjustment. Further, this study hinted that children with difficult temperaments may be more vulnerable to the effects of caregiving quality than other infants.

13. Temperament and caregiving seem to interact to affect security of attachment. For example, some caregivers may react to the frustrations of caring for a difficult baby by becoming less sensitive and responsive to their baby's needs. Their unresponsive caregiving may then contribute to an insecure attachment.

14. Babies form attachments to both their mothers and fathers, as well as other frequent caregivers. Each parent's sensitivity influences the quality of the infant's attachment to that parent, although the primary caregiver may have the most influence on a baby's attachments overall.

15. Across cultures, there are differences in the proportion of infants who are categorized as securely or insecurely attached. There are substantial cross-cultural differences in specific caregiving practices, such as how much face-to-face interaction adults have with infants,

but across cultures, the connection between sensitive caregiving (especially responsiveness to distress) and security of attachment has been corroborated.

16. Attachment quality can change over time if caregiving quality changes. It is also possible for children with reactive attachment disorder, who have been deprived of adequate adult care as infants, to later form secure attachments. Early attachment launches processes that can have long-term consequences; but the quality of care a child continues to receive can either strengthen or redirect those processes.

17. Early attachment quality has been found to predict later psychosocial functioning, including dependency, self-confidence, and social skills. Moreover, if children have secure attachments with both parents, their later functioning is more positive than if they have a secure attachment with only one parent. However, it is unclear whether the early attachment quality is the cause of later psychosocial adjustment or whether the ongoing quality of the parents' caregiving is the key predictor. The primary influence of early infant attachments may be their tendency to perpetuate themselves. Once a pattern is established between parent and child, it tends to be repeated. However, it can be changed, and if it is, the child's working model of relationships, of self, and of others can also change.

18. Methods for assessing attachment security in adults have been devised, such as the Adult Attachment Interview (AAI). In some studies, parents' own attachment quality has been predictive of the quality of attachment they establish with their infants.

19. The specifics of infant care—such as bottle-feeding versus breastfeeding—may be less important to child outcomes than the sensitivity of caregiving. Focusing on the quality of infant–caregiver relations, rather than the specifics of parenting practices, seems to provide a better understanding of later socioemotional development.

Attachment in Context

20. Attachments are embedded in a system of contexts including parents' relationships, extended family relationships, neighborhoods, and so on. All contexts can affect infants' emotional well-being and attachment security. Children under 5 are especially likely to be exposed to negative experiences in these contexts, including traumatizing events such as maltreatment, accidents, and marital conflict. Attachment security can be a protective factor, but children who have such experiences are also at increased risk of forming insecure attachments.

Practice Using What You Have Learned

MyLab Education Application Exercise 4.1: Case Study: Infant Attachment
MyLab Education Application Exercise 4.2: Case Study: Factors Influencing the Quality of Attachments
MyLab Education Application Exercise 4.3: Early Social Relationships

Case Study

Angela is a White 17-year-old girl who is also the mother of a baby named Adam, now 11 months of age. Both Angela and her baby live with Angela's mother, Sarah, in a small rented house in a semirural community in the Midwest. Sarah, a single mother herself, works as a food server in a local restaurant. Sarah has another child, David, who is 13. Angela's father abandoned the family when she was 7 years old. Wayne, Angela's boyfriend and Adam's father, has also become estranged primarily because Sarah refuses to allow him in her house. She is angry that Angela became pregnant and views Wayne as incapable of, and uninterested in, taking on his share of the responsibility.

During her pregnancy, Angela continued to attend classes at her high school. She dropped out, however, when she was 7 months pregnant. She had grown increasingly depressed about the prospect of caring for an infant, and she found dealing with schoolwork and her pregnancy overwhelming. Following Adam's birth, Angela tried hard to be a good mother to her son. She took on most of the caretaking responsibilities by herself, which gave her some measure of satisfaction. However, she also felt deeply ambivalent. Above all, she resented the restrictions that the baby placed on her life. Adam's frequent crying for no apparent reason was particularly frustrating. According to Angela, Adam cried even when he was not hungry or wet.

Sometimes she handled Adam roughly, when he wouldn't quiet down after a feeding or around bedtime. At other times, Angela was upset that Adam didn't seem to smile enough at her when she wanted to play with him. Sometimes, Adam paid no attention to her when she wanted interaction. At these times, she would raise her voice and hold his face in her hands to make him look at her. She was beginning to feel that she was not a very good mother to her son after all.

Sarah and Angela's already strained relationship grew more hostile as Adam approached his first birthday. Angela felt that her mother wasn't interested in helping her. Angela always idealized her father and believed that it was her mother's frequent outbursts of anger that led to her father's leaving home.

For her part, Sarah believed that her daughter wasn't doing enough to help herself. Angela chose not to go back to school, even though she could have access to school-based child care services. All through Angela's high school years, Sarah had expected her daughter to find a steady job after graduation and to contribute to the family financially. Instead, Sarah found herself in the role of financial provider for another child. She was very angry and hurt that Angela didn't seem to appreciate all she had done for her over the years. Whenever the mother and daughter had an argument, Angela would say that she felt her mother never really cared about her. What was even worse for Sarah was that Angela had begun seeing Wayne again, without her mother's permission. She made it clear to Angela that she and the baby would need to move out if she ever got pregnant again.

Discussion Questions

1. Comment on the quality of the attachment relationship between Angela and Adam and between Sarah and Angela. Do you think that Adam is at risk for developmental problems? Discuss.
2. Using the model of intergenerational transmission of attachment presented in this chapter, discuss the transmission sequence as it applies in this case.
3. What kinds of interventions could you suggest to help the members of this family?
4. How would you engage with a parent who is maltreating a child? What steps would you take to help in this circumstance?

Journal Questions

1. Present five adjectives that describe your early childhood relationship to each parent.
   a. Why did you choose these adjectives?
   b. To which parent did you feel the closest?
   c. What did you do as a child when you were upset, hurt, or ill?
   d. What do you remember about any separation that you experienced as a child?

2. How would your parents describe your temperament as a young child? In what ways is it the same now and in what ways is it different?

3. Consider the intergenerational relationships in your family of origin (e.g., mother–grandmother). What were the qualities of your mother's (or father's) attachments to their parents? What have been the effects on your own attachment? If you have children, consider this question from their point of view.

Key Concepts

Phineas Gage matrix (p. 127)
emotional intelligence (p. 127)
basic emotions (p. 128)
emotion schemas (p. 129)
valence (p. 130)
arousal (p. 130)
orthogenetic principle (p. 130)
self-conscious emotions (p. 132)
emotion regulation (p. 132)
synchrony (p. 133)
still-face paradigm (p. 133)
other-directed coping behaviors (p. 133)
self-directed coping behaviors (p. 133)
social referencing (p. 134)
basic trust (p. 135)
ethologists (p. 136)
attachment theory (p. 136)

proximity maintenance (p. 137)
secure base (p. 137)
safe haven (p. 137)
working models (p. 138)
stranger anxiety (p. 139)
oxytocin (p. 140)
strange situation test (p. 141)
securely attached (p. 141)
anxious ambivalent (p. 141)
avoidant babies (p. 142)
disorganized-disoriented (p. 142)
temperaments (p. 145)
fearfulness or reactivity (p. 145)
irritability or negative emotionality (p. 145)
activity level (p. 145)
positive affect (p. 145)
attention-persistence (p. 145)

rhythmicity (p. 145)
behavioral inhibition (p. 145)
difficult babies (p. 146)
easy babies (p. 146)
slow-to-warm-up babies (p. 147)
genetic vulnerability (diathesis-stress)
   (p. 147)
differential susceptibility (p. 147)
goodness of fit model (p. 147)
Adult Attachment Interview (AAI)
   (p. 156)
intergenerational transmission (p. 159)
developmental traumatology (p. 162)
neuroimmunology (p. 162)
callous-unemotional (CE) traits (p. 165)
reactive attachment disorder (RAD)
   (p. 166)

Chapter 5

The Emerging Self and Socialization in the Early Years

 Learning Objectives

After reading this chapter, you should be able to:

5.1 Explain theoretical views of the self-system including elements of self and factors that influence a child's perceptions of self.

5.2 Describe phases on the continuum of early self-system development in the areas of pre-self, self-recognition, and self-regulation and identify indicators (manifestations) and influencing factors.

5.3 Assess the effects of different parenting styles on a child's self-development and suggest techniques for improving parenting skills to address targeted behaviors.

5.4 Describe how parenting, child temperament, self-regulation, and internalization shape conscience formation and the beginnings of a moral self.

Angie is 4 years old; her sister, Mary, just had her second birthday. Their mother, Jennie, and father, Jim, have been somewhat nomadic over the last few years. It started when Jim decided not to re-enlist in the Army and to try for a good paying job in "sales." He tried large appliance sales, swimming pool sales, lawn service sales, and a few others. Often, when he left a company it was not because he couldn't hold the job but because he was bored, not making much money, and certain that he was leaving to chase a better opportunity, in a different industry and usually in a different location. Between jobs, his family is essentially homeless. Jennie works as a health care aid. She can usually find work wherever they land, and she faithfully follows Jim on his endless quest. They often stay with family or friends in between Jim's jobs, but occasionally they live in their car.

Angie seems to adapt well to every change. She is quiet but attentive, and she rarely disobeys or is out of sorts. Little Mary is a different story. She was highly active and reactive as an infant, and her parents regard her now as "impossible," always getting into things, running off, reacting with temper tantrums when she is prevented from having what she wants, and disregarding the admonitions of the stream of different adults who house the family. The parents manage the two sisters quite differently. They are usually gentle with Angie, showing some warmth and affection, but they tend to just let her play quietly. If she does something "wrong," such as accidentally breaking a lamp, they react with irritation, but Angie is so cautious that such things rarely happen. The parents are occasionally amused by Mary's boisterousness, but more often they respond negatively: yelling at her to eat or to stop crying, pulling her roughly away from what they consider dangerous, often expressing anger or disappointment. Their own lives are unpredictable and difficult, and they usually find Mary's rambunctious impulsiveness a heavy burden.

You can probably see the potential for Angie and Mary to develop rather different ideas about themselves from their different experiences of parenting. Their shared experiences –such as repeated relocations, periods of privation, reactions from people who do (or do not) take them in—are also likely to affect their early self-views.

In this chapter, we will describe the earliest roots of self-development. The role of caregivers is of major significance, but the causal influences are multidimensional. As you can see with Angie and Mary, a child's temperament impacts parents' typical responses and management strategies. And these interactive processes unfold within and are influenced by the context of the family and the broader culture. Let's begin our examination of self-development by considering the rather elusive notion of "self" itself.

The Self-System

5.1 Explain theoretical views of the self-system including elements of self and factors that influence a child's perceptions of self.

"Mirror, mirror on the wall, who is the real me, after all?" Philosophers, poets, wicked stepmothers, and ordinary human beings have pondered versions of this question ever since the ancient Greeks advised, "Know thyself." The search for self embodies within it many of the profound questions at the heart of the human condition: What is the nature of self-awareness? Are we the same or different across situations and over time? How do people come to understand and accept who they are? Modern cultures are not the first to express interest in these matters, but critics have raised concerns that the level of attention directed toward the self has increased in recent decades. Note the amount of press devoted to the ideas of self-concept, self-esteem, self-enhancement, and self-actualization, and you might agree that we have become downright self-centered!

Those of us in the helping professions are no exception to this trend. Even a cursory review of the professional literature in clinical and educational fields reveals an intense interest in topics related to the self. Therapeutic approaches that emphasize self-development are very common. Educational institutions struggle to incorporate self-development into their more traditional academic objectives. Popular magazines are saturated with advice about self-concept and self-esteem. All together, the pieces add up to a crazy quilt: part folklore, part research, part anecdote, and part good intention. Our task in this chapter is to unscramble some of this information and present the self in its developmental context. Helpers need to understand the research findings in this critically important area lest they assume that all of our popular, contemporary notions about self-development are valid.

Traditional Conceptions of the Self-System

What constitutes a self? To address this question, theorists and researchers have had to account for the fact that selves are multifaceted and possess elements of both stability and change. If you have ever said that you are not the same person that you were some time ago, you can understand this point. Writers often use the term **self-system** to replace "self," because the latter seems too unidimensional. The *self-system* includes such things as self-as-agent, self-recognition, self-concept, self-regulation, and self-esteem.

The notion of an independent entity called "self" is such a deeply embedded concept in Western psychology that we tend to take it for granted. It may be surprising to learn that in some cultural views of the psyche, mind and matter are seen as changing continually, and this impermanence is viewed as being influenced by surrounding conditions (Bodhi, 1999). In Buddhist psychology, this is the concept of "no self" (anatta). It does not imply that our conventional use of "self" is not helpful or that you and I are not real in some way. Rather, it emphasizes the transient nature of our phenomenological experience as human beings. The self is constantly being constructed in the moment-to-moment flow of experience. This insight is at the core of recent therapies that offer ways to alleviate the suffering that can come from our human tendency to protect and defend reified concepts about ourselves (Chadha, 2017; Olendzki, 2014). The view of "no-self" is quite different from that of classic Western psychology, which assumes a relatively permanent construct that can be studied over time.

We will begin our look at the nature of the self-system within Western psychology with a brief description of the classic work of James, Cooley, and Mead. William James (1890) made a distinction between the "I" and the "Me," a distinction that still guides contemporary research about the self (Harter, 2013; Prebble, Addis, & Tippett, 2013). That part of the self called "I" refers to the I-self/self-as-subject, as the active agent, or as the knower. It is that part of the self that experiences a sense of subjective self-awareness. The part called "Me" is that part of the self that is the object of self or others' observations, or in other words, the part that is known. One might think of the "Me" part of the self (Me-Self) as the Me-self/self-concept.

More recently, writers have developed alternative ways of categorizing the classic "I–Me" distinction. Among these are Lewis's (1994) subjective and objective self-awareness, Case's (1991) implicit and explicit self, Neisser's (1993) ecological and remembered self, and Gallagher's (2000) minimal and narrative self. All the newer contrasts share the original distinction between the self as knower and the self as known. Furthermore, there is consensus between classic and contemporary theorists that the "I" self emerges first.

The "I" is the side of the self that experiences continuity over time. Even though we all grow and change, we know we embody core elements of the same "self" throughout our lifetime. The "I" also recognizes the distinctiveness of the self as a person compared to other persons. You know where you end and the person sitting next to you begins. Finally, the "I" reflects *agency*; it is the part of the self that engages in self-directed activity, self-control, and contemplation of the "Me." The "Me" includes all those attributes that are used to define the self and that make up the self-concept. In James's typology, these are the "material self," the "social self," and the "spiritual self," ranked in that order of importance from lowest to highest. The material self encompasses a person's physical characteristics and material possessions. The social self includes her social standing, her reputation, and those personal characteristics that are recognized by others, such as gregariousness or stubbornness. The spiritual self, viewed by James as the most precious, incorporates her qualities of character, beliefs, and personal values.

Self-esteem is distinct from self-concept but still part of the "Me." Whereas *self-concept* is a person's knowledge of her personal attributes, *self-esteem* is her evaluation of these attributes. In other words, she assigns a *valence* to her characteristics, judging them to be good, bad, or neutral. James believed that self-esteem is more than just the measure of accomplishments. Rather, he believed that it depends upon the number of successes we enjoy relative to our aspirations, or, in his terminology, pretensions. Pretensions are goals that we choose to meet for ourselves because of their personal importance. For example, if it is highly important to you to be popular and socially active, the lack of a date for an important New Year's Eve party can be a real blow to your self-esteem. However, if you really care more about earning enough money to become rich at an early age, you might consider working overtime on New Year's Eve to be highly congruent with your aspirations. Your dateless condition is less damaging to your self-esteem. Failures or even successes in areas that are relatively unimportant to us may be discounted and will have less effect on self-esteem.

James's ideas about the structure of the self are usually part of contemporary theorizing (e.g., Verschoor & Hommel, 2017). Another early theorist whose ideas suffuse modern work is Charles Cooley (1902). He introduced a developmental perspective that describes how interactions with others help construct the self-system. Using his now-famous metaphor of the "looking-glass self," Cooley described the process of self-development as one that originates from observing the reflected appraisals of others, primarily attachment figures. Cooley hypothesized that this process consists of three steps. As we interact with others, we first imagine how we must appear to the other person on a certain dimension, such as intelligence. Then, we interpret or imagine how that other person evaluates us on that certain dimension. Finally, we experience some emotional response to that perceived evaluation. The resulting interpretation and its affective valence are building blocks for constructing self-knowledge. Our self-representations are shaped and given affective valences by the significant people in our life.

Let's consider a simplified example of a young child's display of affection for a parent. Imagine that Angie or Mary approaches her father to give him a hug. The father, preoccupied with searching the web for new job opportunities, looks annoyed by the interruption. He gives her a quick hug and returns to his search. If this type of sequence is repeated on a regular basis across various situations, the child may come to develop a "self-idea" that she is bothersome and not important enough to interrupt her father. She may begin to construct a vague impression of herself as unappealing or possibly too emotionally expressive or dependent. Because the child perceives the emotion and interprets her father's response as impatient and irritated, her view of the event includes a self-appraisal—presumably that she is irritating—that is incorporated into her self-system. With repeated experience, the youngster comes to regard herself in certain ways by looking at the mirror of her parent's view of her, warped though that mirror might be. The emotional valence associated with this aspect of the child's self-image can be unpleasant or uncomfortable. This self-representation may serve as a standard for her behavior in social interactions (e.g., in her willingness to express her need for attention and affection from others) and inform her sense of right and wrong.

Now imagine this same little girl in another family. She interrupts her father to give him a hug, and he beams, expressing evident satisfaction in his daughter's affectionate nature. This child's self-concept is likely to include a positively valenced sense of being emotionally expressive. The same child and the same behavior could lead to different social responses in different families, setting the child's developing sense of self, relationships, and morality on a different pathway. Thus early attachment and parenting interactions of many sorts have been viewed as instrumental in the development of individual differences in self-concept (Sroufe, 2016).

Although the development of the self is obviously influenced by many factors and is extraordinarily complex, Cooley believed that it was largely the product of social influences. Recent researchers have investigated the possibility that the sequence Cooley proposed can also operate in reverse order, namely that a positive appraisal of oneself can generate positive interpretations of others' appraisals.

George Herbert Mead (1934) expanded on Cooley's work, enlarging the scope of social influence to include the role of language and society in shaping the self-system. He held that children adopt descriptive information about the self, based on what is emphasized in their cultural milieu. They also incorporate those standards, rules, and goals that their family and their culture have determined to be appropriate ways of behaving and thinking. The "ingredients" of people's self-concepts across cultures can be rather different as a result. In a classic study, for example, Markus and Kitayama (1991) found that Japanese participants were more likely to describe themselves by emphasizing their affiliations, such as family membership, whereas Americans used self-descriptors that emphasized their individuality.

These classic formulations of the self as multidimensional, as influenced by the reflected appraisals of significant others and as shaped by the cultural milieu, provide a foundation for current Western thinking about the self-system. As you will find in this and subsequent chapters, conceptions of self and of morality overlap in these models. Damon and Hart (1992) noted:

> Children cannot know themselves without some sense of the other. Nor can they forge their self-identities without an awareness of their own values. Moreover, at all developmental periods, social activities derive from—and in turn shape—judgments about the self, other, and morality. In these and many other ways, self-understanding, social

MyLab Education

Video Example 5.1

As you observe children and teacher interacting during lunch, think about social influences that shape the self-system. Recall the statement by Damon and Hart (1992). "Children cannot know themselves without some sense of the other."

interaction, and morality are intertwined in a developing psychological system that grows and changes throughout the life span. (p. 421)

Self-understanding is one of the key building blocks of personality, social, and moral development. How does this mysterious "self" begin? In the next section, we will review the earliest stages of developing self-awareness.

MyLab Education Self-Check 5.1

The Early Development of the Self-System

5.2 Describe phases on the continuum of early self-system development in the areas of pre-self, self-recognition, and self-regulation and identify indicators (manifestations) and influencing factors.

The Beginnings of the "I" and the "Me"

You learned in Chapter 3 that studying a young infant's ability to think and to understand the world is very challenging. Learning about the infant's developing self-system is equally challenging. A child cannot describe herself as "smart" or "funny" until several years after birth. Does this mean there is no sense of self until then? To find out, we have to look for nonverbal indicators of what an infant is experiencing. As you have seen, when behavior has to be interpreted, researchers can disagree about what those behaviors mean. But on the whole, developmental scientists tend to agree that the self-system gradually unfolds, beginning at birth and continuing throughout life. (Discussions of self-development are part of many of the later chapters in this text.) What are the competencies of the infant that make self-development possible? How do these competencies interact with the social relationships that ultimately give birth to the self?

PRECURSORS OF SELF-AWARENESS IN INFANCY—THE "PRE-SELF" AND THE "I-SELF"

The newborn's capacities for rudimentary information processing and social bonding provide the building material out of which the self is born. For example, one early competency is the infant's ability to imitate. As you saw in Chapter 3, babies can imitate the facial and hand gestures of adults within their first few months of life. When a baby imitates an adult who is clapping his hands, she is detecting, at least at a behavioral level, similarity between herself and the adult model. She probably does not yet have a sense of herself as separate from the other person, but noticing these parallels may help her start the process of building that sense.

There are many other experiences and abilities that should help with that process as well. For example, when the baby acts, she feels the bodily states that go with that action; when another person acts, she does not have the same experience. As Meltzoff (2007, p. 28) suggests, "these first-person experiences contribute to a detailed . . . map linking internal states and behavior," and they support the process of separating the self from others.

As you saw in Chapter 4, sensitive caregivers respond to their infants' signals. They establish predictable, reliable interactive routines as they meet their babies' needs and help them to manage their emotions. The regularity and reliability of caregiver–infant interactions may help babies begin to extract notions of "self-invariance" and "other invariance," which precede self-awareness.

Overall, in the first half year we might say that the infant comes to possess a **pre-self**, composed of early inklings that she has a body, that it is separate from others, and

MyLab Education
Video Example 5.2
A sensitive caregiver responds to this infant's signals, allowing the child to take control of the meal. This type of behavior encourages development of a strong sense of an autonomous self.

that her actions affect events. Gradually, over the second half year, the infant appears to gain more control over when and how she signals the caregiver to provide for her needs. Imagine the lesson learned by an infant who, when she coos and babbles, regularly attracts the smiles and responsive vocalizations of her caregivers. This baby's world, in some small way, begins to come under her control. She might encode the message, "When I am upset or need attention, my parent responds and takes care of me." Clearly, young infants do not represent these ideas linguistically, but rather encode these kinds of organized sequences as procedural models or patterns of the self-in-relationship. Affective responses, such as feelings of love and relief, also become associated with these sensorimotor patterns. The infant's self-system is under construction.

By 8 to 12 months, several cognitive and social developments you have learned about in previous chapters indicate that the I-self is emerging. Babies engage in intentional, planned behavior. To obtain an out-of-reach toy, for example, a baby might first set aside a barrier, or she might vocalize to get a parent's attention, then reach or point toward the toy. Intentional action is considered a hallmark of feelings of agency (e.g., Prinz, 2012; Verschoor & Hommel, 2017). Doing things on purpose, making choices and plans, requires an I-self.

At about the same time, babies show other signs of an increasing sense of self as separate from others. They begin to display separation anxiety, signaling the formation of an attachment to the primary caregiver. For example, they might show distress even at an impending separation from an attachment figure, perhaps by looking anxiously at the door when the babysitter arrives. Many babies cry and cling to a departing caregiver. These behaviors demonstrate the infant's recognition that the caregiver is separate from herself.

As you learned in Chapter 4, attachment theorists like Bowlby assume that the attachment between infant and caregiver gives rise to a sense of security and optimism in an infant, what Erikson described as a burgeoning trust in others and an early sense of self-worth. From this perspective, when the 1-year-old begins to use the caregiver as a secure base from which to explore the environment, we are seeing the emergence of a kind of preliminary sense of self-worth. Once again, the infant's self-development evolves from her experience in relationships.

We also saw in the last chapter that late in the first year, caregivers' facial expressions influence infants' reactions to situations. Suppose, for example, that Mom opens the door to a stranger. Imagine how differently her 1-year-old might react if she sees her mother smile happily versus if Mom looks frightened and wary. Such social referencing not only implies recognition of the separateness of the other person, but it also provides the baby with a context in which she is sorting out experiences of the self from experiences of the other and from the combined experiences of the "we" (Emde & Buchsbaum, 1990). Social referencing demonstrates how transactional the self-development process really is. The child uses the caregiver's emotions to discern meaning in events and to regulate her own feelings in different situations.

Suppose now that the mother reliably responds to the approach of a stranger in one way: either with smiles or with wariness. When caregivers communicate consistent emotional signals about environmental events, infants are also likely to develop certain pervasive emotional dispositions. These emotional dispositions often are integral to a family's or even a culture's "value system," and they can affect how infants learn to approach questions such as "Can I trust other people?" "Is it safe to take risks?" Furthermore, caregivers' emotional signals may affect the process of emotion regulation and emotional self-knowledge well beyond infancy. For example, suppose a family tends to be unsympathetic to indications of incompetence in other people, often expressing anger or blame. When the child herself struggles with a task and fails to complete it despite her effort, she is likely to conclude that she should feel guilty or ashamed (Campos, Frankel, & Camras, 2004).

THE EMERGENCE OF SELF-AWARENESS AND SELF-CONCEPT

At 18- to 24-months-old, toddlers show signs of a benchmark achievement in self-development: They pass the "mirror test" (Lewis & Michalson, 1983). This classic test of **self-recognition** involves surreptitiously marking a child's nose, say with red

MyLab Education
Video Example 5.3
Note the difference between the response of the 12-month-old and the response of the 19-month-old as each faces self in a mirror. The 12-month-old does not recognize himself, but the 19-month-old shows self-awareness.

rouge, and then watching what she does as she looks at herself in a mirror. Children younger than 18 months usually touch the mirror where they see the mark, or they might look behind the mirror. But at about 18 months or soon after, most children reach up to touch their own noses, demonstrating that they understand that their own body is reflected in the mirror.

Another measure of *self-recognition*—seeing oneself as an object in the world—is called the "body-as-obstacle test." It is based on an observation that Piaget reported (1952). His 18-month-old daughter, Jacqueline, was trying to pick up a cloth without success, because she was standing on it. Apparently she figured out that her body was the obstacle, stepped off the cloth, and successfully retrieved it. In a modern version of the body-as-obstacle test, a mother encourages her infant to push a toy shopping cart toward her (Moore, Mealiea, Garon, & Povinelli, 2007). But the infant has been placed on a mat that is attached to the shopping cart, so that the cart will not move. The child has to recognize that her body is creating the problem and step off the mat. Children typically succeed on this task at about the same time that they pass the mirror test. And, once they begin to pass self-recognition tests, they show other signs of self-awareness. For example, they begin to display self-conscious emotions (see Chapter 4), such as pride and embarrassment, that indicate judgments about the self.

The timing of self-awareness seems to be about the same across cultures, but the culture's preferred approach to defining self, reflected in how infants are reared, seems to affect which measure is easier for children. The mirror-test seems to require recognizing the self in a completely individualistic setting, whereas the body-as-obstacle test is more a test of recognizing the self as it relates to context. Ross and colleagues (2017) predicted and found that babies in an individualistic Western culture, Scotland, usually passed the mirror test before they passed the body-as-obstacle test. When Scottish parents were observed caring for their infants, they tended to encourage autonomy, engaging in lots of face-to-face and other "distal" interactions, such as talking with their babies. On the other hand, Ross and colleagues predicted and found that in Zambia, where the culture defines self as embedded in relationships, babies were better at the body-as-obstacle test. Consistent with their culture, the Zambian parents were observed using more "proximal" infant-care strategies, such as keeping their babies close. These parents rarely engaged in face-to-face games or conversational style interactions.

For children whose development is delayed, as in the case of children with Down syndrome, self-recognition usually begins when they achieve a developmental level of approximately 2 years (Reddy, Williams, Constantini, & Lang, 2010). Comparison studies of maltreated and non-maltreated children show no differences in the timing of self-recognition (see Cicchetti, 2016). These studies also suggest that self-evaluation, or self-esteem, begins to emerge along with self-recognition. Maltreated children show considerably more negative or neutral affect when seeing their faces in the mirror than do non-maltreated children, who display more positive affect.

Self-recognition is a clear signal that a child has begun to formulate a conscious concept of self. Roughly after the child's second birthday, an increase in language skills makes possible further elaboration of the self-concept or Me-self. Children begin to describe themselves as "a boy" or "a girl" or as "big" or "little," and they begin to use appropriate personal pronouns to refer to themselves (e.g., Lewis & Ramsay, 2004). These achievements mark a watershed in the development of the self-concept, and caregivers make important contributions by virtue of the labels they apply to children. Parental statements such as "You are a big girl" can now be stored in memory as part of a child's self-knowledge (e.g., Nelson, 1993).

Caregivers' descriptions can be neutral and objective (such as the child's name or personal pronoun) or evaluative and subjective (such as "pretty" or "good"). Toddlers appear to believe both objective and subjective claims about themselves, apparently because the claims come from an authoritative source. In other words, young children cannot discount the negative part of the parental evaluation "bad girl" as due to parental bias or temporary bad mood. When self-description begins, maltreated children tell more negative stories about themselves than other children do (Toth et al., 2013). Such findings imply poor self-esteem, and they show the influence of caregivers' words and deeds on children's earliest self-evaluations. In fact, maltreatment generally seems to blunt the development of self-awareness, especially children's awareness of their inner thoughts and feelings (Harter, 2006).

As toddlers become preschoolers, their self-concepts become more and more differentiated and complex. Consistent with their level of cognitive development, preschoolers generally describe themselves in concrete, physical terms, such as "little" or "strong," whereas older children and adolescents use more abstract words. They also become more skilled at identifying specific aspects of themselves. For example, a 7-year-old might describe herself as helpful, funny, a good soccer player, and smart in reading but not in math. As we shall see in a later chapter, the self-concept continues to become more differentiated with age.

In summary, the self-system begins to develop in earliest infancy. There are many precursors to a conscious concept of self in the first year, a kind of procedural knowledge of the self in action and interaction, or "pre-self." An I-self, a sense of agency, is in place by the end of the first year, but clear awareness of self as a distinct entity, the Me-self, begins with self-recognition in the second year and is followed by explicit self-description in the third year. Self-evaluation or self-esteem is evident as soon as toddlers show signs of self-recognition. See Table 5.1 for a summary of the early phases of self-development.

Throughout infancy and beyond, the self-system is a joint construction of child, caregiver, and cultural and family milieu. We have described some ways in which caregiver–infant interactions seem to contribute to the development of the self. Later in this chapter, we will discuss in greater detail how parenting in the toddler and preschool years contributes to child outcomes, including the development of the self-system.

Roots of Self-Regulation

Up to now, we have described the emerging "I" and "Me." Now we turn our attention to another important dimension of the developing self-system, *self-regulation*. You were introduced to self-regulation in Chapter 3. It is an executive function that helps us to inhibit some impulses and behaviors and to perform other less preferred behaviors in order to achieve our goals. It involves not only controlling our behavior but also managing our emotions. A child who can pull her hand back from the cookie jar when she remembers, "No cookies before dinner," and who forces herself to try some unappealing vegetable dish at dinner because "It's good for you," is clearly engaged in self-regulation. She is controlling her behavior, but she is also finding ways to moderate her excitement (about the cookies) and her disgust (about the vegetables). As children grow, self-regulation becomes more complex. Children begin to be able to manage their emotional reactions and their actions in adjustment to the particular and sometimes subtle variations in their physical and social environment. What is appropriate and effective to say or do varies depending on whether a child is with Grandma at a movie or with a friend at the park. Self-regulation is a critical ingredient for success in all aspects of life, from getting along with others to learning in school or achieving in any arena.

TABLE 5.1 Phases of Self-Development

AGE	DEVELOPING ASPECTS OF SELF	MANIFESTATIONS
0–6 months	Pre-Self	Beginnings of "self-invariance" and "other invariance" embedded in infant–caregiver interactions
8–12 months	Intentional or Agentic Self or "I"	Intentional signaling of caregiver; social referencing; shared referents; beginning self-efficacy; using caregiver as secure base (beginning self-worth and trust)
15–24 months	Objective Self or "Me"	Self-recognition; early self-control; early self-esteem (feelings of autonomy); self-conscious emotions
24–60 months	Self-Monitoring Self	Self-description; self-regulation

Professionals regularly deal with problems involving self-regulation in one form or another. The preschooler who throws tantrums in school, the rebellious adolescent who runs away from home, the young adult who repeatedly loses jobs because she fails to show up on time—all may be examples of individuals who have difficulties in this area. Many other factors contribute to such adjustment problems; however, they all reflect some lack of compliance with specific requests or rules.

Obviously, achieving self-regulation is a rather formidable task for a mischievous toddler or even for a sophisticated high schooler. Even though this may sound like the accomplishment that many parents of tempestuous 2-year-olds long for, it is not realistic to expect a child to be able to master her behavior and emotions in every circumstance. The movement from dyadic emotion regulation to self-regulation of behavior and emotion, permitting harmonious interchange with the social environment, is a painstaking, complex, and long-term process (Thompson, 2014).

Historically, self-regulation has been studied under several headings: as a temperament trait (usually called "effortful control"); as a capacity to delay gratification (usually called "will power"); and as an executive function (usually called "inhibitory control"). Each line of research has focused to different degrees on emotional versus cognitive processes and on automatic versus intentional processes. But researchers are beginning to merge their findings and to learn how the whole complex self-regulatory system develops and works together (e.g., Blair, 2016; Duckworth & Steinberg, 2015; Gagne, 2017).

THE IMPORTANCE OF EMOTION REGULATION

It is absolutely essential to recognize that emotion regulation underlies any ability to control behaviors (Gagne, 2017). In fact, the earliest developmental task of infancy is to establish physiological balance, or control over fluctuating levels of arousal. The affective tension that the infant experiences when her homeostatic "set point" has been altered through hunger, pain, or too much stimulation motivates her to return to a more balanced state. You learned in Chapter 4 that the infant, unable to manage this on her own, signals the caregiver, whose soothing attentions function as critical ingredients in the development of the affect-regulation system. When the toddler or preschooler experiences periods of high arousal or distress, the sensitive caregiver steps in once again to help the child regain some affective control. As we emphasized in Chapter 4, good caregiving in infancy and beyond involves scaffolding the child's developing ability to regulate both emotional and behavioral expression.

THE EARLY PROGRESS OF BEHAVIOR REGULATION

How does behavior regulation come into being? It depends on two major cognitive and emotional advances that emerge in tandem with objective self-awareness or self-recognition: first, representational thought and associated abilities, and second, emotional response to wrongdoing.

Recall from Chapter 3 that by 9 or 10 months, babies show some capacity for representational thought, such as deferred imitation and separation anxiety. By 18 months their representational thought is progressing rapidly, supporting the toddler's ability to understand and produce language. Language is important for self-regulation (Blair, 2016). Toddlers begin to decipher and store parents' requests such as "Don't jump on the furniture," which might be a manifestation of a broader value that property should not be damaged, or "Share your candy with your sister," a version of "Do unto others." These standards or rules might differ somewhat according to the child's family and culture, but every cultural group maintains them (Lewis, 2016b).

Along with the growth of mental representation and language, many other cognitive skills are strengthening, such as the ability to focus attention, to comprehend the caregiver's requests, and to generalize rules to new situations. As these abilities sharpen in the second year, toddlers begin to show signs of governing their own behavior by some rules. Obviously, an infant cannot comply with social conventions precisely because she has no comprehension of them. But a 2-year-old who has the requisite level of cognitive maturity to understand and remember some rules, as well as the motivation to comply, begins to show signs of inhibiting her own behavior in such situations. Over the next several years, the many cognitive skills that support self-regulation advance rapidly. You can see the effects in how children manage tests of inhibitory control, for example, such as the "head-toes-knees-shoulders" test described in Chapter 3. Most children show dramatic improvement from ages 3 to 7 (Montroy, Bowles, Skibbe, McClelland, & Morrison, 2016).

The growth of emotions often linked to violations of standards for everyday behavior appears to begin late in the second year. These are the self-conscious emotions that we mentioned earlier as appearing when children show self-recognition: embarrassment, shame, guilt, and pride. These emotions are different from the emotions of infancy, because they require the ability to consider the self as separate from others and as the subject of others' judgments. Children have to be able to "think . . . about others thinking about them" (Lewis, 2016b, p. 793). Between the ages of 2 and 3, young children often display emotional responses to their wrongdoing and mistakes, suggesting that they have begun to evaluate themselves in ways that they expect to be evaluated by others. At 18 months, a child might take notice of her rule violation but without any discernable emotional response. Consider, for example, the toddler who spills milk on the floor. She may say "Uh oh!" and giggle or point to the spill without much concern. Later, rule breaking becomes associated with some negative affect. This same youngster at 3 may experience a sense of embarrassment, evaluate herself as "bad," and try to hide the evidence (Saarni, Campos, Camras, & Witherington, 2006).

The capacity for emotional response to wrongdoing is an important first step in moral development, which we will examine more closely later in this chapter. For now, we will consider how two emotions connected to wrongdoing, guilt and shame, differ. They do not have equally positive moral effects. As a means of making sense of transgression, children and adults who experience guilt might reason "I did a bad thing" whereas the inner script for those who experience shame might be "I am a bad person." Although guilt is often characterized as problematic, even "crippling," it is usually less intense than shame and can have adaptive consequences. Feelings of guilt have been associated with increases in other-directed empathy, positive reparative action, constructive problem solving, and low defensiveness and anger. Shame, on the other hand, is often more intense and painful, and a person feeling ashamed wants to hide or disappear. It is linked to elevated levels of cortisol and proinflammatory cytokines. Children may cope with the bad feeling by denying wrongdoing and/or blaming other people or situations. Shame is associated with displaced aggression, externalizing behavior, low self-esteem, and a range of psychiatric disorders (see Lewis, 2016b and Tangney, Stuewig, & Mashek, 2007 for reviews).

> **MyLab Education** Self-Check 5.2

Early Socialization: Parenting and the Development of the Self-System

5.3 Assess the effects of different parenting styles on a child's self-development and suggest techniques for improving parenting skills to address targeted behaviors.

Theorists from Cooley (1902) to Bowlby (e.g., 1969/1982) and Erikson (1950/1963) have assumed that many parts of the self-system grow out of our social interactions. As we saw in the last chapter, the available data do suggest that our earliest relationships create a trajectory for the development of self-concept and self-esteem. For example, when babies are securely attached to their mothers, they tend to be appropriately independent as 4-year-olds and to be self-confident and socially skilled as 10-year-olds (e.g., Sroufe, Egeland, Carlson, & Collins, 2005; see Thompson, 2015, for a review).

To briefly review: We know that early caregiving quality can make an important contribution to the quality of babies' attachments. Infants are likely to become securely attached to caregivers who respond promptly and consistently to crying; who react appropriately to babies' facial expressions, eye contact, and other signals; who handle their infants sensitively, and who hold them often during the first year, providing the contact comfort that helps infants modulate their emotions. Such caregiving requires patience and a child-centered approach that can be difficult for any parent sometimes, but is especially challenging if the baby has a difficult temperament or other special needs or if the parent is stressed or depressed. But the effort and self-sacrifice required for parents to create a "good fit," as Thomas and Chess (1977) described it, between their caregiving and a baby's needs does appear to contribute to attachment quality and to the direction that self-knowledge and self-evaluation will take. This process continues after infancy, as the description of self-development in the last section indicates. In this section, we will take a close look at parent–child relationships in the toddler and preschool years. We will focus especially on the characteristics of parenting that may be most conducive to helping young children to develop positive self-esteem and adaptive self-regulatory mechanisms. One way to think about parents is to consider them as having a basic set of caregiving responsibilities or tasks, beyond meeting their children's physical requirements for food, clothing, shelter, health care, and so on.

We just summarized the caregiving responsibilities parents have toward their infants, and these are captured by the first three parenting tasks listed in Table 5.2. You can see in the table that as the infant becomes a toddler, gaining cognitive, communicative, and motor skills, the list of parenting tasks expands. There are new challenges for parents who are trying to be sensitive and responsive and seeking to create a good fit between their care and the child's needs. First, caregivers are faced with the need to grant more autonomy to the child. As toddlers become capable of doing more on their own, they are motivated to practice and expand their growing competencies. The strong dependency that characterizes young babies is gradually replaced by a capacity and need for independent action and mastery. Erikson theorized that toddlers' emerging feelings of worth are benefited when they can use their growing skills to function at least somewhat autonomously, whether it is by feeding themselves or by buttoning their own buttons, or more subtly, by saying "NO!"—that is, refusing to do what someone else requires (see Table 1.2 in Chapter 1). Thus, although the earliest feelings of worth grow out of an infant's trust in others to meet all her needs, those feelings of worth grow in the toddler years when the child begins to experience self-sufficiency, or autonomy, a sense that "I can do it myself."

TABLE 5.2 Parents' Caregiving Tasks

PARENTING TASK	WHEN IT BEGINS (CHILD STAGE)
Regulating emotional arousal	Infancy
Engaging in appropriate stimulation/reciprocal interaction	Infancy
Providing secure base and safe haven	Infancy
Accepting child's growing autonomy	Toddlerhood
Supporting mastery/scaffolding problem solving	Toddlerhood
Socializing expression/containment of emotions	Toddlerhood
Socializing behavior/providing clear rules/setting limits	Toddlerhood
Providing opportunities for broader social contacts	Toddlerhood

SOURCE: Based on Sroufe, L. A. (2016). The place of attachment in development. In J. Cassidy & P. R. Shaver (Eds.), *Handbook of attachment: Theory research and clinical applications* (3rd ed., pp. 997–1011). NY: Guilford Press.

Second, also because the child's behavioral and cognitive skills are growing, the caregiver must begin to **socialize** the child, that is, to prepare the child to be a competent member of society, from providing opportunities to interact with people beyond the family to imposing **discipline**. *Discipline* involves limiting some behaviors and demanding others, so that the child will be safe ("Don't climb on the counter") and so that she will behave in ways that are conventionally acceptable ("You must wear clothes"). Parents generally impose more discipline on the child as they perceive her to be more and more capable of self-control. When parents tell a child to do, or not to do, something, they are depending on the child's ability to initiate or to stop her own actions. The only way to make a young infant do, or not do, something is to rely on physically moving or restraining the child. Parents do a lot of that with infants, but they rely more and more on controlling by request or command during early childhood, as the requisite abilities (such as representational and comprehension skills) develop.

Thus, caregiver–child relationships are reorganized in the post-infancy period, with the additions of children's autonomy seeking, on one hand, and parents' imposition of discipline, on the other hand. What are the important features of this more complex relationship between parent and child? What role does the parent–child relationship play in the child's developing self-system? Let's begin by examining what research indicates are the most important dimensions or features of a parent's behavior in this relationship.

The Dimensions of Parenting Style

Studies of parenting after infancy have a long history and have produced many complicated findings. Remarkably, researchers from very different theoretical traditions have repeatedly identified two major dimensions or aspects of parents' behavior that seem to characterize the quality of parenting. These can be thought of as the primary contributors to what is called **parenting style** (for reviews see Baumrind, 1989, 1993; Bornstein, 2015; Maccoby & Martin, 1983; Pinquart, 2017).

THE WARMTH DIMENSION—PARENTAL RESPONSIVENESS

In the post-infancy period, parents continue to create an emotional climate for their children. Contributing to a positive climate is the **warmth dimension (parental responsiveness)**: listening to the child, being involved and interested in the child's activities, accepting the child, making positive attributions toward the child, being "tuned in" and supportive (e.g., Baumrind, 1989; Bornstein, 2015). In essence, high levels of warmth with toddlers and older children are comparable to high levels of responsive, sensitive care with infants. But some of the child's needs have changed. With toddlers, as we have seen, autonomy needs begin to be important, and responsive parents accept these needs, acquiescing when possible to their children's reasonable demands for autonomy (Baumrind, 1993). So, when 25-month-old Amanda begins to insist that she can dress herself, her mother tries to accommodate her by setting aside extra time for the morning dressing ritual. She also ignores the inconvenience and the sometimes strange-looking results and gives Amanda positive messages about the process: "You're getting to be such a big girl to put on your own clothes!" Her attitude is **child centered**, sidelining parental needs (for time, convenience, and coordinated outfits) when possible to meet Amanda's developmental needs.

Some parents create a more negative emotional climate. Their behavior is often **parent centered**: They show little responsiveness to their children's concerns and are unlikely to do things just to meet those concerns. They may even make hostile attributions when children's needs are out of line with their own. When 20-month-old Jessie wants to feed herself her morning cereal, for example, at first her mother ignores her. When Jessie insists, her mother attends to her demands by making negative attributions, such as "You'll just make a mess" and "Why do you always make things so hard in the morning?" When Jessie accidentally spills the milk, her mother responds in frustration, "I told you that you couldn't do it yourself!"

We have seen that sensitive, responsive parental care in infancy promotes secure attachments. Likewise, parents' warmth and responsiveness with their toddlers and

MyLab Education
Video Example 5.4
Many parts of the self-system grow out of our social interactions. As you observe the play setting in this video, consider how the self-system is influenced by the interactions and opportunities for expression.

preschoolers help maintain secure attachments and increase the likelihood that children will be cooperative when parents place demands on them (Thompson, 2016). In a series of classic studies, for example, toddlers' compliance with their mothers' requests was observed in toy cleanup tasks and in a situation where mothers designated some attractive toys as "off limits." The most enthusiastically compliant toddlers were those who were securely attached to their mothers (according to a separate assessment), and whose mothers maintained a warm, positive emotional climate throughout the sessions (Kochanska, 1995; Kochanska, Aksan, & Koenig, 1995).

What happens when a parent of a securely attached infant becomes a less sensitive caregiver as the child moves into the toddler and preschool years? First, it is worth noting that this is most likely to happen when the parent faces an increase in negative life events (such as a job loss, separation from spouse, homelessness, violence in the home or neighborhood, and so on). Second, if a toddler begins with a secure attachment, she tends to weather insensitive parenting better than if she starts with an insecure attachment. However, even for children with a history of secure attachment, insensitive care in the toddler and preschool period seems especially problematic, as though "the continuing harmony of the parent-child relationship . . . constitute(s) a bridge between a secure attachment in infancy and the development of later personality and working models of relationships" (Thompson, 2016, p. 334).

THE CONTROL DIMENSION—PARENTAL DEMANDINGNESS

The second major dimension of parenting style is the **control dimension (parental demandingness)**. If parental responsiveness means that parents sometimes acquiesce to their children's demands, parental demandingness leads parents to impose discipline. Demanding parents exercise **behavioral control**. They communicate to their children expectations for appropriate behavior that are suitable to each child's level of maturity (sometimes called **maturity demands**). Demanding parents impose clear and consistent standards and rules of behavior, and they enforce them. Interestingly, this dimension of parenting can be either child centered or parent centered. If the parent's concern is the development of self-control necessary for children to feel secure, to behave in ways that gain social acceptance, and to become skillful at social give and take, then discipline has a child focus. If the parents' concerns—for example, for quiet, or convenience, or orderliness, and so on—are primary, then discipline has a parent focus. Of course, parents' disciplinary motives may sometimes combine both kinds of concerns, and the same parents may shift their focus depending on the given situation. For example, Hastings and Grusec (1998) found that parents expressed more parent-centered concerns (such as wanting to be in control) when disciplining their children in public, but parents expressed more child-centered concerns (such as teaching a child not to give up easily) in private interactions.

The control dimension refers to parents' *behavioral control*, which is an important element of responsible parenting. This must be distinguished from **psychological control**, which refers to a kind of intrusiveness and interference on the part of parents (e.g., Barber, Stolz, & Olsen, 2005; Doan et al., 2017). The latter often involves criticizing and/or derogating the child. It is called *psychological control* because the parent seems to be trying to manipulate the child's emotional experiences by promoting feelings of guilt or shame to pressure the child (e.g., "You ruined my day" or "You should be ashamed of yourself"), and/or by making love conditional on the child's behavior (e.g., "I don't like you right now," or "I can't stand the sight of you"). Psychological control has more to do with the emotional climate a parent creates (the warmth dimension) than it does with demandingness.

Four Parenting Styles

We can describe four basic *parenting styles*, or constellations of parenting characteristics, as shown in Table 5.3, by combining and crossing the positive and negative poles of parental responsiveness and demandingness (Maccoby & Martin, 1983). As you will see, these styles are often predictive of child characteristics (Baumrind, 1989, 1993; Pinquart, 2017).

MyLab Education
Video Example 5.5
This caregiver shows both warmth and demandingness as she guides the children through the resolution of a dispute. The guidelines she provides for sharing will help the children develop their own self-control.

TABLE 5.3 Parenting Dimensions and Parenting Styles

PARENTAL DEMANDINGNESS	PARENTAL WARMTH	
	ACCEPTING, RESPONSIVE, CHILD-CENTERED	*REJECTING, UNRESPONSIVE, PARENT-CENTERED*
Exercises Behavioral Control, Makes Increasing Maturity Demands	**Authoritative Style**	**Authoritarian Style**
Does NOT Exercise Behavioral Control, Makes Few Demands	**Permissive Style**	**Neglecting–Uninvolved Style**

SOURCE: Based on Maccoby, E. E., & Martin, J. A. (1983). Socialization in the context of the family. In P. H. Mussin & E. M. Hetherington, *Handbook of child psychology* vol. 4 (4th ed., pp. 1–101).

THE AUTHORITATIVE STYLE

Parents with an **authoritative style** are both highly responsive and highly demanding. So, they create a positive emotional climate for their children, promoting autonomy and supporting assertiveness and individuality. At the same time these parents accept responsibility for socializing their children by expecting mature behavior and by setting and consistently enforcing clear standards. Other qualities also tend to be part of this constellation. These parents are often openly affectionate; they encourage two-way communication with their children (that is, they genuinely listen and pay attention as well as talking themselves). Their communications about expectations and standards are usually clear and come with explanations that go beyond "You do it because I said so" to statements that help children make sense of their parents' demands. Thus, they are strong on behavioral control, but do not use psychological control.

THE AUTHORITARIAN STYLE

Parents with an **authoritarian style** are low on responsiveness, but highly demanding. Thus, they do not create a positive emotional climate nor do they encourage children's individualistic strivings or assertiveness, but they do tend to exercise considerable control, making maturity demands and requiring conformity to rules. A few other qualities tend to be characteristic of authoritarian parents. First, authoritarian parents usually communicate less effectively with their children than authoritative parents. Their communications are more one sided ("I say what will happen; you listen"). They express less affection. And their control tends to be more restrictive, meaning that they often restrict their children's emotional expressiveness and other self-assertive behaviors. In other words, they are likely to exercise not just behavioral but also psychological control. They also are more likely to enforce control by using harsh techniques (see the section on parenting practices below) and are less likely to provide explanations that go beyond "Because I said so."

THE PERMISSIVE STYLE

Parents with a **permissive style** are moderately to highly responsive, but low on demandingness. Thus, they exercise less behavioral control of their children than other parents, making fewer maturity demands. They may be especially "laissez-faire" about restricting aggressive behavior. They are more nurturing and affectionate than authoritarian parents, but usually not as nurturing as authoritative parents.

THE NEGLECTING–UNINVOLVED STYLE

Some parents are both low on responsiveness and low on demandingness, so that they actually invest little time or attention in a child and are largely parent centered in their concerns. Like permissive parents, those with a **neglecting–uninvolved style** seem to neglect their responsibility to socialize the child, but they also express less affection and are not likely to be responsive to their children's needs, perhaps even expressing hostility or making negative attributions to their children. When they do impose limits on their children, they tend to use harsh techniques and little explanation.

Parenting Style and Child Outcomes

Through the long history of research on parenting, small but significant correlations have been found between parenting style, on one hand, and children's typical behaviors, on the other. Briefly, authoritative parenting has been associated with many positive outcomes in young children: adaptability, competence and achievement, good social skills and peer acceptance, and low levels of antisocial or aggressive behavior. Of particular interest to us in this chapter, authoritative parenting seems to promote positive self-development, especially high self-esteem and the capacity for self-regulation.

The children of authoritarian parents are more likely to be irritable and conflicted, showing signs of both anxiety and anger. They are conforming (self-controlled) with authority figures, but are not likely to be socially skillful, and they are susceptible to being bullied and/or to becoming bullies (Ladd & Ladd, 1998; Pinquart, 2017). They tend to have low self-esteem, and although they exhibit self-control with authorities, they may lack self-regulation when they believe that authorities are not monitoring them (Bornstein, 2015).

Permissive parents are more likely to have children who exhibit uncontrolled, impulsive behavior and low levels of self-reliance. They are low on cognitive competence and social agency, and are likely to be aggressive, especially in family interactions. In some studies they have had high self-esteem, apparently when parents are very warm, but many studies suggest that warmth combined with demandingness is more certain to be associated with self-esteem (Maccoby & Martin, 1983).

Finally, the children of neglecting/uninvolved parents are likely to be impulsive, to show high levels of both externalizing problems (e.g., aggressiveness) and internalizing problems (e.g., depression), and to have low self-esteem.

Be cautious in interpreting these relationships between parenting style and child outcomes. The strength of the associations is modest, cueing us that many factors interact with parenting and modify its effects. Researchers have begun to identify a multiplicity of interacting factors, which we will discuss in a later section of this chapter (see Bornstein, 2015; Pinquart, 2017).

Parenting Practices: Methods of Control

Thus far, we have looked at parenting style—parents' combined responsiveness and demandingness—as a source of children's behavior and self-development. Another aspect of parenting concerns the methods of control parents choose. These are the strategies parents use to enforce their demands. Parents' control methods mostly fall into three categories: power assertion, psychological control (which includes love withdrawal), and induction. Power assertion can involve corporal (physical) punishment or the threat of corporal punishment, ranging from spanking on the buttocks to harsh beating with objects. Or, it can involve withdrawal of privileges, from mild forms (such as time-out procedures with toddlers, see Box 5.1), to severe denial (e.g., withholding meals). Power assertion of both types is usually effective for the immediate control of behavior. Children often change their behavior while they feel threatened. But there can be unwanted side effects. Harsh or severe power assertion has been linked to high levels of anger and anxiety in children, and children whose parents use harsh, punitive practices tend to be more aggressive than other children (Baumrind, 2001; Bornstein, 2015; Pinquart, 2017). New research on the effects of "milder" forms of corporal punishment (e.g., spanking) will be reviewed later in this chapter.

If a child is accustomed to power assertive control methods, what happens when the threat is removed (e.g., Mom or Dad is not present or unlikely to find out)? Does the child engage in self-regulation? In other words, will she regulate her own behavior because she is committed to an internalized set of standards? There are conflicting data on this issue. On the whole, power assertion does not seem to be particularly effective in promoting self-regulation. Interestingly, *milder* forms of power assertion are more effective than harsher forms, especially when they do not involve corporal punishment. But the picture is complex and cannot be fully understood without considering other factors, such as child temperament, culture, and overall parenting style. We will return to this issue later.

Box 5.1: Time-Out: Getting It Right

In many Dennis the Menace cartoons, Dennis sits in a pint-sized chair, hugging his teddy bear, facing into a corner, banished for some infraction. Dennis's parents use **time-out** as a disciplinary procedure: During a short span of time, Dennis is required to discontinue his involvement in ongoing activities to quietly sit somewhere apart. The technique involves mild power assertion and is suitable for use with toddlers and preschoolers. There is no pain involved, but time-out gets the attention of young children. Requiring a child to sit in a corner is one approach, but you can choose any place that separates the child from the action, while keeping her in a safe place that is within easy reach of the caregiver. Do not choose a spot where the child might be overwhelmed by feelings of isolation. The purpose of time-out is to eliminate the rewards of misbehavior, not to frighten a child. Indeed, it will work even if the "place apart" is in the midst of things. For example, in one day care center, the time-out chair is in the middle of a busy classroom so that the child is safely in view of the teachers. For the children, just being confined to the chair, unable to participate in the ongoing activities of the class, is sufficiently aversive to be effective.

It seems simple, but it is actually somewhat complex, and parents often fail to fully understand what they need to do to make it work (Drayton et al., 2017). First, to minimize the child's anxious arousal, stay calm. Remember that nearly all young children misbehave sometimes, and more exuberant children may do so more often. For example, many preschoolers occasionally engage in instrumental aggression, such as grabbing toys away from other children (Hay, 2017). You may be frustrated, but your child is usually just being a child. It should be clear that your negative assessment is restricted to the offending behavior; your affection for your child is intact.

To start, it helps to choose just two or three specific, target behaviors that need to be changed. For very young children, reserve time-out for behaviors that are important to control because of safety, such as climbing on the kitchen counter, or because they are antisocial and hurtful, such as hitting or biting. Explain to the child *which* behaviors will lead to time-out, *why* they are unacceptable, and *what alternative behaviors* would be acceptable. It works best if children know the rules in advance so that what will lead to time-out is clear. (Don't forget to provide some positive attention for those more acceptable behaviors.) Don't use time-out for behaviors that have not been previously identified as inappropriate, and when the time-out is over, follow up with a reminder of your reasons for restricting this behavior. As you will see in this chapter, mild power assertion combined with induction can be very effective. Although Dennis the Menace is allowed to have a teddy bear in time-out, it is more consistent to eliminate access to toys, television, and attention from others.

Don't expect everything to go smoothly right from the start. At first a child may refuse to stay in time-out, or she may repeat the offending behavior just to test your resolve. If the child won't stay in time-out, make it *very* brief—just a moment—and gently hold her from behind to create the condition of no attention. Then quickly make eye contact and praise the child for staying in time-out, even though it was only for a moment. Stick it out—it will pay off. Time-out needs only to be long enough to get the point across. The younger the child, the less time is appropriate. One rule of thumb is 1 or 2 minutes for each year of age, so that the maximum time-out for a 2-year-old would be 4 minutes. Longer times are likely to become so aversive that they could defeat the purpose of simply getting the child's attention and creating an opportunity for her to think over her behavior.

At the end of a time-out episode, assurances of your affection are appropriate. This also may be a good time to assist the child with emotion regulation, helping the child to identify her emotions and to consider ways of managing them.

Time-out, like most effective discipline, requires putting aside what you are doing to attend to the misbehavior when it happens. It can be inconvenient, but *immediacy* is important to help young children make the right connection between their behavior and its consequences. Similarly, *consistency* is essential. When a parent's responses are unreliable, it is difficult for a child to learn what the rules are. Just how consistent can a parent be? There are going to be times when you simply cannot follow up on an act of misbehavior. But most times you can, if you make it a priority and if you are careful to use time-out for just a few important behaviors. Suppose, for example, that you are teaching your 4-year-old, Jenny, not to hit her baby brother. In the middle of your grocery shopping, sure enough, Jenny hauls off and whacks him. Immediately, tell Jenny what's wrong with this picture: "Jenny, you know that hitting is not okay. It hurts and it makes people cry, and we don't hit in our family, ever! You have to go to time-out for that." Pick up the baby, take Jenny's hand, leave the cart, and head for the car. In the car, put Jenny in the back seat and sit in the front with the baby. Say clearly, "You are in time-out," and face forward for the designated time. At the end, explain the rule again, tell Jenny that time-out is over, and head back to the shopping cart. In other words, if at all possible, improvise. (No car? Stand silently on the sidewalk for the time-out period.) There are bound to be situations that make immediate and full follow-through impossible. You could have been in the middle of checking out your groceries, for example. But if your usual response is swift and sure, your efforts will pay off (see Drayton et al., 2017; Hecker & Sori, 2016; and the Applications section for more detailed pointers on effective discipline and intervention for parents).

Psychological control, as you have seen, is a set of strategies that tend to go together, including inducing guilt or shame and withdrawing love. Love withdrawal might include a parent's withdrawing attention or affection, expressing disappointment or disillusionment with a child, turning away from a child, cutting off verbal or emotional contact, or enforcing separations from the parent. Psychological control is rarely used alone by parents, but when it is used, it seems to generate high anxiety and is more effective in eliciting immediate compliance than any other method (Doan et al., 2017). As with power assertion, the compliance that psychological control generates is usually short term (Grusec, Danyliuk, Kil, & O'Neill, 2017).

Induction refers to parents' use of explanation: giving reasons for rules ("If everybody touched the paintings they would soon be very dirty from fingerprints") and appealing to children's desires to be grown-up ("Big girls don't take toys away from babies"). "Other-oriented" explanations seem to be especially powerful in promoting empathy ("When you hit people, it hurts them and makes them sad"). But explanations need to be appropriate to the situation. Suppose a parent is trying to explain to a preschooler why her teacher wants the children to raise their hands during group time. An "other oriented" explanation is not likely to work as well as pointing out how confusing things get when everyone talks at once (Grusec et al., 2017).

Using induction seems to be the most effective way to promote the internalization of rules. When a child has *internalized* a rule, she has made it a guiding principle for herself. She will usually then employ that rule to regulate her own behavior regardless of whether authorities are present and whether immediate consequences are likely. For example, Laible and Thompson (2002) observed mothers with their 30-month-olds in contexts where conflicts were likely to arise. These were a clean-up task and a "frustration task" where children had only a too-difficult puzzle to play with while their mothers were busy and while other more interesting toys were off limits. Mothers who used more inductive control strategies, like justification ("We can't touch those toys because they might break"), and fewer punitive or aggravating control strategies, like threats, teasing, and harsh commands, had children who were more likely than other children to exercise self-control in a resistance-to-temptation task 6 months later.

Often, the same parents will use one practice on some occasions and another in other situations, and sometimes parents use multiple practices in the same disciplinary episode (Bornstein, 2015; Fung, Li, & Lam, 2017). Most parents tend to favor using one type of practice more than the others, and when they do, their primary practice is somewhat predictive of certain child outcomes. But, much as we found with rearing practices in infancy, such as breast versus bottle feeding, particular practices may be less important than the overall quality of the parent–child relationship. For toddlers and older children, the meaning that the child attributes to parents' practices is likely to be important and appears to be tied to the emotional climate established by parenting style. In particular, when parents are warm and responsive, their children are more likely to comply with parental demands (Grusec et al., 2017).

Parenting style, then, affects how effective a parenting practice will be with a child. As it happens, certain practices tend to be combined with certain parenting styles. Authoritative parents, for example, are often characterized by extensive use of induction, regardless of what other practices they might sometimes use. The children of authoritative parents are likely to show higher levels of competence, self-esteem, and self-regulation than children exposed to other parenting styles. But what might happen if parents who show most of the qualities of an authoritative style—especially high responsiveness and high demandingness—were to use primarily power assertion to enforce their demands? In the next section, we will consider how parenting style interacts with practice for different children and in different cultural contexts, focusing on how these factors interact in the early phases of self-development, during the toddler and early preschool years. We will revisit these issues in later chapters when we describe self-regulatory and moral development in older children and adolescents.

Moderators of Parenting and Parenting Effectiveness

Authoritative parents seem to get the best results from their children, but are their behaviors really having any influence? Both developmentalists (e.g., Scarr, 1993) and popular writers (e.g., Harris, 1998) have asked whether we are wrong to assume that correlations between parenting and child outcomes imply that parenting style and practice are actually causing children's behavior. Several other possibilities exist. First, the shared biological inheritance of parents and children might account for both the parental and the child characteristics measured in these studies (Scarr, 1993, 1997). For example, the same genetic endowment that makes parents affectionate and responsive might produce children who are cooperative and good-natured. Second, children's predispositions and temperaments may actually cause parents' behaviors rather than vice versa. For example, perhaps children who are "naturally" mild-mannered and compliant, like Angie, usually elicit authoritative parenting, but active, impulsive, negative children, like Mary, usually elicit more authoritarian or neglectful parenting behaviors.

Overall, although some controversy persists on these issues, an accumulation of evidence supports a multidimensional approach to the question of direction of effects in children's social development (Bornstein, 2015). That means that multiple causes are interacting, mutually modifying one another. As in Bronfenbrenner's bioecological model, proximal processes—reciprocal interactions between the child and the people and things that surround the child—as well as distal processes, such as genes and culture, are all playing a role (e.g., Bronfenbrenner & Morris, 2006). In this section, we will consider two important factors in the multidimensional mix: the child's temperament and the broader cultural environment.

THE CHILD'S TEMPERAMENT, PARENTING, AND CHILD OUTCOMES

Recall that during a child's infancy, both parents and infants contribute to the quality of the caregiving relationship. It is harder for mothers to be sensitive and responsive to a baby with a difficult temperament, for example. But when mothers are highly responsive during infancy, the good fit they create between their caregiving and the baby's needs supports the development of a secure attachment even for babies with difficult temperaments. When mothers are not able to create a good fit, the type of insecure attachment that emerges often seems to be at least partly influenced by the baby's temperament (Vaughn & Bost, 2016).

With toddlers and preschoolers, temperament and other child characteristics continue to contribute to the quality of the parent–child relationship. Children's typical behaviors can affect both parenting style and the particular disciplinary practices that parents are most likely to use.

In a classic paper, Bell and Chapman (1986) reviewed 14 studies that demonstrated the influence of children on parents. Many of these studies were at least partly experimental, with adults (usually parents) reacting to, or interacting with, children who were not their own, in situations created by the researchers. The studies examined adults' responses to children's dependence versus independence behaviors, their tendencies to be aggressive or to withdraw, and their responsiveness to adults (e.g., tendencies to smile, chat, imitate, and so on). For example, in one of these studies, Marcus (1975, 1976) showed parents videotapes of a child actor solving a puzzle. The child in the film behaved either dependently (e.g., seeking help, like, "Would this piece go better here or here?") or independently. The adults' reactions were more directive with the dependent than with the independent child. Stevens-Long (1973) examined parents' reactions to unrelated children's aggressive, uncooperative behavior or to anxious, withdrawn behavior. The adults were more likely to command or ignore the more aggressive children, but to verbally help or reward the more depressive children. A number of newer longitudinal studies have corroborated these early findings. For example, child characteristics at one age (e.g., children's low levels of affectionate behavior) have been found to predict changes in parents' behaviors over time (e.g., decreases in parental warmth; Waller et al., 2014). When Hallers-Haalboom and colleagues (2017) studied families with two children, they found mothers' and fathers' sensitivity was sometimes different with each child. When it was, the children's specific characteristics seemed to be important, as we saw with Angie and Mary. Studies such as these paint a picture of a multilayered, complex interactive system between parent and child. The child's characteristics are likely to affect the parent's behavior, and the parent's style and practices affect the child's behavior. But other factors also modify parents' and children's effects on each other. The degree to which the child affects the parent's practices and beliefs depends in part on the parent's initial attitudes toward children and child rearing, as well as the parent's emotional state and ability to manage stress (Bornstein, 2015). For example, parents who have child-centered rather than adult-centered concerns are able to be more supportive and responsive to their youngsters. Parents' emotional states influence how child centered they are likely to be. Depressive mothers report fewer child-oriented positive emotions and concerns than mothers who are not depressed (Dix, Gershoff, Maunier, & Miller, 2004). Similarly, as we saw in the last chapter, parents' own relationship histories and their working models of attachment are likely to influence how they respond to their children and how well they adapt to their children's characteristics.

CHILDREN'S DIFFERENTIAL SUSCEPTIBILITY TO PARENTING STRATEGIES

One illustration of the interactive complexities we have been describing is that children show *differential susceptibility* to different rearing approaches, depending on their early temperament characteristics (e.g., Belsky & Pluess, 2013). As you saw in Chapter 4, difficult, negatively reactive infants are often *more* affected by both sensitive *and* insensitive parenting than infants with easy temperaments. We see similar interactive patterns as children get older. Let's consider the tendency to display aggressive behavior. Children who have difficult temperaments are more likely than children with easy temperaments to show inappropriate levels of aggression with peers and/or adults (Streit, Carlo, Ispa, & Palermo, 2017). But how aggressive they become is more closely linked to parents' disciplinary and interactive style than it is for children with easy temperaments. For youngsters with difficult temperaments, insensitive, negative parent behaviors (e.g., frowning, criticizing, yelling, being physically intrusive) appear to increase their proneness to aggression, whereas sensitive, positive discipline (e.g., being affectionate, praising, using distraction) decreases their proneness to aggression. For youngsters with easy temperaments, even those who seem prone to aggression, parenting differences do not have as much effect as they do for children with difficult temperaments. That is, aggressive tendencies are not moderated substantially by parenting practices (Slagt, Dubas, Deković, & van Aken, 2016).

THE CULTURAL CONTEXT, PARENTING, AND CHILD OUTCOMES

Just as children's characteristics can affect parenting and outcomes, cultural factors, such as the race, ethnicity, and socioeconomic status of the family, can moderate parenting practices and may even alter their effects. The preceding sections have made a strong case for the benefits of authoritative parenting, but most of the supportive research findings have come from U.S. majority samples. Does parenting differ in other parts of the world, or in other ethnic or SES groups, and are these styles effective for other populations? No doubt about it, culture affects parenting. At its core, culture dynamically shapes values, self-regulation, and behavior, and cultures could not continue to exist without some means of transmitting their values and worldviews to younger members. Through socialization, cultures transmit methods of coping with and adapting to specific challenges, a process that fosters resilience in children and youth (Garcia Coll, 1990).

Studying the effects of culture on parenting is a task that is nothing less than daunting. Remember that what we call "culture" is essentially embedded within the environment at every level of the ecological system, from the immediate family to the larger society and its institutions. It is sometimes difficult to avoid conflating culture with geography, SES, or race. Researchers often paint with a relatively broad brush in order to capture key qualities that make one culture different from another, but, in reality, there is wide individual variation within groups (Gibbons, 1998). For example, "Hispanic" or "Latino" culture, broadly construed, reflects Mexican, Puerto Rican, South American, Dominican, Spanish, and other group influences. "European American" culture includes British, Irish, Italian, German, French, Polish, and other influences. So it is important to remember that these labels are generalizations that attempt to capture common underlying dimensions. When you consider all the labels writers have used to distinguish cultures, such as individualistic-collectivist, developing-developed, East-West, rural-metropolitan, immigrant-acculturated, native–nonnative, majority-minority, and so forth, you can see what they are up against.

Despite these difficulties, some underlying cultural structures and values that are particularly salient for parenting have been identified. These structures and values may help to explain observed differences in parenting practices, such as discipline, across cultures. Table 5.4 offers several examples of traditional cultural values, reviewed by Yasui and Dishion (2007), thought to influence parenting from five major ethnic groups in the United States. Definitions for less commonly used words (in italics) are provided as well.

For middle-class White Americans, an authoritative parenting style and the nondirective or inductive disciplinary practices that usually accompany that style— offering suggestions, making polite requests, distracting a child, giving explanations, and so on—are associated with beneficial outcomes for their children. In other cultural

TABLE 5.4 Parenting Values and Effects Across Five Cultures

CULTURAL GROUPS	TRADITIONAL VALUE ORIENTATION	TRADITIONALLY IMPORTANT VALUES	POSSIBLE EFFECTS ON PARENTING
African American	*Communalism*	Individualism, Importance of kinship relationships, Unity, Creativity, Cooperation, Authenticity, Awareness of racial disparities and discrimination	Authoritarian (No-nonsense) parenting; Unilateral decisions made by one parent; Egalitarian (equality of mother and father) family structure
European American	Independence	Autonomy, Individualism	Authoritative; Egalitarian family structure
Latino American	Collectivism	Interdependence, *Familism, Respeto, Personalismo, Machismo, Marianismo*	Authoritarian; Patriarchal family structure; High Parental warmth
Native American	Collectivism	Interdependence, Value of Nature, Harmony, Balance, Extended Family, Respect for elders, Cooperation, Sharing	Permissive; Patriarchal and Matriarchal Structures
Asian-American	Collectivism	Interdependence; *Filial piety, Guan & Chiao shun, Amae,* Conformity, Obedience, Avoiding loss of face, Humility/Modesty	Authoritarian; Structural and managerial parental involvement; Patriarchal family structure

SOURCE: Based on Yasui, M. & Dishion, T. J. (2007). The ethnic context of child and adolescent problem behavior: Implications for child and family interventions. *Clinical Child and Family Review, 10,* 137–179.

Key: _____

Communalism: Emphasis on social bonds and mutual interdependence as well as individuality that contributes to the good of the group.

SOURCE: Boykin, A. W., Ellison, C. M., Albury, A., & Jagers, R. J. (1997). Communalism: Conceptualization and measurement of an Afrocultural social orientation. *Journal of Black Studies, 27,* 409–441.

Familism: A sense of loyalty, solidarity, and identification with family and community.

SOURCE: Marin, G. (1993). Influence of acculturation on familialism and self-identification among Hispanics. In M. E. Bernal & G. P. Knight (Eds.), *Ethnic identity: Formation and transmission among Hispanics and other minorities* (pp. 181–196). Albany, NY: SUNY.

Respeto: Respect for experience of others and deference to authority.

SOURCE: Altarriba, J. & Bauer, L. M. (1998). Counseling the Hispanic client: Cuban Americans, Mexican Americans, and Puerto Ricans. *Journal of Counseling and Development, 76,* 389–396.

Personalismo: Preference for warm, courteous, and personal interactions with others over more formal interactions.

SOURCE: Ojeda, L., Flores, L. Y., Meza, R. R., & Morales, A. (2011). Culturally competent qualitative research with Latino immigrants. *Hispanic Journal of Behavioral Sciences, 33,* 184–203.

Machismo: Traditional gender value for males; emphasis on the masculine role of defending, protecting, and caring for family but sometimes interpreted as dominance and sexual bravado.

SOURCE: Torres, J. B., Solberg, S. H., & Carlstrom, M. S. (2002). The myth of sameness among Latino men and their machismo. *American Journal of Orthopsychiatry, 72,* 163–181.

Marianismo: Traditional gender value for females: emphasis on the feminine role of self-sacrifice, virtue, and caring (using the Virgin Mary as a role model).

SOURCE: Castillo, L. G. (2010). Construction and initial validation of the Marianismo Beliefs Scale. *Counselling Psychology Quarterly, 23,* 163–175.

Filial piety: Moral obligation to respect, honor, and care for parents; considered to be a key value in intergenerational relationships.

SOURCE: Hwang, K.-K. (1999). Filial piety and loyalty: Two types of social identification in Confucianism. *Asian Journal of Social Psychology, 2,* 163–183.

Guan and Chiao Shun: Duty to train or govern children in a loving way for their benefit.

SOURCE: Chao, R. K. (1994). Beyond parental control and authoritarian parenting style: Understanding Chinese parenting through the cultural notion of training. *Child Development, 65,* 1111–1120.

Amae: Characterized within a relationship by the mutual indulgence of each member's needs for love and affection; parental indulgence of children's needs to promote harmony in the relationship.

SOURCE: Rothbaum, F., Kakinuma, M., Nagaoka, R., & Azuma, H. (2007). Attachment and amae: Parent–child closeness in the United States and Japan. *Journal of Cross-Cultural Psychology, 38,* 465–486.

groups, parents who are warm and responsive are often more restrictive of their children's behavior, more directive, and less likely to tolerate discussion about rules. They also are somewhat more likely to use harsher enforcement practices, such as high levels of power assertion and/or psychological control strategies. Generally, the combination of high warmth and harsher discipline is more common among African American, Asian American, and Hispanic American groups, possibly due to different parenting goals.

What impact does this combination have on children? Let's address this question first by looking at the impact of corporal punishment, and then we will consider the effects of psychological control techniques. You should note that severe physical punishments (inflicting bodily injury by beating, kicking, punching, scalding, and so on) are consistently associated with problematic child outcomes, such as aggressive behavior, emotion dysregulation, attention problems, conduct disorders, and depression (Cicchetti & Toth, 2006) and are considered to be maltreatment regardless of culture. The use of more common forms of corporal punishment (e.g., hitting, spanking, and paddling) in schools and homes is more contentious. Corporal punishment has been defined as "the use of physical force with the intention of causing a child to experience pain, but not injury, for the purpose of correction or control of the child's behavior" (Straus, 1994, p. 4). Despite the intent, a growing body of research indicates that there may be harm in these less extreme forms of punishment. In a large early study of mother–child pairs, Straus and his colleagues (1997) asked mothers how often they had spanked their child in the last week when the children were between ages 6 and 9. The researchers measured children's antisocial behavior then and over the course of the next 2 years. More frequent spanking at the first assessment predicted increases in the children's antisocial behavior over the next 2 years. This was true regardless of the family's social class, ethnicity, the child's gender, or maternal warmth.

As we have stated, however, some studies of power assertive discipline have shown culture-specific differences. In European-American samples, there is a linear relationship between amount and harshness of physical discipline and children's aggressive behavior. The more severe the punishment, the more aggressive children are likely to be. For African American children, researchers have not always found the same relationship, or as strong a relationship, between corporal punishment and children's aggression (e.g., Baumrind, 1993; Deater-Deckard, Dodge, Bates, & Pettit, 1996; Lansford, Deater-Deckard, Dodge, Bates, & Pettit, 2004). What might account for these differences among U.S. subgroups?

One possibility is that normativeness reduces negative impact. In other words, if children expect to be disciplined in a certain way, such as by spanking, because most parents in their community or ethnic group use this technique, then they may perceive spanking as normal, and possibly even as a manifestation of their parents' concern for them. Gershoff and her colleagues (2010) found some evidence that children's perception of the normativeness of punishment moderated outcomes in a sample of families from China, India, Italy, Kenya, the Philippines, and Thailand. Remember that a moderating influence would affect how strongly certain types of disciplinary techniques were associated with adverse outcomes. Normativeness diminished the deleterious outcomes of yelling and corporal punishment, but only by a bit. These particular forms of discipline were *always* related to greater levels of aggression in all cultural groups, despite this moderation. Alampay and colleagues (2017) reported similar multicultural results in another large, longitudinal study of parents and children from around the globe.

Another explanation may be that the long-term effects of punishment are moderated by the warmth, affection, and responsiveness of the parent who is doling out the discipline. Several large studies of American children support this idea (e.g., Aucoin, Frick, & Bodin, 2006; McLoyd & Smith, 2002). McLoyd and Smith looked at outcomes across a 6-year period in nearly 2,000 American children. Once again, for all children, African American, European American, and Hispanic, the amount of spanking in the home predicted the level of children's externalizing behavior over time. But mothers' emotional support of their children moderated this link in all three groups. Overall, the moderating effects of normativeness and parental warmth indicate that the meanings that children attribute to parents' control strategies have some impact on how these strategies affect them.

You may be wondering what "spanking" means in some of these studies. Most often, data is collected on the frequency of spanking incidents, but not on how it's done. In response to an argument by Baumrind (e.g., Baumrind, Larzalere, & Cowan, 2002) that "ordinary" spanking (done with an open hand less than once a week) would not be associated with problems related to more severe discipline (e.g., frequent spanking, spanking with objects), 585 families were followed over several years to explore the effects of different forms of spanking (Lansford, Wager, Bates, Pettit, & Dodge, 2012). Some support for Baumrind's argument came from maternal self-reports indicating no differences in externalizing behavior between not-spanked and mildly (with a hand less than once per week) spanked children compared to the harshly spanked group. However, over 50% of mothers initially reporting mild spanking admitted using objects to spank later on. Findings indicated that mild spanking, compared to no-spanking, increased the probability that discipline would escalate into harsher forms in the following year by 50%. In other words, the majority of mothers who spanked continued to do so, and the majority of these mothers increased the harshness of their spanking over time.

A large nationally representative sample of over 11,000 children from White/Non-Hispanic (64%), Hispanic (19%), Black/Non-Hispanic (12%), and Asian (5%) families were studied at kindergarten and again at third grade (Gershoff, 2008; Gershoff, Lansford, Sexton, Davis-Kean, & Sameroff, 2012). Two independent sources of data were provided by parents and teachers, an improvement over studies that relied solely on parents as informants. Teachers reported on children's externalizing behaviors (arguing, fighting, getting angry) and mothers responded to questions such as: *"About how many times, if any, have you spanked your child over the past week?"* Number of times was coded using a 0 (no spanking) or 1 (ever spanked) to 6 (five spanking incidents or more during the prior week). The research focused on spanking and excluded harsher disciplinary methods known to correlate with adverse outcomes. Overall, spanking was shown to be a popular method of discipline, with some differences in frequency of use among the various ethnic groups. After controlling for initial group differences in frequency, spanking was found to predict the same increases in children's externalizing behaviors for White, Black, Hispanic, and Asian American groups. In findings similar to those in the previously described study (Lansford et al., 2012), these results demonstrated a downward spiral. More spanking strengthened a pattern of coercive interaction processes in the families (see Chapter 7 for information on coercive family processes).

Associations between corporal punishment and later mental disorders were reported in the largest representative study to date (Afifi, Mota, Dasiewicz, MacMillan, & Sareen, 2012). Close to 35,000 U.S. adult males and females from the National Epidemiologic Survey on Alcohol and Related Conditions were interviewed by trained investigators. For purposes of analysis, a distinction was made between maltreatment and "harsh physical punishment." Maltreated individuals, defined as those who reported physical abuse (burning, injury), extreme neglect (going without clothes or food), sexual abuse, or witnessing violence, were excluded from this study. Harsh physical punishment, which was the variable of interest, was defined as *either* being pushed, shoved, slapped, or hit by a parent or someone living in the home *at least once* during childhood. Findings indicated that the incidence of a lifetime mental disorder (all mood disorders, all anxiety disorders, drug abuse or dependence disorders, and several personality disorders) was significantly associated with harsh physical punishment as defined above, even after controlling for initial level of family dysfunction and other demographic variables. Interestingly, the odds of harsh physical punishment increased as families' income and educational levels increased. Although the size of the relationship was relatively modest, the implications are great when viewed from a public health perspective. The authors concluded that the rates of mental disorders could be reduced 2% to 7% by eliminating harsh physical punishment.

In sum, despite a few studies that report minimal effects of corporal punishment on children in some cultural groups, the overwhelming preponderance of findings supports the conclusion that this parental control strategy promotes increasing aggressiveness in children. Inflicting pain to gain children's compliance with demands may work in the short run, but it has unwanted consequences. In the Applications section, you will learn more about spanking, its frequency in different cultural groups, and the most recent findings on its effects.

Now we will consider psychological control strategies: shaming, inducing guilt, and making affection conditional on behavior (love withdrawal). Here again, these approaches are more commonly used by some cultural groups than others. In middle-class, European American samples, they have some toxic consequences for children (e.g., high levels of anxiety, risk of depression, low self-esteem). Could the outcomes be different in cultures where these practices are normative and/or combined with parents' high levels of overall warmth? The answer to this question appears to be "No." For example, psychological control is more commonly used among East Asian parents (e.g., Chinese and Chinese Americans) than among European American parents. It seems likely, then, that psychological control is perceived as more normative by children from East Asian groups. Yet, Gershoff and her colleagues (2010), who included several East Asian countries in their study (see above), found that the use of shaming as a way of disciplining children (e.g., "You should be ashamed of yourself") was linked to anxiety disorders regardless of culture. Comparisons of American and Chinese families have found the same negative outcomes for children (Doan et al., 2017; Pomerantz & Wang, 2009; Wang et al., 2007). In the study by Doan and colleagues, mothers and children from suburban communities in the United States and China were compared. The Chinese mothers reported more use of psychological control strategies than the U.S. mothers, as expected. But in both samples, the more psychological control mothers used, the greater was their children's stress response (e.g., cortisol output) during a challenging task.

MyLab Education Self-Check 5.3

Conscience: The Beginnings of a Moral Self

5.4 Describe how parenting, child temperament, self-regulation, and internalization shape conscience formation and the beginnings of a moral self.

You can see that research on parenting supports the many theories of self-development that emphasize the importance of social interactive experiences in the development of the self-system. Parenting style especially has been found to correlate with children's self-esteem—how worthy and competent children feel—and it appears to be linked to self-confidence in social interaction. Children whose parents are child centered, responsive, and warm tend to show high levels of self-esteem, and they are likely to be skillful in social interaction, as evidenced by peer acceptance and teacher ratings of social competence. These findings suggest that Erikson (1950/1963) may have been on the right track when he argued that after initial feelings of worth are laid down in late infancy, these feelings will be reworked by the child as she develops. For example, as toddlers become more capable of self-sufficiency, they acquire needs, such as autonomy and control needs, that sensitive, responsive caregivers accommodate. If a toddler's needs are met in a positive, affirming way, the child will go beyond having global feelings of worth and will acquire more differentiated feelings of competency.

Parenting appears to contribute to other aspects of the developing self-system as well. In particular, parenting style and practice are related to children's self-regulation, including the child's ability to guide her own behavior in socially approved ways when she is not being monitored by adults. As you have seen, parents' use of induction promotes internalization, the process by which children adopt adults' standards and rules as their own. Internalization, in turn, is associated with the development of **conscience**, feelings of discomfort or distress when the violation of a rule is contemplated or carried out. Internalization and conscience formation are both aspects of the broader topic of moral development and will be discussed again in later chapters as we look at the course of moral development in older children, adolescents, and adults.

At this point, let's take a closer look at the complex connections among early parenting, child temperament, the beginnings of self-regulation, and the associated processes of internalization and conscience formation. We have already noted that children can begin to learn self-control when they can understand and remember adults' behavioral commands—when statements such as "No cookies before dinner" have meaning for them—certainly during their second year. You have also learned that 2-year-olds begin to show signs of emotional distress if a standard is violated (Kim, Kochanska, Boldt, Nordling, & O'Bleness, 2014), and soon after, they can show strong reactions if they are tempted to break a prohibition (Emde & Buchsbaum, 1990). At the same time, toddlers begin to show prosocial behavior, such as offering comfort to others in distress (Thompson, 2014, 2015).

Two aspects of parenting seem to promote these processes. First, parents' warmth and responsiveness facilitate compliance (self-control) and promote the development of concern for others (Kim & Kochanska, 2017). Sensitive, responsive parents seem to establish a cooperative, mutually responsive relationship with their toddlers—an ongoing secure attachment—and toddlers are usually eager to maintain such relationships (Aksan, Kochanska, & Ortman, 2006). Second, children's anxiety or emotional arousal seems to play a role in their willingness to comply and in the internalization of standards (Kochanska et al., 2007). Hoffman (1983) proposed that a parent's discipline causes a child to feel **anxious arousal**. The key is for the parent to use strategies that elicit only mild arousal, enough for the child to take notice, but not to make her especially fearful. This is called the **minimum sufficiency principle**. If arousal is minimally sufficient, the child is likely to pay attention, to try to understand, and to remember the parent's "socialization message." She may attribute her own compliance to her acceptance of a rule, which is a step toward internalization of the rule. But if the child experiences intense anxiety during a disciplinary episode, she may pay more attention to her feelings and fail to really process and understand the socialization message. For example, she might notice, and later remember, how scared she is of her parent's loud and angry voice, and then attribute her compliance to her fear rather than to the standard or rule that she could have pondered and learned. Hoffman's ideas help explain why mild power assertion is more effective than harsh power assertion for long-term internalization of rules. Milder strategies may produce minimally sufficient arousal in a child. His views are also consistent with findings that induction is helpful for internalization. Children are more likely to remember and accept rules they can understand.

If anxious arousal is an important ingredient in how children respond to their parents' discipline, individual differences among children in how easily their anxiety *is* aroused should also be important. In other words, temperament differences among toddlers should influence the early development of conscience. For fearful children, gentle discipline that deemphasizes power and emphasizes requests and reasoning should be sufficiently arousing to produce optimal effects. But what about children who are not easily aroused—who seem almost fearless? Do they need harsh discipline to be sufficiently aroused to pay attention? To find out, Kochanska (1995) studied 2-year-olds' **committed compliance**, that is, their eager and enthusiastic willingness to go along with their mothers' requests. Committed compliance in 2-year-olds is predictive of measures of internalization and conscience in the later preschool period (Kochanska, Aksan, & Koenig, 1995). Kochanska found that toddlers' fearfulness is indeed an important ingredient in the effectiveness of mothers' discipline. Highly fearful children, as expected, showed the most committed compliance if their mothers used gentle discipline. Harsh discipline was not as effective. However, neither gentle nor harsh discipline was particularly effective in promoting compliance for the most fearless toddlers. For them, only the security of their attachment to their mothers made a difference. Securely attached, fearless toddlers tended to show committed compliance, but insecurely attached, fearless toddlers were much less likely to do so. And, as expected, committed compliance at age 2 was predictive of moral development at 4 ½ years (Kochanska et al., 2007). We see again that children's temperaments make them *differentially susceptible* to parenting behaviors, helping to explain why correlations between parenting behaviors and child outcomes tend to be moderate. Parenting clearly is important, but it works somewhat differently with different children.

To clarify Kochanska's findings, imagine a 2-year-old, Joel, who tends to be more fearful than the other children in his play group. For example, he holds back and ducks his head when a supervising adult offers him a turn to ride the new "race car" at the neighborhood playground, even though many of the other children are clamoring for a turn. When Joel's mother encourages him gently to participate in a cleanup session, explaining how much help it would be, he is quite cooperative. She tells an observer that she never "yells" at him because he gets so upset that it is counterproductive. José's mother, on the other hand, says that her son seems unfazed by yelling or any kind of harsh control from her. José does not seem to be afraid of anything. He can't wait for his turn to ride the new race car, and the fact that the supervising adult is a stranger is of no concern to him. Fortunately, José and his mother share a warm relationship, and José, too, cooperates enthusiastically when his mother asks him to help with the cleanup. Andrew, another toddler in the play group, seems a lot like José in his fearlessness. He is panting to ride the race car and to try all the toys on the playground, and he marches right up to the supervising adult, asking for help. But there seems to be very little warmth between him and his mother, and when she asks him to help out with cleanup, he ignores her. Even when she gives him a shove and speaks sharply to him, he only halfheartedly moves to pick up a toy and abandons the cleanup effort almost immediately. Unfortunately, Andrew may be on a trajectory toward increasing antisocial behavior problems and poor conscience development. Parents low on warmth who use harsh power assertion to control their fearless toddlers tend to see their children's externalizing behaviors and callousness (lack of empathy, guilt, remorse) increase as their children get older (Kim et al., 2014; Waller & Hyde, 2017).

In sum, parenting helps shape the development of the self-system in early childhood. Which aspects of parenting will be influential depends in part on the particular child. For the development of self-regulation, the quality of attachment, grounded in warm, responsive caregiving, may be all-important for some children. For others, particular parenting practices (methods of control) also play an important role.

MyLab Education Self-Check 5.4

Applications

Because the stages of infancy and early childhood have long been viewed as important ones for later socioemotional development, theories of early attachment, self-development, and parenting provide a theoretical formulation that can help explain the effects of sensitive and insensitive parenting.

Building a Self Through the Attachment Relationship

In Crittendon's (1994, 1997, 2016) view, attachment classifications are linked to operant conditioning processes. Securely attached infants and toddlers receive predictable, soothing care when their physiological needs, fear, aggression, excitement, or anxiety threaten to overwhelm their capacity for homeostatic regulation. These children learn that expressions of their positive, as well as their negative, feelings (anxiety, distress, and anger) are acceptable, because their caregiver tolerates these expressions, and accepts and helps them. In other words, they are positively reinforced for expressing both positive and negative feelings. Let's consider an example that might apply to adult students. Imagine a time when you were close to despair because of all the work you had to do. You had a number of responsibilities to complete at your job, you had family obligations to attend to, and your professors were being unreasonably demanding about their assignments! On top of everything, you felt tired and on the verge of getting your annual cold. Your level of crankiness increased significantly, suggesting that you were starting to lose some emotional control. Now imagine that some loving person in your life approached you, and instead of telling you to "grow up," was able to see through the irritability to the anxieties underneath. This person offered to help shoulder some of your burdens. Emotionally you experienced what amounts to a sigh of relief. You were able to function much better with the support, and your sense of yourself as a valuable and loved person increased greatly. In this supportive context, you would probably even be receptive to constructive suggestions about how you might schedule your time to improve your situation.

Although this example is not a strict analogy to early experience, young children have special needs for caregiver support to help them regulate their emotions and internalize positively valenced self-understanding. Crittendon believes that secure reciprocity with a caregiver allows the child to be open to both cognitive and affective experiences, gradually building procedural models of the self as competent to communicate with the caretaker, able to manage affect with the caretaker's reliable help, and able to accept and express both positive and negative parts of the self. Essentially, the positive message the secure child encodes is that she is a valuable and loved person even when she's not being particularly grown up. These repeated dyadic patterns of attachment are encoded as procedural memories that serve as precursors to the mature self and to the self-in-relationship.

The Emotionally Constricted Self

In contrast, insecure-avoidant infants who learn over time that displays of distress elicit rejection, punishment, or withdrawal become conditioned to inhibition of affect. These infants are, in fact, punished for their emotional displays, so these children come to actively avoid or block out perceptions that arouse their feelings because of the aversive consequences. Crittendon and DiLalla (1988) have reported that even very young children who have been severely abused actively block out information about their own feelings and demonstrate false affect—that is, affect that is superficially positive and incongruent with true feelings. Consistent with the general assumption of attachment theory, this pattern of avoidance is adaptive for an early nonresponsive caregiving environment but may have significantly negative consequences for later functioning. A highly defended or "false self" (Kernberg, 1976; Miller, 1981; Winnicott, 1965) may result from the inhibition of affect because the child distorts or mistrusts the evidence of her feelings. This situation effectively reduces the information that the young child can access in constructing the self and in learning about the world. The message the child encodes is that feeling anger or distress is unacceptable and should be avoided because the expression of these feelings distances the caregiver, emotionally if not physically. The child views the self as able to communicate with caregivers only if her own emotional needs are kept in check. Positive aspects of the self may be expressed, but negative aspects, such as emotional neediness, need to be repressed.

Avoidant children who have learned that emotional expression can be dangerous take on the responsibility of their own emotion regulation without seeking caregiver help. They function defensively to keep the caregiver "close but not too close" (Crittendon, 1994, p. 95). To cope with this style of parenting, they learn a style of relating that involves repressing emotions that might anger or distance their more authoritarian caregivers. Negative affect (feelings of distress, sadness, anger) is not well integrated into the self-system, and a false self develops that is biased in favor of its "good" parts and against its more shameful ones. These avoidant or defended children may appear self-reliant to their parents, who may not be very responsive to their children's feelings anyway. In extreme circumstances, these children may demonstrate what Bowlby called **compulsive caregiving**. This is the pattern of providing emotional or instrumental care for caregivers, creating an imbalance in family relationships called role confusion (Macfie, Brumariu, & Lyons-Ruth, 2015). A pattern of **compulsive self-sufficiency** represents an opposite yet equally unhealthy result. These children are at risk because they appear so self-possessed. A closer look reveals their self-evaluations to be based on others' negative appraisals, including shaming for their expressions of dependency or needs for closeness. Parents of these children can be helped to develop the nurturant side of authoritative parenting by using some of the attachment-related approaches described in earlier chapters.

The Emotionally Volatile Self

Insecure-anxious infants learn that their displays of distress elicit unpredictable results, sometimes positive and sometimes negative. They experience an intermittent reinforcement schedule because inconsistent or neglectful parental responsivity deprives them of a reliable method of communicating with caregivers. They don't know which bid for attention will pay off. Consequently, their emotional experience is complex, characterized by "anxiety of unresolvable arousal in which desire for the attachment figure, distress at her absence, and aggression toward her are all felt concurrently" (Crittendon, 1994, p. 93). Ultimately these children learn they can trust neither their affect nor their cognitions. However, they may learn that escalation of affect often works best in getting their caregivers' attention. Highly coercive strategies (aggressiveness or tantrums) and very coy behaviors (disarming manipulation) may be developed to maintain proximity. The self incorporates messages that reflect its ineffectiveness in communicating its needs to caregivers. The child's aggressive behavior threatens the caregiver ("You must listen to me!"), whereas her coy behavior disarms ("Please don't get angry at me"). Parents of these children might describe them as "out of control."

Not all noncompliant child behavior problems are due to early insecure attachments, however. Children may discover, as they become more independent and more verbal, that coercion works well in getting them what they want. Patterson and others (1982; Dishion & Snyder, 2016) who study the development of noncompliance in children maintain that an intermittent (or inconsistent) schedule of reinforcement sustains the coercive child's behavior problems.

A pattern of **negative reinforcement**, when the cessation of a stimulus increases the frequency of some behavioral response, follows the child's display of intense negativity or misbehavior. For example, a parent might tell her 4-year-old to go upstairs because it is time to go to bed. The little boy, detesting this interruption of his play time, begins to whine. The parent repeats her command several more times only to be met by continued resistance. The parent's patience begins to thin and she escalates into threats, which, according to Patterson's research, are usually not carried out. Instead, the parent appeases the child out of guilt or exasperation. The parent gives up and the child's noncompliance is reinforced. This pattern strengthens the child's coercive interaction style, which, with time and repetition, can become the predominant mode of communication. Ironically, Patterson believes that coercive children do not really want parents to give in. Instead, they crave the predictability that derives from knowing what their limits are and the security of knowing that parents will enforce them. Coercive children, however, need help developing a communication style that expresses their needs more directly so that caregivers will understand and respond appropriately. If left unchecked, child noncompliance can be a significant risk factor for later maladaptive outcomes, such as peer rejection and aggression. In such situations, some parent training is generally a very good idea.

Why Train Parents?

Parent training ([PT]; Patterson, Chamberlain, & Reid, 1982), or parent management training ([PMT]; Brestan & Eyberg, 1998), has the distinction of being one of a relative handful of therapies deemed efficacious for children (Kazdin, 2003; Lee, Horvath, & Hunsley, 2013). Studies have shown that PT is effective in reducing noncompliance and promoting prosocial behavior, especially for children ages 4 through 8. Parent training can substantially strengthen the limit-setting side of authoritativeness, improve the quality of life in the home, and reduce stress for parents who must grapple with children's noncompliance. Table 5.5 provides some examples of skills taught in parent training programs.

TABLE 5.5 Some Examples of Skills Taught in Parent Training Programs

SKILL	EFFECTIVE RESPONSE	INEFFECTIVE RESPONSE
Make directives clear and authoritative; don't turn commands into questions; wait a few seconds before restating the command so the child can comply.	*Please pick up the toys on the floor before lunch.*	*We're going to pick up all our toys now, OK? Would you like to pick up your toys?*
Reinforce good behavior with positive verbal and physical attention (within 5 seconds when child complies with request); avoid criticism, sarcasm, yelling or threatening.	*You're doing a good job picking up your toys.*	*If you don't start picking the toys up this minute, I'm going to throw them all out!*
Ignore minor or simply annoying misbehavior (whining, interrupting, arguing, tantrumming, etc.); redirect attention.	*Let's read our book for a while now.*	*Stop whining! I'm tired of hearing it.*
Use clear consequences (reprimands, removal of privileges, time out) sparingly and only as needed.	*You can't hit your brother because it can hurt him. You have to take a time out now.*	*I told you not to do that! Why can't you just be good and behave?*

In some cases, an added parent management component can make a good therapeutic program even better. For example, in the case of treatments for attention-deficit hyperactivity disorder (ADHD), a multimodal treatment that included medication and behavioral (including parent management) treatment demonstrated an advantage over medication alone for children with comorbid conditions (anxiety or conduct problems), for children with more highly educated mothers, for members of minority groups, and for families who learned to improve their discipline techniques via this training (Pfiffner & Haack, 2014). The principles involved in parent management training have also been used effectively in classroom management.

Parent training is successful, no doubt, because it has a strong theoretical rationale. It draws on a set of well-established principles from operant conditioning and social learning theory that can be used in individual counseling, group counseling, psychoeducation, and consultation. Whereas the benefits of well-delivered programs can be great, they are most effective for families with young children. Given the developmental needs of older children and adolescents, training for their parents should take into consideration adolescents' need for some measure of personal control and autonomy by incorporating skills in decision making and negotiation into the counseling.

Effective parent training programs incorporate a few essential elements (Dishion, Forgatch, Chamberlain, & Pelham, 2016; Kazdin, 1991; Moore & Patterson, 2003).

1. These programs are directed toward parents or guardians; children are not directly involved in treatment. An exception to this is treatment with adolescents, which typically does require the adolescent's participation.
2. Parents are taught to observe and define their children's noncompliance in behavioral terms. They are instructed to note their own part in interaction cycles that reward and sustain noncompliance. The most problematic behaviors and their prosocial opposites are identified.
3. Basic principles of learning theory, such as reinforcement, shaping, mild punishment, generalization, and so on, are taught to parents, used to illustrate the nature of parent–child interactions, and applied in contingent ways to achieve the goals of treatment. These principles provide the basis for therapeutic change.
4. Parents (with a professional's help) put these ideas to the test at home. Target behaviors that parents wish to modify are identified; skills are practiced in sessions using role play, modeling, therapist feedback, and discussion. These techniques are then employed in the home, and the results of the new behavior management strategies are recorded, reviewed, and further developed during subsequent sessions.

Parent management approaches depend upon the careful application of behavioral principles. Therefore, the therapist who uses this modality needs to understand behavioral terms correctly, must be precise about selecting and defining target behaviors, and must be able to identify contingencies that increase or decrease behavior. One method involves asking parents to identify two to four of the child's behaviors that are most problematic. This is often supplemented by the use of more formal observational assessment tools. Moore and Patterson (2003) report that a typical initial concern can be defined as "minding" versus "not minding." Once the parents are helped to notice the context wherein the "not-minding" occurs, principles like positive reinforcement (using tangible objects or the very powerful attention of parents), mild punishments (like time-out or restriction of privileges), and shaping (rewarding closer and closer approximations of "minding" with social praise) can be incorporated into some contingency management system. Contingency management involves presenting and withdrawing reinforcers and punishments in a systematic and consistent way to effect behavioral change. The linchpin of these approaches is the mindful use of positive reinforcement, a particularly potent response from parents when it comes in the form of warm encouragement, acceptance, and attention. A correct understanding of concepts like negative reinforcement, which is central to understanding the coercion cycle (Patterson, 1982) and which is distinct from the concept of punishment, is particularly important as well. When parents use time-out correctly, for example, they are removing the situational rewards that support the child's misbehavior. Daily documentation of progress can be a useful part of the program, helping parents become more consistent in their use of techniques. More information about coercive processes is presented in Chapter 7.

Over the years, many effective programs have built upon these basic principles. Some have been adapted for highly distressed families, such as those affected by addiction and abuse. Programs have also been successfully used and scaled up in community, residential, and foster care systems. Pioneering work done in the 1960s (Bijou & Baer, 1966; Hanf, 1968; Patterson, 2002; Wahler, Winkel, Peterson, & Morrison, 1965) has generated a range of behaviorally based family programs that have helped untold numbers of children and their families in accessible, culturally sensitive and cost-effective ways. (See Table 5.6 for a sample.)

Sometimes, stressed families, who possibly need parent training the most, are unlikely to access it. Many find it extremely difficult to commit to structured meetings or participation in other community-based supports. Limited finances and time, language barriers, and fear of criticism from social service providers can all reduce the chance of engagement. Creative ways to bridge the gap between parent need and resource access are necessary. One approach, the Family Check-Up ([FCU]; Dishion & Stormshak, 2007), has demonstrated that families who took part in this short-term intervention were more likely to avail themselves of other community services, such as the more in-depth parenting programs mentioned earlier. The FCU may be

TABLE 5.6 Evidence-Based Parenting Programs Founded on Behavioral Principles

PROGRAM	SOURCE
Incredible Years	Webster-Stratton, C. H. & Reid, M. J. (2010). The Incredible Years parents, teachers, and children training series: A multifaceted treatment approach for young children with conduct disorders. In J. R. Weisz & A. E. Kazdin (Eds.), *Evidence-based psychotherapies for children and adolescents* (pp. 194–120). New York, NY: Guilford Press.
Parent Management Training	Kazdin, A. E. (2010). Problem-solving skills training and parent management training for oppositional defiant disorder and conduct disorder. In J. R. Weisz & A. E. Kazdin (Eds.), *Evidence-based psychotherapies for children and adolescents* (pp. 211–226). New York, NY: Guilford Press.
Parent-Child Interaction Therapy	Zisser, A. & Eyberg, S. M. (2010). Parent-child interaction therapy and the treatment of disruptive behavior disorders. In J. R. Weisz & A. E. Kazdin (Eds.), *Evidence-based psychotherapies for children and adolescents* (pp. 179–193). New York, NY: Guilford Press.
Triple P–Positive Parenting	Sanders, M. R. & Murphy-Brennan, M. (2010). The international dissemination of the Triple P–Positive Parenting Program. In J. R. Weisz & A. E. Kazdin (Eds.), *Evidence-based psychotherapies for children and adolescents* (pp. 519–537). New York, NY: Guilford Press.
Parent Management Training—Oregon Model	Forgatch, M. S. & Patterson, G. R. (2010). Parent Management Training—Oregon Model: An intervention for antisocial behavior in children and adolescents. In J. R. Weisz & A. E. Kazdin (Eds.), *Evidence-based psychotherapies for children and adolescents* (pp. 159–178). New York, NY: Guilford Press.
Treatment Foster Care—Oregon Model	Smith, D. K. & Chamberlain, P. (2010). Multidimensional treatment foster care for adolescents: Processes and outcomes. In J. R. Weisz & A. E. Kazdin (Eds.), *Evidence-based psychotherapies for children and adolescents* (pp. 243–258). New York, NY: Guilford Press.
Family Based Treatment for Oppositional Behavior	McMahon, R. J. & Forehand, R. L. (2005). *Helping the noncompliant child: Family-based treatment for oppositional behavior*. New York, NY: Guilford Press.

delivered in schools or other community settings, so it is relatively easy to access. First, FCU involves a 3-session phase comprising an interview, family assessment, and feedback meeting (hence, the "check-up"). It is notable that clinicians employ **motivational interviewing** techniques throughout (see Miller & Rollnick, 2002) to identify family strengths and challenges as a way of eliciting parent participation. For example, clinicians might explicitly point out to parents how certain positive behaviors they already demonstrate or family traditions they share *do* benefit their children. Next, parents and therapists work on areas that need improvement, which have been identified in the check-up assessment. These might include setting limits, increasing the frequency of positive comments to children, monitoring behavior, and defining effective discipline strategies or other areas of need. Just as your doctor doesn't prescribe every possible medication to you after your check-up, so every family doesn't need to improve every possible parenting skill. Building on existing competencies, parents and therapists work together to define targets and identify community-based resources that are available to support them. Consequently, the FCU is personally tailored to each family's needs; it is ecologically and culturally valid, strengths-based, and accessible.

Recently, new interventions that address the emotional regulation and attention of the parent have been explored as a means of promoting parenting quality. We know that the presence, warmth, and listening skills of the parent are particularly important influences on the health of their relationships with their children. Parents who are stressed, distracted, or emotionally unavailable, especially when this is a chronic pattern, tend to undermine the quality of relationships and foster children's dysregulation. Recent work in mindful parenting interventions has shown promise in improving parenting quality because of the nature of the attention that is being cultivated. Mindfulness practice can have an impact on relationships because it supports loving attention and helps reduce parental stress. In improving parents' own emotion regulation, all too common in normal and distressed parent–child relationships, child behaviors can improve (Bogels & Restifo, 2014). The use of mindfulness practice has increased in novel programs for parents during pregnancy, birthing, and parenting because it benefits both parent and child (Duncan & Bardake, 2010). We will have more to say about mindfulness in Chapter 14.

As Masten (2014) notes, the family is the context for child resilience, especially in the early years, acting as a protective factor against adversity through the transmission of beliefs and values, rules, routines, and other supports. Research supports that parenting quality moderates child outcomes. Therefore, parenting interventions such as the ones mentioned in this section can serve as potentially powerful influences on the course of later child development.

Noncompliance: Forewarned Is Forearmed

Higher rates of noncompliance appear to occur at certain times throughout the day (7:30 a.m., 11:30 a.m., 5:30 p.m., and 8:30 p.m.; Goodenough, 1931, as cited in Moore & Patterson, 2003). Consider this scene in the Arnold family. Mom, whose shift at work ends at 5:00 p.m., has just returned from the babysitter's house with her 6-year-old twins. Both children are hungry and tired from a long day at school. Yvonne needs help with a homework project. Kenney has a Cub Scout meeting at 6:30 and needs to find some items for the pack's activity. As their mother struggles to put together a meal, the children become more intense in their demands for her attention. Pretty soon, they are fighting with each other. She yells at them to stop, but this only makes matters worse. Yvonne ends up in tears and Kenney runs to his room. No one feels like eating dinner.

What makes scenes like this one so recognizable to so many people? The rates of noncompliance rise when several factors intersect: changes in biological states, a spike in demands for compliance, and simultaneous transitions that are occurring for all members of the system (parents and children). Because these are predictable, the use of contingency management skills, especially positive encouragement, and establishment of consistent routines can help parents navigate these flash points more successfully.

What About Spanking?

Current research is blurring what was once considered a bright line between corporal punishment and abuse, painting a picture of a slippery slope between mild corporal punishment and harsher forms of discipline (Gershoff, 2008). This may be the reality, unfortunately, because most of the corporal punishment meted out by adults is not done in a particularly calm, loving, or reflective way (Holden, Williamson, & Holland, 2014). As you have seen, the use and severity of corporal punishment tend to escalate over time, and most episodes of physical abuse occur in the context of child discipline (Durrant & Ensom, 2012).

So far, you have been reading about the importance of nurturing children to develop strong bonds of attachment and of socializing them in ways that imbue a sense of feeling valued and loved. It may be jarring to think about hitting children as helpful for these purposes. Despite this disconnect, if you also believe that most U.S. parents spank their children, you would not be mistaken. Corporal punishment enjoys wide support in the United States according to recent surveys. In large numbers, women (65%) and men (76%) agree that children sometimes need "a good, hard spanking" (Child Trends, 2015, p. 2). Other surveys show that corporal punishment is used by one third of U.S. parents to discipline infants as young as 10 months of age (Regalado, Sareen, Inkelas, Wissow, & Halfon, 2004) and approximately 65% to 70% of parents use it to discipline toddlers ages 1 to 3 (Maguire-Jack, Gromoske, & Berger, 2012). An analysis of responses to an online survey about spanking showed that over 70% disagreed with professional advice from the American Academy of Pediatrics (1998) that spanking should not be used under any circumstance.

Despite evidence to the contrary, many parents continue to believe spanking is an effective way to control children's aggressive and noncompliant behavior, and methodological problems in many studies complicate matters by leading to varying interpretations of results. Given the concerns expressed by professional associations in the United States and internationally, finding consensus is important. As you recall, meta-analyses, or studies of studies, are helpful because they offer a firmer body of evidence from which to draw conclusions than single studies alone. To address the methodological shortcomings of previous meta-analyses, Gershoff and Grogan-Kaylor (2016) compared the effects of severe physical punishment/abuse (i.e., hitting with objects, etc.) with spanking (i.e., "hitting a child on the buttocks or extremities using an open hand," p. 453) using 75 studies that met a high standard of quality. Less rigorous studies were eliminated, and 52% of the newly included studies had not been part of previous meta-analyses. Results indicated that spanking had deleterious effects on 13 domains and not a single beneficial effect on child well-being, even when considered separately from abuse (see Table 5.7). Spanking appears to have little influence on the goals that parents want most to achieve with discipline—the development of self-regulation and morality.

The growing consensus from research in this area has attracted a high level of international attention. In 1989, the United Nations recognized children's right to protection from physical and psychological violence, including spanking, through the UN Convention on the Rights of the Child (United Nations, 1989). Originally, only six countries out of the total 198 member countries (Somalia, Palestine, the United States, Taiwan, Western Sahara, and Vatican City, which has no child population) did not ratify this treaty. In 2015, five of the remaining countries ratified it, leaving the United States as the only country not to ratify the Convention on the Rights of the Child (treaties.un.org, accessed August 10, 2017). A large group of national organizations in Canada have joined together (Durrant, Ensom, & the Coalition on Physical Punishment of Children and Youth, 2004) to promote the message that physical punishment is ineffective and only serves to threaten children's well-being.

You may be wondering why it is that researchers, professional groups like pediatricians, and international policy makers agree that spanking is not good for kids but many parents are very reluctant to give it up. A creative methodology was recently employed to investigate this question. Using a *Time* magazine article about the association between spanking and aggression (Park, 2010) as a springboard, researchers randomly sampled social media comments from a Yahoo! news site that reported on the article. Disagreement with the article's conclusion was strong (71%). Use of corporal punishment was justified using personal (*I was hit as a child, and I'm OK; I love my child so it's not abuse.*), child-focused (*Children need discipline*), family-focused (*Parents need to be in charge*), strategic (*Spanking is the only thing that works*), societal (*Kids get away with too much these days*), religious (*It's the*

TABLE 5.7 Thirteen Detrimental Outcomes Related to Spanking: Information for Consumers About the Effects of Corporal Punishment on Children

SIGNIFICANT OUTCOME DOMAINS IDENTIFIED IN 75 RESEARCH STUDIES	SELECTED EXAMPLES OF SPANKING'S EFFECTS AS MEASURED ACROSS STUDIES
Moral Internalization	Lower levels of moral internalization: Children more likely to ignore parent, engage in misbehavior, show impaired prosocial behavior, etc.
Child Aggression	Children more likely to engage in aggressive behavior in childhood and later verbal and physical aggression in adolescence, etc.
Child Antisocial Behavior	More disobedience, problems in getting along with others, impulsive behavior, temper tantrums, etc.
Child Externalizing Behavior Problems	More fighting, cheating, etc., as measured on clinical scales of externalizing problems.
Child Internalizing Behavior Problems	Higher scores for sadness, loneliness, and anxiety on clinical scales of internalizing problems.
Child Mental Health Problems	More depression, fearfulness, irritability, poor adjustment, etc.
Negative Parent–Child Relationship	More arguing, fighting, lack of warmth, etc.
Child Impaired Cognitive Ability	Poorer academic outcomes, lower school grades, etc.
Child and Adult Low Self-Esteem	Lower self-esteem in childhood and later adulthood.
Adult Physical Abuse	More likely to become perpetrators of later abuse on own children and/or spouse; more likely to engage in interpersonal or dating violence.
Adult Antisocial Behavior	Greater aggression, delinquency, trouble with the law, etc.
Adult Mental Health Problems	Higher rates of symptoms at young and later adulthood on measures of Anxiety, Depression, Hostility, Interpersonal Sensitivity, Obsessive-Compulsive, Paranoid Ideation, Phobic Anxiety, Psychoticism, and Somatization.
Adult Support for Physical Punishment	Approval of corporal punishment as a discipline strategy.

SOURCE: Based on Gershoff & Grogan-Kaylor, 2016, Spanking and Child Outcomes: Old Controversies and New Meta-Analyses.

parent's duty not to spare the rod), and ideological (*Other people shouldn't tell parents what to do with their own children*) reasons (Taylor, Al-Hiyari, Lee, Priebe, Guerrero, & Bales, 2016).

In the end, conclusive evidence demonstrates that corporal punishment does pose a public health problem of significant proportions, yet long-held assumptions are slow to shift. Research attempts to change people's beliefs about the acceptability of corporal punishment have experimented with creative ways to use empirical knowledge in the service of altering preconceptions. For example, people were invited to read short summaries online describing corporal punishment effects while interacting with the text. For example, readers were asked to estimate the level of association between corporal punishment and various outcomes, like aggression or drug abuse. The program provided immediate online feedback about the correctness or incorrectness of their choices. This very brief exposure to empirical evidence about the effects of spanking was successful in changing attitudes toward the acceptability of corporal punishment for groups of parents and non-parents alike (Holden, Brown, Baldwin, & Caderao, 2014). Future research may help us harness this approach to aid in reducing the social acceptability of corporal punishment for parents and others.

Another significant approach most experts advise is parent education and the provision of alternative strategies for child discipline, but this cannot occur in a vacuum. Studies have long shown that conditions of economic and social stress

in families burden caregivers and undermine the quality of their parenting (Conger & Elder, 1994). Combined efforts to support families economically and educationally may have the best chance of reducing caregiver stress and promoting more positive discipline practices. Also, efforts that educate with sensitivity to cultural context are necessary. The evidence suggests that "any efforts to reduce both spanking and externalizing behaviors would need to target Blacks, Whites, Hispanics and Asian Americans. While the approaches would likely vary by cultural group, the message would be the same—spanking children is not associated with better behavior over time" (Gershoff et al., 2012, p. 843).

The Flexible Work of Parenting

It would be incorrect to assume that the quality of the early attachment relationship will automatically be transformed into a complementary pattern of parent–child relationships in early childhood. That is, it is not necessarily the case that every securely attached baby becomes a securely attached preschooler, and so forth. But, as our discussion of parenting style in the toddler and preschool years illustrates, the elements of sensitive parenting that characterize the infancy period are not much different from those that are right for preschoolers. The specific parenting behaviors might change, but the underlying requirement to be psychologically available and sensitive to the child's developmental needs and capabilities remains the same. For the most part, messages about the self-in-relationship that the child has internalized become the foundation for more mature interactions. Cicchetti and Toth (1994) believe that the negative adolescent and adult self-views that undergird many psychological disorders stem from insults to the self that were experienced during childhood. Consequently, clinicians need to apply primary prevention strategies to strengthen early parent–child relationships.

As children get older, they should be provided with experiences that allow for the growth of mastery, autonomy, and self-efficacy. Parent education and discussion groups can be helpful forums for parents in which to gain support for their strengths and to learn about the developmental needs of toddlers and preschoolers. Parents sometimes construe insensitive parenting to mean actions that are mean or rejecting. But intrusive interference, such as picking up the child to give her a hug when she is absorbed in an activity, or arbitrarily restricting a child's mobility, may also be insensitive to the child's needs if done repeatedly. Of particular relevance to self-concept development is educating parents about the implications of their language when conversing with their children. Insulting or insensitive remarks, particularly those intended to shame the child, should be avoided lest they become part of the young child's self-concept.

The growth of a healthy self-system depends upon an environment that provides the child with love and limits appropriate to her developmental level. When the proximal environment is distorted, as is the environment of defended and coercive children, youngsters will make adaptations. However, their adaptations will come with a cost to the development of a child's true self. Fostering the growth of the authentic self in infancy and early childhood sets the child on a developmental pathway that will support healthy functioning at every stage thereafter.

Summary

The Self-System

1. Some traditional theorists viewed the self-system as multidimensional. William James, for example, distinguished between the self-as-subject, as active agent or "I," and the self-concept, the object of our own observations and evaluations, or the "Me." The "I" is continuously experienced, is distinguished from others, and is an agent of action. The "Me" consists of personal attributes, the material (or physical), social, and spiritual characteristics of self. Self-esteem, the evaluation of one's attributes, can be good, bad, or neutral. The valence assigned to one's own attributes depends on the number of successes we enjoy relative to our aspirations.

2. James Cooley introduced a developmental perspective into theorizing about the self. Self-representations are constructed from our interactions with others, especially caregivers. We build a looking-glass self that reflects our view of how others see us.

3. George Herbert Mead added that language and society contribute to shaping the self-system. There are culturally determined differences in people's preferred ways of viewing themselves. For example, Japanese emphasize affiliations in their self-descriptions, whereas Americans emphasize more individualistic qualities.

The Early Development of the Self-System

4. The pre-self that develops in infancy begins with early inklings of one's body permanence and separateness from others that are derived from the regularity and reliability of infant–caregiver interactions. Procedural representations of interactions are established and may promote a budding sense of mastery by the second half of the first year, if babies' behavior controls caregiving responses. A sense of self as self-in-relationship begins to emerge. Late in the first year, infants engage in intentional action, a sign of the I-self, a sense of agency. By the end of the first year, separation distress and social referencing signal the baby's deepening understanding that the other is separate. Additional indicators include the baby's tendency to explore more readily in the presence of a familiar caregiver. If the caregiver provides a secure base, the baby in a sense has the self-worth or confidence to explore. All of these indicators of a growing sense of the self as separate emerge from and depend on the baby's relationship to others.

5. Self-recognition is demonstrated as early as 15 months in the mirror recognition and "body-as-obstacle" tests. Passing these tests indicates that children are forming a self-concept, or a "Me." After the second birthday, children begin to use self-descriptive words. Self-evaluation or self-esteem advances with self-recognition, with abused children showing signs of poorer self-esteem than non-maltreated children from the beginnings of mirror recognition. Gradually, more differentiated self-descriptions emerge, with preschoolers describing more concrete characteristics, such as "little," and older children beginning to refer to more abstract, less obvious qualities, such as "funny."

6. Self-regulation involves both emotional and behavioral control. Emotional control begins in infancy, when caregiver–infant interactions give babies outside assistance with affective control. The caregiving relationship is the context in which the infant's own capacity for emotion regulation develops.

7. Behavior regulation begins in the second year when toddlers achieve objective self-recognition. The simultaneous

emergence of symbolic or representational thought and other cognitive skills allow the child to begin learning and storing rules or standards of conduct. By late in the second year, self-conscious emotions emerge, such as embarrassment or guilt, emotions that require awareness of self and of others' judgments. Between 2 and 3, children show such emotions when they realize they have broken a rule or made a mistake. Once these capacities are in place, the child can begin to control her own behavior based on others' expectations.

Early Socialization: Parenting and the Development of the Self-System

8. As the infant becomes a toddler, her needs shift from total dependency to growing independence, and the parent–child relationship reorganizes such that sensitive, responsive caregiving begins to include efforts to socialize the child—to shape or control the child's autonomous action, so that she remains safe and behaves in culturally appropriate ways.

9. Two dimensions of parenting style, parents' approach to caring for and disciplining their children, are important. First is warmth or parental responsiveness, which includes affection, acceptance, involvement and interest, and so on. Second is control or parental demandingness, the degree to which parents impose and enforce standards of behavior.

10. Four parenting styles can be described, crossing the positive and negative poles of the two dimensions. Authoritative parents are high on warmth and on demandingness. Authoritarian parents are low on warmth but high on demandingness. Permissive parents are high or moderate on warmth but low on demandingness, and neglecting or uninvolved parents are low on both dimensions. Authoritative parenting is associated with the most positive outcomes in child development, including adaptability, competence, good social relations, low levels of antisocial behavior, high self-esteem, and good self-regulation. The correlations between parenting styles and outcomes are significant but moderate, indicating that such outcomes are also influenced by other factors, not just parenting style.

11. Parents use a variety of methods of control. Power assertion, which involves either physical punishment or withdrawal of privileges, tends to be effective for immediate control of behavior, but may not have longer term benefits, and harsher forms can have some negative side effects, such as increased aggressiveness in children. Psychological control, which includes love withdrawal, generates high anxiety and elicits immediate compliance, but seems to have few effects on long-term self-regulation. Induction, providing explanations and emphasizing benefits to the child and to others, seems most effective for promoting internalization of rules and longer term self-regulation.

12. Are parenting practices actually having an effect, or are there other reasons why parenting is correlated with child outcomes? For example, could it be that the correlation is the result of shared inheritance of traits between parents and children? Data support a multidimensional approach. Parenting, genetics, child temperament, and other factors all contribute to child outcomes.

13. Parenting practices are partly the result of child characteristics, such as temperament traits. For example, adults are more directive with dependent children than with independent children. Also, the effectiveness of different parenting practices is partly a function of a child's temperament. For example, toddler boys with difficult temperaments respond with high levels of aggressiveness when parents use physically intrusive control methods, whereas boys with easy temperaments do not.

14. The broader cultural context seems to have an influence on parenting practices and may have an impact on their effectiveness. Some parenting practices may have different meaning, and therefore different outcomes, depending on ethnicity and culture. The traditional values of various cultures have shaped the ways they parent and discipline their children.

15. Corporal punishment, which inflicts pain on children in order to control behavior, has been shown to predict increases in later externalizing behavior and mental disorders, even in its "milder" forms (i.e., spanking). This finding generally holds up across cultural groups. In some cultures harsh practices are normative, and parents may combine high levels of warmth with corporal punishment. Normativeness and parental warmth appear to moderate the link between corporal punishments and aggression, but not change the direction of effects.

16. Psychological control practices seem to have the same negative effects across cultures (e.g., high levels of child anxiety) regardless of potential moderating factors, such as normativeness.

Conscience: The Beginnings of a Moral Self

17. Children's internalization of rules and values is associated with conscience, feeling distress when one violates a rule. This is the beginning of moral development.

18. Children are more cooperative and compliant when they share a warm, responsive relationship with a parent. Their compliance can also be related to anxious arousal. Hoffman argued that mild arousal can help children pay attention to a rule, but doesn't make them so anxious that they pay attention only to how afraid they are. This is consistent with the finding that mild power assertion practices are more likely than more severe power assertion practices to lead to children's internalization of rules and their long-term compliance. Further, Hoffman's ideas help explain why children who have fearful temperaments respond best to gentle discipline, but children who are fearless are unfazed by either gentle or harsh disciplinary practices. The most important determiner of compliance for fearless children is the warmth of their relationship to the parent.

Case Study

Terry and Bill, married for 5 years, are a Black couple who live in a small suburban community. Terry graduated from high school and worked as a receptionist before her marriage to Bill, a communications company manager. Because both of them believed that mothers should stay at home with young children, Terry quit her job when she had her first child, who is now an intense and active 4-year-old daughter named Dawn. Both parents were very attentive to their daughter and enjoyed caring for and playing with her when she was a baby. As Dawn got older, she became more active and assertive. When Dawn fussed, resisted, or showed frustration, Terry was patient and affectionate with her. She was able to coax Dawn out of her bad temper by making up little games that Dawn enjoyed. Both Terry and Bill liked Dawn's spirited personality. Because her parents wanted her to have access to playmates, Dawn attended a church-related program for toddlers and preschoolers three mornings a week.

When Dawn was 3 years old, Terry gave birth to the couple's second child, a son named Darren. Soon after the baby's birth, the family learned that Darren had a congenital heart problem that would require ongoing medical treatment and a specific regimen of care at home. Darren was an irritable baby. He fussed for long periods and was very difficult for Terry to soothe. Because of Darren's need for medical care and the limitations of Bill's medical insurance, the couple soon found themselves in financial difficulty. Bill began to take on overtime work at the company to subsidize some of the bills and was away from the home several nights a week and part of each weekend.

Terry found the care of two demanding young children and the worries about money to be increasingly more stressful. She was always tired and seemed to have less patience with her family. Although she once had the leisure time to read to Dawn, to take her for walks, and to help her master tasks that proved frustrating, Terry now had to shift her attention to the care of her medically fragile infant. Because Dawn looked so grown-up compared to the vulnerable newborn, Terry began to perceive her daughter as able to do many things for herself. When Dawn demonstrated her neediness by clinging or whining, Terry became abrupt and demanded that Dawn stop. Many battles revolved around Terry's new rule that Dawn have a nap or "quiet time" each afternoon so that mother and baby could get some rest.

One day, Dawn's preschool teacher, Mrs. Adams, asked to speak with Terry. Mrs. Adams noted that Dawn's behavior was becoming a problem in the morning preschool sessions. Dawn had begun throwing toys when she became upset and often refused to cooperate in group activities. Terry was greatly embarrassed to hear about her daughter's misbehavior. Dawn was the only Black child in the small class, and her mother wondered if this was part of the problem. When Terry got home, she put her tearful, clinging daughter in her room for time-out for being bad at school. She loved Dawn, but she could not tolerate this kind of behavior, especially when Darren needed so much of her time. She began to wonder if she and Bill had spoiled their daughter. Terry feared that Dawn would have problems when it came time for her to enter kindergarten if they didn't take a strong stand with her now.

Discussion Questions

1. Explain Dawn's behavior from an attachment point of view. How would you describe Dawn's attachment history?
2. Describe Terry's parenting style. Has the style changed? What suggestions would you make to Terry and Bill about handling this problem?
3. What are some of the contextual influences on Dawn's behavior?

Practice Using What You Have Learned

MyLab Education Application Exercise 5.1:
Self-Awareness in Early Years
MyLab Education Application Exercise 5.2:
Case Study: Parenting Styles, Parent Training
MyLab Education Application Exercise 5.3:
Case Study: Methods of Control

Journal Questions

1. How would you describe your parents' parenting style?
2. What are your views on spanking children? To what extent have your beliefs been influenced by the kinds of discipline used in your family? What would you advise other parents about disciplining their children?
3. How would you describe the impact of cultural changes (such as the use of smartphones, texting, computers, social media, etc.) on caregiver behaviors? In your experience, does their use make it more or less difficult to pay attention to young children with full awareness, acceptance, and presence?
4. Identify a cultural value from your family of origin and describe how this value was reflected in your experience as a family member. If your experience included different or contrasting values and expectations (e.g., from parents, step-parents, etc.), reflect on that as well.
5. What do you believe is the relationship between your early self-development and your later self-esteem?

Key Concepts

self-system (p. 173)
"I-self" or self-as-subject (p. 174)
"Me-self" or self-concept (p. 174)
self-esteem (p. 174)
"looking-glass self" (p. 174)
pre-self (p. 179)
self-recognition (p. 177)
socialize (p. 183)
discipline (p. 183)
parenting styles (p. 183)
warmth dimension (parental responsiveness) (p. 183)
child centered (p. 183)
parent centered (p. 183)
control dimension (parental demandingness) (p. 184)
behavioral control (p. 184)
maturity demands (p. 184)
psychological control (p. 184)
authoritative style (p. 185)
authoritarian style (p. 185)
permissive style (p. 185)
neglecting–uninvolved style (p. 185)

externalizing problems (p. 186)
internalizing problems (p. 186)
method of control (p. 186)
power assertion (p. 186)
love withdrawal (p. 186)
induction (p. 186)
corporal (physical) punishment (p. 186)
withdrawal of privileges (p. 186)
time-out (p. 187)
internalization (p. 188)
normativeness (p. 192)
conscience (p. 195)
anxious arousal (p. 195)
minimum sufficiency principle (p. 195)
committed compliance (p. 195)
compulsive caregiving (p. 197)
compulsive self-sufficiency (p. 197)
negative reinforcement (p. 198)
attention-deficit hyperactivity disorder (ADHD) (p. 199)
contingency management system (p. 199)
motivational interviewing (p. 200)

Chapter 6
Realms of Cognition in Middle Childhood

Learning Objectives

After reading this chapter, you should be able to:

6.1 Describe brain development and concomitant cognitive and behavioral changes in middle childhood and explain atypical variations such as attention-deficit hyperactivity disorder (ADHD).

6.2 Discuss theoretical views of cognitive development that examine conceptual change, logical reasoning, memory, and executive functions in middle childhood, and identify contextual factors that influence children's cognitive and academic growth.

6.3 Analyze children's progress in developing social cognition with specific focus on perspective taking and psychosocial competencies and suggest relevant therapeutic interventions.

Malik is 8-1/2 years old and in the third grade. He lives in a blue-collar, urban neighborhood that borders on a much poorer section of the city. He's on schedule when it comes to learning to read, and he's particularly good in math. There are three kids in his class who are pulled out for an advanced math class, and he is one of them. The school's playground has little to offer except a basketball hoop at one end. The most active and aggressive boys tend to take over that end of the playground during recess. Malik usually spends recess at the opposite end, with a couple of good friends, including his next-door neighbor, Benj. They like to play a complex game of tag, often negotiating and changing the rules.

Malik lives with his mother, father, grandmother, and 3-year-old twin brothers. All of the adults in his family work, and so after school each day Malik lets himself into their row home with his key, fixes himself a snack, and either does his homework or plays video games (usually the latter). He is not permitted outside, or to have friends in, unless one of his parents or grandmother is home to monitor him. His mom arrives home about 5:30, along with his brothers, who spend their weekdays in a child care center. After they talk for a bit, his mom expects Malik to take charge of the twins, playing games or reading to them while she prepares dinner. Malik is good at distracting the boys, and after being on his own for several hours he's usually happy to have their company until everyone else gets home. When dinner is over, Malik has responsibility for taking out the trash, but otherwise, if his homework is done, he watches TV or plays video games with Benj until bedtime.

Development is so rapid during the early childhood years that it is not uncommon for parents to view their elementary school aged child as having grown up, almost overnight. However, children are still far from grown up in middle childhood. They face a whole new set of developmental challenges. Many youngsters begin to spend longer periods away from home, some face hours on their own, and all children must adjust to more rigorous schedules. They must learn to control their behavior, monitor their attention, and acquire formal and complicated academic competencies. They must make friends and learn to navigate the schoolyard, with its greater demands for athletic prowess, social skill, and cooperative negotiation of conflicts. They must also learn the rules of the group and when to abide by them. They must discover what it means to be male or female, not to mention what it means to be themselves. So many challenges await them.

However, children of elementary school age are also more adept at almost every task when compared to their preschool-aged siblings. Observing the eagerness and energy children exhibit in the early school years makes it easy to understand the capacity for industry that Erikson described (see Chapter 1). For most children, the challenges of school and peer group will be mastered gradually, and in many different ways. Armed with foundational skills in language, mobility, self-regulation, and understanding of self and others, the youngster is now poised to assume membership in a larger social network.

Clearly, the years of elementary school, as the years to follow, are marked by ups and downs. These normal fluctuations create opportunities for helpers to provide support or guidance for children, their families, and their teachers. What are the cognitive, emotional, and social needs of children at this stage? What approaches are most helpful given children's developmental level? In the next two chapters, we will attempt to provide you with information that will be useful when working with children at this point in their development. Your understanding of cognitive development, the focus of this chapter, will enable you to understand children's ways of construing the world, helping you appreciate their academic needs as well as the intellectual bases for their friendships, gender roles, moral understanding, and conflicts.

Brain and Behavior

6.1 **Describe brain development and concomitant cognitive and behavioral changes in middle childhood and explain atypical variations such as attention-deficit hyperactivity disorder (ADHD).**

Let's begin by briefly considering the child's changing brain. Changes in brain size and organization accompany the accomplishments of middle childhood. It is tempting to assume that these brain changes are "maturational," that is, triggered by pre-programmed genetic activity. But remember the epigenetic process when you think about brain development: "it is the ongoing interaction of the organism and the environment that guides biological . . . development. Brains do not develop normally in the absence of genetic signaling, *and* they do not develop normally in the absence of essential and contingent environmental input" (emphasis added; Stiles, 2009, pp. 196–197). Put more positively, genes *and* experience dynamically interact to influence emerging brain organization (Stiles, Brown, Hoist, Hoist & Jernigan, 2015). There is no simple answer to the question, "Is this brain/behavioral change genetic or determined by experience?" It is both.

Even though the brain is at 95% of its peak size by age 6, it grows measurably in middle childhood (Blakemore, 2012; Mills et al., 2016). Cortical gray areas increase in volume up to about age 9 or 10, at least partly because the surface of the cortex expands (Mills et al., 2016; Ziegler, Ridgway, Blakemore, Ashburner, & Penny, 2017). There is some dispute about whether the cortex thickens during this period as well, or whether it starts to thin from about age 3 (Walhovd, Fjell, Giedd, Dale, & Brown, 2017). But there is no disagreement that much of the growth of the brain during childhood is due to increases in the volume of white matter (Piccolo et al., 2016; Walhovd et al., 2017). These brain changes slow down by late adolescence, although some continue into adulthood.

Let's consider the growth of white matter in middle childhood. As you learned in Chapter 2, white matter is "white" because of the fatty myelin sheaths that form around the axons, insulating them so that electrical impulses travel faster from one neuron to another. Myelination increases the speed of neural signals dramatically. Also, functional neural networks become more integrated because myelin changes the timing and synchrony of neuronal firing (Giedd & Rapoport, 2010). Overall then, increasing white matter seems to reflect increasing neural connectivity and communication between neurons and between brain areas.

For example, one important area of white matter increase is the corpus callosum. This is the system of connecting fibers (bundles of axons) between the right and left hemispheres of the brain. As the corpus callosum myelinates, the left and right sides of the body become more coordinated. The upshot is that children have much greater motor control, something you can appreciate if you compare the awkward full frontal running of a 3-year-old to the ducking and weaving you might see by Malik and his friends as they avoid capture during a game of tag. Changes in the corpus callosum (along with other brain areas, like the cerebellum) influence and are influenced by the great strides school age children make in both gross motor (e.g., riding a bicycle, skating, climbing trees, jumping rope) and fine motor (e.g., cutting, drawing, writing) skills. Much of this chapter is focused on typical (normative) development in middle childhood, but there are many individual differences among children. Researchers are beginning to link some of these to brain development. For example, children diagnosed with *attention deficit hyperactivity disorder (ADHD)* can show atypical variations in brain development (e.g., Sowell et al., 2003). Between 5% and 10% of school-age children are diagnosed with ADHD based on one or more of a cluster of symptoms that are especially problematic for school performance: poor attentional control (distractibility, problems sustaining attention), restlessness or hyperactivity, and impulsivity (e.g., Martel, Levinson, Langer, & Nigg, 2016). Studies comparing structural MRIs for children with and without ADHD have found differences in several brain areas. These include the frontal lobes, where normative growth is associated with improvements in attention and other higher order cognitive processes. Other areas include the parietal lobes, basal ganglia, corpus callosum, and cerebellum (e.g., Friedman & Rapoport, 2015; Kumar, Arya, & Agarwal, 2017; Wyciszkiewicz, Pawlak, & Krawiec, 2017).

For many children with ADHD, the "difference" is really a delay, especially in the growth of the cerebral cortex. The middle prefrontal cortex shows the greatest delay, with growth for ADHD children lagging behind typically developing children by as much as 5 years (e.g., Shaw et al., 2007, 2012). Fortunately, about half of ADHD cases diagnosed in childhood remit by late adolescence or early adulthood. For those children, it appears that brain development follows a delayed but typical trajectory. For cases of ADHD that do not remit, researchers have found unusual, progressive loss of brain volume in some brain areas, such as the cerebellum (Mackie et al., 2007; Shaw et al., 2013). Note that there is some disagreement about whether ADHD actually comprises more than one disorder, with different frontal brain areas more affected in one type versus another (see Diamond, 2005).

Many children *not* diagnosed with ADHD are behaviorally different from average—they have better or worse attentional control or they are more or less impulsive or active than other children their age. Giedd and Rapoport (2010) suggest that "ADHD is best considered dimensionally, lying at the extreme of a continuous distribution of symptoms and underlying cognitive impairments" (p. 730). In line with this argument, they report that for children who are considered typically developing but more active and impulsive than average, brain changes also take place at a slower rate. Thus, researchers are beginning to identify some neurological differences among children that align with their behavioral differences. In general, helpers need to remember that there is a significant amount of unevenness in brain development in middle childhood, both between and within children (e.g., Berninger & Hart, 1992; Myers et al., 2014). It is not unusual for children to show lagging performance in some skills and more rapid advances in other skills than their age mates.

MyLab Education
Video Example 6.1
This video introduces one case of a young child with ADHD. Note the biological and environmental factors contributing to Eric's diagnosis of ADHD in the doctor's assessment summary.

MyLab Education Self-Check 6.1

Cognitive Development

6.2 Discuss theoretical views of cognitive development that examine conceptual change, logical reasoning, memory, and executive functions in middle childhood, and identify contextual factors that influence children's cognitive and academic growth.

When children leave behind the preschool years, they begin to seem more savvy to adults. As you saw with Malik, they can be given fairly complex responsibilities ("Come straight home from school and lock the door after you're in the house. Don't forget to have a snack and then do your homework."). They can participate in discussions of local or world events, and they often appreciate humor that would have been lost on them earlier. The cognitive developments that underlie these new capacities have been described and studied from several different theoretical traditions. We will first present Jean Piaget's characterization of cognitive change in middle childhood.

Piaget's View: The Emergence of Concrete Operations

Let's review the basic points you have already learned about Piaget's description of cognitive development. One key idea is that knowledge is constructed; it is not just "stamped in" by experience or teaching. Children *assimilate* new information, meaning that they change it, interpreting it in ways that fit in with what they already know or with the way their thinking is structured. Simultaneously, they *accommodate* or adjust their existing knowledge structures somewhat. The result can be that when children are presented with new information, what they actually learn and understand about it often is not completely consistent with reality or with the information that adults mean to convey. Gradually, as new experiences are assimilated and accommodated, children's knowledge and understanding come closer and closer to matching reality.

FIGURE 6.1 Children's images of a round Earth.

Sphere

Flattened Sphere

Hollow Sphere

(a)   (b)

Dual Earth

Disc Earth

Rectangular Earth

SOURCE: Republished with permission of Elsevier Ltd. from *Mental models of the Earth: A study of conceptual change in childhood. Cognitive Psychology*, by Vosniadou, S., & Brewer, N. F. (1992). 24, 549; permission conveyed through Copyright Clearance Center, Inc.

THE CONSTRUCTION OF KNOWLEDGE IN MIDDLE CHILDHOOD

Children in the middle years are confronted with lots of new information every day, especially in school. Let's consider one illustration: the information that the Earth is round. Children all over the world are taught the "round Earth concept" early in elementary school. But the Earth looks flat, so much so that for thousands of years, until Copernicus came along in the 16th century, even scholars believed that it *was* flat. It will not surprise you then that children start out believing that the Earth is flat. So how do they reconcile what they believe, based on what they perceive, with what they are told? Piaget (1929) and many other researchers since have found that children construct some surprising theories as they try to fit the information their elders give them to the concepts they already have.

For example, Vosniadou and her colleagues did a series of studies interviewing children about how the Earth could be round. Figure 6.1 illustrates a few of the ideas Minnesota children in grades 1 to 5 came up with (Vosniadou & Brewer, 1992). It appears that children begin by trying to fit the information that the Earth is round to their naïve view that the Earth is flat. Some children said the Earth was a flat disc—like a coin. Some thought it was a ball that has a flat surface within it and a domed sky overhead. Others saw the Earth as spherical but with a flattened side where people live. The researchers found that the older the child, the more likely he was to represent the Earth as the sphere that scientists believe it to be. But even in fifth grade, 40% of the children still had some other idea of what it meant for the Earth to be round. Similar ideas have been found among school children from countries around the world, including Israel, Nepal, India, Greece, Samoa, Australia, and China (see Hayes, Goodhew, Heit, & Gillan, 2003; Tao, Oliver, & Venville, 2013), and from different subcultures within the United States (e.g., Native Americans; Diakidoy, Vosniadou, & Hawks, 1997).

It appears that what adults teach is not necessarily what children learn. One of the practical implications of Piaget's constructivism is that teachers are likely to be more effective in promoting change in children's naïve concepts if they are mindful of how new information is being assimilated and accommodated by their students. Asking probing questions can be quite useful. Carey (e.g., 2000, 2015) has argued that it helps to know as much about the structure of children's current conceptual ideas or "theories" as possible. Then, teaching can focus on modifying the pieces of the structure that are, in a sense, supporting each other. So, for example, Vosniadou's interviews of children about round Earth concepts uncovered that two important beliefs were connected. First, children saw the Earth as flat. Second, children had a simple idea of gravity: Things fall down, not up, which makes it difficult to understand why things wouldn't fall off the Earth on the "bottom side" of a round Earth. Some of children's strange models of a round Earth were efforts to integrate the round earth concept with both of these ideas.

LOGICAL THINKING AND PROBLEM SOLVING IN MIDDLE CHILDHOOD

You'll recall that despite the gradual construction process that Piaget described, in which knowledge structures are continually changing, he considered there to be stages of thought development, so that within a relatively broad period of time, children's thinking about many different things has some similar organizational properties. We have already discussed some of the characteristics that Piaget attributed to the sensorimotor (0 to 2 years) and preoperational (2 to 6 or 7 years) stages (see Chapter 3). In this chapter, we will consider his view of children's thinking in the *concrete operational stage*, the period spanning the elementary school years from about age 6 to 12.

To understand how Piaget described the thinking of school-aged children, recall the limitations of the younger, preoperational thinker. Generally, preschoolers focus on one salient dimension of a situation at a time, and so they often miss the important relationships among aspects of a situation. Logical thinking is difficult to characterize, but it certainly includes the ability to recognize and take into account all of the relevant information in a problem situation and then to identify how those pieces of relevant information are related to each other. Consider the following simple problem in deductive logic: "All glippies are annoying. George is a glippy. Is George annoying?" To answer correctly, you must take into account a number of pieces of information—that there are glippies, that they are annoying, that there is an individual named George, and that George is a glippy. The important relationship you are then in a position to identify is between George and the characteristics of glippies: If he's one of them, he must be like them. From there you can infer that George is, indeed, annoying.

As we saw in Chapter 3, in very simple situations, even preschoolers can sometimes take into account more than one piece of information at a time. For example, sometimes they can solve very simple deductive inference problems, like the glippy problem (e.g., Blewitt, 1989; Smith, 1979). But more often, their thinking is centered, making it seem quite illogical. Remember the number conservation problems that Piaget invented? Three-year-olds actually think that the number of candies in a row increases if the row is spread out. They focus (center) on the change in length, but they fail to note the corresponding change in the density of the row.

When children are in the concrete operational stage, they usually answer number conservation questions correctly. They may look at the "spread out" row of candies and say "it looks like more," but they can logically conclude that it remains the same number of candies as before. Piaget argued that their logic is dependent on being able to understand the relationship between the row's *increasing* length and *decreasing* density (the candies are not as close together). Because children can decenter (think about more than one dimension of the situation at once), they can discover the relationships among those dimensions.

The compensatory relationship between the length and density of the row of candies is a kind of **reversible relationship**. In essence, one change reverses the effects of the other change. Piaget thought that being able to recognize reversible relationships is especially important for solving many kinds of logical problems, allowing children a deeper understanding of the world around them. For example, preschoolers can learn

MyLab Education
Video Example 6.2
The teacher in this fourth grade class assesses students' prior knowledge before introducing a new concept. This allows him to address possible misconceptions before the lesson and help students accurately assimilate and accommodate the new concept.

MyLab Education
Video Example 6.3
Concrete operational thinkers benefit from visuals and concrete representations of the aspects of a problem. This teacher provides a model for children to think logically about the comparison of fractions.

the following two number facts: "2 + 1 = 3" and "3 − 1 = 2." But only when a child recognizes reversible relationships is he likely to realize that the second fact is the inverse of the first and therefore that they are logically connected. If the first fact is true, then the second fact must be true. To put it differently, knowing the first fact allows the child to deduce the second one if he can think reversibly. When children's thinking becomes efficient enough to decenter, and thus to identify reversible relationships, children can begin to draw logical conclusions in many situations. This is the hallmark of the concrete operational child.

Piaget also identified limits to concrete operations. School-aged children seem to be most capable when the problems they are solving relate to concrete contents, and they seem to expect their solutions to map onto the real world in a straightforward way. But when a problem is disconnected from familiar, realistic content, these children have a difficult time identifying the relevant aspects of the problem and finding how those aspects are related to each other. Here are two versions of the same logical problem. (Logicians call it a *modus tollens* conditional reasoning problem.) The first version is completely abstract—disconnected from any familiar content. The second is framed in terms of familiar, concrete events (adapted from Markovits, 2017). Try to solve the first one before reading the second one.

1. Suppose it is true that if P occurs, then Q occurs. And suppose that Q has *not* occurred. Has P occurred?

2. Suppose that it is true that if a rock is thrown at a window, then the window will break. And suppose that the window is *not* broken. Has a rock been thrown at the window?

The logical relationship among the pieces of information is the same for each problem, and the answer to each is the same: "No." Concrete operational children can usually give the right answer to the second problem, but not the first. You may have found the first problem more difficult too; most of us find completely abstract problems a challenge. But we adults are much more likely to solve them correctly than elementary school children.

Here is another example of how important concrete experience is for elementary school children to think logically. In a classic study, Osherson and Markman (1975) asked children to say whether certain statements were true, false, or "can't tell." The experimenter made statements such as "The [poker] chip in my hand is either green or it's not green." Sometimes the poker chip was visible; at other times the chip was hidden in the experimenter's fist. If the chip were hidden, children in the elementary school years would usually say, "can't tell," asking to see the chip to judge the statement. But the statement's truth was not determined by the actual color of the chip; it was determined by the linguistic elements in the sentence and the relationships between them (e.g., "either-or"). No check with the concrete world was necessary or even helpful. A chip, any chip, is either green or it's not. In other words, the abstract, formal properties of the statement, not concrete objects, were the contents of importance. Concrete operational children find it difficult to think logically about abstract contents, and they seek out concrete or realistic equivalents to think about in order to solve a problem.

Children's tendency to "hug the ground of empirical reality" (Flavell, Miller, & Miller, 1993, p. 139) is especially obvious when they need to think logically about their own thinking. Suppose for a moment that you are a child who believes you have a pair of lucky socks. You think that if you wear your lucky socks, you're more likely to hit a home run playing baseball than if you don't wear them. To test this theory scientifically, you would need to weigh the evidence, pro and con. But before you could do this effectively, you would need to recognize that your belief about your lucky socks is really an assumption or a theory, only one of many possible theories. As such, it could be wrong. Because you already believe your theory, it will seem like a fact to you. You would need to apply careful logical thinking to your own thought processes, first to distinguish your belief from true facts or observations and then to see the relationship between your theory and those facts. However, if you are 8 or 9 years old, you have trouble thinking logically about anything abstract, and theories (or thoughts) are certainly abstract. So, logically evaluating any of your own beliefs or theories is not likely to be easy for you.

As a result, researchers have found that although elementary-school-aged children can think scientifically sometimes, identifying simple theories and checking them against evidence, they make a muddle of it if they already believe a certain theory (e.g., Kuhn & Franklin, 2006; Moshman, 2015). Children get better at evaluating their own theories as they move into adolescence and become capable of what Piaget called *formal operational* thought—logical thought about abstract material. As you will see in Chapter 9, adolescents often extend their logical thought processes to many kinds of highly abstract contents, including their own thinking. As you have already seen though, even adolescents and adults find this kind of abstract thinking a challenge and may make some of the same errors as concrete thinkers.

Even though middle childhood has its cognitive limitations, Piaget was on to something in identifying it as a time when children can be expected to think logically. In every culture in the world, adults seem to recognize that somewhere between ages 5 and 7 children become more sensible, reliable problem solvers. In societies with formal schooling, kids are sent to school to work at serious tasks that will prepare them to take their place in the community of adults. In societies without formal schooling, children are given real work to do by age 6 or 7, tasks that are essential to the community (such as watching younger children, planting, or shepherding).

Piaget's description of the concrete operational child as a logical thinker about concrete contents has proved a useful one, and it seems to capture the typical cognitive characteristics of middle childhood quite well. However, as we saw in Chapter 3, some of Piaget's own research and much of the newer work makes it clear that there are no sharply defined stages in development. Just as adults sometimes have trouble thinking clearly about abstract problems, younger children sometimes solve problems that we might expect only adolescents or adults to manage. Take a concept like "proportionality" in math. It refers to a relationship between two things, such that if one thing changes by a certain ratio the other thing will change by the same ratio (e.g., we might find that the amount of food children eat is *proportional* to how much they grow). Proportionality is an abstract concept that generally is difficult for children to reason correctly about before age 11 or 12 (e.g., Inhelder & Piaget, 1955/1958). But with some materials, especially liquids, even 6- and 7-year-olds find the concept easier to intuit, and they often solve proportionality problems correctly with these materials (Boyer, Levine, & Huttenlocher, 2008).

On the whole, logical thinking seems to emerge over an extended period of development and "must be achieved at successively greater levels of complexity" (Kuhn, 2011, p. 502). Many factors affect how advanced a child's reasoning will be in any situation. Among these are the particular properties of the materials or context (as proportionality problems illustrate); the child's general knowledge; his experience with the technology he is using (see Box 6.1); and his particular expertise (see Ricco, 2015). Expertise refers to how much a child has learned about a specific **domain of knowledge** (that is, a particular subject matter or content area). If a child has a lot of knowledge about a particular domain, say dinosaurs or chess, his ability to think logically about problems within that domain is often more advanced than in other content areas (Chi, Hutchinson, & Robin, 1989). It seems that a child or adult with a lot of domain knowledge is better at identifying the important features of a problem within that domain and at identifying the relationships among those important features (Moran & Gardner, 2006). Thus, logical thinking is at least somewhat *domain specific* (that is, applicable to a particular area of knowledge) rather than strictly domain general and determined by one's stage of development, as Piaget's stage theory implies. For a child who loves experimenting with chemistry sets, reasoning about chemistry is likely to advance more quickly than for a child whose passion is music.

In the next sections, we will consider some other ways of characterizing children's cognitive abilities in the middle years, starting with the information processing approach. We will examine what we have learned about some abilities, combining research from the Piagetian, information processing, and other research traditions.

Box 6.1: Techno-Kids: Cognitive Development in a Wired World

Across from the reference desk at the local public library, Kim, Jeanine, and Serena, third-grade classmates, huddle together in front of a computer screen, looking for information for a group project. They are accustomed to using computers, both at home and at school. As the girls take turns speedily clicking the mouse, scanning screens, jumping from one webpage to another, an elderly woman at the next desk observes them with wonder. She too is using a computer, but the children have a facility and comfort with the equipment that she can only dream about. How else might their "tech savvy" make them different from the woman? Are there developmental consequences for children to having easy access to television, video, computer games, the Internet, or any of the myriad electronic media that are part of our technologically saturated environment? Are the consequences different depending on whether access begins early or late in childhood? What practical advice should helpers give to parents who want to protect their children from harm but also to provide them with the advantages that make sense?

These are among the questions that developmental scientists are tackling, as a technological tsunami engulfs us. Let's consider some of what we have learned so far.

Infants and Toddlers

Babies automatically orient to novel stimuli. Visual electronic media like television, videos, and computer games tend to draw their attention with rapidly changing sights and sounds. There is little evidence that this attentional pull is good for very young children and some evidence that it may be harmful (see Kostyrka-Allchorne, Cooper, & Simpson, 2017). In longitudinal studies of television use, Christakis and his colleagues (Christakis, 2011; Zimmerman & Christakis, 2007) found a link between infant/toddler viewing and later attention problems, even though several other sources of attention difficulties, such as low family income, were controlled in their research. In one study, the more television children watched before age 3, the more likely they were to have difficulty regulating attention at age 7. In a second study, the actual content of television programs turned out to be important. Amount of *educational* television viewing (e.g., *Barney, Sesame Street*) before age 3 *was not* a predictor of attention problems later, but children's *entertainment* television (e.g., cartoons) was. Also, the more violent the content, the more serious the later attention problems were. The researchers hypothesize that a key factor in these content differences may be the pacing of visual and auditory changes. Entertainment programming tends to have shorter scenes with more frequent changes that may "overstimulate the developing brain" (Zimmerman & Christakis, 2007, p. 990). Language use is also much more quickly paced in these programs than the slower "parentese" that young children hear in actual interaction with adults (see Chapter 3); educational programs are more likely to mimic the pacing of parentese.

While some studies implicate early video viewing as a cause of attention problems, not all researchers have found similar associations. In the research where links have been found there may be alternative explanations (Courage & Setliff, 2009). For example, temperament differences in infants and toddlers predict how much video viewing parents allow them to do (Brand, Hardesty, & Dixon, 2011; Brand & Dixon, 2013). Children who are difficult to soothe watch more TV, probably because parents find that it has a calming effect on them. Attention problems at 7 or 8 may be the result of these early temperament differences instead of the amount of early TV viewing children have done.

Do infants and toddlers actually learn from videos that are intended to be educational? Marketers claim great educational benefits, but the evidence does not support these claims (Barr, 2013; Choi & Kirkorian, 2016). For example, DeLoache and her colleagues (2010) tested the effectiveness of a best-selling DVD designed and marketed for infants from "12 months and up." The video shows a variety of house and yard scenes and repeatedly presents labels for household objects. Parents enthusiastically endorse the video in marketing testimonials. Yet babies who watched the video at least 4 times a week over 4 weeks performed no better on a test of the target words than babies who never viewed the video. In a condition where mothers were asked to teach the target words to their babies "in whatever way seems natural to you" over a 4-week period, those children performed substantially better on the final word test than babies who had watched the video. Interestingly, mothers who liked the video also believed that their babies had learned a lot from it, even though they had not, which may account for some of the enthusiastic testimonials on marketing websites!

These findings are consistent with a survey of over 1,000 parents of 2- to 24-month-old children (Zimmerman, Christakis, & Meltzoff, 2007). Parents reported on the children's video viewing (including television) and completed a measure of children's language development. For 8- to 16-month-olds, viewing "educational" DVDs was actually linked to a slower pace of language development, and the more viewing there was the worse the language delay was (even when factors such as SES were controlled; although see Ferguson & Donellan, 2013 for a different interpretation). Sometimes parents interact in positive ways with babies when they watch educational media together. When they do, children seem to learn more, but high quality interactions are much more likely when there is no TV or video playing (Simcock, Garrity, & Barr, 2011). Twelve- to 30-month-olds can learn to some degree from video—for example, they will imitate some of the actions that they see on screen—but they imitate substantially more when they witness live demonstrations of the same actions (Barr, 2013).

In sum, it is still uncertain whether early use of electronic media actually causes harm (such as later attention problems) (e.g., Fields, 2016). But one thing is clear. These media can *displace,* or take time away from, other activities that are more critical for positive cognitive development. Interactions with sensitive, responsive adults are central to the processes of acquiring language skills, building event and autobiographical memories, and learning about emotions, the self, and others. The "full body" exploration of objects and spaces that characterizes early play—smelling, tasting, manipulating, climbing, opening, closing, putting together, taking apart—helps babies and toddlers build a foundation of temporal, spatial, and physical knowledge that prepares them for later developments (see Chapter 3). Unfortunately, even when they are engaged in play with objects, if a television is on in the background, babies frequently turn toward the screen, reducing the length of play episodes and disrupting focused attention (Schmidt, Pempek, Kirkorian, Lund, & Anderson, 2008). Short play episodes and reduced attention during play are "marker(s) for poor developmental outcome" (Schmidt et al., 2008, p. 1148). Despite such concerns, many parents and other caregivers give infants and toddlers access to these media. For example, one startling finding from a large survey of families by Common Sense Media in 2013 is that 16% of infants and 37% of 2- to 4-year-olds in the United States actually had televisions in their bedrooms. Concerns about brain and behavioral development have led the American Academy of Pediatrics (AAP) to recommend no use of digital media (e.g., television, videos, and computer games) for children under 18 to 24 months of age, except for video-chatting (Council on Communications and Media, 2016a). For 18- to 24-month-old toddlers, the AAP suggests that parents might introduce a child to digital media with high quality programming if child and adult watch or play together, but recommends no solo viewing yet.

Children and Adolescents

As children grow older, controlled exposure to electronic media is less problematic for perceptual and cognitive development. For example, television watching by 4- and 5-year-olds does not appear to be associated with long-term attentional problems (Stevens & Muslow, 2006; Zimmerman & Christakis, 2007), although children this age are still likely to have short-term attention difficulties after watching violent programs (Freidrich & Stein, 1973; Geist & Gibson, 2000). On the positive side, preschoolers' experience with some age-appropriate *educational* programming, such as *Sesame Street* and *Dora the Explorer*, is linked to improved school readiness, vocabulary growth and better number skills by kindergarten (Anderson & Kirkorian, 2015), and with better school achievement by adolescence (Kostyrka-Allchorne et al., 2017), even when other characteristics of the home environment and parenting are controlled. Among the features to look for in quality programming for young children are "the use of child-directed speech, elicitation of responses, object labeling, and/or a coherent storybook-like framework throughout the show" (Bavelier, Green, & Dye, 2010, p. 693). Unfortunately, the more exposure to *entertainment* programming in the preschool and elementary school years, including child-directed programming like cartoons, the less likely children are to perform well in school. Just as we have seen with infants and toddlers, part of the problem seems to be that watching television displaces more achievement-related activities. Another problem may be that early television exposure socializes children's tastes, building preferences for superficial, rapid action, formulaic sequences and plots, and reducing the appeal of slower paced, more intellectually challenging entertainment, such as reading and puzzle

solving (Comstock & Sharrer, 2006). What are the costs and benefits when children use interactive media, such as computers and gaming devices? To begin, there is little doubt or disagreement that giving all children means and opportunity to become computer literate is an important educational goal. Learning to use basic computer software and the Internet as tools for acquiring, organizing, storing, and communicating information should be part of every child's experience. Some schools are even teaching basic programming in elementary school, another useful skill for children in today's world. Individuals who lack computer skills will be disadvantaged in many settings, especially the workplace. Also, having access to computer technology and the Internet can benefit academic performance. For example, Jackson et al. (2006) analyzed data from HomeNetToo, a longitudinal project in which low-income families were offered free computers, Internet access, and in-home technical support in return for permission to monitor each family member's Internet use. Children in these families were mostly low achievers in school, but those who used the Internet more during the 16 months of the project had higher GPAs and reading achievement scores at the end (but not at the beginning) than children who used it less. The authors suggest that surfing web pages gave children substantially more reading practice than they would otherwise have had, helping to explain the benefits.

Such benefits do not seem to be limited to low-income children. In another longitudinal study, 1,000 adolescents from a range of backgrounds were surveyed in the 9th or 10th grade and then again in the 11th or 12th grade (Willoughby, 2008). Controlling for factors such as parents' education, moderate use of the Internet (about 1 to 2 hours per day) was more predictive of better school grades than either nonuse or high levels of use. It appears that nonuse is an academic liability in today's schools and that excessive use is also problematic.

Academic performance today depends on achieving a balance between on- and off-screen activities (Anderson & Kirkorkian, 2015). Another study of reading skills helps to demonstrate. As you have just seen, the more that low-income children use the Internet, the better they tend to score on standardized tests of reading, apparently because of the practice that reading web pages gives them. But if screen use *displaces* reading books and other printed matter, then children's reading skills are likely to suffer. In a large study of 8- to 13-year-olds in Great Britain, the larger *proportion* of reading kids did on screen versus with print material, the more poorly they performed on measures of reading (Clark, 2012). That may be because off-screen reading sources often provide more challenging content. Electronic games, whether they are played on a computer or on some other platform, such as an Xbox or Play Station, can help develop the skills that the games use (see Markey & Ferguson, 2017). There is more research on these practice effects with adults than with children, but for skills that have been studied in children the same benefits apply, and they seem to be wide ranging, from improvements in vision and attention to refinements in motor skills. For example, playing action video games improves the ability to find small details in cluttered scenes or to see dim signals (Benady-Chorney, Yau, Zeighami, Bohbot, & West, 2018). Many studies indicate that playing action video games also can improve

(continued)

children's visual-spatial abilities, such as spatial rotation skill. The latter involves looking at an image of a three-dimensional object or scene and recognizing a representation of that object or scene from another perspective, a skill that many games use (Uttal et al., 2013) and that plays an important role in mathematical problem solving (Newcombe, Levine, & Mix, 2015). Some games are designed specifically for educational purposes, such as improving math skills or vocabulary. Some are effective; some are not. Many are not substitutes for other educational experiences, but can be helpful supports. Interestingly, younger children seem to prefer educational games to games designed purely for entertainment.

Research on the cognitive benefits of interactive media for children is in its infancy. There is certainly potential not only for teaching specific knowledge or skills but also for achieving broader cognitive impact (see Adachi & Willoughby, 2017). Imagine a program that asks probing questions and encourages the child to hypothesize solutions, then to test and evaluate hypotheses, and so on. Or consider that many games have multiple levels of skill and require extended practice and intensive effort, rewarding the persistent player with the pleasure of achieving mastery at one level and the opportunity to face the challenge of a new level (e.g., Gee, 2007). These kinds of experiences seem likely to promote good problem solving and learning strategies if they generalize to other situations. But whether they do is not yet clear (see Markey & Ferguson, 2017, for a discussion of when learning from video games is likely to transfer).

Extrapolating from decades of research on children's television viewing, it seems very likely that the *content* of a game or web page, along with the level of parent or teacher engagement in screening, explaining, and discussing that content, is more important than the electronic tool that delivers the content. What we know about television is that educational content can promote learning, and prosocial portrayals encourage prosocial behavior. Violent content can promote aggressive behavior, at least for individuals who are prone to aggression, and, as we noted earlier, may have problematic consequences for the development of attention in very young children. Exposure to explicit sexual content and to sexism (e.g., women washing floors, men washing cars) and pervasive commercial propaganda about what is "fun" and important to own affect children's beliefs and values about sexual behavior, gender, and what is important in life. We also know that when caring, knowledgeable adults help children to choose content and when they join children in their media use, scaffold their problem solving, and discuss and interpret media messages, children are less negatively and more positively affected (see Calvert, 2015).

Guidelines for Parents

When should interactive media be introduced? Experts tend to agree that children under age 2 are better off not being "wired" at all, but opinions about access for preschoolers are much more mixed. On the one hand, organizations like the National Association for the Education of Young Children and the Fred Rogers Center for Early Learning and Children's Media (2012) are cautiously in favor of integrating "developmentally appropriate" exposure to computers and educational software into the preschool classroom. On the other hand, many researchers emphasize the dangers of preschool computer use, especially because time with electronic media displaces social interaction, pretend play, and constructive, creative problem solving in the three-dimensional world (e.g., Healy, 1998). Unfortunately, although some truly constructive computer learning games are available, much of the programming for preschoolers is focused on superficial and largely rote activities. Research on electronic books, for example, suggests that children's attention is often drawn to flashy elements—such as clicking on icons that are peripheral to the story—at the expense of attending to the story. The result is that children's story comprehension is not as good with electronic books as it is with traditional books (Bus, Takacs, & Kegel, 2015; Parish-Morris, Mahajan, Hirsh-Pasek, Golinkoff, & Fuller Collins, 2013). There are also concerns about possible health effects: muscular skeletal injuries, visual strain, and obesity due to inactivity (Alliance for Childhood, 2000). Because of such concerns, the American Academy of Pediatrics (AAP; 2016a) recommends limiting screen time for 2- to 5-year-olds to 1 hour a day. They also urge that adults choose quality programming, and that parents view with children to help them understand the content and learn how to apply it to the real world (Council on Communications and Media, 2016a).

For children older than 6 or 7, the AAP suggests developing a clear plan for family media use (Council on Communications and Media, 2016b). The primary concerns are that parents control content exposure and set time limits on media use so that it does not displace other important developmental experiences. Children should avoid screen use for one hour before bedtime and should not sleep with devices in their bedrooms. Parents also need to monitor whom their children communicate with through the Internet, scaffold children's efforts to master programs, and help children to evaluate not only programming content but also commercial messages, which can be as ubiquitous on the Internet as they are on television.

Parents and educators need to recognize that to make effective use of computers and the Internet in the classroom, teachers must be well trained in their use and know how to judge the value of educational programs (e.g., Roschelle, Pea, Hoadley, Gordin, & Means, 2000). Does the teacher, for example, know how to guide children to information that comes from a reliable, objective source as opposed to a source with an agenda (commercial or cause driven)? Time and money invested in teacher training is at least as important as investments in hardware and software. "The best results from all technology use for children come accompanied by a skilled adult 'coach' who adds language, empathy, and flexibility" (Healy, 1998, p. 247).

A number of authors and organizations provide helpful guidelines and information for parents and educators, who often are not as savvy or comfortable with newer electronic media as children are. Some valuable websites are:

American Academy of Pediatrics (aac.org)
U.S. Department of Education (ed.gov)
Common Sense Media (commonsensemedia.org)
The Children's Partnership (childrenspartnership.org)
Children Now (childrennow.org)
Entertainment Software Rating Board (esrb.org)
Center for Media Literacy (medialit.org)

An Alternative Perspective: The Information Processing Approach

Many interesting studies of middle childhood cognition—especially memory and problem solving—have been done by researchers in the information processing tradition. Information processing theories compare cognitive functioning to a computer's processing of information (see Chapter 1). The structural organization of the cognitive system is thought to be the same throughout development. A typical example of the kinds of structural components through which information is thought to "flow" during cognitive processing is presented in Figure 6.2. In this view, there are no qualitative, stage-like changes that characterize most of a child's thinking or processing. There are some changes with time, however, mostly in the amount and efficiency with which information can be processed. With increasing age, children can work with more information at once, and the strategies that children use to organize, understand, or remember information may also change. However, children apply different processing strategies to different specific contents, such as math, reading, and spatial concepts, so that strategies are not usually considered to be the result of broad cognitive skills that are applied across different domains. Instead, strategies appear to be largely domain specific.

Information processing researchers focus heavily on what children do with information of particular kinds: what they pay attention to, how they encode it, what and how much information they store, what other information they link it with, and how they retrieve it. In other words, information processing theories are focused on the mechanics of thinking. A Piagetian researcher might try to demonstrate that one cognitive achievement, perhaps in math, is related to another, perhaps in social perspective taking, to illustrate the global effects of some underlying stage characteristic. An information processing researcher typically tries to track the specific information handling that underlies a child's increasing mastery of a single domain.

FIGURE 6.2 The information processing system.

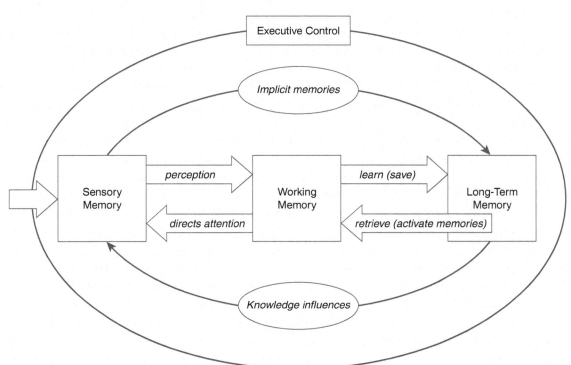

SOURCE: Adapted from Woolfolk, A. (2014). *Educational psychology: Active learning edition* (12th ed.). Upper Saddle River, NJ: Pearson Education, Inc.

The skills that appear to guide the flow of information are called *executive functions (EFs)*, as you saw in Chapter 3. These include *working memory, self-regulation (or inhibitory control)*, and *cognitive flexibility*. Improvements in the efficiency of these skills in particular are seen as supporting other cognitive advances throughout childhood. Longitudinal studies find that good executive functions in childhood are related to many positive outcomes in adolescence (e.g., frustration tolerance) and adulthood (e.g., higher socioeconomic status) (Zelazo & Carlson, 2012). Interestingly, some of the negative consequences of poverty on children's academic performance are related to slower development of executive functions in poor children. As you have seen in earlier chapters, many children in low-income families experience chronic stress, which affects neuroendocrine pathways and the development of the body's typical reactions to stress. This in turn affects how well children can modulate their emotions and exercise control over attention and other higher order cognitive functions (e.g., Obradović, 2016).

As EFs improve, children get better at consciously controlling their thinking (e.g., planning, strategically problem solving), their actions (e.g., inhibiting automatic responses), and their emotions. Self-regulation or inhibitory control is typically quite good by the end of middle childhood. For example, Bunge and colleagues (2002) asked 8- to 12-year-olds to push a button on the left side of a panel if a central arrow pointed to the left and to push a button on the right if the central arrow pointed to the right. It's a simple task—unless the central arrow is surrounded by arrows pointing the wrong way. Then it takes some doing to inhibit the tendency to push the button that all the other arrows point toward. Children were not as good at the task as adults, but they nonetheless were about 90% accurate.

Children show improvement on measures of executive functions through middle childhood and adolescence (Boelema et al., 2014; Zelazo et al., 2013; see Zelazo, Blair, & Willoughby, 2017 for a review). Neural circuits that heavily involve the prefrontal cortex mediate these functions, and their development is dependent on experience or practice. Genetic processes are certainly at work here, but social, cultural, and educational experiences make important contributions (see Hughes, Roman, & Ensor, 2014). The role of experience is clear when we examine cross-cultural differences in executive functions. From early childhood through adolescence, children from Asian countries, such as Japan and China, make more rapid progress in the development of executive functions than children from Western countries, such as Great Britain and the United States, even though adults in these different countries eventually achieve similar levels of performance on EF tasks (e.g., Ellefson, Ng, Wang, & Hughes, 2017; Imada, Carlson, & Itakura, 2013). Culturally based differences in socialization practices may be important here. For example, Asian parents put more emphasis than Western parents on teaching children to inhibit their own desires in order to conform with the collectivist (versus individualistic) norms of their culture. Such practices may encourage earlier development of some self-regulation skills.

Information processing theorists have traditionally paid special attention to the executive function of working memory and its role in cognitive development. This is the part of the cognitive machinery that holds information we are actively thinking about at the moment. It "works" with that information in ways that allow us to maintain our attention, to plan, to solve problems, and to learn. That's why it is depicted so centrally in Figure 6.2.

You will also notice in Figure 6.2 that some information coming in from the senses bypasses working memory. This is because information processing seems to occur at two general levels (e.g., Evans & Stanovich, 2013; Ricco, 2015). The first level of processing tends to be automatic, intuitive, and unintentional. Processes of this type are usually fast, and they do not need working memory. They are sometimes called "bottom up" processes. So, for example, you might automatically jump up when you hear the soft beeping sound of your microwave. You're conditioned to do it and you do not need to make a conscious decision to respond. In comparison, working memory and other EFs govern a second level of processing that is slower, more intentional, and deliberative. These are sometimes called "top-down" processes (e.g., Diamond, 2013). If you are conditioned to react to the sound of your microwave, *not* responding to the sound might actually require that you use your working memory to think through what you want and take conscious control of your behavior.

We will take a closer look at working memory and its development later in this chapter. You will also learn more about the importance and modifiability of executive functions during middle childhood in the Applications section.

Some Other Approaches to Understanding Cognitive Development

The influence of both Piagetian and information processing approaches has fueled a rapid increase in our understanding of cognitive development, and it is not surprising that some theorists have attempted to marry the best components of each. **NeoPiagetians** explain Piaget's stages, or revise the stages, using many information processing concepts (e.g., Case, 1985, 1992; Fischer & Bidell, 2006; Halford & Andrews, 2006; Pascual-Leone & Johnson, 2017). For example, Case (1985) specifies four stages comparable to Piaget's, but explains the transition from one to another partly in terms of increases in the capacity of working memory. Another example, offered by Halford and colleagues (see Halford, 2014; Halford & Andrews, 2006), analyzes many of Piaget's tasks in terms of "complexity theory." Instead of assessing logical problem solving as dependent on how concrete or abstract the contents are, they suggest that the difficulty children have with problems depends on the number of variables that must be related to each other, that is, the size of the "processing load." The idea is that younger children can process fewer variables at once than older children.

Theory theorists (see Carey et al., 2015; Gopnik & Wellman, 2012) suggest that children quite spontaneously construct theories about how the world works: about mind, matter, physical causality, and biology. Many theory theorists argue that humans have some innate knowledge of these domains, even in infancy, which is not consistent with Piaget's view. And theory theorists do not typically agree with the idea of stage-like changes in overall cognitive functioning. But following Piaget, theory theorists are constructivists. They claim that children's understandings in each conceptual domain are re-constructed over time, as children acquire new information. Children's efforts to include information about the Earth being round into their concept of the physical world is an example. Like neoPiagetians, most theory theorists see executive functions as the mechanisms that make re-construction possible. Working memory, for example, makes it possible to hold more information in mind while reflecting on problems within a domain.

Focus on Memory: Why Does It Improve in Middle Childhood?

So far, we have considered major theoretical approaches to explaining cognitive development in middle childhood. We have talked about conceptual change (e.g., the round Earth concept) and the growth of logical reasoning skills (e.g., deductive inference) to illustrate these theories. Now, let's focus on another cognitive ability, memory. By examining how memory improves during the elementary school years, you will be able to see how a whole host of factors contribute to the growth of intellectual functioning.

Let's begin by imagining a child who has just had his annual medical examination. With his parent's consent, an interviewer asks a set of questions to explore what the child remembers about the experience. Some are open-ended questions, such as "Can you tell me what happened when you went to the doctor?" Others are specific yes–no questions, such as "Did she look in your nose?" A subset of the yes–no questions are strange or silly, such as "Did the doctor cut your hair?"

As you might expect, elementary-school-aged children usually answer such questions more accurately than preschoolers do. If you wait for several weeks and then ask about the doctor's exam again, a 3-year-old will forget more of what he could originally remember than a 7-year-old will. In one study, by 12 weeks after the checkup, 3-year-olds' responses to the silly questions were at chance levels of accuracy (meaning that they were saying "yes" to about half of the silly questions), but 7-year-olds averaged about 90% accuracy, despite the delay. The older children's answers had also remained relatively consistent over time, so that if they answered "yes" to a question right after the exam they tended to do so on repeated tests at later times (Gordon, Ornstein, Clubb, Nida, & Baker-Ward, 1991, as cited in Ceci & Bruck, 1998).

Almost all aspects of memory seem to improve with age, at least up through young adulthood. Before we consider some of the cognitive changes that contribute to these improvements, let's briefly define terminology that is commonly used in discussions of memory. Many of these terms were first introduced by information processing theorists, and some are included in the information processing flow model depicted in Figure 6.2.

MEMORY TERMINOLOGY

First, we can describe memory as consisting of different memory stores. **Sensory memory** refers to a brief retention of sensory experience. For about one third of a second, when we first see a scene, we store most of the sensory information that has come in, almost as though our eyes have taken a snapshot of the whole scene. A similar phenomenon occurs with hearing. Interestingly, sensory memory capacity does not seem to change much with age. At least for visual information, even infants' sensory memory is similar to that of adults (e.g., Blaser & Kaldy, 2010).

Working memory is the next storage "unit." It is partly a "short-term store." As you have learned, working memory allows us to focus attention, plan, execute problem-solving strategies, and make inferences. It also organizes information for transfer into **long-term memory**, the almost unlimited store of knowledge. The information we pay attention to in working memory comes from our immediate sensory experience and from long-term memory. For example, suppose you are watching a movie about an African adventure, and an array of color and movement suddenly fills the screen. Your working memory combines the sensory data coming from the screen with information drawn from long-term memory to create a meaningful interpretation: It's a charging zebra. Or suppose your supervisor reminds you that your counseling approach to a client's new problem is similar to one that was not very successful in the past. Your thinking about the strategy (in working memory) combines elements of the supervisor's input with stored memories of prior interactions.

Unlike long-term memory, working memory is thought to have a limited capacity. We can pay attention to, and think about, a limited number of meaningful units of information at one time, and material is lost from working memory in 15 to 30 seconds unless we engage in **rehearsal** (i.e., unless we actually keep working with it, making an effort to pay attention, such as repeating it to ourselves). Explicit learning that results in our ability to recall information later requires working memory. To get new information into long-term memory in a form that we can access later, we must pay attention to it and think about it. For example, you may hear the music playing as the zebra on the screen charges, but unless you pay attention to it, you are not likely to be able to intentionally recall the tune later. Or if you're mulling over another problem while your supervisor gives you feedback, you will be unlikely to recall her comments later. So, much of learning seems to require real work or effort. If you find you have to go back and reread a section of this chapter to commit it to memory, you are making the kind of mental effort that characterizes working memory and accounts for successful learning.

We should note that some learning does seem to bypass working memory. It involves the kind of lower level, automatic processing we mentioned earlier. You can store connections or associations between stimuli that you experience together even when you're not paying attention. Much of infant learning seems to be of this sort. So, even though you weren't paying attention to the music when the zebra was on the screen, hearing that music later might remind you of the zebra, although you probably couldn't say why. This kind of learning is sometimes referred to as implicit.

Learning, or acquiring knowledge, involves the storage of information. **Retrieval** is what we usually mean by remembering, that is, getting information out of storage so we can use it. In Chapter 3, we talked about two kinds of remembering or retrieval: *recognition* and *recall*. Recognition happens when the information to be remembered is immediately available to your senses. For example, you see a clerk from your local grocery store crossing the street in front of you, and you realize that you're experiencing someone who is familiar. Your sensory image elicits information about the clerk stored in long-term memory. We saw in Chapter 3 that some ability for recognition seems to be present from birth, and generally young children's recognition skills are very good, especially for visual-spatial information, such as memory for pictures. (Try playing a game that involves visual memory with a 4-year-old. You might not win!) However, long-term retention of visual-spatial information does improve over the preschool years (Morgan & Hayne, 2011), and recognition of verbally presented information shows even longer-term developmental improvement (Schneider & Bjorklund, 1998).

Recall is more work. The to-be-remembered information is not present, and you must somehow draw it out of long-term memory and re-present it to yourself, as when you must answer an essay question on an exam. Or, as we described in the opening of this section, a researcher asks a child to remember what he experienced when he went to the doctor. When a child has problems with recall, it could be because he did not attend to the information in the first place, because he did not store the information in long-term memory despite having paid attention to it, or because the child does not have adequate strategies for finding the stored information. Clearly, recall depends on many processes.

One feature of human memory is that we can store different kinds of information or knowledge. Knowledge about facts and events, called declarative knowledge, is of two kinds. The first kind is semantic knowledge, which includes factual information ("the Earth is round"), rules ("red lights mean stop"), and concepts ("an elephant is a large, gray animal"). The second kind is episodic knowledge, which refers to our knowledge of the events that we have experienced. When researchers ask children to recall their visit to a doctor's office or when your supervisor asks you to describe a counseling session, they are asking about episodic knowledge. Episodic knowledge is organized around time and space—what happened in what order, where, and when. After we've had several experiences with one kind of event, such as being examined by a doctor, we begin to form a schematic representation of the typical features of such an event and the order in which they happen. This is called a script.

In addition to declarative knowledge, we have nondeclarative knowledge that we cannot adequately put into words and that may not even enter our awareness. For example, you may know how to shift the gears in a standard transmission vehicle, but you might have a difficult time explaining how to do it. Many physical skills are based on this kind of unconscious, nondeclarative knowledge, which we usually call procedural. You may remember that we have used the term procedural knowledge to describe what infants "know" about how to do things or what to expect from interpersonal interactions (see Chapter 5). Early working models of attachment are probably a kind of procedural knowledge. Much of what infants and toddlers know seems to be nondeclarative rather than declarative.

WHAT IMPROVES WITH DEVELOPMENT?

Now that we have a vocabulary of memory terms, let's take a look at how memory seems to work in middle childhood and what improves with age. Perhaps most importantly, working memory seems to expand. Because working memory expands, children's capacity for learning and for retrieving information from long-term memory also expands. So understanding what contributes to working memory development will help us understand how memory in general grows.

Like Piaget, most observers, regardless of theoretical orientation, have noted that older children usually pay attention to more pieces of information at one time than younger children. Their performance on digit span tests illustrates this change in working memory capacity. You may recognize these tests as a typical part of most intelligence tests. A series of digits is presented to the test participant, who must immediately repeat them in the same order. A child of 2 years can usually reproduce about two digits accurately; by the time he is 7, he will probably be able to remember a five-digit string. Adults, on average, can recall about a seven-digit string.

What accounts for increases in working memory capacity with age? There could literally be, somehow, more "room" in the older child's working memory (Cowan, 2016). But many other cognitive changes seem to contribute and may actually be more important. We will consider several of these.

Processing Speed. The first cognitive change that contributes to memory improvement is that children can process information more quickly as they get older. How rapidly children can make a simple response (e.g., pushing a button) to a stimulus (e.g., the onset of a light on a computer screen) increases from early to middle childhood, and it continues to improve until about age 15 (e.g., Kail, Lervåg, & Hume, 2016; Spanoudis, Demetriou, Kazi, Giorgala, & Zenonos, 2015). Piaget attributed the decentering skill of school-aged children (their ability to pay attention to more than one thing at a time) to the speeding up of mental activities with practice, and modern research does support the idea that practice can accelerate information processing (Mackey, Hill, Stone, & Bunge, 2011). In addition, speed of processing can increase with physical maturation—that is, simply as a function of age (Toga et al., 2006). The upshot is that as children get older, they can do more with more information at one time (e.g., Demetriou et al., 2014).

Breadth and Depth of Knowledge. The second cognitive change that affects memory improvement is that as children get older their knowledge about many things increases. They expand their **knowledge base**. Consider the study of children's recall of a medical examination mentioned earlier. One reason that a 7-year-old might have recalled information more accurately than a 3-year-old is that the older child probably knew more about medical exams. By 7, a child has formulated a script of the typical medical exam. When an interviewer asks questions about a particular exam, even many weeks after it happened, the 7-year-old may not actually remember whether the doctor cut his hair, for example, but he knows that doctors don't do that sort of thing in medical exams, and so he answers correctly. In general, older children know more about most events, and so they are more likely than younger children to be able to reconstruct accurately what probably happened in any given situation.

It should be noted that prior knowledge can also lead to false memories. For example, in a series of classic studies by Liben and colleagues, children were shown videos or pictures of people playing roles such as that of a doctor or a nurse (see Liben, Bigler, & Hilliard, 2014). Sometimes the gender of the adult was consistent with traditional expectations—such as a man playing the role of doctor—and sometimes the person's gender and occupation were not traditionally consistent, such as a man playing the role of nurse. Children's preexisting beliefs about gender and work roles—that is, their gender stereotypes—influenced what they later recalled about what they saw. In one particularly interesting study, Signorella and Liben (1984) found that elementary school children with strong gender stereotypes were more likely than children with less stereotyped beliefs to misremember who had played what role in the pictures they had seen when gender and occupation were not traditionally matched. So, for example, if they had seen a woman doctor, the children with strong stereotypes would be likely to remember that it was a man they had seen instead, or that the woman had been a nurse. (See Box 6.2 for other examples of how false memories can be induced.)

So prior knowledge affects your ability to reconstruct what you have experienced. In addition, the more you know about a particular subject, or domain of knowledge, the more easily you can learn new information in that domain and the better you will remember it later. If knowledge in most domains expands with age, then learning and retrieval of information in most domains should get better with age. But age is not what is most important—knowledge is. Suppose, for example, that you show an 8-year-old child a chessboard with chess pieces arranged as if in the middle of a chess game. Later, you ask the child to reconstruct the placement of all the pieces on an empty board—that is, to recall the layout of the pieces. If the child happens to be an "expert" chess player—someone who plays in competitions and is highly knowledgeable about the game—his performance on this recall task will be much better than that of an average adult "novice," who knows how to play but who does not have

Box 6.2: Children's Eyewitness Testimony

The following is an experience reported by Bill, a 4-year-old:

> My brother Colin was trying to get Blowtorch [an action figure] from me, and I wouldn't let him take it from me, so he pushed me into the woodpile where the mousetrap was. And then my finger got caught in it. And then we went to the hospital, and my mommy, daddy, and Colin [older brother] drove me there, to the hospital in our van, because it was far away. And the doctor put a bandage on this finger (indicating). (Ceci, Loftus, Leichtman, & Bruck, 1994, quoted in Ceci & Bruck, 1998, p. 749)

Bill appeared to have a clear memory of this scary event, and he was confident even about details such as where his father was at the time of the accident. But the experience Bill described so convincingly never happened! It was a false memory, induced by a researcher who had read brief descriptions of a set of pictures to Bill each week for 9 weeks. The description for one of the pictures had said, "Got finger caught in a mousetrap and had to go to the hospital to get the trap off." The researcher then said, "Think real hard and tell me if this ever happened to you. Do you remember going to the hospital with a mousetrap on your finger?" In the first session, Bill said he had not had such an experience. By the tenth session, as you have seen, he seemed convinced that he had.

Preschoolers can have some difficulty with **reality monitoring**, distinguishing fantasies from realities. Young children can tell the difference between what is real and what is not and between what it feels like to only imagine something versus to actually experience it (e.g., Flavell, Flavell, & Green, 1987), but they have more difficulty with these distinctions than older children or adults (e.g., Tempel, Frings, & Mecklenbräuker, 2015). In particular, if they imagine an event, they are somewhat prone to say later that it actually happened. One charming and usually harmless example occurs when a child becomes devoted to an imaginary friend. But a young child's problems with reality monitoring can make him more susceptible to suggestion than older children or adults, a serious concern when children serve as eyewitnesses. For example, in child sexual abuse cases, interviewers and therapists have sometimes used a technique called **guided imagery** as an aid to memory. A child might be asked to pretend that an event occurred, then create a mental picture of the event and its details (Ceci & Bruck, 1998; Gilstrap, 2004). Unfortunately, if an adult encourages a child to construct a fantasy about what *might* have happened, the child may eventually come to believe that it *did* happen, even if it did not.

In considering whether children should serve as eyewitnesses, the key issue is, how valid can children's reports be expected to be? In the late 1600s, children's testimony at the witch trials in Salem, Massachusetts, led to the execution of 20 defendants. Young girls testified convincingly that they had seen defendants doing fantastic things, like flying on broomsticks. Some of the testimony was later recanted, and the whole episode created such a negative view of children's testimony that for three centuries child witnesses were not often seen in American court proceedings. Only in the 1980s did many states end restrictions on children serving as witnesses (see Ceci & Bruck, 1998).

Modern memory research has helped increase the acceptance of children's testimony in America. Many studies indicate that what children remember *can* be accurate, although the number of details a child will recall and with what accuracy improves with age. But at any age, a witness's memory for observed events could be incomplete or distorted or simply wrong, sometimes as a result of exposure to suggestion. And in most situations the younger the child, the more susceptible he is likely to be to suggestion (see Ceci, Hritz, & Royer, 2016).

We have seen that preschoolers' difficulties with reality monitoring can be a source of suggestibility, and there are several other sources as well, many of which children might encounter in the course of being interviewed by parents, police, social workers, therapists, and other court officials. When interviewers are biased, they may guide children's testimony, planting suggestions without realizing that they are doing so. So, for example, if an interviewer is already convinced that a child has been abused, she may encourage a child's admission of abuse by asking leading questions, such as, "Where did he kiss you?" instead of open ended questions, such as "What did he do?" The interviewer might also ask the same question repeatedly if the child's initial answers are not consistent with the interviewer's belief. Studies of interview transcripts indicate that even the most well-meaning and concerned interviewers, including parents, use many such tactics to try to get at what they believe, or fear, is the truth (e.g., Bruck & Ceci, 2013). Unfortunately, they may be planting suggestions that can lead the child to reconstruct his memory of an event.

A study by Pettit, Fegan, and Howie (1990) is just one of many that illustrates how effective such suggestions can be with young children. Two actors visited a preschool classroom. They pretended to be park rangers and talked to the children about helping a bird find a nest for her eggs. In the middle of the discussion, one "ranger" knocked a cake off the top of a piano "by accident." The cake was smashed, and there was silence for a few moments in the classroom, creating a rather distinctive event. Two weeks later, each of the children in the class was interviewed about the incident. Before the children were questioned, the researchers gave some of the interviewers an accurate account of what had happened. Others were provided with false information, and a third group was given no information at all. The interviewers' instructions were to find out what had happened from each child, but without asking leading questions. Despite the instructions, the interviewers did ask leading questions—30% of the time—and half of these were misleading. Naturally, the interviewers who had false beliefs about the event asked the most misleading questions. And the children were often misled, agreeing with 41% of the misinformation suggested to them. Apparently, interviewers biased by false beliefs can unwittingly maneuver children into providing false information (see Bruck et al., 2006 for other experimental examples).

(continued)

Elementary-school-aged children are generally less suggestible than preschoolers (Brown & Lamb, 2015; Ceci et al., 2016). For example, their reality monitoring is more adequate, and they are less affected by leading questions. But even older children and adults are not immune to suggestion (Ackil & Zaragoza, 1995; Loftus, 1979). Fortunately, witnesses of all ages can provide more accurate information if they are interviewed under conditions designed to minimize suggestion. Even traumatic experiences can be recalled well by young children under the right conditions. Research on children's eyewitness testimony reveals a number of characteristics that may reduce the influence of suggestion in interviews (Ceci et al., 2016; Lamb, Malloy, Hershkowitz, & Rooy, 2015). Of course, interviewers should ask open ended questions, such as "What happened last night?" and "What happened next?" They should avoid leading questions, as we have seen, and they should keep both the repetition of questions and the number of interviews to a minimum. The interviewer's tone should also be neutral, rather than urgent, aggressive, or accusatory. For example, an accusatory tone may be set by statements such as "Are you afraid to tell?" and "You'll feel better once you've told." In one study, when interviewers made such comments, even children who previously indicated no recall of an event sometimes agreed with questions that incorrectly suggested abuse (Goodman & Clarke-Stewart, 1991).

Sometimes in cases of suspected sexual abuse, investigators use anatomically detailed dolls or human figure drawings as props, encouraging children to show what happened or where they were touched. This technique has been seen as a way of helping children overcome limited language skills or feelings of embarrassment. Unfortunately, the evidence indicates that young children cannot easily use such props symbolically as was hoped (Lytle, London, & Bruck, 2015). Interviewers are now encouraged not to use these props with young children (Lamb et al., 2015). Interviewers should not use inducements such as telling children they can help their friends by making disclosures. In one criminal investigation, for example, investigators said things to children such as "Boy, I'd hate having to tell your friends that you didn't want to help them" and "All the other friends I talked to told me everything that happened . . . . You don't want to be left out do you?" (quoted in Ceci & Bruck, 1998, p. 745). Such pressure might have the effect of encouraging children to produce responses even when they do not recall the events in question. Another interview strategy to be avoided is **stereotype induction**, that is, slanting the interviewee's view of an individual. Sometimes interviewers will encourage children to make revelations by indicating that the alleged perpetrator is a bad person or does bad things. But in studies where this strategy was implemented, young children were found to produce incorrect, negative recollections of such an individual's behavior more often than children who were not exposed to the induction (see Bruck & Ceci, 2012).

As Ceci and Bruck (1998) emphasize, interviewers are motivated by concern about the welfare of the child: "[N]o interviewer sets out with the intention of tainting a child's memory" (p. 730). But even with the best of intentions, an interviewer can elicit questionable testimony. An understanding of the ways in which memory is constructed and reconstructed can help investigators to make eyewitness testimony, especially in children, more trustworthy. To aid in this process, The National Institute of Child Health and Human Development (NICHD) has created a research-based protocol for investigators and interviewers working with children (Brown & Lamb, 2015). The protocol is available at NICHDProtocol.com.

extensive knowledge of the game. In other words, when children are more expert than adults in a domain of knowledge, they can remember more new information from that domain than adults can (e.g., Chi, 1978; Chi & Koeske, 1983). We will see later that other domains of knowledge, such as knowledge about others' perspectives and feelings, improve at this age and enhance social relationships.

Many studies suggest that as you amass knowledge of a subject, you understand new information in that domain more quickly and more completely. Knowledge is not just a list of separate pieces of information. A rich web of well-organized connections forms in long-term store (Marsh, Cantor, & Brashier, 2016). For example, a counselor's concept of "therapy" might be part of a detailed web of stored information such as the one presented in Figure 6.3. We fit new information into this web, allowing us to retrieve it later through many routes and making it more accessible than if there were fewer connections. The processing speed for new information increases, and the depth of understanding is greater. All aspects of memory seem to be positively affected. Of course, ordinarily, the older you are, the more knowledgeable you are, and so the better you are at remembering, particularly in your area of expertise.

One advantage of a rich web of knowledge is that it allows chunking of information in working memory. Chunking links several pieces of information together into a single meaningful unit. For example, suppose you were given the following series of letters to remember: NCISIRSCIAFBI. You might notice that you could divide the series into four chunks that represent federal agencies in the United States: NCIS, IRS, CIA, FBI. If so, you would probably be able to remember all the letters because you converted them to just four pieces of information, which would not exceed your working memory capacity. The more extensive the webs of information in your long-term memory, the more likely you are to find ways to chunk information meaningfully in working memory (Cowan, Ricker, Clark, Hinrichs, & Glass, 2015).

FIGURE 6.3 A conceptual web for the term *therapy*.

Logical Thinking Skills.   A third cognitive change that contributes to memory improvement with age is advanced logical thinking. If older children can think more logically than younger children, they may have a better understanding of at least some of their experiences. Understanding better helps them to remember more about the experience later. Piaget's own research on memory improvement with age focused heavily on the contribution of logical thinking (see Piaget & Inhelder, 1973). In a typical study, he showed children from ages 3 to 7 an array of sticks, arranged in serial order by size. One week later, he asked children to draw what they had seen as a test of their recall. They were also given an opportunity to put a series of sticks in order according to size. This seriation task is a lot like the conservation of number task. It looks simple, but children usually are not completely successful at it until about age 7. In other words, it seems to require the logical thinking of the concrete operational stage. Piaget found that if children did not have the logical thinking skills needed to seriate sticks themselves, they typically could not remember the serial pattern they had been shown a week earlier. Children who could seriate the sticks (mostly 6- and 7-year-olds) showed better memory for the serial pattern. Remarkably, though, when he tested children's memory again at least 6 months later, many of the younger children were now more accurate in their memory drawings than they had been originally, depicting some aspects of the serial order. These findings have often been replicated, indicating that children's memory for some experiences can actually improve over time! How could this happen?

The key here seems to be that memory is often reconstructive. That is, when we recall an experience, we integrate "what we currently experience, what we already know, and what we infer" (Kuhn, 2000a, p. 22). You have already seen that older children may use what they know about doctors' examinations in general to reconstruct a particular doctor's examination. This helps them recall more accurately than a younger child. It also appears that if a child's logical understanding of an event improves from the time he first experiences it to the time his memory is tested, he may reconstruct it more accurately than he could have earlier. As the children in Piaget's study got older, they could understand seriation better, and so when they "remembered" the original stick array, they often inferred that the sticks had been arranged according to size.

Language Skills. A fourth cognitive change that can benefit memory with age is greater facility with language, especially improvements in *narrative* skill, the ability to tell a coherent story. Clearly, one way in which we mentally represent information is in words. As children's vocabularies grow and their skill in describing events develops, their ability to store information about experiences in coherent verbal form also improves (see Reese et al., 2011). As we saw in Chapter 3, this aspect of memory improvement is enhanced by narrative interactions with adults. If parents encourage their children to talk out loud about their experiences, asking questions and helping them with facts about shared events, children are better storytellers. They also have better memory for autobiographical events. On the whole, language skills such as these improve with age and experience, and so older children's memory for events can generally be expected to be better than that of younger children.

Memory Strategies. A fifth cognitive change that can facilitate memory improvement with age is learning to use memory strategies. Strategies are "potentially conscious activities a person may voluntarily carry out" to remember something (Flavell et al., 1993, p. 235). Imagine that we asked you to remember all the names of the children in your class when you were in the fifth grade. After you finished groaning, you would probably take a strategic approach to this retrieval task. That is, you would follow some plan. Maybe you would try to remember all the girls and then all the boys; or maybe all your good friends and then all your enemies; or maybe all the popular kids, then the less popular ones; or maybe you would use a spatial organization strategy, trying to remember the kids in the front row first and work your way to the back of the classroom. Generally, adults approach memory tasks strategically, and when they do, they remember more than if their approach is haphazard. There are a host of strategies that we can call on. Some help us encode new material that we expect to have to remember later. Others help us retrieve information that is already stored. People who are really good at remembering names and phone numbers and other details of experience are generally well practiced at applying strategies.

But what about children? Preschoolers are usually considered nonstrategic in their memory efforts. An interesting example comes from a study of 3- to 8-year-olds who were shown rows of boxes that contained either toy animals or household objects. Boxes with animals had a picture of a cage on top; boxes with household objects had a picture of a house. Children were asked to remember either the locations of the animals or the household objects. The researchers carefully observed the children's actions during a study period, and found that the younger children tended to open all the boxes, whereas the oldest children were more strategic, opening only the boxes with the items that they would have to remember later (animals or objects). In other words, older children selectively attended to the locations that they had to learn about. Younger children did not seem able to use selective attention to help them with the memory task (see Miller, 1994).

Selectively attending to one thing and not to another is very difficult for preschoolers, and so it is not a skill that 3- or 4-year-olds are likely to deploy to aid memory. But sometimes preschoolers seem to use other skills in ways that we might call "pre-strategic." When they know that they will be asked to remember something later, sometimes they do things differently than they might otherwise. For example, researchers gave 4-year-olds a set of toys to play with. They told some children that later they would be asked to remember what some of the toys were. These children tended to play with the toys less and to name them more than children who were not given such instructions (Baker-Ward, Ornstein, & Holden, 1984). So, in other words, they seemed to act in ways that would help them remember.

Systematic use of strategies is much more likely in middle childhood. If you give a group of third graders the job of learning the names of all the states and their capitals, you will probably see them using *rehearsal*—repeating the names over and over. There are a variety of more complex strategies, but children usually do not use them spontaneously until the late elementary school years or even adolescence. For example, a child could use an organization strategy: sorting the items to be learned on some meaningful basis, such as grouping the names by region. Or he might use an elaboration strategy—finding or creating some kind of meaningful link between items. To help remember that Baton Rouge is the capital of Louisiana, he might make up a sentence like "Louise saw a bat," or he might create a mental picture, visualizing a girl named Louise with a bat on her head. At about 9 or 10, children will use organization strategies spontaneously and to good effect. Not until adolescence are they likely to use elaboration without prompting. Strategies that are particularly useful for learning textual material, such as underlining and summarizing main ideas or key points, also emerge late, during adolescence (see Miller, 2014).

Developmental progress in children's use of memory strategies is a bumpy affair. On one hand, children might at first use a strategy quite sporadically, often showing a production deficiency, meaning that they might fail to use it even in situations where it is ordinarily helpful. On the other hand, sometimes children use a strategy, but it does not seem to boost memory; in this case they are said to have a utilization deficiency. Although strategies usually do aid memory performance, when a child first uses a strategy spontaneously, it may be so much work that it takes up a lot of time and attention, minimizing its effectiveness for improving memory. Yet children still may use the strategy. As Siegler (1998) argued, it's as though children intuitively understand the "law of practice"—that practice improves efficiency in the long run—even if there is no immediate profit!

We have been describing the development of children's spontaneous use of memory strategies, but effective use of strategies also can be taught. Children whose parents or teachers instruct them on how to use a strategy are likely to use it on the tasks where they were taught to do so. However, they typically do not generalize the use of a strategy to new situations, and it takes considerable practice to use such strategies efficiently (see Clerc, Miller, & Cosnefroy, 2014).

Metacognitive Skills.   The discussion of memory strategies leads us to a sixth, and final, cognitive change that seems to affect memory. It is the development of metacognition, knowledge of our own mental processes and the ability to reflect on those processes. You learned in Chapter 3 that preschoolers have some awareness of mental processes. Four- to 5-year-olds have a theory of mind that includes understanding that their own thoughts, beliefs, and desires often differ from those of other people, as we have seen. They also have some beginning skills at judging what they know. For example, if we show a 4- or 5-year-old a classmate's picture, even if the child cannot spontaneously recall the classmate's name, he will be able to accurately judge whether he would know the name if he heard it (e.g., Cultice, Somerville, & Wellman, 1983). This kind of self-monitoring and understanding of what you can and cannot accomplish cognitively, and how to accomplish it, improves dramatically across the elementary school years.

Consider changes in children's understanding of their memory processes, which is called metamemory. In a classic study, researchers compared aspects of metamemory in kindergartners and fifth graders (Kreutzer, Leonard, & Flavell, 1975). Fifth graders understood that remembering the gist of a story is easier than remembering it word for word; only half of the kindergartners understood this point. Kindergartners understood some things about memory, such as the value of writing things down if you want to remember them, but not until fifth grade did children realize that there are differences in memory ability from one person to another or from one situation to another. Many researchers have found that whereas preschoolers are usually overly optimistic about how much they are likely to remember about some material, such as a list of words, older children's estimates are usually much more realistic.

Children use memory strategies more, and also more effectively, as they grow in understanding of how their memories work (see Miller, 2014; Schneider & Ornstein, 2015). In one study (Grammer, Purtell, Coffman, & Ornstein, 2011), researchers measured first graders' metamemory skills. For instance, children had to say who would have the hardest time remembering a story about a town: Would it be a person who had never been to the town, a person who had been there two years ago, or a person who had been there 4 weeks ago? Some first graders had better insights into how memory works than others. They realized, for example, that recent visitors to the town might find it easier to remember the story. All of the children were also given training on how to use an organizational strategy to help with recall of a set of picture cards. Over the next year, the children were repeatedly tested on their spontaneous use of the strategy they had been taught. The children with the best scores on the metamemory test at the beginning of first grade were most likely to increase their use of the organizational strategy by the beginning of second grade.

You can see that metacognitive awareness makes it more likely that children will regulate their own learning strategically. But there is a lot to learn about our own cognitive processes, and some of it is difficult for kids in middle childhood. For example, suppose you are trying to learn the information in this chapter for your next exam. You probably understand that keeping track of what you have already learned by testing yourself (monitoring your memory) will help you to allocate your study time well. This is one bit of metacognitive awareness that shows little development through elementary school, at least with challenging material. Elementary-school-aged children don't often spontaneously monitor their learning. In fact, one of the better ways to help children in this age range use memory strategies more effectively is to train them to explicitly monitor what they have learned through techniques such as self-testing (Pressley & Hilden, 2006). In other words, teaching children to keep track of what they have learned seems to be an important element in teaching them how to learn. An important side-benefit to self-testing is that the retrieval practice it provides can actually improve later recall (e.g., Jaeger, Eisenkraemer, & Stein, 2017; Jones et al., 2016).

It's important to note that metacognition is the target of many clinical and educational practices that are collectively known as **self-instruction** or **self-monitoring** (Meichenbaum, 1986) and are a major part of cognitive therapies for children and youth (Kendall, 1993; see Elliott, Gresham, & Witt, 1988). The general goal of such practices is to effect some behavior change (such as control of impulsivity or improvement in test-taking skills) by helping children attend to, regulate, and sometimes change their cognitions. As you will see in the Applications section, interventions can target improvement in three kinds of knowledge: *declarative*, or knowledge about facts, rules, or oneself as a learner; *procedural*, or knowledge about *how* to apply rules and strategies effectively; and *conditional*, or knowledge of *when* to apply the rules or strategies (Schraw & Moshman, 1995). Consider 10-year-old Amelia, who, having missed a day of school, calls a classmate to get her homework assignments. Does she know that if she doesn't write down the page numbers, she won't remember them later (declarative)? Does she rehearse her spelling words both by writing them out and repeating the letters aloud (procedural)? Does she do her science homework first because it is the most difficult for her (conditional)?

This review of memory improvement through middle childhood has, of necessity, touched on many aspects of cognitive development, including advances in processing speed, growth of knowledge, development of logical thinking and language skills, growth of selective attention and other strategic skills, and metacognitive developments. It is clear that "to study memories is to study much of . . . cognition and cognitive development" (Kuhn, 2000a, p. 22).

But memory is more than the product of the cognitive system. It is also influenced by affective and social factors. To illustrate, consider that adult interactions with children seem to figure critically into the development of memory skill. You have just seen that teaching children strategies for learning new material improves children's memory performance. Encouraging children to narrate their experiences helps them develop better autobiographical memories. In other words, scaffolding by adults, in the Vygotskian sense (see Chapter 3), contributes substantially to memory development and to all aspects of cognitive achievement. Let's take a look now at the relationship between cognitive development and education: What do adults do that matters?

Cognitive Development and Formal Schooling

There is a synergy between cognitive development and schooling: Children's cognitive abilities, all of the processes we have been describing, have a major impact on children's academic performance. For example, children's performance on measures of executive functions as they enter kindergarten predicts their academic achievement throughout their schooling (Bull & Lee, 2014; Morgan et al., 2017). At the same time, the experiences children have in school make critical contributions to their cognitive development. Teachers' interactions with children are the proximal source of educational influence (Caro, Lenkeit, & Kyriakides, 2016), but these interactions are shaped partly by the school environment, by the broader community and culture, and by government policies and structures (Rindermann & Ceci, 2009; Rindermann & Thompson, 2014). These contexts are of course affected by (and affect) many economic and social forces, from wealth and wealth distribution to degree of modernization (e.g., access to electricity, motorized forms of transportation, telecommunications, and so on; Gauvain & Munroe, 2012). In Table 6.1 you will see a list of some characteristics that researchers have repeatedly found to predict cognitive competence and academic achievement across countries and regions of the world.

No single factor operates alone, including those listed in Table 6.1. Multidimensional processes are at work, with the impact of each moderated by several others. Student/teacher ratios are a good example. Generally, lower ratios (smaller classes) support better outcomes when other variables are well controlled (e.g., Fredriksson, Öckert, & Oosterbeek, 2013). Having fewer students in a class allows more individual interactions between teachers and students, more oral participation by children, and a greater likelihood that children's learning problems or other special needs will be recognized and addressed. However, the potential advantages of small class size can be reduced by poor teaching or ineffective class management. And the disadvantages of large classes can be offset as well. In many East Asian countries, where class size tends to be rather large, children perform very well academically in comparison to many other countries. The negative effects of high student/teacher ratios appear to be balanced by other characteristics, including strong cultural (and family) expectations that children will be self-disciplined and diligent in school (see Box 6.3). Also, it is often

---

TABLE 6.1 Educating Cognitively Competent Children: Some Factors Associated with Academic Achievement

COUNTRY AND CULTURAL FACTORS

General educational level of adults
Access to quality preschool education
Kindergarten attendance
Valuing/training of self-regulation
Quantity of instruction per year (including after school/weekend instruction)
Achievement tests and "exit exams"
Low grade retention

SCHOOL FACTORS

Strong leadership by principal or head of school
Clear mission and vision shared by teachers and staff
Small class sizes
Communication with parents/encouraging parental involvement
Support and respect for multiculturalism
Consistent behavioral expectations for cooperation and courtesy
Adequate teaching materials, physical facilities
Coherent curriculum across grades
Support for teachers' preparation and training

TEACHER FACTORS

Warmth, positive attitudes
Good behavioral management skills
High academic expectations of each child
Tailoring feedback and input to children's needs
Respect and valuing of children's ethnic differences

Box 6.3: Children of Immigrant Families

In the middle of the school year, Elena's family arrived at their new home. On the first day at her new school, Elena's mother left her with the principal, who walked her to her second grade classroom. Her new teacher introduced her to the class, assigned her to a desk, and asked Jenna, who sat in the seat next to her, to help Elena when she had questions. Elena had just turned 8 years old. She was ordinarily shy, and in this classroom she felt nearly paralyzed. Everyone was a stranger. The classroom routine was different from that of her old school, from the order of daily activities to the books used for reading instruction. The teacher was doing a unit on plants with lessons on science and on geography that the class had been working on for 2 weeks, a topic that Elena had never confronted in school before. Only when a math worksheet was distributed with familiar addition and subtraction problems did Elena feel like she might be able to breathe.

Changing schools is hard on any child. But Elena has just arrived in the United States with her family from Mexico and she speaks only Spanish. Asking questions of Jenna, even if Jenna sympathizes with Elena's predicament, might not help much with the transition. Elena has become one of the 4.6 million **English-language-learner (ELL)** students enrolled in U.S. classrooms. The majority of these children are in grades K to 5, and they speak more than 350 different native languages (McFarland et al., 2017). Even though many are born in the United States, they often have little exposure to English or to American culture prior to the start of school.

A child is considered to be from an **immigrant family** if at least one parent was born outside of the country of residence (Crosnoe & Fuligni, 2012). In the United States, over 40% of such children are Hispanic, their parents having migrated largely from Mexico and Central America. Another 14% have parents who migrated from East or South Asia or the Pacific Islands (Jung, Fuller, & Galindo, 2012). Clearly, these children are a diverse group in many ways besides country of origin and native language. Some are the "1.5 generation," meaning they themselves have immigrated, and others are "second generation," born after their parents arrived in the host country; their parents differ in education and job training; for some, both parents have immigrated, for others only one parent; some have a history of exposure to war, famine, or other disasters in their country of origin, others do not; some have legal status in their host country, others do not.

Immigration is not unique to the United States. It contributes most of the population growth to developed countries around the world, so the needs and developmental progress of immigrant children is a topic of international concern. Leading researchers in this field argue that "international migration is shaping the nature of child development as powerfully as it is changing the nature of the societies involved" (Crosnoe & Fuligni, 2012, p. 1475).

How do children of immigrant families fare? Are they especially vulnerable to academic or social problems because of an accumulation of risk factors (the **immigrant risk model**)? Or, are they relatively more successful than other children because immigrant families have strengths or protective factors that moderate the risks (the **immigrant paradox model**)? In fact, researchers find evidence for both models, and they are beginning to untangle the factors that contribute to vulnerability versus advantage. The circumstances that lead to migration are important. Children whose families enter the new country legally, perhaps seeking new opportunities or pursuing re-unification with other members of their families, may have many fewer problems than children whose families are fleeing violence and/or whose legal status is uncertain. For example, recent migrations from war- or gang-ravaged regions into European and North American countries have often created traumatic circumstances for children. These could lead to life-long cognitive and emotional problems, especially for children who have experienced lengthy separations from their primary caregivers (Bouza et al., 2018). See the discussion of the long-term consequences of chronic stress in Chapter 2.

Other important factors include the characteristics of the country of origin and of the family (e.g., religious values, family size and structure, parents' education). In addition, the family's circumstances once they are settled in the host country are important, such as their socioeconomic status, job opportunities, social supports, available schools, diversity within schools and communities, and racial/ethnic tolerance and discrimination patterns. Let's consider how some of these factors relate to children's outcomes, especially their cognitive and academic outcomes.

Children's Health

Children's health is a key element in their cognitive development, so understanding whether immigrant status impacts health and health care is important. In the United States, when children from Hispanic immigrant families are compared to native children they are often advantaged in physical and mental health, a paradoxical outcome given they are more likely to be socioeconomically disadvantaged (Marks, Ejesi, & García Coll, 2014). Children born to immigrant Hispanic mothers in the United States have fewer birth problems (e.g., lower infant mortality rates, less frequent low birth weight) and fewer acute and chronic illnesses (e.g., asthma). Among the family differences that might account for these health advantages are higher rates of breastfeeding among foreign born mothers, a greater tendency to fully immunize their children, and lower smoking rates (Jackson, Kiernan, & McLanahan, 2012). Interestingly, one study found many similar health advantages for children of immigrant families in the United Kingdom, even though they tended to migrate from different parts of the world (Jackson et al., 2012). However, in the United States at least, the continuing health of children varies depending on the immigration status of the parents even when comparing only low-income families (Ziol-Guest & Kalil, 2012). Children of naturalized citizens tend to do quite well; children whose parents are non-naturalized (either permanent or non-permanent residents) are less likely to be in very good or excellent health as reported by their mothers. This difference corresponds to the likelihood that children are receiving regular dental or medical care. It appears that non-naturalized parents are less likely to have health insurance or to take advantage of health care programs even though their children may be entitled to them. This could happen for many reasons. Language barriers may make it difficult for parents to access information or find suitable health care providers; parents may misunderstand the consequences of seeking assistance for eligible children (e.g., worrying that it might affect their efforts to become citizens or to attain permanent residency); or if some householders do not have legal status, parents may be reluctant to call attention to themselves (Yoshikawa & Kalil, 2011).

Results are mixed on mental health. Some studies have reported better outcomes for children of low-income immigrant families compared to children of low-income native families (Crosnoe, 2006), but others have not. It may depend on the kind of behavioral outcomes that are examined. One study found fewer externalizing problems but more internalizing problems for immigrant children (Jackson et al., 2012). More in-depth longitudinal studies have also found that the most resilient immigrant children in the United States adapt by learning American cultural values, but they also demonstrate high ethnic pride and continue to endorse essential values of their culture of origin in adolescence and beyond (Cruz, King, Cauce, Conger, & Robins, 2017).

Family Function

Much of what you have read in earlier chapters demonstrates that how families function, including their parenting practices, can affect every area of child development. Family functioning varies widely among immigrant families. Differences in migration and demographic history and related cultural practices are important influences. For example, among immigrants to the United States, births to unmarried mothers are much more common for Mexicans (46% of births in 2006) than for Asians (11% in 2006). South Asian parents are more likely than Mexican parents to have completed high school and to be fluent in English. These and other differences influence the likelihood that families will live in poverty once in the United States. Approximately 33% of Mexican families but only 8% of South Asian families live in poverty (Jung et al., 2012).

You are already aware of how problematic the stress of poverty can be for children's development in many domains. Yet immigrant families may buffer the negative effects of poverty on children in some ways. For example, "core socialization norms" in many Hispanic families emphasize "good comportment and respectful communication . . . cooperation and caring for peers . . . and the children's contribution to the collective interest of the family . . . " (Galindo & Fuller, 2010, p. 581). Immigrant Hispanic mothers also tend to describe themselves as mentally healthy (e.g., reporting low levels of depression), perhaps in part because they often feel that they have good social support (either from fathers or other family members) (Jung et al., 2012). Children from such families enter school with academically useful social competencies, such as self-control and low levels of aggressiveness. Kindergarten teachers tend to rate the social-emotional functioning of children from Hispanic immigrant families somewhat lower than children from White native families, but

the differences are quite small (Galindo & Fuller, 2010). Different cultural expectations rather than problematic parenting seem to account for the slightly lower ratings. Hispanic children, who are taught not to pose questions to elders as part of respectful behavior, may seem less socially competent to U.S. teachers who value more verbal engagement and inquisitiveness.

Immigrant families are quite divergent with regard to practices that specifically prepare children for formal schooling. Country of origin makes a big difference here (Koury & Votruba-Drzal, 2014). One large study found that Mexican immigrant mothers read to their preschool children less frequently than native White mothers, but Chinese mothers read more often than the native White mothers (Jung et al., 2012). Differences in parents' education might be key to this finding, because only 33% of the Mexican mothers had more than a high school education, whereas 93% of Chinese mothers did. However, even if Asian parents have very little education, their cultural beliefs and practices appear to be especially helpful for their children's academic lives (Ng, Sze, Tamis-LeMonda, & Ruble, 2017). They tend to view intellectual achievements as a function of hard work, whereas many other groups (e.g., native White families) see intelligence as a fixed capacity. In Chinese and other South Asian groups, a "learning model" is typically the highest cultural value, meaning that learning is seen as bringing "honor, respect, and everything good in life" (Li, Holloway, Bempechat, & Loh, 2008, p. 12).

Typically, Chinese immigrant parents with little education or income are especially focused on promoting their children's learning opportunities. For example, they may work extra jobs and longer hours so that their children can attend Chinese school on weekends. They correspondingly expect their children to work hard; commitment to academic excellence is "nonnegotiable" (e.g., Ng et al., 2017). Interestingly, low-income Chinese parents are unlikely to be involved in their children's school activities (such as helping with homework) because of long work hours and/or lack of the necessary language or academic skills, but they frequently designate an "anchor helper" for that purpose, such as an older sibling or other relative. They also encourage their children to emulate peers who are academically successful, holding them up as role models. And extended family members are expected to "co-parent," reinforcing the value of school achievement, checking up on grades, offering assistance, even if they do not live nearby. As one child of Chinese immigrants said, "My grandparents call a lot; they always ask me how I'm doing in school . . . my entire family, I think they're the most concerned about grades, cause whenever they call, it's always about school . . . They call twice a week from Australia" (Li et al., 2008, p. 21). Perhaps because of the emphasis on learning in their culture, children of Chinese immigrants often perform better in school on average than native White children in the same socioeconomic circumstances.

Supporting Immigrant Children in Schools and Communities

Let's focus now specifically on the academic achievement of the children of immigrant families. You have just seen that the cultural values of the country of origin are important for children's school

(continued)

performance. You have also seen that parenting practices that ready children for school success, like reading to young children, are often related to parents' education. Not surprisingly, parents' education before migration is strongly related to children's academic achievement in the host country (Pong & Landale, 2012). Cultural valuing of academic success and parent education are protective factors, buffering or moderating the impact of more negative factors such as low income.

One negative factor for children of some immigrant groups is the pattern of prejudice and discrimination they might face in the host country. Discrimination is the experience of negative treatment because of group membership, and it can be from peers (e.g., teasing or exclusion), from teachers (e.g., expecting poor performance, grading unfairly, treating children as troublemakers, ignoring or isolating them), or from community members (e.g., preferring residential segregation). Children who perceive discriminatory behavior by teachers and/or peers are often less likely to stay interested in school and to perform at their best (António & Monteiro, 2015). "Weak relations with teachers diminish students' motivation to pursue academic work, and in turn lower teachers' expectations in a self-perpetuating cycle of academic disengagement and under-achievement" (Tienda & Mitchell, 2006, p. 85). Conversely, when teachers maintain high academic expectations for *all* their students and value multiculturalism in the classroom, freely discussing cultural differences and creating an environment of respect, children perceive less discrimination not only from their teachers, but also from their peers, and they are more likely to succeed in school (Brown & Chu, 2012).

Having a strong sense of their own ethnic identity is a protective factor for children, even buffering the negative effects of perceived discrimination (García Coll & Marks, 2012). Positive ethnic identity includes seeing your ethnicity as a central aspect of who you are and positively valuing that aspect of yourself (Fuligni & Tsai, 2016; see Chapter 9 for a more in depth discussion). From elementary school onward, children with positive ethnic identities are more academically motivated and more likely to do well in school. This is especially important in schools where children from immigrant families are in the minority. In schools where immigrant children are in the majority, such as predominantly Hispanic schools in parts of the United States, perceived discrimination and positive ethnic identity are not especially predictive of academic outcome (Brown & Chu, 2012; Greene, Way, & Pahl, 2006).

This brings us to a central, and contentious, factor in immigrant children's academic success: language. Many children from immigrant families are ELL students. In the United States, they may enter school with no knowledge of English or they may have some facility in English in addition to their native language. Generally, ELL students, especially from Hispanic families, perform more poorly academically than native White children when they begin school in the United States. Common sense suggests that helping these children become proficient in English, the language of the classroom and of most tests, should be a high priority. But should they be immersed in all-English classes? Should their families encourage them to speak only English at home?

The most recent research suggests that ELL children are most academically successful when schools and families encourage their bilingualism, helping them to learn English while maintaining or building fluency in the family's native language. What is most effective is teaching children in both their native language and English at school, and encouraging them to use their native language at home. First, there are important cognitive advantages to bilingualism, as you have seen, including greater cognitive flexibility and better executive functioning. Second, children who continue to use their native language maintain strong connections with their families and ethnic communities, supporting a positive ethnic identity, which we have just seen is important for academic motivation. "Language congruence may enhance the parent-child relationship, and, in turn . . . have great implications for children's motivation to succeed academically" (Han, 2012, p. 301). Bilingual education in schools has the best track record across immigrant groups and academic competencies in promoting ELL students' performance. One study reviewed the records of 700,000 U.S. students, comparing outcomes of ELL children in a wide range of programs (e.g., English as a Second Language [ESL] programs, pullout programs, transitional bilingual education, and so on). Four to seven years of bilingual education and support yielded the best results by far, with early academic gaps tending to disappear and children outperforming their native English-speaking peers over time (Collier & Thomas, 2004).

customary in East Asian countries to enroll children in private "cram schools" that offer late day and weekend classes, increasing the amount of instruction and learning time children experience. Interestingly, cram school enrollment in East Asian countries goes up as class size in public schools increases (for cross-country comparisons, see Burhan, Yunus, Tovar, & Burhan, 2017; Caro et al., 2016; Rindermann & Ceci, 2009).

In general, educational factors that promote children's cognitive and academic growth seem to fall into three broad categories: *quantity, stimulation/engagement, and valuing.* First, there is *quantity.* More time in educational settings is valuable, especially early education in preschool and kindergarten. Another such factor is having access to extra learning opportunities, such as reading or math specialists or tutors, or cram schools. Factors that increase the amount of classroom time that is actually dedicated to instruction and learning, such as good classroom management, are also helpful.

Second, *more stimulating, engaging environments* are important, so that factors like educational level of the family and society matter. Minimal use of grade retention helps to reduce boredom, and small classes make it more likely that each child can be engaged in learning activities that meet his needs, with challenging input and individually tailored feedback. Receiving increased amounts of instruction at school is more stimulating than doing lots of homework alone. Positive teacher–child relationships also help motivate children's engagement.

Finally, *valuing learning and valuing the child as learner* is of great importance. Factors that fit this category include prioritizing education in the culture and in the family; having high expectations of each child and believing that challenge and hard work are the keys to success (as opposed to native ability); providing supports for self-regulation; and respecting the value of different backgrounds and interests among learners.

WHAT PROXIMAL INTERACTIONS ARE MOST EFFECTIVE?

Let's now take a look specifically at the kinds of proximal interactions—between teachers and children—that seem to promote children's cognitive development and academic achievement.

General Teacher Factors.   Take a moment to examine the "teacher factors" in Table 6.1. We will look closely at two of these: teacher warmth and high expectations (or demandingness) for each child. These are the ingredients of authoritative teaching, similar to authoritative parenting. Teacher warmth is defined much like parental warmth (Chapter 5). Warm teachers establish a positive emotional climate in the classroom for all students. They are caring and respectful, engaging their students in the process of setting individual goals, listening to them and explaining requests. They also are mindful of children's peer relationships and friendships, requiring that children work cooperatively and treat each other respectfully. Such classroom climates help motivate children's compliance and enthusiasm for learning tasks. Children who see their teachers as warm tend to perform better (see Caro et al, 2016; Rubie-Davies & Rosenthal, 2016).

Teachers who have high expectations encourage each child to exceed his current level of skill by providing challenging work. They are also likely to give the child "tailored" feedback and practice, another factor that promotes learning. Children whose teachers have high expectations make substantially greater academic progress than other children. Unfortunately, teachers' expectations may vary with different children, sometimes depending on a child's socioeconomic status, race, or ethnicity. Lower expectations are correlated with lower warmth, although teachers usually believe that they treat all of their students equally (see Rubie-Davies & Rosenthal, 2016; Sandilos, Rimm-Kaufman, & Cohen, 2017).

People, including teachers, have different **mindsets** about intelligence. *Mindsets* are beliefs about whether intelligence or some ability is a fixed asset or is malleable (see Dweck, 2017). If you think that some people perform well because they are just smart, or math geniuses, or very musically talented, then you have an **"ability" mindset.** You will have limited expectations for some children, especially those you think have done poorly in the past in some skill area. Having high expectations of all students is easier for teachers who believe that intelligence and academic performance can be nurtured and modified. This is a **"growth" mindset.** Teachers with this view believe their students can overcome poor performance with hard work and practice on appropriately challenging tasks. We will have more to say about mindsets in future chapters.

How Teachers Teach and Children Learn.   Research on children's progress in math will help us illustrate how some proximal processes work in the classroom to advance children's academic success. We hope you can see the bidirectionality of these processes: A child's current level of skill, and what he does spontaneously, influences (or should influence) teacher behavior; and a teacher's scaffolding influences the child.

In the early preschool years, the typical U.S. child has several number skills. For example, he can count, he knows there is a one-to-one relationship between number word and item when he counts, and he understands that the order in which items are counted is irrelevant (see Chapter 3). By late preschool, he has informal arithmetic skills such as adding and subtracting small numbers by using counting strategies, like the **counting all strategy.** For example, given two red blocks and three green ones, he will probably count all the blocks to find out the sum. As children in elementary school

MyLab Education
Video Example 6.4
In addition to learning facts and procedures, children need to understand concepts. The children in Ms. Brown's group are demonstrating their understanding of fractions with number lines.

are introduced to more formal arithmetic, with its written numbers and standard, step-wise processes (or algorithms) for computation and recording, they continue to use their informal strategies. They also devise more and more strategies, some invented, some derived from what they are taught (Siegler & Braithwaite, 2017). For example, given a simple addition problem such as 3 + 4, they might use a strategy called the **counting on strategy**, starting with the first number and counting four more numbers from there. Soon, this strategy is likely to be modified so that the child usually "counts on" from the larger number. A **decomposition strategy** may be used sometimes when children know one sum and use it to construct another. For example, if they know 5 + 2 = 7, to figure out 5 + 3, they might just add 1. As children are exposed repeatedly to addition and subtraction facts, they begin to use the most efficient procedure of all: a **retrieval strategy**, pulling the answer automatically from memory.

Acquiring a store of memorized facts, or a knowledge base, is not only efficient, it helps children advance in math problem solving. When a small set of facts in addition, subtraction, multiplication, and division is learned so well that retrieval is automatic (e.g., 2 + 2 = 4), more complex problems become easier to solve, because little or no working memory space needs to be allocated to calculating answers to the simple problems that are always embedded within the harder problems (Willingham, 2009/10).

Some researchers in the information processing tradition have closely followed young school children's progress in discovering and utilizing math strategies. They have found interesting trends that seem to occur across cultures. First, most children use most of the strategies, sometimes using one, sometimes another. Second, children often use a particular strategy on problems where it is especially effective, and more efficient strategies gradually become more predominant. Third, however, even older children (and adults) sometimes use less efficient strategies (Siegler & Braithwaite, 2017). Thus, it appears that cognitive development moves gradually toward greater efficiency but that less efficient strategies are not entirely abandoned. "Bumpy" progress in strategy use seems to characterize the development of many skills, as we have seen already in memory development. As in memory development, the shift toward using more adequate math strategies, more often, seems to depend partly on metacognitive development—the child's growing understanding of his own strategies and his increasing awareness of how effective those strategies are (Kuhn, 2000b). Figure 6.4 shows typical patterns of change in math strategy use as children move through the elementary school years.

FIGURE 6.4 Bumpy progress in math strategy use with age.

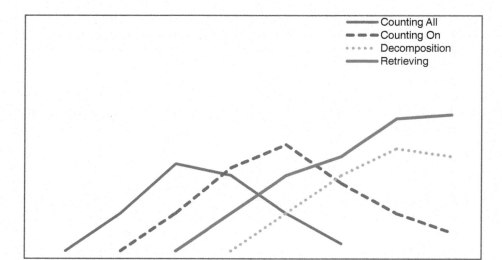

Age

SOURCE: Based on Hopkins, S. L., & Lawson, M. J. (2002). Explaining the acquisition of a complex skill: Methodological and theoretical considerations uncovered in the study of simple addition and the moving-on process. *Educational Psychology Review, 14,* 121-154.

As math learning moves beyond the simplest of problems, teachers help children acquire effective strategies by teaching them step-by-step solution procedures (e.g., in adding two-digit numbers, if the sum of the first column is a two-digit number, carry the tens digit from that sum to the tens column). Children might sometimes construct these more complex procedures themselves, but teaching them these strategies helps children progress more efficiently (Willingham, 2009/10).

However, learning the procedures is not enough. When children assimilate the procedures to a limited understanding of mathematics, they sometimes invent strategies that produce errors. In the information processing tradition, flawed strategies are referred to as "bugs." An example would be a boy who does not yet truly understand the base 10 system, but who thinks that one should always subtract the smaller from the larger number. When he is given the problem

$$\begin{array}{r} 21 \\ -5 \\ \hline \end{array}$$

he subtracts the 1 from the 5 and comes up with 24 (Ginsburg, 1989).

In the Piagetian tradition, some research specifically explores developmental changes in what children understand about what they are taught about mathematics. Children's progress in understanding the base 10 system provides a good illustration of the extent to which their mathematical knowledge is constructed (e.g., Kamii, 1986, 1990; Mix, Smith, Stockton, Cheng, & Barterian, 2017). If we ask a first grader to count a set of 13 blocks and then write down the answer, he will probably be able to comply. But if we circle the "3" and then ask, "Does this part of your 13 have anything to do with how many blocks there are?" a first grader might say, "No." He thinks that only the whole number 13 tells about the number of blocks. When he's in second grade, he might say that the "3" represents a certain three blocks. When in third grade, he may talk about ones and tens, but is likely to say that the "1" in 13 represents one single item, not 10. By fourth and fifth grades, about half of children recognize that the "1" represents a 10 (example from Kamii, 1990). Thus, although a child typically hears about the base 10 system from first grade onward, he seems to assimilate it to concepts that are not correct and only gradually constructs its true meaning.

Findings such as these on children's understanding of math concepts are a reminder of an important tenet of Piaget's view of education: Teaching children facts or procedures is not sufficient for developing the kind of understanding they will need to truly advance in a subject, as was the case in the round Earth study (Vosniadou & Mason, 2012). Teachers need also to probe children's comprehension. It helps to ask questions such as "Does the '3' have anything to do with how many blocks there are?" Such questions both aid teachers in evaluating what kinds of supports a child might need to understand better and may help children begin to recognize inconsistencies in the meanings they have constructed. This kind of probing can also help teachers establish adequate placements for their students.

Care should also be taken in choosing curricular materials and in structuring assessments of students' learning. Without practice and elaboration, advanced or accelerated programs of study may outstrip the abilities of many children and lead them to shallow or rote memorization of facts and procedures instead of deep conceptual understanding. Knowledge of facts and procedures without conceptual understanding is associated with slower, less accurate problem solving even in the early stages of math learning (Rittle-Johnson, 2017).

Thus, education in math requires, *simultaneously*, practice that promotes memorization of facts, exposure to efficient procedures or strategies, and help discovering the conceptual structure of math that makes the facts and procedures what they are. You have just seen that teachers who keep track of what the child can and cannot do are able to then tailor instruction or suggestion to the child's "region of sensitivity" or zone of proximal development—one step beyond the level at which the child is currently performing. Effective teaching also tends to engage children in activities of many different kinds to promote the kind of conceptual understanding that is needed (e.g., McNeil, Fyfe, Petersen, Dunwiddie, & Brletic-Shipley, 2011). For example, it helps to give children many different and *familiar* examples from their experience (e.g., for fractions, sharing an apple by cutting it into equal parts). As children advance, providing familiar examples might become more difficult, but it is often possible to show them familiar situations that are *analogous* to a concept (e.g., an equation is analogous to a balance scale; if you do the same thing to each side, it stays balanced) (Willingham, 2009/10). Using familiar examples and analogous situations is important because, as Piaget argued, children build new knowledge by starting with what they already know. It is also important to understand that approaching the same concept from many different angles is not about catering to "learning styles." Researchers have found *no evidence* for the popular concept that different people learn differently (e.g., some visually, some kinesthetically, some verbally), although they might have different preferences for how information is presented (Willingham, Hughes, & Dobolyi, 2015).

This discussion of proximal processes between teachers and children has focused on teaching math skills. Children learn other academic subjects and skills in similar ways. Consider learning to read, for example. Here too, teachers are most effective when they bring up-to-date knowledge of the skills that are most important for reading acquisition to their teaching, and when they probe their students to determine what children are bringing to the task. Then teachers can provide their students the most effective scaffolding. For instance, you saw in Chapter 3 (Box 3.2, *Early Childhood Education: Helping All Children Succeed*) that oral language skills are critical for reading. These skills include phonological awareness and a good vocabulary (which reflects good general knowledge). Problems in oral language development can slow down reading progress substantially, and they are key contributors to **dyslexia**, severe reading disability (e.g., Snowling & Melby-Lervag, 2016; Taylor, Duff, Woolams, Moaghan, & Ricketts, 2015). With careful probing, a teacher can identify whether a child has any weaknesses in oral language skills and can provide extra opportunities for practice of the needed skills to facilitate the child's appropriate progress.

MyLab Education Self-Check 6.2

Social Cognition

6.3 Analyze children's progress in developing social cognition with specific focus on perspective taking and psychosocial competencies and suggest relevant therapeutic interventions.

One day, Malik and Benj (from the beginning of this chapter) find themselves in conflict over a rule change in their daily game of "tag." Benj insists on keeping the rule the same, but Malik keeps arguing that changing the rule would make the game more fun. Benj, who is usually quiet and calm, stamps his foot with frustration and anger, and he looks perilously close to crying. Malik starts to walk away, but he wants to play and he wants things to be okay, so he finally gives in with a shrug. Later, as they are lining up to go back to class, Malik tells Benj about something crazy his little brothers did the night before, and they troop back to their classroom laughing.

Malik is surprised and hurt by Benj's strong negative reaction to his suggestion. The boys change the rules of their game almost daily, usually without problems. But Malik is able to control his own emotional reaction to Benj's unexpected behavior. He also has a notion that Benj could be having a bad day for reasons he has not shared with Malik, and that this time it's better not to press his point. That guess leads Malik to "cave" for now and to try to lighten the mood between them. Malik's capacity to control his own emotions and to take into account his friend's mental state is an important ingredient in the maintenance of his friendship with Benj.

Just as children's knowledge about the physical world and about logical-mathematical concepts becomes more sophisticated with time, so does their understanding of other people. This latter domain, referred to as social cognition, focuses primarily on the ways people think about other people and how they reason about social relationships.

You have already learned a lot about the foundations of social cognition. As you will recall from earlier chapters, infants and toddlers begin to understand social relationships within the context of the attachments they form. The discriminations infants make between objects and people, their diligent attention to caregivers, their capacity for imitation and social referencing, and their early attempts at communication presage knowledge about people and human psychology. Toddlers try to change the behaviors of others, empathize with others' distress, and use emotion words indicating that they have explicit knowledge of others' mental states. These skills suggest that infants and young children are in the process of learning about social interactions almost from birth (see Carpendale & Lewis, 2015).

Studies of the young child's theory of mind focus on key aspects of social cognition, addressing questions such as "When does the child come to understand that the other has a mind?" and "How does the child use information about mental states to understand people and social relationships?" You have already seen that by their fifth birthday most children realize that others often have different thoughts and beliefs from their own. For example, they now succeed on false belief tasks in which they must anticipate that a person who has not had the opportunity to see an object moved from its original hiding place to a new location might have a false belief about the object's whereabouts (see Chapter 3). Preschoolers' success on false belief tasks has been related to reciprocal communication with peers and to the ability to communicate about internal mental states with friends. As cognitive understanding of mental processes in self and others progresses, children are better able to function in social relationships.

Even though a typical 5-year-old can usually understand that beliefs and other mental experiences can differ from one person to another, he has much to learn about how to interpret others' thoughts, feelings, and desires. This skill, as you learned in Chapter 3, is called *perspective taking*. Studies of social cognition in middle childhood often focus on how perspective taking develops, and how it affects children's friendships, methods of conflict resolution, and appreciation for social rules and conventions. In this chapter, we will focus on how social cognitive skills, especially perspective taking, are related to friendship development.

The Importance of Friendships

No one has to convince helping professionals that the dynamics of social relationships are important ones to understand. Although not every social relationship can be considered a friendship, the special relationships we have with friends teach us about human relationships in general.

During the middle childhood years, friendships take on enormous importance. Long-term studies have found that having at least one mutual friend in middle childhood is an important predictor of mental health in adulthood (Fink et al., 2015). For school-aged children being reared in difficult circumstances, having a good friend serves as a protective factor, moderating some environmental risks. For example, in the Virginia Longitudinal Study of Child Maltreatment (Bolger & Patterson, 2003), 107 children who were abused or neglected were identified through state social service records from a larger sample of 1,920 public school children. Most of the maltreated children were at risk in other ways as well. For example, 92% had low enough family incomes that they qualified for federal food subsidies of some kind. During the course of the study, children were asked whether they had a best friend, and their friend choices were compared to verify that they were reciprocated. Among the measures collected over time were assessments of the children's self-esteem. Children also rated their own competence in a variety of domains. As you might expect, maltreated children perceived themselves as less competent than children who had no history of abuse or neglect. But maltreated children with a reciprocal friend showed substantial gains in self-esteem from grade 3 to grade 5, gains that were maintained through grade 7, and on average they were doing about as well on self-esteem as other children. Unfortunately, maltreated children who did not have a best friend showed declines in self-esteem across the years of middle childhood.

Any child's difficulties in making and keeping friends can consume much of a helping professional's time because of the far-reaching consequences of poor peer relationships and inadequate conflict resolution skills on emotional well-being, academic achievement, and behavior. What is important for helpers to understand is that the skills of friendship are not just behavioral but are heavily dependent on cognitive development. In this section, we will introduce some major theoretical approaches to friendship development that have a basis in cognitive developmental theory. In Chapter 7, the research on larger peer group interaction and peer group status will be reviewed.

How Perspective Taking Develops in the Middle Years of Childhood

The cognitively complex skill of perspective taking develops gradually as children mature, much in the same way that other cognitive abilities change and improve (see Miller, 2012, for a review of research). What contributes to the improvement? First, this ability is tied to other cognitive advances, such as the development of executive functions, and especially working memory. You saw in Chapter 3 that very young children seem trapped in their own perspective; Piaget called it preoperational egocentrism. He theorized that the ability to decenter, to hold in mind more than one piece of information at a time, helps children become less egocentric. Modern theorists, like neoPiagetians and theory theorists, see growth of working memory capacity as critical to this development. Children's performance on executive function tests, especially working memory tests, is correlated with their performance on tests of theory of mind (perspective taking) in preschool (Devine & Hughes, 2014) and in elementary school (Devine, White, Ensor, & Hughes, 2016). In fact, in a study of 9- to 10-year-olds, the size of working memory at age 9 predicted growth in theory of mind test performance at age 10 (Lecce, Bianco, Devine, & Hughes, 2017).

Piaget also theorized that growth in perspective taking skill was critically dependent on interaction with peers. He believed that about the time children enter elementary school in industrialized cultures, they are forced to consider other children's viewpoints to survive the normal give-and-take of the classroom community structure. Before then, children may have been able to rely on parents' or other family members' willingness to meet their egocentric needs and to understand their egocentric communication. Peers are typically less willing and able to do so. The child in elementary school, or even before, is forced to clarify his thoughts and adopt better communication skills in order to be accepted by peers. Piaget saw the major and minor conflicts that accompany this process as essential to a developing awareness of perspectives other than one's own (Flavell, 1963; Piaget, 1928).

Modern research shows that many different kinds of social experiences help children improve their perspective taking skills, not just peer interactions. Parent–child relationships play a role. When children form secure attachments to parents, they are likely to make more rapid progress in perspective taking, although why this takes place is not clear. One reason may be that securely attached dyads engage in more talk about people's thoughts and feelings, both their own and those of others (McElwain, Booth-LaForce, & Wu, 2011), and there is evidence that such talk promotes perspective taking. Another possibility is that securely attached children approach interactions with other children in positive ways, because they have trusting, positive expectations (working models) of social relationships. If that means they have more opportunities to interact with peers, they may (as Piaget theorized) get more practice in perspective taking than children who are less engaging (see Carpendale & Lewis, 2015; Furman & Rose, 2015).

Interactions with siblings also benefit perspective taking skills, at least in Western countries. (This "sibling effect" has not yet been found in non-Western countries; see

Hughes & Devine, 2015.) Children with siblings often perform better on tests of perspective taking than children without siblings. "The juxtaposition of love and hate is a common (and rather unique) feature of sibling relationships" (Hughes & Devine, 2015, p. 16). So brothers and sisters might influence each other's theory-of-mind abilities either through their positive interactions (their close collaboration and support) or through their more negative interactions (teasing and conflict) or both (Carpendale & Lewis, 2015). Imagine a younger sibling hearing this mocking assessment of her play from an older sister: "Yeah it's stretching; really, really, interesting. You know in fact I am amazed. I wonder if I'll ever, ever, see this again. No I don't think I will because it's just so, so rare, so amazing. Wow, I think I'm going to faint" (Hughes & Devine, 2015, p. 16). Not only is the target of this diatribe getting exposure to the fact that not everyone assesses her behavior as benignly as she does herself, but she is getting a lesson in how someone can say one thing and mean another. Interaction with peers, especially friends, is also associated with advances in perspective taking, just as Piaget proposed. For example, young children are more likely to talk about mental states—feelings and thoughts—with friends than even with parents. And such conversations are correlated with advances in interpreting others' mental states, like understanding false beliefs (see Hughes & Devine, 2015).

Perspective Taking and Friendship Development

The healthiest friendships are marked by mutual give-and-take, allowing both partners to feel affirmed, understood, and respected. This kind of give-and-take both requires good perspective taking skills and helps to sharpen these skills. It also both requires and provides practice at managing conflicts. Think for a moment about your own close friendships. Regardless of how overtly agreeable or conflictual these relationships may be, there is always a tension between "what is good for me versus what is good for us" (Barr, 1997, p. 32). No friendship is immune to this underlying dynamic, which surfaces from time to time over the course of the relationship. To sustain friendships, friends must be able to coordinate both individuals' needs and resolve the inevitable conflicts that arise in ways that are mutually agreeable. Any imbalance, such as too much coercion from one partner and too little assertiveness from the other, can undermine the friendship in the long run. In other words, ineffective management of the dysynchrony between the needs of the individual and the needs of the pair puts the friendship at risk.

Even in adulthood, friendships are always "works in progress" that require mutual coordination of perspectives and ongoing balancing of needs. Imagine how short-lived a friendship would be if you typically perceived your friend's momentary insensitivity or inability to participate in some shared activity as a personal insult directed toward you. Your understanding that he might be overextended and thus under stress can help you take a more empathic perspective, despite your own disappointment. Children find this harder to do because they are essentially practicing their perspective taking and other friendship skills. Hurts, betrayals, and conflicts will almost inevitably accompany their friendship development as they struggle to learn to compromise, compete, and cooperate in a civil way. Without this sometimes painful experience, however, children may not learn the intimacy and autonomy strategies they need to reap the benefits of satisfying friendships throughout their lifetimes. Helping professionals who are knowledgeable about the nature of friendship development are in a unique position to facilitate children's progress in this area.

Egocentrism—being unable to see or understand things from a different perspective—is a trap that all of us fall into sometimes, an inevitable part of the human condition. Even when we are aware of the likelihood that someone else has a different perspective, being able to "read" and understand others' mental states is difficult and sometimes impossible. But as you have seen, social relationships, and especially friendships, are important contexts for developing the necessary skills. In the next section, you will learn about a classic theory of friendship development that has stood the test of time and helps organize what we have learned about the relationship between the development of perspective taking and friendship, emphasizing the bidirectional relationship between them. Friendships help children learn perspective taking skills, and better perspective taking skills increase the chances of making friends.

Selman's Stages of Friendship Development

Building on a Piagetian framework, Robert Selman (1980, 2008) identified five stages in the development of perspective taking, beginning at preschool age and continuing through adolescence. Each level of perspective taking skill is linked to a different level of friendship or shared experience, as well as to a different level of conflict resolution (see Table 6.2). Selman's theory highlights the tight interconnections among a child's ability to understand others (perspective taking), his needs for intimacy in relationship (friendship), his skill in balancing personal needs without sacrificing the relationship (autonomy), and his ability to solve conflicts (conflict resolution). A number of studies provide support for aspects of Selman's account (e.g., Diazgranados, Selman, & Dionne, 2016).

As with other stage theories, the age ranges are only rough approximations. What is most important is the sequence and nature of the developmental change. Stage 0, or the "Undifferentiated/Egocentric" stage, is typically manifested in preschool children before about age 5, when perspective taking capacity is quite limited. Youngsters at Stage 0 have little appreciation for the thoughts and feelings of either themselves or others. Friendship is defined in very concrete terms, without an understanding of the other person's psychology. For example, a preschool child might define a friend as someone who lives next to you, who gives you gifts, who shares toys with you, or who likes you. Young children typically establish friendships with children who are like themselves in concrete ways, such as age, gender, race, and ethnicity (see Rubin, Bukowski, & Bowker, 2015). Conflicts between friends are not perceived as disagreements that occur between two parties with two different and legitimate points of view but are viewed as struggles to get one's own way. Lacking much ability to consider another's perspective, children typically resort to flight ("Go away!") or fight ("I'll get you!") strategies to resolve conflicts as they seek to preserve their interests.

In Stage 1, the "Differentiated/Subjective" stage, children from about 5 to about 9 come to understand that others have viewpoints that are different from their own, but they are generally not able to coordinate these perspectives simultaneously. In other words, they can't maintain their own perspective and that of someone else at the same time. So even though they understand that their peers have different points of view, they still may act as though their own perspective or that of an "authority" is correct.

TABLE 6.2 Selman's Stages of Friendship and Levels of Perspective Taking Skills

STAGE	APPROXIMATE AGES	FORMS OF SHARED EXPERIENCE	SOCIAL PERSPECTIVE TAKING	INTERPERSONAL NEGOTIATION STRATEGIES
0	3 to 6 years	Unreflective imitation or enmeshment	Undifferentiated/Egocentric	Physical force; impulsive fight or flight
1	5 to 9 years	Unreflective sharing of expressive enthusiasm	Differentiated/Subjective	One-way, unilateral power; orders or obedience
2	8 to 12 years	Reflective sharing of similar perceptions or experiences	Reciprocal/Self-Reflective	Cooperative exchange; reciprocity; persuasion or deference
3	10 to 15 years	Empathic sharing of beliefs and values	Mutual/Third-Person	Mutual compromise
4	Late teen/adulthood	Interdependent sharing of vulnerabilities and self	Intimate/In-Depth/Societal (generalized other)	Collaborative integration of relationship dynamics (commitment)

SOURCE: Based on Selman, R. L., Watts, C. L., & Schultz, L. H. (1997). *Fostering friendship: Pair therapy for treatment and prevention*. New York, NY: Walter de Gruyter, Inc.

They are able to understand, for example, that they can be the subject of another's thoughts, but they generally do not have the capacity to judge how their behavior is being evaluated by that other person. Dyami, for instance, might understand that his friend Kono has a viewpoint or a perspective on him, but Dyami has little insight into what Kono's view of him is really like. We might say that interpersonal perspective at this age is unilateral or one-way. Yet during this period children do become better able to infer the thoughts and feelings of others, especially when they are encouraged to reflect on them. The child's understanding of physical experience, however, is another thing altogether. In the behavioral realm, two-way reciprocity ("You hit me and I hit you back") is readily understood.

On the psychological level, friendship is still largely a one-way proposition. The child at Stage 1 may understand his own psychological perspective but may fail to do the same for his friend. In other words, friendships may be defined by the behavioral and psychological rewards they provide for the individual child and not in terms of the mutual satisfaction afforded both members of the dyad. Seven-year-old Pavla might describe a friend as someone who helps her with her homework, doesn't fight with her, and doesn't walk away from her when she's upset. Notice the mix of behavioral (homework help) and psychological (social support) characteristics that are directed toward the benefit of one person. Conflicts are also viewed as one-way propositions. The responsibility to resolve a conflict is in the hands of the person who was perceived to have initiated it. There is little understanding of problem solving by mutual consensus.

At Stage 2, the "Reciprocal/Self-Reflective" stage, older children master a critical developmental task. During this period, between late childhood and early adolescence (about 8 to 12), children's friendships become more intense. Children show a more focused interest in same-sex age-mates or "chums." Their "chumships" teach children that the needs and perspectives of other persons must be considered as carefully as their own. Malik shows signs of this kind of social understanding when he considers that Benj may be having a bad day and may need some special consideration.

Children become more cognizant of the perspectives of others and learn to put themselves in another's place as a way of evaluating intentions and actions. Children begin to assume the psychological position of the other, and they start to reflect on their own behavior and motivation as perceived by someone else. Eleven-year-old Keisha, who doesn't really want to go swimming at her friend Amber's house because she'd prefer to spend the afternoon watching TV, might agree to go anyway. Keisha, seeing Amber as a person who is rather easily hurt, reasons that if she declines the invitation, Amber might think that Keisha doesn't like her or that she doesn't want to be her friend. This more sophisticated level of perspective taking ability reflects two-way reciprocity ("I think; you think").

At this stage, children can grasp more highly differentiated patterns of motivations and emotions and make finer discriminations between thoughts and feelings. They can conceive of the fact that people, including themselves, can experience conflicting motives and feelings and can feel one thing but act in a completely different way. In our earlier example, Keisha wants to spend some time alone but she also wants to preserve her friendship with Amber. She may simultaneously feel liking and impatience toward her friend. She may decide to go swimming and cover up her true feelings of disinterest in the activity. Conflict resolution between children at this stage reflects the growing awareness that both parties must give a little to reach a solution.

At Stage 3, the "Mutual/Third-Person" stage, adolescents of about 10 to 15 learn to view each other's perspectives simultaneously and mutually. Rather than simply viewing each other's perspective in a back-and-forth approach ("first me, then you"), adolescents can mentally step back to take the perspective of a "third-party observer" even as they remain a member of the pair. This allows a more detached view of the proceedings, somewhat like the way a disinterested spectator might construe a social interaction. Egocentrism is further reduced insofar as the adolescent can view the interchange between himself and his friend and reflect on it from the outside looking in.

MyLab Education
Video Example 6.5
Based on Selman's stages of friendship development, what stage corresponds to the friendships described in this video?

Friendship at this stage is characterized by mutual support and shared intimacy and is not seen just as a means of obtaining what either party desires as an individual. Consequently, conflict resolution strategies are marked by more attention to the mutuality of the relationship. There is an awareness that problems do not always reside within one of the participants but instead that they are the responsibility of both parties to address. Harmonious resolution of the conflicts that are inevitable in relationships is perceived to strengthen both parties' commitment to that relationship. Adolescents at this stage are more capable of understanding that a friendship could break down because "it just didn't work out between us" rather than because "she wasn't nice to me."

Finally, at Stage 4, the "Intimate/In-Depth/Societal" stage, older adolescents and adults learn to adopt the perspective of the larger society. Perspective taking ability becomes more abstract and complex. Now the individual can assume the perspective of people beyond the limits of the dyad, namely that of a larger social group. This achievement makes possible the understanding of cultural and other group differences and the increasing appreciation of relativity—that no one person's or individual group's perspective is necessarily the only correct one regardless of how deeply valued it might be. Relationships are marked by the individual's increasing ability to balance his needs for intimacy and autonomy while still preserving the friendship. With each new level of perspective taking skill, understanding of friendship improves, interpersonal values are clarified, and social and conflict resolution skills are refined.

Selman's Framework for Friendship

Perspective taking is an important part of social relatedness, but it is not the only determinant. Let's briefly consider how the understanding of others' perspectives is integrated with other skills and characteristics of the child and with features of the child's environment. Selman and his colleagues (e.g., Selman, Levitt, & Schultz, 1997) argue that many layers of interacting influences affect children's success in making and keeping friends (see Table 6.2). Selman's theoretical framework lends itself to clinical applications that are developmentally sensitive. An understanding of the elements of this model can help you assess relative strengths and weaknesses in a child's social relatedness and help you choose relevant interventions.

First, the child brings to the task a variety of *biologically based characteristics*, from temperament (e.g., fearful versus fearless) to neuropsychological maturation (e.g., of motor abilities). Second, the *family and neighborhood culture* matter. For example, is the family home a place where friends are welcome and comfortable? Does the child live in a safe neighborhood where there are other children to play with, who accept the child's ethnicity, and so on? These factors provide a backdrop to children's social functioning, but they may only have strong, direct effects on children's friendships in more extreme (atypical) cases. For example, a child might be so intensely fearful that he never responds positively to the overtures of other children. Or chronic parental discord in a child's home might make it impossible for him to bring friends home. Or a child might lack friends if he lives in a dangerous neighborhood with no nearby peers, and his parents have no time or resources to arrange play dates with children who live elsewhere. Malik is fortunate that his classmate Benj lives right next door; otherwise he might have few opportunities to interact with children outside of school.

At the core of friendship success is a set of processes that make up **psychosocial development**. Selman defines these as "the internal psychological processes of interpersonal understanding, skills, and values that comprise an individual's capacity for interpersonal relationships, including friendships" (Selman et al., 1997, p. 35). **Friendship understanding** refers to a child's changing knowledge of what friendship implies. **Friendship skills** are behavioral skills, such as appropriate assertiveness, good communication, and conflict resolution that maintain and enhance friendships. **Friendship valuing** describes the emotional attachment or investment that the child makes in a friendship. Developmental changes in the child's perspective taking abilities are crucial for growth in each of these three components of psychosocial development. In other words, competence in these three areas will be delimited by a child's cognitive understanding of interpersonal relationships.

To work effectively, helpers need to appreciate what can be reasonably expected from children at each stage of their development. Teaching appropriate social skills, such as making eye contact and communicating effectively, may be irrelevant for children whose level of friendship understanding is very egocentric or for a child who is not particularly interested in being friendly toward another member of his class. On the other hand, learning how to solve conflicts effectively may be very helpful for a child who is invested in a friendship. All three dimensions need to be considered therapeutically so that interventions can be targeted accurately.

There is one other important factor in Selman's analysis of friendship. This is the child's **interpersonal orientation**, or the way the child characteristically interacts on a social level. The most mature interpersonal style is characterized by a flexible *balance* between intimacy and autonomy strivings. Less effective orientations, as identified by Selman, are "**other-transforming**" and "**self-transforming**" social interaction styles.

A child with an other-transforming style characteristically tries to dominate or coerce a friend into meeting his needs. He acts to change or transform the other and can be bullying, aggressive, or manipulative. A child with a self-transforming style typically gives in to reduce the level of tension. He changes his own behaviors or feelings to conform. Selman and Schultz (1990) found that very young children or socially immature older children tend to behave in these extreme ways. Such children are both more labile than other children, sometimes moving from victim to victimizer position depending on the relationship, and more rigid, refusing to compromise their position once established, even at the risk of losing the friendship.

What does it mean for a child to be bossy, impulsive, stubborn, passive, or withdrawn? On its face, each label might prescribe a certain kind of intervention: self-control training for the impulsive child, assertiveness training for the shy one, and so forth. Selman's theoretical model gives us the means to go beyond this level of understanding to unpack the fundamental psychosocial competencies that the child depends on to engage in any social interaction. From this perspective, the bully and the victim can be functioning at the same developmental level of friendship knowledge, skills, and valuing, only using different personal orientations. Assessment of the fundamental properties that underlie friendship expression can be a helpful means of addressing interpersonal problems. We will revisit the topic of peer relationships and the processes that govern them multiple times in subsequent chapters.

MyLab Education Self-Check 6.3

Applications

The middle years of childhood are marked by major advances in reasoning, in memory, and in the comprehension of many domains, including social relationships. From infancy, the child has been navigating the social world, moving from early attachment relationships to the gradually enlarging network of peers in the school setting. There are some fundamental linkages between these early relationships and children's later social interactions. For example, encouraging preschool children to take notice of others' perspectives has been related to empathy, good social problem solving, and perspective taking at school age (Webster-Stratton & Reid, 2004). Success in relating to others rests on having a positive internal working model for social responding, having access to peers in settings that promote mutual respect, and knowing how to resolve conflicts, among other things. And, as we have seen in this chapter, cognitive developments contribute importantly to children's social success at this time. During the school years, children need to be successful in the classroom as well as on the playground. Some general implications related to learning may be useful to helpers.

Knowledge acquisition is a constructive process, built on the foundation of prior learning and experience. Children benefit from instruction that organizes information, relates it to previously learned material, and stresses its meaningfulness. Too many children, critics have noted, are taught in ways that reflect an emphasis on rote memorization of facts without any fundamental understanding of concepts. Therefore, instruction should include some basic elements: gaining the child's attention and motivation; activating what the child already knows about the material to be taught using familiar examples or analogies; presenting the new material in many ways; providing adequate, meaningful, and interesting practice to ensure retention; and giving task-specific feedback that scaffolds the child's progress. Students can also benefit from techniques such as cooperative learning, if teachers or group leaders offer them opportunities to learn how to work effectively together. Cooperative methods should also incorporate some form of individual accountability as well as group recognition for goals achieved (Slavin, 1995).

Keep in mind that normal cognitive development is uneven. Theories of development have suffered, to some degree, from their emphasis on stages. This emphasis can lead to thinking that development proceeds in a rigid series of steps. In the real world, children as well as adults are much more variable. As you have seen, even though Piaget described stage-wise development, he also recognized that variation in skill exists within stages. Specifically, he found that logical skills were applied to some contents (such as number conservation) before other contents (such as weight conservation). This variability in skill level is clearly evident in any classroom. Some students may excel in reading and language arts, yet find math a chore. Others may be gifted athletes who remember detailed plays but who have difficulty remembering facts in social studies. Isn't such unevenness characteristic of adults as well? Most people's panorama of abilities reflects a mix of relative strengths and weaknesses. Teachers can provide opportunities for students to demonstrate abilities in creative ways as a supplement to more traditional forms of teaching and assessment. For example, developing skits, creating poetry or pictures, designing experiments, establishing classroom government, or running a school store are all activities that tap creative and practical intelligence (Sternberg, 1985), which may be areas of relative strength or interest for students.

Understanding and Strengthening the Tools of Learning

If you take the time to examine schools' mission statements, even a cursory review would show a list of goals that repeat themselves across the country: academic excellence, critical and reflective thinking, life-long learning, social responsibility, and so on. What are the mechanisms by which schools achieve these goals? Do such outcomes materialize automatically by virtue of 12 or 13 years of schooling? Can we declare "mission accomplished" or are we able to improve upon outcomes with more fine-grained understanding of the processes involved?

Enter cognitive neuroscience, which promises to help educators unravel some beneath-the-surface processes that contribute to the realization of these goals. As you have been reading, executive functions (EFs) are prime candidates to explain the operations by which children succeed (Zelazo, Blair, & Willoughby, 2017). They are the building blocks we use to learn and self-regulate: working memory, inhibitory control, and mental flexibility. Think about trying to remember what you want to add to a rapid-fire discussion while you ponder others' comments and, quite possibly, allow them to reshape your own. Consider, as well, how you manage the anxiety or irritation you might feel while awaiting your turn to speak. Your eventual comments might be different from the ones you initially had. Your brain does the "work" of holding something in mind as it flexibly accommodates new information, all the while inhibiting distractions and regulating affective states that might interfere with your intended goal: to contribute your ideas to the discussion. This is one example of executive functions in action.

Currently, research is not advanced enough to tell us precisely what kinds of training might strengthen this network of skills. Nor do we know how much practice is needed, nor what types of practice generalize best to tasks beyond the specific skills involved in the training activity. Despite many unanswered questions, there are some clues about what are useful principles of intervention, what might impair EFs, and where the field needs to go next (see Blair, 2017).

Current EF activities and interventions come in many varieties: cognitive training like computer games, physical training like yoga and martial arts, aerobics and other kinds of exercise, and so on. A review of well-conducted research by Diamond and Ling (2015) takes a critical look at current practices to separate those that work from those that do not. Some conclusions from their summary include the following points.

- In general, widespread effects from specific training (like computerized memory training) have not been found to generalize to other domains. For example, playing a computer game that requires the same kind of response over and over can make you better at that response, but it may have no effect on other real-world problems. People do get better at the skills they practice, but typically these skills remain in their narrow lane.

- There is some evidence for dosage effects. That is, the more you practice something, the better your performance becomes. Yet some research indicates that smaller doses of practice are optimal for certain types of skills, presumably because repetition can cause boredom.

- Skills, unlike diamonds, do not last forever. You need to challenge yourself continuously to retain and further develop the skills. Just as you wouldn't expect to stay fit and trim without continued physical exercise, you shouldn't expect the same kinds of EF results without cognitive practice. Simply staying in your comfort zone is apparently not enough. Tackling more and more challenging cognitive tasks seems to be the answer. Once practice stops, benefits decline.

- Contrary to conventional wisdom, aerobic exercise or resistance training, on their own, do not impact executive functions. Once again, the key to EF improvement appears to be some kind of challenging cognitive component. Thus, the marriage of exercise with some mental challenge (planning, teamwork, problem solving, remembering rules, etc.) has shown beneficial effects. Although research on sports and EFs is sparse, this is a fertile ground for future study because success in many team sports depends on the exercise of EF skills. Some school-based programs discussed earlier (like Tools of the Mind) demonstrate the potential of certain educational approaches and structured play to boost executive functions because they support self-regulation, require decision making and planning, and are motivating.

Executive functions, while primarily localized in the brain's prefrontal cortex (PFC), are connected via neural networks to areas that process emotional and motivational information (like the amygdala). Their cross talk is accomplished by means of neurotransmitters, which greatly affect how well EFs operate. If a child (or an adult, for that matter) is emotionally upset, aroused, or stressed, these affective states signal and can ultimately overwhelm the PFC. Then, EFs suffer. When the adult or child is unmotivated or bored,

signaling is too low for healthy EF activity. Thus, a well-modulated and moderately strong level of input in this circuitry supports peak EF functioning. Stress, boredom, poor health, lack of sleep, etc. compromise working memory, attention, and cognitive flexibility because they interfere with the brain's feedback loop (Blair, 2017).

It makes sense, then, for helpers to address the factors that can compromise EF efficiency. Stress is a likely suspect. Mindfulness meditation (more in Chapter 14), which may have great benefits for EFs because of its ability to reduce mental and physical tension, has been making inroads into educational settings (Zelazo & Lyons, 2012). Similarly, interventions that promote social acceptance and belonging, physical fitness, restorative sleep, and health can support cognitive functions. Increasing recess time may be another avenue. Schools in the United States, compared to many other countries, have increasingly reduced recess time in the service of academics, and a majority of U.S. elementary schools still allow withholding recess as punishment for behavioral or academic infractions (Turner, Chriqui, & Chaloupka, 2013). A 2011 study found that U.S. children got an average of 26 minutes of combined recess, snack, and lunchtime (Bornstein, 2011). In Finland, by comparison, students get 75 minutes of recess plus a break of 15 minutes after lessons. In Shanghai, students get 10 minutes of recess for each 40-minute instruction period in addition to lunch and "rest" periods (Chang & Coward, 2015). Students in these countries are academically successful, perhaps because of regular breaks that take their physiology into consideration, help reduce stress, reboot concentration, and support social and emotional skills. Diamond and Ling remind us that "if a program focuses only on training EFs and does nothing to decrease how stressed an individual feels, increase joy, enhance feelings of social connectedness and social support, improve sleep or increase physical fitness, then unmet emotional, social, or physical needs, we predict, will work to oppose any improvement in EFs from the program" (2016, p. 41).

As we have stated previously, buyer beware. There is a burgeoning market for "mind training" tools, many of which are supported by dubious claims. As always, some discernment is probably called for. Not all claims are true, but that doesn't necessarily mean we should throw out the whole idea of strengthening EFs. Finding the best route to this end remains the task for research in the years ahead.

Social and Emotional Learning: The Time Has Come

Would you be impressed with an intervention that improved students' achievement scores by 11 percentile points without even mentioning academics? This is precisely what was found in a large-scale study of social-emotional learning (SEL) programs in schools (Durlak, Weissberg, Dymnicki, Taylor, & Schellinger, 2011). SEL is defined by the Collaborative for Academic, Social and

Emotional Learning (CASEL, www.casel.org) as "the process through which children and adults acquire and effectively apply the knowledge, attitudes, and skills necessary to understand and manage emotions, set and achieve positive goals, feel and show empathy for others, establish and maintain positive relationships, and make responsible decisions" (http://www.casel.org/faqs/). The beneficial academic effects mentioned earlier were demonstrated in a meta-analysis of over 270,000 students who participated in SEL programs in their schools. Improvements in prosocial attitudes and behaviors were also found. Not only were these gains evident in the short run, but a subset of programs studied six months to 18 years after programs ended revealed a pattern of protection resulting in subsequently higher achievement (13 percentile points), lower drug use, fewer conduct problems, and less emotional distress (Taylor, Oberle, Durlak, & Weissberg, 2017).

Programs that fall into the category of SEL are generally considered universal or primary prevention programs. They are integrated into the school day, so that all students participate. Social-emotional skills, such as empathy, self-management, decision making, etc., are considered just as important to school and life success as reading and math instruction, and research bears this out. Effective programs listed in the CASEL guides have some things in common: sequenced lessons, activities and practices focused on explicit social and emotional skills, and active learning techniques, all provided within a caring context that is sensitive to cultural conditions (see Jones et al., 2017). Recently, school districts, professional organizations, school boards, and even state governments are getting on board. The U.S. Department of Education "Every Student Succeeds Act" (ESSA, https://www.ed.gov/essa) requires schools to take non-academic factors into account in the teaching–learning process. Perhaps future expansion of SEL programs will also be fueled by economic arguments such as the one offered by researchers from Columbia University (Belfield, Bowden, Klapp, Levin, Shand, & Zander, 2015). In their analysis, SEL programs showed a substantial economic benefit to society. For every dollar spent on these programs, $11 was returned on the investment.

One comprehensive SEL program with demonstrated effectiveness is Promoting Alternative Thinking Strategies (PATHS), a prevention program that includes 131 lessons for children in Grades K through 5 (Greenberg & Kusche, 2002). PATHS is founded on a holistic approach to the development of emotional well-being, and like good prevention programs, reaches out to include multiple levels of the system (peers, parents, and teachers). The primary goals include the promotion of emotional literacy, self-control, and social problem-solving skills in the context of a positive school environment. The benefits of this program have extended to children from a wide range of ethnic, racial, and social class backgrounds, to children with disabilities, and to children of both genders (Conduct Problems Prevention Research Group [CPPRG], 1999; Greenberg & Kusche, 1998).

The interpersonal cognitive problem-solving portion of this program offers an example of the material we have been discussing in this chapter. This part of the curriculum includes 33 lessons (introduced in grades 3 or 4) that are presented after the units on emotional recognition, self-control, and communicating with others have been completed. The authors note that problem solving is not just an isolated cognitive activity but one that flows from a basic understanding of self and others. The lessons in the problem-solving unit are listed in Table 6.3. To generalize the skills and apply them to everyday life, children are encouraged to write out real problems from their life experience and put them into a "mailbox" on the teacher's desk. These problems are discussed in regular problem-solving meetings. Teachers also build problem-solving practice into other areas, such as academic subjects.

Assessing and Teaching Metacognitive Skills

Despite typical age-related limitations in children's abilities to reflect on their thinking, metacognitive advances do emerge during this period and open up a range of clinical possibilities (Elliott et al., 2013). The major elements of metacognition, which includes the ability to appraise and regulate one's own thinking, have great relevance for educational and clinical efforts to improve skills like problem solving and perspective taking. The role of distorted cognitions in mental health problems is also very well known to clinicians, so understanding children's self-statements can be important in this regard.

One component of metacognition is the ability to know what one is thinking. Several means of assessing cognition have been used in research, including asking people what they say to themselves while they are currently thinking about some task (called "self-talk"), asking them what they were thinking after they completed the task (called "thought-listing"), or, after videotaping an activity and replaying the video, asking them to "dub" the self-talk

---

TABLE 6.3 Problem-Solving Unit of the PATHS Curriculum

STOP!
1. Stop and calm down.
2. Identify the problem (collect lots of information).
3. Identify the feelings (your own and other people's).

GO SLOW!
4. Decide on a goal.
5. Think of lots of solutions.
6. Think about the consequences.
7. Choose the best solution (evaluate all of the alternatives).
8. Make a good plan (think about possible obstacles).

GO!
9. Try my plan.
10. Evaluate—How did I do?
11. If you need to, try again.

SOURCE: Based on Greenberg, M. T., Kusche, C., & Mihalic, S. F. (2002). Promoting alternative thinking strategies (PATHS). In D. S. Elliott (Series Ed.), *Blueprint for violence prevention, Book Ten* (pp. 29–30). Boulder, CO: Center for the Study and Prevention of Violence, Institute of Behavioral Science, University of Colorado. Available from http://www.prevention.psu.edu/projects/PATHSCurriculum.html.

(called "video-mediated recall"). A self-talk instruction might be "When you read this short paragraph [or work on this problem], just remember to say out loud all the things that come into your head." The use of self-talk can help the helper understand how the child understands a particular situation or problem, how he makes attributions about the problem, and how he goes about solving the problem.

The areas of study skills training, academic counseling, or tutoring also depend on a working knowledge of children's cognition. Counselors can attempt to appraise thinking by informal assessment of memory as described in this chapter. In the case of underachievement, students may be helped to understand the study process through prompts such as: "Do you know that studying every night will help you master the material?" (declarative knowledge); "What do you do when you study for a test?" (procedural knowledge); and "When do you think you should memorize definitions and when should you practice problems?" (conditional knowledge). Once the thoughts are revealed, helpers can clarify misconceptions and help children learn more effective study skills. Table 6.4 presents a sampling of self-monitoring questions.

Another rationale for using self-talk procedures is to help children realize the *existence* of their self-talk, its relationship to their feelings and behaviors, and the ways they can modify it to make it more adaptive. This approach is critical to many cognitive-behavioral treatments for anxiety, depression, anger control, and ADHD (see Kendall, 1991). In this latter case, the content of the self-statements is as relevant as the process of self-instruction. In other words, teaching children (and adults, for that matter) to recognize negative self-statements is a necessary first step before instruction and practice in alternatives.

Meichenbaum and Goodman (1971), who pioneered self-instruction training, began by teaching self-control to impulsive children using guided modeling and self-talk procedures. Their approach included the following steps. First, the helping professional models effective self-talk while doing some task or dealing with some hypothetical scenario. Next, the child is asked to repeat the same process while the adult provides overt instruction. Then, the

TABLE 6.4 Sample Self-Monitoring Questions

1. Why am I trying to learn this information? What is the purpose of this exercise or assignment?
2. What do I already know about this subject?
3. Do I already know any strategies that will help me learn this?
4. What is my plan of action?
5. Do I understand the steps I need to take?
6. How should I get help if I need it?
7. How should I correct my mistakes?
8. Am I accomplishing my goals? Am I being successful?
9. How will I know when I've accomplished my goals?

child is asked to redo the activity, first talking out loud by himself and then by subvocalizing (whispering) the instructions. Finally, the child practices using private (nonvocal) self-talk.

One can imagine a situation wherein therapy involves both learning the steps of self-instruction training and modifying the content of maladaptive cognitions. For example, once self-talk assessment has identified a person's negative self-statements ("I can't do math"), training in self-instruction can strengthen the frequency of positive alternatives ("I didn't do well on this problem because I didn't spend enough time studying"). Researchers report that it is not necessary, and is actually undesirable, for people to expect to have only positive thoughts. The ratio of 2 positive thoughts to 1 negative one appears optimal for healthy adjustment (Schwartz & Garamoni, 1989). Depressed individuals, for example, show an equal 1:1 balance (Kendall, 1991). Therefore, tipping the scales in favor of more positive thoughts appears to be a clinically important goal for adults and children alike (Kendall, 2011).

Focus on another element of metacognition, self-regulation of thinking—the "how well am I thinking?" part—helps the individual translate knowledge into action. As in self-instruction approaches, this provides the basis for cognitive problem-solving techniques, which are used to good effect in a variety of clinical and educational settings. Typical problem-solving steps include defining the problem or goal, selecting a plan to solve the problem or meet the goal, monitoring progress toward the goal, and revising goal-directed strategies, if needed.

Summary

Brain and Behavior

1. Changes in the brain both enable and are affected by cognitive and motor developments. In middle childhood, continuing brain growth is partially a function of ongoing myelination. Both gross motor and fine motor coordination benefit from continued myelination of the

corpus callosum, connecting the left and right cortical hemispheres, and the cerebellum, as well as other brain maturation processes.

2. Some differences in cognitive and behavioral development among children are related to differences in brain development. For example, in about half of children diagnosed with ADHD, brain growth is delayed,

especially in the frontal lobes, although most catch up by adolescence or early adulthood. Unevenness in brain development, both between and within children, is to be expected.

Cognitive Development

3. In Piaget's theory, children at the concrete operational stage (6 to 12 years) can decenter, or think about more than one dimension or aspect of a situation at one time. This allows them the possibility of recognizing or constructing the relationships among the dimensions, which is important for logical thinking. Understanding reversible relationships, when one change reverses the effects of another, or one change compensates for the effects of another, is especially important. Recognizing the nature of the relationships among features of an event makes it possible for children to infer underlying realities.

4. At the concrete operational stage, children's thinking is most logical when they are solving problems that relate to real, concrete events. They find it difficult to think logically about abstract contents, like their own thought processes. They find it difficult to distinguish between their own theories or assumptions and objective fact.

5. Whether or not children are able to solve a problem logically in middle childhood depends on factors such as the particular materials or context of the problems. When children have a great deal of experience with a specific domain of knowledge (expertise), they are more likely to think logically about problems in that domain.

6. In the information processing approach, cognition is compared to the functioning of a computer. The organization of the cognitive system stays the same across age, but there are age changes in the amount and efficiency of information flow. "Top-down" processes engage executive functions. They require focused attention and effort. "Bottom-up" processes seem to bypass executive functions, not requiring conscious effort to occur. With increasing age, executive functions improve, including control of emotions, attention, and problem solving. The pace of improvement varies somewhat across cultures, apparently depending on parents' socialization practices.

7. NeoPiagetians are theorists who try to integrate concepts from Piaget's theory and from information processing theory to explain cognitive development. Theory theorists assume that children form theories about the physical, biological, and social world from infancy. Like Piaget and neoPiagetians, they are constructivists.

8. Two kinds of remembering or retrieval are called recognition (realizing that information being experienced now is familiar) and recall (drawing information out of long-term memory and representing it to yourself). Our memories can store declarative knowledge, both semantic (about facts and concepts) and episodic (about events we have experienced). A schematic representation of a frequently experienced event is called a script. We also store nondeclarative knowledge, which is hard to verbalize and is often referred to as procedural, which is "knowing how" rather than "knowing that." Infants' and toddlers' knowledge is largely nondeclarative.

9. Working memory (one of the executive functions) increases in capacity with age, as indicated on digit span tests. This seems to be partly a result of faster information processing, perhaps due to practice, perhaps to maturation, or to both.

10. Children's knowledge base increases with age, and that helps children reconstruct events. They "remember" more accurately because they can infer what must have happened. An expanded knowledge base also helps children learn new information more easily, perhaps because they can fit the new information into a rich web of well-organized connections. Having an expanded knowledge base also benefits chunking in working memory.

11. Advances in logical thinking can help children improve their memories. The better the child understands the original experience, the more likely he is to reconstruct it accurately.

12. Increasing facility with language helps children store memories for events in coherent verbal form and seems to improve later retrieval of those events.

13. Children also improve in the use of memory strategies with age from preschool through middle school. Rehearsal is an early strategy, with more effective strategies such as organization coming later. Children's progress in strategy use is bumpy. They may exhibit either production deficiencies or utilization deficiencies.

14. Children gradually improve their understanding of their own cognitive processes (metacognition), including memory abilities (metamemory), as they approach the end of middle childhood, partly accounting for improvements in strategy use with age.

15. Memory is also influenced by affective and social developments, like motivation to learn and the amount of scaffolding available from adults.

16. Formal schooling is the context in which a great deal of adult scaffolding of cognitive development occurs. Many factors contribute to children's academic success at the country/culture level, the school level, and the proximal, teacher–child interaction level. These factors moderate each other's effects, so that some factors matter more or less depending on the presence of other factors. Overall, effective educational factors fall into three categories: *quantity (amount of instruction/practice), stimulation/engagement,* and *valuing (of learning and the learner).*

17. Teacher factors that contribute to effective teacher–child interactions are much like the most effective parenting factors: warmth and demandingness (high expectations). Teachers with a "growth" mindset see intelligence as malleable, and they are more likely to be demanding with all children regardless of past performance. Teachers with an "ability" mindset see intelligence as a fixed trait and are less likely to challenge children whom they expect to be poor performers.

18. The kinds of proximal, teacher–child interaction processes that matter are illustrated by effective math education. Children usually begin school with informal mathematical skills, such as adopting simple counting strategies for adding and subtracting small numbers. In elementary school, they continue to invent their own strategies as well as adopting the formal procedures and strategies they are taught. Gradually, more efficient strategies win out over less efficient strategies, though again, development is bumpy.

19. Helping children build a knowledge base of memorized math facts and procedures is useful but must be accompanied by support for conceptual understanding. Children assimilate formal procedures to their own concepts, and often misunderstand. Teachers can encourage mathematical development by exploring their students' understanding and by working forward from what children already understand, such as by providing familiar examples of concepts or familiar analogies to more difficult concepts.

20. Children learn other academic skills via similar processes. For example, learning to read requires strong verbal language skills, such as phonological awareness and a good vocabulary. Teachers need to assess these skills and work forward from the child's current capacities.

Social Cognition

21. Learning about social interactions, including how to make and keep friends, and acquiring a theory of mind begins in early childhood and is heavily dependent on cognitive developments. For example, children's perspective taking improves as they acquire the ability to think about their own mental experiences and those of another person at the same time. Growth of executive functions, especially working memory capacity, makes an important contribution. Advances in perspective taking are also a function of experience in social interactions, with parents, with siblings, and with peers.

22. In Selman's five-stage theory of friendship development, improvements in perspective taking affect an individual's friendship understanding, influence his friendship valuing, and affect the social and conflict resolution skills (friendship skills) he develops.

23. In Selman's view, a mature interpersonal orientation balances intimacy and autonomy strivings. Less effective orientations may be other-transforming or self-transforming, and are more characteristic of very young children and of socially immature older children. Both a bully and a victim may be functioning at a similar developmental level with regard to perspective taking skill. Assessing the properties of understanding that underlie relationship skill is a helpful approach to addressing social problems.

Case Study

Alex, the second child of Ernest and Isabel Palacio, a Cuban American couple, is a fourth grader at J. F. Kennedy Elementary School. He has one older sister, Paula, who is in fifth grade, and a younger brother, Thomas, who is 4 years old. Until recently, Alex appeared to be a happy child and a good student in school. Although somewhat reserved, he interacted well with peers, was athletic, and was popular among his classmates.

During the year Alex was in third grade, the Palacios' marriage was seriously affected by Ernest's close relationship with a female coworker. Despite an attempt at counseling, the couple could not resolve their differences. During the summer before his fourth-grade year, Alex's parents separated. The children continued to live with their mother, but maintained a relationship with their father, seeing him every weekend in the apartment he rented nearby.

Both parents tried hard to make this arrangement work for the sake of their children, to whom both were devoted. The fourth-grade school year began fairly smoothly for Alex, who was happy to see his friends again after the summer vacation. His teacher, Mr. Williams, was regarded as tough but usually fair, and Alex seemed to make a good initial adjustment to his class. Ernest continued his employment with an advertising agency and paid for many of the family's living costs. However, the expense of maintaining two residences quickly became burdensome. Isabel, formerly employed as a part-time library aide, needed to find a position that provided a larger income. She began a job as a secretary shortly after the children began school in September.

In December, Isabel fell ill and needed to be hospitalized. Primary care of the children fell to Isabel's mother, the children's grandmother. Ernest took over as much of the caretaking as his work schedule would permit, but he feared that if he took off too much time for family responsibilities, his job would be in jeopardy. Because of these changes in the family, all three children needed to adjust. It became much more difficult for an adult to transport the children after school to music lessons and games, so they had to drop out of some of their activities. As Isabel recuperated, she needed much more rest and general peace and quiet. She could no longer take the children on trips or allow groups of her children's friends to have sleepovers in her home.

Toward the middle of his fourth-grade year, Alex's grades started to slip, and he began to act up. Alex grew apathetic and sullen in class. Mr. Williams was a relatively young teacher in the school district. His first two years of teaching had been spent in the eighth grade of the district middle school. He liked teaching older students and reluctantly accepted the fourth-grade position because of his lack of seniority in the system. Mr. Williams, despite his youth, was a fairly traditional teacher. He believed in giving lots of homework and in placing high expectations for performance on his students. He ran a very disciplined classroom that was based on a system of winning and losing points for behavior. Because Alex did not participate actively in classroom exercises or turn in homework, he continually "lost points."

On one particularly difficult day, Alex and one of his friends got into an argument. Alex accused his friend of picking on him and teasing him in the lunchroom. Mr. Williams tried to intervene by taking both boys out into the hallway and listening to each version of the problem. When the disagreement got louder, Mr. Williams told both boys that they would "just have to work it out." He told them he would take away points and was sending them both to the principal's office. Alex became very agitated and said to his teacher, "Sometimes I feel like throwing my chair at you."

Mr. Williams began to see Alex as a threat and recommended to the principal that the incident be handled as a disciplinary matter. It was the teacher's belief that Alex should be suspended and then referred for a psychological evaluation by the school psychologist because of his "aggressiveness." He insisted that Alex not be returned to his classroom.

Discussion Questions

1. How would you assess the problem?
2. What are the different perspectives involved in this conflict?
3. What actions would you take and what recommendations would you make as a helping professional in this situation?

Practice Using What You Have Learned

MyLab Education Application Exercise 6.1:
Cognitive and Academic Growth: Middle Childhood

MyLab Education Application Exercise 6.2:
Friendship Development

MyLab Education Application Exercise 6.3:
Case Study: Analysis of Perspective Taking Skills

Journal Questions

1. If you can remember struggling with some subject or concept in school, describe the impact of this experience on your sense of competence and industry. If you were counseling a student in this situation, what advice would you have for his parents? His teachers?
2. Describe what your friendships were like in elementary school. Did you have a best friend? What characteristics did he or she possess?
3. Compare and contrast how you solved conflicts as a child in grade school and how you solve them now. How would you assess your level of perspective taking?
4. Provide an example of something at which you excelled in elementary school (academic and non-academic areas are fair game). If possible, connect your skill area to one or more of the executive functions. How much practice was involved in your expertise? Describe your level of motivation for this performance. What kinds of conditions might have strengthened or weakened your performance? How does this framework help you understand the role of EF in school and life?

Key Concepts

reversible relationship (p. 211)
domain of knowledge (p. 213)
"bottom-up" processes (p. 218)
"top-down" processes (p. 218)
neoPiagetians (p. 219)
theory theorists (p. 219)
sensory memory (p. 220)
long-term memory (p. 220)
rehearsal (p. 220)
retrieval (p. 220)
declarative knowledge (p. 221)
semantic knowledge (p. 221)
episodic knowledge (p. 221)
script (p. 221)
nondeclarative knowledge (p. 221)
procedural knowledge (p. 221)
digit span tests (p. 221)
knowledge base (p. 222)

reality monitoring (p. 223)
guided imagery (p. 223)
stereotype induction (p. 224)
chunking (p. 224)
memory strategies (p. 226)
selective attention (p. 226)
organization strategy (p. 227)
elaboration strategy (p. 227)
production deficiency (p. 227)
utilization deficiency (p. 227)
metacognition (p. 227)
metamemory (p. 227)
self-instruction (p. 228)
self-monitoring (p. 228)
mindsets (p. 233)
"ability" mindset (p. 233)
"growth" mindset (p. 233)
counting all strategy (p. 233)

counting on strategy (p. 234)
decomposition strategy (p. 234)
retrieval strategy (p. 234)
dyslexia (p. 236)
social cognition (p. 237)
English-language-learner (ELL) (p. 230)
immigrant family (p. 230)
immigrant risk model (p. 230)
immigrant paradox model (p. 230)
psychosocial development (p. 242)
friendship understanding (p. 242)
friendship skills (p. 242)
friendship valuing (p. 242)
interpersonal orientation (p. 243)
other-transforming (p. 243)
self-transforming (p. 243)

Chapter 7
Self and Moral Development: Middle Childhood Through Early Adolescence

 Learning Objectives

After reading this chapter, you should be able to:

7.1 Explain the differentiated structure of self-concept in middle childhood and early adolescence, identifying influences on self-concept development and factors affecting individual differences in viewing and valuing self.

7.2 Discuss classic and contemporary views of moral development as well as factors that promote prosocial and antisocial behavior and suggest interventions to encourage healthy development in middle childhood and early adolescence.

At 9 years old, Josie is a talkative and active fourth grader. She is a good student when she likes a subject (e.g., science) but she often loses focus with other subjects. If you asked her if she likes school she would probably say that it was "okay," but she would rather be free to play with her friends. She especially loves outdoor activities, and she is good at the sports that she has tried. Josie's family recently moved from the northern United States to a small Southern town, an affluent suburb of a large city. For many reasons Josie is finding the transition difficult. First of all, she and her friends played basketball every day in the park across from her old home. Now, there are few kids in her new neighborhood, and there is no place close by to play basketball. Second, she is experiencing peer rejection at school. Not only is she the new kid, but also she's the only Catholic child in her public elementary school. Unlike her former community, most of the Catholic children in her new town attend private, religious schools, so she is an outsider in multiple ways. She feels like no one wants to be her friend, and several of her classmates routinely make remarks like "You don't belong here," and "Our school is not for Catholics." Josie is flummoxed by these assaults and is unhappy much of the time. She is also starting to see herself as less likeable than she had thought. Adding to her problems, Josie's mother recently discovered that she had stolen a lipstick (a very pretty pink lipstick with sparkles) at the local drugstore. She tried to deny it at first, but her mother was having none of it. Her mother made a bit of a show of making an appointment to meet with the store manager, and then she accompanied Josie to the store to confess her misdeed, return the lipstick, and apologize for her mistake. The store manager spoke solemnly about the problems that thefts cause for others, and then he accepted the lipstick and Josie's apology. Fortunately for Josie, her mother is also looking into moving her to a parochial school, hoping to ease some of Josie's burden.

Honesty, dependability, kindness, fairness, respect, self-control, truthfulness, and diligence. Rare is the adult who would not agree that any one of these traits is desirable for children to attain. The advantage is very basic: Behaving in accordance with these values makes the world a better place for everyone. Josie's life in her new home would certainly be better if respect and kindness were guiding her class-mates' behavior. Certainly, individuals or groups might disagree on the particulars, such as what "being fair" may mean in a given situation. But it is truly difficult to imagine any sizable group of parents, teachers, or helpers who would promote the opposite values: meanness, laziness, dishonesty, irresponsibility, or disrespect, to name a few.

Not too long ago in the United States, there was considerable agreement that inculcating these values, virtues, or behavioral habits was perhaps the most impor-tant responsibility that adults have relative to their children. The public schools had as their express purpose the creation of good citizens—people who, for the most part, valued and practiced these virtues. Consider the advice educator Charles Davis presented in 1852 in a lecture to parents and teachers on their duties toward children:

> Education is the system of training which develops in their right direction and in their proper proportions our physical, intellectual, and moral natures. . . . The moral nature of the pupils will be, with the teacher, a subject of earnest and constant solicitude. What are the first things to be done? To establish his [the teacher's] authority over his school—to ensure the obedience of his scholars—to win their confidence—to gain their respect, and to call into exercise their warmest affections. (Davis, 1852, pp. 6–8)

Hiram Orcutt, writing in a famous manual to parents in 1874, advises thus:

> The child must establish a character of integrity and to be trained to habits of honesty, benevolence and industry or he will be lost to himself and to society. . . . We may not expect benevolence to spring up spontaneously in the heart of the child. . . . Without knowledge and experience, the child cannot appreciate the rights and wants of others, nor his own duty in regard to them. (Orcutt, 1874, pp. 72–73)

If this seems a bit quaint and outdated to you, consider the fact that even in mod-ern times there is evidence for broad consensus among North American parents about what they consider fundamental for children to achieve their life goals. When David R. Shaffer and his students asked young parents what they considered to be the most important aspect of a child's social development, most placed morality at the top of their lists (Shaffer, 2000). They apparently felt that acquiring a moral sense and liv-ing by its dictates were critical for self-development and central to successful adult functioning.

Perhaps this consensus is shaped by our experience of the culture we share. We are benumbed by the repetitious refrain that comes from all manner of media report-ing on a world marred by violence, aggressiveness, hopelessness, underachievement, and declining civility.

Is something happening to the healthy moral and self-development we wish for our children? As you might have already guessed, the issue is complex. The world is changing in many ways at once, and understanding how those changes affect our children's development is among the goals of developmental science. The answers researchers can make available have profound significance for practice, given helpers' investment in their clients' healthy development. In this chapter and the next, we will introduce the topics that are fundamental to understanding social and emotional development in middle and late childhood and provide some guide-lines and suggestions for interventions. We pick up the discussion with the topic of the self.

Self-Concept

7.1 Explain the differentiated structure of self-concept in middle childhood and early adolescence, identifying influences on self-concept development and factors affecting individual differences in viewing and valuing self.

The Development of Self-Concept—An Overview

Imagine that you live across the street from an empty lot. One day, you notice that workers have placed piles of building materials, bricks, lumber, and bags of concrete on the property. After some time, the frame of a large, boxlike house takes the place of the piles of materials. From your vantage point, you can see the empty beginnings of where rooms will be. With more time, the internal structure becomes clear. Walls are assembled; doors and stairways connect the parts. Each section of the new house—living, dining, bedroom, and storage areas—has multiple divisions that provide useful space dedicated to some purpose. The disparate piles have been transformed into a coherent structure, and the once simple structure has become increasingly complex. Finishing touches are made, and ongoing renovations will undoubtedly accompany the life of the home.

This image illustrates how Western science describes the development of the self-concept or the "me-self," from early childhood through adolescence and adulthood. It is important to recognize that self-concept or self-knowledge is very much like any other kind of knowledge, for the self is a cognitive construction. Therefore, knowledge of the self will be constrained by the child's general level of cognitive development and will most likely progress unevenly. As Harter (1999) has pointed out in her description of general cognitive-developmental stages, ". . . it is expected that the particular level of development at which one is functioning will vary across different domains of knowledge" (p. 30), as we noted in Chapter 6.

In addition, remember that the self-concept is multidimensional, like a house with various rooms (see Chapter 5). In many homes, rooms are added on after the initial construction. In contrast to this somewhat static analogy, the self-system is dynamic and changes throughout development. Generally, the child's self-concept proceeds from a rather undifferentiated state or simple structure to a much more differentiated, organized, and coherent structure in adulthood through a process of stage-like changes. Let us consider some of the developments in self-knowledge that occur as children mature.

The preschool child's rendering of herself is something like the lot filled with building materials. Self-descriptors such as "big," "girl," and "nice" are separate, uncoordinated elements in the child's self-portrait because she is cognitively unable to integrate these elements into an organized whole. We know from our discussion of cognitive development (see Chapter 3) that young children's ability to hold in mind several ideas at the same time and to integrate these in some meaningful way is quite underdeveloped. Furthermore, preschool youngsters find accommodating opposing characteristics, such as being "nice" and "mean," or opposing emotional states, such as "happy" and "sad," to be especially difficult (see Harter, 2012, 2016). Nor do young children make much use of perspective taking at this age, as we saw in Chapter 6. In failing to do so, they show limited ability to use the behaviors or perspectives of others as guides for evaluating their own conduct or performance. Stated in other words, they do not use comparisons of themselves with others as a way of assessing their competencies. Consequently, the young child's self-evaluations are often overly positive (e.g., Davis-Kean, Jager, & Collins, 2009). Four-year-old Jamar might insist he has won the round of miniature golf despite hitting the ball outside the lane every time!

Gradually, the early-elementary-school-aged youngster begins to organize the characteristics of the "Me-self" into sets of categories that display some coherence. For example, the child might relate being good at drawing, at coloring, and at cutting as an indication that she is good at art. However, the child still does not accommodate sets of characteristics with opposing features. As one 5-year-old insisted, "Nope, there's no way you could be both smart and dumb, you only have one mind!" (Harter, 2016). Given her tendency to perceive personal qualities as good and to discount the subtlety of coexisting negative attributes, the child's thinking about herself may still have an all-or-nothing quality that is often unrealistically positive. Gradual improvements in perspective-taking ability, however, allow the child to begin to evaluate her own behavior according to others' standards. The child's anticipation of another person's reaction, be it as a reward or a punishment, becomes internalized (Harter, 2012). As others' rules or standards become internalized, they become adopted as self-regulatory guidelines and form the basis for the looking-glass self.

In middle to late childhood (approximately 8 to 10), the child becomes capable of integrating opposing characteristics. For example, Josie may now consider herself "smart" in science but "dumb" in social studies. Her growing working memory capacity also helps her to keep in mind information about herself and her peers and to make comparisons. Her improving perspective taking skills also help her to identify and integrate how others see her into her self-portrait. So, as she brings to bear the cognitive skills that emerge during the middle childhood years, her self-concept becomes more accurately reflective of how she compares to others and how others view her. Self-esteem may begin to decline somewhat as children become more realistic about themselves.

As the child moves into early adolescence, her ability to think more clearly about abstract content helps her to form more abstract trait-like concepts to describe herself, generalizing across more concrete or singular traits. For instance, she might now see herself as "intelligent," including being smart, curious, and creative into this overriding concept. Or, she might start to consider herself an "airhead," combining academic failings, awkwardness in social situations, and the feeling that she never knows what's going on in the world (Harter, 2016).

Self-esteem typically declines in early adolescence for a host of complex reasons. Adolescence is a time of such great change in so many ways—cognitively, physically, and with regard to social and cultural expectations—that self-concept development is profoundly affected. We will save detailed discussion of adolescent self-development for later chapters.

The Structure of Self-Concept

Although we continue to use the term *self-concept*, it is not a unidimensional construct, as we noted in Chapter 5. One's overall sense of self is a composite of several related, but not necessarily overlapping, elements that are evaluated by the individual to determine *self-esteem*, our feelings about ourselves. Although technically they are separate constructs, self-concept and self-esteem are closely intertwined and are difficult to discuss separately. In a classic analysis, Shavelson and colleagues (Marsh & Shavelson, 1985; Shavelson, Hubner, & Stanton, 1976) proposed a useful theoretical view of the self. In this model (see Figure 7.1), children's general self-concept can be divided into

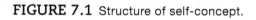

FIGURE 7.1 Structure of self-concept.

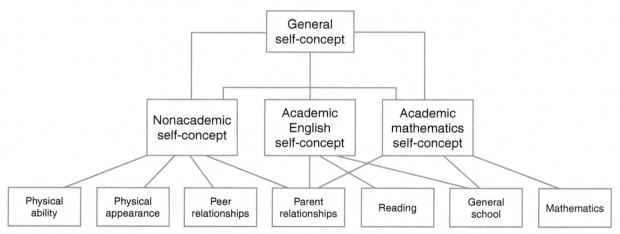

Students have many separate but sometimes related concepts of themselves. The overall sense of self appears to be divided into separate, but slightly related, self-concepts.

SOURCE: Marsh, H. W. & Shavelson, R. J. (1985). Self-concept: Its multifaceted, hierarchical structure. *Educational Psychologist, 20,* 114. Adapted with permission from Lawrence Erlbaum Associates, Inc. and H. W. Marsh. Used by permission of H. W. Marsh.

two main domains: academic and nonacademic self-concepts. Academic self-concept is further divided into specific school subject areas such as math, science, English, and social studies. Other developmentalists have proposed the addition of other components such as artistic self-concept.

The nonacademic self-concept is divided into social, emotional, and physical self-concepts. The last domain is further subdivided into physical ability and physical appearance. Other theories of the self also emphasize multidimensional and hierarchically arranged self-structures (see Rentzsch, Wenzler, & Schütz, 2016). Despite this general consensus, however, many researchers have retained the notion of global self-esteem within their frameworks. This reflects the view that a global sense of self coexists with, shapes, and is shaped by self-appraisals in specific domains.

By grade school, children can articulate their own assessments of their specific competencies as well as a generalized overall perception of themselves. Harter (1985, 1988b) found evidence that different domains of self-concept emerge at different points in the life span (see Table 7.1). The number of dimensions of the self that can be appraised, however, increases dramatically from early childhood through adolescence and adulthood. In middle childhood, the dimensions of importance include academic or scholastic competence, athletic competence, physical appearance, peer acceptance, and behavioral conduct.

Is one domain more important than the others to a child's overall sense of self-esteem? Evidence from many studies clearly documents the powerful association between physical appearance and overall self-esteem (correlations are as high as 0.80)

TABLE 7.1 Domains of Self-Concept Across the Life Span

EARLY CHILDHOOD	MIDDLE TO LATE CHILDHOOD	ADOLESCENCE	COLLEGE YEARS	EARLY THROUGH MIDDLE ADULTHOOD	LATE ADULTHOOD
Cognitive competence	Scholastic competence	Scholastic competence	Scholastic competence		
		Intellectual ability Creativity	Intelligence	Cognitive abilities	
		Job competence	Job competence	Job competence	Job competence
Physical competence	Athletic competence	Athletic competence	Athletic competence	Athletic competence	
Physical appearance	Physical appearance	Physical appearance	Physical appearance	Physical appearance	Physical appearance
Peer acceptance	Peer acceptance	Peer acceptance	Peer acceptance	Sociability	
		Close friendship	Close friendship	Close friendship	Relationships with friends
		Romantic relationships	Romantic relationships	Intimate relationships	
			Relationships with parents		Family relationships
Behavioral conduct	Behavioral conduct	Conduct/morality	Morality Sense of humor	Morality Sense of humor	Morality
				Nurturance Household management	Nurturance Personal, household management
				Adequacy as a provider	Adequacy as a provider
					Leisure activities Health status Life satisfaction Reminiscence
	Global self-worth	Global self-worth	Global self-worth	Global self-worth	Global self-worth

SOURCE: Harter, S. (1990). *The construction of the self: A developmental perspective.* New York, NY: Guilford Press. Used by permission of Guilford Press.

for older children, adolescents, college-aged students, and adults (e.g., Baudson, Weber, & Freund, 2016; see Harter, 2012, for a review). The strength of this association holds up for special student populations such as individuals with learning disabilities and those with academic talents as well. This somewhat disconcerting reality may be due to the fact that physical attractiveness is such an omnipresent, recognizable aspect of the self. It is also true that more attractive individuals receive more positive attention from others (Maestripieri, Henry, & Nickels, 2017). They receive more affection from parents and other adults in infancy. In later childhood and adolescence, teachers have higher expectations for them, and peers show more positive regard for them. As adults, they have more good qualities ascribed to them, and they are generally more successful in life, advancing more rapidly in their careers and earning more income. Thus, physically attractive individuals may be getting a consistently larger number of positive reflected appraisals with which to construct the self than their less attractive counterparts.

It also appears that cultural emphasis on rigid and often unobtainable standards of beauty, particularly for females, contributes to observed differences in self-esteem for males and females, which we will discuss in a later section of this chapter. Beginning around early adolescence, girls report more dissatisfaction with their appearance and their bodies than do boys of the same age. We should note that, increasingly, physical appearance is becoming a central element to male self-valuing as well (Frederick, Sandhu, Morse, & Swami, 2016). In fact, in one large study of Norwegian adolescents, body satisfaction predicted self-esteem equally strongly for both girls and boys (Wichstrom & von Soest, 2016).

Influences on the Development of Self-Concept

We have already presented the earliest influences on the developing self of the infant, toddler, and preschooler (see Chapter 5). What can we add to the story of self-concept development that applies to older children? Are the same processes at work? What can we say about the nature of self-esteem, that evaluative dimension which colors our self-appraisals? As you might suspect, the traditional positions of James (1890) and Cooley (1902) have much to offer contemporary researchers looking for explanations. Recall that William James believed that self-esteem was dependent on the ratio of our successes to our aspirations. Harter (1990) found support for James's position. Children's, as well as adolescents' and adults', global self-esteem is heavily dependent on competence in areas of personal importance. Individuals of all ages are more able to discount weak performance if it occurs in unimportant areas. For example, if it is very important to Ashley (and to her peers and parents) to be athletically competitive, having a relatively weak performance in this area is likely to lower her overall self-regard. On the other hand, if Sharon's goal is to be a stellar student, a weak athletic showing is likely to have less punishing consequences to her global sense of self.

In general, Harter found that the greater the discrepancy between adequacy in some domain and the importance of that domain, the greater the negative impact on self-esteem. This helps explain why some students who display low levels of competence in certain domains may still have high self-esteem overall. Evidence suggests, however, that this reality is not well understood and may even contradict conventional wisdom. Consider a survey of U.S. teachers, school administrators, and school counselors in which approximately 60% of the respondents believed poor academic performance was the major cause of low self-esteem among students (Scott, Murray, Mertens, & Dustin, 1996). Yet, many other attributes are important to children (e.g., social relationships, hobbies, other recreational activities and interests; Tatlow-Golden & Guerin, 2017). In addition, academic success may not be highly valued by everyone. Interestingly, in the same study, 69% of counselors compared to 35% of administrators believed that the self-esteem of underachieving students could be improved by more unconditional validation, a strategy we will examine more thoroughly later in the chapter.

How do children appraise their competencies? For a child at school age and beyond, there are obviously some concrete standards of performance that can be used to infer

MyLab Education
Video Example 7.1
Global self-esteem is related to feelings of competence. How might a growth mindset influence these children's self-esteem and self-efficacy beliefs?

competency, such as getting good grades or being selected for a sports team. Cooley also emphasized the importance of social influences on appraisals of competence. In other words, he believed that self-perceptions can be based on the internalization of approval or disapproval of others in the social network. In one study, for example, 8- to 12-year-olds participated in an online "game" in which a jury of same-aged, anonymous peers ostensibly judged each child's "likeability" in comparison to four other "contestants" (Thomaes et al., 2010). Actually, the researchers randomly assigned a high, low, or intermediate likeability score to each participating child. The children filled out self-esteem questionnaires both before and after the "game." Receiving a low likeability score decreased their self-esteem, and receiving a high score increased their self-esteem. Children with narcissistic tendencies (that is, who had demonstrated extreme, unrealistically positive self-views) before the manipulation actually were the most vulnerable to the negative peer feedback. It does appear that, "As social beings we live with our eyes upon our reflection, but have no assurance of the tranquility of the waters in which we see it" (Cooley, 1902, p. 247).

Children put more stock in how their peers see them as they get older. For example, one study found that sixth graders' self-appraisals match those of their peers more closely than third graders' self-appraisals do (e.g., Cole, Maxwell, & Martin, 1997). For both age groups, parents' and teachers' appraisals also contributed to the process. But the role of the social network involves more than just providing an accumulation of comments or responses from others that become part of the self-concept. The self-system also assimilates and accommodates evaluative data from internal ("How am I doing in reading compared to math?") and external ("How does my reading performance compare with that of my classmates?") sources in ways that involve comparison.

In social comparison, people observe the performance of others and use it as a basis for evaluating their own abilities and accomplishments (Festinger, 1954). When they do this and how they do it vary somewhat depending on context and level of global self-esteem. Social comparison processes are particularly active in situations that are novel or ambiguous or when more objective standards of performance are unavailable. It is fairly obvious that classrooms provide a wealth of material for this ongoing process. Generally, children tend to make comparisons with other children who resemble them in some important ways. Most people, at least in Western cultures, are motivated to maintain moderately positive beliefs about themselves, called the self-enhancing bias (Taylor & Brown, 1988), which is considered a good thing in most cases (McKay & Dennett, 2009).

Strategies for protecting one's self-esteem differ depending on children's level of self-esteem. When self-esteem is low, children may prefer situations that are rich in positive reinforcement. For example, Smith and Smoll (1990) reported that children with lower levels of self-esteem responded most favorably to coaches and instructors who were highly encouraging, and least favorably to those who were least supportive. Children with high or moderate levels of self-esteem showed less variation in their responsiveness to adult reinforcement styles. Researchers (Pyszczynski, Greenberg, & LaPrelle, 1985) have also noted that children will make "downward" social comparisons by comparing themselves to less competent or less successful peers when their own self-esteem is at stake. Such comparisons protect the child from negative self-evaluations. Generally, children and adults with lower levels of self-esteem are more susceptible to the kinds of external cues that carry evaluative messages and are more reactive to social feedback (Campbell, 1990). They are reluctant to call attention to themselves and are more cautious and self-protective. Possibly they feel they have more to lose if they experience negative evaluations from others. This contrasts with individuals with high self-esteem, who demonstrate more self-enhancement strategies and are more likely to call attention to themselves (Campbell & Lavallee, 1993).

What message can we draw from research in the tradition of James and Cooley? Harter (e.g., 2006) concludes that the two theorists' positions operate in an additive way to explain the variation in self-esteem found in older children and adolescents. In other words, both competence *and* support contribute to the final product. The higher the level of competence in important domains and the greater the level of social support, the higher the level of self-esteem is overall.

What is the importance of self-esteem for children's development? As you might expect, positive self-esteem not only is a consequence of competence and social support, but also has consequences for life outcomes. Many longitudinal studies lead to the same conclusion: Self-esteem influences the quality of life from childhood through adulthood (see Orth & Robins, 2014). For example, one longitudinal study followed participants from adolescence through old age (Orth, Robins, & Widaman, 2012). Higher self-esteem early in life predicted more positive and fewer negative emotional experiences over time, as well as more relationship and job satisfaction. Another longitudinal study began when participants were 13 years old and followed them to age 30 (Birkeland, Melkevik, Holsen, & Wold, 2012). The researchers identified three typical trajectories of global self-esteem: consistently high, chronically low, and U-shaped. In the U-shaped group, participants reported positive self-esteem when they were 13 years old and then showed a decline, reaching a low point at about 18 years old. Subsequently, their self-esteem climbed so that by their mid-20s they saw themselves much more positively again. By age 30, self-esteem trajectories appeared to have effects on life satisfaction as well as the likelihood of depressive mood, health problems, and insomnia. The importance of self-esteem is especially evident when we examine outcomes for the group that experienced an adolescent decline and subsequent rise in positive feelings (the U-shaped group). Even though by age 30 their global self-esteem was as positive as the consistently high group, they still reported more negative life outcomes.

Understanding Different Kinds of Self-Valuing: Self-Esteem, Self-Efficacy, and Narcissism

It is important for helpers to understand the distinctions among self-esteem, self-efficacy, and narcissism. Someone with high self-esteem sees herself as a worthwhile person and feels general satisfaction with herself. *Self-efficacy* specifically refers to a person's belief in her ability to control events in her life, especially her ability to overcome challenges successfully (Bandura, 1989). Feelings of self-efficacy often go together with positive self-esteem, but not always. Suppose Toni plays soccer well for her age, and she is recruited to play in an elite league. Unfortunately, she rarely can control the ball against the more skilled players in the new league, and she "messes up" repeatedly. If she has strong self-efficacy beliefs, she is likely to believe that she can improve her skills with hard work, and she will put in extra practice time to make that happen despite her initial experience of failure. But if her self-efficacy beliefs are weak, she is likely to attribute her failure to inadequate ability, and she will not be motivated to work harder. She is more likely to find an excuse to leave the new league, maybe moving back to a team where she can feel like she excels. Her self-esteem might recover, but her approach to difficult challenges will limit her success in the long run.

Self-efficacy beliefs are similar to what Erikson (1950/1963) called a sense of industry (see Chapter 1), which he saw as emerging in middle childhood. A child with a sense of industry believes in her ability to master the skills and tools needed to be productive, and she gets pleasure from facing challenges. You will learn a bit about what kinds of interactions support self-efficacy in the Applications section of this chapter, and we will look again at self-efficacy beliefs and the experiences that strengthen them in Chapter 12.

What about *narcissism*? Narcissus, a figure from Greek mythology, fell in love with his own beautiful reflection, and wasted his life pining after his own reflected image. In the past it was not uncommon for self-concept researchers to define narcissism as "excessive self-esteem," but the evidence now shows that these are different characteristics, developing from different experiences. People who score high on measures of narcissism "feel superior to others, believe they are entitled to privileges, and crave respect and admiration from others" (Brummelman, Thomaes, & Sedikides, 2016, p. 8). Narcissists feel that they are better than other people; they often try to dominate or use others to meet their own needs and seek to be the center of attention. If others are admiring and respectful, they feel great; but if not, or if they are humiliated, they often lash out aggressively. Narcissists are more likely to behave delinquently to get what they want than non-narcissists.

In contrast, people who score high on measures of self-esteem are happy with themselves, but they don't see themselves as superior. They are more likely to try to build good relationships with others than to dominate them. It's not impossible to have narcissistic tendencies and to have high self-esteem (or at least to report that you do; see Brookes, 2015), but most narcissists are vulnerable to slights or criticism, suggesting that their apparent self-esteem is fragile.

How do children develop narcissistic traits? One longitudinal study provides some clues (Brummelman et al., 2015). Children ranged from ages 7 to 11 at the initial assessment, and the researchers re-evaluated the children and their parents every 6 months after that for two years. Children rated statements that could reveal narcissism (e.g., "Kids like me deserve something extra") and self-esteem (e.g., "Kids like me are happy with themselves as a person"). Both children and parents rated statements about parents' warmth and affection (e.g., "My mother lets me know that she loves me" or "I let my child know that I love her"), and parents rated statements that could reveal tendencies to "overvalue" their children (e.g., "My child is more special than other children").

The researchers found very different pathways to narcissism compared to self-esteem. Corroborating other research, warm, supportive parenting predicted high self-esteem as children matured. But children's narcissism was not related to parents' warmth. Narcissism was predicted by parents' overvaluing of their children. Always keep in mind, of course, that causal processes are multidimensional. Parenting behaviors interact with other child and environmental characteristics. So, for example, narcissistic traits are also more likely to develop in children who are more impulsive than other children (Cramer, 2017). In the Applications section, you will learn about the pitfalls of praise that overvalues a child or that can otherwise be problematic for a child's self-development.

Gender, Race, Ethnicity, and Self-Esteem Differences

GENDER

Much attention has been paid to the apparent decrease in self-esteem experienced by females around the time of their entrance to middle school. This phenomenon has been called the "loss of voice" by Gilligan and her colleagues (Brown & Gilligan, 1992), who purport that a girl experiences a gradual silencing of an authentic, imperious, and often willful self in order to identify with certain culturally prescribed roles of women as self-sacrificial and pleasing to others. Speaking one's mind, at least for women in certain contexts, can be threatening to the relationships that are such an important part of their lives. These authors argue that suppressing one's voice becomes the only possible way of maintaining important connections to others. In time, they conclude, women become disassociated from their true selves and may lose touch with their own opinions and feelings. Comparably negative claims of gender bias or silencing have been directed toward schools for "shortchanging" girls by giving them less attention than boys and for attributing their academic failure to lack of ability rather than to lack of effort (Ornstein, 1994; Sadker & Sadker, 1991). Popular accounts of these reports have contributed to the notion that the self-esteem of girls plunges precipitously around the early adolescent period, whereas that of boys remains robust.

What actually happens to girls' level of "voice" and to their views of themselves in late childhood and early adolescence? Are gender differences in self-regard real and universal? First, let's consider studies of girls' versus boys' level of voice. Harter and colleagues (Harter, Waters, Whitesell, & Kastelic, 1998) assessed level of voice by asking 9th to 11th graders to rate how able they feel to "express their opinions," "share what they are really thinking," and so on. They also asked the teens about whether others—parents, teachers, male classmates, female classmates, and close friends—listen to their opinions, respect their ideas, and show interest in their views. Finally, the researchers measured "relational self-worth" with different groups of people, asking respondents to say whether they liked or didn't like themselves the way they are around different people in their lives, such as parents or friends. The results support Gilligan's ideas about the importance of voice for self-esteem, but they do not support her notion that girls are more subject to "voice suppression" than boys. Levels of voice were the same for both girls and boys with teachers, parents, and male classmates. But with female classmates and close friends, girls reported a stronger level of voice than boys did! For neither gender did level of voice decline with age, and for both genders, level of voice varied dramatically depending on whether the adolescent felt support for self-expression. For both girls and boys, feelings of self-worth varied with level of voice: In social contexts where kids felt like they could express themselves freely, they felt more self-worth.

Many more recent studies buttress the conclusion that girls are *not* more likely than boys to lose their "voice" in adolescence (see Faraday, 2010). For example, a large-scale survey of 10- to 30-year-olds examined their reported general willingness to "go along" with peers even when they do not agree with them. Females overall reported more self-reliance: They were less likely to change their behavior to conform with peer pressure than males (Steinberg & Monahan, 2007).

Now, what about the claim that girls' overall self-worth declines in late childhood and early adolescence? Many studies of developmental change in self-esteem establish that for *both* girls and boys, self-esteem begins to decline in late childhood, levels off in late adolescence and begins a slow, moderate climb in young adulthood, peaking in the sixth decade of life and then declining again (see Helwig & Rupricht, 2017; Orth, 2017). And, there is a gender difference. As you can see in Figure 7.2, girls' self-esteem drops more in late childhood than boys' does, and there is a small but significant difference between females and males until late adulthood. For example, one group of

FIGURE 7.2 Self-esteem for males and females across the life span.

SOURCE: Robins, R. W., Trzesnlewski, K. H., Tracy, J. L., Gosling, S. D., & Potter, J. (2002). Global self-esteem across the life span. *Psychology and Aging, 17,* 428.

researchers looked carefully at the data from two large studies of global self-esteem, which included a combined total of 155,121 participants (Kling, Hyde, Showers, & Buswell, 1999). They found that males showed higher self-esteem. Another group of researchers who included nearly a million participants found the same gender difference in countries around the world (Bleidorn et al., 2016). The level of difference is typically small, however, compared to gender differences in aggressive behavior and activity level (Hyde & Else-Quest, 2012). The idea that girls' self-esteem plunges dramatically at adolescence relative to that of boys is overstated. Other studies even indicate that gender gaps in self-esteem for specific competency areas favor girls in some domains (e.g., behavioral conduct) and boys in other domains (e.g., sports); they usually appear in early elementary school, and do not increase in magnitude at adolescence (Gentile et al., 2009; Jacobs, Lanza, Osgood, Eccles, & Wigfield, 2002). For both girls and boys, weight and physical attractiveness are important predictors of self-esteem as early as 9 years old, but more so for girls (Harter, 2012; see Chapter 9). In fact, decline in body satisfaction with the onset of puberty appears to make an important contribution to declining self-esteem in early adolescence (Cribb & Haase, 2016).

The small but stable gender difference in global self-esteem should be taken seriously, but Kling and her colleagues (1999) caution that inflating the significance of the self-esteem slide may create a self-fulfilling prophecy. Adults who believe that girls have lower self-esteem than boys may convey this impression to girls in subtle but powerful ways. Girls may internalize this message and alter their self-appraisals accordingly. In addition, championing the self-esteem deficits of girls may lead some to conclude that boys do not have self-esteem problems. Clearly, there are gender role strains for boys as well. For example, they are more likely than girls to feel social pressure to conform to gender stereotypes (Yunger, Carver, & Perry, 2004). Also, as noted earlier, boys are more vulnerable to peer pressure than girls (e.g., Steinberg & Monahan, 2007). Boys who are not athletically inclined can suffer greatly in social status and self-esteem relative to their peers (Kilmartin, 1994). In Chapters 8 and 9, we will examine other facets of the link between gender and self-evaluation.

RACE AND ETHNICITY

For many years it was assumed that the self-esteem of minority group children would be lower than that of White children because of their minority status in North American culture. This interpretation was based on Cooley's idea of reflected appraisals and social comparison processes. Members of oppressed groups, for example, would be more likely than members of non-oppressed groups to internalize the discriminatory appraisals of others in constructing their sense of self. Similarly, social comparisons would be more negative when oppressed minorities held themselves to the standards of the majority culture (see Zuckerman, Li, & Hall, 2016). Large studies of self-esteem have challenged these interpretations by demonstrating a slight but relatively consistent self-esteem advantage for Black Americans, the minority group most extensively studied, over White Americans (Gray-Little & Hafdahl, 2000; Twenge & Crocker, 2002).

Several explanations have been proposed to account for this phenomenon. Crocker and Major (1989) posit that, to maintain their self-esteem, members of historically marginalized groups engage in three complementary processes. They attribute negative feedback directed toward them to the prejudice that exists in society. They make social comparisons to members of their own group rather than to members of the advantaged majority. Finally, they tend to enhance the importance of self-concept domains in which members of their group excel, while discounting the importance of domains in which their members do not excel.

Black Americans are also less likely to show a gender difference in self-esteem. Zuckerman et al. (2016) suggest that specific aspects of Black American culture and experience may be important here. For example, within the Black community, appearance standards for women are somewhat different than in the White majority culture, and they may be easier to reach. Also, Black males may be more marginalized or stigmatized by the majority culture than Black females are. When Gray-Little and Hafdahl

(2000) summarized the existing data on this subject, they concluded that Blacks and other minority groups demonstrate a higher level of ethnocentrism than do Whites. In other words, racial identification is a more salient component of self-concept for members of these groups (see Chapter 9). Black Americans, in particular, may benefit from this emphasis on their desirable distinctiveness within the larger society (Orth, 2017). In fact, strong racial or ethnic identity correlates positively with level of global self-esteem (Harris-Britt, Valrie, Kurtz-Costes, & Rowley, 2007).

It is important to realize, however, that these results cannot be generalized to members of all minority groups, nor even to all members within a single minority. Gray-Little and Hafdahl (2000) make the important point that race is a complex construct, confounded with socioeconomic status, culture, gender, and other important variables. Using race as a dividing criterion to compare groups is appealing because it seems so simple, but it may mask great within-group variability. How individual differences arise within cultural/racial groups is now an important focus of research. For example, Bean, Bush, McKenny, and Wilson (2003) found that maternal support and acceptance are key factors in both academic achievement and the development of global self-esteem in African American youth, more so than paternal support. These researchers suggest that mothers play an especially central role in many African American families, and mothers' influence on youngsters' self-esteem is commensurate with that role.

Cross-Cultural Differences in the Development of the Self

As you have seen, very young children learn about themselves largely in the contexts of relationships with parents and other caregivers (Chapter 3). As children get older and their perspective taking skills improve, peer assessments, peer acceptance, and social comparisons become increasingly more important. The construction of self-concept is a social process, and any social process is conditioned by culture. The judgments, beliefs, values, and expectations of others—parents, teachers, and peers—are embedded in sociocultural meanings and practices. For example, parents in a culture that emphasizes individuality might value "knowing your own mind," identifying your own interests, and learning how to make your own choices. If so, their parenting practices are likely to promote independence, encouraging children to formulate and express their own opinions, interests, and needs, and to participate in family decision making. Parents from a more collectivist culture that emphasizes interdependence might place more value on conformity, respect for others, and group harmony. If so, their parenting practices might discourage children from identifying or expressing their own opinions and interests, but rather encourage them to be obedient and to concern themselves with supporting the needs of the family.

Such cultural differences suggest that the "self" that develops in one culture will be different from the self that would develop in a different culture. To illustrate, let's examine self-concept and self-esteem in individualistic as compared to collectivist cultures. Table 7.2 lists just a few of the values and expectations that characterize each of these cultural types. Western societies, and especially the United States, are typical of individualistic cultures, whereas Eastern societies, such as China and Japan, and many other regions of the world are more collectivist. Such categorizations are often overly simplistic, however, as we noted in Chapter 1. There are elements of both individualism and collectivism in all societies, and there are many shared values across cultures. For example, relationships with others are central to human functioning in all cultural environments, but the typical approaches to relating may vary. In more individualistic cultures, for example, people may feel comfortable seeking relationships with new partners, whereas in collectivist cultures, loyalty to in-group members (such as family) is often the primary path to meeting relationship needs. Needs for autonomy also appear to be important across cultures, but what contributes to feelings of autonomy may differ substantially. For example, in a more collectivist context, accepting the choices that trusted others make for you may feel as "right" for the individual as making your own choices does in a more individualistic setting (see Miller, Goyal, &

TABLE 7.2 Individualistic and Collectivist Cultures: Differences in Values and Emphases

INDIVIDUALISTIC	COLLECTIVIST
Becoming autonomous and self-reliant is important; this includes separating from others and following one's unique course, making one's own choices.	Relatedness rather than autonomy is emphasized; personal choices are subordinated to the needs of the group.
Personal opinions, ideas, experiences, and feelings are important; their open, articulate expression is valued.	Perspective taking and identifying group needs are more valued than self-expression.
Social relationships serve personal goals.	Social relationships are more important than personal goals; social harmony with close others (in-group) is the ultimate value.
Achievement and competitive advantage are closely linked; they indicate ability and are self-enhancing; failure is negative.	Achievement is an indicator of both hard work and social support; failure provides information about avenues for self-improvement.

Wice, 2017). It is also important to recognize that there are cultural differences among subgroups within countries and regions (e.g., among socioeconomic, racial, or ethnic groups), and there can be substantial differences among individuals and families within groups (e.g., Carey & Markus, 2017).

See Table 3.5 (Chapter 3) and Table 5.4 (Chapter 5) for examples related to caregiving behaviors and parents' values.

When there are cultural differences in patterns of social behavior, what effects do they have on children's developing self-concepts? In more individualistic contexts, independence is a central element of the self. Separateness, personal choice, and standing out from others are part of this independent pattern (e.g., Markus, 2017). "Standing out" is often made possible through achievement, and having pride in one's achievements is expected. That would suggest that seeing yourself as better than others in some ways would be important, and therefore seeing yourself in a positive light (high self-esteem) would also be important. Sure enough, from middle childhood onward, North Americans are more likely than people from Eastern cultures to report high self-esteem and to use self-enhancement strategies, such as downward comparisons, to help maintain their positive self-views (Heine & Hammamura, 2007). Even by age 4, Western children refer more to themselves in their narratives, and they make larger drawings of themselves, than children from more collectivist cultures (Schroder, Tõugu, Lenk, & De Gee, 2011). Western children are also more willing to express their own opinions and reactions, including emotional ones (Harter, 2012).

Children and adults in many Eastern societies are more likely than those from Western societies to incorporate the characteristics of close family and friends into their self-concepts rather than emphasizing their own uniqueness (Markus, 2017). A striking illustration of this comes from a study of the neural processes involved in self-representation (Zhu, Zhang, Fan, & Han, 2007). Participants judged whether traits (e.g., brave, childish) were true of themselves, true of their mothers, or true of distant others (President Clinton for U.S. participants; a former Chinese premier for Chinese participants). fMRIs indicated that when Chinese individuals made judgments about themselves the same area of the cortex was activated as when they made judgments about their mothers. Different cortical areas were activated when they judged more distant others. For U.S. participants, the cortical areas activated when they judged themselves were distinct from the areas that were activated when they made judgments about either their mothers *or* distant others.

Rather than being concerned with self-esteem as it is usually measured (e.g., rating oneself high on statements such as "I am proud of who I am"), people in Eastern cultures place more value on self-criticism and self-effacement (Diener & Diener, 2009). Negative self-evaluations are less likely to be associated with emotional problems (such as depressive tendencies) and more likely to spur self-improvement efforts (Heine et al., 2001). Hard work and achievement are important indicators of self-improvement, but they are seen as intimately related to others' efforts, not just one's own. Pride in personal accomplishments is often interpreted as arrogance; self-respect depends more on having harmonious relationships.

FIGURE 7.3 Cultural differences in views of the self.

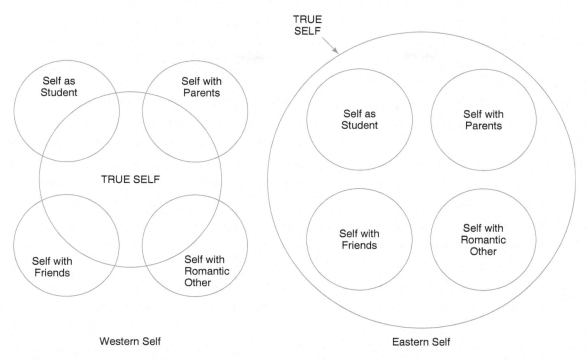

SOURCE: Harter, S. (2011). *The construction of the self: Developmental and sociocultural foundations* (2nd ed.). New York, NY: Guilford Press. Used by permission of Guilford Press.

Overall, in Eastern cultures the concept of the self *includes* relationships with others; a person's roles in, and duties to, the in-group are part of the self. Relationships for Western children and adults are not as central to self-concept. They are more like voluntary connections that serve personal needs, and they can be given up or changed (Markus, 2017). Western children and adolescents may strive to be like someone else, but that kind of identification process (see Chapters 9 and 10) is not the same as incorporating relational processes into the self-concept. A study of thousands of people's Facebook habits seems to demonstrate these cultural differences (Hong & Na, 2017). The researchers found that Eastern participants gave more "likes" than Western participants, suggesting more attention to others. Western participants made more "status updates" than Eastern participants, suggesting that they focused more on their individual behavior. Figure 7.3 illustrates some of these differences in self-concept for developing independent and interdependent self-schemas.

MyLab Education Self-Check 7.1.

The Moral Self

7.2 Discuss classic and contemporary views of moral development as well as factors that promote prosocial and antisocial behavior and suggest interventions to encourage healthy development in middle childhood and early adolescence.

One important ingredient in self-development is the acquisition of values. Colby and Damon (1992) found that adults who lead exemplary lives tend to have very clear beliefs about what is right, and they consider those beliefs to be a central feature of their own identities. Their self-esteem hinges on acting in responsible ways, consistent with their beliefs. As early as age 5, a child's view of herself as a moral person predicts good behavior (Kochanska, Koenig, Barry, Kim, & Yoon, 2010). For children in the middle years, behavioral conduct is an important self-concept domain that is linked to global self-esteem. Generally, moral beliefs are increasingly central to self-definition as children get older, influencing them to act in responsible ways, but as Damon (1995) points out,

> the development of the self can take many paths, and persons vary widely in the extent to which they look to their commitments and convictions in defining their personal identities. . . . For some . . . morality may always remain peripheral to who they think they are. (p. 141)

In this section, we will examine some theories and research on how the moral self develops and why for some it is more compelling than for others.

Let's begin by specifying what we mean by a moral sense, or morality. First, it is a capacity to make judgments about what is right versus what is wrong, and second, it is preferring to act in ways that are judged to be "right." In other words, morality involves both an "evaluative orientation" toward actions and events (Damon, 1988) and a sense of obligation or commitment to behave in ways that are consistent with what is right. Early on, this sense of obligation is partly influenced by rewards or punishments from parents, teachers, and other adults. Gradually, a slate of standards and principles—a *conscience*—is internalized (see discussion of self-regulation in Chapters 4 and 5) and becomes the primary guide to action, so that a moral adult could even behave in ways that are disapproved by others if she judged the behavior to be right (Krettenauer & Victor, 2017).

It is also important to recognize that moral development and religious experience are not the same thing. Religions do, of course, address issues of morality, and they prescribe standards of conduct. But moral development is part of normal self-development in all individuals, regardless of whether they are practitioners of a religious faith or whether they receive formal religious training.

As we noted in the introduction to this chapter, it is not surprising that parents regard the development of morality as a critical concern. Even though there are cultural and historical variations in the specifics of what is construed as moral, the meaning of morality generally includes some social interactive principles or propensities that are necessary to the successful functioning of all societies and of individuals within society (Damon, 1988; Killen & Smetana, 2008; Sachdeva, Singh, & Medin, 2011; Turiel, 2015). First, concern for others is important, as well as a willingness to act on that concern by sharing, forgiving, and other acts of benevolence. Second, a sense of justice and fairness, including a willingness to take into account the rights and needs of all parties, is part of a moral sense. Third, trustworthiness, defined primarily as honesty in dealings with others, is critical to most discussions of morality. Finally, self-regulation (self-control) is essential. To live by standards requires a capacity and willingness to inhibit one's own selfish or aggressive impulses under some circumstances, that is, to avoid misbehavior. This is one aspect of self-regulation. Also, to be a useful member of society, or even to fully develop one's talents or abilities, requires effort and persistence regardless of discomfort or difficulty. This is a second aspect of self-regulation—a willingness to do things that are not much fun, such as work and practicing skills, even when play is more enticing. For example, there may be no exciting way to learn multiplication tables. Hard work and self-control are necessary to achieve long-term goals at any point in the life span. Research on the development of morality has largely focused on this set of fundamentals: concern for others, justice, trustworthiness or honesty, and self-control.

Elements of Morality

Morality requires a complex interweaving of three elements—emotions, cognitions, and behaviors—that do not always work together in perfect harmony. Consider the following true-life experience. Several decades ago, in a blue-collar city neighborhood, 10-year-old Carmen headed for a local grocery store to buy some items for her mother. Her family never saw her alive again. But some other folks later did see her. They were motorists, driving at high speeds on an inner-city expressway, heading home in the evening rush hour. They remembered seeing a girl who looked like Carmen, running naked along the edge of the expressway with a man following her. Apparently, she had escaped from his car when he parked along the side of the road. But none of the motorists stopped, and the man caught the girl. Her raped and beaten body was later found in a remote location.

In the days and weeks following Carmen's disappearance, first one motorist and then another either phoned police anonymously or came forward openly to describe what she or he had seen, although none had reported the incident when it happened. The city's inhabitants were horrified both by the crime and by the failure of the witnesses to help or to come forward immediately, but none were more distressed than the witnesses themselves. Their moral emotions—empathy and sympathy for the girl and her family, shame and guilt at their own failure to come to the girl's aid—were experienced by many as overwhelming. These feelings in many cases were triggered from the beginning, when they first saw the naked child. Why did their behavior not match their feelings? Many witnesses reported confusion and disbelief when they passed the strange scene, and though they felt concern for the girl and guilt at their own inaction, they reasoned that there must be a sensible explanation, one that would make them feel foolish if they made the extraordinary effort to stop. Others indicated that it was impossible to process the events—so unexpected and atypical of their ordinary experience—in the split second of decision making, and they had only "put it all together" when they heard about Carmen's disappearance on the news. Others thought that someone else would take care of it—after all, hundreds of motorists were passing the same spot—or that the risks of helping were too great.

Most adults believe that their behavior is usually consistent with their beliefs or feelings. But the witnesses to Carmen's plight illustrate that even adults with strong moral feelings do not always think clearly about moral issues or behave in ways that are consistent with their moral sense. Some of the earliest research on children's moral development indicated that children are particularly prone to such inconsistencies. Hartshorne and May (1928–1930) observed 10,000 children between the ages of 8 and 16 in a wide variety of situations where they had opportunities to lie, cheat, or steal. For example, children could raise their scores on a test by sneaking a look at an answer key, cheat on a test of strength, pilfer some change, or tell lies that would place them in a good light. In every situation, the researchers had devised techniques to surreptitiously detect cheating, lying, or stealing. They found that children's knowledge of moral standards did not coordinate with how likely they were to cheat or to help others to cheat. They also found that children's honesty varied from one situation to another. Some children cheated in academic tasks, for example, but not on tests of athletic skill. Hartshorne and May concluded that moral conduct is usually determined by the particular situation and is not coordinated with moral reasoning or training. However, more recent research, with more adequate measures of children's emotions and cognitions, indicates that emotions, cognitions, and actions do tend to become more synchronized with age and that their interrelations are influenced by many factors, including training.

Before we consider these many factors, let's take a brief look at some classic theories of moral development with which you may be familiar, theories that emphasize either emotions or cognitions as the most important source of moral behavior. How do these theories fare in light of modern research?

Some Classic Theories of Moral Development

FREUD'S PSYCHOANALYTIC THEORY

In Freud's (1935/1960) psychoanalytic theory of moral development, the behavior of very young children is driven by the inborn impulses of the id, which are completely self-serving desires for sustenance and release, such as hunger or the need to defecate.

The superego, which emerges in the preschool period, is the source of moral emotions, such as pride in good behavior and shame or guilt about bad behavior, and once a child has a superego, it is these emotions that impel moral functioning, like an internalized system of rewards and punishments. Freud argued that the superego develops when a complex set of id-driven motives and emotions come into conflict with parental authority. Specifically, beginning at about age 3, vague sexual desire for the opposite-sex parent puts the young child in competition with the same-sex parent, who is much more powerful than the child and thus a frightening competitor. The child's solution to this no-win situation is to identify with the same-sex parent. Identification with the (imagined) aggressor is a solution for two reasons. First, by trying to be like the angry parent, a child wins the parent's approval and affection. Second, by pretending to be the parent, the child attains some vicarious satisfaction of her or his sexual longing for the other parent. The critical element of this situation for moral development is the identification process itself. Identification includes both imitation of the parent's behaviors and, most important, internalization of the parent's standards and values, creating the child's superego.

As we will see in the next chapter, the identification process described by Freud is an explanation of both moral development and sex role development in young children. Unfortunately, research fails to support its predictions. With regard to moral development, attributing moral emotions to the emergence of the superego, sometime between ages 3 and 5, is not consistent with findings that many toddlers show signs of empathy and shame as early as 18 to 24 months, beginning when they demonstrate self-recognition while looking in a mirror. By age 3, sympathy, pride, and guilt appear to be part of the emotional repertoire as well (see Chapters 4 and 5; Lewis, 2016b). In addition, even toddlers perform prosocial actions based on empathy (Kim & Kochanska, 2017) and sometimes they seem eager to comply with a parent's rules, even if the parent is not around (Kochanska, Tjebkes, & Forman, 1998; Turiel, 2006). Such early signs of conscience development undermine the psychoanalytic view that early behavior is driven only by selfish impulses. Finally, and perhaps most important, Freud argued that children develop a conscience because they identify with a parent whom they fear. Yet, as we saw in Chapter 5, parents who intimidate their children are least successful in fostering the development of conscience. Rather, warmth, affection, and support are more likely to be characteristic of parents whose children show signs of mature conscience formation—self-control in the absence of authority figures (Goffin, Boldt, & Kochanska, 2017; Thompson, 2015). We should note that psychoanalysts since Freud have increasingly explained conscience formation as linked to the bond between child and parent, that is, more as a function of the strength of attachment and the need to keep the parent close than as a function of fear (Emde, Johnson, & Easterbrooks, 1987).

THE COGNITIVE THEORIES OF PIAGET AND KOHLBERG

Whereas Freud focused on the impetus that emotions provide to moral behavior, cognitive theorists have emphasized the importance of changes in logical thinking as a source of moral development. To understand how children think about rules and standards of conduct, Piaget (1932/1965) presented children with moral dilemmas and asked them to both judge the behavior of the protagonists and explain what should be done. He also played marbles with children and asked them to describe and explain the rules of the game. Piaget proposed that preschoolers are premoral in the sense that they seem unconcerned about established rules or standards, making up their own as they go along in a game of marbles, for example, and having little regard even for their own rules. At about age 5, Piaget described children's morality as heteronomous. They regard rules as immutable, existing outside the self, and requiring strict adherence. So, 5-year-old Jasmine might argue that a rule should never be broken, even if some greater good might prevail or even if all the participants in a game agree to the change. When her older sister crosses the street without waiting for a "walk" signal, rushing to help a neighborhood toddler who has wandered into the street, Jasmine might insist that her sister should have waited for the signal no matter what. She might also judge that a boy who broke 15 cups trying to help his mother get ready for a party deserves more punishment than one who broke one cup while actually misbehaving. In heteronomous morality, the letter of the law must be followed, and failure to do so requires punishment. In fact, Jasmine might believe in immanent justice, expecting that misbehavior will eventually be punished, even if no one knows about it, as though some higher authority is always watching.

Piaget argued that heteronomy is based on the child's experiences in relationships with parents and other authority figures, where rules seem to come from above and must be obeyed. But in middle childhood, both experience with the give-and-take of peer relationships and advances in perspective taking skill help children to see the rules of behavior differently. As children and adolescents have more experience in egalitarian relationships with their peers, their moral thinking becomes more autonomous, meaning that they begin to understand that rules are based on social agreements and can be changed. Advancements in perspective taking skills, which also are benefited by interactions with peers, help young people understand that rules and standards are not just a function of authoritarian dictates but that they promote fair play and cooperation, serving to establish justice. They can also be set aside for some greater good or changed through negotiation. So, by about 9 or 10, Jasmine could support her sister's violation of their parents' rule about not crossing the street, recognizing the greater importance of protecting a younger child. Also, she would probably be more consistently well behaved than she was earlier, because, in Piaget's view, she has a better understanding of the value of rules and standards for social interaction.

Kohlberg (e.g., 1976, 1984) further investigated children's moral reasoning from late childhood into the adolescent and early adult years. His theory goes beyond Piaget's, offering a fine-grained analysis of changes in the older child's, adolescent's, and adult's reasoning about moral issues (see Table 7.3 for a comparison of ages and stages in Piaget's and Kohlberg's theories). Unlike Piaget's dilemmas, which focused on everyday challenges familiar in the lives of children, Kohlberg's stories were outside ordinary experience and raised broad philosophical issues. Perhaps the most famous of these is the story of Heinz, whose wife is very ill and will die without a certain medicine, which Heinz cannot afford. The druggist who makes the product refuses to sell it, though Heinz offers all the money he has managed to raise—about half of the retail cost—which would more than cover the druggist's expenses. The druggist argues that he discovered the drug and plans to make money from it. In desperation, Heinz breaks into the druggist's establishment and steals the medicine.

Kohlberg was not interested in whether participants judged Heinz's behavior to be right or wrong, assuming that reasonable people might disagree. He focused instead on the reasons they gave for their judgments. He found there to be three levels of moral reasoning, each characterized by two stages. At the first level, elementary school children usually show preconventional morality, roughly corresponding to Piaget's heteronomous level, in which what is right is what avoids punishment, what conforms to the dictates of authority, or what serves one's personal interests. Then, young adolescents move to conventional morality, more consistent with Piaget's autonomous level, in which what is right depends on others' approval or on the need to maintain social order. Finally, by adulthood, some people move to postconventional morality, in which right is defined by universal principles or by standards of justice, not by the particular rule in question (see Table 7.3 for further elaboration of the stages within each level).

Although individuals at different levels of moral reasoning might come to the same conclusion about what is "right," their explanations reveal that they come to their decisions by different routes. Compare the "pro-stealing" decisions of Jay and Jesse when given the "Heinz" dilemma to resolve. Jay, a preconventional thinker, bases his choice on personal need:

> Heinz should take the drug, because the druggist won't really suffer, and Heinz needs to save his wife.

Jesse, a conventional thinker, bases her decision on the importance of others' agreement or approval:

> Heinz should take the drug, because nobody would blame him for wanting to keep his wife alive. They might blame him if he didn't.

TABLE 7.3 Piaget's and Kohlberg's Stages of Moral Development

APPROXIMATE AGES	PIAGET'S STAGES	KOHLBERG'S STAGES
Preschool	*Premoral Period* Child is unconcerned about rules; makes up her own rules.	
		Preconventional Level
5 to 8 or 9 years	*Heteronomous Morality* Child is a *moral realist:* Rules are determined by authorities; are unalterable, moral absolutes; must be obeyed. Violations always punished.	*Stage 1: Punishment and Obedience Orientation* Child obeys to avoid punishment and because authority is assumed to be superior or right. Rules are interpreted literally; no judgment is involved.
8 or 9 to 11 or 12 years	*Autonomous Morality* Social rules are arbitrary, and promote cooperation, equality, and reciprocity; therefore, they serve justice. They can be changed by agreement or violated for a higher purpose.	*Stage 2: Concrete, Individualistic Orientation* Child follows rules to serve own interests. Others' interests may also need to be served, so follow the principle of fair exchange, e.g., "You scratch my back, I scratch yours."
		Conventional Level
13 to 16 years		*Stage 3: Social-Relational Perspective* Shared feelings and needs are more important than self-interest. Helpfulness, generosity, and forgiveness are idealized.
Late adolescents/young adults		*Stage 4: Member-of-Society Perspective* The social order is most important now. Behaviors that contribute to functioning of the social system are most valued, e.g., obeying laws, hard work.
		Postconventional Level
Some adults		*Stage 5: Prior Rights and Social Contract* The social contract now is most valued. Specific laws are not most valued, but the process that they serve is, e.g., democratic principles, individual rights.
Some adults		*Stage 6: Universal Ethical Principles* Certain abstract moral principles are valued over anything else, e.g., above specific laws. Social order is also highly valued, unless it violates highest moral principles. (Theoretical; Kohlberg's subjects did not achieve this stage.)

MyLab Education

Video Example 7.2

Young children tend to state that people should not cheat because they'll be punished, whereas older children and adolescents are more likely to consider the reasons one might cheat as well as possible alternative actions. How would you classify each of these four children, according to the theories presented by Piaget and by Kohlberg?

There is some research support for the general trends in moral reasoning suggested in the work of Piaget and of Kohlberg. Consistent with Piaget's view, for example, when young children judge moral culpability they usually pay more attention to consequences (e.g., the number of cups broken by a child who is helping his mother prepare for a party), whereas older children pay more attention to intentions (e.g., whether the child was helping or misbehaving). Consistent with Kohlberg's view, young people around the world progress through the stages of the preconventional and conventional levels of moral reasoning in the same, invariant order. Cross-cultural differences are more likely to be found at Kohlberg's higher stages: The few who reach Stage 5 of the postconventional level are most often Western, middle-class, urban adolescents and adults (for reviews, see Gibbs, Basinger, Grime, & Snarey, 2007; Jensen, 2008; Snarey, 1985).

Perhaps most important, the roles of perspective taking and peer interactions in the growth of moral reasoning skills, emphasized both by Piaget and by Kohlberg, have been supported. For example, advances in perspective taking skills such as those described in Chapter 5 generally precede, although they do not guarantee, advances in moral reasoning (Jambon & Smetana, 2014; see Killen & Smetana, 2015). Also, when children discuss moral issues with their peers they are more likely to think carefully about the ideas and to advance in their reasoning than when they discuss those issues with adults (Kruger, 1992; Kruger & Tomasello, 1986). Perhaps challenges from a peer may seem less threatening and create less defensiveness than challenges from adults (Walker & Taylor, 1991).

LIMITATIONS OF CLASSIC COGNITIVE THEORIES

Despite the support that these cognitive approaches to explaining moral development have received, their usefulness is limited in several ways. First, young children have a greater capacity for moral reasoning than Piaget's theory indicates. For example, although young children judge people's actions by their physical consequences (such as how many cups are broken) more than older children do, still they are capable of focusing on the intentions behind behavior if those intentions are made salient (Zelazo, Helwig, & Lau, 1996). In one study, even preschoolers could tell the difference between intentional lying and unintentional mistakes, and they judged real liars more harshly than bunglers (Siegel & Peterson, 1998).

Another important challenge to Piaget's theory is the finding that young children do not necessarily treat all rules and standards as equally important just because they are specified as such by parents or other authority figures. Moral philosophers point out that some standards, called **moral rules**, address fundamental moral issues of justice, welfare, and rights, such as rules about stealing, hurting others, or sharing. Other standards, called **conventional rules**, are more arbitrary and variable from one culture to another and are a function of social agreement, such as gender norms or rules about appropriate dress, forms of address, and table manners. Finally, there are areas of functioning that individuals or families might have standards about—such as choices of friends or recreational activities or participation in family life—which are not governed by formal social rules in Western societies. We'll call these **personal rules** (Nucci, 2014; Turiel, 2015). Piaget assumed that young children treat all rules as "handed down from above," that is, as determined by authority figures. But even by age 3, children are more likely to judge violations of moral rules as more serious than violations of conventional rules (Smetana & Braeges, 1990). By ages 4 or 5 children believe that moral rules should be obeyed despite what authority figures might say (e.g., Crane & Tisak, 1995). For example, at 5, Jasmine believed it would be wrong to steal even if there were no laws against it and even if a friend's mother said it was okay. As children get older, they make clearer and clearer distinctions between moral and conventional rules, so that by age 9 or 10 children accurately categorize even unfamiliar rules (Davidson, Turiel, & Black, 1983). Turiel (1978) reexamined data from Hartshorne and May's (1928–1930) classic study of children's honesty and found that the participants were much more likely to cheat in academic tasks than they were to steal when given an easy opportunity. He argued that children probably saw the academic tasks as governed by conventional rules, whereas stealing more clearly violates a moral rule.

By adolescence, children assume that their parents have a right to regulate and enforce moral behavior. They usually accept parents' regulation of conventional behavior as well, although there is more conflict with their parents in this domain than in the moral arena. Finally, with regard to personal issues such as appearance, spending, and friendship choices, adolescents balk at parental regulation, often arguing that parents have no legitimate authority in this domain (Rote & Smetana, 2016; Turiel, 2017). Interestingly, Arnett (1999) argues that parents may push for their right to control personal behavior more as a function of how they judge that behavior (e.g., in some instances they may see it as crossing over into the moral domain) than because they are reluctant to grant their children personal freedom. So, in other words, parents and adolescents may differ in how they categorize rules and regulations. We address this issue again in Chapter 10.

Given what you have learned about cultural differences in self-concept development, you might wonder if children and adolescents make the same distinctions about personal, conventional, and moral domains of behavior in collectivist cultures as they do in the United States and other Western societies. The general answer to that question is "Yes." As Jensen (2008) notes, "children in many parts of the world recognize that not all issues are of the same hue" (p. 295). Even in the preschool years, children across cultures make a distinction between some foundational moral rules (e.g., it's wrong to hit or rob an innocent child) and more conventional or personal ones (e.g., it's wrong to eat soup with your fingers). If moral rules are in conflict with conventional rules, the moral rules are likely to win, regardless of culture. For example, in a study of both Korean and U.S. children, 5-, 7-, and 9-year-olds were willing to violate gender norms (e.g., boys wearing dresses) if the behavior were in service of a higher moral purpose (e.g., helping others; Conry-Murray, Kim, & Turiel, 2015). But there is also substantial disagreement across cultures about the categorization of some behaviors. For example, in some parts of the world honoring a deathbed promise is a moral imperative, whereas Westerners are more likely to see it as a conventional rule.

Like Piaget's theory, Kohlberg's view may have some important limitations. When moral issues beyond the legalistic ones studied by Kohlberg are examined, both adults' and children's reasoning seems to include factors not described by Kohlberg. Gilligan (e.g., 1977, 1982) has argued that moral development follows different trajectories for males and females. She views Kohlberg's legalistic moral dilemmas and his approach to scoring people's reasoning as biased toward representing a more typically masculine approach to morality. Her concern is that Kohlberg's theory and the research it inspires tends to disregard the "different voice" women use in their approach to moral decision making. Males, she argues, are more likely to use a justice focus (sometimes called the **morality of justice**), whereas females are more likely to use a caring focus (**morality of caring**).

In her own research on moral reasoning, Gilligan (1977; Gilligan & Attanucci, 1988) included more practical dilemmas that are representative of the complex problems real people face, such as struggling with how to deal with an unplanned pregnancy. Although she found no significant differences in moral orientation (care vs. justice) between males and females, she did report some tendency in her data for men to focus on issues of justice and for women to focus on caring issues. However, her major finding has been that both women and men are concerned about both justice and caring and that together these concerns contribute to mature moral reasoning. A substantial body of research supports this conclusion (see Turiel, 2006). Perhaps the most valuable contribution of Gilligan's critique of Kohlberg's work is that she raised awareness of the need to study real-life moral problem solving and addressed the role that concerns about caring play in moral judgments. You will not be surprised to learn that concerns about care are universal, but that people in different cultures often focus on different aspects of care in their moral reasoning. For example, in many Eastern cultures, children and adults are more likely to emphasize the importance of role-based duties, whereas Westerners more often refer to interpersonal feelings when discussing care concerns (Miller, 2006).

Many researchers have studied children's thinking about real-life dilemmas in a child's world and have found that children consider matters of fairness even at ages when Kolhberg's scheme assumed they would not (Damon 1988; Sloane, Baillargeon, & Premack, 2012; Killen & Smetana, 2015). For example, in studies of sharing and distributive justice, preschoolers and young school-aged children rarely justify acts of sharing on the basis of concern about punishment, as one might expect if they were at Kohlberg's preconventional stage. Rather, they talk about fairness, and if their actions do not quite measure up to what we might consider fair, they at least seem to feel a need to somehow explain why their selfish choices might actually be fair.

To illustrate, Damon (1988) describes a conversation between a 4-year-old and a researcher who asks the child if she would share some poker chips with an imaginary friend. The child initially decides to keep seven of nine chips, including all the blue ones and some of the white ones, and gives her friend "Jenny" two white ones. She explains that her "friend" is younger and that she herself has a blue dress, so clearly she should have the blue ones, and also that she is 4 and so should have four of the white ones. Even though the child's reasoning cannot disguise her blatant self-interest, she seems to feel an obligation to share (she gives away some white ones), and she wants to believe that she is being fair.

Even toddlers appear to have an incipient sense of fairness, showing surprise when rewards are not distributed evenly to equally deserving individuals (Sloane et al., 2012). Younger children seem to be most focused on equal distribution. But older children, still at a preconventional level of reasoning in Kohlberg's scheme, often try to balance a complex set of concerns in deciding what is fair, and these concerns are not captured by Kohlberg's descriptions. Children may now take into account hard work, poverty, talent, in-group versus out-group membership, and issues of equality when trying to assess the best ways of distributing property or remuneration (Rutland & Killen, 2017; Shaw, Chosen-Hillel, & Caruso, 2016; see Killen & Smetana, 2015 for a review). Which of these many factors children focus on most is influenced by culture. For example, Schäfer and her colleagues (2015) looked at how 4- to 11-year-olds from several cultures distributed rewards after completing a "fishing" task with a peer. Across cultures, older children considered merit (how many "fish" each child caught) more often than younger children. But children from a competitive, Western (German) culture emphasized merit much more heavily than children from an egalitarian culture (a forager society in rural Namibia). These Namibian children chose to distribute rewards more equally regardless of merit. Another limitation of Kohlberg's work seems to be his assumption that moral reasoning is the prime determiner of children's moral behavior. As we have seen, moral reasoning is only imperfectly coordinated with action. Yet helpers who work with parents and teachers are often most concerned with encouraging children's moral behavior. In the next section, we will examine the many factors that influence children's prosocial or antisocial behavior.

Children's Prosocial Behavior

When a child voluntarily acts in ways that seem intended to benefit someone else, we credit her with prosocial behavior or altruism. Although prosocial behaviors are observed even in toddlers, they tend to increase with age, from preschool to grade school ages and continuing into adolescence (Eisenberg & Fabes, 1998). Altruistic tendencies are different from one child to another, and individual differences tend to be somewhat stable across age. In other words, a child who shows prosocial inclinations as a preschooler is somewhat more likely than other children to produce prosocial behavior in grade school.

Sharing, comforting a friend, helping a neighbor carry her groceries, collecting canned goods for victims of a flood—all are examples of simple prosocial behaviors that we might see from a child. You can probably see that whereas behaviors such as these benefit others, they can be motivated in many ways, and they could even provide some social reward to the benefactor. Sharing, for example, can help a child maintain a pleasant interaction.

When 15-month-old Michelle went trick-or-treating for the first time, as soon as an indulgent neighbor would put a treat in her bag, Michelle would reach into the bag and offer the neighbor a treat as well. She seemed to be sharing, literally, for the fun of the social exchange. When a child successfully comforts a crying friend she might be trying to regain her playmate's company. Or when she participates in an organized effort to provide relief to flood victims she may be hoping for positive attention from teachers or parents. For developmentalists, labeling an action altruistic or prosocial only specifies that it benefits someone other than the actor, not that unselfish motives are necessarily involved. Let's consider what factors have been found to influence the development of prosocial action in children, with an eye toward understanding how helpers might be able to promote children's prosocial tendencies.

EMOTIONS AS A SOURCE OF HELPING BEHAVIOR

In many cases, our emotional reactions to others' distress can be an important source of helping behavior, and the emotion of empathy may be the linchpin (Hoffman, 1982; Kagan, 1984). Empathy can be thought of as "feeling with" another person—recognizing her emotional condition and experiencing what she is assumed to be feeling. Hoffman (1982) argued that children have a biological predisposition toward empathy, the earliest hint of which may be the contagious crying of some infants—that is, their tendency to cry when they hear other babies crying. If their mothers show distress, many toddlers will try to offer comfort (Kim & Kochanska, 2017). In fact, offering comfort when others show distress is common in chimps as well as humans (Cronin, 2012).

Sympathy, an emotion related to empathy, involves "feeling for" another: having concern for the other person, but not necessarily sharing the feelings of the other. Both empathy and sympathy seem to propel some prosocial acts from the time that toddlers begin to clearly differentiate self from other (Vaish, 2016). Children's empathic responses are also associated with their tendencies to inhibit antisocial behavior, as we will see in the next section. Toddlers' early helping behavior may be the result of their empathic feelings, but they still have little capacity to take another's point of view. Hoffman, for example, described the charmingly egocentric effort of a 13-month-old who sought out his own mother to comfort a crying toddler, even though the other child's mother was readily available.

Empathy and sympathy are evident in young children. However, their tendency to lead to effective prosocial action increases substantially with age, especially after the preschool years. Children's improving perspective taking skills are an important ingredient. One reason appears to be that better role-taking ability can help a child be more sensitive to subtle indicators of how another is feeling, which thereby increases the child's own empathic response. Also, increased understanding of another's emotions and thoughts should help a child assess what kind of prosocial action, if any, is likely to be beneficial (Eisenberg, Spinrad, & Knafo-Noam, 2015).

In late childhood, the scope of empathy expands, probably influenced by increasing abilities to think about abstractions. Whereas younger children can empathize with particular people whom they observe, older children and adolescents can empathize with whole groups of people who are living in unfortunate circumstances, such as all those suffering from a famine, or from the abrogation of their rights, and so on (Hoffman, 1982).

Clearly, as important as prosocial emotions may be for altruistic behavior, other influences interact with those emotions in complex ways. These include not only advances in cognitive abilities such as perspective taking and abstract thinking but also individual temperamental and personality characteristics, parenting practices, and peer experiences. Also, prosocial behavior involves more than helping another in need. Behavior such as Michelle's spontaneous sharing of her Halloween treats often occurs in the absence of any apparent need on the part of the other and therefore seems not to rest on emotions like empathy or sympathy. Let's take a look at some of the other factors that can influence prosocial action.

COGNITIVE CONTRIBUTIONS TO PROSOCIAL BEHAVIOR

Let's first consider how reasoning about other people's needs (called **needs-based reasoning**) changes with age, and then we will look at its relation to children's prosocial behavior. In needs-based reasoning, a person must weigh her own personal needs against those of others. For example, Eisenberg and her colleagues have posed moral dilemmas to children in which a child's needs are in competition with the needs of another. In one story, a child, on her way to a party, comes upon another child who has fallen and broken her leg. The first child must decide whether to continue on to the party, which is very important to her, or to find the parents of the injured child. (Compare this dilemma, focused on caring and concern, to Kohlberg's problems in social justice, like the story of Heinz and the druggist.) Eisenberg has found that preschoolers tend to be **hedonistic**—concerned for their own needs. By early elementary school, many children express recognition that another person's need is a good reason for helping—they are **needs oriented**—but they often do not express sympathy, nor do they talk about feeling guilty for not helping. By later elementary school, children begin to express recognition that helping is what is required or socially approved. At the next stage, in late elementary school or adolescence, expressions of sympathy for others, guilt about inaction, and, to some minimal degree, reference to duty, become part of the reasoning process. Finally, some adolescents begin talking about the relationship of helping to one's self-respect and about the need to be consistent with one's values. For these young people, it appears, moral values are becoming a core aspect of their self-concept (Eisenberg, Spinrad, & Sadovsky, 2006).

We have seen in our discussion of the cognitive theories of moral development that moral reasoning is somewhat related to moral behavior. If the kind of moral reasoning that is assessed is similar to the kind of moral behavior, there is a stronger (but still moderate) relationship between reasoning and behavior. This is particularly true of needs-based reasoning and altruistic behavior. In middle childhood and adolescence, more advanced levels of needs-based reasoning tend to be associated with certain kinds of prosocial behavior. Specifically, if the behavior requires some real personal sacrifice, such as volunteering some free time after school, kids whose moral reasoning is more advanced are more likely to participate. Prosocial behaviors that incur little or no cost, such as helping a teacher to pick up the papers she has just dropped, are likely to occur regardless of a child's moral reasoning (Eisenberg et al., 2015).

Interestingly, moral reasoning, which is likely to benefit from interaction with peers (Killen & Smetana, 2015), tends to be more advanced in popular children with good social skills, at least for boys. Bear and Rys (1994) found that boys who tended to be aggressive and to have poor peer relations were also low in needs-oriented reasoning. One explanation may be that children with poor social skills have fewer opportunities for positive peer interactions, contributing to a lag in the development of their moral-reasoning skills (see the discussion of bullying later in this chapter). A number of intervention programs designed to promote children's moral functioning, including prosocial behavior and self-control, are focused on using peer discussions. For example, Gibbs (1987; Gibbs, Potter, & DiBise, 2013) describes a technique using small, peer group discussions aimed at encouraging empathic responding in delinquents. Actual problem incidents are re-created and discussed, and both peers and adults provide feedback to a participant about their own emotional reactions to the incident and to the participant's attitudes and emotions. Many violence prevention programs incorporate components designed to foster empathy development.

It is important to note that for younger children whose moral reasoning is not very advanced, their tendency to engage in prosocial behavior is especially dependent on their prosocial emotions, empathy and sympathy, and the internal arousal they feel when help seems to be needed (Hepach, 2017; Vaish, 2016). Moral reasoning is not a key motivator. When children and adolescents have more advanced levels of prosocial reasoning, their reasoning is better matched to prosocial action regardless of how strong their prosocial emotions are, and it appears to be a more important motivating force (Eisenberg, Spinrad et al., 2006; Malti, Gummerum, Keller, & Buchmann, 2009). These findings demonstrate that different children can follow different paths to prosocial conduct, suggesting that counselors and other helpers should be able to gain inroads in moral development via more than one route.

TEMPERAMENT, PERSONALITY, AND PROSOCIAL BEHAVIOR

As we saw earlier, children who are prosocial in one situation are somewhat more likely than other children to be prosocial in other situations. Also, there is some consistency in the tendency to behave altruistically from early childhood through later childhood. These kinds of observations imply that temperamental or personality variables that are relatively stable across place and time might foster an "altruistic personality" (Eisenberg et al., 2015; Hill & Roberts, 2010). What might these characteristics be?

First, children's relative sociability or shyness might be an influence. Children who score low on social anxiety (behavioral inhibition or shyness) are a little more likely to help others than children who score high on this trait, especially when no one has requested their help, when assisting another requires initiating a social interaction, or when helping involves a stranger (Broeren, Muris, Diamantopoulou, & Baker, 2013).

Second, as we saw in our discussion of moral reasoning, socially competent children who are popular with peers tend to show greater empathy and prosocial behavior (Eisenberg et al., 2015). It is difficult to sort out which is cause and which is effect in this relationship, but it seems likely that social competence and prosocial behavior are mutually causal, with several other intervening influences involved as well. Children who are empathic, for example, may do better at perspective taking, making them more appealing social partners, and may have closer friendships. The opportunities this creates for peer interaction help boost their perspective taking skills, which in turn benefit their moral reasoning and empathy, and so on.

Another of these feedback loops may underlie a third link between personality and altruism: Older children and adolescents with positive self-esteem generally tend to be more helpful to strangers than other children. Feeling competent and secure may help a child both focus her attention on others and believe that her help will be effective. But helping others also seems to foster kids' feelings of competency and self-worth (Fu, Padilla-Walker, & Brown, 2017).

Assertiveness is a fourth personality variable tied to prosocial behavior. This characteristic helps illustrate that even though there is some tendency for individual children to be prosocial in many situations, there is also a great deal of situation-specific altruism. Assertive children, who will, for example, defend their possessions, are likely to be prosocial in situations in which no one has asked them to help, probably because offering assistance is, at least in part, an assertive act. Children who are unassertive are usually prosocial when it is requested of them, not when they must take the social initiative themselves. Their prosocial behavior seems to be based more on compliance than that of assertive children. It should be noted also that children whose behavior goes beyond assertiveness to being domineering are actually *less* likely than other children to behave altruistically, regardless of the situation (Eisenberg & Spinrad, 2014). Although assertiveness is positively linked to prosocial behavior, aggressiveness is not. Especially after the preschool years, aggressive children are less likely than others to behave prosocially (Eisenberg et al., 2015).

Finally, a child's capacity for self-regulation, which helps the child modulate her emotional reactions, may be important. You will recall that self-regulation includes effortful control, inhibiting a response that is "dominant" to perform a response that is less compelling. Eisenberg and Fabes (1992) hypothesized that although empathic emotions can motivate prosocial behavior, they can also be counterproductive if a child is overwhelmed by them. If the child cannot moderate such emotions, she might focus attention on her own discomfort, and doing so might reduce the chances of a sympathetic response to someone in need. Valiente and colleagues (2004) tested this hypothesis with 4- to 8-year-olds. Children watched a film about a girl who is burned in a fire and later endures cruel teasing by peers because of her scars. After the film, participants were asked about their "self-focused emotions"—feeling upset, scared, and so on—and about their sympathetic emotions—feeling concern, sadness for others, and so on. The children were also measured for effortful control. For example, they were asked to put together a puzzle "blind." The wooden shapes were covered by a cloth and children manipulated the pieces under the cloth (although it was possible to cheat by peeking at the pieces). How much time children persisted on puzzle solving without cheating or becoming distracted was the measure of effortful control. The higher children's scores were on effortful control, the better able they seemed to be at controlling their self-focused emotions during the film and the more sympathy they expressed.

PARENTS, PEERS, AND PROSOCIAL BEHAVIOR

In Chapter 5 we began an examination of parenting behaviors and of the development of self-control, compliance, prosocial behavior, and conscience in infants and preschoolers. We observed that these aspects of moral development are, on the whole, most effectively launched when parents are authoritative in their style: on one hand, warm, responsive, and sensitive in their caregiving and, on the other hand, demanding, requiring that children live up to standards and values appropriate to their level of maturity. The methods of control that seem to foster internalization of those standards and values in the long run involve mild power assertion, sufficient only to capture the child's attention but not to arouse a lot of anxiety, and induction (explaining why it is important to share, for example). It should be noted that parents who are demanding without warmth and sensitivity (the authoritarian style) may actually interfere with prosocial development. At least for toddlers, this parenting style has been associated with reductions in children's empathic responding (Eisenberg et al., 2015; Thompson, 2015). Extremes of negative parenting, resulting in child abuse, seem to suppress prosocial behavior. When abused toddlers and preschoolers see another child in distress, for example, they very rarely respond with sympathetic gestures. Rather, they are likely to respond with hostility and/or fear (Anthonysamy & Zimmer-Gembeck, 2007; Main & George, 1985).

In middle childhood and beyond, the same conclusions about what elements of parenting are most effective in promoting prosocial behavior (and inhibiting antisocial behavior) still apply (Padilla-Walker, Gustavo, Christensen, & Yorgason, 2012). There are also a number of other specific characteristics of parenting that seem to foster children's altruism. First, when parents have strong prosocial values, their children and adolescents are more likely to behave prosocially (Eisenberg et al., 2015). Similarly, adults who show unusual prosocial tendencies, such as rescuers of Nazi victims in Europe during World War II, frequently report having had parents who strongly valued caring and helping behaviors (Oliner & Oliner, 1988).

Second, adult modeling of prosocial behavior seems to influence children's altruism. On the whole, models who are perceived by children as competent; models who have long-term, nurturant relationships with children; and models who express happiness after prosocial behavior (rather than receiving tangible rewards for their behavior) tend to foster children's prosocial behavior (Eisenberg et al., 2006).

Finally, providing children with opportunities for prosocial action seems to help encourage a commitment to altruistic action. Eisenberg calls this "the foot in the door effect" (Eisenberg et al., 2015). For example, Eisenberg, Cialdini, McCreath, and Shell (1987) found that starting in middle childhood, children who are encouraged to donate in one context are more likely to engage in helping behavior later in another context. This was mostly true for children who valued being consistent. It may be that once children begin to form a stable self-concept, they are more likely to value consistency, and that practicing prosocial behavior then fosters further prosocial activities as children seek to maintain a coherent self-concept. But there are probably other benefits to practice in some contexts, such as gaining increased feelings of competence and obtaining social approval (Eisenberg et al., 2006).

Children's Antisocial Behavior

Antisocial behavior may look quite different as children grow and change, but it is generally distinguished by its intent to harm or injure another or by the perpetrator's disregard for the harm it might cause others (Dodge, Coie, & Lynam, 2006; Krahé, 2013). It might involve acts like cheating, lying, and stealing or it might include physical, verbal, or social attacks (aggression). There are some typical developments in the likelihood of antisocial behavior, but there are substantial individual differences as well. As in the development of any general category of behavior, the processes that contribute are many and varied. We will examine two types of antisocial behavior to illustrate: lying and aggression.

LYING

As you have already seen, honesty and trustworthiness are important moral values in cultures around the world. Even preschoolers seem to see honesty as a moral imperative, and they generally assume that adults do not lie. Yet, most people, including children, do lie: They make false statements in order to deceive (Lavoie, Nagar, & Talwar, 2017). Sometimes they lie for prosocial reasons: to be polite ("You can have that cookie, I'm too full"), or to gain a social foothold ("I'd love it if you could teach me more about wrestling"), or to protect others from hurt or harm ("Your new hairstyle looks really good"). Lying that is intended to hurt someone else ("You know that everyone hates you") is a form of aggression, and we will consider that later. Let's look now at the kind of lying that parents and teachers are likely to see as a violation of trust: when a child breaks a rule or directive and tries to cover it up.

This kind of lying begins by age 2 and becomes most likely in middle childhood. Researchers who study lying sometimes rely on parental reports or on children's own reports of lying, or they might observe children in natural settings. But many studies set up experimental situations designed to make misconduct very tempting (temptation paradigms). For example, a young child might be told not to look inside a gift bag while the researcher is gone. An older child or teen might be left alone completing a test. While the child is "alone" she is actually being observed or recorded using hidden cameras or two-way mirrors. Now comes the real test: If the child gives in to temptation, she is questioned later to see if she will lie or confess.

As you saw in the classic Hartshorne and May (1928-1930) study, many children transgress in these situations. And younger children are more likely to give in to temptation than older children. Transgressors are also likely to lie afterward. The percentage who lie increases with age until about age 6, and the percentage begins to decline with age after about age 10. Typically developing adolescents are more likely to tell the truth than to lie, as their moral judgments begin to come into line with their behavior and their sense of moral identity (see Figure 7.4; Evans & Lee, 2011, 2013; Lee, 2013). Observational studies of children's attempts to deceive in natural settings consistently find the same trends with age (Evans & Lee, 2014). It is worth noting here that these age trends do not hold for prosocial lying. Teens are actually more likely to lie to protect someone else's feelings or to fit into a group than younger children are (Popliger, Talwar, & Crossman, 2011). They are also more likely to think that this kind of lying is morally acceptable (Lee, 2013).

You won't be surprised to learn that many cognitive and social factors contribute to these trends. As their perspective taking skills improve in early childhood, children lie more and they are able to do it more convincingly (e.g., not revealing what they shouldn't know, like what's in the gift bag; Ding, Wellman, Wang, Fu, & Lee, 2015). For example, a child who can pass the false-belief task, usually by age 4 to 5, understands that other people do not necessarily know what she knows, and she is more likely than a younger child to try to deceive. The growth of executive functions is also linked to lying. In a study of 8- to 16-year-olds, improvements in working memory did *not* affect a child's decision to lie, but they did affect how sophisticated the child's deception was (Evans & Lee, 2011). Prosocial lying is also related to perspective taking and executive functions: As these cognitive skills improve, prosocial lying also becomes more likely (Williams, Moore, Crossman, & Talwar, 2016).

It is during middle childhood that children are the most likely to lie in order to cover up their misdeeds. But throughout this age period, their views of lying and what to expect from it are evolving. Preschoolers expect people to feel good after lying. They usually focus on what the transgressor can get from the lie and the fact that she can avoid punishment. But by 7 to 9 years, children expect people to feel better if they confess than if they lie, suggesting that moral judgments (that lying is wrong) are starting to come more into line with emotional expectations (feelings of guilt), if not with behavior. Older children are also more likely than younger children to think that parents will respond well to their confessing the truth (Smith & Rizzo, 2017). It may be worth noting that parents tend to think that they can tell when their children are lying, but their actual accuracy in controlled experiments is at chance level once children reach middle childhood, regardless of whether parents are judging their own or other

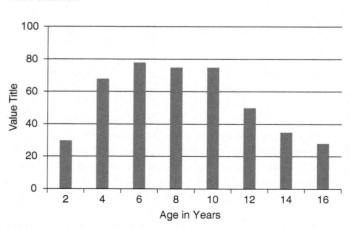

FIGURE 7.4 Percentage of children who lie after misbehavior.[a]

[a]Percentages are approximate, based on averaging data from many studies that have used temptation paradigms.

people's children (Evans, Bender, & Lee, 2016). Interestingly, when children are asked to *promise* to tell the truth, they are more likely to do so (Evans & Lee, 2010). Overall, developmental changes in the frequency of lying for typically developing children provide an excellent example of how moral reasoning, emotions, and behavior become more coordinated—and nuanced—with age.

AGGRESSION

Aggression is characteristic of all mammalian species. It seems to be linked to the emotions of anger and frustration, and it clearly has some adaptive survival functions, such as facilitating self-protection in the face of threat (Dodge et al., 2006). Anger expression can serve a communicative function even in infancy. In one study, researchers restrained infants by grasping and holding their forearms about 6 inches in front of their bellies. As early as 7 months some babies' anger showed clearly on their faces, which they turned toward their mothers as if to say, "Hey, I don't like this!" (Stenberg & Campos, 1990).

Some displays of aggressive behavior are normative in early childhood. This behavior might be directed toward adults who serve as sources of frustration as children seek autonomy, or toward peers as children compete for attention or resources (e.g., toys; see Hay, 2017). Temper tantrums with parents and power struggles with peers are not unusual. For example, observations of 12- to 18-month-olds indicate that nearly half of peer interactions involve some conflict (Caplan, Vespo, Pedersen, & Hay, 1991). Physical aggression usually declines substantially from ages 2 to 4. For example, in one large-scale U.S. study "[t]he most frequent form of early aggression, hits others, occurred in about 70% of the sample at ages 2 and 3, but declined to 20% by ages 4 and 5" (National Institute of Child Health and Human Development [NICHD], 2004, p. 42). At the same time, verbal aggression tends to increase. As children grow in language facility, "using their words" becomes a more typical way of bullying others or expressing anger.

In elementary school, not only does overall aggressive behavior continue to decline for most children, but also the nature of aggression changes. At this point, instrumental aggression (using force or threat to obtain possession) tends to give way to aggression that is person directed and more hostile (i.e., more strongly focused on hurting the other). This type of aggression can involve physical attacks but increasingly it involves "social aggression" or relational aggression, which is aimed at damaging peer relationships. Relational aggression might include social rejection, spreading rumors and lies, teasing, demeaning and humiliating the other in front of peers, and so on. A great deal of research has been directed to relational aggression in recent years, partly because of the role it seems to have played in some school shootings, in which the shooter has been found to be a frequent victim of relational aggression (see Markey & Ferguson, 2017). Some research has found that girls are more likely to use relational aggression than boys, but other studies find just the reverse pattern, or no difference in its use by gender (Spieker et al., 2012). What is clear is that girls are less likely than boys to use physical forms of aggression (Nivette, Eisner, Malti, & Ribeaud, 2014).

Typically, aggression declines with increasing age, just as prosocial behavior tends to increase, although, as we will see in later chapters, some forms of aggression may increase somewhat in adolescence. Many of the same factors that facilitate prosocial development contribute to the decline of aggressive tendencies, such as feelings of empathy and sympathy, authoritative parenting, improvements in self-regulation, peer experiences that help children to increase their perspective taking skills, and advances in cognitive skills in general (Eisner & Malti, 2015). For example, empathy is linked to the inhibition, or control, of aggression (Joliffe & Farrington, 2006). Presumably, when someone initiates an aggressive act, the ability to empathize with the distress of the target person can help inhibit continued aggression in that situation, and the anticipation of a target's distress may inhibit future episodes of aggressive behavior. A focus on the other, rather than the self, seems to be a key element of self-control in these situations.

The role of social cognition (especially perspective taking skill) in the typical decline of aggression has been studied in some detail. Its importance is especially obvious when we look at more aggressive children, whose thinking styles fundamentally involve the misattribution of negative motives to others. In Figure 7.5 you will see an illustration of the social information-processing that Dodge and his colleagues have

MyLab Education

Video Example 7.3

One girl's aggressive behavior disrupts the group activity in this first grade classroom. What actions indicate that she is attempting to learn self-control?

FIGURE 7.5 Social information-processing model.

SOURCE: Based on Crick, N. R., & Dodge, K. A. (1994). A review and reformulation of social information-processing mechanisms in children's social adjustment. *Psychological Bulletin, 115,* 74–101.

suggested is required to interpret others' behaviors and make decisions about how to respond in social situations (see Crick & Dodge, 1994, for a review). Let's imagine Brian waiting in line for a drink at the school water fountain. Two other youngsters, involved in a clandestine game of tag in the hallway, bump into him and knock his backpack to the floor. How might he respond?

Dodge's model suggests a typical sequence of mental activity for aggressive children. First, the child encodes cues selectively, focusing on situational cues that suggest threatening content. This tendency may develop as a response to harsh discipline, which enhances the hypervigilance needed to protect oneself from ever-present threats to personal security (Dodge, Bates, & Pettit, 1990). Brian might attend more to the boy's body coming close and bumping him rather than to the smiles on the other boys' faces.

The child next interprets or attributes meaning to the cues. A biased interpretive style, called **hostile attributional bias (HAB)** or hostile attribution of intent, characterizes aggressive individuals who tend to perceive threats even in neutral situations (Dodge et al., 2015). For example, Brian might conclude that the boys knocked the backpack off intentionally because they dislike him. The next step is to clarify goals. In Brian's emotionally aroused state, the primary goal might be to get even with the other boys for the perceived insult. For aggressive children, schemas or mental guides for social interaction may be organized around aggression. In other words, these individuals use aggressive schemas to make sense of or to figure out what has transpired socially. Because the situation is likely to be viewed through the lens of perceived hostility and because more socially acceptable responses have not been practiced, the likelihood of aggressive responding is high.

Brian next proceeds to access a behavioral response from his repertoire. Then he evaluates the response and enacts the behavior. Brian, still rather impulsive, is quick to respond in anger. He may start to punch the other boy for the perceived violation. For a child like Brian who is impulsive, who has experienced the benefits of aggression, or who has learned that aggression is a preferred means of problem solving, aggressive responding may become natural.

Underdeveloped self-control and weaknesses in verbally expressive means of problem solving could add to the tendency to aggress. Children who fail to make normal strides in their ability to regulate their own emotional responses, especially anger, and whose concern for self is not adequately balanced by concern for and understanding of other people, are at risk for poor and declining academic performance over time and for experiences of peer victimization (e.g., Schwartz, Lansford, Dodge, Pettit, & Bates, 2013). They are also at risk for developing conduct problems in childhood and more serious criminal behavior as they move through adolescence and adulthood. See the Focus on Developmental Psychopathology in this chapter for a discussion of the development of conduct disorder and externalizing problems generally.

BULLIES AND VICTIMS

The problem of peer victimization (bullying) in childhood and adolescence is especially important for teachers, counselors, and other helping professionals to understand. Bullying is aggressive behavior, physical or verbal or through social media, that targets a specific victim over a period of time. It typically involves intimidation, coercion, or social exclusion. Victims might be physically attacked, threatened, or forced to act; they might be socially excluded and/or made the targets of gossip or unflattering publicity (e.g., compromising pictures posted on social media); or they might have their belongings taken or damaged (Eisner & Malti, 2015; Saarento & Salmivalli, 2015).

How frequent is peer victimization? Estimates vary depending on measurement techniques and location. In one large study of Canadian children, 38% of fourth graders reported being victimized. The percentage declined as the children got older (Brendgen, Girard, Vitaro, Dionne, & Boivin, 2016). A longitudinal study of Midwestern U.S. children also showed declines in victimization from second through eighth grade, although there was less decline after children reached middle school (Sugimura, Berry, Troop-Gordon, & Rudoph, 2017). The percentage of children who were victims was not reported, but children's victimization scores suggest that it was a fairly frequent experience. In a very large national survey of middle school children in China, more than half reported being victimized within the previous month (Qiao et al., 2010). Overall, victimization appears to be common among children and adolescents, but the frequency declines as children mature.

Who bullies? And who are their victims? As we noted above, in some cases, aggressive children are at risk of being both bullies *and* victims. Many children who are targets of direct aggression, either physical or face-to-face verbal aggression, engage in such behavior themselves and are sometimes targets because they do. Also, children who jockey for position among peers by using relational aggression (using rumors or other tactics to exclude or demean a victim) are at increased risk of being targets of retaliation of the same sort (Casper & Card, 2017).

Some bullies do not suffer victimization themselves. These "pure bullies" are often socially competent, with good perspective taking skills. They are good at both engaging and manipulating others, and they are likely to be strong and healthy. Usually, they are liked by some peers and disliked by others (Isen, McGue, & Iacono, 2015; Wolke, Copeland, Angold, & Costello, 2013).

There are also "pure victims"—children who are targeted by aggressors but who do not victimize others. These children may be withdrawn, and they are usually more socially awkward than their age mates. They may be physically weaker than other children and/or more likely to react by getting upset or running away (Wolke et al., 2013). Generally, unlike bully-victims, these children have more internalizing problems (e.g., depression, anxiety) than externalizing problems (various forms of misbehavior). But like bully-victims, they often do not have friends who will stand up for them (Casper & Card, 2017).

Peer victimization can have negative, long-term consequences. Many bullies experience increasing difficulties in both making friends and getting along with teachers. Some are at risk of developing conduct disorders (see the Focus on Developmental Psychopathology in this chapter).

Risks for victims include not only depression and anxiety, but also failure to learn critical social skills. For example, Troop-Gordon and her colleagues (2017) followed over 600 children from several small Midwestern towns from second through sixth grade. Every year the researchers asked the children and their teachers to answer a series

MyLab Education
Video Example 7.4
The problem of bullying is important for helping professionals to understand. Observe the procedures and the rhetoric used in the dialog between a school counselor and student in a bullying case.

FIGURE 7.6 Children's use of effortful engagement strategies.

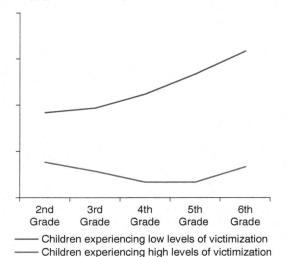

— Children experiencing low levels of victimization
— Children experiencing high levels of victimization

SOURCE: Based on data from Troop-Gordon, W., Sugimara, N., & Rudolph, K. D. (2017). Responses to interpersonal stress: Normative changes across childhood and the impact of peer victimization. *Child Development, 88*, 640–657.

of questions about how frequently they were bullied (e.g., "How often do you get teased by another kid?"). (It's noteworthy that teachers and children's reports were highly consistent.) The children were also asked to answer questions about how they reacted to bullying. The possible kinds of reactions fell into four categories. The first, "effortful engagement" (e.g., "I do something to try to fix the problem or take action to change things"), is considered the most adaptive. The remaining three reaction types are considered less adaptive: "effortful disengagement" (e.g., "I try to believe it never happened"); "involuntary engagement" (e.g., "I keep remembering what happened or can't stop thinking about what might happen"); and "involuntary disengagement" (e.g., "I just have to get away, I can't stop myself").

Boys and girls who experienced only low levels of victimization reported more and more use of effortful engagement strategies as they got older (see Figure 7.6). In other words, they improved through middle childhood in their tendency to cope effectively with social conflict. But children who experienced high levels of victimization showed a *decline* in effortful engagement through this period, and they increasingly reported the three less effective social problem solving strategies.

We will look more closely at both the determinants and longer-term consequences of children's peer experiences in the next chapter. For now, let's consider the role that teachers might play in peer victimization, given that much of bullying occurs in school. Researchers have identified some characteristics and behaviors of teachers that can make a difference (Troop-Gordon, 2015). First, it is important for teachers to be aware of the harmful effects of victimization. Some teachers view bullying as normal for children, maybe even something that helps "toughen them up." Or, they may acknowledge that physical aggression is a problem, but they fail to recognize the costs of relational aggression (Kowalski, Giumetti, Schroeder, & Lattanner, 2014). If teachers see victimization as "normal," victims are not likely to go to teachers for help. When they do, such teachers may suggest that victims stay away from children who bother them or that they settle their problems on their own. Unfortunately, when teachers fail to act, victimization usually increases, and the emotional consequences for the victims also increase (Troop-Gordon & Ladd, 2015).

What kinds of teacher behaviors can improve the climate of a classroom and reduce bullying? There is much yet to learn on this subject, but some things are clear. First, teachers need to see victimization of all kinds as unacceptable. Also, teachers are more effective if they are tuned into the social dynamics of their classrooms, and if they accept that they can have an impact on those dynamics. Simple strategies include reorganizing a classroom so that a victim is separated from her aggressor. This usually works while the children are separated, and it can have longer term benefits for the victim by giving her opportunities to form relationships with other children. Adopting school and classroom level intervention programs designed to change the peer ecology can be effective, depending on the time and effort that the school invests (Polanin & Espelage, 2015). These programs are usually aimed at raising teachers' awareness of the costs of peer victimization and helping them to identify social processes at work among their students. Such programs also help children to recognize forms of aggression, empathize more with victims, and learn appropriately assertive ways of intervening rather than standing by (e.g., Oldenburg et al., 2015; Troop-Gordon, 2015; see Nickerson, 2017, for a review of evidence-based interventions).

MyLab Education Self-Check 7.2.

Applications

A strong sense of self-worth and a sturdy moral compass are elements widely viewed as important for building and participating in a civil society. Some have recently argued that the two have parted ways and that, in Western cultures, the self has been emphasized over concern for the common good. Baumeister and Bowden (1994) put it this way: "[T]he modern growth of selfhood has included a love affair with it. Whereas, for centuries, morality and self-interest were regarded as mortal enemies, the modern individual has increasingly linked the self to positive values. Finding oneself, knowing oneself, cultivating oneself, and benefiting oneself are seen not only as moral rights, but even, increasingly, as moral duties" (p. 144). The unquestioning and unqualified pursuit of self-esteem is an example of this trend. It's true that low self-esteem has been implicated as a key element in a wide variety of problems manifested by children, adolescents, and adults, including anxiety (Battle, Jarratt, Smit, & Precht, 1988; Keane & Lodes, 2017), low academic motivation, and diminished achievement (Carlson & Lewis, 1993; Duru & Blakis, 2017). Abundant research has demonstrated that low self-esteem is a feature of depression (Beck, 1963; Peterson, Maier, & Seligman, 1993) and that ruminating on one's deficiencies both prolongs and amplifies the depressive state (Nolen-Hoeksema, Morrow, & Fredrickson, 1993).

Therefore, self-esteem *is* an important therapeutic target. However, there is disagreement about the direction of effects. Does low self-esteem cause problems like academic failure, depression, or aggression or does the experience of failure, for example, lower self-esteem (Baumeister, Campbell, Krueger, & Vohs, 2003)? Parents, teachers, and clinicians have often been advised to boost self-esteem directly. While this might be helpful in some cases, it can also be problematic without a clear understanding of pathways of action. In fact, the goal of pursuing self-validation is viewed from many theoretical perspectives as maladaptive. Praising children for their personal characteristics, which was widely advised beginning in the 1970s, has become controversial. Researchers noted that children who were routinely praised for being smart, for example, could be derailed once they actually failed at something. Certain children's self-esteem, researchers learned, could be fragile and easily threatened, rendering them less likely to take risks, to persevere through difficulties, and to remain flexible and optimistic about setbacks. In other words, their specific feelings of self-efficacy could be at risk. Here are some key considerations for parents and clinicians on this important topic.

- Most adults (85%) believe that low self-esteem in children is a widespread and pernicious problem that can be "cured" by praising them (Thomaes, Brummelman, Bushman, Reijntjes, & Orobio de Castro, 2015). As we note, low self-esteem is associated with many problems, but the indiscriminate application of praise has not been supported by research to be an effective cure.

- A few distinctions need to be made with regard to categories of praise. Praise directed toward personal characteristics (*person or ability* praise, e.g., *"You are smart"*) is different from praise directed toward behavior (*process* praise, e.g., *"You did a good job figuring that out"*). Sometimes praise is used to compare a child to others (*social-comparison* praise, e.g., *"You're so much better at math than your sister"*). Praise also incorporates a dimension of intensity, from modest to exaggerated. *"The story you wrote is very good"* is different in tone and impact from *"The story you wrote is incredibly awesome!"*

- The tendency for parents and others to lavish excessive praise on children seems to be gaining ground. Some researchers relate this to the phenomenon of *parental overvaluation* (Brummelman et al., 2015), which reflects an underlying belief that one's child deserves special treatment and is superior to others. As you saw earlier in this chapter, it's important not to conflate overvaluing with warmth. Overvaluing is related to problematic outcomes whereas genuine parental warmth is wholly beneficial for children's development.

- Researchers have found that specific types of praise influence children's motivation and affect (Dweck, 2006). Children who get a diet of person or ability praise, especially individuals with low self-esteem, are less likely to persist when the going gets tough. Frequent exaggerated and person-centered praise provides a rewarding experience that children learn to expect. However, a corresponding internal message, *"I am outstanding, and I need to be outstanding in order to be valued"* might be developing as well. Failure can become so threatening to a fragile self, dependent upon external validation, that risks are avoided and any criticism is unbearable. Children also may form the "ability" mindset that traits, such as intelligence, are fixed (i.e., part of who I am) and therefore immutable. A helpless orientation may be one result. (See more about mindsets in Chapter 6.)

- Person or ability praise can also influence children's moral behavior. A study of Chinese children in one study showed that those who received praise for the stable trait of ability were more likely to cheat on an experimental task than those who were praised for effort. Presumably, these children acted on a need to maintain their positive self-image as smart and capable. This study reflects the significant contribution socialization makes to children's actual behavior (Zhao, Heyman, Chen, & Lee, 2017).

- Evidence is somewhat less clear for process praise. While some research indicates an association with mastery efforts and increased achievement motivation or self-efficacy (Blackwell et al., 2007), others have found no improvements (Pomerantz & Kempner, 2013). Perhaps something about the characteristics of the child, parent, or even the setting moderates the effects of process praise. Future research will help us clarify this question and lead us to firmer conclusions.

- Children with low self-esteem, compared to those with high self-esteem, are often treated to higher doses of exaggerated praise in the service of improving their feelings of inadequacy (Brummelman, Crocker, & Bushman, 2016). One can certainly understand the good intentions of parents and teachers who do this. However, some research has pointed to a troublesome transactional cycle that develops as a result of this practice. The cycle begins when the adult attributes some worrisome child behavior to low self-esteem. Examples may include the child's disappointment with a low grade or unwillingness to join peers in trying something new. The adult wants to help the child and concludes that offering praise is the solution. At this point, she inflates person praise, believing this to be an effective antidote. When the child doesn't show greater self-esteem or more resilient behavior, the adult concludes that even more praise is called for, increasing the risk that the child will grow dependent upon external praise for self-worth. This transactional cycle ultimately shapes the child's self-perceptions about how she measures up (see Figure 7.7).

While chasing the elusive goal of high self-esteem can backfire, the goal of acquiring mastery in school and in other pursuits is viewed as adaptive (e.g., Rusk & Rothbaum, 2010; see Harter, 2012). As you have seen, Erikson emphasized that when school-aged children successfully tackle the work teachers give them, they build a sense of industry, a "can-do" spirit, which enables them to take on challenges and persevere in spite of difficulty. These faculties have been associated with "grit" (Duckworth, 2016), but they share a lot in common with older constructs like self-efficacy, self-reliance, resilience, and persistence. Dryfoos (1990), in a review of 20 years of research, found no compelling evidence that high self-esteem is a necessary precursor for competence. In fact, much evidence points in the other direction, namely that competent performance results in

feelings of high self-efficacy, and ultimately, self-esteem. From this perspective, feeling good becomes a "delicious by-product" of doing well (Seligman, 1995).

Reducing Hostile Attributional Bias

We humans instinctively create stories about events that help us make sense of things. We assume that these explanations for events reflect "the way things work." Often not directly expressed, they reside in the background of our mental operations and may profoundly influence our behavior. Thus, they are sometimes called implicit theories. A scientific foundation for this phenomenon comes from attribution theory (Abrahamson, Seligman, & Teasdale, 1978; Weiner, 1974), an influential line of reasoning in psychology. For example, cognitive theories of depression have benefitted from knowing about the particular attributional (or explanatory) style of depressed individuals. On three major explanatory dimensions (locus, stability, and controllability), depressed people tend to attribute bad events to something inside themselves (internal), predict that the same bad outcome is likely to reoccur in the future across situations (stable), and express a lack of control (uncontrollable) about outcomes. Non-depressed people are more likely to attribute bad events to external circumstances, to perceive they have more control, and to expect more fortunate outcomes in the future. Needless to say, the former attributional style is associated with low self-esteem.

Research has demonstrated that schemas (including self and relational schemas) are resistant to change and support consistency in perceptions. This is so, in part, because schemas are economical ways to predict and make sense of the world. They help us filter out a lot of unnecessary information, hone in on the data that have functional significance for us, disregard inconsistent information, and focus our attention on information that supports (or is consistent with) existing schemas. One can view hostile attributional bias (HAB) as a relational scheme that has functional significance for a child with a history of coercive interactions. This scheme is not a distortion of reality for someone whose safety once depended on assuming the imminent presence of threats. Obviously, this kind of social information processing bias may severely hurt a child's peer interaction in the present.

HAB is fairly common among preschoolers but diminishes in most children as they get older and learn to understand others' perspectives (Dodge, 2006). Growth in theory of mind skills, like understanding intentionality, helps children separate bad outcomes (e.g., being hit by a ball on the playground) from bad intentions (e.g., being hit by the ball on purpose). Most children also develop skills in emotion regulation, which help them modulate arousal and inhibit the tendency to see mistakes as hostile acts.

Although our theoretical understanding of social information processing somewhat exceeds our present understanding of successful interventions, it may be clinically useful to introduce new ways of interpreting social situations. A classic treatment sequence for many anger management programs includes helping clients to recognize provocative

---

FIGURE 7.7 A transactional model of praise.

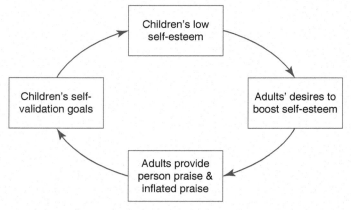

SOURCE: Based on Brummelman, E., Thomaes, S., & Sedikides, C. (2016). Separating narcissism from self-esteem. *Current Directions in Psychological Science, 25,* 8-13.

stimuli or events in the environment, to stop long enough to reduce levels of reactivity using deep breathing or backward counting, to change distorted thinking by using rational self-statements, and to practice more appropriate social behavior and emotion expression (Kendall, 1991).

The difficulty here is that strategies that help children generate alternative interpretations, come up with alternative solutions to problems, or increase perspective taking skills are typically carried out under nonthreatening, non-emotional, intellectualized conditions (called *cold cognitions*). As we all know, those cognitive biases that provoke fights or lead to feeling depressed operate below the level of conscious awareness when personally significant and emotionally charged association networks become activated by some event. Bierman (2004) suggests using real conflict situations with real peers, as opposed to hypothetical ones, when working with children in order to increase the generalizability of treatment effects. Videotaping children in social situations, reviewing the tape with the child, and stopping the action to process "online" those cues the child was attending to and how she was interpreting them may be a way to provide more access to *hot cognitions* (Putallaz, 1983; Rolls, 2013).

All of these interventions depend upon the ability of the child to "mentalize." As you will read in subsequent chapters, the ability to infer one's own mental states and those of others continues to develop over time, particularly in adolescence. Therefore, interventions need to take the capacities of the child into account. Young school-aged children can recognize that people may have different interpretations of events. But children between 10 and 12 are better able to distinguish various mental capacities (e.g., understanding, remembering, paying attention, hearing, etc.) and thus are more capable of diverse explanations for events. Researchers asked children questions that revealed their level of understanding about mental processes and found that recognizing and distinguishing among different types of processes was protective against HAB and aggressive behavior in adolescence (Weimer, Parault Dowds, Fabricius, Schwanenflugel, & Suh, 2017). Presumably, expanding the child's repertoire of possible attributions, such as

understanding that unpleasant things can happen because people make mistakes or because others have different perspectives and desires from you, can reduce automatic hostile inferences. Table 7.4 includes some of these researchers' questions, which can be useful prompts for discussion about mental operations and potentially applicable to psychoeducational interventions. Of course, the child's emotion regulation skills play a critical role, especially in "hot" conflict situations. Therefore, both affective and cognitive processes should be included in any intervention.

Building a Healthy Self

The teachings of James and Cooley have important implications for interventions in this area as well. It seems obvious, but still worth emphasizing, that words can and do hurt. Shaming, sarcasm, demeaning, and name calling by adults are incorporated by children and seep into the fabric of their self-concept. These internal voices can resonate in our psyches throughout adulthood, becoming the root of chronic self-reproach. Often they are coupled with the belief that we are not entitled to the painful feelings these negative messages elicited in the first place. Parents must be helped to understand the powerful looking glass their words create. By the same token, saying no to children should not be expected to hurt their self-esteem. Setting limits authoritatively by saying no when appropriate is necessary; this needs to be disentangled from the idea that negative comments hurt children—an unfortunate conflation of ideas.

Self-worth, particularly as linked to morality and a sense of character, is ultimately something that resides inside us. We have seen that it cannot be acquired in a social vacuum, dependent as we all are on the positive appraisals of significant others (Cooley, 1902). But just as true, it cannot be acquired by cosmetic or superficial means. Children have work to do in this area, and this "industry" is not always easy (Erikson, 1950/1963). It is unrealistic for parents and clinicians to assume that failure should be avoided at all costs, that children can be inoculated against self-doubt by unconditional love, or that being "the best" in some competitive arena (social, academic, athletic, or appearance) guarantees

TABLE 7.4 Selected Interview Questions That Probe for Understanding of Mental Processes with Implications for Attributions

SAMPLE INTERVIEW QUESTION	EXPLANATION THAT DOES INCLUDE MORE IN-DEPTH UNDERSTANDING OF MENTAL PROCESSES	EXPLANATION THAT DOES NOT INCLUDE IN-DEPTH UNDERSTANDING OF MENTAL PROCESSES
Can two people watch the same thing happen and both see and hear everything but remember it very differently?	Yes. One sees things positively and one sees things negatively.	Yes. If one didn't pay attention.
Could somebody hear everything someone said to them but not understand it?	Yes. Could get a different meaning.	Yes. Talking too fast.
If two people looked at two objects very carefully, could one decide that both were very different and the other decide that they were very much the same?	Yes. A knife and fork—one says both silverware and the other says one has one prong and the other has four.	Yes. One sees something like a small design that the other doesn't see.

SOURCE: Based on Weimer, A.A., Parault Dowds, S.J., Fabricius, W.V. ,Schwanenflugel, P.J. & Suh, G.W. (2017). Development of constructivist theory of mind from middle childhood to early adulthood and its relation to social cognition and behavior. *Journal of Experimental Child Psychology, 154*, p 32.

high self-esteem. Parents (and, by extension, therapists) make a critical mistake when emphasizing approval from others over approval from the self. Parents and teachers should be cautioned that very subtle messages can communicate the notion that pleasing others or winning others' regard is what constitutes self-worth in this world. Children should be helped to take personal responsibility for their actions and to choose internally motivated or learning goals (Pintrich, 2000) when possible. They can also be discouraged from excessive competition and overreliance on social comparison. These approaches can have positive effects on the internalization of personal standards and the fostering of a strong private self.

Damon (Malin, Ballard, & Damon, 2015) reminds us that the development of morality is dependent on the contexts we inhabit. He notes that schooling provides an excellent opportunity to support the development of prosocial values and behavior. "Like a broad-spectrum vaccine that can block the growth of many dangerous viruses at once, a child's wholehearted engagement in schooling can stop destructive and wasteful activities before they begin to consume a child's life" (Damon, 1995, p. 195). The emphasis here, we stress, is on wholehearted engagement. Children need personal relationships with teachers who hold high intellectual, moral, and behavioral expectations in settings that are small enough to permit these relationships. They need rigorous and meaningful learning experiences that encourage diligence and depth of thinking, and they need high standards for behavior that actually hold them to account for their behavior. Table 7.5 summarizes the main principles of character education as it ideally looks when

TABLE 7.5 Summary of the 11 Principles of Character Education (CEP)

PRINCIPLES OF CHARACTER EDUCATION (CE)	EXPANDED EXPLANATION	HOW THE PRINCIPLE LOOKS IN A SCHOOL SETTINGS
1. School community promotes core values as foundation of CE.	e.g., respect, perseverance, honesty	Including values in school mission statement and PR materials
2. School defines character to include thinking, feeling, and doing.	e.g., discussing, caring about, and acting on core values are all emphasized	Discussing importance of values and acting on values, i.e., peer mentoring, expressing appreciation for others (e.g. school custodial staff)
3. School uses an intentional, comprehensive, and proactive approach.	e.g., infusing CE into all aspects of school life	Inclusion of values into curricular areas, school rules, and procedures
4. School creates a caring community.	e.g., support for caring relationships among students, staff, and parents across grades and levels	Use of educational practices like cooperative learning and processes like class meetings that foster inclusion and reduce bullying
5. School provides students with opportunities for moral action.	e.g. allowing students to engage in projects and activities that promote in-school common good	Service learning, cross-grade tutoring, responsible student government, caring for environment, etc.
6. School offers meaningful and challenging academic curriculum.	e.g., provides a curriculum that is meaningful and meets the needs of diverse student body; promotion of thinking skills, attitudes and behaviors that support success	Promoting student engagement and motivation for learning through curriculum; identification and responsiveness to student needs; support for critical thinking, self-management, collaboration, etc. within academic curricular areas and in student advisories
7. School fosters student self-motivation.	e.g., fostering intrinsic motivation by emphasizing the innate benefits of good character rather than privileging material rewards	Emphasis on personal honor, integrity, and positive comments that recognize acts of character and offer opportunities to improve rather than coercive forms of management; use of behavioral principles with logical consequences for misbehavior
8. School staff adhere to the same core values that guide students.	e.g., all teachers, support staff, paraprofessionals, and administrators take ownership for the development of CE strategies and help to sustain the program	All participate as members of an ethical learning community, model core values and engage in continuing education about them within a caring, collaborative environment
9. School fosters shared leadership in the CE initiative.	e.g., school members provide guidance and long-range support for initiatives	CE team plans for school activities; student leaders are included in planning and implementation of initiatives
10. School engages family and community members in character-building effort.	e.g., parents are made aware of the CE initiative, are recruited and trained for leadership positions	Programs and activities in the larger community, including businesses, youth organizations, etc. are encouraged to participate and volunteer in school-based initiatives
11. School assesses its climate, staff functioning, and student performance on a regular basis.	e.g., schools engage in self-reflection and requests for feedback about how well they meet the goals of CE	Data is obtained from students and staff about quality and outcomes of CE using a variety of approaches (surveys, grades, artifacts, etc.)

SOURCE: Based on *11 Principles of Effective Character Education*, 2014, www.character.org.

embedded in the school context. These principles offer useful guidance for developmentally appropriate education at every level, given that most children excel when opportunities to develop competence and character are provided within a supportive environment.

Finally, community organizations such as YMCA, sports leagues, and so on, composed of members who live and work in the communities they serve, have a critical part to play. The most successful ones provide a source of care and mentoring to children and require them to abide by strict rules and regulations. In this way, they provide a healthy dose of adjunct parenting by helping youth to internalize values and standards. Opportunities for children to provide meaningful service to others sharpen their sense of purpose and competence and reduce the demoralization that grows from excessive self-centeredness. Adults will provide a more powerful environment for moral development if we communicate some shared values to all our children through our words and deeds. Children learn the important messages best when homes, schools, and communities speak with one voice.

Focus on Developmental Psychopathology

Conduct Problems

Jason, at 3 years of age, is a high-energy youngster who never seems to sit still. He engages in daily bouts of toy grabbing, aggressive play, and fighting. His behavior definitely has an impulsive quality to it: Strike now and think later! Two years later at age 5, Jason is still going strong. He communicates his strong-willed temperament in frequent temper tantrums over household rules. His developing language ability permits him to be more argumentative with adults and peers than he had been earlier. Problems with disobedience occur at home and at school. Jason frequently refuses to go to bed on time, pick up his toys, or take a bath. He rarely sustains attention to an activity for longer than 5 minutes. His mother resorts to spanking out of frustration, but she realizes that this is not effective in getting Jason to change his behavior. In squabbles with preschool classmates, Jason may throw something or hit another child. His teacher finds him a challenge to her patience and her classroom management skills.

Stop for a moment and reflect on 5-year-old Jason's behavior. How would you evaluate this youngster? Do you consider his behavior normal or problematic? Now consider him at age 8. He is in the third grade. His aggressive behaviors have persisted, primarily in the form of fighting and taunting other students. He is not well liked by classmates and has difficulty fitting into the social fabric of the class. His academic performance is marginal, and he finds schoolwork "boring." Jason has begun to steal toys and money from his classmates and has been caught vandalizing property belonging to one of his neighbors. How would you assess Jason's problems now?

If you view Jason's profile as problematic, your assessment is in line with current research on antisocial behavior. Antisocial behavior is a multidimensional term, which is usually characterized by the presence of aggression or the intent to harm another person. Recent formulations have recognized that antisocial behavior in adolescents and adults may also include such acts as risky sexual activity, substance abuse, defiance, cheating, lying, and vandalism (see Frick & Nigg, 2011). Antisocial behavior can be both overt, such as hitting, and covert, such as cheating. When these behaviors are serious enough to warrant a diagnosis in children and adolescents, oppositional defiant disorder (ODD) or conduct disorder (CD) are the most likely classifications depending on the nature, duration, and severity of symptoms. A diagnosis of antisocial personality disorder (APD) is typically reserved for adults (American Psychiatric Association [APA], DSM-V, 2013). In this section, we use the broad construct of conduct problems as a general descriptive term for externalizing problems that include disruptive, impulse control, and conduct disorders.

The scope of the problem. Conduct problems burden society with enormous economic and social costs. However one frames the problem—as aggression, behavior problems, conduct disorder, delinquency, or crime—its effects are borne by victims and their families, by perpetrators whose lives are restricted, and by taxpayers who fund the costs of incarceration, rehabilitation, treatment, and security. Fortunately, rates of violent crime have been decreasing in the United States for some time. From a high point in 1993 (79.8 violent crimes per 1,000 people), violent crime rates for individuals aged 12 or older have fallen to 18.6 per 1,000 in 2015 (U.S. Department of Justice, available from www.bjs.gov/content/pub/ascii/caavv0413.txt). Aggressive behavior remains a problem in schools as reported in the *Youth Risk Behavior Survey (YRBS)*, a biennial report on risk factors affecting middle and high school students' health and safety. Although the overall incidence of many problematic indicators decreased since 1993, students in 2015 reported being in physical fights (22.6%), carrying weapons to school (16.2%), being threatened or injured by a weapon at school (6%), and remaining at home at least one day in the previous month because of threats to safety (5.6%). Students across the United States reported being bullied on school grounds (20.2%) and online (15.5%). Females are victims of physical dating violence (being hit or having something thrown at you) at higher rates (11.7%) than males are (7.4%), and they more often experience sexual dating violence (15.6% for females and 5.4% for males). (All data from Kann et al., 2016.)

Research clearly confirms that conduct problems can start early. A report of the Office of Juvenile Justice and Delinquency Prevention's Study Group on Very Young Offenders (Loeber & Farrington, 2000) states that child delinquents (ages 7 to 12) have "a 2- to 3-fold increased risk of becoming tomorrow's serious, violent and chronic offenders" (p. 738). Although rates of child delinquency are low compared to older offenders, they are nonetheless significant. One in 12 murders committed in 2002 (8%) involved a child offender, implicating them in an estimated 1,300 murders. More tellingly, approximately 48% of crimes committed by juveniles never get reported to the police (Snyder & Sickmund, 2006). Such evidence has led to the contemporary emphasis on prevention and early intervention to reduce the growth of chronic antisocial behaviors and, additionally, to reduce costs of supporting adolescent and adult offenders. Reports from the Dunedin Birth Cohort Study, now in its 40th year, reveals why targeted early intervention is important. In the large cohort being followed by the research team, only 22% of the participants accounted for the bulk of the economic and social burden: 36% of insurance claims, 40% of obese group, 54% of smokers, 57% of hospital stays, 66% of welfare recipients, 77% of father-absence during childrearing, 78% of prescriptions filled, and 81% of convictions for criminal offenses (Caspi et al., 2016).

Pathways of antisocial behavior. Several developmental pathways can eventually lead to antisocial outcomes in adolescence and adulthood. One pathway has a life-course trajectory characterized by the presence of oppositional, noncompliant, and aggressive behavior that begins early, persists and diversifies over time, and becomes increasingly more serious. This **early-starter model** has been called **life-course persistent** ([LCP]; Moffit, 1993b). A second pathway for late starters, whose experience with delinquent activities begins at adolescence, is less likely to

MyLab Education
Video Example 7.5
Nicole and her mother describe a negative, defiant interaction pattern they have developed. Her mother reports, "Usually, she ends up winning"—suggesting that she gives up demands for compliance when the child becomes whiny and demanding.

result in adult criminality. This **late-starter model** called **adolescence-limited** (AL) antisocial behavior, although serious, seems to be more reflective of a difficult or exaggerated reaction to the adolescent period (Moffit, 1993b). Both pathways are more complicated than they seem, and other researchers have identified variations on these two themes. Some children manifest behavioral problems in childhood, but the externalizing difficulties remit in adolescence. This model has been called **childhood-limited** ([CL]; Barker & Maughan, 2009), although some questions remain as to whether these children suffer from more internalizing disorders later on (Moffit et al., 2008). A subset of youth identified in the AL group actually do go on to have adjustment problems in adulthood, reflecting yet another variation called the **adolescent onset model** rather than adolescent limited ([AO]; Fairchild et al., 2013; Kretschmer et al., 2014). If you are confused about all these possibilities, you may be wondering about the point of this kind of research. Remember back to Chapter 1 where we discussed translational research. One of its goals is to identify genetic and early environmental risk factors that combine to orient individuals toward certain trajectories of development so that interventions can be tailored to their unique needs. The search for pathways helps to flesh out this personalized prevention approach.

Most of the evidence for these models comes from studies on males, for males show higher rates of externalizing disorders compared to females across the life span (Moffit, Caspi, Rutter, & Silva, 2001). Some have questioned whether girls exhibit the LCP pattern at all. A report from the longitudinal Dunedin Multidisciplinary Health and Development Study (Odgers et al., 2008), which was initiated in 1972, provides evidence for the existence of this dual pathway in girls as well as boys. When girls show antisocial aggression in childhood and adolescence, they are also much more likely to have comorbid depression and anxiety.

Are outcomes different for individuals on different pathways? One long-term study from Europe followed children from age 4 to age 20 (Sentse, Kretschmer, de Haan, & Prinzie, 2017). The authors report that those in the LCP group had the most serious outcomes in early adulthood. However, levels of externalizing problems were comparable at age 20 for both LCP and a subset of AL groups. This finding supports the idea that some adolescent manifestations of conduct problems arise from a gradually accelerating pattern in earlier years and do not necessarily remit after adolescence.

We should keep in mind, however, that some oppositional behaviors are relatively normal for young children of 4 and 5 years of age (Achenbach & Edelbrock, 1983). Sometimes caregivers fail to appreciate children's normal variations in activity level, intensity, and willfulness. The important thing to remember is that in the less extreme cases these oppositional behaviors tend to recede around age 8. The developmental course that is problematic is one in which these behaviors are maintained into elementary

TABLE 7.6 When Should a Parent Seek Help?

- When child refuses to do what parent asks them to do 8 out of 10 times
- When a teacher or day care provider reports child has a problem with aggression toward peers and has difficulty making friends
- When parents feel they aren't successful in helping child reduce aggression
- When child has developmental problems making it difficult for him or her to learn social skills

SOURCE: Used with permission of Carolyn Webster-Stratton.

school, then enlarged and expanded on in more delinquent ways. A number of risk factors, both internal and external, operate in synergistic fashion to set this LCP trajectory in motion. Like a storm that gathers strength as it moves along, early antisocial behaviors in certain cases are compounded by related problems in families, classrooms, and peer groups that often trap youngsters in a downward spiral. Table 7.6 provides some guidance about when a parent should seek outside help for a child exhibiting oppositional behaviors.

Physiological and Neuropsychological Influences

Certain physiological and neuropsychological characteristics have been explored in the search for risk factors for antisocial behavior. Genetic contributors, delayed neural maturation, sympathetic nervous system arousal, and circadian rhythm patterns have all been candidates for study. Molecular geneticists have discovered the presence of 409 gene variants from 38 genes that have been implicated in high levels of aggression (Liu, Li, & Guo, 2015). Serotonin and dopamine related genes have received particular attention (Ficks & Waldman, 2014).

The investigation of cardiac vagal tone as a biomarker of risk is another promising field of study. The two opposing components of the autonomic nervous system (ANS), the sympathetic and parasympathetic divisions, are mediated by the vagus nerve, which supplies fibers to the heart and other organs and feeds back input to the brain. The vagus nerve helps slow down the heart, acting, among other things, as an arm of the parasympathetic system to keep the ANS in balance (Porges, Doussard-Roosevelt, Portales, & Greenspan, 1996). Vagal tone refers to how effectively the vagus nerve mediates the parasympathetic system. An estimate of vagal tone can be derived from the ebb and flow of heart rate, a measure called respiratory sinus arrhythmia (RSA). Studies have shown that reduced vagal tone/low RSA is associated with aggression, hostility, and depression in children, adolescents, and adults (Beauchaine, 2001; Raine, Fung, Portnoy, Choy, & Spring, 2014).

Certain heritable personality characteristics have also come under scrutiny. In particular, the constellation of callous-unemotional traits (lack of empathy and remorse, fearlessness, shallow affect, and lack of concern about behavioral consequences) appear in a small subset (about 25% to 30%) of children whose conduct problems start early and continue through adulthood (Frick & Ray, 2015). This group had the most negative outcomes of all. Their aggression was power-assertive, vengeful, and premeditated, and treatment outcomes for this group were poor. Another genetically influenced characteristic, trait impulsivity, is also associated with mental health problems of children, youth, and adults. Trait impulsivity arises from deficiencies in subcortical systems related to irritability, or the tendency to manifest a chronically angry or grumpy mood marked by intermittent angry outbursts (Copeland, Brotman, & Costello, 2015). Chronic underlying dissatisfaction propels individuals to act out in frustration and to engage in reward-seeking behaviors that can be destructive. Impulsivity is a strongly heritable vulnerability that underlies a range of externalizing disorders and compounds problematic effects of inadequate early environments (Beauchaine, Zisner, & Sauder, 2017). As you can see in Figure 7.8, impulsivity contributes to attention-deficit hyperactivity disorder (ADHD), oppositional defiant disorder (ODD), conduct disorder (CD),

FIGURE 7.8 Impulsivity as a vulnerability trait: Behavioral syndromes and timing of emergence.

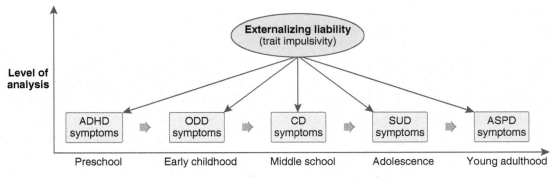

SOURCE: Based on Beauchaine, T.P., Zisner, A.R, & Sauder, C. L. (2017) Trait impulsivity and the externalizing spectrum. *Annual Review of Clinical Psychology, 13*, 343-368.

substance use disorder (SUD), and antisocial personality disorder (ASPD) (DSM-V, 2013).

Other biological markers related to problems with aggression are lower baseline levels of cortisol and lower morning-to-evening cortisol ratios compared to normal, nonaggressive samples. This abnormal cortisol pattern, observed in antisocial males and females, has also been associated with the tendency to sleep late and to stay up late, called "eveningness" as opposed to "morningness" (Carskadon, Viera, & Acebo, 1993). Recent evidence suggests that the tendency toward eveningness exists prior to the delayed phase preference changes ushered in at adolescence, and thus may represent a stable temperamental dimension of risk for externalizing problems. Susman and her colleagues (2007; Susman, Peckins, Bowes, & Dorn, 2017) report that eveningness was associated with rule-breaking and conduct problems in boys and to relational aggression in girls, as has been observed in older groups.

Adverse Environmental Influences

Hostile attributional bias (HAB) tends to be practiced over and over in ambiguous circumstances once the child has learned its value. Rates of HAB and aggression, partly acquired in social contexts, shape perceptions of threat. Attributional patterns are sometimes handed down intergenerationally and within social groups because of actual threatening circumstances like political struggles that go on for generations. Children who evidence HAB are more likely than those reared in non-harsh circumstances to become anxious, hypervigilant, and chronically reactive (Pettit, Lansford, Malone, & Dodge, 2010). Dodge and his colleagues (Dodge et al., 2015) studied boys and girls over 4 years (mean age of 8.3 at year 1) living in 12 different social groups in 9 countries. Their purpose was to determine if HAB, acquired through socially reinforced patterns of understanding ambiguous circumstances and interpreting intent, represented a universal psychological mechanism for explaining later aggressive behavior. Children from Thailand, Italy (Naples and Rome), Colombia, China, Sweden, Kenya, Jordan, the Philippines, and the United States were studied. The U.S. group, all from Durham, North Carolina, included African American, European American, and Hispanic youth. Mothers of all participants independently rated their children's level of externalizing behavior over four years of the study to provide behavioral evidence of aggression. In support of the hypothesis, children across the globe who made hostile attributions after provocation were more likely to show increasingly aggressive responses. Thus, one fundamental way to understand the growth of interpersonal aggression and violence across the world is potentially through the lens of social cognitive patterns for processing provocation.

Conditions such as poverty, substandard housing, low levels of parental education, teen parenting, parental substance abuse, membership of family or friends in gangs, large family size, inadequate educational opportunities, exposure to violence, and frequent residential moves exert great stress on family resources and are related to the development of antisocial behavior potentially by means of previously described mechanisms (Shaw & Shelleby, 2014). Such conditions increase the likelihood of hostile, harsh parenting; they heighten the risk of physical abuse, which is clearly related to later aggressive behavior (Cicchetti, 1989); and they are associated with chaotic home environments (noisy, lacking in routine, crowded), which also predict children's disruptive behavior (Jaffee, Hanscombe, Haworth, Davis, & Plomin, 2012).

More proximal influences include the characteristics of the parent–child relationship. Much of the current research on the early antecedents of antisocial behavior focuses on parent–child socialization practices. Patterson's influential model of **coercive family interaction** describes how children learn to act aggressively (see Figure 7.9). Based on the concept of negative reinforcement, Patterson and his associates have shown that young children learn to escape aversive consequences (such as turning off the TV) by whining, complaining, having tantrums, and so on, which cause parents to give up their demands for compliance (e.g., Snyder & Patterson, 1995). As soon as parents or caregivers cooperate with the child by backing off, the child reinforces the adults by stopping the unpleasant behavior (whining or crying). Sooner or later, these parents learn that the best way to escape or avoid the unpleasant situation their children create is by giving in to their children's demands. Thus,

FIGURE 7.9 Example of coercive parent–child interaction.

Parent asks child to turn off TV.

Child whines, cries, argues, or has tantrum.

Parent threatens or repeats command.

Child screams, refuses, escalates tantrum.

Parent relents and withdraws request.
Negative reinforcement of child's tantrums

Parent backs off, allowing child to watch TV.
Positive reinforcement of child's noncompliant behavior

aggressive children reinforce parental cessation of demands by providing their parents with some short-lived peace and quiet. In such coercive interaction sequences, fairly typical in families of antisocial children, children are trained in the effectiveness of aggressive noncompliance and learn powerful parent-control strategies.

Both child and parent characteristics appear to contribute to these coercive cycles. Processes that foster and evolve from early insecure attachments (Fearon, Bakersman-Kranenburg, van IJzendoorn, Lapsley, & Roisman, 2010) are important, along with temperamental differences in children's proneness to anger (Kochanska, Barry, Stellern, & O'Bleness, 2009; Kochanska & Kim, 2012). Longitudinal studies have found that with insecure toddlers who are anger-prone, parents tend to use ever-increasing power-assertive discipline strategies, and that by school age their children are rated both by themselves and by teachers as oppositional, disruptive, and callous. But securely attached toddlers who are anger-prone do not usually follow this negative pathway. For anger-prone toddlers, "early insecurity appeared to act as a catalyst for the parent–child dyad embarking on a mutually adversarial path toward antisocial outcomes, whereas security defused such a maladaptive dynamic" (Kochanska & Kim, 2012, p. 783).

Implications for Treatment

The best treatments for conduct problems are multidimensional, targeting individual, family, educational, and peer-related contexts. Despite this consensus, treatments are often based on "magic-bullet" approaches, as evidenced by court-mandated requirements for individual psychotherapy, group therapy, boot camps, wilderness programs, and the like. Such therapeutic efforts have very limited effectiveness in reversing conduct problems (Henggeler, Schoenwald, & Pickrel, 1995) and sometimes make problems worse. One famous study demonstrated that group treatments for antisocial youth pose a large iatrogenic increase in the rate and type of behavior problems. In other words, treating antisocial youth in group settings potentiates their antisocial behavior and enlarges their antisocial skill set through peer reinforcement of deviant behavior or "deviancy training" (Dishion, McCord, & Poulin, 1999). This finding received corroboration with a bit of a twist. Adolescents in mixed groups (with deviant and nondeviant peers) were found to display higher rates of deviant behavior and positive attitudes toward drug use than those receiving treatment in a homogeneous high-risk group setting (Poulin, Dishion, & Burraston, 2001).

Research has made three points crystal clear: (1) Early conduct problems in children are serious; (2) they need to be treated early; and (3) intervention needs to be multifaceted.

The Incredible Years ([IY]; Webster-Stratton et al., 2001) is a preschool prevention program for at-risk children (ages 2 to 10) and their families that is intended to prevent conduct problems before they take root. Parent training has three levels: basic (parenting skills, discipline), advanced (parent communication and anger management skills, conflict resolution), and school (home–school relationships, supporting educational achievement). Parents meet in small groups to discuss topics, watch videos of common problems, and role-play solutions. The curriculum for children, Dina Dinosaur Social Skills Curriculum, utilizes "child-size" dinosaur puppets and video vignettes to engage children in learning and practicing social and emotional skills. A third level of prevention includes a program for teachers that uses video, group discussion, and practice to help teachers learn effective management techniques for difficult behavior problems. All three curricula emphasize developing positive interpersonal relationships and effective emotion regulation skills. Program effectiveness studies show clear and sustained improvements in reducing conduct problems (Webster-Stratton & Hammond, 1997; Webster-Stratton & Reid, 2003), in improving school readiness and reducing classroom disruptive behavior in low-SES children (Webster-Stratton, Reid, & Stoolmiller, 2008), and reducing ADHD symptoms in preschool children (Jones, Daley, Hutchings, Bywater, & Eames, 2008).

The Fast Track program (Conduct Problems Prevention Research Group, 2015; 2013) is a successful research-based intervention for school-aged children that combines a universal curriculum (PATHS) with additional layers of intervention involving small friendship groups for children at risk for externalizing problems and training groups for their parents. Another approach, Multisystemic therapy ([MST]; Henggeler & Sheidow, 2012) is an intervention that provides family-based services for adolescent offenders who are at risk for out-of-home incarceration. MST has been successful in reducing recidivism and need for placement (Curtis & Ronan, 2004). Comprehensive school-based programs to reduce hostile attributional bias and promote effective conflict resolution have also shown promise. The Resolving Conflict Creatively Program (RCCP), which began in 1994 in the New York City public schools, has now been implemented in more than 400 urban, suburban, and rural schools in the United States (Brown, Roderick, Lantiere, & Aber, 2004). Aber and his colleagues (Aber, Jones, Brown, Chaudry, & Samples, 1998) showed that when students were taught a lesson by teachers with training in the program, the students demonstrated less dramatic increases in hostile attributions and fewer aggressive behaviors than comparison groups over time. Encouraging research reports from programs like the ones mentioned here provide clinicians with excellent guidance in how to address conduct disorders effectively.

Summary

Self-Concept

1. Although preschoolers can describe themselves, they have difficulty coordinating the different aspects of themselves. Also, they do not accommodate the opposition of some traits, such as "nice" and "mean," and they usually see themselves in an overly positive light. By middle childhood, the Me-self is becoming a more organized structure, although children still tend to emphasize the positive. Gradually, more trait-like concepts of self emerge, social comparison begins building on perspective taking skills, and self-esteem tends to decline a bit.

2. During middle childhood and beyond, the self-concept can be divided into multiple domains, such as academic and nonacademic, and each of these can be further differentiated. A global sense of self and self-esteem may coexist with these more differentiated assessments of self. Appearance is particularly associated with overall self-esteem, especially for girls.

3. Global self-esteem depends on competence in areas of importance to the individual, as William James suggested. In evaluating their own competencies, children may use concrete standards (e.g., making a team), but they are also influenced by social processes, as suggested by Cooley. They internalize the assessments of others, and they engage in social comparison, evaluating their own abilities and accomplishments against those of others who resemble them in some important way. They tend to be motivated by a self-enhancing bias, sometimes making downward social comparisons when their self-esteem is at stake. Children's self-appraisals come more and more into congruence with others' appraisals as they get older.

4. Positive *self-esteem* refers to feeling worthwhile and having a general sense of satisfaction with one's self, without feeling better than others. *Self-efficacy* is the more specific belief in one's ability to overcome challenges, along with a willingness to keep trying. This is similar to Erikson's notion of *industry*, referring specifically to seeing oneself as a competent worker and enjoying the challenge of work. *Narcissism* is different. It is seeing the self as special and entitled, and it usually is associated with needing to be the center of others' admiring attention. Positive self-esteem is linked to parental warmth whereas narcissism is associated with parental overvaluing.

5. There is a small but stable gender difference in self-esteem favoring males in late childhood and early adolescence, but little evidence of a self-esteem slide for girls. Level of voice is one predictor of self-esteem, but girls' and boys' levels of voice do not appear to differ at adolescence.

6. Older views that marginalized groups would have lower self-esteem than mainstream groups due to the internalization of discriminatory appraisals are not supported by current research. African Americans, for example, have a slight self-esteem advantage over White Americans. In general, strong racial or ethnic identity correlates positively with level of global self-esteem, although findings vary from group to group and from individual to individual.

7. In different cultures, the judgments, beliefs, values, and expectations that influence self-concept are likely to differ. For example, individualistic cultures value independence more than collectivist cultures, which value interdependence more. As a result, both self-construals and the bases of self-worth evaluations tend to be different as well. For example, in individualist cultures, being proud of oneself, an element of self-esteem, is important and predicts positive outcomes if it is not overly inflated (narcissistic). But in collectivist cultures, having harmonious relationships is more important for self-respect. Pride in oneself is seen as arrogance, and self-criticism in the service of self-improvement is more valued.

The Moral Self

8. The meaning of morality varies across individuals, groups, and cultures, but generally includes fundamental principles necessary to successful functioning of society: concern for others, a sense of justice and fairness, trustworthiness or honesty, and self-control.

9. Emotions, cognitions, and behaviors are all part of morality, and are not always well coordinated.

10. In Freud's psychoanalytic theory, conscience emerges between ages 3 and 5, when children identify with the same-sex parent. In the process, children internalize the same-sex parent's values and rules, forming a superego. Much evidence is inconsistent with this view. For example, moral emotions and prosocial behavior begin as early as toddlerhood.

11. Piaget and Kohlberg propose cognitive theories, arguing that moral development is influenced by developmental changes in logical thinking and emerges in a series of stages. Although there is some clear support for these views, there are inconsistent findings. For example, Piaget assumed that preschoolers treat all rules as inviolable, determined by authorities. But even 3-year-olds judge violations of moral rules, such as rules about stealing, more seriously than violations of conventional rules, such as how one should dress.

12. Altruism may be motivated in many ways. Emotional reactions, such as empathy and sympathy, are important motivators. Even toddlers show signs that

empathy can propel prosocial action such as sharing or comforting, but such emotions are much more effective motivators after the preschool years, as perspective taking ability improves.

13. Needs-based reasoning can also affect prosocial behavior and shows predictable developments with age. It also tends to be more advanced in popular children with good social skills, especially boys. Also, younger children whose moral reasoning is needs oriented are not as likely as older children to engage in prosocial behavior unless they also experience prosocial emotions. For older children whose reasoning is needs oriented, the presence of such emotions is not so important.

14. Personality characteristics also affect tendencies toward prosocial behavior—characteristics such as sociability, social competence, positive self-concept, assertiveness, and effortful self-control.

15. Parents who use an authoritative parenting style with high levels of warmth and demandingness seem to promote prosocial behavior. Also, when parents have strong prosocial values their children are likely to follow suit. Providing children with opportunities to practice prosocial behavior increases further prosocial behavior, referred to as the "foot in the door effect."

16. Antisocial behavior includes acts like cheating, lying, and stealing, as well as aggressive behavior that can be physical, verbal, and social.

17. Most people lie, even though it is considered morally unacceptable in many situations. Lying to cover up misdeeds increases from early to middle childhood as children's perspective taking skills and executive functions improve, and begins to decline in early adolescence as children's moral reasoning and behavior become more coordinated. Prosocial lying (e.g., to avoid hurting someone's feelings) continues to increase into adolescence and is often perceived by teens as morally acceptable.

18. Physical aggression, like hitting, is common in 2- and 3-year-olds but declines substantially by ages 4 and 5 and continues to decrease in middle childhood. Forms of aggression also change with age. Instrumental aggression gives way to person directed forms, such as relational aggression (e.g., spreading rumors, teasing).

19. Many factors contribute to declines in aggression with age, such as improving perspective taking skills. For children who show high rates of aggression, social information-processing often appears to involve a hostile attributional bias. That is, these children tend to misattribute negative motives to others. Hostile attributions lead them to defend themselves or to extract revenge. Such children are using aggressive schemas to make sense of social interactions.

20. Peer victimization is a fairly common experience in middle childhood and tends to decline with age. Some children are bully-victims, others are just bullies or victims. Peer victimization tends to decline with age as aggression declines, but not for all children. Both bullies and victims are at risk for a range of social, emotional, academic, and conduct problems, so that interventions, especially at the school and classroom level, are vital.

Case Study

Kevin Miller, a White fifth-grade student at Greentree Elementary School, is in the principal's office with his parents. Mr. Dolan, the school principal, has just informed Mr. and Mrs. Miller that Kevin's fifth-grade trip privilege will be revoked because of an accumulation of disciplinary offenses. Kevin's behavior in fifth grade has become progressively more disruptive. This time, he has managed to create enough problems for his teachers to prevent his participation in the end-of-the-year event, which was planned as a reward for the students' effort and achievement.

Kevin is a very intelligent and physically attractive youngster with particular interests and abilities in sports and computer games. In second grade, he was identified as a candidate for the school's gifted student program, yet he invests little energy in schoolwork. He tells his teachers that he finds the assignments boring and can find no reason to involve himself in the learning process. He does little studying, but he manages to get by with a C+ average. In class, he talks to other students when he should be working, makes disrespectful comments to his teachers, and basically tries to get away with doing what he pleases most of the time.

Kevin relishes his position of power in the group. Many students in the class look up to Kevin because of his engaging bravado. They like him because he is often funny and provides a diversion from class work. Other students find him a nuisance who distracts the teachers from their instruction. Students know that if they work with Kevin on a group project, they may have a good time, but it will come with a price: getting in trouble with their teachers.

Kevin's parents have a long history of conferencing with the school principal and counselor. Over the years, problems have increased from some concerns about his attention span in the early grades to more serious issues. In fourth grade, Kevin was caught cheating on a test proctored by a substitute teacher. Kevin claimed that he was falsely accused because the teacher "didn't like him." At the beginning of fifth grade, Kevin responded to his English teacher, who was trying to get him to focus on a classroom writing assignment, with a profane comment. When confronted about his behavior, Kevin was convinced that he did not do anything seriously wrong. His explanation was that he was joking, and he suggested that the adults should "lighten up."

Kevin's parents believe it is their job to stand up for their only son and support him, even though they are unhappy about his frequent problems at school. The Millers describe their son as "lively and creative" and "smarter than they are" in some areas, such as computer literacy. Encouraged by the school counselor, they initiated private counseling for Kevin at the end of fourth grade. Kevin has seen his counselor sporadically for almost a year. Both parents believe that Kevin is a good boy whose irrepressible spirit and intellect get him into trouble with those who misunderstand him.

Faced with this new consequence, Kevin is quite upset. He was looking forward to the class trip and believes that the punishment is extreme. The Millers understand the principal's reasoning, but they also disagree with the punishment. They indicate that they will request a meeting with the superintendent to have the decision changed. They express the view that most kids behave like Kevin sometimes. From their perspective, Kevin should be allowed to express himself and to have the autonomy to make choices about what he does. They emphasize his persistence and interest in activities that engage his attention. They come close to faulting Kevin's teachers for failing to motivate him.

The district superintendent, after considering the case, decides that depriving Kevin of the trip would jeopardize any relationship teachers would be able to develop with him in the future. Kevin's consequence is changed to an in-school suspension; he is allowed to participate in the class trip.

Discussion Questions

1. What are the issues involved in Kevin's case? What assessment can you make of his moral development and his self-concept?
2. If you were his counselor, what would you recommend to promote healthy development?

Practice Using What You Have Learned

MyLab Education Application Exercise 7.1:
Differentiated Structure of Self-Concept

MyLab Education Application Exercise 7.2:
Influences on Self-Concept

MyLab Education Application Exercise 7.3:
Moral Development

Journal Questions

1. Give an example of a moral principle you learned as a child. How and when did you learn it? Provide an example from your own experience of an inconsistency between your level of moral reasoning and your behavior.
2. If you can remember struggling with some subject or concept in school, describe the impact of that experience on your sense of competence and industry. How have you resolved this struggle?
3. Comment on your view about the self-esteem controversy. Do you think fostering self-esteem by praise is well founded or problematic; does it encourage a failure orientation or a mastery one according to your experience? What was your own experience as a child? Can you identify your own orientation (mastery/failure) in general? If possible, provide a specific example from elementary school to illustrate how your own self-efficacy developed.
4. How did your peers contribute to your understanding of yourself? Explain.
5. Describe an example of hostile attributional bias from your life or your experience. What problems facing society might be fueled by this particular type of social information-processing? What might be an effective intervention for this problem from your perspective?

Key Concepts

academic self-concept (p. 256)
nonacademic self-concept (p. 256)
social comparison (p. 258)
self-enhancing bias (p. 258)
downward social comparisons (p. 258)
self-efficacy (p. 259)
narcissism (p. 259)
industry (p. 259)
self-esteem slide (p. 262)
identification (p. 265)
premoral stage (p. 268)
heteronomous stage (p. 268)
immanent justice (p. 269)
autonomous stage (p. 269)
preconventional morality (p. 269)

conventional morality (p. 269)
postconventional morality (p. 269)
moral rules (p. 271)
conventional rules (p. 271)
personal rules (p. 271)
morality of justice (p. 272)
morality of caring (p. 272)
prosocial behavior or altruism (p. 273)
empathy (p. 273)
sympathy (p. 274)
needs-based reasoning (p. 274)
hedonistic (p. 274)
needs oriented (p. 274)
antisocial behavior (p. 277)
instrumental aggression (p. 279)

relational aggression (p. 279)
social information-processing (p. 279)
hostile attributional bias (HAB) (p. 280)
oppositional defiant disorder (ODD) (p. 287)
conduct disorder (CD) (p. 287)
antisocial personality disorder (APD) (p. 287)
early-starter or life-course persistent model (p. 288)
late-starter or adolescent-limited model (p. 288)
childhood-limited model (p. 288)
adolescent onset model (p. 288)
coercive family interaction (p. 290)

Chapter 8
Gender and Peer Relationships: Middle Childhood Through Early Adolescence

 Learning Objectives

After reading this chapter, you should be able to:

8.1 Describe biological processes in sex determination, differentiation in male and female prenatal development, sex-related vulnerabilities to hereditary diseases, and mortality rates.

8.2 Identify and describe key elements that contribute to gender role development and, having examined your own schemas about gender identity (stereotypes, expectations), respond effectively to children's gender-associated needs and problems.

8.3 Recognize the role, influence, and relevance of peer relationships in childhood and adolescence, and analyze children's functioning within their peer groups and structure interventions that meet needs for acceptance and belonging.

It's recess time for the third graders at Columbus Elementary. Nine-year-old Eloise and three of her girlfriends take turns jumping rope, while other small clusters of girls are playing hopscotch or sitting and talking. One pair whispers conspiratorially, occasionally giggling and glancing up at Eloise and her friends. Another girl, Shayla, skips across the grass alone and then sits on a swing, watching three friends play a climbing game on the modern jungle gym. The game has something to do with a TV show they saw the night before. Dmitri and a crew of boys are playing a variant of tag, in which whoever is "it" must not only catch someone else (who will then become "it") but also dodge the assaults of players who risk being caught as they race past and punch the boy who is "it" in the back or arms. Another boy watching on the sidelines, Jacob, suddenly jumps into the tag game, punching the player who is "it." The others gather round, shoving and yelling at the intruder. When Jacob says, "I can play if I want to," Dmitri shouts more loudly than the rest, "Let him play, but he's gotta be it." In the remaining 10 minutes of recess, Jacob catches three different boys, but the captives are forcibly freed by Dmitri and the others, and Jacob never escapes being "it" despite his bitter protests. Moments before recess ends, he stomps off in a rage, cursing at the others.

As the third graders move off the playground, recess begins for the higher grades. Soon a group of sixth graders, seven boys and one girl, are playing basketball on the paved court; another larger group, all boys, is playing soccer on a grassy field. Most of the sixth-grade girls are standing around in circles, talking.

We could watch a large assembly of elementary school children on any playground in the United States—the roof of a private Manhattan school; the small, fenced yard of a Chicago public school; or, as in this example, the ample playing fields, paved courts, and wood-chipped, well-equipped play area of a sprawling school in an affluent Seattle suburb. Despite the constraints of the setting, some key elements of the children's behavior would be strikingly similar. Like Eloise, most of the girls would be playing or talking in clusters of two or three, separately from the boys. The boys would be playing in larger groups, and often their play would consist of some mostly good-natured roughhousing. Some children would probably be alone. They might stand apart, like Shayla, or they might push their way into a group where they are not welcome and then find themselves in conflict with others, like Jacob. Occasionally, a child of one sex might play comfortably with a group of the opposite sex, but generally she or he will be a quiet, peripheral member of the group. More often than not, this child will be a girl. Sometimes, groups of boys will interfere with the play of a cluster of girls, most often to chase them or to upset their game. The girls might chase the boys back, always with their girlfriends along for support.

These patterns will be familiar to anyone who has ever participated in, or observed, a children's recess. In this chapter, we will examine two major features of child development that contribute to these patterns. The first is gender role development in childhood and early adolescence, including the formation of a gender identity and the acquisition of gender-related behaviors. (We will discuss a related but separate construct, the emergence of sexual orientation, in Chapter 9.) The second is the formation and influence of peer relations in the lives of children and young adolescents, including both the degree to which children are able to establish satisfying relationships with their peers and the nature and influence of broader peer groups. Gender role development and peer relations have traditionally been separate disciplines in the developmental sciences, and to some degree we will discuss them separately here. It is becoming increasingly clear, however, that peer interactions differ as a function of gender and that peer processes contribute substantially in shaping gendered behavior.

For helpers, understanding the processes of gender role development can be a key element in providing valid supports to children and adults as they struggle with identity issues, self-acceptance, and self-esteem. Many coping difficulties, both externalizing and internalizing problems, are more typical of either one gender or the other in our society, or they have different features and implications depending on the gender of the client.

It also has become increasingly obvious that a major function of counselors, teachers, and other helpers who work with children and adolescents is to identify and intervene with individuals whose peer relationships are distorted. In fact, estimates suggest that up to 75% of children referred for counseling services experience difficulties getting along with their peers (Parker, Rubin, Erath, Wojslawowicz, & Buskirk, 2006). Many developments—including perspective taking, as we have already seen, and gender role development, as we will see in this chapter—are now recognized to be at least partly a function of peer group interaction. Establishing and maintaining satisfying relationships with peers and finding a place among broader peer groups are salient to children themselves and are considered central developmental tasks of middle childhood and adolescence. Victims, bullies, and loners in the world of childhood are at risk for long-term social problems as well as emotional and behavioral difficulties (Rubin, Bukowski, & Bowker, 2015).

The Biology of Sex

8.1 Describe biological processes in sex determination, differentiation in male and female prenatal development, sex-related vulnerabilities to hereditary diseases, and mortality rates.

You may recall from Chapter 2 that humans have 23 pairs of chromosomes in the nuclei of their cells. In females, the 23rd pair, called the sex chromosomes, consists of two large X chromosomes. In males, the 23rd pair is mismatched: There is one X chromosome and one much smaller Y chromosome. (Go back to Figure 2.2 to see the difference.) When a woman produces an ovum (egg) with only half the typical number of chromosomes, one from each pair, the egg contains one of the woman's X chromosomes. Sperm also contain only one member of each pair of chromosomes, so half of the sperm a man produces will carry an X and half will carry a Y chromosome. The role of heredity in sex determination begins at conception. If an X-carrying sperm fertilizes the egg, the zygote will have an XX pair and will develop into a female. Fertilization by a Y-carrying sperm will give the zygote an XY sex-chromosome pair, and a male will be the outcome. Unlike other chromosome pairs, the X and Y differ not only in size, but also in function: Most of the genes on the X are not matched on the Y, and vice versa.

The chromosomal differences have some impact right from the start. For example, cells carrying the XY chromosome pair have a higher metabolic rate than XX carrying cells, so they divide more quickly and their prenatal growth is faster (e.g., Pergament, Todydemir, & Fiddler, 2002). But the major differentiation of males and females begins at about 5 weeks after conception. By this point, the fetus has developed a pair of "indifferent" or unisex gonads that could become either ovaries or testes. We'll begin by following the process of differentiation into male structures. The key is a gene located only on the Y chromosome, called the **SRY gene** (sex-determining region of the Y chromosome). The SRY gene codes for a transcription factor that binds to regulatory DNA, which turns on genes that start the production of other proteins responsible for the development of gonads into testes. The cells of the testes begin to produce many masculinizing hormones, including **anti-Mullerian hormone (AMH)** and testosterone, one of several male hormones called **androgens**, which circulate throughout the body and influence the development of many different kinds of tissue.

All fetuses develop two sets of ducts, called the **Mullerian ducts** and **Wolffian ducts**, which can differentiate into reproductive structures. Testosterone and other hormones stimulate the *Wolffian ducts* to develop into male structures, such as the seminal vesicles. AMH causes the deterioration of the *Mullerian ducts*, which could have developed into internal female parts: the fallopian tubes, uterus, and upper part of the vagina. By the third month, androgens are influencing the growth of male external genitalia from a whole set of "indifferent" structures. For example, the indifferent **genital tubercle** becomes a penis; in the absence of androgens it would have become a clitoris. Similarly, an area of genital swelling develops into a scrotal sac; without the androgens it would have become the labia majora (see Figure 8.1).

You can see that the presence of the SRY gene in the male begins a cascade of changes that result in a male reproductive system. Much of the process depends on high levels of circulating androgens, produced by the testes. Without the SRY gene and the male hormones, the default developmental path for all the indifferent structures is in the female direction (ovaries, clitoris, and so on). In females, the Mullerian tubes survive and evolve into female reproductive structures, and the Wolffian tubes deteriorate without androgens to stimulate their further development.

Females produce some androgens (both in the ovaries and the adrenal glands), just as males produce the female hormone, estrogen (from androgens as it happens; females produce estrogen more directly in their ovaries). The key to the determination of physical sexual characteristics is the amount and timing of androgen production. "If these hormones are not present in adequate amounts or over the correct temporal intervals, the natural tendency to retain female characteristics prevails" (Ward, 1992, p. 158), which is what happens in individuals with two X chromosomes. Males' androgen production begins surging at 5 weeks of gestation; the surge ends at about 28 weeks. There is another surge just after birth, peaking at 1 to 2 months, and then declining. Females' estrogen production surges a bit during this same post-natal period, which is sometimes called "mini-puberty" (see Hines, Constantinescu, & Spencer, 2015). After 5 months, both androgen and estrogen production is equally low for boys and girls until actual puberty. After puberty, males produce high levels of testosterone throughout adulthood, much higher than females, until a gradual decline begins at middle age (andropause). Females generally produce higher levels of estrogen than males until menopause.

FIGURE 8.1 Prenatal differentiation of male and female external genitalia from the same structures.

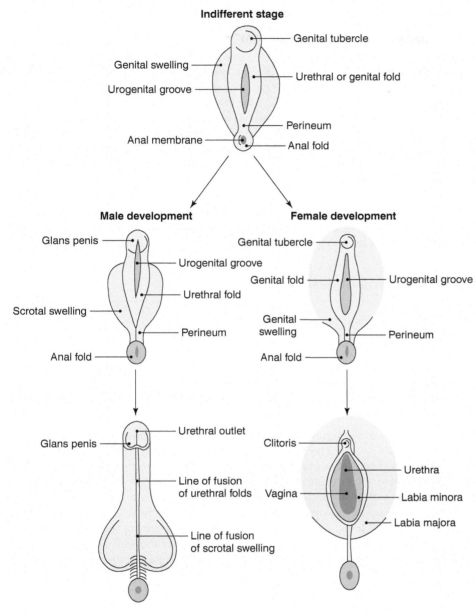

It is frequently reported that male conceptions far outnumber female conceptions (e.g., Pergament et al., 2002), though recent analyses with more comprehensive samples indicate that the sex ratio at conception is likely to be equal for males and females (Orzack et al., 2015). The challenges in accurately estimating sex ratio at conception arise from changes over prenatal development in the likelihood of fetal death for males versus females. As previously understood, recent estimates indicate that more male than female embryos are spontaneously aborted during early pregnancy, often before the mother realizes she is pregnant, and that more male than female fetuses are miscarried late in pregnancy. In mid-pregnancy and overall, however, there are more females than males miscarried (Orzack et al., 2015), resulting in an actual birth ratio of about 105 males to 100 females.

Much remains to be understood about these developmental changes in the prenatal sex ratio, though the prenatal vulnerability of males at certain times is known to be partly a function of their susceptibility to hereditary diseases. This vulnerability continues into childhood. The problem for males is the mismatched sex chromosomes. The smaller Y chromosome does not carry most of the genes that the X chromosome does. There are a slew of X-linked recessive disorders, such as hemophilia, baldness, color blindness, night blindness, Duchenne's muscular dystrophy, fragile X syndrome (which involves intellectual disability), and so on, and males are much more likely to have these disorders than are females. To understand why, consider color blindness. Normal color vision is influenced by a gene on the X chromosome that is ordinarily dominant over any defective allele. Thus, even if a girl (who has two X chromosomes) has a defective allele that could cause color blindness on one of her X chromosomes, she will not be color-blind as long as she has a normal color-vision allele on her other X chromosome. If she happens to inherit defective alleles from both parents, then she will be color-blind. In other words, for females only, color blindness, and all of the other X-linked recessive disorders, function like all inherited diseases caused by recessive, defective gene alleles (see Chapter 2). For males, the process is different. If a boy inherits a defective gene allele for color vision on the X chromosome, which comes from his mother, he will be color-blind because his Y chromosome, inherited from his father, bears no matching gene. This is true for all the X-linked recessive diseases. The result is that females tend to be carriers and males are more likely to be affected.

MyLab Education Self-Check 8.1.

Gender Role Development

8.2 Identify and describe key elements that contribute to gender role development and, having examined your own schemas about gender identity (stereotypes, expectations), respond effectively to children's gender-associated needs and problems.

Let's now take a look at the development of cognitive, social, and behavioral phenomena related to one's gender. The first part of our discussion of gender role development deals with gender identity, a person's awareness of his or her own gender assignment and understanding of its meaning. It is often assumed in both society and psychological research that a child's gender identity, or sense of self as a girl or boy, will align with her or his assigned biological sex based on XX or XY chromosomes at birth (Fast & Olson, 2018; Lee, Houk, Ahmed, & Hughes, 2006). However, we will also discuss circumstances such as those for intersex and transgender individuals when this may not be the case. The second part of our gender role development discussion centers on *gender differences in behavior*. We will consider some of the processes that might account for these phenomena, and later we will examine how a helping professional could use this information to benefit clients.

Gender Identity

Augustina was the youngest girl in a family of nine children. Her parents had emigrated from Italy to the United States before she was born in 1913. When she was an elderly woman, Augustina recalled that as a young child, she had firmly believed she would be a man when she grew up. She remembered that sometime in her preschool years she was aware of being a girl, but she was excited about the prospect of becoming like her older brothers, whom she saw as confident, swaggering, well-dressed young men to whom her mother deferred and who could stand toe-to-toe with her imposing father. (In the cultural tradition of her family, men were more privileged and powerful than women.) She could also remember a feeling of bitter disappointment that hung with her for many months after she realized, sometime later, that she was destined to remain female and that she would inevitably become a woman.

Augustina's story illustrates some elements in the progress of *gender identity* for young children, although most children do not associate negative feelings with the process but seem to wholeheartedly accept their status. The first step in the process is learning to categorize oneself as male or female. By late in their first year, babies seem to make perceptual distinctions between the sexes. They can distinguish pictures of men from pictures of women (Poulin-Dubois & Serbin, 2006), and they can distinguish the voices of men from those of women (even when the voices are matched for pitch; Miller, 1983). Toddlers (about age 2) begin to show signs that they can discriminate some actions as more typical of one gender or the other. For example, they look longer (as if surprised) at a man putting on makeup than a woman doing so (Hill & Flom, 2007).

Children show some skill at labeling males and females and at understanding labels such as *lady* or *man*, *girl* or *boy* late in their second year (e.g., Zosuls, Ruble, Bornstein, & Greulich, 2009). Some children produce a gender label for themselves before age 2. The majority know a self-label by age 2½, and they can identify others who fit into the same category as they do (Maccoby, 1998; Martin & Ruble, 2009). Furthermore, children around age 2 show preference for objects and people associated with their own gender (Zosuls et al., 2009).

As Augustina's experience illustrates, however, knowing your gender category today may not mean that you understand that it will stay that way forever. A second step in the process of identity formation is **gender stability**—the understanding that over time, one's gender category usually stays the same: Boys grow into men, girls grow into women. A third step appears to be recognizing that gender category membership is permanent, that it could never change, even if one's behavior or appearance were changed to resemble the other gender. This is called **gender constancy** (Slaby & Frey, 1975). Most children seem to have gender stability by 3 to 4 years old—a girl knows she was a girl yesterday and expects to be one again tomorrow. But even older preschoolers may not understand gender constancy. For this, children must realize that even if major surface changes were made—in hairstyle, dress, and behavior—the gender of the individual would not also change.

Controversy swirls around the question of when gender constancy develops. In some studies, preschoolers who are shown pictures of, say, a boy dressed up like a girl, with a long-haired wig and a dress, often express the belief that the boy has changed into a girl (DeLisi & Gallagher, 1991; Fast & Olson, 2017; Kohlberg, 1966). In other studies, even some 3-year-olds seem to have a pretty clear sense of gender constancy (e.g., Bem, 1989; Johnson & Ames, 1994). But it is safe to say that until about the time of school entry, a child's understanding of this concept can be fragile, and he can show uncertainty about the permanence of gender categories. This uncertainty may be more common, and not necessarily inappropriate, among children who are transgender themselves or siblings of transgender children, which we discuss more in a later section (Fast & Olson, 2017). By school age, children know their gender, and they understand that it is consistent across situations and permanent over time (e.g., Ruble et al., 2007). Still, there are many other dimensions to gender identity that continue to evolve, like the child's comfort with his gender, as you will see in Box 8.1.

Box 8.1: Beyond Gender Constancy: Gender Identity, Social Adjustment, and Ethnicity

Sebastian is a boy and he knows it. He understands that this gender category is essentially immutable. But at age 6, his gender identity is only beginning to develop. As he gets older, his self-knowledge will grow in many ways, as we saw in Chapter 7. This growth in self-awareness will come partly from his own active social comparisons and partly from the input and feedback that he receives from others. In this process, Sebastian's sense of himself as a member of the "boy" category will differentiate. He will identify and evaluate his gender-typical behavior in many arenas, for example, "Do my interests match those of other boys?"

or "Do I act like the other boys in my class?" Besides developing a more detailed and complex sense of himself as a boy, he will integrate much of this information into more general considerations of his gender typicality, such as, "Overall, am I a good fit with my gender category?" (Egan & Perry, 2001; Martin, Andrew, England, Sozuls, & Ruble, 2017).

Do these more complex gender identities have any effects on children's psychosocial adjustment? Perry and colleagues (e.g., Egan & Perry, 2001) set out to study this. They discovered that in the United States, the impact of gender identity on adjustment

(continued)

can depend on whether children are members of the White majority or an ethnic/racial minority.

Let's begin by considering what the researchers learned about White children. In studies of hundreds of third to eighth graders, they measured various dimensions of gender (Carver, Yunger, & Perry, 2003; Egan & Perry, 2001; Yunger, Carver, & Perry, 2004). Three turned out to be especially important: felt gender typicality (compatibility), contentedness with gender assignment, and felt pressure to conform to social expectations for one's gender. These dimensions were related to children's psychosocial adjustment, including peer acceptance, internalizing problems, and self-esteem.

To measure children's self-perceptions on dimensions of gender identity, researchers met with each child individually and read a set of statements, asking the child to rate how true the statements were. To assess Sebastian's felt gender compatibility, for example, one of the statements he would have rated is as follows:

"Some boys don't feel they are a good example of being a boy,	BUT	Other boys do feel they are a good example of being a boy."	
Very true for me	Sort of true for me	Sort of true for me	Very true for me
☐	☐	☐	☐

To measure his contentedness with his gender assignment, Sebastian would rate statements like "Some boys wish it'd be okay for them to do some of the things that usually only girls do BUT other boys never wish it would be okay for them to do some of the things that only girls do." A statement about felt pressure for sex-typing would be "Some boys think their parents would be upset if they wanted to learn an activity that only girls usually do BUT other boys don't think their parents would be upset if they wanted to learn an activity that only girls usually do" (Egan & Perry, 2001).

Other measures focused on children's interest in stereotypical male (e.g., "using tools to make things") and female (e.g., "baking") activities and traits, their "intergroup bias" (whether and how strongly they valued their own gender over the other), their global self-esteem, and their perception of their own social competence. As a sociometric assessment of peer perceptions, classmates of participants indicated which children they liked the most and which they liked the least. In one study, peers indicated whether statements representing internalizing problems (e.g., "He says bad things about himself") or externalizing problems (e.g., "She hits and pushes others around") were true of participants.

Children varied widely on how they perceived their own gender typicality, how satisfied they were with their gender, and how much pressure they felt to conform to gender stereotypes. As you might expect, how typical children felt and how content they were with their gender were both correlated with their actual gender-typical activities and traits. But you might be surprised to learn that the correlations were only modest. Children do not all use the same criteria to judge what is typical for their gender and how closely they personally match gender norms. They construct their own meanings for gender categories. These meanings are certainly affected by cultural stereotypes and norms, but they are also somewhat unique for each child.

Longitudinally, there was some tendency for children to increase in felt gender typicality over time; boys also showed a tendency to increase in gender contentedness, but girls did not. Girls at all ages felt less typical and less content with their gender than boys did, but they also reported less pressure to conform than boys. Yet for both boys and girls, the connections between gender identity and social adjustment were largely the same. Youngsters who reported feeling that they were not very typical of their gender had lower self-esteem than those who felt more compatible with their gender. Perhaps children with low felt gender typicality fear rejection by peers or others, or they might just feel inadequate and out of step. Such feelings seem warranted: Children who felt less typical both considered themselves less socially competent and were less well liked by peers than youngsters who felt more typical.

We might expect that children who are dissatisfied with their gender assignment would be especially prone to social adjustment problems, such as depression or low self-esteem. This is often the case, especially among children who fall at the extreme end of gender discontent (e.g., Martin, Andrews, England, Zosuls, & Ruble, 2017; Pauletti, Menon, Cooper, Aults, & Perry, 2017). But in the Perry studies of White children in the United States, and with more recent investigations building on this work, the determination of whether dissatisfaction with gender assignment was problematic depended on if children felt pressured by others (adults or children) to conform. In one study, children who scored low on gender contentment also tended to have internalizing problems, like self-deprecating behavior and social anxiety, but only if they felt that they were under pressure by others to conform to gender stereotypes (Yunger et al., 2004). In recent studies, rejection and bullying by peers that was related to gender nonconformity partly accounted for links between low gender typicality and negative social and emotional outcomes, especially for boys (Jewell & Brown, 2014; Smith & Juvonen, 2017).

Some theorists have argued that when acceptance depends on fitting gender stereotypes, children are likely to limit the range of activities they explore and the talents that they choose to develop (e.g., Bem, 1981). As a result, children who feel strong pressure to conform have less opportunity to develop in ways that are maximally satisfying—that fit their preferences and inclinations—and they tend to be unhappy, anxious, and discontented with themselves. Although the research by Perry and colleagues supports this position to some extent, it also makes clear that felt pressure for gender conformity interacts with other aspects of gender identity in complex ways. High felt pressure is most problematic for children who sense that they do not fit in, either because they perceive their talents and interests to cross gender boundaries or because they are not as comfortable with their gender assignment as other children. Later in this chapter we further discuss issues related to gender nonconformity and transgender identity.

Egan and Perry (2001) argued that "children's adjustment is optimized when they (a) are secure in their conceptions of themselves as typical members of their gender yet (b) feel free to explore cross-sex options when they so desire" (p. 459). In addition, children who describe their identities as consistent with both male and female qualities, sometimes referred to as *androgynous*, also tend to show healthy adjustment (Martin et al., 2017; Pauletti et al., 2017). But do the same gender identity processes affect social adjustment for children in minority groups? Corby, Hodges, and Perry (2007) investigated, using the measures from Perry's earlier studies with White, Black, and Hispanic fifth graders from lower middle class neighborhoods.

In general, gender identity seemed to have less impact on social adjustment for the minority group children. For example, although gender *contentedness* was just as important for Black children's adjustment as it was for White children, it was not especially important for Hispanic children. Also, even though Black and Hispanic children felt *more* pressure for gender conformity than White children did, it did not seem to cause adjustment problems. In fact, Hispanic boys who felt a great deal of pressure to conform had fewer internalizing problems than other boys!

What can we make of these differences across U.S. subcultures? Corby et al. (2007) remind us that for children growing up with minority status, many features of experience, and many aspects of self-concept development, are different than for children with majority status (see Chapter 9). Even though gender seems important to all groups (e.g., minority children also feel pressure to conform to gender expectations), in different developmental contexts it may not have the same meaning or power. For example, formulating a racial or ethnic identity or coping with minority status may have more influence on adjustment for some groups than gender identity dimensions or they may interact in complex ways with developing gender identity (Leaper, 2015; Rogers, Scott, & Way, 2015; see Chapter 9). Clearly, we have much more to learn about the ways that culture moderates the effects of gender identity on children's social adjustment.

What influences affect the formation of a gender identity? How do children come to make gender a part of their self-concept? Like every other important behavioral development, many factors contribute: social, cognitive, and biological.

THE ROLE OF SOCIAL PROCESSES IN GENDER IDENTITY

When babies are born, adults assign them to gender categories based on their genital characteristics. From the first, young children hear themselves described as male or female. They are told, "You're a big girl to help Daddy like that," "Mommy loves her sweet boy," or "You don't want to be a mean girl who makes her friend cry!" Children are literally surrounded by verbal reminders of their assigned gender. It's not surprising, then, that between 2 and 3, at the same time that they are learning other labels for themselves such as "naughty" or "nice" (see Chapter 5), nearly all children have learned their own gender label.

Research with **intersex** children suggests that social assignment to a gender category can influence gender identity. Intersex children have either ambiguous genitalia or genitalia that are inconsistent with their sex chromosomes. These individuals are described medically as having Disorders of Sexual Development (DSD), a controversial term that refers more broadly to congenital conditions in which development of chromosomal, gonadal, or anatomic sex is atypical (Anderson, 2015; Hughes, Houk, Ahmed, & Lee, 2006; Sandberg, Gardner, Collen, & Mazur, 2017). In one example, biologically male children, with one X and one Y chromosome, have suffered surgical damage to their genitals during infancy, sometimes as a result of a botched circumcision. Faced with this difficult situation, some parents have raised these children as girls from infancy onward. One boy was reassigned by his family as a "girl" at age 7 months (Bradley, Oliver, Chernick, & Zucker, 1998). Physicians provided treatments with female hormones at puberty so that female secondary sexual characteristics would develop, such as enlarged breasts. At the most recent follow-up, in early adulthood, the young woman still accepted her female identity and was comfortable with her female role. (Note that the results in this case do not indicate that such a solution would be right in all cases. See the discussion below of another boy whose penis was ablated in infancy, and the very different outcome he experienced.)

Another type of intersex condition, **congenital adrenal hyperplasia (CAH)**, occurs when biological females with two X chromosomes are exposed to high levels of androgens during prenatal and postnatal development. The overproduction of androgens by their own adrenal glands is caused by a defective gene. Although CAH females usually have the internal organs of a girl, their external genitalia may be masculinized. They may, for example, have an enlarged clitoris that looks like a penis, and they have sometimes been misidentified at birth as boys. When they are properly diagnosed, a set of medical interventions can minimize the overproduction of androgens postnatally, and the genitalia can be surgically altered to resemble those of a girl. But John Money and his colleagues, who did extensive studies of children with CAH, concluded that if the diagnosis is not made before the age of 2½ to 3, a child's gender identity can be very difficult to alter (Erhardt & Baker, 1974; Money & Dalery, 1977; Money & Erhardt, 1972) and more recent studies seem to confirm this finding (Endendijk, Beltz, McHale, Bryk, & Berenmaum, 2017). Critics of Money's research program have questioned some of his evidence for the social construction of gender and caution against early gender assignment without the possibility of individual choice (Reis, 2007). Today, early misidentification of CAH girls is much less likely, and the American Academy of Pediatrics recommends that CAH girls identified as such in infancy should be raised as girls. It should be noted that sexual assignment or reassignment in infancy that involves surgery is becoming more and more controversial (see further discussion in the upcoming section "The Role of Biology in Gender Identity").

When CAH females are raised as boys their gender identity is inconsistent with their biological sex, and yet most accept their gender assignment. Of course, their social assignment to the status of male may not be the only factor that supports their acceptance of a male identity. Their exposure to androgens appears to have a masculinizing effect on their behavior as well as on their genitalia, and this biologically generated difference in behavior may make a male identity a comfortable "fit" for some CAH females. Indeed, as you will see shortly, research with intersex children demonstrates that nature and nurture operate in tandem with regard to the development of gender identity.

THE ROLE OF COGNITION IN GENDER IDENTITY

Forming a concept of oneself as either a boy or a girl is a cognitive task. Some theorists have argued that one's gender identity changes partly as a function of general developments in cognitive ability, especially logical thinking (e.g., Kohlberg, 1966). As we have seen, when children first categorize themselves as boys or girls, they may have done little more than learn a label. Their understanding of the implications of that label is limited. Gradually, they begin to recognize that there is stability to their category membership and, finally, that their category membership is constant, based on underlying properties that do not change when superficial perceptual characteristics alter. In a sense, gender is something that is conserved (at least under normal circumstances), much like number is conserved when candies in a pile are made to look different by spreading them out in a row. We have seen (Chapter 3) that a full understanding of number conservation typically is achieved between 5 and 7 years and seems to be based on the development of logical thinking. Gender constancy may also be dependent on the logical thinking skills that emerge as children reach middle childhood.

Although developments in logical thinking may be important, there are other cognitive factors that can influence the progress of gender identity, such as having accurate information about how gender is decided. As we pointed out earlier, adults assign babies to a gender category based on their genitalia. But unless young children are explicitly taught about the importance of genitals to gender assignment, they are likely to be unaware of the typical genital differences between the sexes. References to gender categorization are pervasive in our society, and they are a large part of children's daily experiences. Not only do children frequently hear themselves being categorized, but also they witness many references to other people that contain gender labels, such as "This man will help us find the toy department." However, most of these references are not based on observation of people's genitals. They depend on people's other physical attributes, such as size and shape, and on more superficial characteristics, such as clothing and hairstyle. It's not really surprising, then, that young children are sometimes oblivious to the genital basis for gender assignment or that they might initially assume that gender categories are determined by superficial properties.

Researcher Sandra Bem (1989) tells the story of her son, Jeremy, who was informed about genital differences between boys and girls and about the importance of genitalia in gender assignment. One day, he chose to go off to nursery school wearing barrettes in his hair. When another little boy repeatedly insisted that Jeremy must be a girl because he was wearing barrettes, Jeremy just as vehemently insisted that he was a boy, because "wearing barrettes doesn't matter; being a boy means having a penis and testicles." Jeremy was even provoked enough at one point to pull down his pants to demonstrate. The other boy was not impressed. He said, "Everybody has a penis; only girls wear barrettes."

A study by Bem (1989) illustrates that when children do have knowledge of the genital basis of gender assignment, as Jeremy did, they are fortified with information that may help them to avoid some confusion about gender constancy. She presented 3- to 5-year-olds with two large photographs of nude toddlers. One was a boy (Gaw), and one a girl (Khwan; see Figure 8.2). Bem gave the pictured toddlers Thai names so that most North American youngsters would find them unfamiliar and would not associate them with gender. Children were asked to say whether a pictured toddler was a boy or a girl, and then were asked to explain how they knew. If no genital information was offered, the researcher probed by asking questions such as, "Can you point to anything about Gaw's body that makes Gaw a boy?" Nearly half of the children showed no awareness of the relevance of genitalia for specifying sex. The children who did know about genitals also seemed to have a better grasp of gender constancy. When they were shown pictures of Gaw or Khwan with cross-gendered clothes or hairstyles, they asserted that their genders had not changed.

It appears, then, that when adults provide appropriate scaffolding, giving children accurate information about how gender is assigned, children's understanding of their own gender identity is more advanced.

THE ROLE OF BIOLOGY IN GENDER IDENTITY

If children are assigned to a gender based on their genitalia and if genitals are usually a product of underlying biological processes, then biology plays at least an indirect role in gender identity. But does biology have any other influence, beyond affecting the genitalia? That has proven a difficult question to answer, but there are some indicators that "feeling like a male" or "feeling like a female" may to some degree be related to factors other than social assignment to a gender category, and these factors could be biological.

Again, research on intersex individuals provides some clues. Consider the case of another biological male who had an identical twin, but suffered surgical damage to his penis in infancy (Colapinto, 2000; Diamond & Sigmundson, 1997; Money & Tucker,

FIGURE 8.2 Photographs used to measure gender constancy in Bem's (1989) study.

"Gaw"   "Khwan"

SOURCE: Bem, S. L., (1989). Genital knowledge and gender constancy in school children. *Child Development*, *60*, pp. 653, 654. Used by permission of John Wiley and Sons.

1975). As with the child we described earlier (Bradley et al., 1998), the parents raised this twin as a girl. Yet by age 10, unlike the child described by Bradley and colleagues, the girl twin was expressing dissatisfaction with her female gender assignment. At age 14, when she was told of her medical history, she took a stand: She refused hormone treatments that feminized her appearance. Instead she received male hormone treatments and surgical reconstruction of the penis. By the time he was 25, the former girl was a married man. Tragically, he committed suicide at age 38, having experienced a long history of adjustment-related difficulties (Colapinto, 2000).

The case of the identical twin is no more than suggestive that biology can outdo social influences in affecting gender identity. First, this child's parents did not commit to a gender change until he was 17 months old. By puberty, this child had a somewhat masculinized appearance, despite receiving female hormones. Because of her appearance, she experienced substantial bullying by her peers, a social factor that could have influenced her gender uncertainty and distress. Further, we cannot say how effective her own family had been in accepting her status as a girl and thus how unambiguous her socialization experiences had been. However, cases such as these raise the possibility that biology can exert an influence on how "male" or "female" one feels, or at least on how comfortable one is with a particular gender assignment. We should note that the results of this case appear to be quite different from the one reported earlier (Bradley et al., 1998).

Intersex children sometimes undergo gender assignment or reassignment at birth because of conditions that cause malformations of genitalia. Large-scale studies of such children have produced conflicting results. In some, social reassignment of XY males to female identities, or of XX females to male identities, seems to work well (see Zucker, 1999, for a review). In more recent studies, although the majority accept reassignment comfortably, a sizeable minority of children have been reported to reject reassignment by the time they reach adolescence (Dessens, Slijper, & Drop, 2005; Kolesinska et al., 2014; Meyer-Bahlberg, 2005; Reiner & Gearhart, 2004; Sandberg, Gardner, Callens, & Mazur, 2017), suggesting that socialization may not be as powerful as once thought in the development of gender identity.

As such, ongoing controversy surrounds decisions about if and how to assign gender for intersex individuals at birth, and whether and how to intervene medically, though recommendations incorporating ethical principles and current knowledge have been put forth (Anderson, 2015; Lathrop et al., 2014; Lee et al., 2016). Many researchers and theorists have argued for recognition and cultural acceptance of intersex statuses (Diamond & Butterworth, 2008; Savin-Williams & Ream, 2007; see also Byne et al., 2012). Blackless and colleagues (2000) report that some type of sexual nondimorphism is present in up to 2 out of every 100 live births. For many people, gender identity simply does not conform to the dichotomous model of gender as either male or female. Models and theories that account for continuous variation in gender identity and gender differences may better describe the broader picture of gender development across individuals (Diamond & Butterworth, 2008; Reis & Carothers, 2014; Savin-Williams, 2016).

GENDER NONCONFORMITY AND TRANSGENDER CHILDREN

As introduced in Box 8.1, an important aspect of gender identity involves the extent to which individuals feel they are typical of their assigned gender. Some children feel so different from their biological sex and assigned gender that they believe they are or wish they were the opposite gender. When these feelings involve extreme dissatisfaction with and distress related to their gender, children may be diagnosed with *gender dysphoria*, which was previously called *gender identity disorder* (APA, 2013). For example, James was born male based on genes but insisted beginning at the age of 2 that she was a girl, choosing to go by the name of "Nora" and insisting on wearing girl's clothing and growing her hair long. Though they were unsure of the best way to respond, Nora's parents accepted her identity as female and did their best to warmly support her choices. Nora maintained this belief and more female-stereotypical behaviors throughout childhood and puberty into adolescence, when she and her parents began considering medical interventions.

MyLab Education
Video Example 8.1
By the age of two or three years, conflict can emerge between biological sex assigned at birth and gender identity. Though skepticism regarding transgender identity exists among the general public, helping professionals need to understand diverse aspects of gender identity.

The term transgender refers to individuals like Nora, who believe that their biological sex does not correspond to their gender identity. For many, this means that they describe their gender identity as "opposite" that of their biological sex. Recent studies suggest that about 0.3% of people in the United States are transgender according to this definition (Russo, 2016). This conflict between biological sex assigned at birth and gender identity can emerge as early as 2 or 3 years of age. In addition to describing oneself as the opposite gender, earliest signs of developing transgender identity involve gender nonconformity, or failing to adhere to gender-based societal expectations for feelings, behaviors, and appearance (Martin-Storey, 2016). Considering the development of gender identity, it is essential to recognize that many young children demonstrate gender nonconformity to some degree, and that even among those who describe themselves as feeling "opposite" to their assigned biological sex at some point as young children, only a small minority continue to identify as transgender following puberty, like Nora. (Some other children who show gender nonconformity— but not all, by any means—later have homosexual or bisexual orientations, which we discuss in Chapter 9.) Those children who do persist in transgender identity through adolescence and into adulthood are described as "insistent, consistent, and persistent" in their firmly held belief that their gender identity differs from their assigned biological sex (Olson, 2016; Steensma, McGuire, Kreukels, Beekman, & Cohen-Kettenis, 2013).

While recent attention to transgender children in the media, legal proceedings, and school board rulings have increased their visibility, much skepticism regarding transgender identity exists among the general public and some professionals. Critics question whether these young children are confused about or delayed in their gender development, and whether they simply may be pretending when they describe their genders as opposite (McHugh, 2014; Zucker et al., 1999). Researchers seeking to address these questions recruited a sample of transgender children ages 5 to 12 who had "socially transitioned" such that they were living according to their gender identity rather than their natal sex (Olson, Key, & Eaton, 2015). The researchers compared transgender children to cisgender (non-transgendered) youth on measures of both implicit and explicit gender cognitions. Results showed a clear pattern: The transgender children looked the same as peers when matched by expressed gender, and very different from peers when matched by natal sex (Olson et al., 2015). In a similar study, preschool-aged transgender children did not differ from controls matched by age and expressed gender on any measures of gender preferences, beliefs, or behaviors except cognitions about gender constancy. Interestingly, the transgendered children's cisgender siblings also differed from controls on gender constancy, as they were more likely to say that other people's gender may not be stable over time (Fast & Olson, 2017). Based on these studies, the researchers concluded that transgender children are unlikely to be confused, delayed, or pretending in reference to their gender development or gender identity.

Transgender youth face approximately two to three times the risk of psychological difficulties such as depression, anxiety, and suicidality or self-harm compared to their cisgender peers (Martin-Storey, 2016; Russo, 2016), presumably resulting from distress related to many factors such as feeling or being treated differently from others, or lack of acceptance from family, peers, or society more broadly. As described in Box 8.1, children who experience bullying related to gender nonconformity face risk for social and emotional difficulties (Jewell & Brown, 2014; Smith & Juvonen, 2017). This victimization may be even more severe for transgender children. While knowledge of the long-term outcomes for transgender children is currently limited, available research indicates that transgender children do best when their parents, schools, and peers accept their gender identities (Martin-Storey, 2016; Olson, 2016). Furthermore, some medical interventions that temporarily and reversibly delay changes associated with puberty may alleviate distress for transgender youth in early adolescence (Spack et al., 2012). In the Applications section of Chapter 9, we discuss additional concerns about, and interventions for, transgendered youth. Overall, you should note that our understanding of the developmental trajectories of transgender children requires much more research to arrive at recommendations for best supporting their healthy development.

Gender and Behavior

Many of us believe that males and females have at least some different behavioral tendencies, and some people believe that there are major differences in the distribution of personality traits between the sexes. Such beliefs about sex differences are called **gender stereotypes**. Researchers have found evidence for some of the differences that people believe in, but other stereotypes seem to arise from expectations that have no basis in fact. In this section, we will first take a look at some of the gender differences that have been found, especially in children. Then, we'll consider some of the theoretical explanations that have been proposed for gender differences. That is, when they actually exist, how do they develop?

GENDER DIFFERENCES IN BEHAVIOR, PERSONALITY, AND PREFERENCE

In 1974, Maccoby and Jacklin did a careful review of the scientific literature on gender differences. They surprised most observers by concluding that there were only four behaviors, skills, or tendencies that clearly differed for males and females: physical aggression, language skills, math skills, and spatial skills. Even in these domains, some behaviors differed across the life span (e.g., aggression) and others only during certain developmental periods, such as after puberty (e.g., certain math skills). Since 1974, researchers have acquired a valuable analytic tool for assessing the effects of variables such as gender. In a **meta-analysis**, the results from a large number of studies on the same question—such as, "Are there gender differences in physical aggression?"—can be combined to produce an average estimate of the magnitude of difference in a population (Glass, 1976).

The results of many meta-analyses are now available, and the list of "real" gender differences has lengthened (see Table 8.1). In addition, our knowledge of gender differences is now more fine-tuned. With regard to math, for example, among top-performing students, boys have an advantage over girls in complex problem solving. This is more likely to be true when problems can be solved using spatially based strategies. Yet, boys are also more numerous than girls among *underperformers* in math, and girls tend to outperform boys on computation (see Halpern et al., 2007, for a comprehensive review). We also have been collecting data for long enough, and in enough circumstances, that we know that these differences can change historically; that is, there are cohort effects. To add to the complexity, these effects can vary from one context to another. For example, historical change has affected math skills such that males and females in the United States today do not differ on most tests of math achievement before grade 12 (e.g., Hyde, 2014), even though they did differ over two decades ago (e.g., Hyde, Fennema, & Lamon, 1990). The gender gaps that continue to exist seem to vary from one culture to another. The male advantage in complex problem solving (which has reduced in magnitude but continues in the United States today as a gender difference on math SAT test performance) differs by country and culture. The more a country is characterized by a cultural acceptance of male privilege, the more boys outnumber girls among top performers in that country (Bergold et al., 2017; Guiso, Monte, Sapienza, & Zingales, 2008; Reilly, Neumann, & Andrews, 2015). In countries where cultural attitudes strongly favor gender equality, such as Iceland, there are as many (or more) girls as boys among top math performers. One very large meta-analysis included the test data of nearly 500,000 14- to 16-year-olds in 69 nations. The analysis identified specific societal indicators of equality that are linked to disappearing math performance differences between boys and girls (Else-Quest, Hyde, & Lynn, 2010). These indicators are equal enrollment in school; larger shares of research jobs held by women; and larger numbers of women lawmakers (parliamentary representatives).

It is just as interesting to note the differences that have *not* been found as those that have. Among the common gender stereotypes, for example, are that females are more sociable, more dependent, and more prosocial than males and that males are more competent at analytical tasks. Although occasional studies have reported findings that are consistent with these expectations, in most studies such differences have not been found. Similarly, arguments that males and females differ in moral reasoning have received a great deal of popular and scientific attention. As we mentioned in Chapter 7, Gilligan (e.g., 1977, 1982) proposed that males are more likely to focus on issues of

TABLE 8.1 A Sampling of Gender Differences

TRAIT OR QUALITY	MORE TYPICAL OF	TIME OF ONSET
Developmental vulnerability (learning disabilities, illness, accidents, etc.)	Boys	Prebirth
Activity level	Boys	Infant
Happy, excited mood	Boys	Infant/toddler
Risk taking	Boys	Infant/toddler
Physical aggression	Boys	Toddler
Faster reaction time	Boys	Preschool
Competitive play	Boys	Preschool
Domineering discourse style	Boys	Preschool
Dominance seeking; clear group hierarchy	Boys	Preschool
Spatial skill: mental rotation	Boys	Middle childhood
Antisocial aggressive disorders	Boys	Middle childhood
Satisfaction with one's gender assignment	Boys	Middle childhood
Math problem solving	Boys	Middle childhood
Homosexuality, bisexuality	Boys	Adolescence
Preference for gender-typed toys	Both	Toddler
Preference for same-gender playmates	Both	Toddler
Quiet, calm mood	Girls	Infant
Language onset (vocabulary)	Girls	Toddler
Collaborative discourse style	Girls	Preschool
Empathy and compliance	Girls	Preschool
Academic achievement	Girls	Middle childhood
Emotional expressiveness	Girls	Middle childhood
Relational aggression (refusing friendship, exclusion from group)	Girls	Middle childhood
Depression	Girls	Adolescence
Social sensitivity	Girls	Adulthood

KEY: Prebirth—Conception to birth; Infant—0 to 1 year; Toddler—1 to 3 years; Preschool—3 to 6 years; Middle childhood—6 years to puberty; Adolescence—Puberty to 18 years; Adulthood—18 years onward.

justice or fairness in their moral reasoning, but females are more concerned with issues of interpersonal responsibility and compassion. However, the evidence indicates that boys and girls show no differences in their tendencies to focus on such issues and that both men and women raise both kinds of issues when they solve moral problems or judge moral maturity (e.g., Walker & Pitts, 1998). Occasionally, adolescent and adult females have been found to raise more concerns about people's needs than adolescent or adult males in addressing real-life dilemmas, but people of both genders raise such concerns quite frequently (Baez et al., 2017; Capraro & Sippel, 2017; Turiel, 2006).

When gender differences arise consistently, they tend to be minor. For example, gender differences in emotional expression overall are significant but small, with girls demonstrating more positive expressiveness and internalizing emotions like anxiety and sadness while boys demonstrate more externalizing emotions, like anger (Chaplin & Aldao, 2013). Figure 8.3 illustrates the considerable overlap between males and females on those traits that show some gender difference. Some researchers have argued strongly that gender differences are too small to be important in development, especially considering that the average difference between genders is much smaller

FIGURE 8.3 Typical pattern of differences for characteristics that show a sex difference.

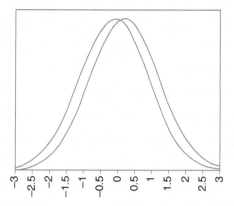

Depending on the characteristic, either boys or girls might have the higher average scores.

than the range of differences within each gender (Hyde, 2014). Furthermore, some researchers argue that gender differences should be conceptualized as more dimensional, differing across all people, than categorical, differing between just male and female groups (Reis & Carothers, 2014).

However, average individual differences between the genders may not be the important story in gender role development. More and more, developmentalists are recognizing that although boys and girls do not behave much differently in laboratory measures of personality or on individual abilities, they do spend their time differently. Specifically, girls spend their time interacting primarily with girls, and boys spend their time mostly with boys. In settings where there are both males and females of similar ages available, such as schools and playgrounds, and where there is freedom to choose one's companions, this gender segregation process begins by about age 2½ for girls and by about age 3 for boys, and it increases with age (see Martin, Fabes, Hanish, & Hollenstein, 2005). Gender segregation characterizes children around the world, in both industrialized and nonindustrialized societies (e.g., Omark, Omark, & Edelman, 1973; Whiting & Edwards, 1988). When children are about 4, the time they spend with same-sex peers is triple the time they spend with other-sex peers (Fabes, Martin, & Hanish, 2003). By the time children are 6, they spend 11 times more time with same-sex peers! During elementary school, sex segregation intensifies, and it begins to ease off only after puberty, when, drawn together by sexual interest, children begin to participate more readily in mixed-gender activities. During middle childhood, mixed-gender interactions, called **borderwork**, tend to be quite limited (Maccoby & Jacklin, 1987; Thorne, 1986, 1994). In fact, there seem to be unwritten "rules" that govern when it is acceptable for boys and girls to engage in mixed-gender interactions. Alan Sroufe and his colleagues (Sroufe, Bennett, Englund, Urban, & Shulman, 1993) observed 10- and 11-year-olds at a summer camp, for example, and identified a set of six rules that seemed to determine when children would cross the boundaries of their single-sex groups (see Table 8.2).

When children segregate by gender, other behaviors also tend to diverge. For example, suppose that Carissa and Duane, both 6 years old, are equally active when they play alone on the playground. They climb on the jungle gym with about average vigor for children their age, and they are more inclined to skip and jog from place to place than either to walk or to run full tilt. When Carissa plays with her girlfriends, her activity level stays about the same. But when Duane plays with a group of boys, he is notably more active than when he plays alone: He moves more vigorously on the jungle gym or runs with greater intensity. Boys tend to increase their activity level in the company of other boys (Maccoby, 1998).

Children do somewhat different things in their same-gender groups. Perhaps most notable is that boys' play in groups is more physical and more aggressive than girls' play. This is true in all primate species, across cultures, and from the earliest ages

TABLE 8.2 Rules Governing Mixed-Gender Interaction, or Borderwork

Rule:	The contact is accidental.
Example:	You're not looking where you are going and you bump into someone.
Rule:	The contact is incidental.
Example:	You go to get some lemonade and wait while two children of the other gender get some. (There should be no conversation.)
Rule:	The contact is in the guise of some clear and necessary purpose.
Example:	You may say, "Pass the lemonade," to persons of the other gender at the next table. No interest in them is expressed.
Rule:	An adult compels you to have contact.
Example:	"Go get that map from X and Y and bring it to me."
Rule:	You are accompanied by someone of your own gender.
Example:	Two girls may talk to two boys, though physical closeness with your own partner must be maintained and intimacy with the others is disallowed.
Rule:	The interaction or contact is accompanied by disavowal.
Example:	You say someone is ugly or hurl some other insult or (more commonly for boys) push or throw something at them as you pass by.

SOURCE: Sroufe, L. A., Bennett, C., Englund, M. and Shulman, S. (1993). The significance of gender. *Child Development*, *64*, p. 456. Reproduced with permission by John Wiley and Sons.

that youngsters play together (Ruble, Martin, & Berenbaum, 2006). When Carissa and her friends ride the wheeled vehicles in the play yard of their after-school child care center, they ride around carefully to avoid hitting each other. But when Duane and his friends are in the drivers' seats, their favorite thing to do is ram into each other—the harder the better (e.g., Dunn & Morgan, 1987; Fabes et al., 2003).

Good-natured physical roughness is called **rough-and-tumble play**, an almost exclusive property of boys' play with boys. Most boys are not consistently aggressive across situations. That is, physical aggressiveness is not so much a personality trait that you see when a child is in any situation—with adults, girls, or boys—although it can be for some children. More typically, it emerges when boys are with boys. Thus, it becomes an important defining feature of boys' social groups, which differ in specific ways from girls' social groups. Boys often use rough-and-tumble play to help establish dominance hierarchies within their groups, with more dominant boys less likely to back down and less often aggressed against. Generally, boys play in larger groups than do girls, who are more likely to play in twos and threes, and the boys' groups are more clearly structured hierarchically. Although girls' groups usually have their more and less dominant members, the rankings are not very stable, and leadership does not depend on toughness as much as on other leadership qualities, such as social skill (Maccoby, 1998; Martin & Fabes, 2001).

Girls' and boys' groups differ on other dimensions as well (Ruble et al., 2006). Boys compete with each other more than girls do. As preschoolers they compete for resources, such as attractive toys, and in middle childhood they compete in structured games. Girls' interactions tend to be more cooperative and to involve much more turn taking. These characteristics of gendered groups are integrally related to the kinds of activities that bring boys and girls together. In particular, boys seem to spend time with other boys who have shared interests, especially starting in middle childhood, and they are more likely than girls to be interested in sports and games and in adventure. For example, when boys pretend, their play tends to involve heroic or warlike themes (e.g., Coyne, Linder, Rasmussen, Nelson, & Collier, 2014).

Girls often seem to get together just to be together, and their choice of companions is based more on personality (Erwin, 1985). On the whole, they tend to have broader interests than boys, and they are more interested in boys' activities than boys are in girls' activities. Girls do have stronger tendencies than boys to enact family or school experiences in their play, and increasingly from preschool onward, girls' pretend play themes have to do with adornment and beauty—being models or brides, doing glamorous or romantic things (Storli & Sandseter, 2015).

As you can see, girls' groups and boys' groups have different cultures to which the members, regardless of their individual characteristics, must adapt. A good example of this difference is the degree to which they use *collaborative* versus *domineering* discourse techniques (Leaper & Smith, 2004). In **collaborative or affiliative speech**, more often used in girls' groups, children's responses are keyed to what someone else has said, expressing agreement or making further suggestions, often in the form of a question rather than declarative or imperative sentences, which seems to soften the suggestion. For example, Carissa might say to a friend as they plan a game, "You want to be the mommy. Why don't we both be the mommy sometimes?" In **domineering or power-assertive speech**, more typical of boys' groups, commands and restrictions are common, as when Duane says, "Don't move that block; build the road there!" It is important to note that both boys and girls will use both kinds of discourse. It is the predominance of one type over the other that differs between their groups. On the whole, girls' discourse strategies are more "conflict mitigating" and boys' strategies are more "egoistic"—threatening, demanding, interrupting, or ignoring of another's remarks (Maccoby, 1998).

Where do gender differences in behavior come from? There are theories that emphasize the importance of biology, of cognitive processes, and of socialization pressures. As always, all three are important. Some theorists emphasize the interaction of the three as children spend time in same-gender peer groups. It seems that gender segregation in childhood, perhaps the most pervasive gender difference, may be both an outcome of some gender differences and a source of others.

THE ROLE OF BIOLOGY IN GENERATING GENDER DIFFERENCES

You learned earlier in this chapter that genetic differences between males and females normally influence the differential development of reproductive organs. You have seen that the prenatal release of masculinizing hormones (androgens) plays a major role in this process. Do masculinizing hormones also affect the developing nervous system, thus influencing postnatal behavior? In animals, there is evidence that prenatal hormones do affect neural structures (e.g., Martel, 2013), and in both animals and humans, there appear to be effects on early behavior. For example, male rats whose exposure to prenatal androgens is delayed not only show a slight demasculinization of their genitalia but they also show more feminized play behaviors as pups (e.g., Ward, 1992; Ward & Stehm, 1991).

In humans, girls with CAH who are overexposed to prenatal (and sometimes postnatal) androgens have been found to exhibit more **tomboyism**—playing with boys and preferring boys' toys and activities—than non-CAH girls (for reviews see Berenbaum, 2004; Constantinescu & Hines, 2012). Findings such as these are open to several interpretations. For one, parents of girls with CAH may have doubts about their daughters' sexual identity that could affect their daughters' behavior; for another, these girls have many unusual experiences, such as genital surgeries and ongoing medical treatments, that could affect their behavioral development, and so on (see Collaer & Hines, 1995). However, the somewhat masculinized behaviors of CAH girls may also indicate a role for prenatal (or postnatal) hormones in some of the typical behavioral differences found between boys and girls. Two studies provide somewhat more convincing demonstrations of a role for prenatal androgens in the masculinizing of girls' behavior. The first is a large study of normally developing children. At 8 years old, both boys and girls were rated as more masculine in their activities if their mothers had had higher than average amounts of testosterone (an androgen) in their blood during pregnancy (Auyeung et al., 2009). The second is a study of 3- to 10-year-old CAH girls and their unaffected (non-CAH) siblings (Pasterski et al., 2005). The children were observed in toy play alone and also with each of their parents. The CAH girls made more spontaneous male-typical toy choices (e.g., trucks) than their unaffected sisters, even though their parents encouraged sex-typical toy play with their children and actually provided more positive feedback to CAH girls than to unaffected girls for play with female toys (e.g., dolls).

At puberty, hormonal changes and hormonal differences between boys and girls may cause some behavioral differences that emerge at about that time. For example, although depressive symptoms increase for both girls and boys after puberty, they increase more for girls; boys show more increases in aggressive, delinquent behaviors than girls (see Table 8.1 and Chapter 9). Could these differences in problem behavior be linked to hormones? It is a sensible question to ask, and some connections have been identified. For example, there is a link between boys' androgen levels and their aggressiveness (Buchanan, Eccles, & Becker, 1992). But androgens appear to more directly affect attempts to achieve social power (dominance seeking), which leads to aggression only in some people and some situations (Josephs, Sellers, Newman, & Mehta, 2006; Rowe, Maughan, Worthman, Costello, & Angold, 2004). Another complication in interpreting hormone–behavior connections is that whereas androgens may increase aggressiveness, one's experiences, such as bullying, may change hormone levels (e.g., Vaillancourt, deCatanzaro, Duku, & Muir, 2009). In particular, for males, aggression and dominance seeking can increase testosterone, an androgen (see Cacioppo & Berntson, 1992). So it is still not clear whether hormone levels cause or result from behavior and experience during and after puberty.

Research on brain structures has identified some sex differences (e.g., Ruigrok et al., 2014), supporting the idea that brain differences may underlie some gender differences, but many of the findings are controversial (see Grabowska, 2017). Among the differences for which there is some evidence is the presence of greater lateralization in males than in females, that is, greater differentiation in the functioning of the two hemispheres of the brain, with language functions more clearly governed by the left hemisphere in males (e.g., Friederici et al., 2008). Even in children as young as 16 months, patterns of brain activation appear to be more lateralized for word comprehension in boys than in girls (as measured by functional magnetic resonance imaging, or fMRI; Molfese, 1990). But here again, findings are unclear. For example, one large fMRI study of older children found no sex difference in lateralization of language processing (Plante, Schmithorst, Holland, & Byars, 2006). If females *are* less lateralized, using more of both hemispheres for language functions, it could account for the female advantage in language. But this, and other brain differences, if they exist, could just as easily be the result of different experiences. That is, when behavioral differences develop, they may *cause* differences in brain function rather than being the *result* of such differences. Given what we have learned about brain development (see Chapter 3), it seems likely that the causal links work both ways.

One other note of caution about relating brain differences to gender differences in behavior should be presented. Sometimes brain differences clearly are *not* related to behavioral differences (see Grabowska, 2017 for a review). For example, in one study, intelligence as measured by standardized intelligence tests was correlated with more gray matter (thicker cortex) in the frontal and parietal lobes for men, but in women intelligence was correlated with more gray matter in different parts of the frontal lobes. There were no differences in these same men and women on intelligence. As the authors put it, "men and women apparently achieve similar IQ results with different brain regions, suggesting that . . . different types of brain designs may manifest equivalent intellectual performance" (Haier, Jung, Yeo, Head, & Alkire, 2005, p. 320).

THE ROLE OF COGNITION IN GENERATING GENDER DIFFERENCES

When Ben was 5 years old, he loved to sit with his mother early in the morning while she dressed for work. He especially enjoyed watching her comb her hair and tie it back with a ribbon. One day he asked if he could have a ribbon in his own hair. His mother, who tried to encourage nonsexist ideas in her children, tied a ribbon in Ben's hair, and he spent some happy moments admiring himself in the mirror. But soon he grew still, staring at his image, and he finally asked, "Do boys wear ribbons in their hair?" to which his mother responded, "Not usually." Ben grasped the ribbon and tore it off his head, pulling strands of hair along with it. Then, bursting into tears, he ran from the room. Despite his mother's neutrality, Ben was angry and humiliated that he had done a "girl" thing. Several cognitive theories of gender differences have been proposed to explain behaviors such as Ben's. We will examine them next.

Cognitive-Developmental Theories. Cognitive-developmental theorists such as Kohlberg (1966) have argued that when children acquire an understanding of gender constancy, partly as a function of advances in their logical thinking skills, they are intrinsically motivated to learn all they can about what it means to be male or female, and they are eager to behave in gender-appropriate ways. In other words, children actively seek to act in accordance with their gender identity, whether or not they experience social pressure to do so. This process is often referred to as **self-socialization**. The anecdote about Ben illustrates the power of such a cognitively based motivational system. There is also research evidence to support a cognitive basis for at least some of children's gendered behaviors, although contrary to Kohlberg's notion, a full understanding of gender constancy does not seem to be required. Rather, establishing basic gender identity (i.e., learning one's own gender category) seems to be sufficient to foster a drive to learn about gendered behavior and a tendency to make gender-typical choices (Weinraub et al., 1984). Once gender stability is established, children are increasingly likely to make gender-based choices over what may be more attractive choices, as Ben did (Martin, Ruble, & Szkrybalo, 2002; Ruble et al., 2006).

Cognitive-developmental theories also suggest that when children achieve gender constancy, their thinking about gender differences should become more "flexible" and less stereotyped. They now understand that superficial characteristics can change without changing one's underlying gender category. Therefore, children should be able to see that gender role stereotypes, such as girls wearing dresses and boys wearing pants, are social conventions, not moral imperatives or requirements for maintaining gender identity. Indeed, children's thinking about gender does become more flexible in middle childhood, as you will see in a later section (Conry-Murray & Turiel, 2012; Halim, 2016). Some researchers theorize that young adolescents become somewhat more rigid in their thinking about what's permissible for people of different genders (Ruble et al., 2006). The **gender intensification hypothesis** suggests that one way young teens cope with the demands of establishing an adult identity is to fall back on stereotyped notions of masculinity or femininity (Hill & Lynch, 1983), but there is little evidence for this position, especially for U.S. adolescents today (Priess, Lindberg, & Hyde, 2009).

Gender Schema Theories.   Cognitive theorists in the information processing tradition emphasize the role of **gender schemas** in influencing the behavior of children and adults (Bem, 1981; Markus, Crane, Bernstein, & Siladi, 1982). A gender schema is a network of expectations and beliefs about male and female characteristics. Schemas affect what we pay attention to, what we interpret, and what we remember about events. So, for example, if elementary school children hear stories or see pictures of men or women engaged in behaviors typically associated with the other gender—such as a woman doing carpentry work—they are likely to remember the pictures later in ways more consistent with their gender schemas. In this example, they might later remember that they heard about, or saw, a *man* working as a carpenter (Liben & Signorella, 1980, 1993; Welch-Ross & Schmidt, 1996).

Gender schemas affect both how children evaluate behavior and the kinds of behaviors they choose for themselves. In one study, when preschoolers were told either that a boy or a girl had spilled some milk, they judged the behavior more negatively if they believed the child was a boy, apparently based on a "boys are bad" stereotype (Giles & Heyman, 2004). Many studies demonstrate the power of stereotypical beliefs on children's behavior. For example, when children are shown novel toys described as "girl" toys, girls play with the toys more and remember them better than if the same toys are described as "boy" toys; the reverse is true for boys (Martin et al., 2002). Recent studies of preschool-aged children have demonstrated that children who consider their gender identity both very important and very positive are most likely to insist on wearing gender-typed outfits, such as pink frilly dresses for girls and sports-themed shirts for boys (Halim et al., 2014).

Gender schema theorists suggest that the schemas children have for their own gender affect what behaviors they choose to learn about and what behaviors they choose for themselves, but they do not account for the exact mechanisms by which schemas are constructed. Social experiences and available role models presumably affect gender differences by affecting what children know or believe to be gender appropriate.

But, according to these theorists, it is the schemas, not the social experiences directly, that motivate children to adopt sex-typed behavior. In the studies of gender-typed outfits described above, differences in children's tendencies to dress in a gender-typical manner were unrelated to their parents' preference for such dress (Halim et al., 2014). There is evidence that knowledge of stereotypes influences children's interests and judgments about what they are good at even when the gender difference is not real. For example, in a large U.S. sample of 6- to 10-year-olds, by second grade children endorsed the stereotype that boys are better than girls in math. Soon after, boys were more likely than girls to see themselves as good at math, even though gender differences in math achievement were absent or even favored girls (Cvencek, Meltzoff, & Greenwald, 2011; Voyer & Voyer, 2014). Research has not yet established clear links, however, between cognitive schemas and actual behavior.

Children's Knowledge of Gender Stereotypes. In general, cognitive theorists assume that the acquisition of knowledge about gender stereotypes influences the feminization and masculinization of children's behavior, regardless of whether others reward or otherwise pressure children to adopt gender-typed behavior. From this perspective, it is important to learn what children know about gender stereotypes and when they know it if we want to understand the development of gender differences.

Two-year-olds show little awareness of gender stereotypes. For example, Gelman, Taylor, and Nguyen (2004) recorded parent–child discussions of pictures depicting children and adults engaged in various activities. In the following exchange between a 2-year-old girl and her mother about a picture of a child playing with a toy truck, the little girl attributes ability not to gender categories but to individuals:

> Mother: Who can play with toy trucks?
> Mother: Hm?
> Child: Um, you.
>   (Later . . .)
> Mother: Yeah, well who else?
> Child: Maybe Daddy.
> Mother: Daddy, yeah.
> Child: Maybe John.
> Mother: Yeah.
> (*Source:* Gelman et al., 2004, pp. 103–104)

But by age 3, most children know something about gender-related preferences for toys and activities, and 4- to 6-year-olds have gendered expectations about people and their behaviors. In fact, 4-year-olds tend to be quite "sexist," regardless of whether their parents explicitly encourage such stereotyping. Contrast the above exchange with this dialogue from the same study between a 4-year-old boy and his mother about a picture of a male dancer:

> Mother: Who can be a ballet dancer?
> Child: I don't know.
> Child: Why is that a boy?
> Mother: Well, can a boy be a ballet dancer?
> Child: No.
> Mother: Why not?
> Child: (sighs)
> Mother: I've seen boy ballet dancers.
> Child: I don't think so.
> (*Source:* Gelman et al., 2004, p. 106)

By school entry, about age 5 or 6, knowledge of gendered activities and occupations is quite extensive (Liben, Bigler, & Krogh, 2002; Signorella, Bigler, & Liben, 1993). In middle childhood, children become more aware of psychological stereotypes, such as expecting boys to be more competent, and they begin to expect that a person with one gender-typical trait or behavior will have others as well. By age 10, children are aware of differences in the ways males and females are evaluated in their culture.

In particular, they recognize that females and many female-typical behaviors are devalued (Lindsey, 2015). Stereotypes of gender inequality may also be conveyed to very young children through media portrayals (Halim et al., 2017; Leaper, 2015). Such awareness may help explain why females show a greater susceptibility to depression than males beginning in early adolescence.

Although knowledge of stereotypes increases dramatically in middle childhood, awareness that people vary in the degree to which they fit their gendered categories also grows. The following example of an exchange between a 6-year-old and her mother illustrates the child's incipient (if grudging) understanding that gender assignment does not necessarily dictate traits, abilities, or preferences:

Mother: Does Cynthia ever play with trucks?
Child: Sometimes.
Child: Girl trucks.
Mother: What are girl trucks?
Child: Pink ones.
Mother: Does Cynthia have pink trucks?
Child: Yeah.
Mother: Really?
Child: (nods "yes")
Child: Well she has pink cars but not pink trucks.
Mother: So she drives the cars while you and Brian drive the trucks?
Child: Yup.

(*Source:* Gelman, S. A., Taylor, M. G., & Nguyen, S. P. (2004). Mother–child conversations about gender. *Monographs of the Society for Research in Child Development, 69* (Serial No. 275). Republished with permission from Wiley-Blackwell.)

However, knowledge of stereotypes does not necessarily lead to conduct in keeping with those stereotypes (Liben & Bigler, 2002). Similarly, individuals may vary in their behavior (both consistent with and inconsistent with stereotypes) depending on context (Bandura, 1986). For example, gender differences in emotional expression are more pronounced when children are interacting with their peers and with adults other than their parents than when interacting with parents and family (Chaplin & Aldao, 2013). Similarly, while both boys and girls tend to play with gender-typed toys, this occurs more frequently in lab or "public" settings than at home. Furthermore, the strength of gender differences in the tendency of children to play with gender-typed toys has diminished over time, suggesting that gradual shifts in societal expectations are influencing these behaviors (Todd et al., 2017).

Research also indicates that factors other than gender knowledge affect some gender differences. For example, cognitive theories explain children's preferences for same-gender playmates as a function of the human tendency to value members of one's own in-group over members of an out-group. Once children identify themselves as male or female, they should quickly begin the gender segregation process. But even though boys tend to learn their own gender category a bit earlier than girls do, girls show same-sex playmate preferences earlier than boys do. As Maccoby (1998) suggested, knowledge of one's own gender identity may be a necessary but not a sufficient condition for gender segregation. In the next section, we will examine some of the social influences that may directly affect the development of sex differences, including children's preferences for same-sex playmates.

THE ROLE OF PARENTING IN GENERATING GENDER DIFFERENCES

A number of theories, in many different traditions, have argued that parenting practices play a special role in the development of gender differences.

Freud's Psychoanalytic Theory. One of the oldest theories on social influence for gender role development is Freud's psychoanalytic theory (e.g., Freud, 1935/1960; see also Chapter 1). Freud argued that at about age 3, children begin to have vague sexual needs that impact how they relate differently to their mothers and fathers.

In brief, boys experience sexual attraction to their mothers and competition with their fathers. Fear of retribution from their fathers motivates boys to identify with and imitate them. Similarly, girls identify with and imitate their mothers. Thus, both boys and girls become gender-typed in their behavior and form a superego (see Chapter 7). Although many aspects of Freud's tale of sexual desire, competition, and fear in young children have become deeply embedded in our culture, efforts to validate the theory have been unsuccessful. For example, one prediction we can make from Freud's theory is that traditional family structure—mother and father both present in the home and sexual partners—should be necessary for children to experience normal gender role development. Yet, gender role development is not impeded in children who come from single-parent homes, nor even in children who come from homes where both parents are the same gender (Farr et al., 2017; Golombok & Tasker, 1996; Patterson, 2004).

There is also little evidence that children model themselves after a single identification figure. Rather, research indicates that children will model themselves after others whom they perceive to be like themselves (e.g., same gender; Bussey & Bandura, 1984), as the cognitive theorists predict, and whom they perceive as competent. It also helps if the model is not scary or punitive, but rather is perceived as nurturant (Bandura, 1977).

Social Learning Theories. Social learning theorists argue that many parents and other adults influence children's gender-typed behaviors, both by modeling such behaviors and by providing differential treatment of boys and girls that teaches them to behave in gendered ways.

What evidence is there that adults actually do behave differently toward children based on gender? First, we should note that in many ways, boys and girls are not treated differently. Meta-analyses indicate no differences in how much parents interact with their sons and daughters, in how much parents encourage them to achieve, in how much parents encourage help seeking, in how much warmth or responsiveness parents show, or in how effectively parents communicate or reason with them (Lytton & Romney, 1991; Mesman & Groeneveld, 2017).

However, there are some important differences in parental behaviors. In what have been dubbed "Baby X" studies, adult participants interact with a baby they do not know (e.g., Seavey, Katz, & Zalk, 1975). When participants think they are interacting with a boy, they are more likely to handle the baby in active ways, such as bouncing; when they think the baby is a girl, they handle it more gently. Participants more often describe boys as big and strong, but they use terms like sweet and pretty more often with girls. Mothers are gentler in handling their infant girls compared to boys (Fausto-Sterling et al., 2015). As children get older, mothers talk more, use more supportive speech, and discuss emotions more frequently with their daughters (Dunn, Bretherton, & Munn, 1987; Leaper, Anderson, & Sanders, 1998). Also, when discussing emotions with their children, both mothers and fathers convey gender-stereotypical messages that boys experience more anger whereas girls experience more happiness and sadness (Van der Pol et al., 2015). Across cultures, girls are more often asked to help with infant sibling care, although across many cultures both boys and girls are recruited to care for young children (Best, 2010). There are other parental differences as well, with fathers more likely than mothers to have different expectations of their sons than their daughters (Endendjik et al., 2014). Fathers are more likely to be disapproving of gender non-conformity in their sons than in their daughters, more likely to roughhouse with their sons, and more likely to be negative or confrontational with them (Maccoby, 1998). In the United States, this is true for Black, White, and Latino fathers, who also engage in more literacy activities with their daughters than their sons by the time their children are 2 years old (Leavell, Tamis-LeMonda, Ruble, Zosuls, & Cabrera, 2012). A recent study demonstrated that fathers of girls have a stronger neural response to happy expressions than neutral expressions by their daughters, whereas fathers of boys had stronger responses to neutral expressions by their sons (Mascaro et al., 2017).

MyLab Education
Video Example 8.2
Although young children recognize gender differences and can articulate gender stereotypes, parental and other environmental influences have a big influence on gender-typical behaviors as children develop their own gender concepts.

Another study found that fathers' stereotypical gender-role attitudes and differential treatment of girls versus boys fully explained later observed gender differences in aggression (Endendijk et al., 2017). In some Western societies, boys typically experience stronger pressure to conform to gender-stereotypic behavior than do girls because the sanctions are more severe when boys deviate from such norms (Sandnabba & Ahlberg, 1999).

Other differences in adult socialization practices with boys versus girls may be particularly important in laying the groundwork for later gender differences in psychopathology. Keenan and Shaw (1997) reviewed a number of findings that are consistent with such a conclusion. They report that preschool girls, in contrast to boys, are more often reinforced by their parents for compliant behavior and more often ignored for attempts to direct interaction in free-play situations (Kerig, Cowan, & Cowan, 1993). Parents also socialize children to deal with conflict in different ways. Girls are more frequently encouraged to yield to peers in conflict situations, for example, by giving up a desired toy (Ross, Tesla, Kenyon, & Lollis, 1990). Girls are also taught, to a greater degree than boys, to take others' perspectives and feelings into account in situations involving conflict (Smetana, 1989). Preschool teachers have sometimes been found to react more negatively to girls than to boys for high levels of activity, including activity levels during play, and more positively to girls than to boys for dependency behaviors (Fagot, 1984). In sum, these authors conclude that early socialization experiences may help channel the development of internalizing behaviors in girls and externalizing behaviors in boys. Consistent with this theory, a more recent study found that parents tend to be more lax in response to externalizing behavior by boys and internalizing behavior by girls but more over-reactive to the opposite—externalizing behavior by girls or internalizing behavior by boys (Kim, Arnold, Fisher, & Zeljo, 2004).

Some research also suggests that parents' socialization behaviors can subtly vary depending on factors such as family composition and cultural background (Leaper, 2002; Ruble et al., 2006). For example, in families with both male and female children, a mother's behaviors are more affected by the gender of the child she is relating to than in families with only girls or only boys (McHale, Crouter, & Whiteman, 2003). African American mothers convey less traditional gender-typed attitudes to their children than European American mothers, whereas Latina mothers convey more traditional attitudes (Ruble et al., 2006). Compared to heterosexual parents, gay and lesbian parents are generally more flexible about boys' play that does not conform to gender stereotypes (Goldberg, Kashy, & Smith, 2012).

When we evaluate typical differences in parents' socialization practices, we have to ask, to what extent are adults' behaviors causing gender differences in children, as social learning theorists would argue, and to what extent are they responding to already existing gender differences? As we have seen so many times, the causal processes are most likely reciprocal. For example, parents make more attempts to "down-regulate" boys' emotional responses in the preschool years (Block, 1978), but boys may also be slower to develop self-regulatory skills than girls. It seems likely that parents are influenced in part by the fact that boys have more impulsive emotional outbursts and in part by their desire to teach boys not to display weakness (Maccoby, 1998). Another example is that parents talk more to their daughters than to their sons. This may influence girls' language development, but girls' vocabulary growth begins earlier than boys', and toddler girls are more talkative than toddler boys, which may help influence parents' behavior as well (Leaper & Smith, 2004).

THE ROLE OF PEER INTERACTIONS IN GENERATING GENDER DIFFERENCES
We have already emphasized how intensive the gender segregation process is, beginning as early as 2½ years of age, and becoming by middle childhood the most extreme gender difference that there is: Girls spend much of their unstructured time with girls, and boys with boys. As we have seen, gender segregation may be influenced by cognitive processes, such that when children become aware of their gender identity, they value members of the same in-group more than members of the out-group.

The main cognitive explanation for gender segregation is that children choose to play with members of their own gender because they share interests in the same gender-typed behaviors (Mehta & Strough, 2009). This follows from well-documented gender differences in play styles and toy choices. However, recent investigations have questioned whether interest in shared activities actually drives gender segregated play beyond simpler explanations.

In two related studies of preschoolers, Martin et al. (2013) demonstrated that, while children did select peers with similar activity interests to some degree, gender similarity in selection of playmates was actually more important than the type of activity the children were engaged in. The researchers hypothesized that children are attracted to same-gendered peers because they expect greater enjoyment from interacting with members of their own gender. This hypothesis was supported by later studies, showing that children experience *gender-based relationship efficacy*, such that they not only expect more enjoyment, but also have more confidence in their ability to engage with same-gendered peers (Andrews et al., 2016; Zosuls et al., 2014). Once children choose to play with same-gendered peers, those peers function as role models and children experience socialization for gender-typed activities (Leaper, 2015; Maccoby, 1990, 1998; Martin et al., 2013). Initial differences in children's play styles are then magnified in same-gender peer groups.

In other words, within their gendered peer groups, children develop interaction styles that are more differentiated than either biology or parenting would predict (see Martin et al., 2005). Martin and Fabes (2001) observed 3- to 5-year-olds' play-partner choices over a 6-month period. They found that "sex segregation was pervasive" among the 61 study participants. Over 80% of the children had clear same-sex play-partner preferences, even though teachers encouraged gender equity, and the stability of these preferences increased over the 6 months of the study. The results also demonstrated that same-gender peers seem to have a socializing influence on children. Stereotyped sex differences, such as activity level differences, "developed or increased over time" (Martin & Fabes, 2001, p. 443). Most interesting was that there was a **social dosage effect**: Children who spent more time in same-gender groups showed greater increases in gender-related behaviors even after only a few months. The social dosage effect also has been reported in studies of older children and adolescents (McHale, Kim, Dotterer, Crouter, & Booth, 2009).

In adolescence, when boys and girls begin to build cross-gender groups and relationships, their different interaction styles can create difficulties. For example, in studies of mixed-gender problem-solving groups, young women can be at a disadvantage. They tend to express agreement with others more often than young men do, consistent with their gendered discourse style. Unlike their experience in all-female peer groups, though, they may never get their chance to speak because males do less turn-taking and are more domineering. Overall, girls tend to have less influence on the outcome (Carli, 1990). Similarly, in heterosexual dyads, males do not offer as much support to their partners as females do for the expression of feelings. As you might expect, males seem less well prepared for the mutuality of intimate relationships, perhaps because of the discourse style they acquire in their larger, less intimate childhood groups (Leaper, 1994).

Gilligan (e.g., 1993) and Pipher (1994) describe females as "losing their voice" when they reach adolescence because they feel pressure to adapt themselves to what others want them to be. As we saw in Chapter 7, there is little evidence that girls' level of voice is compromised in this sense at adolescence (Harter et al., 1998; Steinberg & Monahan, 2007). Perhaps, instead, the more cooperative discourse style of females, in the face of the more egoistic male style, makes girls and women less powerful agents when interacting with males than when they are interacting with other females. These different styles may become particularly relevant in the context of romantic relationships (see Chapter 10) and other adult contexts where men and women ideally should function as equals, such as in the workplace (Kendall & Tannen, 1997). In Box 9.2, we present another situation where girls seem to face disadvantage despite equivalent ability: the pursuit of STEM studies and careers.

Box 8.2: Gender Differences in STEM Fields: Why Do So Few Girls Pursue Math and Science Careers?

In the fields of both psychology and education, experts have turned their attention to the persistent gender differences in individuals pursuing STEM scholarship and careers. STEM refers to *science, technology, engineering, and mathematics*—fields historically and currently dominated by men. Though rates of bachelor's degrees awarded to women in domains of science have increased substantially in the past 50 years, these rates remain low, around 20%, in fields such as computer science, physics, and engineering (Liben, 2016). Our understanding of gender development indicates that these differences observed in early adulthood likely have their origins in childhood. Given that girls demonstrate comparable or even superior academic achievement in domains of math and science to boys (Voyer & Voyer, 2014), we are compelled to consider what factors other than ability may push so many capable and talented girls away from STEM pursuits.

Gender stereotypes and *stereotype threat* are likely culprits. Stereotype threat refers to the fear of being judged based on some negative stereotype, such as the unsupported stereotype that girls are not as good at math and science as boys. Girls who experience stereotype threat may perceive themselves as incapable, or may worry that others consider them not well suited to math and science fields (Miyake et al., 2010). Some recent studies support the idea that girls' perceptions of their abilities may impact their attitudes towards math and science. With two samples of German students in grades 5 through 10, Goetz et al. (2013) examined gender differences in math anxiety relative to performance based on grades. They found that, although girls achieved comparable grades and had similar levels of anxiety during math class and math exams, they had higher levels of trait anxiety related to math than boys. In other words, girls perceived themselves to have less global competence and ability for math than did boys.

Similarly, Tarampi, Heydori, and Hegarty (2016) investigated the possibility that apparent gender differences in spatial perspective taking arise more from stereotype threat and negative expectations than from actual differences in ability. This is important because gender differences in spatial abilities are thought to be one factor explaining the male advantage in fields like engineering and physics. The researchers had male and female undergraduates attempt perspective taking tasks that were framed either as spatial tests, likely to favor males, or as tests related to empathy, likely to favor females. The demands of the task were similar, though, and males only outperformed females in the spatial condition (Tarampi et al., 2016). Other work with adult samples has demonstrated that gender roles influence gender differences in spatial abilities, such that differences are greater among males who adhere more strongly to masculine gender identities (Reilly & Neumann, 2013).

It also has been hypothesized that, because spatial perspective taking is not taught explicitly in academic curricula, boys' advantage may arise from differences in experience outside of school. Specifically, boys spend more time on average playing sports and video games than girls do, and both sports and many video games popular with boys provide practice in spatial perspective taking. When girls are exposed to tasks that coach these skills, they perform as well as boys do on tests of spatial perspective taking (Uttal et al., 2013). Thus it has been recommended that more explicit instruction on spatial perspective taking in school may reduce or even eliminate these gender differences. Questions about how differences in the typical experiences of boys and girls may influence STEM interests relate to consideration of broader social environments, like cultural differences in gender equity.

In a large study involving data from 49 countries, Goldman and Penner (2016) found that differences in math self-concept were more important than differences in achievement for predicting the desire to enter math-related careers. Furthermore, though more gender-egalitarian countries showed smaller gender gaps, they also had fewer boys and girls overall who were interested in math (Goldman & Penner, 2016). In addition, in a study of 1.5 million 15-year-olds from 75 countries, Stoet and Geary (2013) demonstrated that gender differences in math achievement tended to track with the opposite gender differences in reading achievement, with males also demonstrating more variability in performance than females. Greater variability for males among both high and low math achievers also has been documented as early as preschool (Lonnemann et al., 2013) and maintained through elementary school to 12th grade (Bergold et al., 2017; Reilly, Neumann, & Andrews, 2015). These studies suggest that possible biological and social influences on gender differences in achievement may be more complex than the simple explanation of differences in gender equity, particularly considering that, on average, girls' achievement is superior to that of boys in the majority of countries (Stoet & Geary, 2015).

Regardless of the challenges in understanding exactly what drives these differences, it remains the case that overall gender differences in ability and achievement are small in magnitude, and certainly much smaller than the gender differences in STEM participation in higher education and eventual careers. As such, researchers and educators are working to develop interventions that might combat stereotype threats to encourage girls towards math and science pursuits (Liben, 2016). Of course, it is also important to consider other factors that may influence motivation for women to pursue STEM careers, such as discrimination and preference for other fields that may be perceived as more welcoming to women or more "family friendly" (Hyde, 2014). Further discussion of factors that influence career choices, such as personality and social class, can be found in Chapter 12.

A MULTIDIMENSIONAL THEORY OF GENDER DIFFERENCES IN BEHAVIOR

As we have seen, several different explanations for gender differences in behavior have some empirical support, but all of them have some important limitations as well. Clearly what is needed is a multidimensional theory that accounts for multiple causal influences and that specifies how these influences transact to produce gender differences. A social-cognitive theory proposed by Bussey and Bandura (1999; see also Bandura & Bussey, 2004) takes a more complex approach to gender differences than the causal explanations we have considered so far. Bussey and Bandura specify three categories of variables that interact reciprocally to help shape the development of gender role, including gender differences in behavior. These factors include personal influences (cognitive conceptions of gender, affective, and biological features of the person), behavioral influences (learning of and execution of activities that are gender linked), and environmental influences (family, peer, and societal). All these influences interact reciprocally to mold the motivational and self-regulatory structures that determine behavior. For example, family and societal influences contribute to children's knowledge base about gender and gender-linked competencies by serving as models and by providing rewards or sanctions for gender-appropriate or inappropriate behavior. In addition, both proximal and distal social forces help shape children's patterns of expectations about how genders behave, their beliefs about how these behaviors will be evaluated by others, and their constructions about their own competence to enact the behaviors in gender-appropriate ways.

Although Bussey and Bandura (1999) specify that affective and biological features of the person are important, in their more detailed analyses of how various causes interact in gender role development, they tend to emphasize social (especially parental) and cognitive factors. They suggest that, at least initially, adult sanctions and direct teaching contribute most to the production of behaviors that are considered gender appropriate. As you have seen, research attests to the important role that children's early socialization experiences play in the development of gender-linked behavior. While there are clear differences across cultures in the specifics of gender-appropriate behavior, most cultures do place restrictions on what individuals of different genders should and should not do. Yet these behaviors are not shaped just by patterns of external contingencies. Children grow increasingly more adept at monitoring and evaluating themselves according to both personal standards and the circumstances of the contexts in which they find themselves. Thus, cognitive factors play a larger role as children get older. Self-regulatory functions become progressively more internalized and direct children's behavior in ways that maximize self-satisfaction and minimize self-censure (Bandura, 1986). Children learn to anticipate the consequences of their actions and can thus predict the responses their behaviors will elicit from others. These emerging capacities for self-monitoring and prediction are linked to the development of internalized standards for performance, largely based upon how others in the social world have responded to the behavior, the models that have been observed, and what has been taught directly. Gender-linked behavior is thus maintained by ongoing social influences operating through psychological mechanisms such as motivation, expectancy for success, and self-efficacy. These internal mechanisms have been constructed in the process of interacting with a world in which gender is a highly salient social category.

Social-cognitive theory specifies that socialization by others and the self is embedded in cultural context. Not surprisingly, many gender differences described in this chapter are attenuated or even reversed in some cultures. For example, boys are typically more competitive than girls in the United States, Canada, and Mexico, but not in India. And in Israel, boys tend to be less competitive than girls (Strube, 1981). One of the cultural factors important for evaluating some gender differences is how egalitarian a society's attitudes and institutions are. As you saw with math achievement, the more egalitarian the society, the fewer gender differences we tend to find.

Bussey and Bandura (1999) provide an attempt to take into account some of the complexity of interacting causal processes in gender role development, but much more work is needed to construct a theory that includes all the influences that we have seen to be important. Future theorists, for example, need to integrate the recent findings on peers' power to affect the development of gendered behavior. In the next section, we will take a broader look at the whole arena of peer relationships and the place of peers in the lives of children.

MyLab Education Self-Check 8.2.

Peer Relationships

8.3 Recognize the role, influence, and relevance of peer relationships in childhood and adolescence, and analyze children's functioning within their peer groups and structure interventions that meet needs for acceptance and belonging.

In 1958, the Primary Mental Health Project, a program for early identification of at-risk students, was initiated in the first grades of several schools in Monroe County, New York. Data from social work interviews with mothers, classroom observations, teacher reports, other school records, and psychological evaluations such as intelligence, personality, and achievement tests were compiled for each of the children in the hope of identifying variables that would predict later adjustment difficulties. Based on these multiple measures, children were given either a "red" or "non-red" tag. Red-tagged first graders were those whose behavior, educational achievement, and social-emotional functioning reflected moderate to severe maladaptation. Out of the total of three academic-year samples (1958–1959, 1959–1960, and 1960–1961), approximately one third of the youngsters received red tags (Cowen et al., 1963).

In a separate and fortunate development, the Medical Center of the University of Rochester initiated a county psychiatric registry concurrent with the school-based project. This registry provided an ongoing, longitudinal record of most persons in the county who were diagnosed with mental health problems and who had received treatment. These two unrelated sources of information made it possible to track the histories of the children in the Primary Mental Health Project 11 to 13 years later by means of registry entries (Cowen, Petersen, Babigian, Izzo, & Trost, 1973).

As they moved into early adulthood, individuals who had been red-tagged as children showed up in the registry in disproportionate numbers. They represented more than two out of every three individuals on the list of those needing psychiatric care. You already know from reading the previous chapters that there is evidence for continuity of behavioral and emotional problems over time, so this is not too surprising. What is intriguing about this story, however, is what predicted these later problems best. In other words, what kinds of measures separated youth who ended up in the registry from their age-mates who did not? If researchers had known the answer to this question, they might have been able to identify and treat children before more serious problems surfaced.

Remember that the researchers administered intelligence, personality, and achievement tests; obtained behavior rating scale data; amassed grade and attendance information; and interviewed parents. They also asked the children to nominate their peers for various hypothetical roles, half positive (e.g., the lead character) and half negative (e.g., the villain) in a "Class Play" exercise (Bower, 1960). Researchers found through retrospective comparison that individuals on the county registry performed slightly less well than their age-mates on most assessment measures, but not significantly so. There was, however, one important exception: The extent to which children were nominated by their grade school peers for negative roles in the class play significantly predicted later membership in the registry. Children far and away outpredicted the adults in recognizing those children destined for later psychological problems. What did these children know?

As we have seen in our discussion of gender role development, peers are a significant force in the lives of children. The story of how effectively grade school children's feelings predicted their peers' later mental health outcomes introduces us to the fascinating world of the peer group, its dynamics in childhood and adolescence, and its relevance to later outcomes. In particular, it implies that peer relationships in childhood are significant predictors of later mental health and social adjustment.

The Peer Group, Social Competence, and Social Skills

What makes for good peer relationships? To answer this question, we need to understand something about the nature of peer groups and the distinctions researchers make between social competence and particular social skills. The study of the peer group may be distinguished from the study of simple social interactions or even the study of friendship relationships in ways that are familiar to helping professionals working in therapeutic settings. Group counseling, for example, differs from individual counseling not only because there are more people involved in the process but also because the interrelationships and dynamics become much more complex.

> Groups are more than mere aggregates of relationships; through emergent properties such as norms or shared cultural conventions, groups help define the type and range of relationships and interactions that are likely or permissible. Further, groups have properties and processes, such as hierarchical organization and cohesiveness, that are not relevant to descriptions of children's experiences at lower levels of social complexity. (Rubin, Bukowski, & Parker, 1998, p. 623)

Social competence, a criterion for peer group acceptance, is a broad construct that is not restricted to one set of prescribed behaviors. Affective responses, such as empathy and valuing of relationships, and cognitive processes, such as perspective taking (see Chapter 5) and ability to make mature moral judgments (see Chapter 7), play a part in the repertoire of the socially adept individual. It is impossible to assess the social competence of a child without considering his skill in relating to others at every relationship level. Social but "nonfriend" interactions, as well as friendship relationships, are embedded within the larger peer group structure, each influencing and being influenced by the other levels of social exchange. Remember, then, that a child's success or lack of success within his peer group is not independent of basic interaction skills or the kinds of friendship skills we discussed in Chapter 6.

Good **social skills** are important contributors to socially competent behavior at every level of interaction. They may be defined as discrete, observable behaviors such as making eye contact, using suitable language, and asking appropriate questions that promote effective social interaction and contribute to the broader construct of social competence. Social skills training approaches grew out of the recognition that students who have peer group problems lack certain essential social skills or behave in ways that are counterproductive to smooth social exchange. Consequently, modeling, coaching, and reinforcement processes are used to teach students how to interact more adaptively in very basic ways.

Both correlational and experimental studies of social skills training programs lend modest support to their usefulness in improving peer acceptance (see Antshel & Remer, 2003; Beelman, Pfingsten, & Losel, 1994; Bierman, 2003; Quinn, Kavale, Mathur, Rutherford, & Forness, 1999). One possible reason for their limited effects is the unidirectional approach typically employed in these interventions. In other words, treatment often assumes that the socially troubled individual owns the problem. There is evidence, however, that if children are disliked, peers also process information about them in biased ways. For example, children interpret negative acts as intentionally malicious when committed by disliked children but not when committed by popular children (Dodge, Pettit, McClaskey, & Brown, 1986; Veenstra, Lindenberg, Munniksma, & Dijkstra, 2010). Bierman (1986, 2003) found that greater success could be achieved by combining social skills training for individual children

MyLab Education
Video Example 8.3
Around the world, children find friends among their peer groups, favoring others of the same gender and with similar interests.

with attempts to enhance the cooperative nature of these children's peer groups. Thus, addressing the context within which the socially unskilled child functions, along with the transactional nature of his social interactions, allows for more lasting improvements. Social competence, including particular social skills, helps children experience success in friendship relationships. The same holds for children's success in the larger peer context.

Peer groups are complicated webs of social relationships, including friendship dyads, cliques, and crowds. These complex social networks emerge and take on great significance for children as early as middle childhood (Gifford-Smith & Brownell, 2003). In contrast, the social worlds of preschoolers and early elementary school children are less intricately constructed. By middle childhood, voluntary social or friendship groups of three to nine members, called cliques, become more common, although they are still rather informal. At this age the group's structure is flexible, and member turnover is common. The importance of cliques reaches a peak in early adolescence, followed by a general decline in importance over the course of high school (called degrouping; see Shrum & Cheek, 1987). Crowds are larger, reputation-based groups, composed of numerous cliques, which become more important in mid-adolescence (Dunphy, 1963). The significance of both cliques and crowds for adolescent development will be discussed in Chapter 10.

The peer group serves many important functions for children and adolescents. It provides opportunities for practice in communication, conflict resolution, joint goal setting, cooperative learning, and shared decision making. Important interpersonal goals—such as the development of empathy, tolerance for others, and a sense of belonging—are met within groups of peers. Skills acquired in activities such as team sports may provide training for certain competitive aspects of adult work roles (Lever, 1978). The peer group is like a real-world laboratory where children can try out and improve their skills for living with and getting along with others.

Zarbatany, Hartmann, and Rankin (1990) explored the function of competitive activities (sports, physical games) and noncompetitive activities (talking on the telephone, watching TV) within peer groups of early adolescents. These authors found that the two kinds of activities were important for facilitating different aspects of socioemotional development and social competence. Whereas participation in competitive activities provided opportunities for self-understanding by defining personal strengths and weaknesses, participation in noncompetitive activities enhanced a sense of acceptance and belonging in relationship to others.

Analysis of the World of Peers

Sarah is a sixth grader who attends middle school in a midsized school district. The school is a mix of White, Black, Hispanic, and Asian youngsters whose families live and work in the surrounding communities. Some parents work in the new technology industry developing on the outskirts of the town center. Others are employed in the one manufacturing plant that still operates downtown.

Sarah is a talented member of her school's track team and sings in the concert choir. She is active in her school's student council as well. She has a few close friends whom she has known since early elementary school. Sarah is the one whom they depend on if they need some advice or help. She loves to spend time with her friends, texting, talking on the phone, and going to movies.

Recently, Sarah's social life has become more important to her than ever. She spends a great deal of time in consultation with her friends, discussing what to wear and planning social activities. She pays a little less attention to her schoolwork now that she has so many other things to think about in her life. However, she still manages to maintain a B+ average. What can we say about Sarah and her place on the social map of middle school?

The attempt to answer this question presents us with an interesting challenge. We have noted the complexity of peer group structures, so you may have already guessed that there are several levels of analysis. In general, researchers have approached this question from two complementary yet distinct perspectives: analysis of the individual group member's characteristics within the peer group network and analysis of the different groups that exist within the larger universe of peer groups. The first approach would help us understand Sarah's status within her peer group and would typically depend on sociometric assessment. The second approach would help us understand the number and nature of the peer groups in Sarah's school and would depend on more ethnographic means of analysis.

Measurement of Individuals Within the Peer Group

SOCIOMETRY

Before we can understand the kinds of categories that describe children's status within peer groups, we need to appreciate the means by which these differences were first identified. Sociometry, the classic way of assessing social competence, had its origins in the work of Moreno (1934), who used children's nomination of their peers to evaluate peer status. Moreno viewed group processes as a mixture of positive forces (attractions), negative forces (repulsions), and indifference (absence of attraction or repulsion). He proposed that the interpersonal relationships within a group could be mapped out on the basis of knowing these social forces. Since this introduction by Moreno, sociometric techniques have diversified and have been applied in a variety of ways. McConnell and Odom (1986) offer the general definition of sociometric measures as "tests in which children make preferential responses to statements about peers in their social group" (p. 217), resulting in a score that defines a child's social status.

Typically, children might be asked to select the classmate or classmates they would most like to play with, work with, or sit next to in class. Although many varieties of analysis have been used in sociometric studies, such as weighting the nominations, the most straightforward approach is to count the number of positive nominations or mentions a child receives. This number, then, reflects the child's social preference score. Sociometric techniques are most useful when they also include negative nominations, or children's mention of peers with whom they do not want to work or play. Researchers have found that children who are rejected by peers cannot be identified without the inclusion of negative nominations (Hartup, Glazer, & Charlesworth, 1967). Social preference scores may range from highly positive to highly negative.

A second score, called social impact, is computed by adding up the total number of nominations, both positive and negative. This measure indicates the degree to which the child gets noticed within his group (see Marks, 2017).

SOCIOMETRIC CATEGORIES

Based on their scores on the dimensions of social impact and social preference, children can be classified into a variety of sociometric categories. Contemporary researchers most often use the methodology and categories identified by Coie and his associates (Coie, Dodge, & Coppotelli, 1982), which include five subgroups: popular, average, neglected, rejected, and controversial. Popular children receive many positive nominations and few negative nominations from their peers (high preference, high impact). Generally, they are well-liked members of the group and have relatively high visibility among their peers. Remember, however, that the term *popular* refers to a specific sociometric category and has a slightly more forgiving meaning than does the contemporary use of the term. In other words, a student considered popular in sociometric terms might not be given the label "popular" by his peers, who would probably interpret the label to mean high in social status and power (Asher & McDonald, 2009). This is referred to as "perceived popularity" and has a very different meaning (Cillessen, Schwartz, & Mayeaux, 2011).

Average children are those who receive an average number of positive and negative nominations (near the mean for the group on preference and impact). *Neglected* children are those who receive few nominations, either positive or negative. This latter group is characterized by its low level of social impact. Students who fall into the *rejected* category receive many negative and few positive nominations. They

FIGURE 8.4 Dimensions and types of social statuses.

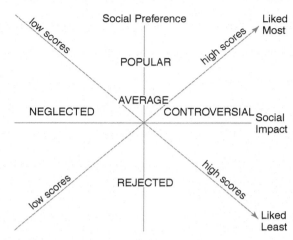

The relationships between positive and negative social choice measures, the dimensions of social preference and social impact, and five types of social status.

SOURCE: Based on Coie, J. D., Dodge, K. A., & Coppotelli, H. (1982). Dimensions and types of social status: A cross-age perspective, *Developmental Psychology*, 18, 557–570.

are typically disliked (low preference) but have generally high visibility (high impact). The final category, called *controversial*, identifies a relatively small group of students who receive many positive and many negative nominations (high impact, average preference). They have been named controversial because they get mixed reviews from their peers and share many of the characteristics of both popular and rejected children. They are seen by some peers as aggressive, but by others as class leaders. They may be perceived as popular, or high in social status, by their peers. These categories are presented graphically in Figure 8.4.

Individual Characteristics Related to Sociometric Status

What are the children in these categories like? Although it is tempting to think of each group as homogeneous in personality and behavior and thus clearly separable from the others, this kind of simplicity does not fit well with the facts. For example, all rejected children do not behave in aggressive ways. Rejected children who do behave aggressively do so only some of the time. Popular children, despite their positive qualities, are not perfect or necessarily liked by all. They may also experience peer-related problems from time to time.

In this section, we will describe general identifying characteristics of the groups, with greatest emphasis on popular, rejected, and neglected categories, the three groups most frequently studied. The controversial category has been more difficult to examine because of its much smaller size and lack of measurement stability. Remember that the categories suggest general tendencies to behave or to process social information in certain ways much, but not all, of the time.

POPULAR

Popular children are notable for their use of perspective taking skills. Upon entering a group, these children can adopt the group's frame of reference and join in without calling undue attention to themselves or to their own needs (Putallaz & Wasserman, 1990). They can be assertive, but they are not deliberately antagonistic or disruptive to others (Newcomb, Bukowski, & Pattee, 1993). In this, they demonstrate high levels of self-regulation and self-control. Popular children also manifest greater cognitive and social problem-solving ability than do children from other groups. Black and Hazen (1990) studied the language patterns of popular preschool children and found that these children were particularly adept at communicating clearly with others and following others' conversations. A recent meta-analysis demonstrated that popular young children tend to show good theory of mind, which likely facilitates their social skills (Slaughter et al., 2015). Positive correlations have also been found between popular status and self-esteem (Gruenenfelder-Steiger, Harris, & Fend, 2016), self-efficacy (Ladd & Price, 1987), and school enjoyment (Eggum-Wilkens, Valiente, Swanson, & Lemery-Chalfant, 2014). For college students, high sociometric status (being liked and admired by peers) is a powerful predictor of feelings of well-being (Anderson, Kraus, Galinsky, & Keltner, 2012).

In general, popular students tend to be prosocial, cooperative, intelligent, and capable of working well with others. They are likely to enjoy close, dyadic relationships with friends, although the domains of popularity and friendship are not necessarily overlapping. In other words, popularity is not a prerequisite for friendship. Sociometrically average and neglected groups also develop friendships. Peer acceptance and friendship make separate contributions to children's overall adjustment. For example, loneliness in adolescence is more closely associated with lack of friendships than with low peer acceptance (see Rubin et al., 2006).

Certain other attributes, such as physical attractiveness (Langlois & Stephan, 1981) and scholastic competence (Coie & Krehbiehl, 1984; Kiuru et al., 2015), are also associated with popular status. If you think about Sarah, the sixth grader from our earlier example, you might conclude her sociometric status to be popular.

REJECTED

The children who are rejected by their peers have received a great deal of research attention. Rejected children are the least socially skilled of all the groups and also the most heterogeneous category. Originally, researchers took the position that aggression was the primary attribute of children in this social group. In fact, being aggressive is still the most commonly cited behavior associated with being rejected by peers (e.g., Haselager, Cillessen, van Lieshout, Riksen-Walraven, & Hartup, 2002). However, it soon became clear that children can be rejected not only because they aggress against their peers (rejected-aggressive group) but also because they withdraw from them (rejected-withdrawn group).

The characteristics of rejected children contrast sharply with those of the popular group. Instead of modulating negativity, as is the case with popular children, rejected-aggressive youngsters demonstrate high levels of instrumental aggression, verbal negativity, and disruptiveness. You might wonder whether these children are rejected because they are aggressive or they act aggressively because they have been rejected. Several longitudinal studies demonstrate a causal link between aggression and subsequent rejection. This evidence is different from most sociometric research findings because it helps to explain what causes a child to be rejected. Over a period of several days, Dodge (1983) observed the interactions of small groups of children who initially did not know each other. After each play session, children were asked to complete a sociometric measure for their group. As the experiment progressed, some children began to take on popular status, whereas others were rejected. As in other studies of this type (Coie & Kupersmidt, 1983; Kupersmidt, Burchinal, & Patterson, 1995), aggression was the characteristic that best predicted rejection by the other children when all other differences were controlled.

In addition to aggression, rejected youngsters are more likely to demonstrate lower levels of perspective taking, self-control, and positive social interaction skills. Particular deficits in information processing, marked by perceptions of hostile intent or hostile attributional bias (see Chapter 7), are significant features of their social cognition. Once rejected, these youngsters are prevented from engaging in the very kinds of social interactions that might help them develop more positive social skills. If you remember Jason, our example from Chapter 7 Applications, you might imagine him fitting into the rejected category. Peer rejection also predicts later bullying behaviors towards peers, and in fact, the pathway from rejection to bullying is stronger than that from bullying to rejection among boys (Sentse, Kretschmer, & Salmivalli, 2015). Controversial children also demonstrate high levels of aggressive behavior, but they possess correspondingly positive attributes, such as greater sociability and cognitive ability, that buffer their abrasive characteristics and may make them attractive to their peers.

As we indicated earlier, however, aggression is not characteristic of all rejected children. Even though estimates indicate that approximately 50% are aggressive (Bierman, 1986), another 10% to 20% are extremely withdrawn (Parkhurst & Asher, 1992). Interestingly, social withdrawal begins to elicit the disapproval of peers in middle to late childhood. Whereas isolation in early childhood is not nearly so stigmatizing (Coplan, Ooi, & Nocita, 2015), presumably because it is not very important at this age, extreme social withdrawal in middle to late childhood is perceived as deviant and may provoke rejection by the group (Rubin, Coplan & Bowker, 2009).

Rejected-withdrawn children are more socially anxious than other groups and likely to behave in socially inappropriate ways. Poor perspective taking skills and general social ineptness may lead these youngsters to behave in ways that are considered odd, infantile, unpredictable, or potentially embarrassing to peers. Consequently, popular peers may ostracize them, just as they ostracize their more aggressive counterparts, for failing to fit in. Children in the rejected category are at special risk for peer victimization (Hanish & Guerra, 2004; Sentse et al., 2015). Both rejected-aggressive and rejected-withdrawn children do have social networks, but their social groups are smaller and are characterized by lower levels of intimacy and interaction (e.g., Ladd, Kochenderfer-Ladd, Eggum, Kochel, & McConnell, 2011). Overall, it is important for helping professionals to recognize that rejected children are a heterogeneous group.

NEGLECTED

Neglected children can be distinguished from children in the average group primarily because they have somewhat lower levels of peer interaction. In their meta-analysis of peer relations studies, Newcomb, Bukowski, and Pattee (1993) reported some differences between neglected and average groups. Sociometrically neglected children are less aggressive than average children, are less likely to be highly visible within the peer group, and show less sociability, but they are perceived by their peers as relatively likeable. These authors conclude that neglected children are simply not choosing to participate very actively within their group of peers. Unlike rejected-withdrawn children, peers do not make them feel especially anxious (Coplan et al., 2015; Ladd et al., 2011). Children in the neglected group are similar to those in the average group in their ability to have friendships and are as likely as other children to have a best friend (Rubin et al., 2009). They may have a few close friends and may engage more fully in activities in other contexts, or they may simply prefer spending time alone. Therefore, even though this group has certain sociometrically distinctive characteristics, neglected children are similar to average children in many respects. Being neglected, as distinct from being in the rejected-withdrawn subgroup, which also incurs high levels of peer neglect, does not seem to be associated with developmental problems (Rubin et al., 2006).

AVERAGE

Average children, as you might have guessed, receive an average number of nominations. They are at neither extreme on the impact or preference dimensions. They show lower levels of social competence than popular children and less aggression than rejected-aggressive youngsters. As with the neglected group, no problematic outcomes are associated with this sociometric category.

Gender and Cultural Differences

Differences between boys and girls across sociometric classifications have received relatively little research attention (Rubin et al., 2006; Ruble et al., 2006). Some studies have found that, on average, girls are more likely to be popular than boys (Paulus,

2017). Male bullies tend to be less accepted than female bullies, and female victims face more rejection than male victims (Sentse et al., 2015). While both boys and girls who show more gender-typical behavior tend to be more popular, there is greater intolerance of gender-nonconforming behavior for males than for females. Boys are more likely to be rejected for behaving in feminine ways, whereas girls who behave in masculine ways are more likely to be accepted by their peers (Jewell & Brown, 2014; Pauletti et al., 2014; Smith & Juvonen, 2017; Yu et al., 2017). Perhaps for this reason, socially withdrawn girls are less likely to be rejected than similar boys. It seems that shyness and social anxiety is perceived as more normative for girls (Doey, Coplan, & Kingsbury, 2014).

Much of the data on peer relations and social status groups is drawn from research in the United States and Canada. Yet it seems very likely that peer relationships, including judgments of social behavior that affect acceptance from or rejection by peers, would vary in different cultural contexts. Only limited information exists on cultural differences in peer group classifications, and some of it indicates that differences in values do have important effects. In some studies in China, for example, popular children are likely to be cautious, restrained, and shy (Chen, Rubin, & Li, 1995), whereas in North America such children are often rejected. Shy, socially anxious Chinese children are more likely to meet with approval and cooperation when they make social gestures, whereas North American children are likely to be ignored or victimized. Interestingly, some recent work indicates that things may be changing in China. Shyness and social withdrawal put children more at risk for social problems and feelings of depression than they once did (see Rubin, Coplan, Chen, Bowker, & McDonald, 2011). Yang, Chen, and Wang (2015) argue that over time, cultural change in China has weakened the link between shyness and popularity.

Generally, across both Western and non-Western cultures, aggression is associated with peer rejection, and helpfulness is associated with popularity (e.g., Chang et al., 2005; see also Rubin et al., 2006). However, aggressive behavior is not necessarily associated with rejection in North America. When aggressive children are more socially competent in other ways (e.g., good at perspective taking), they may be considered part of the controversial category we have just discussed, and may even be perceived as popular, especially as children get older (e.g., Rodkin & Roisman, 2010; see Chapter 10). Research in China indicates that aggression is more severely sanctioned there, and that aggressive children are more likely to feel isolated, perhaps because of greater emphasis on maintaining harmony (see Rubin et al., 2011). And yet, a nationally representative study involving over 9,000 middle school children in China found bullying to be a significant problem, with over 25% of both boys and girls affected (Cheng et al., 2010). Overall, it appears that despite some cross-cultural variation, aggressive behavior in children is a universal problem, with consequences for the perpetrators and the victims.

Even though all children, regardless of culture, are likely to experience some peer conflicts, societies differ in how adults intervene. In societies that value individualism, such as the United States, children are often encouraged to verbally defend themselves, to negotiate, and to seek fairness for themselves, often with an adult acting as arbitrator. In more collectivist cultures, such as China and Japan, children at odds with peers are not likely to be singled out or to be encouraged to act on their own behalf. Rather, adults are likely to expect the peer group to manage the conflict and to establish harmony among themselves, bringing each child's behavior into line with group expectations (e.g., Tobin, Wu, & Davidson, 1989; see also Greenfield, Suzuki, & Rothstein-Fisch, 2006). There is an important lesson here for helping professionals:

> In a multi-cultural society such as the United States . . . there is a tendency for each interactant to see the other's behavior through the implicit lens of his or her own value system. It is therefore important for educators and clinicians to be aware of the potential differences between children to help each child to better understand that children may have different perspectives on proper peer interaction, and that these differences can be acknowledged, respected, and even appreciated. (Greenfield et al., 2006, p. 684)

Stability of Categories and Outcomes

Once classified, do children maintain their status in the peer group throughout childhood and adolescence? Many researchers have studied the long-term stability of these sociometric classifications (Asher & Dodge, 1986; Newcomb & Bukowski, 1984) and have found that the most extreme categories (popular and rejected) are also the most stable, at least over short periods (Rubin et al., 2006; Sentse et al., 2015). Both neglected and controversial status categories show instability even in the short term. Those studies that have looked at the long-term stability of sociometric classifications have produced mixed results. In general, the impact of peer group classification is moderately stable, particularly for the broad dimensions of acceptance and rejection, with the category of peer rejection being the most stable of all. Denham and Holt (1993) propose that this stability stems from children's early experience with each other. Once a child's reputation has been formed on the basis of early social interaction, his reputation endures despite evidence to the contrary.

What are the long-term outcomes for children who belong to these different categories? Recently, a number of prospective or follow-up studies have used early peer group designations to predict later performance on various measures of adjustment, much like that of the Rochester Registry. The broad-based categories of early acceptance and rejection have been studied most frequently and provide the most consistent results.

Not surprisingly, peer acceptance has been associated with myriad positive outcomes, both psychologically and academically. The outcomes change dramatically, however, for rejected-aggressive children, who often have poorer academic records, are more likely to repeat grades, are absent more frequently, face greater risk of dropping out, and report more criminal behavior and drug use (see Coie, Terry, Lenox, & Lochman, 1995; Ladd & Burgess, 1999; Prinstein, Rancourt, Guerry, & Browne, 2009). The strongest linkages, by far, have been found between early aggression and peer rejection on one hand, and later externalizing problems on the other hand—the early-starter model of antisocial development described in Chapter 7 (see Dodge et al., 2003).

Researchers have also investigated outcomes for rejected-withdrawn youngsters and have found evidence for later internalizing problems such as depression and loneliness (e.g., Rubin, Coplan et al., 2009). This is especially true for children who have no friendships (see Rubin et al., 2006). A prospective study by Ladd and Burgess (1999) followed three groups of children from kindergarten through second grade: aggressive, withdrawn, and those with a comorbid profile of aggression and withdrawal. Consistent with predictions from developmental psychopathology, the children with multiple risks were predisposed to the most severe and enduring outcomes. The children who exhibited aggression and withdrawal in kindergarten were the most likely of all the groups to have troubled relationships with teachers and peers in second grade, to report more loneliness and dissatisfaction, and to express greater feelings of victimization.

Measurement of the Peer Group: Another Level of Analysis

Let us turn our attention to peer groups, the cliques and crowds we referred to earlier. These are networks of like-minded individuals who become associated with a specific set of norms, dress, and behaviors, like "jocks" or "brains." When we examine peer processes from this angle, we do not focus on the accepted or rejected status of particular children. It is certainly possible to be a popular member of a group of jocks as well as a popular brain. These peer groups appear to develop more significance in late childhood to early adolescence for the reasons specified in previous sections of this chapter. Moreover, adolescents may be better able to recognize and describe their peer groups effectively because they become increasingly proficient in thinking abstractly about categories as a function of their cognitive development.

Brown (1990) noted that the term *peer group* has been used rather loosely in the past, often applied to the whole spectrum of peer relationships, from dyadic friendships to membership in large crowds. This lack of clarity compromises our understanding of the role that each type of relationship plays in development. We use the terms *peer group* and *clique* somewhat interchangeably here, consistent with the view that these units are small enough to allow for regular interaction among members and to serve as the center of most peer-related interaction. Crowds, as we noted earlier, are larger collectives, composed of multiple cliques, which serve as social categories for students rather than as actual friendship groups. You might think of crowds as actual peer "cultures" that represent approaches to behavior, attitudes, and values. In Chapter 10, we will take a closer look at crowds. As we noted already, crowds are a more potent force in the lives of middle and late adolescents than for elementary schoolchildren and early adolescents.

Peer group analysis at the level of cliques and crowds can be done in various ways. In general, identification of peer groups or cliques requires students to specify who "hangs around" with whom in their classroom. Based on this information, maps of the social structure of classrooms or schools can be drawn using social network analysis (Knoke & Yang, 2008). Peer groups also can be described based on characteristics of their structures, such as *connectivity*, which describes how many individual links exist between different members of the groups; *reciprocity*, which considers how many of these links are mutual; and *cohesion*, which refers to the strength of these within-group linkages (see Rubin et al., 2015).

Why Do Cliques Form?

Perhaps you are wondering why cliques surface in middle childhood and take on such significance in the first place. Common terms such as *in-group, clique, pecking order,* and even more pedantic ones like *status hierarchy* make many adults uncomfortable, particularly when these terms are applied to children. This is so because these descriptors imply a set of winners and losers in the game of social relationships. Adults often prefer to believe that children are less critical and more tolerant of each other than these descriptors suggest. But like it or not, there is strong evidence for the existence of stable status groups among children and adolescents.

What motivates the development of distinct cliques? Two major forces are at work: first, the need to establish an identity, and second, the need for acceptance (approval) and belonging. As we shall see in Chapter 10, peers play a central role in the process of identity or self-development. The search for the self rests largely on comparing oneself to and distinguishing oneself from others by processes of social comparison (see Chapter 6). One's own identity becomes more distinct to the degree that it can be contrasted with that of another. Children who tend to dress, act, or otherwise express themselves in similar ways gravitate towards each other. Together, they form a type of social group that provides some identity to its own members and a basis of comparison to, and for, others. A group's identity is based on shared activities, values, appearance or dress, and behaviors (Ellis & Zarbatany, 2017; Killen & Rutland, 2011). Recognizing and understanding group characteristics helps early adolescents construct a map of the social world and provides them with a knowledge base about human differences.

Individuals' needs for acceptance and belonging also help explain the significance of the peer group. Children as well as adults want to be liked by their associates and will typically engage in the kinds of behaviors that result in their friends' praise or approval (Hartup, 1983). In addition to this kind of external social reinforcement, youngsters are also motivated by more internal goals. Berndt and Keefe (1996) argue that children and adolescents are intrinsically motivated to identify with their friends in behavior, dress, and academic achievement because they get satisfaction from emulating their friends' characteristics and being part of a group, not because they fear retribution if they fail to conform.

Peer Groups' Influence on Behavior

Our understanding of peer group processes must accommodate the power of both their beneficial and their potentially harmful aspects. As a helper, you have undoubtedly read about peer pressure. If you are also the parent of a middle or high school-aged child, you may have lost some sleep over it. Adults frequently blame early to late adolescent behavior and misbehavior on peer pressure, a notion that almost always has a negative connotation. They may imagine that children and adolescents are forced to conform to peer group standards to avoid humiliation or punishment. No one disagrees that peers become increasingly more influential as children mature. However, studies also show that the influence of peers is primarily indirect rather than overtly coercive (Ellis & Zarbatany, 2017). For example, clique influence seems to be greatest for members who are uncertain about their place within the group or have less access to the resources associated with their clique. Furthermore, peers can motivate students to engage in beneficial as well as risky behaviors, such as prosocial behavior, academic achievement, and avoidance of drugs (Hoorn, Dijk, Meuwese, Rieffe, & Crone, 2016; Steinberg & Monahan, 2007; Wentzel, Baker, & Russell, 2012; Witvliet et al., 2009).

Of course, not all peer group effects are positive or benign. The peer group delimits the range of opportunities by its very nature as a group with norms and roles. Within any peer culture, the range of acceptable activities is circumscribed. For example, the peer group determines who may be included as a member, how leisure time is spent, and how the members should dress and behave. In some cases, peer group members may use both indirect (e.g., teasing) and direct (e.g., confrontation) means to promote adherence to these group norms (Ellis, Zarbatany, Chen, Kinal, & Boyko, 2017). Unfortunately, the norms for certain groups may support deviant, antisocial behavior.

Many interventions that address typical developmental problems make the implicit assumption that peer pressure is a cause of most early to late adolescent difficulties. Many of these intervention models are built upon "resistance" training, which attempts to prepare children to do battle with dangerous peers. But is this the way it really works? And do these assumptions make sense?

It may be possible to shed some light on this issue, and to improve interventions as well, by reviewing a few principles of peer group dynamics. First, peer groups or cliques are generally homogeneous. There is a well-documented tendency for peer groups to exhibit homophily, or a degree of similarity among members on behavioral or attitudinal attributes of importance. This is why you can often identify the members of a group by the way they dress or on the basis of what they do after school. Second, groups are formed based on processes of influence and selection (Cohen, 1977; Kandel, 1978). Basically, *influence* refers to the fact that the peer group can cause an individual to conform to the norms of the group. For example, if a youngster is part of a peer group that disparages getting good grades, the child presumably reduces his investment in doing homework in order to be accepted by the group. Researchers have found that the influence of the group is not usually a result of coercive pressure, however. Instead, normative social processes, like positive reinforcement, observational learning, and in some cases discussion and information exchange seem to be important (e.g., Harakeh & Vollebergh, 2012). "The idea of a group of friends putting pressure on a single child to do whatever they want the child to do is a myth" (Berndt & Murphy, 2002, p. 283).

Less attention has been paid to the complementary process, called *selection*, in which individuals choose to affiliate with others who share similar behaviors or attributes. For example, youth who are highly motivated academically are drawn to peers who are similar in this respect. As children mature, they become more able to select the environments that suit them, perhaps influenced by their genetically based predispositions (Scarr & McCartney, 1983) and their increasing understanding of autonomy and identity (see Chapter 10).

Contrary to conventional wisdom, which emphasizes the importance of peer influence, many recent studies have found that selection processes are at least as important in the formation of peer groups. For example, Shin and Ryan (2014) investigated how sixth-grade students' peer groups affected their academic motivation, school engagement, and achievement. They found evidence for an initial selection process, with students selecting a peer context early in the school year that reflected their unique level of motivation and academic self-efficacy as well as achievement level. Furthermore, students were influenced by their peer groups such that they became even more similar to their friends over the academic year in achievement and engagement. Ennett et al. (2006) looked at this issue as it relates to adolescent substance use, including marijuana and cigarette smoking. Once again, they found support for both selection and influence processes. Adolescents were drawn to cliques where substance use was the norm if they already used substances or viewed substance use as desirable (selection). But it was also the case that nonusers in substance-using cliques were more likely to begin than were nonusers in nonusing cliques (influence).

What is important to remember is that both processes contribute to peer group formation and maintenance. Overemphasis on peer influence processes may compromise our understanding of other dynamics, such as motivation to affiliate with similar individuals. Once established, peer groups constitute important social contexts for young people that reinforce certain ways of thinking and behaving. Obviously, peer groups differ in the degree to which they provide a healthy developmental context for children and adolescents, yet their impact can be profound regardless of their benefit or harm. Paxton and her associates (Paxton, Schutz, Weitheim, & Muir, 1999) studied female cliques that varied in their levels of concern about body image and eating. Those girls who showed higher levels of eating-related disorders also inhabited more negative social environments, which appeared to amplify their distorted ideas about body image. More recent work has confirmed the importance of peer group dynamics for development of body dissatisfaction, indicating that peer groups characterized by high levels of teasing based on appearance and perceived importance of thinness and overall appearance are most detrimental (Webb & Zimmer-Gembeck, 2013).

As children mature into adolescents, much more of their time is spent in the company of their peers. The body of research on peer relationships teaches us that we would do well to consider the peer network in our conceptualization of problems and in the structuring of our interventions. A study by Mahoney speaks clearly to this final point. Reasoning that some positive modification in environment could alter the course of development for at-risk students, Mahoney (2000) studied the trajectories of 695 boys and girls from elementary school to young adulthood. He specifically focused on the role that participation in extracurricular activities in school played in ameliorating the difficulties of those participants who were most at risk. Not too surprisingly, most of the students who participated in extracurricular activities (one or more years of involvement in sixth through tenth grades) graduated from high school and did not become involved in criminal activity as young adults. This result was most obvious for students in the highest risk category.

What was surprising, however, was that this benefit was limited to those high-risk students whose peer groups also participated in the activity. There was no appreciable gain from participation unless the youngster's peer group shared in the activity. Participation in positive, highly organized, and supervised activities enriched the adjustment of the whole group, reinforcing more socially adaptive behavior for everyone. It may be that raising the index of positive adaptation for the whole group attracts more adaptive members (selection) while providing a context that promotes healthier activity (influence).

MyLab Education
Video Example 8.4
In this video, various groups of children in early adolescence gather and engage in different activities. Consider the processes of influence and selection in the formation of such groups.

MyLab Education Self-Check 8.3.

Applications

As children mature, they are exposed to influences from many contexts, and the relative power of these influences shifts with development. Friendships, peer groups, and other extrafamilial settings such as school play increasingly important roles.

Focusing on children's relationships with their peers has become a major clinical objective, given what we now understand about their importance. First of all, functioning well within a peer group is one of the most significant accomplishments in children's lives (Parker et al., 2006). Good peer relationships operate as a powerful protective factor, providing children and adolescents with experiences of friendship, opportunities for problem solving, and enhancement of perspective taking and empathy skills. The opportunity to feel validated by others in your age group, who share many of your ideas and feelings, contributes to a sense of self-worth, relatedness, and security (Rubin et al., 2015). Second, problematic peer relationships are risks because they elicit or maintain maladaptive behavior and deprive youth of the kinds of protective effects mentioned above. Peer group problems figure prominently in developmental models of antisocial behavior (the early-starter pattern). As you recall from Chapter 7, accumulated evidence supports links between early childhood characteristics, such as difficult temperament or poor emotion regulation, and family factors, such as poverty, harsh or inconsistent parenting, and the development of coercive family interaction patterns. These, in turn, fuel social information processing deficits that set the stage for aggression towards peers and problems with teachers once children enter school. Lack of academic success and chronic peer rejection reduce motivation to do school work and promote positive identification with aggressive and deviant groups. Conduct disorder, possibly continuing as adult antisocial behavior, can be the final outcome of this developmental trajectory. Fortunately, not all children with these high-risk profiles demonstrate adult aggressive outcomes; approximately half show no disorders in adulthood (Cairns & Cairns, 2000). Yet we are well advised to take peer problems seriously because they figure so prominently in the histories of children with externalizing behavior problems, which are the most frequent referral problems in outpatient clinics (McMahon, Greenberg, & CPPRG, 1995).

Assess Carefully

Helpers should keep in mind that there is more than one route to peer rejection. Understanding rejection profiles can help us tailor our interventions to be most effective. Although we tend to group rejected children together or divide them into aggressive and withdrawn types, Bierman (2004) emphasizes that we can differentiate the social behaviors that contribute to rejection into at least four constellations: aggressive/disruptive (fighting, stubbornness, threatening, lying, meanness); inattentive/immature (disruptive, irresponsible, dependent, poorly organized); low levels of prosocial behavior (uncooperative, temperamental, bossy, humorless); and socially anxious/avoidant (solitary, withdrawn, nervous, cries easily). As you have seen, it is possible for aggressive children to be rather well liked if, for example, their aggression (dominance and competitiveness) is balanced by strengths in areas like athletics and a sense of humor. Rejection is more likely when aggression comes in the form of being a "sore loser" or a "hothead." Meanness without provocation, inability to regulate negative affect, deliberate disruption of peer group activity, and low rates of cooperative behavior are danger signals. Peer and teacher ratings of behaviors or direct observation in naturalistic settings are useful for assessment because aggressive children do not always report feelings of distress and may overestimate their own popularity.

Rejected-withdrawn children typically do not show aggression. These children annoy others by their strange or immature behavior, social awkwardness, and failure to "get" the rules governing social conventions. Because these are the children who are most likely to be bullied by their peers, self-reports of their own distress, loneliness, or social anxieties provide the most reliable estimate of problems. Some overlap in symptoms can exist in peer-problem profiles. Some victims can also be aggressive, for example, the "provocative" as opposed to "passive" victims described by Olweus (1993) (see also Cook, Williams, Guerra, Kim, & Sadek, 2010). These children retaliate aggressively to the taunts and teasing of their peers who are irritated by their obnoxiousness. It is important to recognize that rejection and peer victimization can lead to increases in aggression, especially for boys. Careful observation and evaluation are required to understand the dynamics of each of these social categories for treatment purposes.

Skills Are Not Enough

Rejected children have obvious deficits in what are popularly called social skills. Historically, the clinical approach to peer problems was based on a behavioral-psychoeducational model, focusing on manipulating the antecedent conditions and consequences of discrete behaviors, such as reinforcing children to make eye contact or approach a peer group. Evidence has demonstrated that these prescriptive teaching approaches fell far short of their mark. The focus on isolated skills does not generalize to naturalistic settings (Gresham, 1981) and does not appreciably alter the quality of peer relationships for rejected children (Asher, Markell, & Hymel, 1981). Given advances in developmental knowledge, emphasis has turned to promotion of social competence, a more broad-based concept that involves the "capacity to coordinate adaptive responses flexibly to various interpersonal demands, and to organize social behavior in different social contexts in a manner beneficial to oneself and consistent with social conventions and morals" (Bierman, 2004, p. 141). The key is that children need to learn to regulate their social behavior in contexts that are constantly changing. Thus, social interaction process skills might be construed as the overarching goal, even though one might also teach component skills when appropriate. Of note here is that many of the concepts we have been discussing, such as social information processing, emotion regulation, perspective taking, empathy, and so forth play an enormous role in the pursuit of satisfying peer relationships. So, if teaching single skills is not advised and advancing social competence is preferred, what can we do to help?

Include the Peer Group

Interventions are most successful when they take into account the transactional nature of these problems, considering what elicits the difficulty and what sustains it. For example, one of the reasons behavioral skill-based approaches are not successful is because these interventions fail to change the target child's level of peer acceptance, even when the child's actual level of prosocial behavior has increased (Dodge, Coie, Pettit, & Price, 1990). Children acquire reputations in their social groups, generally pointing in either the "good" direction if the child is well liked and socially adept or in the "bad" direction if the child seems socially unskilled. Remember that children tend to see things concretely, in black-and-white terms, and that they will perceive new information selectively so that their schemas remain consistent. Interactions with the target child after a schema for that child has been constructed are marked by attention to evidence that confirms the disliked child's antisocial characteristics (called **confirmation bias**; Gurwitz & Dodge, 1977) and discounting of evidence that indicates a departure from his antisocial role. Children also interpret ambiguous or neutral behavior in ways that are consistent with their schemas (Peets, Hodges, Kikas, & Salmivalli, 2007). Because these social forces operate to maintain homeostasis, they are quite resistant to change.

Efforts to enhance social competence should target not only the peer-rejected child but also the child's peer group (Mikami, Lerner, & Lun, 2010). Peers can be encouraged to initiate more positive interactions with a rejected child through cooperative activities. They may also be taught to clearly communicate that they will not tolerate aggression. The goal should be to create "niches of opportunity" (Bierman, 2004, p. 44) wherein the disliked child can behave more prosocially to modify the peer group's stereotypical schema.

Bierman and Furman (1984) found that combining cooperative activities with other social competence interventions had more lasting effects than cooperative activities alone. Olweus's Bullying Prevention Program (Olweus & Limber, 2010) also takes a comprehensive approach. This program approaches bullying as a problem that resides in the whole system, not just within the bully or victim. Consequently, this universal intervention targets all individuals in a school through classroom meetings and activities that focus on effects of bullying, parent meetings, teacher training, and outcome assessment. It is very important for helpers to offer well-researched universal programs in schools, given that 70% to 80% of the children who need mental health treatment get their only services there (Burns et al., 1995).

Treat the System

Perhaps the most important clinical consideration that follows from recent research in the peer relations field is that interventions need to be directed simultaneously to multiple targets. One exemplary model based on the principles of prevention science is Fast Track, a 10-year, broad-based program that integrates both universal (school-based PATHS curriculum for all children) and targeted interventions (parent groups, social skills training for children, academic tutoring, and home visitations for high-risk children and their families). Interventions are theoretically driven by the developmental early-starter model of conduct disorder and designed to conform to the principles of prevention science. To assess the effectiveness of this program, participating schools have been randomly assigned to intervention and control conditions for purposes of outcome assessment. Assessments from kindergarten through grade 9 have indicated that treated children are significantly less aggressive, disruptive, and noncompliant than controls (CPPRG, 2007).

The backbone of the technique used with children in this program is described as social competence coaching (Bierman, Greenberg, Coie, Dodge, & Lockman, 2017). A few guidelines for effective coaching programs (from Bierman, 2004) can be useful for helpers:

1. The content of interventions should include important research-based domains of social competence that offer children a variety of behaviors, which can be flexibly applied to many different social situations. These domains include: social participation (how to join peers and feel comfortable in peer contexts, etc.), emotional understanding (how to identify and express feelings, etc.), prosocial behavior (how to interact cooperatively), self-control (how to cope effectively with frustration, etc.), communication skills (listening and speaking appropriately, etc.), fair-play skills (being a good sport, etc.), and social problem-solving skills (similar to the steps of the problem-solving models discussed in Chapter 6).
2. These skill domains should be taught by incorporating each of the following four steps: (a) presenting skills through modeling, discussion, giving examples and nonexamples; (b) allowing children to practice skills using role plays or other structured exercises; (c) providing feedback on children's performance by means of discussions, self-evaluations, and so on; and (d) fostering generalizations of skills to the real world of peer relationships. For this last goal, the more the actual peer group is involved in activities, the better one is able to create niches of opportunity for the child with social problems.
3. Create a positive environment so that changes can be practiced and sustained. The warmth and reinforcing qualities of the counselor or coach help reduce anxiety, motivate participation, and increase group cooperation.

Gender and Risk

What, if any, are the special needs and problems of children that attach to gender? Certain clinical syndromes are more frequently reported among boys, including ADHD and learning disorders. Risk for internalizing disorders like anxiety and depression in adolescence are clearly greater for girls, as are risks for eating disorders and sexual abuse (American Psychiatric Association, 2000). Externalizing disorders are more often reported in boys, except for adolescent conduct disorder (Johnston & Ohan, 1999). However, some have suggested that we may have failed to recognize the distinct trajectory of girls' aggression that emerges by late childhood (Crick & Grotpeter, 1995). Girls tend to display a pattern of nonconfrontational, relational aggression (social ostracism, spreading rumors, alienation of others) along with direct confrontational approaches. In contrast, boys escalate their use of direct confrontational aggression at adolescence as the peer group's demands for masculine behavior increase. The fact that boys' aggression has been more visible should not diminish the importance of girls' antisocial behavior for treatment and prevention because of its links to later interpersonal problems with partners and children, anxiety, and depression (see Pepler et al., 2010).

The forms that problem trajectories take are also influenced by gender-role expectations, particularly for youth whose behavior challenges gender norms. As described in this chapter, gender nonconformity places children and young adolescents at particular risk for distress and difficulty, particularly if they experience intolerance or rejection by family or peers. Transgender children and teens show dramatically elevated rates of anxiety, depression, self-harm, and suicidality. Fortunately, public attention to the issues of transgender children has increased their visibility and facilitated access to support and services for these children and their families, though controversy still surrounds the issue at every level. While much additional research is needed to establish best practices for intervening with these individuals, early evidence points to the importance of acceptance without undue pressure for children's gender nonconforming behavior. Special attention must also be paid in schools and other peer contexts to protect gender nonconforming children from bullying and other forms of victimization.

Gender-role stereotypes and expectations also have important clinical implications for youth who identify strongly with their gender and aim to conform. If girls' expression of emotions is tolerated, or even encouraged, then boys' emotional expression is actively discouraged. You have learned that behaviors considered appropriate according to gender are more restrictive for boys than for girls and that parents often reinforce different behaviors for their sons and daughters.

Some authors, who provide clinical insights into the particular challenges faced by boys, argue that the "boy code" that is enforced in the masculine socialization process works like a gender straitjacket. They argue that just as some girls' voices may be suppressed in certain contexts, some boys' voices also go unheard (see Box 8.3). The boy code requires learning that feelings of fear, weakness, and vulnerability should be suppressed in order for them to appear brave and powerful. Although we may be primed to notice symptoms of depression in girls because they fit our conceptions of what depressed behavior looks like, we may miss the cues in boys. Adults need to avoid shaming boys for expressions of vulnerability and to provide them with the time and safety they need to open up. We should not take boys' stoicism as a given.

Evidence from many studies that have examined gender differences in behavior demonstrates that for most characteristics there is actually very little gender difference. Therefore, we need to remember that girls and boys have many similar qualities and needs. Feelings, either good or bad, should not be off-limits because one happens to be a boy or a girl. Counselors can help by examining their own schemas or constructions about what it means to be male and female. That way, we will not selectively attend to information that fits our schema while we discount other important information. For healthy development, both genders need safe spaces in which to exercise their power and to express their vulnerabilities.

Box 8.3: Meeting the Special Needs of Boys

Although boy babies are on average more active and intense in their reactions than girls, there is little consistent evidence of difference in emotion or emotional expression in the first two years (Blakemore, Berenbaum, & Liben, 2009). By 3 to 4 years old, some differences in emotional expression are emerging, at least in U.S. samples, with boys beginning to hide feelings of sadness and fear more than girls (Kyratzis, 2001) and with girls beginning to hide feelings of pride more than boys (see Else-Quest, Higgins, Allison, & Morton, 2012). Way (2011) points out that learning to hide emotions linked with vulnerability, as boys seem more likely to do, can be an impediment to friendship and intimacy, even though friendship is as important to males as it is to females.

Pollack (1998) and Kindlon and Thompson (1990) make the case that boys need support if they are to preserve their emotional lives in a culture that undermines and constrains the expression of emotion among males. Too often, the only messages boys hear are those that advise them to be strong, competitive, and unemotional. These authors emphasize that this state of affairs is supported by multiple systems, from peer groups to adults, that do not take kindly to expressions of male vulnerability. In fact, boys are well schooled from their very early years in a "boy code" (Pollack, 1998) that prizes courage, activity, and strength, and devalues sensitivity and empathy. Sometimes the code prescribes that boys engage in bullying or be "silent witnesses to acts of cruelty to others" (Kindlon & Thompson, 1990, p. 82). In relation to adults, highly active and rambunctious boys are often more likely than girls to receive harsh punishment. As we have seen, harsh punishment is related to increases in aggression and reductions in empathy. The collective consequence of these gendered experiences can be the numbing of emotional awareness and its guarded expression.

These authors advocate that parents, teachers, and other helpers concerned about boys' development need to support the full range of boys' emotional expression by building upon their special strengths. One way is to capitalize on boys' task orientation by encouraging good problem solving. Another way is to respect their preference for activity by providing appropriate opportunities to exhibit strength and skill. Advocating a more oblique approach to the expression of emotion, Kindlon and Thompson (1990) suggest using indirect questions with boys that presuppose underlying emotional complexity, such as "I know you were disappointed about not getting a part in the play last year. Do you want to take the risk and try out again?" (p. 241) rather than "What do you want to do?" Above all, adults need to avoid harsh and shaming punishment, combat the culture of bullying, and model that it is

acceptable for men to be both caring and strong. Thus, boys will be given permission to be strong and caring as well.

Boys may feel especially ill at ease in the culture of psychotherapy where emotional expression is often de rigueur. For counselors who work with young male clients, Kiselica (2003) offers some practical guidelines for making psychotherapy "male-friendly." Several of his suggestions are listed below.

- Be flexible about where to meet and how long to hold sessions.
- Display magazines or other reading material in your office that may be of interest to boys, such as sports magazines.
- Avoid face-to-face seating arrangements in favor of a side-by-side setup; offer a snack before starting the counseling session.
- Become acquainted with contemporary teenage slang or be honest enough to ask what the boy's words mean if you are not familiar with the vocabulary.
- Pay attention to the boy's cues regarding pacing the session; be mindful of the boy's comfort level with respect to sensitive topics.
- Avoid asking too many questions; take the heat off from time to time by focusing on more practical problems like making a team or finding a job.
- Support autonomy strivings and motivation to continue therapy by scheduling appointments directly with the male client, if possible.
- Use appropriate humor and self-disclosure to facilitate engagement.

Summary

The Biology of Sex

1. The sex chromosome pair consists of two XX chromosomes in females but an XY pair in males. Development in a male direction is initiated by expression of the SRY gene on the Y chromosome, which triggers the transformation of the indifferent gonads into testes. Testes produce masculinizing hormones, including androgens, which influence the development of internal and external reproductive organs and some brain structures. In the absence of the SRY gene and the masculinizing hormones, the natural course of development is in the female direction, beginning with the indifferent gonads becoming ovaries.

2. Males are more vulnerable than females to a host of hereditary diseases because of their susceptibility to X-linked recessive disorders. One result is that many more males fail to survive the prenatal period, and males have higher mortality rates at all ages postnatally as well.

Gender Role Development

3. The first step is learning to label oneself as male or female by about age 2½. Next comes gender stability, by 3 or 4 years, which means realizing that gender doesn't fluctuate over time. Finally comes gender constancy, realizing that gender cannot change. This may not emerge until age 6 or 7, although there is controversy on this issue.

4. Social processes, involving active teaching by others, influence learning one's gender identity. Intersex children, whose genitalia are either ambiguous or inconsistent with their biological sex, often acquire the identity that is socially assigned even if it is inconsistent with their biological sex.

5. Cognitive development may also influence the acquisition of gender identity. For example, logical thinking may help a child understand gender constancy. Also, being given accurate information about what is and isn't important for gender assignment is helpful.

6. Biological sex may also influence children's gender identity, even when social input is inconsistent with biology. Some intersex individuals have eventually rejected their assigned identity, apparently feeling more comfortable adopting an identity that is consistent with their biology.

7. Meta-analyses of many different behaviors, personality characteristics, and preferences have identified some that usually vary between males and females. Certain characteristics are found across the life span, whereas others typify specific developmental periods. Some have changed historically, such as differences in math problem solving. The average differences between males and females are usually quite small.

8. Perhaps more important than the small gender differences in laboratory measures of behavior is that boys and girls spend their time differently: boys more often with boys, and girls with girls. Gender segregation begins as early as 2½ years old for girls and 3 years old for boys and increases with age. In their segregated groups, girls and boys behave differently. For example, boys are more active and engage in more aggressive play when they are with boys than with girls or adults. Girls' play and talk is more cooperative or collaborative, whereas boys' play and talk is more competitive and domineering.

9. Where do gender differences come from? Biology seems to play a role in some traits. For example, girls exposed prenatally to male hormones have stronger male play preferences in childhood than other girls.

10. Cognitive developmental theories argue that children are motivated to acquire gender-appropriate behavior once they identify themselves as male or female. Gender schema theories also hypothesize that children choose to act in ways that are consistent with their gender schemas, that is, their networks of expectations and beliefs about male and female characteristics.

11. Parenting processes are also thought to contribute to gendered behavior. Social learning theorists assume that parents play a more direct role, teaching children to adopt gendered behaviors through the use of rewards and punishments. There are some differences in the ways parents treat girls and boys, and there are differences in the kinds of pressures they place. But there are many similarities as well.

12. Peers appear to play a role in engendering gender-typed behavior. Children spend a great deal of time in their gender-segregated peer groups, and in these groups some preexisting gender differences appear to be magnified. Recent research indicates that the more time preschoolers spend in gendered groups, the more gender-typed their behavior becomes (the social dosage effect).

13. Clearly what is needed to explain gender role development is a multidimensional theory that considers all the contributing elements: biology, cognitive processes, and parent and peer socialization pressures.

Peer Relationships

14. In a longitudinal study of children at risk for later mental health problems, one early risk factor stood out as highly predictive of later problems: peer rejection.

15. Evaluating social competence involves examining social skills at every level of social interaction, both within friendships and outside them. Interventions designed to improve specific children's social skills have moderate success, but they might have more success if both the disliked child and the children with whom the target child interacts were included.

16. Peer groups include dyads, cliques, and crowds. The clique and crowd structures begin to emerge in middle childhood and are crystallized in early adolescence. They play a role in the development of self-understanding, and they provide a sense of acceptance and belonging.

17. In sociometry, children's status among their peers is measured. Children in a class are asked to select which children they would most, or least, like to interact with in different contexts. Each child can be categorized on the basis of a social preference score (number of positive less negative nominations) and a social impact score (total nominations, positive and negative).

18. Popular children have high social preference and social impact scores. They have strong social skills, tend to be well-adjusted emotionally, and are cognitively and academically competent as well.

19. Rejected children may be either aggressive or withdrawn, and neither group demonstrates the positive social skills of the popular children. They have low social preference scores but high social impact scores.

20. Neglected children have especially low social impact scores but are not perceived negatively by their peers and tend to show competent development. They may choose not to participate centrally in group activities.

21. Controversial children have some of the qualities of popular children and some of the qualities of rejected children. They are seen by some as leaders and by others as disruptive. Some controversial children may be perceived as "popular," or socially influential, by their peers.

22. Average children score in the average range on both social preference and social impact. They have less social competence than popular children, more than rejected children.

23. Preferred qualities in peers seem to differ somewhat across genders and cultures. For example, boys, especially as they approach adolescence, are more likely to be rejected for cross-gendered behavior than girls. Shy, socially anxious behavior may be valued more in some cultural contexts than others. Aggressive behavior is generally sanctioned in all cultures, and bullying is found to be a problem cross-culturally, but there are differences as well. In the United States, children are expected to defend themselves in conflict situations,

and adults serve as arbitrators. In more collectivist cultures, children who "fight back" are seen as behaving inappropriately, and peers are expected to help resolve conflicts.

24. Popular and rejected categories show the most stability over time and have fairly predictable long-term consequences: positive for popular children, negative for rejected children. The strongest links are found between rejected-aggressive status in childhood and later externalizing problems.

25. Cliques play a role in identity development. Children with similar characteristics form groups that provide some identity and a basis for social comparison. Cliques also serve needs for acceptance and belonging.

26. Peer groups are formed and maintained both through influence and through selection processes. Influence is largely indirect (e.g., teasing) rather than directly coercive (e.g., confrontation) and can cause an individual to conform. Selection refers to the fact that individuals choose to affiliate with others like themselves.

Case Study

Hyun-Ki and his family emigrated from Korea 3 years ago and now live in a large city on the West Coast. His parents moved to this location because they had relatives living in the same city, and they wanted the economic and educational opportunities that they believed the United States could afford their family. Both parents immediately found work in their relatives' small business.

The family lives in a modest home in a working-class neighborhood. The daughters, 16-year-old Sun and 17-year-old Cho, attend the local public high school, and they are diligent, academically advanced students. Hyun-Ki, a fifth grader, is the youngest child. He is quiet and socially reserved. He is also physically slight for his age, shorter than most of the boys and all the girls in his grade. His heavily accented English is somewhat difficult to understand, and he is sensitive about his speech. Consequently, he does not often volunteer to answer questions in class.

Although there are many ethnic groups represented among the students in his class, Hyun-Ki seems to get the brunt of the teasing, even from other Asian American students. When he enters the classroom, students snicker and deride him. "Look what he has on today!" they call out. They make fun of his speech and his reserved ways. When he walks down the hallway to his locker, he is aware of the disparaging looks he gets from some groups of students. Hyun-Ki has a Korean friend whom he sees every Sunday at church. The two boys enjoy spending time together after the service. Hyun-Ki and his friend share an interest in nature and biking. Hyun-Ki wishes he had a friend like this in his own classroom.

Mrs. Marshall, Hyun-Ki's teacher, has assigned a class project that is to be done by small groups of students. Peter,

a boy in Hyun-Ki's group, is an outgoing and popular student who is considered one of the class leaders. He has called Hyun-Ki on the phone several times to discuss the project and is always friendly and pleasant toward him. In school, however, it is a different story. Peter is often part of the group of students who make fun of Hyun-Ki when they pass him in the hall. Hyun-Ki cannot understand why Peter is so nice to him on the phone and so mean to him at school.

Mrs. Marshall observes that Hyun-Ki is not participating very actively in the cooperative group assignment. From the teacher's perspective, Hyun-Ki is "too quiet" and has not contributed sufficiently to get a passing grade for the project. She also notes Hyun-Ki's reluctance to participate in the regular class discussions. She fears that Hyun-Ki's educational needs are not being met in her classroom. Hoping to intervene on the boy's behalf, Mrs. Marshall refers Hyun-Ki to the school's child-study team, whose role is to evaluate the special needs of students in the school.

Discussion Questions

1. How does your knowledge of the topics of gender role development culture and peer group processes contribute to your understanding of Hyun-Ki's situation?

2. How could you help Hyun-Ki's parents and teachers understand the situation? How would you suggest they help him?

3. What prevention efforts would you like to see initiated in this school?

Practice Using What You Have Learned

MyLab Education Application Exercise 8.1:
Case Study: Gender Role Development

MyLab Education Application Exercise 8.2:
Sociometric Categories

MyLab Education Application Exercise 8.3:
Case Study: Interventions for Rejected Children

Journal Questions

1. Gender-role training can be a straitjacket for both girls and boys. Reflect on the gender messages you received as a child and adolescent. Which ones were particularly restrictive? How did these messages affect the decisions you made in your life? Do you think gender-based messages have changed for more recent cohorts of children and adolescents?

2. Identify a gender-related issue that you are personally struggling with at the present time. How are you dealing with it? What resources would be helpful for you in dealing with it?

3. How would you assess your own peer status as an elementary school student? As a middle or junior high school student? As a high school student? What was the most difficult thing you experienced as a child or adolescent in relation to your peers? What could have made the situation better?

4. Give a personal example of an experience you had with peer pressure or peer influence. Has the nature of peer pressure changed?

Key Concepts

SRY gene (p. 298)
anti-Mullerian hormone (AMH) (p. 298)
androgens (p. 298)
Mullerian duct (p. 298)
Wolffian duct (p. 298)
genital tubercle (p. 298)
X-linked recessive disorders (p. 300)
gender identity (p. 300)
gender stability (p. 301)
gender constancy (p. 301)
intersex (p. 303)
congenital adrenal hyperplasia
    (CAH) (p. 303)
transgender (p. 307)
gender nonconformity (p. 307)
gender stereotypes (p. 308)

meta-analysis (p. 308)
borderwork (p. 310)
rough-and-tumble play (p. 311)
collaborative or affiliative
    speech (p. 312)
domineering or power-assertive
    speech (p. 312)
tomboyism (p. 312)
self-socialization (p. 314)
gender intensification hypothesis (p. 314)
gender schema (p. 314)
social dosage effect (p. 319)
social skills (p. 323)
dyads (p. 324)
cliques (p. 324)
crowds (p. 324)

degrouping (p. 324)
sociometry (p. 325)
social preference (p. 325)
social impact (p. 325)
popular (p. 325)
average (p. 325)
neglected (p. 325)
rejected (p. 325)
controversial (p. 325)
rejected-aggressive (p. 327)
rejected-withdrawn (p. 327)
homophily (p. 332)
influence (p. 332)
selection (p. 332)
confirmation bias (p. 335)

Chapter 9
Physical, Cognitive, and Identity Development in Adolescence

 Learning Objectives

After reading this chapter, you should be able to:

9.1 Describe sequential processes in adolescent physical development from hormones that trigger events to corresponding changes in the brain and body and explain how environmental and hereditary factors affect timing of puberty.

9.2 Explain behavioral and emotional changes in adolescence, including a discussion of mood, depression, and the emergence of adult sexuality, and identify factors that shape these changes as well as vulnerabilities that pose threats.

9.3 Describe changes in cognitive functioning in adolescence, characterized by Piaget as formal operational thought, and examine broad implications of these cognitive advances including the effects of egocentrism on adolescent life.

9.4 Assess levels of exploration and commitment in adolescent identity formation and support healthy and developmentally appropriate identity construction.

Rebecca recently had her 13th birthday. Her Aunt Cathy, who has just returned from a year abroad, hardly recognizes her. When she saw her last, Rebecca was a cute, pug-nosed little girl with a sunny disposition and an easy laugh. Now she is 3 or 4 inches taller. But her rapid growth is not what surprises her aunt; it is the qualitative change in both her appearance and her manner. Her slim, child's body is softening and changing shape. Her breasts are emerging, her hips spreading. And her face is, well, a little weird. Suddenly she has a big nose and a pimply complexion. Although she seems genuinely happy to see her aunt, within the first hour of her reunion with the family Rebecca begins interjecting sarcastic remarks into the conversation, and she petulantly rolls her eyes at comments made by other members of her family. Little of what is said escapes her biting criticism. When her mildly exasperated father gently suggests that she should spend some time studying for tomorrow's test, she suddenly seems near tears, whining, "I always have more to do than anyone else!"

Clearly, Rebecca has entered the land of puberty and has begun her trek across the divide from childhood to adulthood. Strictly speaking, puberty is a process of sexual maturation. When it is complete, boys and girls are fertile: Males can impregnate females, and females can conceive. But as most of us can recall from our own journey, puberty is related to a wide range of emotional, behavioral, and social changes as well.

From Shakespeare's Romeo and Juliet to Salinger's Holden Caulfield to Margaret, the teenager in Judy Blume's novel who poignantly asked, "Are you there, God?" we have enjoyed many memorable literary examples of adolescents' coming of age. In many cultures and throughout many different historical periods, adolescence has evoked a certain fascination. We endow it with meaning and celebrate it as the time when innocent, dependent children are transformed into young adults. However, one reason this life stage is so interesting is that, in reality, it defies easy description. What are the tasks of adolescence, and are they completed by a certain chronological age? Are these tasks the same for all adolescents, or are there some that are culture or gender specific? Is adolescence a period of storm and stress or a relatively smooth transition? Should adolescents rebel against convention to define their uniqueness, or is rebellion a sign of maladjustment? Is legal adult status a real indicator of adulthood, or should we look to other indicators of cognitive and emotional maturity? And what is *really* happening within the adolescent brain? These are some of the topics we will discuss in the next two chapters.

Because of its child-to-adult metamorphosis, writers have long recognized the centrality of identity development to the adolescent period. Erik Erikson (1950/1963, 1968) is possibly best remembered for his writing on the topic of identity. Sometimes, however, his emphasis on the shaping of identity in adolescence, which has been the popular interpretation of Erikson's work, inadvertently suggests that there is no real sense of identity beforehand.

As we consider this important task of adolescence, we should note that Erikson was careful to emphasize the epigenetic nature of human development. The human being, like any other growing organism, has a "ground plan" (1968, p. 92) composed of parts that unfold or come into ascendancy at certain times, to eventually become a coherent whole. Success at each new developmental task requires qualities and skills acquired from the work of prior life stages and depends upon relative mastery of earlier tasks as a basis for moving ahead. Thus, far from being divorced from the child's earlier sense of self and self-in-relationship, adolescent identity is a synthesis of earlier elements with new, more cognitively and emotionally mature aspects of the self-system.

We begin our look at the adolescent period by exploring the physical, emotional, and cognitive changes that mark this time of life. Building on the growth and maturation of these systems, we will then consider how they support the process of adolescent identity development. In Chapter 10, you will learn about how adolescents' interactions in their families, in their schools, and with their peers are impacted by the fundamental processes discussed in this chapter.

Physical Development

9.1 Describe sequential processes in adolescent physical development from hormones that trigger events to corresponding changes in the brain and body and explain how environmental and hereditary factors affect timing of puberty.

The physical changes that startled Rebecca's Aunt Cathy are just what we see on the surface. Recent discoveries about the adolescent brain have revealed changes that are less obvious externally but no less dramatic.

A Glandular Awakening

It has been said that "Puberty begins with a *Kiss*" (e.g., May & Cotton, 2014). That is, it begins with kisspeptin, a signaling chemical produced in the hypothalamus. It is called *kisspeptin* because it was discovered in Hershey, Pennsylvania, home of the famous Hershey Kiss™ (Cortés, Carrera, Rioseco, del Río, & Vigil, 2015). Kisspeptin combines with receptors in the hypothalamus to trigger a cascade of events in many parts of the brain and body (see Figure 9.1 for a guide to some of the structures involved and the direction of effects). The hypothalamus produces **gonadotropin releasing hormone (GnRH)**, which stimulates the pituitary and sets the reproductive axis into motion. The pituitary releases **follicle-stimulating hormone (FSH)** and **luteinizing hormone (LH)** that circulate through the bloodstream and stimulate other endocrine glands to increase their hormone production. These glands include the **gonads**—**testes** in males, **ovaries** in females—that now increase their production of both masculinizing hormones (**androgens**, such as **testosterone**) and feminizing hormones (**estrogen**).

Both masculinizing and feminizing hormones (as well as **progesterone**, which is involved in the reproductive cycle) are released in males and in females, but they are produced in different ratios. Increases in androgen production are much higher in boys than in girls, whereas estrogen production increases much more in girls. In combination with other hormones circulating in the blood, they cause a series of changes in children's bodies that promote the maturing of both **primary sexual characteristics** (those directly involved in reproduction, such as the genitalia) and **secondary sexual characteristics** (physical traits not directly involved in reproduction but indicative of sex, such as enlarged breasts in females and deeper voices in males). Early, outward signs of puberty are usually the appearance of pubic hair in both sexes, the growth of the scrotum and testes in boys, and the budding of breasts in girls. **Menarche** in girls (first menstruation) and **spermarche** in boys (first ejaculation) usually occur near the end of puberty and are often treated as important social markers of sexual maturation. But fertility—ovulation in girls and adequate sperm production in boys—may not be achieved for a year or more after these outward manifestations of maturity (Cortés et al., 2015). Table 9.1 gives you an overview of some of these changes and the typical order of their appearance in boys and girls.

FIGURE 9.1 Key structures affecting changes during puberty.

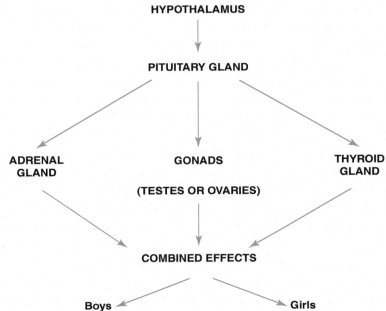

SOURCE: Adapted from Arnett, J. J. (2013). *Adolescence and emerging adulthood* (5th Ed.). Upper Saddle River, NJ: Pearson Education, Inc. Used by permission of Pearson Education.

TABLE 9.1 Typical Sequence of Physical Changes with Puberty

BOYS		GIRLS	
CHARACTERISTIC	**AGE OF ONSET (YEARS)**	**CHARACTERISTIC**	**AGE OF ONSET (YEARS)**
Growth of testes, scrotal sac	9.5 to 13.5	Growth of pubic hair	8 to 14
Growth of pubic hair	10 to 15	Growth of breasts	8 to 13
Growth spurt	10.5 to 16	Growth spurt	9.5 to 14.5
Growth of penis	10.5 to 14.5	Menarche	10 to 16.5
Change in voice	11 to 15	Growth of underarm hair	10 to 16
Spermarche	12 to 14	Changes in sweat & oil producing glands	10 to 16
Growth of facial & underarm hair	12 to 17		
Changes in sweat & oil producing glands	12 to 17		

SOURCE: Adapted from Arnett, J. J. (2013). *Adolescence and emerging adulthood* (5th Ed.). Upper Saddle River, NJ: Pearson Education, Inc. Reprinted and Electronically reproduced by permission of Pearson Education, Inc., New York, NY.

The timing of puberty appears to be affected by genetic factors: Identical twins usually begin and end the process within 2 to 3 months of each other, and mothers' and daughters' ages at menarche are correlated (Brooks-Gunn, 1991; Day, Perry, & Ong, 2015; Golub, 1992; Mustanski, Viken, Kaprio, Pulkkinen, & Rose, 2004). But environmental factors are clearly important as well. For example, there has been a downward shift in the average age of menarche in many countries (Li et al., 2017). Today, the average age is just under 13 years, with slight variations across racial and ethnic groups, whereas in 1850 it was approximately three years later.

Because menarche and spermarche occur later in the maturational process, changes in breast development and pubic hair can be useful markers of pubertal onset. A study conducted in Cincinnati, New York, and San Francisco of over 1,200 girls ages 6 to 7 showed high rates of early puberty. At age 7, early breast development was found for 23% of African American girls, 15% of Hispanic girls, and 10% of Caucasian girls. By age 8, the rates had jumped to 42.9%, 30.9%, and 18.3% respectively. The findings for Caucasian girls represented the greatest increase relative to studies conducted 10 years earlier, even though the absolute numbers were lowest for this group. Since early puberty in girls is a risk factor for later breast cancer, cardiovascular problems, elevated BMI, insulin resistance, and a number of mental and behavioral health issues, this study prompts serious concern about the public health issues associated with the trend toward earlier pubertal timing (Biro et al., 2010).

Signs of early puberty have been increasing in U.S. boys as well. In a comparable study, the approximate age for early signs of genital development in boys was 10.14 for non-Hispanic White boys, 9.14 for African American boys, and 10.04 for Hispanic boys. The results from this study showed pubertal onset occurring 6 months to 2 years earlier (depending upon groups) than data reported 20 years before (Herman-Giddens et al., 2012).

What might be causing this phenomenon? One influence seems to be declining physical activity and increasing intake of high-calorie foods (Herman-Giddens, 2017). Body fat affects the timing of puberty in girls, such that higher ratios of fat are associated with earlier onsets. Whether body fat affects pubertal timing in boys is less clear, although some studies indicate that it does (Lee et al., 2016; see Li et al., 2017). Several mechanisms seem to be involved, including the overproduction of leptin, which is a hormone produced in fat tissue that can affect GnRH levels in the hypothalamus (Fu & Zhou, 2014). Children whose body fat is unusually low, such as those who are malnourished, are likely to begin puberty later than other children.

One intriguing association between environment and timing of puberty is that the onset of puberty tends to be earlier in families where there is substantial conflict or other significant sources of stress (Rickard, Frankenhuis, & Nettle, 2014). This conclusion derives from studies of adolescents around the world. For example, Polish boys and girls living in crowded urban conditions begin puberty earlier than those living in rural areas (Hulanicka, 1999). Puberty is accelerated for Finnish boys and girls reared in father-absent homes as compared to other children (Mustanski et al., 2004). New Zealand girls from divorced families start menstruating earlier than girls whose parents are married (Moffitt, Caspi, Belsky, & Silva, 1992; Tither & Ellis, 2008). Early childhood abuse has also been associated with early menarche (Boynton-Jarrett et al., 2012). A large, longitudinal study of Australian children found that extreme socioeconomic disadvantage put children at high risk for early onset of puberty. Compared to children in better circumstances, low SES boys showed a four times greater frequency of early onset. For low SES girls, the frequency was two times greater, even though the effects of overweight were controlled (Sun et al., 2017). There could be multiple reasons for the correlations between environmental stress and puberty, but one is likely to be that stress affects hormone production.

The effects of environmental stress, at least the effects of chronic socioeconomic disadvantage, may be moderated by protective social factors, such as secure attachments. For example, in a longitudinal study of U.S. children, low SES was linked to early menarche (Sung et al., 2016). But if low SES girls were securely attached to their mothers as infants, they were less likely to experience early menarche than if they were insecurely attached.

Overall, aspects of nutrition and stress may also interact with chemical exposure to disrupt pubertal processes. Certain chemicals used in industrial production (called endocrine-disrupting chemicals or EDCs) interfere with endocrine functions. These chemicals have been linked to changes in pubertal timing and have been shown to affect fat metabolism. EDCs include flame retardants, pesticides, certain pharmaceutical agents, lead, mercury, phthalates found in plastic, and so forth. They have been related to pubertal abnormalities in studies of animals and humans and warrant further investigation according to experts (see Fisher & Eugster, 2014).

The Growth Spurt

Puberty corresponds with the **adolescent growth spurt**, a rapid increase in size accompanied by changes in the shape and proportions of the body. Over about a four-year span, the average increase in height is about 10 inches for both boys and girls; boys gain about 42 pounds on average and girls about 38 pounds. Different parts of the body grow at different times. Facial features like the nose and ears usually grow before the skull does, accounting in part for Rebecca's strange appearance. It is likely that when her head growth catches up with her features, she will no longer seem to have a big nose. Hands, feet, and limbs usually grow before the torso, which can create awkwardness and adds to the odd look. There can even be asymmetries in growth between the two sides of the body, with one breast or one testicle growing before the other (Hofmann, 1997; Tanner, 1990).

Some aspects of the growth process play out differently for girls and boys. For girls, the growth spurt begins and ends about two years earlier than for boys (Herting & Sowell, 2017). Besides other obvious differences, such as increased breast size and greater pelvic spread in girls and broader shoulders in boys, there are gender differences in internal growth. The size of the heart and lungs increases more in boys, for example, and boys also develop thicker bones and more muscle tissue than girls. Many of these changes contribute to average differences in physical strength and endurance between the sexes. Adolescent and adult males are typically stronger than females of the same general size. Thus, the adolescent growth spurt increases both internal and external **sexual dimorphism**, physical differences between the sexes (Malina, 1990).

The Changing Brain

The adolescent brain is an instrument of change. Its plasticity is its most remarkable characteristic (Giedd, 2015). It is not so much that the brain is growing but that its circuitry is changing. Because it is reorganizing, the teen brain seems especially open to new experiences and learning opportunities, and especially vulnerable to adversity (Byrne et al., 2017; Schultz & Sisk, 2016). We will briefly summarize some changes and then examine how they relate to teen behavior.

The availability of new technologies is rapidly altering our understanding of the processes that contribute to neural reorganization during adolescence. Longitudinal studies of humans and other mammals show that puberty's hormonal cascade helps trigger and moderate changes in brain structure and function (Gur & Gur, 2016; Juraska & Willing, 2017; Schultz & Sisk, 2016). Hormones can modify the brain by influencing the onset or offset of genes. By doing so, they alter protein synthesis, which is important for all neuro-maturational processes.

Let's consider gray matter changes first. Gray matter volume, which appears to peak in early to middle childhood, begins to decrease with puberty (Mills et al., 2016). Pruning of cortical synapses is one likely reason (Kilford, Garrett, & Blakemore, 2016). You will recall that pruning involves carving away unused or dysfunctional synapses (connections between neurons). The pruning we described in the sections on infancy and early childhood take place primarily in the sensory and motor cortices of the brain. In adolescence, pruning occurs primarily in areas of the brain that are related to higher-order functions, especially in the prefrontal cortex.

As gray matter volume decreases, white matter increases because of continuing axon myelination. As a result, the relative proportion of white to gray matter rises during the teen years (Mills et al., 2016). As you know, myelination allows faster information processing. Axons transmit impulses up to 100 times faster after myelination than before, and neurons with myelinated axons can fire up to 30 times more frequently (Giedd, 2015). The upshot is more efficient information processing. Myelin also "fine tunes" the timing of signals arriving at any single neuron from multiple parts of the brain. When multiple synapses are activated simultaneously, it is more likely that a neuron will fire and then activate other neurons, further up the line. Firing also strengthens the synapses with the activating neurons. This makes learning, the building or strengthening of associations, more likely. So, while some synapses are pruned, others are strengthening, and brain circuitry is reshaping in response to the environment. Overall then, white matter expansion means more learning and more complex circuitry within structures (e.g., within the prefrontal cortex) and between structures (e.g., between cortical and subcortical regions; Casey, 2015; Giedd, 2015).

There are other important brain changes that are launched at puberty as well. For example, there are large shifts in the production of neurotransmitters and the enzymes that metabolize them. In particular, puberty initiates a slow decrease in serotonin levels and a rise in dopamine levels (Casey, 2015).

Imbalance in Adolescent Brain Development

Brain researchers are finding that adolescence is also a time of uneven brain development; that is, different regions mature at different rates. However, the complexity of the processes is so great that researchers do not always agree on what structures or functions are changing the most quickly, nor do they agree on what the behavioral consequences might be (e.g., compare Shulman et al., 2016, to Romer, Reyna, & Satterthwaite, 2017). The bulk of evidence indicates that subcortical areas, such as the limbic system (amygdala, hippocampus, etc.) and the closely related nucleus accumbens, mature at a faster pace than other regions. These subcortical structures are important for what some call "hot" processes—emotional reactivity, attraction to peers, and the pleasures of risk and reward. The prefrontal cortex, the seat of "cool," more rational processes, changes at a slower, steadier pace (see Figure 9.2). The prefrontal cortex is also important for emotional and social processing, but it plays a planning and control function, adding a contemplative element to emotional reactions, to social interaction, and to the evaluation of risk and reward (Giedd, 2015).

There is a variety of evidence to support the notion of more rapid subcortical maturation. For example, dopamine is a neurotransmitter that is important in many brain areas, and it is critical for learning, processing emotions, and anticipating and experiencing reward. Studies of animals show that subcortical structures like the ventral striatum (part of the nucleus accumbens) reach a peak of responsiveness to dopamine (indicated by the density of dopamine receptors)

FIGURE 9.2 A model of timing of functional maturation of the emotional and cognitive control systems of the brain.

SOURCE: Based on Casey, B. J., Getz, S., & Galvan, A. (2008). The adolescent brain. *Developmental Review, 28*(1), 62-67. Used with permission from Elsevier.

by early adolescence. But the prefrontal cortex does not reach its peak responsiveness to dopamine until early adulthood (Casey, 2015). It is important to keep in mind that despite its more protracted development, the prefrontal cortex still makes substantial maturational progress during the teen years. Improvements in executive functions, in learning, and in logic can be remarkable (Juraska & Willing, 2017; see the next section on Cognitive Development). But the neural circuitry that connects the prefrontal cortex to the subcortical, "emotional" brain is in flux and may not fully develop until the maturation of the two systems comes more into alignment. As a result, some researchers argue that sometimes a teen's choices in emotionally and socially charged situations, especially those involving peers, risk, and/or reward, are driven more by subcortical structures, or "hot" processing, than by the "cool" regulatory processes of the prefrontal cortex (Casey, 2015; Cohen et al., 2016).

In addition, you might recall from Chapter 4 that the "emotional" brain governs both an avoidance system (avoiding harm) and an approach system (approaching pleasure). These two behavioral systems may not develop at the same pace. The avoidance system is led by the amygdala, which is an important driver of the stress response (see the next section). As you know, this system helps us to interpret stimuli as potentially dangerous and to react in ways that avoid punishment or pain. The approach system, which identifies potentially rewarding situations, is driven by the ventral striatum. Ernst (Ernst, Pine, & Hardin, 2006; Ernst, 2014) proposed a triadic model of neural development to explain increased sensation seeking and risk taking in the teen years. First, the regulatory prefrontal cortex is maturing more slowly than the subcortical structures, as we already described. But also, at the subcortical level, the approach system has a greater effect on teens' behavior than the avoidance system does. Both systems are maturing, but either the amygdala is developing more slowly than the ventral striatum, or the circuitry that allows each of them to moderate the other's responses is lagging.

As you can see, imbalance in brain development might help explain why adolescents tend to score higher than other age groups on **sensation seeking** (Harden et al., 2017). *Sensation seeking* is defined as "the need for varied, novel, and complex sensation and experiences and the willingness to take on physical and social risk for the sake of these experiences" (Zuckerman, 1979, p. 10). If sensation seeking is rewarding, and the emotional brain, especially the subcortical approach system, is maturing more rapidly than regulatory circuitry, then teens might literally anticipate and experience more pleasure from risky behavior than other age groups do. They might also be less able to regulate their behavior in potentially rewarding situations (Casey, 2015). In Chapter 10, you will learn more details on how typical risk taking is for this age group, and how peers, gender, and other individual differences seem to affect it.

The Adolescent Brain and Stress

Before we take a closer look at teen behavior, let's examine in more detail what happens to the stress response and the hypothalamic-pituitary-adrenal (HPA) axis during adolescence. You'll recall from Chapter 2 that when we perceive a stressor, the amygdala triggers a chain of reactions in the hypothalamus, the pituitary, and the adrenal glands. The adrenals release cortisol, which travels through the bloodstream to many organ systems, causing the body to ready itself for "fight or flight," whatever it takes to avoid harm. Under ordinary conditions, cortisol circulates back to the amygdala and the hippocampus, and it binds with receptors there, ending the stress response so that the body can get back to equilibrium and normal functioning.

The HPA axis matures in multiple ways during adolescence (Trotman et al., 2013). First, the basal rate of cortisol production increases, and it remains higher in adulthood than it is in children. Second, the HPA axis grows more sensitive to stressors, secreting more stress-induced cortisol than it did during childhood. In other words, the stress system becomes more responsive, and it remains that way through young adulthood (Holtzman et al., 2013).

One often-cited experiment illustrates this altered stress responsiveness. Stroud and colleagues (2009) assessed HPA axis and cardiac functions in children (ages 7 to 12) and adolescents (ages 13 to 17) who were exposed to either performance or social stressors. To induce performance stress, participants had to make a 5-minute speech, answer mental arithmetic questions, and copy a picture from its mirror image in front of a small audience. Social stress was induced with a social rejection interaction: Confederates gradually excluded the participant during a conversation. Although the teens did not report feeling more distress than the younger children, they had stronger physiological reactions on all stress-related measures, including cortisol production.

We have been describing typical changes to HPA responding during adolescence. Given how much reorganization the teen brain undergoes, you won't be surprised to learn that severe, unpredictable, or chronic stress can have especially negative effects for this age group. For example, in one study, 16-year-olds who reported experiencing severe social adversity (e.g., violence or bullying) showed a blunting of their stress response by the time they were 19 years old (Laceulle, Nederhof, van Aken, & Ormel, 2017). Animal studies have also found that structures in the limbic system and the prefrontal cortex can show permanent stress-induced atrophy, hypertrophy, or other atypical changes as a result of severe stress during the adolescent period, affecting performance on a variety of behavioral measures (Eiland & Romeo, 2013; Holtzman et al., 2013).

MyLab Education Self-Check 9.1.

Behavioral and Emotional Changes

9.2 Explain behavioral and emotional changes in adolescence, including a discussion of mood, depression, and the emergence of adult sexuality, and identify factors that shape these changes as well as vulnerabilities that pose threats.

The physical changes we have catalogued correspond with many types of behavioral change. You will be reading soon about cognitive developments and about the teen's reconceptualization of self (identity development) as she experiences the physical transformation puberty initiates. In this section, we will focus on some of the specific behavioral and emotional effects that have been identified, the vulnerabilities that emerge in adolescence, and the advent of adult sexuality.

Sleeping—Or Not

Puberty's physiological changes affect Circadian rhythms and homeostasis. The timing of daily hormone release from endocrine glands is delayed, and that shifts the adolescent's sleep-wake cycle to later times, as much as 1 to 4 hours later. Sleep homeostasis, the sleep regulating system, also changes, so that after puberty adolescents can resist sleep pressure (i.e., tolerate the need to sleep) more than before puberty (Hagenauer, Perryman, Lee, & Carskadon, 2009; Hummer & Lee, 2016; Tarokh, Saletin, & Carskadon, 2016).

These biological changes mean that adolescents prefer to go to sleep later at night, and they prefer to sleep later in the morning than they did before puberty. This sleep pattern is called **delayed phase preference**. This preference, along with other adolescent experiences—increased autonomy to control bedtime, more time spent on homework, commitments to extracurricular activities, late night opportunities to socialize via texting and other social media—conspire to make bedtimes later and later. But wake up times, at least during the school week, are usually quite early, and the result is that many teens are sleep deprived.

The thing is, adolescents actually need a good deal of regular sleep, between 8 and 10 hours per night, according to the National Sleep Foundation (2017). In one longitudinal study, when teens were able to sleep as much as they wished up to 10 hours, they averaged 9.25 hours per night (Tarokh et al., 2016). On school days, most teens get considerably less sleep than they need. Most middle and high schools begin earlier than elementary schools, and because adolescents go to bed late, they simply miss out on adequate sleep. They not only are sleep deprived, but their sleep routines tend to vary a great deal.

Unfortunately, both sleep deprivation and variability are problematic for the developing brain. "[S]leep itself may play an active role in sculpting the adolescent brain" (Tarokh et al., 2016, p. 184). For example, in one longitudinal study, researchers asked boys and girls to complete daily sleep diaries for two weeks, once when they were approximately 14 years old and again one year later (Telzer, Goldenberg, Fuligni, Lieberman, & Gálvan, 2015). The participants recorded when they went to bed at night, when they woke up in the morning, and the total time they slept. A few months after the second diary was completed, the teens underwent an imaging procedure called DTI, which can reveal the organization and structural integrity of white matter in the brain. The more variable the teens' sleep time was at 14 years old, the less white matter integrity their scans showed a year and a half later.

At any age, sleep deprivation is associated with poorer performance on executive function tests, learning tasks, and emotion regulation measures (Bryant & Gomez, 2015; Tarokh et al., 2016; Telzer, Fuligni, Lieberman, & Gálvan, 2013). And of course, insufficient sleep makes it more likely that you will be sleepy when you need to be alert. In one well-controlled experiment, 13- to 17-year-olds were allowed to sleep only 6.5 hours per night for five nights. In a school-like context, they learned less, and their attention wandered more frequently, than controls whose sleep was not limited (Beebe, Rose, & Amin, 2010).

So, what can we do to protect teens' sleep in the modern world? One possibility is to start school later in the morning, a solution recommended by the American Academy of Pediatrics (Adolescent Sleep Working Group, Committee on Adolescence, & Council on School Health, 2014). Shifting to later start times tends to increase teens' sleep duration, and longer sleep is associated with better attendance, improved grades, feeling less unhappy, and less risk of driving accidents (Lewin et al., 2017; Minges & Redeker, 2016; Wahlstrom et al., 2014; Wahlstrom, Berger, & Widome, 2017). Even a 30-minute later start seems to improve things for adolescents (Owens, Belon, & Moss, 2010).

Parents can also take steps to help their teens. Table 9.2 offers some practical recommendations. One caution: Many people assume that sleep deprivation effects can be managed by "catching up" on weekends. But delaying wake time on weekends is associated with later daily release of melatonin (a sleep hormone) over the next week, making later sleep times even more likely (Bryant & Gómez, 2015). Sleep regularity is a more effective protection.

Emotions and Mood

You have seen that increased sensation seeking and reward sensitivity can be among the consequences of adolescent brain changes. There are other emotional changes as well. Recall the story of Rebecca at the beginning of this chapter. Part of what surprised her aunt was how moody Rebecca had become. Parents whose children have gone through puberty often warn parents of younger children to "Enjoy them while they're

---

TABLE 9.2 Teen Sleep Recommendations for Parents

- Set bedtimes for 10:00 p.m. or earlier.
  (If the schedule is regular, teens will fall asleep as easily as they do at later times.)

- Restrict technology use before bedtime and in the bedroom.

- Limit caffeine and energy drinks, especially in the evening.

- Keep sleep schedules consistent.

- Consider advocating for later school start times.

SOURCE: Adapted from Bryant, N. B. & Gomez, R. L. (2015). The teen sleep loss epidemic: What can be done? *Translational Issues in Psychological Science, 1,* 116–125.

young; you don't know what you're in for!" Parents of adolescents often assume that hormones are the underlying cause when their adolescents seem emotionally unpredictable, making comments such as "Her hormones are raging!"

Given that hormones influence brain restructuring and changes in stress responding in the teen years, this is a reasonable statement. But remember, any developmental outcome is usually the result of many contributing factors. Adolescents are adjusting to a host of profound changes that can and do affect their moods: new cultural expectations for mature behavior, more difficult academic tasks, the prospect of making critical life decisions, major changes in friendships and peer experiences, dramatic appearance changes, intensified sexual impulses, and so on.

A pioneering study illustrates that teenagers tend to be moodier than other age groups. Larson and Richards (1994) used a technique called the experience sampling method (ESM) to gauge adolescents' moods in natural settings. A sample of teens and their mothers and fathers wore pagers throughout their waking hours. When the pagers beeped, the participants made notes about what they were doing, thinking, and feeling at that moment. In the course of a day, adolescents reported more mood disruptions, more feelings of self-consciousness and embarrassment, more extremes of emotion, and less overall happiness than the adults. In addition, their emotional reactions to the very same events tended to be more intense than those of their parents.

Many experimental studies have demonstrated that adolescents are more responsive to emotional stimuli than younger or older groups are. For example, they show greater pupil dilation to emotion-related words and they tend to remember proportionally more emotion-related words in delayed recall tasks than younger children (Silk et al., 2009). Whereas adults show increased amygdala responses only to images of fearful faces, adolescents show greater amygdala activation to both fearful and neutral faces (Thomas et al., 2001).

So, adolescents are often more emotionally reactive than children or adults. Regarding threats, you have seen that teens have a more intense stress response than younger children. Their responses to threats also can be qualitatively different from those of other age groups (Casey, 2015). For example, Pattwell and colleagues (2012) presented children (ages 5 to 11), adolescents (ages 12 to 17), and adults (ages 18 to 28) with colored squares (neutral stimuli) while blasting a loud, aversive noise (frightening stimulus). Participants of all ages quickly began to show a conditioned fear response to the colored squares, based on physiological measures. Participants then experienced several "extinction" trials: The colored squares were presented *without* the aversive stimulus. The fear response was extinguished for both children and adults, but the adolescents continued to react to the colored squares as though they were frightening. It appears that adolescents may have more difficulty than other age groups suppressing emotional responses to threatening cues when in fact those cues no longer pose a problem.

Consider one more example of emotional difference in adolescence. Sebastian, Viding, Williams, and Blakemore (2010) manipulated girls' social stress by asking them to play a 3-minute computer game called "cyberball." The girls experienced either inclusion or ostracism as a function of being "thrown" the ball or ignored by two other players. Compared to adult studies using this manipulation, both young (ages 11 to 13) and mid (ages 14 to 15) adolescents reported greater negative mood, and younger girls also showed significant increases in distress. Even a short experience of social stress markedly affected their moods.

Such emotional developments are normal for adolescents. But exaggerated emotional responding can be a risk factor for the development of mental illness when combined with other potential risks (e.g., family dysfunction, childhood trauma, genetic susceptibility, and so on). As you have seen before, risk factors potentiate each other. The diagnosis of serious mental disorders rises dramatically in the teen years. The "intersection of stress and the developing adolescent brain may represent a 'perfect storm' in the context of dysfunctional emotional development" (Romeo, 2010, p. 249). First episodes of psychosis, including bipolar disorder and schizophrenia, often occur in the later teen years or soon afterward (Holtzman et al., 2013). Half of social anxiety disorder cases are first diagnosed by age 13, with 90% being diagnosed by age 23 (Kilford et al., 2016). Rates of clinical depression increase in adolescence as well.

Depression in Adolescence

Let's take a closer look at the rise in depression during adolescence. Compared to much lower rates in childhood, about one third of teens experience depressed mood, defined as a subclinical level of depression, at any given time (Petersen, Compas, Brooks-Gunn, Ey, & Grant, 1993). Rates of clinical depression are also higher for teenagers than for children. In fact, by mid-adolescence, clinical depression rates reach adult levels. As we have noted before, both depressed mood and clinical depression occur more often in females than in males, beginning in adolescence. Depending on the measurement techniques used, large studies report major depression rates for 12- to 19-year-olds ranging from 5% to 20%, with girls' rates as much as triple that of boys (SAMHSA, 2017; Thapar, Collishaw, Pine, & Thapar, 2012).

What accounts for the adolescent rise in depression rates? As with most behavioral outcomes, there appear to be multidimensional processes at work here. Physical changes brought on by puberty interact with other causal factors to affect adolescent emotions and behavior, especially mental health.

We will examine these multidimensional factors by considering why girls are more susceptible to depression than boys. Sex differences in circulating hormones may directly contribute to sex differences in depression rates (Hamilton, Hamlat, Stange, Abramson, & Alloy, 2014). But most developmentalists argue that social stressors can play as great or a greater role in the mix of causes. Both boys and girls experience increased stress of various kinds after puberty. But on the whole, it may be that girls face more challenges in early adolescence than boys do (Petersen, Sarigiani, & Kennedy, 1991). That is, girls must deal with more stressors simultaneously. In comparison to their male counterparts, females report experiencing more stressors from early adolescence onward (Compas, Howell, Phares, Williams, & Giunta, 1989; Wichstrom, 1999).

Let's start by looking at what happens when puberty is "off time," especially when the onset is early. Going through puberty before one's peers can create social and emotional problems, especially for girls (Galvao et al., 2014; Mendle, 2014). Even though early and late maturers are subject to the same hormonal influences once puberty begins, early maturers are more susceptible to depression, suicidal thoughts, panic attacks, substance use, and many other problems. The reasons must depend on factors other than hormones.

For example, partly because most girls begin puberty before most boys, an especially early-maturing girl is bigger than most of the other children her age. She is also heavier and so is more likely than other girls to be unhappy with her body in a culture that prizes slimness (Wichstrøm & von Soest, 2016). Early sexual maturation (e.g., breast development) can also make her a target for teasing or innuendo from peers or even outright rejection by less mature girls (Hamilton et al., 2014).

Parents of early-maturing girls often worry about their daughters being at risk for sexual experiences that they are not ready to handle, and they may limit their daughters' independence in ways that are grating. Their concerns may not be exaggerated. Behavior problems for early-maturing girls are more likely if the girls become involved with older boys, which is more probable with low levels of parental supervision (Skoog & Stattin, 2014). Early-maturing girls are also more likely to be targets of sexual victimization and partner violence than other girls (Mendle, 2014).

For early-maturing boys, the picture is less clear. Older studies indicate that early puberty might be helpful to boys, giving them an edge in socially approved activities such as athletics, or in romantic relationships, given that their pubertal timing may be more in line with that of typical girls. Late-maturing boys could be at a disadvantage in such activities. This is probably true in some cases, but newer, longitudinal studies often find that early-maturing boys have some of the same disadvantages as girls. Being different is a social liability and can lead to peer rejection. Early-maturing boys, like girls, show less social competence than their "on time" peers as they move through adolescence (Westling, Andrews, & Petersen, 2012). On the whole, it appears that for boys as well as girls, early puberty creates some risk of both internalizing and externalizing problems, although the list of negative consequences is longer for girls than for boys (Hamilton et al., 2014; Mendle, 2014).

Box 9.1: The Limits of Guilt in Adolescence

Steven Drizin, a defense attorney who works with juvenile clients, provides the following case description:

> In November 1999, a Michigan jury convicted thirteen year old Nathaniel Abraham of second degree murder in the shooting death of Ronnie Greene, a crime committed when Abraham was only eleven years old. Under Michigan law, Judge Eugene Moore could have sentenced Nathaniel as a juvenile, as an adult, or given him a blended sentence that treated Nathaniel initially as a juvenile and then later as an adult if he failed to rehabilitate himself with services provided in the juvenile system. Judge Moore gave the boy the break of his life, sentencing Abraham as a juvenile and sparing him a sentence of between 8 and 25 years in prison. But the boy, who fidgeted and doodled during the judge's twenty-minute speech, didn't appreciate the judge's generosity. Reportedly, he turned to his attorney after the judge had concluded, and asked, 'What happened?' (Drizin, 2003, p. 8)

Drizin suggests that Nathaniel's response to his trial illustrates an important reason for treating juvenile offenders differently from adults: They are not necessarily fully capable of understanding the proceedings of a trial, participating in their own defense, or of making the many decisions that are required of an adult defendant.

The first juvenile justice system was established in Illinois in 1899. Within 25 years, in every part of the United States there were two systems of justice for individuals charged with crimes, one for adults and the other for juveniles (usually defined as those under the age of 18). The juvenile system emphasizes rehabilitation rather than punishment, and it reflects that focus even in the terminology that is used: "*petition* instead of *indictment*, *respondent* instead of *defendant*, and *disposition* instead of *sentencing*" (Trivits & Repucci, 2002, p. 694). The emphasis on rehabilitation is based on the belief that juvenile offenders are immature, not fully formed, and so can be reshaped or reformed. Further, the state's role is a parental one, to provide the right environment for future development.

But by the 1990s, "a legislative tsunami was washing over the United States" (Wilcox, 2003, p. 12). In one state after another, laws were altered to allow juveniles, especially adolescents, to be tried in adult criminal court, facing the same penalties that adults would face. A sense that predatory teens with well-established and irremediable character flaws were victimizing citizens and getting off too lightly in the juvenile justice system seemed to prevail. This "tough on crime" attitude overwhelmed the reasoning that had inspired a different approach to juveniles a century before. Yet an appreciation for that reasoning has re-emerged, and is reflected in U.S. Supreme Court decisions in the early years of this century. The Court ruled in 2005 that sentences of capital punishment are unconstitutional for any defendant under age 18. They later limited sentences of life without parole. In 2010, these were deemed unconstitutional for individuals under 18 for crimes other than homicide. In 2012, states were first enjoined from automatically sentencing juveniles to life sentences even when the crime was homicide; in 2016, states were required to revisit such sentences delivered prior to the 2012 ruling (Steinberg, 2017).

In making these landmark decisions, the U.S. Supreme Court took into account information that was presented by developmental scientists on adolescents' cognitive functioning, on brain development, on identity development, and on social interactive processes, like peer relations (Cohen & Casey, 2014; Steinberg, 2017). Such research has been brought to bear on two critical questions. First, are teens as fully culpable as adults when committing the same crimes? And second, are adolescents competent to participate in the adult justice system?

Adolescent Culpability

Even when an individual is found guilty of a crime, her guilt can be mitigated under the law. "**Mitigation** places the culpability of a guilty actor somewhere on a continuum of criminal culpability and, by extension, a continuum of punishment" (Steinberg & Scott, 2003, p. 1010). Mitigation does not mean excusing the crime. The perpetrator is held responsible, but she is considered less than fully blameworthy. If by virtue of being an adolescent a guilty party's culpability were mitigated, then the punishments that would be appropriate would be altered as well. Indeed, interventions aimed at rehabilitation rather than punishment might be the wisest course.

Steinberg and Scott (2003) indicate that there are roughly three sources of mitigation in adult criminal law. The first is **diminished capacity**, which could be due to mental illness, emotional distress, intellectual impairment, or "susceptibility to influence or domination" (p. 1011). The second, **compelling circumstances**, occurs when an individual faces such pressure that even an ordinary, reasonable person could be expected to give in, such as acting in the face of extreme need or under threat of injury. The third source of mitigation is when the crime represents **uncharacteristic behavior** on the part of the perpetrator, as in the case of a first offense or when the crime is "aberrant in light of the defendant's established character traits and respect for the law's values" (p. 1011).

Are teens as fully culpable as adults? Steinberg (2017; Schulman & Steinberg, 2016; Steinberg & Scott, 2003) argues that if we look at the developmental evidence, adolescents should be considered less culpable on the basis of all three sources of mitigation. First, their cognitive and psychosocial development is likely to affect their choices in ways not characteristic of adults. In essence, their decision making tends to be immature (or we could say impaired) in comparison to that of adults, suggesting *diminished capacity*. Reasoning ability improves throughout adolescence into adulthood. By mid-adolescence, many youngsters do well on tests of formal logic if they are given hypothetical problems that have logical solutions under conditions of low emotional arousal (like the scientific problem solving described later in this chapter). But as you will see in Chapter 11, teens do not perform as well as young adults on the more ambiguous problems of real life, especially when they are emotionally invested in an issue (Blanchard-Fields, 1986). In addition, teens' decisions in real-life situations may be influenced by their psychosocial immaturity and lack of experience. As you will see in Chapter 10, adolescents are particularly susceptible to peer influence, they are high risk takers, and their self-control is not fully developed. Their capacity or tendency to think about future consequences is beginning to develop, but is quite limited. Teens heavily weigh short-term gains in their decision making and tend to discount long-term considerations (e.g., Halpern-Felsher & Cauffman, 2001). When they are asked to imagine themselves or their circumstances in the future, teens use a much shorter time frame than adults do (e.g., Nurmi, 1991).

Adolescent characteristics that suggest diminished capacity from a legal standpoint appear to be linked to immature, and changing, neurological processes. As this chapter makes clear, the teen brain shows gradual maturing of precisely those regions that affect long-term planning, judgment, decision making, regulation of emotion, impulse control, and the evaluation of risk and reward. Change in these areas continues throughout adolescence and into young adulthood.

Not only could adolescents be considered less culpable than adults on the basis of diminished capacity, but also they are more vulnerable to *compelling circumstances*. As Steinberg and Scott (2003) argue, "ordinary adolescents may respond adversely to external pressures that adults are able to resist" (p. 1014). For many of the reasons already indicated, they may be more easily provoked to aggressive responses by perceived threats. Their emotional lability and intensity seem to make many situations more stressful for adolescents than for adults. Also, their need for peer support and approval makes them especially susceptible to peer influence, whether in the form of direct pressure or as a result of the adolescent's own concern for fitting in.

Finally, adolescents' criminal actions may well qualify as *uncharacteristic behaviors* on the grounds that a teen's character and identity is relatively unformed. Identity formation is a major developmental task in adolescence and can involve assessment and reassessment of every aspect of the developing self, including the moral self. Teens who are immersed in this process often experiment with (or "try on") behaviors that are potentially dangerous, like drug use or antisocial acts, but for most adolescents this delinquent activity is relatively short-lived. It is referred to as "adolescence limited" behavior (see Chapter 10).

One arena in which this adolescence limited behavior has been observed is the perpetration of sex offenses. Trivits and Repucci (2002) examined recidivism rates across a wide range of studies of adolescents and adults convicted of sex crimes, such as rape, child molesting, and exhibitionism. On the whole, adolescents' recidivism rates over many years ranged from about 8% to 12% and were substantially lower than those of adult offenders, which ranged from about 20% to 40%. Other studies have reported similar differences in recidivism rates between adolescents and adults (e.g., Caldwell, 2010).

As Trivits and Repucci point out, sexual offenses may tend to have very different etiologies in adolescents as compared to adults, and patterns of sexual behaviors are likely to be less established among adolescents. Sexual misconduct in teens may often represent the kind of experimentation described earlier, associated with the fact that the adolescent's identity and character is very much a "work in progress." Adolescent sex offenders are also more likely than adults to respond well to treatment (Harris, Walfield, Shields, & Letourneau, 2016).

Adolescent Competence to Stand Trial

The same characteristics that may mitigate adolescents' culpability raise questions about their competence to be processed in the system of justice designed for adults. In this system, a criminal defendant must be competent to stand trial, meaning that she must be able to assist her counsel in preparing her defense, understand the court proceedings well enough to participate, and be capable of making decisions about her rights, like whether or not to waive a jury trial or to accept a plea bargain. Fortunately, a research consortium, the MacArthur Research Network on Adolescent Development and Juvenile Justice, is undertaking studies that are designed to assess the degree to which teens have these capabilities. In one study (reported in Grisso et al., 2003, and in Steinberg et al., 2003), 1,000 juveniles (ages 11 to 17) and 500 young adults (ages 18 to 24) participated. Half of the participants were either in juvenile detention centers or adult jails, and the other half were drawn from the community (and matched for socioeconomic status, ethnicity, and so on). Each of them completed two measures. One was designed to assess competence to stand trial, including factors such as "understanding" (e.g., comprehension of courtroom procedures) and "reasoning" (e.g., recognition of information relevant to a legal defense). The other measure was designed to identify the kinds of choices that might be characteristic of the different age groups with regard to legal decisions. Participants heard stories about individuals charged with crimes and were asked to make decisions for them (e.g., about how to respond to police interrogation, whether to disclose information during consultation with an attorney, and how to respond to a plea agreement that would involve a guilty plea and testifying against other defendants).

The results support the conclusion that juveniles from ages 11 to 15 are significantly less competent than young adults to stand trial, whereas 16- to 17-year-olds are not significantly different from young adults. Substantially more young teens showed impairments in understanding or reasoning about court-related matters in comparison to young adults. Only age and intelligence were significant predictors of competence—gender, ethnicity, current status as an offender, and socioeconomic status were not important.

A similar pattern was obtained on the measures of decision making. Younger teens, ages 11 through 15, were significantly more likely to make decisions based on what authorities dictated. "Thus, compared with older adolescents and young adults, adolescents aged 15 and younger are more likely to recommend confessing to the police rather than remaining silent and accepting a plea bargain offered by a prosecutor rather than going to trial" (Steinberg et al., 2003, p. 10). The researchers looked at what considerations were involved in making these decisions and found that, compared to older adolescents and adults, younger juveniles often failed to identify or to adequately evaluate risks or to take into account the long-range, as opposed to short-term, consequences of their choices.

In general, the results support Drizin's (2003) judgment that juvenile offenders, at least those under the age of 16, are substantially less likely than adults to have the ability to function adequately in the adult justice system.

Other stressors, beyond the impact of early puberty, can contribute to sex differences in depression rates. We will consider a few of the challenges that seem to especially affect girls regardless of pubertal timing. First, by age 11, children are aware that the female gender role is less valued than the male role. They believe that there are greater restrictions on behavior for females and that there is gender-based discrimination (Brown & Bigler, 2005). They recognize that females are seen as less competent than males, and that traditional female occupations are less prestigious than male occupations (Ruble, Martin, & Berenbaum, 2006). As they integrate these beliefs into their self-concept, girls may begin to feel less worthwhile than boys, or at least less appreciated. Second, although both boys and girls are concerned about **body image** (their concept of, and attitude toward, their physical appearance), girls worry more than boys about appearance and weight after puberty (Dion et al., 2015). And, adolescents' dissatisfaction with their bodies is predictive of declining self-esteem and depressive symptoms (Solomon-Krakus et al., 2017).

We should note, as we did in Chapter 7, that ethnicity moderates body satisfaction. For example, African American youth are more likely to report positive body images than White youth. Body ideals among African Americans are more consistent with actual body characteristics, which serves as a protective factor for adolescents (Paxton, Eisenberg, & Neumark-Sztainer, 2006). For other ethnic groups, especially for girls, thinness as a body ideal is well established by early adolescence (Carey, Donohue, & Broderick, 2014). As Harter (2006) points out, such "images of female attractiveness are very punishing in that they are unattainable by the vast majority of girls and women in the culture" (p. 556).

Third, girls historically have more often had lower expectations of success than boys (Ruble, Gruelich, Pomerantz, & Gochberg, 1993). Despite much cultural change, lingering inequalities may still affect girls' beliefs about their future possibilities as they navigate adolescence.

Fourth, girls may be more stressed by the burgeoning of their sexuality and their sexual desirability. The traditional **double standard**, by which female sexual behavior is judged more harshly than male sexual behavior, has clearly diminished over the last half century, as the rates and acceptability of premarital sex have increased among teens of both sexes. Yet, in the United States there is still a tendency for girls who have engaged in sex between ages 11 and 16 to experience increased peer rejection over time, whereas the opposite is true for boys (Kraeger, Staff, Gauthier, Lekowtiz, & Feinberg, 2016). Girls and young women who have had multiple sexual partners are still considered to be more immoral than boys and young men who have (Crawford, 2003; Jones, 2016). Thus, even though girls' acceptance of and experience with sexuality is increasing rapidly, they are still more subject to ambiguous messages about the acceptability of sex and seem to be more uncertain about what is appropriate for them in a world of shifting values (Collins & Steinberg, 2006). In addition, the physical and social consequences of sexual activity are greater for girls. They are still the ones who get pregnant.

Fifth, after puberty, girls and boys start interacting more in mixed-sex groups and in heterosexual dyads. In these contexts, the differences in their discourse styles may create more stress for girls. You'll recall from Chapter 8 that girls tend to acquire a more cooperative discourse style and boys a more domineering style during childhood. One result is that when adolescent girls socialize with boys, they are less likely to influence the outcome of a discussion (Maccoby, 1990). Also, boys do not offer as much support to their conversation partners as girls do (Davies, 2003).

Sixth, early adolescent romantic involvement is also linked to depression, especially for girls. **Sexual debut** refers to age of first intercourse, and in the United States an *early* debut is usually defined as before age 15. For girls (but not boys) who experience an early debut, depression tends to increase over time, and self-esteem tends to decrease (Golden, Furman, & Collibee, 2016). In early adolescence, especially for girls, even typical romantic behaviors, such as flirting and kissing, are associated with increased depressive symptoms (Steinberg & Davila, 2008). Why this is so is not yet understood. Girls tend to report more feelings of guilt and shame than boys do (Golden et al., 2016), so issues such as a lingering double standard and low levels of support from male partners may certainly be important (Davila, 2008). (We discuss sexuality and sexual debut more fully later in this chapter.)

Seventh, because puberty comes earlier for girls, they are more likely than boys to simultaneously face both the changes of puberty and the difficult transition to secondary school (i.e., junior high or middle school; Petersen, Kennedy, & Sullivan, 1991; see Chapter 10 for a discussion of this transition).

Girls may be more subject to depression than boys not only because they face more challenges but also because they often adopt a coping style, **rumination**, that increases the risk of depression (Hilt, Armstrong, & Essex, 2017; Nolen-Hoeksema, 2012). *Rumination* may be defined as a stable, emotion-focused coping style that involves responding to problems by directing attention internally toward negative feelings and thoughts. Ruminating about problems includes both cognitive (self-focused cognitions) and affective (increased emotional reactivity) elements. Ruminative strategies may include isolating oneself to dwell on a problem, writing in a diary about how sad one feels, or talking repetitively about a negative experience with the purpose of gaining increased personal insight. In general, however, ruminative focusing on problems while in a depressed mood may actually make the depression worse.

This type of heightened focus on negative feelings and issues increases the duration and intensity of depressive episodes, particularly in adolescent and adult females, who are much more likely to exhibit this style of coping than are males (Butler & Nolen-Hoeksema, 1994; Hilt et al., 2017). Adolescents and adults who ruminate are more likely to experience depression.

There are other coping styles that seem to help minimize depression, or at least do not exacerbate it. These include, for example, **distraction**, which involves diverting attention away from a problem towards more positive thoughts or actions. Males appear to be more likely to use such approaches than females (Broderick & Korteland, 2004; Nolen-Hoeksema, 1987). However, gender role also influences how children and early adolescents cope with problems. A ruminative coping style is most pronounced among girls and some boys whose gender roles are stereotypically feminine. These individuals identify themselves as relatively passive and nondominant, and they are less likely to cope by using active problem solving or distraction. Having a ruminative coping style, or being uncomfortable with or incapable of psychological distraction, may be a particularly heavy burden for feminine-identified boys, for whom such behavior is clearly contrary to the peer group's expectations for appropriate masculine behavior (Broderick & Korteland, 2004).

The Emergence of Sexuality and Sexual Preference

Sexual pleasure is a part of human functioning even in early childhood. Preschoolers and school-aged children may fondle their own genitals for the pleasure of it, and many engage in sex play with others. "Playing doctor," for example, has been known to involve disrobing or fondling the genitals of other children. On average, children begin to show sexual attraction at **adrenarche**, when the adrenal glands increase their activity just before puberty, at about age 10 (Diamond, Bonner, & Dickenson, 2015). However, the strength and urgency of the adult sex drive, emerging as a function of puberty, is a new experience to young adolescents. They are more sensitive to, and interested in, sexually relevant stimuli than younger children. Despite having spent most of childhood spontaneously segregating into single-gender groups, young adolescents begin to seek out opportunities to socialize in mixed-gender groups (Maccoby, 1998; Rubin, Bukowski, & Bowker, 2015). Faced with their increased sexual interest, most adolescents begin to explore their sexuality.

The earliest and most common activity throughout adolescence is sexual fantasizing, and the next step tends to be masturbation. It is reported more by boys than by girls, but this seems to be more socially and culturally determined than driven by any differences in sexual desire (Diamond et al., 2015; Fortenberry, 2013). Girls with more education about how their bodies function are more likely to engage in masturbation (Bancroft, Herbenick, & Reynolds, 2003) as are girls living in countries with greater gender equality (Peterson & Muehlenhard, 2007). Although some religions and cultures frown on masturbation, and adolescents often report feeling guilty or ashamed about masturbating, it actually seems to be associated with some valuable health outcomes. It benefits the development of sexual self-awareness and as a result, more satisfying partner relationships. It also provides youth with an option for sexual release that doesn't carry the health risks of pregnancy and sexually transmitted diseases (STDs) (Diamond et al., 2015).

Partnered sex tends to begin with kissing and fondling (making out) and for some, moves on to oral-genital contact, which is more often received by boys than by girls (Chandra, Mosher, Copen, & Sionean, 2011). Participation in oral-genital sex is increasing in frequency, but little is really known yet about how typical it is for teens, or what effects such practices might have on them (Fortenberry, 2013). Some young people see it as a way of maintaining their virginity or as safer than intercourse. Unfortunately, when teens define activities other than intercourse as not really "counting" as sex, they seem to be less likely to use condoms or other protection. That may be why adolescents who take a virginity pledge have STD rates as high as those who do not take a pledge (Bruckner & Bearman, 2005). Another problem may be that if males are more often recipients of oral-genital stimulation than females, kids of both genders may begin to see girls more as givers than as receivers of sexual pleasure (Diamond et al., 2015).

The most often researched sexual activity is coitus, which is defined as penile-vaginal intercourse. Data on sexual debut usually refers to first coitus. This aspect of adolescent sexual behavior is important, of course, because of the implications it has both for social adjustment and for health. Around the world, sexual debut is most likely to occur between the ages of 12 and 24, and for most young people by age 20 (Diamond et al., 2015). In the United States, "debut is considered 'early' if it occurs prior to age 15, 'normative' if it occurs between 15 and 19 years of age, and 'late' if it occurs after 19 years of age" (Golden et al., 2016, p. 1). Table 9.3 indicates gender, ethnic, and grade differences among U.S. high school students reporting ever having had intercourse in a large, 2015 survey Similar annual surveys indicate that percentages have steadily declined for all gender and ethnic groups since 1991, perhaps in part because of increases in other types of sexual behavior (Kann, McManus et al., 2016).

Sexual maturation is a key determiner of sexual behavior, but many other factors come into play. Adolescents are often moved to engage in sexual behavior out of curiosity or because of their peer culture (Collins & Steinberg, 2006). Peers can affect teens' sexual behavior in many ways. One large meta-analysis of peer influence studies showed that adolescents are more likely to have sex if their peers are sexually active, if their peers approve of having sex, or if their peers pressure them to be sexually active (van de Bongardt, Reitz, Sandfort, & Dkovic, 2015).

MyLab Education
Video Example 9.2
Josh says there's no peer pressure to have a girlfriend, but he also says that some classmates brag or lie about having a sexual relationship. On this topic, consider the range of perspectives among adolescents.

Table 9.3 Percentage of U.S. High School Students by Gender, Race, and Grade Endorsing "Ever Had Intercourse"

	BOYS	GIRLS
Ethnicity/Race		
White	39.5	40.3
Black	58.8	37.4
Hispanic	45.1	39.8
Grade		
9	27.3	20.7
10	37.9	33.5
11	51.2	48.2
12	59.0	57.2

SOURCE: Kann, L., McManus, T., Harris, W. A., Shanklin, S. L., Flint, K. H., Hawkins, J. . . . Zaza, S. (2016). Youth risk behavior surveillance—United States, 2015. *MMWR Surveillance Summaries, 65*(SS06), 1–174.

Myriad other influences—from social class and ethnicity to religious background, geographic setting (urban versus rural), popular culture (as portrayed in movies, music, teen magazines, and Internet sites), the quality of sex education in schools, and personality factors—play a part in when and whether adolescents become sexually active (Baams, Overbeek, Dubas, & van Aken, 2014; Collins & Steinberg, 2006; Madkour et al, 2014). Clearly, sexuality is a normative part of adolescent development, but early sexual debut is associated with more negative outcomes. Pregnancies and STDs are more likely with early debut than with normative or late debuts, and so is depression, especially in girls. The causal relationship between early debut and depression seems to be bidirectional. That is, early debut predicts the onset of depression, and depression in young adolescents increases the likelihood of early debut (Davila, Capaldi, & La Greca, 2015).

Sexual Orientation

A central feature of sexual development in adolescence is the emergence of sexual orientation, referring to a preference for sexual partners of the opposite sex (heterosexuality), the same sex (homosexuality; "gay" males and "lesbian" females) or both (bisexuality). Researchers often refer to individuals who identify as either homosexual or bisexual as nonheterosexual. Most adolescents eventually identify themselves as heterosexual. For example, in a recent Youth Risk Behavior Surveillance (YRBS) survey of high school students across the United States, approximately 89% identified as heterosexual. Girls were more likely to identify as bisexual (9.8%) than lesbian (2%), which is a pattern that is also typical of large adult samples. Boys were about evenly divided between identifying as bisexual (2.4%) or as gay (2%), whereas by adulthood, males are more likely to be exclusively homosexual than bisexual. The survey also inquired about type of sexual contact in which youth engaged. Most students reported only heterosexual contact (median = 48%). A smaller proportion (1.7%) reported sexual activity only with same-sex partners, 4.6% reported bisexual contact, and 45.7% reported no sexual contact (Kann, Olsen et al., 2016).

Young adolescents are especially likely to have some sexual contact with members of the same sex, primarily displaying and touching genitals, and engaging in mutual masturbation. These activities seem to be partly a function of opportunity, because young adolescents still spend more of their time with same-sex than opposite-sex peers. For most youngsters, these sexual contacts are not indicators of a homosexual orientation (Diamond et al., 2015). For example, in one large longitudinal study, only 1 in 5 girls and fewer than 1 in 25 boys who reported same-sex contact during their teens actually identified as nonheterosexual by the time they were in their 20s (Savin-Williams & Ream, 2007). Adolescence is a time of exploration and sensation seeking when it comes to many kinds of behavior, including sexual behavior.

For some, more often for girls, adolescence and young adulthood is also a time of sexual fluidity, meaning change in sexual interest in same-sex versus opposite-sex partners. In one longitudinal study, females who identified initially as nonheterosexual were interviewed repeatedly from age 16 to 23. Many participants changed their reported sexual identity to "adjacent" categories, such as from bisexual to heterosexual, or from lesbian to bisexual (Diamond, 2008).

If heterosexuality is by far the most typical pattern for adolescents and adults, and one that clearly benefits the survival of the species, what causes homosexuality or bisexuality? Available theories that postulate social causes have no empirical support. The most famous of these is Freud's account (e.g., Freud, 1935/1960). As you will recall from Chapter 8, Freud proposed in his psychoanalytic theory that 3- to 5-year-olds compete with the same-sex parent for the attentions of the opposite-sex parent. To avoid the punitive consequences of such competition, Freud believed that boys eventually identify with their fathers and girls with their mothers, imitating the behaviors and internalizing the values of that parent. According to Freud, this identification process explains why most children eventually adopt a heterosexual orientation. It is just one more way in which the child becomes like the same-sex parent. Homosexuality or bisexuality results when something goes wrong with the identification process: The process cannot unfold in the usual way because there is only one parent in the home, the same-sex parent is too weak or shows little interest in the child, or the opposite-sex parent lacks sufficient warmth to be attractive or is too dominant.

Freud's theory of identification is not supported by the evidence. Adults who are homosexual or bisexual are not more likely than heterosexuals to come from one-parent homes or to have weak fathers or dominant mothers. Even modeling by parents does not seem to affect children's sexual preference. Children raised by homosexual partners (lesbian or gay couples) are no more likely to become homosexual themselves than children raised by heterosexuals (Miller, Kors, & Macfie, 2017; Patterson, 2017).

Other theories that pose social causes are also unsupported. One view, for example, is that homosexuality is "socially contagious," that is, when it is encouraged by removing legal or moral restrictions or by sexual recruiters (enticements by others), nonheterosexuality spreads. Although tolerance does increase the open expression of homosexuality, there is currently no scientific evidence that rates of heterosexuality and nonheterosexuality differ across cultures or religious groups (Bailey et al., 2016).

There is better evidence for nonsocial influences on sexual orientation. One well-supported finding is that nonheterosexual adults are likely to have been gender non-conformists in childhood, showing a strong and persistent tendency to behave like the other sex, such as in playmate or toy preferences (Karson, Kung, & Hines, 2017). Both retrospective interview studies and longitudinal studies following individuals from childhood to adulthood have demonstrated this behavioral thread, although there are, of course, many exceptions. Children often show signs of gender nonconformity by age 2, and it usually does not seem to be a function of parents or others pushing the child to act in gender atypical ways. This suggests that there are often differences among children that emerge early in development and are precursors of heterosexual and nonheterosexual attraction later.

Such findings suggest that biological causes are at work, causes that are likely to result from the coaction of genes and early (perhaps prenatal) environment. There is good evidence for genetic influence. If one identical twin is nonheterosexual, there is a significantly greater chance that the other twin will be nonheterosexual (a higher concordance rate) than we find between less closely related family members, including fraternal twins (Chaladze, 2016). The same is true for males and females, although the concordance rates appear to be lower for female twins (Burri, Spector, & Rahman, 2015). Sexual orientation researchers have identified some candidate genes, but there is still much to learn about which genes are important and how they might influence sexual orientation (e.g., Sanders et al., 2015). Prenatal hormones appear to play an organizing role. You will recall that male fetuses produce androgens in large quantities while female fetuses usually do not. Androgens, especially testosterone, masculinize the developing reproductive systems and brains of mammals. And exposure to androgens, especially testosterone, during prenatal development has been linked to the development of sexual orientation. There are several lines of evidence for the importance of prenatal androgens. We will give you just a couple of examples.

First, some girls are exposed prenatally to these masculinizing hormones, either by overproduction of them (such as in the case of congenital adrenal hyperplasia or CAH; see Chapter 8) or from some environmental source. These girls are later often found to have a greater frequency of homosexual experiences and fantasies than female relatives who have not experienced such exposure (Hines, 2011; Pasterski et al., 2015). Second, for males, delayed exposure to masculinizing hormones during prenatal development has been found to affect sexual behavior in many nonhuman mammalian species. It is reasonable to assume that the processes are the same in humans. For example, if a mother rat is stressed during pregnancy, the hormones she produces can delay the release of androgens in her male rat fetuses. When her male offspring reach adulthood, they show homosexual tendencies—higher frequencies of female sexual posturing and lower frequencies of male sexual behaviors, such as mounting—than males whose mothers were not prenatally stressed (see Chapter 8; Hernández-Arteaga et al., 2016; Ward, 1992).

Another prenatal influence on homosexuality in males is fraternal birth order (FBO). Epidemiological evidence shows that homosexual males tend to have disproportionately higher numbers of older brothers compared to heterosexual males (Blanchard, 2017). Each additional older brother increases the chances of a man being homosexual. The explanation for this robust finding suggests a possible role for immunology. It appears that the maternal body begins to develop antibodies to male-linked (Y-chromosome) proteins during pregnancy. This antibody response accumulates with each successive male pregnancy and has an effect on prenatal brain development, perhaps by blocking the function of those Y-chromosome proteins in the fetus. Certain differences in areas of the brain, like the hypothalamic nuclei, have been related to sexual differentiation (Swaab, 2008). Bogaert (2006) found that this FBO effect held up across cultures and socioeconomic groups.

You should note that all of the potential causes of nonheterosexuality that are currently supported by evidence involve nonsocial processes. Even the FBO effect is not a function of being reared with older brothers, because there is no such effect if the older brothers in the home do not share the same biological mother, and there is an FBO effect even when biological siblings are raised in different households (Diamond et al., 2015). And, it is worth repeating that no potential cause appears to operate alone (for example, not all later-born sons with brothers are homosexual). There is obviously much to learn about the processes that lead to same-sex attraction. Regardless of how biology and environment transact in the determination of sexual preference, most nonheterosexuals, like most heterosexuals, feel that their sexual orientation is not something they have chosen but that it is a part of what they are "naturally" (Bailey et al., 2016).

MyLab Education Self-Check 9.2.

Cognitive Development

9.3 **Describe changes in cognitive functioning in adolescence, characterized by Piaget as formal operational thought, and examine broad implications of these cognitive advances including the effects of egocentrism on adolescent life.**

When were you first introduced to the mysteries of algebra? When we asked a U.S. class of college sophomores that question, a few thought they might have been given a taste of algebra as early as fifth grade (at age 10 to 11). But the majority said it was either seventh or eighth grades (that is, between ages 12 and 14). The National Council on the Teaching of Mathematics (2000a, 2000b) recommends introducing the more concrete elements of algebra in grades 5 through 8, as a generalization of arithmetic with some precursors to that as early as grade 3. But the Council suggests that the more abstract concepts are better introduced in grades 9 through 12.

Why do curriculum planners wait so long to introduce most aspects of algebra? Simple equations solving for x can be solved using basic mathematical operations such as adding, subtracting, multiplying, and dividing. In a culture known for its desire to do things faster and better, often pushing children along as quickly as possible, why do we wait until fifth or sixth grade to teach them to solve even simple equations? The answer seems to be, "because it does not work if we begin earlier." We make no faster progress if we introduce algebra in second grade than if we wait until later. The juggernaut seems to be that even the simplest algebraic equation involves the use of a symbol for the unknown, the x. You may recall your first algebra teacher defining those letters that appear in equations as "symbols for unknown numbers," representing "any possible number." When we ask children to use those letters to substitute for unknown numbers, we are asking them to reason logically about an abstraction, something that cannot be represented in concrete terms. The x can be defined or exemplified only in words or by other symbols. There is no concrete example of "an unknown number."

In middle childhood, the period Jean Piaget referred to as the stage of concrete operational thought, children clearly can reason logically. They have the capacity to hold several pieces of information in mind at one time and to discover the relations among them. But, as we saw in Chapter 6, they seem to reason most effectively if the information they are working with can be represented readily in the concrete, real world, or at least if parallels can be found in the real world. In early adolescence, we begin to see this limitation of middle childhood recede. More and more, youngsters seem able to leave the ground of reality and to spin a logical tale with abstract contents such as probabilities, hypothetical possibilities, and statements that are contrary to one's belief or even to fact.

Formal Operational Thought

Suppose you have two canisters of hard candy (see Figure 9.3). Your favorite flavor is lemon, the yellow candies. You know the first canister has 1 green candy and 2 yellow ones. The second canister has 5 green and 5 yellow candies. To get a candy, you must shake one out of a canister, sight unseen. Which canister should you shake to be most certain of getting a yellow candy?

You are faced here with a probability problem. With the first canister, you would get a yellow candy 2 out of 3 times, or 67% of the time. With the second canister, you would get a yellow candy 5 out of 10 times, or 50% of the time. These odds make the first canister your best choice.

An 8-year-old would probably choose to take her chances with the second canister, arguing that it contains more yellow candies. But the absolute number of candies is not important in this case. Rather, the important features to compare are the relative proportions of yellow candies in each canister, which determine the probability of getting a yellow candy. The proportion of yellow candies is an abstraction, one that is difficult for an 8-year-old to reason about when faced with the concrete reality of a larger number of yellow candies in the second canister (see Piaget & Inhelder, 1951/1976).

Even as an adult, you may not have known which canister to choose. Perhaps you got confused about how to calculate the probabilities. Perhaps you were momentarily distracted by the concrete reality that is convincing to the 8-year-old—there are more yellow candies in the second canister. But now that you have run through this kind of problem and seen how it works, you are likely to see the importance of the more abstract concepts—the proportion of yellow candies in each canister—as opposed to the actual numbers of candies. Given another problem like this one, you have a good chance of figuring it out correctly. An 8-year-old, however, would not be likely to attack the next problem any differently, even with explanation and training. The 8-year-old's difficulty is not just inexperience with the probability concept; it is a failure to understand and reason effectively about an abstraction.

The problem of the yellow candy illustrates several characteristics of the **formal operational stage** of thinking that Piaget and his colleague, Barbel Inhelder, identified as beginning at about 11 or 12 years (e.g., Inhelder & Piaget, 1955/1958). First, formal thought rises above particular contents and focuses on relationships that govern those contents—that is, on abstractions. In the candy example, the proportion of yellow to green candies, not the number of yellow candies, in each canister is what you had to reason about. Second, formal reasoning involves coordinating multiple relationships. In the candy example, the successful problem solver must discover the relationship between the two proportions, which are themselves relationships. Third, formal thought can be difficult even for adults. We all find logical thinking to be easier when the information we must contend with is more concrete. As a result, even adolescents and adults who are capable of formal thought do not always use it effectively (Gray, 1990). It helps if we have experience and training in solving a particular kind of problem or if we have familiarity with the subject matter (the domain of knowledge), just as we saw with younger children in Chapter 6 (Lehrer & Schauble, 2015). Across a number of studies using a variety of tests of formal operational thinking, researchers report that about 30% of young adolescents (about 13 years old) show a tendency to apply formal reasoning in some situations, and about 60% of older adolescents or young adults (college students) do so (Gray, 1990; Kuhn, 2010; Ricco, 2015).

FIGURE 9.3 From which canister are you more likely to get a yellow candy?

Y = Yellow Candies
G = Green Candies

As we have seen before, changes in cognitive ability usually occur gradually, not in startling stagelike shifts. The development of formal reasoning is no different, so that we see glimmerings of formal thought in middle childhood. The kinds of problem-solving strategies that children use at ages 9 or 10 are likely to be more elaborate than at ages 6 or 7, and they may even involve operating on relatively abstract contents (Kuhn & Franklin, 2006; Ricco, 2015; Zimmerman, 2007). But formal thinking is more likely to emerge in adolescence.

Information Processing: Sharpening Executive Functions

In Chapter 6 you learned that neo-Piagetians and "theory" theorists assume that more elaborate reasoning skills are constructed over time with the help of advances in information processing abilities, specifically, executive functions. Improvements in executive functions that we see in middle childhood continue at a somewhat slower pace through adolescence. They are linked to maturation of the prefrontal cortex and the building of more elaborate cortical circuitry (Müller & Kerns, 2015). For example, extensive ongoing axon myelination after puberty helps increase processing speed, and with it, working memory continues to expand (Demetriou et al., 2014). Another change is improvement in inhibitory ability, which primarily affects attentional control. Throughout middle childhood and early adolescence, children continue to get better at ignoring irrelevant stimuli (e.g., what is perceptually salient) during problem solving and focusing instead on what is important. This includes suppressing already learned information and responses in order to allow for new understandings and the practice of new responses (although reward sensitivity can disrupt teens' inhibitory control, as you will see in Chapter 10).

All of these processing changes do seem to contribute to what Piaget called formal thinking: the ability to identify, organize, and draw inferences about complex abstract content. Changes in executive functions have been found to be closely linked to the development of reasoning skills through the teen years (Demitrou et al., 2014; Kail et al., 2016). However, while these processing changes may be necessary, they do not seem to be sufficient (Makris, Tachmalzides, Demetriou, & Spanoudis, 2017). Growth in knowledge, advancing metacognitive understanding of effective strategy use, and intentional efforts to acquire, compare and organize information are all important as well (Ricco, 2015).

Educators have long recognized that more can be expected of adolescents; because of this, as with algebra, more abstract subject matter is likely to be introduced to the curriculum after about age 12. In science classes, where younger students may be given laboratory assignments that consist of simple demonstrations, adolescents are often expected to generate and test hypotheses with thorough rigor (see the next section). In literature, teachers require students to begin to analyze works of fiction on multiple levels, going beyond the sequence of events that creates the story and looking for ironic, satiric, and metaphoric themes. These themes are abstractions, relationships among words on a different plane from the literal meaning. Some of us remember pining for the simpler, easier days when a story was just a story!

The capacity for formal thought can influence many aspects of adolescent life, from the approaches teens take to academic tasks to their views of religion and politics, their self-evaluation, and their relationships with parents and peers. In the following sections, we will look at some examples of these wide-ranging implications.

Scientific Problem Solving

Suppose a high school physics teacher posed the following problem to her class: A pendulum is a swinging object at the end of a length of string. The important characteristics of a pendulum are the weight of the object, the length of the string, the force of the push that starts the swing, and the height of the dropping point. Some pendulums swing faster than others. *Your job is to figure out whether the length of the string makes any difference in the rate at which the pendulum swings.*

MyLab Education
Video Example 9.3
Formal operational thought occurs gradually and involves the ability to reason abstractly and focus on relationships rather than concrete concepts. Many adolescents achieve formal thinking and are able to solve problems like the example in this video. Compare the thinking required to solve this problem (focused on abstract relationships) with problems involving concrete concepts.

To solve this problem effectively, a student would need to understand the "control of variables strategy" (CVS). She would need to change the hypothesized cause of rate of swing—the length of the string—without letting any other important variable change simultaneously. Then, if a pendulum's rate of swing changed (which it would), the only possible explanation for that change would be the change in length, and she could conclude that length of the string changes the rate of swing. CVS is the essence of experimental procedure. A potential cause is changed, whereas all other potential causes (or variables) are controlled (held constant). Some elementary-school-aged children figure out CVS on their own when given problems like this one; most do not. But those who don't discover it themselves can be successfully trained to see its value and to use it consistently (Bullock, Sodian, & Koerber, 2009; Ricco, 2015).

If we change the problem, as follows, it becomes much more difficult, and most children do not do well on it until adolescence, either spontaneously or with training: A pendulum is a swinging object at the end of a length of string. The important characteristics of a pendulum are the weight of the object, the length of the string, the force of the push that starts the swing, and the height of the dropping point. Some pendulums swing faster than others. *Your job is to figure out why some pendulums swing faster than others* (problem adapted from Inhelder & Piaget, 1955/1958).

Consider how some high school students respond. One student makes a good start. She approaches the problem like this: "I think it could be any of the four characteristics that is important. First, I will try changing the weight of the object; then I'll change the length of the string; then I'll vary the force of the push; then I'll try changing the dropping point." The student makes a change in the weight with no effect on rate of swing. Then she changes the length of the string. Voila! The rate of swing changes. She stops her assessments and announces that she has found the solution: length of the string.

Another student approaches the task by changing more than one characteristic at a time. When she changes weight and length together, the rate of swing changes. She concludes that the rate of swing is a result of the combined effects of weight and length.

A third student tests each of the four characteristics and, of course, finds that changing the length affects rate of swing. But she continues her assessment, combining changes in pairs of characteristics: weight plus length, weight plus force of push, weight plus height of dropping point, and so on. Even though each pairing that includes a change of length affects the rate of swing, she continues her tests. She moves on to combine changes in weight plus length plus force of push, then weight plus length plus height of dropping point, and so on until she has tested every combination of three changes, and finally tests a combination of changes in all four characteristics at once. Only combinations in which length of string is changed affect rate of swing—no other combinations make a difference. Finally, she reports her conclusion: Length of string alone is the determining factor.

Only the third student has solved the problem using combinatorial logic, a type of formal operational thought. She has generated every possible hypothesis. Then, she has tested each hypothesis by holding constant all the factors that are not posited to contribute to the rate of swing by that hypothesis, so that by systematic examination of the results of all the tests she can eliminate all but the hypotheses that must be correct.

The first and second students provide two examples of concrete operational thinking. There is a degree of systematicity to their generation of hypotheses, but not a complete generation of all possibilities. Their conclusions are also too closely tied to concrete outcomes. When the "length of string hypothesis" works for the first student, she stops her testing, even though it remains possible that other characteristics could be involved or that some combination of characteristics could negate the effects of changing the string length. When the combination of weight and length works for the second student, she ends her investigation, drawing the false conclusion that the combination is important.

Adolescents who approach scientific problems by considering every possibility and then carefully testing each one are using formal operational reasoning. The pattern of results among all the tests is what drives the conclusions, not any particular concrete observation.

In effective scientific problem solving, we see another characteristic of people who use formal operational thought. They can generate and think about possibilities. What is real is just one of a full set of possibilities. These possibilities can be generated only in the realm of thought—they are abstractions, not dependent on observations. This is a metacognitive understanding, and it is essential for scientific problem solving. Specifically, if we understand that when we generate theoretical explanations for phenomena, those theories are just possibilities, we can understand that their value is not only in how plausible they seem, but importantly, in what kind of evidence supports them, or could support them. As we noted in Chapter 6, even adults often fail to treat their own theories as just one in a set of possibilities. Even for individuals capable of formal thought, scientific reasoning often runs aground on the shoals of belief, so that evidence is distorted or ignored instead of carefully analyzed for overriding patterns. In other words, our motives and emotional commitments can sidetrack our logical reasoning (Kuhn, 2010). It appears that those of us who overcome these common difficulties have learned to logically analyze our own thought processes (Bensley & Lilienfeld, 2017). When we have favorite theories (e.g., strong beliefs about the value of capital punishment or ideas about the best approach to bilingual education), we must take our own thinking about those theories as the subject of our formal reasoning, and we must monitor our own thought processes as we evaluate evidence, to ensure that we are maintaining logical consistency. As you will see, skill at such self-monitoring clearly advances in adolescence. However, the stronger our emotional commitment to an idea is, the harder it is to engage in such self-evaluation effectively and the less likely we are to do it (Kuhn & Franklin, 2006). Helpers often struggle to help clients see problematic situations in logical, objective ways to facilitate good decision making.

Researchers are looking into ways of helping children and adolescents develop their formal reasoning, and by extension, their scientific problem solving skills. One strategy was incorporated into a set of educational standards called Next Generation Science Standards (NGSS), established by an independent reform organization composed of business and political leaders in the United States (Lehrer & Schauble, 2015; NGSS Lead States, 2013). This strategy incorporates training in reasoning, in domain knowledge (e.g., chemistry facts, behavioral facts, etc.), and in practical methods of science at all grade levels, assuming that all three interact to advance children's understanding of how to investigate problems. With regard to reasoning, the NGSS recommends that even in primary grades, children should be engaged in argument from evidence, so that the process of learning to distinguish opinions from evidence, assess the relevance of evidence to a problem, and so on, can become more familiar than traditional curricula have made possible. The motivation for such recommendations is clear: As we have just seen, even adults often have difficulty sorting out theory and evidence. The hope is that scaffolding scientific thinking by exposure to, and practice with, argument structure can help scientific thinking develop more effectively by adolescence. Some recent research does support this idea, at least with early adolescents (e.g., Papathomas & Kuhn, 2017).

Constructing Ideals

Adolescents who are capable of generating possibilities, without regard for present reality, have acquired a powerful new cognitive tool that can be used to construct ideals: logically organized possible systems. As Cowan (1978) puts it, such individuals are "adept at generating ideas about the world as it could be" (p. 291). They might mentally construct an ideal political system, or religion, or school. They might also construct an ideal self, teacher, parent, or friend. Any of these ideal systems can make the real, imperfect forms seem shabby and inadequate by comparison. For some adolescents, this new capacity for constructing ideals leads to a zeal for reform. It may also contribute to a skeptical attitude toward childhood religious beliefs or toward parental politics and values (Cowan, 1978; Piaget, 1964/1968). A family belief system can become for the adolescent just one of many possibilities. Thus, the capacity to entertain possibilities and to construct ideals appears to contribute to a critical attitude, and to a skepticism about the justifications that others often give for the status quo. Rebecca's critical attitude in conversation with her family may be linked to her ability to construct ideals and her impatience with anything real that does not measure up.

The "cure" for a critical attitude is experience (Cowan, 1978; Piaget, 1964/1968). Ideals, by definition, are not real. They are perfect possibilities. But real systems and people are never perfect. Adolescent idealists are not familiar yet with the enormous complexity of putting ideas into action and with the actual limitations of the concrete world. Until they gain more experience with the difficulties, they are likely to be critical, even unforgiving. In essence, the adolescent's failure to understand the real limits of her ideas is a form of egocentrism. Interestingly, this seems to apply to her judgments not only of others but also of herself. The increase in depression in adolescence may in part be affected by a tendency to be discouraged by one's own imperfections: The real self never quite measures up to the ideal (Harter, 2006). An interesting feature of this new, self-critical attitude is that it is self-generated. Even when an adolescent's appearance or behavior does compare favorably to the standards that others hold, she may judge herself to be inadequate, based on her idealized version of the self. Such misplaced self-criticism can be very frustrating to adults who deal with adolescents, and it can play a role in some serious disorders, such as anorexia (Harter, 2006; Thew, Gregory, Roberts, & Rimes, 2017).

Advances in Metacognitive Skill: Thinking About Thought

In middle childhood, children gain some metacognitive skill, that is, some understanding of their own cognitive processes. They get better and better, for example, at assessing when they have studied a list of words enough to remember them on a test. But planful, organized thinking about one's own thought processes involves logical thinking about an abstraction—thought. The capacity for formal operational thinking seems to give this process a strong boost. Adolescents are much more likely than children to "be introspective in an analytic mode, to think critically about themselves and about the way that they think and behave" (Cowan, 1978, p. 289).

On the positive side, improved metacognitive skill benefits scientific thinking as we have just seen. Such skill also contributes to more careful planning and evaluation of one's activities. For example, once Rebecca sits down to study for her exam, she may test herself to determine what she has learned so far, evaluate the study strategies she has been using for their effectiveness, and allocate her study time planfully, spending the most time on the information she knows least well (Glogger, Schwonke, Holzäpfel, Nückles, & Renkle, 2012).

On the more negative side, the self-evaluation and self-monitoring that come with improved metacognitive skill may also contribute to other forms of egocentrism that seem to emerge at adolescence. Elkind (1968), elaborating on some of Piaget's (1964/1968) ideas about adolescents, describes the young teen as intensely self-focused. In a sense, her new capacity for introspection, for evaluating her own mental processes, contributes to an inward focus that is distorting. Although she understands that others have minds of their own and that they have their own concerns, her own fascination with herself, enhanced by the compelling and unpredictable physical changes she is undergoing, leads her to mistakenly assume that others are as intrigued by and concerned about her as she is. Elkind calls this assumption the adolescent's **imaginary audience**. Because she is so sure that others are as interested in her as she is, she feels extremely self-conscious, acutely aware of her looks and her behavior in the presence of others (Ranzini & Hoek, 2017). Another feature of the adolescent's self-focus is a distorted view of her own importance. Elkind calls this assumption the **personal fable**. Perhaps partly because they see themselves as a focus of others' scrutiny and interest, adolescents often seem to feel that they are special—that their experiences and concerns are unique. The personal fable may also include fantasies of having a special destiny, an important role to play in the lives of others or on the world stage. A feeling of being invulnerable, even immortal, called the **invincibility fable**, can be a part of this fantasy, perhaps contributing to increases in risk taking at adolescence. Adolescents may reason, for example, that others who drive drunk may get hurt in auto accidents or that others who engage in cyberbullying will get caught, but they don't believe that they themselves would suffer these consequences (Cingel, Krcmar, & Olsen, 2015; Lin, 2016).

The notions of imaginary audience and personal fable are useful, but researchers have raised a number of questions about where they originate and when they recede. Elkind (1968) characterized these egocentric developments as a product of formal operational skill, and he suggested that they diminish in later adolescence as a function of interpersonal experience. Sharing ideas and feelings with others, especially peers, helps an adolescent do a better job of perspective taking and helps her to recognize that others are focused on themselves and that her experiences are not unique.

Studies indicate that adolescents' self-focused thought is not as closely associated with the emergence of formal operational skills as Elkind suggested (Lapsley, FitzGerald, Rice, & Jackson, 1989). Lapsley (1993) argues that the social realities of adolescence—the need to separate from parents, to form an adult identity—are at least as important in explaining the egocentrism of the adolescent. He contends that the imaginary audience may be an expression of intense anxiety associated with individuation and that the personal fable may be a useful fantasy for reducing some of that anxiety.

Of course, adolescents may be more anxious than other age groups for many reasons as we have seen, and anxiety tends to increase egocentrism. In one series of experiments, researchers induced anxiety in some participants and other strong, negative emotions (e.g., disgust, anger) in others. Those who experienced anxiety (but not the other emotions) showed increases in multiple measures of egocentrism (Todd, Forstmann, Burmer, Brooks, & Galinsky, 2015).

Whatever the cause or causes of adolescent egocentrism, recent research suggests that it is not a phenomenon that belongs exclusively to teens. Several studies have found that elements of the imaginary audience (extreme self-consciousness) and of the personal fable (a sense of invulnerability) continue into adulthood, sometimes not showing much decline even then (Ranzini & Hoek, 2017). There is little disagreement that these egocentric tendencies begin in adolescence. It may be, however, that some of us are stuck with them far beyond our teen years.

The newer work on adolescent egocentrism reminds us that even if cognitive change contributes to these processes, the adolescent's cognitive abilities do not operate in a vacuum. They are among the many causal elements in a multidimensional mix. Adolescence brings a remarkable confluence of change into a child's life: change in thinking skills, biochemical and brain functioning, physical shape and size, peer and parental expectations, and educational structures and requirements. In addition, adult responsibility lurks just around the corner. In the next section, we return to the issue of how the child's self-concept evolves, in the midst of all this change, into an adult identity.

MyLab Education Self-Check 9.3.

Identity Development

9.4 Assess levels of exploration and commitment in adolescent identity formation and support healthy and developmentally appropriate identity construction.

Some Basic Considerations

The sweeping and transformative changes that adolescence brings to body, brain, sexual, and cognitive functioning are all readying children to take their places in the world of adults, when they must take responsibility for themselves and become contributing members of society. In preparation, "'life,' through its many agents (e.g., family, peers, teachers), asks adolescents many new questions (e.g., What do you want from life? How do you see your future?)" (Negru-Subtrica, Pop, Luyckx, Dezutter, & Steger, 2016, p. 1926). That's what forming an identity is about: figuring out, as Erik Erikson put it, "What do I want to make of myself and what do I have to work with?" (1968, p. 314).

The concept of identity, or **ego identity**, was first elaborated in Erikson's theory of personality development (e.g., Erikson, 1968). His theory is not so much about traits, like the temperament characteristics we discussed in earlier chapters (e.g., activity level, inhibition or shyness, etc.). We will return to discussing such traits in later chapters. Rather, Erikson focuses on what has been called the "doing" side of personality (Luyckx, Teppers, Klimstra, & Rassart, 2014; see Chapter 1). From infancy onward, children face new tasks in each "stage" of development that help them to see themselves in new ways that motivate their behavior. With adequate social support, infants acquire basic feelings of trust and self-worth (I am valued and valuable), toddlers begin to feel autonomous (I can do things myself), preschoolers feel safe taking social initiative (I can assert my needs with others), and older children achieve a sense of industry (I can work effectively).

Adolescent identity formation incorporates and expands on all of these feelings about self, as well as other forms of self-knowledge that develop through childhood, such as social, academic, and physical self-concept (see Chapter 7). The process also draws on the beliefs and expectations that have been handed down to the child by her family and the larger culture. In identity formation, a teen or young adult identifies the passions, strengths, and values that fit together to provide her with a framework for her future life course. In other words, identity formation is the construction of a guide to relationships, career, and political and religious choices in adulthood.

Erikson labeled the process of identity formation a "crisis" of "identity versus identity confusion." But his view of the process is more accurately characterized as a specific challenge or task that asserts itself in adolescence. If adequately resolved, then the individual sees a path forward. If she fails to resolve the task, she remains in a state of confusion about herself and her future. But Erikson cautioned against thinking of life stages in terms of either-or propositions. In the case of identity, individuals make choices and have experiences that take them closer to or further away from a meaningful sense of self until one kind of resolution (e.g., identity achievement) predominates over the other (e.g., identity confusion, also called "diffusion").

Erikson argued that the formation of an identity in adolescence is not the end of the story. Anyone who has counseled both youngsters and adults will recognize that growth and change of self-representations and commitments can take place throughout the life span. What makes this particular period of the life cycle remarkable are the impressive strides young people make during adolescence and young adulthood in developing the essential core of how they will be as adults. All of our life stories are subject to revision by time, place, and circumstance. However, a core sense of self that "fits" becomes clearer as the years unfold. Erikson captures the tension between continuity and change by writing that "ego identity could be said to be characterized by the actually attained but *forever to-be-revised* sense of the reality of the Self within social reality" (1968, p. 211).

Erikson also emphasized the power of social contexts to shape development. He saw cultural milieu as formative to personality development, and so his view is consistent with the contemporary notion that those values held in highest regard within a person's cultural context strongly affect the nature of her self-representations, worldviews, and commitments.

We take a closer look at how some cultural contexts relate to identity formation in the Applications section of this chapter.

Identity Status

James Marcia (1993; Kroger & Marcia, 2011) noted that embedded in Erikson's notion of identity formation are two processes: **exploration** and **commitment**. *Exploration* is "actively questioning and weighing various identity alternatives before deciding which values, beliefs, and goals to pursue" and *commitment* is "making identity choices and engaging in activities to implement them" (Crocetti, 2017, p. 145). Therefore, there are actually four identity statuses that could characterize a person, depending on whether exploration and commitment have or have not occurred.

The first two statuses are Erikson's poles: In **identity achievement**, a period of exploration has occurred and is followed by commitment; and in **identity diffusion**, neither exploration nor commitment has occurred. Another status is **foreclosure**, in which a teen makes a commitment without any exploration, perhaps simply adopting a choice that is dictated by family or culture. And the last status is **moratorium**, when no commitment has been made but the teen is actively engaged in exploration.

Figure 9.4 illustrates the relationships among the two processes (or dimensions) and the four statuses. Think of Rebecca from the beginning of this chapter. At this time, Rebecca is passionately Catholic. With regard to religious belief, she is in *foreclosure*, because she is committed to Catholicism but she has done no exploring. Her family is Catholic, and she wholeheartedly accepts the religion of her childhood. She has two friends from Catholic families, however, who are in *moratorium* with regard to religion. They spend hours together arguing about whether God exists, and each of them has taken special interest in attending services at other churches, at a synagogue and a mosque. One of them is also reading up on Buddhism. When they make a choice— either for a religion or against any religion—they will be in identity achievement. Finally, another friend, when asked about her religious views, shows no interest. She says she hasn't thought about it, and it's not important to her. She appears to be in identity confusion, adrift on a sea of uncertainty, neither exploring nor committed.

At any one time, the same adolescent may be characterized by different statuses with regard to religion, political beliefs, career direction, and so on. Rebecca, for example, is definitely in *moratorium* when it comes to politics. Her parents take liberal views on most issues. But Rebecca challenges them whenever those issues come up, asking lots of questions and often playing "devil's advocate" by arguing the opposite position. She reads newspaper editorials and debates the issues with her friends as well, trying out different positions at different times.

The construction of identity in adolescence and beyond builds on or incorporates many of the components of self-concept developed earlier, such as social, academic, and physical self-concept. Identity may be construed as an overarching construct, with each domain representing a more specific aspect. Just as individuals vary in their level of self-esteem across domains, individuals will also show variation in the nature of their identity formation and in the timing of developmental progress. Thus, Rebecca can be foreclosed in the area of religious identity but in moratorium in her political views.

Erikson (1950/1963) considered moratorium the essence of the adolescent mind and in so doing, he helped make sense of the transitory, inconsistent, and often incomprehensible nature of many adolescent behaviors. It is an uncomfortable state to be in, but the prize to be gained from this trial and error process is an identity that has been

FIGURE 9.4 processes and statuses.

personally constructed. This **constructed identity** is not based upon a predetermined set of expectations, but represents either a personal redefinition of childhood and early adolescent goals and values or perhaps something very different from them. (That is, it would not be unusual if Rebecca eventually adopted political views very similar to those she was raised with, but she might not.) In moratorium, the future may be perceived as difficult, exciting, or even anxiety producing, but the process allows the future to be shaped by one's own decision making.

Both moratorium and identity diffusion are statuses characterized by confusion and uncertainty, but a teen in diffusion is not engaged in any motivated effort to clear up the confusion. Although this state of affairs is fairly common in early adolescence, Erikson argued that diffusion can be highly problematic later on in young adulthood. Persons whose identity is diffused may not trust their ability to find and commit to a meaningful path in life, or they might deny their need to do so. They may lack a sense of optimism about the future and, "many a sick or desperate late adolescent, if faced with continuing conflict, would rather be nobody or somebody totally bad, or, indeed, dead" (Erikson, 1968, p. 176). Alternatively, they may situate themselves within a highly controlling environment that dictates the conditions of their behavior and the nature of their views, such as joining a gang.

Culture may limit identity status. Western cultures tend to make possible many different options for most identity domains, so that periods of moratorium are common among Western youth. In very traditional cultures, there may be few or no options with regard to future directions or belief systems, and therefore youth may more typically be foreclosed. Similarly, members of ethnic or racial subcultures within Western societies sometimes see their options as much more restricted than mainstream youth.

Dividing identity statuses into just four types is clearly somewhat arbitrary when an individual could be functioning anywhere on the two dimensions of exploration and commitment. Not surprisingly then, some researchers have added other statuses to the four originally outlined by Marcia. For example, Crocetti (2017) suggests that there are two kinds of exploration: exploration for breadth (searching out and trying different alternatives, like Rebecca is doing with her political views), and "in-depth exploration." Teens who have made a commitment usually continue with in-depth exploration, which includes reflecting on the meaning of their commitment and figuring out how their talents and potentials fit. In-depth exploration can help to solidify the young person's commitment and identification with a goal. But it occasionally can lead to uncertainty and reconsideration of the commitment. Crocetti refers to this state of affairs as a "searching moratorium" status, different from moratorium, when no commitment is present. For simplicity's sake, we will continue to refer to the four identity statuses described by Marcia.

Another process that is important for some youth is referred to as "ruminative exploration," sometimes called "the dark side" of identity development (Beyers & Luyckx, 2016). We will look at this process in more detail in the Applications section of this chapter.

Assessing Identity Formation

In order for us to study identity development, it must be translated into something that can be measured. One early measure, designed by Marcia (1964), was a semi-structured **Ego Identity Interview** that assessed three domains of identity: vocational choice, religious beliefs, and political ideology. Marcia selected these domains because Erikson viewed occupation and ideology, both political and religious, as expressions of one's identity. Various forms of this measure have been developed since, with different forms including a variety of other domains, such as work/family priorities, gender-role attitudes, parenthood, and beliefs about sexual expression. The interview format consists of general questions such as "Should one believe in God or not?" "What type of work would you like to do?" and "What do you see as the advantages and disadvantages of being single versus being married?" followed up by more specific probes. (See Marcia et al., 1993, for other items from the interview.) Participants can be categorized for identity status in each of the individual domains assessed, and they can be assigned a "global identity status" based on all of the interview information (e.g., Carlsson, Wängqvist, & Frisén, 2016).

Some researchers use questionnaires to measure an individual's current degree of both exploration and commitment in multiple domains. Participants are asked to rate how true statements are of themselves, such as "Today I felt that I could better look for a different best friend," as an indicator of *exploration* in the interpersonal domain, or "Today, I felt confident about myself because of my best friend," as an indicator of *commitment* in the interpersonal domain (e.g., Becht et al., 2017).

Another approach to evaluating identity formation is to ask individuals to tell stories about themselves and their lives, using open-ended questions that serve as prompts (Adler et al., 2017). Prompts can be quite diverse, but they often involve questions about high points, low points, or turning points in a person's life that might have affected how they think about their future careers or about relationships, and so on. Researchers then code the resulting narratives for different aspects of content, such as feelings of agency (sense of being in control of one's life), or communion (importance of harmony with others). This narrative identity approach is designed to determine the content of domains of identity and, if used in a longitudinal study, evaluate how that content changes over time. This contrasts with the interview and questionnaire approaches described above, which are designed to measure whether identity status is changing and to identify the sequence of changes.

PERSONAL AND BEHAVIORAL CHARACTERISTICS AND IDENTITY FORMATION

Not surprisingly, an adolescent's personality and cognitive characteristics affect and are affected by her identity formation, especially how likely she is to engage in exploration or to stick with a commitment (e.g., Luyckx, Teppers, Klimstra, & Rassart, 2014). Much of the early research on identity focused on the behavioral and cognitive correlates of each global identity status. For example, researchers found that those who have reached an achieved identity status are more likely to see themselves as having control over events ("internal locus of control"), whereas diffused individuals are more likely to feel they have little internal control and that external processes govern their lives (Dellas & Jernigan, 1987). Youth who have made commitments, especially those who are largely in a foreclosed status, tend to be less anxious than those in a state of diffusion, and those in moratorium are the most anxious (Marcia, 1967; Sterling & Van Horn, 1989). More egocentric adolescents seem to engage in more exploration and to have a greater likelihood of reaching identity achievement, especially males (O'Connor, 1995).

More recent work links identity status or degree of exploration and commitment to other personal and behavioral characteristics, such as religiosity, risk taking, prosocial behavior, delinquency, openness, and conscientiousness. Foreclosure is more strongly associated with religiosity (defined as strength of religious faith) than the other identity statuses. Individuals in identity diffusion report more risk taking and less prosocial behavior than individuals in other identity status groups. Youth whose commitments decline over time are more likely than others to engage in delinquent acts, while those whose commitments increase tend to engage in fewer delinquent acts (Mercer, Crocetti, Branje, van Lier, & Meeus, 2017; Padilla-Walker, Barry, Carroll, Madsen, & Nelson, 2008). Some associations between personal characteristics and identity formation are specific to particular domains. For example, early conscientiousness tends to predict commitment to educational goals (Klimstra, Luyckx, Germeijs, Meeus, & Goossens, 2012).

Overall, adolescents and young adults who have acquired a stable and coherent sense of self and of their future path (global identity achievement) tend to see their lives as more meaningful than those who have not (Negru-Subtirica et al., 2016). Making commitments is also associated with many aspects of positive well-being and adjustment, from low levels of internalizing and externalizing problems to high academic achievement (Crocetti, 2017). Not all individuals who remain in identity diffusion over time (that is, fail to engage in exploration or to make commitments) by adulthood are troubled individuals. But many do suffer psychological distress and are typically less autonomous and more influenced by external pressures than other young people (Carlsson et al., 2016). In the Applications section of this chapter, we will examine more closely the relationship between identity formation and mental health.

Developmental Sequence in Identity Formation

Theorists since Erikson have hypothesized that there is a normative course to identity formation, with foreclosure, or sometimes diffusion, more typical of younger adolescents, and periods of moratorium and identity achievement becoming more common in older adolescents and young adults (Erikson, 1968; Marcia, 1967; Stephen, Fraser, & Marcia, 1992; Waterman, 1993a). These theorists argue that a shift from diffusion to either foreclosure or moratorium is progressive. Other progressive shifts are from foreclosure to moratorium and from moratorium to achievement. They assume that any commitments made early in adolescence, either with or without a previous period of moratorium, are more likely to change later than those commitments made in later adolescence or early adulthood. Because moratorium is really a transitional status, in which a person is actively engaged in the search for an identity but feeling unsettled and anxious, this status is expected to be the most "unstable," that is, the most likely to change.

What do studies of identity formation actually find? In 2010, Marcia and his colleagues (Kroger, Martinussen, & Marcia, 2010) did a meta-analysis of 124 studies from 1966 to 2005. Longitudinal studies following the same participants over some period of time (ranging from 9 months to 9 years) with measures of global identity status found that about one third of the participants made progressive changes during the time of the study. About 15% made regressive changes, and about half showed no change. Unfortunately, there were not many longitudinal studies available, and they covered such a variety of age ranges that it is hard to conclude more than that progressive changes in identity status are more likely than regressive changes.

Many more cross-sectional studies were available, with different participants tested at each age level. In these studies, younger adolescents showed more diffusion and foreclosure than older groups. The proportion of individuals in moratorium increased across the teen years, and a greater proportion of late teens and young adults showed identity achievement than younger teens. So generally, the notion of progressive change in identity formation was supported, but the authors note that there appears to be a great deal of fluctuation even in diffusion and foreclosure over the whole period, from the early teens through the mid-twenties (Kroger et al., 2010).

Newer longitudinal studies are confirming that change tends to be progressive, but there is a great deal of variability (e.g., Becht et al., 2017; Meeus, 2011). One finding in studies that include repeated measurements over short periods (even day to day) is that teens commonly engage in repeated cycles of exploration (especially in-depth exploration), often tweaking or reconsidering commitments in various domains (Mercer, Crocetti, Branje, van Lier, & Meeus, 2017). Another finding is that, as Erikson suggested, meeting new people, having new experiences, and undergoing major life changes (such as entering college) are likely to trigger cycles of re-evaluation (Magolda & Taylor, 2015).

Identity Development and Diverse Groups

Do individuals differ in their identity development processes because they are members of certain groups? There is intense clinical and research interest in the specific identity development patterns of groups differing in gender, race, ethnicity, and sexual orientation. This body of work has developed as an offshoot of more classic identity research for a number of reasons. As you have seen, scientists and practitioners are becoming more acutely aware that past research often has been male-centric and/or ethnocentric. Most developmental scientists are now convinced that it is critical to sort out which processes and trends are generalizable across groups, and which are not. More specifically, how does group membership moderate development and impact intervention efforts?

Demographic trends that project a growing multicultural citizenry and social movements that emphasize gay, lesbian, and women's rights, as well as pride in one's ethnic heritage, have sparked increased attention to these issues. Critical of traditional, monocultural approaches, counselors and other helpers have also called for recognition and integration of diverse perspectives into practitioner training and therapeutic practice because of the relevance of gender, race, and sexual orientation to personal well-being and to client–counselor interaction (Hook, Davis, Owen, & DeBlaere, 2017; Sue, Arrendondo, & McDavis, 1992).

One of the first ways in which the message of diversity was promulgated was through an array of identity development theories based on group differences. Developmental schemes were proposed for identity formation of Blacks (Cross, 1971), Hispanics (Bernal & Knight, 1993), Asian Americans (Sue, Mack, & Sue, 1998), Whites (Helms, 1990), women (Parks, Carter, & Gushue, 1996), and lesbians and gays (Cass, 1979). An example of the proliferation of early theories can be observed in Eliason's (1996) summary review. She described 11 different theories of "coming out" or identity development for lesbian, bisexual, and gay individuals published in the social science literature. Similarly, Helms (1990) described 11 models of Black identity development.

Clearly, scholarly work in this area was long overdue. The effects of race, culture, class, and gender on development are highly significant. To their credit, these early identity theories broadened our perspective and continue to encourage a more inclusive look at developmental processes. In this section, we will try to examine some of the general issues that pertain to the literature on gendered and racial or ethnic identity development, search for some commonalities, and look at some newer empirical work.

GENDER AND IDENTITY

Is the identity formation process different for males and females? Depending on what facet of the process we look at, the answer to this question changes. If we examine the general progress of identity formation, such as movement from more diffused or foreclosed statuses to more moratorium and achieved statuses, the patterns are the same in most studies that include gender comparisons. However, some have found that girls and young women engage in more in-depth exploration and more ruminative exploration than boys and young men do (Luyckx et al., 2014). Other studies indicate that the whole process of adolescent identity formation might begin sooner and be further along at earlier ages for females than for males (Schwartz & Montgomery, 2002), but not all studies find such differences. If there is a difference in time course, it may be at least in part a function of the earlier onset of puberty that is typical for girls (Norona, Preddy, & Welsh, 2015).

Given some of the behavioral differences we find between girls and boys, one possibility is that there are also differences in the content of gender identity. Some theorists have speculated that some domains are differentially important to males and females. These domains should then be more central to identity and get more attention in the identity formation process for members of one gender than for the other.

There is a long research history of looking for such differences, and the results are equivocal at best. For example, let's consider the domain of religion. In late adolescence and young adulthood, religious involvement tends to decline (e.g., attending services) for both males and females. There *are* some gender differences in religious behavior. For instance, young women are more likely to pray, or meditate, or turn to religion for comfort, which could be an indicator that religious identity is more important to young women than to young men. But the importance of religion more generally (for example, in terms of service attendance) does not seem to differ for males and females (Norona et al., 2015; Stoppa & Lefkowitz, 2010).

The possibility of gender differences in identity formation seems most likely in the interpersonal domain. Some theorists propose that for girls and young women, intimacy, social relationships, and communal experiences are more central than they are for boys or men (Eagly, 2013; Gilligan, 1982; Sneed et al., 2006). One argument is that "boys and young men are socialized to maintain a degree of separation from others, whereas girls and young women are socialized to maintain connection with others" (Norona et al., 2015, p. 66), so that when they are constructing their identities, the need to maintain a sense of self as separate and/or as connected is quite different for each.

Research across several decades provides some support for the greater importance of interpersonal domains for girl's and women's identity development and for the fact that relational issues may be more central for women's development than for men's (Block, Gonzalez, Schmader, & Bacon, 2018; Furman & Rose, 2015).

For example, Meeus and Dekovic (1995) did a cross-sectional study of 3,000 Dutch adolescents. They found that in the interpersonal domain, girls were much more involved than boys in exploration, and they showed more signs of commitment, such as experiencing more personal satisfaction from relationships. Other studies indicate that adolescent girls generally have closer friendships than boys do (in the sense that they share more, talk over problems more, have higher expectations of being cared for and understood, and so on), and they are more vulnerable to distress when friendships end (Furman & Rose, 2015). Both adolescent and adult females express more relationship-themed fears about their futures than do males (Anthis, Dunkel, & Anderson, 2004).

Such findings do not imply that other domains, such as vocation, are unimportant or even less important for girls and women. Nor should they suggest that relational issues are unimportant for boys and men. For example, with their closest friends, males report similar levels of intimacy as females, such as self-disclosing personal information (Radmacher & Azmitia, 2006). When we look at the content of male and female narratives, we find that beginning in childhood, girls include more themes of relationships in their stories than boys do, but in late adolescence, such differences in autobiographical stories tend to subside. In fact, both young women and young men tell stories that emphasize the importance of relationships and emotional connections, and for men, themes of masculinity and autonomy decline (Fivush & Haden, 2003; Norona et al., 2015). It might be useful to interpret the overall findings this way: When studies do identify differences in aspects of self-definition that are more important to one gender than to another, girls and women are more likely to assign interpersonal, communal aspects of themselves a higher priority than boys or men are. However, whether or not they do, the interpersonal domain is central to both males and females.

A major question in identity formation is the degree to which the domain of gender is seen by young people as centrally important to who they are and therefore the degree to which it engages their exploration and commitment processes. We addressed some of the key issues related to this question in Chapter 8. We will not repeat them here, except to remind you that gender is a salient social category from the earliest years. For example, Rogers and Meltzoff (2017) asked 7- to 12-year-olds in low-income, racially diverse U.S. schools to select identity labels that were true of them from the following set: boy, girl, son, daughter, student, Asian, Black, Hispanic, White, athlete. Children were then asked to rank the labels they had selected in order of importance. Labels representing gender were ranked third overall, after family and student labels, but gender was ranked more important than race or ethnicity. It appears then, that of the social categories that "define" children as they enter adolescence, gender is quite salient.

RACIAL AND ETHNIC IDENTITY FORMATION

The study by Rogers and Meltzoff (2017) implies that race/ethnicity may not be as important as other domains to self-definition as children enter adolescence. For example, having Mexican heritage may be less important to a young Mexican American girl than the fact that she is the oldest daughter in her family, is smart in school, has lots of friends, and is the best soccer player on her team. However, a wealth of research indicates that this identity domain increases in importance during adolescence and young adulthood for most members of minority or marginalized groups (Meeus, 2017).

Theorists (e.g., Cross, 1994) have long speculated that ethnic/racial identity (ERI) development tends to progress much like other aspects of adolescent identity, with an early phase of diffusion, during which ethnic identity is either unrecognized or not considered very important, as the Rogers and Meltzoff findings seem to suggest. In most theories, this period is followed by a moratorium-like stage, typically triggered by some experience that thrusts the importance of one's race or ethnicity to the forefront. This stage is characterized by ambivalence or conflict, as the individual explores and comes to terms with her race or ethnicity. For many young adolescents, it is a time when the racism or cultural oppression that exists in society takes on personal significance.

MyLab Education
Video Example 9.4
Ethnic/racial identity (ERI) may progress like other aspects of adolescent development. Consider the effects of experiences based on racial and ethnic stereotypes during this period of identity development.

Experiences based on racial and ethnic stereotypes clearly can be salient and central to adolescent development. Here is how author Beverly Daniel Tatum (1997) explains the struggle that her 10-year-old son will likely have:

> When David meets new adults, they don't say, "Gee, you're Black for your age!" If you are saying to yourself, of course they don't, think again. Imagine David, at fifteen, six-foot-two, wearing the adolescent attire of the day, passing adults he doesn't know on the sidewalk. Do the women hold their purses a little tighter, maybe even cross the street to avoid him? Does he hear the sound of the automatic door locks on the cars as he passes by? Is he being followed around by the security guards at the local mall? As he stops in town with his new bicycle, does a police officer hassle him, asking where he got it, implying that it might be stolen? Do strangers assume he plays basketball? Each of these experiences conveys a racial message. At ten, race is not yet salient for David, because it is not yet salient for society. But it will be. (p. 54)

In a looking-glass society that sorts people on the basis of race, ethnicity, and appearance and then reflects back to them the measure of their worth, early adolescence is a time when many youngsters such as David, who are members of minority or marginalized groups, confront the negative stereotypes and discriminatory practices of others head on. In a startling real-life example of such experiences, the first African American president of the United States, Barack Obama, tells the story of his own White grandmother, who admitted to him that she often had been fearful when she saw a Black man walking toward her, for no other reason than that he was Black. How do minority youth respond to such discriminatory views and behavior? Theories suggest that some adolescents may immerse themselves in their racial or cultural groups or even actively reject the dominant culture during this period.

Researchers have documented a host of negative effects that discriminatory experiences can have on physical and psychological health (Benner, 2017). For example, in one longitudinal study, 16- to 18-year-old African Americans who reported experiencing racial discrimination in the previous year showed more signs of "wear and tear" on biological systems at age 20 (e.g., blood pressure and cortisol changes) than those who did not (Brody et al., 2014). In a review of studies, Lewis, Cogburn, and Williams (2015) found that the more discrimination experiences African Americans reported, the more likely they were to develop mental health problems such as mood, anxiety, and substance use disorders.

The major risk that discrimination represents in the lives of minority group members seems to be moderated by the ethnic/racial identity commitments that develop in adolescence and early adulthood. Strong ethnic identity serves a buffering role, protecting self-esteem during stressful inter-racial interactions (Yip & Douglass, 2013). We will discuss how to promote the protective role of ERI more fully in the Applications section of this chapter.

For now, let's examine what the normative processes seem to be in the adolescent's formation of ERI, and what the evidence is for its protective role. In most theories, the highest stage is achieved when the individual, having actively explored what her ethnicity means, affirms her identity as a member (commitment). Phinney (1990, 2000, 2003) argues that ERI development can be seen as reflecting the same four statuses that characterize other aspects of identity, indicating the degree to which individuals have explored the meaning of their ethnicity/race in their lives. She asserts that the resolution—identity achievement—is twofold: (1) reconciling the differences that exist between the ethnic minority group and the dominant group, and (2) coming to terms with the lower status of one's group within the larger society. She also states, however, that this achievement does not necessarily need to coexist with a high level of involvement in one's own cultural group. The overall pattern of stages is similar to formulations of homosexual/bisexual identity development as well. Cross and Fhagen-Smith (2001), referring specifically to African American identity, suggest that adolescents can go through a process of exploration of what race means, and thereby achieve ethnic identity. Or if their families use positive racial socialization practices, they may have a foreclosed identity, which can be a positive result. But if they fail to commit to a racial identity during adolescence, they may, as you have seen, be more vulnerable to stress when they do experience discrimination.

Studies of various minority groups in different countries generally support these theoretical ideas. For example, Supple and colleagues (Supple, Ghazarian, Frabutt, Plunkett, & Sands, 2006) identified such a process in Latino adolescents in the United States. They described the stages of identity formation as exploration (engagement with cultural activities and roles), resolution (coming to understand the meaning of identifying with one's culture), and affirmation (accepting and identifying with oneself and one's group). For their participants, exploration and resolution were primarily related to parental socialization efforts. However, affirmation of cultural identity depended as well on the interaction of parenting quality and environmental context, such as neighborhood safety. Highly supportive parenting, in the context of neighborhood security, was positively related to ethnic identity affirmation. Low-quality, harsh parenting in the context of more dangerous surroundings showed the opposite effect. For Latino adolescents, strong ethnic identity operated as a protective factor and contributed to better academic performance. The authors conclude that ethnic identity is shaped by a number of interacting variables and is enhanced by the quality of the micro and exo-systems.

Other research seems consistent with this view. When minority group membership is central to high school and college students' identity, that ethnic identity appears to both increase sensitivity to (awareness of) discrimination and protect psychological well-being in the face of discrimination (Neblett, Shelton, & Sellers, 2004; Greene, Way, & Pahl, 2006). Yip, Seaton, and Sellers (2006) found that for African American adolescents, college students, and adults, having an achieved ethnic identity status was associated with racial centrality (seeing race as an important aspect of self) and with private regard (seeing one's race as positive). For college students, achieved status also appeared to be a protective factor against depression.

Many parents engage in ethnic/racial socialization practices that help young people build strong ethnic identities (Dunbar, Leerkes, Coard, Supple, & Calkins, 2017; Meeus, 2017). These practices typically have several key features: (1) teaching about culture, cultural values, and participating in cultural activities, (2) preparing children for the possible experience of discrimination and schooling them on ways to cope emotionally with such experiences, and (3) providing them with opportunities for mainstream cultural experiences and egalitarian relationships with others from different groups (Boykin & Toms, 1985; Dunbar et al., 2017). In general, messages about racial and ethnic pride and participation in activities that reflect shared heritage lead to many positive increases in competence, identity, self-esteem, academic achievement, and less antisocial behavior (Wang & Huguley, 2012). So do parenting strategies that help children feel safe about confiding their experiences and concerns (Brody, Miller, Yu, Beach, & Chen, 2016). Helping children accept their negative emotions and training them to manage those emotions with, for example, encouragement, problem solving, and comfort is also important (Dunbar et al., 2017).

Arming youth against the threat of racial discrimination has more mixed results. For example, preparing African American children for experiences of discrimination strengthened their connections with family members but lowered their academic performance and heightened depression and feelings of hopelessness in some studies (Davis & Stevenson, 2006; Reynolds & Gonzalez-Backen, 2017). Some research indicates that adolescents' expectations about discrimination can foster hostility and antisocial behavior (Hughes et al., 2006). It is possible that teaching children about the realities of discrimination, which appears to be protective, needs to be decoupled from the promotion of mistrust and/or coupled with school and community efforts to promote trust (Yeager, Purdie-Vaughns, Hooper, & Cohen, 2017). Providing opportunities for mainstream activities and fostering cross-racial friendships are related to better social skills and overall adjustment (Graham, Taylor, & Ho, 2009). A number of longitudinal studies indicate that inter-group contact and cross-group friendships can increase exploration of ERI, and that increased ethnic commitment is associated with positive and diverse peer relationships (Gonzalez et al., 2017; Rivas-Drake, Umaña-Taylor, Schaefer, & Medina, 2017).

All of these processes are embedded within larger contexts. For example, there are some minority group youth who do not seem to benefit much from developing a strong ethnic identity. Dmiitrova et al. (2017) found that Roma adolescents in Eastern Europe are better served by a strong family identity. Roma adolescents with strong ethnic commitments tend to do more poorly on measures of well-being than those with weaker ethnic identities. The authors speculate that particularly harsh national policies aimed at the Roma minority in places like Bulgaria and Kosovo might play a role in disrupting the protection that ethnic identity often affords.

ISSUES IN THE STUDY OF ETHNIC OR RACIAL AND SEXUALITY DEVELOPMENT

There are many methodological complexities involved in studying gender, racial, and ethnic identity development that we should mention. In the area of sexuality and gender development, for example, we have noted previously that there is considerable disagreement and uncertainty about what the categories of gender and sexual orientation are or should be, especially given that for many individuals a multiplicity of categorizations seem to apply. Even terms such as *race, ethnicity*, and *culture* are often used by different authors to signify different things, which adds to the confusion. The term *sexuality development* has replaced *sexual development* over the past two decades, which reflects the fluidity and interconnectedness of physical and psychological development over the course of coming to understand one's sexuality.

MyLab Education
Video Example 9.5
Identity formation for immigrant students is influenced by families, school experiences, teachers, and peers. Based on insights expressed by immigrant students in this video, consider broader applications to all groups of adolescents who diverge from mainstream patterns in their identity development.

Assuming that members of a race or ethnic group are homogeneous on variables such as ethnic identity is another problem. In a study of Latino/Latina adolescents living in the United States, Umana-Taylor and Fine (2001) found evidence for heterogeneity of ethnic identification among Colombian, Guatemalan, Honduran, Mexican, Nicaraguan, Puerto Rican, and Salvadoran participants. These authors concluded that grouping individuals from these Latino/Latina cultures into one collective ethnic group masked some real differences. They suggest there is a need to consider generational status, immigration history, and nationality in order to refine our understanding of ethnic identity. More recent work has begun to acknowledge these issues, and investigators often take pains to avoid overgeneralizing their findings from one group to another (Meeus, 2017).

Is "whiteness" a racial characteristic or a social-cultural one? Whatever stance you take on this issue, it is generally a good idea for people to consider the place of their own race, culture, and ethnicity in their self-definition. For members of the dominant White culture, race is often a nonissue in conceptualizations of identity, and many writers have pointed out that Whites are largely unaware of themselves in racial terms. In other words, White people often fail to recognize how their being White (i.e., the "in-group") in a society stratified on the basis of race influences their attitudes and behaviors towards themselves and towards members of other racial groups (i.e., the "out-groups"). Although White youth do report some ethnic identity exploration, especially if they have cross-cultural friendships, ethnicity is not typically a key domain of identity exploration for Whites in Western societies (Else-Quest, 2015; Russell, Liebenberg, & Ungar, 2015). A failure to construe ethnicity/race as an important aspect of self, experience, and place in society is a failure of perspective taking, and it appears to help sustain the problems of White dominance or privilege.

Another important methodological challenge is that group membership typically involves the intersection of multiple categories. Young people construct a gender identity, one or more ethnic/racial identities, a sexual identity, and so on. Each identity almost certainly moderates each of the others, so that exploration and commitment are likely to be relatively unique for each individual. Sorting out what, if any, developmental patterns and processes characterize different intersectional groups is an important goal of developmental researchers who study identity formation (Ghavani, Katsiaficas, & Rogers, 2016). See Box 9.2.

Box 9.2: Choosing an Identity: The Case of Multiracial Youth

Carlos was born in California. His mother is part Filipino and part Mexican. His father is White. In ninth grade, he filled out a questionnaire that asked him to "Select the major ethnic group that best describes you." Carlos picked "White." How did he make his choice?

That was the question that Melissa Herman (2004) addressed as she examined questionnaire data from nearly 9,000 adolescents surveyed in California and Wisconsin schools in the 1980s. Students were asked to "select the one major ethnic group that best describes you" with the choices being Black, Native American, White, Asian, Hispanic, and Pacific Islander. Students were also asked to select the ethnic background(s) of their parents, and in this case they were given the opportunity to select more than one answer. From the data the children provided on their parents, Herman was able to identify nearly 1,500 kids with multiracial or multiethnic backgrounds. Herman's study continues to be the most comprehensive investigation of multiracial and multi-ethnic youth in the United States.

Americans are frequently asked to identify race or ethnicity on questionnaires, from political surveys to SAT exams, and in many of these situations they are not given the choice of identifying themselves in more than one way. Herman looked for the factors that seem to influence the choices that young people make when forced to choose. The questionnaire they completed also probed the teens' views of themselves and their ethnicity with questions on global self-esteem, on perceived importance of ethnic background for self-definition, on overall feelings about their ethnic background (from strongly negative to strongly positive), and on perceived ethnic discrimination (e.g., "How often are teachers unfair or negative to you because of your ethnic background?"). In addition, data were collected from other sources. The respondents' yearbook pictures were coded for apparent race by a group of independent observers. Demographic information like socioeconomic status was assessed by looking at parents' education level and at U.S. Census Bureau information on average income in a census tract.

Herman also looked at context variables. Did one or both parents reside with the adolescent? If just one, which one? Which ethnic group characterized the adolescent's friends? What was the ethnic makeup of the student's neighborhood and school?

Herman categorized students as either monoracial or biracial, using a complex formula to determine biracial status if they reported more than two racial backgrounds for their parents. Biracial minority White adolescents, especially those whose minority category was "Black," were more likely to identify with their minority category than to identify as White, a finding reported by other researchers as well (e.g., Quintana, 1999). All groups felt positively about their ethnic background, and biracial adolescents' feelings were about the same as those of

monoracials. For example, monoracial Asians and biracial Asian Whites reported similar feelings about their ethnicity, although both were somewhat less positive than most other groups. Interestingly, although both monoracial non-Whites and biracial kids reported experiencing ethnic discrimination, they also had self-esteem scores that were comparable to those of Whites who reported experiencing little or no discrimination. In fact, monoracial Blacks had somewhat higher self-esteem scores than Whites, although monoracial Asians had somewhat lower scores.

How did students decide what racial identity to report? As we saw already, the majority of biracial adolescents identified with their minority category. Those biracial teens who identified as "White" were more likely than others to look White to observers or to live with a White parent. There were some effects of larger contexts as well, mostly for Hispanic White biracials. For these kids, living in a more affluent or White neighborhood predicted identifying as White. Ironically though, attending a largely White high school predicted identifying as Hispanic. Perhaps for some teens, under some conditions, being in the minority highlights their distinctiveness and makes a non-White category identification more likely. There were other findings that were specific to certain biracial groups. For example, Native American White biracials, even those who looked White to observers, almost never identified as being White.

Biracial adolescents' perceptions of the importance of ethnicity issues in their lives were among the strongest predictors of their identity choices. First, if a minority White biracial teen reported experiencing a good deal of ethnic discrimination, she was more likely to identify as non-White. Second, if she felt that ethnicity was an important aspect of her identity, she was also more likely to identify as non-White. Similarly, Quintana (1999) reported that for college students, sensitivity to ethnicity issues was a key factor in deciding their ethnic identity. Most of her respondents identified as non-White, they said, because they felt it was "the right thing to do." They cited reasons such as the history of oppression of non-White groups or their loyalty to a non-White parent (who was likely to be the parent with whom they had most contact). It is not clear from these data whether focus on ethnicity causes adolescents to adopt a minority identity or the reverse. More than likely, it is a bidirectional process, such that kids who are sensitive to ethnicity issues (e.g., who experience or have concern about racial discrimination) are prone to adopt a minority status, and kids who adopt a minority status are more likely to confront and be sensitized to issues like discrimination. In contrast, Whites do not usually perceive racial status to be an important aspect of their own identities, and they tend not to recognize the privilege it conveys. Herman found this to be true of both White monoracials and of biracials who identified as White in her study.

MyLab Education Self-Check 9.4.

Applications

Identity: The Long and Winding Road

A sense of identity is related to psychological well-being because one's personal goals are met through its expression, and meaning is found in its pursuit (Negru-Subtirica, Pop, Luyckx, Dezutter, & Steger, 2016). Adolescents, much more than younger children, are able to identify their own goals, create meaning from their actions, and chart their own course (Pittman, 2017). Some of the behaviors adolescents use to express themselves are very different at age 14 than those they exhibited at age 8. Sometimes teenage behaviors may appear strange and annoying, but they might not be dangerous. Helping parents and others understand the developmental appropriateness of non-destructive personal expression can be very reassuring. In other cases, when healthy alternatives for autonomy-seeking are lacking, teenagers might try to meet their fundamental needs in ways that are potentially harmful. Supporting adolescents' exploration of healthy and developmentally appropriate routes for expressing independence, for feeling part of a social group, and for experiencing satisfaction in accomplishment are important goals for educators, therapists, and parents.

Despite the fervent wishes of many parents that their teenagers "find themselves" quickly, the trajectory of identity development, outlined in this chapter, is far from linear. In fact, it may be more nuanced and dynamic than previously believed. Contemporary opportunities for exploration are abundant compared to those available to prior generations whose roles in life were more constrained. The current situation presents both advantages and challenges because youth need to find their place in a complex and globalized world seemingly possessed of unlimited choices. Aspects of personality interact with family, school, community, and culture in the construction of identity, and each offers raw material that adolescents use to shape a self (Crocetti et al., 2015; McAdams & McLean, 2013). Some of these "big-picture" influences, like the culture in which adolescents grow up, are important for how commitments come to be made (see Table 9.4). Professionals may wish to consider these macro-influences when working with young people. It's important not to expect one standard developmental sequence but rather to support the emerging coherence and meaningfulness of each client's unique identity construction.

TABLE 9.4 Identity Development from an International Perspective: The Influence of Culture and Context

COUNTRY	SNAPSHOT OF CULTURE AND CONTEXT	SNAPSHOT OF CULTURAL EFFECTS ON SPECIFIC DIMENSIONS OF IDENTITY	SOURCE
Belgium & the Netherlands	Belgian and Dutch universities offer low cost tuition to everyone, but do not provide freshmen with broad exposure to different academic areas (e.g., general education). College major depends upon one's choice of an educational track in high school (roughly at age 14–15). Belgian (but not Dutch) students tend to return to their homes on weekends.	Educational identity development must begin early in both countries. Belgian students who did more experimenting with educational alternatives (longer moratorium) were likely to experience more parental pressure to choose a career, often because they had ongoing parental contact. Subsequently weaker overall commitment to an educational identity was noted for this group.	Klimstra, Luyckx, & Meeus, 2012
China	Chinese youth are coming of age in an era of increasing globalization. Youth attempt to integrate both local and global influences into identity construction. Confucian values like shame and filial piety contrast with individualistic Western values.	Some research shows that youth with strong "local" ethnic identity, as opposed to stronger "global" identity, report more life satisfaction and may have a stronger basis for exploration in other areas (e.g., career). Strength of Chinese collectivist values related to family responsibility and shame calls into question Western typologies for assessing identity statuses with their implicit bias toward autonomy.	Cheng & Berman, 2012
Italy	Youth live at home for a prolonged period (mean age of independent living is 29.5 for females and 31 for males) with few financial responsibilities and substantial freedom. Italian government subsidies are limited compared to other countries but only about 28% of youth actually express financial concerns as the reason for remaining with parents. This phenomenon has been called the "delay syndrome." In some sectors, job opportunity is poor.	Italian youth spend more time in moratorium, exploring and reconsidering their choices, than many other cultural groups. Such exploration is generally supported by Italian families. Youth ultimately consolidate their identity within the family rather than by separating from it. High job insecurity and unemployment in Italy presumably influence youths' conception about the power of personal agency to combat social realities. Virtual reality (e.g., gaming or social networking) is used as a strategy for dealing with insecurity about the postmodern future, delaying commitment.	Crocetti & Meeus, 2014
Arab adolescents in Israel	The minority Arab community living in Israel was once part of the Palestinian majority before Israel's founding in 1948. Arab youth grow up cognizant of social and political tensions between the Arab and Israeli communities, often marked by violent clashes, and are aware of the discrimination against them.	Collective identity development is shaped by strong familial loyalty and adoption of parental social and political views. Given the prevailing conflict between minority and majority citizens living in Israel, the adoption of a strong collective Arab identity may be a way of preserving a cultural heritage in a hostile environment. A similar process may be happening in other countries where religious minorities face discrimination.	Aboud-Halabi & Shamai, 2016

Where Do I Fit?

Achieving coherence or a good-enough fit with one's social networks, vocational choices, sexuality, and racial, ethnic, and spiritual values results in healthy identity expression. Research has shed light on what obstructs successful resolution of the search for this good fit. Striving to make early college decisions or committing to a career path while in high school may be developmentally inappropriate goals for many adolescents who lack the life experience necessary to make personally meaningful choices. Although teenagers who make these decisions may appear mature to observers and may establish themselves as role models for their peers, their behavior may actually reflect a pseudo-maturity that is more akin to premature foreclosure in certain domains, such as vocational identity.

Commitment generally follows a period of exploration. As you have learned, initial exploration (exploration in breadth: *I think about a number of possibilities for my future*; Luyckx et al., 2008) precedes another form of exploration (exploration in depth: *I talk to people about the plans I have or the choices I made for my future*) that is usually done after some commitment is made. It's possible to reaffirm the commitment or seek healthier commitments by virtue of this process. Yet, researchers have identified a "dark side" to exploration. One type that is associated with maladaptive outcomes is called ruminative exploration (*It's hard to stop thinking about the plans I want to follow in my life*). Longitudinal research shows that all types of exploration can be related to meaning making, but some youth may get stuck in maladaptive ruminative exploration, which is related to lower well-being, depression, and unresolved questioning of commitments.

Consider, for example, a high school student who begins to consider careers in various scientific fields as he makes his way through school (breadth of exploration). Over time, he recognizes that environmental science is interesting and meaningful to him, actively investigates fields of study leading to career opportunities (depth of exploration), and chooses to pursue a degree in this area. His best friend also wanted a career in science during high school, but now at university, he is conflicted about making enough money to support the life he wants as an adult. He has chosen a major in science but can't seem to settle on a direction. Because of persistent doubts, he adds some courses in finance to his schedule. He ruminates about being unhappy in the future because he doesn't see himself working in either of these areas. After three years, he hasn't accumulated enough credits to continue in either science or finance and drops out of school in frustration.

Current research suggests that ruminative exploration is a risk factor for successful identity development because it undermines commitments that might contribute to coherence and meaning. Therapists can be helpful to these youth by scaffolding adaptive versus maladaptive forms of exploration, by helping clients reduce chronic self-judgment and indecisiveness, and by supporting mindsets of persistence versus failure (Beyers & Luyckx, 2016).

Navigating Special Challenges

For adolescents from marginalized or other disadvantaged groups, the process of resolving the challenge posed by Erikson (1968), "What do I want to make of myself, and what do I have to work with?" may be more complicated than for others. The constricted opportunity experienced by some adolescents because of societal discrimination, cultural intolerance, poverty, or lack of support can make the identity domains of relationships, school, and work "closed" domains, accommodating little positive exploration. Prevention and/or intervention in this situation might depend upon opening up opportunities for exploration as well as supporting commitments.

Given the salience of racial and ethnic group membership for minority individuals, the emergent identity development process in adolescence, and the benefits that attach to a healthy sense of self-worth in general, culturally sensitive efforts have been advanced that combine goals of fostering pride in one's group affiliation with meeting developmental challenges adaptively. As we describe in this chapter, one's ethnic/racial identity (ERI) is constituted from features of identity specific to race or ethnicity, processes of identity construction related to these elements, attitudes and feelings about one's racial/ethnic membership, and understanding of society's views about one's group (Umaña-Taylor et al., 2014). Positive ERI has been related to psychological well-being among Black, Latino, Native American, Pacific Islander, and Asian American groups, although the results are not always consistent (see Rivas-Drake et al., 2014). Even stronger associations have been found between ERI and school achievement and self-efficacy, although some negative associations were also noted. In some studies, for example, strong ERI was negatively associated with achievement for African American youth (Worrell, 2007) and had no effect on achievement for Asian American students (Farver, Narang, & Bhadha, 2002). Effects of strong ERI on health outcomes of youth, like risky sexual behavior and drug use, were more inconsistent than for those related to positive mental health and achievement. ERI presents some challenges to measurement, so this may explain some of the inconsistencies. It also appears that the greatest benefits accrue to those who are interested in and who value their racial/ethnic identity in the first place. For them, positive effects from supportive programs are greatest. Some individuals are less connected to their ERI and view it as less salient than other identity dimensions like family or personal relationships. Meeus (2017) points out that ERI, unlike other identity domains, cannot be freely chosen from a range of possibilities. Strong ethnic identity is more likely the product of identity maintenance (in-depth exploration) or of a growing interest in one's heritage. Yet, even though individual differences in the personal relevance of specific domains exist, there seems to be sufficient evidence, especially in the achievement area, to support the cultivation of positive ERI among minority group youth.

Because adolescents have greater ability, compared to younger groups, to engage in perspective taking from the perspective of group affiliation (group consciousness), cultivating these assets in youth programs may offer unique opportunities. For minority youth whose identity development can be compromised by racial and ethnic bias, youth programs can be effective vehicles for the promotion of ethnic and racial heritage as a shared cultural asset (Lerner, Lerner, Bowers, & Geldof, 2015). Meta-analyses report benefits for African American youth when interventions explicitly incorporate cultural values into their curricula (Brittian Loyd & Williams, 2017). In addition to teaching conventional communication and social skills, some programs incorporate African cultural values (e.g., *umoja*–unity, *nia* - purpose), traditions and rituals (e.g., naming ceremony, rites of passage), African history lessons, skits about famous cultural figures, discussions about racism (e.g., coping with bias), and health and wellness information (e.g., natural hair care). Such programs were effective in increasing positive ERI in their participants. One reason may be their fundamental message: that African American values and cultural traditions are assets to be recognized and celebrated. More research needs to be done before other questions can be answered definitively, such as whether teachers and youth need to be racially and ethnically matched for program success and which psychological processes related to identity construction are actually impacted by the program.

Some programs are family-based. One example of a culturally sensitive 7-week program that supports adolescent identity development is the Strong African American Families Program (SAAF; Brody et al., 2004). This prevention program, originally studied with rural African American mothers and their young adolescent children, is based on strengthening parent and youth protective factors. The goal of the program is to prevent young African American adolescents from engaging in drug use by targeting improved family communication about race, sexuality, drug use, etc. Of primary interest here is that adaptive racial socialization is considered a protective factor based on evidence that minority children who receive explicit information about the nature of racial prejudice, adaptive ways of dealing with discrimination, and the clear message that they can be successful despite this reality have better academic success and more positive expectations about the future (Hughes & Chen, 1999).

Presumably, these active socialization practices assist adolescents in managing their personal encounters with racism and help reduce internalization of negative messages as their sense of personal identity matures. One trial of the 7-week program included seven separate meetings for mothers and adolescents (Brody et al., 2004). Parent sessions covered topics about involved parenting, racial socialization, and communication about sexuality and alcohol use. Youth sessions covered such topics as following family rules, setting goals for the future, adaptive ways of handling racism, and resistance strategies for alcohol and drugs. Joint parent–child sessions were also held once a week. Outcome assessment revealed increased goal-directed future orientation and more negative attitudes about drug and alcohol use for youth participants and improved communication skills for parent participants 7 months after program completion. A recent follow up (2017) showed that youth who had participated in the program showed lower risk factors for smoking at age 20 (Chen, Yu, & Brody, 2017).

Helping Sexual Minority Youth

Sexual identity development cannot be disentangled from other aspects of identity like gender, race, and culture, which is why current research is embedding its study in these intersections. For simplicity, we focus here on the special needs of sexual minority youth, even as we are mindful that all the potential complexities of concurrent identity domains present questions to be clarified in future research.

Just as a supportive environment, provision of cultural information, recognition, affirmation of differences, and understanding of cultural barriers are important for helpers and others to provide for ethnic and minority youth, the same can be said for sexual minority youth. When LGBTQI adults (Lesbian, Gay, Bisexual, Transsexual, Queer, & Intersex) from a community sample were asked about their experiences with health care professionals, their responses provided prescriptions for the medical community about what they wanted. Three of the themes include the following advice: (1) Providers should be comfortable enough to show authentic respect, not treating people differently based on sexual identification; (2) providers should not generalize or make assumptions about sexual identity, preferences, or behaviors; and (3) providers should address barriers to care, provide resources, and recognize the obstacles faced by these individuals (Alpert, Cichoski Kelly, & Fox, 2017). The context may be different for younger individuals, but the core of the message is certainly the same.

As sexual minority youth move through the central developmental processes of sexual questioning and disclosure to others, outcomes may depend upon family acceptance or rejection, the complexities of gender and ethnic/racial status, and social support or ostracism. Many sexual minority youth are struggling to come to terms with their own sexual orientation often *before* they understand what the issue really is. At first, conflicts might be expressed as feeling "different." This feeling can exist in the context of societal condemnation or actual threats and rejection, a state of affairs that exacerbates the sense of isolation, especially when the condemnation is based on religious grounds (Gibbs & Goldbach, 2015). The need for affirmation, understanding, and social support is obvious.

Currently, the timing of "coming out" (about age 14) is earlier than it has been in past generations possibly because of greater social awareness and acceptance. One dark side to early self-identification and disclosure, however, is the potential for increased bullying by peers. Younger adolescents tend to view sex roles as rigid and can be quite punishing of deviations from sexual norms, even in areas as superficial as dress and mannerisms (Mulvey & Killen, 2015). Only 18 states have passed laws that protect students from bullying and harassment due to gender identity and sexual orientation (see www.glsen.org/article/state-maps). Yet, a 2016 survey found that 85% of sexual minority youth reported being called names or threatened. Around 70% did not participate in school functions because of harassment (Kosciw, Greytak, Giga, Villenas, & Danischewski, 2016). Adverse consequences of bullying by peers are alarming.

Victimization is related to increased involvement in disciplinary actions in school, higher dropout rates, and involvement with the juvenile justice system (Palmer & Greytak, 2017). Homophobic bullying, sadly, does not remit to the same degree over the course of schooling as other forms of bullying. Consequently, sexual minority youth experience bullying for longer periods of time (Robinson, Esplenage, & Rivers, 2013). Consider this situation in combination with the devastating effects of parental disapproval. The fact that between 30% and 43% of youth serviced in drop-in centers, shelters, and street outreach programs self-identify as LGBT signifies the real-world impact of family rejection and abuse (Durso & Gates, 2012).

On so many fronts, sexual minority youth are at great risk. Rates of depression, anxiety, substance abuse, PTSD, and suicidal ideation are higher than for heterosexual individuals (Russell & Fish, 2016). Suicidal attempts are reported by 31% of LGBT youth, compared to 4.1% of the general population, often because they perceive themselves to be a burden to their families (Baams, Grossman, & Russell, 2015). Some research indicates that bisexual youth are in the highest risk category; compared to homosexual youth, they express even more suicidality and depression (Marshall et al., 2011).

One evidence-based approach to supporting sexual minority youth is to establish school climate policies that provide them with acknowledgment, respect, and protection. Gay-Straight Alliances and other student-led clubs that offer education and support in combination with teacher professional development can be a lifeline for struggling students (Snapp, Watson, Russell, Diaz, & Ryan, 2015). Studies also indicated that good relationships with supportive peers and romantic partners can help reduce the deleterious effects of discrimination and homophobia on identity development.

Professionals who work with sexual minority youth can help them by attending to the special dimensions of their adolescent experience and by being alert to the risks associated with sexual minority status. The following clinical guidelines are offered by Telingator and Woyewodzic (2011).

1. As a helper, consider your own attitudes, anxieties, and judgments insofar as they influence the quality of the professional relationship.
2. Be aware that social stigma and fear of rejection can make a young person try to hide sexual identity and discount sexual feelings.
3. Allow for openness around the issues of sexuality, sexual attractions, and gender identity so that the young person experiences a place that is safe for honest self-exploration.
4. Consider that sexual identity development is a fluid process that may manifest in changing attractions and orientations over time.
5. Help the adolescent identify real and reliable sources of support among family, friends, and community members and assist the young person in accessing them.
6. Family support is the key protective factor. Work with the adolescent's family to strengthen attachments that will protect against risk. Clinical work with the family may involve supporting family members themselves and helping them understand fears and uncertainties about their child's sexual identity.

One more important element should be added: the use of language. The examples in Table 9.5 are taken from work of Cicero and Wesp (2017), who offer suggestions about working with transgender youth.

TABLE 9.5 Some Ways to Communicate with Transgender Youth

CIRCUMSTANCES	EXAMPLES
Names and forms of address (if gender identity is not known)	If you are uncomfortable about not knowing the person's gender identity: "How would you like to be addressed?" "Is it OK to call you . . . ?" "Do you have another name you like to go by?"
Personal Pronouns	Instead of using an incorrect pronoun or when the person prefers a gender neutral pronoun (ze, hir, hirs). "I wanted to check before I assumed—What are your pronouns?" "I have never used that pronoun before. Can you help me pronounce it?"
When completing documents or speaking to parents or guardians	Be respectful to the individual by asking preference. The family may use a different name. "When I call (or when I write this report), which name should I use?" "What is the name on the school records?"

SOURCE: Cicero, E. C., & Wesp, L. M. (2017). Supporting the health and well-being of transgender students. *The Journal of School Nursing*, 33(2), 95-108. SAGE Publications, Inc.

The Path Ahead

Some adolescents manage to make the transition to young adulthood in ways that evidence only mild or sporadic periods of upset, whereas others appear to be on a long roller-coaster ride. The temperament and capacities of the adolescent, the contributions of earlier experience, and the fit between the individual and the spheres that influence her will uniquely affect the adolescent experience. Despite the widely different ways that adolescents engage in the process of exploration, Erikson (1968) believed that the reward for the search was the achievement of "fidelity," or something to hold on to.

In other words, the adolescent who is in search of a way to be in the world may appear confused, lost, and bewildering to others. Yet, this process is a necessary part of the moratorium that precedes the achievement of greater stability. As Josselson (1994) points out, this search is fundamentally a dialogue that the adolescent does not engage in alone. The success of adolescents' search for fidelity depends upon the community's fidelity to adolescents as they search.

Focus on Developmental Psychopathology

Eating Disorders

Food occupies a privileged place in human society. It supports life and social connectedness, offers pleasure, and communicates cultural and religious values. Maslow (1954), in his famous hierarchy of needs, puts food solidly at the foundation of the pyramid because of its importance to basic survival. Why, then, do some individuals refuse to eat or eat in such disordered ways as to create enormous emotional and physical suffering? These disturbances, called eating disorders (APA, 2013), are not a new phenomenon. Bulimic behaviors were seen in the ancient societies of Greece and Rome. Anorexia, or self-starvation, was associated with fasting in the Middle Ages (Brumberg, 1988). But during the latter part of the 20th century, media images of shockingly emaciated anorexic figures and heartbreaking stories of bulimic binging and purging have raised public consciousness about these aberrant patterns of eating, to both fascinate and repel us.

Rates of eating disorders are increasing, especially when considering the number of subthreshold cases (Swanson, Crow, LeGrange, Swendsen, & Merikangas, 2011). The DSM-V *Feeding and Eating Disorders* include anorexia nervosa (AN), bulimia nervosa (BN), binge-eating disorder (BED), avoidant/restrictive food intake disorder (ARFID), rumination disorder, pica, and a category for subthreshold disorders of AN, BN, BED, purging disorder, and night eating syndrome (NES) (APA, 2013). Eating disorders affect fewer males than females, with ratios estimated at 1:10, but some rates are as high as 1:3 (Carlatt, Camargo, & Herzog, 1997; Hudson, Hiripi, Pope, & Kessler, 2007). Rates for children younger that 12 are also increasing (Zhao & Escinosa, 2011). Eating disorders are frequently accompanied by other psychiatric conditions, especially affective and anxiety disorders. In particular, AN is associated with very high rates of inpatient hospitalization and suicide. Some suggest the consequences of bulimia may also be quite severe (Crow, 2013).

Anorexia nervosa, a disorder characterized by refusal to maintain adequate body weight (below 85%) for age and height, has two subtypes. The restricting type maintains a malnourished state by not eating or by caloric restriction. The binge eating/purging type also shows marked weight loss, but the course of disease is punctuated by bursts of binging and/or purging. Binges are typically followed by some type of compensatory action (self-induced vomiting, use of laxatives or diuretics, or extreme exercise routines). Those who have AN have highly distorted cognitions about body shape and size.

The disease is deadly. Keel and colleagues (2003) report that those with anorexia are 57 times more likely to die from suicide than are their peers who do not have eating disorders. Although for years anorexia was regarded as a disease affecting mid- to high-SES White females, incidence is also increasing within minority groups (Decaluwe, Braet, & Fairburn, 2003).

Bulimia nervosa is characterized by repeated binge eating and compensatory behaviors at least once a week for three months. Those who have BN may remain at normal weight but only do so by relying on purging, laxative use, or excessive exercise. Furthermore, like those who have anorexia,

MyLab Education Video Example 9.6

Teens with anorexia often mention feeling pride in their ability to control themselves and their eating. This girl has been in treatment for two years with various therapists, a psychiatrist, and a nutritionist. Why might she, more so than others struggling with similar eating disorders, have a good chance of moving past this disorder?

they share cognitive distortions about body shape and size and the tendency to base their self-esteem on these dimensions. Bulimia manifests in purging, which includes regular self-induced vomiting or use of laxatives, enemas, and so on, and non-purging, which includes excessive fasting or exercise. Binges are marked by perceived lack of control over the eating behavior.

Etiology and Risk Factors for Eating Disorders

Many theories have been proposed to account for the puzzling phenomenon of disordered eating, including genetic, personality, family systems, cultural, and developmental explanations. Clearly, eating disorders represent a good example of multiply determined disorders, for no one causal factor is sufficient to explain their emergence (Kaye, Klump, Frank, & Strober, 2000). Currently, the search is on for pathways that explain how these factors interact to result in eating pathology.

There is evidence for the influence of genetically transmitted risk of AN and BN, which cluster in families. Research in molecular genetics is underway in order to identify the particular genes associated with risk, and to identify potential epigenetic processes involved in etiology. At this point, more research is needed to clarify the specific pathways and to identify possible gene candidates (Trace, Baker, Penas-Lledo, & Bulik, 2013). Researchers have also recognized that the hormonal and neurotransmitter abnormalities associated with AN and BN may result from malnutrition or even pre-morbid psychiatric conditions like depression, anxiety, and substance abuse, so direction of effects needs to be carefully examined (Kaye et al., 2000).

The personality characteristics of individuals with eating disorders have been the subject of great interest. While both AN and BN types share preoccupations around food/eating, distortions in body image, and low self-esteem, certain differences have been described that appear to predate

diagnosis and persist even after recovery (Casper, 1990). Anorexics have been described as perfectionistic, conformist, obsessional, high in self-control, and rigid in their thinking. Restricting food intake fits into this constellation of personality traits and provides a source of control and security. Some bulimics, in comparison, may be impulsive, prone to self-mutilation and substance abuse, and dependent upon food to regulate dysphoric moods. Other bulimics have been described as self-effacing and guilt-prone. Their pattern of food restriction after binging is viewed as a means of alleviating guilt for over-indulgence. The line between AN and BN, however, is not completely clear; both disorders can share symptoms. For example, 25% to 39% of bulimics have a history of anorexia (Kaye et al., 2000). The role of family dynamics in the development of eating disorders has also been examined, largely through clinical case reports. In classic conceptualizations, overcontrol or enmeshment is said to be prevalent in families of girls with anorexia, whereas parental undercontrol and conflict is more prevalent in families of girls with bulimia (Minuchin, 1974). However, results from empirical studies have demonstrated inconsistent evidence for this distinction (Archibald, Linver, Graber, & Brooks-Gunn, 2002). Some evidence for the role of culture, with its emphasis on narrowly defined standards of beauty and the "thin" ideal, has also been implicated in eating pathology in vulnerable individuals (Kaye et al., 2000).

Stice (2016) attempts to bring clarity to this somewhat confusing field by summarizing methodologically rigorous studies of EDs, all of which include baseline info that preceded the onset of disorders. In this way, emergence of disorders was distinguished from other confounding features, like maintenance of the disorder or other diagnoses. Table 9.6 summarizes this information.

Different etiologies are identified from which distinct patterns of disordered eating arise. Thus, an important consideration is the need to separate what contributes to the

TABLE 9.6 Risk Factors for Eating Disorders

EATING DISORDER TYPE	RISK FACTORS THAT *PREDICTED* ONSET OF DISORDER	RISK FACTORS THAT *DID NOT PREDICT* ONSET OF DISORDER
Anorexia Nervosa (or Subthreshold AN)	Premature birth, low birth weight, co-birth, instrument delivery, childhood eating conflicts, unpleasant mealtime experiences, low body mass index (BMI), perfectionism, and low dieting were all correlated with onset.	Internalization of the thin-ideal, body-dissatisfaction, cultural pressure for thinness or pre-disorder fasting were not correlated with onset.
Bulimia Nervosa (or Subthreshold BN)	Thin ideal internalization, dieting in adolescence, weight concerns, body dissatisfaction, negative affect, mental health care, early puberty, and lack of social support were predictive.	Perfectionism, maturity fears, interpersonal distrust, problematic family dynamics, childhood eating conflicts, digestive problems, and fear of loss of control over eating were not correlated.
Binge Eating Disorder	Same as BN	
Any Eating Disorder (Mixed) (Array of risk factors resembles binge eating and BN risks rather than AN possibly because BN and BED are higher incidence disorders.)	Body dissatisfaction, negative affect, internalization of the thin-ideal, dieting, and lack of family support were most consistent predictors.	Parental pressure for thinness, family dysfunction, emotional eating, lack of social support, and perfectionism.

beginnings of an eating disorder and what maintains it once it is present. Other questions involve untangling the many variables that contribute to onset and maintenance. For example, negative affect may present an indirect risk factor for eating pathology. When the capacity for emotion regulation is not up to the task of managing distress, one's perceptions of the world, oneself, and one's future can appear very bleak. Dissatisfaction spreads, and emotions become dysregulated. Pathological behaviors (e.g., binges) are more likely to occur in these circumstances. Dieting has also been demonstrated to promote binging through mechanisms of negative affect, which can arise from the physical and emotional stress of caloric deprivation. Other studies, however, find that dieting curbed impulses to overeat and actually restrained binging. It is possible that some unexplained individual difference contributes to these distinct trajectories.

The array of risk factors appears to operate similarly in predicting eating disorders in adolescent boys (Ricciardelli & McCabe, 2004), although variables implicated in the development of masculine body image, notably the influence of male peers and athletic participation, also need to be considered (Bardone-Cone, Cass, & Ford, 2008). A recent longitudinal study showed different trajectories for males and females who have bulimia. Although similar risk factors were operating for both groups (e.g., body dissatisfaction, alcohol use, anxiety, and depression), girls' risk of developing bulimia was greatest in mid-adolescence, whereas risk peaked for males in the early 20s (Abebe, Lien, & von Soest, 2012).

Prevention and Treatment Issues

A recent review of 91 published papers on treatments for EDs offer the following recommendations for clinical practice (Lock, 2015). Overall, family-based therapy with a behavioral focus (FBT, Lock & LeGrange, 2015) or Maudsley Family Therapy (Wallis, Alford, Hanson, Titterton, Madden, & Kohn, 2013) are the only well-established treatments for AN. Initially, these structured approaches focus on weight gain and recruit the adolescent and the family as nonjudgmental partners who work together to accomplish this goal. Gradually, control over eating is returned to the adolescent. Once satisfactory weight has been re-established, insight-oriented psychotherapy or therapy focused on family dynamics can be helpful, whereas general Cognitive Behavior Therapy (CBT) with a nonspecific focus on thoughts and feelings has not yet been sufficiently tested to draw conclusions for AN patients (Lock, 2015).

Both FBT and Cognitive-Behavior Therapy-Guided Self-Help (Barakat et al., 2017; Schmidt et al., 2007) are possibly efficacious for treatment of BN. Components of this CBT online program include self-monitoring activities using a food diary, regular eating using the three-hour rule (planning regular meals and snacks so that food deprivation does not exceed capacity to tolerate), and interactive online sessions designed to deliver classic CBT themes. Treatments for youth who have BED have not been sufficiently studied, even though the need is clear. CBT and Interpersonal

Therapy (IPT, Klerman et al., 1984, see Chapter 11) have some empirical support for adults, as does Dialectic Behavior Therapy (DBT) (Safer, Robinson, & Jo, 2010). For youth, IPT and DBT have preliminary support, but more research is needed.

ARFID differs from the diagnoses just mentioned because body dissatisfaction or weight concern is not present. Those who have this disorder are averse to new experiences, may be overly sensitive to tastes and textures, and may have phobias related to certain foods. No clear treatment options meeting standards of efficacy are available at present, so individual behavioral plans are recommended (Locke, 2015).

One promising approach to treatment of EDs lies in modifying their underlying cognitive characteristics. Inefficient neurocognitive functions such as cognitive inflexibility (inability to shift attention from one thing to another) and weak central coherence (absorption with details to the neglect of the "big picture") are present in individuals with EDs and may explain the obsessiveness and hyperfocus on food issues. Efforts to modify these cognitive deficits, especially with youth, may be a useful complement to existing treatments (Lock, 2015).

Stice and Shaw (2004) offer some empirically based guidelines for prevention programs based on meta-analysis of evidence from 15 available programs. One major finding was that universal prevention programs were not as effective as selective interventions in producing beneficial results and reducing remission. The authors speculate that programs targeted to those at-risk or already experiencing some symptoms may be more effective because participants are more motivated to seek help. Also, universal prevention, typically provided before problems arise, may be directed toward an age group lacking the cognitive skills necessary to benefit. Consequently, programs offered to adolescents who were 15 years old or older were more successful than those offered to younger participants. Programs provided exclusively for females were more effective than combined programs. Brief programs were more effective than longer programs, provided that they offered more than a single session. Program content was less critical, but the strongest results were obtained from those that targeted the risk factors mentioned above, for example, interventions to alter maladaptive attitudes towards thinness and negative affect.

Recently, interest in mindfulness and acceptance-based treatments (see Chapter 14), such as Mindfulness-Based Stress Reduction (MBSR; Kabat-Zinn, 1994), Mindfulness-Based Cognitive Therapy (MBCT; Segal, Williams, & Teasdale, 2002), Dialectical Behavior Therapy (DBT; Linehan, 1993), and Acceptance and Commitment Therapy (ACT; Hayes, Strosahl, & Wilson, 1999), have been adapted for various problem areas, including eating disorders (see Telch, Agras, & Linehan, 2001). All these approaches share an emphasis on the cultivation of nonjudgmental awareness of present experience in the service of developing emotion regulation skills or the "Wise Mind" (Linehan, 1993).

All have demonstrated effectiveness in reducing negative affect and may thus target a central causal factor in eating pathology.

Mindfulness-based Eating Awareness Therapy (MB-EAT; Kristeller & Hallett, 1999) is a group treatment designed for binge-eating disorder that utilizes elements of MBSR and MBCT. Guided eating-related meditations and mindful eating exercises are an integral part of the program. The tools offered by the program help participants develop greater awareness of satiety mechanisms and eating behaviors without the critical judgments that often surround food.

Mindful awareness, as is taught in the program, fosters self-acceptance and emotion regulation and helps reduce the need to use food for emotional nourishment. In a recent comparison with a psychoeducational/CBT intervention, MB-EAT was more effective in reducing binge eating and other clinical symptoms (Kristeller, Wolever, & Sheets, 2014). After four months, 95% of those in the mindfulness group improved and no longer met criteria for BED diagnosis compared to 76% of those in the CBT comparison. The benefits were related to the degree participants practiced mindfulness on a regular basis.

Summary

Physical Development

1. Puberty begins when the pituitary gland produces hormones that stimulate hormone production in the gonads. These and other circulating hormones promote the maturing of both primary and secondary sexual characteristics. The timing of puberty is affected by both genes and environmental factors such as nutrition and various stressors.

2. The adolescent growth spurt parallels puberty and includes large increases in height and weight. Different parts of the body grow at different times, such as the arms and legs before the torso. Gender differences in growth increase both internal and external sexual dimorphism.

3. Puberty's hormonal changes trigger and moderate developments in brain structure and function. Changes include decreases in gray matter volume (partly via pruning), especially in the prefrontal cortex, and increases in white matter due to myelination. Large changes in the production of neurotransmitters and the enzymes that metabolize them are also important.

4. Subcortical structures that comprise the "emotional brain" seem to mature at a more accelerated rate than the prefrontal cortex or the "rational brain." The circuitry that connects these structures may not mature fully until subcortical and cortical developments are more in alignment. The imbalance in brain maturation may underlie some characteristic teen behaviors, such as increases in sensation seeking.

5. The stress response and the HPA axis also mature in adolescence. Cortisol production increases, and the HPA axis becomes more responsive to stressors. Severe, chronic, or unpredictable stress can have especially negative effects for teens.

Behavioral and Emotional Changes

6. Adolescent sleep is affected by hormonal changes, causing delayed phase preference (later sleep onset and offset). This and early school start times, as well as other factors, can lead teens to get inadequate sleep, which can have negative effects on the rapidly reorganizing brain.

7. The many changes adolescents experience have effects on mood and emotion. In comparison to other age groups, teens show more mood disruptions, more negative mood, more emotional reactivity, and more difficulty suppressing responses to threats.

8. Exaggerated emotional responding combined with other risk factors puts teens at risk for diagnoses of serious mental disorders, such as first episodes of psychosis.

9. At adolescence, girls are more susceptible to depressed mood than boys are, apparently because of differences in stress and methods of coping with stress. Among the stressors girls experience more than boys are the devaluing of the female role; worries about appearance and weight; fewer expectations of success; the double standard regarding sexuality; the use of a cooperative discourse that makes them less influential in mixed-sex groups; and earlier puberty, which means that girls are more likely to be making school transitions and coping with the onset of puberty simultaneously. Unusually early pubertal onset increases the risk of depression further, as does early sexual debut. Girls are also more likely than boys to deal with stress using a ruminative coping style, which increases the risk of depression relative to the distracting style, which is more characteristic of boys.

10. Sexual activity and exploration, both with the opposite sex and with the same sex, increases at puberty. Sexual maturation is primarily responsible, but familial, social, and cultural factors are also important.

11. Sexual orientation becomes manifest in adolescence. Approximately 89% of teens identify as heterosexual. Sexual fluidity (shifts in sexual attraction between same and opposite sex) is more common in adolescents than in other age groups. There is no evidence that social causes (e.g., parenting practices) influence sexual orientation. Evidence does exist for nonsocial causes, such as genetic factors and prenatal hormone levels.

Cognitive Development

12. At Piaget's fourth stage in the development of logical thinking, 11- or 12-year-olds begin to be able to think logically about abstract contents, discovering relationships among relationships. Formal thought is difficult even for adults and is easier to apply in domains of knowledge with which we have some expertise.

13. Information processing skills, such as executive functions, continue to improve in adolescence, linked especially to maturation of the prefrontal cortex. These skills are closely tied to improvements in reasoning ability.

14. When a formal operational thinker approaches scientific problems, she generates and considers every possible solution, then tests each one. The pattern of results among all the tests determines the conclusions. Generating and evaluating possibilities is a hallmark of formal operational thought.

15. With formal operations comes the ability to construct ideals, such as ideal political systems or ideal people. Young adolescents do not understand, however, that the real always falls short of the ideal. This failure to understand the limits of ideas is a form of adolescent egocentrism, and it contributes to a critical attitude toward anything that is less than perfect, including the self.

16. Other aspects of adolescent egocentrism are derived from a distorting inward focus, which is partially a function of an improved capacity to think about one's own thinking. Self-focus may be a function of other factors as well, such as the need to form an adult identity. The imaginary audience and personal fable of adolescents are thought to be results.

Identity Development

17. Erikson's notion of an adolescent identity crisis is better characterized as a search for answers to questions such as "What do I want to make of myself, and what do I have to work with?" Identity attainment does not imply that no further change occurs; identity is always to some degree in revision. Identity is also a product of the cultural contexts that shape development.

18. Marcia describes two processes, exploration and commitment, that result in four possible identity status categories. Diffusion characterizes adolescents who lack both exploration and commitment. Moratorium describes adolescents who are actively exploring but have made no commitments. Adolescents in foreclosure have not experienced exploration but have made commitments. Achievement comprises individuals whose development has involved exploration and has reached commitment. Each identity status is associated with certain personal and cognitive characteristics.

19. Assessment of identity status can involve a semi-structured interview procedure in which status within several domains is assessed. For example, Marcia's original Ego Identity Interview assessed status in vocational choice, religious beliefs, and political ideology. Questionnaires are typically designed to determine the degree to which adolescents are either exploring a domain or have already made commitments. And narrative methods ask participants to tell stories about their lives so that the content of their identity formation process can be probed.

20. A number of personal and behavioral characteristics are associated with identity statuses. For example, persons in moratorium are more anxious than those in other statuses.

21. There is no fixed sequence of identity statuses, but longitudinal research has found some developmental trends. The number of achievements increases over time, foreclosures decrease, and diffusions decrease or remain the same. The number of moratoriums does not increase or decrease.

22. Research on gender differences in identity formation has produced inconsistent results: Some studies find gender differences; some do not. When differences are found, women, as a group, are more likely to assign interpersonal, communal aspects of themselves a higher priority.

23. Ethnicity or race is not a salient feature of self-concept as children enter adolescence. At that time, for teens in minority and marginalized groups, this aspect of identity begins to take on greater importance, sometimes triggered by experiences of discrimination. Studies of many groups indicate that ethnic/racial identity (ERI) development follows a course comparable to that of other identity domains. Strong ERI tends to be a protective factor, supporting well-being even when discrimination is experienced. Parent socialization practices often encourage strong ERI in minority youth.

Case Study

Dean is a White 16-year-old. He is a sophomore at George Washington Carver High School. He lives with his father and his stepmother in a semirural community in the South. His father and mother divorced when Dean was 8 years old, and both parents remarried shortly after the breakup. Dean's mother moved to another state, and, although she calls him from time to time, the two have little contact. Dean gets along well with his father and stepmother. He is also a good "older brother" to his 5-year-old stepbrother, Jesse.

Dean's father owns and operates an auto-repair shop in town. His wife works part time, managing the accounts for the business. She is also an active contributor to many community projects in her neighborhood. She regularly works as a parent volunteer in the elementary school library and is a member of her church's executive council. Both parents try hard to make a good life for their children.

Dean has always been a somewhat lackluster student. His grades fell precipitously during third grade, when his parents divorced. However, things stabilized for Dean over the next few years, and he has been able to maintain a C average. Neither Dean nor his father take his less-than-stellar grades too seriously. In middle school, his father encouraged him to try out for football. He played for a few seasons but dropped out in high school. Dean has a few close friends who like him for his easygoing nature and his sense of humor. Dean's father has told him many times that he can work in the family business after graduation. At his father's urging, Dean is pursuing a course of study in automobile repair at the regional vo-tech school.

Now in his sophomore year, Dean's circle of friends includes mostly other vo-tech students. He doesn't see many of his former friends, who are taking college preparatory courses. Kids in his class are beginning to drive, enabling them to go to places on weekends that had formerly been off-limits. He knows many kids who are having sex and drinking at parties. He has been friendly with several girls over the years, but these relationships have been casual and platonic. Dean wishes he would meet someone with whom he could talk about his feelings and share his thoughts.

Although he is already quite accustomed to the lewd conversations and sexual jokes that circulate around the locker room, he participates only halfheartedly in the banter. He has listened for years to friends who brag about their sexual exploits. He wonders with increasing frequency why he is not attracted to the same things that seem so important to his friends. The thought that he might be gay has crossed his mind, largely because of the scathing comments made by his peers about boys who show no interest in girls. This terrifies him, and he usually manages to distract himself by reasoning that he will develop sexual feeling "when the right girl comes along."

As time passes, however, he becomes more and more morose. His attention is diverted even more from his classwork. He finds it more difficult to be around the kids at school. Dean starts to drink heavily and is arrested for driving under the influence of alcohol. He is sentenced to a 6-week drug education program and is assigned community service. His parents are disappointed in him because of this incident, but they believe he has learned his lesson and will not repeat his mistake. Dean's father believes that his son will be fine as soon as he finds a girlfriend to "turn him around."

Discussion Questions

1. What are the issues facing Dean at this point in his development?
2. Enumerate the risks and the protective factors that are present in his life.
3. How would you, as his counselor, assess Dean's situation? What approaches could you take with this adolescent? What kinds of psycho-educational interventions might you consider within the school setting?

Practice Using What You Have Learned

MyLab Education Application Exercise 9.1:
Cognitive Development: Formal Operational Thought

MyLab Education Application Exercise 9.2:
Identity Development

MyLab Education Application Exercise 9.3:
Case Study: Helping Sexual Minority Youth

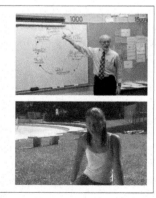

Journal Questions

1. Recount an example of the imaginary audience or the personal fable from your own adolescence. How can this knowledge help you in counseling young people?
2. Were you an early, an on-time, or a late-maturing adolescent? What impact did your physical development have on your adjustment and your peer group relationships?
3. Remember back to the time when you were 18 or 19. Using Marcia's identity categories, assess your own status in the following domains: relationships, career, religious or political ideology, ethnicity, and sexual orientation.
4. Reflect on the development of your cultural identity. How has this aspect of your self-system influenced your life?
5. Can you remember a life circumstance or event when you felt that you were the victim of discrimination? How did you feel during this time? Write what you remember about your thoughts and feelings during this experience. How might this help you relate to other marginalized individuals?

Key Concepts

puberty (p. 342)
kisspeptin (p. 342)
gonadotropin releasing hormone (GnRH) (p. 343)
follicle-stimulating hormone (FSH) (p. 343)
luteinizing hormone (LH) (p. 343)
gonads (p. 343)
testes (p. 343)
ovaries (p. 343)
androgens (p. 343)
testosterone (p. 343)
estrogen (p. 343)
progesterone (p. 343)
primary sexual characteristics (p. 343)
secondary sexual characteristics (p. 343)
menarche (p. 343)
spermarche (p. 343)
leptin (p. 344)
adolescent growth spurt (p. 345)
sexual dimorphism (p. 345)

sensation seeking (p. 347)
delayed phase preference (p. 348)
experience sampling method (p. 350)
depressed mood (p. 351)
mitigation (p. 352)
diminished capacity (p. 352)
compelling circumstances (p. 352)
uncharacteristic behavior (p. 352)
body image (p. 354)
double standard (p. 354)
sexual debut (p. 354)
rumination (p. 355)
distraction (p. 355)
adrenarche (p. 355)
sexually transmitted disease (STD) (p. 356)
coitus (p. 356)
sexual orientation (p. 357)
heterosexuality (p. 357)
homosexuality (p. 357)
bisexuality (p. 357)

nonheterosexual (p. 357)
sexual fluidity (p. 357)
formal operational thought (p. 360)
ideals (p. 363)
imaginary audience (p. 364)
personal fable (p. 364)
invincibility fable (p. 364)
ego identity (p. 366)
exploration (p. 366)
commitment (p. 366)
identity achievement (p. 367)
identity diffusion (p. 367)
foreclosure (p. 367)
moratorium (p. 367)
constructed identity (p. 368)
Ego Identity Interview (p. 368)
narrative identity (p. 369)
ethnic/racial identity (ERI) (p. 372)
ethnic/racial socialization practices (p. 374)

Chapter 10
The Social World of Adolescence

Learning Objectives

After reading this chapter, you should be able to:

10.1 Explain the instability of adolescent autonomy and the shift from parent to peer dependency.

10.2 Describe the structure and characteristics of peer relationships in adolescence and explain how they shape social identity.

10.3 Describe adolescent views of parental authority and discuss common sources of parent–adolescent conflict as well as the positive and negative effects of various parental approaches.

10.4 Identify elements of schooling that support adolescents' developmental needs and promote academic success across ethnic/racial groups.

10.5 Discuss research-based evidence of positive and negative effects of extracurricular activities, jobs, and media consumption on adolescent behavior and attitudes and suggest guidelines that reduce risks and promote beneficial outcomes.

10.6 Analyze various views of risky adolescent behavior including adolescent reasoning and adult concerns and suggest appropriate patterns of parenting and intervening in the context of managing risks.

10.7 Weigh contrasting views of adolescent problem behavior including attitudes about adolescent self-sufficiency and adult/societal responsibility.

Sixteen-year old Ashley is having a hard time falling asleep again. Her phone beeps incessantly with new text messages, which she reads immediately. After coming home from school, she checked Instagram and discovered a photo of her new boyfriend partying with girls in the grade above hers. This upset her so much that she couldn't finish her homework and got into another argument with her mother about cleaning her room. Ashley thinks her mom wouldn't understand and that sharing this embarrassing discovery with her would only start another disagreement. A week ago, her mother overheard Ashley talking with a friend about obtaining birth control, and that sparked a real battle. She hasn't told her parents about her new boyfriend because she fears it will create a lot more drama in her life, which she really doesn't need right now.

Instead, she has been texting her friends most of the night and has gotten their advice. Her close friends have agreed to go with Ashley to confront the older girls about the humiliating photo. She'll tell her mother she's going to the library to study and can't be home for dinner. She's a little worried about the social studies presentation scheduled for the next day, because she hasn't had time to prepare. But right now, she can't concentrate on anything else.

The search for identity is considered the primary developmental task of the adolescent period. In this chapter, you will find that the outcome of an adolescent's search is very much affected by the social world. Peers play a critical role, and so do parents, schools, neighborhoods, technology, and the larger culture. All are influenced by the social, political, economic, and historical context in which the adolescent's identity is formed. Despite the power of macrosystem influences, much of the day-to-day action affecting adolescent social development occurs within the peer context. Although benefits to autonomy accrue from increased social exposure, certain kinds of peer-related experiences, like being rejected or being exposed to deviant behavior, have been associated with both internalizing and externalizing problems (Lansford, Dodge, Fontaine, Bates, & Pettit, 2014). Parents and families are an especially powerful influence, although the changes that occur over the adolescent period shift relationships with parents to ones that are characterized by greater mutuality than in earlier stages of development. Increasing needs for autonomy result in less disclosure to parents, especially about personal information. Parents, like Ashley's, may have no idea about some of the concerns their children face in school and in other social settings. Despite this, the importance of family relationships for adolescents remains constant. Just how these relational shifts play out, what benefits they offer to adolescents, and what potential pitfalls they present will be discussed in the following sections.

Adolescent Autonomy and Social Identity

10.1 Explain the instability of adolescent autonomy and the shift from parent to peer dependency.

Theorists have long argued that one's identity develops within the context of interpersonal interactions (Cooley, 1902; Mead, 1934), and peers are particularly important in the construction of identity at adolescence (Erikson, 1968). To understand fully the function of peers, let's look again at what happens when a child enters adolescence. The body changes in appearance; adult sexual needs emerge; hormonal shifts may heighten irritability; the capacity to reflect on the future and on the self expands, bringing its own brand of egocentrism; and demands for autonomy increase. All of these changes are supported by dramatic alterations in the adolescent brain. These profound shifts can produce a state of instability and anxiety unique to adolescence:

> The adolescent is at sea. Previous boundaries and guideposts are no longer functional. In earlier developmental periods, expansion and growth exist within a context of familiar motion and exercise. The adolescent condition is different, however. The adolescent is possessed of new physical and intellectual capabilities that are both mystical and mystifying. . . . The allure of the adult world calls, and is strong, even as the safety of childhood is close and still beckons. Yet neither fits; the one is outgrown, the other not yet encompassable." (Seltzer, 1982, p. 59)

The adolescent's passage to adulthood is in some ways parallel to the infant's passage to childhood status. To exercise their developing skills and to explore the beckoning world, infants must give up the security of the caregiver's continual presence and care. Most attachment theorists believe that toddlers manage the stress of this separation by referring to their working model of the other, a kind of mental representation of the caregiver, which provides feelings of security and makes independent exploration possible. For adolescents, the task of establishing adult independence requires

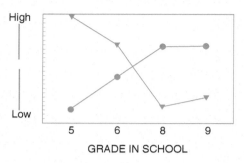

FIGURE 10.1 Parents, peers, and adolescent feelings of autonomy.

Autonomy from peers ▲

Autonomy from parents ●

SOURCE: Based on Steinberg, L. & Silverberg, S. B. (1986). The vicissitudes of autonomy in early adolescence. *Child Development, 57*, 847. Reproduced with permission of Blackwell Publishing Ltd.

separating from caregivers on a new plane, a process traditionally called the "second" individuation (Blos, 1975).

In a classic study, Steinberg and Silverberg (1986) asked 10- to 16-year-olds in the United States questions about their relationships with parents and age-mates. As most studies have found, children between fifth and eighth grades showed a marked increase in agreement on items assessing emotional autonomy from parents, such as "There are some things about me that my parents don't know" and "There are things that I would do differently from my mother and father when I become a parent." When the students in this study were asked "What would you *really* do?" if a friend suggested either some antisocial act such as cheating or some neutral act such as joining a club, they showed a marked decrease between the fifth and eighth grades in their ability to resist peer influence, as you can see in Figure 10.1. Studies indicate that increasing susceptibility to peer influence is greatest for antisocial or risky behaviors, and more likely for boys than for girls (Sim & Koh, 2003). Resistance to peer influence begins to rise in middle adolescence, increasing most between 14 and 18 years, with continuing, shallower gains in young adulthood (Steinberg & Monahan, 2007). Overall, it appears that between the ages of 11 and 14 children transfer at least some of their emotional dependency from their parents to their peers.

The Peer Arena

Why do peers become so important? Adolescents spend much more of their time with peers, so proximity is an important factor. Peers are of similar chronological age and educational status and may share similar feelings of aloneness and loss of past certainties. Social psychologists established long ago that people under stress tend to affiliate with others perceived as having similar experiences (Schacter, 1959); so adolescents' shared sense of instability makes the peer group a likely target of affiliation. The sometimes difficult movement toward identity can, at least in part, be shared.

Peers are thus a source of support and a reflection of the adolescent's own concerns. Teens compare themselves to others and develop themselves through modeling other's behaviors, appearance, and attitudes (Seltzer, 1982). A formerly quiet boy might imitate the wisecracking style of a friend, a girl may explore the mysteries of the occult espoused by a classmate, or a mediocre student might work for hours on a special project, mimicking the approach of a more successful peer. In early adolescence, the imitation is rapid, intense, and undifferentiated, but toward later adolescence, some features actually become more stable and will form the foundation of the young adult's identity. These reasons underscore the importance of the adolescent social network, within which adolescents co-construct their identity.

MyLab Education Self-Check 10.1.

The Structure of the Peer Network

10.2 Describe the structure and characteristics of peer relationships in adolescence and explain how they shape social identity.

By early adolescence, a typical youngster is part of a nested set of peer relationships that seem to form concentric circles. He spends most of his time with a few close friends, the innermost circle. In the case that opens this chapter, these are the friends who will accompany Ashley to confront the girls who flirted with her boyfriend. A larger clique of about 6 to 10 members forms a less intimate second circle, composed of friends who eat lunch or go to class together. The clique's boundaries are somewhat permeable, and the membership may fluctuate. Finally, the much larger third circle is the adolescent's crowd. What crowd members share is not necessarily friendship, but instead similar interests, attitudes, behaviors, and appearance. Brown (1990) defined adolescent crowds as large "reputation-based collectives of similarly stereotyped individuals who may or may not spend much time together" (p. 177).

Crowds reflect the individual's social status. And, they "demarcate different values and lifestyles that can form the core of an individual's identity" (Brown, Herman, Hamm, & Heck, 2008, p. 530). Many studies suggest that association with a crowd can be linked to youngsters' healthy or unhealthy eating, drug and alcohol use, sexual behavior, academic commitment, achievement, and even the types of psychiatric symptoms they display (Moran, Walker, Alexander, Jordan, & Wagner, 2017).

A classic example of the impact of crowds on adolescent behavior was provided by Steinberg and his associates (Lamborn, Mounts, Steinberg, & Dornbusch, 1991; Mounts & Steinberg, 1995; Steinberg, 1996; Steinberg, Fegley, & Dornbusch, 1993; Steinberg, Lamborn, Darling, Mounts, & Dornbusch, 1994; Steinberg, Lamborn, Dornbusch, & Darling, 1992). More than 20,000 adolescents and their families from nine public high schools in Wisconsin and northern California were studied. Students came from ethnically and socioeconomically diverse communities (more than 40% were ethnic minorities) and from a variety of family structures (intact, divorced, and remarried). Student data were collected over a 3-year period from 9th through 12th grades. Teens answered questions about their emotional adjustment, academic achievement, and behavior, as well as the parenting practices of their families and their peer associations.

Steinberg and his colleagues found a characteristic crowd structure that many other large-scale studies of U.S. teens have confirmed (Barber, Eccles, & Stone, 2001; Brown et al., 2008). Roughly 20% of students belonged to popularity-conscious crowds ("populars" and "jocks"), who were moderately achievement oriented and might engage in some illicit behavior, such as drug use. About 20% belonged to "alienated" crowds ("druggies" or "burnouts"), who were even less invested in academic success and who might be involved in heavy drug use and delinquent behavior. "Average" crowds, comprising about 30% of students, were not openly hostile to academics but, like the populars, were only moderately concerned about grades. In majority White high schools, some crowds were defined primarily by ethnicity (roughly 10% to 15% depending on the school), and academic achievement differences existed among these ethnically defined crowds. Less than 5% of high schoolers belonged to crowds characterized by high academic achievement. These students were unlikely to use drugs and were more likely to form strong ties with teachers. Membership in the largest, most appealing, and preferred crowds (populars, jocks, and average) was related to more modest academic achievement. Most students in these crowds, representing about 50% of high schoolers, earned Bs on average.

Distinct crowd structures also exist in other cultures. Researchers in Denmark, for example, found four major crowd categories: Alternative, Urban, Conventional, and Achievement-Oriented (Delsing, ter Bogt, Engels, & Meeus, 2007). Alternative crowds ("punks," "metal heads," "goths") tended to display more nonconformist, rebellious behavior than more conventional crowds. The Urban crowd was characterized by an orientation to musical and cultural activities typically found in urban areas ("hip-hop," "rasta"). The Conventional crowd was made up of "normals," rural, and religious youth. The Achievement-oriented crowd ("posh," "brains") was oriented toward academic and financial success. Affiliation with the two nonconventional crowds (Alternative and Urban) was associated with higher rates of delinquency, aggression, and depression.

In Singapore, where the cultural rules for dress and behavior are stricter and where a relatively strong norm for conformity exists, adolescents also identify with different crowds. Sim and Yeo (2012) identified seven primary crowd orientations from a large number of suggestions obtained from open-ended questions ("Nerd," "Gangster," "Athlete," "Computer Geek," "Joker," "Ordinary," and "Loner"). "Gangsters" were generally rebellious in the ways they dressed, were rude toward others, and were disinterested in academics. You may suspect some overlap between these crowds and those seen in U.S. schools, notably with jocks, brains, delinquents, and nerds. While groups in both cultures show a similar distinction between conventional and unconventional, there are also notable differences. Because of the cultural value

MyLab Education
Video Example 10.1
Adolescents spend most of their time with their inner circle of friends but are aware of the cliques in their schools. Whether by choice or by default, most teens also associate with a larger group—a clique with whom they have much in common.

placed on academic achievement and filial piety, "nerds" in Singapore were primarily identified with academic achievement rather than social awkwardness, and thus were viewed much more positively. Although socializing and "partying" are common features of the "popular" crowd in the United States, a comparable "popular" group did not emerge in Singapore. The authors suggest that this is due to the relative absence of these types of activities among Singaporean youth. "Nerds" and "gangsters" were the largest and most commonly identifiable crowds. "Athletes" came in a distant third, a much less recognizable group compared to those in U.S. schools. Although the sample in this study did not represent the whole of Singapore, findings are interesting in light of how cultural values and practices shape adolescent behavior and identify formation.

Interest in how crowd affiliation affects adjustment has currently extended to students in the post–high-school years. Hopmeyer and Medovey (2017) identified four groups (athletic, social, scholastic, and countercultural) among their college sample. Athletic crowd members ("jocks") were oriented towards sports and fitness activities. Social crowd members ("partiers") were attracted to the parts of campus life that involved entertainment and recreation. Scholastic members ("academics," "ethnics") identified with scholarly and political pursuits, while the countercultural group ("stoners," "slackers") showed more deviant patterns of behavior. Social adjustment was assessed to be higher among scholastic and athletic groups, whereas more loneliness was reported in the countercultural group. Crowd affiliation was also related to achievement (Hopmeyer, Troop-Gordon, Medovoy, & Fischer, 2017). Scholastic crowd members showed higher levels of achievement and belongingness. Social crowd affiliation was related to belongingness but also to engagement in risky behaviors. In contrast to high school samples, athletic affiliation was not related to achievement and showed little relationship to risky behavior. Most disadvantaged were countercultural members who showed the greatest levels of social isolation and the most substance misuse.

While any taxonomy applied to crowds is appealing, some suggest this approach may be oversimplified. Cross and Fletcher (2009) have pointed out that definitions of crowds are fuzzy, and pathways to crowd affiliation are unclear. Does the adolescent himself select his crowd, or is it assigned to him by the peer group? Steinberg (1996) suggests three determining factors: children's personalities and interests as they enter adolescence, the types of crowds available, and the ways that parents attempt to manage their children's peer relationships. Research findings also show that adolescents operate according to the principles of group dynamics that govern any social group— namely, they often choose to participate in shared norms, roles, and expectations, a process called **peer selection** (Cohen & Prinstein, 2006). They are influenced by peers, and sometimes that **peer influence** is related to negative control tactics by their peers, such as teasing and threats of rejection. Under the powerful influence of peers, teens may willingly engage in peer-sanctioned behavior. Research has shown that deviant peers mutually influence each other (Gifford-Smith, Dodge, Dishion, & McCord, 2005), a process called **deviancy training**.

Some students are hard to classify into the crowd structure. Some may fit into more than one crowd, and some students change crowd affiliations over time. The study of **social identity complexity** (Roccas & Brewer, 2002), which is a measure of overlapping alignment with more than one peer crowd or network, shares some similarities with identity development theories covered in previous chapters. Many young people identify with multiple groups. For example, the 10th grade honor roll student and standout football player of Latino origin may consider himself a jock, a nerd, and also a member of a minority group. The nature of this young person's experience, possibly due to the composition of his school and neighborhood, makes it more likely that he sees himself as having multiple, somewhat fluid, affiliations (Miller, Brewer, & Arbuckle, 2009). Students with higher social identity complexity (multiple affiliations) showed less in-group/out-group bias, more positive relationships with out-groups, and greater personal well-being (Knifsend & Juvonen, 2014). Here it appears that the composition and the social structure of the school are quite important, either amplifying or constraining opportunities to develop cross-group friendships. Diverse, multiethnic schools can be beneficial to youth in advancing the complexity of their social identities, reducing bias, and fostering positive intergroup attitudes.

MyLab Education
Video Example 10.2
By early adolescence, a typical youngster is part of a nested set of peer relationships. Notice the structure of the peer network described by the adolescent in this video.

MyLab Education Self-Check 10.2.

The Role of Parents

10.3 Describe adolescent views of parental authority and discuss common sources of parent–adolescent conflict as well as the positive and negative effects of various parental approaches.

Adolescents rework their views of their parents, deidealize them, and loosen, somewhat, their emotional dependency (Steinberg & Belsky, 1991; Steinberg & Monahan, 2007). Figure 10.2 illustrates the typical decline between the ages of 11 and 17 of adolescents' willingness to acknowledge the legitimacy of their parents' claims to authority or to endorse the notion that they (the children) are obligated to follow parental dictates. These data are from a large sample of Chilean youth, but young people in many countries, including the United States, show similar patterns of decline, with the steepest drop coming in early adolescence (Darling, Cumsille, & Martinez, 2008). Thus, it appears that in early adolescence the mental representation or concept of the parent becomes more peripheral to the child's self-system. However, a teenager's increasing individuation and sense of autonomy does not come without a price. As adolescents experience a loss in feelings of security, their sense of uncertainty can increase.

Psychological separation from parents does not mean cutting ties in some dramatic fashion, even though stereotypes about adolescence might imply this. We know that emotional attachments persist across the life span, and there is more than one pathway through the adolescent period. Cultural assumptions of interdependence and virtues such as filial piety can help shape alternative narratives of adolescence with respect to parent–child relationships. While the movement towards separation and independence becomes stronger over the course of early adolescence in many countries, the same is not completely true for adolescents in China. For example, U.S. adolescents report more conflicts, less emotional closeness, and a reduced sense of obligation to parents compared to their Chinese counterparts (Pomerantz, Qin, Wang, & Chen, 2009). Filial piety, which involves the sense of repaying and honoring parents for their role in child rearing, appears to influence the developmental course of Chinese early adolescents substantially. Pomerantz and her colleagues (2011) found that Chinese adolescents' sense of obligation to parents increased over 7th and 8th grades compared to a declining pattern among U.S. youth (see Figure 10.3). The trend toward increasing levels of obligation to parents was associated with better grades, greater mastery of learning, and improved self-regulation.

MyLab Education
Video Example 10.3
Camila, at age 16, states that friends say she and her mother seem like "best friends," but she then goes on to describe a variety of disagreements that she has with her parents. How does she try to exert her independence, and how do her parents respond?

FIGURE 10.2 Adolescents' likelihood of endorsing parental legitimacy and their own obligation to obey, by age.

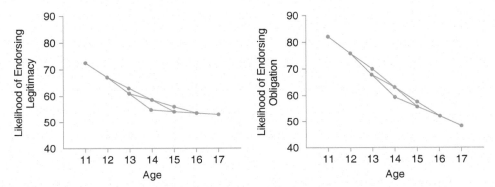

SOURCE: Darling, N., Cumsille, P., & Martinez, M. L. (2008). Individual differences in adolescents' beliefs about the legitimacy of parent authority and their own obligation to obey: A longitudinal investigation. *Child Development, 79*, 1103–1118. Reproduced with permission of Blackwell Publishing Ltd.

FIGURE 10.3 Obligation to parents across two cultures.

U.S. and Chinese adolescents show differences in their academic motivation as a function of their intention to please parents.

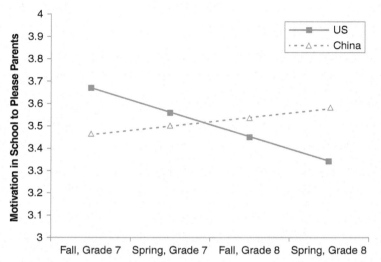

SOURCE: Pomerantz, E. M., Qin, L., Wang, Q., & Chen, H. (2011). Changes in early adolescents' sense of responsibility to their parents in the United States and China: Implications for academic functioning. *Child Development, 82,* 1136–1151. Reproduced with permission of Blackwell Publishing Ltd.

It is important to note, however, that Confucian cultural values, such as filial piety, did not necessarily imply parental dominance. Some contemporary Chinese parents also encourage adolescents' personal autonomy and decision making, which they perceive as a way to prepare youth for success in a rapidly globalizing world (Wang, 2014). And even in more individualistic cultures, becoming independent and personally responsible is not necessarily accompanied by emotional detachment from parents (Collins & Laursen, 2004; Offer, 1969).

Because I'm the Parent, That's Why . . .

Although not necessarily intense, conflict with parents is a very common feature, especially in early adolescence. Some research shows that frequency of conflicts peaks in early adolescence but the intensity of conflict increases into middle adolescence across many cultures (Smetana, 2015). Much of it centers on dissimilar perspectives about who can or should control behavior. What are the different ways that parents and their teenage children perceive authority? This topic applies to the work of helping professionals, who often negotiate family conflicts, and has, fortunately, been the subject of much research attention (Darling, Cumsille, & Martinez, 2007; Darling et al., 2008; Smetana, 2006). As reasoning, social cognition, and the press for autonomy increase, adolescents perceive authority to be more or less legitimate depending upon the nature of its domain and who gives the advice. As we introduced in earlier chapters, both moral and social conventional domains concern behavior that has consequences for self and others. Parental authority in the *moral* domain, concerned with issues of right and wrong (e.g., stealing and cheating), is generally viewed by adolescents across cultures as quite legitimate. The *social-conventional* domain, or what is deemed appropriate in certain circumstances, varies by culture and may be considered less consequential. Standards of neatness or table manners fall into this category. Parents often report conflicts in this area because violations of social-conventional norms add to family workload (like not taking out the trash) or potentially embarrass them (like styles of dress). The *personal* domain involves issues perceived to affect only the self, and they are more likely to be contested by adolescents when they come into conflict with parents. Some personal issues may not involve potentially harmful effects (like hair style or certain clothing preferences). However, one class of personal issues, called *prudential* issues, can involve safety and health concerns (like drinking and smoking).

Smetana and her colleagues (Smetana et al., 2009) call some issues *multifaceted* because they involve personal choice as well as potentially risky consequences. Ashley's choice of boyfriend is an example. Whom one chooses as a friend would seem to be a personal decision, but the possibility of risky sexual behavior moves the needle into the prudential range. The fact that Ashley asks for friends' advice suggests that she sees her choice of action as primarily personal in nature. In some studies, romantic relationships have been studied as a separate class of multifaceted issues, given their salience in adolescence (Smetana & Rote, 2015).

Adolescents report conflicts about autonomy in personal issues, or control over their own body, personal preferences, and privacy. For teens, gaining control over this personal domain is a way of establishing autonomy and therefore is an important identity issue (Smetana, Crean, & Campione-Barr, 2005). Parents tend to believe that they, as parents, have more authority over teen behaviors than their children do (Smetana, 2011). Parents may feel they *should* have this level of control because of their responsibility for children's well-being. It is in the highly charged area of multifaceted concerns, where adolescent personal and parental prudential concerns collide, that most disagreement occurs (Smetana et al., 2006).

There are some normative patterns in adolescent behavior that confirm teens' typical strategies for handling conflict with parents. Research has consistently found that teens become more secretive as they get older (Cumsille, Darling, & Martinez, 2010) and that parents become less knowledgeable about their children's lives (Masche, 2010). Adolescents report a number of strategies to deal with information they consider personal or subject to parental disapproval: sharing information only if asked, omitting details, avoiding the conversation, and lying (Bakken & Brown, 2010).

Similarly, adolescents have a number of reasons to justify these information management strategies. They don't want to disappoint or worry their parents, they don't want to be restricted, or they just don't think their parents have the right to know (Smetana, 2008). Adolescents learn to discriminate between those aspects of peer relationships they want to share and those they wish to keep to themselves. Studies show that they are most likely to disclose information about activities with peers but less likely to disclose details about the quality of these relationships (Chan, Brown, & Von Bank, 2015). Youth protect relationship details and negative information about their peers because of loyalty to them as well as to avoid the risk of parents' curtailing their access. Adolescents use their more advanced moral reasoning ability to differentiate among goals when making decisions about what or what not to disclose. Most parents, however, overestimate how much information their children actually do share with them (Smetana, 2008).

With increasing age, adolescents perceive more and more aspects of peer relationships to fall within the personal domain, thus not requiring parental oversight. Youth in highly individualistic cultures like the United States may have more areas that they believe to be personal than do youth in other cultures. However, it is the norm for teens across the world to view important aspects of their lives as something they have a right to manage independently (Ahmad, Smetana, & Klimstra, 2015). A small cross-cultural study investigated information management in African American and Hmong low-income samples (Bakken & Brown, 2010). Unlike the African American families in this study, the Hmong families were recent immigrants/refugees to the United States who faced language and cultural barriers. The African American parents had a long history in the United States and were more knowledgeable about cultural norms. Hmong adolescents perceived their parents to be more restrictive and less able to help them with some of the challenges they faced. Understandably, Hmong parents wanted to protect and preserve the values of their culture, but frustrations and difficulties of life in a new country affected both parents' and adolescents' experience. Hmong adolescents justified withholding information from parents on pragmatic grounds (e.g., because they wouldn't understand) and also because they wanted to maintain good relationships with their parents. Hmong adolescents didn't want to worry parents by disclosing some aspects of teenage life in the United States. Younger African American adolescents believed that their parents had the resources to find out whether they were telling them the truth. Compared to older African American adolescents, younger adolescents engaged in more disclosure. African American parents believed that they needed to balance their children's growing need for autonomy with their parental inclination to protect them from experiences of racial discrimination. Although African American youth could understand parental protectiveness, they were secretive about some things to preserve their own growing autonomy. Both universal aspects of adolescent autonomy-seeking and culturally specific rationales for information management were noted in this study. Even though the authors conclude that lying to parents is typically not a good idea, "more careful work is revealing that adolescents are both thoughtful and strategic in deciding what information about peers to share with parents. Often, they consider not only the quality of the parent–child relationship and the best interests of their parents but also their obligation to maintain confidence of peers" (Brown & Bakken, 2011, p. 155).

Raising Adolescents

Let's revisit the case of Ashley's unsuspecting parents. Without knowing about her boyfriend or that upsetting photo, they will probably allow her to go to the library to study. This raises an issue that strikes fear into the heart of every parent of an adolescent: *What is my child not telling me? How can I control what I don't know?* This common dilemma raises questions about the determinants of effective parenting in adolescence, when parent–child relationships are changing and new rules are in order.

For years, conventional wisdom has advised parents to monitor adolescents' behavior in order to ensure less deviance during a potentially difficult developmental transition. Originally, parental monitoring was conceptualized as parental behaviors that track a child's whereabouts, friendships, and activities so as to offer guidance when needed (Dishion & McMahon, 1998). Studies done over the last half of the 20th century that investigated the antecedents of deviant behavior showed that parental monitoring was related to lower rates of delinquency and other problematic behaviors (Loeber & Stouthamer-Loeber, 1986). Helping professionals came to believe that parental monitoring was an important protective factor and routinely advocated for this practice. But what does monitoring mean? What does it mean in Ashley's situation? Parents frequently question adolescents directly about their lives and activities, a process called parental solicitation by researchers. Monitoring and solicitation techniques might be easy when adolescents are open and chatty about their lives. In other circumstances, monitoring might conjure up images of detective work, involving close supervision, interrogation about peers, and an intense and exhausting parent-driven process. It seems reasonable to clarify what value monitoring offers by parsing its components to take a more fine-grained look at this construct. In their important contribution to this area of research, Kerr and Stattin (2000; Stattin & Kerr, 2000) revealed that it was parental knowledge (knowing what is going on in the child's life), not monitoring/solicitation per se, that was associated with healthy outcomes for teens. Table 10.1 shows each dimension as assessed in research with parents and youth.

Longitudinal work that separated parental monitoring from parental knowledge was done to explore connections among monitoring, knowledge, and later delinquency

TABLE 10.1 Parental Monitoring Unpacked

	PARENTAL CONTROL	PARENTAL KNOWLEDGE	PARENTAL SOLICITATION	YOUTH DISCLOSURE
Parents	If your child comes home late, do you require him or her to explain what he/she did and whom he/she was with?	Do you usually know when your child has an exam or paper due at school?	How often did you start a conversation with your child about what they do in their free time?	Does your child usually tell you about school when he/she gets home?
Youth	If you come home late, do your parents require you to explain what you did and whom you were with?	Do your parents usually know when you have an exam or paper due at school?	How often did your parents start a conversation with you about what you do in your free time?	Do you usually tell your parents about school when you get home?

SOURCE: Adapted from Margaret Kerr, A Reinterpretation of Parental Monitoring in Longitudinal Perspective, *Journal of Research on Adolescence, 20*(1), 39–64.

(Kerr, Stattin, & Burk, 2010). Results corroborated what other cross-sectional studies had observed. Greater disclosure by youth increased parental knowledge, which was associated with less delinquency. Parental control, sometimes referred to as active parental monitoring and solicitation, did not elicit youth disclosure, and in some cases, reduced it substantially. Active parental monitoring, despite its good intentions, did not affect delinquency outcomes.

Research with African American youth has reported some beneficial effects of parental monitoring on reducing risky behavior (Lamborn et al., 1996; Lansford, Deater-Deckard, Dodge, Bates, & Pettit, 2004; Walker-Barnes & Mason, 2001). Especially in unsafe environments, parents who may be perceived as more controlling were more successful in protecting their children from exposure to community violence (Moed, Gershoff, & Bringewatt, 2017). However, this recent work clearly separates the effects of behavioral control from harshness. Parental harshness had deleterious effects on violence-exposed youth, actually driving them away from home and what protections it could provide. Clearly, we need to understand these distinctions in order for helpers to be able to provide sound advice to parents about monitoring their adolescents.

You might recognize, in this discussion, some of the themes presented in earlier chapters on parenting. Just as in childhood, the quality of the relationship with parents is extremely important, but this relationship must adjust as the child matures. Let's review the characteristic of optimal parenting style to see what this means during adolescence. Two dimensions define all parenting. First is parental warmth or responsiveness. By being warm, involved, and accepting of their children's needs and feelings, responsive parents seem to encourage their children's self-acceptance, confidence, and assertiveness. They take their children's feelings and expressed needs seriously and are willing to explain their own actions, particularly when they impose limits on the child. The second dimension is parental control or demandingness. Demanding parents apparently foster self-discipline and achievement by making appropriate maturity demands on their children. They provide consistent supervision and consequences for misbehavior, when needed. According to a large body of research, the most effective parenting style, authoritative parenting, combines high responsiveness and high demandingness and is associated with most beneficial outcomes (Baumrind, 1991; Sorkhabi & Middaugh, 2014). Treating responsiveness and demandingness as two distinct dimensions, three other categories of parenting style can be derived. Besides authoritative, there are authoritarian, **indulgent** (also called permissive), and **dismissive** (also called neglecting or uninvolved) styles (Maccoby & Martin, 1983). In the large-scale study of 14- to 18-year-olds by Steinberg and his colleagues (1994), teenagers whose parents were authoritative showed higher achievement, greater resilience, and less internalizing and externalizing behavior compared to those from neglectful homes.

In general, research on parenting styles from as early as the 1940s (Baldwin, 1948) has produced results that are consistent with the large-scale studies of today, supporting the notion that both responsiveness and demandingness are beneficial. Overall, responsiveness seems more closely tied to adolescents' self-confidence and social competence, and demandingness is more closely associated with "good" behavior and self-control. Some work indicates that it can be useful to consider responsiveness as comprising two separable factors. **Acceptance** is being affectionate, praising the child, being involved in the child's life, accepting the child's strengths and limitations, and showing encouragement and concern for the child's needs; it is correlated with children's self-esteem and social adjustment. **Democracy** is the degree to which parents encourage children's psychological autonomy by soliciting their opinions or encouraging self-expression, and it is most closely linked to children's self-reliance, self-confidence, willingness to work hard, and general competence (Steinberg, 1996). *Democracy*, important during adolescence, is the opposite of "psychological control," which we described in Chapter 5: a parent's tendency to subvert an adolescent's autonomy by invalidating his feelings, constraining his verbal expression, criticizing, inappropriately curtailing activities or peer interactions, and violating personal privacy.

Parental Control

Parental monitoring strategies might be conflated with psychological control in some circumstances and, thus, might help explain some inconsistent research findings. One important lesson from this research is that parental monitoring, like many other complex constructs, needs to be defined before drawing conclusions. The distinction between behavioral and psychological control is increasingly made in research to describe parenting and monitoring practices (see Table 10.2).

Psychological control is associated with both internalizing and externalizing problems and disorders (Barber et al., 2005; Pinquart, 2017). Within African American single-mother families, adolescents whose mothers used psychological control as part of their parenting were more likely to develop both internalizing and externalizing problems and engage in more risky behavior (Kinkaid, Jones, Cuellar, & Gonzales, 2011). As mentioned previously, harsh or psychologically controlling parental practices such as severe punishment, restrictions, and coercion were associated with increases in exposure to violence in a multiracial New York City sample of youth (Moed et al., 2017). Similar adjustment difficulties were observed for Chinese adolescents with controlling parents (Wang, Pomerantz, & Chen, 2007; Xiang, Liu, & Bai, 2017). Overall, this body of work indicates that the danger of parental psychological control and harsh parenting practices to adolescent development exists across cultures. On the other hand, lack of behavioral control or behavioral monitoring has been associated with externalizing problems, as we have seen in the case of neglectful parents. Remember that adolescents view parental authority or control as legitimate in certain domains but not others. When adolescents view prudential issues to be within the personal domain, the distinction between psychological and behavioral control can become murky. Consider a mother who is upset that her son is spending a lot of time with a friend, whom she knows smokes cigarettes. She attempts to restrict the amount of time they spend together, a type of behavioral control. Her son, on the other hand, perceives that she doesn't like his friend, registers her displeasure with him, and feels that she is trying to tell him what to do, a form of psychological control. Clearly, the effectiveness of parental control tactics may be dependent upon the domain to which they are applied (Arim, Marshall, & Shapka, 2010).

Conflicting results about parental monitoring can confuse helpers and parents as they search for answers about parenting youth. Building on the two-component model of parental monitoring described above, Flemish researchers provided an even more refined model of parenting that could be used to consider parental conflict-management approaches (Janssens, Goossens, Noortgate, Colpin, Verschueren, & Van Leeuwen, 2015) in the hopes of defining best practices. Their five-factor model includes dimensions that range from positive and non-controlling to more negative control. The first dimension, *support*, refers to parental emotional availability, interest, and acceptance. Three kinds of behavioral control are distinguished: *proactive* (establishing rules for guiding behavior), *punitive* (dominant), and *harsh punitive* (dominant and physical) control. The fifth factor is *psychological* (intrusive, coercive, critical, manipulative) control. Although these advances offer more clarity about the nature of parental monitoring and help us understand beneficial and deleterious practices, we still have much to learn. Both relationship (parent–child) and individual (within child) variables need to be explored over time to better understand what helps prevent specific youth from engaging in specific problem behaviors (Keijsers, 2016).

TABLE 10.2 Some Differences in Parental Control Characteristics

PARENTAL PSYCHOLOGICAL CONTROL	PARENTAL BEHAVIORAL CONTROL
Communicates the message that she/he is trying to change the child in some way.	Asks the child about plans, including who will drive, supervise, attend a function, etc.
Reduces conversation, looks upset or hurt if child misbehaves.	Establishes curfews.
Wants the child to see things (or others) the same way as parent does or expects child to value the same things.	Checks homework (at an age-appropriate level).

SOURCE: Adapted from Barber, 2002; Barber, 2005.

MyLab Education Self-Check 10.3.

Adolescents in School

10.4 Identify elements of schooling that support adolescents' developmental needs and promote academic success across ethnic/racial groups.

Secondary school reform is the focus of contemporary debate (National Center for Educational Statistics, 2002; National Research Council and Institute of Medicine, 2004; Smith, Cannata, Cohen-Vogel, & Rutledge, 2016). Some educational innovations, such as applications of positive behavior management techniques, have shown some success (Bradshaw, Pas, Debnam, & Johnson, 2015), yet problems in secondary schools persist. Despite the fact that dropout rates have fallen in the United States, dropping out still remains a concern because of its effects on long-term indicators of social and economic well-being. Approximately 7% of U.S. students between the ages of 16 and 24 were not enrolled in school in 2014, nor had they earned a high school diploma, compared to 12% in 1990 (Kena et al., 2014).

Educational institutions have been challenged to adjust in order to support the developmental needs of adolescents (Carnegie Council on Adolescent Development, 1996). Curricular changes, structural redesigns, and promotion of student engagement are potential targets for improvement (Dolph, 2017; van Rooij, Jansen, & van de Grift, 2017). This effort derives both from accumulated evidence that demonstrates a stage-environment mismatch between adolescents and their schools (Eccles et al., 1993; Eccles & Roeser, 2009) and from the recognition that many contemporary adolescents face a host of social and academic problems that threaten their well-being (National Center for Educational Statistics, 2002, 2012).

Take a moment to bring to mind your own adolescent self. How would you describe your time in middle and high school? What was most important to you at that time in your life? It is likely that your mind did not immediately leap to memories of your academic subjects, nor to your class assignments. You may recall feeling a bit disengaged from schooling as other aspects of your teenage experience took center stage. Many researchers have noted a decline in academic orientation and motivation starting in the early adolescent years that for some individuals continues throughout high school or culminates in dropping out (Eccles & Roeser, 2011; Gutman, Sameroff, & Cole, 2003). Traditional instructional practices such as whole-group lectures (Feldlaufer, Midgley, & Eccles, 1988), ability grouping (Oakes, Quartz, Gong, Guiton, & Lipton, 1993), and competitive rather than cooperative activities and assessment (Ward et al., 1982) all occur more frequently in middle and junior high schools than in the elementary grades. These practices have been linked to low levels of student motivation and heightened social comparison. For example, just as adolescents become exquisitely sensitive to their place in the peer scene, school-based evaluative policies such as "tracked" academic classes may make differences in ability more noticeable to the adolescent's peers and teachers, leading to decreased status for some (Oakes, 2005). Compared with elementary schools, middle or junior high schools place a heavier emphasis on discipline and teacher control, and they provide relatively fewer opportunities for student decision making (Midgley, Feldlaufer, & Eccles, 1988). As they do at home, adolescents question authority, often perceiving school rules to be unfair (Yang et al., 2013). The large size of most middle and secondary schools is another factor that may detract from personal, mentoring relationships between students and available adults. Ravitch (1983) writes that the trade-off for bigger, more "efficient" schools means "impersonality, bureaucratization, diminished contact between faculty and students, formalization of relationships among colleagues, a weakening of the bonds of community" (p. 327).

Elkind (1984) asserted that the adolescent's identity formation is enhanced by being surrounded by a relatively small group of adults who know the student well and who, over time, are able to support the movement toward responsible autonomy.

MyLab Education
Video Example 10.4
Teacher-student relationships are critical to adolescents' academic engagement. Notice the strategies the sociology teacher uses to relate to students in this high school sociology class.

Students who perceived their teachers as caring and supportive were more likely than were students of less nurturant teachers to show greater academic effort and to express more prosocial goals. Interestingly, when students described teachers "who cared," they named characteristics that were quite similar to those of authoritative parents (Gregory & Weinstein, 2004; Woolley & Grogan-Kaylor, 2006). Interest in translating parenting research about authoritative practices to school settings has emerged as a way to improve student engagement and achievement. Authoritative school climate theory (Gregory & Cornell, 2009), originating from Baumrind's seminal work, advocates both teacher–student relationship improvement and provision of clear rules and high academic expectations.

Both elements, responsiveness and demandingness, make important contributions to success in schools as well as in homes. In a study of middle school students, Wentzel (2002) found that teachers' high expectations for their students was predictive of students' achievement and motivation to learn. In addition, negative feedback or criticism from teachers, even in combination with high expectations, was found to be most clearly associated with diminished motivation and poor achievement. This finding applied to all students in her sample, regardless of gender, race, or ethnicity. She points out that "by creating a context free of harsh criticism *and* [italics added] one in which students are expected to do their best, teachers might be better able to convey information clearly and efficiently, encourage student engagement, and focus students' attention on academic tasks" (p. 298). Similarly, a large study of school climate in over 300 U.S. high schools found that high expectations (demandingness) on their own were not the answer to increased student motivation and engagement. The quality of the student–teacher relationship appears to be a critical ingredient. In high schools with high expectations, the dropout rate was almost 35% higher than in schools with high expectations *and* high levels of student support (Jia, Konold, & Cornell, 2016).

The level of involvement by parents in the schooling of adolescents also influences achievement outcomes. Despite longstanding support of parental involvement as a critical ingredient in school success (e.g., U.S. Department of Education, 1990) particularly for poor and minority children (Comer, 1988), involvement can decline at the middle and high school levels (Steinberg, 1996; Stevenson & Stigler, 1992), especially in more hands-on ways like volunteering and supervising homework. Steinberg has indicated that approximately one third of the students in his study said their parents were uninformed about their school performance, and another one sixth said that their parents did not care. More than 40% of participants said their parents did not attend any school function or activity. This parental unresponsiveness seems closely tied to the child's age and possibly to parental beliefs about an adolescent's right to autonomy. Parents and teachers tend to view various dimensions of involvement (e.g., monitoring homework and use of time, helping at school, attending meetings and conferences, plus serving as a partner with the school in decision making) as appropriately decreasing once the child has made the transition out of the elementary grades (see Stewart, 2008). More recent work suggests that some types of parental involvement remained stable over the course of middle and high school. For example, parents continue to communicate the value of education and to express expectations for academic achievement as it relates to their children's future goals (Bhargava & Witherspoon, 2015).

How much of this phenomenon is part of some universal adolescent rejection of schooling and how much might be due to social and cultural beliefs and expectations? Research from China can offer some clues. Chinese youth surpass American youth in academic achievement, and the trajectory of decreasing academic motivation and involvement observed in U.S. adolescents around middle school is typically not seen in this population (Qu & Pomerantz, 2015; Wang & Pomeranz, 2009). What explains most of the gap between Chinese and American seventh and eighth graders' academic motivation appears to be a fundamental difference in perceived responsibility to parents. Recall that filial piety is a deeply held cultural value that influences parent–child relationships and beliefs about adolescence itself. Whereas American youth tended to minimize responsibility to parents as a feature of adolescence, their Chinese counterparts saw gratitude and obligation to parents as more central. Both groups endorsed independence as an adolescent characteristic, but American youth endorsed it more strongly (Qu, Pomerantz, Wang, Cheung, & Cimpian, 2016). It may be that Chinese youth take a slightly different pathway to maturity, one that emphasizes interdependence.

Despite highly successful academic outcomes, this approach might not come without some personal cost. Chinese mothers, in contrast to Western parents, were found to use more psychological control practices and to regard their children's performance as a reflection of their parenting quality (Ng, Pomerantz, & Deng, 2014). Unfortunately, the deleterious consequences of psychological control are not mitigated by cultural attributions. Adverse emotional consequences were found for both American and Chinese adolescents whose parents engaged in psychologically controlling parenting practices (Pomerantz & Wang, 2009).

In their classic study of ethnic difference across the United States, Steinberg, Dornbusch, et al. (1992) found some fundamental similarities across White, Black, Hispanic, and Asian American ethnic groups. First, not surprisingly, hard work was linked to academic success regardless of ethnicity; students who put in the most time on homework, for example, were the best school performers. Second, teens across all ethnic groups were equally likely to believe that getting a good education pays off. But the researchers also found some surprising differences in beliefs about the negative consequences of not getting a good education. Asian American students were most likely to believe that poor academic preparation could limit their job options later, whereas African American and Hispanic youngsters were the most optimistic; that is, they were the least likely to believe that poor academic preparation would hurt their job prospects.

These differences in belief systems were reflected in the degree to which various ethnic peer groups supported academic achievement: Asian crowds were usually highly supportive, whereas African American and Hispanic crowds were not. Unlike White students, minority students sometimes have little choice of which crowd to join, especially when they go to a school where White students are in the majority. They may see themselves as having access to one or a few crowds defined primarily by ethnicity. Steinberg, Dornbusch, et al. (1992) found that for all ethnic groups, the most successful students were those whose parents and peers supported academics. When peers were at odds with parents, the crowd's support, or lack of it, for homework and hard work was the better predictor of a student's day-to-day school behaviors. As Steinberg (1996) noted, even Asian students of disengaged parents are often "saved from academic failure" by their friends' support of academics (p. 157). Yet African American youngsters with authoritative parents often face giving up or hiding their academic aspirations to keep their friends because the crowds they join not only fail to support school effort but also may even criticize it as an attempt to "act White" (Fordham & Ogbu, 1986). Indeed, at a very vulnerable age some Black adolescents may feel compelled to choose either to give up high academic standards, greatly limiting their future opportunities, or to face being cut off from peer groups that help define their ethnic/racial identity (Ogbu, 2003).

MyLab Education Self-Check 10.4.

Leisure, Work, and Media

10.5 Discuss research-based evidence of positive and negative effects of extracurricular activities, jobs, and media consumption on adolescent behavior and attitudes and suggest guidelines that reduce risks and promote beneficial outcomes.

Outside of school, leisure activities occupy much of an adolescent's time. Leisure activities can promote skill mastery, such as sports participation, hobbies, and artistic pursuits, or they may be more purely recreational, such as playing video games, watching TV, daydreaming, or hanging out with friends. Figure 10.4 shows how youth spent their leisure time compared to older adults on an average day in 2015.

FIGURE 10.4 Average hours spent per day in leisure and sports activities, by youngest and oldest populations.

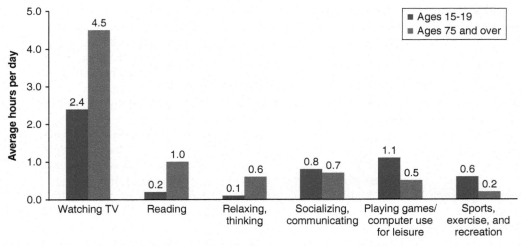

SOURCE: U.S Bureau of Labor Statistics—Available at https://www.bls.gov/tus/charts/chart10.pdf

In general, young people who are involved in extracurricular activities sponsored by their schools and community organizations—athletics, social service, school newspaper staff, student government, band, and so on—are more likely to be academic achievers and to have other desirable qualities than students who are not involved in sponsored activities (Barber, Abbott, Blomfield, Neira, & Eccles, 2014). Longer and more intensive involvement is associated with better long-term effects, including greater educational, civic, and occupational success even in adulthood (Gardner, Roth, & Brooks-Gunn, 2008). Participation in extracurricular activities does appear to be protective against **binge drinking** and drug use as well (McCabe, Modecki, & Barber, 2016). These good outcomes may arise because of exposure to adult mentors who provide a disciplined structure. Developing positive friendships through extracurricular activities provides another important pathway by which activity involvement influences later outcomes (Simpkins, Eccles, & Becnel, 2008).

Although there are general benefits to extracurricular participation, the kind of benefit varies somewhat by activity and not all the outcomes are positive. One longitudinal study followed over 1,000 Michigan youth for 14 years, beginning when they were in the sixth grade, and kept track of, among other things, their extracurricular involvements (Mahoney et al., 2005). High school participation in either prosocial activities or sports was associated with long-term educational achievements (e.g., going to college). But although kids who participated in non-sport activities were unlikely to use alcohol or other drugs in high school, those who participated in sports were more likely than most other teens to use alcohol in high school, perhaps because of peer modeling or because sports participation is also related to high stress (Larson, Hansen, & Moneta, 2006). A study of Canadian youth showed that participation in in-school, non-sport activities (volunteering, music, art, drama, yearbook, etc.) was associated with better self-esteem, lower anxiety, higher achievement, and more prosocial behavior compared to non-participation. Weekly participation in in-school sports, however, was associated with a greater probability of failing a grade (Guèvremont, Findlay, & Kohen, 2014). While more research is needed to further understand these distinctions between non-sport and sport activities, the general consensus from researchers is that participation in extracurricular activities can provide benefits to youth.

Teens in the Workplace

Adolescents also spend time doing work for pay. Figure 10.5 shows a breakdown of employment as a function of school enrollment (Child Trends, Databank, 2016).

Are there benefits to these early jobs for teens? It seems reasonable to propose some developmental advantages. Having adult responsibilities might help adolescents

FIGURE 10.5 Percentage of youth (ages 16–24) employed, total, and by school enrollment: 1993–2015.

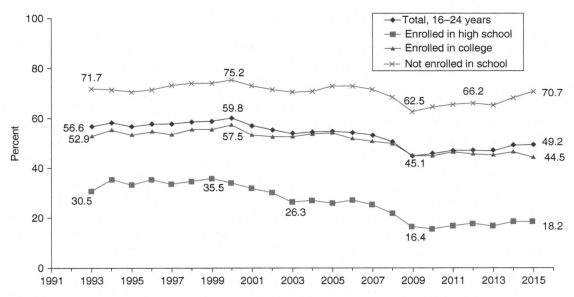

SOURCE: U.S. Department of Labor. Archived Bureau of Labor Statistics News Releases (Various Years). Available at http://www.bls.gov/schedule/archives/all_nr.htm#HSGEC

feel independent and grown up, enhancing self-esteem. Searching for work and being employed might provide training that is hard to come by in any other way, such as learning how to find a job, learning one's own job preferences, and clarifying one's work values. Parents often assume that working will help adolescents to learn to manage their money and their time. Mortimer et al. (1999) report that teens who work generally endorse many of these presumed benefits, seeing their jobs as helping them to be more responsible, to manage their time and their money, to establish a work ethic, and to learn social skills. Adolescents also list some negative outcomes, primarily feeling fatigued and having less time for homework and leisure activities. But on balance, they see their work in a positive light.

Do adolescents who work need to work—to save for college or even to help ease financial burdens at home? During the Great Depression, economic hardship did send adolescents into the workplace, and working was apparently linked to more responsible use of money and a more "adult" orientation (Elder, 1974). But the culture has changed dramatically since then. Whereas in 1940 only about 3% of 16-year-olds still in school were employed, by 1980 the government estimated that more than 40% were working. Of course, relatively more youngsters complete high school today than in 1940. Middle-class teens are more likely to be employed than those from lower socioeconomic groups, and their money is unlikely to be saved or contributed to family expenses. Rather, working teens more frequently spend their money on materialistic pursuits: wardrobes, entertainment, drugs, and alcohol (Steinberg et al., 1993).

Cultural change has also affected the kinds of jobs adolescents acquire. In 1940, many teens worked on farms or in manufacturing, in jobs where they were supervised by adults (frequently adults who were family members or were known to their families), and they often received training that was directly relevant to the jobs they would have after high school. Today, teens are much more likely to work in retail establishments, including restaurants, and to be under the direct supervision of other young people rather than adults. It appears that the work teens do today is often less educational than it was in 1940, and it may have less long-term career value (Aronson, Mortimer, Zierman, & Hacker, 1996; Staff & Schulenberg, 2010).

Researchers report that there are both positive and negative consequences of paid employment while in high school. In general, these results are related to hours of employment—the more hours the teenager worked, the more problematic were the effects in most cases. A troublesome finding is that long hours of employment (especially 20 or more hours per week) were associated with increases in problem behaviors like theft (e.g., giving away store products to friends), school misconduct, and alcohol and drug use, including cigarette smoking (Mihalic & Elliot, 1997; Mortimer et al., 1999). The effects of work on schooling and school involvement are also mixed. Several large-scale studies have found no effects on students' grades, but negative effects on total educational attainment. Years of schooling tend to be reduced for students who invest long hours in their jobs. Other studies have found negative correlations between working and grades even for relatively few hours of work (Largie, Field, Hernandez-Reif, Sanders, & Diego, 2001). Bachman, Safron, Sy, & Schulenberg (2003) found that negative associations between schooling and work appear to be bidirectional—for example, teens with less school involvement are more likely to seek jobs, and once they are working substantial hours, teens become even less involved in school. Monaghan, Lee, and Steinberg (2011) found that part-time work of moderate intensity (less than 20 hours per week) was not associated with either positive or negative outcomes, nor with psychological benefits for adolescents.

Scholarly research on paid employment during adolescence has yet to reach firm conclusions because the issue is not a simple one. Variables like SES, race/ethnicity, peer relationships, work quality, number of hours worked, and personal characteristics (e.g., motivation for school and for work) all play a role in determining outcomes. Hwang and Domina (2017) analyzed a large, mixed racial sample from the National Center for Educational Statistics (NCES) to explore some of the interrelationships among employment during high school and post-secondary outcomes. In general, some limited employment (less than 5 hours per week) during the high school years was linked with better post-secondary student outcomes (Associate or B.A. degree) compared to those of non-employed students or those with high-intensity (more than 20 hours per week) jobs. Some of these relationships were more nuanced and moderated by race. For example, high-intensity work was associated with more negative educational attainment for White students. For Black students, however, high-intensity work was not associated with poorer educational outcomes. The authors speculate that differential selection may help explain this finding. Black high school students who are employed at high-intensity jobs may have some specific personal characteristics that contribute to their academic success.

Adolescents and Media

No doubt about it, media also plays a major role in the life of contemporary adolescents, and its use is increasing rapidly for both children and youth (see Figure 10.6). A peek into the ways young people consume electronic media paints a picture of just how rapid this change has been. The rise in popularity of social media is clearly evident in the lives of adolescents, many of whom report feeling "constantly connected" to some online device (Lenhart, 2015). Almost three quarters of adolescents report using more than one social media site regularly. Many share information and photos through apps and texts, and watch TV on their phones. The word "consume," often used in regard to media, is an interesting and apt choice because researchers have long been concerned about the effects of a steady diet of technology on the brains and behaviors of young people. In the most recently available nationally representative study by the Kaiser Family Foundation (2010) and its reanalysis by race (Rideout, Lauricella, & Wartella, 2011), U.S. 3rd to 12th graders increased their total daily media consumption from 6 hours and 21 minutes in 2004 to 7 hours and 38 minutes by 2009, approximating the hours of a typical adult work day. Media usage takes up even more time than work, however, because it continues during the weekend. Rates of all media consumption (music, computers, video games, TV, and movie) except for print media increased over the three waves of the Kaiser study. What percentage of 3rd to 12th graders have a TV in their bedrooms? If you guessed slightly more that 7 out of 10 youth have TVs (71%), you are correct. Cable TV and video game consoles are present in 50% of bedrooms. Computers are also very common. Most children, age 8 and older, watch an average of 2 hours of TV per day and have a wide variety of shows to watch, given the popularity of streaming services (Rideout, 2015).

But how does this kind of media exposure affect children and adolescents, and how much of a threat is it? High levels of media use have been associated with a

MyLab Education
Video Example 10.5
As portrayed in this video, texting and social media influence adolescent relationships with parents and friends. What are the concerns, and how do parents balance autonomy and control?

FIGURE 10.6 How much media do children and adolescents consume?
Types and Extent of Media Use Among U.S. 3rd to 12th Graders.

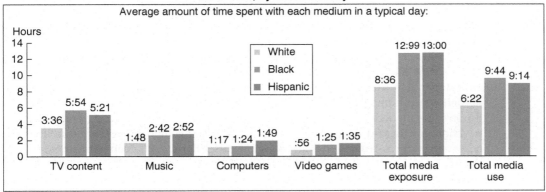

SOURCE: The Henry J. Kaiser Family Foundation (2010, January 1). *Generation M2: Media in the lives of 8- to 18-year-olds.* From http://www.kff.org/other/poll-finding/report-generation-m2-media-in-the-lives/. Used by permission.

number of health risks for children and adolescents, including obesity, sleep problems, underachievement, early initiation of **risky behaviors** like smoking and drinking, cyberbullying, sexting (sending sexually explicit messages or images via text message), and depression (AAP Council on Communication and Media, 2016). When researchers asked teenagers and their parents about the number of social media accounts the youth used, they found relationships between the number of media platforms used and symptoms (Barry, Sidotti, Briggs, Reiter, & Lindsey, 2017). Parents reported higher levels of attention problems, oppositional behavior, and depressive symptoms in their high-media-use children. Teenagers themselves reported more loneliness and fear of missing out when they had more social media accounts. Twenge and her colleagues (Twenge, Joiner, Rogers, & Martin, 2017) conclude that changes in ways adolescents use their leisure time (e.g., increasing screen-time versus nonscreen-time activities) have been implicated in the rise of depression and suicide-related behaviors since 2010, especially for girls. We will present some guidelines for parents and helpers about teen Internet use in the Applications section.

A substantial part of the average media diet includes violence, and quite a lot is known about exposure to violence through TV, movies, and other media outlets. The link between viewing televised violence and behaving aggressively for certain individuals has been well researched and is generally accepted (Comstock & Scharrer, 1999). Modeling processes (see Chapter 1) are presumed to account for much of this relationship. Recent interest in the role of media as a socializer of values expands upon social learning principles to include constructivist conceptions of how individuals make sense of their environments. In other words, people use what they perceive as raw material from which to construct ideas, beliefs, and guiding principles. Violent video games have become a source of concern for many people because they offer a double whammy:

viewing violent acts and engaging with virtual activities in an active way. One longitudinal study (Willoughby, Adachi, & Good, 2012) followed Canadian adolescents over the course of their high school years to investigate relationships between playing violent video games and later aggressive behavior. Even after controlling for other media use, quality of parenting, academic and school variables, sports involvement, depression, and deviant behaviors, the relationship between a steady diet of violent video game play and aggressive behavior was significant. Furthermore, the authors did not find support for the idea that more aggressive youth elected to play more violent video games (a selection effect). On the contrary, playing the violent games themselves was associated with increased levels of aggressive behavior for both boys and girls. There appears to be something unique about the violent video game effects insofar as the same increase in aggression was not seen in those youth who played nonviolent video games.

Violent video games are now played by adolescents around the world. A new diagnostic category, not yet official but requiring further research, is Internet Gaming Disorder (DSM-V, 2013), which is characterized by addiction-like symptoms related to excessive Internet game playing. Does violent video game play have the same causal relationship to aggressive behavior and cognitions across cultures? The answer appears to be yes. Results from a large meta-analysis of studies from Western countries and Japan showed that increased violent video game play was a causal factor in increasing aggressive behavior and cognitions and in reducing prosocial behavior and empathy (Anderson et al., 2010). Neither gender nor age significantly moderated this relationship. This finding is important because it updates other analyses and strengthens the view that repeated practice shapes brain and behavior via processes of experience-dependent learning. This is a timely and practically important issue for parents, helpers, and public policy makers. The authors conclude that playing video games doesn't just involve moving a joystick. Players "are indeed interacting with the game psychologically and emotionally. It is not surprising that when the game involves rehearsing aggressive and violent thoughts and actions, such deep game involvement results in antisocial effects on the player. Of course, the same basic social–cognitive processes should also yield prosocial effects when game content is primarily prosocial . . . Video games are neither inherently good nor inherently bad. But people learn. And content matters" (Anderson et al., 2010, p. 171).

Recently, a task force was convened by the American Psychological Association to summarize the body of evidence and draw some conclusions about the effects of violent video games on aggression. This large meta-analysis was carried out by expert researchers on aggression with the goal of making recommendations for public policy (Calvert et al., 2017). Results largely strengthened earlier findings and suggested additional questions that need to be answered, especially as effects may differentially affect diverse youth. Table 10.3 summarizes some of the task force's major conclusions. We should note that this is a complex issue to study, and some researchers cite data that

TABLE 10.3 Findings from APA Meta-analysis of Studies on Violent Video Games

FINDING	TAKE-HOME MESSAGE
Violent video game exposure is consistently related to aggressive behavior, aggressive thoughts, aggressive feelings, reductions in empathy, and decline in prosocial behavior. Exposure is also related to aggression desensitization.	Violent video games are a clear risk factor for aggression.
Studies that controlled for preexisting factors, like inherited antisocial traits, prior antisocial behavior, parenting conflict, depression in child or parent, or having deviant friends, also show a strong relationship between violent video games and aggression.	Violent video games contribute uniquely and separately to aggression, in addition to other preexisting or concurrent factors.
It is not possible to ascertain the links between exposure to violent video games and later criminality at this point.	More research is needed in this area.
The size of effects of violent video games is the same for teens, college students, and adults. No dose-response relationship has been identified.	Violent video games affect adolescents and adults. Research with children under 10 is lacking. We don't know yet what specific amounts of playing violent video games are most dangerous.
Major gaps are present in the literature with regard to race, gender, and SES as well as in video game properties (e.g., 1st vs. 3rd person perspective).	More research is needed in these areas.

SOURCE: Adapted from APA Task Force, Calvert et al., 2017.

suggest lesser effects of violent video games in promoting violence among teens (Markey & Ferguson, 2017).

Another area of particular concern for adolescents is the learning of sexual messages and attitudes. Studies using correlational methods have found relationships between frequent viewing of televised portrayals of sexuality with more distorted cognitions, more liberal attitudes about sex, and more tolerance for sexual harassment (Strouse, Goodwin, & Roscoe, 1994). Frequent consumption of sexualized media has also been linked to increased sexual behavior—that is, more sexual partners and earlier sexual initiation than for individuals without such media exposure (Brown et al., 2002). This may have something to do with the perception that "everybody's doing it." Researchers have found that people's expectations or constructions about what is normative influence what they choose to do. Adolescents who believe that teens in general have frequent sexual experiences engage in riskier and more frequent sexual activity themselves (Whitaker & Miller, 2000).

A study by Ward (2002) employed both correlational and experimental methods to study whether television's messages influenced attitudes about sexuality in a multiethnic sample of older adolescents. This study confirmed that the three beliefs investigated in this study—that men are driven by sex, that women are sex objects, and that dating is a recreational sport—were very strongly related to heavy TV viewing and to personal involvement with TV. High personal involvement was measured by individuals' goals for TV (entertainment and a way to learn about the world), discussions about TV shows with others, and identification with TV characters, among other things. Outcomes of the experimental part of the study revealed that females more strongly endorsed the stereotypical beliefs after viewing sexual TV clips than did women who saw nonsexual episodes.

Interestingly, this pattern was not the same for males. Males' agreement with the three stereotypes was already much higher than women's, so it may not have been realistic to expect this experimental manipulation to generate higher rates of agreement. Another possibility is that males' attitudes might be differentially influenced by exposure to other types of media, such as music videos.

National monitoring studies report that dating violence is a significant concern in the teen population (Kann et al., 2014). Among all high school students surveyed, over 10% reported being physically victimized by someone they dated. Girls were at higher risk, with 14.4% reporting being the victim of sexual violence. Girls appear to suffer more serious consequences than males, although problematic outcomes were seen for both males and females reporting physical/sexual victimization (Bonomi, Anderson, Nemeth, Rivara, & Buettner, 2013). Unfortunately, the problem is pervasive. Four out of 10 young adults report having had an experience of sexual violence or nonconsensual sex during their lives (Halpern, Spriggs, Martin, & Kupper, 2009). No matter when it occurs over the life span, interpersonal violence leaves its mark—as we have amply described throughout this text. Movies and TV appear to be leading purveyors of sexual information for youth (Ybarra, Strasburger, & Mitchell, 2014) although Internet, games, and other media also play a role.

> **MyLab Education** Self-Check 10.5.

Risk-Taking Versus Risky Lifestyles in Adolescence

10.6 Analyze various views of risky adolescent behavior including adolescent reasoning and adult concerns and suggest appropriate patterns of parenting and intervening in the context of managing risks.

Andy and Ben are talking about drinking and driving. They describe a typical "party"—one that involves lots of alcohol and not much parental supervision. They frequently drive home from these unsupervised events, believing that they are "responsible drivers" because they're so good at drinking and driving and have never had any accidents. It's not that Andy's and Ben's parents are intentionally neglectful. The teens just don't share this information with their parents. Andy and Ben simply believe they are very good at doing what they want to do without getting into trouble. They tend to think that other teenagers, those who aren't as smart or clever, might get into trouble, but not them. Are the behaviors Ben and Andy describe normal or deviant? Are they part of a passing phase or predictive of future problems? Should we crack down on these behaviors or look the other way? These questions pose real problems, not only for parents and helpers but also for social policy makers in fields such as education, mental health, and criminal justice. These behaviors epitomize a paradox at this stage of development.

Adolescence is associated with major cognitive advances and gains in physical strength and vitality. Peer relationships flourish as a way to support adolescents' transition into adulthood. Risk taking is a developmentally appropriate propensity as it serves autonomy-related goals. Contravention of adult norms by experimentation with deviant behaviors has always been part of the adolescent experience and is, in fact, statistically normative (Barnes, Welte, & Dintcheff, 1992; Jessor, Donovan, & Costa, 1991; Reyna & Farley, 2006). Yet, adolescence is also notable for the onset of many physical and mental health problems that are preventable and that persist into adulthood, interfering with educational achievement and work productivity in long-lasting ways (Costello, Foley, & Angold, 2006; Spear, 2010). Most of the threats to well-being derive from emotional and behavioral dysregulation in the context of potentially risky environmental circumstances (see Chapter 9).

Rates of morbidity and mortality increase by 200% to 300% in adolescence, largely due to risky behaviors (Victor & Hariri, 2016). Most major mental health disorders have their start in adolescence, making this stage of life a prime target for prevention and intervention efforts (O'Connell, Boat, & Warner, 2009). Recently, rates of certain harmful behaviors have decreased or are holding steady but some are increasing among the adolescent population in this country. Compared to 2011, levels of marijuana use, illicit drug use, and first-time alcohol, marijuana, and cigarette use were lower for adolescents, ages 12 to 17, overall. Rates of depression were higher in 2015 than in 2011. About 3 million adolescents experienced at least one major depressive episode in 2015. U.S. assessments indicate that emotional, mental, or behavioral disorders affect 17% of youth. Disorders that are most prevalent, from higher to lower rates of incidence, are substance abuse disorder, anxiety, depression, and attention-deficit hyperactivity disorder. Juvenile crime rates have dropped overall since spiking in the 1990s (2015, retrieved from https://www.ojjdp.gov/ojstatbb/crime/JAR.asp on Nov 16, 2017). In 2010, the incidence was 55% lower than it was at its peak in 1994 (Puzzanchera, Adams, & Hockenberry, 2012; U.S. Bureau of Justice Statistics, 2000).

Attention has been focused on risky behaviors in adolescence for some time, given accumulating research on the adolescent brain, the flowering of translational science to inform treatment and prevention, and the economic and social costs associated with adolescent morbidity and mortality rates. Some of these factors, like increased attention and treatment, might help to explain why certain behaviors have been reduced or, at least, held in check. Researchers have also been able to refine our understanding of risk, thus setting the stage for more precise and well-targeted interventions (Romer, Reyna, & Satterthwaite, 2017). The popular notion that any risky behavior can set the adolescent on the path to ruin has been challenged by a more nuanced understanding of risk-taking itself. Most adolescents will take some risks, especially in the context of potentially rewarding outcomes, but they also learn from these adventures because of executive functions that continue to increase over the course of adolescence. Some adolescents engage in risky behavior without thinking, manifesting an underlying trait impulsivity that may continue from childhood and culminate in adoption of risky lifestyles. These underlying differences point youth in different directions. Understanding these distinctions can make future prediction and treatment efforts more effective.

Interestingly, statistical trends towards stable or decreasing drug use, criminal offenses, and sexual behavior are suggestive of results from a large survey that

MyLab Education
Video Example 10.6
Autonomy-related goals may result in greater risk-taking during adolescence. As you consider the risks taken by the 16-year-old girl in this video, think about the scope of influences leading to her behavior and the interventions involved in dealing with her dilemma.

examined the decline in some activities by teenagers overall (Twenge & Park, 2017). The results of large samples of adolescent generations from the past four decades (1976–2016), totaling 8.44 million U.S. adolescents, suggest that level of participation in adult activities (drinking, driving, working for pay, dating, sex, etc.) can be construed as a measure of "developmental speed." As predicted by life history theory (Figueredo et al., 2006), a "fast life" strategy prioritizes reproduction and activities that maximize separation from parents, in the service of independence. Engaging in adult activities during adolescence, such as the ones mentioned above, would be more representative of youth on a fast life trajectory. A "slow life" strategy privileges delayed gratification and later reproduction. The historical and social context within which an adolescent's generation exists is strongly determinative of fast or slow life strategy. More societal resources allow for slower developmental speed because the environmental investment in children, like extended educational opportunities and parental attention, is greater. At times when survival is at risk, life spans are shorter and the reproductive push is maximized. Twenge and Park (2017) report that the current generation of adolescents is noticeably less engaged with many adult activities, compared to earlier generations (see Figure 10.7).

While speculative at this point, these data suggest that the nature of adolescence may be changing. No support was found for alternative hypotheses to explain the observed declines, such as more school responsibility limiting the time available for adult behaviors. To the contrary, earlier generations actually spent more time on schoolwork. One historical shift that might be an influence on lower rates of dating and going out is Internet use, which can substitute for in-person social contact. This study represents an early exploration into developmental shifts that may be in process. Its findings complement recent observations about early adult transitions described in the next chapters.

FIGURE 10.7 Percentage of 12th Grade student participation in adult activities over time.

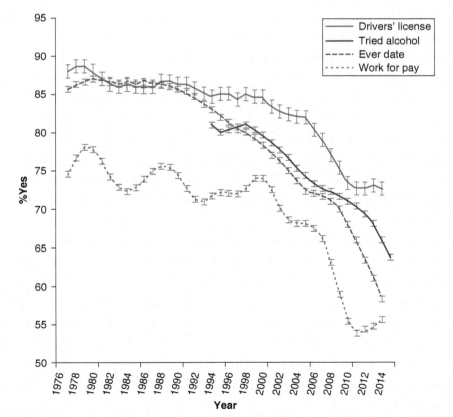

SOURCE: Twenge, J. M. & Park, H. (2017). The Decline in Adult Activities Among U.S. Adolescents, 1976–2016. *Child Development*, pp. 1–17.

Who Takes More Risky Risks?

One thing is clear from the study of development: No adolescent is the same as any other, and some adolescents are more vulnerable. Despite the declines, problems associated with risky behavior among teenagers have not disappeared. For some adolescents, risky behaviors become risky lifestyles. Various writers have used different terms to refer to these behaviors, including *reckless, problem, deviant, antisocial,* and *delinquent.* Here we use the adjectives somewhat interchangeably, although risky and reckless connote slightly more benign behaviors than do deviant, antisocial, or delinquent. Even so, separating these activities into bad and not-so-bad is tricky because, as we shall see, they all pose potential dangers. They vary on a continuum of severity and, when severe, tend to appear in clusters in the lives of teenagers at risk.

Is adolescence-limited antisocial behavior the same as reckless behavior in adolescence? The answer may be a matter of degree. Certainly, some teenagers go to more extreme lengths, have more accumulated risk factors and fewer protective ones in their lives, and thus suffer more than others from the consequences of their behavior. But the paradox we introduced earlier seems to apply here. Behaviors traditionally considered deviant are increasingly becoming part of the experimental repertoire of teens who are considered well adjusted. Hersch (1998) closely followed the activities of adolescents in a suburban high school for several years. She got to know the students well, becoming an "insider" in the world of adolescents, and was able to document the escalation of dangerous pursuits as a normal part of contemporary adolescent life. "Behaviors once at the fringe of adolescent rebelliousness have not only permeated the mainstream culture of high school but are seeping into the fabric of middle school" (p. 156). As Jessica, an eighth-grade student interviewed by Hersch said, "This [smoking, using drugs, having sex] is *what you are supposed to do* [italics added]. . . . It's our teenage phase. You are only a kid once" (p. 156). Researchers who followed adolescent males with childhood-persistent and time limited antisocial behavior to age 26 found that problems had persisted, to a greater or lesser degree, for both groups (Moffitt, Caspi, Harrington, & Milne, 2002). The authors conclude that antisocial behavior, regardless of when it emerges, should be treated and taken seriously.

Peer and Parent Influences on Risky and Deviant Behavior

How do peers affect adolescents' risky behavior? We know that teenagers are more likely to take risks when they are in the company of their peers (Gardner & Steinberg, 2005), but why is this the case? What power do peers exert, and how do they do it? A very careful look at peer influence mechanisms on one risky behavior, smoking, can provide a window into this process. Liu and her colleagues (Liu, Zhao, Chen, Falk, & Albarracín, 2017) reviewed 75 carefully done longitudinal studies from 16 different countries to explore how peers affect smoking initiation and maintenance. Countries were evenly representative of those with more individualistic (e.g., United States) and more collectivist (e.g., Middle East) orientations. The findings reveal some key relationships. Adolescents were about twice as likely to begin smoking (initiation) if their friends smoked. Friends provide opportunity, models, and means for risk taking. Adolescents not only initiated smoking but also continued to smoke if their friends did. Personal friendship mattered a lot when smoking was initiated. Perhaps teens are more likely to adopt the behaviors and attitudes of peers they feel close to and want to please. Once smoking began, however, it mattered less that teens felt close to other smoking peers. Selection effects might propel smokers into certain smoking crowds, and other smokers might trigger processes that reinforce the behavior. Both initiation and continuation of smoking are strongly affected by peers. Finally, youth from collectivist cultures were more attuned to conforming to group norms, and their smoking initiation and continuation was more strongly affected by peers than that of youth from individualistic cultures. The important role played by motivational factors, like seeking closeness with friends, is an important discovery and has implications for research and prevention. For example, these findings caution against anti-smoking campaigns that inadvertently communicate high levels of smoking among the intended target population. This message might convince youth that they need to smoke to be like their friends. It is also important to remember that these results apply to one specific risky behavior, smoking, and more research is needed before generalizing the conclusions.

Egocentrism, Development, and Risk

Cognitive features like adolescent egocentrism also play a role in risky behavior by supporting the fiction that risky behavior is exciting but not potentially catastrophic. Arnett (1992) implicates adolescents' weaknesses in reasoning about probability, a kind of formal operational thinking, as particularly important here (see Chapter 9). Drawing upon Piaget's ideas, Arnett argues that

> [I]n every judgement of probability, there is a reference, implicit or explicit, to a system of distributions or frequencies. Adolescents' perceptions of these systems are skewed by their desire for sensation and by the personal fable that convinces them of their immunity from disaster. . . . But even if an adolescent were exceptionally proficient at estimating probabilities, on a given occasion, the likelihood of disaster resulting from drunk driving, or sex without contraception, or illegal drug use, or delinquency/crime is, in fact, statistically small—even when applied to others, and seen through the lens of sensation seeking and egocentrism, the perceived probability fades even further. (p. 350)

Recent empirical research supports some aspects of Arnett's analysis but not others. Adolescents who perceive the risks of certain behaviors seem to be somewhat less likely than others to ever engage in those risky behaviors; but adolescents who *do* engage in risky behavior actually seem to be well aware that they have put themselves at risk! There seem to be complicated processes at work here (see Reyna & Farley, 2006). It appears that some teens put themselves at risk because they are responding to triggers that cue big, short-term rewards; they do not do a cost/benefit analysis. This is what you would expect if the emotional system were activated without benefit of control from the executive system. However, even when adolescents feel vulnerable and *do* engage the cognitive control system, their approach to evaluating risk may keep them from being as risk averse as they should be. Reyna and Farley (2006) suggest that when probability analyses are new to adolescents, they are likely to do cost/benefit assessments that favor risk taking, just as Arnett suggests. They often perceive the relative costs, which are usually low probability, as well worth the potential rewards. Adults, on the other hand, think about risk situations differently. They are more likely to assess risky behaviors, like having sex with a casual partner without a condom, as completely unacceptable, because *if* there were negative consequences, however low the probability, they would be catastrophic. As Reyna and Farley put it, adults eventually develop a more global or categorical approach to risk assessment, a sort of automatic response to the "gist" of the situation, rather than painstakingly weighing the probabilities of positive and negative outcomes. To illustrate, in a study of adolescents' versus adults' reaction time to questions such as, "Is it a good idea to set your hair on fire?" or "Is it a good idea to swim with sharks?" Baird and Fugelsang (2004) found that adolescents responded much more slowly than adults, as you would expect if they were actually taking a risk/benefit analysis approach. They did not respond more slowly to other, non–risk-related questions.

Are there any benefits for humans to having an adolescent period that involves increased sensation seeking and risk taking? In one view, recklessness in adolescents, especially in males, once had a strong fitness value (e.g., Nell, 2002; Steinberg & Belsky, 1996; Steinberg, 2008). Nell, for example, argues that in the evolutionary history of the human species, young males who were willing to risk their own safety to fight for territory and for dominance won the most desirable mates. The legacy of this evolutionary history is that, even today, adolescent boys are prepared, even more so than girls, to take risks and to engage in aggressive behavior. Research on the dopaminergic remodeling of the limbic and paralimbic systems that takes place at puberty indicates that "it is more pronounced in males than in females" (Steinberg, 2008, p. 87), providing a neurological basis for greater risk taking in males during adolescence.

Another somewhat related view is that adolescent limited antisocial behavior is adaptive because it promotes individuation and self-determination. Goldstein (1990), for example, suggests that risky behavior is instrumental in relieving the maturity gap that afflicts adolescents who are caught in a time warp between physical and social maturity. To possess the symbolic trappings of adult status (sexual intimacy, material possessions, autonomy, and respect from parents), adolescents mimic the behavior of more advanced, and often more antisocial, peers, borrowing those elements that elicit respect from others and that affirm personal independence.

Arnett (1992) theorizes that reckless behavior is more a fact of life in cultures with broad socialization as opposed to narrow socialization practices. Societies with broad socializing practices permit and encourage high levels of individual freedom of expression, have fewer social constraints, expect less community responsibility, and thus tolerate a wider variety of socially deviant behaviors. Cultures with narrow socialization practices, more characteristic of nonindustrialized cultures, exert more control over the expression of behaviors that violate social standards, and they expect more conformity from young members of the society.

So is reckless behavior among adolescents the price we must pay for living in a society that encourages freedom of expression? What kinds of trade-offs should we be willing to tolerate? Even though adolescent-limited antisocial patterns usually attenuate sometime in early adulthood, when more conventional roles of employee, spouse, or parent are assumed, we should not conclude that this pattern poses no risk at all. To be sure, Moffitt (1993a) notes that risky behavior, while enhancing peer involvement, may also ensnare adolescents in situations that can ultimately prove quite harmful, such as fostering drug dependence or depressing academic achievement. As Reyna and Farley (2006) argue, no matter how normative risk taking may be in adolescence, both its immediate and long-term consequences can be so substantial that it is a matter of great social concern. Developing effective, empirically based interventions to eliminate the most consequential of the risks should be a high priority. Steinberg advocates a commonsense solution: making risky options less available to youth until they have greater maturity in making decisions.

What can a parent do to prevent risky lifestyles? In this chapter, we have discussed the importance of parent–teen relationships during this period of life. Parents don't have control over their child's friends, but they do have the power to provide the kind of parenting that maximizes their child's well-being.

A nationally representative sample of over 4,000 seventh and eighth graders in the United States (Jaccard, Lushkin, & Kaploun, 2017) illustrated the complexities of the adolescent–parent–peer relationship. The authors attempted to identify youth who were most likely to drink in the future as a function of how much they lied to their parents. Results from this prospective study revealed that teens who perceived their mothers as warm were less likely to lie to them, allowing parents to engage in more supportive roles and limit future drinking risk. Parental control was not directly related to knowledge volunteered by adolescents. Instead, the quality of the disclosure to parents depended upon how supportive the teenager perceived the relationship to be. These authors' results "challenge the common interpretation of parental monitoring as representing unilateral tracking/ surveillance practices. Rather, parents craft styles, roles, and relationships with their adolescents so that youth will volitionally share honest accounts of their whereabouts, activities and companions, inviting some parental guidance in the process" (p. 105).

Results from a nationally representative sample serves to underscore these conclusions with regard to delinquency (Harris-McCoy, 2016). As we have seen, lack of parental behavioral monitoring has been associated with involvement in risky behavior and delinquent activities. However, excessive control during adolescence, for all the reasons we have outlined in this chapter, is also associated. While conventional wisdom has often drawn straightforward conclusions, the relationship is more complicated. Using data from a sample of over 17,000 adolescents to explore the relationship between parenting and juvenile delinquency, the best fit was a curvilinear relationship (see Figure 10.8). Both too little and too much parental oversight are problematic. Some parental control is always needed, but it should not be rigid or inflexible. Importantly, warmth, support, and emotional connection need to be present in the parent–child relationship in order to provide the young person both roots and wings.

FIGURE 10.8 Curvilinear relationship between levels of parental control and delinquent outcomes.

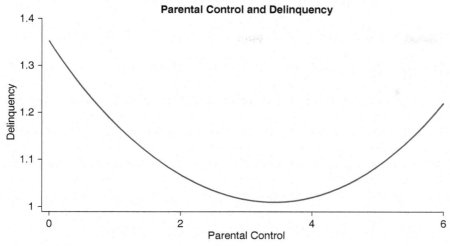

Parental Control and Delinquency

SOURCE: Harris-McKoy, 2016.

MyLab Education Self-Check 10.6.

Society's Role in Adolescent Problem Behavior: Then and Now

10.7 Weigh contrasting views of adolescent problem behavior including attitudes about adolescent self-sufficiency and adult/societal responsibility.

Let's reflect again about the continuum of narrow to broad socialization. At which point along the continuum would you place contemporary U.S. culture? Although there are certainly regional and ethnic variations, it is likely that you identify contemporary socializing practices as quite broad. Adolescents, and even younger children, seem to have a lot more freedom now than they have had in the past. However, we can also consider this question from a slightly different perspective, focusing not just on freedom but also on support. How much support does our contemporary culture provide for young people? How is level of support related to engagement in risky behavior? Has our collective level of responsibility changed in any way from that of the past decades, or is this idea just a nostalgic myth?

Siegel and Scovill (2000) provide a comprehensive look at the approach U.S. society has taken toward young people from the 1920s onward. In the 1920s, society viewed deviant adolescent behavior—as much a problem then as it is now—as an expression of youthful energies gone awry. In addition, social deviancy was considered an alternative pathway that some teenagers used to meet normal developmental goals, such as autonomy and relatedness, when more socially conventional means were unavailable to them. Consequently, it was generally believed that society as a whole was responsible for providing more productive outlets for adolescent energies. Many institutions and organizations were established to encourage teenagers to participate in socially constructive activities, to provide them with structured adult contact, and to facilitate prosocial interactions among youth themselves. Some examples of these organizations, most initiated before the 1920s, include Boy Scouts and Girl Scouts, Campfire Girls, Pioneer Youth of America, 4-H Clubs, Junior Achievement, Kiwanis, Order of the Rainbow for Girls, and Optimist International Boys' Work Council. Institutions dedicated to special interests, such as the National Recreation Association, the Girls' Service League of America, and the Sportmanship

Brotherhood, as well as religiously affiliated groups such as the YMCA, the YWCA, the Knights of King Arthur, and the Ladies of Avalon, were also established. All were united in their purpose of providing guidance and character-building activities for youth.

Today, as Siegel and Scovill (2000) point out, many of these age-appropriate community support systems have disappeared or have more limited scope. Consequently, the social envelope, which in the past strengthened families and schools and provided a safety net for youth who lacked family support or good educational opportunities, is weak or even absent. Many academic and recreational opportunities, often available free of charge to past generations of children and adolescents as part of their neighborhoods or communities, now come with a price tag. What has happened to cause this shift in attitudes and priorities?

Society's view of the cause of adolescent problem behaviors undoubtedly shapes its attitudes towards responsibility, prevention, and treatment. Contemporary society leans towards perceiving the source of deviancy as something within the individual adolescent rather than within society at large.

> While problem behavior was largely "socialized" through the 1960's, it has become "medicalized" in the 1990's. In an age in which we have been led to believe that there is a "magic scientific bullet" for nearly all physiological and social problems, we have "medicalized" problem behavior. An unspoken corollary of the "intrapsychic" view is that if the locus of the problem is in the adolescent, then parents and society are off the hook. The genetic or biological perspective provides that out: "There's nothing we could do; our child was born a delinquent." (Siegel & Scovill, 2000, p. 781)

No one should interpret these comments as suggesting that we return to either–or, nature–nurture thinking. As we have seen repeatedly, within-person and within-family influences on behavior are strong, and they contribute significantly to developmental outcomes. Remember that families themselves are nested within neighborhoods, communities, and social contexts that need to be supported. What these authors recommend is a serious examination of the personal needs and rationalizations we adults may use in interpreting adolescent problem behavior. If, as a society, we emphasize adolescent self-sufficiency and sophistication and deemphasize adolescent needs for adult time, guidance, structure, and connection, then we do them, and ourselves, a great disservice.

Applications

Helping Teenagers and Their Families

Adolescence is the life stage characterized by the highest overall level of risk taking. Some risk taking is a healthy expression of autonomy in the service of identity development. Some risky pathways lead in less adaptive directions. Helping professionals who work with adolescents spend a good deal of their time attempting to encourage healthy behaviors and to discourage or reduce harmful ones. Clearly, there is no shortage of work in this area given the cultural possibilities for exploration in potentially dangerous areas like drugs, alcohol, sexuality, violence, and truancy that are open to younger and younger generations. What is the best way to make headway with adolescents given their natural proclivity to take risks? First, we need to recognize that adults can't prevent all risky behaviors. But assuming the attitude that "they'll grow out of it" can be ill-advised as well, given the convergence of research on the power of cumulative risk to affect later outcomes. Below we introduce some ideas that draw upon the developmental knowledge presented in this chapter to help professionals in their work with youth and their families.

- In general, advocating for authoritative parenting and providing the information and support parents need to get the job done can have wonderfully beneficial effects on adolescents. Encouragement and support should be given to adults who are trying to maintain connections with their adolescents, especially for teenagers at risk.

- Communication is important, and adolescent disclosure to parents is related to warm, supportive relationships—not directly to monitoring. Adolescents who feel supported and accepted are more likely to disclose because they feel more emotionally connected.

- Steinberg (1994) found that parents of adolescents go through their own perilous transition and that 40% of them experience strong feelings of powerlessness, rejection, and personal regrets when their children become adolescents. Watching teenagers struggle with the problems of adolescence is painful, particularly when they behave egocentrically, when they are emotionally volatile, when they act as if they do not want or need our help, or when they actively rebel against the limits we have set. A certain amount of egocentrism appears to go with the adolescent territory. It is often quite a bit easier for parents and other adults to respond authoritatively, with love and limits, to children when they are young. Something in the nature of their open dependence makes adults feel needed, valued, and important. The task often gets harder during the teenage years, at least in cultures and families that value independence and opportunities for personal expression. Being an adult authority figure in an adolescent's life may entail some hard times, when love and patience are put to the test. Sometimes adolescents' self-absorption seems impenetrable. In what may mirror adolescents' own sense of separateness, adults also can feel isolated. Whereas sharing stories of problem behaviors is rather common among parents of younger children, parents of adolescents are often uncomfortable doing so (Sandmaier, 1996). Therefore, in addition to reconnecting adolescents to their families, helping professionals can help support and reconnect adults to each other.

- Despite adults' best efforts, teens will not disclose everything to parents, because developing a sphere of personal autonomy is an important developmental goal. Helping parents to become aware of their own needs for control and their own levels of anxiety when confronted by adolescent challenges is important in some cases. Parental reactivity, in the guise of harsh punishment, coercion, criticism, or other form of psychological control, is associated with greater adolescent secrecy and communication breakdown. Establishing rules and monitoring behavior is best done from a less reactive and more dispassionate stance. Adolescents, keenly attuned to social cues, can pick up on parental anxiety, which can spiral into conflictual interactions. The new field of mindful parenting has much to offer parents in this area because it provides helpful ways to learn and practice these skills (see Chapters 5 and 14 for more information about mindfulness).

- In some especially difficult situations, teenagers have managed to convince the adults around them that they are their equals and that they are entitled to wield much of the power. Some adults are inclined to avoid the grueling job of limit setter and enforcer because they may feel worn down, may have their own personal struggles to contend with, or may simply not know what to do. Sometimes parents take their cues, despite their better judgment, from other teenagers' more permissive families. Adults who are responsible for adolescents need to be committed to authoritative practices for the long haul. Despite their protestations, the last thing adolescents need is for parents, teachers, or counselors to disengage from them or abdicate their authoritative role. In particular, research has shown that involved and vigilant parenting has been critically important in protecting poor African American youth from potentially dangerous outcomes like delinquency (Brody et al., 2001).

- Ways to encourage parental involvement in education are also important. Many parents who have had unpleasant school experiences themselves resist dealing with school personnel despite their concern for their children. Sometimes schools present formidable obstacles, either real or perceived, to parents who wish to obtain help or information. Helpers can facilitate communication by advocating for parents, by explaining policy and procedures, and by working to develop good relationships with school personnel. Steinberg (1996) found that the most effective parental involvement strategy was to "work the system" on behalf of the student (for example, contacting the school when there is a problem, meeting with teachers or counselors, etc.). When school personnel encourage and facilitate this kind of participation instead of viewing it as an intrusion, it can be very helpful to the adolescents they serve. For difficult teens who are failing in school, coordinating both systems (home and school) creates a powerfully watchful force that signals caring and demandingness. Some schools have created confidential hotlines to allow students to get their friends help if needed. Other implications drawn from the literature include supporting a wide variety of extracurricular activities that provide positive outlets for teens and limiting the number of hours spent in paid employment.

- Efforts to change peer networks directly appear less realistic. Peer groups by their very nature represent adolescent attempts to establish independent social networks and to provide a supportive structure that is an alternative to parent and family (Eckert, 1989). Peer society is influenced by so many factors (individual personalities, availability of types, social context, ethnicity, media, and so forth) that single proximal interventions are likely to be difficult. Consequently, calls for changes in the broader societal context and in the more immediate family and school environment are thought to be the best way to exert influence on the chemistry of the peer groups formed. This is not to suggest that adults should necessarily leave peer groups alone. Indeed, schools and communities are in a unique position to provide guidance, activities, mentorship, and opportunities for service. Other strategies, such as Social and Emotional Learning programs in high schools, peer mediation and peer counseling programs, and a variety of extracurricular opportunities can be useful approaches for teens because they capitalize on the power of the peer group.

- Certainly, not all media use is problematic, but recent cautions are well advised. Violent video game play is a risk factor for aggressive behavior, emotions, and cognitions (like hostile attributional bias). Excessive screen time use has been associated with internalizing problems including depression, suicide, loneliness, obesity, sleep problems, cyberbullying, and poor academic achievement. Twenge and colleagues (2017) reported a dose-response relationship between screen time and suicide-related risk. Suicide-related risks included (1) feeling extremely sad or hopeless, (2) seriously considering suicide, (3) making a plan, and (4) making an attempt. In their study of over 500,000 13- to 18-year-olds, 33% of teens who spent at least 2 hours a day using electronic devices reported at least one suicide-related risk compared to 29% who spent one hour per day. At five hours per day, close to 50% endorsed at least one suicide-related risk. Figure 10.9 shows the relationship between exposure and risk. Use of devices such as smartphones and computers are significant, albeit modern, risks that demand new kinds of responses. Professionals should stay abreast of research in this area in order to care for their clients using the best available information. They should take teenagers' online experiences of cyberbullying, social comparison, and exclusion as well as dosage of exposure very seriously given that social media reality *is* reality for many contemporary youth. This is a case wherein adolescents are best *not left to their "own devices."* Parents and society as a whole need to be involved in harnessing these new technologies for good instead of harm (Underwood & Ehrenreich, 2017). Parental communication about safety issues related to media use may be helpful because this discussion lies within the prudential domain.

- Remember that adolescents are trying to find their place in the larger world *while* maintaining the attachments that have been their source of comfort since birth. The connections change and expand, but the underlying emotional needs remain the same. For youth who have been traumatized, whose family relationships have been damaged or for those drawn into risky patterns of

FIGURE 10.9 Pattern of relationships between suicide risk factors and electronic device use in youth ages 13–18.

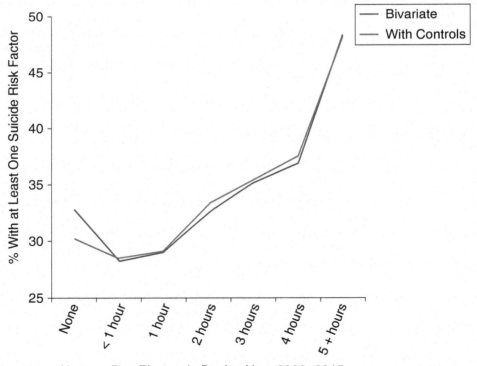

SOURCE: Based on Twenge, J. M., Joiner, T. E., Rogers, M. L. & Martin, G.N. (2017). Increases in depressive symptoms, suicide-related outcomes, and suicide rates among U.S. adolescents after 2010 and links to increased new media screen time. *Clinical Psychological Science.*

Key: *Bivariate* = Correlations between depressive symptoms and E-Device use. *With Controls* = Partial correlations controlled for sex, race/ethnicity, SES, grade and U.S. region with E-Device use.

behavior, family therapy can be a very effective intervention. Table 10.4 summarizes four approaches with substantial research support to help at-risk youth and their families.

The Personal Meaning of Risk

It would be easy if adolescents bought the argument that risky behaviors should be avoided. Some adolescents are inclined to do so, but many others seem impervious to adult logic. Those in the latter group, who may act without thinking, might be more likely to show up in a counselor's office. Although we have discussed many of the theories about why adolescents take risks in general, it is important from a helping perspective to consider the personal motivation that drives a young person and, in so doing, to uncover the personal meaning of risky behavior for that individual. Counselors know how important empathy is for the success of therapeutic relationships. It is good to be mindful that, at its core, real empathy incorporates perspective taking. In work with adolescents, adults cannot assume that mature perspective taking

skills are present or that adolescent perspectives will necessarily resonate with their own adult points of view. Consequently, until we become aware of our own perspective and differentiate it from that of our adolescent clients, attempts to reason with youth across this "great divide" can be ineffective.

In individual counseling, a good place for the therapist to start might be with the questions "How does this young person perceive the risky behavior?" and "What purpose does it serve?" Although not yet fully developed as an intervention strategy, Selman and Adalbjarnardottir (2000) describe a method for understanding adolescents' reasoning about risky behaviors that is based on social perspective taking. In their study, a developmental lens was applied to themes that emerged from extensive interviews with Icelandic adolescents about their alcohol use. The interview questions used in this study included two semistructured protocols, the Risky Business Interview (Levitt & Selman, 1993) and the Relationship Interview (Schultz, 1993), both composed of open- and closed-ended prompts. The use of these instruments underscores the central connection

---

TABLE 10.4 Selected Family Therapies for Adolescents

THERAPY	TARGET POPULATION	THEORETICAL ORIGINS AND KEY FEATURES	RESOURCES FOR MORE INFORMATION
Brief Strategic Family Therapy (BSFT)	Well-established program for youth with behavior problems, drug and alcohol use, delinquency, association with antisocial peers, and unsafe sexual behaviors.	BSFT focuses on changing repetitive patterns of interaction within family systems that maintain problematic interactions, using strategic and functional family therapy techniques drawn from the pioneering work of Salvador Minuchin and Jay Haley. Treatment is short term (12–16 once per week sessions).	Szapocznik, J., Hervis, O., & Schwartz, S. (2003). *Brief Strategic Family Therapy for adolescent drug abuse*. Bethesda, MD: National Institute on Drug Abuse. Minuchin, S. (1974). *Families and family therapy*. Cambridge, MA: Harvard University Press. Haley, J. (1976). *Problem-solving therapy*. San Francisco, CA: Jossey-Bass.
Multisystemic Therapy (MST)	Well-established treatment for juvenile delinquents, youth with conduct, substance abuse, emotional, social problems.	Based on Bronfenbrenner's bio-ecological model, MST targets individual, family, school, peer, and contextual influences at the same time. Primary target is the family that mediates other improvements. Treatment is personalized to the family and provided through home visits.	Henggeler, S. W. (2010). Efficacy studies to large-scale transport: The development and validation of multisystemic therapy programs. *Annual Review of Clinical Psychology, 7*, 351–381. Bronfenbrenner, U. (1979). *The ecology of human development: Experiments by nature and design*. Cambridge, MA: Harvard University Press.
Multidimensional Family Therapy (MDFT)	Well-supported treatment for juvenile delinquency and antisocial behavior.	Theoretical background is in family, developmental and systems psychology. It is intended to create new, more adaptive lifestyle decisions for teens with risky lifestyles. Treatment is provided in diverse settings (e.g., juvenile justice settings).	Liddle, H. A. (1995). Conceptual and clinical dimensions of a multidimensional, multisystems engagement strategy in family-based adolescent treatment. *Psychotherapy: Theory, Research, Practice, 32*, 39–58.
Attachment Based Family Therapy (ABFT)	Adolescent trauma, suicidality, and depression.	Treatment focuses on repairing or strengthening trust in attachment relationships, using features of contextual therapy. Trauma experiences are addressed. Attachment relationships are the primary vehicle by which change occurs. Treatment may be short term (e.g., 14 sessions).	Diamond, G. S., Diamond, G. M., & Levy, S. A. (2014). *Attachment-based family therapy for depressed adolescents*. Washington, DC: American Psychological Association Press. Bowlby, J. (1969). *Attachment and loss: Attachment (Vol. 1)*. New York, NY: Basic Books. Boszormenyi-Nagy, I. K. & Krasner, B. R. (2013). *Between give and take: A clinical guide to contextual therapy*. New York, NY: Routledge.

between risky behavior and the world of peer relationships in adolescence.

In this research study, verbal responses of adolescent participants were coded to produce highly nuanced portraits of social perspective taking, meaning making, and relationships. However, a few general implications can be adapted for clinical purposes to help us better understand adolescent thinking and behavior.

Recall that perspective taking develops in stage-like shifts from unilateral/noninclusive awareness of multiple perspectives to contextualized/highly inclusive awareness. The coordination of multiple perspectives gradually improves with time and experience. The theory posits that adolescents are likely to make more risky choices, especially in social contexts, when they lack the ability to coordinate their own perspectives with those of parents and other significant adults. Coordination of perspectives on risk actually involves the reciprocal interplay of three related competencies: (1) the adolescent's level of general knowledge about risks and their place in social interactions, (2) the variety of risk-management strategies that are available to the adolescent, and (3) the adolescent's level of awareness about the personal meaning of risky behavior. The last of these skills, personal meaning, is considered the "linchpin between understanding of factual knowledge and actual behavior—and between adolescents' perspectives on risk and relationship. Even individuals with sophisticated levels of understanding and a full repertoire of high-level social strategies are vulnerable to addictive influences of alcohol—especially if genetically disposed—if they do not have a mature perspective on what drinking means to them personally" (p. 62).

Consider the example of an adolescent who believes that adults prohibit alcohol because they don't want kids to drink, that kids should just go ahead and drink anyway to have fun with their friends, and that drinking makes kids "cool." Here we see a unilateral, undifferentiated perspective demonstrated in rule-based thinking (adults try to control people and drinking is cool) and in one-way, nonmutual problem solving (just do what you want to do). Another adolescent with more highly developed perspective taking skills might say that adults don't want kids to drink because kids might not be able to handle alcohol, that kids should go out with friends but stick to their own decision not to drink if they have to drive, and that drinking makes social situations easier so it might be hard to stop. Here the notion of intent to protect children, the costs as well as benefits of alcohol, and the possibility of more reciprocity in problem solving are apparent.

The authors hold that more mature functioning depends upon adolescents' ability to allow aspects of others' perspectives, even if these perspectives complicate the issue, into the thinking process. In other words, both the advantages and meaning of risk must be weighed simultaneously against the possibility of harm to oneself and to important

relationships. This presents a difficult cognitive challenge for adolescents who, when confronted with such dilemmas, begin to wade into the muddy waters of ill-defined problems (see Chapter 11). Recall that formal operational skills, which are marked by increased capacity to reason about abstract ideas simultaneously and to engage in introspection, are still developing throughout the adolescent period. In general, the younger the adolescent, the less well developed are these skills.

Interventions that provide factual information in isolation address only one part of the equation. Interventions that focus on changing behaviors also may not work if the adolescent does not "see" the point of changing the behavior and thus is not motivated to do so. Information and risk management skills need to be tied to personally meaningful real-world social contexts where costs and benefits of risk taking are acknowledged to coexist.

What are some specific ways to help adolescents become more reflective about their behaviors in the peer arena? Using the interviewing methods employed in this research as a springboard, helpers can start a dialogue with adolescent clients that focuses on coordinating their subjective points of view with the realities of alcohol (or other risks) and the wishes of adults who are important to them. The kinds of questions included in the interviews focus on perspective taking deficits and are intended to move the adolescent toward more differentiated perspectives (see Table 10.5).

Professionals might apply these questions to the individual's actual risky behavior or employ videotaped or narrative vignettes as the basis for discussion. In addition to the questions in the table, other probes can help clinicians assess the maturity of adolescents' differentiation of feelings: "If you feel happy about drinking with your friends but you don't like it when your parents get angry about it, how do you feel overall? Can you have mixed feelings? How can feelings be mixed?" Others assess levels of self-reflection: "Can a person fool himself into thinking that he doesn't care about getting into trouble?" and "Is there a difference between fooling yourself and fooling another person? What is it?" (Questions are from Selman, 1980.)

The goal is to introduce some dissonance into the discussion to promote reflection and increase motivation to consider alternative ways of handling risks. The ultimate goal is more careful decision making. In practice, this approach blends developmental knowledge with an approach similar to motivational interviewing (Miller & Rollnick, 1991). Considering that many adolescents would be appropriately classified in the precontemplative stage (Prochaska & DiClemente, 1982) with regard to the risks they take, introducing some doubt in the context of a warm and supportive helping relationship might help them gain new perspective and assist them in managing the inevitable risks of adolescence.

TABLE 10.5 The Risky Business Interview: Psychosocial Components, Issues, and Key Questions

PSYCHOSOCIAL COMPONENTS	ISSUES	KEY QUESTIONS
Understanding of the risk (here "drinking")	Initial (past) experiment	Why do you think someone your age starts to drink beer or other alcoholic drinks?
	Current purposes	Why do people your age like to drink these days?
	Further consequences	What can happen to people your age if they continue to drink? Is it more difficult for some people to stop drinking than others? Why?
Interpersonal strategies (from hypothetical dilemmas with parents[a] and peers)	Definition of the problem	What is the problem in this dilemma?
	Alternative strategies	What are some ways they can solve these problems?
	Best strategy	What is the best way to solve this problem?
	Evaluation	How would they know the problem is solved?
Personal meaning of the risk	Past motivation for experimenting	When you first began drinking, why did you decide to give it a try?
	Present attitude	What are the reasons for your drinking *now*?
	Further orientation	Do you think at some time you might decide to change your drinking habit? If you decided to stop drinking, do you think you could stick to that decision if you wanted to? How do you know?

[a]Gunnar/Gudrun goes to a party one weekend evening and comes home late and drunk. His/her dad is waiting for him/her when he/she comes home and is very angry. He tells Gunnar/Gudrun that he/she is to be grounded for a month. Gunnar/Gudrun feels this is too severe a penalty and that he/she is old enough to decide for himself/herself whether he/she drinks or not. How can Gunnar/Gudrun deal with his/her father?

SOURCE: Selman, R. L. & Adalbjarnardottir, S. (2000). A developmental method to analyze the personal meaning adolescents make of risk and relationship: The case of "drinking." *Applied Developmental Science, 4*(1), 47–65. Reprinted by permission of Taylor & Francis Ltd.

Adolescent Suicide

Among our most important public health concerns, suicide is increasing worldwide and is a leading cause of mortality among young people (Stone et al., 2018). Researchers are concerned with the constellation of suicidal thoughts and behaviors (STB) because of their potential to lead to actual suicide. Despite the very real risk STBs present, comparatively little is known about the most effective treatments for youth (Asarnow & Miranda, 2014). Many risk factors have been identified, and every day clinicians need to assess how serious the threats may be. Suicide rates differ by gender, age, and across cultural groups. Table 10.6 displays some culture-specific approaches to the problem of STBs (Goldston et al., 2008).

Consistent with a risk and protective factors model, we would hope to have the ability to identify reliable risks in order to craft effective STB prevention programs for all groups across the life span. However, a thorough meta-analysis of 50 years of research on risks for suicidal thoughts and behaviors produced disappointing results (Franklin et al., 2017). After exhaustive analysis, the authors of this report conclude that available studies do not allow for conclusive evidence about the predictive power of risk factors because of deficiencies in the studies thus far.

Although most clinicians would agree that individuals who have suicidal ideation or behavior are depressed,

MyLab Education
Video Example 10.7
Suicide is a leading cause of mortality among adolescents. Counselors like the one in this video need to assess the seriousness of threats in individual situations.

depression is not, in itself, a strong and independent predictor of suicide. Many people who experience depression do not show suicidal ideation or behaviors. More accurate prediction probably depends on combining large numbers of factors, including depression. It is most likely that suicide is the endpoint of a number of different pathways (equifinality) that are unique to different groups, like women, youth, the elderly, patients with mental disorders, veterans, etc. Each of these groups might share certain risk profiles in combination with individual characteristics that could, once identified, predict suicide with greater precision. Because of extreme emotional volatility of individuals with

TABLE 10.6 Adolescent Suicide Risk Across Cultures

CULTURAL GROUP	PURPORTED RISKS	SPECIFIC PROTECTIVE FACTORS	HELP-SEEKING BEHAVIORS	PREVENTION AND TREATMENT
African American	Perceived discrimination; deindustrialization of inner cities leading to economic and social disadvantage; heightened sensitivity to inequities despite progress of civil rights movement; perceived pressure to adopt majority values; adoption of "cool pose" attitude of appearing invulnerable; disproportionate numbers of victim-precipitated suicide (e.g., shooting by gang or police) as a more culturally acceptable way to end one's life.	Religious orientation that supports meaning in life despite hardship; cultural capital and belonging to an interdependent social group.	Low rates of seeking help possibly due to distrust of professional mental health system; lack of adequate health coverage; culturally inappropriate screening; an ethic that values personal expenditure of effort to cope with problems. Higher rates of help-seeking directed to members of clergy.	Gatekeeper model utilizing the Black church; training clergy and others to recognize risk and make referrals. Example: HAVEN program (Molock et al., 2008)
American Indian and Alaska Native Youth	Isolation of life on a reservation associated with poverty and social limitations; high rates of alcohol and substance use disorders; particular sensitivity to suicide contagion because of isolation; residual effects of ethnic cleansing trauma; high rates of complementary life-threatening/risky behaviors.	Spiritual orientation; traditional cultural values and identity provide grounding.	Distrust of the mental health system; stigma associated with seeking professional mental health services; more adults and adolescents sought help from traditional community healers.	Tribes often strive to maintain their cultural integrity, so generic approaches may not be effective; programs should integrate cultural values of the group. Example: Western Athabaskan Natural Helpers Program (May et al., 2005)
Asian American/ Pacific Islander	Emphasis on interdependence and group harmony may serve to suppress conflict, leading to depression; loss of face and stresses of immigration for some may influence suicidal behavior.	Language fluency, ethnic pride, and social support from families serve as protective factors for some groups.	Tendency not to disclose feelings may manifest in reporting more physical (rather than psychological) symptoms; long delays in accessing treatment may make problems more severe; loss of face may be a barrier to help seeking.	No empiricallysupported prevention programs at this point; ethnically matched therapists and centers and family involvement tends to result in longer treatment duration.
Latino/Latina	Familism may lead to stress that puts youth at odds with peers; traumatic immigration experiences and acculturation may be risks; culture-specific dissociative experiences (ataques de nervios) may precipitate suicide attempts.	Familismo also serves to bolster pride, family cohesion and sense of security.	Less likely to seek professional help due to language and structural barriers; value of parental involvement in treatment may be difficult with limited numbers of bilingual helpers, especially for recent immigrant families.	No empirically supported prevention programs at this point; adaptations of CBT and interpersonal therapy for depression included parental involvement consistent with value of familismo; adaptations required for specific Latino groups rather than treating all the same.

SOURCE: Based on Goldston, D. B., Molock, S. D., Whitbeck, L. B., Murakami, J. L., Zayas, L. H., & Nagayama Hall, G. C. (2008). Cultural considerations in adolescent suicide prevention and psychosocial treatment. *American Psychologist, 63,* 14–31.

suicidal inclinations, it may also be more useful to assess risks like hopelessness as "states" (over minutes, hours, or days) rather than as traits.

Obviously, more research is warranted to find profiles or algorithms that are more reliable than symptom lists. In the meantime, the authors provide a strong caution: Those risk factors identified by expert consensus at present *should be maintained* as practice guidelines. The fact that more research is needed does not obviate the need to pay attention to risk factors, however imperfect they might be. At present, some risks for suicidal ideation include: prior suicide ideation,

hopelessness, depression, abuse history, and anxiety. Risks for suicidal attempts include: prior nonsuicidal self-injury, prior suicide attempt, certain mental health diagnoses, and prior psychiatric hospitalization. Risks for actual suicide include: prior psychiatric hospitalization, prior suicide attempt, prior suicide ideation, lower SES, and stressful life events.

As discussed in an earlier section, there may be a new risk for suicide unknown to prior generations that is shaping our understanding of this serious social problem (Twenge et al., 2017). The sharp uptick in use of electronic communication among youth may be affecting their well-being during a sensitive period of development. Teenagers who spend more time on screen activities were significantly more likely to report more depressive symptoms and suicide-related behavior than those whose time was spent on nonscreen activities. Among the nonscreen activities included in this study were homework, reading print media, participation in social, athletic, and religious organizations, etc. Authors hypothesize that there is something unique to screen use. It might reduce feelings of belongingness and emotional connection that are supported by in-person interaction.

It Takes a Village

Successful negotiation of the adolescent period depends upon the interaction of a number of variables—biology, social environment, perceptions, personality, and behavior. The fact that so many influential systems touch on adolescents' lives and that some systems, such as the peer network, can be resistant to adult intrusion makes it critical to use a wide-angle lens when evaluating and treating teenagers.

The world's youth population is now close to two billion, presenting us all with challenges for education and health care as well as opportunities to strengthen the future adult work force in productive ways. Many global institutions have recognized the need to pay attention to this growing demographic. For example, the United Nations Commission on Population and Development selected adolescents and youth as its 45th session theme in 2012 (United Nations, www.un.org/en/development/desa/population/theme/adolescents-youth). Advocates encourage a holistic, life-course approach to adolescent health and well-being, rather than an approach that focuses on single-problem issues, such as drug abuse. Arguably, advances in understanding adolescent brain development, developmental psychology and psychopathology, and the long-term consequences of harmful behaviors and contexts have added a sense of urgency to this agenda. Additionally, the gains in prevention science have made delivering on this growing knowledge base a more realistic possibility.

Increasingly, professional training in prevention science and evidence-based practice is being recommended for those who work with children and youth (Catalano et al., 2012). This requires understanding specific risks and protective factors faced by adolescents within their cultural context, which informs and contributes to the effectiveness of interventions.

Recently, we have witnessed an increased interest in supporting positive youth development. In general, these efforts recognize the importance of providing resources at all levels of the system (Larson & Tran, 2014). Although positive youth development has been described in a variety of ways, some essential elements exist: the presence of caring adults and mentors on a regular basis, schools that build academic competence and offer vocational preparation, an atmosphere of hope, encouragement of positive values, and high but achievable expectations (Lerner, Fisher, & Weinberg, 2000). Clearly, professionals and nonprofessionals alike need to join forces to create the kinds of communities that offer these opportunities for everyone.

Larson and Tran summarize the challenges for youth in this way:

> As a result of this deep complexity, producing one's own development requires young people to address a wide variety of—often unstated—bio-psycho-social-cultural challenges. These include basic "developmental tasks" first introduced by earlier theorists (Erikson 1950; Havighurst 1953). These tasks: Who am I?, what are my values?, learning self-regulation, achieving autonomy-with-connection with family, and preparation for adult work roles consist of untidy puzzles that adolescents need to figure out. Many involve working out tensions and contradictions (e.g., personal desire with morality, reconciling obligations to self vs. to other). In the 21st century, young people face added developmental challenges associated with growing up in increasing fluid and heterogeneous societies. As adolescents awaken from the protective shell of childhood, their daily lived experiences confront them with more complex worlds, with more contradictions and challenges. (p. 1013)

Helping young people solve the untidy puzzles that await them will take team effort. Neither families nor schools, two of our major socializing institutions, can do this alone. A few general guidelines from Siegel and Scovill (2000; see Table 10.7) summarize and reemphasize important points.

1. Take the social and cultural context seriously. Don't rely on intrapsychic interpretations alone when identifying or assessing problems. Don't blame everything on the adolescent brain. Adolescents do not engineer all their problems, despite how appealing that argument might appear.
2. Consider adolescent problem behavior as a means to an end. Table 10.7 provides some suggestions to help clinicians understand the functions that problem behaviors serve.
3. Construct healthy and attractive alternatives to help adolescents meet their developmental needs, including social as well as educational alternatives. Not all adolescents fit into the traditional academic mold for success, yet they want success and they are worthy of it.

TABLE 10.7 Risk Taking in Adolescence: Examples, Functions, Damaging and Healthy Practices

EXAMPLES OF ANTISOCIAL OR PROBLEM BEHAVIORS	POSSIBLE FUNCTIONS OF BEHAVIOR (I.E., OUTCOMES TEENS MAY BE SEEKING)	DEVELOPMENTAL TASK	DEVELOPMENTALLY DAMAGING PRACTICES	DEVELOPMENTALLY HEALTHY ALTERNATIVES
Skipping school, disobeying teachers	Expression of frustration with inability to succeed in school setting	Competence	Large schools, high student to teacher ratios in classrooms, ability grouping	Provide individualized programs where youth with a wide range of skills can be successful
Engaging in pseudoadult behaviors such as drinking, drug use, and early sexual activity	Means of coping with anxiety, frustration, and fear of inadequacy—seeking to be recognized as competent, capable, respected through mimicry of pseudoadult peers	Transition to adulthood	Lack of connectedness with adults created by lack of parental presence at home, few opportunities to develop relationships with adults at school or in the community, little one-on-one time with adults	Teach alternative methods for coping with stress, presence of adult role models, opportunities to learn career skills, involvement in mentoring or apprenticeship programs
"Teenage behaviors" (e.g., outrageous clothing, music, use of profanity), violation of minor rules such as curfew, status offenses	Means of making a personal statement (how I'm different, important, angry, etc.) seeking to be recognized as an individual of worth, capable of making a unique contribution	Identity, autonomy, individuation	Targeting of teens as consumer group by media, lack of opportunities for teens to make a positive contribution to family and society	Allow teens to participate in rule making; allow teens to participate in decision making; increase the types of contributions teens can make to society; increase variety of socially sanctioned clubs at school
Joining a gang, involvement with delinquent peers	Means of meeting the need to belong (I want to be part of something)	Intimacy, relationship building	Lack of opportunities to meet and interact with prosocial peers, coercive family interactions	Teach relationship enhancement skills, conversation skills, empathy skills; provide alternative niches or ecologies with prosocial peers and adults
"Acting out" (e.g., causing trouble at school, getting into fights, making threats, theft, running away)	To be heard or understood; to bring attention to perceived inequity of treatment	Identity, competence, industry	Failure to listen to teens, not allowing teens to participate in rule and decision making, doing things "to" teens rather than "with" them	Provide strong adult role models who listen to teens; teach youth to identify and express anger and other emotions (rational self-talk); teach negotiation skills; include teens in decision making
Smoking, having sex, drinking, status offenses	Way of asserting/affirming the transition from childhood to adulthood—seeking to be recognized as a person with an opinion that counts; attempting to establish a role for oneself	Transition to adulthood	Double standard of behavior for adults and teens	Create more formalized markers to acknowledge transitions; recognize the cost to children/adolescents when adults fail to "walk the way they talk"
Speeding, riding on the hoods of cars, "sensation seeking" (Zuckerman, 1979)	Way to avoid boredom and seek excitement—seeking a way to not feel put down, ignored or unimportant	Competence	Few community centers, clubs, or other environments where adult-monitored youth activities are provided	Develop exciting, adult-monitored activities for adolescents (e.g., midnight basketball)
Playing "chicken" with yourself and others, shoplifting, vandalism	Means of testing personal limits and status—seeking competence, finding something to be "in charge of"	Identity	Few opportunities for teens to succeed and to learn adult skills (e.g., career skills, communication skills) or to make a contribution to society	Create environments where adolescents can gain confidence and excel in something; broaden the scope of what defines success for adolescents beyond academics and sports
Violent behavior, law violations, conduct disorder	Expression of opposition to or outrage at adult authority—seeking control and power over disruptive/unsafe environment	Trust vs. mistrust, safety needs	Failure to protect children from poverty, child abuse, neglect, mistreatment, physiological disadvantages	Early childhood intervention has been most successful here; prognosis in adolescence is poor

SOURCE: Siegel, A. W. & Scoville, L. C. (2000). Problem behavior: The double symptom of adolescence. *Development and Psychopathology, 12,* 786–787. Used with permission by Cambridge University Press.

Summary

Adolescent Autonomy and Social Identity

1. The profound physical, cognitive, and social changes that accompany entry into adolescence can create a state of instability. Establishing independence requires some separation from caregivers on a psychological level. Simultaneously, teens increase their affiliation with and dependency on peers, who become more central to their social world.

The Peer Arena

2. Peers are a source of support, of social comparison, and of identification. Adolescents borrow from their peers' ways of behaving and thinking and provide an arena for identity formation.

3. Peer contact is helpful to adolescents because it provides support on the road to greater autonomy. However, some kinds of contact, like peer victimization and exposure to deviant behavior, can result in internalizing and externalizing disorders.

The Structure of the Peer Network

4. Most adolescents have a few best friends, who are part of a clique of individuals who tend to do things together. Larger groups composed of many cliques comprise crowds, whose members may not be friends but share interests, attitudes, behaviors, and appearance.

5. Most American high schools are characterized by fairly similar crowd structures, consisting of populars and jocks, some alienated groups such as druggies, an average crowd, and an academically high-achieving group.

6. Crowds influence their members, but they are also freely selected by their members, who choose to participate in shared norms, roles, and expectations. Both selection and influence processes operate.

7. Crowds also exist in other cultures and in post-secondary settings, but specific groups (e.g., jocks, etc.) and outcomes related to membership may differ.

8. Youth who belong to multiple crowds have higher social identity complexity, which is related to more prosocial intergroup relationships and less in-group/out-group bias.

The Role of Parents

BECAUSE I'M THE PARENT, THAT'S WHY…

9. Parent–child conflicts increase during adolescence. Conflicts often arise around issues of control; parents and teens may hold different perceptions of rights and responsibilities. Parents are perceived to have more legitimate authority in the moral domain than in the personal domain. Prudential issues often are in dispute because they overlap with legitimate safety concerns and areas of privacy and personal choice.

10. Teens become more secretive as they get older and avoid sharing information because they may not want to upset their parents or be denied access to friends or activities. Youth protect information by not sharing some details with parents, avoiding conversations, or lying.

RAISING ADOLESCENTS

11. Research has focused on whether certain kinds of parenting at adolescence may be more predictive of positive outcomes and have found that both warmth (responsiveness) and control (demandingness) are as important with adolescents as they are with younger children. This kind of authoritative parenting is associated with, among other things, higher achievement, self-confidence, self-esteem, social adjustment, and self-control.

12. Parental knowledge is related to adjustment and less risky behavior than parental monitoring. Parental monitoring does not directly improve disclosure and may impede it. Warm and supporting parental relationships with adolescents are more predictive of adolescent sharing. Parental monitoring has several dimensions, including control. Psychological control is particularly harmful to youth across cultures.

Adolescents in School

13. Declines in academic orientation and motivation are noted in early adolescence and may be associated with shifting school structures and processes as children enter middle school or junior high school. Larger classes and schools, whole-group lectures, and heavy emphasis on competition are among these practices. Also, some kinds of parental involvement decline sharply at secondary school levels, despite evidence that it remains just as important for teens' achievement as for that of younger children.

14. Schools have attempted to translate the research findings on authoritative parenting to schools. Those secondary schools that prioritize affective and motivational supports, like warm teacher–student relationships, have better outcomes than those with high expectations alone.

15. Participation in crowds that support academic achievement can be helpful for those students whose parents are disengaged. This suggests the role that crowds can play in many important outcomes.

Leisure, Work, and Media

16. Involvement in school- or community-sponsored out-of-school activities is associated with better achievement and adjustment overall. However, some deleterious effects, like poorer achievement, have been related to some kinds of extracurricular activities.

17. Like leisure, research on paid employment for adolescents is mixed. In general, some paid work can be helpful, but spending substantial hours working is associated with lower school achievement, less involvement in school activities, more drug and alcohol use, and more delinquency. Some cultural differences have also been found.

18. High rates of media use are associated with obesity, sleep problems, underachievement, early initiation of risky behaviors like smoking and drinking, cyberbullying, sexting (sending sexually explicit messages or images via text message), and depression. More positive outcomes include ability to be connected to others and to access helpful information.

19. Playing violent video games is a clear risk factor for aggressive thoughts, feelings, and actions. TV and movies are prime outlets for sexual information for youth. Other forms of interpersonal violence, like dating/sexual victimization, are a serious problem for adolescents.

20. Adolescents, their peers, families, and schools are affected by the larger culture, and vice versa. Present culture may not be very "adolescent friendly" due to loss of community and a focus on individualism and material success. Negative media forces seem to shape attitudes and beliefs. Teens are increasingly exposed to violence, sex, and commercial messages through the media, affecting what they view as normative and acceptable behavior. Thus, media messages often compete with other, more traditional messages from families and schools, and research demonstrates that media messages do influence teens' beliefs and behaviors.

Risk-Taking versus Risky Lifestyles in Adolescence

21. Risky behavior increases sharply during adolescence, peaking at about age 17. Some rates of risky behavior have declined or held steady since 2011. Other problems, like depression, have increased. A moderate level of parental control, compared to little control or very high levels of control, is related to less risky behaviors in adolescents.

22. Risky behavior may also provide some advantages in the teen years, making it, in some cases, adaptive. It can sometimes serve as an indicator of individuation and self-determination and as a source of peer acceptance. Thus, risk taking has both positive and negative aspects. It may be inevitable in cultures with "broad" socialization practices, which encourage high levels of individual freedom.

23. Some research suggests that a developmental shift might be occurring. Youth are engaging in adult (sometimes risky) behaviors less frequently than in previous generations as well as in more solitary time with media. This is hypothesized to be due to a slow life strategy that is related to longer periods of education and later childbearing.

Society's Role in Adolescent Problem Behavior: Then and Now

24. Although the United States provides high levels of freedom to adolescents, it may not provide adequate supports to ensure that risk taking is within reasonable limits and that positive youth development is supported. In the 1920s, concerns about adolescent risk taking fostered a sense of community responsibility to provide adequate supervision and healthy outlets for young people, and a number of youth-oriented institutions sprang up offering free services to teens. Today such community support systems are often in short supply, and costly when they are available. The current approach seems to be based on a reconceptualization of the issue. Risky behavior is now viewed as a problem of the individual rather than a problem of society.

Case Study

Mark Spencer is a White, 16-year-old sophomore at a suburban public school. He lives with his mother, father, and older brother in a middle-class community. Mark has attended the local public schools since kindergarten, and until 8th grade he was an above-average student who frequently made honor roll. Mark's father Doug commutes to his job at an insurance company and in recent years has increased his hours at the office as his company has downsized and shifted responsibilities to remaining employees. His mother Joanne works as a secretary at a local real estate agency. Mark's brother Dave is a senior who is also an above-average student and who has been very active in intermural sports, especially soccer and baseball.

During middle school, Mark had a strong interest in scouting and was particularly involved in camping and developing survival skills. Several of Mark's friends in the scout troop left scouting in the 7th grade and began spending more time hanging out with girlfriends and playing sports. Mark continued scouting until 8th grade, but teasing from his friends became unbearable, and he finally gave up. Mark was shy with girls and not particularly interested in sports, so he was left with little in common with his middle school friends. At the same time, his grades began to slip.

When Mark's parents expressed concern about his poor grades, he told them that his teachers were jerks and his classes were boring. Although Doug and Joanne tried to encourage him to study more and to continue scouting or to try sports, Mark would generally react angrily, and his parents would back off to not upset him further. By 9th grade he was spending more and more time alone, playing video games and watching television in his room. When Mark turned 16, he begged for a car, and his parents agreed. Because they were so busy, Doug and Joanne felt it would be helpful to give Mark more independence, and they hoped it would increase his social acceptance. Mark was one of the first students in the sophomore class to turn 16, and he found that his old friends' interest in him was piqued when he began driving his new car to school.

Mark began to hang out with his old friends, and began smoking, drinking, and experimenting with drugs. His grades slipped further, although with almost no effort he was able to maintain a C average. Once again his parents became concerned about his grades, particularly because college loomed. They even threatened to remove the television from his room, but, as usual, they backed down when confronted by his anger. Doug and Joanne were also loath to rock the boat when Mark finally seemed to be enjoying his social life. He was no longer moping around the house, watching TV, and worrying his parents.

When Mark asked to be allowed to drive his friends to a concert in a nearby city, with plans to spend the weekend at the home of a friend's uncle, his parents disagreed about how to handle his request. Joanne was afraid of giving him so much freedom and worried about the safety of the group. Doug, remembering how restrictive his own parents were, argued that "you're only young once" and that "you have to hope that what you've taught them up to now will stick, because that's all you can do. At 16, kids are really on their own."

The weekend trip was a disaster. After the concert, the group partied at the uncle's home, without adult supervision. Neighbors called the police about the noise. Parents were notified after the police found evidence of underage drinking. Mark persuaded his parents that he did not know the uncle would be away and that he had no control over his friends' drinking. Doug and Joanne gave Mark the benefit of the doubt, but a month later, Joanne found a bottle of vodka hidden in Mark's room. Both parents realized that they needed to seek help.

Discussion Questions

1. Consider the developmental path that Mark has followed. Describe the elements that have been influential in shaping this adolescent's experience.
2. Describe and comment on the parenting style used by Doug and Joanne. Evaluate the parents' approach to Mark throughout his early adolescence and suggest ways they might have responded differently.
3. What role could the school have played in modifying the course of Mark's development?
4. What specific suggestions for treatment might you make for Mark and his family?

Practice Using What You Have Learned

MyLab Education Application Exercise 10.1
The Role of Parents

MyLab Education Application Exercise 10.2
How Schools Support Adolescents'
Developmental Needs

MyLab Education Application Exercise 10.3
Case Study: Risky Adolescent Behavior

Journal Questions

1. Compare and contrast the social world of adolescents today with that of your own adolescence. What similarities and differences do you find?
2. Recall a situation or interaction in which you felt a measure of psychological control (shaming, coercion, criticism, invasion of privacy, etc.). Describe your feelings in that situation and your response to the person in control. What effect did this have on the relationship, on your motivation, on your behavior? How would you address this with clients or parents if it should present itself?
3. How much information did you share with your parents as an adolescent? Describe your motivation for disclosure or nondisclosure. In which way can you relate to the material about secrecy and disclosure in this chapter?
4. Identify one action step that you could take to improve the lives of adolescents with whom you are in contact. If you could change their school (academically, structurally, or otherwise), what changes would you make, and why?
5. Consider your own level of media consumption. What portion of your day is spent consuming media? What are its benefits to you? What are its drawbacks? How does the prevalence of media in our culture affect our ability to sustain attention? What advice would you give parents who are concerned about their adolescent's media use?

Key Concepts

peer selection (p. 392)
peer influence (p. 392)
deviancy training (p. 392)
social identity complexity (p. 392)
parental monitoring (p. 396)
parental solicitation (p. 396)

parental knowledge (p. 396)
indulgent parenting (p. 397)
dismissive parenting (p. 397)
acceptance (p. 397)
democracy (p. 397)
binge drinking (p. 402)

risky behaviors (p. 405)
life history theory (p. 409)
maturity gap (p. 412)
broad socialization (p. 412)
narrow socialization (p. 412)

Chapter 11
Physical and Cognitive Development in Young Adulthood

 Learning Objectives

After reading this chapter, you should be able to:

11.1 Describe physical development in young adulthood and contrast the effects of healthy versus unhealthy lifestyles.

11.2 Compare dominant views of the changes young adults experience in cognitive functioning and suggest problem-solving approaches that apply the postformal or relativistic thinking needed for the unstructured problems they face.

Garrett is 20 years old. During high school, he was enrolled in college prep and "honors" classes. Despite the challenging course work in his private school, it was pretty easy for him to keep up a low A average. He wrote his papers in one draft and barely studied for exams. He was much more interested in winning tennis competitions and partying with his friends. Good scores on college entrance exams helped gain him admittance to an elite university. His parents were thrilled: Maybe he would settle down and actually complete the premed curriculum he signed up for. But Garrett is not quite "settled down." Early in his second year, for example, Garrett fell off the roof of his fraternity house after climbing up on a drunken dare. His parents' health insurance covered the costs of the hospitalization and rehab, and he lived at home for most of his recuperation. Back at school now, still in a leg cast for the multiple fractures to his leg, he spends much of his time playing poker and getting into what he considers hilarious predicaments while having sex with his latest girlfriend. He's getting by in his classes without working too hard, but he can see that the more advanced courses coming up in the curriculum are going to take some serious work. At the moment, Garrett spends little time worrying about that future, while his parents keep paying his tuition and hoping for the best.

Is Garrett an adult? Scholars are likely to disagree about the answer to this question. Most would agree that the onset of adolescence is marked by the changes of puberty. But there are no easily observed physical changes that signal entry into adulthood. Instead, adulthood is a social construction. One or more culturally determined criteria usually must be met before one's maturity is established, and the criteria vary depending on the observer and the culture.

In the past, sociologists emphasized the achievement and timing of marker events as criteria for adulthood. These have included completing formal education, entering the adult workforce, leaving the family home, getting married, and becoming a parent (Juárez & Gayet, 2014). Around the middle of the last century, a large proportion of the U.S. population achieved many of these marker events between the ages of 18 and 24 (Rindfuss, 1991). However, if we evaluate our hypothetical student, Garrett, according to these traditional marker events, he would not be an adult despite being in the "right" age range.

From a sociological perspective, it seems to take longer to grow up today than it did at earlier points in history for many reasons. Some of these include the demand for a highly educated workforce and the increased cost of this education (Jacobs & Stoner-Eby, 1998), the difficulties inherent in earning enough to support children and in achieving stable employment (Halperin, 1998b), and the frequency of early, nonmarital sexual activity and the availability of contraception (Warner et al., 1998). All have had profound effects on the timing of life events. On one hand then, some markers of adulthood are considerably delayed. For example, the median age for marriage in the United States was about 22 or 23 in 1976. By 2016, the median age for marriage had risen to about 28, a difference of more than 5 years in 4 decades (see Figure 11.1). On the other hand, other indicators of adulthood, such as the onset of sexual activity, occur much earlier than they did in the past.

FIGURE 11.1 Median age at first marriage: 1890 to 2017.

SOURCE: U.S. Census Bureau, Decennial Censuses, 1890 to 1940, and Current Population Survey, Annual Social and Economic Supplements, 1947 to 2017.

FIGURE 11.2 "Do you feel that you have reached adulthood?"

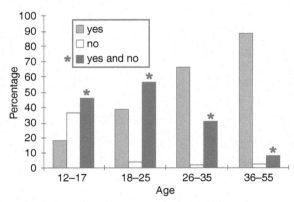

SOURCE: Arnett, J. (2000). Emerging adulthood: A theory of development from the late teens through the twenties. *American Psychologist, 55*, 472. Reprinted by permission of the American Psychological Association.

Such shifts in the timing of marker events appear to have delayed the onset of adulthood, especially in Western societies, where these shifts have most often occurred and where the pathways to adulthood are remarkable in their variability, so that specifying when adulthood has been achieved is difficult. One approach is to ask young people themselves. In a seminal study, Arnett (2000) asked young people in the United States to rate the importance of criteria in several areas (such as cognitive, behavioral, emotional, biological, and legal criteria, as well as role transitions and responsibilities) as definitions of adult status. He also asked participants whether they felt they had reached adulthood. A majority of respondents in their late teens and early twenties answered both "yes and no." Perhaps Garrett would say something similar. As you can see in Figure 11.2, the proportion of young people in Arnett's study who judged themselves to be adults gradually increased with age, with a clear majority of participants in their late 20s and early 30s doing so.

Similar findings have been reported in other U.S. studies, including studies of religious (e.g., Mormons) and ethnic (e.g., Latino) minorities, and in studies of young people throughout the world, from Canada to Argentina to several European and Asian countries (Nelson & Luster, 2015). Can this delay in identifying oneself as an adult be attributed to the timing of role transitions? Apparently not. Most young people in the countries and cultures that have been studied do not consider chronological age and role transitions such as marriage and parenthood, on their own, to be significant markers. For example, Arnett's (2000) respondents indicated that the two most important qualifications for adulthood are first, accepting responsibility for the consequences of one's actions, and second, making independent decisions. Becoming financially independent, a traditional marker event, was third. Consequently, the subjective sense of being an adult may be more important than the accomplishment and timing of discrete tasks.

Across cultures, independence and autonomy are typically endorsed as important to feeling like an adult, but relational factors are also scored high on most young people's lists of criteria for adulthood: having and keeping relationships and meeting obligations to family. As one research team put it, "independence and interdependence are not mutually exclusive" (Syed & Mitchell, 2015). There are cultural differences, of course. Young people from collectivist cultures often score relational factors nearer to the top of their lists than Westerners do. For example, in Argentina, being able to care for children and becoming less self-oriented are especially emphasized by college students (Facio & Micocci, 2003). In China, young working women highly rank being able to support their parents (Zhong & Arnett, 2014).

Given that young people from 18 to 29 years old so often feel that they have not yet met their own criteria for reaching adulthood, Arnett (2000, 2015) proposes that this period be considered a distinct stage of life called emerging adulthood. *Emerging adulthood* is a sociological phenomenon and it is made possible by the kind of economic development that characterizes developed countries. If the labor of young people is not urgently needed for the economic well-being of their families, and if many occupations require extended years of education, then work is postponed, marriage and childbearing are likely to be delayed, and self-exploration can continue. Arnett (e.g., 2002, 2015) has argued that increasing globalization is spreading the experience of this new stage from Western societies to other parts of the world. *Globalization* is "a process by which cultures influence one another and become more alike through trade, immigration, and the exchange of information and ideas" (Arnett, 2002, p. 774), a process that has shifted into high gear with advances in telecommunications and transportation. In developing countries, young people increasingly move from rural communities to urban centers as they pursue expanding economic opportunities. More occupational and lifestyle options are available, and self-development tends to continue well past the teen years.

Emerging adulthood is typically a more unstable time than adulthood. As they try to find their places in the adult world, emerging adults "move around a lot, go from job to job, and test out love and intimacy in a variety of ways" (Syed & Mitchell, 2015, p. 90). According to the U.S. Census Bureau (2012c), the average person changes jobs seven times between the ages of 18 and 27, but only half that often between the ages of 27 and 44. Moving at least annually during college is not uncommon for emerging adults, nor is moving in and out of the parental home or setting up housekeeping one or more times with a romantic partner, whether in college or not. A sense of life being in flux seems to characterize many young people in this period.

The social world of emerging adults usually expands beyond immediate family, friends, and neighbors. While this presents new challenges for all young people whether they attend college or enter the work force, for some groups it may involve special new stressors. For African Americans, for example, this often means moving into a much more ethnically diverse world than the schools and neighborhoods of their childhood. In college, fewer instructors or students are likely to be Black; in work environments, few employers and co-workers will be Black. Consciousness of one's minority status is exacerbated by the fact that discrimination against African Americans in hiring and housing are still a reality in the United States (Rich, 2014). Arnett and Brody (2008) argue that dealing with identity issues with these added sources of stress may intensify the process. "We believe that identity issues are especially acute for African American emerging adults due to the injection of discrimination and prejudice, and that this may explain a range of puzzling findings" (p. 292). One is the change in substance use during emerging adulthood. It is important to note that African American adolescents and adults engage in less substance use than White adolescents. But for some substances (tobacco, marijuana) there is a greater increase in use during emerging adulthood for African Americans than for Whites. And in rare cases, there is a crossover effect; that is, Black substance use may reach greater levels than White substance use. For example, by about age 26, Black female users of marijuana either match or begin to exceed the frequency of use of White female users. Figure 11.3 illustrates some changes in alcohol, cigarette, and marijuana use across emerging adulthood from a longitudinal study of over 14,000 U.S. participants (Keyes et al., 2015).

FIGURE 11.3 Sample age changes in substance use by White and Black emerging adults: a) alcohol, b) cigarettes, c) marijuana.

SOURCE: Adapted from Keyes, K. M., Vo, T., Wall, M. M., Caetano, R., Suglia, S. Martins, S. S., . . . Hasin, D. (2015). Racial/ethnic differences in use of alcohol, tobacco, and marijuana: Is there a cross-over from adolescence to adulthood? *Social Science & Medicine, 124,* 132–141.

Another puzzling finding concerns suicide rates in the United States. As with substance use, males are much more prone to suicide than females, and Whites are over twice as likely to commit suicide as Blacks. White males show a steady rise in suicide rates through much of adulthood, with the sharpest rise after age 65. But for Black males the peak suicide rate occurs much earlier, between ages 25 and 34 (Centers for Disease Control and Prevention, 2015). Arnett and Brody speculate that "there are uniquely formidable challenges to forming a Black male identity" in the United States and that for some the strain may become intolerable during early adulthood (2008, p. 293).

Research on other ethnic minorities in the United States supports the idea that moving into a more ethnically diverse world after adolescence both extends the process of identity formation and increases its complexity. Fuligni (2007) looked at the children of Asian and Latin immigrant families and found, as you would expect, culture-specific concerns among young adults. The children of the immigrant families had a stronger sense of "family obligation" than European American offspring. They expected to support and assist their families in many ways (e.g., caring for siblings, providing financial support, living near or with the family) and they believed that they should consider the family's wishes when making important decisions. Interestingly, the researchers found that these kinds of values, while strongest in the immigrant children, also increased in young adulthood for all ethnic groups, including the European Americans. Apparently, the importance of connection, as well as autonomy, becomes clearer after adolescence. Immigrant children were most likely, as young adults, to experience a much more expanded social world if they went to college than if they did not, and this happened most often for those of East Asian background. With these young people, Fuligni found a trend toward the kind of extended identity development that characterizes emerging adulthood. Their sense of obligation to family did not disappear, but it competed with new aspirations, "to be able to be doing something that I like" and "to be the person you're supposed to be" (p. 99).

Is a stage of emerging adulthood a good or a bad thing? Could it be viewed as a tendency for modern youth to simply avoid taking on adult roles and responsibilities, nurtured by overprotective, indulgent parents? Arnett argues that in fact, there could be a grain of truth here: Many young adults seem to "find it burdensome and onerous to pay their own bills and do all the other things their parents (have) always done for them" (2007, p. 71). But he generally sees the ambivalence of young adults as a recognition of the value of an extended period of self-development to help them prepare more adequately for taking on adult roles in a complex society. He points out that few emerging adults fail to "grow up." By age 30 nearly all are stably employed, and three quarters are married and have a child. There is also evidence that as adolescents move into young adulthood today they are not substantially different from their counterparts in the 1970s. For example, high school seniors now and then report similar levels of loneliness, anti-social behavior, self-esteem, and life satisfaction (Trzesniewski & Donnellan, 2010).

But some researchers are not as sanguine about this new stage (see Syed, 2015). For example, Hendry and Kloep (2007) express concern that young people are more often inadequately prepared for adulthood than they are benefiting from an extended transition into adulthood. Modern parents, they suggest, tend to both overindulge their children and to pressure them to excel, rather than assuring that their children are adequately educated in basic life skills (see the Applications section on "helicopter" parenting). Twenge (2013) examines cross-sectional data comparing different cohorts of college students and argues that the self-esteem movement has produced a generation of more narcissistic individuals who are less willing to take responsibility for their lives and less concerned about others than previous generations have been. Although such views may all have "grains of truth," only continuing research on this interesting new stage can resolve the issue.

In this and the next chapter we will examine some of the key characteristics of life after adolescence, primarily for young people in the United States. We will refer to the period from about 18 to 30 as **young adulthood**, although we acknowledge Arnett's argument that many 18- to 25-year-olds are better described as "emerging adults." The early years of young adulthood are often an extended period of transition involving exploration of potential adult identities.

We will begin by examining the physical characteristics of young adults and then move on to consider the cognitive changes that are likely in this period of life. In Chapter 12, we will explore the complexities of forming intimate, enduring adult attachments, maintaining or revamping family relationships, and making vocational commitments. That is, we will look at some of the myriad processes involved in taking one's place as a contributing member of an adult community.

MyLab Education
Video Example 11.1
Gary grew up in a Vietnamese American family, who had certain expectations for his future. He describes clearly the stress that arises when need for autonomy and desire to meet family obligations come into conflict in young adulthood.

Physical Development in Young Adulthood

11.1 Describe physical development in young adulthood and contrast the effects of healthy versus unhealthy lifestyles.

Brain Development

In Chapter 9, you learned that the onset of puberty initiates changes in the brain, such as gray matter thinning due in part to pruning, and massive increases in white matter as myelination proceeds. You also learned that there can be some imbalance in brain development, with subcortical and cortical areas maturing at different rates, and the circuitry that connects them lagging as well. The changes in structure and function that begin with puberty continue well into young adulthood. The greater flexibility—and vulnerability—of the adolescent brain carries forward into the mid- to late-twenties. Improvements in executive functions, learning, and thinking continue, both resulting from and influencing ongoing brain changes. Susceptibility to the onset of major mental disorders is extended into this life phase as well (Taber-Thomas & Pérez-Edgar, 2015).

Let's consider just one example of this ongoing maturational process. Inhibitory control, one of the executive functions, involves stopping ourselves from making a "usual" response in order to make a different response (see Chapter 3). Remember the Stroop test, in which you have to stop yourself from automatically reading the color word in order to name the color of the letters? Imaging studies show that in adults, tasks that require inhibitory control activate parts of the prefrontal cortex and several other cortical areas, all on the right side of the brain. In adolescents, different cortical areas on both sides of the brain are activated during these tasks, suggesting that the adult circuits are not fully developed yet. And, teens' performance on these tasks is not as good as that of adults (e.g., Vara, Pang, Vidal, Anagnostou, & Taylor, 2014).

But when does performance actually reach top levels? Knežević and Marinković (2017) addressed this question by comparing three age groups ("early 20s," "mid-20s" and "early 30s") on a standard inhibitory control task. They also looked at event related potential (ERP) patterns as the participants completed the task. Only the "early 30s" group performed at top levels. The two younger groups were less accurate, and their responses were more rapid and impulsive. The ERP patterns helped corroborate that the oldest group was engaging in more reflection than the younger groups. Such data clearly demonstrate that brain development continues in young adulthood, supporting advances in functioning.

Reaching Peak Physical Status

By age 18 to 20, most people have reached their full physical growth. Sometime between 18 and 30, all our biological systems reach peak potential. For example, we can see, hear, taste, and smell as well as we ever will; our skin is as firm and resilient as it can be; the potential strength of muscle and bone is as great as we will ever experience; and our immune systems provide us with the most effective protection we will ever have from diseases ranging from the common cold to cancer. Not all physical capacities reach their peak simultaneously. Visual acuity, for example, reaches a maximum level at about age 20, with little decline for most people until about age 40. But auditory acuity appears to peak before age 20 and may show some declines soon after (Saxon & Etten, 1987; Whitbourne & Whitbourne, 2016).

There are certainly individual differences among us in the achievement of peak physical status—for example, some people reach their full height by age 15, whereas others may not finish growing until age 18 or 20. There are also substantial differences among different physical skills in the timing of peak performance, which is usually assessed by looking at the records of "super-athletes" (e.g., Cotterill, 2017; Tanaka & Seals, 2003). Schulz and Curnow (1988) examined athletic performance records for superathletes in a wide variety of sports. On one hand, they found that maximal performance for most sports is reached within the young adult period; on the other hand, they found that the average age of greatest skill (e.g., winning an Olympic gold medal in track or achieving a Number 1 world ranking in tennis) is different from one sport to another, and sometimes depends on which particular skill is examined within a given sport. For example, the average age at which Olympic swimmers win gold medals is 19; professional golfers typically do not achieve a Number 1 ranking until age 34. For a professional baseball player, the average age for "most stolen bases" is 23, but the mean age for "hitting the most doubles" is 32.

The differences in age of peak performance suggest that the relative importance of practice, training, knowledge, experience, and biological capacity varies from one skill to another. Skills that are based on muscle strength, flexibility, and speed of movement and response tend to peak early. Abilities that are heavily dependent on control, arm–hand steadiness, precision, and stamina tend to peak later. Overall, the greater the importance of cognitive factors in performance—factors such as strategy knowledge and use—the later a skill will top out (Cotterill, 2017).

Superathletes are those whose performance of a skill seems to match their full potential. Most of the rest of us are not concerned about achieving maximal skill, but we usually are motivated to maintain our physical capacities at high levels—including not only performance skills, but also sensory abilities, good health, and youthful appearance—during and beyond the early adult period. Clearly, biology plays a role here. For example, regardless of activity level, muscular strength begins to decline somewhat by about age 30. But research supports the importance of lifestyle in this process. There are good habits that help maintain peak or near-peak functioning and appearance, and there are bad habits that can erode functioning (Whitbourne & Whitbourne, 2016). For example, regular exercise can help both younger and older adults maintain muscle and bone strength and can keep the cardiovascular and respiratory systems functioning well. Smoking, poor diet, and a sedentary lifestyle accelerate loss of peak cardiovascular and respiratory functioning and loss of muscle and bone. Smoking or any excessive drug or alcohol use can diminish functioning in a variety of physiological systems. For example, smoking contributes to more rapid wrinkling of the skin, and alcohol causes damage to the nervous system, the liver, and the urinary tract.

"Eating right" is part of a healthy lifestyle. It means having regularly spaced meals (including breakfast) that are low in fat and that sample a range of food groups, allowing a proper balance of nutrients. Failure to eat right contributes to obesity, to depressed mood, and to many aspects of physical decline. Obesity is epidemic in the United States and other Western countries, and weight gain is especially likely between the ages of 20 and 40 (Haftenberger et al., 2016; Ogden, Carroll, Kit, & Flegal, 2014). Longitudinal studies that have followed participants for 40 to 50 years have made clear that people who fail to follow healthy lifestyles in their young adult years suffer from poorer health later and that they are less satisfied with their lives in late adulthood when compared to people who do adopt healthy habits in young adulthood (Belloc & Breslow, 1972; Mussen, Honzik, & Eichorn, 1982).

None of this information is likely to be new to you. Many Americans, including young adults, are aware of the benefits of a healthy lifestyle and of the liabilities that bad living habits pose. Do they heed what they know? We learned in Chapter 10 that adolescents often act in reckless ways that compromise their health and wellness. Often young adults are not much better. Consider their alcohol use. In an interview study conducted by the U.S. Census Bureau (Lee et al., 2018), 41% of 20- to 24-year-olds reported heavy drinking, often binge drinking (i.e., having at least five drinks in a row for men, 4 for women). Many young adults indicate that their drinking has caused them problems, such as having unplanned or unprotected sex, getting hurt, or causing property damage (Brook & Willoughby, 2016; Hingson, 2010). Both human and animal studies of adolescents and young adults indicate that the ongoing development of memory and learning abilities may be inhibited in binge drinkers (An, Loes, & Trolian, 2017; Lacaille et al., 2015). In Figure 11.3a you can see that steep rises in alcohol use during the teens and early 20s tend to level off by the mid-20s (Keyes et al., 2015). Such changes occur as young adults' reasons for drinking begin to change. In one study, "To have a good time with my friends" was the most common reason given by younger participants, but it gradually declined after age 20 and was surpassed by the desire "to relax or relieve tension" as participants approached age 30 (see Figure 11.4; Patrick & Schulenberg, 2011). This study also indicated that being in college is

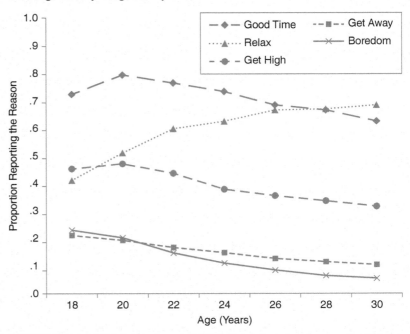

FIGURE 11.4 Frequency of endorsement of five reasons for drinking in the young adult years.

SOURCE: Patrick, M. E. & Schulenberg, J. E. (2011). How trajectories of reasons for alcohol use relate to trajectories of binge drinking: National panel data spanning late adolescence to early adulthood. *Developmental Psychology, 47*, 314. Reprinted by permission of the American Psychological Association.

a contributing factor to substance abuse in the United States, because college students drink more alcohol and smoke more marijuana than same-age peers who have never attended college.

In addition to substance use problems, attending college appears to have negative health effects in general. In one survey, over 20,000 college students completed a questionnaire in the fall of their first year of college and again one year later (Keup & Stolzenberg, 2004). Over the course of that year, they reported substantial declines in their emotional well-being, in their physical health, and in their health habits (e.g., reduced levels of exercise). Fromme et al. (2008) also found that between high school and the end of freshman year of college, young people reported substantial increases in alcohol and marijuana use, as well as sex with multiple partners. There was some variability depending on whether students lived at home (less increase) or not, and whether they came from urban (less increase), rural, or suburban high schools, but in all groups there *was* an increase.

The unhealthy, underregulated lifestyles of many young adults are probably an outgrowth of multiple factors: poor application of problem-solving skills to practical problems (see the next section on cognitive development); perhaps a continuing sense of invulnerability that began in the adolescent years, which may be exacerbated by the fact that young adults can bounce back from physical stress far more readily than they will in later years; and the stresses of leaving home and facing the social and academic demands of college or the workplace—all steps that create new challenges to one's identity.

MyLab Education Self-Check 11.1

Cognitive Development in Young Adulthood

11.2 Compare dominant views of the changes young adults experience in cognitive functioning and suggest problem-solving approaches that apply the postformal or relativistic thinking needed for the unstructured problems they face.

Each year, millions of young people participate in a rite of passage that marks their entry into young adulthood, the transition to college. Although not all adolescents go on to higher education, statistics indicate the numbers continue to increase. A century ago, fewer than 5% of young adults attended college in the United States; today, more than 65% do (National Center for Education Statistics, 2016). So, at least for a sizable subset of American youth, the college experience represents a major influence on their cognitive and social development.

We can all picture the scenes: students piling out of cars driven by their anxious parents, descending on dorms at the beginning of the semester, bustling across campus as fall's first colors begin to tint the foliage, eagerly anticipating the educational challenges that await them in their classes, gathered late into the night talking and laughing with their newfound community of peers, relishing the heady freedom of young adulthood.

If these images remind you of far too many movies you have seen, it may be because they have been overly romanticized, due in equal parts to advertising and to nostalgia. Below the attractive exterior these images suggest lies a core set of developmental challenges that await individuals at this time of life. For the most part, these tasks involve continuing the hard work of carving out an identity, now all the more pressing because of one's status as an "adult." Moreover, most of the work takes place outside the protected environments of home and high school, even though continuing attachments to family remain important, as we shall see in the next chapter.

In this section, we will examine the changes in cognitive functioning that appear to characterize many young adults. Most of the research on young adult development has been done on college students and focuses on the kinds of change that one can expect to find among people with the opportunity to continue their education beyond high school, delaying many other adult responsibilities. As we noted earlier, more than half of young Americans fall into this category. We know very little about cognitive change in those individuals who move directly from adolescence into the world of work. In the next chapter, we examine some of the special issues that may apply to this segment of our young people.

Unquestionably, early adulthood is a time of great learning. Whether in college or on the job, young people are faced with being the "novices," the "unknowledgeable," or the "inexperienced" when they enter the world of adults, and they spend a great deal of time building their knowledge base and becoming more expert in particular domains of knowledge, such as computer science or philosophy or mechanics. Not surprisingly, at the end of four years of college, students perform better on tests of general knowledge than they do as entering students, and the majority judge themselves to be "much stronger" than they were as first-year students in their knowledge of a particular field (Astin, 1993). Comparable change measures are not available for young people who enter the workforce after high school, but it seems reasonable to assume that after four years on the job, some of which may be in job training programs, at least their knowledge of a particular field would have increased.

On the whole, longitudinal research on intellectual change across the life span indicates that many skills (such as executive functions, as we noted earlier, spatial orientation abilities, and inductive reasoning skills) improve throughout young adulthood, with measures of knowledge acquisition or breadth, such as understanding of verbal meanings, showing the most improvement in this time frame (Brysbaert, Stevens, Mandera, & Keuleers, 2016; Schaie, 2013). As long as opportunities to learn exist, the acquisition of knowledge seems to proceed rapidly during early adulthood. In later chapters, we will look in more detail at the typical progress of specific intellectual abilities throughout adulthood.

Logical Thinking: Is There Qualitative Change?

Is growth of knowledge and skill the only kind of cognitive change that we can expect to find in early adulthood? Or, as in childhood, does the nature of one's thinking and problem solving change as well? Piaget's analysis of structural shifts in children's logical thinking skills ends with the description of formal operational thought in the adolescent years (see Chapter 9). Formal operational thinking allows us to think logically about abstract contents. We can discover and understand the implications of relationships among pieces of information that may themselves be abstract relationships—such as proportions, for example. But many theorists have speculated that more advanced forms of rational thought are possible and emerge sometime in adulthood.

Several schemes, many borrowing heavily from Piaget's seminal work, attempt to describe the cognitive shifts that might occur in the adult years. Among these theories are those that propose a stage of adult cognitive thought that has variously been called **postformal** or **fifth-stage thinking**, implying an extension of Piaget's sequence of stages. Some of these theories actually elaborate a number of substages in the movement from formal operations to postformal thought. We will describe two of these theories—Perry's (1970/1999) and Kitchener's (Kitchener & King, 1981; King & Kitchener, 2015)—in detail in later sections to illustrate the possible processes of change in young adulthood.

Some theorists disagree with the concept of a fifth stage of cognitive development. They often argue that the formal operational system of thinking is powerful enough to address any kind of logical problem. They are more inclined to see qualitative differences in adult problem solving and logical thinking not so much as an indication of a stage beyond formal operations but as a sign that the kinds of problems adults must solve are different from those that children are usually trained and tested on. As a result, adults must adapt their existing problem-solving skills to the new kinds of problems they face in adulthood (e.g., Labouvie-Vief, 2015; Schaie, 1977–1978). Part of what people may learn as they confront adult problems and responsibilities is the limits of their own problem-solving abilities. That is, they may grow in metacognitive understanding, recognizing that in some circumstances logical thinking will lead to a clear solution but that in other circumstances they must make decisions based in part on values, needs, and goals (e.g., Chandler & Birch, 2010; Kuhn, Zillmer, Crowell, & Zavala, 2013; Moshman, 2015).

In sum, theorists disagree about whether adult problem solving represents a fifth stage in the development of logical thinking or is a reflection of the fact that life presents adults with new problems. In the latter view, adults do not achieve a new rational system but learn to recognize the limits of their existing problem-solving systems and to evolve new strategies for applying them. Despite some disagreements, nearly all theorists agree that problem solving takes on a different look and feel in adulthood. In the following sections, we will summarize a few theoretical descriptions of adult logical thinking, and we will examine some of the research demonstrating that indeed, something changes as people face life's grown-up challenges.

Schaie's View of Adults Adjusting to Environmental Pressures

Schaie's (1977–1978; Schaie & Willis, 2000) theory emphasizes the importance of new roles, needs, and responsibilities in determining adult intellectual functioning. Schaie does not argue for postformal thought but for shifts in cognitive functioning, or in the use of knowledge and skills, that are straightforward adaptations to the new demands that adults face at different times of life. According to Schaie, we can think of the child and adolescent years as a time when the individual is sheltered from much of life's responsibilities. Schaie calls this the acquisition stage of cognitive development, when youngsters can learn a skill or a body of knowledge regardless of whether it has any practical goal or social implications. Practical problems and goal setting are monitored by parents and others who take on the responsibility for making decisions that will affect the child's life course. The child has the luxury of learning for learning's sake or problem solving just to sharpen her logical thinking skills. Many of the problems she confronts in this phase are those with pre-established answers.

In young adulthood the protections of childhood rapidly recede and the individual is faced with taking responsibility for her own decisions. The problems she must solve—such as how to maintain good health, what career path to choose, whom to vote for, or whether to marry—usually do not have pre-established answers. Many theorists have described them as ill-defined or ill-structured problems. Not only do they have no pre-established answers, but the "right" answer may be different depending on circumstances and on the perspective of the problem solver. Further, when we solve such problems we often do not have access to all the information that might be helpful.

Young adults are in the achieving stage of cognitive development, when an individual must apply her intellectual skills to the achievement of long-term goals, carefully attending to the consequences of the problem-solving process. Schaie assumes not that additional thinking skills are emerging beyond formal operational abilities but that previously acquired skills are being sharpened and honed on very different kinds of problems, such that the solution to one problem must be considered and adjusted relative to other life problems and goals. For example, an adult who is contemplating a divorce must contend with a number of issues: her future happiness, her economic status, and the well-being of her children, just to name a few.

According to Schaie, each new stage of adult life brings new kinds of problems, with different skills more likely to play an important role in one stage than in another. In middle adulthood, the responsible stage, ill-defined problems are still the norm, but problem solving must take into account not only one's own personal needs and goals but also those of others in one's life who have become one's responsibility: spouse, children, coworkers, members of the community. Schaie suggests that the greater impact of one's problem solutions leads adults to become more flexible in their thinking and to expand their knowledge and expertise and use those qualities more widely than before. For people who take on supervisory functions at work and in the community, the extended impact of one's problem solving is even greater than for others, and the responsible stage becomes the executive stage, requiring that one focus heavily on learning about complex relationships, multiple perspectives, commitment, and conflict resolution. Such individuals must sharpen skills in integrating and hierarchically organizing such relationships.

People's responsibilities usually narrow in early old age as their children grow up and retirement becomes an option. This is the reorganizational stage, when flexibility in problem solving is needed to create a satisfying, meaningful environment for the rest of life, but the focus tends to narrow again to a changed set of personal goals and needs. Practical concerns, such as planning and managing one's finances without an income from work, require applying one's knowledge in new ways.

As people move further into their elder years, called the reintegrative stage, they need less and less to acquire new domains of knowledge or to figure out new ways of applying what they know, and many are motivated to conserve physical and psychological energy. Schaie suggests that elderly people are often unwilling to waste time on tasks that are meaningless to them, and their cognitive efforts are aimed more and more at solving immediate, practical problems that seem critically important to their daily functioning.

A legacy-leaving stage may also characterize people whose minds are sound but whose frailty signals that their lives are ending. Such people often work on establishing a written or oral account of their lives or of the history of their families to pass on to others. Consider Jean, who used her considerable organizational ability to construct a detailed genealogy to pass along to her only son. The activity gave her a sense of satisfaction, purpose, and meaning. Clearly, these goals require substantial use of long-term memory and narrative skill, more than problem-solving skills, but as Schaie points out, such accounts do require decision making, or the use of judgment, about what is important and what is not.

This discussion of Schaie's theory has involved describing cognitive functions beyond early adulthood. We will return to the later stages in Chapters 13 and 14. For now, Schaie's depiction of cognitive functioning as heavily affected by the environmental pressures people face at different times of life should help set the stage for understanding other theories of young adult cognition. Most theories emphasize that advancements or changes in problem solving are embedded in the new experiences faced during adulthood.

Schaie's description of environmental pressures clearly is focused on typical middle-class experiences in Western cultures, and there are findings that support his stage view with Western participants. For example, a series of studies done with Swiss adults demonstrated that given the same ill-defined problems, younger adults focused more on strategies that maximized their personal gain (consistent with the achieving stage) and middle adults were more likely than young adults to use strategies that could maximize their contribution to a public good (consistent with the later stages of Schaie's scheme) (Freund & Blanchard-Fields, 2014).

Schaie would probably be the first to acknowledge that adults in other cultures, or in some North American cultural groups, might show different shifts in the polishing or use of cognitive skills through life, depending on the unique demands that their environments impose. For example, we noted earlier in this chapter that young Chinese working women rank being able to take care of their parents as very important for considering themselves adults; young women in the United States rarely rank this factor very high on their lists of criteria for judging adult status. Keep in mind as you read the following accounts of postformal thought that they are almost entirely based on observations of members of the majority culture in Western societies and that it remains to be seen whether these conceptions adequately characterize adult cognitive development in other cultures.

Postformal Thought

Many theorists argue that the realities of adult experience actually lead to new forms of thought (e.g., Basseches, 1984; Commons & Richards, 1984; Giri, Commons, & Harrigan, 2014; Mustakova-Possardt & Basseches, 2014; Sinnott, 1998; Sinnott, Tobin, Chrzanowska, & Hilton, 2017). The full flower of postformal thinking may not be realized until middle adulthood or even later, but the experiences of young adulthood

MyLab Education
Video Example 11.2
Amanda is still figuring out her adult roles and responsibilities. Which stage of Schaie's theory of development would you say best characterizes her?

contribute to the reconstruction of logical thinking. As we saw with formal operations, not all individuals will necessarily reach postformal operations. If they do, we can expect them to "skip in and out" of this type of thinking (Sinnott, 1998).

Sinnott (1998; Sinnott et al., 2017) captures many of the features of postformal thinking described by others. For Sinnott, the essence of postformal thought is that it is **relativistic thought**: "[S]everal truth systems exist describing the reality of the same event, and they appear to be logically equivalent" (1998, p. 25). The knower recognizes both the consistencies and the contradictions among the multiple systems of truth, or systems of formal operations, and, depending on her goals and concerns, in many situations she will make a subjective commitment to one; in other situations, she may seek a compromise solution that integrates some of each perspective, but will not lose sight of the inherent contradictions.

For example, advanced study of a science often reveals that more than one theoretical system can account for much of the data, although perhaps not all of it. Let's use Sinnott's example from mathematics to begin our demonstration:

> The knower may be aware that both Euclidean and non-Euclidean geometries exist and that each has contradictory things to say about parallel lines. In Euclidean geometry parallel lines never come together; in non-Euclidean geometry, parallel lines eventually converge. These are two logically contradictory truth systems that are logically consistent within themselves and logically equivalent to one another. A mathematician bent on knowing reality must decide at a given point which system he or she intends to use, and must make a commitment to that system, working within it, knowing all along that the other system is equally valid, though perhaps not equally valid in this particular context. (Sinnott, 1998, p. 25)

Here is a more personal example adapted from Basseches:

> Mary . . . and Judy are . . . mothers of daughters. Each mother has held a set of values which have guided her efforts to raise her daughter. Now, the daughters have grown up and each of them is rejecting many of her mother's values.
>
> Mary is very troubled. She sees only two possible interpretations. If her values are right, she has failed as a parent . . . If her daughter's values are right, the way Mary has lived her life is wrong . . .
>
> Judy . . . reasons that human values change . . . as old values interact with changing environmental circumstances . . . [I]n acting according to their values [people] change the world, and the changed world in turn leads to the development of new values . . . Judy says to herself: instead of assuming either that I am wrong or that my daughter is wrong, I can try to see what I can learn for my future life from her values borne of her experience. I can also see how she has learned from my values and transformed them to keep up with the times. (Basseches, 1984, p. 1)

Mary's absolutism makes the conflict irreconcilable; Judy's approach is relativistic and dialectical. She contextualizes the problem by taking an historical perspective, allowing her to truly accept that neither set of values is the only right way.

In the behavioral sciences and the helping professions, we are quite familiar with the phenomenon of competing truth systems. For example, a counselor may be aware of multiple theories to account for snake phobias. One might be biologically based, another based on assumptions about the symbolic meaning of snakes in a person's life, and another a behavioral theory arguing that irrational fears are classically conditioned. Suppose she understands the logic of each theory and knows that each is supported by a set of evidence. Yet, in a therapeutic situation, she must make a commitment to one of these systems of "truth" for the purposes of developing a therapeutic plan that will achieve relief for her client as quickly as possible. As Sinnott argues, for her purposes that system then becomes her "true description of the world," but if she remains aware of the inherent contradictions among the different systems and realizes that each has some claim on being true, her thinking has postformal characteristics. Truth is relative, but one truth system may be more valid than another, depending on our goals. This example illustrates that descriptions of postformal thinking have parallels in the descriptions of "reflective practice" presented in Chapter 1.

Chandler (1987; Chandler, Boyes, & Ball, 1990; Chandler & Birch, 2010) agrees that adults faced with the ill-defined problems of life begin to

> abandon the empty quest for absolute knowledge in favor of what amounts to a search for arguably good reasons for choosing one belief or course of action over another . . . an endorsement of the possibility and practicality of making rational commitments in the face of the clear knowledge that other defensible alternatives to one's views continue to exist. (Chandler et al., 1990, p. 380)

But Chandler and his colleagues disagree that such thinking actually is more advanced than formal operational thought. They are more inclined to see it as a result of self-reflection, a growing metacognitive awareness that is the product of "an ongoing effort to reflect on the status of the general knowing process" (p. 380) and to understand its strengths and its limits.

Whether relativistic thinking is truly postformal is perhaps less important than when and under what circumstances it emerges. Let's consider in greater detail two descriptions of cognitive change in the college years and the research in which they are grounded. In each of these theories, the final accomplishment is relativistic reasoning like that described by Sinnott. But each draws on data from studies of young adults to specify in detail how thinking might be restructured and why it is, especially for college students. They each describe a series of stages that we might consider sub-stages in the progression from early formal operational thought to a postformal kind of thinking.

PERRY'S THEORY OF INTELLECTUAL AND ETHICAL DEVELOPMENT IN THE COLLEGE YEARS

William Perry's (1970/1999) theory may be the oldest effort to examine the changes in thinking that characterize people as they transition to adulthood. It also remains perhaps the most authoritative, and other theoretical efforts tend to be quite similar (see, for example, King and Kitchener's review of multiple approaches, 2015). For this reason, we provide you with some detail about Perry's theory, and we follow that with a brief summary of one other similar position, that of Kitchener (King & Kitchener, 2015).

Perry focuses on the cognitive and moral development of college students. He was a professor of education at Harvard and founder of the Harvard Bureau of Study Council, a counseling and tutoring center. Using many of Piaget's ideas, Perry proposed a stage-based theory that depicts the typical intellectual and ethical transitions experienced by students in higher education settings, from absolute adherence to authority to beliefs founded on personal commitment. Perry's theory examines the changes that occur over time in the structure of young adults' knowledge, or, put another way, the changes in their expectations and assumptions about the world.

Perry's original study involved hundreds of volunteer Harvard and Radcliffe students from 1954 through 1963. The theory was constructed from extensive interviews of students as they moved through their college years. In general, interview questions were open ended, such as "Why don't you start with whatever stands out for you about the year?" (Perry, 1970/1999, p. 21), allowing students maximum freedom to talk about their experiences. Initially, Perry considered the differences in students' thinking or worldviews to be a function of their personality differences. It was only after careful reflection on many transcriptions that Perry and his team of raters began to consider the possibility of a developmental sequence. He states, "We gradually came to feel that we could detect behind the individuality of the reports a common sequence of challenges to which each student addressed himself in his own particular way" (p. 8). Although Perry acknowledged that specific forms of knowing do vary across domains of knowledge (as we saw in our examinations of cognitive development in childhood), he believed it was possible to identify a dominant position or overarching form of thought for a given individual at a given time.

Perry constructed a sequence of nine "positions," or stages, ranging from extreme dualistic thinking to high levels of personally committed beliefs. What happens in between is the stuff of intellectual growth during the college years. Few students, if any, enter college at the first position, and few leave having achieved the ninth position. Like Piaget's theory, Perry's is a theory of continual movement and transition. Students "rest" for a time at each of the positions, but the dynamic clearly moves forward. From his perspective, the experience of a liberal arts college education accelerates the growth process, particularly in a society that values pluralism, because students are invariably confronted with diversity of thought, values, and beliefs.

To understand Perry's ideas, let's consider each of the positions and the three alternatives to growth (see Table 11.1 for a summary).

Position 1: Strict Dualism.   Strict dualism is really a downward extrapolation of higher stages, given that virtually no one enters college at this level. Strict dualistic thinking implies a rigid adherence to authoritarian views, a childlike division between in-group (the group that includes me, my family, and authorities who have the "right" idea) and out-group (the group that is "wrong" or has no legitimate authority). Individuals in this stage simply never think to question their belief that authority embodies rightness. Because most adolescents have struggled with parents over autonomy issues and have experienced peers and teachers who, at the very least, have exposed them to various viewpoints, it is unlikely that many students would enter college with this extremely simplistic view of the world.

Position 2: Multiplicity (Prelegitimate).   Multiplicity (prelegitimate) is characterized by the student's first encounters with multiplicity, that is, multiple ideas, answers to life's questions, or points of view. Students now find themselves face to face with

TABLE 11.1 Moving Toward Postformal Thought: Descriptions by Perry and Kitchener.

PERRY FROM DUALISM TO RELATIVISM	KITCHENER EMERGENCE OF REFLECTIVE JUDGMENT
Dualism	
Position 1: Strict Dualism There is right vs. wrong; authorities know the truth.	**Stage 1** Knowing is limited to single concrete instances.
	Stage 2 Two categories for knowing: right answers and wrong answers.
Position 2: Multiplicity (Prelegitimate) Multiple ideas exist; some authority knows what's right.	**Stage 3** Knowledge is uncertain in some areas and certain in others.
Position 3: Multiplicity (Subordinate) or Early Multiplicity Multiple perspectives are real and legitimate.	**Stage 4** Given that knowledge is unknown in some cases, knowledge is assumed to be uncertain in general.
Position 4: Late Multiplicity A. *Oppositional Solution:* Either "authority is right" or "no one is right." B. *Relative Subordinate Solution:* Some opinions are more legitimate (better supported); outside guidance may be needed to learn how to evaluate and to reach this conclusion.	**Stage 5** Knowledge is uncertain and must be understood within a context; can be justified by arguments within those contexts.
Relativism	
Position 5: Contextual Relativism Respectful of differing opinions, but belief that ideas can be evaluated based on evidence.	**Stage 6** Knowledge is uncertain; constructed by comparing and coordinating evidence and opinions.
Position 6: Commitment Foreseen Preference for a worldview begins to emerge despite awareness of legitimacy of other views.	**Stage 7** Knowledge develops probabilistically through inquiry that generalizes across domains.
Positions 7, 8, and 9: Commitment and Resolve "Flowering" of commitment; resolve to continue reflecting.	

SOURCES: Based on Kitchener, K. S., Lynch, C. L., Fischer, K. W., & Wood, P. K. (1993). Developmental range of reflective judgment: The effect of contextual support and practice on developmental stage. *Developmental Psychology, 29,* 893–906; and Perry, W. G. (1970/1999). *Forms of ethical and intellectual development in the college years: A scheme.* San Francisco, CA: Jossey-Bass.

uncertainty when exposed to a mass of theories, social experiences, and information. Their confusion is exacerbated because they lack the structure to accommodate the sheer volume of ideas. Despite their confusion, however, individuals at this stage maintain the belief that some "authority" possesses the ultimate truth or right answers. It is just up to the individual to find it. It is not uncommon, according to Perry, for students to sort through and organize confusing or contradictory information by creating mental dichotomies. For example, they may distinguish between "factual" courses, such as those in the sciences, and "vague" courses, such as those in the humanities. Students who pursue fields that are relatively clear-cut, at least at the early stages of study, may experience confusion when they later have to confront the multiplicity inherent in advanced levels of study. (Remember our examples of multiple truth systems in advanced sciences.) As a student in one of our advanced classes complained on a course evaluation:

> This Psychology stuff is so interesting, but the Professor ruins it. She won't tell us what the facts are. She throws theories at us, and maybe evidence that supports a theory—but then she usually says there is also some evidence against the theory, or evidence that fits another theory. It's confusing and frustrating.

Position 3: Multiplicity (Subordinate) or Early Multiplicity.   In the stage of multiplicity (subordinate), the individual grudgingly acknowledges the reality and legitimacy of multiple perspectives. For example, it becomes more difficult to deny that reasonable people can differ in their perspectives on life, and people who hold different views are not so easily dismissed as being wrong. Some of the students' beliefs in a just world—that the world is fair and people in it get what they deserve—are now reevaluated. Students realize that working hard on assignments or putting many hours into studying does not necessarily guarantee wished-for results. They may observe other students doing far less work than they do and getting better grades. They may be distressed by their inability to understand "what the professors want." They are nudged toward the sometimes painful realization that even their professors and other authority figures around them don't have all the answers. They may also be distressed by the fact that their teachers continue to evaluate them, despite not having the "right" answers themselves.

Position 4: Late Multiplicity.   Late multiplicity was the modal position of Harvard and Radcliffe students in the original study in the latter part of their first year. Perry's research identified two possible epistemologies or adaptations to the problem of multiplicity at this point in development. In effect, students at this stage now fully realize that even experts differ among themselves in regard to what is true. Students handle the realization in one of two ways. One response, identified as oppositional, is characterized by legitimizing multiplicity as one pole of a new kind of dualism. The right–wrong dualism of Position 1 moves to one end of a new continuum, with multiplicity on the other end. Individuals taking this view of the world succeed in maintaining a dualistic either-or structure in their thinking. In other words, either "authority is right" or "all opinions are equally right." One student in Perry's study captured the essence of this position when commenting to the interviewer about his English course: "I mean if you read them [critics], that's the great thing about a book like *Moby Dick*. Nobody understands it" (1970/1999, p. 108). The viewpoint that nobody possesses the truth, thus rendering all people's opinions equally valid, can provoke students to irritation when they believe their work or the content of their ideas has been evaluated unfairly.

The second alternative, called relative subordinate, is less oppositional. Students with this perspective begin to understand that some opinions are more legitimate than others, presaging the relativism of Position 5. The value of a perspective is now understood to be related to the supporting arguments and evidence for the position. However, the consideration of alternative points of view is still done primarily under the guidance of authority. A Perry interviewee reported that his first set of grades in a literature course was mediocre because he could not understand the kinds of thinking required:

> Finally I came to realize, about the middle of the second term, that they were trying to get you to look at something in a complex *way* and to try to weigh more factors than one, and talk about things in a concrete manner. That is, with words that have some meaning and some relevance to the material you were studying." (1970/1999, p. 112)

Often students receive explicit guidance that helps them weigh opinions or compare and contrast ideas. Instruction such as this fosters the kind of metacognition—awareness of how rational arguments are constructed and weighed—that is the foundation of later relativistic thinking.

Position 5: Contextual Relativism. The move to Position 5, contextual relativism, represents a major achievement in intellectual development. The first four positions are variants of a basic dualistic structure. The later positions represent a qualitatively different way of looking at the world. Kneflekamp (1999) reports on a common misunderstanding of Perry's theory, which confuses the "anything goes" quality of late multiplicity with the concept of relativism. He recalls what Perry himself used to say: "Relativism means *relative to what—to something—it implies comparison, criteria, and judgment!*" (pp. xix–xx). The individual can no longer accept the fiction that everyone's ideas are as good as everyone else's. Although she respects the rights of others to hold diverse views, the student at this stage possesses sufficient detachment to "stand back" on her own and consider ideas and values more objectively than before. In a very real way, the student develops the habit of thinking that relies on some standard of evidence that is appropriate to the domain in question. Students' new analytic abilities allow them to appreciate the merits of diverse perspectives and to find convincing elements in multiple points of view. Thinking relativistically, or thinking about knowledge in context, becomes more habitual.

Authority figures are seen more as colleagues than they were before, as people grappling with the same conflicts that beset students, only with more experience in dealing with those conflicts. They are figures no longer to be opposed but to be respected, as this third-year college student from the study illustrates:

> I think when I was younger, when people in general are young, there's [*sic*] so many problems that they feel they don't have to face, and that's why they're indifferent to them. Either it's something that somebody else—the hierarchy, like the family—worries about, or it's something in the future that isn't any problem yet. And then you, when you mature you begin facing these problems for yourself, and looking at them, and then the family just becomes a help to people . . . with more, with a lot of experience. To help you, and not to take the brunt of the problem or something that's *your* worry. (Perry, 1970/1999, p. 138)

Position 5 also represents a watershed stage for religious belief, the point of demarcation between belief and the possibility of faith. No longer can an individual's religious belief rest on blind adherence to authority. Real faith, Perry purports, has been tested and affirmed in the context of a relativistic world. This implies that those who hold viewpoints other than one's own may be wrong, but no more wrong than oneself, given that the student now rejects the idea of absolute truth. With some effort, individuals come to respect and tolerate those who hold different viewpoints even while they struggle to clarify their own beliefs.

Position 6: Commitment Foreseen or Anticipation of Commitment. With commitment foreseen, we hear echoes of Erikson's discussion of identity development (see Chapter 9). Thinking at this stage incorporates a measure of moral courage, as the individual begins to affirm what it is she believes in, all the while knowing that reason will never provide absolute proof that her ideas or perspectives are right or are better than those of others. Commitments to a set of beliefs, to a field of study or career, to relationships, and so forth, like the constructed commitments we discussed in Chapter 9, can take place "after detachment, doubt, and awareness of alternatives have made the experience of choice a possibility" (Perry, 1970/1999, p. 151). This way of thinking incorporates not only respect for diverse ideas and understanding of their rationales but also emerging, personally chosen, preferences for worldviews. One student captures this element of Position 6:

> It seems to me that so much of what I've been forced to do here, this taking of two sides at once, just suspends my judgment. There is a value in it, in seeing any perspective, or any one particular facet of, of a problem. But there's also a value in, in being able to articulate one side more than another. (p. 157)

One notices a general trend in thinking toward personal meaning making or reflective thinking.

Positions 7, 8, and 9: Commitment and Resolve. Perry discusses Positions 7 (initial commitment), 8 (multiple commitments), and 9 (resolve) together. Taken as a group, they suggest a flowering of the commitments anticipated in Positions 5 and 6. Changes in thinking are more qualitative than structural. According to Perry, 75% of students in the study had a level of commitment at Positions 7 or 8 at graduation. Despite its place at the end of the line, Position 9 does not imply a static resolution of existential conflict. On the contrary, it characterizes a state of courageous resolve to continue the work of reflecting on one's commitments throughout adulthood.

Perry also accounted for individuals who refrain from taking the intellectual challenge necessary for growth through these stages. Fallback positions include temporizing, retreat, and escape. *Temporizing* refers to delaying movement to the next stage. *Escape* characterizes a movement back to relativism when the demands of commitment prove too taxing. *Retreat* occurs when individuals revert to dualistic thinking in times of stress in order to seek the intellectual security of absolute right or wrong, a position that is unavailable at the level of committed relativism.

Perry characterized his theory and the research that supported it as focused on intellectual and ethical development, and his work does pertain to these things. However, it is more fundamentally a study and characterization of epistemological development. That is, it examines young adults' increasingly complex conceptions of where knowledge comes from, and of the nature of truth and reality (Erdynast, Chen, & Ikin, 2016). As such, it has relevance for how students might approach learning and problem solving in any domain (social, ethical, scientific, and so on) as their understanding of the nature of knowledge changes. Some researchers have used Perry's framework to explore the connection between students' beliefs about knowledge and their approach to learning. For example, in an early study, Ryan (1984) found that relativists were more successful in their college classes because they tended to use more constructivist approaches to studying course material. They paid attention to context, constructed meaningful interpretations of textual information, and summarized main ideas. Dualists were more likely to focus on memorization of factual information, in keeping with their belief in "right" versus "wrong" information. These differences were significant even when the effects of scholastic aptitude were eliminated statistically.

Some more current work, although not necessarily inspired by Perry's theory specifically, is consistent with the idea that as college students become more relativistic in their views of knowledge, their learning strategies change. For example, in a series of three studies, Yoder, Mancha, and Smith (2014) found that students in the later years of college are more willing to attend to information that violates their own beliefs than first year students are. The researchers asked students to complete a reading on political issues. On a later test, first year students remembered better any information from the reading that was consistent with their own beliefs. Older students, however, remembered more information that was *inconsistent* with their own views, suggesting that they focused especially on understanding ideas that were different from their own as they read. Problem-solving strategies also change as thinking becomes more relativistic. For example, relativistic thinkers are more likely than dualistic thinkers to provide legitimate evidence to support their thinking and problem solving (Kuhn, 1992, 2001; Kuhn & Franklin, 2006). Dualists also take a more narrow view of problem-solving tasks, breaking them down into unrelated, discrete parts and ignoring some important aspects. Relativists are more likely to consider the whole problem, processing and taking into account all of its components before attempting a solution (Wilkinson & Maxwell, 1991). Relativists are also more likely than dualists to approach problems by evaluating evidence and its sources critically, rather than accepting claims made "authoritatively" (McGinnis, 2016).

Reasoning about moral dilemmas in the Kohlberg tradition (see Chapter 7), however, actually seems to regress somewhat for some young adults as they begin to progress through Perry's stages (Eisenberg et al., 2002; Padilla-Walker, 2015). Kohlberg (Colby & Kohlberg, 1987) at first thought this might be due to the stress of the transition to college, but newer analyses suggest that it may be a function of early relativistic thinking: a kind of "over-reaching" tolerance that makes some young adults hesitate to commit to their own values in approaching a moral dilemma (Padilla-Walker, 2015).

KITCHENER'S MODEL OF THE DEVELOPMENT OF REFLECTIVE JUDGMENT

As we noted earlier, and as helpers know all too well, many problems of adulthood are ill defined. An ill-defined problem has neither one acceptable solution nor one agreed-on way to solve it. Should a talented athlete stay in college or accept an attractive job offer? Should a young woman pursue a high-powered career that will leave little room in her life for marriage and child rearing? How can a young adult deal with the pressures of both academics and her social life? Moreover, how do helpers deal with the messy issues that come to them on a daily basis?

Kitchener and her associates (Kitchener & King, 1981; King & Kitchener, 2015) have proposed a seven-stage theory outlining the development of reflective judgment, how people analyze elements of a problem and justify their problem solving (see Table 11.1). They presented individuals with a standard set of ill-structured problems from the social and physical sciences and questioned them about the reasoning they used in coming to conclusions about the problems. Like Perry, these researchers found a predictable, sequential progression that moved from a belief in the existence of absolute, fixed certainty to a kind of contextual relativism.

For Kitchener, different stages of thinking can be differentiated on the basis of three dimensions: certainty of knowledge, processes used to acquire knowledge, and the kind of evidence used to justify one's judgments. As you can see from Table 11.1, the early stages (1 through 3) are characterized by a belief in the existence of certainties and the use of personal justification ("This is just the way it is") or reliance on authorities for guidance. Individuals in the early stages also tend to use personal observation as evidence of the rightness of their judgments. Individuals in the middle stages (4 and 5), similar to Perry's multiplists, perceive knowledge as uncertain. They believe in the supremacy of personal opinion and tend to make judgments based on idiosyncratic kinds of reasoning. Those in the later stages (5 through 7) resemble Perry's contextual relativists in that they tend to make judgments based on a set of rules or logic in combination with personal reflection.

For example, one reflective judgment problem concerned whether certain chemicals in foods, such as preservatives, are good or bad for us. In the following prototypical example of a Stage 5 response to such a problem, you can see that the speaker sees knowledge as uncertain and contextually dependent; but she does not yet have a sense that evidence can be weighed probabilistically (as in Stage 7):

> I am on the side that chemicals in food cause cancer, but we can never know without a doubt. There is evidence on both sides of the issue. On the one hand there is evidence relating certain chemicals to cancer, and on the other hand there is evidence that certain chemicals in foods prevent things like food poisoning. People look at the evidence differently because of their own perspective, so what they conclude is relative to their perspective." (Kitchener, Lynch, Fischer, & Wood, 1993, p. 896)

Some research demonstrates that reflective judgment is related to level of education (Dunkle, Schraw, & Bendixen, 1993; Kitchener & King, 1981) as well as to the kind

MyLab Education
Video Example 11.3
Many problems in adulthood are ill-defined. Such is the case with college student Laura who faces difficult decisions as she seeks a career path.

of training one has received (Lehman, Lempert, & Nisbett, 1988; Papathomas & Kuhn, 2017). Graduate students, for example, reason at higher levels than college undergraduates, and graduate students in psychology, a discipline that emphasizes probabilistic reasoning, show higher levels of proficiency on such tasks than graduate students in chemistry, medicine, or law. Specific kinds of training or support appear to improve skills in reasoning and judgment. In one study, individuals from middle through graduate school were provided with prototypic statements like the one quoted above, with each statement modeling successively higher levels of reflective judgment, and then they were asked to explain the reasoning in the prototypic statement. The results indicated that after such modeling and practice, participants' own levels of reasoning on such problems had advanced.

One classic study illustrates that reflective judgment in social and personal issues tends to lag behind problem solving in domains that do not relate to one's own personal concerns (Blanchard-Fields, 1986). In this study, participants ranging in age from 14 to 46 were presented with two accounts of each of three events. One event that had little personal relevance for most people was an account of war (the Livia task) by two opposing parties (see Kuhn, Pennington, & Leadbeater, 1982, for a full description of the task). The remaining two events were characterized as "a visit to the grandparents" and "the pregnancy," and both events were rated by participants as emotionally involving. In the first of these, a teenage boy and his parent each present a story about a time when the boy was required to accompany his parents on a visit to his grandparents. The two stories are inconsistent in emotional tone and in many details (see Box 11.1 for the full text of the competing accounts). In the second emotionally involving event, a woman and a man each take a different stance on the woman's pregnancy, she favoring an abortion, he against an abortion. For each of the three events, study participants were asked to explain what the conflict was about and what happened. They also responded to probe questions such as "Who was at fault?" and "Could both accounts be right?" The participants' understanding and analysis of the events were scored based on six levels of reasoning, combining features of Perry's (1970/1999) and Kitchener and King's (1981) levels of cognitive maturity. Performance on the Livia task was better at earlier ages than performance on the more emotionally involving tasks. Performance continued to improve on all tasks from adolescence to young adulthood and from young adulthood to middle adulthood.

The following are examples of performance for these three age groups on the emotionally involving "visit to the grandparents" event (from Blanchard-Fields, 1986).

> **Level 2.** This was the average level of response for adolescents on the two emotionally involving events. It is close to an absolutist conception of reality.
>
> There's a lot more said by John of what they did and they had an argument and the parents did not say it like—how he talked, and that he wanted to be treated like an adult. It seems more right because I don't like the parents' talk. (p. 327)
>
> **Level 3.** This level was about average for young adults in this sample. They recognized that different perspectives appear valid, but they tended to cling to the possibility that there may be an absolute truth, even in such ill-defined situations.
>
> Yes [they could both be right]. I think you'd have to have a third person not involved emotionally with either party. They'd be able to write without feeling, the facts, just what happened. (p. 327)

Note that "just what happened" suggests one correct interpretation of events.

> **Level 4.** This level was about average for middle-aged adults. They were not biased toward one side or the other, and the idea that more than one truth might exist was intimated, but there was still a strong sense that one can identify an essential similarity or truth despite the different perspectives.
>
> I think the accounts, as far as the actual events, are pretty much the same. The important differences are in the presentation . . . the important differences are in their

perceptions of what was going on. The actual "this happened" are the same, but the interpretation of it is different. (p. 328)

Level 6. Perhaps you will recognize this relativistic view as one that helping professionals are trained to assume in highly personal matters. There is no hint here that one experience of the event was more valid than the other.

> They'd have to be able to really share [to resolve this conflict] . . . this way with each other, and even deeper, in terms of getting into some of their fears and some of their angers. They have to be able to accept it in each other, and maybe, they can resolve the conflict, only if they can accept feelings in each other. (Blanchard-Fields, 1986, p. 328)

Only a few participants, all of them middle-aged, responded at Level 6 in this study. As Kuhn et al. (1995) point out, "topics in the social sphere both engage people and challenge them. They are easy to think about *but hard to think well about*" (p. 120, italics added). In Box 11.2 we consider some of the mistakes in problem solving that researchers have found to be quite common, even among adults. You will notice that these tend to occur in situations that can be very personally involving, so they have particular relevance to helping professionals.

Box 11.1: A Visit to the Grandparents: Two Perspectives

Blanchard-Fields (1986, p. 333) presented adolescents and adults with three tasks, each consisting of two discrepant accounts of the same event. Participants were interviewed to assess their reasoning about the events. The following are the two accounts for the task called "A Visit to the Grandparents."

Adolescent's Perspective

I'd been planning on spending the whole weekend with my friends. Friday, in school, we'd made plans to go to the video game arcade and the school carnival. We were all looking forward to a lot of fun. Saturday morning my parents surprised me by telling me that we were going to visit my grandparents that day. They reminded me that they'd planned this a long time ago. But how am I supposed to remember those things? So, we ended up in one of those big arguments with the typical results; I gave in and went with them. The worst part was when they lectured me on why it was my duty to go without ever once looking at my side of it. When we finally got to my grandparents, I had to do everything they wanted to do. I had to answer silly questions about school, play their games, and see their old slides and movies. It eventually blew up in an argument between me and my parents over the legal age for drinking.

Even though I was being as polite as I could, it was boring. I felt forced into everything. I just can't wait until I am free and out on my own. I was really angry with them. So, on the way home I told them that I wanted to be treated more like an adult; that I wanted more respect from them and I wanted them to take my

plans seriously. They seemed to agree with this and decided that I was now old enough to make my own decisions.

Parents' Perspective

Two months had gone by since we had visited the grandparents. We try to visit them at least once a month, but everyone gets so busy that a month slips away very quickly. This time, we planned the visit far enough in advance so that everyone would come. When we tried to get John ready to go with us on Saturday morning, he put up a battle. After all, he hadn't seen his grandparents for a long time. They are getting old and won't be around much longer. We tried reasoning with John, stressing the importance of family unity and obligation as well as consideration of others. Certainly, in the future, he would regret not spending more time with his grandparents after they've gone. Although John was reluctant to go, he finally came with us and actually seemed to really enjoy himself. Since he seemed to be having a good time, we were surprised by how angry he became when we all got into a discussion about the legal age of drinking.

Even though he was reluctant to go with us at first, he seemed to have a good time, to enjoy the family closeness. He showed respect for his grandparents and seemed to understand how good it made them feel to see him. What this means to us is that he's old enough now to enjoy being with adults more and to learn from them. On the way home we agreed that John should take a more active part in discussions about family matters.

SOURCE: Blanchard-Fields, F. (1986). Reasoning on social dilemmas varying in emotional salience: An adult developmental perspective. *Psychology and Aging 1*, 325–333. Reprinted by permission of the American Psychological Association.

Box 11.2: Helper Beware: Decision-Making Pitfalls

Our ability to think our way logically through problems improves and expands throughout childhood and adolescence. As this chapter indicates, problem-solving skill continues to improve in adulthood as well, especially for ill-defined problems. We have also seen in this chapter that effectively using our logical abilities to make decisions can be especially difficult when we deal with social or emotional issues that have personal relevance. Among the many kinds of logical fallacies that commonly ensnare adults are some that may be especially problematic for helping professionals and their clients (Stanovich, 1998, 2016; Stanovich & West, 2014).

Suppose you want to encourage a client to consider beginning an exercise program. You are concerned that her sedentary lifestyle is contributing both to her depression and to other health problems. When you introduce the idea, however, she counters, "That won't help. I have a neighbor who has run 20 miles a week for all the years I've known her, but she had to be hospitalized last year because she was suicidal." The logical error that your client is making is sometimes called **"the person who" fallacy**. She is refuting a well-documented finding, like the correlation between regular exercise and well-being (both physical and emotional), by calling on knowledge of a person who is an exception. Especially when dealing with psychological and social issues, matters in which most of us have great personal interest, "people tend to forget the fundamental principle that knowledge does not have to be certain to be useful—that even though individual cases cannot be predicted, the ability to accurately forecast group trends is often very informative. The prediction of outcomes based on group characteristics is often called aggregate or **actuarial prediction**" (Stanovich, 1998, p. 149). So, for any individual, a prediction about the effectiveness of a treatment is more likely to be accurate if we base that prediction on general findings for people with that individual's characteristics than if we base it on one or a few other individuals whom we have known or observed.

Like many logical mistakes, "the person who" fallacy involves failing to step back and consider how well the evidence supports one's theory. Your hypothetical client has a theory that exercise will not relieve her depressive symptoms, perhaps motivated in part by her distaste for exercise. She is aware of one instance in which the prediction of her theory appears to have been correct. She fails to recognize that a single case is an inadequate test of a treatment's effectiveness. One outcome can be influenced by multiple factors, many of them unknown. Also, your client completely ignores the evidence *against* her theory: Proportionally, more people experience long-term emotional benefits from exercise than not. In other words, probabilistically, regular exercise has a good chance of helping.

Part of the reason that "the person who" fallacy occurs is because of the **vividness effect**. When we are trying to make decisions, some salient or vivid facts are likely to attract our attention regardless of their actual value as evidence. Even when other facts are available the *vividness* of personal experience or

of the personal testimony of other individuals can be greater than that of any other information that we might access. Wilson and Brekke (1994) documented the strength of the vividness effect in a study of consumer behavior. Participants in the study were told they would be given free condoms and that they could choose between two brands. They were also given access to two kinds of information about the condoms to help them choose a brand. One was an extensive analysis of survey data on the performance of condoms from a *Consumer Reports* magazine and the other was a pair of student testimonials. Objectively, the data from the *Consumer Reports* analysis were more useful in this case, but most participants asked for the testimonials as well, and when the testimonials were in conflict with the survey research, about one third of the participants were swayed by the testimonials. Thus, even in a situation in which *both* carefully collected group data *and* individual testimony were readily available, the vividness of the less appropriate individual testimony was hard for many participants to resist.

The insidiousness of vividness effects is especially problematic when testimonials are one's source of evidence for the effectiveness of a treatment. When your client's Cousin George swears that his son was relieved of his depression by "Dr. Olivino's oil immersion therapy," the appeal of Cousin George's testimonial may be irresistible to your client, especially when she observes for herself that George's son does indeed appear to be doing quite well. Unfortunately, people can be found to offer testimonials for any therapy or treatment that has ever been offered. One reason for the ready availability of testimonials is, of course, the **placebo effect**. People sometimes improve with attention or in the course of time, no matter what the medical or psychological intervention. The actual effectiveness of a treatment can only be determined in careful studies in which some participants are given the treatment and some are given a dummy, or placebo, version of the treatment. Typically in such studies, a substantial percentage of participants given the placebo control will improve, and typically they are convinced that their "treatment" is responsible. Clearly, the actual effectiveness of a treatment approach cannot be determined by testimonials. The only useful indicator of the effectiveness of a treatment is whether treatment participants are benefited more than placebo controls.

Counselors, too, often find the vividness effect hard to resist. For example, our own experience with individual cases often looms larger in our decision making about probable treatment outcomes than the actuarial evidence that is available to us from controlled studies of a treatment's effectiveness.

How can we protect ourselves and our clients from making poor decisions based on "the person who" fallacy and the vividness effect? Increased metacognitive awareness—that is, awareness of one's own thinking—seems to be the key. For example, educating clients to see that personal experience or the testimony of others can be limited in its generality, despite its vividness, can help them resist the appeal of such evidence. More generally, we can encourage clients to understand the

(continued)

decision-making process itself. When we try to decide whether a treatment should be pursued, we are actually evaluating the *theory* that a particular treatment alternative will cause improvement. Our task is to specify all the possible theories (treatment options) and to evaluate the evidence for each. When people have a favorite theory, they often do not realize that it is just a theory. As Kuhn (1991) points out, they think *with* their theory, not *about* their theory. In other words, the theory guides their thought and what they pay attention to instead of being an object of thought and evaluation. So, for example, if your client believes that Dr. Olivino's oil immersion therapy works, she will pay more attention to examples that support her theory and may either fail to look for, or will ignore, counterevidence. In such a case, her **belief bias** is standing in the way of a full, rational analysis of the problem (Markovits, Brisson, de Chantal, & Thompson, 2017; Kuhn, Ramsey, & Arvidsson, 2015).

Helping clients make better decisions, then, will include encouraging them to recognize that they are working with a theory, not a fact. A theory must be justified by evidence, and *all* the available evidence, both pro and con, should be considered. In addition, alternative theories (treatment options) and the evidence for them should be considered. Testimonials or personal experiences are not likely to become less vivid in this process. But when our clients are armed with knowledge about the shortcomings of such data, they may become more cautious about using them as evidence.

MyLab Education Self-Check 11.2

Applications

On the cusp of adulthood, individuals in their late teens and 20s confront a number of new developmental milestones. The serious tasks of consolidating an identity, solidifying a career path, and realizing the capacity for intimacy (Erikson, 1968; Keniston, 1971) are both challenging and time consuming. One competency required for each of these tasks is the ability to make decisions and choices given a wide array of possible alternatives. Helpers are frequently called on to assist clients in making decisions, and, to some, this is the quintessential role of the helper. Decision-making (Krumboltz, 1966; Stewart, Winborn, Johnson, Burks, & Engelkes, 1978) and problem-solving (D'Zurilla, 1986; Egan, 1975) models are widely used among clinicians to help people with personal and career-related issues.

Such models have in common a series of general steps, including (1) defining the problem, (2) setting realistic goals, (3) developing a variety of possible solutions, (4) assessing the costs and benefits of each alternative solution, (5) selecting and implementing one alternative, and (6) reviewing the effectiveness of the solution after implementation (Nezu, Nezu, & Lombardo, 2003). On its face, this strategy appears to incorporate some aspects of postformal thinking, specifically the relativistic, pro-and-con nature of solutions to fuzzy problems, for it is rare to find solutions to difficult problems that don't have potential disadvantages as well as advantages. But it can also suggest to more dualistic thinkers that problems are "well defined" and have correct solutions, if only someone can figure them out. Although most professionals understand that any solution or decision incorporates some good and some bad, their clients may not.

Given what we know about the importance of belief systems, the helper might be remiss if she did not consider the client's epistemology, or her beliefs about the nature of knowledge, when working on decision making—or other problems, for that matter. In other words, seeing a dilemma through the client's eyes requires an appreciation of the way she views truth, knowledge, and meaning in life.

If a client tends to see the world in absolute terms, she might be confused as to why alternatives are even being considered! Twenty-year-old Hannah recently moved into her boyfriend Mike's apartment near the college campus where both are students. She is upset that Mike wants to spend so much time with his friends, playing basketball and going to bars. Hannah resents the fact that he doesn't spend his free time with her, and, to make matters worse, she believes drinking alcohol is a moral failing. Because the tension between the two is so great, Hannah consults a counselor for advice about how to change Mike's behavior. Hannah becomes indignant when the counselor asks her to consider the advantages of allowing Mike to socialize with his friends and to reflect on her role in the relationship problems. "Mike is the one with the problem," Hannah states emphatically. "I came here to find out how to get him to stop drinking and to spend time with me." Hannah's perspective on truth at this point is rather dogmatic: Drinking is evil and people who drink are wrong. Hannah will become frustrated if the counselor presses her to adopt a relativistic stance too quickly, and she may seek out another "authority." She will probably not return to this counselor.

Growth in critical thinking skills is a generally recognized educational goal. From early elementary school, teachers prize critical thinking skills. However, many students come to higher education lacking these tools (Larmar & Lodge, 2014). **Critical thinking (CT)**—the ability to think clearly, make good judgments, use evidence, and reflect on the quality of one's thinking processes—is a form of relativistic thinking (Halpern, 2014).

In general, relativistic thinking is considered to be more sophisticated than dogmatic thinking because most problems in life involve uncertainty as well as some measure of uncontrollability. Expectations that complex problems should have clear-cut solutions can complicate the problem-solving process by increasing individuals' anxiety when simple answers prove inadequate. The ability to generate solutions, assess advantages and disadvantages of each, and then integrate aspects of several solutions into one presumes a level of epistemic knowledge that has come to terms with the ambiguity of real-world problems. Yet as Perry and others have demonstrated, this skill develops gradually; it does not necessarily come with a high school diploma. Professionals who are knowledgeable about cognitive development can help clients resolve specific problems and help them acquire more general skills in decision making, such as knowing when and where a strategy is effective.

Level of epistemological thinking also influences academic success. Studies have demonstrated that students who are dogmatists do more poorly academically than those who have more flexible thinking styles. It appears that moving toward thinking in more expert ways, especially in certain fields, requires grappling with uncertainty (James & Brookfield, 2014). Research has also demonstrated that students who believe that learning should be quick, that prolonged concentration is a waste of time, and that memorization of concrete facts is sufficient for learning demonstrate poor performance on mastery tests despite reporting high levels of confidence in their ability (Schommer, 1990). Students who perform better on mastery tests are more likely to disagree with the view that knowledge is certain and that single, simple answers are most reflective of reality (Schommer, 1993; see Muis, 2007). Skills in reflective thinking are also correlated with greater understanding of multicultural issues (King & Howard-Hamilton, 1999).

Can educational approaches enhance critical thinking? Given its importance to real-world functioning, it would be helpful to know which strategies work best. A meta-analysis of 31 studies reached some conclusions (Niu, Behar-Horenstein, & Garvan, 2013). While interventions such as specific teaching approaches did improve CT ability overall, the effects are quite modest, for the most part, and specific to subject area (e.g., science). These weak effects may be partly due to the challenges of measuring critical

thinking, especially as a cross-disciplinary construct, and more definitive conclusions await future research. It's also important to recognize that growth in cognitive development is not a rapid process at any stage of life; thus improvements in CT skills may take time. Small post-intervention improvements may reflect this reality (Franco, Butler, & Halpern, 2015).

It does appear that students can learn to think more critically when they are motivated because of some personal connection to the material. Addressing students' epistemologies—that is, their attitudes and beliefs about the nature of truth, what constitutes factual information and what does not, and how evidence is evaluated directly—can be particularly important across multiple disciplines. Making explicit connections between subject matter and students' lives can also be helpful. Ding and Mollihan (2015) found that non-science majors in an introductory science class shifted their thinking from beginner to more expert views by the end of the course. In contrast, science majors, who took their own version of the introductory course, actually regressed to more novice-like views post-course. Because the majors' course was so heavily abstract, the authors posit that even good science students were not able to relate the information to their real-world experience and goals. Some points to take away from all these studies include the following (see Schneider & Preckel, 2017):

- Discussion groups, clear presentation of information, use of case studies, and reflection assignments can all be used to generate connections between abstract subject matter and real-world applications. College student achievement is improved when teachers offer conceptually challenging tasks and provide careful scaffolding for these assignments.

- Critical thinking interventions that last longer (more than 12 weeks) are more effective in enhancing skills than those of shorter duration.

- Well-designed and implemented programs to support critical thinking skills can be more effective than simply offering students a course in a certain subject. Perhaps the explicit detail and consideration of what CT skills are and how to practice them are particularly reinforcing features.

- Incorporating critical thinking skills into the academic curricula over a long period of time can be a useful alternative to specific CT interventions. This approach takes into account the discipline-specific nature of skills in use. However, more research is needed to understand which aspects of this approach are most effective.

Stonewater and Stonewater (1984) proposed a model based on Perry's theory that balances a bit of challenge (to introduce disequilibrium) along with support and engagement to improve greater critical and reflective ways of thinking. They suggest that individuals who are closer to the dualistic end of the continuum need more carefully controlled exposure to diverse ways of thinking and can benefit from the provision of adequate structure as a framework for incorporating new ideas. For example, students who find the process of career selection overwhelming may be aided by a very specific set of activities that guides them through the exploration process. Students who are at the stages of dualism or early multiplicity may find that knowing what questions to ask or what criteria to investigate allows them to engage in the confusing career decision-making process with a supportive road map. In a process very consistent with Piaget's ideas, individuals will not be able to accommodate new ways of thinking if the complexity of the information is too great and the support is not sufficient. Likewise, individuals will not be motivated to accommodate at all if the challenge is minimal and support is overdone.

King and Kitchener (2002) offer specific suggestions for teachers and others who work with emerging adults. Several of these ideas can be useful in promoting reflective thinking about academic and psychoeducational content. First, demonstrate respect for young adults' thinking, keeping in mind that they are most likely to open up to new ways of reflection in a supportive atmosphere. Second, provide opportunities for young adults to gather information about an issue, evaluate the quality of that information, and draw conclusions based on that data. Third, teach young adults to explicitly examine the epistemological assumptions they use in making decisions about ill-defined problems.

The theories of cognitive development described in this chapter make another important contribution to the practicing clinician. They help us understand that certain kinds of thinking, sometimes labeled "irrational," may not be attributes of a dysfunctional personality style but rather the manifestation of a developmental stage. Construing clients' thinking and judgments from this perspective allows us to be more forgiving of their idiosyncrasies and more supportive about their potential for growth and change. Sometimes, clients with fairly rigid belief systems may not have been exposed to the kinds of contexts that encourage them to examine beliefs carefully or to consider alternative explanations. Or clients who hold less mature perspectives may be retreating from the confusion of too many ideas and too little support. For example, more anxious college students make greater use of ineffective problem-solving strategies like avoidance, blaming self or others, denial, and so on. Training in effective problem-solving skills can reduce their anxiety, increase well-being and may have beneficial implications for cognition and achievement (Stillmaker & Kasser, 2013). Here the helper has a good opportunity to assess the person's thinking and to provide a balance of support and challenge that facilitates progress from a dualistic, polarized belief system to one that is more cognitively complex (Sanford, 1962).

Putting Things Off

The road to adulthood is marked by a point when individuals are no longer bound by the externally controlled routines of home and school. This freedom can be exhilarating, but many are set adrift by the lack of structure. Feeling unsafe and framework-less once again, many young people search for the certainty of "right" answers and struggle with the challenge of organizing large blocks of unstructured time to work on tasks that may have no clear-cut boundaries. In the past, they could rely on authoritative sources to provide guidelines and directions. Now, the need to become more self-reliant increases dramatically.

One problem that arises frequently at this point in the life span is procrastination. This problem has the power to derail, even if temporarily, emerging adults' potential success in academic and work environments. Procrastination is a multidimensional construct having motivational, behavioral, cognitive, and personality components, and may be the end product of diverse pathways. Those who investigate procrastination as a dispositional, traitlike characteristic (Paunonen & Ashton, 2001; Schouwenburg, 2004) report that procrastinators share low levels of trait conscientiousness (see the section on personality in Chapter 13), rendering this group more likely to be disorganized, poor at planning, and lacking the self-regulation needed to accomplish things in a timely way. Several subtypes have been identified within the general population of procrastinators. Those with low levels of conscientiousness and high levels of neuroticism tend to be fearful, anxiety-prone, and perfectionistic. These perfectionistic procrastinators abide by the "procrastinator's code" (Burka & Yuen, 1983), that specific cognitive tendency to equate failure in one area to a generalized sense of failure in all aspects of the self. An unrealistic set of perfectionistic standards and irrational beliefs, namely that failure is a fate worse than death, may fuel their avoidant behavior.

Those whose combination of personality traits includes low conscientiousness, low neuroticism, and high extraversion are more likely to procrastinate without the worry. These individuals also avoid tasks they consider unpleasant and prefer to engage in more satisfying pursuits but do not do so because they are averse to failure. Some have also identified a "rebellious" type of procrastinator who resists authority and asserts independence through procrastination. In counseling situations, care should be taken not to try to fit everyone who procrastinates into one of these "types" or to assume that patterns of dilatory behavior in certain contexts necessarily reveal the nature of that person's personality. Most of us have avoided aversive tasks at one time or another, and sometimes we may procrastinate in one setting (academic) but not in another (job). We suggest, as well, that there are developmental reasons for the ubiquity of procrastination at this stage of the life span. The landscape of emerging adulthood can be perceived by some as a frontier with open-ended possibilities and many high-stakes choices. The skills of decision making and self-management are honed in the identity development process, which proceeds concurrently with entry into college, military service, or the world of work. Procrastination may be the manifestation of confusion or lack of certainty about how to proceed. Although this is a growing area of research, we still need more evidence to sort out information about the nature of procrastination and ways to intervene to reduce it.

Behavioral approaches such as instruction in time management and organizational skills are very popular (Tuckman, Abry, & Smith, 2002). These techniques can be useful in helping students learn to segment tasks into manageable components, develop timelines and benchmarks for task completion, and provide themselves with regular feedback about performance. Other approaches blend behavioral elements with specific components that address underlying psychological needs. For example, van Essen, van den Heuvell, and Ossebaard (2004) developed a self-management course that facilitated self-reflection about personal reasons for procrastination as the basis for change. Rational Emotive Behavior Therapy (REBT) principles were incorporated to address the irrational beliefs that supported procrastination. These authors reported that the program was effective in enhancing self-efficacy and reducing procrastination. For perfectionistic procrastinators, helpers may find stress-management interventions such as guided relaxation training and systematic desensitization procedures helpful adjunctive therapies (Flett, Hewitt, Davis, & Sherry, 2004).

Helicopters Overhead

Some contemporary writers have suggested that young adult difficulties with problem solving and decision making have their origins close to home (Gibbs, 2009). Perhaps we are witnessing a change in parenting behavior that is qualitatively different from that seen several decades ago. Many researchers agree that the phenomenon of over-parenting (also known as "hovering" or "helicopter parenting") afflicts the current generation of young adults. By and large, this change centers on how much less responsibility contemporary generations are expected to carry. Is this topic more than just fodder for a lively dinner table conversation? A variety of popularized definitions render the concept a bit muddy, but researchers have identified several characteristic fingerprints (Segrin, Woszidlo, Givertz, Bauer, & Murphy, 2012).

Overparenting young adult children includes the following parental behaviors: providing excessive advice; manifesting emotional over-involvement or enmeshment; showing hyper-vigilance and anticipation of potential problems or concerns facing the young person; controlling the young person's sense of self-direction; and offering excessive tangible resources like money, goods, and time (Segrin, Woszidlo, Givertz, & Montgomery, 2013). These characteristics distinguish overparenting from classic enmeshment because "helicopter" parents behave in ways that prevent—or try to prevent—their young adult children from failure or harm by virtue of excessive amounts of support. Although it is natural for parents to be concerned about their children, inordinate anxiety about potential threats or preoccupation with children's achievement may reflect personal feelings of inadequacy, desire for vicarious experience of success, sadness about parenting failures, or regrets about missing parenting opportunities that will never come again. These associations have been explored by researchers (Segrin et al., 2013). Interestingly, the overparenting style was not included in original parenting typologies (see Chapter 5), possibly because helicopter parenting is developmentally inappropriate in ways that were not popular when Baumrind did her famous work.

Overparenting has been linked to a number of problematic outcomes for post–high school youth. Table 11.2 presents some of these relationships.

TABLE 11.2 Selected Outcomes Associated with Overparenting with Young Adult Children.

OUTCOMES RELATED TO OVERPARENTING OF COLLEGE-AGE YOUTH	SOURCE
Lower well-being; greater prescription medication use for anxiety/depression and use of pain pills for recreational purposes.	LeMoyne, T. & Buchanan, T. (2011). Does "hovering" matter? Helicopter parenting and its effects on wellbeing. *Sociological Spectrum, 31,* 399–418.
Lower quality parent–child communication, less family satisfaction and greater young adult child entitlement.	Segrin, C., Woszidlo, A., Givertz, M., Bauer, A., & Taylor Murphy, M. (2012). The association between overparenting, parent-child communication, and entitlement and adaptive traits in adult children. *Family Relations, 61,* 237–252.
Higher depression and lower life satisfaction.	Schiffrin, H. H., Liss, M., Miles-McLean, H., Geary, K. A., Erchull, M. J., & Tashner, T. (2014). Helping or hovering? The effects of helicopter parenting on college students' well-being. *Journal of Child and Family Studies, 23,* 548–557.
More critical family environment; parental regard more conditional upon academic performance; effects generalize to social difficulties in other interpersonal relationships.	Segrin, C., Givertz, M., Swaitkowski, P., & Montgomery, N. (2015). Overparenting is associated with child problems and a critical family environment. *Journal of Child and Family Studies, 24(2),* 470–479.
Greater interpersonal sensitivity (e.g., excessive sensitivity to social feedback, to others' behavior, and to negative evaluation by others either perceived or real).	Scharf, M., Rousseau, S., & Bsoul, S. (2017). Overparenting and young adults' interpersonal sensitivity: Cultural and parental gender-related diversity. *Journal of Child and Family Studies, 26(5),* 1356.
Indirect association between overparenting with poorer college adjustment. Overparenting undermines adjustment by reducing self-efficacy of young adult students.	Darlow, V., Norvilitis, J. M., & Schuetze, P. (2017). The relationship between helicopter parenting and adjustment to college. *Journal of Child and Family Studies, 26(8),* 2291–2298.

Despite the risks of overparenting, it is important to resist an extreme overcorrection. Young adult children do need to feel connected and supported by parents. Many young adults, especially from collectivistic cultures, recognize their parents' good intentions even though the documented outcomes are adverse across the different cultures studied (Kwon, Yoo, & DeGagne, 2017; Scharf, Rousseau, & Bsoul, 2017). Developmentally appropriate emotional connection should promote the young person's autonomy while not undermining her sense of competence. Parents may need to explore their own motivations for overparenting, possibly with the support of a helping professional. They can be assisted to redirect their energy into more constructive ways to stay connected. Providing encouragement to young adult children to explore, experience, and learn as much as they can during a stage when identity is still being constructed can promote healthier parent–child relationships. It goes without saying that some young adult children may need more support from parents than do others, especially if they are in danger or have experienced some serious setback. So it is always a good idea for professionals to understand the family context and the young adult's specific needs before making family recommendations.

This being said, all parents need to come to terms with the inevitable truth that their children grow up and need to realign relationships with them. In healthy parent–child bonds, relationships become less vertical (parent in control) and more horizontal (both parent and child as adults). For parents, this shift in control does not necessarily imply distance or loss but rather a realignment that makes emotional connection sustainable over the life span.

Growth and Change in Professionals' Epistemology

Don't be alarmed if you recognize that some aspects of your own thinking might seem dualistic or authority-oriented. Perry noted that new learning in any discipline can evolve in a similar stage-like way. Table 11.3 presents Stoltenberg and Delworth's (1987) model of stages in counselor development. As you can see, Level 1 counselors operate somewhat like dualists. They tend to be dependent on supervisors to tell them the "right" way to conceptualize cases. Level 1 counselors try to fit clients into categories and often rely on canned strategies. In general, they also tend to attribute too much pathology to their clients because of their own anxiety level. Level 2 counselors vacillate between dependence on supervisors and personal autonomy. Because they have more experience with difficult cases, they may be less optimistic about the possibilities for change in certain circumstances. As with multiplists, exposure to competing theories of human behavior and therapy undermines confidence in the validity of each. Counselors at this level are more skillful yet also more confused about their own efficacy. At Level 3, helping professionals are more independent and also more tolerant of divergent opinions. They come to accept the ambiguity that is inherent in the helping process. They are creative problem solvers and more objective in their assessment of their clients. In the fluid way they utilize the discipline's knowledge base to adjust to the needs of the client, these counselors truly embody the characteristics of reflective practice.

TABLE 11.3 Client Conceptualizations at Stages of Counselor Development.

Level 1

Self- and Other-Awareness—Emotional and cognitive self-focus. *Indications:* Diagnoses/conceptualizations will be "canned" or stereotypical, trying to fit clients into categories. Incomplete treatment plans will focus on specific skills or interventions, often quite similar across clients. Treatment plans may not reflect diagnoses.

Motivation—High, with strong desire to learn to become effective diagnostician and therapist. *Indications:* Willing student, will seek out additional information from books, colleagues, and other sources.

Autonomy—Dependent. *Indications:* Relies on supervisor for diagnoses and treatment plans. Locus of evaluation rests with supervisor.

Level 2

Self- and Other-Awareness—Emotional and cognitive focus on the client. *Indications:* Realizes treatment plan is necessary and logical extension of diagnosis. May resist "labeling" client into diagnostic classifications. Treatment plans may prove difficult due to lack of objectivity. May reflect various orientations yet lacks integration.

Motivation—Fluctuates depending on clarity regarding various clients. *Indications:* May be pessimistic, overly optimistic or confident at times.

Autonomy—Dependency-autonomy conflict. *Indications:* May depend on supervisor for diagnoses and treatment plans for difficult clients, may avoid or resist supervisor suggestions concerning others. Confident with some less-confusing clients. More resistance to perceived unreasonable demands of supervisor, threats to tenuous independence and therapeutic self-esteem.

Level 3

Self- and Other-Awareness—Emotional and cognitive awareness of client and self. *Indications:* Able to "pull back" affectively and cognitively, monitor own reactions to client. The client's perspective and a more objective evaluation will be reflected in conceptualizations. Treatment plans will flow from diagnoses, taking into account client and environmental characteristics. Reflects therapist's own therapeutic orientation.

Motivation—Consistently high, based on greater understanding of personality-learning theory and self. *Indications:* Not as susceptible to pessimism or undue optimism. Diagnoses and treatment plans consistently thought through and integrated.

Autonomy—Independent functioning. *Indications:* Seeks consultation when necessary. Open to alternative conceptualizations and treatment approaches but retains responsibility for decisions. Makes appropriate referrals.

SOURCE: Stoltenberg, C. D. & Delworth, U. (1987). *Supervising counselors and therapists: A developmental approach.* San Francisco, CA: Jossey-Bass. Used with permission by John Wiley & Sons, Inc.

It bears repeating that good clinical judgment relies on good critical thinking skills. It is not uncommon, even for professional helpers, to base their decisions on misinformation, lack of rational examination of claims, or preferred ways of thinking. Kahnemann (2011) described two modes of thinking: Type 1, based on intuition and overlearned rules of thumb, and Type 2, based on a slower and more reflective analysis of information. The problem is not confined to laypeople. Large numbers of adults (72%) and a smaller group of neuroscientists (6%) agreed that people only use 10% of their brain (Herculano-Houzel, 2012). Approximately 81%

of helping professionals endorsed a relationship between a full moon and abnormal behavior (Owens & McGowan, 2006) and 90% agreed that matching teaching to learning style improved performance, despite no evidence for these claims. Clinicians should be aware of personal tendencies to over-rely on quick, gut-level, unreflective Type 1 thinking. Some measure of professional humility is probably in order. Bensley and Lilienfeld (2017) remind us that "evaluating claims requires not only reasoning skills and the dispositions to use them but also the metacognitive ability to recognize when beliefs may be wrong and require revision" (p. 379).

Focus on Developmental Psychopathology

Depression

Most people have some familiarity with the concept of depression, from professional training and work with clients, from widespread coverage in popular media, or from all-too-common personal experience. Unfortunately, depression can be trivialized and misunderstood by those who have not lived through its torment. The novelist William Styron (1990), who suffered from clinical depression himself, takes issue with our limited understanding of this terrible ordeal. He described the experience as "a howling tempest in the brain" (p. 37), not at all consistent with the standard comments of people who have not experienced it, such as "We all have bad days" or "You'll pull out of it."

This misunderstanding might be clarified if depression were specified more clearly. Some advocate differentiating between a depressive symptom (e.g., sad mood), a depressive syndrome (e.g., sad mood plus anxiety), and a depressive disorder (Rutter, Tizard, & Whitmore, 1970). According to formal diagnostic criteria, depression is a serious mood disorder that has several presentations, including unipolar, bipolar, dysthymic, and cyclothymic forms. Some of the core features for major depressive disorder (MDD) include sad affect, anhedonia, fluctuations in weight and/or sleep, psychomotor changes, fatigue, cognitive impairments, feelings of guilt or worthlessness, and suicidal thoughts or acts. At least five symptoms must be present for at least two weeks, be clinically significant, and impair normal functioning in order to qualify for diagnosis (APA, 2013). Although this seems simple enough, diagnostic problems do result from the counting up of symptoms because normal mood fluctuations can be misconstrued as clinical depression. Evidence is building that it is the *number and intensity* of symptoms and not the presence of symptoms alone that should distinguish between depressed and nondepressed individuals (Angst & Merikangas, 2001; Slade & Andrews, 2005). **Bipolar disorder** is characterized by the presence of

impulsivity, irritability, overactivity, and euphoria (characteristic of mania and hypomania), along with periods of depressed mood, feelings of worthlessness, and low energy. People suffering from bipolar illness are at particular risk of suicide and self-harm (Mitchell & Malhi, 2004).

The various manifestations, symptom sets, risk factors, and courses of depression have led researchers to consider depression as a heterogeneous category of disorders (Chen, 2000; Chen, Eaton, Gallo, Nestadt, & Crum, 2000). Because all types of depression include alterations in mood, others argue that depression is best represented as a spectrum disorder, with unipolar depression on one end, atypical depression in the middle, and bipolar disorder at the other end (Akiskal & Benazzi, 2007). Although it is clear that children experience depression, the question of whether depression in childhood is qualitatively different from depression in adolescence and adulthood has not been resolved (Weiss & Garber, 2003). Nolen-Hoeksema (2008) sums up the issue, writing that "the notion that there is a coherent entity we call depression that will be identifiable in the body is just wrong, or at least, not very useful" (p. 178). Fundamentally, symptoms that collectively manifest as depression appear to arise from high levels of negative affect and stress.

Prevalence and Comorbidity

According to global estimates, approximately 300 million people suffer from depression. Depression is the world's greatest contributor to overall disease burden, and rates have increased more than 18% worldwide since 2005 (World Health Organization, 2017). Depression is a costly problem as well. Over $1 trillion are lost every year, according to WHO Estimates (WHO, 2017), because of depression's links to substance abuse and other disabling health conditions. As we have noted, depression is not just a problem for adults. Rates of depression among U.S. youth ages 12 to 20 have increased dramatically from 8.7% in 2005 to 11.3%

MyLab Education
Video Example 11.4
Feliziano, who has bipolar disorder, describes his experience with the depressive phases of his disorder. He recognizes that depression isn't a cognitive problem—he has no "reason" to be depressed. Rather, depression is a mood disorder.

in 2014 (Mojtabai, Olfson, & Han, 2016). This troubling finding underscores an earlier observation that depression has been appearing in successively younger generations since 1940 (Cross-National Collaborative Group, 1992; Kessler et al., 2003). A similar trend has been observed for bipolar illness (Chengappa et al., 2003). This phenomenon, called the "Birth Cohort Effect," cannot simply be explained by genetics, since genes presumably do not change so rapidly. Furthermore, earlier and earlier spikes in depression are supported by objective measures such as increases in hospitalizations and suicides.

Females are diagnosed with disproportionately higher rates of depressive syndromes and serious disorders than males from mid-adolescence through late adulthood (Compas et al., 1993). The recent increase in depression in youth is largely due to increases among females (Mojtabai, Olfson, & Han, 2016). Before puberty, boys' rates of depressive symptoms and disorders are equal to or higher than those of prepubescent girls (Nolen-Hoeksema et al., 1992). Both genders are diagnosed with bipolar disorder in equal numbers, an exception to the sex-based trends found in **unipolar disorders** (American Psychiatric Association, 2000). Females are also more likely than males to ruminate about their sad moods when depressed, to admit feeling sad, and to seek help (Nolen-Hoeksema, 2002). However, we can't assume from this evidence that males do not also suffer from depression in high numbers. Addis's (2008) Gendered Responding Framework of depression offers a way of understanding how male gender norms interact with the experience of negative affect. In this framework, males' experience of negative affect (grief, sadness, dysphoria) may be handled through distraction, anger, or avoidance because of prototypical masculine role expectations. Males, too, feel sad and upset, but they may learn, through social conditioning, to express their vulnerabilities in ways that don't neatly map onto available checklists of depressive symptoms.

Increasingly, depression is seen as a heterogeneous group of disorders that frequently coexist with other illnesses (Ballard et al., 2017). In children, anxiety, impulse-control, and conduct disorders have been found to manifest prior to

depression and show high comorbidity with depression later on (Kessler et al., 2003). Some evidence has suggested that anxiety disorders are precursors to later depression. Other evidence suggests the opposite—that the presence of depressive disorders predicts later anxiety disorders. Regardless of what appears first, if one disorder predicts the other in a strong, unidirectional, and prospective way, it would be considered a **prodrome** (i.e., a prior manifestation of the later disorder). If each disorder predicts the other with relatively approximate strength, then both are simply risk factors for the other, not early manifestations of the other disorder. Jacobson and Newman (2017) investigated these relationships in a large meta-analysis of over 88,000 adults and concluded that evidence supported the latter, bidirectional risk pattern. All types of anxiety disorders predicted later depressive disorders and vice versa roughly at the same magnitude. Depressive disorders, however, were a prodrome for phobias and prospectively predicted this class of anxiety disorders quite strongly. This kind of evidence shapes decisions about prevention and treatment. In other words, trans-diagnostic treatments for anxiety and depression may effectively reduce the impact of both disorders, given their bidirectional relationship. Specific treatments for depression, however, may be advisable before the onset of phobias, given the predictive nature of this association.

The Perplexing Search for Causes

Despite enormous research efforts, the specific causes of depression remain unknown most likely because the heterogeneity of the disease and the complexity of interacting influences make simple answers unlikely. However, some variables are clearly correlated with risk. Genetic/familial predispositions, early adverse life experiences, hormonal changes in puberty, cognitive and motivational processes such as attributional and coping style, number and intensity of stressors, and absence of protective factors like social support all have influential parts to play (Rutter, 1986). Much attention has focused on three main neurotransmitter systems: dopamine associated with loss of pleasure, norepinephrine associated with psychomotor retardation, and serotonin associated with depressive ideation (Sapolsky, 2004). There is no clear consensus about which system is most critical nor is there any clear understanding of whether there is too much or too little of some neurotransmitter in the brains of some depressed individuals. The question is complicated: Does a neurochemical imbalance cause depression or does depression (e.g., stress, trauma, distorted cognitions, etc.) cause a change in the chemistry of the brain? There is good evidence for the latter view, particularly in the case of early life stress.

In Chapter 2, we described the HPA axis as central to the body's stress response. Remember that the perception of a stressor causes the hypothalamus to trigger a cascade of neurochemical changes, via corticotrophin-releasing factor (CRF), that operate in a coordinated way to respond to threat. As it turns out, CRF is released from nerve terminals that also communicate directly with the serotonin, dopamine, and noradrenergic (epinephrine) systems, modulating the release of these neurotransmitters (Austin, Rhodes, & Lewis, 1997). Early exposure to adversity can alter the development of these systems and sensitize children so that it doesn't take much subsequent stress to activate the neurochemical pathways associated with depression (Graham, Heim, Goodman, Miller, & Nemeroff, 1999; Rudolph & Flynn, 2007). Even a genetically based biochemical imbalance can be an underlying diathesis that can be activated by adverse life experiences. This may help explain why early onset of depression during childhood is associated with more recurrences of depression, and more severe and comorbid symptom presentation among young adults (Ramirez, Ekselius, & Ramklint, 2015).

Sapolsky (2004) argues that the ability to recover from stress distinguishes who becomes depressed when stressed and who does not. The presence of a gene variant that limits the effectiveness of a neurotransmitter system to recover (like the 5-HTT gene mentioned in Chapter 7) may play a key role in determining who is most at risk. Certain medications, especially SSRIs (selective serotonin reuptake inhibitors), assist in the recovery of neurotransmitter systems and may explain their success in symptom reduction for some patients. It is important to emphasize, however, that reliable differences in neurotransmitter levels in the brains of depressed and non-depressed individuals have not been found, and medications are ineffective for a substantial percentage of depressed individuals (Leventhal & Martell, 2006).

Burke and colleagues' (Burke, Davis, Otte, & Mohr, 2005) meta-analysis of studies on recovery from stress reviewed differences between depressed and non-depressed individuals in cortisol reactivity. Remember that cortisol levels, which increase under perceived stressful circumstances, are designed to decrease when stress remits. This is the pattern of effective stress regulation. Persistently high cortisol levels suggest a blunted stress response that has been implicated in depressive disorders. Burke et al. (2005) found that impaired recovery from stress, as measured by elevated cortisol patterns, was observed in depressed, but not in non-depressed adults. Among adolescents, dysfunctional cognitive patterns, blunted cortisol recovery, and lower heart rate recovery were all found to characterize depressed youth (Shapero, McClung, Bangasser, Abramson, & Alloy, 2017). Treatments can thus target both psychotherapeutic (cognitive thinking style) and biological (stress regulation) mechanisms.

All of these biopsychological processes are mediated by epigenetic changes at the most basic level of genes. In earlier chapters, we discussed how the stress system develops, how it can be sensitized to stress by early experience. In Chapter 14, we will further elaborate on sensitization with regard to stress. Epigenetic processes serve to alter the actual chemistry of genes and leave their mark. These processes help us understand why depression is a recurrent illness. With regard to unipolar and bipolar disorders, genetic changes produced by events "above the genome" increase

the individual's sensitivity to stress and precipitate depressive episodes. Post (1992, 2016) refers to such changes as a kind of genetic memory that results in behavioral sensitization. At the beginnings of a depressive course, the first 5 to 7 episodes are generally related to some stress in the person's life. After that, depressive episodes can be triggered by the perception or anticipation of stress, irrespective of actual events (Stroud, Davila Hammen, & Vrshek-Schallhorn, 2011; Treadway et al., 2015). Refinements in our understanding of the particular epigenetic mechanisms can help inform psychopharmacological treatments that target epigenetics processes while psychological treatments can address perceived stress.

Pathways of Risk

The recognition that serious adversities experienced in childhood are related to later depression is nothing new (Goodman, 2002). Early adverse experiences, such as parental loss, family disruption, and neglectful/abusive parenting, have long been considered serious contributors to psychopathology. To shed light on how these experiences might exert their impact, Duggal, Carlson, Sroufe, and Egeland (2001) followed a group of at-risk low-SES children from birth to age 17.5. During the group's first 3.5 years, the researchers conducted observations of mother–child interaction style so as to assess attachment-related constructs. A high percentage (19% of 168 children) demonstrated clinical depression in childhood and 18% did so in adolescence, rates higher than expected from epidemiological estimates. Two different pathways to depression were observed. Depression that presented first in childhood was best predicted by the accumulation of adverse family circumstances and characteristics. Think of these children as being born into very difficult or inadequate family circumstances. In this pathway, it was the *combination* of number and types of stressors on mothers, insensitive and emotionally unsupportive parenting, maternal depression, and abuse that was shown to "interfere with responsiveness to developmental needs, increasing the probability of depressive symptoms" (p. 159). Adolescent-onset depression, in contrast, was best predicted by maternal depression and lack of early supportive care, rather than the aggregate of factors that predicted prepubertal depression. Interestingly, gender differences emerged in pubertal depression pathways. Maternal depression, assessed when children were 7 or 8, predicted pubertal depression best for females, possibly because of sex-role identification processes. For males, unsupportive early care in infancy and early childhood was the strongest predictor of depression in adolescence. As the authors conclude, "for males, it seems to be what the caretaker did rather than who the caretaker was during childhood that is most relevant to depressive symptomatology in adolescence" (p. 160). All of these unfortunate circumstances could facilitate the particular cognitive vulnerabilities associated with depression: hopelessness, low self-worth, negative expectations, and cognitive distortions, to name a few (Garber & Flynn, 2001). Findings such as these highlight the complex processes involved in the development of vulnerability to psychopathology.

A parent's death during the childhood years is an especially stressful event. A large study of Swedish young adults whose parents died of natural (illness) and external (accident, homicide, or suicide) causes during their childhood was carried out to explore later mental health outcomes (Berg, Rostila, & Hjern, 2016). The rate of hospitalizations for depression in the young adult years increased two- to threefold among those whose parents died from external causes during their childhoods, suggesting a more urgent need for prevention and intervention for this group. In contrast, only a slightly elevated risk for later mental health consequences was found for those whose parents died of natural causes, presumably because the individuals had both time and support to prepare themselves.

Treating Painful Passages

Stressors that occur after childhood and adolescence can also precipitate the emergence of depression in vulnerable individuals. The role transitions involved in moving out of the home into the larger world of adult responsibilities are one example. While not all emerging adults experience depression or even depressive symptoms, the challenges that are part of the developmental work of constructing an adult identity can take their toll on the mental health of individuals within this age group. The separation and losses involved in the predictable life transitions and changes in interpersonal relationships that occur at this stage are stressful and can make already vulnerable individuals more vulnerable. Emerging adulthood typically involves a major separation from home—physically, psychologically, or both. For some, the combination of leaving family and friends, disruptions in romantic attachments, stresses of academic or work responsibilities, and the day-to-day challenges of caring for oneself may seem overwhelming. A stark reminder is the fact that the highest prevalence rate for depression across the entire life span occurs during the ages of 15 to 24 (Blazer, Kessler, McGonagle, & Schwartz, 1994).

The stress of the passage into adulthood can be especially intense for minority students in the United States, as you saw earlier in this chapter. Apparently as a result, minority college students can be more at risk of suffering from depression than majority students. The direct experience of racism and discrimination is not the only source of students' minority stress. Minority status often brings with it other problems, such as "interethnic difficulties (e.g., difficulty in making White friends), within-group conflicts (e.g., being viewed as "acting White"), and achievement stress (e.g., feeling less intelligent or less capable than others, or the pressure of high expectations for college success from one's family)" (Wei et al., 2010, pp. 411–412). An important factor that can reduce depression risk for minority students is **bicultural competence**, which involves having social skills for getting along in both the majority and minority culture "without compromising . . . one's sense of cultural identity" (LaFromboise, Coleman, & Gerton, 1993, p. 404). These skills include knowledge of beliefs and values in both cultures, a belief that one can function well in two cultural groups and maintain one's cultural identity, good communication skills, a repertoire of appropriate role behaviors in each culture, and so on. Minority students who perceive themselves as having such skills report fewer depressive symptoms and more feelings of psychological well-being (David, Okazaki, & Saw, 2009; Wei et al., 2010). Supporting bicultural competence may be an important added ingredient in any kind of treatment for minority students.

There are effective treatments for some individuals who suffer from depressive disorders. These include pharmacological, cognitive-behavioral (CBT), interpersonal (IPT), and mindfulness-based cognitive (MBCT) therapies. Unfortunately, depression does not always remit completely for approximately 50% of individuals with MDD. This is the case despite conventional treatment with two courses of different SSRIs (Wisniewski, Gaynes, Rush, Fava, Trivedi, & Warden, 2009). Treatment-resistant depression appears to be related to genetics, abnormalities in immune and neural functions, presence of bipolar symptomatology, certain personality traits like low sociability and high anxiety, and high allostatic load (Murphy, Sarris, & Byrnes, 2017). This is an important finding because we need to recognize that the effectiveness of psychopharmacological medications has been overblown in some of the literature and in advertising. These authors propose that the course of depression should be factored into treatment decisions because some treatments may be more helpful in earlier or later stages.

In young adulthood, the foundations of interpersonal therapy may have particular relevance for development, insofar as the struggle involved in making normal life transitions is one of the primary factors assumed to cause the disorder. Interpersonal therapy (Klerman, Weissman, Rounsaville, & Chevron, 1984; Weissman, Makowitz, & Klerman, 2000) assumes that depression is affected by and affects interpersonal relationships, and aspects of the depressed person's social network are of primary importance in understanding and treating the disorder.

The theoretical foundations of the interpersonal approach derive from the work of Sullivan (1953a, 1953b) and Meyer (1957), among others, who emphasized the here and now social contexts of the depressed individual over causes of depression that were intrapsychic and rooted in the distant past. While IPT does not dismiss the cognitive processes that support depression, irrational, distorted thinking is not the primary focus of treatment. Therapeutic change is purported to come via several interpersonal processes: social support, stress reduction in areas of interpersonal functioning, and development of emotion regulation and interpersonal skills (Lipsitz & Markowitz, 2013). The causes of depression are presumed to be four broadly defined interpersonal situations: grief, role disputes (conflicts with significant others), life changes/role transitions, and significant interpersonal deficits. Using a time-limited approach (roughly up to 20 sessions) and functioning as a supportive ally, the therapist assesses symptoms, connects depression to one of the four major problematic areas, and assigns the client a "sick role" (Parsons, 1951). Assigning a sick role legitimizes the client's needs for support from others who may be included in the therapeutic process, temporarily frees the client from unmanageable responsibility, and allows the person to focus on recovery during the restricted period of therapy. During the intermediate stage of therapy, the therapist takes a moderately directive role and helps clients make real changes in relationships and renegotiate their roles in interpersonal contexts. In the case of difficult role transitions, such as the transition to adulthood, clients are helped to mourn the old "adolescent" role by reviewing what was good and bad about it, clarify feelings about the new role, and explore opportunities that the new role offers. When anxieties about one's ability to manage the new life stage successfully surface, expectations about what "being an adult" might be are discussed and readjusted if necessary. Sources of social support are identified and recruited and incentives for taking on new developmental challenges are created. The final stage of therapy acknowledges termination as a loss but also focuses on sustaining the gains made in therapy in the post-therapy social environment. Some techniques used in IPT include those common to supportive psychotherapies: questioning, clarification, support of emotional expression, behavior change strategies, and development of a strong therapeutic alliance. IPT has also been adapted for use with younger depressed adolescents (Mufson, Moreau, Weissman, & Klerman, 1993).

A key point in the interpersonal conceptualization of depression is its transactional emphasis. Unfortunately, it has been repeatedly demonstrated that depressed people suffer more frequent rejection from others than do nondepressed counterparts (Segrin & Abramson, 1994) and thus need to exert more effort and display more skill in order to overcome this social tendency. However, the life events that may have precipitated depression in vulnerable individuals in the first place, such as a move to a new school, reduction in contact with family and friends, and increased maturity demands, can produce symptoms (chronic fatigue, poor concentration, indecisiveness, sad mood, anhedonia, etc.) that make engaging in positive social interactions an enormous effort (Coyne, 1999). The vicious cycle is obvious. Regardless of theoretical bent, it is very important for helpers to pay serious attention to the environmental contexts that sustain depression. As Coyne warns, "depressed individuals' statements about themselves and their relationships get interpreted as enduring cognitive structures, a sociotropic trait, or working model of relationships, and these *reified entities* are then given causal priority over any interpersonal processes" (1999, p. 368). Even though IPT is an individual approach to counseling, including significant others in some manner in treatment can be done.

Both CT and IPT have been shown to be effective for many individuals across multiple studies (Lemens et al., 2017). In Chapter 14, we will discuss mindfulness-based approaches to stress reduction and depression. Offering therapeutic strategies that emphasize certain features of depression, like dysfunctional cognitions or impaired social functioning, they make significant contributions to prevention and remediation of this costly and painful family of disorders. In order to benefit from treatment, primary care screening for depression, especially for females who are at greatest risk, is a priority worldwide. Early screening for adolescents is also important because it might forestall more serious episodes of this recurring condition. Advances in psychopharmacology and improved understanding of the etiology of depressive disorders also offer the hope of reducing this global health burden (Cuijpers, Beekman, & Reynolds, 2012; Salk, Hyde, & Abramson, 2017).

Summary

1. Specifying exactly when an individual reaches adulthood is surprisingly complex. Sociologists look to marker events, such as completing one's education, entering the workforce, leaving the family home, and so on. Young adults tend to emphasize accepting responsibility for their own behavior and making independent decisions. Relational factors are also important, such as meeting obligations to family. In today's society, the period from about ages 18 to 29 may be described as a time of emerging adulthood, as young people try to carve out their places in the adult world.

Physical Development in Young Adulthood

2. Brain changes that begin at puberty, such as gray matter thinning and white matter expansion, continue well into the third decade. These contribute to continuing improvements in cognitive functions, such as learning and inhibitory control.

3. Between ages 18 and 30, all biological systems reach peak potential. There are individual differences in when people reach peak potential, and there are differences among different systems and skills in the timing of peak status. For different skills, these differences reflect differences in the relative importance of practice, training, knowledge, experience, and biological capacity. Males and females also peak at different times.

4. Lifestyle affects the achievement and maintenance of peak or near-peak functioning. Healthy lifestyles include getting regular exercise, eating a healthy diet, and avoiding unhealthy behaviors such as smoking and drug use. Such behaviors in young adulthood are reflected in poorer health later in adulthood, yet many young adults have unhealthy, underregulated

lifestyles, probably as a result of poor application of problem-solving skills, continued feelings of invulnerability, the fact that young adults "bounce back" quickly from physical stress, and the many stresses they face.

Cognitive Development in Young Adulthood

5. Young adulthood is a time of great learning. We have clear data on the growth of knowledge in the college population (roughly 60% of young adults today), but it seems likely that rapid growth of knowledge characterizes all young adults as they gain training and experience in their vocations and avocations.

6. Logical thinking also appears to change beginning in young adulthood. Theorists and researchers disagree as to the nature of the change. Some propose that a more advanced kind of thinking, postformal or fifth-stage thinking, emerges. Others argue that the formal operational abilities of the adolescent period represent the most advanced form of thinking for humans but that adults learn to apply this kind of thinking to the more ill-defined or ill-structured problems that adults face. As part of this process, they may also gain better understanding of the limits of their own problem-solving abilities. That is, they may grow in metacognitive understanding.

7. Schaie argues against a new kind of adult thinking. Rather, he argues that at different times of adult life people face different kinds of problems, and different skills are brought to bear on those problems. He describes seven stages in adults' intellectual functioning, with each new stage a result of shifts in the challenges people face.

8. Theorists who argue that there is a stage of postformal thought suggest that it may not reach full development until middle adulthood, but its emergence begins in young adulthood. Most theorists, such as Sinnott, describe postformal thought as relativistic. The same reality can be described within several different truth systems, all of which are valid from one perspective or within some context. The postformal thinker recognizes the validity of different truth systems. She may make a subjective commitment to one in some situations or seek a compromise in other situations.

9. Perry's stage theory of intellectual and ethical development in the college years describes a sequence of steps in the movement from more absolutist or dualistic thinking (there is one right answer, other answers are wrong) to relativistic thinking (there is more than one correct way to view the same issue). In addition to Perry's own longitudinal interview study, a number of researchers have provided some evidence for aspects of Perry's theory. For example, students' beliefs about knowledge have been found to relate to their approach to learning, as Perry's theory predicts.

10. Kitchener provides a seven-stage theory of the development of relativistic thinking, calling it reflective judgment. Research in which subjects are given ill-defined problems indicates that in the early stages of adult thinking, individuals believe in the existence of certainties. In the middle stages, people perceive knowledge as uncertain. In the later stages, they base their judgments on a set of rules or logic in combination with personal reflection. Essentially, they are relativistic.

11. Some research indicates that reflective judgment is related to level of education and to the specific kind of training people have received. Graduate students in psychology, for example, tend to show more proficiency than graduate students in other disciplines. Evidence also indicates that people are benefited by modeling of forms of thinking more advanced than their own.

Case Study

Angela, a young Black woman, comes from a close-knit and very religious family that has always taken great pride in her accomplishments. Despite some minor rebelliousness during high school, Angela maintains close ties to her family and considers her parents and younger sister to be her best friends. A solid student all through school and a leader in her church's youth ministry, Angela knew for a long time that she wanted to go to college to be a teacher. Angela's father attended community college for two years, and her mother graduated from high school. Both parents were delighted when Angela became the first member of the family to pursue a baccalaureate degree.

Now in her first year at a state university in the South, she is getting used to college and to life in a dormitory. She enjoys the freedom and the challenge of college but is also experiencing some problems getting along with other students. Her roommate, a young White woman named Jen, poses a particular dilemma for her. It bothers Angela that Jen never goes to church, never prays, frequently spends the night at her boyfriend's apartment, and is an outspoken agnostic. Jen makes various comments about what she has learned in her religion and philosophy classes that trouble Angela, who firmly believes that Jen lacks a proper moral center. Angela has tried to convince Jen about the importance of belief in God and the consequences of her disbelief, but to no avail. Because it is important to Angela to maintain her beliefs, she starts to avoid being in the room when Jen is there and considers finding a new roommate.

During the spring semester, Angela develops a serious infection that confines her to bed and makes her unable to attend classes or to care for herself. She is both surprised and pleased when Jen comes to her assistance. Jen runs errands for her, brings her meals, and does her laundry. Even Jen's boyfriend pitches in to help Angela make up her missed assignments. She is touched by their generosity and confused about how this goodness can coexist with a nonreligious perspective on life. These are the kind of people she had thought were immoral. When the time comes to plan for next year's housing arrangement, Angela is uncertain. Her friends in the ministry counsel her to find a more appropriate roommate. Yet Angela cannot reconcile Jen's kindness toward her with what she believes to be an immoral lifestyle. This disjunction causes her great distress. She decides to seek out a counselor in the University Counseling Center to help her with her decision.

Discussion Questions

1. Discuss Angela's level of development according to the various theories presented in the chapter.
2. As a counselor in a university setting, how would you respond to her problem? How would you take her cognitive development into account?

Practice Using What You Have Learned

MyLab Education Application Exercise 11.1:
Schaie's View of Adults Adjusting to
Environmental Pressures

MyLab Education Application Exercise 11.2:
Problem-Solving with Postformal Thinking

MyLab Education Application Exercise 11.3:
Case Study: From Dualism to Relativism

Journal Questions

1. Give examples of your own thinking at one or more points in your life that reflected dualism, multiplicity, and relativism.

2. In what respect and in what areas have you achieved the stage of committed relativism? Discuss this process from your personal experience.

3. Describe your transition to college. What aspects of this adjustment were particularly difficult for you? If you were a helper working with similar problems, how would you approach them?

4. Discuss your response to the section on overparenting. What was your experience with your own family like as a young adult? How might your experience influence your attitudes, sensitivity, or lack of sensitivity to the parent–adult child relationships you observe in practice today?

Key Concepts

marker events (p. 428)
emerging adulthood (p. 429)
globalization (p. 429)
crossover effect (p. 429)
young adulthood (p. 431)
postformal or fifth-stage thinking (p. 435)
acquisition stage (p. 436)
ill-defined or ill-structured problems
    (p. 436)
achieving stage (p. 436)
responsible stage (p. 436)
executive stage (p. 436)
reorganizational stage (p. 437)
reintegrative stage (p. 437)
legacy-leaving stage (p. 437)

relativistic thought (p. 438)
strict dualism (p. 440)
multiplicity (prelegitimate) (p. 440)
multiplicity (subordinate) (p. 441)
just world (p. 441)
late multiplicity (p. 441)
oppositional (p. 441)
relative subordinate (p. 441)
contextual relativism (p. 442)
commitment foreseen (p. 442)
initial commitment (p. 443)
multiple commitments (p. 443)
resolve (p. 443)
temporizing (p. 443)
retreat (p. 443)

escape (p. 443)
epistemological (p. 443)
reflective judgment (p. 444)
"the person who" fallacy (p. 447)
actuarial prediction (p. 447)
vividness effect (p. 447)
placebo effect (p. 447)
belief bias (p. 448)
critical thinking (CT) (p. 449)
bipolar disorder (p. 453)
unipolar disorder (p. 454)
prodrome (p. 454)
bicultural competence (p. 456)

Chapter 12
Socioemotional and Vocational Development in Young Adulthood

 Learning Objectives

After reading this chapter, you should be able to:

12.1 Using the conceptual framework of attachment theory, analyze interpersonal relationships of young adults, identify their challenges, and suggest approaches for resolution/improvement.

12.2 Determine level of compatibility between an individual's personal characteristics and the demands of a chosen career and suggest effective approaches to enhance the process of career development.

Katie and Phil were in love. Their families lived in the same small, middle-class community. They had known each other since middle school, but they didn't start dating until one summer during college. As they got to know each other better, Phil really appreciated Katie's practical, good-hearted ways, and Katie loved Phil's gregariousness, sense of humor, and devotion to his family, especially to his spirited nieces and nephews. They planned a future together. Katie worked in a retirement community during her college summers, and she treasured the time she spent with her grandmother and with Phil's irascible grandfather, who lived to 101. When she completed a Bachelor's in Nursing, she went straight to her dream job in a facility for the infirm elderly. She loved the work, and Phil shared her happiness in finding a satisfying career. But Katie and Phil both knew that her career choice would not make them wealthy. They hoped that Phil's might. Phil saw himself following in his older brother's footsteps. With a finance degree from a good university (his mom's employment there gave him and his siblings tuition waivers), he took a corporate position, aspiring to climb the ladder to executive success. After college, Katie and Phil each lived with their parents to save for a wedding and their own home. But one year into his finance career, Phil was sure that he was headed down the wrong path. He hated his job. He needed to be active and interactive, to be problem solving in a more direct, hands-on way. So he quit. His parents blanched, but they kept supporting him as he thought through his next steps, and they cautiously postponed plans for their retirement. Despite Phil's stubborn insistence that this was the best way for him to move forward, Katie remained committed to him and to their relationship, although they both began to feel the strain as one year of searching for a better career stretched into two. Finally, after really listening to Phil explain what he felt he needed, Katie's dad came up with an idea. He worked for the electric company, and one of the jobs available was line crew manager. It was complicated work that required on-the-ground, rapid problem solving, organizational skills, computer savvy, and a capacity to stay focused and calm and to help crew members do the same, often in emergency situations. Phil was intrigued, and with a good word from Katie's dad, he landed the job. He knew it wouldn't make him wealthy like his brother, but the fit was good, and Katie and Phil moved forward with more modest life plans than they had originally mapped out.

What is required for a happy, well-adjusted adult life? For Sigmund Freud, both love and work are powerful methods by which we "strive to gain happiness and keep suffering away" (Freud, 1930/1989, p. 732). Love, he felt, might bring us closer to the goal of happiness than anything else we do. The disadvantage of love, of course, is that "we are never so defenseless . . . never so helplessly unhappy as when we have lost our loved object or its love" (p. 733). Work, from Freud's perspective, not only helps justify our existence in society, providing the worker with a sense of security within their social network, but it also can be a source of special satisfaction if it is "freely chosen—if, that is . . . it makes possible the use of existing inclinations" (p. 732).

For Erikson (e.g., 1950/1963), both intimacy (love) and generativity (work) are arenas for expressing and developing the self, dominating the concerns of adults in their young and middle years. True intimacy and generativity require achieving an adult identity and are part of its further enrichment and evolution. "Intimacy is a quality of interpersonal relating through which partners share personal thoughts, feelings, and other important aspects of themselves with each other" (McAdams, 2000, p. 118). True intimacy is marked by openness, affection, and trust. Generativity is a motive or need that can be filled through one's vocation or avocations, through child rearing, or through community service. It includes productivity and creativity (Erikson, 1950/1963). Generativity is also a trait that people can be described as having when they are contributing members of society. Generative people tend to have prosocial motives, aiming to engage in behaviors that benefit future generations (McAdams & Guo, 2015). For most adults, achieving generativity is central to their belief in the meaningfulness of their lives. Erikson considered young adults to be especially driven by needs for intimacy, middle adults by needs for generativity. Modern research suggests that both are powerful influences on behavior throughout adulthood, although intimacy needs may predominate early and generativity needs later.

More recent conceptions of how adults achieve happiness, mental health or "wellness" are quite consistent with the importance that Freud and Erikson placed on love and work. Close relationships with lovers, friends, and family, as well as the opportunity to make productive use of one's time and talents, figure prominently in nearly all modern theorizing about what people need to be happy and well-adjusted (see Chapter 14; Ryan & Deci, 2017). From a developmental perspective, then, the period of young adulthood should be a time when identity issues are resolved sufficiently to allow a person to make significant progress on two major tasks: The first is establishing and strengthening bonds with people who will accompany him on his life journey, and the second is becoming a productive worker.

Love

12.1 **Using the conceptual framework of attachment theory, analyze interpersonal relationships of young adults, identify their challenges, and suggest approaches for resolution/improvement.**

Making connections with others in adulthood—establishing intimacy with a mate, making friends, reworking family ties—has been studied from many perspectives. One promising developmental approach examines the impact of attachment style, which is assumed to have its roots in infancy and childhood, on the formation and functioning of adult relationships.

Adult Attachment Theory

Attachment theory has enjoyed a prominent place in the child development literature since the groundbreaking work of John Bowlby and Mary Ainsworth (see Chapter 4). Following an explosion of studies on childhood attachment, researchers began to train their sights on attachment theorists' suggestion that early bonds with caregivers could have a bearing on relationship building throughout the life span. Today, attachment theory provides a useful framework for conceptualizing adult intimacy. The abundance of research in this area makes it the most empirically grounded theory available for explaining the formation and nature of close interpersonal relationships throughout adulthood (Zeifman & Hazan, 2016).

As we saw in Chapter 4, attachments are a special kind of social bond. According to Bowlby (1969/1982), the attachment between infant and caregiver serves survival needs, and has four defining features: *distress at separation*, which ensures *proximity* to the caregiver, who is a *safe haven* in case of threat, and who acts as a *secure base* for exploration. The attachment figure, then, is a preferred provider of emotional warmth and affect regulation.

How the attachment process unfolds is a function of the caregiving relationship. Depending on the caregiver's sensitivity and responsiveness, an infant becomes securely or insecurely attached to that caregiver. To the extent possible, he adapts his behavior to the caregiver's style to get his needs met, and he begins to internalize a working model of how relationships operate.

Despite diminishing demands for physical caretaking as individuals age, adults continue to need the emotional and practical support of significant others. As we have noted, Erikson identified the achievement of intimacy as the central task of early adulthood. In his view, even though adults are much more independent than children, they still need to establish and maintain intimate connections to people who will provide them with love and care. Although you may never have thought of your adult relationships with significant others, including your bonds to your parents, as attachment relationships, many researchers believe that they are precisely that. Let us look more closely at the various manifestations of attachments in adulthood and consider a framework for organizing the existing research.

Research Traditions in Adult Attachment

Attachment theory has provided a framework for understanding many kinds of individual differences in adults' behavior, from how they react to bereavement and loss (Schenck, Eberle, & Rings, 2016), to their responses to stress in general (Simpson & Rholes, 2012), to their choices of religious practices (Granqvist & Kirkpatrick, 2016), to their manner of social information processing (Dykas & Cassidy, 2011). Among helping professionals, attachment theory has been used to explain conflict resolution in interpersonal relationships (Rholes, Kohn, & Simpson, 2014), family dysfunction (Wiebe & Johnson, 2016), and psychopathology (Stovall-McClough & Dozier, 2016), and it provides a basis for therapeutic interventions (Berlin, Zeanah, & Lieberman, 2016; Josephs, 2018).

Our focus here is on two major research traditions (Crowell, Fraley, & Roisman, 2016; Simpson & Rholes, 1998). First, there is a body of work that examines the outcomes of a person's attachment to his primary caregiver in infancy, once the person becomes an adult. This has been referred to as the "nuclear family tradition." Investigations center on whether our earliest attachments to primary caregivers endure throughout life, how they might affect the quality of caregiving we give to our children, and whether parents in any sense "pass on" their own attachment statuses to their children. A parallel line of research, sometimes called the "peer/romantic partner tradition," focuses on the peer attachments of adults. In this work, investigators try to answer questions about how early attachments impact the quality of romantic and friendship relationships in adulthood, and conversely, how adult relationships might influence changes in attachment statuses.

The two bodies of work are grounded in attachment theory, but they have often used different methods and measurement techniques, sometimes even coming up with their own terminology, as you will see. As a result, it is not always easy to see how the findings from one tradition cohere with those from the other. Both research traditions generally support the notion that attachment patterns affect how adults behave, from caring for children to interacting with friends and romantic partners. After the first two decades of research on attachment in adults, Bartholomew and Shaver (1998) remarked:

> When we step back from the details of specific measures and measure-specific findings, the results produced by attachment researchers are all compatible with the possibility that various forms of adult attachment arise from a continuous but branching tree of attachment experiences, beginning in infancy and developing throughout the life course. (p. 42)

The more recent decades of research have only served to strengthen that conclusion. We will continue our discussion of adult attachment by focusing on each approach in turn. First, we will consider how the nuclear family tradition contributes to our understanding of adult caregiving. Then we will present an overview of significant contributions from the peer/romantic partner tradition.

The Nuclear Family Tradition: The Past as Prologue

Does the nature of your attachment to your caregiver predict your behavior in adulthood, influencing the quality of attachment you will form with your own children? This is the intriguing question that is at the heart of the nuclear family line of research. We briefly examined this issue in Chapter 4. Now we'll take a closer look.

You may recall that the primary instrument used to measure the attachment representations of adults vis-à-vis their early caregivers is the Adult Attachment Interview (AAI) developed by Main and Goldwyn (1984; see Hesse, 2016). It is composed of a series of 18 open-ended questions with follow-up prompts that are transcribed verbatim by a trained interviewer. Table 12.1 provides a sampling of some of the questions in the protocol. The questions concern memories of relationships with mother and father; recollections of stressful events such as separations, loss, harsh discipline, or abuse; interpretations of parental behaviors; and evaluation of the effects of these early events on the interviewee's later development. Follow-up prompts to interviewee's answers are critical, requesting more detail and/or explanation, such as "Why did you describe your father as 'strict'?" "Can you give me an example of a disciplinary episode you recall?"

Main and her colleagues hypothesized that the primary task for the interviewee is to resurrect emotionally loaded memories of early childhood experiences while simultaneously presenting them in a coherent fashion to an interviewer. Because the questions deal with very complicated, personal, and often intense issues in a person's early history, they may never have been articulated by the individual prior to this interview experience. The rapidity of questioning, combined with the nature of the items and the interview setting, are thought to elicit material often heretofore unconscious, yet

TABLE 12.1 Sample Questions from the Adult Attachment Interview Protocol

1. To begin with, could you just help me to get a little bit oriented to your family—for example, who was in your immediate family, and where you lived?

2. Now I'd like you to try to describe your relationship with your parents as a young child, starting as far back as you can remember.

5. To which parent did you feel closer, and why?

7. Could you describe your first separation from your parents?

11. Why do you think your parents behaved as they did during your childhood?

SOURCE: Based on Hesse, E. (2016). The Adult Attachment Interview. Protocol method of analysis, and selected empirical studies: 1985-2015. In J. Cassidy & P. R. Shaver (Eds.), *Handbook of attachment: Theory, research, and clinical applications* (3rd ed., pp. 5).

highly descriptive of the adult's state of mind regarding early attachments to primary caregivers. The assumption is that by adulthood, security has become a characteristic of the individual. Representations of different relationships—like relationships with mother versus father—tend to coalesce, and a single working model of attachment can be tapped (Hesse, 2016).

Interviews are scored according to Grice's (1975) criteria for coherent discourse: truthfulness as supported by evidence, succinctness, relevance to the topic, clarity, and organization of responses. Additional scoring criteria include the coder's assessment of the interviewee's early attachment quality as well as an assessment of the language used in the interview (e.g., angry, passive, derogating). Four qualitatively different classifications, or attachment styles, are then assigned to adults based on their verbatim transcripts. These are secure or insecure (which includes three subcategories: dismissing, preoccupied, and unresolved) categories. Different classifications of insecurity are thought to reflect the different strategies and rules of information processing that the person has developed to manage the anxiety of early relationship failure, loss, or trauma. Let us examine each of these categories in turn.

Autonomous (secure) adults provide a transcript that is coherent and collaborative. They answer questions with enough detail to provide sufficient evidence without giving excessive information. For example, incidents of caregiver insensitivity are described matter-of-factly, without embellishment or defensiveness. Secure adults also demonstrate the ability to integrate and monitor their thinking, summarize answers, and return the conversation to the interviewer. They seem to be less egocentric in their presentation than insecure individuals, and they demonstrate good perspective taking skills. Secure individuals acknowledge the importance of attachment-related experiences in their development. Their memories of the parenting they received match up with the specific instances they present to the interviewer as illustrations. The emotions they express, both verbally and facially, are consistent with the content of their remarks (Crowell et al., 2016).

Can adults be classified as secure if they have had less than favorable experiences as a child? Some individuals do come from circumstances of early adversity but describe their painful backgrounds truthfully and believably, while acknowledging the stressors their own parents faced. This ability to reflect on a difficult past realistically, yet with a certain level of generosity towards parents, results in a special classification called **earned secure**. Such adults appear to have come to terms with less than optimal early experiences, quite possibly with the help of a secure spouse or partner. Individuals in both secure categories typically have children who are securely attached to them (see Chapter 4 for a detailed discussion of children's attachment categories).

Dismissing (insecure) individuals provide transcripts that are characterized by markedly low levels of detail and coherence. They are likely to describe parents as very positive or idealized; however, they do not support their evaluations with any specific evidence. Whatever details these dismissing respondents offer may actually contradict their generally favorable presentation of parental behavior. They tend to minimize or avoid discussion of attachment-related issues and downplay the importance of close relationships. When discussing nonemotional topics, dismissing individuals generate coherent and comprehensive records and can talk at some length. Responses to attachment themes, in contrast, lack elaboration. Failure to remember is often cited as a reason for the impoverished answers. Adults classified as dismissing tend to have children who are in the avoidant attachment category.

The dismissing style has been linked to early experiences of rejection or other trauma and the development of repressive personality styles. Do these individuals simply hide their distress, or have they managed to actually suppress their attachment needs? Some evidence using an information processing approach indicates that these individuals, over time, function with the goal of avoiding emotional thoughts and other reminders of unpleasant emotional experiences, such as parental unavailability. This motivated avoidance may lead to less cognitive elaboration of attachment themes and a reduction of behaviors that would encourage intimacy, such as sharing intimate conversation, mutual gazing, cuddling, and so on.

However, it is unlikely that the system has been deactivated completely. Dozier and Kobak (1992) provide interesting evidence that dismissing individuals do react strongly to emotional issues. These researchers interviewed college students using the AAI while measuring their rates of skin conductance. Dismissing subjects, although outwardly appearing unfazed during questioning, had significantly elevated levels of skin conductance, as compared to baseline levels, when asked questions about the emotional availability of their parents and the effects of early attachments on their self-development. Roisman et al. (2004) replicated these results cross-culturally, studying European Americans, Chinese Americans, and Chinese nationals who were students at a midwestern American university.

Many more recent studies, done with a range of physiological measures, consistently support the conclusion that dismissing individuals have strong reactions in emotional situations (see reviews by Gander & Buchheim, 2015; Mikulincer & Shaver, 2016). During the AAI, they seem to effortfully engage in diversionary tactics, called "deactivating" or "minimizing" strategies, to deal with the anxiety generated by the topics. Such strategies do not suppress strong physiological reactions, but they do seem to impede a dismissing person's ability to understand and recall his own and others' emotions (Stevens, 2014). In the AAI interview, dismissing people have trouble remembering childhood experiences, and they often provide rather general descriptions of their parents. In other contexts, their deactivating strategies lead to odd "disconnects" between their feelings and behavior. For example, in a study of couples' conversations, when *secure* individuals showed physiological signs of distress (increased skin conductance), they also expressed emotions to their partners that were consistent with distress, such as anger or hurt. But *dismissing* individuals were actually more likely to express positive feelings to their partners when their physiological reactions signaled that they were feeling distressed (Seedall & Wampler, 2012).

Individuals in a third group, classified as preoccupied (insecure), typically violate the rule of collaboration on the AAI interview. These individuals provide very long, incoherent, egocentric responses that shift from topic to topic. They perform in ways that suggest they are overwhelmed by the emotional memories elicited by the interview questions and are sidetracked from the task of responding succinctly. Such speakers often sound angry, sad, or fearful, as if they have never resolved the painful problems of their childhood. Parents may be remembered as intrusive or egocentric. Preoccupied individuals' transcripts paint a picture of substantial enmeshment or preoccupation with parents, registered by angry, accusatory language or by conflicted descriptions that connote ambivalence and confusion about early relationships. This feature of the preoccupied attachment style has been referred to as "hyperactivating," and there is emerging evidence that individuals with hyperactivating responses to the AAI are more likely than others to show heart rate increases in situations that arouse the attachment system (Roisman, 2007). Both their facial expressions and their self-reported emotions during the AAI are often inconsistent with the childhood memories they describe. For example, distressed facial expression might be combined with their description of a positive experience (Roisman et al., 2004). Linguistic features of their transcripts include run-on sentences, idiosyncratic uses of words, and juxtaposition of past and present tense, as though early problems continue to persist in the present. The children of preoccupied adults often have anxious-ambivalent attachments.

Individuals in the fourth category, called unresolved (insecure), produce transcripts characterized by marked lapses in logical thinking, particularly when these individuals discuss loss or other traumatic memories. One example of a lapse in reasoning might be an interviewee's mention of a deceased parent as still living. Hesse and Main (1999b) have suggested that these abrupt shifts may be related to temporary changes in consciousness, possibly due to the arousal of unintegrated fear. Individuals in this category may also receive a secondary classification of dismissing or preoccupied. The children of unresolved individuals show a higher frequency of disorganized attachment patterns than other children.

A fifth category, cannot classify, is used when protocols do not meet the criteria for other categories. Only a very small number of cases fall into this classification. Data on AAI classifications and psychopathology demonstrate that psychiatric disorders are clearly associated with insecure status and that, in particular, unresolved status is the clearest predictor of emotional disturbance (Lyons-Ruth & Jacobvitz, 2016; Stovall-McClough & Dozier, 2016).

Most longitudinal studies have found that a person's attachment behavior in infancy, as measured by the strange situation test, predicts whether he will be scored as secure or insecure on the AAI as an adolescent or an adult (Hesse, 2016). As we saw in Chapter 4, however, a child's attachment status can become more or less secure if he has either positive or negative experiences with close relationships after the infant–toddler period. People can either "earn" security, as we have already noted, by experiencing later supportive relationships or can develop insecure representations of attachment. Adults who were secure as children can later demonstrate insecure states of mind because of intervening, highly stressful events such as parental loss, divorce, abuse, illness, or psychiatric disorder. Such findings suggest that deviations from the predicted pathway are most likely explained by lawful rather than random discontinuity (Crowell et al., 2016), although more longitudinal studies with larger numbers of participants are needed.

IN SEARCH OF THE WORKING MODEL

Perhaps you are wondering if the attachment representation categories that are derived from adults' AAI performances could simply be measures of general linguistic style. If so, then interviews would have no particular relevance to attachment, and their predictive value for children's attachment characteristics might be coincidental. Crowell et al. (1996) investigated whether the different linguistic features used to make AAI classifications also characterize individuals on other measures of discourse. Using the Employment Experience Interview, he examined a group of adults who had been assigned AAI classifications. The Employment Experience Interview had the same structure as the AAI and was coded using the same criteria. Note that the only difference between the two was in the nature of the questions: one was about job skills and the other early attachment relationships. Results showed differences among the transcripts (e.g., vague vs. clear discourse). However, the interesting finding was that respondents' classifications were different on each measure. In other words, an adult who might be judged "secure" on the employment interview could be "insecure" on the AAI. The researchers concluded that there is something unique about the attachment questions. They appear to provide a window into a person's state of mind concerning interpersonal representations.

The power of attachment theory rests on the concept of the inner working model. The AAI was designed to tap an adult's representation of attachments to primary caregivers. The assumption is that the individual's narrative reflects partly unconscious representations. Results are not considered to be a direct measure of an individual's attachment to any one person, but rather are an indicator of the individual's state of mind regarding attachment-related issues. Like an algorithm for our close interpersonal associations, the working model is thought to provide rules for processing information about relationships and for behaving in relationships.

Researchers agree that the working model of relationships that one has as an adult cannot simply be a carbon copy of the one that was formed with the primary caregiver in infancy. It is a cognitive structure or schema (often now described as a prototype) that must evolve with time and experience, becoming more elaborate, incorporating new elements into the original version in dynamic, qualitatively transformed ways. Like all cognitive schemas, our working models of relationships help us understand, predict, and act on information that is only fragmentary. The obvious advantage is that they allow us to process information and to respond quickly. The downside is that we may fail to accommodate real differences in present relationships, and we may behave in these relationships in ways that are adapted to quite different circumstances (Bretherton & Munholland, 2016).

For example, consider Sheila, whose mother was depressed and dependent. As a youngster, Sheila felt that her mother's needs always came before her own. Because even the simplest task was a chore for her mother, Sheila began taking on the care of the household and her younger siblings in order to spare her mother. Sheila grew increasingly competent as a caretaker, which, in turn, caused her mother to depend on her even more. As a young adult, Sheila has difficulty getting close to people. She bristles when any friend or romantic partner, in an attempt to get close to her emotionally, talks about a personal problem. She quickly changes the subject of conversation. Sheila's relationships in adulthood appear to be affected by the legacy of her earlier attachments. She exaggerates other people's reliance on her and fears she will be overcome by their needs, despite any real evidence for this.

As we have seen, adults' attachment representations predict the quality of their attachments to their children (see Chapter 4). This link suggests that attachment representation is a determinant of parental caregiving behavior. Does attachment representation also affect the way that adults interact with other adults? If the working model, in fact, functions like an algorithm for close relationships, individual differences in attachment representations should also affect adults' ability to relate to others in romantic and friendship relationships. This is the subject of our next section.

The Peer/Romantic Relationship Tradition

Any reader of romance novels can testify that the topic of adult love relationships has considerable appeal. In the research community as well, quite a bit of time and energy has been devoted to understanding the formation and development of adult pair-bonds. Researchers have examined specific issues such as mate selection, relationship satisfaction, conflict resolution, relationship dissolution, and so on, and have produced a wealth of findings in each of these areas. Studies have also been done that show consistent individual differences in adults' approaches to romantic relationships, sometimes called "love styles" (Lee, 1973). Similarly, there are theories about the elements of love, such as Sternberg's (1986) passion, intimacy, and commitment, and the ways they function in relationship formation. **Passion** refers to erotic attraction or feelings of being in love. *Intimacy* includes elements of love that promote connection and closeness, whereas **commitment** refers to making a decision to sustain a relationship with a loved one. We will discuss these elements further in the next chapter.

An early investigation by Shaver and Hazan (1988) contributed significantly to the growing body of knowledge on adult relationships by anchoring the fledgling field within the conceptual framework of attachment theory. These researchers tried to integrate the disparate threads of data into a comprehensive theory of relationships. Today, research conceptualizing adult pair-bonds as attachments represents the second influential offshoot of attachment theory.

FEATURES OF ADULT PAIR-BONDS

Do adult pair-bonds qualify as bona fide attachment relationships? Although there are some dissenting opinions (e.g., McAdams, 2000), many researchers answer yes. Bowlby (1969/1982) defined a behavioral system as a set of behaviors that serve the same function or goal. Human beings are equipped with multiple behavioral systems, meeting multiple goals, which interact in coordinated ways. The attachment system is one of these. In early childhood, attachment behavior—which includes proximity maintenance, separation distress, and treatment of the caregiver as both a safe haven and a secure base—is the most important behavioral system because it serves the ultimate goal of survival. When security is threatened, the attachment system is triggered, and proximity-seeking behaviors increase. But when security is felt, other behavioral systems, such as exploration, can be activated.

In adulthood, as in childhood, particular behavioral systems are organized to meet specific needs. Attachment (based on the need for felt security) is just one of the adult behavioral systems serving psychosocial needs, which also include caregiving, sexual mating, and exploration. Because of their structure and function, pair-bonds in adults provide an effective way to integrate three of the basic systems: caregiving, attachment (felt security), and sexual mating. The support provided by the secure base of an attachment relationship enhances exploration in adults, just as it does in children (Feeney & Woodhouse, 2016; Jakubiak & Feeney, 2016). Zeifman and Hazan (2016) argue that "infant-caregiver and adult romantic relationships share unique psychological properties . . . and serve similar functions from an evolutionary standpoint . . . (They) confer benefits that are distinct from those associated with other relationships" (p. 416). Infant–caregiver bonds and adult pair-bonds are notably similar in the kinds of physical contact they involve, such as mutual gazing, kissing, cuddling, and so on, and in the goals they serve (support, emotional closeness, etc.). Adult attachments, however, do differ from childhood attachments in the following three ways. First, the attachments adults have with adults are structured more symmetrically than are parent–child bonds. Both partners mutually provide and receive caregiving, whereas the parent is the unilateral source of caregiving for the child. Second, adults rely more than children do on "felt security" rather than on the actual physical presence of the attachment figure. Longer periods of separation can be tolerated by adolescents and adults because they understand that attachment figures will be dependable and available when they need contact. Third, adult attachments typically involve a sexual partner or peer rather than a parent figure.

THE PROCESS OF RELATIONSHIP FORMATION IN ADULTHOOD

How does the attachment system of early childhood become transformed into the attachments of adulthood? Zeifman and Hazan (2016) chart the progress of attachments by tracing the behaviors that serve the goals of the system. In infancy, as we have stated, all four functions of the attachment system (proximity maintenance, separation distress, secure base, safe haven) depend on the presence of an attachment figure, and infant behavior towards the caregiver clearly is adapted to meet these goals. As children get older, behaviors towards peers appear to serve some attachment functions as well. For example, children transfer some proximity-seeking behaviors to peers by early childhood. Children begin to spend more time with age-mates and seek them out as preferred playmates. By early adolescence, needs for intimacy and support are often met within the peer group, as you saw in Chapter 10, suggesting that needs for a safe haven in times of distress are directed to peers as well as parents. By late adolescence and early adulthood, romantic partners may satisfy all the needs of the attachment system.

In a now classic study, Hazan and Zeifman (1999) asked children and adolescents from 6 to 17 years old a number of questions that tapped attachment needs. Researchers asked the participants whom they preferred to spend time with (proximity maintenance), whom they turned to if they were feeling bad (safe haven), whom they disliked being separated from (separation distress), and whom they could always count on when they needed help (secure base). Results of this study supported shifts away from parents to peers, apparently preparing the way for adult attachment behaviors. The great majority of respondents sought proximity to peers instead of parents at all ages. Between the ages of 8 and 14, participants' responses indicated a shift towards use of peers for safe haven as well. Most children and adolescents identified parents as their secure base and the source of their separation distress. However, among those older participants who had established romantic relationships, all four attachment needs were met in the context of their pair-bonds. In a second study that included adults ages 18 to 82, the same researchers found that the majority of adults reported that their proximity-seeking and safe-haven behaviors were directed towards peers, especially romantic partners. Secure-base behaviors and feelings of separation distress tended to remain directed more towards parents until romantic relationships had proven themselves to endure, usually by two years into the relationship. Zeifman and Hazan (2016) suggest that romantic relationships require about two years to become "full-blown attachments." Their findings also show that nonromantic relationships can serve attachment functions in adulthood. These include relationships with

FIGURE 12.1 Age changes in attachment and close relationships.

	TARGET OF ATTACHMENT BEHAVIORS	
DEVELOPMENTAL PHASE	**Parents**	**Peers**
Infancy	proximity maintenance safe haven secure base	
Early Childhood	safe haven secure base	proximity maintenance
Late Childhood/ Early Adolescence	secure base	proximity maintenance safe haven
Adulthood		proximity maintenance safe haven secure base

SOURCE: Hazan, C. & Shaver, R. (1994). Attachment as an organizational framework for research on close relationships. *Psychological Inquiry, 5*, 1–11. Reprinted by permission of Lawrence Erlbaum Associates.

friends, siblings, or parents. But the majority of adults eventually see their romantic partners as their chief attachment figure. See Figure 12.1 for a model of the attachment transfer process across age.

INDIVIDUAL DIFFERENCES IN ADULT ATTACHMENTS

The preceding discussion describes what might be considered normative processes involved in the development of adult attachments. Remember, however, that individuals differ in their states of mind regarding attachment experiences, that is, in their internal working models. Do these different "states of mind" predict different approaches to peer or romantic relationships in adulthood? To shed light on this question, we must recall that each tradition of attachment research has its own way of looking at these issues. Even though researchers in both traditions start from the same premise, namely that adults' attachment styles will resemble Ainsworth's infant attachment typology, the typical measures used in the peer/romantic relationship tradition are different from those of the nuclear family tradition. Adult romantic relationship research began with self-report or questionnaire measures that were presumed to tap conscious, rather than unconscious, expectations about relationships. The sheer volume of work done in the area of measurement prevents a comprehensive discussion of this topic in this chapter. However, we will present an introduction to certain key issues and describe some important instruments. The interested reader is referred to Crowell and colleagues (2016) for a more thorough presentation.

The first influential measure of adult romantic attachment, developed by Hazan and Shaver (1987), asked adults to identify which of three statements (see Table 12.2) best captured their approach to and beliefs about romantic relationships. Descriptive statements represented avoidant, anxious-ambivalent, and secure classifications. As

TABLE 12.2 Three Attachment Prototypes in Peer/Romantic Tradition

Avoidant. I am somewhat uncomfortable being close to others; I find it difficult to trust them completely, difficult to allow myself to depend on them. I am nervous when anyone gets too close, and often, love partners want me to be more intimate than I feel comfortable being.

Anxious-ambivalent. I find that others are reluctant to get as close as I would like. I often worry that my partner doesn't really love me or won't want to stay with me. I want to get very close to my partner, and this sometimes scares people away.

Secure. I find it relatively easy to get close to others and am comfortable depending on them. I don't often worry about being abandoned or about someone getting too close to me.

SOURCE: Based on Hazan, C., & Shaver, P. R. (1987). Romantic love conceptualized as an attachment process. *Journal of Personality and Social Psychology, 52*, 515. Reprinted by permission of the American Psychological Association.

measurement was refined and attempts to integrate the fields of nuclear family and adult peer attachments increased, researchers recognized that the category called "avoidant" from Hazan and Shaver's instrument did not correspond to the "dismissing" category of the AAI. The avoidant person clearly acknowledged anxiety about getting too close to another, whereas the dismissing individual reported no subjective distress.

Faced with the needs to include both aspects of avoidance, Bartholomew and her colleagues (Bartholomew & Horowitz, 1991; Bartholomew & Shaver, 1998) proposed a new conceptual framework consisting of four categories across two dimensions. Figure 12.2 illustrates this typology which operationalized Bowlby's view that working models of the self and of others are interrelated. People are thought to develop expectations about how reliably their significant others will behave in close relationships, as well as expectations about how worthy or unworthy they are of care and support. Four categories of attachment orientation are defined by crossing the working model of self with the working model of others.

In Bartholomew's typology, secure individuals have internalized a positive sense of themselves along with positive models of others. In general, they expect others to be available and supportive of their needs in close relationships. They are comfortable with emotional closeness but are also reasonably autonomous. Individuals classified as *preoccupied* hold positive models of others but negative models of themselves. Others are viewed as not valuing the preoccupied person as much as he values them. Preoccupied attachment is marked by emotional demandingness, anxiety about gaining acceptance from others, fear of and hypervigilance to cues of rejection, and excessive preoccupation with relationships.

The avoidant category is subdivided into two, based on reports of felt distress. *Dismissing* individuals are characterized by a positive model of the self but a negative model of the other. Denying the need for close relationships permits these adults to maintain a sense of superiority while devaluing the importance of others to their well-being. Self-sufficiency is preferred, and anxiety about attachment relationships is inhibited. A fearful attachment is the product of negative models of both self and others. For individuals with this style, attachments are desirable but seen as out of reach. Their desire for close relationships with others is thwarted by fear of rejection, and ultimately they withdraw. A high level of distress surrounds attachment themes.

The use of categories such as the ones we have just described is intuitively understandable and attractive but poses a number of problems. There is a danger of failing to recognize that individual differences often exist on a continuum, reflecting the degree to which a certain tendency is exhibited (e.g., high to low levels of anxiety), as opposed to differences in kind (highly anxious vs. not anxious). Therefore, measurements that place people in quadrants will undoubtedly mask the continuity that actually exists along the underlying dimensions. This kind of categorization may actually underestimate the real continuity of attachment patterns from childhood to adulthood and diminish the strength of associations between attachment research from the parental and romantic traditions. It may be convenient to use a typology, but a number of studies suggest that attachment scales are really measuring two continuous dimensions: avoidance and anxiety (e.g., Brennan, Clark, & Shaver, 1998; Crowell et al., 2016; Fraley & Roisman, 2014).

For helping professionals, a dimensional perspective may make it easier to think of individuals as operating within a range of possible behaviors. Specific attachment patterns should be viewed as tendencies to perceive and act in certain ways but not as guarantees that individuals will always operate according to type. So clinicians and other helpers should avoid "typecasting" clients on the basis of attachment categories that are fixed and orthogonal, a practice that can distort clinical judgment by acting as a cognitive bias or stereotype. It may be more helpful to keep in mind that the most basic issues involved in relationships concern a person's level of anxiety about social

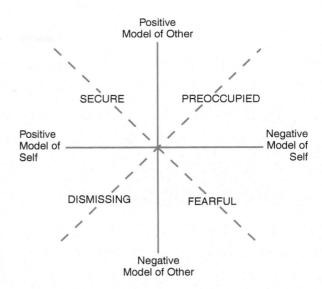

FIGURE 12.2 Bartholomew's typology: A four-category model of adult attachment categories.

SOURCE: Bartholomew, K. & Shaver, P. (1998). Methods of assessing adult attachment: Do they converge? In J. A. Simpson & W. S. Rholes (Eds.), *Attachment theory and close relationships* (pp. 25–45). New York, NY: Guilford Press. Used by permission of Guilford Publications, Inc.

interaction and his level of approach or avoidance. The prototypical classifications may best represent individuals with very pronounced characteristics at the extremes of the anxiety-avoidance dimensions. It is probably more accurate to think of people having particular attachment styles rather than classifications, which is a less forgiving term. It may also be helpful to keep in mind that there is wide variability in behavioral expression of anxiety and of approach-avoidance in relationships.

RESEARCH ON YOUNG ADULT DYADIC RELATIONSHIPS

Western research in the peer/romantic tradition has uncovered a number of interesting aspects of dyadic relationship patterns that are related to attachment style. The focus of most of this work has been the exploration of how individual differences in attachment orientations play out in areas of social interaction. Let us take a brief look at some of the results of these investigations in areas of concern to young adults: partner selection, satisfaction with and stability of relationships, communication and conflict resolution styles, and engagement in casual sexual contact. When appropriate, we will also consider how gender differences mediate these relationships.

MyLab Education
Video Example 12.1
Research has uncovered interesting connections between attachment style and young adult dyadic relationships. Consider how these research findings might relate to the dilemma of the young woman in this video.

Partner Selection.   What contributes to romantic interest in another person? In particular, does the attachment status or style of either potential partner influence who chooses whom? Researchers approach this question in two primary ways. First, they use experimental studies, presenting participants with vignettes describing potential romantic partners and asking them to rate their attraction or interest in dating those individuals. This technique allows the experimenter to hold constant other factors that are known to affect partner selection, such as the physical attractiveness or career success of the potential partner, while examining the impact of behavioral descriptions that suggest the potential partner's attachment style as secure, avoidant, or anxious. Researchers can look at whether the participants' own attachment status, or the attachment status of the prospective partner, affects their choices.

These studies consistently show that people are most attracted to others who are secure, regardless of their own attachment status (Finkel & Eastwick, 2015; Pepping, Taylor, Koh, & Halford, 2017). In many studies, the next most appealing potential partner is an anxious person—someone who craves intimacy. Finally, people claim to least prefer avoidant partners, who avoid intimacy. But there is also some evidence that "like chooses like." Everyone is more likely to choose a potential mate who seems secure, but anxious individuals favor other anxious individuals more than avoidant ones, and in a few studies, avoidant individuals favor avoidant individuals somewhat more often than anxious ones (Holmes & Johnson, 2009; Pietromonaco & Beck, 2015).

These experimental studies examine people's initial attraction, when they have minimal information. A second kind of study looks at the characteristics of existing couples, those whose relationship has endured for several months or even years. First, as you might expect, secure individuals, who neither avoid intimacy nor are desperately in search of it, are more often paired with other secure rather than insecure partners (Holmes & Johnson, 2009; Pietromonaco & Beck, 2015). Katie and Phil, introduced at the beginning of this chapter, seem to be a clear example of such a pair. However, pairings of insecure individuals are often *not* what you might expect from the experimental studies of initial attraction.

Attachment theory predicts that insecure people will usually select partners who confirm their expectations or working models of close relationships. Avoidant partners, who are fearful or dismissing of intimacy, would expect partners to cling and overwhelm them with their demandingness. Anxious partners, who crave closeness, may expect rejection and believe that their needs for intimacy will go unmet. Thus, an avoidant individual might pair with an anxious one, fulfilling expectations of both partners. In other words, the theory predicts that "complementary pairings" between insecure individuals would be more common than "similarity pairings."

Several studies have documented the fact that avoidant-avoidant and anxious-anxious pairings are rare. For example, in an early study of 354 heterosexual couples, not a single couple showed either of these patterns. Consistent with attachment theory, similarity pairings seem to violate people's expectations from their working models, and therefore are not very likely to endure. What is far more likely is the complementary pairing of avoidant with anxious mates, and studies of both heterosexual and homosexual couples have found a preponderance of such matches among insecure individuals (Mohr & Jackson, 2016; Pietromanco & Beck, 2015).

At this point, although the findings match the predictions of attachment theory, it is unclear whether romantic partners always enter relationships with these complementary attachment styles or whether something in the nature of the relationship alters the attachment style. As you will see in Box 12.1, attachment styles can change with experience in a romantic relationship, but the probability of change is not large.

Intimacy, Satisfaction, and Stability of Relationships. Consistent with attachment theory, the attachment styles of romantic partners help predict their emotional closeness and mutual acceptance—the intimacy of their relationships. The quantity and quality of both caregiving and sexual experience are affected. Highly avoidant partners tend to provide less physical comfort to their partners and their care tends to be less sensitive and nurturing. With primary romantic partners, they engage in sex less frequently than secure people, even though they might be more inclined than others to have casual, uncommitted sex (see below). Highly anxious partners are more controlling and intrusive in their caregiving than secure partners, and they are more likely to view sexual relations as a way of avoiding rejection and strengthening their attachment (Birnbaum, 2016; Mikulincer & Shaver, 2016).

Not surprisingly, feelings of commitment and relationship satisfaction are also tied to people's attachment styles. Some studies assess attachment status at one time and follow up later with assessments of partners' interactions and/or feelings about their relationships (Holland & Roisman, 2010; Holland, Fraley, & Roisman, 2012). Secure individuals tend to experience more positive and less negative emotion, to have more harmonious interactions with their partners, and to report greater satisfaction in their relationships than those who are insecure. They also report more trust, commitment, and interdependence. Katie and Phil illustrate how two secure partners are likely to support one another through difficult transitions. For example, Katie's trust and commitment were sustained despite setbacks and changes in the life course the couple had planned. Highly avoidant partners report weaker interdependence and less commitment; highly anxious people are more likely to say that their relationships lack trust. There are also some interesting gender differences. Avoidant males experience less distress when their relationships end than others, but that is not the case for avoidant females. Perhaps this is due to the commonly held perception that women are primarily responsible for maintenance of personal relationships and so they feel more accountable for the partnership's success.

Overall, when both partners are insecure, relationship satisfaction tends to suffer, and anxious attachment seems to be especially problematic (Feeney, 2016; Mikulincer & Shaver, 2016; Sobral, Teixeira, & Costa, 2015). The lowest levels of satisfaction are usually reported by couples composed of avoidant men and anxious women (e.g., Kirkpatrick & Davis, 1994). Yet these matches are typically about as stable as matches between more satisfied, secure partners. The couples who are most vulnerable to breaking up seem to be those made up of anxious men and avoidant women. Once again, this may have something to do with women being the stereotypical tenders of relationships. Avoidant women may be less skilled at accommodating, or less motivated to accommodate, the needs of the more dependent partner. Anxious women, overly concerned with possibilities of abandonment, might be more willing to do what it takes to maintain a relationship with an avoidant partner, perhaps explaining the high level of stability in these relationships.

Communication Style and Conflict Resolution. Consider for a moment a problem that you experienced at some time in one of your close relationships. Now reflect on how you dealt with that problem. Was your response typical of the way you usually deal with relationship problems? You undoubtedly know, by virtue of your training, that when faced with a relationship's inevitable glitches, it is a good idea to be open, nondefensive, reasonably assertive, and yet flexible enough to compromise. Keeping a clear head so that problem solving can be effective is another requirement. Easier said than done, you're probably thinking! Why is it often so hard to do this well?

Box 12.1: The Benefits of Love: Stability and Change in Adult Attachment Styles

A child's attachment status can change if the caregiving environment changes. We saw in Chapter 4, for example, that major disruptions of family life, such as parents' divorce or loss of employment, can impact the quality of care a child receives and alter the security of the child's attachment. Is an adult's attachment style open to revision? If so, it seems likely that such change would happen primarily in the context of major relationship shifts—after marriage, or with parenting, or because of the dissolution of an intimate partnership. Crowell, Treboux, and Waters (2002) studied stability and change in young adults' attachment representations after they were married, expecting that although stability might be the rule, the intimacy and intensity of marital relationships could be especially conducive to positive change for some individuals.

One hundred fifty-seven couples, averaging about 24 years old, were recruited for the study when they sought marriage licenses in one county of New York State. None was previously married and none had children. They had already been together for an average of 51 months, although most (about 67%) were still living separately, usually with their parents. These young men and women were tested 3 months before and 18 months after their weddings. At each assessment they were given an attachment classification based on an Adult Attachment Interview (AAI). In addition, participants completed a "Family Behavior Survey," answering questions about amount of happiness, discord, and aggression in their relationship. Finally, each partner participated in a "Current Relationship Interview." In these interviews, they were required to use adjectives to characterize their own and their partners' behaviors, and they had to provide examples that supported those descriptions. They also talked about what factors were important aspects of, and influences on, their relationships, and about qualities of their interaction in different circumstances, such as when one partner was sick or upset.

From these interviews, the researchers assigned each participant a relationship rating. A relationship, like an attachment status, could be classified as "secure," "dismissing," "preoccupied," or "unresolved." Individuals whose relationships were secure, for example, were likely to report examples of shared comfort and support, saw their partnership as an opportunity for both partners to grow, and spoke coherently about the importance of attachment elements, like emotional closeness. In dismissing relationships, individuals tended to express support for their partners only conditionally, that is, only for concerns that they regarded as important. They also talked more about the material or personal goals they had for their relationship (e.g., we'll be buying a house together) than they did about factors like their emotional bond. In preoccupied relationships, partners spoke of feeling anxious about their partners' expressed concerns and about the relationship, sometimes manifesting that anxiety as anger or confusion.

As expected, for the majority of participants (78%), attachment status remained stable through the marriage transition.

This was especially true of those who began with a secure attachment. The relationships formed by secure partners were also more secure. As we would expect from other studies, the partnerships of secure individuals were more intimate from the beginning, and they had fewer difficulties, like arguments or verbal aggression, during the first 18 months of marriage. According to attachment theory, a working model of attachment *should* be fairly stable by adulthood, representing a characteristic state of mind in relationship contexts that affects the behavior of the individual and that in turn affects the responses of the relationship partner. As we have seen, these mental and behavioral patterns begin in infancy, evolve through childhood and adolescence, and become more entrenched with time. As a result, we should not only expect stability in the attachment status of the typical adult, but also find that his relationships tend to reflect his attachment style.

As you know, attachment theory states that working models *can* be influenced by new input. If a new relationship provides truly different interactive experiences from those that have come before, then change is possible. The researchers found that nearly all secure individuals remained secure at the end of the study, but over 20% of individuals who were insecure at the beginning of the study were secure by the second assessment. Those who changed were more likely to have been classified as preoccupied than as dismissing at the beginning of the study. It may be that because dismissing individuals tend to avoid intimacy, they are less likely to experience the kinds of support that can transform one's expectations of relationships. The "became secure" participants were no more likely than the "stable insecure" participants to be paired with a secure partner, suggesting that "a committed, devoted, but insecure partner can be as effective as a secure partner in fostering growth and change, and may even be relatively tolerant and supportive of a partner's secure-base 'missteps'" (p. 476). The telling difference between the "became secure" and the "stable insecure" groups was that the "became secure" group had more positive relationships, even before the wedding. They were more intimate, happy, and passionate, and there was somewhat less discord than in the relationships of the "stable insecure" participants. The "became secure" group also tended to have more education and to have lived away from parents prior to marriage. "This suggests that experiences and opportunity in such settings (e.g., exposure to new ideas, new people, and new relationships), as well as physical and psychological distance from parents, facilitate the reconceptualization of childhood attachment relationships" (Crowell et al., 2002, p. 476). If we think of the parent–child relationship as a child's "first love," it does indeed seem that love can be sweeter the second time around.

Can therapeutic interventions promote more secure attachments? For romantic partners who struggle because of insecure attachment styles, successful couples' therapy does seem to modify partners' working models of relationships, helping them shift from insecure to more secure approaches and expectations (Coy & Miller, 2014). For example, emotionally focused couple therapy (Johnson, 2004) is an evidence-based treatment that tracks and highlights for couples the negative patterns that emerge from their expectations and styles of interaction. It has been shown to help couples restructure their conflict-induced behaviors (Wiebe & Johnson, 2016; see the Applications section). In addition, studies measuring attachment pre- and post-therapy for couples who have completed the full therapeutic protocol have found increases in security scores and decreases in avoidance and anxiety scores on attachment measures (e.g., Moser et al., 2015).

One reason is that conflict and communication in close relationships frequently have one or more subtexts: love, loss, trust, and abandonment, to name a few. In short, conflicts are stressful, they elicit emotions, and, perhaps, they can trigger the patterns of emotion regulation learned in the earliest of attachment relationships. Many studies have documented the advantages of attachment security for interpersonal communication (Feeney, 2016; Mikulincer & Shaver, 2016). Secure individuals display more reciprocity and flexibility in communication. Greater self-disclosure characterizes the communication of secure and anxious groups as compared to avoidant ones. Several studies also document the advantages of having a secure orientation when it comes to solving problems (Pistole, 1989). In general, secure individuals are more apt to compromise in ways that are mutually beneficial. Avoidant individuals tend to be more uncompromising, whereas anxious individuals tend to give in.

What actually happens when a couple has to deal with conflict in the relationship? According to attachment theory, the conflict produces stress, which activates the attachment system, makes the working models more accessible, and influences how affect gets regulated. Simpson, Rholes, and Phillips (1996) asked 123 heterosexual couples, who had been dating from 6 months to 2 years, to discuss problems in their relationships. Participants were videotaped, and their interactions were rated by observers. Secure individuals were less defensive than insecure ones, and they held the most favorable views of their partners after discussing a major problem. Avoidant participants kept the greatest emotional distance in the discussion. Presumably uncomfortable with the expression of emotion, they appeared to minimize personal involvement. By the same token, they did not display evidence of anger, distress, or less positive views of their partners. Avoidant men provided less warmth and supportiveness to their partners, consistent with theoretical predictions. In contrast, avoidant women did not display this pattern in this study. The strength of society's mandate that women be relationship caretakers might, in certain circumstances, override avoidant dispositions. But this is not the case in every close relationship. With friends and colleagues, both male and female adolescents and adults with avoidant styles do less to build or maintain closeness and they provide less emotional support than more secure individuals (Phillips, Simpson, Lanigan, & Rholes, 1995; Shomaker & Furman, 2009; Sias, Gallagher, Kopaneva, & Pedersen, 2012).

Ambivalent partners in the study by Simpson and colleagues (1996) reacted with the most negative emotion to the discussion of problems, displaying high levels of stress and anxiety during the interaction. They also reported feeling more hostility and anger towards their partners after the session. Consistent with attachment theory, these individuals expect their partners to fail at meeting their needs in stressful situations. Rholes and his colleagues explain the phenomenon in this way:

> Conflict elicits a cascade of unpleasant feelings in ambivalent persons, and it should raise doubts about the quality and viability of their current partner and relationship. Moreover, if fears of abandonment become salient, ambivalent partners ought to derogate the partner and relationship to minimize or "prepare for" potential loss. Persons who are not ambivalent, in contrast, may not experience conflict as aversive, but as an occasion in which open communication and the joint, constructive sharing of feelings can occur. (Rholes, Simpson, & Stevens, 1998, pp. 181–182)

Attachment style affects more than just a couple's interactions in conflict situations. It also affects their physiological responses. We noted earlier that dismissing and preoccupied individuals appear to have distinctive physiological responses in situations that arouse the attachment system, such as participation in the AAI. Dismissing people tend to show increased electrodermal reactivity (i.e., increased skin conductance), which is associated with effortful emotional inhibition, whereas preoccupied people may show increased heart rate, which is associated with higher behavioral activation. Roisman (2007) observed both young engaged couples (ages 18 to 30) and older couples (older than 50, married for at least 15 years). After completing the AAI, the couples were asked to identify and discuss a problem area in their relationship and to try to resolve it. In these conflict discussions, dismissing individuals showed increased electrodermal reactivity and preoccupied individuals showed increased heart rate, regardless of age or length of relationship. In contrast, secure individuals showed little physiological change in these mildly stressful conversations. (Similar findings are reported by Holland & Roisman, 2010.) The physiological data are consistent with the idea that dismissing adults are motivated to avoid their partners when they are asked to resolve problems in the relationship, whereas preoccupied adults tend to be emotionally overinvolved in their relationships.

What's Love Got to Do with It? The Hook-Up Culture and Attachment Style. As you have seen, one of the characteristics of emerging adulthood is the delay of important transitions, such as marriage. Experimentation with different forms of romantic relationships and marriage delay increased over the last half century as reliable birth control methods became more available. Casual sex has become common for many young adults, described with terms like *hook up*, *one-night-stand*, *friends-with-benefits*, and *booty call*. We refer to any of these as casual sexual relationships, meaning that they are not part of formal romantic relationships (Claxton & Van Dalman, 2015). In essence, the participants are not romantic partners such as "boyfriend and girlfriend" or "exclusive" couples. In surveys of college students, between 50% and 80% report having had casual sex, although most sexual behavior still occurs with romantic partners (Vrangalova, 2015). Although most studies have surveyed college students, casual sex is also commonly reported in studies that include noncollege young adults (Lyons, Manning, Longmore, & Giordano, 2014).

Casual sex seems to have both positive and negative impacts in the short term, and many reasons seem to contribute. For example, in one study adults were asked about their "morning after" feelings following one-night stands (Campbell, 2008). They rated 6 positive and 6 negative statements for how well the statements matched their own feelings, and they were invited to add further comments of their own. Both men and women endorsed feeling flattered and successful as the result of a desirable partner's interest. Neither men nor women seemed to expect more from the relationship, or to see it as a way to test out the possibility of a longer term relationship. Women were typically less positive about the experience overall than men. In particular, they were more likely to endorse feeling used, whereas men were more likely to endorse feeling like a "user." Women's written comments suggest that they tended to feel used because they were disappointed by men's behavior after the event, feeling rejected if the partner made an abrupt departure or failed to express appreciation. Overall, surveys indicate that positive feelings are linked to free and intentional choice, and having a pleasurable experience, including being well treated afterwards. Feelings of sadness or regret are more often associated with participating without clear intention or to prove something, or because of external pressure. Regret was also associated with having unfulfilling sex or with feeling mistreated by the partner (Garcia, Seibold-Simpson, Massey, & Merriwether, 2015).

There is still much to learn about how casual sexual experiences influence the formation of long-term relationships. One longitudinal study examined college students' attitudes about casual sex and about committed love relationships both early and late in their freshman year (Katz & Schneider, 2013). Those who reported having casual sex showed a tendency to become more sexually permissive and more comfortable with casual genital contact over time. However, their attitudes towards love and its potential importance in their lives did not change, regardless of participation in casual sex. Other researchers have found that most young adults, regardless of their sexual experiences, still pursue committed love relationships and want to marry (Shulman & Connolly, 2015).

How does attachment style relate to casual sex? First, we should note that in today's culture, when large proportions of young adults have engaged in casual sex, it is not exclusively the province of people with one or another attachment style. However, there are trends. First, as you might expect, avoidant individuals, especially males, are more likely to have promiscuous attitudes, regardless of whether they are engaged in committed relationships. They tend to use sex to avoid emotional intimacy, expecting to enhance their self-esteem or to impress their peers (Birnbaum, 2016). Avoidant men (but not women) are also more likely than other men to be sexually coercive in dating situations (Karantzaset al., 2016). The destructive effects of an avoidant attachment style appear to be exacerbated by male sex role norms that glorify sexual conquest and invulnerability. Female sex role norms that emphasize the importance of nurturing may reduce women's feelings of sexual entitlement, even for avoidant women (Birnbaum, 2016).

Anxious attachments also seem to influence women and men differently when it comes to casual sex. Women with anxious attachment styles seem to be more likely than other women to confuse sex with love. Compared to secure or avoidant women, they begin having sex earlier, they have more positive attitudes towards casual sex, they engage in more of it, and they are more likely to give in to coercive tactics (Birnbaum, 2016). Anxious men seem to feel especially vulnerable in the traditional role of sexual initiator, perhaps because they risk interpersonal rejection. They tend to view casual sex *less* positively than other men, and they have fewer sex partners over time (Cooper et al., 2006). However, they have a somewhat greater tendency to force sex on a partner than secure men, perhaps because they sometimes feel desperate for proximity when they perceive a partner as unresponsive (Birnbaum, 2016).

In general, attachment theory serves as a useful template for conceptualizing the universal human needs served by close, interpersonal relationships as well as the systematic differences individuals display in all of their personal associations. Clinicians are already very familiar with the notion that certain qualities of family relationships experienced early in life tend to get repeated in later relationships. Although not derivative of attachment theory per se, psychoanalytic and some family therapy approaches, such as Bowen's (1978), advise clients to examine the nature of conflicted childhood relationships within their family of origin in an effort to achieve insight and gain the freedom to make more adaptive relationship choices in the present. Other therapeutic approaches, such as Johnson's (2004; Wiebe & Johnson, 2016) emotionally focused couple therapy, are aimed at helping couples recognize the problematic interactive behaviors that are linked to their long-standing attachment styles (see Box 12.1 and the Applications section).

MyLab Education Self-Check 12.1

Work

12.2 Determine level of compatibility between an individual's personal characteristics and the demands of a chosen career and suggest effective approaches to enhance the process of career development.

For most young adults, the launching of a vocational life is as important a developmental task as the process of forming or reforming attachments. What are the key elements in a successful launch? A large body of theory and research has addressed this question. The theories share in common a general notion that career success and satisfaction depend heavily on matching the characteristics of an individual and the demands of a job. If this notion is correct, then self-knowledge is a critical element in career decision making. Thus, not only is establishing an occupational role an important part of identity or self-concept development, it is also an emergent property of that process. The stronger our sense of who we are as we become adults is, the more likely we are to make good career choices. Two classic theories of career development will illustrate this.

Some Theories of the Career Development Process

HOLLAND'S THEORY OF PERSONAL ORIENTATION–ENVIRONMENT TYPES

Holland's (1997) theory is the most widely applied approach to explaining how personal interests and behavioral inclinations relate to vocational development. The assumptions of his theory have a great deal of empirical support, and the measurement techniques he constructed are widely used in the vocational counseling field, including by college career counselors. Holland suggests that by early adulthood each individual has a **modal personal orientation** (also called a **personal style**): a typical pattern of interests and preferred style or approach to dealing with social and environmental tasks. Holland proposed that most people can be categorized as having one of six modal orientations (described in Table 12.3), which can be seen as part of each individual's personality. (We will discuss other aspects of personality in Chapter 13.) According to Holland, a job or career typically makes demands on an individual that are compatible with one or more of these interactive types. That is, a job can be construed as creating an environment within which a certain personal orientation will lead to both success and happiness. For example, one of the personal orientation types is "social." A social type is likely to be sociable, friendly, cooperative, kind, tactful, and understanding and is often a good match to occupations that involve working with others to educate, to cure, or to enlighten them—such as counseling or social work (Ferreira, Rodrigues, & Costa Ferreira, 2016). A contrasting type is the "enterprising" individual. He too is likely to be sociable, but more domineering, energetic, ambitious, talkative, and attention getting. He is also likely to be more effective in vocational tasks that involve maneuvering others to achieve goals, such as reaching a certain level of sales, or more efficiently delivering services as a salesperson, for instance, or as an executive. Thus, each type of modal personal orientation, such as social or enterprising, is also a type of vocational environment. Usually, neither individuals nor environments fall neatly into only one "type." Holland and his colleagues have developed coding systems for rating both individuals and environments. In these systems, three-letter codes indicate the most characteristic style for the individual or the environment, as well as the second and third most characteristic styles. So, for example, a person (or environment) might be coded *RIS*, meaning primarily *realistic* (R), secondarily *investigative* (I), and finally *social* (S). See Table 12.3 for some characteristics of these types for individuals.)

MyLab Education
Video Example 12.2
A career counselor applies Holland's theory of personal orientation-environment types to help Laura, a college student, reflect and narrow her diverse set of career interests. What personal style most closely matches Laura's interests and behavioral inclinations?

Consider Phil from the beginning of this chapter, who found that his first job was not a good fit. Suppose he had gone to the career counseling center at his college. Career counselors have available a number of different assessment questionnaires that can be used to help determine interests and identify typical personal styles. Phil might have found that his typical styles included "Social." You will recall that his first job was in finance, a position that required spending hours alone with spreadsheets. Phil had the cognitive ability and academic training to manage the work, but the job's minimal requirement for interpersonal engagement did not converge well with his personal style.

Studies spanning several decades have corroborated two important claims of Holland's theory. First, the interests and behavioral inclinations that comprise personal style are relatively stable over time, from adolescence through middle adulthood (Schultz, Connolly, Garrison, Leveille, & Jackson, 2017; Stoll et al., 2017). They can and do change for some individuals, but early personal style tends to persist for most. Second, a good fit (convergence) between modal orientation and job characteristics is correlated with job satisfaction, performance, and stability, as well as feelings of personal well-being (Nye, Su, Rounds, & Drasgow, 2017; Phan & Rounds, 2018; Wille, Tracey, Feys, & Fruyt, 2014). Some early studies of specific occupations provide good examples. Gottfredson and Holland (1990) studied young adult bank tellers for 4 months after they were first hired. Congruence between an individual's personal style and job type was clearly correlated with job satisfaction. In two studies of school teachers, Meir (1989) examined several kinds of congruence or fit: between personal style and job type, between personal style and outside activities (avocations), and between the

TABLE 12.3 Some Characteristics of Holland's Personality Types

REALISTIC	INVESTIGATIVE	ARTISTIC
Conforming	Analytical	Complicated
Dogmatic	Cautious	Disorderly
Genuine	Complex	Emotional
Hardheaded	Critical	Expressive
Inflexible	Curious	Idealistic
Materialistic	Independent	Imaginative
Natural	Intellectual	Impractical
Normal	Introverted	Impulsive
Persistent	Pessimistic	Independent
Practical	Precise	Introspective
Realistic	Radical	Intuitive
Reserved	Rational	Nonconforming
Robust	Reserved	Open
Self-effacing	Retiring	Original
Uninsightful	Unassuming	Sensitive
SOCIAL	**ENTERPRISING**	**CONVENTIONAL**
Agreeable	Acquisitive	Careful
Cooperative	Adventurous	Conforming
Empathic	Ambitious	Conscientious
Friendly	Assertive	Dogmatic
Generous	Domineering	Efficient
Helpful	Energetic	Inflexible
Idealistic	Enthusiastic	Inhibited
Kind	Excitement seeking	Methodical
Patient	Exhibitionistic	Obedient
Persuasive	Extroverted	Orderly
Responsible	Forceful	Persistent
Sociable	Optimistic	Practical
Tactful	Resourceful	Thorough
Understanding	Self-confident	Thrifty
Warm	Sociable	Unimaginative

individual's particular skills and opportunities to use those skills on the job. All three kinds of congruence predicted the participants' reported feelings of well-being. A person's happiness seems to be linked to the fit between his personal style and both his work, as Holland predicted, and his leisure pursuits. It appears that creating a good match in one arena can help compensate for a lack of congruence in another.

One intriguing area of research on person–job fit explores how employees can actively improve fit by shaping their jobs to some extent. In this process, called **job crafting**, employees may initiate change in a number of different ways: by the kinds of tasks they choose or projects they launch, by negotiating with employers to modify

MyLab Education
Video Exercise 12.3
Studies indicate that convergence between modal orientation and job characteristics is correlated with job satisfaction, performance, and stability. In this video, identify comments made by the professional that indicate a good fit between the job and the individual's personal orientation.

job content, by proactively seeking feedback, by changing aspects of their jobs that involve relationships, and so on (Hakanen, Peeters, & Schaufel, 2017; Tims, Bakker, & Derks, 2012). You might think that job crafting opportunities would be limited to high level positions that allow employees a great deal of autonomy, but the data suggest that it happens at all levels of employment, especially among workers with good self-esteem, feelings of *self-efficacy* (see discussion later in this chapter), and self-regulation skills (Bakker, 2011). Also, people who are highly engaged and enthusiastic about the *potential* of their jobs to fit their needs seem to be more likely to work to change them (Hakanen et al., 2017). In one example, some nurses added the task of relating with and seeking information from patients' families to their specified tasks of patient care, improving the fit between their social needs and their job requirements (Wrzesniewski & Dutton, 2001). Lower ranking employees do seem to have different obstacles to face in job crafting than higher ranking employees. In particular, they are more likely to have to change others' expectations in order to modify their jobs to fit their own personal styles (Berg, Wrzesniewski, & Dutton, 2010; Petrou, Bakker, & den Heuvel, 2017).

SUPER'S DEVELOPMENTAL APPROACH

Super (1990) agrees with Holland's notion that a satisfying work life is most likely when an individual's personal characteristics are well matched to the demands of a job. His theorizing about career development, however, focuses less on specifying personal style or job types and more on describing the developmental processes that determine both the emergence of one's vocational self-concept and the multiple factors that influence job choices throughout the life span. Vocational self-concept is part of one's total identity. It includes ideas about which qualities of the self would (or would not) provide a match to the requirements of an occupation. Vocational self-concept is a function of two things: first, a person's view of his personal or psychological characteristics, and second, how he assesses his life circumstances, such as the limits or opportunities created by economic conditions; by his socioeconomic status; by his family, friendship network, and community; and so on.

Super described a series of typical life stages in the development of vocational self-concept and experience, beginning in childhood. In the growth stage (up to age 14 or so), children are developing many elements of identity that will have a bearing on vocational self-concept, including ideas about their interests, attitudes, skills, and needs. In the exploratory stage, which includes adolescence and young adulthood up to about age 24, vocational self-concept is tentatively narrowed down, but often career choices are not finalized. General vocational goals are formulated in the earlier part of this stage (crystallization), gradually leading to the identification of more specific vocational preferences (specification), and finally to the completion of education along with entry into full-time employment (implementation). In the establishment stage, from about ages 25 to 44, work experiences provide the laboratory within which the matching of vocational self-concept and job settings is tried out, sometimes reevaluated, sometimes confirmed, and eventually stabilized (stabilization). From about ages 45 to 64, in the maintenance stage, an individual makes ongoing adjustments to improve his work situation, often achieving more advanced status and seniority (consolidation). If not, this can also be a time of increasing frustration with work. Finally, in the decline stage, right before and after age 65 for most people, the career winds down, with retirement planning and actual retirement taking precedence over career advancement and consolidation. Note that although these are typical life stages, at least partially verified by longitudinal research (e.g., Super & Overstreet, 1960), an individual can go through additional sequences of crystallization, specification, implementation, and stabilization when life circumstances change. These "mini-cycles" of reevaluation can be initiated by any number of events: disappointment with a career choice, job loss, changes in family life, and so on. Note that in Super's description young adulthood is an intensive time for vocational development. It is when people move through the three phases of the exploratory stage and into the establishment stage (Marshall & Butler, 2015). Perhaps Super's most important insight is his recognition that career development is a continuing process. It serves as both a source and an outgrowth of an individual's overall personal growth. For Super, a career is the life course of a person encountering a series of developmental tasks and attempting to handle them in such a way as to become the kind of person he or she wants to become. With a changing self and changing situations, the matching process is never really completed. (Super, 1990, pp. 225–226)

Research indicates that many aspects of the person in addition to personal style, and many aspects of the job, beyond compatibility with one's interests and talents, influence how rewarding a job is, and how successful an individual is likely to be. On the person side, personality traits such as *conscientiousness* (see Chapter 13) are important, as well as cognitive and scholastic abilities, and personal health (Volodina, Nagy, & Köller, 2015). On the job side, quality of supervision, participation in decision making, interaction with others on the job, geographic location, pay, and a number of other factors are also correlated with satisfaction and work engagement (Mauss, Li, & Angerer, 2017; Rhoades & Eisenberger, 2002). However, theories and research such as those of Holland and Super make the powerful suggestion that even when all these other factors are acceptable, a person's work responsibilities can be incompatible with his or her personal characteristics. Under these circumstances, although a hardworking individual could succeed in meeting his responsibilities, real satisfaction and the opportunity to truly excel are likely to elude him. The interdependence of career and self-development is an important focus of some career counseling approaches. McAuliffe (1993; McAuliffe & Emmett, 2017), for example, describes a developmentally oriented career counseling system that has an Eriksonian flavor. He argues that a central role of the counselor is to help clients address the following key question: "Who am I becoming and how shall I express this emerging self?" He points out that many clients may begin counseling with a different, but less helpful, way of conceptualizing their career issues. Some, for example, may be asking themselves, "What does my community, my family, my ethnic or religious group expect of me?" That is, they frame the issue such that their career, and their self-definition, is embedded in interpersonal relationships, not authored from within. Perhaps for this group, career identity represents a closed, rather than a constructed, facet of their identity (see Chapter 9). Other clients, especially those facing some career threat, such as downsizing, may begin with the question, "How do I maintain the current form I am in?" With this conceptual framework the self is embedded in what the person has always done, so that new career paths, expressing other needs or dimensions of the self, are not imaginable. The task for helpers may be to facilitate the development of a new, personally constructed sense of self as worker.

For many clients, then, career counseling may need to begin with help in reframing the way one construes the self. In McAuliffe's words,

> it is the counselor's challenge to assist clients in their transformations of meaning making. . . . For example, for the young adult college student whose seemingly simple dilemma is to choose between pursuing a parent-approved pre-medical track or to consider the internal voice that draws her to the social sciences, counseling would operate on two levels: one to weigh the pros and cons of various fields of study and the other to support and challenge the person so that the tacit assumptions about "who's in charge" become conscious, so that the dissonant voice that implicitly calls the person to author his or her own career can be considered. (1993, pp. 25–26)

McCauliffe and Emmett (2017) suggest that for career counselors, too, a key to successful counseling is examining their own expectations about what makes a match between self and career, so that they are open to alternate constructs. They argue that practicing open-mindedness is especially important in today's world, where both the people and the emerging work options are increasingly diverse.

The Realities of Career Development in Young Adulthood

For young adults launching a work life, many variables influence the speed and form of that process. Consider the prospects of two 18-year-olds, Akil and Jarod, who have just graduated from high school. Akil comes from a middle-class family. His parents take

MyLab Education
Video Exercise 12.4
A young teacher talks about her lifelong desire to be a teacher. Consider the developmental processes unfolding over a period of years and shaping her vocational self-concept.

MyLab Education
Video Exercise 12.5
When Mak's early career expectations crumbled, he combined his interests, skills, and education to establish a fulfilling career.

great pride in being the first ones in their own families to have graduated from college and to provide their children with a comfortable middle-class life. They expect their children to attend college and to select careers that will help them maintain or even improve on their socioeconomic status. They have several children to educate, but they are quite savvy about how to finance a college education, having put themselves through college, and they are convinced that college is a necessity for career success. Akil sees college as a necessary step on his way to a professional career, although his future plans are not specific. He expects his college experience to help him figure out what profession to enter.

The expectations that Jarod and his family have are quite different. Jarod's mother earns low wages working for a janitorial service, and she often puts in overtime to help make ends meet. Neither she nor Jarod's father (from whom she is estranged) completed high school, and both are quite proud that Jarod has. However, they have never even considered the possibility of college for Jarod. As they see it, he has completed his education and should now be able to earn a living. His mother expects him to find his own apartment to relieve the crowding in her small place. Many of Jarod's friends are enrolling in the local community college, but Jarod is not eager for more schooling. He is simply hoping to find a job, any job, one that will give him a start, providing an opportunity to learn a skill and to find a niche.

Even if these two young men happen to have similar interests and personal styles, their careers are likely to follow very different trajectories, largely because of the differences in their socioeconomic class, their families' views of education, and the opportunities that they perceive to be available to them. In the following sections, we will consider what the typical course of career development is for individuals like Akil and Jarod. We will specifically examine the characteristics of the process when young people move on to college from high school and when they do not. We will also consider the impact of other major factors on one's early career experiences, such as immediate environment, social class, race, and gender.

COLLEGE TRAJECTORIES: ASPIRATIONS AND OUTCOMES

In the United States, the percentage of high school students who say they plan to earn a bachelor's degree has skyrocketed in the past half century. Nearly 70% of students who graduated from high school in 2016 were enrolled in college by October of that year (U.S. Bureau of Labor Statistics, 2017). Young adults entering college have many hopes and expectations for the college years. Some of their concerns are incidental to the educational setting and are focused on either maintaining or establishing social networks or finding intimate relationships—the pursuit of *love*. But many of their hopes are relevant to *work*, their vocational lives. In 2016, over 80% of first-year students expected the college years to be a time of self-development, when they would learn more about things that interest them and become more clear about the course their adult lives might take. Even more students, 87%, considered college attendance to be a very important factor in getting a better job. Such practical career concerns fluctuate somewhat with economic conditions. For example, as unemployment soared after the great recession of 2008, the percentage of students endorsing "getting a better job" as a very important reason for attending college increased. It reached a peak of nearly 90% in 2012 and then started to decline somewhat as the economy improved. It is interesting to note that with this decline came an increase in the percentage of students (to over 75% in 2016) indicating that "gaining a general education and appreciation of ideas" was also a very important reason for their attending college (Eagan et al., 2017).

The first vocationally relevant decision that students make is the choice of a major. Those students who are career oriented tend to decide on an occupation first and then select a major, whereas students more focused on self-development tend to select a major first and then consider possible occupational choices (Goodson, 1978). A majority of students change their majors at least once during college, although the changes they make are usually among related disciplines (Herr, Cramer, & Niles, 2004). There are substantial cohort differences regarding which majors and occupations are more popular with students. Historically, majors in business, psychology, education, and engineering have been among the most popular, but even these show relatively large shifts. For example, 25% of freshman planned a business major in 1985; by 2015, only 12% did. Education as a major choice saw a similar decline, from 10% of freshman in 1985 to 4% in 2015. In the same time period, other majors have been more or less steadily on the rise, such as the biological sciences (from 4% to 15% of freshmen choices). Engineering was strong in 1985, dipped to 8% in 2005, and has steadily risen since, to 13% of freshman choices (Eagen et al., 2016).

Career intentions have shown corresponding changes (Eagen et al., 2016). For example, interest in medical careers (physician, dentist, nurse) has risen, but interest in business careers has declined. We have seen that theorists such as Holland and Super argue that career choices often are, and should be, based on one's personal characteristics. What other factors, besides self-concept or personal style, might influence the choice of a major in college, and ultimately the choice of a career? First, cohort changes in choice of majors indicate that social and economic conditions influence choice of major. This includes economic upturns and downturns, change in the kinds of goods and services that are in demand, shifts in population size and composition, advances in technology, and developments in political and legal philosophy, such as in the area of civil rights law. For example, increasing interest in biological science majors and in health careers is probably linked to changes in the employment landscape, with service sector jobs increasing dramatically over the last several decades, including health care jobs (U.S. Bureau of Labor Statistics, 2018).

Some of the most interesting changes in majors and occupational choices across recent decades are gender specific and appear to reflect political and social trends in our beliefs about the role of women in society. The Higher Education Research Institute at UCLA reports that the proportion of women majoring in traditionally male-dominated STEM fields (science, technology, engineering, and mathematics), as well as prelaw and business fields, increased substantially in the last three decades of the twentieth century, as hiring patterns in related fields became less gender biased than they once were (Dey & Hurtado, 1999).

Many colleges and universities are now exploring ways of strengthening that trend, as well as recruiting minorities into such fields, especially STEM (Figueroa, Hurtado, Cobian, Wilkings, & Lewis-White, 2016), because despite cultural shifts, women and minorities are still underrepresented in these fields (Harackiewicz, Canning, Tibbetts, Priniski, & Hyde, 2016). In the next sections, we will consider some of the difficulties that these groups encounter.

SOCIAL CLASS, ETHNICITY, AND RACE

In addition to the influence of social, civil, and economic changes, other more stable factors appear to play a role in choice of major among college students and in occupational trajectory among all young adults. As the stories of Akil and Jarod indicate, socioeconomic status (SES) is important in shaping the expectations of young people, heavily influencing the educational choices that they make and the jobs to which they aspire. Research indicates that other family and environmental factors, such as race and ethnicity, also affect the choice of whether to go to college. Individuals from minority and low-SES groups are less likely than other groups to make the college choice. If an individual enrolls in college, are a student's career aspirations affected by such variables? Some indicators suggest that the answer is yes. To illustrate, the probability of retention, staying in college long enough to graduate, is related to SES (National Center for Education Statistics, 2016). The influence of SES on retention is probably multifaceted. Often, low-income high school students expect to go to college, and are encouraged to do so, but their high schools often do not provide adequate academic preparation (e.g., little or no access to AP courses or SAT preparation), and they may offer little access to counseling services designed to inform students of what will be required of them as they move on to college (Rosenbaum & Rosenbaum, 2015; Westrick, Le, Robbins, Radunzel, & Schmidt, 2015). Students who enroll in a 2- or 4-year institution often find that they must take remedial classes that are a financial drain and do not provide college credit. Lower SES students also have more problems paying for college, and they may receive less support from teachers, family, and friends to remain in college than higher SES students do (Gregory & Huang, 2013; Ryland, Riordan, & Brack, 1994).

FIGURE 12.3 Percentage of U. S. students who enrolled at 4-year colleges and universities in 2010 who graduated within six years.

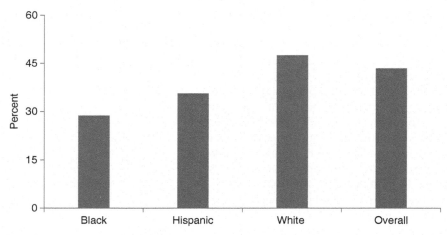

SOURCE: Adapted from Shapiro, E., Dundar, A., Huie, F., Wakhungu, P., Yuan, X., Nathan, A., & Hwang, Y. A. (2017). *A national view of student attainment rates by race and ethnicity—Fall 2010 cohort* (Signature Report No. 12b). Herndon, VA: National Student Clearinghouse Research Center.

Being of minority status is also linked to lower rates of retention (Shapiro et al., 2017). Black and Native American students are at particular risk for dropping out, a problem that may be partially a result of the stress of dealing with minority status, such as feeling unwelcome or unsupported in predominantly White institutions (e.g., Newman & Newman, 1999). How engaged and involved students feel in academic and social activities is clearly connected to retention and graduation rates (Stephens, Hamedani, & Destin, 2014; see Figure 12.3). A student's internal sense of validation—a feeling that the institution and its representatives believe in and will support the student's ability to succeed—may be especially important here (Figueroa et al., 2016; Hurtado, Cuellar, & Guillermo-Wann, 2011). Institutions vary in how likely they are to create an inclusive educational environment where both faculty and staff engage in behaviors that support the success of individual students. What kinds of behaviors are important? A study of nearly 4,500 students from a wide range of 2- and 4-year institutions uncovered several key experiences that promoted students' feelings of validation (Hurtado et al., 2011). First, students felt academic validation in the classroom when their instructors indicated that they were keyed into students' level of understanding, would provide students with adequate feedback, valued students' in-class contributions, were available to meet outside of class, encouraged questions and participation, and demonstrated concern for students. Students felt general interpersonal validation when faculty *and* staff showed interest in them, recognized students' achievements, believed in their potential, and encouraged students to get involved in campus activities (see also, Luedke, 2017). Unfortunately, minority students consistently reported experiencing substantially less validation, both academic and interpersonal, than White students.

Do factors such as SES affect a student's choice of a college major? There is indirect evidence that they can. As we have already seen, low-income and minority students are under-represented in STEM majors. STEM fields tend to be dominated by White men and are seen by some as characterized by a competitive, "survival of the fittest" mentality (Figueroa et al., 2016). Minority students who don't either look or act like the typical STEM major may feel like they don't belong in those fields, or they may not be as likely as more mainstream students to be encouraged by mentors towards a STEM field.

Other characteristics of the college environment also seem to influence choice of major or career (Astin, 1993). For example, students are more likely to select college teaching as a career if they attend smaller colleges that provide high levels of student–faculty interaction, opportunities for independent research, and written evaluations of students' work. African American students are more likely to choose premed if they attend a traditionally Black college. Membership in a fraternity or sorority is linked to greater tendencies to select business or prelaw as a major. Of course, whether one attends a small college or a Black college, or joins a sorority or fraternity, is probably influenced by preexisting characteristics of the student. For example, extroverts appear to be more attracted to Greek life on campus than introverts (Sher, Bartholow, & Nanda, 2001). Therefore, it is difficult to say whether such features of college life have a causal influence on students' major or career choices or whether students who favor such environments also tend to prefer certain fields of study. It seems likely that the causal connections work both ways.

One role that the college experience seems to play in choosing a major and ultimately a career is that it provides opportunities to try out different choices with relatively little cost. Some students enter college aspiring to be lawyers or physicians or engineers, for example, only to find that the prelaw, premed, or engineering course work is not suitable to their interests or abilities. Such majors often lose enrollment as students move through their college years. Other majors tend to draw increasing numbers over the college years. Education and business majors are among these. Interestingly, some of the more academically challenging fields, such as scientific research and college teaching, also increase their draw somewhat after students get a taste of college (Astin, 1993; Pryor & Bright, 2012).

Since a student's choice of a college major is associated with college success as well as career choice, career counseling in college should begin with advisement on choice of a major. Unfortunately, leaving this task to relatively untrained faculty advisors seems to be insufficient for helping students to make good choices. Herr et al. (2004), in their text on career guidance throughout the life span, argue that career guidance professionals at the college level should provide students with assistance in selecting a major. In pursuit of this and other career goals, even first-year students should have help available in self-assessment and self-analysis, as well as in decision making.

It is clear that a college education plays a critical role in occupational opportunity. One's highest educational degree is the single most important predictor of level of job entry, and level of job entry weighs more heavily than IQ or job skill in predicting career advancement. But the value of a college education goes beyond its contribution to career development. For example, being a college graduate means a greater likelihood of being healthy or of having a successful marriage. Some of the effects of higher education are probably due to the income opportunities it creates and so are career linked; others may be related to the development of critical thinking skills and flexibility in problem solving that it seems to foster (Amato, Booth, Johnson, & Rogers, 2007; Kapan, Fang, & Kirby, 2017).

THE FORGOTTEN HALF IN THE "COLLEGE FOR ALL" ERA

The forgotten half was the name given by the William T. Grant Foundation Commission on Work, Family, and Citizenship (1988) to 18- to 24-year-olds who do not go to college. They comprised just under half of the total young adult population in the United States in 1988. They were described as

> the young people who build our homes, drive our buses, repair our automobiles, fix our televisions, maintain and serve our offices, schools and hospitals, and keep the production lines of our mills and factories moving. To a great extent, they determine how well the American family, economy and democracy function. They are also the thousands of young men and women who aspire to work productively but never quite "make it" to that kind of employment. For these members of the Forgotten Half, their lives as adults start in the economic limbo of unemployment, part-time jobs, and poverty wages. Many of them never break free. (1988, as cited in Halperin, 1998a, cover)

Follow-up reports sponsored by the William T. Grant foundation (Halperin, 1998a, 1998b; Rosenbaum, Ahern, Becker, & Rosenbaum, 2015) and data collected by federal agencies (e.g., National Center for Education Statistics, 2016) show that the high school dropout rate has declined since the original report, and the numbers of high school graduates entering 2- or 4-year colleges has increased, so that 86% of young adults now attend college at some point within 8 years after high school. Graduation rates for those who begin college have improved, but still only somewhat over half complete a degree. Unfortunately, the employability of young people without a college degree has declined relative to those with one (see Figure 12.4). Further, over several decades the real income of young adults in the United States has declined, and the most serious losses have been experienced by those with the least education. Poverty rates have increased for those at every educational level, but especially for those without a college degree (see Figure 12.5 for U.S. poverty rates by education in 2016).

FIGURE 12.4 Percentages of U.S. adults (ages 25 to 34) who were employed (1990 to 2015) by level of education.

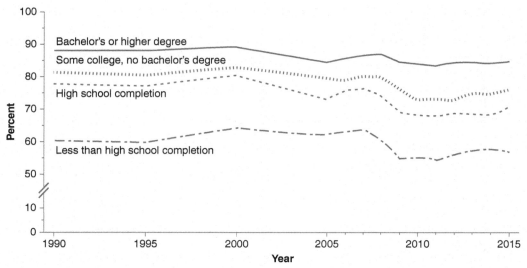

SOURCE: Adapted from the National Center for Education Statistics (2016). *Digest of Education Statistics: 2015*. Available at https://nces.ed.gov/programs/digest/d15/

Interestingly, the many basic attitudes of young adults towards work and family do not differ regardless of whether they go to college. Young people usually rank good pay and opportunities for advancement as highly desirable features of a job. They also want their work to make a meaningful contribution to society. As for their social aspirations, young people of all backgrounds generally consider having a good marriage and having children to be important life goals for them (Hill & Yeung, 1999; Shulman & Connolly, 2015).

Despite the broad similarities in the goals of college and noncollege youth in the United States, the chances of achieving these goals are substantially reduced for the latter group. As we have already seen, education is a key predictor of employment success, career advancement, and general success in life, so that when a young person chooses to end education with high school, he limits his options and opportunities. "Until the last few decades, young people without an education beyond high school were often able to find family-sustaining work in service industries or manufacturing operations. Today, they face lives of grinding economic struggle, virtually shut out from jobs that will allow them to build assets and support children of their own" (Pennington, 2003, p. 60). A number of other factors also affect the degree to which a young person's goals are likely to be achieved. These factors include socioeconomic status, as was the case with Jarod. Even when young people fail to attend college, coming from a family of relatively high socioeconomic status provides opportunities and advantages that youth from lower SES families usually do not have. Another important factor is race, which can have a profound impact on the probability of employment across all education

FIGURE 12.5 Percentage of adults (age 25 and older) living in poverty in the U.S. in 2016.

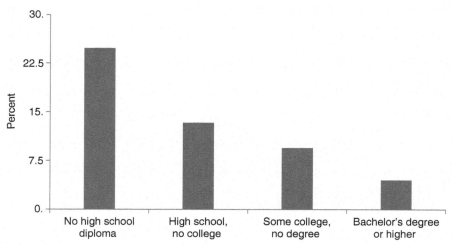

SOURCE: Data from Semega, J. L., Fontenot, K. R., & Kollar, M. A. (2017). *Income and poverty in the United States: 2016* (Report # P60-259). Available at https://www.census.gov/library/publications/2017/demo/p60-259.html.

levels. Finally, a variety of "behavioral obstacles," including having a child early or out of wedlock and engaging in criminal behavior, are important determiners of whether young adults will make significant strides towards meeting their goals. Among noncollege youth, those most at risk of slipping into poverty, for example, are Blacks with criminal records who come from low-income families (DeFina & Hannon, 2013; Halperin, 1998b). As we have discussed earlier, these outcomes may be the result of histories of accumulating and interlocking risks.

Although many factors can contribute to a slide into poverty, adequate educational preparation is clearly the most effective avenue to avoiding poverty and to achieving the typical goals that young people have for work and family. The problems faced by noncollege youth in America are partly a function of a disorganized and inadequate system for training adolescents and young adults for the kinds of skilled employment that are personally rewarding and that can provide an adequate income to support a family. As you have already seen, it is often difficult for high school students from lower income groups to get information that helps them prepare for the rigors of college (Rosenbaum et al., 2015). Young people face similar obstacles in obtaining information on how to prepare themselves for particular jobs and occupations. Recommendations for improving the lot of noncollege youth begin with ideas for improving basic skill training in public schools, including the teaching of such traditional academic skills as reading, writing, math, and speaking abilities, as well as thinking skills, self-management, and social skills. The particular concern is to improve the quality of secondary education for students who go through general or vocational (noncollege preparatory) tracks in high school. These programs are often criticized for having watered-down, boring curricula (Bailey, Jeong, & Cho, 2010; Duncan & Murnane, 2014).

Next, reports on the forgotten half encourage providing high school students with better access to extensive vocational counseling; information and support for moving into post-secondary training designed to culminate with technical certificates or associates degrees; and with opportunities for work-based learning (Rosenbaum et al., 2015). They also suggest increasing the participation of employers in providing training and apprenticeship programs, using the community college system to create expanded opportunities for technical training, and creating community-based resources to provide young adults with information about pathways into specific occupations (Duncan & Murnane, 2014; Neumark & Rothstein, 2005; Pennington, 2003).

For some young adults, special training programs designed for economically disadvantaged participants who face multiple risks can be quite effective. In one longitudinal study of over 8,000 adolescents, beginning when they were 12 to 17 years old, high school mentoring programs, co-op programs, school enterprise programs, and internship/apprenticeship programs all had beneficial effects on employment and college attendance for males after graduation. For females, there were fewer benefits, but internship/apprenticeship programs led to better earnings after high school (Neumark & Rothstein, 2005). Similarly, the American Youth Policy Forum evaluated a large number of programs launched in the United States over several decades (see Partee, 2003; Hooker & Brand, 2009). The most successful of these helped young men and women move on to postsecondary education or to quality employment opportunities, simultaneously supporting the young adults they served and reaping economic and social benefits for their communities. For example, Job Corps, a public–private partnership administered by the U.S. Department of Labor, returned about $2.00 to society for every $1.00 invested. Private programs like Strive, operated in New York City's Harlem, helped at-risk young adults sustain employment over multiple years. Like other effective interventions, these programs tend to have certain characteristics in common, such as implementation quality (e.g., sufficient and sustained resources, strong leadership, and professional staff development); caring and knowledgeable teachers, counselors, and mentors; high standards and expectations; and a holistic approach, meaning that they address multiple needs (e.g., providing child care and transportation, life skills and assertiveness training, individualized attention, and so on).

FIGURE 12.6 Incarceration rates (per 100,000 people) in countries around the globe.

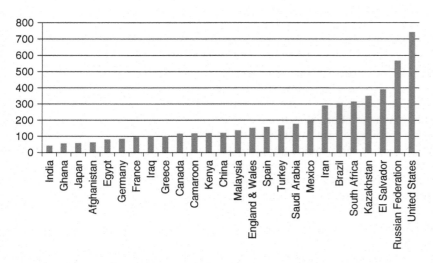

SOURCE: Based on National Center for Education Statistics. (2011). *America's youth: Transitions to adulthood*. Washington, DC: U.S. Department of Education. Retrieved from http://nces. ed.gov/pubs2012/1012026/chapter3_3.asp.

Many researchers note that there is a particularly sinister trend that affects the forgotten half. Arrest and imprisonment for minor crimes (e.g., drug possession) have increased dramatically since the early 1970s, especially for males, such that the United States now far outdistances every other country in the world in incarceration rates (numbers of prisoners per 100,000 people; see Figure 12.6). The number of young men incarcerated in U.S. prisons more than doubled between 1986 and 1995, and continued to rise slowly until 2009, when the number leveled off and started to decline slightly (National Research Council, 2014). Minority males have been especially affected. By 2008, for example, 1 in every 15 Black males, age 18 and older, was in prison, compared to 1 in every 106 White males (The Pew Center, 2008). The disparity in minority versus White incarceration rates for males has decreased somewhat in more recent years, but it remains substantial. The rate of incarceration for both White and minority women is low in comparison, but it has shown a rise in recent years as well (National Research Council, 2014).

The impact of high incarceration rates for both individuals and communities was aptly articulated by Laub decades ago:

> For some segments of society, crime control policy . . . has regressed to the point that imprisonment is the major governmental intervention in the transition to young adulthood. . . . This means that segments of the population are cut off from voting, employment, and community organizations. This disenfranchisement will further contribute to increased unemployment and undermine family life. (Laub, 1999, p. 49)

Given that friendships, family ties, and a sense of belonging in a community play a significant role in a young adult's hope for the future and chances for upward mobility, school- and community-based vocational training and counseling seem like much better alternatives than jail for many adolescent and young adult delinquents. When we consider that young adult incarceration has cascading negative effects for the families of those who are jailed as well, the importance of implementing alternative interventions is strikingly clear (National Research Council, 2014).

WOMEN VERSUS MEN

Traditionally, gender has been a significant factor in career development. In 1957, Super found that a variety of career patterns characterized adults in the mid-20th century in the United States. For men, the "conventional career pattern" included a period or periods of "trial work," that is, trying out possible jobs and then launching into a stable career. The conventional career pattern for women, however, involved entry into work as a stopgap after high school or college. Once married, women tended to shift to full-time homemaking. Even in 1957, there were other patterns for both men and women that were common enough not to be considered atypical, but most of the alternative patterns also displayed gender differences. For example, women sometimes followed the "double-track career pattern," first establishing a career and then adding a second career as homemaker. Or they might show the "interrupted career pattern," first establishing a career, then marrying and becoming a full-time homemaker, and then shifting back to a career when home responsibilities were less pressing. Interestingly, none of the patterns Super characterized as typical of men included double-tracking or any kind of interruption based on family or homemaking concerns.

How important is gender in career development today? As we have already seen, there have certainly been substantial changes relevant to gender in our culture since 1950. These changes have grown out of the civil rights movement and the women's rights movement in particular, and are also linked to technological changes such as the availability of reliable contraceptives and an increase in the use of machines to do heavy labor. Many work-related gender differences have diminished, and some have even disappeared or reversed. For example, women now enter college in larger numbers than men do, whereas up until about 1980, men outnumbered women (National Center for Education Statistics, 2018). As we have already noted, women now often choose majors in college that traditionally were the preserve of men, such as premed and business. Women earn as many or more graduate degrees as men. Half of all MDs are now earned by women, as well as the majority of doctoral degrees overall. Women constitute nearly half of the employed labor force, and in 2013, women filled about 51% of executive, administrative, and managerial positions in the United States, more than doubling their representation in these kinds of jobs over recent decades (U.S. Bureau of Labor Statistics, 2014). Still, the representation of women in various jobs within these categories is often linked to gender traditions. Women are particularly underrepresented in STEM fields that are math intensive (Simon, Wagner, & Killion, 2017). They are overrepresented in fields that involve primarily caregiving, such as nursing, social work, education, and child care (U.S. Bureau of Labor Statistics, 2014). Historical changes favoring greater gender equity have occurred even in these fields, however. For example, women earn nearly one third of the PhDs in mathematics today (as compared to about 6% in 1960); males are entering fields such as nursing and child care in increasing numbers as well.

Yet, gender continues to be a powerful predictor of vocational interests, more so than other individual differences, such as race or ethnicity (Morris, 2016). Although men and women use most of the same criteria to evaluate potential careers (they try to match their interests and they carefully consider professional advancement and income opportunities), women are more likely than men to consider relationships with people (opportunity for and kinds of) and altruistic concerns as important factors in selecting a career. A greater focus on relational/social elements of career choice may help explain why women with exceptional math ability are more likely to choose paths to social and health science careers than careers in the physical sciences (National Science Foundation, 2015). It is also interesting to note that women with outstanding math skills also tend to have outstanding verbal skills, whereas that is less likely to be true for men. As a result, such women may see themselves as having a wider range of good career options (Wang, Eccles, & Kenny, 2013).

Gender differences in career choice are also influenced at least in part by gender-role beliefs and lifestyle preferences (McDonald, 2018). Both men and women anticipate that marriage and parenting will be important to their lives, for example, but men give greater priority to their role as breadwinner in the family, and women give greater priority to their role as caregiver. Overall, women seem more concerned with work–life balance. For example, in surveys of young, high-ability adults (e.g., graduate students), women say that they work fewer hours per week than men, and when asked about how many hours per week they are willing to work on their ideal job, they choose fewer hours than men (Amon, 2017; Robertson, Smeets, Lubinski, & Benbow, 2010).

In a survey of Australian college and noncollege young people (ages 16 to 26), the majority of both females and males endorsed the notion that women (but not men) need to plan on careers that allow flexibility of work hours. They also expected women to seek careers that would tolerate interruption for periods of child rearing (McDonald, 2018). Even though respondents of both genders seemed to accept the importance of equality and some were even pondering taking on nontraditional roles, those who wanted to have children usually saw women as the more suitable caregiver. And, male respondents often expressed a disinclination to give up the traditional role of primary wage earner. Consider just two fairly typical comments:

Female undergraduate, age 22: I would expect my husband to play a role in their upbringing, aside from working full-time, aside from an economic point of view. But I think personally as a mother, I wouldn't want to work full-time . . . That's not the type of mother, personally I want to be. (McDonald, 2018, pp. 33–34)

Male vocational student, age 17: I couldn't look after the kids all the time. I like having a job. I like earning money. It would just feel out of place . . . I guess it's a sexist stereotype, but I would rather it that way as terrible as that may sound . . . (McDonald, 2018, p. 34)

Different role expectations are nowhere more evident than in the typical patterns of career development. There have been several noteworthy changes in career patterns for women, and to some extent for men, but these changes continue to reflect the tendency for women to focus more than men on family and child-rearing concerns at every stage of career planning. For example, despite the fact that both men and women have the right to take parental or family leaves in some companies in the United States (a right that is mandated by law in many European countries), it is relatively rare for a man to exercise that right. The most dramatic change in women's career patterns since the 1950s has been the great increase in women's choice of a double-track pattern. To illustrate the enormity of the change, in 1950, most mothers of children under age 6 were full-time homemakers (88%). In 2009, more than 63% of U.S. mothers of preschoolers were employed, and the percentage of employed mothers has continued to rise (U.S. Bureau of Labor Statistics, 2011; 2014).

Mothers who work are described as having two careers because they typically take more responsibility for child care and daily household tasks than fathers who work, although there is an increasing tendency for men to share somewhat more equitably in homemaking responsibilities and to make job-related decisions that take into account their parenting role (Amon, 2018; Bond, Thompson, Galinsky, & Prottas, 2002). Men have also become more likely to take their wives' careers into account in making other job-related decisions, such as whether to relocate.

Despite some improvements, old habits do die hard. Women, for example, still make less money than men (U.S. Bureau of Labor Statistics, 2017). Unsurprisingly, researchers find that one contribution to earnings differences is the degree to which people endorse gendered separation of roles. In fact, women who endorse this view tend to earn less than other women, and men who endorse this view tend to earn more than other men (Judge & Livingston, 2008). "Overall, . . . although gender role attitudes are becoming less traditional for men and for women, traditional gender role orientation continues to exacerbate the gender wage gap" (Judge & Livingston, 2008, p. 994). Organizational structures, possibly constructed and maintained to build in certain privileges for select groups, are slow to change. Research has demonstrated that women in male-dominated occupations are not viewed as favorably as men, despite comparable skills. Their work is evaluated more negatively than that of men, and they face more exclusion from the kinds of informal networks and social activities that often pave the way for advancement in the workplace (Eagly & Johannesen-Schmidt, 2001; Pringle et al., 2017). Clearly, both traditional gender roles and the realities of secular change are influencing career patterns for both women and men. We will revisit the issue of dual careers and parenting in the next chapter.

Work and the Development of Self-Concept

As we have now seen, theorists in the arena of career development see an individual's vocational self-concept as critical for the evolution of a successful, satisfying career. Both Holland and Super specify the importance of self-knowledge in career development: accurate assessment of one's own style, interests, and characteristics. Super also emphasizes that one's vocational self both emerges from one's broader sense of identity and contributes to it. Thus, it seems that self-concept is a central force behind career development and is, in turn, a product of it. These ideas have formed the backbone of many career counseling approaches. In the following sections, we will consider how feelings and attitudes towards the self as a worker develop. What do these aspects of identity contribute to work and its role in the life of an adult and vice versa? We begin by recapping Erik Erikson's ideas about how work and self-concept are related in development.

ERIKSON'S THEORY OF IDENTITY DEVELOPMENT

In Erikson's (1950/1963) view of the developing self-concept, children begin to formulate a sense of themselves as workers when they first confront serious work. In both nonindustrial and industrial societies around the world, children are expected to begin to work by the time they are 5 or 6 years old. In nonindustrial societies, they work alongside adults, caring for younger children, doing household tasks, helping with farm animals, working in the fields, or hunting. They are expected both to contribute to the productive efforts of the community and to learn the skills they will need as full-fledged adults. In most industrial societies today, children's work begins in school, where they are expected to achieve competence in basic skills, such as reading and arithmetic, that will serve them in nearly any adult work they might take on.

You may recall from Chapter 7 that Erikson expected these early work experiences to provide a child with a feeling of *industry*, which is both a belief in his ability to master the skills and tools needed to be productive and a sense of "the pleasure of work completion by steady attention and persevering diligence." Feelings of industry help the child to be "an eager and absorbed unit of a productive situation" (1950/1963, p. 259). The child can, unfortunately, also slip into feeling inadequate and inferior if he cannot seem to master the skills that are required of him and begins to be discouraged about how effective he can be in contributing to productive work efforts. Feelings of inferiority can also begin at this point if social barriers, such as those experienced by the poor, limit a child's opportunities to try out challenging work, provide substandard educational opportunities, or lead him to question his abilities.

Thus, for Erikson, the elementary school years are a crucial time for establishing a strong sense of industry. In adolescence, teens work on fashioning an adult identity, which includes developing a sense of direction for their vocational lives. This process continues, as we have seen, well into young adulthood. Identity formation is influenced by the attitudes towards self that evolved in childhood. We can expect that young people who bring to this process a strong sense of industry will find the task of vocational self-development less cumbersome than those who are plagued by self-doubt.

As you know, Erikson theorized that in adulthood the process of self-concept development continues. Individuals with a sense of who they are and what they can do are motivated to use their lives and their skills to leave a legacy for the next generation. Erikson called this a need for *generativity* and hypothesized that generativity motives have a strong influence on one's work life as adults move into middle age. Concepts akin to what Erikson called "industry" and "generativity" have been the focus of intensive study in several different research traditions. In the following sections, we will take a closer look at some findings on the importance of these two aspects of self-concept for young adults.

The Importance of Industry.   As you learned in Chapter 7, a sense of industry as Erikson describes it is similar to what Bandura and his colleagues have called *self-efficacy*, a person's belief in his ability to exercise control over events that affect his life (Bandura, 1989). A positive, optimistic sense of personal efficacy, like a feeling of industry, motivates a person to work hard at a task and to persevere even in the face of obstacles. There is evidence that high levels of achievement usually depend on "an optimistic sense of personal efficacy" (Bandura, 1989, p. 1176).

Closely related to Bandura's work on self-efficacy is research by Dweck and her colleagues who have studied mastery orientation and the helpless pattern in school children and in college-aged adults (Dweck & Allison, 2008; Haimowitz & Dweck, 2017). These are two different orientations to failure. Individuals with a mastery orientation move forward optimistically even when they fail. They assume that they *can* succeed with further effort. They construe failure as a challenge rather than as an obstacle. Individuals with a helpless pattern, however, often begin to denigrate their abilities when they encounter failure and typically stop applying themselves or trying to improve their performance. Dweck emphasizes the importance of our *mindsets*, that is, theories of intelligence or ability in influencing how we deal with failure (Dweck, 2017; Haimovitz & Dweck, 2017; see Chapter 6). She has found that mastery-oriented people are likely to have a "growth" mindset, seeing intelligence as a dynamic and malleable quality that can be increased by hard work and instruction. People who show a helpless pattern more often have an "ability" mindset. They see intelligence or ability as a fixed, concrete thing: "You can only have a certain amount of it, so you'd better show that it's enough and you'd better hide it if it isn't" (Dweck, 1999, p. 20).

When individuals with different orientations to failure move out of work environments where they have been successful and into more challenging situations where they encounter more experiences of failure, they show different degrees of progress and different emotional reactions. Mastery-oriented people dig in and try harder and by that very effort make success more likely in the future. Helpless people tend to turn away from the new challenges. They seek tasks where they feel more certain they can succeed, settle for mediocre performance, or give up altogether. They also tend to feel more stress and shame when they find the new work they are faced with difficult. This pattern has been observed in children moving out of elementary school, where teachers often protect children from failure, into the more impersonal and competitive environment of a middle or junior high school (e.g., Blackwell, Trzesniewski, & Dweck, 2007; Sorich & Dweck, 1996). It has also been found with young adults as they move through challenging college programs (Grant & Dweck, 2003; Robins & Pals, 1998). In both kinds of transitions, individuals with ability mindsets performed less well than those with growth mindsets, and they found their experiences in the new situations more emotionally distressing. This was true despite the fact that both groups entered the new environments with equally good credentials.

Findings like these might have particular significance for the patterns of career development observed among women and minorities. Gender differences in the choice of a career in male-dominated fields have been linked to lower self-efficacy in women, especially women who perceive themselves as highly feminine. Whereas women in general tend to have lower self-efficacy beliefs for "masculine" occupations requiring quantitative or leadership skills, males have about the same sense of efficacy for both masculine and "feminine" career options (Betz & Schifano, 2000; Good, Rattan, & Dweck, 2012).

A closely related factor affecting self-efficacy for women and other minority group members is **stereotype threat**, the fear that a stereotype might be true or that one will be judged by that stereotype (Spencer, Logel, & Davies, 2016). When people are reminded of stereotypes that pertain to their own category (e.g., women, Blacks), they often show increased stress and reduced performance. For example, when researchers showed an engineering conference video to male and female STEM students, females reacted differently depending on the gender stereotype cues in the video (Murphy, Steele, & Gross, 2007). Specifically, in a version of the video with no stereotype cue, equal proportions of men and women were depicted as attending the conference. In another version of the video, many more men were depicted than women, cuing the stereotype that engineering is a masculine profession. Men appeared to pay no attention to the cues, but women who watched the more stereotypical video were more physiologically reactive (e.g., their heart rates increased) and they reported both a lower sense of belonging and less willingness to attend the conference. In another study of gender stereotype threat, Krendl, Richeson, Kelley, and Heatherton (2008) used functional brain imaging techniques to demonstrate that creating a threat by calling attention to a gender stereotype literally changed how women's brains functioned as they solved math problems. College students were asked to solve math problems both before and after the researchers reminded them that "research has shown gender differences in math ability." Men's functioning was unaffected by the stereotype induction. For women, performance on the math problems declined somewhat, and the parts of the cortex that they recruited to solve problems were different before and after the threat induction. Beforehand, they used neural networks that are typically associated with math learning, but afterward they showed more activation of neural regions associated with social and emotional processing. Such studies show us that when environmental cues trigger "ability" mindsets, people's performance tends to suffer (Cimpian, Mu, & Erickson, 2012).

Why does stereotype threat impact performance? One important reason is that working memory space that should be available for learning or problem solving is partially taken up with concerns about being judged negatively (Armstrong, Gallant, Li, Patel, & Wong, 2017). People under threat use up precious working memory space with worry about making mistakes, feeling too anxious, looking stupid to others, and so on. The following study illustrates that people are often paying close attention to their own anxiety when they are experiencing stereotype threat. In one condition, female participants were given a threat-cue: they were told that females' reaction times are slower than males' (Johns, Inzlicht, & Schmader, 2008). They then performed the task of identifying the position of a dot on a screen as quickly as possible. If the dot were preceded by an anxiety word in the location where the dot would appear, women who were given the threat-cue actually responded more quickly to the dot than they did if the dot were preceded by a neutral word in the same location. Women who were not given the threat-cue did not show this increased attention to anxiety-related stimuli. They responded with the same speed whether the dot was preceded by an anxiety word or a neutral word. In this particular study, being hypervigilant to anxiety was helpful to performance, but in most situations, it simply uses up memory space that is needed for the task at hand.

As we noted earlier, African American college students are more likely than White students to drop out of college. We also saw that when African American students attend Black colleges, they are more likely to pursue some particularly challenging majors, such as premed, than when they attend predominantly White colleges. Aronson and Fried (1998) posited that African American students are burdened by the stereotype that Blacks are less intelligent than Whites. Being in school with White students may produce a tendency to evoke this stereotype and may make some Black students more susceptible to a helpless pattern, interfering with their achievement. In a now classic study, Aronson and Fried provided undergraduates with a training program that they hoped would reduce stereotype threat. The researchers hoped to foster a mastery orientation and thereby help improve achievement. Through film and lecture, citing scientific research, they instructed both Black and White undergraduates at Stanford University on the processes by which intelligence can actually be cultivated and changed. The training emphasized that when people take on new tasks and learn new skills, there is neuronal growth so that they literally become smarter. To make sure that students had consolidated the information, participants were required to explain the incremental view of intelligence in letters to elementary school children. By the end of the school year, African American students who had been taught the incremental theory showed significant increases in achievement, reflected in their grade point averages. These students also were enjoying school more and felt more academically oriented than African American students in a control group, who had not been part of the incremental theory training.

There is evidence that many interacting variables in one's development affect the feelings of industry or positive self-efficacy or mastery orientation that people carry into adulthood. Such variables ultimately influence the likelihood of long-term achievement. These variables include parenting styles (Kim et al., 2018; Pinquart & Kauser, 2017), teacher expectations and practices (Park, Gunderson, Tsukayama, Levine, & Beilock, 2016; Rubie-Davies & Rosenthal, 2016), stimulation and opportunities for personal challenge in one's home environment (e.g., van Doorninck, Caldwell, Wright, & Frankenberg, 1981), security of attachments (Kerns & Brumariu, 2016), and, as we have just seen, gender and cultural stereotypes. Dweck and her colleagues have also demonstrated that parents' and teachers' approaches to children's successes and failures play a role. For example, praising the whole person for success ("You're a smart girl" or "You're a good boy") tends to foster helplessness, apparently because it focuses attention on ability explanations rather than process or incremental explanations of performance. Praising process ("You found a good way to do it") fosters a mastery orientation (Haimovitz & Dweck, 2017; see Chapter 7 Applications).

The Importance of Generativity.　　How important are generativity needs in career development? As we have seen, Erikson described generativity as most influential in middle adulthood, but research indicates that young adults are also influenced by generativity as they plan and launch their work lives (Mackinnon, Pasquale, & Pratt, 2016).

A seminal study by Stewart and Vandewater (1998) examined two broad features of generativity—generativity desire and generativity accomplishment—and found that the desire for generativity is quite strong even in early adulthood and actually declines through middle and late adulthood. Desire was defined as expression of generativity goals, such as caring for future generations ("I'm concerned about the planet"), wanting to produce something of lasting value ("I want to write a major piece of nonfiction"), and being concerned about being needed ("It's nice to discover that my kids still come to me for advice and help"). In two cohorts of women who were studied longitudinally, such desires were strong through early adulthood, peaking in the early 30s and then declining. Generative accomplishment peaked later, in middle adulthood. The authors propose that "healthy early adulthood includes the formulation of generativity goals or desires, while healthy midlife includes the subjective experience of the capacity to be generative as well as the beginning of a sense of satisfaction in generative accomplishment" (p. 94). Stewart and Vandewater's results seem consistent with the finding, noted earlier, that even right after high school, young adults from all walks of life are likely to say that they would like their work to make a meaningful contribution (Hill & Yeung, 1999). We will look again at generativity issues in the next chapter, as we consider the development of adults in midlife.

MyLab Education Self-Check 12.2

Applications

The search for intimacy in adulthood demonstrates the continuing human need for social connectedness. The deepest aspects of a person's emotional life as an adult are often expressed within the confines of pair-bonds. The importance of these associations is evidenced by the fact that referral problems for helpers commonly involve interpersonal relationships. As we have seen, early attachment experiences can act as templates for the intimate relationships of adulthood. In particular, they may influence our willingness to rely on others (approach) to meet our needs for intimacy and to help us manage stress. They can also affect how trusting we are that others will meet these needs (anxiety) or the degree to which we avoid relying on others for intimacy (avoidance). These representations are intimately linked to how we view ourselves, and, as Erikson emphasized, how worthy we believe we are of being loved. Attachment theory provides a dynamic theoretical framework to explain the simultaneous pulls for intimacy and autonomy that can make interpersonal behaviors seem puzzling and contradictory. As the poet David Whyte puts it, "We are strange, difficult creatures who long for both freedom and belonging at the same time, and often run a mile when the real thing appears" (Whyte, 2001, p. 234).

Attachment in Counseling Contexts

The major theoretical tenets of attachment theory and their extensions to adult pair-bonds have implications for individual, marital, and family therapies in some of the following ways. For helpers who utilize an attachment perspective, the therapeutic bond is the primary mechanism of change. The therapist functions as the secure base, provides the client with appropriate responsiveness and availability, and offers opportunities to explore models of self and others. Traditional views of therapy have long held that early attachment patterns carry over into therapeutic relationships (transference) and that therapy provides a chance for a corrective experience (Alexander & French, 1946). The way to revise insecure internal models, according to Bowlby (1988), is through the power of another, more secure and more responsive, base. In a review of attachment-based therapies, Berry and Danquah (2016) delineate the working-alliance features that demonstrate client-therapist attachment and permit a corrective experience. Clients often view therapists as wiser and more knowing than themselves; seek proximity in regularly scheduled contacts; experience the therapeutic relationship as a secure base to return to when stress occurs in their lives; and report separation anxiety with breaks in contact (e.g., vacation) and eventual termination. Effective attachment-based therapies can help clients move towards greater attachment security (Taylor, Rietzschel, Danquah, & Berry, 2015). If handled competently by the therapist, pre-existing issues of loss, separation, lack of connectedness to others, and maladaptive stress response patterns, which emerge as treatment progresses, can be processed within the therapeutic context to help clients revise their early, dysfunctional patterns of relating.

Some research suggests that the client's attachment to the therapist is the variable most strongly related to the working alliance, a significant predictor of therapeutic outcomes. Client–therapist attachment is even more important than client's typical attachment style, a finding that held true even for non-relationship-focused treatment modalities like CBT (Taylor et al., 2015). Experts in attachment-informed therapies advise that the working alliance be strengthened and a secure base established prior to engaging in exploring issues like prior relationships with early attachment figures (Berry & Danquah, 2016). Gradually, over the course of therapy, clients can be helped to understand that their ideas of self and others might not conform to the reality of present circumstances. This involves helping clients reflect on and articulate their feelings about current interpersonal encounters or conflicts, explore how they handle such situations, and draw connections between prior experiences in close relationships and present patterns of relating.

As in all therapeutic relationships, the therapist has to manage transference and countertransference. Although this concept was Freud's contribution to the psychodynamic literature, many theoretical orientations acknowledge the presence of therapist-client transference in their theoretical models, e.g., client-centered, gestalt, existential, CBT, behavioral, and multicultural therapies (Gelso & Bhatia, 2012). Transference is the "patient's experience and perceptions of the therapist that are shaped by the patient's own psychological structures and past, involving carryover from and displacement onto the therapist of feelings, attitudes, and behaviors belonging rightfully in earlier significant relationships" (Gelso & Bhatia, 2012, p. 385). Countertransference refers to the same phenomenon directed towards the client by the therapist.

Dozier, Cue, and Barnett (1994) found that the therapists' level of attachment security was related to countertransference processes. In other words, secure therapists were more likely to respond empathically to the dependency needs of their dismissing or avoidant clients. They were able to see the needs hidden beneath a detached or a rejecting exterior, whereas insecure therapists were more likely to be driven away by the negativity. Secure therapists were also better able to manage clients with ambivalent attachment styles. They were less likely to get trapped into "taking care of" these clients by responding to their obvious needs rather than attending to the more important, underlying ones.

Therapists need a high level of personal awareness to work effectively in relationship-based therapies. For example, being mindful of one's own need for closeness and distance can help prevent therapists from inadvertently activating client avoidance or dependency (Brisch, 1999). With anxious clients, therapists need to monitor arrangements to avoid starting late, postponing sessions, taking frequent vacations, or creating other situations that trigger the client's needs for care. These events can be easily interpreted as rejection. For the avoidant client, too much emotional closeness or too much emotional probing in the stages of therapy may trigger anxiety as well and prompt premature termination.

Another central task for the therapist is to use attachment theory as a basis for understanding client behavior. "The qualities Ainsworth called for—sensitivity in perceiving the patient's signals and the capacity to interpret them correctly and react to them appropriately and promptly—are just as necessary in the therapeutic situation and are just as helpful there as they are in the creation of attachment between mother and child" (Brisch, 1999, p. 79). Remember that attachment is a flexible construct; many different behaviors can signal similar intent. Bowlby noted that when people feel threatened by loss of or separation from the secure base, the attachment system is activated and responds in protest. If protest behaviors prove ineffective in restoring connection, despair and detachment may follow. We have seen in earlier chapters what these behaviors look like in children. In adult partners whose attachment systems are activated due to conflict, protest can include crying, pleading, controlling, nagging, criticizing, or seeking reassurance. Despair behaviors might include detachment, withdrawal from the partner, or anhedonia. These behaviors have been frequently reported in depressed individuals with respect to their partners (Anderson, Beach, & Kaslow, 1999; Coyne, 1976).

Interpreting behaviors as expressions of attachment needs shifts the ownership for marital or family problems away from only one member of the system. The therapist appraises what the verbal or nonverbal behaviors communicate about the felt security or insecurity of the dyad. Emotionally distressed individuals or couples, viewed from this perspective, may be chronically "on alert," never quite sure that their bids for connection will be read accurately by intimate others, expecting rejection, and prepared to respond to threats of rejection by escalating demands or defensive withdrawal. Their real need for emotional closeness is hard to see when their bids for intimacy are accompanied by irritable, critical, or dismissing acts that are sometimes incorrectly interpreted by their counselors as resistance or regression.

If working models are to be changed, it is probably a slow process. Revising representational models happens by engaging in a curative, therapeutic attachment that takes time, patience, and dedication. Slade (1999) draws our attention to the limitation of certain kinds of short-term, problem-centered therapies that are not well suited to reworking fundamental models of social and emotional relationships. Obviously, helpers should avoid over-diagnosing attachment-related problems because there is such wide individual and cultural variation within the range of normal functioning. Some people's relationships appear distant or enmeshed to observers, but they may be perfectly satisfactory to the couple involved. Clinicians should also resist viewing attachment style as a monolithic, trait-like characteristic that resides within a person. Working models of self and relationship are always shaped in context.

Attachment Applied to Couples and Families

For distressed couples, especially those prone to interpersonal violence, attachment constructs can be used to help partners reconnect in more adaptive ways. Researchers have noted that individuals with an anxious attachment style (avoidant or preoccupied) often choose partners who have the opposite way of manifesting anxiety (e.g., preoccupied with avoidant). Especially when under stress, one partner's anxiety (proximity-seeking) can be met by the other partner's distancing (avoidance). Over time, these patterns can solidify, become highly resistant to change, and even lead to violence (Schneider & Brimhall, 2014). Internal scripts about abandonment, lack of comforting, and loss of emotional control might trigger individuals to resort to maladaptive interactional cycles. One partner might seek connection in escalating criticism while the other withdraws emotionally or resorts to violence to get some distance. From this perspective, violence can be a behavioral enactment of an earlier experience of trauma. If conjoint therapy is safe for both partners (Stith, McCollum, Amanor-Boadu, & Smith, 2012), attachment-based therapies can help partners better manage anxieties, frustrations, and threats to security with greater awareness of how their own interactions serve to trigger these automatic patterns.

Emotionally focused couple therapy ([EFT]; Johnson, 2004) utilizes attachment theory to work with the underlying emotional needs that lead to conflict. Therapy focuses on creating a strong working alliance; prioritizing safety and validation for each partner; reframing conflicts as dysfunctional interactional patterns; exploring deep, underlying attachment-related emotions like fear; and using enactments between partners to help them move into more adaptive cycles of communication (Sandberg et al., 2015). EFT has been helpful in unlocking couples' understanding of how their needs for closeness and autonomy perpetuate conflicts and contribute to their distress (Dalgleish, Johnson, Moser, Lafontaine, & Wiebe, 2015; Wiebe & Johnson, 2016).

Another example of an empirically supported treatment that integrates attachment theory with interpersonal therapy (see Chapter 11) is attachment-based family therapy ([ABFT]; Diamond, 1998; Diamond, Russon, & Levy, 2016), a model typically used for families with adolescent children. According to ABFT, the major components of therapy are (1) alliance building, (2) reattribution, (3) teaching effective parenting, and (4) reattachment. Alliance building involves creating a relationship that provides a safe place for the therapeutic work and a source of ongoing support for family members. The target of alliance building, typically the relationship between therapist and client in individual

TABLE 12.4 Career Counseling Interview (CCI)

INTERVIEW QUESTIONS	PURPOSE
1. Whom did you admire when you were growing up? List three heroes/role models.	The underlying hypothesis is that clients admire qualities that they already possess. Answers shed light on clients' strengths, primary life goals, and preferred solutions to problems.
2. What attracts you to your favorite magazines or TV shows?	This question indirectly assesses clients' interests and preferred activities. Answers point to areas of work that clients might prefer.
3. What is your favorite book/movie? Tell me the story.	This question assumes that people gravitate to stories that are emotionally compelling and reflect potential scripts for their own lives. Answers may reflect a client's main presenting problem.
4. What is your favorite saying or motto?	This question explores the potential advice that clients offer to themselves. Answers reflect a client's inner wisdom.
5. What are three of your early recollections (between ages 6 and 10)?	Purportedly, clients' remembrances reflect their early understanding of how they fit into the world and suggest current life problems or themes that need to be addressed.

SOURCE: Based on Savickas M.L. (2013). Career construction theory in Brown S.D., Lent R.W. (Eds.), *Career development and counseling. Putting Theory and research to work* (2nd ed.), Wiley, Hoboken, NJ , pp. 147–186.

counseling, is the relationship among family members. The therapist does, however, build personal alliances with parents and their adolescent to ensure a safe haven for expression of emotions and to provide the empathy needed for parents and children to feel heard and understood. The task of reattribution involves helping family members conceptualize their conflicts in more positive ways. Questions take an attachment perspective by orienting clients' attention to a family member's need for connection. An example would be asking parents, "When your child feels so bad that she acts out, what is getting in the way of you being a resource for her?" (Diamond et al., 2003). The therapist helps make explicit the connections between negative emotions and problematic behaviors. This strategy can evoke parents' motivation to help rather than to blame. Effective parenting education may be part of the therapy if appropriate. Finally, the task of reattachment is accomplished by supporting communication and conflict resolution skills. The ultimate goals are to repair attachment relationships, strengthen emotional connections, and support family members' ability to recognize and acknowledge each other's needs for closeness and autonomy.

The Importance of Work

Finding a place in the world of work is another important challenge at this time of life. Historically, the helping professions have contributed significantly to the theory and practice of career development. A central tenet of this field is that finding a career is more than a simple choice. This task, like so many others, is a process that requires self-understanding and the ability to use self-knowledge to make informed decisions. Kegan (1982) believed that vocational development is a function of people's levels of self-awareness and the kinds of meaning they attribute to themselves as workers. His theoretical ideas have some things in common with Perry's scheme, which was described in Chapter 11.

According to Kegan, adolescent vocational aspirations are heavily influenced by family and peers. From their foreclosed position, adolescents often construe their early career aspirations as the "right" choice. When confronted with confusing or contradictory feedback about their skills or when given opportunities to pursue other career paths, they may cope by becoming even more rigidly entrenched in the pursuit of their original career goals. They mistake the form of the career (such as medical school) with the underlying functions it serves (such as prestige and service). In other words, vocational identity is construed as a position rather than as an aspect of one's self. Individuals at this stage may resist revising a career goal, even when personal experience or feedback from others challenges its suitability. With maturity, individuals can reflect on this dissonance, integrate the contradictions, and reach a new level of self-understanding and acceptance. They can also identify career goals that are a better fit with their underlying dispositions and goals. Counseling can be particularly helpful for those who need guidance in self-exploration and who may need to reconstruct new meanings about career. With individuals working longer, this need may extend well into later decades of life that were once considered time for retirement (Lytle, Clancy, Foley, & Cotter, 2015).

Using a narrative, meaning-making approach to career issues, the Career Counseling Interview ([CCI]; Savickas, 2013) creates a life portrait through interview questions that construct a narrative around important life themes. The interview is conducted over two sessions to allow the story of the client's life to be explored in depth. Counselors can help the individual construct meaningful connections between self and work through this autobiographical portrait. The life themes, once fully explored, can enhance clients' ability to process work-related problems, make career choices or other decisions, and move towards greater awareness of preferred work environments (Hartung & Vess, 2016; Savickas, 2009, 2015). Table 12.4 lists the five basic questions of the CCI and a brief rationale for each.

It's also clear that work-life balance is critically important to career satisfaction (Whiston & Cinamon, 2015). Our families and social lives satisfy many of our needs for affiliation, but so does our work. Family stress can spill over into the workplace and vice versa. Thus, work and family are not separable arenas, but rather aspects of living that are closely intertwined. Helpers are encouraged to consider both work and family as interconnected spheres rather than operating "as if" work were a compartment able to be set aside at the end of the day. With the increasing connectedness technology provides and with growing job-related demands, workers can anticipate that the press for interventions to promote work–life balance will only increase.

Building Self-Efficacy

One important component of success in life and work is the set of beliefs a person has about his ability to be successful. Self-efficacy is a construct that is meaningful in many different domains of development, as we have seen. It has rather recently been integrated into a model of career decision making (social cognitive career theory [SCCT]; Lent, Brown, & Hackett, 1996) that is based on Bandura's (1977, 1997) self-efficacy theory. In this approach, client beliefs about how successful they will be in certain roles and work settings are given a prominent position in the career decision-making process. Our sense of self-efficacy shapes our best guess about whether some outcome is likely to be successful and, thus, influences the level of exploration we are willing to undertake in regard to pursuing that outcome. Self-efficacy level also influences our willingness to sustain effort in achieving desired outcomes and to learn the skills that might be needed for successful accomplishment of some goal. One's sense of self-efficacy is shaped by past experiences with success and failure as well as by opportunities to try things out. These opportunities can be constrained by social class, gender, age, race, disability, the quality of educational experience, or family and peer influences.

Helpers can be both tutors and coaches in this process, scaffolding the development of a personal sense of efficacy in regard to many of life's important challenges. Because self-efficacy beliefs influence functioning in a whole host of ways, from making decisions (What major shall I select?) to behavioral performance (Shall I ask this person for a date? Or my boss for a raise?), it is a useful target for clinical intervention. Bussey and Bandura (1999) describe four major ways to instill a strong sense of self-efficacy.

1. Construct and try out graded mastery experiences that are tailored to the individual's level of ability and that maximize the chances of success. To do this effectively, helpers need to listen to clients explain why they try or don't try certain activities and what they think are their roadblocks to success. In relation to career counseling, Betz (2004) suggests asking clients what they would choose to do if they could do "anything," what skills they need to improve their career opportunities, and what they feel is standing in the way of improving their skills. These kinds of questions can reveal something about how clients view their own capabilities and limitations and thus provide a guide for selecting specific corrective experiences.
2. Discuss or provide models who demonstrate success in an area of difficulty for the client. Successful models encourage individuals to believe in their own capacity for success and provide skills and know-how to the motivated observer.
3. A third way to enhance self-efficacy is to apply social persuasion. This might be done by challenging erroneous beliefs about lack of ability, making attributions for failure to lack of effort (incremental) rather than lack of ability (fixed), and providing support as well as realistic, helpful suggestions for improvement.
4. Finally, attempt to reduce coexisting factors that lower self-efficacy, such as stress, depression, or features of the environment, like restricted opportunity structure, whenever possible. By means of these processes, clients revise versions of their expectancies, which can lead to changes in behavior.

"As they (clients) continue to accumulate more and more of such success experiences, processing this information within the therapy session helps them realign their anticipatory thoughts and feelings with an appropriate self-evaluation of the outcome of their response. Eventually, a new behavior pattern, together with a greater sense of self-efficacy, begins to emerge" (Goldfried, 1995, p. 113).

Adjusting to the World of Work

Finding productive work enhances our lives, but choosing a career is only one step in the career development process. People also need to adjust to the demands of the workplace.

Classic career counseling theories have taken the view that Hershenson's (1996) work adjustment is most likely to occur if the ongoing characteristics of the individual (work values, skills, goals, habits, etc.) mesh with the day-to-day demands of the job (behavioral expectations, skill requirements, available rewards, and opportunities). For example, an organizational position that is highly structured and requires adherence to routine may be unsatisfying to an individual with high needs for autonomy and little motivation to work in a corporate culture. Helping clients consider the person–environment dimensions of a career can promote more successful adjustment.

Unfortunately, finding the ideal fit, although a desirable goal, is not always realistic. The workplace is harsh and unsatisfying for many people due to job-related threats to health, lack of job security, lack of control over tasks performed, and pressure to increase productivity with limited time and resources.

Work stressors are deeply rooted in the nature of workplaces and the culture that drives them, even for those who work in jobs they prefer. A new generation of challenges has emerged over recent decades, leading to increased need for individual and societal interventions. The growth of technology and global markets have created pressure on employers to enlist cheap labor; restructure traditional benefits; increase part-time, temporary, and contingent work; and increase demands for productivity (Seigrist & Wahrendorf, 2016). Overall, this phenomenon has proved unsettling at best and harmful at worst. "With the advent of new technologies and new societal demands, employment sectors in high income countries shifted from industrial mass and lean production towards service delivery and information/communication technology-driven jobs. Although physically strenuous work and exposure to main occupational hazards of industrial production continue to pose serious challenges to workers' health and safety, the *threats of a health-adverse psychosocial work environment* are becoming more widespread and more visible with this shift, and they contribute to a growing burden of work-related diseases" (Siegrist & Wahrendorf, 2016, p. 5).

Researchers have proposed that work stress results from an imbalance between the effort a worker expends and the reward he obtains. High effort combined with low reward is a formula for stress, especially for people who have no choice about their jobs, who are overcommitted to work (high effort) because of their need for approval, or who are in highly competitive positions (Siegrist & Wahrendorf, 2016). Workplace stress accounts for over a third of work-related illness and more than half of sick days. In addition, workplace stress is related to depression, cardiovascular problems, diabetes, sleep problems, and increased workplace bullying (Despréaux, Saint-Lary, Danzin, & Descatha, 2017).

Personal health management and stress reduction can be useful approaches for professionals dealing with client workplace stress (see Chapter 14). Self-efficacy is a particularly powerful vehicle for enhancing workers' health behaviors. Compared to employees who were offered a standard menu of health benefits (e.g., access to wellness programs), participants in a self-management plus self-efficacy workplace intervention called *Act Healthy* (Schopp, Bike, Clark, & Minor, 2015) showed improved health behaviors and greater self-efficacy to sustain those lifestyle changes. Mindfulness-based approaches for workplace stress are also promising (Grover, Teo, Pick, & Roche, 2017). When working with individual clients, helpers can target aspects of work stress that would benefit from specific interventions. Several dimensions of workplace stress can serve as a basis for the assessment. These include sufficient time to do one's job, overall workload, opportunities to develop skills, decision-making power, coworker cooperation, supervisor support, material compensation, rewardingness and satisfaction of one's job, trust in supervisors and company, and fair and just treatment (Mauss, Li & Angerer, 2017).

It should be emphasized that, as helpful as individual interventions might be, collective action to improve workplace conditions may be more realistic in the face of widespread workplace shifts. Helpers can take an advocacy position on issues related to work, such as government or company policies that support workplace improvements and benefits like high-quality child care. Given the importance of love and work in adults' lives, understanding and supporting successful adjustment in these two areas is a worthy task for clinicians.

Summary

1. Freud characterized love and work as the means by which adults strive for happiness. Erikson described intimacy—closeness to another that is marked by trust, openness, and affection—as the goal of young adulthood, and generativity—creating, producing, and contributing to the human community—as the goal of middle adulthood. Recent conceptions of mental health or "wellness" also emphasize both having close relationships and feeling competent and productive as essential ingredients for happiness.

Love

2. Attachment theory provides one framework for conceptualizing adult intimacy. It suggests that early bonds with caregivers could have a bearing on relationship building in adulthood and that intimate adult relationships provide some of the same benefits as infant–adult relationships: a secure base, safe haven, and emotional warmth.

3. Two traditions or lines of inquiry characterize adult attachment research: the nuclear family tradition, exploring how early attachments might affect the quality of caregiving that an adult gives his own children, and the peer/romantic partner tradition, which focuses on the peer attachments of adults.

4. The Adult Attachment Interview (AAI) consists of questions about early memories of relationships with parents. Autonomous (secure) adults provide a coherent, collaborative narrative, acknowledging the importance of attachment-related experiences in their development. Individuals described as earned secure appear to have come to terms with painful backgrounds. They reflect on their past realistically, acknowledging their parents' perspective. Autonomous adults tend to have securely attached children.

5. Dismissing (insecure) adults describe parents positively but provide either no evidence or contradictory evidence. Generally, they downplay the importance of early relationships. Their children tend to form avoidant attachments.

6. Preoccupied (insecure) individuals provide long, incoherent, egocentric monologues. They seem overwhelmed by the interview questions and are often angry, sad, or fearful. They seem preoccupied with parents, who are remembered as intrusive or egocentric. Their children often have anxious-ambivalent attachments.

7. Unresolved individuals produce narratives with notable lapses in logical thinking. Their children have a tendency to show disorganized attachment patterns. Insecure adults are the most likely to be emotionally disturbed.

8. Longitudinal studies find that an individual's infant attachment status (as measured by the strange situation test) predicts his AAI status, although intervening events can shift that status from secure to insecure or vice versa.

9. AAI narratives are different from other interview narratives with the same interviewees, suggesting that the AAI specifically reflects a person's state of mind regarding interpersonal representations. This working model of attachments is assumed to be a schema that has evolved with time and experience and that serves as a guide for understanding, predicting, and acting.

10. Adult pair-bonds integrate three basic behavioral systems: caregiving, attachment, and sexual mating. The attachment system involves proximity seeking and separation distress and serves safe haven and secure base functions. Attachment functions gradually transfer from parents to peers and, eventually, to romantic partners. Proximity seeking begins to shift as early as the preschool years. Between 8 and 14 years, peers also provide safe haven. Eventually attachments to romantic partners involve proximity seeking and separation distress, and they also serve safe haven and secure base functions.

11. The measurement procedures and typologies in the peer/romantic relationship tradition have been different from those in the nuclear family tradition. Several typologies have been proposed, and in the most recent work it is suggested that people may be better characterized as differing along two continuous dimensions, one having to do with their degree of anxiety about close relationships and the other with their approach-avoidance tendencies. It appears to require about 2 years for a romantic relationship to serve all 4 attachment functions.

12. Partner selection can be predicted to some degree by the attachment characteristics of the partners. Although at zero acquaintance, people expect to be attracted to people with similar attachment styles, actual pairings are somewhat different. Secure individuals do tend to pair with secure partners, but anxious individuals are more likely to pair with avoidant than with anxious partners; avoidant-avoidant pairs are also uncommon. Whether individuals always enter relationships with these characteristics or sometimes evolve these styles within their relationships has not been determined.

13. Partnerships between secure individuals seem to involve more positive and less negative emotions than other pairings. Male avoidant individuals show less distress during breakups than other males, but females of all attachment types show similar levels of distress. Anxious partners are most stressed by conflict within a relationship.

14. Many young adults participate in casual sex, encounters outside of romantic relationships. The effects of casual sexual experiences on the formation of long-term relationships are unknown, but they do not seem to affect the widespread intention of young adults to form committed relationships and to marry.

15. Attachment style is related to the likelihood and frequency of casual sex. For example, it is more common among avoidant men and anxious women.

Work

16. In Holland's theory of career development, people are categorized as having one of six modal personal orientations or personal styles, part of their personality. Jobs or careers make demands that are compatible with one or more of these orientations. A good fit (convergence) between modal orientation and job characteristics benefits job satisfaction and feelings of well-being.

17. In Super's theory, the focus is on the development of a vocational self-concept, part of one's total identity. He describes five stages in its development, from the growth stage in early childhood through the decline stage in people of retirement age. Super emphasizes that career development is a continuing, lifelong process. Many career counseling approaches emphasize the important relationship between career and self-development, with self-discovery an important ingredient in career satisfaction.

18. College students' first vocationally relevant decision is choice of a major. Whereas personal characteristics and interests influence the choice, so do cultural changes (e.g., economic shifts) and cohort characteristics. Ethnic and socioeconomic differences appear to influence not only who attends college but also the likelihood of college retention and career choices. Career counseling in college should begin with advisement on choice of a major.

19. For the "forgotten half," those who do not attend college, the chances of achieving career goals shared by all young adults (e.g., good pay, opportunities for advancement, opportunities to make a meaningful contribution to society) are substantially reduced. As with college students, factors such as socioeconomic status and ethnicity affect these chances as well.

20. Career opportunities for noncollege young people could be improved if there were more systematic and effective resources for them, such as basic skill training in public schools, extensive vocational counseling, and opportunities for work-based learning. Some well-designed training interventions for high-risk groups have been successful, such as the Job Corps program.

21. Traditionally, women with careers have followed different career paths from men. Substantial changes have occurred, such as women outnumbering men in college. But there are still gender differences: Some careers are still highly gendered, and women are still more likely to consider the impact of career choices on their relationship opportunities and future child rearing responsibilities, although men are increasingly attending to such concerns as well.

22. Self-concept and self-understanding are central features of many theories of career development. How do basic feelings and attitudes towards the self as a worker develop? Erikson describes a sense of industry, belief in one's ability to work productively and expectation of satisfaction from work, as beginning in middle childhood, when children have their first work experiences. Generativity becomes important in adulthood, as people become motivated to leave a legacy for the next generation.

23. Bandura has studied self-efficacy, beliefs in one's own ability to affect events, as motivating people to work hard and persevere even in the face of failure. Such beliefs are correlated with high levels of achievement.

24. Mastery orientation is similar to self-efficacy and to a sense of industry. Mastery-oriented individuals move forward even when they fail, apparently because they are "growth" theorists, believing that hard work and instruction can affect ability. Conversely, people who show a helplessness pattern, who give up when they fail, tend to be "ability" theorists, seeing ability as fixed.

25. Differences in self-efficacy beliefs, or mastery orientation, may have significant effects on minority groups and women. Stereotype threat, the fear that an inferiority stereotype might be true, can influence achievement. In some research, stereotype threat has been reduced and achievement improved when individuals have received intensive training on the scientific evidence for the malleability of intelligence and ability.

Case Study

Tayib, who is 29 years old, works as a paralegal in a public defender's office. His parents came to the United States from India before he was born. Tayib's extended family in India are highly educated people, and his parents encouraged him to get a good education as well. Although he considered going to law school, Tayib never felt confident enough to pursue this goal. In his current place of employment, many coworkers rely on his conscientiousness. He feels that others, including his superiors, often take advantage of him by giving him the most difficult cases to sort out and the shortest deadlines for getting them done. He was recently passed over for a promotion by his boss, who decided to fill the higher level post by hiring someone from outside the department. He feels unsatisfied in his position, but he thinks that his chances for advancement may be best if he remains in civil service. His parents encourage him to find a position with more prestige and a better income.

Tayib has been dating Rachael, a 27-year-old White woman with a young son, for the past 6 months. Rachael works as a public relations executive in one of the corporate offices in the city. Rachael and her son, Luke, share an apartment with one of Rachael's girlfriends. This has been her living arrangement since the breakup of her relationship with Luke's father, Kevin, 3 years ago. The couple were never married, a factor that led to strained relationships with her own mother and father.

Tayib and Rachael are both interested in finding someone with whom they can have a serious relationship. Lately, however, their relationship has not been going as smoothly as it did in the beginning. As Luke's fourth birthday approached, Rachael wanted to plan a celebration for him. Tayib had already taken Luke and Rachael to an amusement park as a birthday present for the youngster. Rachael decided to have a special birthday dinner for Luke and invited her parents and Tayib. Tayib, in the midst of an important project at work, declined the invitation.

Rachael feels totally rejected by his refusal to attend the dinner. She cannot understand why she and Luke mean so little to Tayib. She believes that she does everything she possibly can in order to keep Tayib interested in her. She prepares meals for him, works on her appearance, listens to him talk about problems at work, calls him to let him know she cares about him, and tries to accommodate her schedule to his. She wonders now if she will ever find someone who wants to make a commitment to her. Tayib can't understand why Rachael is so upset about the dinner. Since she is a working woman with a child to support, he feels that she should understand how important it is to have and keep a job. Tayib begins to wonder if she really understands what is important to him. Although the two do not discuss this incident directly, they both feel tension growing in the relationship.

Discussion Questions

1. What are the issues involved in this case?

2. From an attachment perspective, what inferences can you draw about the relationship styles of Tayib and Rachael?

3. What are the challenges each person faces at this point in his or her development? How would you help them cope with these challenges?

Practice Using What You Have Learned

MyLab Education Application Exercise 12.1: Case Study: Individual Differences in Adult Attachments
MyLab Education Application Exercise 12.2: Case Study: Convergence of Personal Style and Job Demands
MyLab Education Application Exercise 12.3: Vocational Self-Concept

Journal Questions

1. Write a brief relationship autobiography describing how you behaved, thought, and felt about one significant relationship. How would you describe your own attachment style?
2. Describe how you solve conflicts in your closest relationship. How do you deal with stress in this relationship? Explain how these patterns relate to what you experienced in your family of origin.
3. How has your own career history changed since you held your first job? What were the influences (both internal and external) on your career trajectory? How would you evaluate your sense of self-efficacy regarding your career?
4. Think about your current job (or a former one). Assess your job on the dimensions of workplace stress using a scale from 1 (strongly agree) to 5 (strongly disagree). If you disagree, explain why and include any actions you could take to improve your situation.

1 . . . . 2 . . . . 3 . . . . 4 5
Strongly agree   Somewhat agree   Strongly disagree
a. I have enough time to get the job done.
b. My workload is reasonable.
c. I am involved in decisions that affect my work.
d. I have the opportunity to develop my skills and knowledge.
e. The people I work with cooperate to get the job done.
f. My manager listens and responds to my ideas and concerns.
g. My total compensation (e.g., salary and benefits) adequately reflects my job performance.
h. I am satisfied with the career opportunities available in our company.
i. There is open and honest two-way communication at this company.
j. My job performance has been evaluated fairly.

Key Concepts

intimacy (p. 462)
generativity (p. 462)
autonomous (p. 465)
earned secure (p. 465)
dismissing (p. 465)
preoccupied (p. 466)
unresolved (p. 466)
cannot classify (p. 466)
passion (p. 468)
commitment (p. 468)
secure (p. 471)
avoidant (p. 471)
fearful (p. 471)
modal personal orientation (personal style) (p. 478)
job crafting (p. 479)
vocational self-concept (p. 480)
growth stage (p. 480)

exploratory stage (p. 480)
crystallization (p. 480)
specification (p. 480)
implementation (p. 480)
establishment stage (p. 480)
stabilization (p. 480)
maintenance stage (p. 480)
consolidation (p. 480)
decline stage (p. 480)
retention (p. 483)
forgotten half (p. 485)
mastery orientation (p. 491)
helpless pattern (p. 491)
stereotype threat (p. 492)
generativity desire (p. 494)
generativity accomplishment (p. 494)

Chapter 13
Middle Adulthood: Cognitive, Personality, and Social Development

Learning Objectives

After reading this chapter you should be able to:

13.1 Using life span developmental theory as a framework, describe healthy coping and functioning in middle adulthood and suggest adaptive approaches to maximize gains and minimize losses.

13.2 Explain the link between early temperament traits and later personality characteristics and, recognizing the relative stability of personality, suggest interventions that promote social maturity in middle adulthood.

13.3 Describe sources of predictable and nonnormative change in adult development, explaining adaptations to gains and losses, and identify significant developmental influences.

13.4 Identify factors that threaten primary relationships and generativity in midlife and discuss resources and interventions that support successful adaptation in these areas of development.

Amanda and Anthony, an African American couple, are both 50. They have been married for 20 years, and they agree that their relationship is strong and loving. Amanda, who did not attend college, currently works as an administrative assistant for the CEO of a small company. When their children were younger she worked as a classroom aide in the local elementary school so that she would have a shorter working day. Anthony is the security supervisor at a large university hospital, and he enjoys the work. His career was interrupted once when the rural hospital where he had his first security job closed. He was out of work for five months, and the family was forced to move to a larger urban area in order for him to find another position. Anthony feels valued in his current job, although he works very hard, putting in long hours at times, to keep it that way. The couple has three children, ages 12, 13, and 15. Through the years of their marriage, Amanda and Anthony have had similar ideas about child rearing, presenting a united front on matters of discipline and sharing the many responsibilities of child care. They have also shared household chores, albeit in somewhat stereotypical ways: Amanda does most of the meal prep and house cleaning, they both have grocery shopping and laundry duties, and Anthony takes care of their small yard and all house and car repairs. There are two "bones of contention" that create recurring friction between them. First, they have different ideas about how conservative they need to be in their spending, with Anthony often buying impulsively (like an expensive new fishing rod or other gear for his hobbies) without consulting Amanda, who worries about saving for the kids' education and for retirement (and, heaven forbid, another employment setback). Second, the way they split their household duties was established when Amanda had shorter working hours and less responsibility at work. Now she works long days, and her boss, who appreciates her organizational skills, counts on her more and more to keep his busy office running smoothly. She finds the job (and her boss's respect and recognition) quite gratifying, but she wants Anthony to take on more of the house cleaning to help balance the longer hours. She also argues that clipping hedges or changing the car's oil occasionally are way less taxing than the day-to-day need to keep bathrooms clean and dishes washed. Anthony feels that he needs time to unwind and pursue his hobbies, so that he can work as effectively as possible at his job. And, after all, he points out, he does earn the higher income. Unfortunately, the strain of their intensified disagreement about this issue comes at a time when the children are all moving into adolescence and presenting their parents with the many challenges their stage of development brings.

What is the nature of development at midlife? This is a perplexing question because adult lives are complex and multifaceted. Adults seek out jobs, select them, and sometimes ascend to positions of responsibility in their fields of work. Adults also change employment voluntarily to work in other settings or in other careers. Some adults lose their jobs and may experience unemployment or underemployment. Some work at multiple jobs. Adults take on leadership, executive, or mentoring roles in their communities. Adults move from one location to another, historically now more than ever before. They marry, cohabitate, divorce, date, and often go on to marry again. Some adults have children and grandchildren; others are childless. Adults may have responsibilities for the care of their own aging parents. Those who are parents or stepparents have to deal with the ever-changing developmental needs of their children. Adults are also affected by the close relationships they share with partners or friends. They may experience financial difficulties. They may sustain illness themselves or experience the illness or loss of loved ones. Some adults experience catastrophic events, such as wars, accidents, or natural disasters. Many more deal with chronic adversities such as discrimination of one sort or another, mental problems such as depression, or simply the gradual physical changes involved in the aging process. Moreover, many of these events occur simultaneously.

The complexity of people's experience and functioning is what is most striking about middle adulthood. How are we to make sense of all the variables operating in adult lives? Is there some coherent scheme that helpers can use to understand development in the adult years? In Chapter 1, we examined some of the many theoretical approaches that explain developmental processes, including stage models, such as Erikson's or Piaget's, and incremental models, such as learning and information processing accounts. As we have seen throughout this book, these approaches to development can be quite helpful in understanding some aspects of psychological functioning, but modern theorists typically turn to multidimensional models, which are focused on the complexity of interrelated causal processes in development. Recall in Bronfenbrenner's multidimensional model, for example, the description of proximal processes in development—reciprocal interactions between an "active, evolving biopsychological human organism and the persons, objects, and symbols in its immediate environment" (Bronfenbrenner & Morris, 1998, p. 996). These proximal processes are modified by more distal processes, some within the organism, such as genes, and some outside the organism, such as the family, the workplace, the community, the broader economic and political context, and other aspects of the culture.

As we saw in Chapter 1, multidimensional theories of adult development, called *life span developmental theories or models*, address all the fundamental questions of development, including the role of heredity and environment in adulthood and the extent to which adult characteristics are continuous with previous traits and propensities versus how much genuine change there is in adult behavior. Life span developmental models (e.g., Baltes, Lindenberger, & Staudinger, 2006) make one fundamental assumption in addressing such questions—that from birth to death, adaptation continues. The development of psychological functioning does not end or become fixed when adulthood is reached, but goes on until death. The reciprocal interaction of many biological and environmental factors forms an ever-changing "architecture" or scaffolding that supports the development of behavioral and mental functioning (e.g., Baltes et al., 2006). Thus, middle adulthood is not some kind of holding pattern before the slide into death. An adult's cognitive and socioemotional functioning continues to evolve through her 30s, 40s, 50s, and beyond.

Life Span Developmental Theory

13.1 Using life span developmental theory as a framework, describe healthy coping and functioning in middle adulthood and suggest adaptive approaches to maximize gains and minimize losses.

Life span developmental theory provides an overarching framework for understanding how middle adult life is linked to the childhood years, on one hand, and to old age, on the other. It can be construed as a kind of macrotheory under whose umbrella all the processes of ontogeny, or the development of organisms, fall into place. This orientation offers a clear benefit to those in the helping professions. First, it provides a way of organizing developmental processes across the life cycle. Think of the multiplicity of challenges and possibilities in adult life, some of which we mentioned at the beginning of this chapter. Rather than viewing them as disconnected parts of a life story, helpers can interpret the choices people make and the ways they adapt as reflecting some degree of lawful continuity. Second, life span developmental theory emphasizes the importance of learning about successful or effective development. Thus, this perspective fits well with therapeutic or psychoeducational goals. Let's now consider some of the elements of life span developmental theory.

Gains and Losses in Development: The Changing Architecture of Biology and Culture

Natural selection through many generations has created a biological trajectory that tends to optimize development in most typical environments, allowing the majority of individuals to grow up and become fully functioning adults who can contribute to the success of the species by reproducing. Of course, basic cultural supports—adequate parenting, nutrition, education, protection from environmental hazards, and so on—are fundamental for the success of this process as well. As individuals move through adulthood, the *biological* supports for life weaken because the reproductive process is complete, and the selection pressure that the need for reproductive success creates for a species is no longer operative. Thus, biological dysfunctions are more likely. "Evolution and biology are not good friends of old age" (Baltes, 1997, p. 368). During middle adulthood (defined here as ages 30 to 55), people begin to depend more and more on *cultural* supports for adequate functioning. Indeed, "old age" exists primarily because of modern culture. Advances in economics, nutrition, general knowledge, technology, and medicine have compensated for the weakening of the biological supports for life. As a result, from 1900 to 1995, the average life span increased in Western societies from about 45 years to around 75 years! For the U.S. population, life expectancy at birth increased to 76.6 (males) and 81.2 (females) by 2015, with some notable racial disparities. For example, Hispanic males (79.3) and females (84.3) have the longest life expectancies, and Black males (71.8) and females (78.1) the shortest, although ethnic/racial gaps have been narrowing in recent decades (National Center for Health Statistics, 2017).

Viewing development as a life span process makes clear that development or change in functioning with age involves both gains and losses for the individual. Gains are most obvious early in life; losses are more obvious later. But once we are sensitized

FIGURE 13.1 The shifting relationship between gains and losses across the life span.

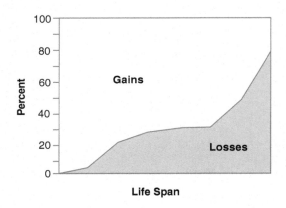

SOURCE: Based on Baltes, P. B. (1997). On the incomplete architecture of human ontology: Selection, optimization, and compensation as foundation of developmental theory. *American Psychologist, 52*, 366–380.

to the fact that development involves both, we begin to notice that gains and losses characterize change throughout life. Thus, children, not just adults, experience some losses in the normal course of development. One familiar illustration is characteristic of language development. As an infant, you were capable of hearing and producing all of the kinds of sound distinctions that are used across all human languages. But as you learned your native language, you became less adept at discriminating and producing sounds that were not part of that language. If you were introduced to a second language after the preschool years, you probably had trouble producing sounds that were not part of your native tongue, and so you probably speak the second language with a "foreign accent." Another example, suggested by Baltes (1997), is that as adolescents strive for personal autonomy, their relationships with their parents are often strained, as we have seen. The intimacy of the parent–child relationship is diminished for both partners as the adolescent struggles to achieve an adult identity.

Of course, loss is more obvious to us in adulthood as biological declines occur. We saw in Chapter 11, for example, that our biological systems, like our sensory abilities and our immune functions, all reach peak potential between ages 18 and 30. Many of these systems begin to decline soon after (see below). But the increase in losses through adulthood should not mask the fact that the gains also continue. For example, in Chapter 11 we discussed the gains in postformal thinking that seem to characterize some people as they move into middle adulthood. Other examples of gains will become clear throughout this chapter. However, the relative balance of gains and losses clearly shifts across the life span, until eventually losses outstrip gains for most people in old age (see Figure 13.1).

Development as Growth, Maintenance, and Regulation of Loss

Life span developmental theory defines development as a process of adapting to the constant flux of influences in our lives (Baltes, 1997; Baltes et al., 2006). One kind of adaptation is growth. We grow when we add new characteristics, understandings, skills, and so on to our behavioral repertoire. So, for example, an adult might grow by becoming more expert at some task at work, or she might acquire a more balanced and thus empathic perspective on her relationship with her parents. Another kind of adaptive functioning is maintenance or resilience, finding ways to continue functioning at the same level in the face of challenges or restoring our functioning after suffering some loss. For example, an adult might maintain the concept of herself as a poet—despite repeated rejections of her work—by persistently revising and resubmitting her work until eventually a piece is published. Or despite the death of a partner, she might eventually reestablish intimacy in her life by returning to social circulation and finding a new partner. A third kind of adaptation is regulation of loss. Like maintenance, this form of adaptation involves reorganizing the way we behave. But unlike maintenance, regulation of loss involves adjusting our expectations and accepting a lower level of functioning. Suppose that a woman who prides herself on her ability to remember names, faces, and telephone numbers suffers a reduction in learning ability as she ages. She adapts by using strategies that include writing down essential information that she previously would have recalled. She accepts that she will never have at her fingertips the breadth of information that she had before, but by using her new strategies she ensures that she will remember what is really necessary.

According to life span developmental theory, all three adaptive processes—growth, maintenance, and regulation of loss—are part of development from infancy through old age. What changes is the relative probability of each. Growth is much more

MyLab Education

Video Example 13.1

How does a fifty-year-old manage the shift in balance of gains and losses? The man in this video, formerly very athletic, describes his transition into middle age. Consider how his experience shows the three adaptive processes—growth, maintenance, and regulation of loss.

characteristic of children than it is of the elderly, and regulation of loss is much more characteristic of the elderly (see Figure 13.2). The middle adult years appear to be a time when the balance is shifting among the three adaptive processes. All three processes occur across the life span. Children experience the need to compensate for loss through maintenance or regulation, and adults of all ages experience growth. However, knowing the relative proportions of each, given a client's stage of life, may provide professionals with a frame for understanding presenting problems. We will have more to say about how these processes affect coping with stress in Chapter 14.

Defining Successful Development at Any Age

As adulthood proceeds, the more physical and psychological resources an individual has, the greater her likelihood of adapting well. Consider the nature of developmental success at different times in the life of Emma, now a 91-year-old woman. Emma never married or had children, which she experienced as a loss. In her young adulthood, she compensated for her childlessness by dedicating her considerable talents to teaching poor urban children in public schools. In middle adulthood, she became an administrator, developing innovative programs for young children and mentoring teachers in the public school system. In her early old age, the physical demands of a daily work schedule became too great, so she retired. This change diminished her power to influence the lives of young children in the public schools. But she managed the loss, maintaining her view of herself as a child advocate, by serving on the governing boards of nonprofit organizations that provide services for children. Now, Emma suffers from a number of biological losses—poor vision, breathing problems, and general frailty—and she has confined her living space to her small apartment. A good deal of her functioning involves regulating her biological losses by living a quiet, sedentary life in her small space and depending on some outside help, which she has the means to pay for as a result of careful financial planning. But she also continues to grow: She has learned to use a computer, and she has begun to write for her own enjoyment. She also maintains her contacts with friends through e-mail, video chats, phone calls, and visits.

At each stage of her life, Emma found ways to manage losses through maintenance or regulation and to continue to grow. The balance of losses and gains in her life has now clearly shifted so that much of her adaptive energy is dedicated to managing losses. With the help of technological supports, such as the computer, Emma has minimized the overwhelming losses of her late life and has continued to maximize her gains, to the extent possible. She provides an example of successful development even in old age.

Our description of successful development will sound familiar to most helpers because it is clearly continuous with what we think of as healthy coping. The life span developmental view helps us see that healthy coping evolves and changes throughout life. What is adaptive coping at one stage of life may be less adaptive at another. In the following sections, we will consider some relatively stable influences on adult life as well as the sources of change. As we look at these influences, we will begin to identify what resources the mature individual brings to the task of development and which of these resources might most effectively contribute to success. In Chapters 14 and 15, we examine additional aspects of the adaptive developmental process that characterizes adult life.

FIGURE 13.2 The relative increase in maintenance and regulation of loss and the relative decrease in growth as adaptive processes across the life span.

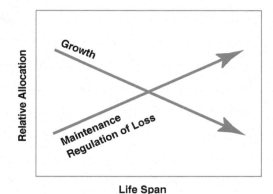

SOURCE: Based on Baltes, P. B. (1997). On the incomplete architecture of human ontology: Selection, optimization, and compensation as foundation of developmental theory. *American Psychologist, 52,* 366–380.

MyLab Education Self-Check 13.1.

Influences on Adult Development: Sources of Stability

13.2 Explain the link between early temperament traits and later personality characteristics and, recognizing the relative stability of personality, suggest interventions that promote social maturity in middle adulthood.

Personality

The popular *Up!* series of films produced by the British Broadcasting Company (BBC) documented the lives of several men and women at 7-year intervals, from the time they were 7 years old to age 56. The series set out to investigate the truth of the proverb: *Give me a child until he is 7, and I'll show you the man.* The eight documentaries clearly depict many changes that occur over the intervening 49 years. Yet they also illuminate the thread of stability that runs through these individual lives. For example, Nick, who at age 7 expressed the desire "to find out all about the moon," became a professor of science in adulthood. Sue, who was a vibrant, independent youngster, is now a fun-loving, independent woman. What kind of continuity is typical of people in general? What are the sources of relative stability in development from childhood through adulthood?

Longitudinal studies have found substantial stability in personality characteristics across the life span (McAdams & Olson, 2010; Roberts, Walton, & Viechtbauer, 2006). In much of this research, personality is construed as a set of traits that may be likened to the temperament characteristics of infants (see Chapter 4). Perhaps the most influential—and well supported—trait theory of personality has been developed by McCrae and Costa (2008; Costa & McCrae, 2017) who specifically assume that traits are biologically based, inherent tendencies that persistently influence thoughts, feelings, and behavior throughout life.

What are these traits that appear to be so stable? In the 1980s, researchers recognized that the thousands of words referring to personality characteristics could be reliably boiled down to five, which McCrae and Costa called the **Five Factor** or **Big 5** model of personality (Costa & McCrae, 2017; McCrae & Costa, 2008). These five traits represent the most basic dimensions of personality: **neuroticism (N)** or **emotional stability**, **extraversion (E)**, **openness (O)**, **agreeableness (A)**, and **conscientiousness (C)**. Each trait or dimension is actually a cluster of characteristics or qualities that are correlated – they tend to go together. Table 13.1 provides additional detail on these dimensions, describing some of the qualities of individuals at the "high" end of each dimension. For example, "energy level" and "talkativeness" tend to go together: If someone is very energetic, she is also likely to be very talkative, and vice versa. Both characteristics are part of the same personality trait or dimension, extraversion. It is also worth noting that the characteristics making up different traits are usually not correlated with each other. So, for example, "warmth" (part of the agreeableness trait) is not correlated with "outgoing" (part of the extraversion trait). That means that someone who

TABLE 13.1 The Big 5 Personality Traits

TRAIT	CHARACTERISTICS
Neuroticism	Tense, touchy, self-pitying, unstable mood, anxious, self-conscious
Extraversion	Outgoing, active, assertive, energetic, talkative, enthusiastic
Agreeableness	Warm, sympathetic, generous, forgiving, kind, affectionate, compliant
Conscientiousness	Organized, planful, reliable, responsible, careful, efficient, self-controlled
Openness to experience	Creative, artistic, curious, insightful, original, wide-ranging interests, positive orientation to learning

SOURCE: Based on McCrae, R. R. & John, O. T. (1992). An introduction to the five-factor model and its applications. *Journal of Personality, 60*, 175–215.

is high on warmth is no more likely to be an extravert (high on extraversion) than she is to be an introvert (low on extraversion).

Across many cultures and subcultures, characteristics cluster into the same five personality traits (DeBolle et al., 2016; Ispas, Iliescu, Ilie, & Johnson, 2014; McCrae & Terracciano, 2005; Rollock & Lui, 2016). There are, however, cultural differences in how people typically score on each dimension or trait. For example, in a summary of cross-cultural findings, Putman and Gartstein (2017) report that Europeans and people from the United States are characterized by somewhat higher levels of extraversion and openness than people from Asian and African cultures. Northern Europeans tend to score higher than Southern Europeans on neuroticism and conscientiousness.

Regardless of country or culture, there are some typical shifts in these traits with age. First, as people get older, they usually increase in social maturity. That means they become more *agreeable*, more *conscientious*, and less *neurotic* (that is, more *emotionally stable*) (Bleidorn, 2015; Roberts, Wood, & Caspi, 2008). This normative trend is considered quite positive, given that more socially mature personality traits predict more positive life outcomes, such as greater economic success, better relationships, better health, and greater longevity (Roberts et al., 2017). This pattern of increasing social maturity may be in part a matter of genetic unfolding (McCrae et al., 2000), but there is also evidence that typical experiences in early adulthood, such as needing to take on adult responsibilities, contribute to this process. For example, cross-cultural comparisons show that personalities mature earlier in cultures where young people have to take on adult role responsibilities early (Bleidorn et al., 2013).

Second, there is more relative change in personality traits early in development than later (Briley & Tucker-Drob, 2014). In other words, *individual differences* in personality tend to *stabilize* with age, usually by about age 30. This means that a person's ranking on personality traits, relative to other people the same age, is more likely to change earlier rather than later in development. Suppose Amanda (from the introduction to this chapter) was average on conscientiousness compared to her age mates at age 12. Her *ranking* (relative to others in her cohort) could have gone up or down during adolescence and young adulthood. Let's suppose that it went up, so that by age 30 Amanda actually scored higher on conscientiousness than most of her cohort. After age 30, if Amanda is like most people, her *relative* conscientiousness probably didn't change much—it stabilized. She *and* the rest of her cohort probably continued to grow more conscientious, but her *ranking* on conscientiousness stayed the same as it was at 30.

Given that personality traits usually change with age, albeit only a little, is it possible to encourage changes? Helping professionals often hope that their interventions will advance at least some aspects of social maturity—agreeableness, conscientiousness, and neuroticism/emotional stability. Do therapeutic and educational efforts actually change people's personality traits? Roberts and his colleagues (2017) addressed this question by doing a meta-analysis of a wide range of studies that examined the outcomes of both clinical and nonclinical interventions. Few of these interventions were intended to change specific personality traits. But each of them included outcome measures that assessed at least some characteristics that are aspects of personality traits, such as sympathy and warmth (agreeableness) or anxiety and anger (neuroticism/emotional stability). Also, aspects of every Big 5 trait were measured in at least some studies (from 44 studies that measured characteristics of openness to 199 studies that measured aspects of neuroticism). There were two critical findings. First, scores on measures of trait characteristics did change in a positive direction on the average, particularly for neuroticism and extraversion characteristics. Second, these positive changes were evident as early as 2 to 4 weeks into most interventions. So, even though most longitudinal studies find only small typical changes in personality over relatively long periods of time, Roberts and colleagues demonstrated that active therapeutic and educational efforts can bring about positive personality changes and can do so relatively quickly.

The Link to Temperament

Where do individual differences in adult personality traits come from? You may recall from Chapter 4 that infants and young children show early individual differences in behavioral tendencies that together are referred to as a child's temperament. As with adult personality, some behavioral tendencies are correlated with each other even in infancy, clustering into overarching traits or dimensions. Although not all researchers agree about the number or composition of the clusters, three that are commonly identified are: *emotionality* (quality and intensity of mood, especially negative mood and soothability), *control* or *self-regulatory tendencies* (such as attentional control/persistence, comfort with low intensity activities), and *surgency* (activity level, approach vs. avoidance, pleasure in anticipating reward or in high intensity activities, sociability) (Rothbart, 2011; Shiner et al., 2012). Like personality traits, these early characteristics are assumed to be biologically based reactivity patterns, and evidence is accumulating for the importance of genetic and epigenetic contributions to the physiological processes involved (Beekman et al., 2015; Saudino & Micalizzi, 2012; see Chapter 4).

Do early temperament traits contribute to later personality? One possibility is that early tendencies differentiate and integrate over time into more mature self-systems (Rothbart, 2011). So, for example, early manifestations of positive approach, such as smiling and laughing, could be precursors of more mature forms, such as social extraversion. Early persistence might contribute to later effortful control and conscientiousness. Infant tendencies toward irritability and problems soothing might predict higher neuroticism in adulthood. If we measure temperament traits and personality characteristics in adolescents or adults we find exactly these kinds of correlations (Shiner, 2015; Shiner & DeYoung, 2013).

However, the most convincing evidence comes from longitudinal studies, some of them focusing on a short-term period, comparing infant temperament to personality characteristics in later childhood, for example. There are also a few much longer term studies, beginning in infancy or early childhood and following participants well into adulthood. Quite consistently, these studies find that earlier temperament traits predict some later personality characteristics (Shiner, 2015; Shiner & DeYoung, 2013; Slobodskaya & Kozlova, 2016).

For example, Caspi (2000; Caspi et al., 2003; Schaefer et al., 2017; Slutske, Moffitt, Poulton, & Caspi, 2012) investigated the continuity of temperament in a cohort of New Zealanders from age 3 onward. The sample for this study consisted of all children born in Dunedin, New Zealand, between April 1972 and March 1973. Temperamental characteristics were assessed at various points by means of parent report, clinical examiner ratings, and self-report. Data on home environment, school, employment, and social history were also gathered. The assessment measures reflected the typologies, developed by Chess and Thomas, that were available in 1972 (Chess & Thomas, 1987; see Chapter 4): undercontrolled or *difficult* (impulsive, restless, negative), inhibited or *slow-to-warm-up* (introverted, fearful), and well-adjusted or *easy* (see Chapter 4).

The results paint a picture of moderate personality stability over time. At age 21 and again at age 32, the 10% of children identified at age 3 as undercontrolled were more likely than other groups to be aggressive, sensation seeking, impulsive, and prone to gambling and troubles with the law. They also tended to experience higher levels of interpersonal conflict in family and romantic relationships. Even if the surface features of behavior changed over time, these undercontrolled children were more likely to grow up to be adults whose behavior reflected a similar lack of control and problematic adjustment. The inhibited children (8% of the sample) at 21 were more likely than the other participants to have suffered from depression. As adults, they were more shy, fearful, and nonassertive, and less connected to sources of social support.

Several possible explanations might account for trait stability over time. First, genes probably play a role in stability of personality. Studies of twins indicate that identical twins are more similar in personality than other siblings, and that about 40% of that similarity seems to be attributable to shared genes (Vukasović & Bratko, 2015). Remember, however, that we do not inherit trait patterns per se. As multidimensional models of development predict, personality features are also shaped by both biological and socio-contextual circumstances. The transactional interplay between individual and context is what sculpts personality.

Viewed from this perspective, personality or trait consistency will be highest if other variables, in addition to biology, provide support or scaffolding for that consistency. For example, the individual's environment should remain consistent. A classic study by Helson and Roberts (1994) is illustrative here. Eighty-one women from Mills College were followed from ages 21 to 52. Those women whose level of ego development showed no change or whose level of ego development even slightly decreased over the years of the study were the least likely to have experienced disruptive experiences or high levels of responsibility. They seemed to have found comfortable niches for themselves that required little accommodation or change. Personality could remain fairly consistent over time, because these women appeared to have selected environments that suited their personalities in the first place. Or they may have behaved in ways that communicated their reluctance to change, thus eliciting compliance from others.

Yet another possible explanation for continuity is that certain kinds of personality styles show more consistency than others. Hampson (2008) reports that high levels of conscientiousness in childhood tend to predict well-being in adulthood, and she speculates that conscientious individuals may "gravitate to niches that are compatible with their attributes, including relatively safe environments for work and leisure . . . and are likely to evoke positive reactions in other people, which will serve over time to sustain these traits and related behaviors" (p. 265). These conclusions have been supported in other studies as well (Burt & Paysnick, 2012; Schaefer et al., 2017). Generally, people who possess resilient characteristics tend to be more stable and consistent throughout life.

MyLab Education Self-Check 13.2.

Influences on Adult Development: Sources of Change

13.3 Describe sources of predictable and nonnormative change in adult development, explaining adaptations to gains and losses, and identify significant developmental influences.

Although personality characteristics can be a relatively stable set of influences on the adult's development, there are many changes to which an adult must adapt. Some changes may be strongly age determined or *age graded*, such as physical changes that come more or less inevitably with time. Some changes are more a function of historical circumstance and are called *history-graded changes*. These include events that we share with our whole cohort, like living through the Great Depression or the Iraq War. Some circumstances that affect people's lives can be unique to cultural groups. Finally, there are changes that apply specifically to our own lives. These are *nonnormative changes*, often accidents of fate, like being in a train wreck or winning the lottery.

Age-Graded Changes

We will consider three kinds of age-graded changes. The first two are the physical and cognitive changes that have been documented as a function of aging in adulthood. The last concerns shifts in the relative importance of various life tasks that seem to occur with age. These shifts in life tasks, described by theorists such as Erik Erikson and Daniel Levinson, are generally thought to be a product of one's psychological response to reaching adulthood and facing the typical burdens and challenges that life presents to all of us. All three kinds of change represent challenges to our adaptive functioning as we get older.

PHYSICAL CHANGES IN ADULTHOOD

Bodily changes may be the most obvious ones in adult life. By about age 30, as people enter middle adulthood, there begins a shift from adolescing, or growing up, to senescing, or "growing down" (Levinson, 1986). Although there are physical declines that most people are aware of fairly early in this process, such as some skin wrinkling or hair loss, most declines are much more subtle, such as a decrease in the effectiveness of immune processes or in cardiovascular functioning. For the most part, people continue to feel that they are at peak or near peak levels of physical functioning until they are 40 or older. In their 40s and 50s, most people become more aware of physical losses. In the United States, the majority of middle adults enjoy good health, but this period is one in which many individuals, especially those in lower socioeconomic groups, begin to deal with chronic illnesses and other health problems that can limit their activities. In the 40s, 7% of adults have some kind of disability; by the early 60s, 30% do (Lachman, 2004).

Most sensory systems decline in sensitivity or acuity, although there is considerable variation among the systems and among individuals. The aging of the visual and auditory systems is probably best understood (Li-Korotky, 2012; Owsley, 2011). Visual acuity declines with age but is maintained at near peak levels until about age 40 and then it noticeably wanes. Individuals who never before wore glasses or contact lenses are likely to need them now, and those who required some visual correction in the past begin to experience more frequent prescription changes, or they now need bifocals or trifocals. Middle adults also begin to notice that they need more light than their younger friends in order to see well, and they may begin to notice that it takes longer to adapt to lighting changes than it used to. They are most likely to be bothered when there is a sudden change in lighting: coming out of a dark movie theater into daylight or encountering the headlights of an oncoming car on a dark road. Changes in the neurons of the retina, as well as changes in the cornea and lens of the eye, all contribute to these growing problems.

Similar declines in hearing or auditory sensitivity begin in the 30s. Sensitivity to high-frequency (high-pitched) sounds declines earlier and more rapidly, and the losses are usually greater in men than in women. Note that women's voices are therefore more difficult to hear in the later years than are men's, so that men are more likely to have difficulty hearing women than vice versa. There is much individual variation in the degree and kind of hearing loss, but most individuals find their lives somewhat affected by the end of middle age (Frisina, 2009; Humes, 2015). A national survey in the United States indicated that 15% of 50- to 59-year-olds and 31% of 60- to 69-year-olds suffered from at least mild hearing impairment (Bainbridge & Wallhagen, 2014). Impairment is more common in Whites and Hispanics than in Blacks, and in men than in women. And, as with many physical disabilities, impairment is more common among lower than higher SES groups (Anderson et al., 2017).

Among the functional systems that show developmental changes sometime in middle adulthood is the reproductive system. As with the sensory systems, noticeable changes tend to begin in the 40s and 50s. The menstrual cycle usually begins to shorten and becomes somewhat more erratic by the time a woman is in her late 30s. The female climacteric, the gradual reduction of reproductive ability, ending in menopause, the cessation of menstruation, usually begins in the 40s and continues for at least 10 years (Clayton & Harsh, 2016; Foxcroft, 2009). The climacteric is largely a function of a reduction in circulating estradiol, a form of the primary female hormone, and estrogen, produced by the ovaries. Having less estradiol eventually influences many other changes: the thinning and coarsening of pubic hair, the thinning and wrinkling of the labia, and changes in vaginal chemistry that can cause dryness and a greater likelihood of vaginal infections. Women commonly experience other physical symptoms as well, such as fatigue, headaches, insomnia, nightsweats, and hot flashes—sudden sensations of intense heat along with sweating that can last for as long as a half an hour. One reason for such symptoms is that lowered estrogen triggers the release of other hormones and these have widespread effects on the body, such as altering its temperature control mechanisms.

TABLE 13.2 Frequency of Sexual Activity by Age and Gender

	M	F	M	F	M	F	M	F	M	F
AGE	**18–26**		**27–38**		**39–50**		**51–64**		**65+**	
N	254	268	353	380	282	295	227	230	212	221
>1/wk	53%	46%	60%	49%	54%	39%	63%	32%	53%	41%
"rarely"	13%	17%	9%	12%	8%	21%	8%	21%	11%	22%

SOURCE: Based on Kellett, J. M. (2000). Older adult sexuality. In L.T. Szuchman & F. Muscarella (Eds.), *Psychological perspectives on human sexuality* (p. 357).

Despite these changes, and despite a general slowing of sexual response times, sexual functioning and sexual pleasure seem to be affected very little for most women (Avis, Stellato, Crawford, Johannes, & Longcope, 2000; Stroope, McFarland, & Uecker, 2015). Many researchers have found only small declines, if any, in the frequency of female sexual activity in middle age (see Table 13.2). Women report less sexual activity than men at every age. A key ingredient for maintaining an active sex life is having a sexual partner, and women are more likely than men to be without a partner (DeLamater & Koepsel, 2015). They are more likely to be widowed than men, and they are less likely to re-partner after either the death of a spouse or a divorce. In one large U.S. study, 89% of 57- to 64-year-old men reported having a sexual partner, compared to 74% of women. Although 78% of men ages 75 to 85 still had partners, only 40% of women did (Waite, Laumann, Das, & Schumm, 2009).

For men in the middle years, changes in the production of *testosterone*, the primary male hormone, are not as dramatic. Some controversy has existed over whether testosterone production declines at all in healthy men, but longitudinal studies in recent years confirm that small average declines do occur, starting as early as the 20s, a process referred to as **andropause** (Ammini, Somsundaram, & Goswami, 2017). Men with health problems, such as cardiovascular disease and overweight, are likely to show a larger drop in testosterone. Lower testosterone levels are thought to contribute to some aspects of physical aging in men, such as loss of muscle mass and bone density. Some erectile dysfunction is also experienced by about 50% of men between 40 and 70 years old, but this seems to be more related to changes in the circulatory system than to hormones. Healthy men remain fertile through old age, even though reproductive structures like the testes, seminal vesicles, and prostate gland do undergo some changes. These changes have little effect on sperm production, but they result in reduced amounts of seminal fluid by the 40s and 50s and a steady decline in the volume and force of ejaculations. Yet, as with women, whereas sexual response times begin to increase in middle age, sexual functioning and sexual pleasure can be maintained (see Table 13.2). For a man with an available sexual partner, how sexually active he will be in his older years is closely correlated with how strong his sex drive was in his younger years (Kellett, 2000) and with his general physical health (Lee, Nazroo, O'Connor, Blake, & Pendleton, 2016). For both men and women, understanding that sexual activity need not be derailed by the normal changes in sexual function that come with age (e.g., slower responses, erectile changes, vaginal dryness, and so on) can be key to maintaining a satisfying sex life (DeLamater & Koepsel, 2015).

In today's popular culture, personal worth is linked to physical beauty, defined in part as a youthful, fit appearance. In such a climate, the most problematic physical changes of middle adulthood for some people can be the wrinkling and sagging of the skin and an increase in body fat (Bessenoff & Del Priore, 2007). Weight gain is not inevitable in middle adulthood, but rather is directly linked to overeating, poor nutrition, or inadequate exercise. Chronic stress and inadequate sleep have also been related to weight gain (McEwen & Karatsoreos, 2015; Roberts, Campbell, & Troop, 2014). Unfortunately, the typical habits of many Americans result in their gaining weight throughout middle adulthood, mostly around the waist and hips. Among the factors contributing to the wrinkling and sagging process are changes in the layers of the skin. For example, elastin, a substance in the cells of the dermis, or middle layer of skin, allows the skin to stretch and contract as we move. After age 30, elastin gradually becomes more brittle, reducing skin elasticity. Areas of the body containing fat, such as the arms, legs, torso, and breasts, usually begin to sag by the 40s and 50s.

COGNITIVE CHANGES IN ADULTHOOD

Age-graded changes in cognitive functioning are experienced throughout adulthood. An enormous research literature exists on adult cognitive change. We humans, including developmental researchers, seem to worry a great deal about what kinds of intellectual declines we can expect as we get older and how we might avoid them. Early findings from cross-sectional studies (Schaie, 1994) showed that most intellectual skills declined fairly steadily after age 25. But in such cross-sectional studies, different ages are represented by people from different cohorts. Many factors contribute to what appear to be age decrements. This is so because different cohorts are often different in breadth of educational, economic, and cultural opportunities (Flynn, 2012; Gerstorf, Ram, Hoppmann, Willis, & Schaie, 2011). Prospective or longitudinal research, which follows people over time, suggests a more complex picture of intellectual change in adulthood. Although some abilities begin to decline early, many cognitive capacities seem to show improvements with age and indicate only small average declines after ages 55 to 60.

One way to make sense of the mixed pattern of improvement and decline through adulthood is to categorize cognitive skills with regard to how heavily they depend on two kinds of underlying intellectual resources: *fluid* and *crystallized* intelligence (Horn & Cattell, 1966). **Fluid intelligence** is also called the **mechanics** of intelligence (Baltes et al., 2006), and refers to basic operational characteristics that seem to directly reflect how well the "hardware" of the nervous system is working, affecting the efficiency of processes like reasoning. Fluid, or mechanical, functions include such things as processing speed and inhibitory mechanisms. They are the most likely kinds of intellectual processes to show declines sometime in middle adulthood. For example, information processing speed may begin to slow down as early as age 30 and it declines fairly rapidly after age 40, so that we are slower to take in information as we get older and slower to respond to it (Kievit et al., 2016; Tucker-Drob, 2011). Inhibitory mechanisms show decrements by about age 40, so that in some tasks, older adults are more easily distracted by irrelevant stimulation than younger adults (Dey, Sommers, & Hasher, 2017).

Executive functions (EFs) are closely linked to fluid intelligence. EFs—working memory, self-regulation (inhibitory control), and cognitive flexibility—are recruited when we effortfully pursue goals, rather than when we function more automatically or intuitively. You have seen in earlier chapters the importance of EFs for the development of skills that support children's and adolescents' academic success. They are important for adult functioning as well, including job success, good quality of life, and even marital harmony (Diamond, 2013). EFs involve activation of the prefrontal cortex, and they affect strategic planning and problem solving, creative thinking, maintaining attention on what is important in a situation, adapting to changing circumstances, avoiding impulsive actions, and so on. EFs show some declines in middle adulthood. These declines are related to changes in fluid intelligence, especially changes in processing speed and ability to gate out irrelevant stimuli.

Working memory provides a good example here. You know that *working memory* stores information that we are thinking about or working with at the present moment. It has a limited capacity, so that only a restricted number of information units can be retained there at one time, and usually only for 15 to 30 seconds, unless we actually keep working with them, that is, unless we make an effort to pay attention to the information. To put it a different way, working memory is the active, attentive part of the mind, where we consciously think and learn. In late middle adulthood, working memory capacity seems to decline. Fewer pieces of information can be attended to at one time, and either problem solving or learning or both can be somewhat affected as a result. Imagine a situation in which you look up and dial a 10-digit phone number, and then you immediately attempt to redial the number. Suppose that at age 30, you could

MyLab Education
Video Example 13.2
Fluid functions decline somewhat in middle adulthood. A woman in her forties describes the decline in her fluid intelligence and the effect on executive functions.

remember about 6 of the digits when you redialed. At age 50, given the same kind of memory task, you would probably remember only 5 of the digits. Clearly, what we are describing here are not catastrophic losses. The modest change is more a nuisance factor than anything else. Most people, by about age 50, notice that they have a little more difficulty than they used to recalling the name of a new acquaintance or solving a complex problem that requires attending to several pieces of information at once. Declines in fluid intelligence seem to make the difference. Slower processing speed may make it harder to keep as many pieces of information in mind simultaneously as we once could or make it difficult to work our way through to the end of a problem before some of the information that we need has disappeared from short-term storage (Mella, Fagot, Lecerf, & de Ribaupierre, 2015). Reduced inhibitory control is also important. For example, we might experience at times "a kind of 'mental clutter' in which extraneous thoughts and plans can interfere with, and possibly crowd out, goal-relevant thoughts and plans" (Zacks, Hasher, & Li, 2000, p. 297).

Another intellectual resource is called **crystallized intelligence** or the **pragmatics** of intelligence (Baltes et al., 2006). It is the compilation of skills and information we have acquired in the course of our lives. Crystallized intelligence, or pragmatics, is a little like the pile of software programs that most of us accumulate for our computers. Our knowledge of language, of how to do a job or to play an instrument, the strategies we have learned for memorizing information or solving problems—all forms of declarative and procedural knowledge (see Chapter 6)—are included. Crystallized intelligence is less likely than fluid intelligence to show declines with age and, for some individuals, can increase even into old age. For most people in middle adulthood, and for most abilities, declining fluid resources are usually balanced or outweighed by continuing steady increases in crystallized resources (Baltes et al., 2006). It is only after about age 60 that losses in fluid intelligence may be great enough to contribute to overall declines in intellectual functioning.

Problem solving in middle adulthood provides a good illustration of the interactive influences of mechanics and pragmatics in overall functioning. As you have just seen, working memory *is* disrupted by mechanical declines with age. Working memory is where we solve problems, but age-related declines in working memory affect problem solving most when either the information that is relevant to the solution or the problem-solving situation is new. When middle adults are solving familiar, everyday problems or problems in areas of their own expertise, the crystallized resources at their disposal often help them to be more effective than younger adults (Salthouse, 2012).

Learning and long-term storage of information also reveal the complex interrelations of mechanics and pragmatics with age. Although the limitations of working memory make it more difficult to get new information into long-term memory, we nonetheless do continue to learn in middle and late adulthood, storing new information from our experiences despite our reduced efficiency. Thus, both younger and older adults add new information to episodic memory—memory for personal experiences—but younger subjects typically learn more with greater ease (Addis, Wong, & Schacter, 2008; Vidal-Piñeiro et al., 2017). To put it differently, we are somewhat less likely, as we get older, to remember specific daily experiences, such as where we parked the car at the shopping mall. However, information already learned appears to be maintained as well as in our younger years. In fact, an older person's semantic memory, her store of factual information, seems to have a richer network of interrelationships as a result of her greater experience, allowing her to retrieve information through many more routes than a younger person can (Salthouse, 2012). As Pak and Stronge (2008) point out, younger adults may have the edge in games that require speedy responding (e.g., a video game), but older adults often outperform younger ones on memory games (e.g., *Trivial Pursuit™* and *Jeopardy™*).

Charness and Bosman (1990) describe an interesting example of the differential effects of age changes in fluid and crystallized intelligence on performance in adulthood. They describe two kinds of chess competitions. In tournament chess, participants make their moves quickly, after deliberating for about 3 minutes. In correspondence chess, the participants can have 3 days to make a move. Clearly, tournament chess makes greater demands on processing speed, whereas correspondence chess seems to draw much more completely on one's knowledge and experience. Not surprisingly, then, top performers win their first world championship in tournament chess at much younger ages, about age 30 on average, than they do in correspondence chess, where the average first-time champion is 46! It is not unusual for middle-aged chess devotees to adapt to declines in fluid intelligence by shifting their focus from tournament chess to correspondence chess as they get older.

In Chapter 15 we will look more closely at cognitive changes in late adulthood, focusing especially on how older adults compensate for losses in fluid intelligence and on the debate over the growth of wisdom.

LIFE-TASK OR LIFE-COURSE CHANGES IN ADULTHOOD

People experience another kind of age-graded change as they move through adulthood. Life-course changes, brought on by shifts in the life tasks that seem most important to us at different times of our lives, have been described by many different theorists. Although each of these theorists tends to emphasize somewhat different aspects of the life experience, you will see commonalities in their observations as we briefly summarize a sampling of these descriptions.

You may recall that Schaie (1977–1978; Schaie & Willis, 2000; see also Chapter 11) proposed a series of stages in adult life, each of which requires the development of new ways to apply and use one's intellectual resources. These changes are directly related to shifts in family roles and in the life tasks that we face as we grow older. In the *achieving stage* of young adulthood, individuals must learn to use logical thinking skills to plan the achievement of long-term goals. In the *responsible stage* of middle adulthood, individuals must learn to use problem-solving skills not only to achieve their own goals but also to help coordinate their needs with those of others for whom they are responsible at home, at work, and in the community. In the *reorganizational stage* of one's elder years, the focus narrows again to reaching personal, practical, day-to-day goals as an adult, devoting thinking skills to managing losses. Finally, in late adulthood, people move into the *reintegrative stage*, when their goals are primarily to conserve energy, and perhaps into a *legacy-leaving stage*, when they use their cognitive resources to help them leave behind a written or oral account of their experience or wisdom.

Schaie emphasizes the shifting allocation of intellectual skills across adulthood, as people confront different kinds of problems related to their age and stage of life. Most other theorists emphasize changes in personality. They do not focus on personality traits, which, as we have seen, are relatively stable in middle adulthood and beyond, but rather they describe structural changes in self-concept and in self-expression.

Perhaps the best-known theory of life-course changes in self-concept is Erik Erikson's, by now quite familiar to you. Erikson (e.g., 1950/1963) describes three stages in self-development in adulthood, based on the kinds of life tasks that become most important to people as they find themselves fully matured and facing the fact that this is the one life that they have to live. Very briefly, in young adulthood, intimacy (vs. isolation) is one's quest: finding a way to validate and expand one's own sense of self by committing to a shared life with others. In middle adulthood, generativity (vs. stagnation) becomes most important, giving one's own life purpose by producing and building for the next generation, through work, community service, or child rearing. By old age, establishing ego integrity (vs. despair) becomes life's task. Ideally, a process of life review helps the elderly adult to develop a sense that her own life is "something that had to be," that she has lived a life that has order, meaning, and dignity (see Chapter 1, especially Table 1.2).

Erikson argued that different concerns reach ascendancy in different age periods. Vaillant (1993; 2012) suggested that two more adult life stages should be added to Erikson's scheme, reflecting that forming deep bonds, becoming productive, and finding meaning in one's life are recurring themes throughout adulthood. In one's mid-20s, career consolidation (vs. self-absorption) is a key focus of self-development. In this phase of life, in addition to ongoing intimacy concerns, making a commitment to work that brings personal satisfaction, regardless of its other rewards, rather than just having a job, becomes important. The most positive development for this period is that such a commitment emerges as an important part of one's identity.

MyLab Education
Video Example 13.3
In the responsible stage of middle adulthood, life focus and life tasks change. The mother in this video, now in her late thirties, focuses her time and energy on her children and the needs of the family, including more responsibility with aging parents.

Vaillant also described a stage that comes near the end of Erikson's generativity stage, in late middle adulthood. This he called the keeper of meaning (vs. rigidity) stage, when the adult expands her generative concerns beyond just making a productive contribution, in order to actually preserve something that is part of the culture. In this sense, adults seek ways to establish the meaningfulness of the work or contributions they have made. For example, Tien, a woman who worked as an aide at her children's day care center, might move on after her own children are grown to join a child care advocacy group in her community, hoping to ensure that future generations of children in her region will have access to the high-quality child care she was able to provide her own children.

As we saw in Chapter 12, research indicates that both intimacy and generativity are central to the lives of young adults. Later in this chapter we will discuss research on how these concerns tend to play out in the arenas of marriage, family life, parenting, and work during the middle years of adulthood.

Several other theorists have proposed stages in adult personality development that repeat many of the themes we see in Erikson's work. They all emphasize that people have fundamental concerns or needs that shift in importance from one adult stage to another. We will briefly describe Levinson's theory here; some additional theories (e.g., Gould, 1978; Loevinger, 1976) are included in schematic comparison in Table 13.3.

In Levinson's account (Levinson, 1986; Levinson & Levinson, 1996), a person's life has structure at any given time. One's life structure is a pattern of relationships between the self and the external world, such as relationships to one's "spouse, lover, family, occupation, religion, leisure, and so on" (Levinson, 1986). There may be many components to the life structure, but Levinson found that at any one time there are usually only one or two really significant, defining components for the self, usually marriage-family and/or occupational components. Levinson identified three major adult stages, or eras: early, middle, and late adulthood. Each of these eras begins with a 5-year transitional period and is marked by a smaller mid-era transition, when the life structure's effectiveness for serving the person's goals is reexamined and may be altered.

Whereas Erikson and Vaillant suggest that certain life tasks occur in a relatively predictable sequence (e.g., first, intimacy needs are greater, then generativity needs), Levinson (1986) argues that life events unfold in many ways depending on a particular individual's life circumstances, gender, and culture and that specific concerns are not necessarily more important in one era than in another. What is predictable, he argues, is the sequence of age periods for building and changing first one life structure and then another. The experience of life changes from one era to the next. Put a different way, what is inevitable in adulthood is that a person will establish and then revise her life structure at particular times as she ages.

In sum, many theorists have identified life-course changes affecting self-concept or self-expression during adulthood. There is by no means complete agreement among these theorists on the character of these changes. For example, following Jung (1963), Levinson (1986) and Gould (1978) describe the midlife transition as a frequently tumultuous time, a period of major upheaval and self-evaluation, not unlike adolescence. You may have heard it referred to as a "midlife crisis." Their research, consisting of longitudinal interview studies of relatively small and somewhat selective samples of adults, tends to support these claims (Gould, 1978; Levinson & Levinson, 1996). But in much larger interview and questionnaire studies, many researchers have found little evidence of widespread midlife distress, although they have found indications of shifting concerns at midlife (Bell, 2014; Lachman, Teshale, & Agrigoroaei, 2015). Crisis-level distress seems most likely to occur as a function of major life events, like financial problems or job loss, which can happen at any time. Individuals who score high on the personality trait of neuroticism are particularly likely to suffer acute distress.

Regardless of such disagreements, there is some similarity among the theoretical descriptions of adult life-course changes. The available empirical work supports the general idea of such change. Some longitudinal research also indicates that major aspects of self, such as intimacy, may be reworked with every major life change, rather than being fully resolved at specific times in the life course (Whitbourne, Sneed, & Sayer, 2009).

Studies of how social networks change over time illustrate this point (Carmichael, Reis, & Duberstein, 2015; Wrzis, Hänel, Wagner, & Neyer, 2013). As we have seen in previous chapters, networks of friends increase in size during adolescence and young adulthood, providing a source of information and support in the quest for adult identity and intimacy. But as adults experience key life events, such as the transition to parenthood and job entry, social networks contract. Friends are fewer, but they are also closer. It appears then that adults rework and intensify their capacity for intimacy in response to such normative life events.

Despite the enormous variation in the immediate details of adult lives—from culture to culture, from cohort to cohort, from family to family, and from individual to individual—there appear to be some life changes that are widely experienced. These changes lead each of us to reformulate, or at least reevaluate, ourselves and our lives periodically. Much more research is needed to establish the specifics of these changes and whom they do and do not affect.

For professionals, awareness of potential stage changes can help enrich our understanding of clients. For example, suppose a 45-year-old woman comes to a counselor looking for help with marital problems she has tolerated for 20 years. We might be inclined to wonder why she is coming now and how likely it is that change can be effected after so many years of entrenched behavior patterns. The answers to both questions may be partly a function of life stage. Many theorists see the 40s as a time when reassessment of one's life structure is very likely and when willingness to act on the basis of one's individual propensities, rather than strictly in adherence with social expectations, increases (see Table 13.3). Vaillant (1977) suggests that generativity needs are likely to reorganize, so that direct caregiving to one's spouse or children is less likely to meet an individual's needs than opportunities to seek broader meaning in life by finding ways to preserve the culture. Thus, not only is it a likely time for this woman to reassess her life, but also it may be a time when she will be open to trying new ways of meeting her needs.

History-Graded Changes

The historical events that affect our whole cohort are another source of change in adult lives. People are partly a product of the historical context in which they develop. Imagine that you were a young adult parent trying to support your children during the Great Depression in the 1930s or the Great Recession of the late 2000s. You would take a job wherever you found one, no matter how difficult the work, and you would

---

TABLE 13.3 Adult Life Stages: Some Theories of Self-Development

APPROXIMATE AGE PERIOD	ERIKSON	VAILLANT	LOEVINGER	GOULD
Adolescence	Identity (vs. Identity Diffusion)	(like Erikson)	Conscientious—Conformist	Separating from parents: becoming independent
Young Adulthood	Intimacy (vs. Isolation)	(like Erikson)	Individualistic	"Nobody's baby": becoming a competent, self-maintaining adult
Middle Adulthood (Early)	Generativity (vs. Stagnation)	Generativity—Career consolidation (vs. Self-Absorption); producing	Autonomous	Opening up: exploring inner consciousness; coming to deeper understanding of self and needs
Middle Adulthood (Late)		Generativity—Keeper of Meaning (vs. Rigidity); giving, mentoring		Midlife: finding the courage and resourcefulness to act on deeper feelings; awareness of pressure of time
Late Adulthood	Ego Integration (vs. Despair)		Integrated	Beyond midlife: establishing true autonomy; becoming inner-directed rather than governed by roles; "I own myself"

probably be grateful for it. What effect might years of deprivation and struggle have on your tendency toward conscientiousness? Or, think about moving through early adulthood during the social upheavals and sexual revolution of the 1960s. Do you think this experience might have some effect on your openness to experience? History-graded events, also called **cohort effects**, provide a context for development and also influence it directly (Kiang, Tseng, & Yip, 2016).

The year of your birth marks your entry into a cohort of peers who accompany you through age-graded developmental changes (toddlerhood, puberty, and so on) within the context of a specific set of historical events (wars, technological shifts, etc.). The effect of history is particularly linked to a person's age and stage of life (such as coming of age in a time of war, when you could be drafted into military service). In addition to age-graded and history-graded changes, we also progress through stages of the family life cycle as child, parent, grandparent, and so on. Researchers who take a **life-course perspective** remind us that development is influenced by the intersection of chronological age (life time), family-related roles (family time), and membership in a birth cohort (historical time; Elder, Shanahan, & Jennings, 2015). If society experiences an economic recession that results in a lengthy period of corporate downsizing, a young father who has just completed a training program in computer repair might see his chances of getting a well-paying job shrink. He may have to wait to buy a first house, ultimately limiting the lifetime equity he can accrue. Because his family must continue to reside in a low-cost apartment, his preschool son might also be affected because of missed educational opportunities that would have been available with a move to a more advantaged school district. Note that despite the important implications of the economic downturn for this young parent's life, his own grandparents, who are retired and receiving a fixed pension, would not be much affected.

Twenge (2000) provides an example of how sociocultural and historical context influences the personality development of cohorts of individuals. She reviewed published reports of child and adolescent anxiety from 1952 to 1993 to see if levels had changed over these years. Her distressing finding showed that the average child in America during the 1980s scored higher on anxiety than child psychiatric patients from the 1950s. Further analysis allowed her to demonstrate that these increases were associated with the breakdown of social connections and with increases in physical and psychological threats. Economic recessions were not related to the increase in anxiety. Twenge's results imply that recent cohorts are living in a world that is less favorable to their positive development than the world in which their own parents grew up. A context that provides for fewer or weaker social bonds at the same time that threats are expanding heightens the sense of vulnerability for these young people, who are truly growing up in an "age of anxiety." Twenge and her colleagues (2014) did a similar analysis of trends from 1972 to 2012 in U.S. adults' "trust in others," defined as belief in the ability, reliability, and honesty of other people. For every generation sampled (the post–World War II "baby boom" generation, "genXers," and "millennials"), there was a steady decline in trust that was linked to a specific economic change: the rise in income inequality, that is, the widening gap between rich and poor. This historical change appears to be corroding adults' fundamental beliefs about other people.

THE SOCIAL GRADIENT AND LIFE-COURSE DEVELOPMENT

What has been absent from some formulations of history-graded effects is the role of culture. Sociocultural effects on development are not restricted to time-limited incidents, nor do they necessarily exert the same influence on all members of a generation. Developmental change also results from structural features of society. For individuals and families, one's place on the rungs of society's status and economic ladders has long-term consequences. Lower status contributes to poorer life outcomes on a number of measures, especially to disturbingly higher rates of illness as people age (see Figure 13.3). Socioeconomic status (SES) is a complex concept that has typically been assessed using indicators like education, income, and zip code. Historically, researchers often considered it a nuisance variable that needed to be statistically controlled so that the "real" differences could emerge. Nuisance variables are hypothesized to be extraneous to the effects researchers intend to investigate. More contemporary views recognize that SES effects are real, direct, and powerful. Increasingly, researchers are adopting the term **socioeconomic position (SEP)**, instead of SES, because it reflects a more systems-centered approach and recognizes the contributions of societal stratification on development. Because the most common impulse within society is to organize itself in a hierarchical fashion, those at the bottom usually end up with restricted access to resources and opportunities. This step-wise top-to-bottom phenomenon is called the **social gradient**. Marmot and Wilkinson (2009) explain how SEP impacts life chances:

> Social organization also structures advantage and disadvantage longitudinally. Advantage or disadvantage in one phase of the life course is likely to have been preceded by, and to be succeeded by, similar advantage or disadvantage in the other phases of life. A child raised in an affluent home is likely to succeed educationally, which will favour entry to the more privileged sectors of the labour market, where an occupational pension scheme will provide financial security in old age. At the other extreme, a child from a disadvantaged home is likely to achieve few educational qualifications and, leaving school at the minimum age, to enter the unskilled labour market where low pay and hazardous work combine with no occupational pension, which ensures reliance on welfare payments in old age. (p. 41)

Life at the bottom of the social ladder is not easy. Across the world, the poor suffer most in terms of morbidity and mortality compared to their more advantaged peers (Anderson et al., 2017). Figure 13.3 depicts the linear increase in incidence rates for disease by SES level.

The study of SEP represents an example of a multidimensional, life-course approach to development that incorporates societal/cultural considerations. The impact of socially embedded influences can be studied at the individual or group level, at sensitive periods of development, and longitudinally across the life span. Neuroscientific research is also targeting the processes through which SEP becomes embodied via brain pathways that mediate its effects (Gianaros & Manuck, 2010). Figure 13.4 presents potential ways to measure SEP at different stages of the life span.

For the most part, life circumstances associated with low SEP include economic hardship (not having necessary resources like food and shelter), loss of job, income, housing or material possessions, debt, evictions, and insecurity. Now, consider the effects of systematic discrimination. What might membership in a socially devalued

FIGURE 13.3 The social gradient in health.

Rates of selected illnesses (osteoarthritis, chronic diseases, hypertension, and cervical cancer) per 100,000 as a function of socioeconomic status.

(a) Osteo- arthritis	(b) Chronic Disease	(c) Hyper- tension	(d) Cervical Cancer
25	150	16	30
20	125	14	25
15	100	12	20
10	75	10	15
5	50	8	10

SOURCE: Based on Matthews, K. & Gallo, K. (2011). Psychological perspectives on pathways linking socio-economic status and physical health, *Annual Review of Psychology, 62*, 501–530.

FIGURE 13.4 Measuring the socioeconomic trajectory over the life span.

Examples of life-course measures for socioeconomic position.

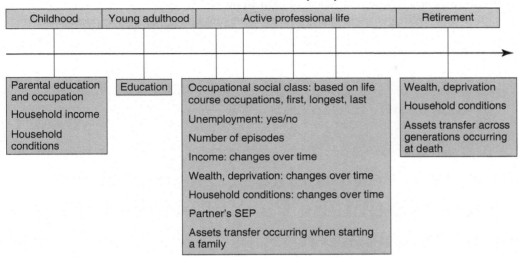

Life course socioeconomic trajectory

| Childhood | Young adulthood | Active professional life | Retirement |

Parental education and occupation

Household income

Household conditions

Education

Occupational social class: based on life course occupations, first, longest, last

Unemployment: yes/no

Number of episodes

Income: changes over time

Wealth, deprivation: changes over time

Household conditions: changes over time

Partner's SEP

Assets transfer occurring when starting a family

Wealth, deprivation

Household conditions

Assets transfer across generations occurring at death

SOURCE: Based on Galobardes, B., Lynch, J., & Smith, G. D. (2007). Measuring socioeconomic position in health research. *British Medical Bulletin, 81–82,* 21–37.

group add to the list of hardships? Would it matter if the individuals felt they had adequate resources to cope with discrimination? Life course researchers are also beginning to examine the long-term impact of racial discrimination on life span development, especially in health-related areas. Just as the sociocultural influences of one's era may create an "age of anxiety," so too might they affect disease processes. The disparities in health among different racial and ethnic groups have been well documented (National Academies of Science, Engineering, and Medicine, 2017). Effects of race frequently co-vary with socioeconomic status, but the particular contribution of racial discrimination appears to increase the damaging effects. Reliable data have shown that for certain historically disadvantaged groups, especially African Americans, the health disparities are stark. Heart disease, diabetes, strokes, hypertension, and obesity occur at much higher rates for African Americans than for all other major racial/ethnic groups (Zonderman, Mode, Ejiogu, & Evans, 2016). The search is on for a comprehensive understanding of how poverty and racism "gets under the skin" by altering physiological reactivity to result, ultimately, in these dramatic health disparities (McEwen, 2012). A clearer understanding of the mechanisms will increase our repertoire of effective prevention strategies (Braveman & Gottlieb, 2014).

Nonnormative Changes

Just as history-graded changes can significantly affect the development of a whole cohort, individual lives are also changed by unexpected events. These events are called nonnormative events, "bolt from the blue" experiences that we don't anticipate, yet that can have powerful developmental effects. Crises such as traumatic illnesses, accidents, imprisonment, the untimely death of a loved one, or even positive events such as winning a lottery can be considered nonnormative. They create new sets of circumstances for people, and these have the potential to alter developmental trajectories (Boyce, Wood, Daly, & Sedikides, 2015; Leikas & Salmela-Aro, 2015).

Imagine a woman at age 45 who has worked hard as a parent and homemaker and looks forward to seeing each of her children move into adult independence. A car accident suddenly leaves her 19-year-old son a quadriplegic. The financial resources she and her husband had carefully saved for their

PCN Black/PCN Photography/Alamy Stock Photo

What do you think might be the nonnormative and cohort effects of the events of September 11, 2001, on people's lives?

retirement and their children's college years are soon gone, and the mother's dreams of opening a small craft shop are dashed. She is a somewhat introverted woman, but the special needs of her son create circumstances that move her to take initiative with lawyers, insurance companies, and government agencies. Literally, her personality and the whole course of her life begin to move in a new direction. So middle age, like the "ages" before it, is both continuous and changing. Stable personality traits are influenced by age, life stage, history, and unplanned events as people continue to adapt to life.

MyLab Education Self-Check 13.3.

Key Developmental Tasks of Midlife: The Continuing Pursuit of Intimacy and Generativity

13.4 Identify factors that threaten primary relationships and generativity in midlife and discuss resources and interventions that support successful adaptation in these areas of development.

In middle adulthood, as in young adulthood, loving relationships and productive, meaningful work continue to be critical elements in the construction of a satisfying life. As you know, Erikson saw intimacy—broadly defined as sharing oneself with another—as a more prominent concern in young adulthood and generativity—defined as the need to create and produce—as a more central focus of middle adulthood. However, it is clear from available research that although the relative balance between these two concerns may shift (see Chapters 12 and 14), both remain important in middle adulthood and beyond. In the following sections we will further explore intimacy issues by examining how marital relationships form, develop, and sometimes fail during adulthood. We will continue our discussion of generativity by considering the parental role from the adult's perspective, and we will touch on other generativity issues in the middle years, having to do with work and community.

Intimacy: Marriage and Other Primary Relationships

One of the most valuable adaptations we humans can make is to establish and maintain close interpersonal relationships. In adulthood, close ties take on a variety of forms, and the number and diversity of forms is increasing. Marriage has provided the traditional structure within which such relationships exist. Approximately 49% of the U.S. population were married in 2016, a figure down from 62% in 1990 (U.S. Bureau of the Census, 2018; see Figure 13.5). More than one third of all households in the United States were single-person households. Cohabitation was also on the rise. Although there has been a steep rise in the number of people living alone or as unmarried partners, a large majority of the population is likely to marry at least once.

The definition of "family" has indeed become more inclusive in the 21st century and refers to more than the traditional nuclear family with its own biological children. Particularly since the social changes initiated in the 1960s, people have felt more free to meet their needs for intimacy and connection in a variety of ways. Extended, multigenerational families, adoptive and foster families, same-sex unions, remarried or blended families, single-parent families, and "families" composed of several people living together without legal ties are all examples of new trends in family formation (e.g., Pew Research Center, 2017). To illustrate, one third of the children adopted in the

FIGURE 13.5 Percentage of U.S. population over age 15 in different marital status categories in 2016.

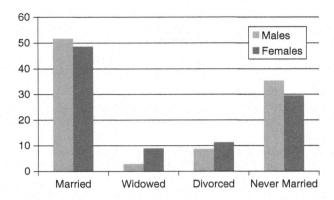

SOURCE: U.S. Bureau of the Census (2018). America's families and living arrangements: 2016, Table A1. Retrieved from https://www.census.gov/data/tables/2016/demo/families/cps-2016.html

United States in 2001 went to single women (Coontz, 2005). Some individuals will be part of several different kinds of families as they progress through their lives.

Clearly, psychological wellness does not depend upon any one specific relationship configuration. It is important for helping professionals to expand their definition of family and to work towards ways of promoting optimal functioning for each of these forms. As Coontz (2005) has argued, "moving in lockstep through a series of predictable transitions is no longer a route to personal security. Each man and woman must put together a highly individualized sequence of transitions . . . a 'do-it-yourself' biography" (p. 277). Regardless of whether people are married, helpers must offer resources that promote healthy relationships and, where children are involved, to improve parenting.

Despite greater social acceptance of alternative family styles, researchers have discovered that good marriages or primary relationships confer a number of physical and psychological benefits that other states may not provide (Perelli-Harris & Styrc, 2018). When researchers compare married to unmarried adults, they typically find that married people report higher levels of sexual and emotional satisfaction and happiness and lower rates of mental illness, drug or alcohol abuse, and physical illness (Hoppmann, Gerstorf, Willis, & Schaie, 2011; Robles, 2014; Waite & Joyner, 2001).

Do cohabiting partners accrue the same benefits? Some studies find more depressive symptoms, poorer relationship quality, or less overall satisfaction in cohabiting than in married couples. But other studies have found similar patterns of well-being in both cohabiting and married couples (Musick & Bumpass, 2012; Perrelli-Harris & Styrc, 2018). It seems likely that many benefits are similar, such as the day-to-day economic and social support that comes with having a partner. On the other hand, whereas marriage is seen by many as a lifetime commitment, for many couples cohabitation is not; it is more of a "trial run." Therefore, cohabitation is accompanied by more uncertainty about the future than marriage. In addition, there are long-term economic benefits to marriage in the United States that may be less available to cohabiting partners, such as assurance of retirement income for surviving spouses. In one study, single mothers who were the sole support for their children for a period of 10 years or more during their lifetimes were 55% more likely to live in poverty at ages 65 to 75, regardless of their current marital status (Johnson & Favreault, 2004).

Tolerance for alternative family arrangements is growing, and as this cultural shift progresses, the benefits of cohabitation and marriage may be coming more and more into alignment. More research is needed to understand how alternative relationship forms affect well-being in a changing world. One thing that is clear at this point is that many factors mediate and moderate the benefits of marriage and other intimate partnerships. One factor is gender. For example, women overall are likely to be less satisfied with their marriages over time than men. Two thirds of divorces filed after age 40 are initiated by women (Hacker, 2003). Another factor is socioeconomic status or position. Consistent with the generally more negative outcomes of lower SEP, for example, women without high school degrees are more likely to divorce (60% rate) than women with college degrees (33% rate) (Coontz, 2005).

Although we use marriage as the prototypical vehicle to illustrate the development of intimacy over the adult life span, we acknowledge that this is not the only road, nor even the best one, for many people. We do not underestimate the importance of friendships nor devalue single status in adulthood. However, as you have seen, demographics show that most people, male and female, heterosexual and nonheterosexual, will marry or participate in some kind of committed relationship for at least some period of time in their lives. (See Box 13.1.) In some Latin American cultures, there is a historical acceptance of long-term consensual unions (Landale & Fennelly, 1992) even though couples are not formally wed. After divorce, people tend to find new partners. Kreider (2006) estimated that in the United States over half of individuals are likely to remarry within 5 years. Between 2008 and 2012, about 17% of U.S. adults were in second or later marriages (Lewis & Kreider, 2015). Although the traditional marital and family life cycle may not be the best descriptive fit for everyone, there are aspects of its stages that can help us understand many kinds of close adult relationships. The nature of intimate relationships, inside or outside marriage, is defined by mutual sharing of joys and sorrows, reaching compromises and working out problems, and developing a sense of "we-ness."

Box 13.1: Changing Families: Gay and Lesbian Couples and Their Children

In 2002, Steve Lofton and Roger Croteau, residents of Florida, achieved media fame when they tried to adopt a 10-year-old boy who had been their foster child since infancy. These men were surrogate parents to five foster children at the time, including several with special needs, but state law prohibited adoption of minor children by gay adults. Lofton and Croteau eventually lost their court challenge to Florida's adoption laws, and the child they had raised was put up for adoption by strangers, despite the child's wish to stay with his foster parents (Patterson, 2004).

Lofton and Croteau are among a growing cohort of gay and lesbian adults who head households, form families, and raise children. They have challenged both custom and law by asking for the opportunity to marry and/or to raise their biological or adopted children. In 2015, the U.S. Supreme Court ended decades of state-by-state battles for marriage rights by declaring same-sex marriage legal throughout the country. It is now also possible for nonheterosexual adults to petition for adoption in all 50 states. Families with nonheterosexual individuals or same-sex couples at the helm are increasing in number throughout the Western world. What are the developmental consequences of these newly constituted families, both for the adults and for the children they raise?

Characteristics of Committed Relationships Between Gay and Lesbian Adults

Although media images of gay and lesbian relationships often suggest they are unstable and dysfunctional, "research has documented that many contemporary lesbians and gay men

establish enduring intimate relationships" (Peplau & Fingerhut, 2007, p. 418). In a review of existing literature, Herek (2006) found that across many studies, 40% to 70% of gay men and 45% to 80% of lesbian women were in committed relationships, many of which had lasted for at least a decade (see also Herek, Norton, Allen, & Sims, 2010). By 2017, approximately 61% of cohabiting gay and lesbian couples were married, up from about 38% just prior to the Supreme Court decision of 2015 (Jones, 2017).

Same-sex couples appear to be similar to heterosexual couples in many ways. Clearly, they face some different stresses, such as continuing social stigma associated with their sexuality (Gates, 2016). But on the whole, the stability of their relationships depends on the same factors as the stability of heterosexual relationships: "positive attraction forces, such as love and satisfaction, the availability of alternatives, and barriers to leaving a relationship, such as psychological, emotional and financial costs" (Peplau & Fingerhut, 2007, p. 412). In a five-year study that controlled for factors such as age and education, relationship satisfaction was the same for married heterosexual and cohabiting homosexual couples at the start of the study, and for both types of couple, satisfaction declined somewhat over time, at similar rates (Kurdek, 1998). More recent cross-sectional comparisons also find greater similarities than differences between same-sex and different-sex couples on a wide range of measures indicating marital satisfaction and mental health (e.g., Ellis & Davis, 2017; Kornblith, Green, Casey, & Tiet, 2016).

Social support from family and friends is an important ingredient in the health and well-being of couples, especially couples with children, whether married or cohabiting, and whether same-sex or different-sex. In 2004, Kurdek found that same-sex couples generally received less support from relatives than heterosexual couples, and they were more likely to rely on friendship networks. But in newer studies, consistent with substantial increases in public acceptance of same-sex unions (McCarthy, 2015), same- and different-sex couples who are adoptive parents have reported similar levels of support from their families and friends (Sumontha, Farr, & Patterson, 2016). It also seems that when partners make legal commitments to one another, via civil unions or marriage, families tend to be more supportive, although it is difficult to say whether couples with supportive families are more likely to legalize their relationships or whether families become more supportive once couples legalize their relationships (Balsam et al., 2008).

There are some differences between same-sex and heterosexual couples. Same-sex couples, especially lesbian couples, are more likely to endorse equal power in their relationships, and they tend to be more egalitarian in the way they divide household chores, decision making, and child rearing duties (Herek, 2006; Farr & Patterson, 2013). It may help that partners in same-sex couples have been socialized into the same gender roles, making their communication styles more similar (Garanzini et al., 2017). There are some differences in exclusivity and frequency of sexual relations as well (Peplau & Fingerhut, 2007; Whitton, Weitbrecht, & Kuryluk, 2015). Gay men are less likely to restrict sex to their primary partner than lesbian or heterosexual women or heterosexual men, and male couples are more likely to openly agree to be non-exclusive than female couples or male-female couples. For all types of couple, the frequency of sexual relations is quite variable, usually declining over time. However, on the average, gay couples have more frequent sex than heterosexual couples, who have more frequent sex than lesbian couples (Peplau & Fingerhut, 2007). In a longitudinal study, Balsam et al. (2008) found that for lesbian couples, having more sex was an important predictor of relationship quality, more so than for gay or heterosexual couples. The authors suggest that it may be especially important for lesbian couples to overcome whatever problems they face in maintaining a good sexual relationship.

The Children of Gay and Lesbian Parents

Many gay and lesbian adults have biological children from prior heterosexual relationships. Others use artificial insemination, surrogacy, or some combination of modern technologies in order to have biological children. And many others adopt. As you have seen, adoption is now legal for same-sex couples across the United States, although obstacles remain. For example, at this writing, in 7 U.S. states, child welfare agencies can refuse services or placement to nonheterosexual individuals or to same-sex couples if such placements conflict with their religious beliefs (Movement Advancement Project, 2018).

Are there any special risks or protective factors that affect children raised by same-sex couples? A growing body of research, some of it longitudinal, some of it using large representative samples, compares outcomes for children reared by homosexual and heterosexual couples. Many more studies include lesbian than gay couples, but both groups are represented in the literature. In general, the findings are quite consistent: The risk of

problematic outcomes is no greater for children of homosexual parents than for children reared by heterosexual couples (see reviews by Gates, 2015; Goldberg & Gartrell, 2014; Meezan & Rauch, 2005; Patterson, 2017). Meezan and Rauch (2005) summarize four key findings:

- The parenting styles of homosexual parents are like those of heterosexual parents, although gay and lesbian parents are somewhat more likely to report using strategies consistent with an authoritative parenting style (high levels of warmth and control). Despite the stereotypic concern that gay fathers might be more likely to sexually abuse their children, gay men are no more likely than heterosexual men to sexually abuse children (Patterson, 2004).
- Children of lesbian and gay parents do not seem more confused about their gender identities than children of heterosexual parents (Bos & Sandfort, 2010). Some studies (but not all) find that they engage in less gender stereotypic toy play than children reared by heterosexual parents, perhaps because their parents are likely to be more liberal in their attitudes toward gender nonconformity (Goldberg & Gartrell, 2014). The vast majority of children grow up to be heterosexual, regardless of their parents' sexual orientation, and it appears that base rates of homosexuality are about the same for children of homosexual and heterosexual parents. Daughters in lesbian-headed households are more willing to accept others' alternative sexual identities, more likely to have homosexual friends, and more willing to say that they would consider same-sex relationships. Both boys and girls in lesbian-headed households are also more likely as children to express concern that they might become homosexual, a concern that disappears in adolescence. The teenage children of lesbian couples are no more likely to engage in same-sex sexual exploration than the children of heterosexual couples (Goldberg & Gartrell, 2014).
- No differences have been found in the cognitive abilities, self-esteem, and social or emotional development of children reared by homosexual parents.
- The majority of studies find no difficulties with peers related to the social stigma of having homosexual parents, although parents worry that their children will be ridiculed, and children sometimes engage in behaviors that keep their families' characteristics hidden. But often, children of same-sex parents rely more on direct confrontation, such as telling the other party that their comments are unacceptable or seeking support from teachers or peers, strategies that are recommended for managing bullying in general (see Chapter 7; Goldberg & Gartrell, 2014). Rivers, Poteat, and Noret (2008) also found that children of same-sex couples report using fewer school-based supports than children of heterosexual couples. Apparently, school staff are unlikely to acknowledge alternative family structures, and children often feel that school-based supports are not really intended for them. However, such practices may be changing as public acceptance of nonheterosexuality increases.

Overall, gay and lesbian parents appear to be as successful at child rearing as heterosexual parents. Consider one

(continued)

study that included lesbian and heterosexual couples and their children. The children were all conceived through artificial insemination arranged through the same sperm bank, so that one parent was biologically related to the child and one was not. When children averaged 7 years old, both parents and children were assessed using a variety of scales. The results did not depend on the parents' sexual orientation but on the same risk and protective factors that appear to affect all parents and their children. "Family process variables such as parental adjustment and couple adjustment were more strongly related to children's outcomes than were family structural variables such as parental sexual orientation or relationship status" (Fulcher, Sutfin, Chan, Scheib, & Patterson, 2005, p. 294).

THE FAMILY LIFE CYCLE

Marriages (and other primary relationships) change as partners age and the demands of family life ebb and flow. The family life cycle, a normative, stagelike sequence of traditional family development in intact marriages, has been described in several ways. For example, Duvall (1971) described a historically typical sequence of stages, from early marriage, to early childbearing, to parenting children through various age periods, to launching children, becoming "empty-nesters," and subsequently facing old age. Carter and McGoldrick (1999) developed a similar description and specified the tasks that accompany each stage (see Table 13.4). In the next section, we borrow from this latter description to highlight some important transitions and challenges facing families. Then we take a closer look at marriage itself and address theories of marital satisfaction and dysfunction.

STAGES OF THE FAMILY LIFE CYCLE

Finding a mate is a task that typically involves a relatively lengthy period of experimentation, especially in Western cultures. Mate selection has been likened to a "winnowing

TABLE 13.4 Family Life Cycle Stages, Transitions, and Tasks

FAMILY LIFE CYCLE STAGE	EMOTIONAL PROCESS OF TRANSITION: KEY PRINCIPLES	SECOND-ORDER CHANGES IN FAMILY STATUS REQUIRED TO PROCEED DEVELOPMENTALLY
Leaving home: single young adults	Accepting emotional and financial responsibility for self	a. Differentiation of self in relation to family of origin b. Development of intimate peer relationships c. Establishment of self in respect to work and financial independence
The joining of families through marriage: the new couple	Commitment to new system	a. Formation of marital system b. Realignment of relationships with extended families and friends to include spouse
Families with young children	Accepting new members into the system	a. Adjusting marital system to make space for children b. Joining in child rearing, financial and household tasks c. Realignment of relationships with extended family to include parenting and grandparenting roles
Families with adolescents	Increasing flexibility of family boundaries to permit children's independence and grandparents' frailties	a. Shifting of parent–child relationships to permit adolescent to move into and out of system b. Refocus on midlife marital and career issues c. Beginning shift toward caring for older generation
Launching children and moving on	Accepting a multitude of exits from and entries into the family system	a. Renegotiation of marital system as a dyad b. Development of adult-to-adult relationships between grown children and their parents c. Realignment of relationships to include in-laws and grandchildren d. Dealing with disabilities and death of parents (grandparents)
Families in later life	Accepting the shifting generational roles	a. Maintaining own and/or couple functioning and interests in face of physiological decline: exploration of new familial and social role options b. Support for more central role of middle generation c. Making room in the system for the wisdom and experience of the elderly, supporting the older generation without overfunctioning for them d. Dealing with loss of spouse, siblings, and other peers and preparation for death

SOURCE: Carter, B. & McGoldrick, M. (2005). *The expanded family life circle: Indvidual, family and social perspectives* (3rd ed.). Upper Saddle River, NJ: Pearson Education, Inc. Used by permission of Pearson Education, Inc.

process" by which people go through the step-by-step elimination of ineligible candidates until they settle on a partner (Blackwell & Lichter, 2004). According to this view, people initially select potential dates on the basis of physical attractiveness and personality characteristics from a pool of available, eligible candidates. Further sorting or filtering out follows on the basis of homogamy, or similarity to oneself in religion, SES, race, education, and so on (Horwitz et al., 2016; Luo, 2017). We saw in Chapter 12 that similarity in attachment style is also likely to increase attraction, especially for secure individuals, although insecure individuals are more likely to maintain relationships with individuals who have complementary styles of attachment.

What about love? In the United States, most people believe that love is the most important consideration when choosing a mate (Sprecher & Hatfield, 2017). You might be surprised to learn that this belief is not universal. For example, a cross-cultural study by Buss (1989) found that people from various cultures considered other factors to be more important. Males in South Africa saw maturity and ability to keep house as more significant than love in choosing a partner. And Chinese women valued emotional stability and the desire for a family as important criteria for mate selection.

Sternberg's (1986, 2006) view of love, composed of the three elements of passion, intimacy, and commitment, which were introduced in Chapter 12, may help us understand these differences. The romantic ideal of love portrayed in many movies and songs embodies the element of passion. This is the aspect of love most closely associated with sexuality and romance. Love that includes passion without intimacy or commitment is called infatuation. Intimacy refers to feelings of attachment or emotional closeness. It characterizes one's willingness to trust another, to value her support, and to care about her well-being. (Note that Sternberg defines "intimacy" differently from Erikson, who defines it more broadly.) According to Sternberg, when intimacy is present in a relationship without the other elements, a state of liking exists, which is similar to friendship.

The third element, commitment, is present when partners agree to love each other or make a commitment to sustain that love. Maintaining a commitment without intimacy or passion results in the state of "empty love." Sternberg proposed that any of the three elements can be either present or absent in a relationship, accounting for eight different kinds of love (see Table 13.5). He has expanded on these ideas by suggesting that people hold implicit narratives for love or "love stories," which direct their choice of a mate and the course of their relationships (Sternberg, 2006). Sternberg posits that those who have matching scripts, or similar implicit narratives, stand the best chance of having a compatible relationship. Each script emphasizes certain elements, such as emotional maturity or the commitment factor, as more important than

Table 13.5 Sternberg's Eight Kinds of Love

| | ELEMENTS* | | |
KINDS OF LOVE	INTIMACY	PASSION	DECISION/COMMITMENT
Nonlove	−	−	−
Liking	+	−	−
Infatuation	−	+	−
Empty Love	−	−	+
Romantic Love	+	+	−
Companionate Love	+	−	+
Fatuous Love	−	+	+
Consummate Love	+	+	+

*Element present (+) or absent (−)

SOURCE: Based on Sternberg, R. J. (1986). A triangular theory of love. *Psychological Review*, *93*, 123.

others, and "love scripts" are heavily influenced by cultural values. In contemporary U.S. culture, elements of romance and sexual passion are typically central to the definition of love and are considered very important for relationship satisfaction and mate selection. Love, it seems, is a social construction and we are strongly influenced by the conceptions of love that are taught by our culture.

Once the members of a couple make a commitment to each other, they begin to develop a new marital or relationship system that is a creative synthesis of the couple's original family systems. Marriages, then, are more than the joining of two individuals. The couple must develop a sense of "we-ness" that is not so rigid that it isolates them from their original family systems nor so weak that it dissolves under pressure from them.

With time, the couple may become parents, creating a new rung on the generational ladder and reaching a new stage in the family life cycle. Caretaking responsibilities then must be integrated into the marital relationship, and each partner needs to adjust to the new parental role. As children move through the adolescent period, the family needs to adapt to children's increasing demands for independence. They must learn how to provide the stability and flexibility that characterize authoritative parenting for adolescents.

Next, a couple must deal with the transition of launching their children and renegotiating the marital relationship. Adult children need to balance the attachments they have with parents with those they form outside the family. Parents need to strive for acceptance of their adult children's extrafamilial attachments as well as of their careers and other personal choices. Overall, all generations need to work toward two goals: tolerance of independence and maintenance of connections. Among families in later life, the transitions involved in grandparenthood, loss of spouse, and physical decline produce further challenges that must be dealt with flexibly.

MARRIAGE AND ITS DISCONTENTS

Recall that the great majority of individuals marry at least once during their lifetimes. Clearly, many of these unions do not last "till death do us part." People still divorce in record numbers despite a modest decline in the divorce rate since 1979. It is surprisingly difficult to determine accurately the likelihood that a marriage will end in divorce, but common estimates based on census data in the United States are that 40% to 50% of first marriages and up to 60% of remarriages end in divorce. These rates do not account for the number of unions that break up without benefit of legal divorce.

Women typically experience a 45% drop in standard of living following a divorce. Each year approximately one million children witness the dissolution of their parents' marriages and subsequently often share in their mothers' reduced circumstances. Yet divorce wreaks more than financial hardship for children. Researchers have documented increased emotional and behavioral problems, such as underachievement, antisocial behavior, and depression in children and adolescents after divorce (Gahler & Palmtag, 2015; see Box 13.2). Given that divorce is sometimes the best or the only alternative to a troubled marriage and that not every child of divorce suffers dire consequences, we should nonetheless consider how to help prevent what is so often a powerfully negative event in people's lives.

WHAT MAKES A MARRIAGE FAIL?

In the United States, the legal grounds for divorce are usually "irreconcilable differences." What makes a difference irreconcilable? How do some people manage to reconcile their conflicts whereas others do not? Are the differences due to the nature of the conflicts or to something about the individuals themselves? These are some of the questions that marital and family researchers have attempted to answer. Increasingly, researchers have relied upon longitudinal studies to describe the course of marriage and to help them identify predictors of distress and divorce as they develop over time. On a more fine-grained level, they have also explored the nature of distressed and nondistressed couples' interactions so that therapeutic recommendations can be made. We will focus on some important research findings in both of these areas to give

MyLab Education
Video Example 13.4
Following her divorce, Pam faces the challenges of raising two children, discovering emerging problems for her daughter, and recognizing mistakes she made in dealing with the problems. How can parents in similar situations take steps to reduce the risks faced by children like Laurel?

Box 13.2: When Parents Divorce

Georgia and Jim, an affluent White couple, were married for 12 years. Georgia had an impairment that made it impossible for her to drive, although she competently handled most aspects of child rearing and homemaking. She felt isolated in a suburban neighborhood without public transportation, living far from her extended family. Jim brushed aside Georgia's frustrations. He felt that suburban environments were best for children. He believed that he was more than generous with his time as the family "chauffeur," and that Georgia was dismissive of the benefits of his successful career. Jim made lots of time for his family, somewhat enjoying his power as transportation guru, and he was jealous of his relationship with the beautiful and gregarious Georgia. He feared what "too much freedom" might bring. Georgia defied Jim's controlling strategies in a variety of ways. Vitriolic battles ensued, with mutual accusations of disloyalty, brutality, and unfaithfulness.

The couple's children, ages 3, 5, and 9, were caught in the headlights as their parents' fears and frustrations drove a once vital marital relationship into a brick wall. Divorce proceedings were marked by repeated custody and financial court battles. Eventually Georgia moved the children to an urban condominium; Jim found a house with some acreage two hours away. The oldest child, Emily, was continually torn by conflicting loyalties, as both parents treated her as a confidante and ally in their battles. At the worst of times, Emily, still a pre-adolescent, was often in charge of her younger siblings overnight, while their mother explored her newfound freedom. Emily was strictly enjoined not to reveal this arrangement to anyone, especially her father. Her father was not much more responsible: At times he insisted on extensive visits from his children, during which he pumped them for information about their mother, and at other times he "punished" their mother by refusing to see the children or to send support payments.

Although this family's story has unique features, it also has many characteristics that are relatively common to the divorce experiences of children: longstanding parental conflict that continues after divorce and to which the children are witnesses and unwitting pawns; parents so stressed and absorbed by their problems that their parenting breaks down in critical ways; dramatic changes in the living arrangements of the children. Although not true in this case, many custodial mothers experience a substantial decline in their standard of living; it is not unusual for mothers and children to slip into poverty. It is not surprising that "children often report their parents' marital transitions to be their most painful life experience" (Hetherington, Bridges, & Insabella, 1998, p.170).

Are There Any Consistent Developmental Consequences for Children of Divorce?

Overall, children whose parents divorce (or divorce and remarry) have higher rates of behavioral, emotional, and cognitive problems than children whose parents maintain a stable marriage (the "continuously married"). As we review some of these outcomes,

however, keep in mind that the impact of divorce on children in specific cases depends on multiple characteristics of the children, the parents, the family, and the community, which all interact in complex ways. Understanding the impact of divorce requires a multidimensional or systems perspective. Individual studies of the consequences of divorce sometimes yield inconsistent results, some finding serious, long-term consequences for children, and others suggesting only temporary problems. Fortunately, meta-analyses and reviews of large numbers of studies have begun to clarify not only what problems tend to occur, but also how the complex blending of risk and protective factors contributes either to sustaining these problems or to mitigating them. The following summary is primarily based on large-scale longitudinal studies (such as Amato & Anthony, 2014; Anthony, DiPerna, & Amato, 2014; Gahler & Palmtag, 2015; Weaver & Schofield, 2015), and on meta-analyses and reviews (Amato, 2001, 2005; Greene et al., 2012; Hetherington et al., 1998; Hetherington & Kelly, 2002; Lansford, 2009).

What Are the Most Likely Problems for Children of Divorce?

Compared to children of continuously married parents, the children of divorce tend to have lower grades and achievement test scores. They are more likely to display externalizing problems (e.g., conduct problems) and/or internalizing problems (e.g., depression). They are likely to have fewer friends and less peer support, and their self-esteem is likely to suffer. As children get older, new problems may emerge. Adolescents and young adults can have more difficulty establishing and maintaining intimate relationships. They are more likely to be sexually active at earlier ages and to have out-of-wedlock children. Dropping out of school, trouble finding and maintaining employment, illicit drug use, and other forms of delinquency are all more common for youth from divorced families, regardless of ethnicity. In adulthood, children of divorce have more trouble staying married, partly because of other outcomes of divorce (like early child bearing) and partly, it appears, because their marital interactions are more likely to involve negative exchanges, such as criticism and contempt. Divorce rates tend to be higher for adults who experienced their parents' divorce during childhood. Intergenerational transmission of marital strife and divorce even extends to the third generation, with the children of the children of divorce more likely to divorce (Amato & Patterson, 2017).

How Common Are These Problems and Why Do They Occur?

It appears that 20% to 25% of children whose parents divorce have one or more of these problematic outcomes, while only about 10% of children of continuously married parents have them (Hetherington et al., 1998). The increased risk for children of divorce is clear, but it is also clear that the majority of children

(continued)

of divorce are able to overcome the difficulties that their parents' marital changes create for them. Children who have adjustment problems in the first year or two after a divorce often show improvements thereafter, although new developmental challenges, such as becoming an adolescent, can precipitate new problems. Among the risk and protective factors that contribute to differential outcomes are individual factors, like parents' personalities and children's temperaments, and family factors, like how much conflict children witness as well as the post-divorce financial arrangements and re-marriages of their parents.

For example, children's characteristics matter. An intelligent child with an easy temperament and good social relationships is likely to weather the storm of divorce, even in very difficult circumstances, more effectively than a child with a difficult temperament or one with a history of cognitive or social problems. Both boys and girls are negatively affected by divorce, but some girls show remarkable resilience, rising to the challenge of increased responsibility, especially in a mother-headed household. Boys are less likely to do so. Yet boys adjust better to a mother's remarriage, apparently benefiting from a stepfather in the home, whereas girls tend not to adjust well to living in stepfamilies (Hetherington et al., 1998; Weaver & Schofield, 2015).

Another important factor is children's exposure to parental conflict both during the marriage and after a divorce. Children whose married parents are chronically in conflict, creating a hostile household environment, often do *better* if their parents divorce, especially if they are less exposed to conflict after the divorce *and* their parents' distress is reduced (Amato, 2005). Conflict, whether before or after divorce, in which children are "caught in the middle" because their parents fight about them, communicate through them, or denigrate each other to the children is especially harmful (Davidson, O'Hara, & Beck, 2014). Parental conflict appears to have *direct* consequences. It increases children's anger, sadness, fear, and insecurity (e.g., Davies & Woitach, 2008), and these negative emotions are related to later behavior problems (e.g., Crockenberg & Langrock, 2001). But perhaps more important are the *indirect* consequences. Parents in conflict tend to interact with their children less effectively. They behave more negatively and less sensitively toward their children than other parents (Cox, Paley, & Harter, 2001). Even infants suffer the effects: Their attachments are less secure and their emotion regulation is less adequate when their parents frequently argue (Crockenberg, Leerkes, & Lekka, 2007). In a 30-year study of personality development, Block and Block (2006) found that boys who were going to experience their parents' divorce in their future tended to be undercontrolled (e.g., aggressive) before the divorce, suggesting that for some children, family dysfunction begins to take its toll well before divorce.

Many risk factors seem to have effects by influencing the quality of the parenting children receive. Divorced or divorcing parents tend to be less sensitive and responsive to their children's needs and less likely to control and monitor their children than continuously married parents (Hetherington & Kelly, 2002). Responding to children's increased distress and insecurity can be a challenge that parents are ill equipped to handle when they themselves are highly stressed. We have seen that one risk factor, parent conflict, affects children partly by reducing parenting quality. Parents' emotional distress also puts children at risk (e.g., chronic anger, anxiety, depression, loneliness, and so on) at least in part by affecting the quality of parent–child interactions.

Another risk factor for children is parental remarriage. Children's adjustment problems tend to increase, and some of this increase is due to declines in parenting quality associated with remarriage. Even though parents may experience emotional and material benefits from repartnering, their own stress often increases as they face new challenges, such as managing new financial arrangements, new relationships and new family roles (e.g., step-parenting). It is not unusual for step-parents to assume disciplinary authority too quickly, before children have had a sufficient opportunity to build the kinds of ties that make discipline effective (e.g., warm, affectional, trusting bonds) (Browning & Bray, 2009).

Another risk factor, separation from the noncustodial parent (usually the father), seems to be a problem more because of changes in the quality of the parent–child relationship than because parent and child spend less time together. The noncustodial parent is likely to find his or her new role quite difficult to navigate, often failing to appropriately enforce controls in order to avoid alienation from the child. Studies of divorced fathers and their children indicate that fathers with more education are more likely to remain highly involved with their children than less educated fathers, and that if mothers are employed, fathers are more likely to stay involved (Kalmijn, 2015). If noncustodial parents maintain an authoritative style with their children, despite having less time with them, children are protected (DeGarmo, 2010). "Competent, supportive, authoritative noncustodial parents can have beneficial effects for children, and these effects are most marked for . . . parents and children of the same sex" (Hetherington et al., 1998, p. 173). Even if parents are in conflict and one parent provides poor quality care, good quality parenting by the other parent serves as a protective factor against negative child outcomes (Mahrer et al., 2016).

Clearly, parenting quality and consistency are not all that is important for long-term child outcomes after divorce. Some factors—such as the temperament of the child, the child's intelligence, and the problems of moving into poverty—have direct or moderating influences on outcomes. But parenting quality turns out to be a critical mediator of many of the effects of parents' marital transitions on children's outcomes. Fortunately, it is a factor that is amenable to intervention (Symons, 2010). Many family courts now offer or require mediation and/or education that is aimed at highlighting to parents the importance of understanding the needs of their children and making those needs a priority in their divorce agreements. At least one comprehensive court related intervention, "The Collaborative Divorce Project" (Pruett, Insabella, & Gustafson, 2005), has demonstrated significant benefits. Compared to controls, intervention parents were more accepting of each others' importance in parenting their children, parents' conflict and distress were reduced, fathers' involvement was increased, fathers were more reliable in making child support payments, and teacher ratings of children's cognitive functioning was improved. If Georgia and Jim had been required to participate in such a program, perhaps Emily and her siblings would have been protected from some of the negative consequences of their parents' divorce.

helpers a framework for understanding the life of a marriage, the behaviors that lead to successful outcomes, and the behaviors that may foreshadow divorce.

Let's begin by considering what happens to relationship quality over time. Early studies of marital satisfaction—how partners perceive the quality of their relationship and how happy they are with it—indicated consistent U-shaped patterns. Couples' satisfaction declined shortly after the marriage, stabilized or reached a low point when children were adolescents, and recovered initial levels of satisfaction when children were launched (Burr, 1970; Rollins & Feldman, 1970). This description is often repeated and tends to be popular and compelling with the public. But it appears to be an artifact of the cross-sectional designs of the early studies. The marriages of the older cohorts in those studies were the ones that had survived, and they were therefore probably among the more satisfying, whereas many less satisfying unions had dissolved. Longitudinal studies consistently paint a very different picture (Karney, 2015). For example, Vaillant and Vaillant (1993) followed a sample of Harvard graduates and their spouses over 40 years. Average ratings of satisfaction gradually declined over the entire course of the marriage for both partners, with somewhat greater declines in women's ratings. Interestingly, when the couples were asked to recollect the course their marriage had taken over time, they described their marital satisfaction as following a U-shaped function, declining after their first child was born and improving after the children had left home. But their actual ratings through the years showed that fluctuations in the family life cycle did not predict changes in overall marital satisfaction.

The average declines in marital satisfaction that researchers have found actually mask the fact that if we look closely at patterns for individual couples, there is a great deal of variability. All studies that have looked for individual differences have found several trajectories. For the largest proportion of couples in these studies, satisfaction begins high and actually stays fairly steady or declines only slightly over time. For about one quarter to one third of couples, declines in satisfaction are quite steep, and these couples account for most of the overall average decline. These couples are usually less satisfied with their marriages from the start. These are the couples who are at most risk of divorce, although couples within every trajectory are at some risk (Anderson, Van Ryzin, & Doherty, 2010; James, 2015; Lavner & Bradbury, 2010, 2012; Lorber, Erlanger, Heyman, & O'Leary, 2015). Partners from low-income and minority groups are somewhat more likely than middle- or upper-middle-class Whites to be among those who begin marriage with lower levels of satisfaction and show substantial declines over time (James, 2015; Karney, 2015), perhaps because day-to-day stressors are often greater for these groups.

Why, at least for some, does marital satisfaction decline? Let us consider three contemporary hypotheses about marital success and breakdown for some possible answers. Imagine three hypothetical newlywed couples, the Grays, the Browns, and the Greens. Mr. and Mrs. Gray are very much in love. Even when they are in the presence of other people, they behave as if they see only each other. They are highly affectionate and romantic, and their courtship was a whirlwind of exciting events. The Grays believe that they are each other's soul mate, possessing few, if any, negative characteristics. They have no doubts about the happiness that awaits them in marriage.

The Browns are also an affectionate couple. Their view of each other, however, is not quite as rosy as that of the Grays. Their engagement period was a long one because both husband and wife worked to save up enough money to buy a house. Shortly after the wedding, Mrs. Brown noticed that her husband was becoming less willing to part with any of his income for furniture or other items for the house that she considered important. This has already become a source of tension in the marriage.

The Greens met each other through an online dating website because each was having difficulty meeting eligible romantic partners. Mrs. Green was very insecure in social situations and worried constantly that she would never find a husband. Mr. Green did not want to get married so soon, but he consented because he was afraid that he might lose his chance. Their courtship was a rocky one from the start.

As you read about each of these couples, did you think one or more of them would be more likely to divorce than another? If so, why? Your answers might illustrate popular hypotheses about why marriages succeed or fail. Those who espouse the **disillusionment model** might choose the hypothetical Grays as the couple most likely to experience marital breakdown. This view posits that overly romantic idealizations of marriage and blissfully optimistic views of one's partner set people up for eventual disappointment. Such fantasies cannot coexist for long with the reality of married life (Casad, Salazar, & Macina, 2015). The rise in divorce rates and incidence of cohabitation might be partially attributable to the fact that young adults today have high expectations for the emotional benefits of marriage, expecting a strong and lasting romantic love (Balestrino, Ciardi, & Mammitti, 2013). However, another possibility is that the Grays are not especially likely candidates for divorce because they will work hard to maintain their favorable beliefs about each other, despite the inevitable challenges of marriage. Their positive illusions are supportive of the relationship; thus they may be reluctant to abandon them to face reality. This perspective is called the **maintenance hypothesis** (Karney & Bradbury, 1997). A number of studies have found that people do sometimes use cognitive strategies to help them maintain positive views of their partners despite negative experiences (Karney, 2015). One strategy is to discount the importance of specific problem domains (e.g., "he's always late"), and to elevate the importance of positive domains (e.g., "he gives me such thoughtful gifts"). Another strategy is to interpret specific negative behaviors as due to special circumstances rather than as indicative of a more general problem. For example, in a study using partners' daily diary reports, most people described specific partner behaviors that they evaluated negatively (Neff & Karney, 2009). But for many, those evaluations did not affect their global assessment of the partner. Instead, they made causal attributions for specific transgressions that helped them "make allowances" and be forgiving.

Perhaps you thought that the Browns were the most likely couple to divorce because of the growing tension in the marriage. Another perspective on marital breakdown, built on **social exchange and behavioral theories**, proposes that increasing problems and mounting conflicts gradually escalate to overwhelm the originally positive perceptions spouses held for each other (Karney, 2015). Over time, partners who experience chronic conflict and who fail to negotiate it adequately may begin to see each others' characteristics, even their strengths, as having significant costs, draining energy and causing the conflicts (Kashdan et al., 2017).

In truth, no marriage escapes conflict. Recall Amanda and Anthony from the introduction to this chapter. Despite the strength of their relationship, they have conflicts over managing money and household tasks, which are rather common areas of disagreement. For most couples, the steepest slide in marital satisfaction is likely to occur during the early period (Gottman & Levinson, 2000). Approximately half of all divorces occur within the first seven years of marriage. In these early years, couples must adjust to each other, work out routines for household tasks, pool resources, and if they have children, take care of them. Several studies have implicated the transition to parenthood as the culprit in the loss of marital satisfaction. For example, many new parents experience a sharp drop in positive interactions and a dramatic increase in conflict as well as a decrease in marital satisfaction following the birth of the first child (Belsky & Kelly, 1994; van Scheppingen, Denissen, Tambs, Chung, & Bleidorn, 2017). But even couples who remain childless report declines in satisfaction in the early years of marriage. Several prospective studies of young couples' marriages have found much higher rates of divorce among childless couples than among those with children (Cowan & Cowan, 1992; Shapiro, Gottman, & Carrere, 2000). Thus, the existence of conflict in a marriage is simply not a good predictor of its prognosis, but the way couples handle it may be, as we will see later on.

Finally, let's consider the Greens. You may have predicted this couple's marital demise because they seem to bring more personal problems into the marriage in the first place. **Intrapersonal models**, which draw on theories of attachment or personality, emphasize the contribution of one's personal history or temperament to the success or failure of relationships. In some studies, intrapersonal variables like a person's tendency to make positive or negative attributions about her partner and her expectations about the future of the relationship have been found to affect relationship quality over time (McNulty & Karney, 2004). Other important factors are how quickly an individual recovers from conflict and her emotion regulation abilities

(Salvatore, Kuo, Steele, Simpson, & Collins, 2011). Personality traits are also important. One particularly robust finding from many investigations of marriages is that higher neuroticism is related to lower levels of marital satisfaction and higher levels of relationship dissolution (Mund, Finn, Hagemeyer, & Neyer, 2016). More neurotic individuals may be easily overwhelmed by the conflicts that are inherent in family life and, therefore, more prone to marital distress. Higher levels of extraversion, agreeableness, and conscientiousness are linked to better marital outcomes (Mund et al., 2016).

KEEPING LOVE ALIVE

Although the models we have described all may contribute something to our understanding of marriage, each by itself is inadequate to explain its complexity. The marital trajectory seems to be affected by intrapersonal (traits, expectations), interpersonal (problem-solving skills), situational (life stresses, environmental conditions), and developmental (transitions, role change) factors (Karney, 2015). A comprehensive, multidimensional theory of marriage or other committed relationships has yet to be developed. Nevertheless, we can learn a great deal from the research that has been done, particularly during the last decade, to help us improve the relationships of our clients.

Some of the most helper-friendly information comes from the "love-lab" of John Gottman, who has a unique approach to the study of marital dynamics. Gottman and his colleagues have spent years observing and videotaping couples interacting with each other to understand, from the inside out, what makes marriages work or fail. Gottman (1993, 1999; Gottman & Gottman, 2015) used this descriptive approach as a step toward building a theory of marital stability and dissolution that can be closely tied to clinical application.

Three fundamental ideas are important in understanding Gottman's research. First, he conceptualizes marriage or any primary relationship as a new system that represents a synthesis of the pre-existing elements of each partner's personal history and temperament. Second, he draws upon systems theory to describe marriage as a relational system that seeks a stable or homeostatic steady state (von Bertalanffy, 1968). This steady state is maintained over time by the couple's unique balance of positive and negative elements in areas of interactive behavior, perception, and physiology. Behavior refers here to a couple's interactions and accompanying affect; perception refers to self-perceptions and attributions directed to partners; and physiology refers to the autonomic, endocrine, and immune system functioning of the partners. Third, he premises his approach on research done in the last few decades, which consistently documents a ratio of high negative to low positive behaviors in distressed/divorcing couples as opposed to nondistressed/stable couples.

Thinking about a marital relationship as a ratio of positive and negative factors is somewhat like considering the relationship to have a typical kind of "weather," for example, sunny, calm, cloudy, stormy, and so forth. The marital climate or stable steady state is made up of uninfluenced (intrapersonal elements like neuroticism) and influenced (couple's interaction) elements. From a systems perspective, a marital union tends towards stability in its positivity to negativity ratio over time. Obviously, contextual features and crises also play a part in the nature of relationships, but these factors are not emphasized because they are less predictable.

Gottman and his colleagues developed ways to measure levels of positivity and negativity in couples' behavioral interactions, in their perceptions of each other, and in their physiological states, such as arousal or calmness, using observational coding systems, measures of physiological responding, and questionnaire and interview data. Over several extensive longitudinal studies, they set out to predict which couples would divorce and which would remain together. Moreover, they sought to determine whether particular elements were associated with marital breakup or success (see Gottman, 1994a; Gottman & Levenson, 2000).

In general, making this kind of marital "weather report" has surprising predictive ability. Assessments done at the beginning of a marriage, including those made from videotapes of the first three minutes of a newlywed marital conflict discussion, predicted later outcomes with a high degree of accuracy (Carrere &

Gottman, 1999; Carrere, Buehlman, Gottman, Coan, & Ruckstuhl, 2000; Gottman & Levenson, 2000). What turns out to predict marital dissolution best? A high level of **negative affect reciprocity** is a distinguishing feature. This construct refers to the likelihood that negative emotions in one partner will follow from the other partner's negativity. You may think of it as the likelihood that partners will bring out the worst in each other. This is accomplished through the combined influences of information processing biases (e.g., seeing the other's qualities as negative), heightened physiological arousal (e.g., interpreting arousal as anger), negative behavioral interactions (e.g., being critical and defensive), and failing to respond to a partner's bids for attention.

But a number of fine points bear mentioning. As it turns out, conflict and angry feelings are part of all intimate relationships, so simply trying to avoid conflict won't help. Furthermore, not all negative affect is equally deleterious to relationships. Anger can play a constructive function when it is a justifiable reaction to a partner's behavior or reflects airing of grievances (Gottman, 1994b). The trick is to distinguish between functional and dysfunctional types of negativity. Other researchers have drawn similar distinctions (e.g., Markman, Stanley, & Blumberg, 1994), but, for the sake of simplicity, we will present Gottman's definitions here.

The four kinds of negativity that do the most damage to relationships and that are highly predictive of divorce are criticism, defensiveness, contempt, and stonewalling (see Table 13.6). The presence of these **"four horsemen of the apocalypse"** (Gottman, 1999), particularly contempt, can be very destructive. But suppose you recognize some of these elements in your own close relationship? Does this forecast an inevitable breakup? You may be somewhat relieved to know that Gottman found criticism, defensiveness, and stonewalling even in happy marriages. In couples headed toward divorce, however, these three behaviors were more frequent, contempt was also present, and there was much less positive affect in the relationship overall. Most important, the distressed couples he observed were not skilled in repairing the relationship after conflict occurred. Instead, prolonged periods of unrelieved distress, accompanied by heightened physiological arousal, fueled negative perceptions of the partner, overwhelmed spouses' positive feelings for each other, and led to a state of isolation and loneliness. Over time, if negativity surpassed positivity, it contributed to the derailment of the relationship.

With the accumulation of stresses and losses that we all experience in adulthood, it makes sense that good coping skills would be an essential component of personal and interpersonal wellness. Therefore, a critical part of marriage maintenance (and probably that of any close relationship) is the capacity to repair the frayed relationship after conflict. Gottman observed that the particular type of conflict style that couples demonstrated did not matter as much as the amount of overall positivity in the relationship (humor, interest, affection, and validation) and the couples' ability to soothe hurt or angry feelings. Some couples tended to avoid conflict and others embraced it with gusto, whereas some discussed their differences with the validating ("I hear what you are saying . . . ") style of counselors. Surprisingly, all three types could be very happily married if the steady state ratios of positivity to negativity in their relationships were 5 to 1. In other words, if a marital climate has substantially more periods of sun than rain, the chances of long-term success are pretty good.

TABLE 13.6 Gottman's Four Horsemen of the Apocalypse

1. *Criticism:* Implying that one's partner has some global deficiency that is part of his/her personality: "You always . . . ; You never. . . . "
2. *Defensiveness:* Failure to take responsibility and defending oneself against criticism: "Who me? . . . I do not!"
3. *Contempt:* A statement or nonverbal behavior that puts down the partner while elevating the speaker to a superior position (such as insulting, using hostile humor, or mocking the partner).
4. *Stonewalling:* Verbal or nonverbal behaviors that communicate impassiveness (looking away, looking bored).

SOURCE: Based on Gottman, J. M. (1999). *The marriage clinic: A scientifically based marital therapy.* New York, NY: Norton.

Generativity: Making a Mark at Midlife

Establishing generativity is the primary developmental task of middle adulthood according to Erikson (1950/1963). Generativity has been described as having several components (Hofer et al., 2016). As we saw in Chapter 12, two primary components are desire and accomplishment. Desire refers to wanting to be creative, productive, or giving, and accomplishment means actually feeling that you are creative, productive, or giving. Generative desire is more characteristic of young adults, but generative accomplishment is more typical of middle adults.

THE EXPERIENCE OF CHILD REARING

For many people, raising children is a significant part of adult life. Parents experience more stress than nonparents, but they usually view their parenting role as a generative process (Marks, Bumpass, & Jun, 2003). The nature and quality of the parenting experience, including the parent's feelings of generativity, change substantially as both children and parents grow older.

Each major period or stage of a child's life creates new challenges for a parent, challenges that the parent is more or less prepared to face depending on her age and stage of life, her personality and coping skills, her socioeconomic status, and the available support systems. For example, the gratifications of parenthood and marriage are usually greater for older rather than younger first-time parents. Older parents tend to have a more fully developed self-concept and greater self-esteem, are more advanced in their careers, have more money, and are more likely to find balancing work and family responsibilities easier to negotiate. Older fathers spend more time caring for their children than younger fathers, a factor that not only increases satisfaction with parenting but also improves satisfaction for both partners. Older dads also tend to be less physical with their young children (e.g., less tickling and chasing), and to engage their children in more cognitively stimulating activities than younger dads (Parke, 2002). Research on mothers indicates that age is not a factor in how likely mothers are to meet their infants' health, safety, and survival needs; younger mothers are as effective as older mothers in feeding, holding, and establishing positive emotional bonds. Yet older mothers tend to have more basic knowledge about children and parenting than younger mothers (Bornstein, 2015). Older mothers are likely to use fewer punitive measures to control their children's behavior, and their children have fewer behavioral and emotional problems than other children, at least until the teen years (Trillingsgaard & Sommer, 2016). Even with social class controlled, older moms provide more cognitive stimulation to their infants. They talk to them more and use more diverse vocabulary, and they provide more exploratory opportunities (Bornstein, Putnick, Suwalsky, & Gini, 2006).

Not surprisingly, very young first-time parents (under 20) are at greater risk than other groups to find that the stress of parenting outweighs its satisfactions. They typically complete fewer years of education than older parents and have lower incomes. They are more likely to divorce than other groups, and their children are more likely to experience developmental problems (Bornstein, 2015; Mollborn, 2016). We should note that some of the problems of teen parenthood are a function of the social disadvantage that many teen parents experience before they become parents. Fortunately, the teen birth rate has declined dramatically in Western countries in recent years, especially in the United States, where the rate decreased by 50% between 1995 and 2013 (Mollborn, 2016).

Although late-life child bearing is associated with many positives, as you have seen, there are risks as well. For example, the children of older parents are more likely to be born with chromosomal abnormalities or other genetic anomalies (Kong et al., 2012; National Down Syndrome Society, 2018). Clearly, the impacts of parenting on parents and children, like all other developmental outcomes, are a function of many interacting risk and protective factors.

The normative experience of parents as they move through each stage of parenting is that the challenges bring both intense new stresses and delightful new pleasures (Nelson, Kushlev, & Lyubomirsky, 2014). For example, in the newborn period, first-time parents often feel distressed and overwhelmed and are likely to experience a decline in marital satisfaction (van Scheppingen et al., 2017). Caring for an infant is far more demanding than most people expect it to be. Distress is linked to insufficient sleep; money worries; anxieties about the baby's dependency and vulnerability; feelings of uncertainty about one's caretaking skill; difficulty balancing the needs of self, partner, and baby; and disillusionment with the "yucky" side of infant care (such as mounds of laundry, endless spit-up, and baffling crying fits just when it's time for the parents to eat dinner). Simultaneously, however, most parents of newborns report feeling like they have now truly grown up, that their lives have new purpose and meaning, and that they have a strong sense of shared joy (Nelson et al., 2014). The transition to parenting involves tasks and demands that are transformative for many first-time parents. For example, gender role attitudes tend to become somewhat less egalitarian and more traditional as mothers and fathers attempt to adapt to their new roles (e.g., Katz-Wise, Priess, & Hyde, 2010). For both mothers and fathers, personal identity becomes somewhat less focused on work and more on family, although the shift in work salience tends to be greater for mothers.

The parent of the toddler or preschooler must begin to discipline a child who is still very dependent but who is skilled enough to need continuous supervision. Because a toddler is a proficient climber, for example, a parent can no longer put her in a crib to keep her safe while the parent takes a quick shower or talks on the phone. Parents begin to have conflicts with their children when the child, who has little capacity to take the parents' perspective, resists their disciplinary efforts. Also, partners often find themselves in conflict about their children as they negotiate disciplinary styles, time commitments, and divisions of labor. And parents feel physically exhausted as they try to keep up with energetic, active youngsters who have little self-control. Although many parents experience this period as especially stressful, there are new pleasures as well (Edwards & Liu, 2002). Children begin to talk, to participate in organized activities, and to do things on their own, such as feeding themselves. Their temperaments are blossoming into personalities, and a new little self becomes part of the family system. Most parents experience these developments as intriguing and as a source of pride, despite the heavy dose of frustration that these advances can bring.

Up to middle childhood, parents spend a good deal of time with their children and tend to be immersed in caregiving activities (Bornstein, 2015). But when children move into middle childhood, parents spend less time with them and the family waters are often somewhat becalmed. If there is a honeymoon period between parents and children, this is it. The child's thinking is more logical, she has a growing capacity to take another's perspective, and she can in many situations keep herself safe, so that supervision can be reduced. At the same time, the child does not yet feel much ambivalence about her dependence on her parents, and parents still enjoy the role of preferred companion. There are plenty of challenges in this period, of course. Outside factors—such as peers, teachers, and the media—are increasingly influential. Helping children learn to interpret and negotiate the outside world and to deal with the stress it creates can be difficult (e.g., Collins, Madsen, & Susman-Stillman, 2002).

Parenting usually becomes more demanding when children reach adolescence (Bornstein, 2015). Mothers with early adolescent children (middle school age) report greater feelings of stress and lower life satisfaction than at other times in their children's life cycle (Luthar & Ciciolla, 2016). The child's push for independence, parental worries about the child's risk taking and sexual maturity, and the child's often critical and rejecting attitudes are tough to bear, even when parents are well versed in the needs of adolescents. Many parents reach their 40s and 50s when their children are reaching adolescence, so that they are beginning to confront their own physical aging and perhaps engaging in a "midlife review" at the same time. Steinberg and Silk (2002) report that adolescent development and parental distress about midlife are interacting factors. For example, parents whose teens are actively dating and involved in mixed-sex activities are more likely to express midlife concerns and to feel less satisfaction with their lives than parents whose teens are not yet dating. Parent and adolescent bickering over mundane matters and adolescents' de-idealization of parents can also take a toll on parents' well-being.

MyLab Education

Video Example 13.5

Each major stage of children's lives creates new challenges for their parents. In this video, Julie describes challenges of parenting three sons at the ages of three, six, and eight.

The **launching period**, when emerging adults begin to move away and become more self-sufficient, brings some new challenges. On the whole, by the time adult children are in their 20s, parents begin to feel the benefits of fewer parental responsibilities—less stress and greater feelings of well-being—and their relationships with their children improve. We often hear about how sad parents are, especially mothers, when their young adult children depart, leaving an "empty nest." In a summary of decades of data, Bouchard (2014) reported that although parents often anticipate that the transition will be difficult for them, only a small proportion describe especially negative feelings. These are more likely for mothers who experience a substantial drop-off in community activities without children at home. It seems that it is the absence of alternative roles that causes the transition to an "empty nest" to be difficult for mothers, rather than children's departure per se. In fact, mothers, who typically do more of the day-to-day child rearing, are more struck by the relief they experience from those duties than fathers are. Their greater involvement may also lead them to prepare more and to do more planning for the next phase of their lives. Fathers (at least in Western cultures) are more likely to report negative feelings than mothers, especially fathers with traditional gender expectations and roles. They seem to struggle more with the concept of their adult children becoming autonomous, which modifies their role as decision maker and changes the structure of the family. For both mothers and fathers, feelings of well-being and generativity are strongly correlated with their children's functioning. If adult children are seen as personally and socially well-adjusted, parents are likely to experience greater self-acceptance, purpose in life, and feelings of mastery (Ryff, Lee, Essex, & Schmutte, 1994).

You won't be surprised to learn that cultural context and historical events can affect how the launching period is experienced by parents. In today's world, Chinese empty-nesters are likely to have poorer relationships with their adult children and to report higher levels of loneliness and depression than parents whose adult children live at home. In a culture where family support for older people is a valued tradition, the migration of young adults from rural to urban areas that characterizes modern China probably contributes to these findings (Bouchard, 2014).

What happens when adult children have launched, or at least by cultural standards, should have launched, but return to live with their parents? The U.S. Bureau of the Census (2017) indicates that more young adults (ages 18 to 34) live with a parent than with a spouse today than have done so in the past. In many cases, children have moved back in with parents after attending college, cohabiting with a partner, or sharing an apartment with friends. These "boomerang children" are typically single, and about one fifth have children themselves. Many characteristics of both parents and children, such as personality traits and health status, influence the impact of co-residence on parents. One important factor is how normative the experience is seen to be. In one study, middle aged parents answered questions about their marital quality at two time points, just before the Great Recession in 2008 and five years later, when co-residing adult children had become much more common (Davis, Kim, & Fingerman, 2016). In 2008, parents of adult children who were co-residing reported lower marital quality than other parents of adult children. In 2013, when co-residence was more normative, there were no such effects on parents' marital quality. However, if children had "boomeranged" because of serious problems, such as divorce or job loss, parents apparently were more stressed, and their marital quality was likely to suffer.

The typical parent is exiting middle age when her children are entering it. Parents whose children are over 30 years old may find the quality of their relationships changing further, such that they now tend to relate to their children more as equals. Adult children often begin to identify with their parents, appreciating more profoundly what an adult's life is like than they ever could have before. Exchange of support seems to become more and more complementary. However, the relationship is still not likely to be completely egalitarian. Assistance and support, such as financial help, are still more likely to be provided by the older generation to the younger one (Birditt, Fingerman, & Zarit, 2010; Byers, Levy, Allore, Bruce, & Kasl, 2008).

As adults move through middle age, they sometimes find themselves in the role of **kinkeeper**, the person in an extended family who helps the generations maintain contact with one another (e.g., Sinardet & Mortelmans, 2009). They may also take on new family responsibilities involving care of an ailing parent or another elderly relative. Most adults in the United States enter midlife with one or both parents living, but by the end of midlife, 77% have lost both parents and many have participated in some way in their parents' terminal care (Lachman, 2004). Women are much more likely to play these roles than men in most cultures, although many men take on some kinkeeping or caregiving responsibilities. These tasks can be particularly challenging if they coincide with the adolescence of one's children. People who carry these double responsibilities are described as being in the sandwich generation (Bornstein, 2015; Hamill & Goldberg, 1997). Many factors affect how stressful this position is, such as the coping style of the sandwiched individual, educational, financial, and cultural factors, and the availability of other family help, especially the support of the partner. As with the challenges of parenting, kinkeeping and elder care can put caregivers at risk for physical and mental health problems (Hsing-Yi & Chiou, 2010). Yet it can also bring emotional rewards, such as feelings of mastery and meaningfulness. See Box 15.1 in Chapter 15 for a fuller discussion.

WORK AND COMMUNITY INVOLVEMENT

Our careers begin in young adulthood, but it is in the middle adult years that people usually feel they are becoming expert in their work. The full fruits of a career are likely to be experienced in this stage of life, and for many, identity is heavily affected by work (Williams, Berdahl, & Vandello, 2016). Incomes for both men and women tend to reach their peak, and top levels of management and professional advancement are most likely to characterize people in this age period as well. Work intensity and time invested in work usually increase in the first half of middle adulthood and then begin to taper off, as many people begin to strike a balance between time spent working and time spent with family and friends and in community service. This shift seems to be motivated for some people by increased confidence in their productivity and their value in the workplace, allowing them to invest more energy and effort into other aspects of their lives. For others, the shift may be motivated by a sense that their work will not bring them the satisfactions they may have once expected or dreamed about (Levinson, 1986).

This temporal pattern, of course, varies considerably across individuals and life circumstances, such as social class and marital status. It is also linked somewhat to gender. In married couples, women who continue to work after having children generally give more priority to child rearing over career responsibilities (McElwain, Korabik, & Rosin, 2005). Men are less likely to do so, although fathers are more likely to modify the intensity of their work effort in dual-earner couples, which now represent the most typical arrangement in the American middle class. With this change has come a shift in role structures, with men becoming more active, involved parents and taking on more household responsibilities, although women still shoulder more of these burdens (Connelly, 2016). There is some evidence that for more recent cohorts of U.S. parents, self-esteem goes up for fathers who adjust their work schedules to accommodate family needs, even though they are likely to worry about negative effects on their careers. "Stay at home" dads are rapidly growing in number, but they still comprised fewer than 5% of fathers in 2015 (Chesley & Flood, 2017). And, just like mothers who choose to give up careers to care for children, "stay at home" dads tend to miss the daily adult interactions they had in the workplace (Cynkar, 2007). For mothers in recent cohorts, self-esteem tends to decline if they cut back on employment to take care of family responsibilities; older cohorts of men show a similar tendency (Carr, 2002). Note the impact of historical context on the interplay of social roles and psychological functioning.

The picture is a little different in Western versus non-Western countries. In one analysis (Chandra, 2012), work–life balance was more likely to be considered the responsibility of employers in Western countries. Employee assistance programs, flexible work schedules, and so on have become more common in the United States and Europe, and both genders share in the benefits. In Asian countries, the problem of balancing home and work was perceived to be an issue for women who retained primary responsibility for household duties. Individuals were expected to take responsibility for balancing jobs and family. In many cases, women were expected to limit their career options in the service of motherhood, which was considered their preeminent role.

Western researchers have found that participating in multiple roles (active parent, spouse, worker, caregiver to aging parents, and so on) makes middle adulthood hectic. Professionals frequently work with middle adults who are struggling to find effective ways of resolving what is called "work-life" or "work-family" conflict, meaning that responsibilities in the work and family domains are at least somewhat incompatible (Bennett, Beehr, & Ivanitsakya, 2017; Fellows, Chiu, Hill, & Hawkins, 2016). Amanda and Anthony, from the introduction to this chapter, are clearly experiencing work-family conflict, and they disagree on how to address it. Amanda's longer work hours and the needs of their adolescent children are squeezing time that Amanda once gave to housework, and Anthony is reluctant to give up his leisure time activities to help compensate. You can see in this couple lingering and long-standing gender role influences. Women tend to see a well-kept house as a reflection on their worth; men do not (Chesley & Flood, 2017). One solution might be for Amanda and Anthony to step a little further outside of their gender roles and compromise. Perhaps Amanda can accept that less housework will be done in a week, and Anthony can reduce some of his leisure activities to contribute more to daily household tasks.

Despite the challenge of such conflicts, when couples reach mutually acceptable agreements, multiple roles can contribute to life satisfaction, to mental health, and to better relationships (ten Brummelhuis & Bakker, 2012). Generally, in dual career households, the degree to which both parents modify their work and leisure time and share child care and household duties is a significant factor in determining marital satisfaction and feelings of spousal commitment, especially for women (Shockley & Allen, 2018; Unger, Sonnentag, Niessen, & Kuonath, 2015).

One of the benefits of participating in multiple roles is **role buffering**: If one role is a source of psychological stress or failure experiences, success and satisfaction in another role may compensate. For example, when women interrupt their careers to take on full-time parenting, they may in midlife restart their careers or start new ones, especially after their children reach adolescence. For them, the intensity of work involvement may be greater than it would otherwise be at this stage of their lives, and it can be out of phase with their husbands' work involvement, because they are at an earlier point in career development. Yet, the opportunity to be productive in another setting seems to provide a buffer against some of the stresses involved in parenting an adolescent (Larson & Richards, 1994).

We need to be careful not to oversimplify the impact of multiple roles on well-being, however. Social class and gender interact in complex ways to influence how multiple roles affect adult lives (Ahrens & Ryff, 2006; Perry-Jenkins, 2016; Williams et al., 2016). For example, for highly educated men with high status careers, professional role is likely to be central to their identity, and they are likely to consider very long work hours as essential (e.g., physicians and lawyers). These men tend to score better on measures of mental health when they have fewer roles. Blue-collar men more often see their jobs as "a means to an end," allowing them to provide well for their families. They are also more likely to choose, when possible, to limit work time to allow time for family and other pursuits. These men tend to do better when they do play multiple roles (e.g., parent, community volunteer). For women, these patterns are reversed: Highly educated women often do well when they have multiple roles, but blue-collar women with multiple roles are likely to do more poorly. Clearly, income, kind of work, gender role expectations, historical context, cohort, and culture underlie and modify such trends. As always, it is important for helping professionals to be mindful of the possible differences that their clients bring to the table around the issue of work-life balance.

Money and promotion are the external markers of achievement for middle adults, but a sense of generative accomplishment appears to be more dependent on how creative and productive we feel. The latter experiences are in turn related to how challenging the work is and to the level of interest and expertise that we bring to the work

(Csikszentmihalyi, 1999; Deci, Olafsen, & Ryan, 2017). McAdams (2006; Mansfield & McAdams, 1996) explains generativity as constituting both **agency** and **communion**. Agency "involves generating, creating, and producing things, ideas, people, events, and so on as powerful extensions or expressions of the self" (Mansfield & McAdams, 1996, p. 721). Agentic generativity, then, depends on self-knowledge, a sense of identity, and the opportunity to work on tasks that match our interests, values, and skills; these are all key features of successful career planning, as we saw in Chapter 12. Generativity also involves communion, expressed "in the adult's desire to care for the next generation, even to the point of sacrificing his or her own well-being for the good of those who will follow" (pp. 721–722). Behaviors involving giving, offering, and contributing are aspects of communion. Research indicates that adults who are identified by others as "generative" tend to combine both agency and communion in the concerns that they express and in their occupational and community behaviors (Mansfield & McAdams, 1996). See Box 13.3 for a further discussion.

Box 13.3: Men, Women, and Leadership

In high school, Regina loved math and science, and as a first-year college student she signed up to be a chemistry major. Regina liked her courses, but she also loved to party, and hours in the lab, along with grinding competition with premed students in organic chemistry, were not much fun. She began to feel that she was floundering: How could she combine her sociability with her sharp, analytic intellectual style to carve out a future? To satisfy distribution requirements she signed up for an economics course her second semester, and the rest is history. Regina became a very successful economics major, and by the time she was a senior, was being wooed by several major banking institutions for their management training programs. It was the early 1970s in corporate America, and recruitment of at least some women for executive management tracks was beginning to be "politically correct." But a foot in the door is only that. What did it take for Regina to become one of the top ranking banking executives in the United States by the time she was 50?

Early research on gender and leadership seemed to indicate that women and men have different "leadership styles." This research often involved bringing together strangers to accomplish some goal and assigning one participant as leader. Under these conditions, gender seems to make a big difference: Men are more "task oriented," focusing on doing whatever will get the job done, whereas women tend to be more "interpersonal," putting more time and effort into the quality of the social interaction. But in a meta-analysis of leadership style research, Eagly and Johnson (1990) found that when actual managers who occupy the same organizational positions are compared, both women and men are characterized by task-oriented, not interpersonal, styles. They did find one sex difference in leadership style, however. Women were more likely to be democratic, whereas men were more likely to be autocratic.

Social role theory, like that of Eagly and her colleagues, paints a complex picture of what contributes to leadership development and success for women and men in today's world (Eagly, 2007; Eagly & Heilman, 2016; Koenig & Eagly, 2014). When an individual fills a role, like a leadership role, the role itself influences their behavior. But their occupational role is only one of many social roles they are fulfilling. Another important one is their gender role, which is composed of a set of expectancies, or "shared beliefs that apply to individuals on the basis of their socially identified sex" (Eagly & Johannesen-Schmidt, 2001, p. 783). Understanding leadership behavior and its effectiveness, for men or women, requires understanding how the demands of these various roles are met within the particular organizational context.

As we saw in Chapter 8, expectancies or stereotypes about gender differences may or may not actually be real, and even when they are substantiated by empirical measures (e.g., males on average are more physically aggressive than females), average sex differences in behavior or traits tend to be small. The range of differences among individuals of the same sex is much greater than the average differences between sexes. But social role theorists argue that the importance of sex differences is not just a function of their real size but of the impact they have on people's expectations of their own and others' behavior, as well as on how people interpret behavior. One example comes from research on the widely held gender stereotype that women are more emotional than men, that is, that women lack emotional control (Brescoll, 2016). In a study on anger expressed in the workplace, Brescoll and Uhlmann (2008) found that in simulated job interviews, when women professionals expressed anger, their reactions were attributed to internal characteristics (e.g., "She's an angry person" or "She is out of control"), but when males expressed anger, their reactions were attributed to external circumstances.

Two aspects of gender roles that are important in the discussion of leadership are *agency*, which is more strongly ascribed to men, and *communion*, which is seen as more characteristic of women. As you have seen in the discussion of generativity, *agency* is a kind of powerful "get things done" expression of self. It can be captured by descriptors like *assertive, ambitious, dominant, controlling, forceful, independent,* and *confident*. *Communion* involves expression of concern for others. Descriptors like *affectionate, helpful, sensitive to others, sympathetic,* and *nurturing* apply.

Social role theory predicts that how a woman or a man will behave in a managerial or other leadership position is largely constrained by the nature of the position. They do not discount the influence of individual characteristics, like personality traits, but they emphasize that regardless of the individual filling the role, certain task requirements must be met, such as supervising the work of others, planning, gathering information, and disseminating it. These responsibilities require agentic behavior, and managers tend to behave agentically regardless of gender, as the meta-analysis by Eagly and Johnson illustrates. People also adjust their agentic behavior depending on whether they are interacting with subordinates or with a boss. Moskowitz, Suh, and Desaulniers (1994) used an experience sampling method to monitor managers' interpersonal behavior at work for 20 days. The same individuals were highly agentic with their subordinates, but less agentic with their superiors. It seems clear that managerial status predicts agentic behavior. But in the Moskowitz et al. study, the same participants' communal behavior was affected by their gender role, not by their managerial status: Women behaved more communally than men, especially with other women.

It appears, then, that women and men may tend to display different leadership styles, not with regard to whether they are task oriented or agentic, but with regard to how they treat people in the process. In other words, although their agentic behavior is constrained by their managerial role, their communal behavior is constrained by their own or others' expectations with regard to gender. Eagly and her colleagues propose that an important reason for this gender difference is that when women are leaders, there is an incongruity in role expectations that does not hold for men. *Agency* is important for leadership and is also expected of men. Therefore, people are likely to accept a domineering, even autocratic, management approach from men. Women must be agentic as leaders because the role requires it, but agency is incongruent with the female gender role and may tend to be perceived negatively by others as a result. In other words, many people may feel ambivalent about yielding power to women. Therefore, for many leadership positions, women will be more successful if they exercise their authority with special attention to at least some communal aspects of the process. They may have to be more democratic, inviting others to participate more in decision making, whereas men may have more freedom to be authoritarian if they choose. Fortunately, women are more likely than men to have developed skill using a collaborative, negotiating style, as we saw in Chapter 8.

Research on leadership in many cultural contexts supports this analysis (Eagly & Antonakis, 2015; Eagly, Makhijani, & Klonsky, 1992; Eagly & Johannesen-Schmidt, 2001; Wang, Chiang, Tsai, Lin, & Cheng, 2013). One meta-analysis examined a large set of studies in which participants were asked to rate others' leadership skills (Eagly et al., 1992). In all of these studies, the behaviors of men and women leaders had been equated by the researchers. In one type of study, for example, the same behavioral descriptions were ascribed to a woman for some participants and to a man for other participants. Interestingly, participants gave significantly lower ratings to women who behaved autocratically than to men.

In a large international study of actual leaders, researchers assessed the behaviors and effectiveness of 2,874 female and 6,126 male managers, looking at ratings by subordinates, peers, superiors, and by the managers themselves (Eagly & Johannesen-Schmidt, 2001). The most effective managers of either gender were characterized by the same leadership behaviors: acknowledging good performance by followers (giving performance-based rewards), developing and mentoring their followers, attending to followers' individual needs, and inspiring their followers' optimism and excitement about the future as well as their respect and pride in their leader. Women managers outscored men on all of these behaviors, especially the most communal of them (e.g., attending to the individual needs of their followers). The least effective managers were those who focused on their followers' mistakes, procrastinated in solving problems, and were absent or uninvolved at critical times. These were not common behaviors for any of these managers, but they were more common for men than for women.

Why were women leaders more likely than men to engage in the most effective managerial behaviors? Eagly and Johannesen-Schmidt (2001) offer two explanations. First, women probably have to meet a higher standard to be successful managers. "Men may have greater leeway to remain in leadership roles, despite poor performance" (p. 793). Second, the behaviors that are especially effective for leaders—for example, individualized consideration, rewarding positive performance—"may involve being attentive, considerate, and nurturing" (p. 793), communal behaviors that women may be more likely to engage in because of gender role expectations. Another meta-analysis suggests that a larger proportion of women than men in leadership positions are "transformational leaders." Such leaders are characterized by their ability to gain the trust of employees, to innovate, and to empower others (Eagly, Johannesen-Schmidt, & van Engen, 2003).

The studies we have reviewed thus far suggest that men are less likely than women to be penalized for autocratic, domineering behavior in leadership positions. But this situation may not hold for all racial and ethnic groups, at least in the United States (Rosette, Koval, Ma, & Livingston, 2016). In one study, researchers asked participants to rate the performance of a leader who was confronting a subordinate employee (Livingston, Rosette, & Washington, 2012). The leader was presented in one of two ways: either as demanding and assertive (dominant) or as encouraging and compassionate (communal). A photograph portrayed the leader either as a Black man or woman or as a White man or woman. Participants tended to rate communal leaders more positively than dominant leaders, regardless of race or gender, consistent with the research we have just reviewed. But dominant leaders were rated differently depending on race and gender. If the leader were White, a dominant man was seen as a better leader than a dominant woman, as you might expect. But the reverse was true when the leader was portrayed as Black. A dominant woman was given much higher scores than a dominant man. Although research examining the intersection of race and gender roles in the workplace is in its infancy, this study suggests that minority group members may face very different sets of gender role expectations than Whites.

McAdams and his colleagues have developed a variety of measures of generativity. For example, on a 20-item questionnaire respondents rate the degree to which statements are true of them, such as, "I have a responsibility to improve the neighborhood in which I live" (McAdams & de St. Aubin, 1992). In a measure of generative goals, respondents are asked to describe 10 "personal strivings," and the responses are coded for "generative imagery" (McAdams, de St. Aubin, & Logan, 1993). Using these techniques, people who rate high on generativity are more likely to use authoritative, child-centered parenting styles, and they are more actively involved in political, religious, and social reform activities. They report higher levels of self-esteem and happiness, and they experience overall better mental health than people who score low on generativity (McAdams & Guo, 2015).

One of the more interesting differences between midlife adults who score high versus low on generativity measures is in the kind of narrative they produce when asked to tell their life stories. McAdams (McAdams & Olson, 2010) argues that the narratives we create about our lives are reconstructions that are based on the real events in our lives but that they also indicate our characteristic ways of making sense of things. They contribute to and reflect our identities and our sense of well-being. Generative adults, for example, tend to tell life stories with "redemption" themes. That is, even though the individual may describe many serious difficulties, her story often progresses from describing an emotionally negative event or bad scene to an emotionally positive or good outcome. Conversely, adults low on generativity tend to include more "contamination" sequences in their life stories. These are descriptions that go from good or positive experiences to negative outcomes.

Generative adults also are more likely to describe themselves as "sensitized to others' suffering at an early age" and as "guided by a clear and compelling ideology that remains relatively stable over time" (McAdams & Bowman, 2001, p. 14). Overall, there is a progressive structure to the generative adult's life story that suggests a reasonably coherent sense of a self who is moving in a positive direction and who feels able and willing to make a difference. In particular, such individuals seem to be able to move on despite sometimes serious setbacks. People low in generativity by midlife, however, seem to be stuck, "unable to grow." McAdams and Bowman (2001) describe one woman who, at 41, is still setting goals that are markedly like those she set as a young woman—"to graduate from high school" and to be "better able to take care of myself." She tells the interviewer that she is "desperately seeking" herself. Unfortunately, her persistent expectation that what appears to be good will turn out bad—reflected in the many contamination sequences she includes in her life story narrative—seems to make her quest overwhelming.

Generativity seems to be foreshadowed in the personality characteristics that emerge in adolescence and young adulthood. Petersen and Steward (1996) found that individuals who as adolescents already had strong power and achievement needs, combined with strong needs for affiliation, were most likely to demonstrate generativity when they reached middle adulthood. The Big 5 personality traits can play a role as well. Aspects of extraversion (which is somewhat agentic) and agreeableness (especially altruism, which is strongly communal) are correlated with generativity (Cox, Wilt, Olson, & McAdams, 2012). Finally, as we pointed out above, identity development contributes to generativity. For example, self-knowledge can help a person make choices, such as career and community activities that provide a good match to her skills and interests, so that she can maintain her intrinsic motivation to produce and create.

MyLab Education Self-Check 13.4.

Applications

The middle years are a challenging period of life. Adults have to contend with jobs, children, partners, and themselves, as well as the unexpected crises that occur. They bring very different experiences and dreams into adulthood. It is impossible to establish a life-stage trajectory that could take into account all this diversity with any level of precision. However, there do seem to be powerful themes, such as the quest for intimacy and generativity that characterize most adult lives.

We have seen that many theorists (e.g., Erikson, 1950/1963; Levinson, 1986; Vaillant, 1977) have attempted to specify these themes and their typical progress, though they all seem to recognize that we cannot expect every life story to unfold in some inevitable sequence of events or experiences. These same theorists have also described psychological requirements for healthy functioning as people move through adulthood. One consistent message that these authors communicate in various ways is this: Adults have to grow up. Growing up is not always easy and often not much fun, particularly in an age and in a society that heavily invests in the notion of personal satisfaction, youth, and freedom of choice. However, the very nature of the life cycle makes certain changes inevitable, and once those changes are accepted, they can be the source of great personal satisfaction and pride.

Adult Commitments

For most married people and other intimate partners, both joyous and painful experiences make up the fabric of close relationships and both wax and wane over the course of the life span. Some of these changes are predictable: when a new baby arrives, when children become adolescents, when adult children marry, when parents age and die, when partners experience age-related declines or the onset of illness. Some changes are due to unpredictable events: the sudden loss of a job or the demands of a new one, an unexpected illness, a relocation, a war or economic recession.

Professionals who work with couples can find it helpful to identify the sources of stress as coming from nonnormative or normative causes. Couples in crisis, for example, may be reeling from an unexpected and sometimes traumatic stressor that has taken its toll on the relationship. On the other hand, changes involved in predictable life events, such as steadily accumulating time demands or eroding incomes of working families with children, can affect the quality of relationships just as significantly and may not be quite as obvious to the people involved. Furthermore, changes that come with daily give and take, such as increased realization of a partner's flaws and idiosyncrasies combined with greater awareness of personal needs and preferences, can set the stage for relationship conflict.

Various methodologies have been employed to address couple difficulties, including behavioral approaches to improving communication and problem-solving skills, cognitive techniques for changing negative thoughts, affective or emotion-focused methods for teaching partners to own and express feelings more effectively, and intrapsychic models that relate present problems to early attachment histories. Specific modalities like Behavioral Couple Therapy ([BCT], Atkins, Dimidjian, & Christensen, 2003), Integrative Behavioral Couple Therapy ([ICBT], Jacobson & Christensen, 1996), and Emotionally Focused Couples Therapy ([EFT]; Johnson, Hunsley, Greenberg, & Schindler, 1999) have demonstrated empirical support and long-term effectiveness in helping distressed couples (Johnson & Lebow, 2000).

The Science of Couple Relationships

Fortunately for helping professionals, the science of couple relationships has progressed over recent decades to reveal some "rules" about how intimate human relationships work. Certainly, researchers don't claim to understand all the dynamics that operate for each couple, but they do offer clinicians a scientific base of information and a generic frame for viewing the individuals they see in the consulting room. Finkel, Simpson, and Eastwick (2017) recently organized years of research on couple relationships into four broad areas of interest. The results are presented in Table 13.7.

So, we can deduce that relationships are complex, interdependent, and changing. They have the power to alter working models over time and are affected by the responsiveness and conflict management style of the dyad, for better or for worse. Their trajectory and quality is impacted by partner characteristics, culture, coping, needs, and expectations. This information raises the question: With so much complexity, what can helpers hope to change? Luckily, just as our understanding of relationships has improved, so has our understanding of effective therapeutic principles. Most approaches try to accomplish some basic goals (Benson, McGinn, & Christensen, 2012).

1. First, it's important to help couples shift the way they see the presenting problem. Therapists can facilitate movement from a personal/one-sided view to a systems perspective. Recall the example of Hannah from Chapter 11 who was quite upset with her boyfriend's occasional drinking with friends. Drinking is bad, in her view, so she perceived Mike to be the source of their relational conflict. Now imagine Hannah and Mike married for 12 years, with the same conflict. Interestingly, the content of couples' problem discussions remains remarkably stable over time. Fully 69% of the time, couples' arguments are about a problem that has existed in the relationship for a long time (Gottman, 1999; Gottman & Silver, 2015). These "perpetual problems," which have to do with partners' personalities,

TABLE 13.7 What Do We Know from Years of Research on Couple Relationships?

QUESTIONS STUDIED	OVERALL FINDINGS	ILLUSTRATIVE EXAMPLE FROM RESEARCH
What is a relationship?	✓ Relationships are *more than just the sum of both parts*.	✓ Relationships reflect unique patterns that arise from partner interaction. Partners' combined commitment to the relationship contributes to overall sense of togetherness beyond each person's individual commitment.
	✓ When partners operate in *interdependent* ways, they tend to become more aligned in thinking, motivation, affect, and behavior.	✓ Higher relationship commitment may be evidenced by more plural pronouns like "we, us, and our."
	✓ Relationships change and develop over the long term, during which couples *revise their working models* of the relationship.	✓ Partners update information about each other as a function of daily, monthly, and yearly interactions. Over time, this can lead to internalized conclusions that one's partner is reliable and worthy of trust.
How do relationships operate?	✓ Partners *evaluate positive and negative* relationship qualities.	✓ People in relationships constantly evaluate their quality, using a two-dimensional set of characteristics (positive and negative). Most relationship variables are labeled in terms of the positive endpoint (highly intimate, low trust, etc.).
	✓ Relationship quality is enhanced by partner *responsiveness*.	✓ People who perceived their partners to provide high-quality, individually tailored support are happier, healthier, and have greater well-being than those who do not.
	✓ Partners' ways of *coping* with events (e.g., conflicts) have downstream effects on relationship stability and quality.	✓ If a transgressing partner does not make satisfactory amends for the transgression, the victim tends to be less satisfied in the relationship quality.
	✓ Committed partners tend to engage in more *relationship-enhancing* (even self-deceptive) processes.	✓ Committed partners are more likely to believe they have a better relationship than others, and more likely to make sacrifices for the relationship.
What do partners bring to the relationship?	✓ People bring *temperamental characteristics and traits* to the relationship.	✓ High or low self-esteem, neuroticism, and rejection sensitivity, among other characteristics, have the potential to influence the quality of the relationship. Neuroticism, in particular, is related to a wide variety of relationship problems.
	✓ People bring different *goals and needs* into the relationship.	✓ The ability to coordinate and achieve goals and meet needs is related to satisfaction.
	✓ People bring a set of *standards and expectations* into a relationship.	✓ Relationship satisfaction is increased when standards are met or exceeded.
How do contextual factors influence relationships?	✓ Partners *evaluate* relationships in *different contexts*.	✓ Various situations arise in relationships that provide opportunities to evaluate the partners' commitment.
	✓ People consider *options* to the existing relationship.	✓ The presence of an alternate partner, or the alternative of no partner, can threaten relationship quality.
	✓ *Stress* affects the relationship.	✓ Both chronic (e.g., financial strain) and acute (e.g., accident) stress can affect a relationship depending upon the couple's coping capacity.
	✓ *Culture* shapes relationships.	✓ Relationships are profoundly influenced by cultural norms and traditions and are embedded within extended families.

SOURCE: Based on Finkel, E. J., Simpson, J. A., & Eastwick, P. W. (2017). The psychology of close relationships: Fourteen core principles. *Annual Review of Psychology*, 68(1), 383–411. Copyright 2017 by Annual Reviews. All rights reserved.

may be expressed in the partners' different behavioral styles or ways of approaching issues such as money, sex, or in-laws. As we have learned, there is evidence for continuity in many temperamental characteristics, and they constitute relatively stable features of individuals' behavior and cognition throughout their life span. Based on his work, Gottman (1999) suggests that therapists "encourage couples to think of these relationship problems as inevitable, much the way we learn to deal with chronic physical ailments as we get older. The chronic back pain, the trick knee and tennis elbow or irritable bowel do not go away, but we learn to have a dialogue with these problems. We keep trying to make

things a little better all the time, but we learn to live with these problems and manage our world so as to minimize them. . . . So it is in all relationships" (p. 57).

2. The second goal, across modalities, is to help couples reduce the amount of emotional distress and negativity in their relationships, especially when there is conflict. Perhaps Hannah still becomes extremely upset when Mike occasionally stops to meet his friends for a drink after work. She accuses him of hurting her and betraying his moral principles as soon as he returns home, prompting a familiar cycle of blaming (Hannah) and withdrawing (Mike). Emotions such as anger are highly arousing and can escalate into a cascade of

negative feelings that shut down real communication. Gottman (1994b) describes in precise detail how these escalating emotions affect interaction:

> From the data gathered in our lab, we've seen how quickly discussions fall apart as soon as one spouse's heart rate begins to soar. Because physical responses are such an accurate barometer of your ability to communicate at a particular moment, tracking your arousal level during intense conversation will help keep your discussions on track as well. (p. 176)

This requires that each person be aware of his or her own physiological and emotional reactions. This as a multi-step process in actual practice: becoming aware of one's reactivity and taking steps towards regulating it effectively. Awareness can be fostered by helping clients learn to take their pulse rate as a measure of physiological arousal, to learn to ask for and take time-outs, and to engage in relaxation activities in order to return to baseline levels of arousal, a process that takes an average of 20 minutes after becoming aroused. Gottman notes that this is a particularly important step for males who typically get physiologically "flooded" with emotion more quickly than women and who take longer to return to baseline (Levenson & Gottman, 1985). Higher levels of physiological arousal during conflict is associated predictively with more unhappiness, so soothing and restoring methods are very important. Partners who are agitated during conflict, with accelerated heart rates, sweating palms, and rapid breathing secrete more adrenalin and other chemical mediators of the stress system, making listening and showing empathy, let alone some humor, virtually impossible. Fight or flight mode gives us tunnel vision and fosters a perception that we are "under attack" by our partner (Gottman & Gottman, 2017).

Couples who live under conditions of sustained interpersonal stress, marital conflict, and dissatisfaction are at risk for mental and physical illness. Significantly, intimate relationships affect partners' health synergistically, as a function of shared experiences, interactions, and transmission of emotional states. Poor marital quality has been related to depression, sleep disorders, metabolic syndrome, and diabetes (Kiecolt-Glaser & Wilson, 2017). Thus, efforts to improve couples' relationship quality has long-term public health benefits.

3. Next, therapists across modalities help clients manage, understand, and express emotions. Emotional suppression intensifies problematic interaction patterns, and over-reactivity can lead to aggression. Partners can become trapped in destructive patterns of relating that create persistent distress. In the demand–withdraw pattern (Eldridge & Christensen, 2002), a very common communication pattern, one partner withdraws to escape the demands of the other and, as a result, demands escalate and withdrawal is reinforced. Mike might be helped to express his disappointment with the couple's communication in the safety of the therapy setting. Hannah might be helped to learn self-soothing techniques for managing her anxiety about the dire consequences of Mike's occasional drinking. The target of therapist intervention will undoubtedly depend upon the nature of the problem as well as the therapist's orientation. However, most couple therapists, regardless of orientation, know to set clear limits on hostile and aggressive displays in therapy sessions to guard against further erosion of the partnership. Counselors are often called upon to help couples work on empathy-building, particularly when their attachment relationship is weakened due to neglect, injury, or prolonged conflict. Sometimes old wounds reemerge in the present and need to be readdressed. Success in relationships often depends upon "the wounded partner being able to express deep hurts and losses and the other partner staying emotionally engaged and actively responding to these emotions with compassion and comfort" (Johnson, 2003, p. 373). Browning's (1998) empathy-expansion procedure helps partners address a long-standing relationship hurt through a specific process facilitated by the therapist. Through a sequence of steps, the counselor coaches one partner to recognize and apologize for the injury that has been causing the impasse. The goal is to enhance empathic responding and to give the aggrieved partner real validation for his or her pain. Clearly, this is most appropriate for couples who are motivated to put past hurts behind them and who are willing to "do whatever it takes" to mend the relationship.

Gottman and Gottman (2017) have found that for unhappy couples, conflict opens the door to a negative state of mind that is hard to escape. The authors describe it as "stepping into a quicksand bog. No matter how hard they tried, they only sank deeper and deeper into negativity, eventually escalating to the Four Horsemen" (p. 14). Contributing to a couple's positive "bank account" in non-conflictual times through giving validation, providing assurances, showing interest, and sharing humor and affection can strengthen the emotional connection that provides some insurance against intermittent negativity. In particular, a husband's playfulness and enthusiasm were related to his wife's willingness to be more affectionate when the couple did experience a conflict.

4. Improving couple communication is the fourth principle. Both Mike and Hannah can also learn communication skills that will help them deal with conflicts more effectively in the future. The emphasis on improving communication has a long-established history in marital therapy and in relationship education (Halford, Markman, Kline, & Stanley, 2003). The goal of such interventions is generally to help individuals express their feelings and disagreements in ways their partner can understand. What is critical here appears to be reducing the tendency to come out swinging when conflicts arise. Called "harsh startups" by Gottman and Silver (1999), a conversation about a problem that starts with criticism, contempt, or sarcasm is likely to become an argument that deteriorates quickly. This speedy buildup of emotional negativity results in feelings of being flooded and can lead one or both partners to protect themselves by stonewalling. Taking a "softer" approach when addressing potentially

difficult issues can reduce defensive responding and maintain a more positive state.

5. Teaching couples to focus on positive aspects of the relationship and to practice relationship maintenance skills on a regular basis is the final goal. Relationship maintenance refers to those actions and interactions that sustain the desired quality of relationship or repair a relationship once there is a rupture. Mike can learn ways to verbalize his commitment and show affection to Hannah, and both partners can talk more openly about shared goals. Simply stated, relationships tend to flourish when the psychological atmosphere is positive, and they tend to deteriorate when it becomes negative. Because stress and disagreements are an inevitable part of all long-term relationships, successful therapies appear to blend skills of conflict management with those of positive relationship enhancement. Among the Zulu, a person is traditionally greeted with a word that is roughly translated to mean "I see you." The response to this greeting is "I am here." Notice the direction of this interchange: Until you see me, I am not here. We are psychologically "here" because we are seen and known by intimate others, much in the way Cooley describes the looking-glass phenomenon. In the intimate world of close relationships, individuals do not need so much for their partners to solve their problems as for their partners to see and validate what they're going through. It appears that relationship satisfaction is related not only to how conflicts are resolved but also to the quality of the emotional connection constructed bit by bit though the mundane interchanges that fill couples' lives. These aspects of a relationship appear to be amenable to therapeutic intervention, whereas many of the cultural, contextual, historical, and personality variables we have discussed are not amenable to intervention. Maintenance skills, however, offer couples the possibility of relationship change.

The Importance of Work

Generativity is not only manifested in building relationships and caregiving. It also is shown in one's efforts to contribute something to society through work. Most adults find work to be an important expression of their talents and abilities. Our working lives are deeply connected to our sense of personal identity. The experience of nonnormative work-related events, like job loss, can affect well-being and, in some cases, permanently alter one's life course. Job loss represents a particular challenge to the normative expectations that most adults hold about their lives: to provide for themselves and their loved ones consistently and independently. When workers lose their jobs, a singular expression of their generative capacity is compromised (see Fouad & Bynner, 2008). A longitudinal study of more than 24,000 German respondents over 15 years found that for people who experienced episodes of unemployment, their lives were never quite the same (Lucas, Clark, Georgellis, & Diener, 2004). Workers experienced a decline in overall life satisfaction following job loss and a trending upward towards pre-unemployment levels of satisfaction after reemployment.

Nevertheless, their sense of life satisfaction did not return to baseline, even many years after being reemployed.

Job loss and unemployment are related to mental and physical health problems (Daly & Delaney, 2013; Paul & Moser, 2009; Wege, Angerer, & Li, 2017). Individuals who were unemployed in young adulthood reported greater weight gain, smoking, decreased physical activity, and poorer overall health than those who had been consistently employed (van der Noordt, Ijzelenberg, Droomers, & Proper, 2014). Unfortunately, the effects of job loss or gaps in employment do not necessarily remit after some time but contribute to declines in mental and physical health around retirement age (von Bonsdorff, Kuh, von Bonsdorff, & Cooper, 2016). Although financial strain is the most significant reason for depression following job loss, Price, Choi, and Vinokur (2002) have shown that the effects on physical and mental health are mediated by the erosion of a sense of personal control that accompanies the reduction of financial resources. Furthermore, these elements operate transactionally. As the authors indicate, "While job loss and financial strain may influence depression, depression, in turn, may reduce access to opportunities to reduce financial strain through reemployment. Thus, chains of adversity are clearly complex and may contain spirals of disadvantage that reduce the life chances of vulnerable individuals still further" (2002, p. 310). The ripples extend to children, as well, who suffer from more behavioral and academic problems when their parents are under financial strain (Conger, Ge, Elder, Lorenz, & Simons, 1994).

Helpers who work with people experiencing job loss need to take into account such psychological consequences, namely increased stress, anxiety, and feelings of hopelessness, as well as physical problems that may arise, as they help clients deal with this stressful event. Sometimes, individuals might try to cope through behaviors like excessive use of drugs or alcohol. Prevention programs offer some demonstrated success in curtailing the downward spiral of disadvantage following job loss. Self-efficacy skill training appears to play an important part in effective programs. Participants in the JOBS project (Akkermans, Brenninkmeijer, Schaufeli, & Blonk, 2015; Vinokur, Schul, Vuori, & Price, 2000) as well as in Cognitive-Behavioral programs that help alter negative thinking and bolster regulatory self-efficacy (Rose et al., 2012) showed success in finding reemployment, demonstrated fewer symptoms of depression, and reflected better overall adjustment than nonparticipants. There are three main elements to the JOBS program: (1) building skills for the job search, such as improving resume writing, learning to "think like" the employer, networking, and contacting potential employers; (2) increasing participants' sense of self-efficacy through graded exposure exercises, role-modeling, and reinforcement of effective behavior; and (3) inoculating participants against setbacks that they might encounter in the job search process by identifying possible barriers while practicing the skills needed to overcome the obstacles (Price & Vinokur, 1995).

Although the ultimate goal of counseling may be to find new employment, it is important to remember that the clients' confidence may be badly bruised and in need of shoring up. This might help explain why some clients do not pursue reemployment in active ways like sending out resumes or going on job interviews. It may be their way of avoiding further damage to self-esteem (Price, 1992). It also suggests why fostering self-efficacy is so important (Lagerveld, Brenninkmeijer, Blonk, Twisk, & Schaufeli, 2017).

Creative interventions, not as task-specific as job searching, may also ameliorate the downstream physical and mental health effects of job loss, discontinuity, or strain that persist into later life. Professionals are fortunate to be able to draw on the rapidly growing body of research in integrative health. As we will discuss in Chapter 14, the mind and body are not separable. Pain, fatigue, poor diet, lack of exercise, substance use, and chronic illness go hand in hand with daily stress, taking their toll in unique and cumulative ways. The challenges of shift work and non-stop responsibility can put adults at risk. Helping clients prioritize reasonable self-care can augment active job seeking steps.

Sleep, in particular, seems to be an underappreciated resource for physical and mental health and personal effectiveness. Naiman (2017) reports on the epidemic of sleep deprivation in the United States that is raising alarms from health professionals. Lack of sleep, particularly the critically important REM (rapid-eye movement) phase of sleep associated with dreaming, contributes to problems with memory, immunity, weight control, and mood. Associations have also been reported between REM sleep deprivation and cardiovascular problems, diabetes, Parkinson's disease, and dementia. Causes for this widespread problem have been identified as increased substance use (alcohol, marijuana), sleep medications that privilege light sleep over deep REM sleep, antidepressants and other medications, the ubiquity of artificial light at night, and insufficient time devoted to sleep. Helpers might explore sleep issues with adults and provide information about good sleep hygiene as an important foundation for personal well-being and ability to care for others.

Off-Time

Adulthood is a time when individuals may have to contend with the realization that events or accomplishments that they once wished for have not been achieved. Individuals of all ages may feel distressed by a sense that they did not meet their developmental goals or expectations "on-time." Feeling "off-time," as it relates to such things as getting married, having children, reaching career goals, or other normative achievements, reflects the fact that we all have a set of age-related expectations for the appropriate timing of major life events. This phenomenon is called the social clock. Clinicians should be sensitive to this particular source of distress in the lives of their clients to help them cope more effectively. Certainly helpers can support client strivings to find outlets for generative needs that might be met in flexible ways. Even the strains of caring for children or older relatives can be reframed as valuable contributions. For clients without such responsibilities, other outlets might be explored.

Couples may voluntarily choose not to have children or may find themselves childless involuntarily. Although societies are becoming increasingly accepting of personal decision in this area, sometimes subtle and not-so-subtle biases arise that communicate pressure and/or judgment about a child-free life. One way of therapeutically helping those individuals or couples who feel distressed is to recreate narratives that reflect alternative paths to generativity. These may consist of other, more accessible, forms of caring and creative expression as well as deepening of existing relationships (Moore, Allbright-Campos, & Strick, 2017).

Becoming generative can be viewed as a way of growing up, by taking and accepting responsibility for oneself and for dependents, by forgiving past generations for what they may have done, and by working to leave a legacy. As we have learned, flexibility and adaptability in the face of life's demands support this process. One developmental task involves the shift in expectations that may occur gradually over this time from adolescent idealism to mature acceptance of reality (Gould, 1978).

Adulthood means getting far enough outside oneself to do as Margaret Mead urged:

> "to cherish the life of the world," that is, to connect with life itself rather than just with oneself, to overcome the narcissism of our youth and make give-and-take connections from which we can feel the pain and pleasure of others rather than crouching selfishly and alone in our own protective skins. . . . The maturing function of psychotherapy is to get people past a narcissistic state where they notice only what other people do and how it makes them feel, and move them into a mature state where they notice what they do and how it makes other people feel. (p. 257)

Focus on Developmental Psychopathology

Post-Traumatic Stress Disorder

Human beings are born with the capacity to experience fear, one of our primary emotions. Fearfulness has evolutionary significance and is necessary for survival. Imagine how long our ancestors would have survived had they not become attuned to the signs of predators and other threats. But is there a difference between fear and anxiety? And when does anxiety become an anxiety disorder? Fear may be considered a hard-wired response to an immediate threatening stimulus, the kind that makes your palms sweat, your heart race, and your stomach tie itself into a knot. Fear triggers the "fight or flight" changes of the body-mind first proposed by Walter Cannon (Bracha, Ralston, Matsukawa, Williams, & Bracha, 2004; Cannon, 1929). Anxiety has been viewed as that uneasy sense of imminent danger. In other words, we get anxious about the possibility of something fearful happening.

In learning theory terms, both classical and operant conditioning processes are in play. Stimuli that actually cause fear or pain, such as loud noises or electric shock, can become associated with other neutral stimuli. In the end, these classically conditioned stimuli elicit the same physiological fear response as the original stimuli because of powerful learned associations. Termination of aversive stimuli results in escape learning, and escape behaviors are reinforced by virtue of their power to provide relief. Ultimately, avoidance conditioning patterns develop whereby individuals tend to avoid settings or situations that *may cause* distress because they have learned a set of anticipatory cues. Avoidance is strengthened through the process of negative reinforcement. Consider a woman who, as a result of early experiences of punishment or love withdrawal for expressing anger towards parents or others, has learned to suppress these threatening feelings. Such early aversive consequences can result in long-term patterns of conflict avoidance as well as avoidance of her own subjective angry feelings. The process is a maladaptive turn of events. What was once adaptive, avoiding pain and discomfort, becomes a generalized operating principle in circumstances that may not be particularly threatening. The maladaptive result, called "experiential avoidance," or anxious apprehension and avoidance of one's own real experience, can be quite problematic (Hayes, 2004). The harmful effects of emotional avoidance and suppression have increasingly been recognized (Hayes, 2016). Opportunities to become more assertive and less anxious in social situations are effectively shut down through avoidance patterns.

When fear and anxiety become overwhelming, individuals can develop anxiety disorders, which cause significant restriction in their lives and persistent intrusion into their states of mind. Unfortunately, anxiety disorders are very common. Across the world, estimates of anxiety disorders range from approximately 4% to 25% (Remes, Brayne, van der Linde, & Lafortune, 2016), with certain groups more affected than others: women, young adults, chronic illness sufferers, and people in North American, North African, Middle Eastern, and European regions. Anxiety also accompanies many other mental illnesses, including depression, schizophrenia, and substance abuse. Previously, anxiety disorders were defined as the class of disorders that shared the characteristic feature of anxiety. DSM-V has revised its diagnostic criteria for anxiety disorders due to better understanding of their causes. Those that remain in the anxiety disorder category include panic, phobia, and generalized anxiety disorders. **Post-traumatic stress disorder (PTSD)** is now in a class of disorders called Stressor and Trauma-Related Disorders, given its clear association with traumatic events (APA, 2013).

PTSD reflects an extreme, persistent, and pathological expression of human stress system physiology (Bernardy & Friedman, 2015). PTSD, together with dementia and substance-induced disorders, is one of the very few diagnostic categories in the DSM whose onset has a clearly identifiable cause, namely the experience of a traumatic event. However, as we shall see, not everyone who is exposed to trauma develops PTSD. From a developmental perspective, it is a good example of the interaction of genetic and environmental influences on psychopathology.

The scientific study of trauma and its effects is a relatively recent phenomenon. Perhaps the incidence of horrific events around the globe, such as wars, abuse, terrorist attacks, and natural disasters, as well as a more refined appreciation of the effects of stress on biopsychosocial processes have sharpened our awareness of the sequelae of such traumas. When PTSD was introduced into the DSM-III in 1980, it was criticized as a conglomeration of symptoms that were patched together to constitute a mental illness in order to procure needed treatment and benefits for Vietnam veterans (Kirk & Kutchins, 1997). Critics of the diagnosis claimed that it was one more example of the psychiatric establishment creating a mental illness out of a normal human response to unusually terrifying events. Researchers have sought to test the charge that PTSD is a Western social construction and have found that individuals throughout the world who have been exposed to traumatic incidents express the symptoms of PTSD (Keane, Marshall, & Taft, 2006). In a population survey across 24 countries, 70% of individuals reported experiencing at least one traumatic event in their lifetimes (Benjet et al., 2016). Although not everyone will go on to suffer from PTSD, cross-national estimates indicate approximately 6% of the trauma-exposed sample meet diagnostic criteria for this disorder (Koenen et al., 2017). Cultural differences in symptom expression, coping style, and stressor profiles (e.g., discrimination) may present unique risks for PTSD development in racial and ethnic minority subgroups. Unfortunately, the suffering caused by PTSD tends to endure. Schnurr and colleagues (2000) found that complete PTSD symptomology continued to plague 32% of soldiers exposed to mustard gas a full 50 years after their exposure in World War II.

Diagnostic Features

For diagnosis of PTSD, a person must have experienced, witnessed, or been confronted with an event so traumatizing that it results in symptoms of *re-experiencing, hyperarousal, cognitive alterations*, and *avoidance*. Such events could include the experience of war, torture, rape, or physical/sexual abuse, to name a few. Some suggest that witnessing such events or being a relative or helper of trauma victims is also sufficient for traumatization, a phenomenon called secondary or vicarious traumatization (McCann & Pearlman, 1990). Symptoms of *re-experiencing* might be manifested by the presence of flashbacks, recurrent dreams, or heightened fear and anxiety when exposed to internal or external trauma-related cues. Symptoms of *hyperarousal* might include irritability, lack of concentration, hypervigilance, sleep problems, or heightened startle response. Symptoms of *avoidance* include behaviors that serve to allow victims to avoid people, places, or things that could trigger an association with the trauma. Avoidance tactics may also extend to avoiding thoughts and feelings that elicit memories of trauma, possibly in an attempt to down-regulate the intensity of re-experiencing. Symptoms also include *altered cognition and mood* related to the traumatic event.

Who Develops PTSD?

Let's consider the interesting question of who develops PTSD. Researchers suggest that the development of this disorder rests upon a combination of factors: biological vulnerability, psychological vulnerability, and the experience of trauma. Binder et al. (2008) found that an early history of childhood trauma/abuse in addition to certain genetic variants was important in predicting the later PTSD symptomatology. We should be cautious, however, about interpreting genetic findings to imply a determinative relationship between certain genes, trauma, and later PTSD. Consistent with the principal of multifinality, twin studies show that genes found to be related to PTSD were also associated with anxiety, depressive, and substance abuse disorders (IOM, 2012).

As we have discussed in earlier chapters, patterns of cortisol receptors are shaped in the developing brain by early experience, and the experience of abuse may make individuals' neurophysiology more sensitive to the effects of stress over time. This understanding appears to be supported by evidence from combat veterans who served in Afghanistan. Berntsen and colleagues (2012) found that the experience of adversity in childhood was a better predictor of which soldiers developed PTSD than the trauma experienced in deployment.

Difficulties in executive functions, low intelligence, and education level prior to a traumatic incident have also been associated with the risk of developing PTSD (IOM, 2012). Executive functions involve the capacity to inhibit distractions and voluntarily direct attention to certain objects of attention. Some research suggests that compromised ability to disengage attention from stimuli that are highly salient can make it difficult to disengage from later traumatic memories, exacerbating symptoms of PTSD (Aupperle, Melrose, Stein, & Paulus, 2012). Early anxiety and depression, patterns of antisocial behavior in childhood, lack of social support, sexual victimization (especially for women), and sexual minority status are particular pre-existing features that also confer greater risk (Sayed, Iacoviello, & Charney, 2015).

It is reasonable to think that more numerous and more serious experiences of trauma would predict PTSD with greater precision. However, research results on this issue have been inconsistent. Therefore, other variables that might moderate the impact of trauma on survivors have been the subject of investigation. One possibility is sleep quality/insomnia, because sleep disturbances make it difficult to regulate emotions, consolidate memory, and control stress reactivity; all are important functions that are disturbed in PTSD. Evidence in support of sleep's moderating role was found by researchers who studied veterans from Iraq (Cox, McIntyre, & Olatunji, 2017). Veterans with the most combat exposure and the most severe insomnia reported the highest frequency of re-experiencing symptoms. Low levels of insomnia did not predict re-experiencing despite the level of trauma. These results suggest that amount of trauma exposure alone does not predict symptoms. Rather, insomnia may function like prolonged stress exposure and impede the adaptive consolidation of traumatic memories that could inhibit recovery (Cox, Tuck, & Olatunji, 2017). Current research attention on sleep as an underappreciated risk factor is timely, not only for PTSD, but also for suicidal behaviors and other mental health disorders (Ribeiro et al., 2012).

Features of Treatment

Just as we are discovering what causes PTSD to develop in certain individuals, some consensus is developing around which therapeutic elements are helpful in public health and clinical interventions for PTSD (Lee, Schnitzlein, Wolf, Vythilingam, Rasmusson, & Hoge, 2016; Hobfoll et al., 2007). The first element is to address safety. This means providing a safe place for victims, promulgating media messages of safety and resilience rather than those of continuing threat, limiting exposure to media that evoke threatening cues, restricting the amount of talk about traumatic events to reduce hyperarousal, and using techniques to ground individuals in their immediate, safer reality, once they are out of imminent danger.

Another element is calming. Victims should receive prompt, practical assistance for their most pressing needs (e.g., food, shelter, etc.) and accurate information about the well-being of their loved ones. Psycho-education about the effects of stress and trauma, relaxation training with imagery, cognitive restructuring, cognitive diffusion, and mindfulness practices and coping skills training might be employed. These interventions are useful in helping individuals better regulate stress physiology and interrupt the development of avoidance behaviors, which, as we have already noted, can seriously impair functioning and integrate memories of traumatic events. One approach, psychological debriefing, is not recommended because of equivocal empirical findings and the possibility of enhancing hyperarousal for some victims by virtue of retraumatization (Sayed et al., 2015; van Emmerik, Kamphuis, Hulsbosch, & Emmelkamp, 2002). Recent research indicates that the benefits of empiricallysupported trauma-focused psychotherapies are significant and long lasting. Consequently, these are recommended as the first line treatment choice (Lee et al., 2016). It is notable that such trauma-focused therapies have been demonstrated to be more effective and to have fewer side effects than available and commonly prescribed medications for PTSD.

Efforts to support self and collective efficacy are also important. Specifically, promoting individuals' sense of efficacy in relation to coping with trauma is important. Interventions should draw on local community supports to provide a caring network for victims. Emphasis on setting reasonable goals for rebuilding lives after trauma promotes a sense of personal control, healthy adaptation, and resilience. A closely linked principle is connectedness. Interventions and community reorganization efforts (in the case of mass trauma) should be structured to bolster connections among survivors and their social networks. Victims should be educated in how to access what they need, materially and interpersonally, through partnerships with families, social agencies, churches, and so on. Supports should be clear and reliable so as to assure trauma survivors of predictable assistance.

Finally, efforts should include the element of instilling hope. Hope counteracts the tendency of victims to perceive their future as foreshortened, to question their ability to survive, and to succumb to resignation and even despair. Approaches that help individuals deal with irrational fears and unrealistic expectations, de-catastrophize, and identify existing strengths permit hope to take hold in the midst of great suffering. However, the authors caution helpers not to encourage victims to see benefits and meaning in a traumatic event before they are ready to do so. Hobfoll, Canetti-Nisim, and Johnson (2006) found that benefit-finding as a therapeutic technique was related to increases in PTSD symptoms, greater defensiveness, and potential for retaliation, possibly because benefit-finding may be perceived as an attempt to minimize the real struggles and hardships associated with traumatic events.

Summary

Life Span Developmental Theory

1. The complexity of adult development makes it clear that multidimensional models are needed to adequately understand the processes of change. Life span developmental models focus on both hereditary and environmental influences and on the continuities and changes that characterize adults. They emphasize that adaptation continues from birth to death.

2. In life span developmental theory, Baltes describes the architecture of biology and culture, a web of interacting organismic and environmental influences on development. During childhood, he argues, optimal development is strongly supported by the processes of natural selection, such that most people reach adulthood and can contribute to the success of the species by reproducing. But biological supports weaken by middle adulthood, as selection pressures decline. Thus, from middle adulthood on, more cultural supports are required to ensure optimal development.

3. Throughout the life span, change involves both gains and losses, but the relative balance of gains and losses shifts as people move toward old age. Adaptation throughout life involves growth, maintenance or resilience, and the regulation of loss. But growth is more common in childhood, whereas regulation of loss is more common in old age. Successful development, or healthy coping, at any age is the relative maximization of gains and the minimization of losses, but coping changes as people age.

Influences on Adult Development: Sources of Stability

4. The Big 5 personality traits are neuroticism/emotional stability, extraversion, openness, agreeableness, and conscientiousness. There are two kinds of developmental change in adult personality traits with age. First, people gain social maturity over time, meaning they tend to increase in agreeableness and conscientiousness and decrease in neuroticism. Second, by about age 30, individual differences tend to stabilize: A person's ranking on a trait, relative to others in her cohort, tends to stay constant.

5. Both clinical (e.g., therapeutic) and non-clinical (e.g., educational) interventions can enable personality changes, such as decreasing neuroticism.

6. Adult personality traits are somewhat correlated with temperament in childhood. Although heredity is implicated in the development and stability of traits, a relatively stable environment is probably equally important.

Influences on Adult Development: Sources of Change

7. Age-graded change refers to change that comes as a function of time. Some predictable physical changes in adulthood include declines in sensory ability and in reproductive ability (much more for women than for men). Appearance changes as skin wrinkles and sags, and weight gain is common though not inevitable.

8. Cognitive changes with age are best studied with longitudinal methods. A mixed pattern of improvement and decline occurs, related to differences in fluid intelligence (mechanics) versus crystallized intelligence (pragmatics). Fluid or mechanical processes, such as processing speed and inhibitory mechanisms, begin to show declines in middle adulthood. Crystallized resources, including all forms of declarative and procedural knowledge, are not as likely to decline, and for many people they increase throughout middle and even old age. Only after about age 60 do losses in fluid intelligence somewhat outweigh crystallized gains for the average individual.

9. The relative losses and gains are illustrated by memory effects. The capacity of working memory declines with age, which can affect problem solving negatively, as fewer pieces of information can be held in mind simultaneously. Semantic memory, however, continues to expand with age, as we learn more and more information, and often older adults solve problems better than younger ones because they are more likely to have expertise they can bring to the task.

10. Life-task or life-course changes are age-graded changes in the tasks and responsibilities that confront us or seem important as we age. Theorists such as Schaie, Erikson, Vaillant, Levinson, Jung, Gould, and so on have all described stages or phases in life-task change. Despite the significant differences in the lives of individuals, there do seem to be relatively predictable sequences of change in our concerns as we move through adulthood.

11. History-graded changes affect the development of a whole cohort. A life-course perspective emphasizes that

development is influenced by chronological age, family-related roles, and membership in a birth cohort. Thus, the same historical events can have different effects on members of different cohorts. For example, recent cohorts of children are experiencing a time of increased breakdown in social connections. Apparently as a result, they experience more anxiety than older cohorts did as children.

12. Nonnormative changes refer to unexpected events, such as an accident or untimely death of a loved one that can alter developmental trajectories.

13. Socioeconomic position (SEP) (similar to SES) is an important developmental influence. Health, longevity, and many other developmental outcomes differ as a function of SEP.

Key Developmental Tasks of Midlife: The Continuing Pursuit of Intimacy and Generativity

14. Adults involved in a primary relationship such as marriage are generally happier than single adults. Other relationships, such as friendships, are also important sources of life satisfaction. Critical features of such relationships involve sharing, working out problems, and developing a sense of "we-ness."

15. The family life cycle begins with mate selection, a kind of winnowing process based largely on homogamy and compatibility. Love is also seen as important in our culture. Sternberg described three elements: passion, intimacy, and decision/commitment. Once a commitment is established, a blending of family systems is involved, not just a joining of individuals. Other stages in the more typical family life cycle include becoming parents and then the transition of launching and renegotiating the marital relationship.

16. A high percentage of marriages end in divorce in the United States, often creating financial hardship for the wife and emotional and behavioral difficulties for children. For many people, marital satisfaction persistently declines over the life of a marriage. Theories about the causes of marital harmony and discord include the disillusionment model (when romantic notions are dashed, marriages fail), the maintenance hypothesis (romantic couples work to maintain their illusions and therefore their marriage), and the social exchange and behavioral theories (marriages fail when problems and conflict escalate to become overwhelming because of inadequate strategies for coping with conflict). Intrapersonal models draw on attachment theory and notions about temperament to explain marital success or failure.

17. Studies of marital dynamics suggest that marriages are successful or satisfying to the extent that positive factors outweigh negative factors, including interactive behaviors, perceptions, and physiology (e.g., endocrine functioning). High levels of negative affect reciprocity (likelihood that negativity in one partner will be followed by negativity from the other) is especially predictive of marital dissolution. What are termed the *four horsemen of the apocalypse* are especially problematic: criticism, defensiveness, contempt, and stonewalling.

Generativity: Making a Mark at Midlife

18. Each period of a child's life presents new challenges to parents. A parent's age, SES, personality and coping skills, and support systems all contribute to how satisfying parenting is (e.g., older parents generally find parenting more rewarding than younger parents).

19. Most parents find their task both stressful and rewarding. Infants are far more difficult to care for than most people expect, but they also bring joy to most parents. Toddlers, combining new skills with poor self-control or understanding, need very close supervision, so they are time and energy consuming. As their unique "self-hood" begins to blossom, they also become more interesting. In middle childhood, parenting is usually much easier as children become logical thinkers but are still relatively unambivalent about their dependence on their parents. Adolescent children are usually experienced as more demanding and difficult as they push for independence, take more risks, and de-idealize their parents. The launching period usually is positive, as parents have fewer responsibilities and their children become more self-sufficient, although many factors, such as parents' work and other roles, influence how the transition is experienced. Parents of middle adults relate to their children more as equals, although assistance and support still tends to flow more from parent to child.

20. Sometimes middle-aged adults find themselves with dual caregiving responsibilities—parents to their children and caretakers for their aging parents. This sandwiched position can be very stressful, depending on factors such as the availability of other sources of support.

21. In middle age, people generally feel they have reached the peak of their career in terms of expertise, income, and advancement. Work intensity and time invested increase in the first half of middle adulthood and taper off thereafter, with most people increasing time spent with friends and family. This pattern can vary dramatically across individuals and is linked to gender. A rise in dual-career couples in recent decades is linked to increases in men's involvement in family roles. Middle adults usually function in many roles, which can increase stress but also allows for role buffering. How multiple roles affect well-being depends in part on gender and social class.

22. A sense of generative accomplishment depends on how creative and productive adults feel. Two kinds of generativity have been described: agency (creating, producing) and communion (wishing to care for the next generation). People who score high on measures of generativity report higher levels of self-esteem and happiness than others. A coherent sense of a self, moving in a positive direction, seems to characterize people who score high on generativity.

Case Study

Lien is a 46-year-old Vietnamese American woman. She has two adult children, a son and a daughter, as well as one granddaughter. She lives in a small apartment near her mother, now in her late 60s. Lien visits her mother several times a week to check on her health and her emotional state. Although Lien's mother, Mrs. Nguyen, is relatively self-sufficient, a recent medical check-up suggested some early warning signs of a neurological disorder. Lien's mother expects attention from her daughter and will let her know when she feels she's being neglected. Lien has always been very responsible and concerned about the well-being of her family members. Even though this takes a lot of her time, she faithfully attends to her mother's needs without complaint. Now, with the threat of a potentially deteriorating health problem, she is more concerned than ever about her mother's health and her own ability to cope.

Lien and her husband, who was born in Vietnam, settled with their young children in a state on the West Coast. Although Lien met and married her husband in the United States, he always wanted to go back to Vietnam, a place he considered his real home. After 10 years, he left the family to return to his home country, because he missed his extended family. He also worried that he could not make enough money to support two children. Single now for 16 years, Lien feels that she would like to meet someone with whom she could share her life. This is a new feeling for Lien. Until recently, she was too distracted with the problems of raising her children and getting her small business started to think about herself. Now she feels that she only has a limited

amount of time left to pursue some of her own wishes. She can envision herself like her mother, old and alone, and that prospect disturbs her. She has started to attend social functions at her church and has accepted some social invitations from members of the close-knit local community.

Lien's life has recently become more complicated. Her daughter, Annie, and her 2-year-old granddaughter, Emily, have moved in with her. The relationship between Annie and her husband, Dave, deteriorated after Emily's birth, and the couple fought frequently. Annie accused Dave of spending too much of his paycheck on frivolous things and not spending enough time with her family. Dave, in response, withdrew even further, spent more time with his friends, and continued to spend money as he pleased. Annie finally took the baby and threatened not to come back.

Discussion Questions

1. What are the developmental stresses (age-related) and contextual stresses (nonnormative) in Lien's life at the present time? Consider her age, family role, and cultural context.
2. What are Lien's sources of strength? What internal and external factors might support her resilience in the face of difficulties?
3. What is the potential impact of Annie's return on her mother at this stage of her life?
4. How might you help Annie and Dave if they came to you for counseling?

Practice Using What You Have Learned

MyLab Education Application Exercise 13.1. Development as Growth, Maintenance, and Regulation of Loss

MyLab Education Application Exercise 13.2. Generativity: The Sandwich Generation

MyLab Education Application Exercise 13.3. Children of Divorce

Journal Questions

1. If you can, ask your parent or a member of your family to describe you using the Big 5 personality traits. Which of your personality traits have remained stable over time? Which have changed?
2. Consider a major event that has occurred in your lifetime (like a war, recession, revolution, major shift in technology, etc.). What effect has this had on your life? Now think of someone from an older or younger generation. Do you think the effects will be similar to or different from your own? What is the impact of developmental timing on history-graded change?
3. Think of a committed couple you know well. You could also reflect on a relationship of your own. What are the major challenges of the relationship? How do the partners handle conflict? What relationship maintenance behaviors are present? How could these behaviors be strengthened? What part or parts of couple therapy would be the most important to this couple?
4. What are the normative and nonnormative challenges you are facing now? How are you coping with each? What other coping strategies could you try?

Key Concepts

ontogeny (p. 505)
growth (p. 506)
maintenance or resilience (p. 506)
regulation of loss (p. 506)
Five Factor Model (Big 5) (p. 508)
neuroticism (emotional stability) (p. 508)
extraversion (p. 508)
openness (p. 508)
agreeableness (p. 508)
conscientiousness (p. 508)
social maturity (p. 509)
adolescing (p. 512)
senescing (p. 512)
climacteric (p. 512)
menopause (p. 512)
andropause (p. 513)

fluid intelligence (mechanics) (p. 514)
crystallized intelligence (pragmatics) (p. 515)
ego integrity (vs. despair) (p. 516)
career consolidation (vs. self-absorption) (p. 516)
keeper of meaning (vs. rigidity) (p. 517)
life structure (p. 517)
cohort effects (p. 519)
life-course perspective (p. 519)
socioeconomic position (SEP) (p. 520)
social gradient (p. 520)
family life cycle (p. 526)
homogamy (p. 527)
disillusionment model (p. 532)
maintenance hypothesis (p. 532)
social exchange and behavior theories (p. 532)

intrapersonal models (p. 532)
homeostatic steady state (p. 533)
negative affect reciprocity (p. 534)
"four horsemen of the apocalypse" (p. 534)
launching period (p. 537)
kinkeeper (p. 537)
sandwich generation (p. 538)
role buffering (p. 539)
agency (p. 540)
communion (p. 540)
social role theory (p. 540)
integrative health (p. 547)
social clock (p. 547)
post-traumatic stress disorder (PTSD) (p. 548)

Chapter 14
Living Well: Stress, Coping, and Life Satisfaction in Adulthood

 Learning Objectives

After reading this chapter, you should be able to:

14.1 Identify needs that must be met for adults to have subjective and psychological well-being, and suggest approaches that meet needs and support life satisfaction.

14.2 Assess levels of stress and the effects of stress on the individual and suggest interventions for coping, building resilience, and cultivating physical and emotional wellness.

John, age 48, is a marketing executive. Because of his company's recent merger, his job description has changed, and some of his previous responsibilities will now be shifted to subcontractors. In order to maintain his role in the company, he has been offered the opportunity to relocate from the firm's urban headquarters to a more rural area in another state. Alternatively, he could accept a downsized position in the company headquarters with a salary reduction. His only child is in college, so he and his wife have some flexibility should they wish to move. John has always been told that he was effective at his job, and he considered his income, which provided for a good life in the city, proof of his high-status position in the firm. Clients liked him, and he felt successful despite some ups and downs over the years. A younger colleague was promoted over him recently, and John believed it might have happened because this person was more familiar with media marketing and other technological innovations. At the urging of his wife, John scheduled a medical check-up to ask about his chronic fatigue. His doctor advised him to make some lifestyle changes because test results indicated borderline metabolic syndrome. John doesn't exercise regularly, except for an occasional game of golf with clients, and he has trouble sleeping. Every January he makes a resolution to lose weight, but it's been getting tougher each year. It's so much easier to eat fast food or take-out from the local restaurants after a busy day. The changes in his job situation have hit him hard, and he finds himself worrying much more about his future. But when he is honest with himself, he admits he's often questioned whether his job was all that satisfying in the first place. Even though John considers himself too old to try another career, he knows there are other things he'd like to do with his life.

Although young adults often feel as though life is still "about to happen," during middle adulthood people see themselves as having "grown up." Their lives have all the trappings of adults in their culture. For North Americans this is likely to mean they are married or have a life partner, have children, are owners or leasers of major possessions like a car or a house, and have substantial commitments to their work, place of worship, or other community organizations.

So how does it feel to be all grown up? Are most people satisfied with their lives? What does it take to be happy as an adult? Western philosophers have debated the ingredients of "the good life" since the days of the ancient Hebrews and Greeks. Religious traditions throughout the world champion virtues that constitute "right living," and that lead to true happiness, either in this life or the next. For helping professionals, the question of what constitutes well-being is at the heart of their work. Although ameliorating psychopathology is an important clinical objective, it is subsumed by the broader goal of promoting well-being, happiness, and the fulfillment of human potential.

Happiness is currently a focus of intense research interest, at both individual and societal levels of analysis (Diener, 2000; Myers, 1993; Veenhoven, 1984). **Subjective well-being (SWB)** is frequently used synonymously with happiness, possibly because its dimensions have been well studied (Busseri, 2015), and we use these terms synonymously in this chapter. The most commonly used measurements of SWB incorporate three separable factors: overall life satisfaction, and frequency of positive and of negative moods (Diener, Emmons, Larsen, & Griffin, 1985; Diener et al., 2009). Measuring life satisfaction usually involves asking people to rate their level of agreement with statements like "So far I have gotten the important things I want in life" or ranking one's place on a ladder where the top rung is the very best life possible and the bottom is the worst (Cantril, 1965; see Box 14.1).

Box 14.1: Question from Cantril's Ladder

Best possible life

Worst possible life

Please imagine a ladder with steps numbered from zero at the bottom to ten at the top. Suppose we say that the top of the ladder represents the best possible life for you and the bottom of the ladder represents the worst possible life for you. On which step of the ladder do you feel you personally stand at the present time?

SOURCE: Based on Bjørnskov, C. (2010). How Comparable Are the Gallup World Poll Life Satisfaction Data? *Journal of Happiness Studies 11* (1), 41–60.

Frequencies of positive and of negative affective experiences are measured by asking people to rate how many times they felt a variety of emotions (e.g., joyful, angry, good, or bad) over a certain period of time. The life satisfaction estimate of SWB represents the cognitive aspect of happiness whereas reports of positive-negative experience represent its more emotional elements. Retrospective self-reports are not the only methods used in this kind of work. Box 14.2 presents a description of another promising way to assess emotional experience.

Because of the complexity of this topic and its overlap with constructs like happiness and meaning, there is still some disagreement about SWB measurement and conceptualization. Additional research is needed going forward to clarify structural dimensions of SWB and to distinguish it from other closely related concepts (Metler & Busseri, 2017).

A rapidly growing body of studies from the social science literature has led to some surprising revelations about what is really important for people to sustain a sense of well-being as they negotiate the complex and frequently stressful realities of adulthood. It should be noted, however, that this is an active research area, so available findings are not necessarily conclusive. More robust measures will most likely lead to a stronger knowledge base (Tay, Chan, & Diener, 2014).

Box 14.2: Measuring What Makes People Happy

In most cases, the constructs of life satisfaction and subjective well-being are studied by asking respondents to complete questionnaires. Participants might be asked to respond on a scale of 1 to 10 to questions like "I believe that I make enough money" or "I am getting what I want out of my life." Such survey results can be very enlightening, but they cannot answer some of the most interesting questions about people's lived experience in a real-time context. For that data, researchers can utilize the technique called the *experience sampling method (ESM)*. As you learned in Chapter 9, those who use this methodology give participants beepers that are programmed to beep at various points during the day. The beep alerts participants to record what they are doing and how they are feeling at that moment. This strategy is a good way to observe lives as they unfold. However, it can be expensive and intrusive to participants. Furthermore, events are recorded as discrete snapshots instead of as a reflection of the ebb and flow of well-being across situations.

Kahneman and his associates (Kahneman, Krueger, Schkade, Schwartz, & Stone, 2004) developed an alternative approach called the **day reconstruction method (DRM)**, which combines elements of experience sampling with elicitation of memories of affective experience. One major difference is that DRM does not require beepers or present-moment reporting of experience. Instead, participants are asked to recall the previous day and to construct a running account or diary that describes the day's events. The instructions direct participants to "think of your day as a continuous series of scenes or episodes in a film. Give each episode a brief name that will help you remember it (for example 'commuting to work', or 'at lunch with B?')" (p. 1778). After the day's "scenes" are remembered and described, participants respond to more structured questions about each one, including how they felt while each was happening. Indices of positive affect (happy, friendly, enjoying myself) and negative affect (frustrated, depressed, hassled, angry, worried, criticized) are gathered. The result is a chronology of daily events linked to subjective ratings of positive or negative feeling.

This method was used to gather information about the life satisfaction of a sample of 909 racially diverse, middle-class women. The average age of participants was 38 years. Results demonstrate that this method can access information that other methods generally cannot. For example, most surveys of life satisfaction report that people believe their children to be a source of great happiness. In this study, the activity of *taking care of children* ranked close to the bottom of enjoyable activities. Only working, housework, and commuting had lower positive ratings. The authors suggest that this finding may be due to the fact that DRM taps experience instead of the kind of global beliefs that are assessed in traditional life satisfaction surveys. Respondents may feel less constrained by socially appropriate or "belief-based generic judgments" (Kahneman et al., 2004, p. 1777) such as the valuing of children. With this method, they report on the reality of their lived experience. Activities that were associated with the most positive affect were intimate relations, socializing, and relaxing. This methodology reveals how enjoyable people's lives are on a day-to-day basis instead of global estimates of life satisfaction.

Similar to other research reported in this chapter, the life circumstances of these women, such as income, religion, and education, made only modest contributions to the affective quality of their daily lives. What did matter? Things that made for a happy day were related to their personality and mental health (like absence of depression) and, notably, the quality of their sleep! The authors found very large differences in women's enjoyment of home-related activities as a function of good or poor sleep, which had a surprisingly powerful impact on the quality of their satisfaction and enjoyment of life overall. In the work arena, job pressure exerted a similarly large effect. Although factors like job security and the presence of adequate benefits were important predictors of job satisfaction, they did not influence women's daily enjoyment at work. What made for a happier workday was less pressure to work quickly and more opportunities to talk with coworkers. Overall, life satisfaction, based upon results of this study, was determined by the difference in net negative and net positive affect. This study suggests that it may be the little things in our day-to-day lives that can make us happy.

Although this method is intuitively interesting, some problems with reliability, conflation of responses with mood, and external events, and so forth have been observed. In particular, refinement of experience sampling methods using electronic devices may make these methods a better way to collect real-time data on current experience (Diener & Tay, 2014).

Life Satisfaction: What Is a Well-Lived Life?

14.1 **Identify needs that must be met for adults to have subjective and psychological well-being, and suggest approaches that meet needs and support life satisfaction.**

Worldly Goods and Well-Being

First, let's consider the importance of money. Although we would probably all concede some truth to the saying "money can't buy happiness," research indicates that most of us *believe* that even a little more income would improve our lives and make us happier (Myers, 2000). On the whole, happiness and income are correlated, but the relationship is complicated.

Easterlin's famous paradox (1974, 1995) contradicted the conventional notion that happiness increases concurrently with income, giving rise to a surge of research on this topic. Easterlin found that the percentage of North Americans who claimed to be very happy remained level or declined slightly even as per capita income and standard of living rose steadily from the mid 1950s through the late 1990s (see Figure 14.1).

At the same time, rates of depression and other pathologies soared. Extrapolating on Easterlin's paradox, Myers (2000) called the inverse ratio of affluence to pathology "the American paradox." The materialistic goals that motivate many Americans do not appear to guarantee happiness, and they seem to have some toxic side effects. Over 25 years of cross-national data on values revealed that U.S. values were most materialistic, compared to trends from the six other nations (United Kingdom, Germany, France, Spain, Italy, and Sweden). In contrast to the United States, these European countries prioritized family, friends, and socially valuable work over money and possessions. Table 14.1 shows the U.S. ranking on various aggregated variables assessed over a quarter century (Bartolini & Sarracini, 2017).

Research on the relationship between wealth and happiness has produced some contradictory conclusions, with some data supporting Easterlin's analyses and some data refuting it. Discrepancies in research findings may be related to aforementioned measurement issues and to different ways of conceptualizing the research questions.

FIGURE 14.1 Economic growth and happiness in the U.S.

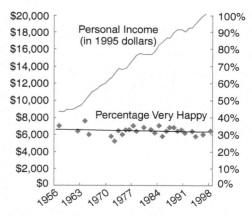

SOURCE: Based on Myers, D. G. (2000). The funds, friends, and faith of happy people. *American Psychologist, 55*, 56–67.

TABLE 14.1 U.S. Summary Ranking on Values Related to Materialism Compared to Other Nations over 25 Years

VALUE	RANKING OF U.S. COMPARED TO 6 COUNTRIES	
Importance of friends in life	5	Less valued
More emphasis on family life	6	Least valued
Importance in a job of meeting people	6	Least valued
Importance in a job of having pleasant people to work with	6	Least valued
Importance of leisure time in life	5	Less valued
Importance in a job of not having too much pressure	5	Less valued
Importance of having an interesting job	5	Less valued
Importance of having a job that meets one's abilities	5	Less valued
More emphasis on individual self-actualization	6	Least valued
Importance of having a useful job for society	5	Less valued
Importance of having good pay	4	Valued
Decreasing emphasis on money and material possession in the country	2	U.S. reported lower materialism levels at the beginning of the 25 year period and Europe reported higher levels. At the end of the period, U.S. emphasis on money increased, far exceeding declining European trends.
More emphasis on a simple and more natural lifestyle in the country	5	Less valued

1 = best trends (smallest increase or greatest decrease of materialism)

6 = worst trends (smallest decrease or greatest increase in materialism).

SOURCE: Republished with permission of Springer from Twenty-five years of materialism: Do the US and Europe diverge? *Social Indicators Research*, by Bartolini, S., & Sarracino, F. (2017), 133(2), 787–817; permission conveyed through Copyright Clearance Center, Inc.

Or, contradictory evidence may be due to the presence of certain moderating variables. We need to probe these questions, despite their difficulty, because the answers are important for countries, communities, and businesses that aspire to increase the well-being of citizens (Frey & Stutzer, 2002; Piekałkiewicz, 2017).

Let's consider some evidence that supports Easterlin's original finding. It is true that the poor are not as happy as the rich. But people with adequate though modest incomes report nearly the same levels of life satisfaction as the wealthiest individuals, both within and between cultures and subcultures (see Table 14.2). Even people who have a sudden economic windfall, like those who win a lottery, "typically only gain a temporary jolt of joy from their winnings" (Myers, 2000, p. 61).

Now for some contradictory findings. Stevenson and Wolfers (2013) tested Easterlin's claim by examining well-being data from 155 countries. Their work did not show a satiation effect at which point the effects of income on happiness stabilize or even decline. Rather, their analyses revealed a steady linear relationship between income and measures of well-being. These results have also been supported by others (Lien, Hu, & Liu, 2017). So does this mean that wealthier people are happier and more satisfied with their lives after all? Clearly, differences in outcome measures of happiness, well-being, and life satisfaction are likely sources of variability. It also appears that asking more nuanced questions might ultimately knit these disparate threads together. For example, do certain conditions in countries or communities moderate the relationship between wealth and well-being?

Decoupling actual household income level from GDP (a summary measure of national economic productivity), Diener, Tay, and Oishi (2013) showed that actual household income level was related to all dimensions of SWB. Over the course of this 7-year study, individuals' satisfaction with rising incomes was more than a transitory blip, suggesting these increases had a long-lasting cumulative effect. The rise in family income appeared to affect SWB if it offered increased purchasing power and was accompanied by optimism about the future. Compared to earlier studies indicating that increased incomes did not augment happiness (Diener, Lucas, & Scollon, 2006; Diener & Seligman, 2004), this study may represent an advance because of the size and representativeness of the sample as well as the use of consistent measurements. It's important to note, however, that the observed relationship between income and SWB did not occur unless the *average* person in the country, not just its wealthy citizens, experienced the income gains. Some have also suggested that the 7-year period covered in this analysis was not long enough to test effects sufficiently.

TABLE 14.2 Life Satisfaction for Various Groups

GROUP	RATING
Forbes magazine's "richest Americans"	5.8
Pennsylvania Amish	5.8
Inughuit (Inuit people in northern Greenland)	5.8
African Maasai	5.7
Swedish probability sample	5.6
International college-student sample (47 nations in 2000)	4.9
Illinois Amish	4.9
Calcutta slum dwellers	4.6
Fresno, California homeless	2.9
Calcutta pavement dwellers (homeless)	2.9

NOTE: Respondents indicated their agreement with the statement "You are satisfied with your life" using a scale from 1 (complete disagreement) to 7 (complete agreement); 4 is a neutral rating.

SOURCE: Diener, E., & Seligman, M. E. P. (2004). Beyond money: Toward an economy of well-being. *Psychological Science in the Public Interest, 5,* 1–31. Reprinted by permission of Blackwell Publishing.

So rising incomes appear to make people happy if a number of other conditions are met. To parse this even further, Mikucka and colleagues (Mikucka, Sarracino, & Dubrow, 2017) studied effects of income on happiness in countries with developed and developing economies as well as countries in transition (i.e., moving from poverty to self-sufficiency). Their results support Easterlin's finding for countries with well-developed economies, whereas the opposite held true for countries in transition. In places where people were transitioning out of poverty towards economic stability, increased income was associated with all aspects of SWB. For countries with developed economies, higher incomes were associated with greater SWB only when social trust and reduced income inequality also existed. Social trust is a form of social capital, or "networks of shared norms, values and understandings that facilitate cooperation within or among groups" (Organization for Economic Cooperation and Development [OECD], 2001, p. 41). Once a basic standard of living is achieved, it appears that money is not enough to ensure happiness. When social trust is lacking and income inequality is great, people's sense of connection and ability to trust others, both profound sources of satisfaction and security, can fray. The important role that income inequality plays in societal well-being has been demonstrated in other studies as well (Oishi & Kesebir, 2015). Rich countries appear to have a lot to gain in terms of the well-being of their populations when trust is high and inequality is reduced.

Finally, in another nuanced look at these interrelationships, Kahneman and Deaton (2010) analyzed Gallup poll data in a way that separated life satisfaction scores from emotional experience. When people were asked to evaluate the quality of their life on the Cantril ladder, their evaluations ascended in relationship to their income and educational level. Think of this as being asked to appraise your life from afar. Presumably, the higher your status and income, the higher your subjective assessment of life satisfaction might be. From this perspective, John might assess his pre-merger life satisfaction to be quite high. However, when asked to assess the emotional warp and woof of life, the joys, sadness, stresses and strains, people's income level failed to correlate with their actual experience of happiness after reaching approximately $75,000 in yearly income, even if they were very wealthy. This figure might be higher now, if the study were repeated, given rising costs of living. Nonetheless, the point is that after a certain income threshold, one's emotional life does not change much and well-being satiates. Conversely, living below a certain income level, in poverty or near poverty, significantly decreased life satisfaction and increased sadness and stress.

This paradox may have many sources; we will mention a few. First, it may be linked to what is described as the "hedonic treadmill" (Brickman & Campbell, 1971). When people are driven to strive for material gain, they are often quickly habituated to each new level of wealth and thus can't be satisfied (Kasser & Ryan, 1996). Pittman (1985) argued, "Wealth is addictive. It enticingly offers happiness, but it cannot provide satisfaction, so those who attain some of it keep thinking more of it will provide satisfaction" (p. 470). Ironically, the more an individual strives for further material gain, the less attention he is likely to give to other pursuits that are more strongly linked to satisfaction, like having supportive social relationships.

Second, the lifestyle that affluence makes possible may reduce some of the forces that ordinarily help create supportive relationships (Luthar, 2003). For example, people who can buy services from the marketplace, such as child care and elder care, are less likely to turn to family, friends, and neighbors for those kinds of support (Putnam, 2000). Further, people living in affluent societies rarely need to rely on others for physical support in "tough times," such as help with food, clothing, and shelter, and so opportunities for friends and neighbors to demonstrate "genuine friendship" by making sacrifices for one another are minimal. Absent such opportunities, it may be more difficult for people to feel that others in their lives can be relied upon. This emotional distance can reduce empathy and generosity, and increase cynicism and objectification of others, further compromising relatedness.

Third, having material resources allows people to make choices and to control much of their lives. But the more control people have, the more likely they are to expect a "perfect" life (Schwartz, 2000). Of course, perfection is impossible to achieve. However, when people fail to do so, they blame themselves, creating fertile ground for depression and regrets. They may also blame others for their disappointments, accumulating a backlog of grievances. Because materialistic cultures foster the belief that material gain brings happiness, affluent people who do become depressed often feel confused and guilty, making it difficult to reach out to friends and share their distress (Wolfe & Fodor, 1996).

Simon's (1955) influential work on decision making elucidated how "maximization" (i.e., having more choices in a wealthy society, but being less satisfied) could help explain this paradox. "Maximizers" (Nenkov, Morrin, Ward, Schwartz, & Hulland, 2008; Schwartz et al., 2002) can be identified by virtue of their heightened exploration of alternatives, difficulty with decision making, and high standards. Compared to "satisficers" (i.e., those who believe that "good enough" is acceptable), maximizers never settle for second best. They expend much more effort to achieve their desired outcome compared to satisficers, who balance desirability with feasibility (Luan & Li, 2017a). The unwholesome consequences of the maximizing style, unhappiness, pessimism, depression, and lower self-esteem, have been well documented. These outcomes appear to be related to maximizers' entrenched belief that *there actually is* an objectively "best" choice, if only they can find it. Clearly, one can never know, in a world of virtually unlimited choice, that the decision you end up making is objectively the best one. Thus, disappointment, second guessing, and dissatisfaction can ensue (Luan & Li, 2017b).

Finally, some research with a U.S. sample examined the contributions of income to positive and negative emotional experience. Wealth can reduce the chances of experiencing some kinds of sadness in everyday life (like food insecurity, loss of housing, lack of medical care, etc.) because it allows for real and perceived control over certain adverse events. Greater wealth, as we have seen, had little relationship to positive emotional experience (Kahnemann & Deaton, 2010; Kushlev, Dunn, & Lucas, 2015). The same pattern of results was found for a German sample (Hudson, Lucas, Donnellan, & Kushlev, 2016). Wealth, while providing some protection from sadness, does little to enhance happiness and may even reduce it. The focus on wealth may diminish the capacity to savor mundane events and to experience the pleasures found in the simple things of life. John, our marketing executive, probably should consider the social and personal costs of staying at or leaving his company before making a decision solely based on income.

Overall, material gain is a source of well-being, but decision-making style, personality, cultural context, and supportive relationships can also be. In the sections that follow we will explore several additional factors that are positively correlated with well-being. We'll begin with the characteristics of the individual himself.

Personality and Well-Being

Could personality be more important than external conditions for explaining life satisfaction? Personality traits like extroversion and neuroticism are correlated with subjective well-being measures, much more so than external factors like wealth (Diener, Oishi, & Lucas, 2003; Realo, 2016). Extroverts, who tend to focus interest on things outside the self, are happier than introverts, who focus more attention on their own interior experience. Not surprisingly, neuroticism, which includes tendencies to be self-conscious, anxious, hostile, and impulsive, is negatively correlated with happiness. Conscientiousness, which includes planfulness and self-control, is positively correlated with later life well-being in some studies (Bogg & Roberts, 2013) but less so in others (Harris, Brett, Starr, Deary, & Johnson, 2016).

These relationships are difficult to assess directly, although stable personality traits may play a moderating role in health and well-being during life. Personality can operate by influencing what information people pay attention to and remember. Information that is congruent with an individual's personality is more likely to be fully processed. For example, extroverts process rewarding stimuli for longer periods than introverts (Derryberry & Reed, 1994). In addition, people who approach situations differently may construe the same life events in different ways (Lyubomirsky, 2001).

Could personality moderate the impact of money on happiness? It appears that it does. Let's consider a person high in neuroticism. By definition, he feels the slings and arrows of daily life more intensely. When income level does not match expectations, this perceived lack might have a more powerful impact on his overall well-being than it would for a less anxious person. High neuroticism is linked to more active social-comparison processes (Olson & Evans, 1999) that can also exaggerate perceived deficiencies. Studies of adults from large representative samples in Germany, Australia, and the UK bear this out. Soto and Luhmann (2013) found that income had a more powerful influence on SWB for individuals high in neuroticism than it did for their more extroverted and less anxious peers.

Reciprocity appears to exist between personality traits and well-being, with each side fostering the other. People with higher baseline levels of agreeableness, extraversion, conscientiousness, and emotional stability experience more positive and less negative affect. Over time, this sustained emotional pattern results in even higher levels of agreeableness, conscientiousness, and emotional stability (Soto, 2015).

Relationships and Well-Being

As we saw in Chapter 12, many theorists, like Freud and Erikson, have emphasized the importance of "love" for happiness. Evidence strongly supports this view. Regardless of personality characteristics, social relationships appear to be essential ingredients of well-being. Both extroverts and introverts report more pleasant emotions in social situations (Pavot, Diener, & Fujita, 1990). *Receiving* social support is clearly linked to better coping with life's stresses, as you will see later in this chapter, but having opportunities to *give* social support is also a key ingredient in happiness. Life is more stressful for people who have limited opportunities to be a source of support to others or who experience limited success in their efforts to do so (Brown, Nesse, Vinokur, & Smith, 2003).

A wide variety of converging evidence links the quality and quantity of social relationships with life satisfaction in adulthood. In a study of "very happy people," Diener and Seligman (2002) found that *all* of their happiest respondents had "excellent" social relationships. People with more friends also experience greater happiness than people with fewer friends (Hintikka, Koskela, Kontula, Koskela, & Viinamaeki, 2000). Women with at least one confidante are less susceptible to depression than women with no confidantes (Antonucci, Lansford, & Akiyama, 2001), and Hammen (1996) suggests that without strong, positive interpersonal bonds, both men and women are particularly vulnerable to depression. Marriages (and comparable long-term intimate partnerships) are a major source of companionship in Western societies. In surveys that include tens of thousands of people from the United States and many other countries, married women and men report more happiness than unmarried people (Wadsworth, 2016). Being married is also associated with a lower risk of depression (Myers, 2000).

Do social relationships cause happiness, or are happy people more likely to be involved in social relationships? There is evidence that it works both ways. People who are more secure, who have more positive attitudes and better social skills are more likely to successfully make friends, develop confidantes, and create long-term partnerships, as we have seen in our earlier discussions of friendship and marriage. But when we study life satisfaction within individuals over time, we find that social relationships do affect people's happiness as well. The same people are happier when they are with others than when they are by themselves. For example, Kahneman and colleagues tracked women's affective states during 15 daily activities—like exercising, resting, commuting, and so on—and found that emotions were more positive when people were with others than when they were alone (Kahneman et al., 2004; see Box 14.2). People whose closest relationships end, as with divorce or death of a partner, may show precipitous declines in well-being. Their life satisfaction recovers only slowly and not usually to the same level as before the loss (Diener & Seligman, 2004; see also Figure 14.2).

The importance of social relationships for well-being and health is consistent across cultures (Holt-Lunstad & Smith, 2012). When people feel supported by family, friends, and community they weather life's difficulties more effectively. But fine-grained analyses demonstrate that the way people derive support from their interpersonal connections differs across cultural groups.

FIGURE 14.2 Life satisfaction before and after divorce or death of a spouse.

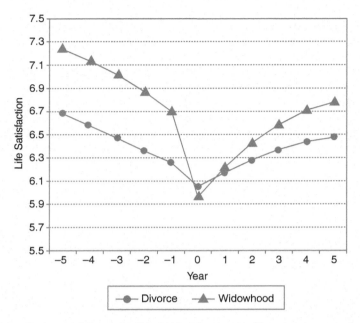

SOURCE: Based on Diener, E., & Seligman, M. E. P. (2004). Beyond money: Toward an economy of well-being. *Psychological Science in the Public Interest, 5*, 1–31.

A useful way to explore this issue is to review support-seeking behavior in individualistic and collectivistic cultures. As you would expect, people from U.S. cultures with Northern European, Protestant roots definitely value family relations but manifest different operating patterns with regard to them. Spending time with family on one's own terms, moving away from home for college or career, voluntarily beginning or ending relationships, and choosing partners and professions independently all reveal an individualistic orientation (Schug, Yuki, & Maddux, 2010). People from collectivistic cultures tend to view themselves as more interdependent. Yet, there are important differences even within collectivistic cultures that influence their manner of support seeking, emotion regulation, health, and well-being. Campos & Kim (2017) reviewed evidence of some key differences in support seeking that are of interest to helpers. These authors highlighted East Asian and Latino groups because, although both are collectivistic, they show how different patterns of support seeking affect well-being. For East Asians, **harmony collectivism** is the norm. While family relationships are primary, care is taken to avoid causing interpersonal conflict or burdening others. High levels of positive emotions towards others are not manifested directly but rather through more practical expressions, like offering advice, solving problems conjointly, or offering practical help. Moderating emotions is the preferred strategy. In collectivistic Latino cultures, direct expression of positive emotions is valued within relationships, a style called **convivial collectivism**. In these cultures, lively and explicit expression of positive emotion serves to create family cohesion. Life decisions often take family into account, time is spent celebrating important events, and high levels of assistance and support are provided. Expressive affirmation of family connections is preferred.

So much of how people relate emotionally is based on cultural experience and assumptions, making it critical for helpers to exercise *cultural humility* when appraising these patterns (Campos & Kim, 2017). Kim et al. (2008) posit that:

> People in more individualistic cultures share the cultural assumption that individuals should proactively pursue their well-being and that others have the freedom to choose to help according to their own volition. In contrast, people in the more collectivistic cultures may be relatively more cautious about bringing personal problems to the attention of others for the purpose of enlisting their help because they share the cultural

assumption that individuals should not burden their social networks and that others share the same sense of social obligation. (p. 519)

Work, Achievement, Generativity, and Well-Being

As theorists like Freud and Erikson proposed, work experience and the general sense of oneself as a competent worker are also important predictors of happiness. Feeling that one is making progress towards challenging goals, both in work and in nonwork settings, is thus correlated with well-being (see Ryan & Deci, 2003). Similarly, scores on measures of generativity are predictors of well-being (Ackerman, Zuroff, & Moskowitz, 2000). As we have seen, generativity is a sense that one's skills and efforts are creatively or productively contributing to the world—to family, coworkers, community, or future generations.

MyLab Education
Video Example 14.1
Mary at age 42 is happy and seems to have balance between work and the rest of her life. She has a good job, two wonderful children, and looks forward with wonder. What will the next 20 years bring?

Work experiences in general are often associated with subjective well-being. In the study by Kahneman et al. (2004) comparing affective states during daily tasks, people generally reported positive emotions at work, although not as positive as during sex or socializing after work. *Congruence* between personality characteristics and the skills and qualities required for a job is part of what makes work satisfying. But there are also many characteristics of the workplace itself that contribute to happiness. Opportunities for personal control, the variety of tasks, the support of the supervisor, interpersonal contact and coworker relationships, good pay and fringe benefits, respect, and status can all influence the degree of satisfaction people derive from work (e.g., Chiaburu & Harrison, 2008; Warr, 1999).

We should remember that balance between work and the rest of one's life is probably the best prescription, no matter how engrossing work might be. Some research suggests that the old adage "all work and no play" actually does lead to a diminished life. Whillans and colleagues (Whillans, Dunn, Smeets, Bekkers, & Norton, 2017; Whillans, Weidman, & Dunn, 2016) found support for the fact that people who prioritized time over money were happier. Helping people consider the trade-offs they make for their work, as in John's case, can be an important goal for helping professionals.

Universal Needs and Values and Well-Being

In sum, material success, beyond a basic level of comfort, is not the primary ingredient in creating the good life for adults. Personality characteristics that support an "other" rather than a "self" orientation do seem to help promote happiness. Good social relationships are particularly important, and productive work opportunities support life satisfaction as well. What can we deduce from this overview of factors that either do or do not promote well-being?

One approach to understanding and integrating these and other findings on well-being is to propose that what really counts is living a life that meets our most fundamental and universal needs. Extrapolating from the insights of philosophers through the ages, the views of personality theorists from many different traditions, and the available research, modern theorists propose that there are basic psychological needs, and meeting these needs is the source of well-being. Waterman (1993a), for example, argued that people need to express their "true selves." If their activities are congruent with their own deeply held values and they are fully engaged, then people can achieve a state of "personal expressiveness," meaning that they feel intensely alive and authentic. Waterman devised measures of personal expressiveness and found that they correlated highly with traditional measures of subjective well-being. But subjective well-being, with its emphasis on happiness and positive emotion (what has also been called **hedonic well-being**) was not exactly the same as the kind of feeling that Waterman called personal expressiveness. The latter has been called **eudaemonic well-being**, and describes feeling a sense of purpose, growth, and mastery.

Ryff and her colleagues (e.g., Ryff & Keyes, 1995; Ryff, 2017) differentiated psychological or eudaemonic well-being from subjective well-being, defining it as the striving to realize one's true potential. They list six fundamental elements of psychological well-being: autonomy, personal growth, self-acceptance, life purpose, mastery, and positive relatedness. Questionnaire measures of these six aspects of experience are highly correlated with measures of positive affect in which individuals are asked to describe how intensely they usually experience 20 different positive feeling states (e.g., interest, excitement, strength, etc.; Urry et al., 2004).

In what is called **self-determination theory**, Ryan and Deci (2000; see also Deci & Ryan, 2008; Ryan, Huta, & Deci, 2008) have also argued that self-realization is at the core of eudaemonic well-being. They suggest that life satisfaction is derived from the fulfillment of fundamental psychological needs for **autonomy** (feeling that one's behaviors are self-endorsed), **competence** (expressing one's talents and skills), and **relatedness** (opportunities to feel cared for and valued by others). These psychological needs, like hunger and other basic physiological needs, are energizing. Their relative salience and the ways in which they are satisfied can be different across the life span and in different cultures. But there is cross-cultural evidence that satisfaction of these needs supports feelings of well-being in general (e.g., Deci et al., 2001; Ryan et al., 1999). A recent meta-analysis of studies from health care settings showed that promotion of autonomy, competence, and relatedness by providers had positive effects on patient physical and mental health (Ng et al., 2012). In extensive studies of U.S. adults, hedonic and eudaemonic well-being were significantly related to lower rates of metabolic syndrome, less smoking, lower levels of alcohol use, healthier diet, and more exercise (Boylan & Ryff, 2015).

Despite our best intentions to meet hedonic and eudaemonic needs in some balanced way, life decisions, once made, may privilege certain needs over others. Previously we noted the tradeoffs that may exist when career success is pursued singlemindedly. Although attainment of status and increase in income from a career can be satisfying, lack of time and demands of a stressful position may compromise life satisfaction (Abele, Hagmeier, & Spurk, 2016). People who have highly demanding careers may find their needs for competence and autonomy amply met but they suffer from the inability to cultivate relationships. Or, like John our marketer, they may feel limited in exploring other options. Research on well-being demonstrates that some skills of living are modifiable, thus raising the intriguing question of whether hedonic and eudaemonic needs should be the targets of intervention for many normative health and lifestyle-related issues of midlife (Ruini, Albieri, & Vescovelli, 2015).

The Importance of Meaning, Religion, and Spirituality

MEANING AND WELL-BEING

Many observers of human nature have proposed that the well-lived life is one that is grounded in the conviction that life has meaning. Park and Folkman (1997) define *meaning* as simply the perception of significance, and they propose that the need to find meaning may be intrinsic to human beings. They differentiate between "global meaning," a sense of what the universe and human existence is about, or what is universally true, and a sense of "situational meaning," which is finding a purpose for one's own life. Generally, they see the second category as heavily dependent on the first.

Baumeister (1991) argues that we humans have a need to understand our lives, to see them as making sense, and he proposes four reasons why people seek meaning. First, they feel a need for their lives to have a purpose, which basically is synonymous with having goals. Such goals help people place their current actions in context, providing a connection between past, present, and future. In other words, they help us see our lives as coherent and making sense. Second, when people have a sense of meaning in their lives, they feel like they have control, that what they do is consistent with a purpose they endorse, helping them meet what self-determination theory describes as the need for autonomy (see Ryan, Huta, & Deci, 2008). Third, a sense of meaning helps people define what actions are legitimate and what actions are not. In this way, people can justify their actions and construct or identify values, morals, and ethics to help guide their behavior. Fourth, a sense of meaning helps people value themselves, fostering self-worth. Baumeister also suggests that becoming part of a social group helps people feel valued and valuable and enhances their sense of meaning.

As we have seen, despite the growth of wealth in the United States and other affluent nations in the last several decades, depression and other mental health problems have been on the rise (Diener & Seligman, 2004). When materialism substitutes for a philosophy of life that provides a deeper sense of meaning and purpose, it may block the development of true life satisfaction. Some of the reasons for seeking meaning that Baumeister proposes are associated with the basic self-actualization needs or values that Ryan and Deci and others have specified, such as needs for autonomy and relatedness. In fact, one way to construe self-realization is that it means to find your true meaning or value—where and how you fit into a larger whole. Because religious traditions are in large part institutionalized meaning systems, they can help people establish global meaning, which in turn can support the creation of situational meaning.

Spirituality and Meaning

For many people around the world, religion and spirituality offer a profound source of meaning and contribute to a sense of purpose. Personality theorists have sometimes argued that spirituality is built into the human psyche. Carl G. Jung in particular felt that religion and spirituality are expressions of an innate need "to find meaning in life, to create a sense of wholeness or completeness, and to connect with something larger than the individual self" (Compton, 2005, p. 210). Modern researchers make a distinction between spirituality and religion (or religiosity). A person can have a spiritual side or spiritual strivings without practicing a particular religion, although the two are closely allied for many people (Hill et al., 2000). Both are concerned with "a search for the sacred" (Zinnbauer, Pargament, & Scott, 1999), which means attempting to identify, articulate, or move towards an understanding or association with a divine being, divine object, or some kind of ultimate reality or truth (Hill et al., 2000). Religion also involves affiliation with "a covenant faith community" that has prescriptive and revelatory teachings and may include rituals, all of which are intended to support the search for the sacred and to encourage morality (Dollahite, 1998). Religion also may serve nonsacred goals, like creating a social identity (Hill et al., 2000). The empirical study of spirituality and religion is beginning to paint a picture of the role that both play in adults' everyday psychological functioning.

RELIGIOSITY AND WELL-BEING

A majority of the world's population report that religion is an important part of their lives (Diener, Tay, & Myers, 2011). Large numbers of children across the globe are socialized within the context of some religious framework that provides beliefs, principles, and practices aimed at fostering a happy, meaningful, and moral life (King & Boyatzis, 2015). In fact, large representative studies do show that religion increases SWB for people in the United States, even after their life circumstances are taken into account (Lim, 2015). Across the world's four major religions—Hinduism, Christianity, Buddhism, and Islam—adherents tended to report higher SWB in each of its three dimensions compared to nonreligious counterparts. But are there certain life circumstances that moderate this relationship? Diener and colleagues (2011) showed that economic development and security contribute to religiosity both at individual and societal levels. In countries where life circumstances were more difficult, levels of religiosity tended to be high and being religious added to SWB. Nonreligious individuals in religious societies tended to report the least SWB, especially in terms of social support and positive affect. An inverse relationship was found for relatively advantaged countries where, in general, level of need was low and security was high. In these societies, organized religion was rated as less important to overall happiness. Nonreligious individuals in economically developed, nonreligious societies also reported high levels of SWB. It is possible that the positive relationship between religiosity and SWB observed in the United States is due to this country's economic advantage and moderate religiosity (Diener et al., 2011).

In addition to life satisfaction and meaning, religious affiliation has been associated with better health outcomes, such as reduced coronary disease, lower blood pressure, less suicidality and lower overall mortality (Masters & Hooker, 2013). Bailey's (1998) work with Christian-identified groups in Great Britain distinguished between explicit (church-attending Christian) and implicit (non-church attending) groups in order to assess whether religiosity provided some of these advantages to both groups. Those considered implicitly religious endorsed the statement "You don't have to go to church to be a Christian." Members of the implicitly religious group had experienced religious upbringings and endorsed participation in rites of passage rituals for major life events, like baptisms and funerals, despite not attending services or engaging in daily prayer. Both implicit and explicit religiosity was associated with more positive well-being, although church attendance offered some protections, particularly against suicidality, that were not seen for the implicitly religious group (Francis & Penny, 2013; 2016).

Does religion contribute to increased positive emotions? Both Eastern and Western religions and philosophies prescribe regulation of negative or destructive emotions, like anger and envy. Some religious movements (e.g., charismatic movements) also emphasize cultivating strong positive emotions, but others foster moderation of all emotional reactions (Emmons & Paloutzian, 2003). In traditional Buddhist teachings, the presence of compassion and serenity and the absence of destructive emotions, like envy and anger, are cultivated through meditative practices. Davidson and his colleagues (2003) have found that areas of the brain associated with positive mood showed increased activity during the practice of meditation. They have also found that the most experienced practitioners, such as Tibetan monks, show the most extreme shifts towards positive emotional states.

Many less striking studies have demonstrated that adherence to religious practices by people of many different faiths is moderately correlated with measures of emotional well-being in the United States. For example, widowed women who worship regularly report more joy in their lives than those who do not (e.g., Siegel & Kuykendall, 1990). Indeed, after many kinds of negative life experiences—divorce, unemployment, death of a child, and so on—religious people seem to recover more happiness more quickly than the nonreligious (e.g., Ellison, 1991). These benefits are more likely to accrue to people who are active religious participants (attending services, praying, meditating) than to those who describe themselves as pro-religious but are not active practitioners (Berthold & Ruch, 2014). In survey assessments of spiritual commitment (e.g., asking whether people agree with statements like "My religious faith is the most important influence in my life," or "I feel very close to God"), those who score highest are also more likely than those who score lowest to rate themselves as "very happy" (Myers, 2000).

BENEFITS AND CHALLENGES OF RELIGIOSITY

Another important reason why religious belief benefits people may be that religious communities provide their members with social support, a critical ingredient in well-being (Myers, 2000). The role of religion in fostering hope and optimism may also be important. Seligman (2002) describes a survey of religious congregations in which level of hope was the best predictor of feelings of well-being. Diener and colleagues (2011) also suggested that religion may increase happiness through the mechanisms of social support, feelings of respect, purpose, and meaning.

It should be noted that religions, like all human institutions, also have their darker side. Although some religious doctrines and practices foster positive feelings, such as hope and compassion, others foster emotions and attitudes, such as guilt and fear of retribution, which can be harmful in excess. Some religious doctrines and beliefs encourage a distrust or intolerance of others, especially outgroup members, or promote retribution or revenge against those who are construed as evil or guilty (Chatters, 2000). For some individuals, religion engenders profound personal struggles and doubts about beliefs and practices that can lead to depression, anxiety, and health problems (Ellison & Lee, 2010). Freud, having seen the dark side, assumed that religion must be "corrosive to happiness" (Myers, 2000, p. 63). Indeed, current evidence suggests that only positive elements of religious doctrine are correlated with well-being (Pargament, Smith, Koenig, & Perez, 1998). U.S. Muslims who used positive religious coping after the attacks of September 11 showed more resilience compared to peers who engaged in negative religious coping. Those who coped positively called on a basic sense of trust in the divine and perceived the tragic events as out of their control. Those who used negative coping were more likely to view the challenges they faced after the attacks as a punishment for their lack of devotion (Abu-Raiya & Mahoney, 2011).

Several categories of problems related to spirituality or religion, called religious/ spiritual struggles (Exline, Pargament, Grubbs, & Yali, 2014; Wilt, Grubbs, Exline, & Pargament, 2016), are important for helpers to recognize. Just as cultural competency is considered essential for ethical practice, so may be religious competency, given its central role for so many clients. Struggles in this area have been linked to depression, anxiety, and lower well-being (Abu-Raiya, Pargament, Krause, & Ironson, 2015; Wilt, Grubbs, Pargament, & Exline, 2017). Religious/spiritual struggles may include (1) divine struggles (concerns about God's punishment or anger directed towards God because of past disappointments, etc.), (2) demonic struggles (beliefs that one is being tormented by evil spirits), (3) interpersonal struggles (differences with others in beliefs about religion or resentment towards organized religion in general), (4) doubt-related struggles (issues related to existence of God or loss of faith), (5) moral struggles (concerns about disobeying commandments or other perceived failures), and (6) ultimate meaning struggles (questioning whether one's life has meaning). Each of these kinds of struggles should be taken seriously by helpers, even if helpers themselves do not share clients' belief systems.

SPIRITUALITY, RELIGION, AND PERSONALITY

One question that researchers have asked is whether there is a link between spirituality or religiosity and personality. Do personality characteristics, like the Big 5 (see Chapter 13), affect the degree to which people are drawn to spiritual exploration or religious involvement? One meta-analysis found that across a large number of studies, high agreeableness and conscientiousness were associated with religiousness (Saraglou, 2002). Personality traits of neuroticism and openness have also been linked to greater frequency of religious/spiritual struggles (Wilt et al., 2017). One interesting set of studies by Piedmont and colleagues suggests that there may even be a sixth personality trait that specifically relates to spirituality or spiritual transcendence, which can be defined as the ability to view life from a perspective that transcends space and time and to achieve a sense of fundamental unity with nature. Spiritual transcendence is viewed as a motivating force that directs individuals' behavior towards specific ends, such as caring for others, and so forth. These investigators consulted theological experts from many different Eastern and Western faith traditions to develop an assessment of spiritual transcendence that seemed to be common to all faiths. They then developed the "spiritual transcendence scale," which required individuals to rate how true spiritually based statements are of them, statements such as "I find inner strength and/or peace from my prayers or meditations" and "I feel that on a higher level all of us share a common bond." Piedmont has found that adults' scores on spiritual transcendence improve prediction of important characteristics like interpersonal style above and beyond their scores on the Big 5 personality traits (Lace, Haeberlein, & Handal, 2017; Piedmont, 2007).

DEVELOPMENTAL SHIFTS IN SPIRITUALITY AND FAITH

In what ways does the understanding and experience of spirituality and faith change across the life span? Fowler (1981) interviewed over 350 individuals, ranging in age from 3 to 84 years, exploring their past and "life-shaping experiences," their values and commitments, and their religious thoughts and feelings. From these interviews, he derived a description of six stages in the development of faith. His definition of *faith* is "our way of finding coherence in and giving meaning to the multiple forces and relations that make up our lives" (p. 4). Faith and religion are not synonymous in his view. People with no religious commitments still develop faith, construed as "an orientation of the total person, giving purpose and goal to one's hopes and strivings, thoughts and actions" (p. 14). He acknowledged that because his interviewees were all reared in Judeo-Christian traditions, it remained to be seen which elements of his descriptions represented universal features of faith development and which were specific to Western culture. As always with stage theories, the ages are approximate and there is substantial variability, with some individuals moving more slowly than others, and many not progressing past the first few stages. Fowler found only one person who had achieved Stage 6. Note that the most advanced middle-aged adults in this model can be expected to move through Stages 4 and 5, as they come to understand the inherent inconsistencies in any spiritual perspective and how profoundly unknowable ultimate truth is. As you will see in Chapter 15, Fowler's description of these stages is consistent with features of a definition of *wisdom*.

Stage 1 (0 to 6 years): Intuitive-projective

At these ages children are intuitive, egocentric, and not logical. Their understandings of sex, death, and taboo begin, and they may be overwhelmed by a sense of danger with regard to doing what's wrong versus right.

Stage 2 (7 to 12 years): Mythic-literal

At these ages children can narrate a life story of sorts. They tend to repeat what they have been taught by parents and other close adults about truths and beliefs, which then serve as their morals and rules. They still literally see God as a father, and they see distinct categories of right and wrong.

Stage 3 (13 to 20 years): Synthetic-conventional

By adolescence, the individual is constructing a life story. A "they" beyond the family is ascribed the authority to dictate values and beliefs, so faith remains conformist at this stage. Beliefs are not yet understood to be abstractions, and when others have different beliefs, they are judged to be wrong.

Stage 4 (21 to 30 years): Individuative-reflective

Authority is shifting from the "they" to the self. People can recognize inconsistencies and conflicts in the beliefs and morals they have been taught, and they can think critically about them. People take responsibility for making commitments to a worldview, lifestyle, beliefs, and attitudes. They see those commitments as individual, belonging to self.

Stage 5 (31 to 60 years): Conjunctive

In early midlife, some individuals begin to see both sides of a problem at once and are able to resolve the conflicts in their beliefs using dialectical (postformal) thinking. The individual begins to appreciate the unknowable—what must be the unfathomable complexity of ultimate truth.

Stage 6 (over 60): Universalizing

Transcending specific belief systems and part of a universal community, this individual lives in a way that is transformed by core values. Fowler (1991) described the transformation in this way. "Gradually, across the stages, there has been a widening of that process of taking the perspectives of others until, finally, those persons who can be described by the universalizing stage have completed the process of decentration. In a real sense we could say that they have identified with or they participate in the perspective of God. They begin to see and value through God rather than from the self. This does not mean that the self is not valued: The self is included in God's loving and valuing of all creation. But the self is no longer the center from which one's valuing is done. It is done from an identification with the transcendent . . . This decentration from self . . . leads to . . . a universalization of her or his capacity for care, for love, and for justice (p. 15).

Culture and Well-Being

So far, we've identified multiple influences on well-being: money, personality, relationships, achievement, values, meaning, and religion. Cross-cultural research offers us the opportunity to examine the relative influence of such factors on happiness among people all across the globe. Some have even suggested that there may be different definitions of what constitutes happiness across cultures. Chinese culture, for example, prizes peace of mind (peaceful, calm) over the kinds of positive experience (elated, excited) valued in Western cultures (Lee, Lin, Huang, & Fredrickson, 2013). Such cultural differences have important implications for assessment of SWB and for analyses of research results.

As you have seen, money is related to happiness, but groups that differ widely in income ("Richest Americans" and African Maasai) report similar levels of SWB (see Table 14.2). Researchers noted that the Maasai take great pride and satisfaction in their culture and its long history, possibly overriding the importance of excessive material goods in their prescription for happiness (Biswas-Diener, Vitterso, & Diener, 2005). Diener and colleagues (Diener, Ng, Harter, & Arora, 2010) asked people around the world whether they had friends or family to count on in times of need. Relative to the previous day, participants were also asked to report the level of respect they felt from others, the opportunities they had to learn something new, and the amount of control they had over their own time. These affective components were strongly related to well-being. Table 14.3 offers findings from a small group of countries.

If you look closely at the findings from this study, you'll notice that no country takes first place across all rankings. Generally, most people in the world report being relatively happy except for those who live in extreme circumstances. But take a closer look at Denmark, a high-income country that has consistently ranked near the top on cognitive and affective measures of SWB and has been called "chronically happy" (Biswas-Diener, Vitterso, & Diener, 2010; Gallup, Inc., 2007). The most recent U.N. happiness study gave the nod to Norway, but differences in rankings between the top two countries were very small (see Table 14.4).

What might account for the rising tide of happiness in Scandinavia? Using multiple measures of life satisfaction, income, affect, and social resources, researchers discovered that high levels of past, present, and predicted future happiness were best explained by relatively greater income equality in Scandinavia compared to the United States. In other words, Denmark's poorest citizens were much more satisfied than their low-income peers in the United States, a phenomenon the researchers called "The Danish Effect." Citizens of the United States were higher in emotionality (both positive and negative) than the Danes. However, while positive emotionality was higher for advantaged U.S. citizens, negative affect was also higher among the more disadvantaged. The Danes were less emotional by comparison and tended to show less extreme highs and lows in overall satisfaction. Perhaps their reported happiness has something to do with contentment, which is defined as an emotional state with a more modest level of arousal compared to other states associated with happiness like excitement, euphoria, or even with the experience of pleasurable events. Contentment has a long history in philosophy and many spiritual traditions. In contrast to some conceptions of happiness, contentment is not based on transitory mood states but arises from a sense of connection to oneself and the world and is marked by emotional features found in equanimity and acceptance (Cordaro, Brackett, Glass, & Anderson, 2016; McKenzie, 2016).

TABLE 14.3 Dimensions of Well-Being Across the Globe

COUNTRY	INCOME/GDP—GROSS DOMESTIC PRODUCT	SOCIAL-PSYCHOLOGI-CAL VARIABLES	WELL-BEING	POSITIVE FEELINGS	*LOW* NEGATIVE FEELINGS
United States	1	19	16	26	49
Denmark	5	13	1	7	1
Israel	20	56	11	61	64
New Zealand	22	12	9	1	22
South Korea	24	83	38	58	77
Costa Rica	41	6	18	4	38
Sierra Leone	87	80	87	87	86

(1 = highest reported well-being; 89 = lowest reported well-being in ranking for 89 countries sampled)

Selected Rankings of Countries (Out of 89) on Income, Well-Being, Social-Psychological Variables and Affect.

SOURCE: Based on Diener, E., Ng, W., Harter, J., & Arora, R. (2010). Wealth and happiness around the world: Material prosperity predicts life evaluation, whereas psychological prosperity predicts positive feelings. *Journal of Personality and Social Psychology, 99,* 52–61.

TABLE 14.4 Top 20 Countries Rankings* on Happiness (2014–2016)

1. Norway	11. Israel
2. Denmark	12. Costa Rica
3. Iceland	13. Austria
4. Switzerland	14. United States
5. Finland	15. Ireland
6. Netherlands	16. Germany
7. Canada	17. Belgium
8. New Zealand	18. Luxembourg
9. Australia	19. United Kingdom
10. Sweden	20. Chile

* Rankings determined by summary measure combining per capita GDP, social support, healthy life expectancy, freedom to make life choices, generosity, and perceptions of corruption.

SOURCE: Helliwell, J., Layard, R., & Sachs, J. (2017). *World Happiness Report 2017* New York, NY: Sustainable Development Solutions Network.

MyLab Education Self-Check 14.1

Stress, Coping, and Well-Being in Midlife

14.2 Assess levels of stress and the effects of stress on the individual and suggest interventions for coping, building resilience, and cultivating physical and emotional wellness.

In Chapter 13 you saw that nonnormative events are often the source of traumatic loss regardless of when they occur during the life span. The normative changes associated with growing older produce more predictable losses. Even when adults are healthy and self-sufficient, the physical changes of midlife and late life raise their awareness of getting older.

Clearly, the capacity to adapt to stress and challenge with resilience is critical to survival at every stage of the life span. Resilience refers to the presence of healthy coping and adaptation *in spite of* challenges and risks, or in the words of Ryff and Singer, "the capacity to flourish under fire" (2003, p. 15). Resilience can also be described as "bouncing back" after the inevitable struggles and setbacks of life. To understand and foster resilience, we must consider the nature of the risks and protective factors that mark each individual's life and attend to the ways that these might change as a function of age. We will also consider some important contributions to fostering resilience from research in positive psychology.

Midlife brings its own set of challenges, not the least of which is the recognition of "time left to live," slowly accumulating losses related to getting older, and often great demands in the areas of the family and workplace. Some research suggests that stress is higher among young and middle-aged adults than it is for older adults (Chiriboga, 1997). Older adults are often more skilled at managing their emotions and sustaining joy. But it may also be that the life space adults occupy in their middle years is filled with more conflicting pulls on time and attention than it is for older individuals. Middle-aged adults are frequently in positions of increased responsibility and authority at work; they may have obligations to children and grandchildren; they may also take on the physical, emotional, or financial care of aging parents. All these situations can increase risk load. These circumstances are a defining characteristic of the sandwich generation, namely that group of individuals described in Chapter 13 who have caregiving responsibilities for generations both younger and older than themselves.

Who, then, are the resilient people? Questions about who thrives and why they do so defy easy answers. True to the principles of multifinality and equifinality, eventual life outcomes are dependent upon a whole array of variables that interact in complicated ways. What we are learning, however, is that pathways to adult disorder and well-being are not random but have their roots in the experiences of childhood and each succeeding stage. And, as with earlier parts of the life span, there are multiple pathways to well-being as well as to disorder.

The Wisconsin Longitudinal Study (Singer & Ryff, 1999), one early, comprehensive study of adult development, offers a look at the lives of adults who graduated from Wisconsin High Schools in 1957. This study of 10,317 men and women provides extensive information about participants' education, IQ, employment, marriage/family status, experience of stressful life events, accomplishments, goals, social support, and history of depression gathered over three data collections. Participants, parents, spouses, and siblings of original participants have contributed to data collections in 1957, 1964, 1975, 1992, 2002, and 2011 (Carney, 2014). Such a rich body of information offers many windows into adult development.

One subgroup that was studied intensively was the group of resilient women. *Resilient women* were defined as those who had experienced depression sometime during their lives but who had subsequently regained a high level of well-being (Singer, Ryff, Carr, & Magee, 1998). Aggregating the life stories of this group, the authors identified four pathways to wellness following the experience of adversity. Their life stories reflected a diversity of experiences in the following major areas: educational level of parents; alcoholism in the home as a child; marriage or cohabitation with an alcoholic as an adult; being a single parent; upward or downward mobility at work; and comparisons with parents and siblings with regard to education, finances, and occupation.

One group of resilient women had more cumulative advantages than the other groups, namely, educated parents, family financial stability, stable marriages, and so on. These women, however, did experience stressful life events, like the death of a parent or the onset of chronic illness, that presumably were related to their depression. A second group experienced more childhood adversity, including growing up in a family where there were problems with alcoholism. Women in this group also experienced similar losses and illness in adulthood. A third group was advantaged in childhood but experienced important setbacks in adulthood, like involuntary unemployment or divorce. The fourth group had lives that incorporated mixtures of advantages and disadvantages throughout early childhood and adulthood. What this work most clearly illustrates is the presence of multiple pathways to resilience. All four groups of women had at least one experience with depression, yet found their way out of it to reclaim a sense of well-being. Although not directly assessed in this sample, the ways in which these women perceived their difficulties and dealt with them most likely played a role in their resilient outcomes.

Another analysis of the Wisconsin Study data sought to examine the later life health and satisfaction of participants who took traditional and nontraditional ways of moving into adulthood in the 1950s and 1960s (Reifman, Oblad, & Niehus, 2017). Groups were clustered around marriage, children, and educational attainment. *Fast-starters* married early, had children, and did not go on to higher education. A *very educated/partnered* group went on to obtain higher education degrees and marry, but they tended to have children later. *Educated/singles* resembled the former group except that they did not marry. The *moderately educated/family oriented* group attended some college, married, and had children early. People who served in the military or otherwise worked before marrying comprised additional cohorts. Some of these trajectories were considered quite nontraditional in the 50s and 60s (e.g., very educated groups, especially for women) even though they bear close resemblance to today's emerging adults. Studying their pathways can reveal potential consequences of social timing and life decisions on later well-being.

When participants were in their 50s and 60s, both *very educated/partnered* and *moderately educated/family oriented* groups scored lowest on symptoms of depression. The authors hypothesize that possible success in meeting professional and personal needs might have played a part in their good fortune. *Fast starters* reported more depression later on, despite their success in family-related areas. Perhaps their lack of education put limits on their income down the road and affected their well-being. It's also important to consider the impact of historical economic conditions in the 1980s and 1990s when interpreting this finding. *Educated singles* displayed high levels of professional satisfaction but also relatively high levels of depressive symptoms. Possibly, their violation of societal expectations to marry and have children, so prevalent when they were young adults, may have contributed to unhappiness in this area over time.

The stressful circumstances of middle age frequently include a taxing set of demands related to managing family and work in the context of diminishing resources, such as time and energy. When circumstances exist that buffer the effects of competing role demands, such as good social support and adequate income, these demands may be perceived as less stressful. However, when the demands are too great given available resources, **role strain** (Goode, 1960) can occur, taking a toll on health and well-being. Perrone and Worthington (2001) found that having more resources, including income and social support, was associated with greater marital satisfaction among their sample of dual-income couples and presumably compensated for some of their work strains. Some others have demonstrated that multiple roles can be beneficial when they buffer the negative effects of one role with the protective function of a more satisfying one. Rozario, Morrow-Howell, and Hinterlong (2004) found that older caregivers with multiple productive roles reported more positive health outcomes compared to those without such roles.

Social support, as found in marriage or other close relationships, can be a potent protective factor in managing stress and promoting health. In a sample of middle-aged rural adults, Wickrama and associates found that unsupportive or distressed marital relationships were linked to early onset of hypertension for both husbands and wives. Problematic relationships with children contributed independently to the early onset of hypertension for mothers, but not for fathers. Husbands' satisfaction with employment, particularly the opportunity for advancement in the workplace, was negatively related to early onset of hypertension (Wickrama et al., 2001). These results suggest that chronic exposure to stressors in relationships can have direct negative effects on health and that these effects may be further exacerbated by gender-salient roles and expectations.

Work, children, spouses, friends, money, health, family . . . it's obvious that there are many challenges in adulthood, and some of these are certainly outside of our control. But what part can our attitudes play in supporting resilience? Let's review some features of stress and coping and then explore what research is learning about the role of a healthy mind in living well.

Stress: A Review

The nature and effect of stress on individuals is important to review because of its clear impact on emotional and physical health. Some have argued that the term *stress* is vague and open to many interpretations (Kemeny, 2003); consequently we adopt the recommended term *stressors*. Stressors have been divided into two varieties: **life events** (Holmes & Rahe, 1967) which are discrete, often traumatic, events that have a clear onset (like a death or accident) and **daily hassles** (Lazarus & Folkman, 1984), which are chronic, problematic situations (like day-to-day care of a sick relative or chronic illness). Research has suggested that chronic daily stress is very important in the development of psychological (Compas, Davis, Forsythe, & Wagner, 1987) as well as physical symptoms (Selye, 1980). For example, the stress of keeping a job while caring for a sick child or older relative may cause a person to go without sleep for a prolonged period of time. As a result the caregiver might succumb to illness herself due, in large part, to physical exhaustion. In some cases, stressors aggregate in people's lives, often subsequent to a traumatic event, and with this accumulation, their power amplifies the allostatic load (Garmezy, 1993). Caregivers like the one just described can lose a job, thus causing them to forfeit access to health care coverage and enough income to maintain a house or an automobile. Such cycles of disadvantage can exert a powerful impact on the lives of children as well as adults and have been consistently linked to the onset of physical and mental health problems (Turner & Lloyd, 1995).

Early models of diathesis-stress presumed premorbid conditions or predispositions that rendered individuals vulnerable to some disorder under certain circumstances (Monroe & Simons, 1991; Zuckerman, 1999). Individual vulnerability or diatheses were viewed as inherited traits or acquired through learning (as in the case of self-defeating cognitions or early attachments). These underlying vulnerabilities might or might not manifest depending upon individuals' experience. A related psychological model that has been useful in explaining how cumulative stressors create vulnerability is called kindling-behavioral sensitization. This model has contributed to understanding mechanisms of drug addiction, epilepsy, and affective disorders (Post, 1985, 2007, 2016). Think of "sensitization" as increasing reactivity such that, after multiple, intermittent doses of something like a drug, a stressor, or some emotional experience, a chemical memory of the exposure remains. Chronic exposure is more likely to produce tolerance or lower sensitivity. Intermittent exposure, however, results in sensitization, a gradual increase in sensitivity to stressful triggers resulting in progressive illness severity or illness incidence, even in the absence of a trigger.

Research has now advanced beyond theoretical formulations to clarify what these processes look like at the cellular level. We now know that there are multiple pathways for epigenetic modifications. Certain experiences, like substandard early caregiving, can alter genes related to stress system functioning by silencing or dampening genes' expression (see Chapter 2). Many genetic markers can be affected, and various types of genetic modifications are presently being studied. One process, methylation, has been associated with development of depression and PTSD after trauma (Zovkic & Sweatt, 2013). An initial episode of depression may be triggered by stressful life events (Dohrenwend & Dohrenwend, 1974), which leaves residual neurological changes in neurotransmitters, receptors, etc. that render him more reactive to stressors. Following this experience of sensitization, subsequent episodes of depression can occur spontaneously or with very little external provocation (Kendler, Thornton, & Gardner, 2001). Studies with animals show that some epigenetic traces can be left even in the absence of trauma experience or exposure to parental behavior, purportedly via alterations in sperm transmitted intergenerationally. When male rats were exposed to drugs like cocaine before mating, their offspring showed the same epigenetic modifications even though they had not been exposed to the male parent nor administered any drugs (Bale, 2015).

Stress and Growth

Those who flourish despite challenging circumstances might enjoy the protections of biology or environment, but explanations are far from crystal clear at this point. Nonetheless, these questions are attracting the attention of many contemporary researchers who are interested in understanding what contributes to positive development. One approach has been provided by Tedeschi and Calhoun (2004), who offer evidence for a phenomenon they call post-traumatic growth. This is defined as "positive psychological change experienced as a result of the struggle with highly challenging life circumstances" (p. 1). People who evidence post-traumatic growth, following experiences like bereavement, accident, illness, and so on, are marked by demonstrable improvements in psychological functioning that exceed pre-traumatic event levels. Some of these gains include an altered set of priorities about life, a greater appreciation for one's life, closer and more positive relationships with others, improved sense of life's possibilities, and heightened spirituality (Tedeschi & Calhoun, 1996). These authors provide evidence that post-traumatic growth is related to certain personality traits, notably extroversion and openness to experience, and to a lesser extent, dispositional optimism. Growth following trauma is believed to occur via the mechanism of cognitive processing, which refers to qualitative shifts in schemata about the self and the

MyLab Education
Video Example 14.3
Personal growth following loss involves qualitative shifts in schemata about self and the world.
For the couple in this video, the qualitative shifts in their views of relationships allow them to rebuild after loss.

world that need to occur to accommodate the enormously traumatic event. "This process is likely to involve a powerful combination of demand for emotional relief and cognitive clarity, that is achieved through construction of higher order schemata that allow for appreciation of paradox" (Tedeschi & Calhoun, 2004, p. 15). Others have pointed out that part of this process also includes the construction of positive illusions, like the belief that trauma makes one a better person (Taylor, 1983). These cognitive distortions may protect traumatized individuals by reinforcing their sense of mastery and self-worth along with soothing the acute stress (Maercker & Zoellner, 2004). Monumental positive experiences, like the birth of a child, can also enhance growth in comparable ways and should not be discounted as a vehicle for positive development (Aldwin & Levenson, 2004).

Coping with Stress

Given that everyone deals with stressors in their lives, that they critically influence our health, and that many of them derive from the aging process itself, the question becomes how best to manage inevitable stressful circumstances. We suggest that management of stress is essentially the same thing as coping. Many typologies have been developed to explain the nature of coping, and a voluminous body of research has been devoted to the question of whether coping in certain ways makes a difference in outcomes. The highly influential model proposed by Lazarus and Folkman (1984) makes a basic distinction between efforts aimed at changing the situation (problem-focused, problem-solving) and those directed towards emotion management (emotion-focused, tension-reduction). The two-dimensional model of primary and secondary control (Rothbaum, Weisz, & Snyder, 1982; see also Chapter 15) emphasizes the role of controllability of stressors as a determinant of coping responses. The repression-sensitization model (Byrne, 1964; Krohne & Rogner, 1982) describes coping behavior as a trait-like characteristic or style of coping that has two primary manifestations. The first (sensitizing) is marked by typically heightened perception of threat and increased attention to stressful information; the second (repression) is characterized by appraisal of stressors as less threatening and/or avoidance. This conceptualization bears some resemblance to other models such as approach-avoidance (Roth & Cohen, 1986), monitoring-blunting (Miller & Green, 1984), and rumination-distraction (Nolen-Hoeksema, 1987).

At present, researchers have recognized that some of these dichotomous distinctions fail to capture the real nature of coping, which does not manifest in mutually exclusive categories. Virtually all coping needs to accommodate cognitive (decision making) as well as emotional (anxiety management) aspects. Therefore, attempts to compartmentalize coping into sets of behaviors that address problem fixing or feeling better do not acknowledge that some coping falls outside these boundaries (such as seeking social support) and that categories are not mutually exclusive (such as taking a "mental health" day that allows you to avoid an unpleasant meeting and makes you feel more relaxed at the same time). Lazarus himself (1996) stated that treating problem- and emotion-focused coping as two highly distinctive types leads to oversimplification of the nature of coping itself. These distinctions are also problematic because they do not consider the function or intention of the coping behavior. In a review, Skinner and her colleagues state:

> If the ways that an individual copes are assembled based on the specific stressor(s) and situational constraints, then any way of coping can be locally adaptive. For example, if a set of stressors is actually uncontrollable, it may be adaptive to give up (to conserve resources). Or if an important goal is arbitrarily blocked, it may be adaptive to attack the obstacle (to defend the goal). In this sense, given the right circumstances, every possible way of coping can be appropriate, normative or right. (Skinner, Edge, Altman, & Sherwood, 2003, p. 231)

Hobfoll (1989; Hobfoll, Stevens, & Zalta, 2015; Hollifield, Gory, Siedjak, Nguyen, Holmgreen, & Hobfoll, 2016) presents a theory of coping with stressors that is relevant to midlife and aging because it emphasizes the centrality of loss experiences. His theory, called conservation of resources (COR) theory, posits that the primary stress trigger is loss through a primary loss event (bereavement, injury), transitions that involve loss (children leaving home, retirement), threats to aspects of the self (demotion, lack of acknowledgment for accomplishments), or challenges that incorporate some aspects of loss (job promotion that involves a move to a new location). Even though some of these events might have positive elements, the experience of stress, according to this theory, is the consequence of the loss component.

Researchers have demonstrated that people tend to weigh resource loss as more important in their lives than resource gain (Kahneman & Tversky, 1984; Tversky & Kahneman, 1974). In other words, negative events in people's lives appear to produce more powerful physiological, emotional, and cognitive consequences than do positive events. Resource loss is a critical predictor of distress following traumatic events, such as those due to natural disasters (Freedy, Saladin, Kilpatrick, Resnick, & Saunders, 1994), as well as in more chronic, day-to-day stressful events (Siegrist, 1996). That is, "losses make us hurt more than gains make us feel good" (Schwartz, 2004).

To deal with loss in its multiplicity of forms, individuals tend to act in ways that conserve their resources. Resources may be understood as things that people value in and of themselves or things that enable people to achieve or obtain that which is important to them (Baltes, 1987; Hobfoll et al., 2015). Resources can include objects (material possessions like a home or car), conditions (marriage, job status), personal characteristics (self-esteem, hope), or energies (time). When stressed, people seek to minimize the cost to their net resource capacity. Individuals also seek to increase their resources during nonstressful times, to accumulate a reserve. These ideas bear some resemblance, from a behavioral perspective, to the "sickness" response of the body under attack that was previously described.

Do the conceptual frameworks proposed to explain coping apply equally well to all cultural groups? It is true that the physiological mechanisms of the stress response are universal. But what about the ways individuals appraise and respond to the threats they perceive in their worlds? Even within groups, there is room for differences in assessment of what is stressful and how best to deal with it. The existence of relatively systematic preferences in coping behaviors within cultural groups, however, might indicate emic (culture-specific) dimensions of coping (Campos & Kim, 2017). In cultures that are more individualistic, an autonomous, direct approach to problem solving best fits the context. In more collectivistic cultures, managing one's own response to difficulties might be preferred over attempts to change the situation. Such a response could be seen as striving to maintain harmony within the group, as we have seen. Selecting a coping response has a great deal to do with the values, beliefs, and attitudes of one's cultural framework. It also has to do with the nature of the stressors that individuals face. Research has begun to identify unique cross-cultural variations. Table 14.5 contains examples of differences in coping responses to a national tragedy, the World Trade Center attacks of September 11, 2001. This field is emerging as one of particular interest to professionals engaged in helping clients manage stress by capitalizing on cultural strengths.

Stressors and the Body-Mind

Historical theories of stress and coping have been helpful in conceptualizing psychological frameworks for understanding these processes, for generating research questions, and for creating interventions that have benefitted many people. However, evidence from interdisciplinary work now offers a much more integrated way of framing stress and coping as universal mind-body functions that are part of the human operating system. While identification, interpretation, and resolution of stressful situations might look different for different events, and between individuals, groups and cultures, the underlying psychophysiological mechanisms are quite similar.

It is worthwhile to revisit the body's way of reacting to stressors and examine how they affect a variety of physiological systems to appreciate these processes more fully. As you may recall from Chapter 2, stressors engage the body's autonomic nervous system, activating the HPA axis, causing the release of hormones into the bloodstream, and preparing the body to respond to the perceived attack. Although this process

TABLE 14.5 Examples of Cultural Influences on Coping in the United States After the World Trade Center Attacks

SAMPLE STUDIED AND METHOD	STYLE OF COPING	COPING STRENGTHS RELATED TO CULTURE	COPING CHALLENGES RELATED TO CULTURE	SOURCE
Interviews from first-generation immigrants from **South Asia** who lost a relative. (Group of 11 included participants from India, Bangladesh, and Guyana.)	Use of relational coping; use of distraction; reliving memories of the deceased; emotional coping (getting angry); cognitive coping (making sense of it); religious/spiritual coping; avoidance; use of indigenous healers	Use of fatalistic beliefs that "suffering is part of destiny" to cope; reliance on community (including indigenous healers and kinship members); increased reliance on religious ritual	Inability to perform cultural rituals (e.g., burial practices) impeded the grieving process; loss of a potential income earner shifted the collective balance vis-à-vis roles in family; being targeted as the "enemy" affected well-being	Inman, Yeh, Madan-Bahel, & Nath, 2007
Interviews from first-generation **East Asian** immigrants who lost a relative. (Group of 11 included participants from China, Philippines, and Korea.)	Primary use of collectivistic ways of coping and support-seeking within the family; some use of distraction (focus on work, cooking, and going out)	Reliance on family and indigenous sources of support; use of spiritual and religious practices	Did not utilize mental health system due to shame and norms about emotional expression; sense of forbearance (bearing up) impeded self-disclosure	Yeh, Inman, Kim, & Okubo, 2006
Interviews from Indian-American **Sikh** males (N = 5) living in NYC.	Primary use of social support; religious coping; increased communication with Sikh community and family members, especially wives	Use of service as a way to cope (*seva* = selfless acts for others' benefit); emphasized nonviolence (not responding to hate with hate); educated others about their religious beliefs	Misidentification by others (due to uncut hair/turban/beard) as anti-American; physical and verbal threats and abuse	Ahluwalia & Pellettiere, 2010
Self-report assessments from 138 **Muslims** living in the United States.	Primary use of social support and religious and spiritual coping; some utilized avoidant coping (social isolation), which was related to depression	Increased religious practices (fasting, prayer, reading Qura'n); reached out to communities of faith for support; provided education about Muslim faith	Physical attacks, anti-Muslim comments; endured special security measures; experienced bullying, discrimination, and violence directed to personal property (setting fire to home)	Abu-Raiya, Pargament, & Mahoney, 2011

serves us well in emergency situations or in relatively short hormonal bursts, there are costs associated with chronic activation of the system (McEwen et al., 2015; Sapolsky, 1992). For example, during the acute phase of the body's stress response, immune system functioning is depressed.

Remember that stressors mobilize the body's energy resources to enhance certain functions (such as motor and sensory abilities, all the better to see and run away from the big, bad threat). The immune system, intended to surround and destroy attacking foreign bodies such as viruses or bacteria, requires mobilization of the body's energy to do its work as well. Our immune system operates through a process of inflammation to limit the spread of such harmful pathogens and to repair their damage.

Each of these important processes requires that the body's energy be directed to different ends (Maier, Watkins, & Fleshner, 1994). During a stressful event, energy reserves need to be devoted to the immediate fight-flight-freeze response and any alternative expenditure of energy, such as that required for reproductive system functions, is suppressed in service of the more immediate need. If homeostasis does not resume following the acute stress-response phase, the ill effects of chronic stress result. Chronically increased levels of cortisol, the body's primary stress hormone, are linked to cardiovascular decline in middle-aged and older adults (e.g., Hawkley & Caccioppi, 2007). High levels of cortisol can also dysregulate immune functions and reduce the body's capacity to protect itself against disease. You may have noticed, for example, that when you are dealing with some ongoing stressor, you might be more likely to catch a cold or flu, an example of the process of immunosuppression. This occurs because cortisol inhibits the proliferation or blunts the responses of certain types of cytokines (e.g., Kemeny, 2003; Robles, Glaser, & Kiecolt-Glaser, 2005).

Another immune system process, inflammation, is also affected when the body confronts chronic stressors (Kiecolt-Glaser, Derry, & Fagundes, 2015; Stein, Naudé, & Berk, 2018). Chronic stress exposure increases cortisol production, but also desensitizes the immune cells' ability to respond to cortisol's instructions to inhibit inflammatory processes. Consequently, high concentrations of proinflammatory cytokines, which are related to maladaptive inflammation, go unchecked. Many disease conditions, such as cardiovascular disease, allergies, rheumatoid arthritis, and other autoimmune disorders, have been associated with unregulated inflammatory processes (Kemeny, 2003; Steptoe, Willemsen, Owen, Flower, & Mohamed-Ali, 2001). These immune-related effects have been demonstrated in a study of adult parents of children with pediatric cancer. This group, presumably under chronic stress, showed impairment in the capacity of their immune system to downregulate inflammatory processes in comparison to parents of healthy children (Miller, Cohen, & Ritchey, 2002).

Maier and Watkins (1998) conclude from their review of research that psychological stressors, such as traumatic environmental events, operate on the body in much the same way as infectious agents. The effects on the body can include some combination of fever, increased sleep, reduction in eating and drinking, reduced exploration and activity, reduced aggression, reduction in social interaction, cognitive alterations, increased pain sensitivity, increased HPA activity, and depressed mood. Viewed from this perspective, these authors argue that certain types of depression are associated with hyperactivation of the immune response, even though the precise direction of these effects is still unclear. The important point in this discussion is the establishment of the connection between emotional experiences and the dysregulation of body mechanisms (like immune system functioning).

> The argument is not that depression is caused by immune activation. The argument is that whatever does cause depression (e.g., negative cognitions about the self or loss of a loved one) may have access to the same neural circuitry that evolved to mediate sickness and activate that circuitry. Some of the symptoms of depression, particularly the vegetative symptoms, may then be the result of this process and represent essentially *sickness* responses. In addition, as noted earlier, the circuit is bi-directional, and the products of these activated immune cells in turn provide signals to the brain. It is conceivable that this positive feedback circuit could help to maintain depression. (Maier & Watkins, 1998, p. 98)

Evidence has clearly supported the existence of bidirectional communication processes between the brain and the immune systems in relation to stressors, be they psychological or physical (Pert, 1997; Sternberg, 2001). Pert, for example, discovered that opiate receptors for the body's natural opiates, called endorphins, are present on the surface of cells in the immune system (spleen and thymus). This discovery uncovered the connections among the brain, the immune system, and emotions, linking the mind and body in new and exciting ways. As we are learning, the brain and the immune system operate together in a highly orchestrated dance that maintains homeostasis or balance within systems of the body-mind. Originally, it was thought that the brain "talked" and the immune system responded. Now researchers increasingly recognize that the brain also "listens" to the communication of the immune system, which sends its chemical messengers to various parts of the nervous system, including the brain. Findings such as these have helped usher in the field of psychoneuroimmunology, the study of the interactions among the central nervous system, the immune system, and behavior (Cohen & Williamson, 1991).

What may be most important to remember in all this is that the brain, as McEwen points out, is the central organ of stress management. Unless we perceive something to be threatening, our system doesn't kick into gear. Once threat is perceived, at conscious or unconscious levels, the system is activated and can lead to adaptation or contribute to allostatic load. We have seen that stress reactivity can be overactive, a somewhat technical term for being chronically "stressed out." In the next section, we'll discuss some approaches to stress management that incorporate advances in the science of mind-body medicine.

Wellness

With increasing attention to the physiology of stress and its effects on wellbeing, it makes sense to become familiar with one's own stress responsivity and stress triggers.

A general sense of self-efficacy (Bandura, 1989), optimism (Schier & Carver, 1985), self-esteem (Rosenberg, 1979), personal control over important goals (Seligman, 1975), and social support (Sarason & Sarason, 1985) are among the characteristics that are associated with greater physical and emotional health and effective coping. See Table 14.6 for a list of such qualities.

But how do people remember to practice these skills in the midst of stress? What if the stressor is uncontrollable, such as the onset of chronic ailments as people age? Is it just a fortunate few, blessed by temperament, who tend towards resilience? There is currently a strong interest in the pivotal role positive emotions play in the experience of well-being and their role in the stress management process. The encouraging news is that these qualities can be cultivated as well. As we have emphasized, not everyone who is exposed to the same stressor will have the same response. This is due, in part, to the way people appraise threats relative to the way they appraise their capacities to deal with them. The appraisal part of coping is the target for many cognitive and behavioral interventions that are geared towards self-efficacy and that enhance a sense of mastery and personal control. But affective elements are also in play in stress management, coping, and more generally, well-being.

The Affectivity Connection

Human emotional experience can be broadly construed as positive and negative, and recent conceptualizations link positive and negative emotions to separate neurobiological systems (Watson, Wiese, Vaidya, & Tellegen, 1999). **Negative affectivity,**

TABLE 14.6 Psychological Resilience Factors: Attitudes and Behaviors That Can Help Maintain Well-Being During Stress

1. Positive attitude: optimism and sense of humor
   Optimism is strongly related to resilience
   Optimism is partly inherited but can be learned through cognitive behavioral therapy
   Putative neurobiological mechanisms: strengthens reward circuits, decreases autonomic activity
2. Active coping: seeking solutions, managing emotions
   Resilient individuals use active rather than passive coping skills (dealing with problem and with emotions versus withdrawal, resignation, numbing)
   Can be learned: work on minimizing appraisal of threat, creating positive statements about oneself, focusing on aspects that can be changed
   Putative neurobiological mechanisms: prevents fear conditioning and learned helplessness, promotes fear extinction
   Facing fears: learning to move through fear
   Fear is normal and can be used as a guide for action
   Facing and overcoming fears can increase self-esteem and sense of self-efficacy
   Practice undertaking and completing challenging or anxiety-inducing tasks
   Putative neurobiological mechanisms: promotes fear extinction, stress inoculation
3. Cognitive flexibility/cognitive reappraisal: finding meaning or value in adversity
   Traumatic experiences can be reevaluated through a more positive lens
   Trauma can lead to growth: learn to reappraise or reframe adversity, finding its benefits; assimilate the event into personal history; accept its occurrence; and recover
   Recognize that failure is an essential ingredient for growth
   Putative neurobiological mechanisms: alters memory reconsolidation, strengthens cognitive control over emotions
4. Moral compass: embrace a set of core beliefs that few things can shatter
   Live by a set of guiding principles
   For many, moral compass means religious or spiritual faith
   Altruism strongly associated with resilience: selfless acts increase our own well-being
   Putative neurobiological mechanisms: spirituality/religiosity associated with strong serotonergic systems; morality has neural basis, likely evolved because adaptive
5. Physical exercise: engage in regular physical activity
   Physical exercise has positive effects on physical and psychological hardiness
   Effective at increasing mood and self-esteem
   Putative neurobiological mechanisms: promotes neurogenesis, improves cognition, attenuates HPA activity, aids in regulation of emotion, boosts immune system
6. Social support and role models or mentors
   Establish and nurture a supportive social network
   Very few can "go it alone," resilient individuals derive strength from close relationships
   Social support is safety net during stress
   Role models and mentors can help teach resilience: imitation is powerful mode of learning
   Putative neurobiological mechanisms: oxytocin mediates initial bonding/attachment
   "Mirror"/Von Economo neurons involved in neuronal imprinting of human values

NOTE: HPA, hypothalamic-pituitary-adrenal axis.

SOURCE: Haglund, M. E. M., Nestadt, P. S., Copper, N. S., Southwick, S. M., & Charney, D. S. (2007). Psychobiological mechanisms of resilience: Relevance to prevention and treatment of stress-related psychopathology. *Development and Psychopathology, 19*, 889–920. Cambridge University Press.

or the extent to which a person experiences nervousness, fear, anger, sadness, contempt, and guilt, is a part of the behavioral-inhibition system. This circuit is related to withdrawal and avoidance behaviors shaped through evolution to help people keep out of harm's way. Positive affectivity, or the extent to which a person experiences enthusiasm, alertness, joy, confidence, and determination, is part of the behavioral facilitation system, that system intended to allow people to respond to reinforcement and to approach and engage with the environment. Both positive and negative affectivity have trait-like as well as state-like qualities. This means that individuals' emotions may change from happy to sad based on certain events. But it also means that people tend to vary in their baseline levels of positive and negative affectivity or emotional style overall.

Studies of the brain indicate that the left prefrontal cortex (LPC) is activated during the experience of positive emotions, whereas the right prefrontal cortex (RPC) is activated during periods of negative emotion (Davidson, 2000). This prefrontal asymmetry can be measured in individuals in resting states and points to what might be thought of as temperamentally related emotional style. When researchers asked participants to watch film clips designed to elicit positive (animals at a zoo) and negative (a burn victim) emotional responses (having recorded their baseline brain activity prior to exposure to the films), they found reliable individual differences in responses that were predicted by prefrontal activity. Those with higher left frontal activity reported more positive affect in response to the positive stimuli; those with the reverse prefrontal pattern reported more fear and disgust in response to the negative stimuli. These results suggest that people are different in their tendencies to respond to emotional stimuli (Tomarken, Davidson, & Henriques, 1990).

So what does this have to do with stress and coping? As you might imagine, negative affectivity has been associated with greater reactivity to stress (Watson & Pennebaker, 1989). Research also demonstrates that the immune systems of individuals with greater LPC activation were less compromised following a traumatic stressor (Davidson, Coe, Dolski, & Donzella, 1999). In other research, participants viewed an emotionally distressing film while hemispheric activity and hormone levels were measured. Researchers employed a procedure that allowed participants to see the film using only their right or left hemisphere. Results demonstrated that viewing the film using the right hemisphere was associated with a significantly higher release of cortisol than was left-hemisphere viewing. The authors concluded that cortisol regulation may be related to right-hemisphere activation (Wittling & Pflüger, 1990). Cohen and his colleagues found that people who tended to have a positive emotional style were significantly more likely, compared to those with a negative emotional style, to be resistant to the common cold (Cohen, Doyle, Turner, Alper, & Skoner, 2003).

Does this mean that those of us with higher levels of RPC activation are doomed to a life of greater unhappiness? Keep in mind that the impact of negative things is stronger than the impact of good ones in general, so to some degree we are all in the same boat (Baumeister, Bratslavsky, Finkenauer, & Vohs, 2001). The good news is that emotional affectivity is not a zero sum game; in other words, positive and negative affectivity circuits are independent of each other rather than opposite ends of a continuum (Cacioppo & Gardner, 1999; Diener & Emmons, 1985). People do not express only one type of emotionality or the other but can have access to the full range of emotions. So even if we view the pattern of trait-like negative affectivity as a risk factor, emerging research suggests that we can encourage the development of positive emotions through certain practices. As Ingram and Price (2001) conclude, "Even though vulnerability is conceptualized as a trait according to some conceptualizations, vulnerability is not necessarily permanent or unalterable. Corrective experiences can occur that may attenuate the vulnerability, or, alternately, certain experiences may increase vulnerability factors" (p. 12).

What are the protections against encroaching stress sensitivity due to temperament, stressful life events, or age? In general, strengthening emotion regulation, reducing the anxiety induced by threats, and cultivating positive emotions are increasingly viewed as antidotes to stress and health-compromising emotional states like anger and hostility (e.g., Goleman, 2003; Lyubomirsky, King, & Diener, 2005; Hölzel et al., 2011;

Srivastava, McGonigal, Richards, Butler, & Gross, 2006). Some suggest that such emotion-related skills can be shifted from temporary states to more permanent traits with practice (Goleman & Davidson, 2017).

It is important to remember that emotions are complicated, and their effects on health may be moderated by culture. In the West, expression of anger and hostility is clearly related to morbidity and mortality, as indexed by health data such as blood pressure, body mass index, inflammatory markers, cholesterol level, etc. (Chida & Steptoe, 2009; Boylan & Ryff, 2013). In Japan, expression of anger (but not anger suppression or trait anger) was not associated with the same worrisome biomarkers. See Table 14.7 for different ways to assess aspects of anger.

Kitayama and colleagues (2016) analyzed questionnaire and health data from large samples of midlife adults living in the United States and Tokyo while controlling for gender, age, chronic health conditions, smoking, and alcohol use. Anger expression was related to increased heath risk for the U.S. sample but not for the Japanese. The authors suggest that expressed anger among people in the West may be an index of frustration, annoyance, or accumulated life stressors, which may be the source of health risk. Among Japanese, expressions of anger may reflect power, social dominance, or an entitled position rather than underlying frustration. This interesting finding suggests a moderating role for culture on the effects of anger expression, but not for other facets of anger.

MEDITATION FOR THE MIND AND BODY

One of the most promising approaches to cultivating the skills of emotion regulation and well-being is meditation. Meditation is a means of mental training and refers to a "family of complex emotional and attentional regulatory training regimes developed for various ends, including the cultivation of well-being and emotional balance" (Lutz, Slagter, Dunne, & Davidson, 2008, p. 163). While there are many ways to train the mind, through yoga, Qigong, reflection, prayer, and so on, training in mindfulness (called *mindfulness meditation*) is a form of training that has been researched extensively in recent years. Two general categories of mindfulness meditation practice include (1) focused attention (practice in stabilizing attention, noticing distractions, shifting attention, etc.) and (2) open-monitoring (nonreactive meta-awareness of experience). Compassion practices (e.g., lovingkindness, forgiveness) are considered an additional category intended to cultivate wholesome, ethical qualities (Lutz et al., 2008; Vago & Silbersweig, 2012). Traditionally, these practices originated from Buddhist scientific knowledge about the mind and its operations. Recognizing that the distracted, ruminative mind was a primary source of human suffering, practitioners developed skillful means for training the ever-wandering, ever-worrying mind, in order to cultivate the mental habit of equanimity (Olendzki, 2010). Basic breath awareness practice was taught first as a means of developing mental focus and concentration. Once the mind was relatively stable, transitioning to open-awareness allowed for practice in nonjudgmental observation of thoughts, bodily sensations, feelings, and experiences without reactivity or unhelpful narrative. With sustained practice, the mind becomes a refined tool, seeing clearly the traps that propel it into cycles of craving or avoiding, and able to direct thoughts and behavior in ways that diminish stress and amplify well-being.

A new field called mindfulness neuroscience (Tang, 2017; Tang, Holzel, & Posner, 2015) has emerged from the rapidly growing corpus of studies on mindfulness and its effects on the brain and body. Mindfulness practice impacts certain brain-related

TABLE 14.7 Facets of Anger

ANGER EXPRESSION	TRAIT ANGER	ANGER SUPPRESSION	ANGER CONTROL
I slam doors. I say nasty things. I lose my temper.	I am a hothead. I am angrier than I'm willing to admit. I get irritated a great deal more than people are aware of.	I keep things in. I withdraw from people. I boil inside but don't show it.	I take a deep breath and relax. I do something relaxing to calm down. I try to simmer down.

SOURCE: Based on Spielberger, C. D., Forgays D. K., Ottaway S. A. (1998). *Factor Structure of The State-Trait Anger Expression Inventory for Middle-Aged Men and Women in Assessment.* Copyright © Psychological Assessment Resources.

functions, namely attention and other executive functions, emotion regulation, and self-awareness. It also affects the body, by virtue of its ability to shift systems towards parasympathetic dominance. We have seen how the mind (worries) and the body (racing heart) interact in times of stress, so use of mind-body approaches can help restore harmony (Tang & Tang, 2015).

Because the brain is our gatekeeper for stress, improving its ability to respond to events in a more regulated, less reactive way could reduce the harmful impact of a stress system on overdrive. It is also reasonable to conclude that practicing a positive emotional style may serve as an antidote, buffering the effects of stress. You might have thought of emotional style as a hard-wired tendency. Recent research is revolutionizing our way of thinking about emotion and providing support for the view that the brain is somewhat plastic with regard to affective style, more similar to an incremental viewpoint. Although much more work needs to be done in this area, current research offers some tantalizing possibilities.

Much has been written about the nature and consequences of negative emotions. Fear prepares us to escape; anger helps us protect ourselves; sadness allows us to grieve a loss. But what is the evolutionary role of positive emotion? Positive emotions serve to undo or reverse the potentially harmful impact of negative emotions (Fredrickson, 2001). This makes sense if we consider the destructive effects of chronically activating the body's stress response.

Stress revs up the system for a reason, but when the stressor has been avoided or conquered, the stress response system needs to revert to baseline in order to prevent damage. However, as you have read, chronic activation of brain-based stress responses can make the system super-sensitive. Attention becomes hyperfocused on threatening details, and individuals feel as if they are living under siege. Figure 14.3 depicts the cognitive, emotional, and physical outcomes associated with chronic stress.

Mindfulness and positive emotions, states of mind that can be practiced, promote recovery from stress. They allow individuals to let go of distress and replace the narrowed focus on threat with a more expansive attention (*broaden*) (Jäger & Rüsseler,

---

FIGURE 14.3 The downward spiral of stress reactivity.
Chronic activation of the stress response can lead to a downward spiral of negative physical and emotional consequences.

SOURCE: Garland, E. L., Fredrickson, B. L., Kring, A. M., Johnson, D. P., Meyer, P. S., & Penn, D. L. (2010). Upward spirals of positive emotions counter downward spirals of negativity: Insights from the broaden-and-build theory and affective neuroscience on the treatment of emotion dysfunctions and deficits in psychopathology. *Clinical Psychology Review, 30 (7)*, 849–864. Used with permission from Elsevier.

FIGURE 14.4 The upward spiral of positive emotions and resilience.

The experience of positive emotions broadens attention and contributes to building a reserve of personal resources.

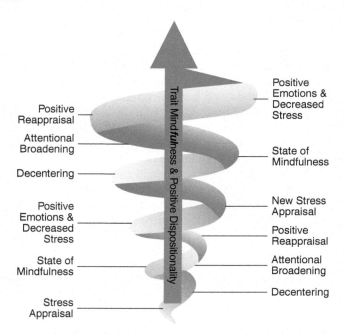

SOURCE: Garland, E. L., Fredrickson, B. L., Kring, A. M., Johnson, D. P., Meyer, P. S., & Penn, D. L. (2010). Upward spirals of positive emotions counter downward spirals of negativity: Insights from the broaden-and-build theory and affective neuroscience on the treatment of emotion dysfunctions and deficits in psychopathology. *Clinical Psychology Review, 30 (7)*, 849–864. Used with permission from Elsevier.

2016). "Because positive emotions arise in response to diffuse opportunities, rather than narrowly focused threats, positive emotions momentarily broaden people's attention and thinking, enabling them to draw on higher-level connections and a wider-than-usual range of percepts or ideas. In turn, these broadened outlooks often help people to discover and build consequential personal resources" (Fredrickson, Cohn, Coffey, Pek, & Finkel, 2008, p. 1045). Accumulating resources may be gained in physical (fewer illnesses), social (more friendships), psychological (increased optimism) or intellectual (mindfulness or creativity) domains. Figure 14.4 illustrates the resiliency process.

Fredrickson and her colleagues (2008) tested the "build" portion of the theory by exploring whether a daily practice of lovingkindness meditation ([LKM]; see the Applications section) would increase participants' experience of positive emotions and add to their repertoire of positive resources to impact long-term well-being. At the end of the 9-week study, the positive emotions experienced by participants in the daily LKM group (such as love, joy, gratitude, contentment, hope, pride, interest, amusement, and awe) were three times as great as they were at week 1. Furthermore, these changes were associated with increased resources like self-acceptance, mindfulness, better health, and improved social relationships. The authors conclude that the path to improved life satisfaction was heavily impacted by positive emotions. "Positive emotions emerged as the mechanism through which people build the resources that make their lives more fulfilling and help keep their depressive symptoms at bay" (p. 1057). A more recent study asked participants to practice either mindfulness meditation or LKM over a 9-week period. Both groups showed significant improvements in positive emotions, regardless of the type of practice they did. Those who practiced more reported more positive emotions, suggesting a general dose-response relationship (Fredrickson et al., 2017).

In a study that investigated the effectiveness of meditation for reducing anxiety and enhancing positive mood, Davidson and his colleagues (2003) explored the effects of a meditation course on brain and immune system functioning. A group of healthy male and female employees at a biotechnology corporation were recruited to participate in an 8-week meditation-based stress reduction program at their workplace, forming a treatment group and a wait-list control. Before beginning the program, participants' brain electrical activity was measured while they were asked to write about a series of positive and negative events in their lives. At the end of the 8 weeks, the same assessments of brain activity were performed. Participants also rated their experience of positive and negative emotions following each group session. Finally, all participants (including the wait-list group) were administered the flu vaccine at the end of the 8 weeks. Blood samples were obtained at 3 to 5 weeks and again at 8 to 9 weeks postvaccination to assess the immune response.

Results demonstrated that meditators showed a significant increase in left prefrontal brain activity, related to the experience of positive affectivity, compared to the control group. Self-report measures reflected a significant decrease in anxiety for those in the program compared to those who did not participate. Interestingly, program participants reported significant decreases in their own experiences of negative affectivity over time, whereas control group members did not. When blood draws were examined, participants in the meditation group had significantly increased concentrations of antibodies in their blood compared to nonmeditators. This finding suggests a greater and more rapid immune system response compared to controls. These findings are promising because they reflect that even a relatively short intervention carried out in a work setting can reduce negative affectivity and anxiety and promote health and well-being.

> **MyLab Education** Self-Check 14.2

Applications

Helping professionals should be proud of their history of fostering wellness in various ways (Keyes & Haidt, 2003). The paths to well-being include the development of mastery and optimism, instruction in effective problem solving and decision making, encouragement of social competence, support for health-promoting behaviors related to diet and exercise, and advocacy for improved environmental circumstances. Some general themes and practice ideas can be distilled from the current crop of research on happiness and life satisfaction. The following list of suggestions comes from the research of well-known experts in the area of well-being. The timing and appropriateness of these suggestions, intended as interventions to increase subjective well-being, should always be considered in the context of client needs and problems.

- Help clients develop social skills. Research demonstrates that social connections are strongly associated with well-being because they foster the basic need for relatedness. Many effective interventions, such as social skills training, social groups, cognitive behavior therapy, etc. can be considered.
- Help clients identify maladaptive thoughts. Cognitive therapy approaches have amply demonstrated how dysfunctional thinking (e.g., "I'll never have any friends"; "Things

never get any better for me") is related to depression, negative affect, and lower well-being. Targeting the ways clients think about their life circumstances can help them modify their outlooks and can lead to greater happiness.
- Introduce some practices to cultivate well-being. Research has shown that exercises like gratitude practices, counting one's blessings, journaling, performing acts of kindness, visualizing one's best self, and reflective/expressive writing, to name a few, can produce increases in positive emotions.
- Discuss client expectations about their well-being. It is important to understand clients' values and preferences for emotional expression. Not everyone expects nor wants to demonstrate high-arousal positive emotions. Perhaps, supporting client contentment may be helpful in shifting perspectives about the kind of happiness that can be sustained.
- Support client lifestyle changes that indirectly lead to greater well-being. Research shows that diet, sleep, exercise, balance between work and leisure, meaningful work, and activities can all lead to greater happiness. In addition, reduction in unhealthy habits can also be a focus of intervention.
- Pay attention to the potentially harmful effects of excessive materialism on well-being. Sometimes, clients'

beliefs about what makes people happy, such as greater wealth, may actually be a source of stress.

- Support workplace efforts to improve personal autonomy, flexibility, and reductions in discrimination. Opportunities to develop and express competence in the workplace can also promote well-being.

- Some community-based programs for adults explicitly focus on promoting greater well-being. The 8-session Lighten UP program, based on Ryff's research, includes the following components (Friedman, Ruini, Foy, Jaros, Sampson, & Ryff, 2017): Focusing on positive experiences in everyday life and reviewing positive events from the past are covered in sessions 1 and 2. Identification of obstacles that impede well-being, such as stress or loss, as well as the automatic negative thoughts and attitudes that sustain unhappiness, are the subjects of sessions 3 and 4. Finally, presentation of cognitive restructuring and other techniques to reduce dysfunctional thinking (session 5), provision of information about domains of well-being (session 6), strategies to improve well-being (session 7), and the connections between well-being and health (session 8) form the core of the program.

Threaded throughout this text is the theme of emotion regulation, that capacity that allows us to regulate levels of emotional arousal. The behaviors and capacities that constitute emotion regulation also include recognition of feelings and appropriate expression and modulation of emotional expression. In infancy and toddlerhood, attachments with caregivers channel youngsters' developing capacity to self-soothe, to tolerate frustration, and to stay for longer and longer periods of time in a regulated emotional state. In childhood and adolescence, social development is promoted by the young person's ability to delay gratification in service of peers, to control impulses that could hurt or antagonize others, and to benefit from capacities for friendship. In emerging and young adulthood, good emotion regulation is associated with better overall adjustment and satisfying communication in close relationships. Conversely, difficulties in emotion regulation have been associated with a wide variety of problems. Recall that temperamental differences in intensity of perceived emotions can make emotion regulation a particular challenge for some children.

Sometimes "emotion regulation" primarily refers to the experience of negative emotions—that is, what we do when we feel bad or when we don't get our own way. Helpers might be heartened by the growing literature indicating that emotional affectivity, both positive and negative, is not immutable and can be shaped by certain practices. All the efforts to support resiliency affirm this conclusion. As Davidson reflects about his own work, "It was the possibility of altered *traits* of consciousness that was particularly appealing to me. Altered traits implied the transformation of consciousness and personality in an enduring fashion to foster increased well-being" (Davidson, 2002, p. 107).

Mindfulness

Within the body of techniques that address stress reduction, interventions that target stress-reactivity—the quick response that often switches on the cascade of potentially harmful biopsychological events described in this chapter—are particularly important. As we've presented, one promising approach is to work with the mind's own plasticity and capacity for reducing negative reactivity and to increase curiosity and interest through present-moment and somatic awareness (Kabat-Zinn, 2003). Interventions and practices of this sort provide an alternative to traditional therapies that emphasize past history, future goals, distraction, or even the restructuring of thinking. In fact, this approach deemphasizes the role of thinking and verbal analysis precisely because "the illusion of language is that one is dealing with the world through thought. In fact, one is actually structuring the world through thought" (Hayes, 2002, p. 104). Varela, Thompson, and Rosch (1991) note the tendency of the mind to reside in the domain of abstraction and refer to this inclination as "the spacesuit, the padding of habits and preconceptions, the armor with which one habitually distances oneself from one's own experience" (p. 25). As we have noted, worrying about something stressful can amplify the stress. Even without the presence of stressors, our minds are constantly engaged in inner conversations that remove us from the direct experience of what is actually happening in the present moment.

The direct experience of the present, as opposed to mental reruns of past events, discursive ruminations about abstract ideas, or fantasy scenarios about future possibilities, is a very different type of mental event. Being present in the moment involves stepping out of the automatic pilot mode that characterizes much of our mental life. With practice in noticing and taking account of the present moment, it becomes possible to disengage from dominating ruminative patterns of thinking. Moreover, it becomes possible to extricate oneself from the attitude of abstraction to reconnect the mind and body. Approaches that foster somatic present-moment awareness help develop the skill of being in the "here and now" without attaching any evaluative valence to the experience. Attention available for discursive thought is deliberately reduced, whereas nonjudgmental acceptance of one's experience and also oneself is increased. Nonjudgmental awareness of present-moment experience improves the capacity to respond to stressors in a more skillful and less reactive way. Mindfulness, then, is a special kind of attention: purposeful, present, open, and nonjudgmental (Kabat-Zinn, 1994).

Mindfulness awareness is acquired through repeated practice. Voluntarily and repeatedly orienting attention to a specific object of focus, like the breath, while gently letting go of distractions enables a deep, compassionate, and first-person level of self-awareness. Attention is directed to thoughts, feelings, and somatic experiences as they arise in real time without trying to change anything. While thoughts and feelings are frequently discussed in therapy, somatic experiences are rarely addressed. Bringing attention to the present moment experience of all three shifts focus away from the past (e.g., memory of troubling incident) and the future (e.g., apprehension of impending trouble), thereby disrupting the connections between automatic cognitive interpretations and patterns of responding (avoidance or over-engagement) through the mechanism of psychological decentering. Nonconscious regulatory processes may come under more conscious control, fostering reflective decision making and reducing prepotent, pre-reflexive reactions. The automatic reactivity that evaluates internal and external experience as "good" or "bad," that is, as something to be sought after or avoided, can be the source of much dysfunction. Patterns of reactivity (e.g., anxiety, boredom, irritation, impulsivity, etc.) that cause regulatory processes to break down can result in problematic behavior. Mindfulness practice allows for the recognition of these mental patterns as they arise, offering more choice about how to respond skillfully.

Let's consider this in the context of something stressful. Our perception of distress can be triggered by internal or external conditions or some combination of the two. When we feel stressed, our response patterns may take the form of avoidance of or overengagement with the distressing object or condition in an effort to reduce distress. For example, we may seek to "numb" feelings of social rejection by drinking, taking drugs, or spending money. Distress is temporarily blunted, relief is provided, and the maladaptive behavior acquires reinforcing properties that strengthen dysfunctional patterns. The maladaptive behaviors not only provide transient relief (positive reinforcement) but also serve to permit escape from emotional pain (negative reinforcement). Alternatively, we might become preoccupied with our stress in ways that strengthen the associations between automatic thoughts and negative affect. An example of this pattern is obsessive worry or rumination, which is constant re-examination or re-experiencing of distressing conditions or events in a misguided effort to resolve problems and regulate emotions. Rumination heightens attention to distress cues, amplifies rather than attenuates distress, and reduces the capacity of working memory to effectively engage in learning (Lyubomirsky & Tkach, 2004). Both approaches to stress management may lock us into harmful patterns that ultimately reduce our happiness and well-being. But what if we could "see" how we relate to the experience of stress, right from our first glimmer of its unpleasantness? Might we be able to tolerate its discomfort a little more? Might we be able to make some different choices about how to respond? This is what mindfulness practice helps us do.

A number of mindfulness-based interventions have been examined for their effectiveness in relieving both mental and physical symptoms (Creswell, 2017). Mindfulness-based stress reduction (MBSR), developed by Kabat-Zinn and colleagues (2005) at the University of Massachusetts Stress Reduction Clinic, is the first and most famous program to be researched. Originally developed as a hospital-based program for stress reduction, MBSR programs have proliferated in recent years to include training for groups as diverse as students, educators, corporate employees, health care professionals, attorneys, inmates, clergy, and athletes. The MBSR course has a structured curriculum that is taught in a group format over 8 weeks and involves daily homework practice. In comparison to therapies that emphasize discussion or analysis, MBSR emphasizes practice in working with attention. A core feature of mindfulness is learning to transform stressful situations by going through them in a skillful way, not trying to avoid or eradicate them. Essentially, to be mindful is to develop skills in attention and moment-to-moment awareness. Therefore, developing the ability to take note of thoughts, feelings, and sensations increases the capacity to work skillfully with negative ones and replace automatic, habitual, and often judgmental reactions with relaxed observing and awareness.

Some of the session themes include noticing the automaticity of thinking and behavior, becoming more aware of bodily sensations, learning how to get "unstuck" from reactive patterns, enhancing stress hardiness, and so forth. The program employs various activities such as walking, sitting, and eating meditation, yoga/mindful movement, and discussion. One of the primary foundations of the program is daily home practice.

MBSR principles have been incorporated into cognitive-behavioral therapy, resulting in a new treatment modality called mindfulness-based cognitive therapy ([MBCT]; Segal, Williams, & Teasdale, 2002). This approach was designed to reduce the risk of depressive relapse. Mindfulness approaches are also a prominent part of Linehan's (1993) Dialectical Behavior Therapy, originally designed for individuals diagnosed with borderline personality disorder, as well as in Acceptance and Commitment Therapy (Hayes, 2004).

Outcome studies on mindfulness-based interventions, like MBSR and MBCT, demonstrate improvements in physical and psychological functioning for individuals suffering from chronic pain, fatigue, insomnia, anxiety, depression and depressive relapse, addictions, and other problems (see Brewer, Elwafi, & Davis, 2013; Gong et al., 2016; Khoury et al., 2013; Lauche, Cramer, Dobos, Langhorst, & Schmidt, 2013; Ma & Teasdale, 2004; Majeed, Ali, & Sudak, 2018; Sun et al., 2016; Zeidan & Vago, 2016). Mindfulness practices improve functioning on a number of important health indices related to longevity and well-being, increased immunity, and cardiovascular system functioning as well (see Allen, Henderson, Mancini, & French, 2017; Black & Slavich, 2016; Creswell & Lindsay, 2014; Gotink, Chu, Busschbach, Benson, Fricchione, & Hunink, 2015; Kok, Waugh, & Fredrickson, 2013). Mindfulness has also been taught to youth as a means of fostering greater emotion regulation and executive functions (Broderick & Frank, 2014; Zoogman, Goldberg, Hoyt, & Miller, 2014). As is the case in many other areas, research on meditation's effects has been criticized for its low quality and inconsistency in outcome measurement. To fully assess the benefits of mindfulness meditation, we need more well-designed studies with active control groups that would enable us to more clearly understand effects. Research into online mindfulness applications is also underway. This application may offer practitioners effective ways to bring interventions to scale. Overall, results on mindfulness-based interventions do show promise, but we need additional high-quality research to expand their use in clinical and community settings (Creswell, 2017).

Forgiveness

Part of the acceptance process must involve forgiveness of past hurts. Increasingly, forgiveness is being accorded more importance in therapeutic contexts as it is shown to contribute to physical and psychological features of well-being (Akhtar & Barlow, 2018). For example, consider this empirical study of the effects of forgiveness or lack of forgiveness on physiology. Witvliet, Ludwig, and Vander Laan (2001) asked participants in this study to imagine a person who had harmed or mistreated them. Participants were then instructed to rehearse unforgiving feelings (like holding the grudge) for a brief period of time while physiological measurements were made. They were next instructed to practice forgiving responses (like empathizing with the offender by trying to take an alternative perspective on the offense) while the same assessments were taken. Blood pressure, facial tension, cardiovascular reactivity, arterial pressure, and sympathetic nervous system arousal as measured by skin conductivity were all significantly higher in the unforgiving condition. Participants reported more negative mood (angry, sad, aroused, etc.) while being unforgiving. Furthermore, negative physiological effects of the period of "holding a grudge" as measured by cardiovascular and sympathetic nervous system indicators persisted into the subsequent stage of the experiment. This finding suggests that the physiological systems activated in the unforgiving state may resist healing, contribute to overall stress, and have implications for overall health.

Forgiveness therapy (Enright & Fitzgibbons, 2000) proposes a series of stages that map the process of forgiveness in a therapeutic setting. The first phase, uncovering, is spent in a thorough examination of the traumatic injury or event. Recognizing and confronting anger or shame, readjusting an old view of a "just world," and coming to terms with the injury are parts of this process. In phase two, the decision phase, injured clients face up to the realization that carrying the burden of rage or seeking revenge may be an unskillful resolution. Here the therapist attempts to motivate clients to see the benefits of forgiveness to physical and emotional well-being. Perhaps for the first time, forgiveness is seen as a possibility. In the work phase, clients might be asked to write about whom it is they wish to forgive. Reframing questions posed by the therapist, such as "What was it like for the offender when he or she was growing up?" encourage perspective taking and empathy, which may plant the seeds of compassion. The authors caution that compassion aids

in the healing process but must unfold in its own time, so therapists should not rush this process. Clients may also be asked to write about the impact that acceptance and forgiveness might have on their lives. In the last phase, called deepening, clients continue to construct a narrative to account for the painful experience, which allows the episode to become integrated into a meaningful life story. Sometimes, sharing one's story with others or working to help others who have been similarly hurt provides a therapeutic resolution.

Worthington offers an alternative therapeutic model (2006) based on the acronym REACH: Recalling the offense; developing Empathy for the offender; offer forgiveness to the offender as an expression of Altruism; make a Commitment to forgive; and Hold on to forgiveness when they experience difficulty. Both models have also been studied in various groups and for various situations and have been found effective across cultures (Hanke & Fischer, 2013; Lin et al., 2014). Forgiveness interventions have shown the ability to improve well-being and reduce depression and stress, although the exact mechanisms are not well understood (Wade, Hoyt, Kidwell, & Worthington, 2013).

Forgiveness does not involve excusing hurtful behavior, necessarily reconciling with the offender, suppressing one's pain, or forgetting the offense. Rather, it involves a shift in thoughts, feelings, and behaviors in relation to offenders in a more positive direction (McCullough, Pargament, & Thoresen, 2000). It generally involves a long and gradual process of transforming the tendency to seek revenge and to let go of enmity. As Kornfield puts it, "Forgiveness means giving up all hope of a better past" (Kornfield, 2002, p. 25).

Self-Compassion: Spirals of Positivity

Looking ahead towards the last of Erikson's psychosocial tasks, we see that everyone needs to come to terms with his or her own life story, regardless of the paths their lives have taken. "Coming to terms" may include forgiving ourselves for real or imagined offenses as well as forgiving those who might have hurt us. The fact that people are developmentally more inclined to take stock in midlife (Erikson, 1968) does not mean that reflection is nonexistent at other points in the life span. However, the salience of this theme in the "second half of life" (Jung, 1963) suggests that self-acceptance is truly a life's work. The world's great religions have all adopted some version of the "golden rule," to love both one's neighbor and oneself. The great philosophical traditions have also championed the values of love for all humanity. But what does it really mean to love oneself? Clearly, this advice has merit not only on theological or philosophical grounds. Self-acceptance and self-compassion offer many advantages for personal happiness, adjustment, and physical health. Empathy for others also makes relationships less confrontational and more satisfying. Perhaps those in the helping professions need to be particularly mindful of their own needs for self-care because they so often share in the emotional experiences of others. Compassion, which may involve some self-forgiveness (Kim & Enright, 2014) is an exceptionally important quality for helpers that can support their work with clients and improve their own psychological well-being (see Germer & Siegel, 2012).

A meditation practice, akin to those described earlier, can be useful to enhance positive affectivity by cultivating lovingkindness. *Lovingkindness* may be defined as an attitude that extends care and empathy towards self and others (Goleman, 2003). This should not be mistaken for some transient sentimental state. Rather it is the basis for a broad-based altruism and a strong positive regard for others. The lovingkindness exercise is essentially a way to practice benevolence directed first towards oneself and then towards friends, neutral acquaintances, and finally enemies. Often people find it easier to be compassionate towards others than towards themselves; indeed, practicing self-acceptance at an affective level may seem strange to many of us in the West.

Disrespect for ourselves and disregard for our basic physical, social, and emotional needs underlies many self-destructive behaviors that take their toll on health and happiness. To cultivate this attitude of compassion in this way, the person first concentrates his attention, repeats inwardly a set of phrases "May I be happy; May I be peaceful; May I be healthy and strong" and so forth, as he generates the emotions of compassion. Research using neuroimaging techniques has shown that such practice produces long-lasting alterations in brain function in areas related to development of positive affective states (Lutz, Greischar, Rawlings,

Ricard, & Davidson, 2004). Savoring the positive moments of life mindfully, expressing gratitude, cultivating optimism, and showing acceptance by not trying to avoid the less pleasant realities of life are all resilience-building strategies. Kok et al. (2013) summarize these points well.

> Most advice dispensed about how people might improve their physical health calls for increased physical activity, improved nutritional intake, and reductions in tobacco and alcohol use. Alongside this good advice, we now have evidence to recommend efforts to self-generate positive emotions as well. Recurrent momentary experiences of positive emotions appear to serve as nutrients for the human body, increasing feelings of social belonging and giving a needed boost to parasympathetic health, which in turn opens people up to more and more rewarding positive emotional and social experiences. Over time, this self-sustaining upward spiral of growth appears to improve physical health. (p. 1131)

Positive practices that help us manage stress and regulate mood are beneficial for clients and helpers alike. One broad implication we can draw from work in this area is that well-being is not just the "absence" of disorder, experienced only some of the time by a fortunate few. Instead, it involves the deliberate cultivation of those elements that make life worthwhile.

Summary

Life Satisfaction: What Is a Well-Lived Life?

1. Subjective well-being, an individual's overall satisfaction with life and general happiness, is usually measured using questionnaires or interviews asking people to rate their lives or their feelings about their lives on a continuum, say from "very happy" to "very unhappy." SWB includes cognitive (satisfaction) as well as affective (positive and negative experience) elements. New ways of measuring daily experience are contributing to this body of research.

2. The well-being of individuals and of national populations is correlated with wealth but its strength depends upon measures used. People who are poor report less well-being than those who are not, but after a certain basic level of income is attained, greater wealth is not strongly associated with greater well-being. Actual increases in disposable income are related to life satisfaction especially in poorer countries. In more developed nations, life satisfaction improves only when social capital and low-income disparity are also present.

3. Values in the United States are more materialistic when compared to values in some other countries. The American paradox, which characterizes many wealthy nations, is that as income and standard of living have increased steadily in recent decades, so have emotional problems such as depression. There may be several reasons, among which are that pursuit of material gain may put many people on a hedonic treadmill. Because they expect more money to make them happier, when it doesn't, they feel compelled to further pursue material gain. Also, the lifestyles made possible by affluence tend to reduce the need for support from others, limiting opportunities for others to demonstrate genuine friendship. Income inequality may play a role because

disadvantaged individuals report more negative experiences. When that control can't create a "perfect" life, people may blame themselves, fostering depression. While having wealth is protective against some negative consequences, like homelessness, it does not add to one's subjective feeling of happiness after a certain point.

4. Some personality characteristics, like extroversion and neuroticism, are strongly correlated with subjective well-being measures.

5. Social relationships appear to be essential to well-being. Giving and receiving social support are both important. People who are happy have better social relationships, but social relationships also play a causal role in creating happiness. Having friends, confidantes, and marriage partners are all linked to well-being. Some cultural groups with strong social connections report high levels of happiness even though income is relatively low. Ways of expressing and maintaining social support differ across cultures. Some primary differences exist between individualistic and collectivistic cultures, but differences also exist within collectivist cultures.

6. Work also is linked to life satisfaction, although prioritizing work over time has been associated with less happiness. People who feel generative report more well-being. Making progress towards goals and having opportunities to exercise skills is associated with well-being, particularly when balanced with needs for relatedness.

7. People may have universal psychological needs that must be met to feel satisfied with life. Among those that have been suggested are needs for autonomy, competence, and relatedness. When such needs are met, people are thought to experience psychological well-being (also called eudaemonic well-being), which is distinguished from subjective well-being (also called hedonic well-being). Although the two kinds of well-being are closely correlated, eudaemonic or psychological well-being specifically involves feeling a sense of purpose, growth, and mastery.

8. Religion/spirituality is an important source of happiness for a majority of people in the world. Many theorists propose that having a sense that one's life has meaning (situational meaning) that is linked to the meaning or purpose of the universe and of humankind (universal meaning) is an important ingredient in well-being. Levels of religiosity vary in terms of a country's economic status and level of strife. Changes in understanding of religion/spirituality follows a developmental course from literal to universal beliefs. Religiosity has been associated with improved health outcomes for practitioners, although religious/spiritual struggles are also relatively common.

Stress, Coping, and Well-Being in Midlife

9. Many stressors affect people at midlife including awareness of limited time left to live, accumulated losses related to aging, and increased responsibilities and obligations in the family and at work that can cause role strain. What determines resilience in this stage of life? Among the protective factors identified in one large-scale study of adults were childhood factors (e.g., educated parents), social attachments (e.g., confidantes and spouses), stable employment, and positive social comparisons with parents and siblings.

10. Two kinds of stressors are life events, which are discrete events, and daily hassles, which are more chronic. The cumulative effect of chronic stressors on the body is called allostatic load. People can experience gradually increasing sensitivity to stressful triggers, called kindling-behavioral sensitization.

11. Classic diathesis-stress models suggest that some individuals have specific vulnerabilities (diatheses) to a disorder that emerge under the right stress conditions. Research now shows how multiple, intermittent doses of a stressor can alter genes, leaving chemical memories of the exposure. Chronic exposure is more likely to produce tolerance or lower sensitivity. Intermittent exposure results in sensitization, which is a gradual increase in sensitivity to stressful triggers, resulting in progressive illness severity or illness incidence, even in the absence of a trigger.

12. Some people experience post-traumatic growth, positive psychological change after struggling with difficult circumstances. Personality traits like extroversion and openness are linked to this kind of change.

13. In response to stress, the body mobilizes energy to enhance functions that would support fight or flight, such as motor and sensory abilities. In response to disease, the immune system also mobilizes energy to fight pathogens. The two systems direct energy to different ends; when under stress, the body inhibits functions that support the immune system, causing immunosuppression.

14. The field of psychoneuroimmunology, the study of interactions among the central nervous system, the immune system, and behavior, indicates that the brain influences the immune system, and the immune system also influences the brain, playing a role, for example, in depression.

15. Management of stress, or coping, has often been conceptualized as constituting binary approaches, such as problem-focused versus emotion-focused coping. But instead of mutually exclusive categories of coping behavior, there may be many ways of coping that work differently depending on the situation. At midlife, stress may be largely a function of loss. To deal with loss, people act in ways to conserve or rebuild their resources.

16. Cultural groups appear to cope in different ways, using strategies that reflect core values such as individualism or collectivism.

17. Among the ways of conserving or rebuilding resources is to cultivate a sense of self-efficacy, mastery, and control. Cultivation of positive affectivity, and reduction of

negative affectivity, is also beneficial. The left prefrontal cortex is activated during the experience of positive emotions, and the right prefrontal cortex is activated during periods of negative emotion. More negative affectivity is associated with greater reactivity to stress. Immune responses are less compromised during stress when positive emotions are increased.

18. The brain is the gatekeeper to stress, so cultivating healthy mental habits can serve as one antidote to health-compromising reactivity. A rapidly growing body of research in the new field of mindfulness neuroscience suggests many benefits to mind-body systems via effects on executive functions, emotion management, and self-awareness. The practice of mindfulness meditation and positive emotions has been shown to promote good health.

Case Study

Luis is a 52-year-old Cuban-American male who has spent the last 24 years in the human resource field. He is currently a supervisor in the billing department of a midsized hospital in the southeastern part of the United States. He worked hard to obtain a master's degree while on the job at the hospital and always had high aspirations for himself professionally. Luis has three children from his first marriage, which ended in divorce. His first wife Anna, who is 50, works as a preschool teacher in a school nearby. Their children's ages are 16, 20, and 22. Both older children started to attend college but may have to drop out temporarily due to financial difficulties. Luis feels that it is his responsibility to support his children's education, and he has been paying as much of their tuition as he can afford. Luis and his second wife live in a modest home in a community close to Luis's job and his church, where he is an active member. Luis's second wife, Sandy, has two boys aged 12 and 14. The younger boy has a serious learning disability and needs extra tutoring and a great deal of parent support to keep up academically. Sandy works part time as a receptionist in a medical practice, allowing her the flexibility to be home when her children return from school. Luis and Sandy support each other and put their family first. Sandy's widowed mother lives nearby and helps with the children on a regular basis.

Recently, Luis has felt that his job is becoming more complicated and demanding. He has noted a dramatic increase in the amount of paperwork required and a distinct decrease in the time allotted to meet deadlines. His supervisory responsibilities have expanded to include workers from another unit, a change that has significantly increased his workload. His long-time assistant, who had taken over the management of many daily office tasks, was recently reassigned. Luis's lower back pain, related to a traffic accident that happened when he was younger, has taken a significant turn for the worse. He is feeling more "on edge" during the day and has resumed taking the painkillers his doctor prescribed. He worries about what would happen if he lost his job, especially with so many people depending upon him. Luis has been instrumental in introducing wellness programs for the hospital employees, and he's even extended some programs to members of his church. However, he feels that these programs are not for him. His employees might not think he's capable of being their supervisor if he admits to needing self-help. And, he's always relied on his faith to get him through hard times.

Discussion Questions

1. Consider Luis's situation: Using a scale from 1 (very low) to 10 (very high), assess his life satisfaction, level of happiness, and overall level of well-being. Identify the risks and protective factors that are present in Luis's life story. What risks and protections are related to his midlife stage, gender, and culture?

2. What role does religion appear to play in Luis's life? Assess the benefits and potential problems associated with this part of his story.

3. Assess Luis's level of stress. Is it acute? Chronic? What is his way of coping? To what degree can he manage his stress more effectively, and how might you help him do this?

Practice Using What You Have Learned

MyLab Education Application Exercise 14.1. Measures of Well-Being

MyLab Education Application Exercise 14.2. Case Study: Wellness and Stress

MyLab Education Application Exercise 14.3. Supporting Well-Being in Midlife

Journal Questions

1. What is your stereotypic view of midlife? Does it or does it not conform to what you have read in this chapter? Explain how your thinking about midlife might have changed.

2. What is your view of a well-lived life? Consider each of the aspects in this chapter (money, social relationships, values, meaning, religion/spirituality, and work) and describe their importance to you. What are your priorities?

3. What does spirituality mean to you? What does "faith" mean to you? Are they the same? How might you help clients suffering from religious/spiritual struggles?

4. Identify which situational stressors make you most reactive. What are your automatic responses (behaviors, emotions, thoughts) to a chronic stressor in your life? How might the mind/body approaches outlined in this chapter help you with your reactivity? How might they help you in your social relationships?

Key Concepts

subjective well-being (SWB) (p. 555)
day reconstruction method (DRM) (p. 556)
social capital (p. 559)
maximizers (p. 560)
satisficers (p. 560)
harmony collectivism (p. 562)
convivial collectivism (p. 562)
hedonic well-being (p. 563)
eudaemonic well-being (p. 563)
self-determination theory (p. 564)
autonomy (p. 564)

competence (p. 564)
relatedness (p. 564)
religious/spiritual struggles (p. 567)
spiritual transcendence (p. 567)
role strain (p. 572)
life events (p. 572)
daily hassles (p. 572)
diathesis-stress (p. 573)
kindling-behavioral sensitization (p. 573)
sensitization (p. 573)

post-traumatic growth (p. 573)
immunosuppression (p. 576)
endorphins (p. 577)
psychoneuroimmunology (p. 577)
negative affectivity (p. 578)
behavioral-inhibition system (p. 579)
positive affectivity (p. 579)
behavioral facilitation system (p. 579)
meditation (p. 580)
mindfulness (p. 580)
mindfulness neuroscience (p. 580)

Chapter 15
Gains and Losses in Late Adulthood

 ## Learning Objectives

After reading this chapter, you should be able to:

15.1 Describe typical physical, cognitive, and socioemotional changes and challenges in late life and identify coping strategies that promote healthy adaptation.

15.2 Explain the process of death and issues associated with dying, including the dynamics of the grief process and grief coping mechanisms, and develop supportive, personalized interventions for coping with bereavement.

At age 81, Helen still maintains her job in a bookstore. As one of the oldest siblings in a large working-class family, she learned early to value hard work and has always been active and productive. Her job provides her with opportunities to maintain her skills as well as the chance to learn new ones, such as the new computerized system her company uses to inventory material. Helen is fortunate in that her health is good, aside from some problems with arthritis that slow down her movement. She recognizes that she must regulate her activity now more than before, reducing extraneous activities so she can be well rested and prepared for work, thus optimizing her performance there. She is an avid fan of crossword puzzles; they are part of her recipe for staying mentally active. When she noticed herself becoming more forgetful, she compensated by writing notes to herself and establishing and following set routines. She travels and volunteers less these days, compared to what she did years ago when her husband was alive. Now she chooses to spend more time with her two children and their young families, and she makes sure to take walks several times a week to keep herself physically active. She knows what she can do, and she focuses on the activities that give her a sense of satisfaction.

Helen's adaptation is a good example of how a person can cope successfully with the challenges of aging. As people move into old age, in their 60s and 70s, or into old-old age, in their 80s and 90s, both gains and losses continue. However, losses may considerably outweigh gains. "Even in young people's lives, not everything goes well. Old age is a genuinely difficult situation with lots of sadness and frustration. Many things do not go well" (Pipher, 1999, p. 26). How can the elderly effectively manage the ever-increasing losses they experience? For example, can their developmental trajectory be a positive one when they experience multiple health problems or find themselves in chronic pain? An important focus of this chapter will be to identify the means by which older adults manage their lives and the extent to which they can grow, maintain themselves, and regulate their losses.

Clearly, different people manage their late-life losses with varying degrees of success. But you may be surprised to learn that for a majority of us, successful development is what we can expect for much of our old age. In what follows, we will first

FIGURE 15.1 The growing aging population across the world.
The numbers of aged are predicted to rise sharply across the world in coming years.

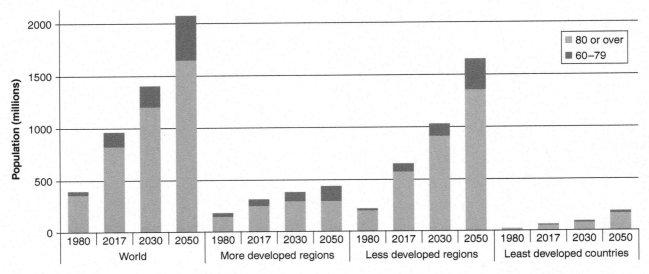

SOURCE: United Nations World Population Aging 2017, United Nations Department of Public Information' retrieved from www.un.org/en/development/desa/population/publications/pdf/ageing/WPA2017_Report.pdf.

review the nature of the losses and challenges that typically confront people in old age. Then we will look at the ways in which older adults cope with these challenges, paying special attention to the processes that seem most important for the life-long experience of psychological well-being. The fact that the world's aging population is rapidly increasing adds a level of urgency to these issues if we are to support healthy development at all points in the life span (see Figure 15.1).

Physical, Cognitive, and Socioemotional Change in Late Life

15.1 Describe typical physical, cognitive, and socioemotional changes and challenges in late life and identify coping strategies that promote healthy adaptation.

Challenge and Loss in Late Adulthood

PHYSICAL CHANGE

A gradual decline from peak functioning is characteristic of most physiological systems beginning as early as age 30. By late adulthood, the losses are usually noticeable and have required some adjustment in expectations or lifestyle. A life-long runner who still entered marathons at age 62 remarked, "At 30, my goal was to win. At 50, I celebrated every race that I finished. Today, I'm delighted to be at the starting line."

Maintaining good physical and mental health becomes more challenging with age, as the immune system grows progressively less effective in staving off cancer and infections, and as the cardiovascular, respiratory, and organ systems decline in their functioning. Rates of chronic illness increase dramatically with age, as does the need for more vigilant health maintenance. Age shifts in the leading causes of death illustrate these changing health concerns. In the United States, accidents are the leading cause of death in adults up to age 45. But at 45, heart disease and cancer take over as the leading causes of death, followed by cerebrovascular diseases and chronic respiratory illness (U.S. National Center for Health Statistics, Health, United States, 2017).

People of any age can suffer from acute or chronic illnesses, such as cancer, heart problems, or diabetes. But the risk of these illnesses climbs dramatically and steadily in our later years.

Among the continuing declines of old age, two are common and often especially debilitating. First are increasing sensory deficits (see Chapter 13). Changes in the visual system can be particularly important for one daily activity: driving. A number of aging changes make driving more difficult, including loss of visual acuity, loss of sensitivity to movement in the periphery, increased recovery time after exposure to glare, and reduced night vision. These changes occur gradually starting in middle adulthood but do not contribute significantly to accident rates until people reach their mid-70s (U.S. Bureau of the Census, 2012; Whitbourne, 2002).

A second important decline in older adults is the onset of arthritis, with its attendant pain, stiffness, and swelling of joints and surrounding tissues. After 65, about half of women and about 40% of men experience the most common form, osteoarthritis, which involves the thinning, fraying, and cracking of cartilage at the ends of bones. Ordinarily, this cartilage helps protect our joints from the friction of bone-to-bone contact. As cartilage degenerates and other joint changes occur, such as the growth of bony spurs and modifications in connective tissues, joints may stiffen and swell. This leads to pain and reduced movement. Being overweight or overusing a particular joint (for example, the knees in sports like running and tennis) can contribute to susceptibility, but ordinary degeneration with age is part of the problem. Osteoarthritis can range from being a painful nuisance to being a source of major disability. It can affect the performance of simple tasks, such as opening a jar or walking, as well as more complex skills, such as playing the piano or swinging a golf club (Hunter, McDougall, & Keefe, 2008).

How older individuals respond to daily physical symptoms has a substantial impact on their overall health over time. Being proactive in seeking help when health problems begin and making a strong commitment to treatment, such as sticking to medical treatment plans or exercise regimens, is important. In a longitudinal study of people above age 60, Wrosch and Schultz (2008) found that the use of such health management control strategies was directly related to health maintenance versus decline. We have repeatedly examined the role of stress in inflammatory and disease-related processes throughout the life span. In old age, stress-related allostatic load contributes to disease burden and lowered quality of life (Prasad, Sung, & Aggarwal, 2012). Of particular significance are studies that implicate stress in telomere shortening. Telomeres are the protective ends of chromosomes that are shortened by physiological and psychological stress as well as age. When stress is chronic, accelerated cell aging has been observed in both children and adults. Shortness of telomeres is associated with earlier mortality (Lin, Epel, & Blackburn, 2011), but some shortening may be reversed with effective stress management strategies such as mindfulness meditation (Deng, Cheung, Tsao, Wang, & Tiwari, 2016). Not all stress is bad, however. Exercise is a beneficial form of physical stress that provides abundant benefits for all age groups. Physical activity may involve sports and regular exercise, but also includes things like walking a pet or gardening. Remaining as active as possible in later life, both through structured exercise and physical activities, helps reduce stress and promotes health. Other mild forms of physiological stress, such as the stress of caloric restriction and exposure to cognitive stimulation, also appear to reduce deterioration in aging individuals (Mattson, Chan, & Duan, 2002).

BRAIN AND COGNITIVE CHANGE

Cognition depends on a healthy and well-functioning brain. This means, among other things, that synaptic connections operate smoothly and the integrity of white matter is preserved. You have seen that healthy brain development proceeds in an organized fashion, with the frontal lobes being the last to mature. As people age, those portions of the brain that matured last tend to be most vulnerable. Vascular problems and atrophy affect the frontal lobes first in late life, although this phenomenon does not account for all the cognitive changes of aging (Mather, 2016). Thus, executive functions, largely controlled by the frontal lobe, are areas that generally show the earliest age-related declines. Continuous decrements on many neurological measures related to cognition like brain volume, cortical thickness, neurotransmitter efficiency, and so forth extend from the decade of the twenties onward (Salthouse, 2009). In this section we'll take a look at these changes and provide a brief review of related material from Chapter 13.

You probably recall that researchers make a distinction between fluid and crystallized intelligence as a way of describing two types of intellectual resources. In previous chapters we called these categories mechanics (fluid) and pragmatics (crystallized). Another way to think about this distinction is to consider fluid intelligence as the processing efficiency of the cognitive system and crystallized intelligence as the product of that processing (Salthouse, 2006). For many years, cross-sectional studies of cognitive aging in adults have reported declines in both fluid and crystallized intelligence (Jones & Conrad, 1933; see Figure 15.2a).

Longitudinal studies paint a different picture. They suggest that crystallized intelligence, as represented by measures of verbal ability and factual knowledge, does not decline until the mid-70s, and the declines are modest thereafter (Schaie, 1996). Many old individuals show no declines in some areas, and some who have maintained good health actually continue to improve on crystallized intelligence measures. For example, in one longitudinal study of 70- to 100-year-olds, vocabulary knowledge increased until age 90 and showed only slow declines thereafter (Singer, Verhaeghen, Ghisletta, Lindenberger, & Baltes, 2003). In contrast, gradual decrements in fluid intelligence, marked by slower processing speed and reduced inhibitory functions, do occur with age. Such declines may limit the efficiency of working memory operations, such as learning and problem solving, but these effects may be balanced by the maintenance or advancement of crystallized intelligence or pragmatics (see Figure 15.2b).

Interestingly, even for people who perform well on cognitive tasks into old age, there appear to be changes in the areas of the brain that are being activated. In brain imaging studies, older adults frequently show less activity of some brain sites and more activity of other sites, especially the prefrontal lobes, relative to younger adults. Also, older adults are more likely to involve both sides of the brain in performing a task whereas younger adults may only use one side. There could be many reasons for these differences in brain utilization, but some evidence indicates that compensation for loss is often involved, helping the older individual to maintain levels of performance. This is a little like using a back-up reserve and can be successful at moderate levels of task difficulty. When the demands exceed capacity, a resource ceiling is reached, which might explain age-related cognitive declines (Reuter-Lorenz & Park, 2014; Sala-Llonch, Bartres-Faz, & Junque, 2015).

Despite the fact that longitudinal results have been the dominant paradigm for interpreting age changes in cognition, some researchers have questioned the accuracy of these results. Salthouse (2009) showed that reanalyzing the longitudinal data while extracting the effects of prior testing or "practice effects" changes the picture. After statistically removing the practice effects, results from longitudinal findings more closely mirror the declines observed in cross-sectional analyses. These findings, however, should not diminish the importance of longitudinal work. They do suggest, however, the need to more clearly identify true maturational change, devoid of practice effects, and to factor in the developmental stage at which the learning occurs relative to when it is lost. Other recent work has indicated that different cognitive abilities may peak at different ages, and that the distinction may be more complex than the simple distinction between fluid and crystallized intelligence (Hartshorne & Germine, 2015).

Craik and Bialystok (2006) offer a framework (see Figure 15.2c) for understanding age changes in cognition that integrates cross-sectional and longitudinal results. These authors use a different way of characterizing cognitive functions: representations and control. Representations are the kinds of schemas or systems of schemas one develops over time to interact with the world. In previous chapters we described Piaget's famous stage theory, a narrative of how representations develop from reflexes to abstract thought across the years of childhood and adolescence. Representational systems can involve declarative (language or world history) or procedural (playing chess or driving a car) knowledge. Representations are the foundation of crystallized intelligence. Control involves the ways one works with knowledge and includes attention,

FIGURE 15.2 Three models of cognitive change throughout the life span.
Part a reflects an inverted u-shaped curve of cognitive development. Performance increases in childhood, is maintained in adulthood, and decreases thereafter. Part b illustrates differing trajectories for fluid and crystallized intelligence. Part c incorporates executive processes informed by neuroscientific findings that show more subtle patterns of maintenance and decline.

(a)

(b)

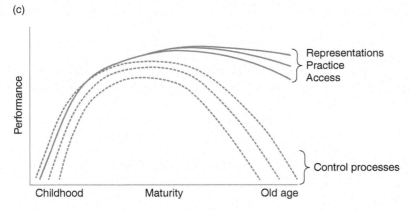

(c)

SOURCE: Republished with permission of Elsevier Ltd. from *Cognition through the lifespan: Mechanisms of change. Trends in Cognitive Sciences*, Based on Craik, F. J. M. & Bialystok, E. (2006). 10, 131–138; permission conveyed through Copyright Clearance Center, Inc.

learning efficiency, and flexibility of working memory, inhibitory control, and processing speed. Both representations and control features interact. Consider how your attention is drawn to certain kinds of information, which, in turn, results in the construction of new schemas or representations of the world. As your understanding grows in a particular domain, so does your expertise.

At older ages, the process of forming new representations is more challenging despite the retention of previously learned representational systems. It appears that using these systems contributes to their maintenance, supporting the proverbial "use it or lose it" advice. But even previously learned representations depend upon control functions in order to be accessed and used. For example, the name of that elementary school classmate you're trying to recall does you no good buried in your memory unless you can access it. Peak levels of cognitive control functions occur in young adulthood, and gradually decrease thereafter.

Craik and Bialystok posit that research on cognition in childhood and late life are separated by differences in language and emphases. "In development, the primary emphasis is on the changes in representations as the child constructs a coherent interpretive basis for understanding the world; in cognitive aging, the primary emphasis is on decline in control processes as they produce impairments of access to existing knowledge, integration of new and existing information, and translation of knowledge into timely and adaptive action" (Craik & Bialystok, 2006, p. 136). But a more holistic approach to cognition and, in particular, to executive functions across the life span can help us map existing knowledge onto new findings in neuroscience. This approach also offers a potential paradigm for studying remediation efforts to increase cognitive reserve (Reuter-Lorenz & Mikels, 2006).

Dementia.   Dementia is a syndrome that affects multiple functional domains due to chronic and progressive disease processes in the brain. Cognitive and emotional skills like memory, judgment, language, self-regulation, and motivation diminish progressively. Alzheimer's disease (AD) is the most common type of dementia, accounting for 60% of all cases. Frontotemporal dementia (deterioration primarily in frontal and temporal lobes), vascular dementia (related to problems with blood flow to the brain), and dementia with Lewy bodies (or protein build-up) also account for many cases. Among these four main types of dementia, there is a great deal of overlap, and combined types are frequent (World Alzheimer Report, 2009). An estimated 46.8 million people around the world were living with dementia in 2015, and rates are predicted to double every 20 years (World Alzheimer Report, 2015). In the United States, it is estimated that there will be over 13 million Americans diagnosed with AD by 2050 (Smith, 2016).

Alzheimer's disease is diagnosed primarily by its clinical characteristics and by excluding other possible causes of dementia. Diagnostic procedures are being improved continually, and skilled clinicians can diagnose quite accurately following a comprehensive evaluation. At this point, however, only autopsy can definitively conclude the presence of AD. Typically dementia progresses in stages. There is a prodromal period, lasting for a year or two, when symptoms like memory loss fall short of a clinical threshold but do present more impairment than normal for that age. In its early stages, AD looks like absentmindedness: forgetting where you recently put something or forgetting an event that happened in the last few days or even the last few hours. Difficulties with decision making, word finding, regulating moods, or completing complex tasks might be present. Some pharmaceutical treatments are currently being tested for symptom reduction at this stage, but, thus far, daily exercise and cognitive stimulation have shown the greatest benefit (Cheng et al., 2012; Morley, 2011).

More general confusion may follow in the middle stage (second to fourth or fifth year). Individuals might have difficulty remembering even very recent events, wander away from home and get lost, or lose the ability to prepare meals or perform other self-care tasks. People at this stage may be quite distressed by their memory loss, perhaps even paranoid if they frequently cannot remember what they have done or where they have put things. They may also conclude that others are responsible for these lapses. A relative of one of the authors, for example, would insist that people had entered her apartment and had turned on her TV when she wasn't looking. Others may become hostile in their frustration and confusion. One elderly man, believing that an intruder had entered his home, assaulted his own son each time the latter visited. In later stages, memory and language problems worsen, disorientation is extreme, and physical coordination deteriorates. Eventually, in the last stage (fifth year and after), Alzheimer's patients are often mute and bedridden, needing full-time care and supervision. The disease eventually causes death (Alzheimer's Association, 2012).

MyLab Education
Video Example 15.1
Alvin, diagnosed with Alzheimer's a year ago, and Susan, his partner and primary caretaker, describe the challenges of living with dementia.

This is not the only course of the disease. Early-onset AD strikes 40- to 50-year-olds, ends in death after about five years, and clearly has a genetic contribution. In all forms of AD, extensive brain changes include the formation of plaques, clumps of insoluble protein that are damaging to neurons, and tangles, twisted filaments of another protein, which may interfere with communication between neurons and even cause cell death (Braak & Braak, 1991). Amyloid precursor protein (APP) and several enzymes that operate on it appear to play an initial role in the development of plaque formation (Ballard, Gauthier, Corbett, Brayne, Aarsland, & Jones, 2011). Related inflammatory processes may also act as important precursors of dementia. These inflammatory processes can start 10 to 20 years before actual symptoms appear (Friedrich, 2013). Early stage studies have also found noticeable brain changes in AD, including thinning in several areas of the brain (Pegueroles et al., 2017). The inability to remember things after an intervening distraction or period of time (either several minutes or longer), called delayed recall, is considered one of the best preclinical signs of approaching AD (Salmon & Bondi, 2009).

Many of us have seen the ravages of dementia in a relative or friend, and we worry that extreme memory loss and disorientation are inevitable consequences of aging. But they are not. Normal aging does not lead to dementia, although the frequency of illnesses and conditions that cause dementia does increase with age. Among these are cardiovascular problems that limit the oxygen supply to the brain for some period of time. These include cerebrovascular accidents, or strokes, in which an artery serving the brain is either clogged or bursts. A single stroke can lead to acute onset of dementia. More typically, many minor strokes (multi-infarct dementia) can gradually do sufficient damage to cause dementia. Hypertension (high blood pressure) or hypertension combined with diabetes, increase the risk of multi-infarct dementia (Venkat, Chopp, & Chen, 2015).

Although AD and other forms of dementia do not affect the majority of older adults, there is some suspicion that the formation of plaques and tangles may occur to some extent as a normal aging process in all of us. Some environments seem to enhance or reduce AD rates. For example, life-long education and intellectual stimulation seem to decrease the risk (Snowdon, 1997; Wilson et al., 2010). Rates of AD and other dementias are substantially higher in low-income compared to high- and middle-income countries (World Alzheimer Report, 2015).

While there are no known treatments for diagnosed AD, advances in research since 2010 have shed light on promising strategies for prevention and intervention prior to diagnosis. Specifically, three different classes of interventions have been identified: cognitive training, general health interventions like blood pressure management in individuals with hypertension, and increased physical activity (National Academies of Sciences, Engineering, and Medicine, 2017; Smith, 2016). The strongest evidence exists for cognitive training and stimulation to delay or slow the progression of age-related cognitive decline. This cognitive training and stimulation can involve formal programs as well as more informal activities or hobbies, like reading, knitting, and doing crossword puzzles. Increased physical activity and exercise may delay cognitive aging in general, and it may also prevent or delay worsening of symptoms in individuals with mild cognitive impairment, a precursor of dementia (Smith, 2016). Other strategies for individuals showing preclinical dementia include cognitive training interventions to encourage active cognition and practice, and also evidence-based treatments like cognitive behavioral therapy for individuals with comorbid depression (Orgeta, Qazi, Spector, & Orrell, 2015).

Perhaps not surprisingly, all the promising avenues for preventing or delaying the development of dementia have more general benefits for the health and well-being of older adults. Mounting evidence supports the importance of regular physical activity for older adults. In a recent longitudinal study of leisure-time physical activities in a sample of over 1,000 older adults, researchers found that engaging in regular moderate to high intensity physical activity predicted slower cognitive declines in areas of processing speed and episodic memory, even when controlling for initial differences in health conditions like high blood pressure and health-related behaviors like smoking (Willey et al., 2016). Other recent work supports the findings that physical activity may

FIGURE 15.3 The relationship between survival scores on an IQ test of verbal meaning in a longitudinal study.

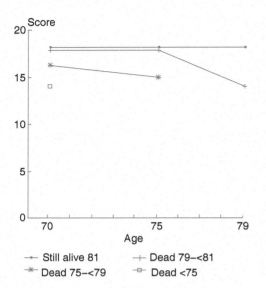

SOURCE: Based on Berg, S. (1996). Aging, behavior, and terminal decline. In James E. Birrens, et al. (Eds.), *Handbook of the psychology of aging* (4th ed.). Burlington, MA: Elsevier Science (USA).

especially slow declines in cognitive abilities associated with the prefrontal cortex and hippocampus (Prakash, Voss, Erickson, & Kramer, 2015) and that higher levels of aerobic physical activity predict greater cognitive benefits, in a dose-response relationship (Vidoni et al., 2015).

Cognitive aging also may be reduced or delayed among older adults with specific cognitive training. A meta-analysis of 49 studies examining approaches to cognitive training, such as computerized practice in domain-specific skills of working memory, demonstrated overall positive effects for improved performance on the trained tasks as well as near-transfer (i.e., very similar) tasks (Karbach & Verhaeghen, 2014). Other studies have indicated that, with practice, older adults can improve their performance on visual and perceptual learning tasks (DeLoss, Watanabe, & Andersen, 2015). It is important to note, however, that these specific training paradigms do not appear to improve more general cognition. Interventions that target multiple aspects of well-being (such as diet and exercise, cognitive training, and engagement in hobbies and social relationships) are most likely to reduce risk for dementia and show measurable benefits for individual older adults (Smith, 2016).

Terminal Drop and Terminal Decline. Terminal drop and terminal decline describe the phenomena of deteriorating cognitive ability as adults approach the end of their lives. In the months and years prior to death, individuals may show a substantial decline in intellectual functioning as indicated by scores on intelligence tests (Berg, 1987; Cohen-Mansfield, Skornick-Bouchbinder, & Brill, 2017). Figure 15.3 illustrates this finding from one set of longitudinal data. Once used synonymously, researchers are now distinguishing between the terms *drop* and *decline*. The former change is more precipitous while the latter suggests a gradual process. Researchers using a large-scale Canadian sample (MacDonald, Hultsch, & Dixon, 2011) found little support for the terminal drop trajectory for aggregated cognitive measures used in this study. Instead, the evidence showed greater support for the model of terminal decline. Abrupt declines in cognition may be observed in certain circumstances, and more research is needed to determine why they occur, given the clinical importance of such meaningful changes. Either way, patterns of cognitive deterioration appear to reflect the individual's declining health status, although there also appear to be some individual differences in deterioration processes linked to genetic susceptibility (Wilson et al., 2007). Interestingly, people often seem to be able to detect in themselves whatever changes in health status are predictive of death. A number of studies have found that when older adults self-rate their health as "poor," they are much more likely to die within the next few years than when they rate their health as "excellent" (DeSalvo, Bloser, Reynolds, He, & Muntner, 2006). This appears to be true when controlling for chronic health conditions for both men and women, though it is less true for African American compared to White older adults (Assari, Lankarani, & Burgard, 2016). Apparently, people often realize when they are going into decline. In Box 15.1, we examine the effect on caregivers when the elderly reach the end stage of their lives.

Autobiographical Memory. One cognitive function that has particular significance for one's sense of self as well as for social interactions throughout the life span is called **autobiographical memory**. This is the remembered self, "representations of who we have been at various points in the past" (Fitzgerald, 1999, p. 143). It draws from several long-term memory systems (see Chapter 6 for an introduction to these systems). When we recall specific experiences in our lives, we are calling on episodic memory; when we remember that we know some fact, we are using our semantic memory; and when we remember how to do something, we depend on our procedural memory. Autobiographical memory has often been treated as synonymous with episodic memory, which is a very important part of it, but our self-recollections are not episodic alone.

Autobiographical memory is important in many ways. It provides us with a "sense of identity in narrative form" (Fitzgerald, 1999, p. 143). It also serves as a source of information about social interactions that have worked or not worked for us in the

Box 15.1: The Burden of Care

In the United States, most older adults are in good enough health to take full responsibility for their own lives and well-being. But with advancing age, the chance of chronic illness or disability increases. For many, there comes a time when full self-care is impossible. Family members provide about 75% of all long-term care for older adults (Qualls, 2016). Between the ages of 85 and 89, over half of older adults receive some assistance from a family member due to health problems or physical limitations (Freedman & Spillman, 2014). For these family caregivers, there may be rewards, but there often are costs as well—psychological, physical, occupational, social, and financial—that together are described as the **care burden**. This burden can bring with it serious consequences for caregivers and sometimes, for patients as well. For caregivers of patients with dementia, for example, quality of life often declines, and their physical and mental health is jeopardized. Care burden also sometimes contributes to the abuse or neglect of the patient, or to generally poor standards of care (Papastavrou, Kalokerinou, Papacostas, Tsangari, & Sourtzi, 2007; Roberto, 2016; Rook, 2015).

Benefits and Burden

A caregiver may reap emotional benefits from her role if she feels confident in her ability to provide care (van der Lee et al., 2014), or if her sense of self-worth is tied in part to "an ethic of responsibility and care" (Martin, 2000, p. 988). In Asian cultures, filial piety (*xaio*) provides an explicit cultural norm that guides caregiving behavior. Children are taught to care for aging parents as a form of gratitude and respect (Wang, 2004). But even in cultures without such explicit norms, children usually care for their parents in old age (Montgomery, Borgatta, & Borgatta, 2000). Good quality caregiving can promote feelings of competency and self-esteem. For some caregivers, there may be financial benefits associated with caregiving as well, as when the primary caregiver anticipates having some priority in the patient's will. In some circumstances, caregiving can be a satisfying aspect of a reciprocal relationship in which the patient continues to serve as a source of emotional and social support to the caregiver. Interestingly, the burden of care is not necessarily reduced by the positive elements of caregiving. For example, caregivers who report strong feelings of general mastery (vis-à-vis their caregiving) have often been found to experience more care burden than other caregivers, perhaps because those who are more effective tend to work harder (Greenberger & Litwin, 2003; Halm, Treat-Jacobson, Lindquist, & Savick, 2006). Relatedly, caregiving at the final stages of the patient's life can be more urgent and intensive, yet at the same time, more rewarding (Gibbons, Ross, & Bevans, 2014).

There are many sources of care burden, such as fatigue, uncertainty about the future, uncertainty about care procedures, increasing demands as needs change, and discomfort with the tasks required. The role strain that caregivers experience, trying to balance the needs of the patient with other responsibilities such as work, parenting, and self-care, is an important part of the problem. The time and energy consumed by both the physical needs of patients and their psychological and behavioral difficulties contribute heavily. How much burden caregivers experience is largely predicted by the degree of physical and/or psychological disability of the patient. Other important predictors of greater burden include living with the patient, more hours spent caregiving, financial stress, and lack of choice about assuming the caregiving role (Adelman, Tmanova, Delgado, Dion, & Lachs, 2014). For caregivers, the psychological and physical consequences of care burden can be profound. The risk of depression and suicide is substantial. Health decline and increased risk of death are common. Emotional turmoil, including feelings of anger, helplessness, guilt, and loss, are typical (National Academies of Science, Engineering, & Medicine, 2016). Furthermore, acting as a caregiver can damage the prior relationship between the family caregiver and older adult, particularly in cases of dementia if aspects of the patient's identity seems to change (Strohminger & Nichols, 2015). Primary caregivers often feel unfairly treated or misunderstood by other family members who are less involved in patient care. Their anger and resentment, and the chances of a long-term rift, are greater when more distant family members justify their lesser involvement by minimizing either the needs of the patient or the sacrifice of primary caregivers (Ingersoll-Dayton, Neal, Ha, & Hammer, 2003).

To appreciate the nature of care burden, consider the following excerpts from the diary of one woman who cared for her husband at home. Her spouse suffered from multi-infarct disease, which resulted from a series of minor strokes. Damage to the brain is progressive, much like Alzheimer's disease. The changes in her husband's interpersonal behavior, linked to his growing confusion and memory loss, clearly constitute the heaviest part of this caregiver's burden.

August 28th:

(Charlie said) . . . "We don't even have any water in the house." Oh no, I thought, not again, but he went on. "And since we don't have water in the house they're going to condemn it for sure."

"They're not going to condemn it," I said. "I told you that before."

"That's all you know about it. You're just dumb and stupid, that's all." He was ranting like a maniac. "I never saw anybody so ignorant." He kept going on and on, but . . . I managed to change the subject.

It's so hard to contend with something like this, to keep loving someone who calls you names and treats you like an enemy. I remember how nice it used to be to sit here in the evening and enjoy the TV together. And how Charlie used to laugh and joke around. I also remember how thoughtful he used to be. How warm, generous and loving, and how close we were. Now, he's so wrapped up in his own mixed up world and in his own thoughts, he hardly pays any attention to what's going on around him, or what I'm doing. He doesn't seem to have a grasp on reality, and yet, his family thinks he's just fine, that he's just a little forgetful.

(continued)

September 15th:

. . . It's 8:30 P.M. He's sitting on the sun porch and he's been crying for over an hour and I don't know what to do. I've tried everything I can think of to quiet him down, but he still just keeps right on crying. When I ask him why he's crying he says, "I don't know." It hurts to see him like this.

March 18th:

. . . I heard loud weird noises coming from the kitchen . . . I hurried into the dinette area just in time to see Charlie raise his arm and throw a handful of ice cubes into one of my cooking pans . . . Water and ice cubes were everywhere.

"What are you doing?" I yelled.

"I have to," he shouted. "We're running out of water."

"We aren't running out of water," I yelled back. "Now, put everything down and leave it alone."

"Get away!" he threatened and he took a swing at me . . .

. . . Every time I tried to stop him, he'd come at me with fury in his eyes, clenched fists, arms swinging, yelling that we were running out of water.

(Shiplett, 1996)

Primary Caregivers

Most primary caregivers are either adult children or the spouse of the patient. Among all racial and ethnic groups, women, especially daughters, are more likely to be primary caregivers. Aronson and Weiner (2007) claim that women today actually spend more total time caring for older parents than they do caring for children. When multiple family members contribute, there appear to be some differences in the tasks that female and male caregivers perform. Women are more likely to provide routine hands-on care, whereas men are more likely to provide help in specific situations. Men are more likely to use formal services than women, and they are less likely to feel a conflict with their employment responsibilities, perhaps because less is typically expected of men as caregivers. Many studies indicate that care burden tends to be greater for women than for men, although this gender difference can be moderated by ethnicity. Specifically, African American women report less care burden than White women, whereas African American men report more care burden than White men. Given that African American households are more likely to include extended family members than White households, it may be that African American women expect to care for frail, elderly relatives, whereas African American men may have less expectation of such responsibilities. African American families may also provide more support to women caregivers than White families.

The aforementioned virtue of filial piety may affect the nature and quality of caregiving among Asian families. A study of Caucasian-Canadian, Chinese-Canadian, and Hong-Kong Chinese caregivers explored the strength of traditional cultural attitudes and caregiving quality (Chappell & Funk, 2012). Contrary to expectations, filial piety did not predict behaviors related to care of basic daily needs because children cared for parents across all cultures examined. However, both Chinese groups were more likely to

provide greater emotional support to aging parents, possibly demonstrating one distinctive effect of cultural socialization. Further research into cultural differences seems especially important if it can help illuminate environmental factors that explain caregiving patterns and mitigate the burden of care (National Academies, 2016).

Helping Caregivers

In their guide for caregivers, Delehanty and Ginzler (2005) remind us of the lesson that airline safety instructions impart: "In the event the oxygen masks deploy due to loss of cabin pressure, put on your own mask first, then assist others." The point is, of course, that a caregiver whose mental or physical resources are depleted can actually endanger herself *and* those who are dependent on her.

Consider these quotes from Mace and Rabins (1999), one from a patient's daughter and another from a patient's husband, both primary caregivers:

My mother would scratch at herself in one spot until it bled. The doctor said we had to stop it. I tried everything until one day I guess I snapped: I grabbed her and shook her and I screamed at her. She just looked at me and began to cry. (p. 218)

Sometimes I couldn't stand it. My wife would get to me so, always on about something, and the same thing over and over. Then I would tie her into her chair and go for a walk. I felt terrible about it, but I couldn't stand it. (p. 217)

Most guidelines for caregivers emphasize the critical importance of "timeouts," regular daily or weekly respites from the constancy of caregiving tasks (Zarit, Bangerter, Liu, & Rovine, 2017). To make timeouts possible, caregivers need access to resources, such as adult day care programs, professional in-home aids, or regular substitutes among family and friends. Avoiding isolation and reserving time for socializing is critical. Many communities, especially through their medical facilities, offer either individual or group interventions to educate and support caregivers. These services teach caregivers what to expect, how to cope, and how to access resources, and they help caregivers to understand their own emotions and the behaviors of difficult patients. Meta-analyses of studies of treatment interventions for primary caregivers found significant benefits of both individual and group approaches (Adelman et al., 2014; Lopez-Hartmann, Wens, Verhoeven, & Remmen, 2012). Interestingly, although women caregivers reported more care burden than men before intervention, women tended to benefit more. Also, there were cultural moderators: Group interventions were more effective than individual interventions for non-White caregivers, but for White caregivers both forms were equally effective.

The impact of the caregiver's role, and the need for support, are poignantly expressed in the words of one husband caregiver as he tried to write a journal about his wife's illness: "I realized that I was telling the story of my own deterioration. I gave up my job to take care of her, then I had no time for my hobbies, and gradually we stopped seeing our friends" (Mace & Rabins, 1999, p. 214). Clearly, helpers can play a role in reducing the costs of care burden, both by advocating for community resources for caregivers and by providing a range of interventions to meet caregivers' needs.

past. When we draw on autobiographical memory to tell stories about ourselves to others, it helps us reveal and share ourselves, get closer to others, create impressions, and even teach lessons (Fitzgerald, 1999; Hyman & Faries, 1992).

One stereotype that people often have about older adults is that they remember more about their early lives than about what has happened to them recently. Studies of autobiographical memory indicate that this belief is only partially true. Elderly people actually do remember their more recent experiences better than earlier experiences, although the stories that they tell about themselves are often well-rehearsed experiences from the distant past.

There are two very salient characteristics of self-memories for adults of all ages. One is **recency**: The strength of a memory declines the more time has passed since the memory was formed. That is, we are more likely to remember something that has happened to us recently than something that happened in the more distant past. One way to study autobiographical memory is to say a word, like "dog," and ask a person to report a specific experience in his life that the word calls to mind. Regardless of the age of the respondent, half of all such cue-prompted memories will be from the most recent 12 months of his life. Eighty percent are from the most recent decade. "The remembered self is largely a now-self, not a distant-self," even for older people (Fitzgerald, 1999, p. 159).

This may sound a bit confusing, given that adults learn new information less efficiently with age. As we saw in Chapter 13, information in working memory is not as easily transferred to long-term memory at later ages. Nonetheless, older people do continue to learn, and recent memories are more readily retrieved than more distant memories.

However, a second salient feature of self-memories is a phenomenon referred to as **"the bump"** or the **"reminiscence bump."** Regardless of age, adults' cue-prompted memories of the self from the young adult period (from about ages 18 to 22) are slightly but reliably overproduced (see Berntsen & Rubin, 2002). That is, more memories are produced from this era than we would predict on the basis of recency (see Figure 15.4). If we explore autobiographical memory in a different way, by asking adults to tell us about their **flashbulb memories**, nearly all of what they tell us comes from the reminiscence bump era (e.g., Fitzgerald, 1988; Koppel & Rubin, 2016). Flashbulb memories in these studies are defined as recollections that are especially vivid and personally relevant. It appears that when people talk about memories that are intense and important to them, they draw very heavily on experiences from young adulthood, even in their old age. If we ask people to tell stories that they would include in a book about themselves, again, a disproportionate number of the narratives come from the bump era (Fitzgerald, 1992). Similar results come from studies in which people are asked to name the most memorable books they have read (Larsen, 2000), the songs they find

FIGURE 15.4 Proportion of reported flashbulb memories by age and time of event for older adults.

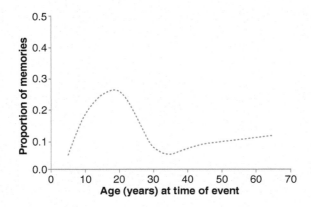

SOURCE: Based on Fitzgerald, J. M. (1999). Autobiographical memory and social cognition. Development of the remembered self-adulthood. In Thomas M. Hess (Ed.), *Social cognition and aging*. Elsevier Science. Burlington, MA: Elsevier Science (USA).

most desirable to listen to (Holbrook & Schindler, 1989; Krumhansl & Zupnick, 2013), or the films that help describe their era (Janssen, Chessa, & Murre, 2007; Schulster, 1996). That is, the elderly refer more often to items from their young adulthood than from any other time of their lives. Fitzgerald (1999) argues that the strength of the reminiscence bump phenomenon for people's most important memories and preferences reveals the significance of late adolescence and young adulthood as a period of intense self-development. This phenomenon might also be explained by the fact that these events tend to be positive in tone and to reflect a bias towards remembering pleasant things (Thomsen, Pillemer, & Ivcevic, 2011). It's also been proposed that these reminiscence events were encoded more strongly in memory in the first place, given their highly emotional charge (Dolcos, Labar, & Cabeza, 2005). In more recent work, however, researchers found that when cue words were provided, older adults tended to recall different memories (Koppel & Rubin, 2016). This suggests that the reminiscence bump for flashbulb memories may have more to do with how older adults retrieve memories rather than with how those memories originally were encoded.

However, the recency effect in cue-prompted memory research makes it very clear that people continue to add to developing their self-stories throughout their adulthood, and that healthy older people have their recent past available to them despite some declines in learning efficiency.

STEREOTYPES AND AGE DISCRIMINATION

Among the challenges that older adults face are stereotyped attitudes and responses from others based on age category rather than on actual unique characteristics. **Age stereotypes** are widely held beliefs about the characteristics of older people. These knowledge structures or schemas can lead to relatively uniform treatment of older people regardless of their own individual characteristics. They are thought to account for certain discriminatory or demeaning practices, such as mandatory retirement and patronizing talk (Hummert, 1999). Despite cultural differences in beliefs about respect for older adults and filial piety between individualistic and collectivist cultures, a recent meta-analysis including participants from 23 countries indicated that age stereotypes do not differ substantially, and that in fact collectivist attitudes may backfire as the aging population grows especially rapidly in countries like Japan (North & Fiske, 2015).

Research on the content of old-age schemas in Western cultures has identified seven common stereotypes. Four of these are negative, such as "severely impaired" or "shrew/curmudgeon," but three are more positive, such as "perfect grandparent" (Hummert, Garstka, Shaner, & Strahm, 1994). A description of each is provided in Table 15.1. A study involving participants from 26 countries asked individuals to assess "typical" adolescents, adults, and old people from their own country on Big 5

MyLab Education
Video Example 15.2
Research on the content of old-age schemas in Western cultures has identified seven common stereotypes, some positive and some negative. The retired teacher in this video most closely depicts which of the stereotypes?

TABLE 15.1 Traits Associated with Stereotypes of Older Adults

STEREOTYPE	TRAITS
Negative	
Severely impaired	Slow-thinking, incompetent, feeble, inarticulate, incoherent, senile
Despondent	Depressed, sad, hopeless, afraid, neglected, lonely
Shrew/curmudgeon	Complaining, ill-tempered, demanding, stubborn, bitter, prejudiced
Recluse	Quiet, timid, naïve
Positive	
Golden ager	Active, capable, sociable, independent, happy, interesting
Perfect grandparent	Loving, supportive, understanding, wise, generous, kind
John Wayne conservative	Patriotic, conservative, determined, proud, religious, nostalgic

SOURCE: Based on Hummert, M. L. (1999). A social cognitive perspective on age stereotypes. In Thomas M. Hess (Ed.), *Social cognition and aging* (p. .178). Burlington, MA: Elsevier Science (USA).

personality characteristics (Chan et al., 2012). Stereotypic views of older people tended to be very similar across all cultures included in this study. Old people were viewed as less active, extraverted, and impulsive compared to other age groups. They were also perceived as more agreeable and more inclined to follow a routine in their daily lives. Other researchers have considered age stereotypes in relation to two broad dimensions of competence and warmth, where studies consistently find that older adults are perceived to be lower in competence (less able and skillful), but higher in warmth (kind and trustworthy), compared to younger adults (Cuddy, Fiske, & Glick, 2008).

Facial features associated with aging play a significant role in activating these stereotypes. The older people appear, the more likely they are to be described in ways that fit a negative stereotype. In one study, participants were asked to match the photographs of people perceived to be in their 60s, 70s, or 80s with trait sets describing either positive or negative stereotypes (Hummert, Garstka, & Shaner, 1997). The older the appearance of the person in the picture, the more likely participants were to match the picture with a negative stereotype. Gender of the pictured person played a role as well. For example, pictures of unsmiling women were more likely to be matched with a negative stereotype than pictures of unsmiling men. Many studies find that people are more likely to perceive men as losing more general competence or agentic ability with age than women, yet they are more likely to judge women as needing more help as they age (Kite, Stockdale, Whitley, & Johnson, 2005). These appearance-based stereotypes can have concrete consequences; in a recent study, employers making simulated personnel decisions were more influenced by age-appearance of potential employees than by their actual chronological ages (Kaufmann, Krings, & Sczesny, 2016).

Also because of age stereotypes, the very same behavior in younger versus older individuals is perceived differently. For example, the seriousness and the causes of a memory failure, such as forgetting the name of a new acquaintance, tend to be perceived quite differently depending on whether the failure is ascribed to a 30-year-old or to a 70-year-old. When younger adults forget, others are more likely to assume that the cause is transient and external, such as "that's a hard thing to remember." When older people forget, others are more likely to assume the cause is something stable and internal, such as a poorly functioning memory (Hummert, 2011; Kite et al., 2005).

When age stereotypes are triggered, the quality of social interactions can be affected. For example, people, including clinicians, often use "patronizing talk" when speaking with older adults. This kind of conversation has many characteristics: simplified vocabulary and sentence structure, slower pace, careful articulation, an overly familiar or overbearing tone, and disapproving, controlling, or superficial content (Draper, 2005; Hummert, Shaner, Garstka, & Henry, 1998). Hummert (1999) has argued that such talk is probably grounded in stereotypic ideas about declining memory and hearing abilities in the aged.

It appears, then, that aging brings with it stereotypic reactions and expectations from others, which seem likely to interfere with satisfying social interactions. Researchers have found that when older individuals perceive themselves as the target of age discrimination, their sense of well-being is negatively affected (Schmitt, Branscombe, Postmes, & Garcia, 2014). Also, the experience of stereotype threat may actually impair performance. For example, O'Brien and Hummert (2006) gave people in late middle age (48 to 62 years old) a memory task, and either implied that they were in the "older" group by saying that their performance would be compared to younger adults, or implied that they were "younger" by saying they would be compared to older adults (over age 70). Participants performed significantly better when they saw themselves as the "younger" group than if they were characterized as the "older" group! Thus, even older people appear to have negative stereotypes about the elderly, having internalized these beliefs when they were younger. Harmful aging self-stereotypes, often operating below the level of awareness, can impact health and well-being (Nelson, 2016). When primed by negative stereotypes of aging, elderly participants showed reductions in cognitive performance, will-to-live, and cardiovascular functioning. Interestingly, more recent work has demonstrated that interventions can increase *positive* age stereotypes, leading to improvements in self-perceptions of aging and physical functioning among older adults (Levy, Pilver, Chung, & Slade, 2014).

Some research also indicates that the conversational styles of older people often include features that may cue stereotypes. For example, older people are sometimes prone to making "painful self-disclosures" to relative strangers about illnesses, loss of a loved one, and other personal problems (Bonnesen & Hummert, 2002). For the elderly, self-disclosures may serve self-presentational goals, such as indicating resilience, but for younger listeners they tend to strengthen stereotypes of the elderly as weak or lonely. Thus, misinterpretations of some characteristic behaviors of older adults probably contribute to stereotypic responses from others (Hummert, 1999).

THE SHRINKING SOCIAL CONVOY

Aging brings with it the more and more frequent experience of social loss. Friends, partners, and relatives may die or suffer from debilitating disorders such as Alzheimer's disease. By their mid-70s, nearly 60% of women and 22% of men have lost a spouse (Rook, 2015). In one study of 85-year-olds, 59% of the men and 42% of the women had lost a friend to death in the past year (Johnson & Troll, 1994). But illness and death are not the only sources of social loss. When people retire they lose daily contact with their colleagues at work. If the older adult is constrained by limited finances or health problems, opportunities to visit others or to be part of clubs or other social activities may be reduced. Adult children may move to geographically distant locations. Older adults may leave behind neighbors and shopkeepers of long acquaintance if they move from a larger home to an apartment, an adult community, or an assisted-living facility. This is especially true for older adults of lower socioeconomic status (Cornwell, 2015). The shrinking of the social network and the pain of bereavement are problems that increase in late adulthood (Rook, 2015).

In Chapter 10, we noted that adolescents are largely segregated into age-bound communities that share language, interests, and a dress code, among other things. Mary Pipher (1999) proposes that the physical, cognitive, and social changes of late life segregate older people as well, in ways that are important for helpers to understand. As we have noted, older people often live in circumstances that separate them from their families and their communities, often because poor health makes independent living impossible. Although these arrangements may provide the benefit of day-to-day care and companionship, they may also prevent older people from interacting with members of younger generations and deprive them of opportunities for service to others. Thus, some of their own developmental needs may be going unmet. "The old look for their existential place. They ask, 'How did my life matter? Was my time well spent? What did I mean to others?'" (Pipher, 1999, p. 15). Social segregation creates islands of culture that discourage intergenerational bonding and may make older people feel less valued and useful to others.

Older adults are restricted in other, less obvious ways. Older individuals may sometimes use language in ways that position them within a cultural group or cohort that is separate from younger generations (such as using "depression" primarily to mean a period of economic downturn rather than a mental health problem). Many elderly people also feel segregated from society because it simply moves too fast. Pipher (1999) recalls the adjustments she needed to make when interviewing her older clients:

> I learned to let the phone ring fifteen times. I learned to wait at doors five minutes after I rang the bell. I had to slow down to work with the old. Their conversation is less linear, and there are pauses and repetitions. Points are made via stories; memories lead to more memories. . . . When I walked the old, I walked slowly and held hands at intersections or when sidewalks were slick. . . . Because their bones break more easily, the old are afraid of falling . . . a broken hip can mean the end of independent living. (p. 27)

In the next section, we will consider how older adults face these and many of the other losses and challenges that we have described. Later in this chapter, we will take a special look at bereavement across the life span, with particular attention to how older adults cope with the deaths of those close to them and with their own dying process.

Maintaining Well-Being in the Face of Loss: Successful Aging

How do aging adults adapt to, or cope with, the increasing losses they face? Baltes and colleagues (Baltes & Baltes, 1990; Baltes, Lindenberger, & Staudinger, 2006) suggest that three processes are key to successful development at any age, and especially in the later years. The first is selection. This is a process of narrowing our goals and limiting the domains in which we expend effort. It is not difficult to see that selection is important at any time in the life cycle. For example, at 20, Len selected a career, limiting the possible directions his life could take but also enabling him to achieve high levels of expertise and productivity by focusing his training and practice on career-related skills. At 62, Len selected family life instead of career. Because he felt his stamina waning somewhat, and despite the many satisfactions he still gained from his work, he decided to retire earlier than originally planned so that he could give more energy to developing relationships with his young grandchildren.

The second process is optimization, finding ways to enhance the achievement of remaining goals or finding environments that are enhancing. Len, for example, traded in his sporty two-door coupe for a larger sedan so that he could take the grandchildren on excursions to movies or museums. He also moved from a small apartment in the city to a place in the suburbs, closer to his children, with amenities such as a yard where he could entertain his family.

The final process that contributes to successful development is compensation. When a loss of some kind prevents the use of one means to an end, we can compensate by finding another means. For example, by age 76, as Len's eyesight began to fail, chauffeuring his grandchildren was no longer possible. He now entertains the youngest ones at his home most of the time, planning special events such as "video marathons" and backyard camping "trips."

Baltes provides the following example of successful development in old age:

> When the concert pianist Arthur Rubinstein, as an 80-year-old, was asked in a television interview how he managed to maintain such a high level of expert piano playing, he hinted at the coordination of three strategies. First, Rubinstein said that he played fewer pieces (selection); second, he indicated that he now practiced these pieces more often (optimization); and third, he said that to counteract his loss in mechanical speed he now used a kind of impression management such as introducing slower play before fast segments, so to make the latter appear faster (compensation). (Baltes, Lindenberger, & Staudinger, 1998, p. 1055)

The three combined processes of successful development are called selective optimization with compensation (Baltes et al., 2006). Table 15.2 summarizes some everyday sayings that seem to promote the three processes of selection, optimization, and compensation, and it provides examples of questionnaire items that have been used to assess these processes.

As previously discussed, meeting basic needs for autonomy, competence, and relatedness substantially determines a person's sense of well-being and life satisfaction, according to self-determination theory (see Chapter 14). Several theorists argue that whatever challenges we face in meeting our needs, there are two broad types of strategies that people use to control their destinies. Heckhausen (Heckhausen, 1999; Heckhausen & Wrosh, 2015) refers to primary and secondary control strategies. When our control efforts are attempts to affect the immediate environment beyond ourselves, we are exerting primary control. The growth of competencies of all kinds serves primary control functions and contributes to feelings of mastery and self-esteem. When we choose to develop some competencies and not others (that is, when we engage in selection, such as choosing a career), we are using a primary control strategy. When individuals freely choose and plan their retirements, they are using primary control strategies (see Box 15.2).

From the perspective of self-determination theory, exercising primary control could serve autonomy, competence, and/or relatedness needs. Secondary control generally refers to our attempts to modify our expectations in the face of things we

MyLab Education
Video Example 15.3
Eighty-one-year-old Thelma engages in all three processes that are key to successful development at her age and stage of life. As she describes her approach to life and her philosophy, identify examples of selection, optimization, and compensation.

TABLE 15.2 Selection, Optimization, and Compensation: Brief Definitional Frames and Examples from Proverbs and Questionnaire Items

STRATEGY	ROLE IN DEVELOPMENT	SAMPLE PROVERB	SAMPLE QUESTIONNAIRE ITEM
Selection	Concerns directionality and focus of developmental outcomes such as goals.	Jack-of-all-trades, master of none. Those who follow every path, never reach any destination. Between two stools you fall to the ground.	I always focus on the most important goal at a given time. When I think about what I want in life, I commit myself to one or two important goals. To achieve a particular goal, I am willing to abandon other goals.
Optimization	Concerns the acquisition and refinement of means and their coordination to achieve goals/outcomes.	Practice makes perfect. If at first you don't succeed, try, try, and try again. Strike the iron when it's hot.	I keep working on what I have planned until I succeed. I keep trying until I succeed at a goal. When I want to achieve something, I can wait for the right moment.
Compensation	Concerns maintenance of functioning by substitution of means in situation of losses of means.	There are many hands; what one cannot do, the other will. When there's no wind, grab the oars. Those without a horse walk.	When things don't work the way they used to, I look for other ways to achieve them. When things aren't going so well, I accept help from others. When things don't go as well as they used to, I keep trying other ways until I can achieve the same result I used to.

SOURCE: Baltes, P. B., Lindenberger, U., & Staudinger, U. (2006). Life span theory in developmental psychology. In W. Damon & R. M. Lerner (Eds.), *Handbook of child psychology Vol. 1. Theoretical models of human development* (6th ed., pp. 569–664). Hoboken NJ: Wiley. Reproduced with permission of John Wiley & Sons Inc.

Box 15.2: Navigating the Transition to Retirement

Beverly, a counseling psychologist and community activist, began to think about her retirement in earnest when she was 57 years old, after a bout with cancer. She recuperated well and her prognosis was good, but the sudden confrontation with ill health helped her to see that she might not always be able to work. Until then, she had vaguely assumed she would work until she dropped. Indeed, at first, she couldn't imagine her life without the challenge of a full schedule of diverse clients and community speaking engagements. But her illness led her to examine her goals for the future more carefully. She decided that eventually she would like to reduce her work commitments to have time for other interests. She had always wanted to explore her artistic talent, and when her long-time partner retired, they both hoped to have more time and energy to pursue the activities they enjoyed together, especially international travel. By the age of 65, Beverly felt she was ready to make the change. She stopped taking new clients and reduced her speaking engagements to one or fewer a month. She began thinking of herself as a retiree.

Most modern adults, both men and women, have been part of the workforce for 30 or more years by the time they retire. Common reasons for choosing to retire include health issues, family care needs, attitudes towards job or career, and desire for more leisure time, as illustrated by Beverly's situation. How do individuals navigate the sometimes dramatic transition from being a worker to being a retiree?

Not everyone who can retire chooses to do so. And when people retire (defined by Wang and Shi [2014] as "exiting from the workforce, which accompanies decreased psychological commitment to and behavioral withdrawal from work" [p. 211]) the strategies people devise for making the shift are quite diverse. Nancy Schlossberg, a retired counselor herself, identified multiple

paths from an interview study of 100 retirees. Some were "continuers" who continued to use their work skills part time or in different settings. Beverly is a continuer; she maintains a small client roster and continues her community activities at a reduced level. "Involved spectators" keep a hand in their previous work but adopt some new role. Schlossberg herself is an example of this category. A former counseling professor, she became an author and consultant who applied her counseling knowledge to developing guidelines for retirees. "Adventurers" leave behind their old work skills and develop new talents or skills, sometimes taking on a new job. "Easy gliders" try to keep their time unscheduled. They seem especially comfortable with the flexibility they have without work or other regular commitments. "Searchers" in Schlossberg's study have not yet found a path that works for them, but see themselves in a trial-and-error phase. "Retreaters" seem to give up on finding a satisfactory lifestyle and become depressed (Dittman, 2004; Schlossberg, 2009).

Some of the diversity in Schlossberg's findings may reflect not only different pathways of retirement but also different **stages of retirement**. Atchley (1976) argued that adjustment to retirement follows a typical progression for many people. Stage 1, **honeymoon**, is a time when people focus on the pleasures of being free from the constraints of old schedules, dress codes, and other work demands. In Stage 2, **disenchantment** occurs when people begin to experience an emotional "letdown" as they face the day-to-day realities of retirement, such as separation from work colleagues, uncertainties about how to feel competent and in control, a sense of diminished generativity and meaningfulness, new tensions that may arise with one's partner, financial concerns, and perhaps, boredom. Stage 3, **reorientation**, can be a time of active trial and error. The retiree seeks solutions for the problems that retirement presents and tries strategies for building a satisfactory life. In Stage 4, **stability** is achieved. The retiree finds a functional path that seems to work. Life span theorists would say that selective optimization with compensation is achieved. Finally, Stage 5 is **termination**, the end-of-life transition, when the individual's health declines and she becomes dependent on others for her care.

There are certainly substantial individual differences in the retirement experience that depend on many factors, such as health, financial security, and marital status. While most of the research considers the process of choosing to retire, it is important to recognize that not all people retire voluntarily. Those who are compelled to retire for other reasons often have substantial health problems or employment issues that influence their retirement experience (Siguaw, Sheng, & Simpson, 2017; Wang & Shi, 2014). As another example, although research on the effects of marital status is limited, it suggests some complex processes at work. In one study, married and remarried women rated themselves as healthier and more satisfied with retirement than unmarried (divorced, widowed, never married) women; yet the two groups scored about the same on overall feelings of well-being (Price & Joo, 2005). Another study examined the retirement status of married partners, and found, in general, that satisfaction was greater when both partners were retired. Also, if one partner were still working, satisfaction of the retired partners tended to be lower if they felt that their decision-making power in the relationship had diminished (Szinovacz & Davey, 2005). This was true for both genders.

Despite the importance of individual circumstances, research suggests that Atchley's stage descriptions do capture some predictable phases of retirement for many people. In addition, there may be several cycles of reorientation and stability, with the same individual renegotiating her retirement strategy several times as her life continues to change with the death of a partner, shifting health status, financial changes, and so on. The longer we live, the more cycles we are likely to experience.

Reitzes and Mutran (2004) found general support for the idea that retirement is a dynamic, and to some degree, stagelike process. Satisfaction was high after 6 months (honeymoon), but had declined after a year (disenchantment) and had increased again after 2 years (reorientation and stability). They also identified a number of individual difference factors that impact how well people adjust to the retirement transition both in the honeymoon stage and thereafter. They assessed 800 men and women who were between the ages of 58 and 64 and who were employed full time (at least 35 hours per week) as the study began. The participants represented a random sample of people in this age range living in the Raleigh–Durham–Chapel Hill, North Carolina metropolitan area, so the sample was diverse with respect to race and socioeconomic status. The participants completed an initial screening, and they were tracked with follow-up phone calls until they retired. About 600 of the original sample had retired within 5 years. Those who were willing to continue the study were reassessed at 6 months, 1 year, and 2 years postretirement.

In addition to providing information on income, pension eligibility, health status, marital status, and so on, at every assessment period the participants completed a questionnaire designed to measure their attitudes towards retirement. At the preretirement assessment, they also completed measures of their self-esteem, the social roles they filled in their current lives (e.g., parent, spouse, widow/widower, divorcee, etc.), and their "friend identity," which captured how they viewed themselves in the friend role. The participant rated herself as a friend on a five-point scale, from (1) passive to (5) active, from (1) anxious to (5) confident, and from (1) unsuccessful to (5) successful. The researchers also collected information on the participants' retirement experience, such as how much retirement planning the participants had done preretirement, what reasons they had for retirement, whether they continued working in any capacity during retirement, and so on.

Reitzes and Mutran found little difference between men and women or among different socioeconomic groups with regard to the basic ingredients of a successful retirement. Several factors at preretirement were strong predictors of positive attitudes towards retirement both early in retirement and later: pension eligibility, high self-esteem, and a positive friend identity. Not surprisingly, pension eligibility allows a degree of financial security that reduces some of the stress of the shift to retirement. As Reitzes and Mutran suggest, individuals with a strong sense of self-worth and who feel confident about their relationships with friends probably are better able to organize and structure new opportunities with confidence. High self-esteem helps people to be optimistic that they will be successful in new activities and pursuits. A positive friend identity would seem to be especially valuable when release from work constraints provides more time for interactions with friends.

Some other factors were very helpful for ensuring a happy honeymoon phase: being in control of the decision to retire (that is, doing so voluntarily), and approaching retirement with a plan of action. People who felt that they had no choice but to retire, because of the conditions of their employment or because of ill health, were not as happy as others in the first year of retirement. The same was true for people who had not carefully considered what they would do in retirement. These individuals were less satisfied at the start, but with time their situations tended to improve, and they were often doing as well as other retirees after 2 years.

One retiree provides a good example of some of these factors at work, and of the typical stages that many retirees experience. Jack just plunged into retirement optimistically with no plan but his usual belief that he could "handle it." For a while he enjoyed finishing some carpentry projects he had never had time for and doing some traveling. But he was deep into disillusionment within a few months. He missed the opportunity to interact with colleagues and he missed the status he had achieved in his work life. With some help from a counselor, he identified the problems and mapped out some alternative solutions. He chose to begin consulting on a part-time basis (often voluntarily for nonprofit organizations), which brought him in touch with a wider range of people and helped him feel generative. At 72, Jack still enjoys good health, and after 4 years of retirement he believes that this is the best time of his life. Recent studies indicate that the majority of retirees, perhaps as many as 80%, experience minimal change or improvements in psychosocial well-being following retirement (Wang & Shi, 2014).

can't change. We are using secondary control strategies when, for example, we change our aspirations and goals because we cannot do everything we used to do or when we minimize the importance of specific needs after failing to achieve a particular end.

> Both primary and secondary control may involve cognition and action, although primary control is almost always characterized in terms of behavior engaging the external world, whereas secondary control is predominantly characterized in terms of cognitive processes localized within the individual. (Schultz & Heckhausen, 1996, p. 708)

When primary control efforts fail or we suffer losses that we cannot overcome, secondary controls are likely to become important. Schultz and Heckhausen indicate that our repertoire of both primary and secondary control strategies will increase with age until late midlife, but that the sheer weight of late-life declines will make primary control decline as well, so that people are likely to use more secondary control strategies in old age. Heckhausen (1997) found, for example, that adults in their 60s demonstrated more flexibility in adjusting their goals than adults in their 20s. When young, middle-aged, and elderly adults were asked to state their five most important goals and plans for the next 5 years, there was a clear shift in aspirations across age (Heckhausen, 1997). Elderly people had fewer aspirations regarding work, finances, and family and more aspirations related to health, community, and leisure pursuits than young adults. Heckhausen argues that these shifts reflect the fact that older people generally have less primary control potential over work, finances, and family. They therefore shift their goals in a compensatory way to those over which they may be able to take some primary control.

On the whole, how well do people in old age adapt to the challenges of late life? There is a tendency for a terminal decline in well-being that is driven by changes associated with impending death such as health decline, cognitive, and physical disability (Gerstorf et al., 2016). Yet, as we suggested earlier in this chapter, generally older people report high levels of well-being. Ryff and Keyes (1995) analyzed measures of six dimensions of well-being from interviews with 1,108 adults. The responses of young (25 to 29), middle-aged (30 to 64), and old (65 or over) adults were compared, and several measures were found to increase over age. Old adults scored higher than both younger groups on a measure of positive relationships. They scored as well as the middle-aged and higher than the young adults on measures of environmental mastery and autonomy, and they scored as well as both younger groups on self-acceptance. Older adults did score lower than the younger groups on two dimensions of well-being: purpose in life and personal growth. Perhaps as a person leaves behind the arenas in which generativity is most directly expressed—work, parenting, and community service—opportunities to feel useful or to grow seem diminished. This conclusion is consistent with findings that elderly women who continue to care for an adult child with disabilities report a much greater sense of purpose in life than elderly women who do not have such responsibilities (Kling, Seltzer, & Ryff, 1997). Generativity issues aside, results of these studies suggested that aging and a sense of well-being were often quite compatible and that some aspects of well-being actually improved in old age. More recent population-based longitudinal studies using Ryff's dimensions, however, failed to find the expected increases in well-being into old age (Springer, Pudrovska, & Hauser, 2011). Some of these differences may be due to methodological problems; thus, more research is needed to clarify maturational trends across specific dimensions of well-being.

Wisdom, Aging, and Culture

Wisdom is often perceived as going hand in hand with advanced age. If that is true, then the well-being elders do manifest may be related to the wisdom they accrue over the years. But what exactly is wisdom anyway? And does everyone achieve it in late life? The search for wisdom has been at the heart of religious and philosophical systems since ancient times. Its study as a Western scientific topic, however, began in earnest only in the 1970s. This may be due, in no small part, to the breadth of the topic and the difficulties posed in defining and measuring it.

Wisdom has been called "expertise in the fundamental pragmatics of life" (Baltes et al., 1998, p. 1970). We have seen that the practical problems adults must face do not necessarily have one right answer. As young adults gain experience with the complexities of such ill-defined problems, the adolescent expectation that logical, absolute right answers always exist may give way to a more relativistic perspective. This perspective acknowledges that there are multiple, contextually embedded truth systems (Perry, 1970/1999). But wisdom encompasses more than cognitive skills. A wise person is an expert in the "psychological art of life" (Staudinger, 1999, p. 343) that includes aspects of motivation, emotion regulation, other-directed versus self-involved orientation, tolerance for ambiguity, and insight. Wise people recognize and deal with the dialectics inherent in human existence (e.g., good and bad, strength and weakness, self-interest and altruism) in a balanced way. They often help guide others to do the same. "Mastery of such dialectics in the sense of wisdom does not mean that a decision for either one or the other side is taken but rather that both sides are essential for grasping human existence. Wisdom embraces these contradictions of life and draws insights from them. It further develops heuristics about when and under which circumstances to focus on which side of each of these opposites (Staudinger & Gluck, 2011, p. 217)." Most recently, Grossman (2017) summarized facets of cognition in wise thinking to include four general components: intellectual humility (or recognizing the limits of one's knowledge), appreciating perspectives beyond the present issue, recognizing the possibility of change in relationships, and compromising or integrating different opinions.

Messages about wise ways of navigating life's challenges are embedded in culture. In fact, researchers often use folk theories of wisdom as a starting point for their work. Transmitted across generations in folk tales and proverbs, these insights have, according to Csikszentmihalyi and Rathunde (1990), universal evolutionary value. Table 15.3 contains proverbs from different cultures, each offering advice about anger and conflict. Do you notice any similar themes? Can you come up with proverbs that present an opposing message? If so, they may be examples of the dialectic we have described.

TABLE 15.3 Wisdom Across Cultures: Wise Counsel About Anger

PROVERB	ORIGIN
He who is slow to anger is better than the mighty; and he who rules his spirit, than he who captures a city.	Old Testament, Book of Proverbs 16:32
Life is short, but troubles make it longer.	Roman Proverb
If you fear something, you give it power over you.	African Proverb
When anger and revenge get married, their daughter is called cruelty.	Russian Proverb
Force, no matter how concealed, begets resistance.	Lakota (Sioux) Proverb
The man who strikes first admits that his ideas have given out.	Chinese Proverb
A knife wound heals, but a tongue wound festers.	Persian Proverb
Holding on to anger is like grasping a hot coal with the intent of throwing it at someone else; you are the one who gets burned.	Indian Proverb (Buddhaghosa)
For what cannot be cured, patience is best.	Irish Proverb
Don't notice the tiny flea in the other person's hair and overlook the lumbering yak on your own nose.	Tibetan Proverb
Two wrongs don't make a right.	English Proverb
He who starts up in anger, sits down with a loss.	Turkish Proverb
Never do anything out of anger; would you hoist your sails during a storm?	Arabic Proverb

SOURCE: Mieder, W. (1993). *The Prentice Hall encyclopedia of world proverbs*. Upper Saddle River, NJ: Pearson Education, Inc. Used with permission from Pearson Education.

TABLE 15.4 Wisdom Problem and Abbreviated Responses

Wisdom Problem
A 15-year-old girl wants to get married right away. What should one/she consider and do?

Low Wisdom-Related Score
A 15-year-old girl wants to get married? No, no way, marrying at age 15 would be utterly wrong. One has to tell the girl that marriage is not possible. (After further probing) It would be irresponsible to support such an idea. No, this is just a crazy idea.

High Wisdom-Related Score
Well, on the surface, this seems like an easy problem. On average, marriage for 15-year-old girls is not a good thing. But there are situations where the average case does not fit. Perhaps in this instance, special life circumstances are involved, such that the girl has a terminal illness. Or the girl has just lost her parents. And also, this girl may live in another culture or historical period. Perhaps she was raised with a value system different from ours. In addition, one has to think about adequate ways of talking with the girl and to consider her emotional state.

SOURCE: Based on Baltes, P. B., & Staudinger, O. M. (2000). Wisdom: A metaheuristic (pragmatic) to orchestrate mind and virtue toward excellence. *American Psychologist, 55*, 122–136.

So, is wisdom universal or is it culture-specific? Perhaps there are some distinctions in the way wisdom is defined that differentiate East and West (Grossman et al., 2012; Takahashi & Overton, 2005). Western cultural views tend to emphasize the cognitive aspects of wisdom, such as breadth of knowledge and ability to analyze. Eastern cultures take a more expansive view, incorporating both cognition and affect into their understanding of wisdom. However, similarities across cultures are greater than these distinctions. Staudinger and Gluck (2011) make clear that the consensus across cultures is that wisdom represents the "perfect integration of mind and character for the greater good" (p. 221).

Is wisdom more likely in old age in all cultures? In a program of research on wisdom by Staudinger, Baltes, and their colleagues, Western participants were told about people experiencing difficult real-life problems and were asked to describe and explain what the fictional people should do. One example of such a real-life problem, along with a response that received a low score for wisdom and one that received a high score, is presented in Table 15.4. Scores for wisdom were based on raters' judgments of how rich the respondent's factual and procedural knowledge seemed to be, whether the response took into account the developmental context, the degree to which the response reflected a relativistic view, and a recognition of uncertainty, as well as attempts to manage uncertainty (Staudinger & Baltes, 1996).

Findings from studies using this technique indicate that wisdom, as defined by Staudinger and Baltes (1996), does seem to require experience and thus is somewhat enhanced by age. The years from 15 to 25 appear to be very important for wisdom acquisition (Pasupathi, Staudinger, & Baltes, 1999, 2001), but after 25, the proportion of people whose wisdom scores are above average does not change substantially. After 75, fewer people continue to function at above-average levels on measures of wisdom (Baltes & Staudinger, 2000). Studies using somewhat different methods have found a tendency for wisdom to increase well into middle adulthood (Blanchard-Fields, 1986, 2007) but also to decline thereafter (Labouvie-Vief, Chiodo, Goguen, Diehl, & Orwoll, 1995). Grossman and colleagues (2010) reported that older Americans displayed wiser reasoning in relation to solving interpersonal conflicts than did younger or middle aged Americans. Furthermore, older adults are more likely to reason wisely in relation to scenarios that are particularly relevant to multiple age groups; in contrast, younger adults are more likely to reason wisely in scenarios most relevant to their current age (Thomas & Kunzmann, 2014).

The developmental trajectory of wisdom acquisition, however, may not be the same for all cultural groups. Let's consider the ways that people deal with conflict. Kunzmann and Baltes (2003) found that individuals scoring high on wisdom tend to prefer cooperative conflict management, as opposed to dominance strategies. They also score high on involvement with others, yet at the same time tend to moderate their emotional reactivity more than other people. They also seem more committed than others to pursuits that have the goal of enhancing the growth and potential of both themselves and other people. Consistent with themes presented in prior chapters, some Eastern cultures tend to privilege harmony and cohesion in social relationships. Their conflict management strategies tend to be indirect and considerate of multiple points of view. Behaviors that assert autonomy and independence, leading to more direct conflict management strategies, are more characteristic of people in the United States. Grossman and his colleagues (2010) reasoned that the sensitivity to social cues young children learn in interdependent cultures may foster an earlier development of wise reasoning skills for solving conflict. Consistent with previous findings, older North Americans in this cross-cultural study gave wiser responses to questions about intergroup conflict than did younger and middle aged Americans. However, younger and middle-aged Japanese participants gave wiser answers when compared to younger U.S. groups, suggesting cultural differences in wisdom development. Elderly Americans reasoned more wisely about intergroup conflict, whereas elderly Japanese were wiser with regard to interpersonal conflict.

Let's take a closer look at some ways of operationalizing wisdom. Theorists from the neo-Piagetian perspective argue that relativistic thinking represents a new, qualitatively more advanced form of logical thinking, called postformal thought. Others regard more relativistic thinking as a function of reflection and experience, perhaps benefited by advancing metacognitive understanding of the limits of one's own thought processes. In the latter view, relativistic thought does not represent a qualitatively different level of functioning, but the outcome of accumulating knowledge. From either perspective, the result for some, though not all, adults is the achievement of wisdom.

Researchers from the Max Plank Institute in Germany ([The Berlin Wisdom Project]; Baltes & Smith, 2008) have been at the forefront of this research agenda. This group posits five criteria for a wise person. The first is a deep fund of factual knowledge about life, human nature, and relationships with others. The second involves well-developed procedural knowledge about how to deal with life and its conflicts. The ability to consider life's challenges from multiple perspectives and to work towards decisions that balance one's own and others' interests are the third and fourth criteria. Finally, understanding that true certainty is impossible for life's ill-defined problems and coming to peaceful terms with uncertainty is the fifth criterion in this typology of wisdom. Identifying criteria makes it a little easier to assess the components of wisdom.

Individuals differ in the degree to which they demonstrate wisdom based on more than just cultural background and age. Correlates of wisdom include crystallized intelligence (Grossmann, Na, Varnum, Kitayama, & Nisbett, 2013), personality characteristics including openness to experience, lack of neuroticism, and concerns for others' welfare (Webster, Westerhof, & Bohlmeijer, 2014; Wink & Staudinger, 2016), emotional regulation (Grossman, Gerlach, & Denissen, 2016), and history of coping well with difficult life experiences (Mickler & Staudinger, 2008; Westrate & Gluck, 2017). In particular, individuals who demonstrate *post-traumatic growth*, or positive psychological change in the course of overcoming adversity, may be especially likely to demonstrate more wise thinking. Interestingly, training or experience in occupations that involve managing and reviewing life's problems also seem to promote wisdom. Clinical psychologists, for example, receive higher wisdom scores than people with similar levels of education who are in fields that do not focus on "the fundamental pragmatics of life" (Smith, Staudinger, & Baltes, 1994, p. 989). Clinical training itself seems to be important, because even when analyses controlled for the contribution of intelligence and personality differences across professions, clinicians had a wisdom advantage (Staudinger, Maciel, Smith, & Baltes, 1998). In employment contexts, experience in leadership roles may also lead to improvements in wise thinking (Yang, 2014).

Social-Emotional Experience in Late Life

Perhaps you are wondering how late-life increases in wisdom might co-exist with cognitive declines. Contemporary research paints a nuanced picture of gains and losses that appear in old age. Evidence supports growth in some areas of socioemotional functioning as long as certain conditions (such as relatively good health and social support) are present. The socioemotional domain seems to be enhanced and better regulated with age. One reason is that older adults choose more carefully the social relationships in which they invest their time. They tend to selectively invest in fewer social relationships, keeping or replacing close, deeply satisfying relationships and eliminating more superficial or peripheral ties (Carstensen, 1998). Figure 15.5 demonstrates that in one study the number of very close social partners stayed about the same for people ranging in age from 69 to 104, but the numbers of less close social partners dropped dramatically (Lang & Carstensen, 1994). Laura Carstensen and her colleagues explain this socioemotional selectivity as a function of people's expectations that the time remaining in their lives is limited (Carstensen & Mikels, 2005; Sims, Hogan, & Carstensen, 2015). In both Western and Eastern cultures, they have found that people of any age will become more selective about whom they spend time with if they perceive their remaining time in life to be constrained (Fredrickson & Carstensen, 1990; Fung, Carstensen, & Lutz, 1999). Because older people (and others who expect their lives to end soon) pay more attention to their feelings, their emotional experiences are more enhanced and complex (Carstensen, 1998). For older adults, emotional characteristics play a greater role than for younger adults in how they categorize potential social partners (Frederickson & Carstensen, 1990). Older adults also remember relatively more emotional information from descriptions of people than younger adults do (Carstensen & Turk-Charles, 1994).

While this selectivity may benefit socioemotional satisfaction, what about cognition? A U.S. study of White and African American older adults living in the community points in a different direction. This study found that the number of social networks an older person had was associated with less cognitive decline, even after controlling for baseline differences in education, SES, health, depression, and intellectual ability (Barnes, de Leon, Wilson, Bienias, & Evans, 2004). The authors concluded that it might be important for older individuals to retain as many social connections and engage in as much social interaction as possible presumably to enhance cognitive reserve. Social relationships promote well-being and mitigate terminal decline, serving a strong protective function (Brandmaier, Ram, Wagner, & Gerstorf, 2017; Gerstorf et al., 2016; Haslam, Cruwys, Milne, Kan, & Haslam, 2016). Relationships with grandchildren may be a special source of social connection and generativity while also promoting cognitive well-being (Burn & Szoeke, 2015; Sneed & Schulz, 2017). Other studies suggest that they play a causal role in preventing onset of dementia (Kuiper et al., 2015) and in promoting recovery after illness, such as stroke (Glymour, Weuve, Fay, Glass, & Berkman, 2008).

Self-reported emotional well-being seems to increase over the years of adulthood, although some decrements after age 60 have been reported (Charles & Carstensen, 2008). Consistently, older adults report more experiences of positive emotions and

---

FIGURE 15.5 Numbers of very close social partners are maintained in old age.

SOURCE: Based on Lang, F. R., & Carstensen, L. L. (1994). Close emotional relationships in late life: Further support for proactive aging in the social domain. *Psychology and Aging, 9,* 315–324.

fewer negative emotions, a phenomenon referred to as the *positivitiy effect*. For example, older age is associated with increases in gratitude (Chopik, Newton, Ryan, Kashdan, & Jarden, 2017) and decreases in regret (Västfjäll, Peters, & Bjälkebring, 2011). Compared to younger adult cohorts, older individuals report more satisfying friendships, marriages, and family relationships. They also report less conflict with others, possibly because of improved emotion regulation over the years (Ali & Alea, 2017; Charles & Piazza, 2007). Older adults also are more likely to remember positive experiences than negative ones, and to attend to positive rather than negative information, when compared to younger adults (Reed, Chan, & Mikels, 2014). Older adults' neural processing of emotional information involves greater activation of the amygdala when viewing positive images as compared to negative images, whereas no such difference occurs for younger adults (Mather, 2016; see also Kisley, Wood, & Burrows, 2007). When older adults think about emotionally arousing experiences in their lives, they show less heart rate reactivity than younger adults, especially for negative emotions like anger and fear (Kunzmann, Rohr, Wieck, Kappes, & Wrosch, 2017; Labouvie-Vief, Lumky, Jain, & Heinze, 2003).

In a variety of cultures, older adults describe themselves as having greater control over their emotions than younger adults do (Gross et al., 1997). Indeed, researchers have discovered age-related changes in emotion regulation strategies such that older adults use fewer maladaptive strategies, and often utilize strategies of acceptance in situations of moderate intensity, anxiety, or sadness (Schirda, Valentine, Aldao, & Prakash, 2016). When older and younger adults listened to taped conversations containing negative remarks, presumably about them, older adults tended to "emotionally disengage" more than younger adults, reporting less anger and less interest in the speakers (Charles & Carstensen, 2008). Older adults also report less negative affect in response to daily stressors than younger adults do (Scott, Ram, Smyth, Almeida, & Sliwinski, 2017). In direct observations of conflict management between spouses, older couples were more skillful than long-married middle-aged couples at interspersing positive, affectionate statements with negative ones and keeping negative expressions to a minimum (Levenson, Carstensen, & Gottman, 1993, 1994). In a recent study where older adults were asked to write narratives about distressing events, the participants seemed to regulate their perceptions by quickly transitioning from negative to positive aspects of these situations (Devereux, Heffner, Doane, Gosser, & Nolan, 2016). It appears that older people may be wise in the ways they deal with emotions: Don't dwell on sorrow, and make happiness last.

Besides focusing on the positive, older people may be more accepting of things they cannot change. Shallcross and her colleagues (2013) explored connections between emotional well-being and acceptance, "the process of deliberately and nonjudgmentally engaging with negative emotions" (p. 734) in an effort to reconcile the inevitable declines of late life with increases in positive affect. Indeed, age-related trends were found for increased acceptance and decreased anger and anxiety among participants ranging from ages 21 to 73. Interestingly, and consistent with other research, sadness did not decrease with age despite the observed growth in positive affect.

While well-being increases up to a point, depressive symptoms also increase in old age. Although overall rates of major depressive disorder (MDD) are lower among older groups, rates of minor depression and subclinical symptoms of depression increase from middle adulthood into very old age (Blazer, 2003; Buchteman, Luppa, & Heller, 2012). It is difficult to establish accurate prevalence estimates because different methodologies and assessments, developed on younger age cohorts, may not reliably capture the nature of late life depression (Edelstein, Drozdick, & Ciliberti, 2010). Co-occuring cognitive declines and physical illnesses also complicate diagnostic efforts. Rates of MDD among community-dwelling adults aged 65 and above range from 1% to 5% (Haigh, Bogucki, Sigmon, & Blazer, 2018) and increase (with median prevalence around 10%) among long-term care residents (Seitz, Purandare, & Conn, 2010). Rates of depressive symptoms that are clinically relevant are much higher. Clinically significant depressive symptoms are estimated to be much more common in older adults in the community, ranging from 10% to 50% compared to about 15% among younger and middle-aged adults (Wittayanukorn, Qian, & Hansen, 2014). Those above age

85 show very high rates ([43.9%]; see Luppa et al., 2011). African Americans showed more severe symptoms than other groups in a recent study (Shellman, Granara, & Rosengarten, 2011) although more research is needed to clarify cultural differences. Symptom recognition is important because of the relationship of depressive symptoms to more serious physical and mental health problems.

A point of controversy regarding depression among older adults involves whether they experience the same types of symptoms and course of disease as younger adults. While results from some studies suggest that older adults report more somatic symptoms like pain, insomnia, loss of appetite, and less guilt, dysphoric mood, and suicidal ideation, these findings are not consistent across studies. It does seem to be the case that older adults are more likely to experience recurrent depression (Haigh et al., 2018). Fortunately, despite the intractability of many health problems in old age, research on the effectiveness of treatment for depressive symptoms has been encouraging. As with younger clients, elderly people, including nursing home residents, respond positively to a variety of psychotherapeutic interventions, including cognitive behavioral, brief psychodynamic, interpersonal, life-review, and problem-solving therapies (Antognini & Liptzin, 2008; Pot et al., 2010).

MyLab Education Self-Check 15.1

Experiencing Loss

15.2 Explain the process of death and issues associated with dying, including the dynamics of the grief process and grief coping mechanisms, and develop supportive, personalized interventions for coping with bereavement.

Death and Dying

In the expectable rhythm of life, most people begin to take the prospect of their own mortality more seriously during middle adulthood. Illness, the deaths of parents, spouses, siblings, or friends, the experience of watching adult children struggle with problems, and many other bumps in the road grow more frequent, and they signal what has already been lost. At some point, we begin to think of time not as unlimited "time to live" but as "time left to live." In old age, the reality of death and loss are inescapable. Even though advances in medicine have extended life and greatly improved its quality for many people, all of us face the certainty of death. And though death can occur at any point in the life cycle, the proportion of individuals who die in late adulthood is much greater than at any other time. Currently, close to 80% of the U.S. population live beyond age 65. Of this group, more than 75% will struggle with heart disease, cancer, stroke, lung disease, or dementia during their last 12 months of life (Lynn, 2000). Despite these statistics, older adults report less anxiety about death and are more realistic about its inevitability than are middle-aged adults (Gesser, Wong, & Reker, 1988; Goranson, Ritter, Waytz, Norton, & Gray, 2017).

Professional helpers will undoubtedly come face to face with the emotionally challenging issues of death and dying in their work. They may be called on to support children who experience a parent's death, relatives or friends of a suicide victim, families struggling to cope with the aftermath of a fatal accident, or individuals facing their own deaths from illnesses such as cancer or HIV/AIDS. Or they may work with the elderly, for whom the prospect of death ever more insistently intrudes into daily life. Death in later life is generally expected. The experience of death for younger persons can be particularly traumatic. Although the older person and his family may have time to prepare themselves for the separation, death at earlier ages defies the natural order. Even though we present the issues of death and dying in the context of later life, many of the issues involved in dying and bereavement are similar across the life span. First we will consider the issues involved in dying. Then we will look at the psychological work of bereavement.

FACING DEATH

Dame Cicely Saunders, founder of the modern hospice movement, recounted a dying patient's words to her: "I thought it so strange. Nobody wants to look at me" (Ewens & Herrington, 1983, p. 5). This remark captures many elements that describe the experience of dying: general reluctance to address the topic of death openly, anxiety about death that informs this reluctance, guilt that emanates from the lack of openness, and the loneliness and isolation of the dying person. If death is a part of every human life, why do many of us avoid discussing it? Death clearly represents unknown territory, and it is difficult to comprehend a more painful or stressful life event than the prospect of dying or of losing a loved one. According to some existential therapists, fear of death is the ultimate source of anxiety and the foundation of most depression and alienation (May, 1979). Some people have also pointed out that the advances of modern medicine, despite their obvious benefits, have encouraged us to think of dying in some of the same ways we conceptualize treatable illnesses (Kane, 1996).

Fortunately, much progress has been made in understanding death and dying relatively recently. Modern U.S. culture is very gradually moving away from one that denies or sanitizes death towards one that supports death with dignity. Courageous pioneers such as Elisabeth Kubler-Ross (1969) have directed our collective attention to the issues facing the dying and the bereaved and, in doing so, have shed much-needed light on their needs and concerns. Faced with a growing population of elderly and prompted by advances in research, the field of medicine has taken steps towards more compassionate care of the dying. An emerging consensus among medical specialties regarding **end-of-life care** is reflected in the development of a set of core principles for providers (see Table 15.5). These 11 principles list the responsibilities of end-of-life caregivers to patients and their patients' families or support systems. Societies such as the American Medical Association and the Joint Commission on the Accreditation of Healthcare Organizations, to name a few, have adopted these principles (Cassel & Foley, 1999). In general, the principles support more humanistic approaches to end-of-life care, including better pain management, continuity of care, and attention to the psychological dimensions of death and dying. These principles are reflected at the practical level in state initiatives such as Oregon's policies to improve end-of-life care (Wyden, 2000).

WHAT IS A GOOD DEATH?

Most people hope for a good death, but what does that really mean? As the poet Robert Frost observed, "Hope does not lie in a way out, but in a way through." You might imagine that dying quickly without unnecessary suffering or dying at home surrounded by loved ones would provide good ways through this final passage. But preferences may be different for different people. In a recent literature review, Meier et al. (2016) considered 36 studies on patient and family members' perspectives on characteristics of a good death, and they identified eleven core themes. The three most

---

TABLE 15.5 Core Principles for End-of-Life Care

1. Respecting the dignity of both patients and caregivers;
2. Being sensitive and respectful of the patient's and family's wishes;
3. Using the most appropriate measures that are consistent with patient choices;
4. Encompassing alleviation of pain and other physical symptoms;
5. Assessing and managing psychological, social, and spiritual/religious problems;
6. Offering continuity (the patient should be able to continue to be cared for, if so desired, by his/her primary care and specialist providers);
7. Providing access to any therapy that may realistically be expected to improve the patient's quality of life, including alternative and nontraditional treatments;
8. Providing access to palliative care and hospice care;
9. Respecting the right to refuse treatment;
10. Respecting the physician's professional right to discontinue some treatments when appropriate, with consideration for both patient and family preferences;
11. Promoting clinical evidence–based research on providing care at end-of-life.

SOURCE: Cassel, C. K. & Foley, K. M. (1999). *Principles for care of patients at the end of life: An emerging consensus among the specialities of medicine.* Used with permission from the Milbank Memorial Fund. Available at www.milbank.org.

commonly identified themes were aspects of the specific dying process, such as where dying would occur and who should be present, a pain-free experience, and emotional well-being, including support as well as the opportunity to discuss the meaning of death. Other themes that presented frequently included religiosity/spirituality, family involvement (including presence and support of family members, not being a burden on family, and family's own support and acceptance of the death), preferences for treatment, ability to die with dignity, quality of life, and relationship of the patient and family with the healthcare professionals. Interestingly, families of patients were more likely than patients to discuss themes of quality of life, dignity, and family involvement, while patients were more likely than family members to discuss themes of religiosity/spirituality, like faith and opportunities to meet with clergy prior to death (Meier et al., 2016).

These findings were consistent with previous work on characteristics of a good death by Steinhauser and her colleagues (2000), who investigated the relative importance of factors that signify a good death in a survey of 2,000 seriously ill patients, physicians, recently bereaved family members, and other care providers. These researchers found that patients also viewed being able to help others as an important contribution to their end-of-life quality, suggesting the significance of generativity across the life span.

Of course, not all individuals have the same preferences for their experiences at the end of life. Contrary to common assumptions, most patients do not express a preference to die at home. In contrast to the value placed on autonomous decision making by many professionals, members of certain cultures prefer to share decision making with relatives because this is perceived as supportive (Brown, Bekker, Davison, Koffman, & Schell, 2016; Morita et al., 2015). Members of Chinese, Pakistani, and Hispanic communities may actively strive to protect their loved ones from knowledge of the full extent of their illness because it is deemed impolite, cruel, or deleterious to health (Talamantes, Lawler, & Espino, 1995). In some Asian communities, a family's desire for extraordinary measures to preserve the life of a relative may reflect the deep reverence they have for their elders. African American patients were more likely than their White counterparts to want all available life-sustaining treatments. They were also less likely to utilize hospice services or to have prepared advanced directives (see below). Wicher and Meeker (2012) suggest that some of these preferences may be shaped by African American cultural and religious perspectives on death. It is important to recognize that there are many ways to define a good death. It is incumbent on caregivers not to make assumptions about their clients, but to ask for and listen to individuals' preferences.

Despite the importance of these individual differences, many studies have demonstrated that **palliative care** (Kelley & Morrison, 2015; Singer, Martin, & Merrijoy, 1999) and the ability to prepare for death (Christakis, 2000; Emanuel & Emanuel, 1998) are two of the most consistently wished-for aspects of end-of-life care reported by patients and families. Palliative care, or comfort care, involves services provided by caregivers from several disciplines. It embodies a comprehensive approach to care that addresses pain management, emotional and spiritual care, and psychological support for caregivers and survivors (Billings, 1998). Palliative care can occur simultaneously with efforts to treat disease, beginning at the time of diagnosis (Kelley & Morrison, 2015).

The philosophy of care embodied in the modern **hospice movement**, which serves people suffering from terminal illness in the last months of life, is a good example of a palliative, patient-centered approach. Considered a hospitable respite for weary travelers in medieval times, hospice is now a place where people on another kind of journey, from life to death, can find peace and comfort. The hospice philosophy of end-of-life care says much about its philosophy of death, primarily about what the dying person needs in order to have a good death (Callanan & Kelley, 1992). Hospice emphasizes the importance of giving patients as much knowledge about their condition as possible so that they maintain some control over their care. The focus is not on curing disease, but on managing symptoms and pain by means of palliative (pain-reducing) medicine. Perhaps more difficult to manage are other aspects of dying: the emotional, social, and spiritual sequelae of illness. In this approach to treatment, patients and their families are assisted in coping with the feelings of depression, anxiety, rejection, abandonment, and spiritual discomfort that may arise from the process of dying and losing a loved one.

Some studies have found that hospice patients are more satisfied with their care than conventional hospital patients (Kavalieratos et al., 2016) and that provision of hospice care in nursing homes improves quality of care there (Baer & Hanson, 2000; Cimino & McPherson, 2014). As noted earlier, there are clear worldwide trends towards improving end-of-life care by incorporating palliative care for all patients, regardless of setting (Lynn, 2000). In some areas, coalitions of hospitals, hospices, medical practices, nursing associations, long-term care facilities, social workers, and pastoral and mental health counselors have been formed to provide high-quality, comprehensive services to seriously ill individuals and their families (Mitka, 2000). Recommendations for the most important components of palliative care have been outlined for a number of different health conditions, such as cancer, dementia, and stroke (Cagle, Pek, Clifford, Guralnik, & Zimmerman, 2015; Holloway et al., 2014; van der Steen et al., 2014).

Having a good death appears to be related to the person's ability to make informed decisions about treatment, a notion congruent with what has been said about the psychological benefits of control. However, even though the importance of this kind of control has generally been acknowledged by practitioners of palliative care, studies suggest that a significant number of patients, even the most highly educated ones, still misunderstand the treatment options available to them. Silveira and her associates (Silveira, DiPiero, Gerrity, & Feudtner, 2000) examined whether knowledge about end-of-life options such as **refusal of treatment, physician-assisted suicide, active euthanasia,** and **double effect** was improved among patients who had signed **advance directives or living wills,** who had experienced previous illness, or who had previously cared for a dying loved one. Refusal of treatment refers to patients' refusal of any food, water, or medical treatment that prolongs life. Physician-assisted suicide involves prescribing medicine that enables patients to take their own lives. Active euthanasia refers to injection of a medication by someone else that causes immediate death. The double effect means giving medication intended to relieve pain even though there is a chance that death can result. Advance directives or living wills are statements, typically in writing, that describe a person's wishes regarding medical treatment in the event of incurable illness.

The results of the study showed that knowledge about end-of-life treatment options was generally poor. It was not improved for those who had signed advance directives or who were ill themselves. Knowledge was somewhat more accurate for those who had cared for dying loved ones. In general, caregivers often wait too long to discuss end-of-life preferences. Decisions may be made in haste, when the dying person is too ill or caregivers too distressed to make reflective choices (Gaster, Larson, & Curtis, 2017; Gleeson & Wise, 1993). It is important, therefore, to initiate conversations about end-of-life decisions well in advance of the stresses of illness.

THE PROCESS OF DYING

In the late 1950s, Elisabeth Kubler-Ross (Kubler-Ross, 1969), a Swiss-born psychiatrist, began to study the ways that people who were dying faced death. At that time, the dying were largely invisible among hospital patients, and she encountered a high degree of professional resistance to her work. When she asked her fellow physicians to recommend to her their dying patients so that she could talk to them, she was told that there were no dying patients in her 600-bed hospital (Ewens & Herrington, 1983). But after meeting people who realized that they were dying and after listening carefully to their stories, she described responses to death that appeared to characterize the process: denial, anger, bargaining, depression, and acceptance. Each of these responses represents a type of coping or defense mechanism for dealing with death. Perhaps it was unfortunate that she referred to these processes as "stages" and linked them together in sequence. Although Kubler-Ross herself (Kubler-Ross, 1974) emphasized that the stages do not always occur in order and that they can and often do occur simultaneously, the use of a stair-step approach is fraught with the kinds of problems we discussed in Chapter 1. Foremost, perhaps, is that a stage sequence can be irresistible to helpers who are looking for fixed, clear guidelines for understanding grief.

Criticism of the model has centered on the overall lack of empirical evidence for the existence of stages (Parkes, 2013; Stroebe, Schut, & Boerner, 2017) and the problems that arise when professionals and caregivers use the stages as a road map by which to evaluate functional versus dysfunctional adjustment to death and dying (Corr, 2015). The belief among some helping professionals that these five responses are the only appropriate ones for the dying represents another limitation of the model as it is applied to practice. Studies of individuals who have received terminal diagnoses do provide some support for the initial manifestation of shock or disbelief as well as for the presence of greater acceptance before death (Kalish, 1985). In general, however, helpers should remember that there is much greater variation in the process than is allowed for by a strict interpretation of these stages, and that individuals who do not experience these stages precisely should not be presumed dysfunctional or maladjusted in their grief. Despite the popularity of Kubler-Ross's stage model of grieving, many professionals and researchers have argued that it should be abandoned due to its theoretical and empirical limitations and the potential for harm when it is considered to be prescriptive, as the "right" way to grieve, rather than descriptive, as some ways that some people may grieve (Corr, 2015; Jurecic, 2015; Parkes, 2013; Stroebe et al., 2017). Perhaps the reactions described by the well-known stage theory can be viewed as some important ways that people cope with impending loss, but by no means is the sequence fixed nor is the range of coping mechanisms exhaustive.

It is helpful for professionals to understand that the dying process may also be distinguished by the nature of illness. Figure 15.6 illustrates some trajectories of dying for patients suffering from three common diseases: cancer, heart disease, and dementia (Eti, 2011). Awareness of these patterns can enhance provision of palliative care. Professionals can better help families understand prognoses and make more informed decisions about treatment.

Bereavement

Life is death kept at an arm's length. Love is grief dressed in its Sunday best. And sadness is the tax assessed on any happiness.

—From **St. James' Park Epistle** by Thomas Lynch

FIGURE 15.6 Trajectories of illness in common diseases of aging.
The trajectories of cancer, organ failure (heart failure), and dementia show different pathways.

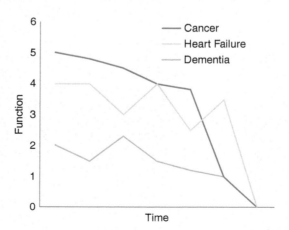

SOURCE: Based on Eti, S. (2011). Palliative care: An evolving field in medicine. *Clinics in Office Practice, 38*, 159–171.

Sadness is not the sole province of the dying person. Those who suffer the loss of loved ones are themselves deeply grieved. Grief is a universal reaction to loss or separation, and, as you recall from the discussion of attachment theory, it takes a number of behavioral forms, such as active distress, protest, and searching for the lost attachment figure. Grief has been described with great poignancy from the earliest times by philosophers, poets, and religious leaders. It has been memorialized in song and codified in ritual. Grief is often so unsettling to observe that it elicits from others a desire to give comfort and solace. Many religious and secular customs have grown up around the grieving process in an attempt to help people survive the rigors of suffering and to give meaning to death. Culture also plays a role in determining how grief is expressed, for example, as an emotional versus a physical set of symptoms (Kleinman & Kleinman, 1985). Box 15.3 describes various rituals from different cultures that demonstrate some of the diversity in people's beliefs about, and experiences with, death.

Helping professionals are often called upon to offer support to people who have experienced the loss of loved ones. An extensive clinical folklore has developed, primarily about the ways that grief should be expressed and the best ways to help people express it. In the 1980s, a vibrant debate commenced when researchers began to question the lack of empirical support for many of these traditionally accepted assumptions about grief. A number of inconsistencies or "myths" about grieving were uncovered in the process (Wortman & Silver, 1989, 2001), and researchers and clinicians have since continued this important dialogue. What follows is a discussion of some classic approaches to grief, an examination of some of the major tenets of bereavement counseling, and a brief summary of evidence from recent studies.

CLASSIC APPROACHES TO BEREAVEMENT

Freud's (1917/1957) theorizing about grief and mourning was very influential in shaping the legacy that came to be known as grief work. In simple terms, Freud believed that individuals who lose a loved one (or object) must withdraw their emotional attachments or energy (or libido) and detach (or decathect) from the lost object. Loss causes great pain, and bereaved people, Freud believed, inevitably need to struggle with the process of letting go. As manifestations of their mourning, they may lose interest in the world, prefer to isolate themselves from others, dwell on thoughts of the deceased, and suffer from depression. Gradually, the reality of loss is accepted. From Freud's perspective, successful resolution involves decathecting, or detaching emotionally, from the former relationship and reinvesting psychic energy into the formation of new attachments.

Freud presented these theoretical ideas on mourning well in advance of some important deaths that were to occur in his own personal life. The loss of his daughter at age 25 and of his grandson at age 4 affected him greatly. He wrote that his life was permanently altered by these enormous losses and that, although acute grief may subside, people "remain unconsolable and will never find a substitute" (Freud, 1929/1961, p. 239). These words suggest that Freud, in his later years, recognized that one does not necessarily recover from grief nor cut the cords of old attachments. However, his earlier notion that active grieving leads to recovery is one idea that he never formally revised and one that has permeated the canon of grief counseling. Other assumptions, that successful resolution of grief necessitates detachment from lost loved ones and reinvestment in other relationships and that abnormal mourning may follow from conflicted relationships, have also influenced clinical practice.

Bowlby's (1969/1982, 1980) highly influential construction of the bereavement process, based on attachment theory, depicts his view of typical human reactions to the experience of separation from or loss of attachment figures. The theory was initially developed to describe the responses of children temporarily separated from their caregivers (see Chapter 4, Box 4.2) and was later adapted to describe permanent separation, or bereavement, in adults. Bowlby's description of various reactions to separation gave rise to popular stage conceptions of dying, such as those of Kubler-Ross (Archer, 1999).

Bowlby's description of the grieving process includes four phases. At first, the loss is met by disbelief, a phase Bowlby called shock. The grieving person may experience

MyLab Education
Video Example 15.5
Bob, age 81, describes losing his 25-year-old daughter. Two of her siblings discuss the experience of learning about their sister's death, and they describe dealing with the loss individually and as a family. How do Bob and his children differ in their bereavement process?

Box 15.3: Funeral Rituals in Different Cultures

In virtually every culture, distinct funeral rituals have evolved that are fascinating reflections of people's beliefs about death. Social anthropologists suggest that these rituals serve to bind a culture together by expressing its "collective representations" about fundamental issues such as life, death, and spirituality (Robben, 2017). To illustrate the diversity of beliefs and the many ways of demonstrating grief, we present a look at funeral practices in four cultures: the Chinese of San Francisco's Chinatown (Crowder, 1999; Hill, 1992), the Luo of Kenya (Nyamongo, 1999), traditional Jewish families (Schindler, 1996), and the San Francisco gay community during the last decades of the 20th century (Richards, Wrubel, & Folkman, 1999–2000).

For the Chinese, a funeral signifies the important transition from family member to ancestor, that beneficent spirit who will look out for the family's well-being from the spirit world. The connection between living family members and their ancestors is so important that, prior to the mid-20th century, Chinese immigrants living in the United States routinely returned their dead to China to be buried next to other family members. The Chinese community in San Francisco practiced elaborate traditional rituals, complete with funeral processions and brass bands. Funerals drew large groups of family members and friends, and they provided an occasion to tell the world about the accomplishments of the deceased. So fundamentally important was this practice that funerals in the Chinese province of Gansu were held *before* the person dies, so that he could be present to hear about the good things he had accomplished in his lifetime (2001, N. Zhang, personal communication).

Chinese funerals in San Francisco may incorporate Christian or Buddhist elements into a ceremony that traditionally consists of five parts: the visit, the service, the procession, the burial, and the dinner. The visit, or wake, allows visitors to view the body of the deceased. Near the body are placed a portrait of the dead person, usually framed with flowers, and items of food, such as chicken, vegetables, rice, and tea, intended to sustain the soul of the person through the journey to the afterlife. Various items such as jewelry, money, and clothing are placed in the coffin for his use as well. The funeral service, usually held the day after the visit, includes prayers and a eulogy. The funeral procession consists of a hearse, the funeral cortege, and a band, which plays hymns and other traditional music. On its way to the cemetery, the procession typically stops at the deceased's home or place of business. The portrait of the dead person is then taken from the hearse and set up facing the building. The mourners bow to pay their respects and may toss "spirit money," pieces of white paper in the shape of bills that are intended to placate malevolent spirits, into the air. Some relatives and friends await the procession at the house and greet the spirit of the ancestor with offerings of food, incense, and candles. At the gravesite, members of the funeral party, males first, followed by females, toss dirt, flowers, coins, or rice into the grave. The ritual is concluded with a formal seven-course meal, because seven is the number for death. At the center of each table is a cup of white rice liquor in honor of the departed.

The Luo live in the western part of Kenya near Lake Victoria. They, like the Chinese, believe that a person who dies becomes transformed from an earthly member of the family into a spiritual one. The funeral ritual is a transformative rite of passage. Death among the Luo is marked by a funeral fire, which is kept burning for approximately one week. The body of a deceased male is prepared by the men of the same clan and lies in state for 4 days, while that of a deceased woman lies in state for 3. After the burial, animals are slaughtered at the site of the funeral fire. Their numbers and kind depend upon the socioeconomic status of the deceased. Relatives and neighbors might contribute some animals for slaughter, knowing that the same will be done for them in their time of bereavement.

During the period of mourning, the sons of the deceased keep company around the fire. Their wives stay together in the house of the deceased, avoiding any sexual contact because of their belief that sexual relations will cause the death of their own sons. The widow of a deceased man is inherited by the dead man's brother, thus transferring her care to another relative and giving him the benefit of an additional laborer.

Traditional Jewish funeral practices emphasize honoring the deceased as well as giving the bereaved time and freedom to grieve. Jewish law is very sensitive to the emotional pain experienced by grieving persons and structures rituals to provide explicit comfort for them. During the funeral service, an emotional eulogy encourages mourners to vent their feelings by crying. A similarly cathartic release is elicited during the recitation of the *Kaddish*, or ritual prayer. Flowers are not customarily given in this cultural tradition because they signify happiness, an emotion that is discordant with the painfulness of death.

Throughout the period of mourning, called *Aninut*, great care is taken to support the bereaved. Jewish law indicates that those who have experienced a loss should be exempt from normal religious obligations, such as studying the scriptures. Customs such as *Kreiah*, or the ritual tearing of garments and the breaking of a shard on the lintel of the deceased's house, provide religious sanctions for outward displays of anger and sadness during the time of mourning. The period of *Shiva*, a 7-day mourning period, is dedicated to visiting and consoling the bereaved. Providing emotional comfort and social support for the survivors is viewed as an important religious obligation that helps to move people beyond the pain of their loss to a state of acceptance. Once the official 12-month grieving period is over, the *Kaddish* prayer is recited again, and excessive outward displays of mourning are expected to cease.

A relatively new culture—that of the gay community in San Francisco—developed its own ways of dealing with bereavement due to the unfortunate increase in HIV/AIDS-related deaths in that community. Because many members of this community died in hospice or home settings, their dying often took the form of a vigil. Family and friends attended the dying person, keeping him as comfortable as possible while saying their good-byes. After death, rituals such as bathing and dressing the body honored the wishes of the deceased and allowed the bereaved to feel connected to the loved one. Photos could be placed around the bedside, and valued objects, such as letters or items of religious significance, were placed near the body. Funeral services could combine elements of formal religious rites with those that signified some personal meaning. For example, planting trees in the loved one's memory, burning incense, playing music, and so forth might be incorporated into the service.

These examples, although certainly not exhaustive, emphasize the healing function of rituals, either traditional ones or those that are newly created. Whatever their type or origin, regardless of their religious or cultural underpinnings, rituals appear to draw people together in their encounter with death. They give voice to fears and to sadness, and they signify love and respect for the persons who have died.

numbness or feelings of unreality. Emotions may be blunted, and some individuals may even appear unaffected by the loss. Others may display emotional outbursts or may experience dizziness or other physical symptoms. The sense of disbelief eventually subsides when the reality of loss sets in. A second phase, protest, follows. Bereaved individuals may experience periods of obsessive yearning or searching for the lost loved one as well as bouts of restlessness or irritability.

The subsequent period, called despair, may be characterized by great sadness; social withdrawal; sleeping, eating, or somatic disturbances; and other symptoms of depression or emotional upset. People may experience flashbacks or intrusive memories of the deceased. They may actively seek support from others by telling and retelling the story of their loss. Yet, as with a child whose attachment figure has left him, the comfort of others cannot replace the presence of the lost loved one. Gradually, the bereaved person begins to adjust to the loss. Bowlby used the term reorganization to describe the last phase of grieving a permanent separation. Taking a position in opposition to Freud's, Bowlby believed that bereaved individuals do not decathect, or detach, from their lost loved ones. Instead, they discover ways to hold on to the memory of the deceased and integrate that memory into their current life and new attachments. They heal, in part, by drawing comfort from the sense of the deceased person's presence (Fraley & Shaver, 1999).

ASSUMPTIONS ABOUT GRIEF WORK AND EMPIRICAL SUPPORT

As we have noted, a number of assumptions about bereavement, many derived from classic theories such as these, have been reexamined in the light of new evidence and cross-cultural information. One of the most prevalent myths is that people need to deal with their loss, by confronting the pain in an active way, for healing to occur. Avoiding the sadness, it is assumed, leads to later emotional problems. The tenets of grief work explicitly encourage bereaved individuals to confront and "work through" their feelings about loss so recovery can take place (Parkes & Weiss, 1983; Stroebe, 1992). This process, often facilitated by therapeutic intervention, might involve reflecting upon one's relationship to the deceased, expressing anger and other negative emotions related to the death, questioning and trying to construct meaning from the death, and ultimately resigning oneself to the loss. Unexpressed grief and unexamined loss, which have not been integrated into one's revised view of the world and the self, are thought to place the bereaved person's long-term physical and psychological well-being at risk. Another assumption is that the normal grieving process evolves in a sequence of stages that take a usually brief but arbitrarily determined period of time, such as 6 months to a year, to complete.

Those studies that have investigated the existence of stages in bereavement find little evidence to support the belief that people grieve in a linear, predictable fashion (van der Waal, 1989–1990; Wortman & Silver, 1987). Although many people do report initial shock and, later, some measure of reorganization, the intervening process does not necessarily follow in a clear sequence of compartmentalized, independent reactions. There is also a great deal of confusion over how long the manifestations of grief should persist before the grief is judged "abnormal." Previous diagnostic criteria (American Psychiatric Association, *DSM IV-TR*, 2000, p. 740) indicated that a clinician may consider a diagnosis of major depression if the depressive symptoms attendant to bereavement persist beyond 2 months. However, it is common for people to show grief symptoms much longer than 2 months. Several studies report gradual declines in depressive symptoms within the first 2 years after loss (Middleton, Raphael, Burnett, & Martinek, 1997; Stroebe & Stroebe, 1993), but depression may persist even longer (Galatzer-Levy & Bonanno, 2012), particularly if the circumstances surrounding the death have been especially traumatic. Such findings have led to criteria for use in the diagnosis of complicated or abnormal grief that allow for longer periods of normal grieving (Horowitz et al., 1997).

Controversy surrounds the decision to allow a diagnosis of depression 2 weeks after bereavement (DSM-5, 2013). At issue is the distinction between normal and complicated (also called chronic, unresolved, pathological) grieving and the decision to treat it as depression needing medication (Zachar, First, & Kendler, 2017). Abnormal grief was viewed by Bowlby (1980) as grief that is either excessive and protracted or absent. At one end of the continuum is chronic grief, which, like a preoccupied attachment, is marked by persistent yearning, anxiety, and unremitting distress. This type of mourning immobilizes bereaved individuals and prevents their return to normal functioning. Absence of grieving, on the other end of the continuum, was viewed by Bowlby and others (Deutch, 1937; Parkes, 1965) as a maladaptive defense against the trauma of loss. In this response, characteristic of a highly avoidant attachment pattern, bereaved individuals suppress grief and try to exclude frightening and painful feelings from consciousness. Despite the lack of consistency in empirical support, the concept of abnormal grief has been accepted in clinical practice (Barlé, Wortman, & Latack, 2017). It is widely assumed that people should demonstrate great distress after a loss and that failure to do so is abnormal, a condition often called the "requirement of mourning" (Wright, 1983).

In general, some recent research has failed to find support for the assumption that to adjust successfully, all people need to work through loss in the highly cathartic fashion advised by advocates of grief work. Contrary to what helping professionals might expect, a certain amount of detachment during the grieving process predicts healthy recovery for some bereaved individuals. Bonanno and Keltner (1997; see also Bonanno & Kaltman, 1999 for a review) provide data demonstrating that minimizing expression of negative emotions can offer some benefit to the bereaved. In this study of individuals whose spouses had died, the remaining partners who manifested a high degree of emotional distress (fear, anger, disgust, and the like) at 6 months after their loss continued to report poorer outcomes after 2 years. Those individuals who had lower initial levels of distress had better health and lower levels of grief after 2 years. Similarly, in a study designed to explore the coping styles of bereaved individuals, Bonanno and his colleagues (Bonanno, Znoj, Siddique, & Horowitz, 1999) reported that some detachment or emotional dissociation was not related to the development of later adjustment problems but was, in fact, predictive of positive outcomes. Neimeyer (2000) concludes from an examination of research that the use of grief-focused interventions with individuals who are not highly distressed risks doing them harm.

Other studies of bereaved individuals (Lund et al., 1985–1986; Vachon et al., 1982), of parents whose babies died from SIDS (Wortman & Silver, 1987), and of individuals who experienced spinal cord injuries (Dinardo, 1971) showed similar results. Those individuals who demonstrated the highest levels of distress initially were also most distressed and less effective in coping with the loss up to several years later. Individuals who showed lower levels of initial distress were generally better adjusted later and were not more likely to experience delayed grief reactions. One conceptual explanation for these findings draws on the framework of individual differences in attachment representations. Specifically, adjustment to loss may be less difficult for individuals whose emotional systems can be deactivated more easily (avoidant) than for those who have difficulty suppressing emotions (ambivalent) (Fraley & Shaver, 1999). Another hypothesis is linked to gender. For example, one study demonstrated that females gave priority to sharing feelings after a loss, while males viewed problem-solving approaches as more important (Hopmeyer & Werk, 1994). Also, extreme levels of distress might indicate longstanding difficulties in emotion regulation or stress system activation. Certainly, much more research is needed to understand fully the significance of individual differences in grieving.

Overall, the evidence presented above should not be interpreted to suggest that outward signs of distress are necessarily unhealthy. Each side of an either-or argument is problematic. Just as a prescription to demonstrate intense grief is not right for everyone, neither is the advice to remain stoic. What we need to understand are the mechanisms that might explain individual differences in grief reactions, in hopes of constructing a more comprehensive theory of grieving. For those who take the stoic approach, perhaps it is not simply detachment, or the temporary psychic space it provides, but also the restricted focus on loss that makes for better overall adjustment. The traditional advice of grief work, which is to confront pain head-on, may be problematic for some people because of the risk of chronically activating systems related to yearning or "pining" for the lost loved one. Rumination, an emotion-focused style of coping, is correlated with poor adjustment. Excessive preoccupation with the deceased or obsessive dwelling on thoughts of pain and sadness may qualify as rumination.

In a longitudinal study of hundreds of bereaved individuals conducted over 18 months, Nolen-Hoeksema and Larson (1999) found that the use of rumination as a way to cope with loss was highly related to depression at each interview point. In addition, people who ruminated tended to have great difficulty finding meaning in the loss, despite the significant amount of time they spent trying to do so. These findings are consistent with the strong association between ruminative coping and depression in general (Nolen-Hoeksema, 1991), and they have been replicated in more recent studies of bereavement, rumination, and depression. It seems that rumination can be detrimental to healthy grieving processes in two different ways: Ruminating can perpetuate distress through negative cognitions, impaired problem solving, and alienation of social support, and it also can serve to distract from challenging aspects of loss, such as its permanency (Eisma & Stroebe, 2017).

You might wonder how a bereaved person can make sense of his loss, another assumed measure of successful grieving, if he does not engage in some rumination. Yet, is it really necessary for people to make sense of the loss to adapt successfully? Davis, Lehman, and Wortman (1997) report that not all people who struggle to make sense of deaths, accidents, illnesses, and other tragedies are able to explain these events in satisfactory ways. Many people do not try to do so, preferring to move ahead with their lives without searching for existential or philosophical meaning.

Davis and his associates (Davis, Wortman, Lehman, & Silver, 2000) reported very consistent findings from several studies that investigated the benefits of meaning-making for later adjustment. In general, individuals who were able to derive meaning from the event relatively early on were least distressed at follow-up interviews. Interestingly, those who were able to find something positive in the experience or who were able to reappraise the loss to extract some benefit from it were the best adjusted. Religious or spiritual beliefs often helped people find meaning in the loss. However, others found that loss precipitated a cascade of doubts about faith because it shattered their views of a just world. Those who did not initiate a search for meaning were also found to have relatively good adjustments. It was the group that struggled for meaning without finding it that suffered most in this study.

Nolen-Hoeksema and Larson (1999) reported significant associations in their bereavement study between the tendency to ruminate and the inability to find meaning in the experience of loss. The highest level of distress at follow-up interviews was demonstrated by the group that struggled continually to make sense of the inexplicable. Certain contextual circumstances may make it more difficult for people to find meaning or benefits from the deaths of loved ones. Among these kinds of deaths are those that occur suddenly (Ingles, Spinks, Yeates, McGeechan, Kasparian, & Semsarian, 2016); deaths of children (Arnold & Gemma, 2008); deaths due to intentional, malicious causes such as homicide (Williams & Rheingold, 2015); and deaths due to the negligence of others, such as those involving motor vehicle accidents (Pearlman, Wortman, Feuer, Farber, & Rando, 2014). Some measure of restitution made by the perpetrators of these acts can be beneficial in reducing the bereaved families' distress and promoting resolution of grief (Davis et al., 2000).

AN INTEGRATED PERSPECTIVE ON GRIEF

As research in this area increases, more sophisticated models of grieving have been developed (Rubin, Witztum, & Malkinson, 2017). One such model that weaves together

FIGURE 15.7 A dual-process model of coping with loss pathways.

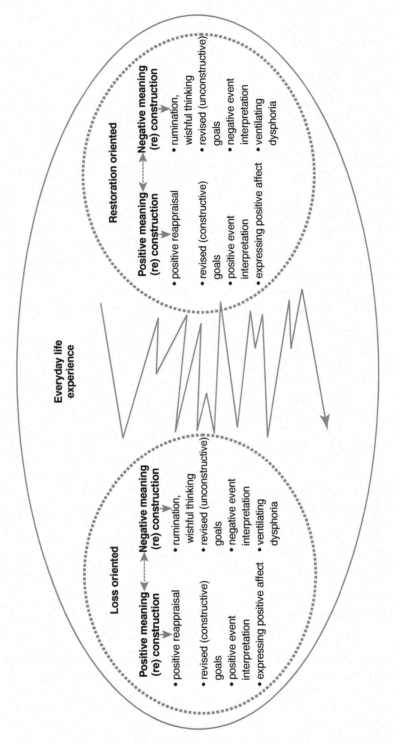

SOURCE: Based on Stroebe, M. S., & Schut, H. (2001). Model of coping with bereavement: A review. In M. S. Stroebe, R. O Hansson, W. Stroebe & H. Schut (Eds.), *Handbook of bereavement research: Consequences, coping, and care* (p. 397).

some of the theoretical and empirical threads described above is the **dual-process model** proposed by Stroebe and Schut (1999; 2010). This conceptualization depicts an interplay of stressors and coping strategies within a flexible, oscillating framework. Specifically, the authors propose that bereaved individuals simultaneously engage in two kinds of coping mechanisms, approach and avoidance, that wax and wane over the course of grieving.

Approach tendencies are reflected in activities synonymous with grief work: confronting the painful reality of death, expressing sadness, and gradually desensitizing oneself to the reminders of loss. Approach tendencies can be tolerated for only so long. They represent loss-focused grief and can lead to rumination or excessive preoccupation and, often, great distress. According to the dual-process model, the loss-focused work of grieving is balanced by parallel activities that represent restoration-focused grief. This type of coping strategy is directed towards handling the practical tasks that need to be undertaken to carry on with daily life. For example, a widow might experience intense periods of grief during which she focuses on memories of her life with her deceased spouse; however, she might also have dependent children who need care. Attending to their needs serves as a distraction, mitigating the periods of loss-related distress. Both loss and restoration coping strategies are part of the grieving process, and Stroebe and Schut view their dynamic oscillation as a healthy regulatory mechanism. Bereaved individuals go back and forth between emotion-focused (loss-oriented) and problem-focused (restoration-oriented) modes of coping. This approach-avoidance interplay protects bereaved individuals from the exacting extremes of unrelieved distress or rigid mental suppression. In general, there is more loss-oriented coping early in the grieving process and more restoration-oriented coping at later points. Traditional conceptions of abnormal grief can be viewed as "disturbances of oscillation" (Stroebe & Schut, 2010, p. 285), either overly loss oriented or excessively avoidant. Figure 15.7 presents a diagram of the dual-process model of coping.

MyLab Education Self-Check 15.2

Applications

This chapter presents information about some key ways people change in later life and how they adapt to or cope with those changes. Coping has been defined as a person's "cognitive and behavioral efforts to manage (reduce, minimize, master, or tolerate) the internal and external demands of the person–environment transaction that is appraised as taxing or exceeding the resources of the person" (Folkman, Lazarus, Gruen, & DeLongis, 1986, p. 572). Adaptive coping, or managing the demands of life relatively well, is at the heart of achieving and maintaining optimal health and wellness. This is certainly true at any age, but perhaps even more so in old age, when the threat of overtaxed resources and the need to tolerate limitations becomes inevitable. Life involves gains and losses. It is naïve to assume that everyone can and will maintain a high quality of life right up to their death. But on the other hand, unnecessarily pessimistic views of old age, fueled by negative stereotypes of older adults, restrict the ways people choose to adapt to aging and limit their sense of control over their lives.

Helpers who are knowledgeable about and skilled in understanding coping mechanisms can promote healthy adaptation, regardless of client age (Ponzo, 1992). Helpers also can advocate within their own professions and other healthcare systems to reduce specific barriers related to negative age stereotypes that older adults tend to face (Nelson, 2016). For example, negative age stereotypes held by healthcare providers can result in the view that older patients are "bothersome," and can lead to older adults receiving different treatments or fewer treatments when their health concerns are dismissed as inevitable due to aging processes. Helpers can seek opportunities to educate families and healthcare providers on the damaging impacts of these aging stereotypes, and also can support older adult clients in advocating for their own care. Furthermore, sources of concrete information about how to cope with getting old (Butler, 2009), how to understand the perspective of elders (Pipher, 1999), and how to deal with dementia (Mace & Rabins, 1999) can help clinicians build their foundation of knowledge. Whitbourne (1989) summarizes the task:

The main point that a clinician must keep foremost in mind when working with an aging client is the need to be flexible. The aging process involves multiple physical, psychological, and social demands that can all potentially impact on the individual's ability to function. Clinicians may be called upon to perform advocacy services, environmental interventions, and interdisciplinary consultations, which they would not ordinarily regard as falling within the domain of "psychotherapy." It is only by maintaining an open approach to the multiple needs of the aged client that the clinician can hope to bring about successful change. (p. 168)

A Good Fit: Adaptations for Professionals

Myers and Harper (2004) offer useful suggestions for clinicians who work with older clients. In general, helpers who work with this population may be younger than their clients. Consequently, more time and sensitivity are required to build rapport with individuals who may be less comfortable with sharing feelings or with asking questions of "authority" figures. Younger professionals also need to be prepared to deal nondefensively with older clients who might view them as unable to understand the lived experience of old age. Lengthening the sessions in individual counseling and increasing the number of sessions

for support groups or other group therapy formats is more important in reducing relapse for older clients than for younger ones. Psychological treatments should be modified as well. Many typical counseling approaches can be accommodated to meet the needs of older clients (Gellis & Kenaley, 2008; Kennedy & Tanenbaum, 2000). Some of these modifications have been summarized in Table 15.6.

The flexibility described by Whitbourne above should extend to the physical environment in which counseling is provided. For example, older clients may have physical limitations that affect their ability to sit for long periods or may need modifications to assessment procedures due to hearing or vision problems. Lyness (2004) advises medical and counseling professionals who work with an older population to screen routinely for depression and other mental health issues because mental health concerns can be the underlying cause of many other presenting problems, and can complicate assessment and treatment for comorbid conditions.

At the end of life, helping professionals can bring a real advantage to patient care: well-honed communication skills. Patient-centered communication that blends empathic listening with provision of information appears to offer patients the greatest support. What are the skills helpers need for delivering bad news when it is

TABLE 15.6 Therapeutic Adaptations for Older Clients

TYPE OF THERAPY	EXAMPLES OF TARGET THERAPEUTIC OUTCOMES	SOME ADAPTATIONS FOR OLDER CLIENTS
Brief Psychodynamic	Resolving survivor guilt; reducing negative attitudes towards self related to aging.	Recognition and skillful handling of age-specific transference issues (e.g., client's view that younger therapist is inexperienced and unable to help).
Cognitive Behavioral	Changing dysfunctional thoughts; active problem solving.	Understanding of older clients' learning styles; recognition of cognitive and sensory impairments that might interfere with learning; use of concrete written material and practice.
Behavioral Therapy for Depression	Improving mood through increasing positive reinforcement.	Provision of methodical and concrete approaches to identify and engage in positive, mood-enhancing experiences and systematically avoid unpleasant experiences.
Interpersonal Therapy for Depression	Improving interpersonal relationships through time-limited approach to problem solving using therapist as supportive resource.	Active therapeutic stance that focuses on solving real problems within the context of old age; provision of ample social support.
Life Review or Reminiscence Therapy	Finding meaning in life at present by reflecting on and integrating past conflicts.	Empathic listening that provides a context for a review of the past; review of memorabilia like photographs, journals, and writing exercises.
Problem-Solving Therapy	Finding ways to view problems more realistically and solve them more effectively.	Careful listening to client's problems, empathy, encouragement and support for trying new solution in a personal context.
Group Therapy	Addressing multiple needs of older clients, particularly clients in institutionalized settings.	Screening of participants to ensure a relatively high degree of homogeneity in cognitive and sensory functioning; provision of structured format; ample positive reinforcement of group members; timing of meeting in midmorning to early afternoon.

SOURCE: Based on Kennedy, G. J. & Tanenbaum, S. (2000). Psychotherapy with older adults. *American Journal of Psychotherapy, 54*, 386–407.

needed? It's important to remember that delivering such life-altering news can be very stressful for professionals who are called upon to communicate it. So, awareness of one's own response to dying and understanding of best practices in this area can be useful. Practicing self-care and compassion for oneself as well as for clients and their families is a powerful resource. Barclay, Blackhall, and Tulsky (2007) offer a very helpful review of key considerations for culturally appropriate communication of difficult information. It's critical for helpers to understand that not everyone wants to hear the same amount of information about prognosis, symptoms, and so forth. Sometimes patients' wishes for information are different from those of their families. Carefully inquiring about how much information is desired as the dialogue unfolds is a good practice. Sometimes separate conversations are indicated, provided that information can be delivered consistently. When prognosis is poor, helpers can help support realistic expectations by discussing ways to manage symptoms, providing emotional support, and connecting the patient and family with resources rather than offering unrealistic promises.

Cultures differ with respect to how directly bad news should be delivered, and it is essential for helpers to be sensitive to cultural norms in this regard. "Here the difference is *not only* about whether to tell the truth, but also about *what it means to tell.* Learning the truth in a more indirect way may be seen as preferable because the ambiguity allows the patient the possibility of hope" (Barclay et al., 2007, p. 963). In general, prior preparation of advance directives can provide an opportunity for discussing preferences for truth-telling while individuals are still healthy. Difficult information should be conveyed with language and pacing that supports patients' understanding. Communication should be caring yet straightforward. The authors suggest pausing to check for comprehension after every three facts. Summarizing the conversation aids understanding as well. Planning for continuing care that includes that patient and/or family can help convey the reality of continuing support through the process.

Healthy Aging and Prevention

The amount of research on aging continues to grow, due, at least in part, to the aging of the world's population. One wave of research is focused on "successful aging," a perspective that assumes that healthy functioning and even the achievement of certain gains is possible in late life. One such initiative is a series of studies called the MacArthur study because of the financial support provided by the John D. and Catherine T. MacArthur Foundation (Rowe & Kahn, 1998). The fruits of 10 years of intensive investigations involving thousands of participants, millions of dollars, and the combined expertise of biologists, neuropsychologists, sociologists, epidemiologists, geneticists, and gerontologists, among others, tell us a great deal about successful aging.

To summarize briefly, enjoying a healthy and productive old age is possible. The more physically and mentally fit older individuals are, the more likely they will age successfully. Clearly, one's lifestyle prior to old age can have a tremendous influence on the quality of later life. A healthy diet and regular exercise, including aerobics and weight training, confers a real physical advantage. Although maintaining healthy habits provides protection from disease and should, ideally, be maintained consistently, the MacArthur study revealed that positive changes in eating and exercise habits, even in old age, can help people live longer and healthier lives. Furthermore, recent research indicates that moderate amounts of physical activity can slow or reduce impacts of cognitive aging. Equally important to successful aging are social relationships. It turns out that older people benefit more from emotional than instrumental support in many cases. So, while it can be very helpful to offer assistance with housecleaning, providing a listening ear may go farther to promote a patient's well-being.

A sense of being productive also is associated with healthy aging. Healthy men and women are three times more likely than those with physical or mental health problems to be engaged in paid work or volunteer activities. However, as we have seen, even people with physical limitations often manage, with some creativity, to engage in activities that keep them in touch with the world. Productive engagement with others, in whatever form it takes, is linked to a sense of mastery or personal self-efficacy. A "can-do" attitude contributes enormously to well-being. Professionals can facilitate the development of self-efficacy by fashioning opportunities for older individuals that reflect their self-endorsed goals and that challenge their capacities without overwhelming them. Helpers also need to provide encouragement to older people to engage in these challenges, give confirming feedback for mastery, and help dispel negative stereotypes that lead to passivity and hopelessness.

MyLab Education
Video Example 15.6
Through her volunteer work in the community, Marie, at age 92, feels productive and remains socially engaged.

When Losses Occur

What should we do to help when the losses of later life occur? Based on recent longitudinal studies, several principles appear to be important. Helping professionals should be aware that grief has many affective, behavioral, and physical manifestations, and that there is wide variation in expressions of mourning at the level of the individual and culture. The oversimplified use of stage theories may suggest that there is one correct way to grieve and one circumscribed time frame in which to do so. One can only imagine how discouraging it must be for a bereaved person to be told that she is not grieving correctly. In our fast-paced world, it is often difficult to let people take the time they need to heal. Helpers should not hold prescriptive rules for how long grief should last, because many people continue to grieve well beyond the limits of several months or even years.

Remember as well that the absence of overt, intense grief is not necessarily problematic. Not everyone who fails to demonstrate great distress or who does not search for meaning in a loss will suffer eventual emotional problems. Furthermore, we often expect people to "recover" from a loss by returning to an earlier level of functioning, despite evidence that this is often impossible.

Difficulties in the grief process may be considered to be an imbalance between too much expression and too little, but even this is mediated by personality, gender, culture, and beliefs. Some interventions that have traditionally been favored by helping professionals, such as active grief work interventions, may not be useful and may actually cause more distress for individuals given to ruminative tendencies. Even support seeking, a style of coping that involves seeking help from other people, may be a source of stress unless those sought after for help are themselves compassionate and willing to listen (Nolen-Hoeksema & Larson, 1999). Efforts to personalize interventions depending upon needs and characteristics of clients are important.

Several sets of tasks have been developed that describe the responsibilities of helpers or other caregivers in times of bereavement (Rando, 1993; Worden, 1982). The following is a brief description of Worden's tasks with evidence-based recommendations derived from the bereavement coping project of Nolen-Hoeksema and Larson (1999). Keep in mind that bereaved individuals differ in their needs, so these recommendations should be considered general guidelines.

1. Bereaved individuals may need support in order to accept the reality of loss. Providing assistance with funeral arrangements and helping to prepare meals or clean up are all useful ways to be of help. It is important not to "push" the person to accept the loss, but to be respectful of the individual's style of coping.

2. Helpers and other loved ones should allow bereaved persons to identify and express feelings if they want to do so. Judicious use of open-ended questions and provisional language ("Sometimes people say that they occasionally feel anxious or impatient. I wonder if you ever feel that way?" Nolen-Hoeksema & Larson, 1999, p. 182) can promote feelings of safety and acceptance.

3. Bereaved persons need to learn how to live without their lost loved ones. For example, they may need to learn restoration-focused tasks previously handled by the deceased, such as managing finances or cooking for children. The helper can scaffold the development of these skills by anticipating possible needs, helping to break them down into manageable tasks, and providing concrete assistance or information.

4. Survivors may need help in finding a place in their lives for the deceased. This may take many forms, depending upon the individual, but generally entails finding a way to maintain some emotional connection. For some people, talking about the deceased is easier and more beneficial than talking about themselves. Silverman (2000) noticed in her work with bereaved children that they were much more articulate when asked to talk about the person who died than they were when asked to talk about their own feelings about the death. She called this process *constructing a relationship to the deceased.*

5. The next task for helpers requires them to be patient and allow time and a nurturing context for grieving. It's worth considering very carefully the risks and benefits of treating grief as an illness that needs medication. While this may surely be advisable in certain cases, it's also possible to turn what is an expectable reaction to loss into a disorder. "Medicalizing normal grief stigmatizes and reduces the normalcy and dignity of the pain, short-circuits the expected existential processing of the loss, reduces reliance on the many well-established cultural rituals for consoling grief, and would subject many people to unnecessary and potentially harmful medication treatment" (Francis, 2010, p. 46).

6. Helpers may need to help normalize grief for the bereaved. Grieving people often report fears about "going crazy" because of symptoms such as visual or sensory hallucinations, panic attacks, and other signs of intense distress. Learning that these are common occurrences in bereavement that will go away in time is very reassuring.

7. Helpers should provide continuing support, as needed, to help survivors weather the trials of grieving and to assist them in examining the effectiveness or ineffectiveness of their coping strategies. Taking notice of strategies that are effective is an empowering exercise because it allows people to recognize that they have some choice. Strategies that are less helpful can be identified, and more useful possibilities can be suggested.

8. Finally, helpers need to identify and find other sources of support if they, for whatever reason, cannot provide for the range of needs described above.

Integrity: The Life Cycle Completed

From Erikson's (1950/1963) perspective, people struggle continuously throughout the life cycle with the "hazards of existence" (p. 274) and should not expect to reach a level of achievement in any of the stages that is completely impervious to conflict. The negative pole of each developmental task represents its counterpoint, a reminder of each stage's dynamic quality (see Chapter 1, Table 1.2). The period of old age is no exception. Facing old age and death are awesome challenges. Yet over a lifetime, the struggles of earlier stages ideally bear fruit. The resulting integrity, that sense of coherence or wholeness that comes from "acceptance of *one's own and only life cycle* [italics added]" (p. 268) is the product of strengths accumulated from each earlier period: hope, self-control, direction, love, devotion, affiliation, and care. Renunciation, the outcome of the final stage according to Erikson, is consummate generativity. It embodies acceptance of the natural order, namely that wisdom which allows us to view death as a stage of life. "Healthy children will not fear life," Erikson wrote, "if their elders have integrity enough not to fear death" (p. 269).

Erikson's view of the life span, then, is less of a straight line and more of a circle, with its final stage a gift of courage and caring for the generations that follow. In his psychosocial view of development, the quality of life from beginning to end is touched by its social intersections. As we are learning, positive relationships keep people well (Ryff & Singer, 2000); they offer long-term protective factors. Nurturing others, so necessary for survival of our species,

returns on the investment at the end of life when we receive others' care. As we age, some have suggested the need to reminisce or review life events as a way of integrating the features of one's identity and achieving integrity (Butler, 1963; Kaminsky, 2014). Part of the benefit of this process, undoubtedly, involves sharing the story with others.

We have provided throughout this text descriptions of various aspects of human functioning: attachments, social networks, cognition, brain development, identity, marriage, adaptation, family ties, and aging, among many others. There is much left to learn about these topics and about how that knowledge can be used to benefit individuals and societies. Research agendas promise to improve even further our working knowledge of the life span and to offer potential avenues for best practice. With this knowledge, helping professionals will be in a unique position to foster resilience, to cultivate compassion for themselves and others, and to create conditions that support well-being for all members of the human family in the face of life's challenges.

Summary

Physical, Cognitive, and Socioemotional Change in Late Life

1. Despite the increasing number of losses older people experience as they move into old age (60s and 70s) or into old-old age (80s and 90s), most individuals manage to adapt to old age successfully.

2. As people age, they experience declines in many physical systems, including the immune and sensory systems. Arthritis, particularly osteoarthritis, is especially common.

3. Cognitive change across the life span shows a nuanced pattern of change. Perspectives from longitudinal, cross-sectional, and integrated models describe maintenance or even gains in some crystallized knowledge (representation) but declines in fluid processes (control) mediated by executive functions. Executive functions are typically the first to show decrements in the aging process. Cognitive functioning in old age is related to overall health, and substantial declines in cognitive functioning, known as dementia, are usually due to cardiovascular accidents or disease processes such as Alzheimer's disease. Brain changes associated with dementia can start many years before symptoms become evident. Current thinking implicates both genetic and physiological influences like inflammation on disease progression. Recent advances in research suggest promising approaches to delay or even prevent the onset of dementia, including cognitive training,

physical activity, and general health promotion. Terminal drop or decline refers to a rapid decline in intellectual functioning shortly before death.

4. Studies of autobiographical memory indicate that, contrary to stereotypic notions, older people remember their more recent experiences better than earlier experiences (recency), even though older adults learn new information less efficiently than younger adults. However, if adults are asked about flashbulb memories, especially vivid and personally relevant recollections, their reports are largely about events in their early adulthood, referred to as the reminiscence bump. That is probably why older people often tell stories about their early years.

5. As people age, their network of friends and family members shrinks. Social loss is exacerbated by negative stereotypes about aging that assume all elderly people share certain negative characteristics. These stereotypes can lead to discriminatory or demeaning practices that interfere with positive social interactions. Stereotypes of aging are similar across cultures. Negative self-stereotypes of aging also affect performance and mood of older individuals.

6. Three processes appear to be important for successful development in old age. Selection involves limiting activities to a few that are particularly rewarding. Optimization involves finding ways of enhancing achievement of remaining goals. Compensation involves finding

new means to achieve our ends. Together these processes are called selective optimization with compensation.

7. There are other, similar ways of describing adaptation processes. In self-determination theory, three needs are said to motivate adaptation at any age: autonomy, competence, and relatedness.

8. Another description of techniques for facing challenges emphasizes two broad strategies. Primary-control strategies are attempts to affect the immediate environment and often increase feelings of mastery and self-esteem. Secondary-control strategies are attempts to change ourselves, such as changing goals. If the latter approach allows a person to then take primary control over some stressor, feelings of happiness and well-being are likely to be enhanced.

9. On the whole, older people seem to cope well with the challenges of late life according to their self-reports. They compare positively with younger adults on some aspects of well-being, such as positive relationships and self-acceptance. Reported well-being does decline in later life.

10. Does increased wisdom help the elderly to cope? Wisdom involves superior knowledge, judgment, emotion regulation, and advice-giving with regard to important questions about life. Research indicates that it is somewhat more likely to characterize older rather than younger adults, although wisdom seems to be as much a quality of the individual person as it is of age. Cross-cultural similarities and differences have been observed in wisdom acquisition and expression.

11. As people age, they pay more attention to their feelings, and their emotions are more enhanced and complex. Positive emotions are as common among the old as the young. Negative emotions, except for sadness, occur less often. Emotion regulation seems to improve with age as older adults use more adaptive strategies for coping with daily stressors. On the other hand, rates of clinically important depressive symptoms and incidence of minor depression increase into old age.

Experiencing Loss

12. Elderly people report less anxiety about death than younger people. Dying adults often must deal with others' reluctance to deal with death and may feel lonely and isolated.

13. A good death for most people includes symptom management and care (such as freedom from pain), practical details (such as knowing what to expect), a good patient–professional relationship, and certain psychological attributes (such as maintaining dignity). But many people have very individual needs and desires as well. For example, some people prefer to die at home, but many do not. Palliative care, such as that promoted by the hospice movement, is important to most people.

14. People who sign living wills or advance directives do not necessarily know more about their end-of-life options, although those who have recently cared for a dying patient are more aware.

15. Kubler-Ross described several reactions to dying that are called stages but that do not necessarily occur for all dying adults and do not occur in any fixed sequence: These are denial, anger, bargaining, depression, and acceptance. The dying process is also influenced by the nature of the terminal illness. Knowledge of typical trajectories can improve effectiveness of palliative care.

16. Both Freud and Bowlby proposed influential theories of the grief process. Freud originally believed that bereaved individuals needed to withdraw from the lost loved one and reinvest emotional energy into forming new attachments. Bowlby used attachment theory concepts to describe stages of the grief process: shock, protest, despair, and reorganization. Assumptions derived from these theories have been disputed by contemporary researchers. In particular, the existence of a stage sequence of grief reactions has not been validated. The concept of abnormal grief and the need for cathartic grief work have been called into question as well.

17. Contemporary models of grieving include diverse ways of coping with loss. The dual-process model of Stroebe and Schut incorporates both loss-focused elements and restoration-focused elements within a flexible framework. Current controversies exist regarding whether to treat grief as a form of depression needing medication.

Case Study

Isabelle and her husband Victor lived together for 53 years in a small, close-knit Italian American section of a big city. Victor made a living for the family working as a forklift operator. Isabelle, a stay-at-home mother when her children were young, returned to work as a sales clerk once the youngest two children entered high school. Isabelle enjoyed her years of full-time mothering, but she also loved the social interaction and camaraderie she found in her job. The family has four grown children, Paul, 51, Sophia, 49, and twins Lenore and Joseph, 45. Paul and his wife own and operate a small restaurant in a nearby suburb. They have two young adult children. Sophia, also married with two children, teaches in a middle school about an hour away from her parents' home. Lenore has recently remarried after a divorce. She lives with her second husband and her three children in the city. Joseph is a salesperson who has never married but lives in another state with his longtime partner, Joanne.

At this time, the family is struggling to come to grips with Victor's recent death. After years of robust health, Victor was diagnosed with pancreatic cancer. During the last 4 months of his life, he was in and out of the hospital as his health demanded. Isabelle tried to care for him as best she could, but it was very difficult. The side effects of Victor's treatment protocol left him feeling ill and in need of constant care. The family members tried to help, but the greatest burden fell to Paul because, in this family, the oldest child is perceived to have the most responsibility.

As time went on and it became clear that Victor was dying, Isabelle mentioned to her children that their father had not wanted any extraordinary measures to be used to keep him alive in his final illness. Victor had never put this in writing, but Isabelle was sure of his wishes. Victor's family physician, a deeply religious man, Victor's older brother, and Joseph all strongly disagreed with this plan. They believed that every effort should be made to save Victor's life. One night, Victor lapsed into a coma and was having trouble breathing. Joseph prevailed upon his mother to allow the physician to insert a ventilator. Joseph's siblings were very upset about this turn of events, for they believed it caused their father unnecessary suffering. Victor died several days later.

Now 4 months after the death of her husband, Isabelle is grieving the loss of her spouse. She lives alone but is seriously contemplating asking her son Paul to let her move in with his family. She quit her job at the department store because she felt she was unable to concentrate well enough

to perform in a satisfactory manner. She has been unable to sleep through the night, and her mind keeps returning to memories of Victor during his illness.

Relationships are strained among the children. Neither daughter speaks to Joseph or Joanne because of their disagreement about Victor's care. Joanne believes that Joseph should "move on" and concentrate on her and their life together. Lenore avoids calling her mother because she does not want to hear her repeat the same troubles over and over again. She uses her hectic schedule as a full-time mother as an excuse. Sophia is somewhat more attentive, but she is also uncomfortable listening to her mother's reminiscences. She wants to believe that her mother is still the same vibrant person she has always known, so she discounts the sadness she hears in Isabelle's voice. Paul is overwhelmed by the responsibility he feels for his family, his business, and his mother. He knows his mother is grieving, but he cannot find a way to make her feel better. For her part, Isabelle feels that she has come to the end of her life as well. She believes that she will end up like many of the other lonely widows she knows in her neighborhood.

Discussion Questions

1. What are the emotional and behavioral responses of each person to Victor's death?
2. Identify the stressors that are operating on this family. Distinguish between those that can be controlled and those that cannot be changed. Develop a list of coping strategies that might be useful in dealing with these problems.
3. As a helper, how would you begin to work with this family? With Isabelle?

Practice Using What You Have Learned

> **MyLab Education** Application Example 15.1. Case Study: Helen, Age 81
>
> **MyLab Education** Application Exercise 15.2. Case Study: Adapting to Changes and Challenges Late in Life
>
> **MyLab Education** Application Exercise 15.3. Case Study: Coping with Bereavement

Journal Questions

1. Identify someone you know whom you believe to be aging successfully. Write a letter to this person (to be given or not) describing how you think the person is dealing with growing old and why you admire the person.
2. What would you do if you had only 6 months to live?
3. What kind of ceremony or funeral ritual would you like to have when you die? Why would you choose this particular type of ritual?

4. Interview someone from a culture that is different from your own. Explore attitudes about the elderly, perspectives on aging and death, and end-of-life rituals or practices that are characteristic of this culture. How are they different from your own?

Key Concepts

arthritis (p. 593)
osteoarthritis (p. 593)
telomeres (p. 593)
representations (p. 594)
control (p. 594)
dementia (p. 596)
Alzheimer's disease (AD) (p. 596)
plaques (p. 597)
tangles (p. 597)
amyloid precursor protein (APP) (p. 597)
cerebrovascular accidents (strokes) (p. 597)
multi-infarct dementia (p. 597)
terminal drop (terminal decline) (p. 598)
autobiographical memory (p. 598)
care burden (p. 599)
recency (p. 601)
reminiscence bump (p. 601)
flashbulb memories (p. 601)

age stereotypes (p. 602)
selection (p. 605)
optimization (p. 605)
compensation (p. 605)
selective optimization with compensation (p. 605)
primary control (p. 605)
secondary control (p. 605)
stages of retirement (p. 606)
honeymoon (p. 606)
disenchantment (p. 606)
reorientation (p. 606)
stability (p. 607)
termination (p. 607)
wisdom (p. 608)
end-of-life care (p. 615)
palliative care (p. 616)
hospice movement (p. 616)

refusal of treatment (p. 617)
physician-assisted suicide (p. 617)
active euthanasia (p. 617)
double effect (p. 617)
advance directives (living wills) (p. 617)
grief work (p. 619)
decathecting (p. 619)
shock (p. 619)
protest (p. 621)
despair (p. 621)
reorganization (p. 621)
complicated or abnormal grief (p. 622)
dual-process model (p. 624)
loss-focused grief (p. 625)
restoration-focused grief (p. 625)

Appendix A
A Practitioner's Guide to Psychological Science

Understanding the Scientific Process

We have argued that information gained from scientific research on development is important for helping professionals to know. Yet, practitioners often do not find research results helpful or relevant to the problems they face with their clients. What is going on here? Is scientific work of practical value? It can be, but only if the practitioner understands the scientific process.

Most of us are enculturated to believe that the sciences provide answers to life's conundrums, and sometimes they do. For example, at one time the causes of diseases such as tuberculosis or polio were a mystery, but biological research has now established that microorganisms are the culprits. The path that biologists followed to achieve this insight was a laborious and time-consuming one, with many wrong turns or apparent missteps. Adequate scientific answers almost always are found at the end of similarly circuitous routes. As a result, practitioners closely allied to any scientific field sometimes find that the best scientific information of today can change tomorrow. In addition, scientists may offer competing answers to the same question until enough work has been done on a phenomenon to validate one answer, or some amalgam of previous answers. It is not unusual for practitioners faced with competing scientific "answers" to begin to wonder, "What good is science?"

Let's address this question by first looking at the nature of the scientific process. Then we will examine how practitioners can effectively use science to achieve their goals.

Psychology as the Scientific Study of Human Behavior

The study of human behavior and its associated mental processes—motivations, cognitions, emotions, and so on—is a topic of great interest to most of us, and it is the subject of many disciplines besides the social sciences. Most of the humanities, such as literature, history, and philosophy, are focused primarily on human behavior. What differentiates these disciplines are the *methods* that they use to gain understanding. For example, the study of *literature* is in part the study of human behavior as seen through the eyes of great writers of fiction. Through their literary work, writers share with us their observations and beliefs about human motivation, morality, social functioning, and so on. *History* examines the unfolding of human behavior in past events, lining up the facts that can be uncovered about the actions of real people in earlier times and speculating about the connections between these actions and their underlying causes. *Philosophers* usually focus their attention on human behavior as well, but their preferred method is rational analysis. For example, a particular philosopher may take human language as her subject matter and attempt to analyze its sources and its implications for the operation of the human mind. The social sciences are like these other disciplines in their subject matter, human behavior, but they use different methods—the methods of science.

The Three Steps in Scientific Investigation

Across different scientific disciplines—psychology, biology, physics, or any other science—the subject matter changes, but the general methods are the same. Some specific techniques may vary, adapted to the particulars of the topics under scrutiny, but three broad steps are alike for all sciences: description, explanation, and verification.

DESCRIPTION

Description is a research step aimed at answering factual questions about a phenomenon, questions such as who, what, when, where, and with whom. Suppose we were interested in understanding the phenomenon of juvenile delinquency. We would begin our scientific exploration by seeking answers to questions such as the following: *Who* engages in juvenile delinquency? (What are the usual ages, gender, socioeconomic status, family characteristics, intellectual characteristics, academic performance, social skills, personality characteristics, and so on, of children identified as delinquent?) *What* kinds of behaviors usually characterize delinquency? (Are most delinquents truants, or nonviolent thieves, or violent murderers, or other kinds of perpetrators?) *Where* and *when* are delinquent acts most likely to occur? *With whom* are delinquents likely to associate and to commit their evil deeds?

EXPLANATION

With an arsenal of facts gained from descriptive research, we are ready to take the next step, **explanation**. At this point, we frame a *theory* or set of *hypotheses* about *how* the facts are related to each other and *why* they occur. Our other theoretical commitments are likely to influence us here. For example, we may tend to make stage assumptions, or we may be more apt to formulate incremental theories. Our theories may be broad in scope, attempting to integrate all the data we've collected, or they may be simple hypotheses, focused on particular aspects of the facts. In formulating a theory, we should meet certain criteria. First, the theory must be *comprehensive*; that is, either it must take into account all of the known facts (for a broad theory) or at least it should not be inconsistent with any of the known facts (for a more simple, focused hypothesis). Second, it must be presented with sufficient clarity that we can make *verifiable predictions* from it.

A note of caution here: It is important to recognize that by definition, a theory or hypothesis is an *inference* rather than an observed fact. Statements about causes are always inferences, because causal relationships cannot be directly observed. We can obtain evidence for them—as you will see in the next step—but we cannot actually *prove* them without a doubt.

VERIFICATION

The gathering of evidence for our theories, or **verification**, is the third step in the scientific method. Verification processes provide means of judging theories *objectively*, on the basis of factual support, rather than *subjectively*, on the basis of how appealing they might be or how well they might fit our biases. At this point again, the scientist turns to research. It is not good enough for a theory to be effective at post hoc explanation, that is, comprehensively explaining the facts we already have. To be really convincing, a theory must generate predictions about events or behaviors that have not yet been observed. Research is designed to test those predictions. If they come true, there is evidence to support the theory. If the predictions fail to come true, there is evidence against the theory. Albert Einstein's theory of relativity revolutionized physics, posing relationships among known facts and suggesting causal processes not previously proposed. It was appealing because it helped explain some findings that had not fit with previous theories. But, like any scientific theory, Einstein's view had to pass the litmus test; could it predict events not previously observed? Despite the abstractness of his principles, the theory did succeed in generating a few predictions about concrete events that had not yet been observed, and these predictions did come true. Thus, Einstein's idea now has the status of being not just a creative explanation of known data, but a theory with supporting evidence.

Suppose, however, that we formulate a theory that sounds good, but its predictions do not come true. Or, as more often happens, some of its predictions come true, and some do not. Or, even more disconcerting, the predictions of our theory come true, but so do the predictions of a very different theory to explain the same phenomenon! This is a situation that drives many students of a science, and allied practitioners, to distraction: scientists providing more than one answer to the same question!

There is a scientific approach to resolving such dilemmas. The next step is to go back to the explanation process, taking the new data we have gained from our verification efforts to craft a new, or at least a modified theory. Then we move forward again to the verification process. Science advances in this fashion, taking the evidence (both pro and con) gathered from testing one theory to help develop a better one, then subjecting the new theory to the same rigorous tests, until eventually we have a theory that encompasses all the known facts and can generate valid predictions.

In our everyday lives, all of us sometimes operate a little like scientists. Suppose there is a phenomenon that concerns us. Perhaps a close friend begins to behave erratically, laughing or grunting inappropriately during conversations, having animated discussions with no one at all, acting irritable or becoming strangely silent. Our first step in confronting this problem is somewhat comparable to the scientist's *description* process. We try to gather more facts about our friend's behavior from coworkers, family, and friends, and we make more observations of our own. Our second step is similar to the scientist's *explanation* process: We try to develop a coherent theory that will explain how these facts fit together and why they are happening at all. Perhaps we hypothesize a schizophrenic breakdown or the onset of a degenerative brain disorder. At this point, however, our approach to our friend's behavior will probably lose its resemblance to the scientific process. Scientists would put all action on hold, make predictions from their theories, and proceed to test the predictions in carefully designed studies (see *Testing Theories Scientifically*). In our everyday lives, however, we are more likely to jump into practical application, such as urging the family to seek medical help. We rarely have the time or the resources to actually verify our theories in systematic ways. We simply act on them and hope that we've made the right guesses. Scientists advance more slowly to action, avoiding practical application until theories are strongly supported by evidence.

Helping professionals, too, use a process closely akin to the scientific method if they follow the tenets of reflective practice. First, as in the scientist's description process, they gather all the information they can about a client and the client's problem. This part of reflective practice includes examining theories and information available from scientific work that might be relevant, as well as considering both standard practices for dealing with similar problems and the practitioner's own experiences. From all of this information, the practitioner formulates hypotheses about the client and about the most appropriate clinical strategy (as in the scientist's explanation process) and then "tests" these hypotheses (as in the scientist's verification process). However, for the practitioner, testing hypotheses occurs in the practice itself, so that, unlike the scientist, helping professionals apply and adjust their hypotheses in the context of practice. In sum, scientifically generated knowledge informs clinical practice not by providing *answers* but by providing *options* for the development of hypotheses that can be tested in application and by suggesting strategies for handling problems.

TESTING THEORIES SCIENTIFICALLY

To understand how scientific research is done, let's consider examples of studies aimed at testing one hypothesis drawn from behaviorist theories in the middle of the last century. The hypothesis was an effort to explain why babies become both more positively responsive to their mothers over time (e.g., smiling more to them than to other people) and why babies seem to become more unwilling to be cared for by others, especially strangers. The argument was that if babies get most of their nurture from their mothers, mothers are rewarding babies' positive social behaviors (smiling and vocalizing) along with babies' more negative help-seeking behaviors (crying). The result, in this view, is that babies *both* learn to behave more socially around their mothers *and* they begin to rely more and more on their mothers to take care of their needs. We will refer to the combination of positive social behaviors and help-seeking as infants' "dependency."

The proposal that "nurturance causes infant dependency" is a simple theory or hypothesis. "Nurturance" is the single postulated cause, or **causal variable**, and "infant dependency" is what is said to be affected by the cause, or the **outcome variable**. Some theories are much more complex, posing more than one cause, suggesting interactions among causes, or speculating about effects on more than one outcome variable. But regardless of how complex a theory becomes, it can be verified only by testing its predictions. There are two general techniques for testing the predictions of any theory—**experiments** and **correlational studies**. These techniques can be as complex as the theories that inspire them, but no matter how complex they become, they are only extensions of the basic experimental or correlational procedures that we will now describe.

Experiments

An experiment is a study in which the researcher purposely changes (or manipulates) the proposed causal variable in order to observe or measure the effects of the manipulation on an outcome variable. In a good experiment, the researcher also takes care that nothing else systematically changes at the same time as the causal variable. This ensures that if the outcome variable does seem to be affected, only the postulated causal variable could be responsible. When a scientist succeeds in eliminating alternative explanations for the changes in the outcome variable, we say that the researcher has exercised *control* over other, possible causes.

When proposed causes of human behavior are put to experimental test, psychologists use standard procedures adapted to the study of people. Rheingold (1956) conducted an experiment to test the hypothesis we have framed as "nurturance causes infant dependency." She studied babies in an orphanage, whose many caregivers usually had time only to meet basic physical needs. Rheingold increased the amount of nurturance babies received from a single caregiver (the causal variable), and she measured babies' dependency with that caregiver (the outcome variable). However, she needed to be sure that no other changes in the babies' lives could account for any observed change in the babies' dependency over time. If Rheingold were studying inanimate objects, she might have been able to make certain that nothing else changed at the same time that she changed the causal variable. But with human infants, it was not possible to simply keep everything else from changing. In most studies with humans, researchers do not have that much power. For example, the babies' nurturance was increased for an 8-week period. But during this period the babies changed in age as well, a process that could not be stopped. There may also have been other, less obvious changes in the babies' experiences. For example, the orphanage could have contracted to buy baby formula from a different vendor, so that the taste and quality of the babies' food could have changed. Rheingold exercised control over all of these alternative explanations of the outcome not by preventing them from changing, but by using a **control group**.

The control group was a second group of babies from the same orphanage nursery who experienced all of the "unstoppable" changes that the first group of babies (the **experimental group**) experienced: They got older in the 8 weeks of the study, and if anything else in the nursery changed, such as the baby formula, it changed for them, too. However, Rheingold did not make any changes to nurturance for these babies. Over time, the experimental group babies showed more positive social behaviors to the primary caregiver as expected, although their negative help-seeking behaviors did not increase. The control group babies showed no change in dependency behaviors, even though they experienced everything that the experimental group babies did except for increased single-caregiver nurturance. Only the change in nurturance could have been the cause of greater dependency in the experimental group babies.

Experiments with humans usually "control" causes other than the postulated causal variable by incorporating control groups to which the experimental group can be compared. The *experimental group* is defined as the group for which the causal variable is purposely changed. The *control group* is a group like the experimental group in every way except that the causal variable is *not* purposely changed. Chemists and other scientists who study the inanimate, physical world need not use control group procedures, but psychologists need this technique because, either for practical or ethical reasons, they cannot necessarily prevent other possible causes from changing during the course of an experiment.

Correlational Studies

Sometimes, both in psychology and in other sciences, predictions cannot be tested using experiments. Remember, in an experiment, the researcher purposely changes the causal variable. But what if the researcher does not have the power to change the causal variable? In some sciences, such as astronomy, this is usually the case. Suppose an astronomer hypothesizes that "meteor showers cause temperature increases in the outer atmosphere of planet X" (a hypothesis invented by a textbook author who knows little about astronomy). To test this hypothesis with an experiment, the astronomer would have to manipulate the occurrence of meteor showers (the causal variable) in the outer atmosphere of planet "X" and then observe or measure atmospheric temperature changes (the outcome variable). But astronomers cannot (at least at the present time) manipulate the occurrence of meteor showers on any planet, so such an experiment could not be done. The alternative, in such a case, is to do a *correlational study*, a technique in which both the causal variable and the outcome variable are measured or observed, and nothing is actually manipulated by the researcher. The research question is, do the two variables change together in the ways predicted by the hypothesis? In this astronomy example, the prediction is that the more intense a naturally occurring meteor shower is, the greater the temperature increase in planet X's atmosphere will be.

A correlational study can determine whether changes in the causal variable are matched by predicted changes in the outcome variable. What a correlational study *cannot* do is tell us whether the changes in the causal variable actually determined the matching changes in the outcome variable. For example, an astronomer would not know if some other variable might also have changed when the meteor shower occurred. If it did, the other variable might actually have caused the increased temperature of planet X's atmosphere. Only experiments, with proper controls, can tell us whether the postulated causal variable is the real cause. But when the predictions

of a theory come true in a correlational study, it is still evidence *for* the theory that made the prediction, because the results are consistent with the theory. And, when the predictions do not come true, it is still evidence *against* the theory, because the results are inconsistent with the theory.

Correlational studies are usually done in the social sciences when experiments are either impractical or unethical. Consider again the hypothesis that "nurturance causes infant dependency." Rheingold was able to purposely change the amount of nurturance orphanage babies received from a single caregiver because she was able to supply the personnel, and no one considered the changes unethical. But if Rheingold had wanted to change the nurturance of babies being cared for by their own parents, it is unlikely that the parents would have considered that reasonable. Parents have their own ideas about the nurturance their babies should get. For this reason, when Ainsworth and her colleagues (e.g., Ainsworth, Bell, & Stayton, 1972; Ainsworth, Blehar, Waters, & Wall, 1978; see Chapter 4) wanted to look at the relationship between maternal nurturance and infant dependency, they did a correlational study. They asked parents only to allow them to watch the nurturing process. Over a period of many months, they observed and measured mothers' nurturance of their infants (the causal variable in this hypothesis) and also measured infants' dependency (the outcome variable in this hypothesis). The hypothesis predicts that the more nurturance that mothers give their babies, the more dependent the babies become. This would be a **positive correlation**: The two variables would change in the same direction, either both increasing or both decreasing. Just as with Rheingold's study, the prediction came true only in part. By late infancy, babies whose mothers had provided the most nurturance were more positively responsive to their mothers, but they were *less dependent* than other babies with regard to help-seeking behaviors. For example, they cried less frequently. So there was a **negative correlation** between mothers' nurturance and these less desirable dependency behaviors. That is, the variables of nurturance and infant help-seeking changed in opposite directions, so that as one increased, the other decreased.

When theories are tested, complex findings like Rheingold's and Ainsworth's are typical. The original theory, as in this case, may be only partially supported, which prompts looking for an alternative theory that can explain all of the data and then testing the new theory. As you see in Chapter 4, Ainsworth and her colleagues found that "attachment theory" could account for the full set of findings, and subsequent studies have supported attachment theory.

No single study, either an experimental or correlational study, is ever a sufficient test of any theory. Theories become more convincing as the stockpile of supporting evidence grows. Sometimes, one study seems to support a theory, but another does not. If the evidence is mixed in this fashion, it's again time to go back to the drawing board and consider how to change or replace this theory in order to explain all of the findings. It can be a "slow slog" as one of our colleagues has described it, but it is the way that enduring theories emerge and that science progresses, providing us with reliable findings that can be applied to real-world problems.

A Special Case: Studying Age Effects

Suppose we have a theory that some behavior or skill changes with age, for example, "In adulthood, aging causes declines in intelligence." We can use only correlational studies to test hypotheses where age is the causal variable, because age is not something that a researcher can directly change or manipulate. So age is observed, and the outcome variable (such as intelligence in this hypothesis) is observed or measured. However, age can be observed in three different ways, and each method has its own advantages and disadvantages.

CROSS-SECTIONAL STUDIES

In **cross-sectional studies**, different ages are represented by different groups of people. For example, a group of 20-year-olds might represent young adults, a group of 40-year-olds might represent middle-aged adults, and a group of 70-year-olds might represent older adults. Then all the subjects would be measured for the outcome variable (such as intelligence). When age and intelligence have been examined in this way, typically intelligence scores have declined with age as our sample hypothesis predicts.

But in cross-sectional studies, what look like the effects of age could be the result of *cohort* differences. Participants in each age group belong to a cohort: They were born in the same historical period, and they grew up at about the same time. People in different age groups belong to different cohorts. When it appears that age is causing some change, such as a decline in intelligence, the change could be the result of other differences among the cohorts. For example, educational approaches and opportunities may have changed dramatically from the time that today's 70-year-olds were kids to the time that today's 40-year-olds were kids, and these changes in education may be the cause of their differences in measured intelligence. Age may have nothing to do with it!

LONGITUDINAL STUDIES

Some researchers study age and its effects by doing **longitudinal** research. Only one group of subjects, all the same age, participates. They are measured several times as they get older. For example, in place of the cross-sectional study we just described, we could do a longitudinal study testing the intelligence of one group of participants several times throughout their lives, starting when they were all 20 years old.

This kind of design eliminates cohort differences because only one cohort is included. In longitudinal studies of overall intelligence, no declines are usually found until after age 50 or 60, and many individuals show increasing scores through much of adulthood, indicating that the steady declines in intelligence often observed in cross-sectional studies are due to cohort effects (see Chapters 13 and 15).

But longitudinal studies have their own disadvantages. First, they can take so long that the original researchers are retired or dead before the studies are completed! Second, age is not the only thing that could be causing the observed changes. Cultural changes could also be a cause of what look like age changes. For example, medical care and nutrition improved dramatically after World War II. If subjects in our imaginary longitudinal study have benefitted from such improvements, they may actually enjoy greater mental alertness as older adults than they did when they were young, helping them to perform better in a testing situation even though other elements of intelligence have not actually improved and may even have declined as a function of age.

Take heart, however, because there is a way to combine the advantages of both cross-sectional and longitudinal studies that helps to isolate the effects of age.

SEQUENTIAL STUDIES

A **sequential** study is like a cross-sectional study in that more than one cohort is included, and it is like a longitudinal study in that each cohort is measured at more than one age. Suppose again that we want to know if intelligence changes with age. We might include three cohorts in our study. Let's say one cohort, born in 1960, is measured at age 60 and again at 70; the second cohort, born in 1970, is measured at ages 50 and 60; and the last cohort, born in 1980, is measured at ages 40 and 50. All subjects are measured in the years 2020 and 2030. Our study will be 10 years long, but we will have information on whether intelligence increases or decreases over each 10-year age period from age 40 to age 70. The subjects who were born first may not have intelligence scores as high as those born later, but we are examining only increases or decreases with age, not absolute scores. And cultural changes will be uniform for all cohorts because they are all being measured at the same times. Cultural changes could still explain results if all groups change the same way from the first to the second testing, but if there are improvements in some cohorts and declines in others, these differences cannot be explained by cultural change and are more likely the result of age.

Qualitative Research Methods

Qualitative research methods afford the developmentalist another, less traditional way of doing research. **Qualitative research** has been defined as "any kind of research that produces findings not arrived at by means of statistical procedures or other means of quantification" (Strauss & Corbin, 1990, p. 17). This definition appears to allow for many types of methodologies and techniques and may seem somewhat ambiguous. One way to clarify the concept is to view qualitative research as a way of answering questions not readily answerable by quantitative methods. For example, qualitative studies can be aimed at providing rich descriptive information about some concept or experience that is not well understood. Rather than using tests or other assessment instruments, the qualitative researcher may choose to interview the participants, make observations, or gather life histories. Although one of the purposes of this kind of research is to build theory, the actual data are not analyzed and tested as in more traditional methods. Instead, the data are the "voices" of the participants, who are allowed to speak for themselves. The data are not categorized according to any predetermined scheme but are allowed to evolve in novel ways. Consider, for example, the question of how middle-aged men cope over time with the death of a spouse when adolescent children are still in the home. A researcher may legitimately choose to study this topic using standardized questionnaires or interviews in an effort to categorize the fathers according to various established typologies of coping behavior. In contrast, a qualitative analysis would probably involve extensive, ongoing interviews without a predetermined typology or way of categorizing the fathers and would allow a "theory" of fathers' coping styles to build over the course of the project.

Daniel Levinson's study of the stages of a woman's life represents a good example of a qualitative research project (Levinson & Levinson, 1996). Using methods he called biographical interviewing and biographical reconstruction, he studied 45 women in order to learn about "the nature of women's development and about specific life issues relating to friendship, work, love, marriage, motherhood, good times and bad times, the stuff life is made of" (pp. 7–8). Levinson's intensive work with these participants resulted in complex, descriptive narratives that provided a framework for a theoretical construction about women's life trajectories.

Qualitative research approaches differ from more traditional methodologies in a number of ways. First, the data, as we have indicated, consist primarily of the words and actions of participants instead of numerical scores or frequencies. Second, the design of a study may change as the study progresses and the "data" are collected and considered. Third, a qualitative researcher may appear to be less objective than the more traditional researcher and may write about the study in a narrative style. Sometimes the data are reported in the first person. Fourth, no hypothesis is used to guide the study. However, a research question identifies the topic of the project, as in "How do middle-aged men, with adolescent children, cope with the death of a spouse?" Other differences exist as well, but these are some of the primary ones. Despite these differences, qualitative and traditional (quantitative) research methods share some similar features. Both approaches can be descriptive and have theory building as their goal (see *Understanding the Scientific Process*). Most importantly, perhaps, both maintain their own rigorous standards for reliability and validity (Lincoln & Guba, 1985).

Qualitative and quantitative methods can enhance each other by approaching a problem from more than one direction. A number of years ago a consortium of editors of developmental psychology journals endorsed the importance of qualitative methods and encouraged researchers to use them in their research projects. They argued that quantitative tools alone "cannot reveal the complex processes that likely give rise to normal and abnormal behavior among different children and adolescents" (Azar, 1999, pp. 20–21).

Caveat Emptor

Helping professionals rely on research to inform their practice with children, adults, and families, and they may be faced with choices about which interventions would be most effective and in which circumstances. Contemporary practice guidelines encourage the use of empirically supported treatments and interventions in all helping professions (Rousseau & Gunia, 2016). Although many programs and practices are advertised as "research based," this term may sometimes be applied loosely and inaccurately, especially when those making the claim do not show any supporting documentation. Helping professionals should be aware that empirically supported treatments need to be shown more effective than a placebo in at least two well-designed and well-controlled studies (or in a large number of single-subject studies). The studies must be carried out using a treatment manual that provides a framework for intervention and allows for replication by others. Reputable research support for interventions can usually be found in published studies that have been subjected to rigorous peer review. The process of review by peers within the research community assures that the reported findings are legitimate and that they have passed the test of scientific research. Such care provides a means of quality control for helping professionals and others who are consumers of scientific research (see Chapter 1 for some resources).

Glossary

"ability" mindset: Believing that when people perform well at a skill or intellectual pursuit, it is because they are "talented" or "smart," that is, they have some native ability that cannot be learned or changed.

academic self-concept: One of two divisions of children's general self-concept, referring to sense of self as an achiever in school subjects. Can be further divided into specific school subject areas such as math, science, English, and social studies.

acceptance: An aspect of parental responsiveness that includes being affectionate, praising the child, being involved in the child's life, and showing concern for the child's needs; correlated with children's self-esteem and social adjustment.

accommodation: In Piaget's theory of cognitive development, the adaptation process by which existing knowledge structures are modified somewhat when an individual is exposed to new information.

acetylation: The attachment of a biochemical called an acetyl group to the histone that binds to DNA, causing a loosening of the histone–DNA bond and therefore an increased likelihood that the DNA will be transcribed, beginning the cellular production of a protein.

acetylcholine: A neurotransmitter that functions in many parts of the brain, including between neurons and skeletal muscles.

achieving stage: In Schaie's theory, the stage of cognitive development when a young adult must apply her intellectual skills to the achievement of long-term goals, carefully attending to the consequences of the problem-solving process.

acquisition stage: In Schaie's theory, the time in cognitive development (during childhood and adolescence) when an individual is sheltered from the majority of life's responsibilities and can learn a skill or a body of knowledge regardless of whether it has any practical goal or social implications.

active euthanasia: Injection of a medication by someone else that causes immediate death.

activity level: The intensity and quantity of movement an individual displays; one aspect of infant temperament.

actuarial prediction: Predicting an individual's outcome based on group characteristics, such as predicting how likely an individual is to suffer a heart attack based on the frequency of heart attacks in large samples of people with similar characteristics (same age, gender, socioeconomic status, etc.).

adaptation: In Piaget's theory of cognitive development, the process by which the human mind constructs its knowledge, both assimilating new information to existing knowledge structures or understandings, and accommodating those structures to create a better fit to what is new.

adolescent growth spurt: Corresponding with puberty, a rapid increase in size accompanied by changes in the shape and proportions of the body.

adolescent-onset or late-starter model: A developmental pathway of antisocial behavior that begins in adolescence and is not likely to result in adult criminality. Although serious, it seems to be reflective of a difficult or exaggerated reaction to the adolescent period.

adolescing: The process of advancing with age, improving or growing.

adrenal glands: Situated at the top of the kidneys, these glands are important in the stress system. They respond to ACTH (released by the pituitary when threats are perceived) by producing cortisol. They also produce epinephrine and norepinephrine as part of the stress reaction. Adrenal glands are also involved in androgen production.

adrenarche: The point just before puberty when the adrenal gland increases its activity and children begin to show sexual attraction.

adrenocorticotropic hormone (ACTH): A hormone, released into the bloodstream during the body's response to stress, which prompts the adrenal glands to release "stress hormones."

Adult Attachment Interview (AAI): A structured interview in which adults describe their memories of the parenting they received and their evaluation of whether and how that parenting influenced their own development. Based on coding of the verbatim transcripts, adults are categorized as having one of four attachment styles: autonomous (secure), dismissing (insecure), preoccupied (insecure), and unresolved (insecure). The security of an adult's attachment style tends to be correlated with the attachment security of his or her own infants.

advance directives (living wills): Statements, typically in writing, that describe a person's wishes regarding treatment in the event of incurable illness.

age-graded changes: Changes to which a person must adapt that are strongly age determined, such as physical changes.

age stereotypes: Widely held beliefs about characteristics of older people.

agency: In cognitive functioning, the ability to act without an external trigger or to engage in self-motivated behavior. In social-emotional functioning, a constituent of generativity that involves generating, creating, and producing things, ideas, people, events, and so on as powerful extensions of the self.

agreeableness (A): One of the Big 5 personality traits that is described using synonyms including *warm, sympathetic, generous, forgiving, kind,* and *affectionate*.

alleles: Different forms of the same gene, such as the many forms of the eye color gene.

allostasis: "Balance through adaption." In this model of stress processes, the central nervous system (CNS) controls multiple interacting regulatory processes so that the best balance for each specific challenge is found, rather than returning to a fixed set point.

allostatic load: The physiological wear and tear on the body that results from ongoing adaptive efforts to maintain stability (homeostasis) in response to stressors.

alternative splicing: A process in which the cell can produce several protein variations from the same protoprotein.

Alzheimer's disease (AD): A brain disease that leads to dementia. Becomes more prevalent with age. Extensive brain changes including the development of plaques and tangles lead to the common symptom characteristics of the disease including absentmindedness, confusion, language and memory problems, disorientation, and problems with physical coordination. The eventual outcome is death.

amygdala: A brain structure that influences motivation, emotional control, fear responses, and interpretation of nonverbal, emotional expressions.

amyloid precursor protein (APP): Protein produced by a gene that is found in the brain, spinal cord, and other organs. Mutations in the gene alter APP and are implicated in early-onset Alzheimer's disease (AD) and plaque formation.

anal stage: In Freud's theory, the second psychosexual stage, beginning in the second year of life, when the anal area of the body becomes the focus of greatest pleasure. During this stage, parenting practices associated with toilet training that are either overcontrolling or overindulgent could have long-lasting effects on personality development.

androgens: Male hormones produced in the testes that contribute to the development of male reproductive organs and may affect some aspects of brain development.

andropause: A decline in testosterone production in men as a function of age.

anterior cingulate cortex (ACC): The front part of the cingulate cortex that partially surrounds the corpus callosum. It influences blood pressure and heart rate and plays a role in both emotion and cognition.

anti-Mullerian hormone (AMH): A hormone produced in the testes during prenatal development that causes the deterioration of the Mullerian ducts, which otherwise would develop into fallopian tubes, uterus, and part of the vagina.

antisocial behavior: Behavior characterized by the presence of aggression or the intent to harm another person. More broadly may include such acts as risky sexual activity, substance abuse, defiance, cheating, lying, and vandalism.

antisocial personality disorder (APD): A personality disorder used for adult diagnosis that is characterized by antisocial behavior of long duration. APD is often preceded by serious conduct problems in childhood and adolescence.

anxious ambivalent: An attachment category describing babies who show a great deal of distress on separation from their mothers, and who may act angry when reunited with the mother, alternately approaching and resisting her, or who may respond listlessly to her efforts to comfort. They seem preoccupied with their mothers and rarely return to exploration after a separation.

anxious arousal: A state that children are thought to experience when parents discipline them. Hoffman proposed that mild forms help a child pay attention to the parent's socialization message, but more intense arousal attracts the child's attention to other concerns, like their own fear.

arousal: The degree of intensity of a felt emotion.

arthritis: A debilitating disease common in the elderly that is characterized by the onset of pain, stiffness, and swelling of joints and surrounding tissues.

assimilation: In Piaget's theory of cognitive development, the process of interpreting new stimulation or information as fitting with what one already knows, sometimes distorting the new information as a result.

attachment theory: According to Bowlby, the infant and his primary caregiver(s) participate in an interactive system that has evolved to keep the infant safe and ensure survival. As the infant changes cognitively and emotionally, an affectional bond with the caregiver emerges in stages, with a full-fledged attachment likely by about 7 or 8 months.

attention-deficit hyperactivity disorder (ADHD): A disorder that is characterized by one or more of a cluster of symptoms that are especially problematic for school performance: poor attentional control, restlessness or hyperactivity, and impulsivity.

attention-persistence: Length of uninterrupted orienting or attention to a single activity and tendency to return to a task after interruption; an aspect of infant temperament.

authoritarian style: An interactive parenting style that combines low levels of warmth (cold emotional climate) with high levels of control or demandingness. Associated with negative emotional tone, poor social skills, and other negative outcomes in children.

authoritative style: An interactive parenting style that combines high levels of warmth (affection, sensitivity and responsivity) with moderate to high levels of control or demandingness. Associated with many positive child outcomes.

autism spectrum disorder (ASD): Developmental disorder that is diagnosed early (typically around age 3). Children on this spectrum are characterized by difficulties in social development, showing impairments in the basic skills necessary for building a theory of mind: joint attention, imitation, and the turn-taking routines needed to cement solid interpersonal relationships. A variety of other symptoms, including impaired language development, mental retardation, special cognitive skills, physical awkwardness, and so on, characterize some children on this spectrum. Generally, even children with good language facility have problems with the pragmatics of language and with communicating effectively with others.

autobiographical memory: What we remember of our own history of experiences, including representations of who we have been at various points in the past. Largely synonymous with episodic memory.

autonomic functions: A set of bodily functions, such as those involving the organ systems, that is outside an individual's conscious control.

autonomous (secure): An attachment category characterizing adults who provide an Adult Attachment Interview transcript that is coherent and collaborative. They integrate and monitor their thinking, summarize answers, return the conversation to the interviewer, demonstrate good perspective-taking skills, acknowledge the importance of attachment-related experiences in their development, and tend to have children who are securely attached.

autonomous stage: Stage of moral development described by Piaget that begins in middle childhood. Children now understand that rules are based on social agreements and can be changed.

autonomy: In Ryan and Deci's self-determination theory, one of three basic or universal needs. Being in control of oneself, or feeling that one's behavior is congruent with one's "true self," meaning that it is intrinsically motivated.

autonomy versus shame and doubt: The crisis faced in the second of Erikson's "Eight Stages of Man," in which the 1- to 3-year-old child may develop feelings of autonomy ("I can do things myself") or of shame and self-doubt, depending on whether his caregiver strikes the right balance between exercising control and being sensitive to the child's new need for independence.

autosomes: The 22 of 23 pairs of chromosomes in humans that are matched (they look and function alike).

average: A sociometric category that includes those children who receive an average number of positive and negative nominations from their peers (near the mean for the group on social preference and social impact).

avoidant: An attachment category describing babies who typically fail to cry when separated from their mothers in a strange situation test. They actively avoid or ignore her when she returns, sometimes combining proximity seeking and moving away, but mostly turning away and often appearing unemotional. In Bartholomew's typology of adult attachments, a category that is subdivided into two types (dismissing and fearful) based on the individual's reports of felt distress.

axon: A long extension, projecting from the cell body of a neuron, which is like a cable attached to a piece of electronic equipment. Electrical impulses travel from the cell body through the axon toward synapses with other neurons.

axon terminals: Structures found at the ends of axons, which contain tiny sacs of neurotransmitters.

babbling: Infant vocal sounds, usually beginning around 6 months of age, consisting of repeated consonant-vowel-consonant sequences such as "bababa" or "doodoodoo." By 9 months of age, they tend to be limited to the sounds permissible in the baby's native language.

basal ganglia: Subcortical nuclei located on either side of the thalamus and involved in many behavioral functions including learning and motivation.

basic emotions: Those core affects that have old neurobiological underpinnings. According to Izard, they include joy/happiness, interest, sadness, anger, disgust, and fear.

basic trust: In Erikson's theory of personality development, an infant's ability to see others as dependable and trustworthy as a result of caregiving that is timely, sensitive to the infant's needs, and consistently available.

behavioral control: Parents imposing and enforcing standards and rules of behavior with their children; the "control dimension" of parenting refers to this kind of control.

behavioral facilitation system: Neural system that regulates approach behaviors, response to incentives, positive affect, and psychomotor activity.

behavioral inhibition: In late infancy and childhood, a tendency towards shyness, manifested as avoidance or distress in new situations. This trait is linked to high reactivity (including irritability in response to new sensory stimulation) in early infancy.

behavioral-inhibition system: Neural system that regulates withdrawal and avoidance behaviors.

behaviorist tradition: Approaches to explaining learning in which behavioral change is seen as a function of chains of specific environmental events, such as those that occur in classical and operant conditioning.

belief bias: A tendency to notice or seek out supporting evidence for one's beliefs while at the same time ignoring or failing to seek counterevidence.

bicultural competence: Competence in dealing with members of one's own and other cultures as reflected in appropriate social and emotional skills.

bidirectional processes: Reciprocal relationships between causal mechanisms. Factors that result in developmental change often moderate each other's influence. For example, genetic influences are moderated by environmental processes and vice versa.

Big 5: See *five factor model of personality*.

binge drinking: Drinking many drinks in a row.

bipolar disorder: An affective disorder that is generally characterized by episodes of mania or hypomania, sometimes alternating with episodes of depression.

bisexuality: A characteristic of individuals who have interest in sexual relations with partners of both sexes.

body image: The concept of, and attitude towards one's physical appearance.

borderwork: Interactions between boys and girls during middle childhood when there appear to be unwritten rules governing when and how the two genders will interact.

"bottom-up" processes: Information processing that is automatic, intuitive, and unintentional, usually occurring quickly and without the need for conscious planning or for working memory space.

broad socialization: Socialization that permits and encourages high levels of individual freedom of expression, has few social constraints, expects less community responsibility, and thus tolerates a wide variety of socially deviant behaviors.

Bronfenbrenner's bioecological theory: A comprehensive developmental model proposed by Bronfenbrenner that takes into account the many levels of influence the environment can have on an individual. The interacting systems in this model are the microsystem, the mesosystem, the exosystem, and the macrosystem.

callous-unemotional (CE) traits: A constellation of genetically influenced qualities that include lack of empathy, manipulative relationships with others, and lack of guilt.

cannot classify: An attachment category characterizing adults who may have psychiatric disorders and who do not fit in any of the other four attachment style categories.

care burden: The physical, emotional, social, and financial challenges that can be experienced by family caregivers.

career consolidation (vs. self-absorption): A life stage that Vaillant added to Erikson's sequence of stages, characterizing the mid-20s, when in addition to ongoing intimacy concerns, one becomes concerned with making a commitment to work that brings personal satisfaction, regardless of its other rewards, rather than just having a job.

carrier: Someone with a gene that is unexpressed in his phenotype but can be passed on to offspring.

causal variable: The postulated cause of a given phenomenon.

central sulcus: A fissure in the cerebrum that is used to locate the parietal lobe, which sits behind this fissure.

centration: A characteristic of preoperational thought in which the child tends to focus on one salient feature of an experience or event at a time.

cerebellum: A brain structure located in the hindbrain that is involved in the planning, coordination, and smooth operation of complex motor activities.

cerebral cortex: The outer layer of the gray matter of the cerebrum, which is the highest and most recently evolved portion of the brain.

cerebrovascular accident (stroke): A cardiovascular problem in which an artery serving the brain is either clogged or bursts.

cerebrum: The highest brain structure, comprising two thirds of the forebrain, and coordinating most other brain activity. Involved in higher brain processes like thinking, language, decision making, and so on.

child centered: Describes caregivers who set aside their own needs (for time and convenience) to meet a child's developmental needs.

childhood-limited model: Anti-social behavior that manifests during childhood and remits in adolescence, sometimes replaced by internalizing problems.

chromosomes: Forty-six tiny strands of DNA, found in the nucleus of each cell of the body, which are the source of biological inheritance.

chunking: The cognitive process of linking several pieces of information together into a single meaningful unit, such as remembering the digits 1, 7, 7, and 6 by thinking of the year 1776.

cingulate cortex: One of the limbic structures involved in processing of emotional information. It receives input from the thalamus and the cortex.

circuits: Series of neurons that are joined via their synaptic connections into groups and are part of larger organizations of neurons.

classical conditioning: A process by which a change in behavior takes place when a neutral event or stimulus is associated with a stimulus that causes an automatic response. As a result the neutral stimulus causes the person to make the same automatic response in the future.

climacteric: The gradual reduction of reproductive ability in women usually beginning in their late 30s when the menstrual cycle begins to shorten and become somewhat more erratic as a result of a reduction in the amount of circulating estradiol.

cliques: Voluntary social or friendship groups of three to nine members characterizing children in early to middle adolescence.

coaction: The intricate pattern by which genes and environment mutually influence one another. The activity of the genes is affected by the environment of the cell that is affected by other levels of the environment including the outside world. One result is that the same complement of genes produces different outcomes in different environments. Also, the same environment can have different effects on outcomes when interacting with different genes.

code switching: Shifting from one form or style of speech to another depending on context, such as shifting from using slang with friends to using more polite forms with authority figures.

codominance: A type of relationship between two alleles of the same gene (located at matching sites on a pair of chromosomes) in which neither allele is suppressed, producing a blended outcome.

coercive family interaction: Patterson's description of how children learn to act aggressively. Aggressive children respond to parental demands by behaving aversively (whining, etc.); parents retreat, rewarding the child's noncompliance, and parents are reinforced with short-lived peace and quiet. Children are trained in the effectiveness of aggressive noncompliance and learn powerful parent-control strategies.

cognitive flexibility: The ability to readily shift one's way of thinking about a problem, categorizing material, or responding to a situation when the more practiced or typical way of dealing with the situation is not effective or appropriate.

cohort effects: Also called history-graded events, they are events that provide a context for development and also influence it directly. The year of your birth marks your entry into a cohort of peers who accompany you through age-graded developmental changes within the context of a specific set of historical events.

coitus: Penile-vaginal intercourse.

collaborative or affiliative speech: A type of speech, more often used among girls, in which children's responses are keyed to what someone else has said, expressing agreement or making further suggestions, often in the form of a question rather than declarative or imperative sentences.

commitment: An element of love that refers to making a decision to sustain a relationship with a loved one.

commitment: According to Marcia, one of the two processes involved in a young person's identity formation; it involves actually making choices (of values, beliefs, goals, etc.) and doing things to implement those choices.

commitment foreseen: Position 6 in Perry's model in which thinking incorporates not only respect for diverse ideas and understanding of their rationale, but also the individual's affirmation of what it is she believes in, all the while knowing that reason will never provide absolute proof that her ideas or perspectives are right or better than others.

committed compliance: Describes toddlers' eager and enthusiastic willingness to go along with parental requests. Predicts measures of internalization and conscience in the later preschool period.

communion: A constituent of generativity that is expressed in the adult's desire to care for the next generation, even to the point of sacrificing her own well-being for the good of those who will follow.

compelling circumstances: Conditions that mitigate the guilt of a criminal defendant because he or she faced such pressure when the crime was committed that even an ordinary, reasonable person could be expected to have acted in the same way, such as acting in the face of extreme need or under threat of injury.

compensation: A process that contributes to successful development. When a loss of some kind prevents the use of one means to an end, the individual finds another means.

competence: In self-determination theory, feeling effective in one's interactions with the social environment and experiencing opportunities to exercise and express one's capacities.

complicated or abnormal grief: A response to bereavement that is generally accompanied by other disorders such as major depression, substance abuse, or post-traumatic stress disorder that is intense and lasts for an extended period of time, greatly interfering with functioning. Abnormal grief may also be marked by a complete absence of grief and the total inability to experience grief reactions.

compulsive caregiving: Describes a behavioral pattern in which children (usually insecurely attached, avoidant children) take emotional care of their parents.

compulsive self-sufficiency: Describes a behavioral pattern in which children (usually insecurely attached, avoidant children) appear very self-possessed, perhaps related to experiences of shaming for expressions of dependency or needs for closeness.

concordance: Similarity in some trait or behavior between members of a twin pair.

concrete operational stage: In Piaget's theory of cognitive development, the period from about age 6 to 12 when children begin to think logically but have difficulty applying logical thought to abstract contents.

conditioned response: In classical conditioning, when a neutral stimulus has been conditioned to produce an automatic response. For example, if an animal hears a tone (neutral stimulus) every time it eats, it may begin to salivate (conditioned response) automatically when it hears the tone.

conditioned stimulus: A formerly neutral stimulus that has become associated with a stimulus that causes an automatic response, thus causing the same automatic response in the future.

conduct disorder (CD): A pattern of serious behavior problems that violate the basic rights of others, such as stealing, aggression, or property destruction. Presently, this diagnosis requires a persistent pattern of aggression in youth.

confirmation bias: When a child's peers have already developed schemas or constructions for him that are built on his social reputation, the interactions with the target child that follow are marked by attention to evidence that confirms the target child's characteristics.

congenital adrenal hyperplasia (CAH): A gender-atypical condition in which biological females with two X chromosomes are exposed to high levels of androgens (male hormones) during prenatal and postnatal development.

conscience: An internalized slate of standards and principles that constitutes a person's primary guide to action. May cause feelings of discomfort or distress when the violation of a rule is contemplated or carried out.

conscientiousness (C): One of the Big 5 personality traits that is described using synonyms including *organized, planful, reliable, responsible, careful,* and *efficient.*

consolidation: In Super's theory, achievement of advanced status and seniority in the workplace that often accompanies the maintenance stage.

constructed identity: The identity not based upon a predetermined set of expectations, but rather representative either of a personal redefinition of childhood and early adolescent goals and values or perhaps something very different from them.

constructivist: An approach to explaining the acquisition of knowledge (e.g., in Piaget's theory). Constructivist theories assume that individuals actively create their own knowledge by interpreting new information in light of prior learning and by restructuring prior knowledge, or by co-constructing knowledge in interactions with others. Individuals are not seen as passive receptors of information who acquire knowledge via external manipulations.

contextual relativism: Position 5 in Perry's model that represents a major achievement in intellectual development because the student now possesses analytic abilities that allow her to appreciate the merits of diverse perspectives and to find convincing elements in multiple points of view. Thinking relativistically, or thinking about knowledge in context, becomes more habitual.

contingency management system: Presenting and withdrawing reinforcers and punishments in a systematic and consistent way to effect behavioral change.

control: According to Craik and Bialystock (2006), similar to fluid intelligence, this refers to the way the brain works with information.

control dimension (parental demandingness): One of two major features of parenting style. The degree to which parents impose discipline, requiring their children to curb some of their behaviors and to perform other behaviors that are suitable to their level of maturity.

control group: In experimental design, a group like the experimental group in every way except that the causal variable is not purposely changed.

controversial: A sociometric category that identifies a relatively small group of children who receive many positive and many negative nominations from peers (high social impact, average social preference).

conventional morality: Kohlberg's second stage of moral reasoning in which what is right depends on others' approval or on the need to maintain social order.

conventional rules: Social rules of conduct that vary from one culture to another and are a function of social agreement, such as rules about appropriate dress, forms of address, and table manners.

convivial collectivism: A form of collectivism (giving the group priority over the individual) that is characteristic of Latino cultures; family relationships are primary and overt, and enthusiastic expression of positive emotions is valued within relationships, tending to create family cohesion.

corporal (physical) punishment: A form of parental power assertion that involves inflicting physical pain or discomfort, such as slapping, spanking, or beating a child.

corpus callosum: A network of fibers that connects the right and left cerebral hemispheres of the brain. Its maturation from early childhood through adolescence contributes to coordination and integration of information and aids in the development of consciousness.

correlational studies: Often utilized when experiments are impractical or unethical, a technique in which both the causal variable and the outcome variable are measured or observed, and nothing is actually manipulated by the researcher. Such studies can determine whether changes in the causal variable are matched by predicted changes in the outcome variable, but they cannot determine whether changes in the causal variable *caused* the changes in the outcome variable.

corticotrophin releasing hormone (CRH): A hormone produced by the hypothalamus that stimulates the pituitary gland to release adrenocorticotrophic hormone (ACTH).

cortisol: A hormone, released during the body's response to stress, that increases blood glucose levels and affects the immune response.

counting all strategy: Rudimentary addition strategy of young children. For example, given the problem of adding 2 plus 3, holding up two fingers on one hand, three fingers on the other hand and counting all of them.

counting on strategy: Addition strategy of young children. For example, given the problem of adding 2 plus 3, starting at 2 and counting 3 more digits on from there.

critical (sensitive) period: A certain time frame in which some developments, such as

first language learning, must take place or the opportunity is missed.

critical thinking (CT): The kind of thinking that includes components of reflection, use of evidence, clarity, and focus, often in the service of decision making.

cross-fostering study: Research that involves separating animal offspring from their biological mothers to be reared by mothers with different genetic or behavioral characteristics in order to assess the effects of biology and environmental factors separately.

cross-sectional studies: A study design in which different ages are represented by different groups of people as opposed to one group of people over time.

crossover effect: Shifts in behaviors such as drug use that is related to age and race, such that the relative frequency of a behavior reverses between or over time. For example, White female marijuana users use more often than Black female users until their mid-twenties when frequency of use for Black female users matches or exceeds that of White female users.

crowds: Large, reputation-based groups, composed of numerous cliques that form in early to midadolescence.

crystallization: In Super's theory, the formulation of general vocational goals in the early part of the exploratory stage.

crystallized intelligence (pragmatics): The compilation of skills and information we have acquired in the course of our lives that can be viewed as the software programs of our nervous system.

culture: Shared traditions, attitudes, values, and beliefs handed down from one generation to the next.

cytokines: These chemical messengers are produced by the body as part of its immune response. These proteins can either promote inflammation or reduce it.

cytoplasm: The jellylike substance that fills a cell between its outer membrane and its nucleus. Cytoplasm comprises an array of organic structures (organelles) and chemicals.

daily hassles: Category of stressor that is chronic and cumulative in its effect.

day reconstruction method (DRM): Method of research in which participants revive memories of a previous day, describe the days' experiences, and rate affective valence of experiences.

deacetylation: An epigenetic change that makes the expression of a gene less likely. It involves the removal of an acetyl group (an organic molecule) from the histones that bind with DNA and results in tightening the binding, typically decreasing transcription of a gene.

décalages: Within-stage variations in Piaget's cognitive stage theory. Children sometimes show more advanced or less advanced functioning in one or another cognitive domain than is typical of their overall stage of development.

decathecting: Detaching emotionally from the relationship one had experienced with a loved one prior to their death and reinvesting psychic energy into the formation of new attachments.

decentration: A characteristic of concrete and formal operational thought in Piaget's cognitive theory. Attending to multiple pieces of information (or multiple aspects of a situation) at one time; a necessary ingredient in logical thinking.

declarative knowledge: Knowledge about facts (semantic information) and events (episodic information).

decline stage: In Super's theory, just before and after age 65, when one's career winds down, retirement is planned and takes precedence over career advancement and consolidation.

decomposition strategy: In addition or subtraction, using knowledge of the answer to one problem to help you figure out the answer to another, such as, if you know that 4 + 4 is 8, to figure out what 4 + 5 is, you might just add 1 to 8.

deferred imitation: Imitation in which children observe the actions of another on one occasion, and then imitate those actions sometime later. In order to do so, the child must be able to recall the observed actions.

degrouping: A general decline in the importance of cliques over the course of the high school years.

delayed phase preference: A shift in sleep patterns characterized by staying up later in the evening and sleeping later in the morning than younger children that has been associated with hormonal changes at puberty.

demand characteristics: Behavioral tendencies that often either encourage or discourage certain kinds of reactions from others.

dementia: Cognitive functioning that is so severely impaired that it negatively affects ability to relate to others and to manage one's own daily activities.

demethylation: An epigenetic change that makes the expression of a gene more likely. It involves the removal of a methyl group (an organic molecule) from either a coded gene or from regulatory DNA. Or, it can involve the removal of a methyl group from histones that bind with DNA.

democracy: An aspect of parental responsiveness. The degree to which parents encourage children's psychological autonomy by soliciting their opinions or encouraging self-expression. Related to children's self-reliance, self-confidence, willingness to work hard, and general competence.

dendrites: Small projections that grow out from a neuron's cell body; they receive transmissions from other neurons.

dentate gyrus: Part of the hippocampus that generates neural stem cells throughout life, playing a role in learning and memory.

deoxyribonucleic acid (DNA): A complex organic substance that comprises chromosomes and genes.

depressed mood: A subclinical level of depression.

description: The first step in the scientific method, aimed at answering factual questions about a phenomenon, such as who, what, when, where, and with whom.

despair: The third phase in the grieving process characterized by great sadness; social withdrawal; sleeping, eating, or somatic disturbances; and other symptoms of depression or emotional upset.

developmental psychopathology: A relatively new and influential field that has applied a developmental focus to the study of abnormal behavior and dysfunction.

developmental traumatology: The study of trauma-induced biological and psychological processes across the life span.

deviancy training: A process by which youth who engage in inappropriate or delinquent behavior mutually influence each other.

diathesis: Underlying predispositions to some disease or abnormal condition.

diathesis-stress: Model for the development of psychopathology that assumes a genetic predisposition (diathesis) that confers particular sensitivity to environmental risk (stress). See also *genetic vulnerability*.

differential susceptibility: Some physiological makeups can make an individual more likely to be affected by environmental influences than other people. For example, a child with a highly reactive temperament might be benefited more than other children by positive parenting but harmed more than others by negative parenting.

difficult babies: A temperament type described by Thomas and Chess. These babies are fearful, irritable, active, display low levels of positive affect, are irregular in biological rhythms, and so on, making them more challenging to care for than other babies.

digit span tests: A test of working memory in which a series of digits are presented and the participant must repeat them in the correct order.

diminished capacity: One source of mitigation in adult criminal law. A guilty actor is considered less than fully blameworthy because of some deficiency at the time of the offense. Perhaps he was mentally ill, emotionally distressed, or intellectually impaired.

discipline: The tendency of parents to limit or demand behavior by exerting or requiring control.

discordance: Dissimilarity in some trait or behavior between members of a twin pair.

disenchantment: The second stage of retirement, when people begin to experience an emotional "letdown" as they face the day-to-day realities of the change, such as separation from work colleagues, uncertainties about how to feel competent and in control, a sense of diminished generativity and meaningfulness, new tensions that may arise with one's partner, financial concerns, and perhaps, boredom.

dishabituation: After habituating to one stimulus, an infant may show reinstatement of the orienting response if the stimulus is changed. This response is dishabituation and indicates that the baby has noticed the difference between the original stimulus and the new stimulus.

disillusionment model: The view that posits that overly romantic idealizations of marriage and blissfully optimistic views of one's partner set people up for eventual disappointment.

dismissing (insecure): An attachment style characterizing adults whose Adult Attachment Interview transcripts provide little detail and coherence. They may describe their parents positively but provide either no evidence or contradictory evidence. They downplay close relationships and tend to have children

who are in the avoidant attachment category. In Bartholomew's typology, these individuals prefer self-sufficiency and maintain a sense of superiority while devaluing the importance of others to their well-being.

dismissive parenting: Also called neglecting, a parenting style that describes parents who are essentially disengaged, scoring low on both responsiveness and demandingness.

disorganized-disoriented: An attachment category describing babies who produce contradictory and even bizarre behaviors in the strange situation test, showing both an inclination to approach the mother when stressed and a tendency to avoid her when she approaches.

distal processes: Factors outside the immediate external environment, including internal forces (genes) and external forces (features of the educational system or of the broader culture), which modify the proximal processes in Bronfenbrenner's bioecological model and other multidimensional theories.

distraction: A coping style that involves deliberate focusing on neutral or pleasant thoughts or engaging activities that divert attention in more positive directions. Distraction can attenuate depressive episodes.

dizygotic (fraternal) twins: Twins who develop from two separate zygotes. Their genotypes are as similar (or different) as any two siblings.

domain of knowledge: A specific subject matter, such as mathematics or chess or history.

domain specific: Describing a level of knowledge or skill that has been achieved in one subject area but not in others, such as being able to think logically about math but not about baseball or biology.

dominant-recessive: A type of relationship between two alleles of the same gene, in which one allele is expressed whereas the other is suppressed.

domineering or power-assertive speech: Discourse containing many commands and restrictions. Tends to be "egotistic," ignoring others' remarks, and often includes threats and interruptions, more typical of males than females.

dopamine: A neurotransmitter and a hormone that serves many functions in the body. As a neurotransmitter, it is involved in several brain processes, including reward systems. Low levels of dopamine production are associated with Parkinson's disease.

dose–response relationship: With regard to problem behaviors in children, mothers who experience fewer stressors during pregnancy tend to have children with fewer internalizing or externalizing problems later, whereas mothers with higher levels are more likely to have children with more problems later.

double effect: Giving medication intended to relieve pain even though there is a chance that death can result.

double standard: The idea that female sexual behavior is judged more harshly than male sexual behavior.

Down syndrome (Trisomy 21): A disorder caused by an extra copy of chromosome number 21 and often characterized by intellectual disability, flattened facial features, poor muscle tone, and heart problems.

downward social comparisons: Comparing oneself to less competent or less successful peers when one's self-esteem is at stake. Such comparisons protect the individual from negative self-evaluations.

dual-process model: The model that proposes that bereaved individuals simultaneously engage in two kinds of coping mechanisms, approach and avoidance, that wax and wane over the course of grieving.

dyads: A social unit or "group" that consists of two people.

dyslexia: Severe difficulty in learning to read that may include interpreting letters or associating sounds to written symbols. Although visual problems may be involved, auditory processing difficulties are often a key factor.

early-starter model: One developmental pathway to antisocial behavior. Oppositional behavior begins in early childhood, persists and diversifies over time, and becomes increasingly more serious.

earned secure: An attachment style characterizing adults who in Adult Attachment Interview transcripts reveal experiences of early adversity, describe their painful backgrounds truthfully, acknowledge the stressors their own parents faced, and come to terms with their early experiences. Their children are usually securely attached.

easy babies: A temperament type described by Thomas and Chess. These babies are placid, not very active, show positive affect, and are regular in their rhythms, making them easier to care for than other babies.

ego: In Freud's personality theory, the second of three aspects of personality, which represents the rational, realistic self that seeks to meet bodily needs in sensible ways that take into account all aspects of a situation.

ego identity: Includes all the dimensions of self-knowledge and serves as the foundation for the behavioral, affective, and cognitive commitments to career, relationships, and political and religious belief systems that will be made in adulthood.

Ego Identity Interview: A standardized, semistructured interview designed by Marcia to assess these core domains of identity: vocational choice, religious beliefs, political ideology, gender-role attitudes, and beliefs about sexual expression through first asking general questions and then following up with more specific probes. Supplemental domains may include hobbies, friendships, dating relationships, role of spouse, role of parent, experiences at school, and issues of work–family balance.

ego integrity (vs. despair): In Erikson's theory, the result of life review in the elderly. Integrity is a sense that one's own life is "something that had to be," and had order, meaning, and dignity. Despair is a sense of hopelessness, that one's life has no coherence or meaning.

egocentric speech: Speech for self, a use of language typical of preschoolers that has no apparent communicative function. Piaget suggested that it serves no useful purpose, but Vygotsky argued that it is the precursor of inner speech and important for problem solving, planning, and self-control.

elaboration strategy: A memory strategy that requires finding or creating some kind of meaningful link between to-be-remembered

items, such as creating a story that includes all the items.

elaborative style: A style that characterizes some adults' conversations with children about past experiences. Adults using this style engage in lengthy discussions providing lots of details, asking questions and encouraging children to provide details as well.

embryo: After conception, the fertilized egg travels down the fallopian tube to the uterus, increasing in size. Once the growing organism attaches to the uterine wall (implantation) it is called an embryo.

emerging adulthood: The time period from about 18 to 25, which is characterized by the shift towards increasing independence and autonomy.

emotion regulation: The set of strategies and behaviors we use to moderate our emotional experiences in order to meet the demands of different situations or to achieve our goals.

emotion schemas: Mental experience that includes feelings, memories, thoughts, images, and noncognitive elements like hormonal shifts that interact with and may amplify a basic emotional experience.

emotional intelligence: The ability to perceive emotions, to identify and understand their meaning, to integrate them with other kinds of cognition, and to manage them.

emotional stability: Among the Big 5 personality traits, this is another label for the *neuroticism* trait or dimension, emphasizing its positive end: *calm, stable, good-natured*.

empathy: "Feeling with" another person, recognizing her emotional condition and experiencing what she is assumed to be feeling.

end-of-life care: Principles that support more humanistic approaches to aiding individuals nearing death including better pain management, continuity of care, and attention to the psychological dimensions of death and dying.

endophenotypes: Biobehavioral processes that are intermediary between the actual genes that contribute to disorders and their expressed behavioral manifestations.

endorphins: Biochemical substances produced by the body under conditions of stress or vigorous exercise that serve to alleviate pain.

English language learner (ELL): A term used to describe school children in the United States from immigrant families for whom English is a second language. Many have little or no exposure to English prior to entering school.

epigenesis: The control of genetic expression by both regulatory DNA and environmental factors.

epigenetic model: A type of multidimensional or systems theory, which assumes that development is the result of complex interactions between genetic and environmental factors. Developmental change is bidirectional with the environment influencing biology and biology influencing the environment.

epigenetics: See *epigenesis*.

epigenome: The full set of factors, from DNA to outside world that controls the expression of coded genes.

epinephrine: Also called adrenaline, it is a substance that is both a hormone and a

neurotransmitter. One place it is produced is in the adrenal glands as part of the body's response to stress. Among its effects is increased heart rate.

episodic knowledge: Knowledge of the events we have experienced, such as what you ate for breakfast.

epistemological: Having to do with knowledge, such as how it is acquired and the nature of truth and reality.

Erikson's psychosocial stages: Erik Erikson's eight-stage model of personality that focuses on explaining attitudes and feelings towards the self and others. The first five correspond to the age periods in Freud's psychosexual stages, whereas three adult life stages suggest that personality development continues until death.

escape: Perry's characterization of the behavior of individuals who revert to relativism when the demands of commitment are too stressful.

establishment stage: In Super's theory, the final stage in the development of vocational self-concept (about 25 to 44), when work experiences provide the laboratory within which the matching of vocational self-concept and job settings is tried out, sometimes reevaluated, sometimes confirmed, and eventually stabilized.

estrogen: A feminizing hormone that is produced by the ovaries in females and to a lesser extent by the testes in males.

ethnic/racial identity (ERI): An aspect of identity that focuses on the ethnic or racial group that individuals see themselves as belonging to; this aspect of identity tends to become more salient and central for members of marginalized groups as they move through adolescence, especially if they experience discrimination.

ethnicity: People are considered to share ethnicity when they have a common ancestry, language, and place of origin, as well as a sense of belonging to the same group.

ethologists: Biologists who do careful observations of animal behavior in natural environments.

eudaemonic well-being: A term synonymous with psychological well-being.

executive functions (EFs): A set of cognitive processes that include *working memory, self-regulation (or inhibitory control)*, and *cognitive flexibility*. Advances in these functions with development make intentional control of attention and behavior possible, such as planning and working toward goals.

executive stage: In Schaie's theory, a stage that some middle adults experience who take on executive functions at work and in the community that extends beyond the responsible stage. This stage requires one to focus heavily on learning about complex relationships, multiple perspectives, commitment, and conflict resolution.

exosystem: In Bronfenbrenner's bioecological model, the level of the environment that children may not directly interact with but that influences them nonetheless.

experience sampling method (ESM): A research technique in which participants are interrupted at random times during the day and asked to report on what they are doing, thinking, and feeling.

experience-dependent: Describes neural growth that is stimulated by environmental experiences and may vary from one individual to another.

experience-expectant: Describes neural growth that requires a certain kind of environmental stimulation that is almost certain to occur in the experience of most members of a species. An example is development of the visual system that requires exposure to light in order to occur.

experimental group: In experimental design, the group for which the causal variable is purposely changed.

experiments: A technique for testing the predictions of a theory in which the researcher purposely manipulates the causal variable to observe the effects of the manipulation on the outcome variable.

explanation: The second step in the scientific method, when the researcher frames a theory or set of hypotheses about how the facts gained from descriptive research are related to each other and why they occur.

exploration: According to Marcia, one of the two processes involved in a young person's identity formation; it involves questioning and weighing alternative values, beliefs, and goals.

exploratory play: Play that involves manipulating objects, checking out their properties, sorting, and/or organizing them. Through exploratory play, children can learn about object properties, spatial relations, numerical relations, categorical relations, and so on. Begins in infancy.

exploratory stage: In Super's theory, the second life stage in the development of vocational self-concept from about 14 to 24, in which vocational self-concept is tentatively narrowed down, but often career choices are not finalized.

externalizing problems: Problem behavior that involves engaging in inappropriate conduct, especially aggressive acts.

extraversion (E): One of the Big 5 personality traits that is described using synonyms including *outgoing, active, assertive, energetic, talkative,* and *enthusiastic.*

false belief tasks: Tasks in which one person has correct knowledge of a situation, but another person (or the same person at another time) has incorrect knowledge, or a "false belief." Used to test children's theory of mind, specifically their understanding of others' mental states.

family life cycle: A normative, stagelike sequence of traditional family developments in intact marriages as partners become parents, rear and launch their children, become "empty nesters," and subsequently face old age.

fast mapping: The rapidity with which young children add new words to functional vocabulary after only one or two exposures.

fearful: In Bartholomew's typology of adult attachment categories, a subcategory of avoidant attachment. Describes individuals who have negative models of both self and others and who see relationships as desirable but out of reach. Their desire for close relationships with others is thwarted by fear of rejection, and ultimately they withdraw. A high level of distress surrounds attachment themes.

fearfulness or reactivity: In infants, proneness to crying or pulling away from new sensory stimuli.

fetal alcohol spectrum disorders (FASD): A range of intellectual and behavioral problems that might occur in children who have been exposed to alcohol during prenatal development.

fetal alcohol syndrome (FAS): A condition found in babies who are exposed to alcohol prenatally. It is characterized by a unique facial configuration (small head, widely spaced eyes, flattened nose) as well as possible intellectual disability and behavioral problems.

five factor model of personality (Big 5): The five most basic dimensions of personality including neuroticism (N), extraversion (E), openness (O), agreeableness (A), and conscientiousness (C).

flashbulb memories: Recollections that are especially vivid and personally relevant because of the emotions associated with them.

fluid intelligence (mechanics): Basic operational characteristics that seem to directly reflect how well the "hardware" of the nervous system is working. Its functions include such things as processing speed and inhibitory mechanisms.

follicle-stimulating hormone (FSH): Hormone that stimulates the gonads.

forebrain: The largest and most recently evolved portion of a mammalian brain; includes the cerebrum.

foreclosure: One of Marcia's four identity status categories that describes individuals who make commitments with little or no exploration of alternatives. They incorporate the values and goals of significant others without reflection.

forgotten half: The name given to 18- to 24-year-olds who do not go to college.

formal operational stage: In Piaget's theory of cognitive development, a stage that begins at about 11 or 12 years, when children are able to engage in thinking that (1) rises above particular contents and focuses on relationships that govern those contents (abstractions), (2) involves coordinating multiple relationships, and (3) can be difficult even for adults.

"four horsemen of the apocalypse": The four kinds of negativity that do the most damage to relationships and that are highly predictive of divorce. They are criticism, defensiveness, contempt, and stonewalling.

Freud's psychosexual stages: The five developmental stages that Freud believed were initiated by changes in the id and its energy levels.

friendship skills: Behavioral skills, such as appropriate assertiveness, good communication, and conflict resolution that maintain and enhance friendships.

friendship understanding: A child's changing knowledge of what friendship implies.

friendship valuing: Emotional attachment or investment that a child makes in a friendship.

frontal lobe: The part of the cerebrum that is situated at the top front part of each hemisphere and controls voluntary muscle movements and higher-level cognitive functions such as planning, goal setting, and decision-making.

gamma-amino butyric acid (GABA): A neurotransmitter that has inhibitory functions.

gender constancy: Recognizing the permanency of one's gender category membership and understanding that it could never change.

gender identity: The awareness of one's own gender assignment and understanding of its meaning.

gender intensification hypothesis: A hypothesis that suggests that one way young teens cope with the demands of establishing an adult identity is to fall back on stereotyped notions of masculinity or femininity.

gender nonconformity: Behaviors, emotions, or aspects of appearance that do not adhere to societal expectations for one's gender.

gender schema: A network of ideas and expectations of male and female beliefs about male and female characteristics that affect what we pay attention to, what we interpret, and what we remember about events.

gender stability: The understanding that over time, one's gender category stays the same: Boys grow into men, girls grow into women.

gender stereotypes: The beliefs and expectations that individuals have concerning the different behavioral tendencies and distribution of personality traits between the sexes.

gene expression: The process by which DNA information is transmitted and translated to cells.

gene regulation: The promotion or inhibition of gene transcription. Intergenic DNA and an array of factors in the cellular environment and beyond are involved in gene regulation.

generalization: The process by which learned behaviors may be extended to new events that are very similar to events in the original learning context.

generativity: A motive or need that can be filled through one's vocation or avocations, through child rearing, or through community service. It includes productivity and creativity. Generativity also describes people who are contributing members of society.

generativity accomplishment: A sense of satisfaction in making a meaningful contribution.

generativity desire: Expression of generativity goals, such as caring for future generations, wanting to produce something of lasting value, and being concerned about being needed.

genes: Functional units or sections of DNA that provide a blueprint or code to the cell for how to produce proteins and enzymes. Found on chromosomes, they come in matching pairs, one from each parent.

genetic counselors: People who help screen candidates for testing that would help determine the risk of genetic disorders for their offspring. Genetic counselors provide information and support to prospective parents regarding their choices about testing, childbearing, and parenting.

genetic vulnerability (diathesis-stress): A physiological makeup (diathesis) that makes an individual more prone to the negative effects of unsupportive parenting or other negative environmental influences (stress) than other people.

genital stage: The fifth and last of Freud's psychosexual stages, when the changes of puberty mean that id energy is especially invested in adult sexual impulses.

genital tubercle: A prenatal structure in both male and female fetuses. In males, it becomes the penis as a result of effects of circulating androgens. In females, it becomes a clitoris.

genome: All of a person's coded and noncoded DNA.

genotype: An individual's genetic endowment, including both expressed and unexpressed genes.

glial cells: Supporting cells in the central nervous system that provide a type of scaffolding for the neurons.

globalization: The process by which, as a result of international communication, transportation, and trade, countries around the world influence one another's lifestyle, economics, and culture, so that similarities among nations increase along with interaction.

glucocorticoid: A set of hormones referred to as "stress hormones," such as cortisol, that play a role in the body's reaction to stress.

glucocorticoid receptors: Receptors located on cells throughout the body and brain that bind with cortisol and other glucocorticoids, triggering an array of physiological responses to stressors.

glutamate: A neurotransmitter that has excitatory functions.

gonadotropin releasing hormone (GnRH): Substance released in the brain that triggers a hormonal cascade related to activity of the reproductive system.

gonads: Testes in males and ovaries in females. Produce eggs (ova) in females and sperm in males. Increase their hormone production at puberty after being stimulated by hormones released from the pituitary gland in response to the maturing hypothalamus.

good stress: Activation of a rapid bodily response to a stressor, followed by an efficient "turning off" of that response.

goodness of fit model: Thomas and Chess's view that when adults provide care that is adjusted to the temperament of an infant or child, even difficult early temperaments are unlikely to lead to later adjustment problems.

grey matter: Brain tissue consisting primarily of neuron bodies, dendrites, and unmyelinated axons, which appears grey.

grief work: A process that explicitly encourages bereaved individuals to confront and "work through" their feelings about loss for recovery to take place.

growth: Developmental change or adaptation to the constant flux of influences on our lives that involves adding new characteristics, understandings, skills, and so on to our behavioral repertoire.

"growth" mindset: Believing that when people perform well it is usually because they have worked hard and/or had good training, and that abilities and skills (such as intelligence) can grow.

growth stage: In Super's theory, the first stage in the development of vocational self-concept lasting until about age 14. Many elements of identity develop in this stage including ideas about their interests, attitudes, skills, and needs.

guided imagery: A technique used to aid memory of an event or person. For example, a child might be asked to pretend that an event occurred, then create a mental picture of the event and its details.

habituation: A decrease in an infant's responses to a stimulus over time, including decreased looking, decreased sucking, a return to a resting heart rate, and so on.

habituation paradigm: A research technique that takes advantage of a baby's tendency to orient to new stimulation and to habituate to repeated or old stimulation. Once an infant habituates to one stimulus a new stimulus can be presented. The baby's reorienting to the new stimulus (or failure to do so) reveals whether or not she perceives or notices the differences between the stimuli.

harmony collectivism: A form of collectivism (giving the group priority over the individual) that is characteristic of East Asian cultures; family is primary, interpersonal conflict or burdening others is avoided; positive emotions towards others are not manifested directly, but care takes the form of giving advice, joint problem solving, or offering practical help; moderating emotional expression is preferred.

hedonic well-being: A term synonymous with subjective well-being.

hedonistic: Preschool-aged children's tendency to be more concerned about their own needs than those of someone else in need.

helpless pattern: An orientation to failure in which individuals begin to denigrate their abilities when they encounter failure and typically stop applying themselves or trying to improve their performance.

hemispheric specialization: The two symmetrical halves of the cerebrum process information from and control opposite sides of the body. They also control some different higher cognitive functions, with the left hemisphere largely responsible for language and the right hemisphere largely responsible for visual-spatial skills.

heteronomous stage: Stage of moral development described by Piaget characterizes children from about ages 5 through 8, when they regard rules as immutable, existing outside the self, and requiring strict adherence.

heterosexuality: A sexual preference for partners of the opposite sex.

hidden object test: A research technique invented by Piaget to assess object permanence in infants from 6 months old. An interesting object, like a small toy, is placed in front of a baby within her reach. As the baby watches, the experimenter covers the object so that it is out of sight. If the baby searches for the object under the cloth she demonstrates that she has a sense of the continued existence of absent objects.

hierarchical integration: The organization and integration of activities and skills from one stage of development into broader, more complex patterns at the next stage.

hindbrain: The part of the mammalian brain that evolved first. Includes the medulla, pons, cerebellum, and reticular formation.

hippocampus: The region of the forebrain that plays a role in emotions, the ability to remember, and the ability to compare sensory information to expectations.

histones: Proteins that wrap around DNA to help form chromosomes.

homeostatic steady state: A stable state maintained over time by a couple's unique balance of positive and negative elements in areas of interactive behavior, perception, and physiology.

homogamy: A standard for mate selection in which one chooses a potential mate based on her or his similarity to oneself in religion, SES, race, education, and so on.

homophily: A degree of similarity among members of a peer group on behavior or attitudinal attributes of importance.

homosexuality: A sexual preference for partners of one's own sex.

honeymoon: The earliest stage of retirement, when people focus on the pleasures of being free from the constraints of old schedules, dress codes, and other work demands.

hospice movement: A patient-centered approach for people suffering from terminal illness that emphasizes the importance of giving patients as much knowledge about their condition as possible so that they maintain some control over their care, and focuses not on curing disease but on managing symptoms and pain by means of palliative medicine.

hostile attributional bias (HAB): A tendency to interpret or perceive what is neutral behavior as threatening. Often characterizes aggressive individuals.

Huntington's disease: A lethal genetic disorder, usually beginning between 30 and 40 years of age, that causes the nervous system to deteriorate, leading to uncontrolled movements, increasingly disordered psychological functioning, and eventually death. Because the dominant, defective alleles causing this disorder do not have their effects until after the childbearing years, it continues to be passed from one generation to another.

hypothalamic-pituitary-adrenal (HPA) axis: The system involved in the body's physical response to stress. When a person experiences or anticipates stress, the amygdala detects the danger and informs the hypothalamus, which communicates the danger to the pituitary gland, which responds by releasing adrenocorticotropic hormone (ACTH) into the bloodstream. ACTH causes the adrenal glands to release the hormones epinephrine, norepinephrine, and cortisol, which travel back to the brain and prepare the body to resist the stressor.

hypothalamus: The brain structure that plays a role in emotions, ability to remember, and ability to compare sensory information to expectations.

I-self or self-as-subject: The part of the self that is an active agent or is the knower. The part of the self that experiences a sense of subjective self-awareness.

id: In Freud's personality theory, one of three aspects of personality. Represents the biological self and its function is to keep the individual alive. It is irrational, blindly pursuing the fulfillment of physical needs or "instincts," such as the hunger drive and the sex drive.

ideals: Imagined, logically organized, perfect systems (such as political systems or persons) that do not match reality.

identification: Trying to become like another person by both imitating the model's behaviors and internalizing her attitudes, standards, and values.

identity achievement: One of Marcia's four identity status categories characterizing individuals whose development has been marked by exploration and then commitment to certain alternatives. Persons in this category have constructed their identity by their own efforts to shape and transform their earlier selves.

identity diffusion: One of Marcia's four identity status categories that often describes young adolescents as they embark on the identity development process. The individual is not actively involved in exploring possible life choices, nor has she made any firm commitments to them.

ill-defined or ill-structured problems: Problems faced in adulthood that lack preestablished answers. The "right" answer to an ill-defined problem may be different depending on circumstances and on the perspective of the problem solver.

imaginary audience: An individual's mistaken assumption that others are as intrigued by and concerned about him as he is. A characteristic feature of adolescents' self-focuses.

immanent justice: The expectation that misbehavior will eventually be punished, even if no one knows about it, as though some higher authority is always watching.

immigrant family: A family in which at least one parent was born outside of the country of residence.

immigrant paradox model: A view that expects children from immigrant families to be more successful than other children of similar SES because immigrant families have strengths or protective factors (such as cultural values) that moderate the risks they face.

immigrant risk model: A view that expects children from immigrant families to be especially vulnerable to academic or social problems because of an accumulation of risk factors, such as low SES, lack of skill with the language of the country of residence, ethnic stereotypes, and so on.

immunosuppression: Suppressed or weakened state of the immune system.

implantation: The process by which a zygote, which has migrated down the mother's fallopian tube into the uterus, becomes attached to the uterine lining.

implementation: In Super's theory, completion of education along with entry into full-time employment that is the final step in the exploratory stage.

incremental models: Theoretical models in which change is considered steady and specific to particular behaviors or mental activities, rather than being marked by major, sweeping reorganizations that affect many behaviors at once, as in stage theories.

indicated prevention: A category of prevention efforts that address individuals who show subclinical symptoms of disorders.

induction: One method parents use to enforce control of children's behavior. Involves use of explanation, giving reasons for rules and appealing to children's desires to be grown-up. The most effective way to promote the internalization of rules.

indulgent parenting: Also called permissive parenting, it is a parenting style that describes parents who are high on responsiveness but low on demandingness.

industry: In Erikson's theory, an aspect of self-concept that develops as a function of the first work experiences in childhood. A belief in one's ability to master the skills and tools needed to be productive and an expectation of pleasure in completion of challenging work.

infant directed speech (IDS): Speech directed to young children, sometimes called *motherese* or *parentese*. In comparison to adult-directed speech, it tends to be slower, higher in pitch, has more exaggerated intonation, shorter sentences, and simpler, less varied vocabulary, among other differences.

infantile amnesia: The difficulty people experience remembering events in their lives before they were 3 or 4 years old.

inferior colliculi: Small structures in the midbrain involved in receiving sensory input from the ears.

influence: The process by which a peer group can cause an individual to conform to the norms of the group.

information processing theories: Theories that tend to liken human cognitive functioning to computer processing of information.

initial commitment: Position 7 in Perry's model that, taken together with multiple commitments (Position 8) and resolve (Position 9), suggests a flowering of the commitments anticipated in Positions 5 and 6. Changes in thinking are more qualitative than structural.

inner speech: Internal, subvocal dialogue that in Vygotsky's theory facilitates thinking.

instrumental aggression: Using force or threat to obtain possession of a desired object or goal.

integrative health: Area of research and practice that addresses the full range of physical, emotional, mental, social, spiritual, and environmental influences that affect a person's health.

intention: A mental state, such as a plan or a desire that is the source of voluntary action.

intergenerational transmission: When parents repeat with their children the patterns of trauma, rejection, and maltreatment that they experienced as children from their own parents.

internalization: The process by which children adopt adults' standards and rules as their own.

internalizing problems: Problem behavior that involves negative feelings about self and other symptoms of depression.

interneuron: One of two main types of neurons in systems of neurons. These have short projections (e.g., short axons) and affect other cells relatively close to the circuit of which they are a part.

interpersonal orientation: The way an individual characteristically interacts on a social level.

intersensory integration (or intermodal perception): The notion that the senses are already somewhat related very early in infancy, perhaps at birth, and that when babies perceive an object in one way, they can construct some notion of the object's other perceptual characteristics.

intersex: One or more categories of gender identity along a continuum from "male" to "female," based on subtle physical variations (nondimorphism) in internal and external reproductive organs, sex chromosomes, and hormones.

intimacy: A quality of interpersonal relating through which partners share personal thoughts, feelings, and other important aspects of themselves with each other. True intimacy is marked by openness, affection, and trust.

intrapersonal models: Drawing on theories of attachment or personality, this model emphasizes the contribution of one's personal history or temperament to the success or failure of relationships.

invincibility fable: A feeling of being invulnerable, or even immortal that can be part of an adolescent's personal fable.

irritability or negative emotionality: The infant's tendency to cry, squirm, and otherwise react with fussiness to negative or frustrating events. An aspect of infant temperament.

job crafting: A process in which employees actively modify the job they perform somewhat to create a better fit to their own interests and skills.

just world: Beliefs that the world is fair and that people in it get what they deserve.

karyotype: A display of the actual chromosomes from human body cells, photographed under a microscope and laid out in matching pairs.

keeper of meaning (vs. rigidity): A stage of life that Vaillant added to Erikson's sequence of stages, characterizing late middle adulthood when the adult expands his generative concerns beyond just making a productive contribution, to actually preserve something that is part of the culture and, in doing so, establish the meaningfulness of the work or contributions he has made.

kindling-behavioral sensitization: Phenomenon characterized by progressive illness severity or illness incidence following an initial illness episode due to increased sensitivity to stressful triggers.

kinkeeper: The person in an extended family who helps the generations maintain contact with one another.

kisspeptin: A chemical produced in the hypothalamus that combines with receptors in the hypothalamus to trigger a cascade of events in many parts of the brain and body, initiating puberty.

knowledge base: An individual's mentally stored information. Adults generally have a larger base for most domains of knowledge than children do.

kwashiorkor: A condition occurring in children who suffer severe protein and calorie shortages, which is characterized by stunted growth, a protuberant belly, and extreme apathy. Although therapeutic diets can reverse some effects, cognitive impairments are likely to persist.

late multiplicity: Position 4 in Perry's model in which students fully realize that even experts differ among themselves in regard to what is true. Students handle this realization by embracing either the oppositional or relative subordinate response to late multiplicity.

latency stage: The fourth of Freud's psychosexual stages, beginning around age 5, during which the id's energy is not especially linked to any particular pleasure or body part, and the potential conflicts among the three aspects of personality are largely latent and unexpressed.

launching period: The time when emerging adults begin to move away from home and become more self-sufficient.

legacy-leaving stage: In Schaie's theory, a late life stage when the mind is sound but frailty signals that life is ending. Individuals often work on establishing a written or oral account of their lives or of the history of their families to pass on to others.

leptin: Hormone found in fat tissue that plays a role in appetite and eating behavior.

life events: Category of stressor that is discrete, often traumatic, and with a clear onset.

life history theory: A view of the causes and outcomes of adolescent engagement in adult activities such as drinking, working for pay, sex, and so on; in this view, a "fast life" strategy (early engagement in adult activities) prioritizes reproduction and early separation from parents and is most likely when resources are scarce; a "slow life" strategy delays reproduction and separation and is more likely when resources are plentiful.

life span development or life span developmental psychology: The study of human behavioral change from conception to death.

life span developmental theories or models: A type of multidimensional theory that emphasizes the continuity of developmental processes from birth through death. Developmental change, seen as adaptation, involves proximal interactions between the organism and the immediate context modified by more distal processes both within the individual and in the environment.

life structure: A pattern of relationships between the self and the external world, such as relationships to one's spouse, lover, family, occupation, religion, leisure, and so on.

life-course persistent model: A developmental pattern of adolescent antisocial behavior that begins in early childhood and continues throughout life. This pattern is generally associated with early conduct problems, aggressiveness, and academic difficulties.

life-course perspective: The view that development is influenced by the intersection of chronological age (life time), family-related (family time), and membership in a birth cohort (historical time).

limbic system: A collection of structures in the brain that includes the hippocampus, amygdala, septum, thalamus, and hypothalamus. These structures produce feelings such as pleasure, pain, anger, sexuality, fear, and affection. Referred to as the "emotional brain" and works in concert with other parts of the brain, such as the frontal lobes.

longitudinal: A study design in which one group of subjects is measured several times as they grow older, eliminating cohort differences.

long-term memory: An almost unlimited mental store of knowledge.

looking-glass self: According to Cooley, a self-concept that develops from the reflected appraisals of others, primarily attachment figures.

loss-focused grief: Confronting the painful reality of death, expressing sadness, and gradually desensitizing oneself to the reminders of loss that can lead to rumination or excessive preoccupation and, often, great distress.

love withdrawal: One method parents use to enforce control of children's behavior. Involves parents withdrawing attention or affection, expressing disappointment or disillusionment with a child, turning away from a child, cutting off verbal or emotional contact, or enforcing separations. Generates high anxiety and elicits immediate compliance.

luteinizing hormone (LH): Hormone that stimulates the gonads.

macrosystem: In Bronfenbrenner's bioecological model, the customs and character of the larger culture that help shape the microsystems.

maintenance hypothesis: The view that couples typically work hard to maintain their favorable beliefs about each other, despite the inevitable challenges of marriage. Positive illusions support the relationship, and people are often reluctant to abandon them to face reality.

maintenance or resilience: In life span developmental theory, a kind of adaptation that involves finding ways to continue functioning at the same level in the face of challenges or to restore one's functioning after suffering some loss.

maintenance stage: In Super's theory, a stage from about age 45 to 64, when an individual makes ongoing adjustments to improve her work situation, often achieving more advanced status and seniority.

making interesting sights last: Occurs when an infant's behavior accidentally produces an interesting event, the child notices the effect, and repeats the action. A precursor to intentional behavior in Piaget's view.

marker events: Events that are used as criteria for adulthood, including completing formal education, entering the adult workforce, leaving the family home, getting married, and becoming a parent.

mastery orientation: An orientation to failure in which individuals move forward optimistically, assuming that they can succeed with further effort. They seem to construe failure as a challenge rather than as an obstacle.

maturity demands: Parents' requirements that children perform behaviors that are suitable to their level of maturity.

maturity gap: A time in adolescence when physical maturity is achieved but social maturity is not. Adolescents may mimic the behavior of more advanced peers to possess the symbolic trappings of adult status (sexual intimacy, material possessions, autonomy, and respect from parents).

maximizers: Decision makers who tend to explore alternatives extensively, have high standards and have difficulty making choices, typically assuming that there is a "best" choice.

Me-self/self-concept: The known part of the self that is the object of one's own or others' observations.

means–end behavior: A type of intentional behavior that characterizes infants by 8 to 12 months. Babies divert their attention from a goal, such as grasping a toy, in order to produce another action that will help achieve the goal.

mediated learning: A central concept in Vygotsky's theory. The child's acquisition of knowledge is "mediated" in the sense that it is highly influenced by the surrounding environment and culture.

mediating variables: Intermediate links in a causal chain. For example, if early poverty causes reading problems in school, and reading problems cause later depression, then reading problems serve as a mediating variable.

mediation: In Vygotsky's theory, the intermediary role of other people in determining the meaning of signs and symbols, like words, which in turn affect the child's thinking.

meditation: Family of techniques intended to train attention and improve regulatory functions.

medulla: A brain structure found in the hindbrain that helps to regulate functions that are basic for survival, such as heart rate, blood pressure, and respiration.

memory strategies: Potentially conscious activities a person may voluntarily carry out to remember something.

menarche: A girl's first menstruation.

menopause: The cessation of menstruation that usually begins in the 40s and continues for at least 10 years.

mesosystem: In Bronfenbrenner's bioecological model, the network of microsystems that relate with and modify one another.

messenger ribonucleic acid (mRNA): The organic compound that cells synthesize by copying strands of DNA. The sequence of bases in a gene is replicated in the mRNA, and then the RNA serves as a "messenger" to the cell from the gene, guiding the cell's construction of a protein.

meta-analysis: An analytic tool for assessing the effects of variables in which data from a large number of studies on the same topic are analyzed together to determine which effects are consistent across studies and what the strength of those effects are.

metacognition: The ability to think about and understand one's own cognitive processes and their effects.

metamemory: A person's understanding of her own memory processes, such as accurately assessing how likely she is to remember all of a list of words she has just studied.

method of control: A technique that parents use to enforce control of their children's behavior. The three primary methods are power assertion, love withdrawal, and induction.

methylation: An epigenetic change that makes the expression of a gene less likely. It involves the addition of a methyl group (an organic molecule) to DNA, either to the coded gene or to regulatory DNA. Or, it can involve the addition of a methyl group to histones that bind with DNA.

microRNAs (miRNAs): Short sections of RNA that can attach themselves to RNA and block the translation of the RNA into proteins.

microsystem: In Bronfenbrenner's bioecological model, the immediate environment where proximal processes are played out.

midbrain: A set of brain structures that are between hindbrain and forebrain and include the superior colliculi, inferior colliculi, and the substantia nigra.

mindfulness: Paying attention on purpose in the present moment with attitudes of curiosity, patience, nonjudgement and openness.

mindfulness neuroscience: The study of the effects of mindfulness on the brain and body; for example, mindfulness practice impacts certain brain-related functions, namely attention and other executive functions, emotion regulation, and self-awareness.

mindsets: Beliefs about whether intelligence or some other ability is a fixed asset or can change with training and practice.

minimum sufficiency principle: Long-term internalization of rules in children is best facilitated by mild power assertion, rather than harsh power assertion.

mitigation: When the perpetrator of a crime is guilty and is held responsible for the crime but is considered less than fully blameworthy. Mitigation applies not only to degree of culpability but also to degree of punishment.

mitochondria: Small organelles within cells that produce energy for the cell's metabolism and overall function.

mitosis: A kind of cell division that produces two new cells identical to the original cell.

modal personal orientation: In Holland's theory, an aspect of personality that is a typical and preferred style or approach to dealing with social and environmental tasks. Most jobs or careers will be compatible with one of the six orientations: realistic, investigative, artistic, social, enterprising, and conventional.

modeling: See *observational learning*.

moderating variables: Causal factors that interact with other causal variables, altering and sometimes even eliminating the effects of other variables altogether.

monozygotic (identical) twins: Twins who develop from a single zygote and have exactly the same genotype.

moral rules: The standards used to address fundamental issues of justice, welfare, and rights, such as rules about stealing, hurting others, or sharing. Rules of behavior that are relatively universal as opposed to being culturally based.

morality of caring: A focus on concern for others (as opposed to establishing justice) when making moral evaluation decisions and when evaluating decisions of others.

morality of justice: A focus on establishing justice (as opposed to concern for others) when making moral decisions and when evaluating decisions made by others.

moratorium: One of Marcia's four identity status categories in which individuals are actively involved in exploring possible life choices, but not having made any firm commitments to them.

motivational interviewing: An interviewing strategy used in some clinical interventions that involves identifying both the client's existing strengths and areas for improvement.

Mullerian ducts: Prenatal structures in both male and female fetuses that can develop into fallopian tubes, uterus and part of the vagina. These are destroyed by anti-Mullerian hormone in male fetuses.

multi-infarct dementia: A number of minor strokes that gradually do sufficient damage to cause dementia.

multidimensional theories: A class of theoretical models in which theorists consider development to be the result of the relationships among many causal components. They generally apply to all domains of development from the cognitive to the social and suggest that there are layers, or levels, of interacting causes for behavioral change: physical/molecular, biological, psychological, social, and cultural. These models may also be called transactional, relational, systems, or bioecological models.

multiple commitments: Position 8 in Perry's model that, taken together with initial commitment (Position 7) and resolve (Position 9), suggests a flowering of the commitments anticipated in Positions 5 and 6. Changes in thinking are more qualitative than structural.

multiplicity (prelegitimate): Position 2 in Perry's model that is characterized by the student's first encounters with multiplicity, that is, multiple ideas, multiple answers to life's questions, or multiple points of view. Individuals in this stage face confusion, yet maintain the belief that some "authority" possesses the ultimate truth or right answers.

multiplicity (subordinate): Position 3 in Perry's model in which the individual grudgingly acknowledges the reality and legitimacy of multiple perspectives. Individuals in this stage find it more difficult to deny that reasonable people can differ in their perspectives on life, and people who hold different views are not so easily dismissed as being wrong.

mutation: A change in the chemical structure of an existing gene, sometimes occurring spontaneously and sometimes occurring due to environmental influences, such as exposure to radiation or toxic chemicals.

myelination: The phenomenon in which glial cells wrap themselves around the axons of neurons, providing an insulating sheath that facilitates the conduction of electrical impulses.

narcissism: Viewing oneself as better than other people; often, people with this trait try to dominate or use others to meet their own needs and seek to be the center of attention.

narrative: A story or event description that conveys the full sense of an experience or gets at the point of an event while taking into account what the listener needs to hear to understand.

narrative identity: A method for studying identity development in which individuals are asked to tell stories about themselves and their lives; usually open-ended questions are provided as prompts.

narrow socialization: Socialization more characteristic of nonindustrialized cultures that exert extensive control over the expression of behaviors that violate social standards and expect substantial conformity from young members of the society.

needs oriented: Describes the understanding that another person's need is a good reason for helping, usually characteristic of children at some time in the elementary school years.

needs-based reasoning: Reasoning about other people's needs in which one must weigh one's own personal needs against those of others.

negative affect reciprocity: A tendency for negative emotions in one partner to follow from the other partner's negativity.

negative affectivity: The state or trait tendency to experience nervousness, fear, anger, sadness, contempt, or guilt.

negative correlation: A relationship between variables in which they change together but in opposite directions, so that as one increases, the other decreases.

negative reinforcement: Withdrawal of an aversive experience, which serves as a rewarding consequence of a behavior. For example, rewarding your dog for sitting on command by removing a restraining muzzle.

neglected: A sociometric category that includes those children who receive few nominations, either positive or negative, from their peers. Neglected children are characterized by their low level of social impact.

neglecting–uninvolved style: An interactive parenting style that combines low levels of warmth (emotional distance) and low levels of control or demandingness, so that parents invest very little time or attention in a child. Associated with many negative child outcomes.

neoPiagetians: Theorists who explain Piaget's stages or revise the stages using many information processing concepts. These theorists attempt to combine the best components of both Piagetian and information processing approaches.

nerve growth factor: A substance found within the brain that is absorbed by neurons and aids in the process of synapse production.

neural pruning: A gradual process in brain development that continues through adolescence into young adulthood in which neurons die off and many synaptic connections are selectively discarded.

neural stem cells: Undifferentiated cells located in the nervous system that can generate neurons and glial cells.

neural tube: A structure that represents the first step in the development of an embryo's central nervous system. It is formed when a sheet of cells from the embryo's upper surface turns inward and curls into a tube.

neuroimmunology: An area of neurobiology that focuses on the relationship between the nervous and immune systems.

neurons: The building blocks of the brain, these nerve cells are specialized for the transmission of electrical impulses.

neuroplasticity: The malleability of the human brain, its capacity to change and grow especially in response to new environmental input. Includes the capacity of neurons to shift functions to compensate for damage to other cells or because they have been transplanted to a different part of the brain.

neuroticism (N): One of the Big 5 personality traits that is described using synonyms including *tense, touchy, self-pitying, unstable, anxious,* and *worrying*.

neurotransmitters: Chemical substances found in the nervous system that communicate messages between neurons when released. The chemical message, once picked up by the dendrites, the cell body or the axon of a neighboring neuron, is read by that cell as a message to "fire" or "stop firing."

neurulation: The prenatal formation of a neural tube that begins the development of the central nervous system.

nonacademic self-concept: One of two major divisions of a child's general self-concept that includes his view of self in the social, emotional, and physical domains.

noncoded genes: Sections of intergenic DNA that do not code for protein production. They function to either initiate or prevent a gene's transcription.

nondeclarative knowledge: Knowledge that one cannot adequately put into words and might not enter awareness, including procedural knowledge, knowing how to do things.

nonheterosexual: A person who identifies either as homosexual or bisexual.

norepinephrine: Also called noradrenaline, it is one of the stress hormones released by the adrenal glands and has no effects on heart rate and other "fight or flight" responses in the body. Also functions as a neurotransmitter.

normativeness: The degree to which a behavior or an experience (such as corporal punishment by parents) is typical of most people in a community or culture.

nucleus: In the brain, a cluster of cells creating a functional structure.

nucleus accumbens: One of the basal ganglia, especially involved in motivation and approach behavior.

number conservation task: A procedure designed by Piaget to test children's understanding of number. Children must be able to recognize that the number of items in a set does not change when the appearance of the set changes; for example, when a row of buttons is spread out or bunched together.

object concept: Understanding of what an object is, including recognition that an object has properties that can stimulate all of our senses and that an object has "permanence"—it continues to exist even when we do not perceive it.

object permanence: The fact that objects have a separate existence from the perceiver; that is, they continue to exist even when no one perceives them.

occipital lobe: The part of the cerebrum, located at the back of each hemisphere that processes visual information.

ontogeny: The development of organisms.

openness (O): One of the Big 5 personality traits that is described using synonyms including *creative, artistic, curious, insightful, original,* and *wide-ranging interests.*

operant: An accidental or random action.

operant conditioning: The process by which a person learns to produce a formerly random behavior (or operant) in response to a cue because the behavior was previously reinforced in that situation.

oppositional: In Perry's theory, a response to late multiplicity characterized by legitimizing multiplicity as one pole of a new kind of dualism and the right–wrong dualism of Position 1 (strict dualism) at the other end of the new continuum. Allows individuals

to maintain a dualistic either-or structure in their thinking.

oppositional defiant disorder (ODD): A pattern of hostile, negative, or defiant behaviors, such as arguing with adults, spitefulness, or throwing tantrums. One type of conduct problem typically seen in children and youth.

optimization: A process of finding ways to enhance the achievement of remaining goals or finding environments that are enhancing that is key to successful development.

oral fixation: In Freud's personality theory, an excessive need for oral pleasures (such as eating or talking) that results from extreme denial or excessive indulgence of them during the oral stage.

oral stage: The first of Freud's psychosexual stages, corresponding to the first year of life, when Freud believed that a disproportionate amount of id energy is invested in drives satisfied through the mouth.

organization strategy: A memory strategy that involves sorting items to be learned on some meaningful basis, such as grouping the names by region.

orienting response: In infants, a set of behaviors that suggest that the baby is attending to a stimulus. May include head turn towards the stimulus, looking, decreased heart rate, and increased sucking.

osteoarthritis: The most common form of arthritis, which involves the thinning, fraying, and cracking of cartilage at the ends of bones.

other-directed coping behaviors: Efforts to deal with stress that appear to be aimed at changing the behaviors of others, such as when infants use facial expressions, movements, and verbalizations that seem designed to get a caregiver to respond positively in an interaction.

other-transforming: An immature interpersonal style in which an individual tries to dominate or coerce a friend into meeting his needs. Acting to change or transform the other; can involve bullying, aggression, or manipulation.

outcome variable: The variable that is said to be affected by the cause of a given phenomenon.

ovaries: Female gonads that primarily produce estrogen and progesterone, but also produce lesser amounts of androgens (such as testosterone). Site of egg (ovum) production in females.

ovum: Reproductive egg cell, containing only 23 chromosomes, produced in and released by the ovaries of females.

oxytocin: A neuropeptide hormone that facilitates social bonding.

palliative care: Comfort care that involves services provided by caregivers from several disciplines embodying a comprehensive approach to care that addresses pain management, emotional and spiritual care, and psychological support for caregivers and survivors.

parasympathetic nervous system (PSNS): Whereas the sympathetic nervous system arouses the body in response to threat, once the threat is reduced this system counteracts the arousal, down regulating the heart and lung activity for example and restoring energy to maintenance systems such as digestion, growth, and reproduction once the threat has passed.

parent centered: Describes parents whose interactions with their children are driven by parental needs rather than focusing on children's needs. Parents with this approach may make hostile attributions when children's needs are out of line with their own.

parental knowledge: When parents actually know what is going on in their children's lives; associated with healthy outcomes for teens.

parental monitoring: Consistent parental supervision.

parental solicitation: A type of parental monitoring that involves directly questioning adolescents about their lives and activities.

parentese: Another name for infant directed speech (IDS).

parenting styles: Approaches that characterize parents' typical interactions with and attitudes towards their children. Four styles have been identified, combining and crossing the positive and negative poles of two parenting dimensions—warmth and control. These styles are often predictive of child characteristics.

parietal lobe: A part of the cerebrum located between the frontal lobe (at the front of the cerebrum) and the occipital lobe (at the back of the cerebrum) and above the temporal lobe (on the side of the cerebrum) of each hemisphere. It processes somatosensory information such as touch, temperature, and pain.

passion: An element of love that refers to erotic attraction or feelings.

peer influence: The individual adolescent's behavior, values, and attitudes are affected and/or determined by peer group norms.

peer selection: Choosing peers based on behaviors, preferences, attitudes, and so on that are similar to one's own.

perceptual narrowing: The process by which infants lose the ability to perceive sound distinctions that are not used in their native language.

period of the embryo: Lasting from the fourth through the eighth week of gestation, the time that most of the body's organ systems and structures are forming.

period of the fetus: Lasting from the ninth week of gestation until birth, the time of rapid growth and further differentiation when the reproductive system forms, gains in body weight occur, and the brain and nervous system continue to develop.

period of the zygote: Approximately a 2-week period from the time of fertilization of a human ovum by a sperm to the time of implantation in the uterine wall.

permissive style: An interactive parenting style that combines moderate to high levels of warmth (positive emotional climate, sensitivity, and responsivity) with low levels of control or demandingness. Associated with impulsive behavior and low levels of self-reliance in children.

"the person who" fallacy: Refuting a well-documented finding by calling on knowledge of a person who is an exception.

personal fable: A distorted view of one's uniqueness that is a feature of adolescents' egocentrism.

personal rules: Rules about areas of functioning that individuals or families might have standards about, such as choices of friends or recreational activities or participation in family life, that are not governed by formal social rules in Western societies.

phallic stage: The third of Freud's psychosexual stages, lasting from age 3 to about 5, in which id energy is focused primarily in the genital region. This stage draws the greatest parental discipline, leads to feelings of guilt and the development of the superego, and can have long-lasting effects on how a child copes with postpubertal sexual needs.

phenotype: The aspect of a genetic blueprint that is actually expressed in the physical and behavioral characteristics of an individual.

Phineas Gage matrix: Syndrome related to injury of the frontal cortex. Consists of cognitive dysfunctions (such as poor planning, inadequate decision-making, inability to take another's perspective, and problems in sustaining employment) and emotional problems (such as shallow affect, lack of an enriched emotional life, lack of passion and initiative, and a diminished sense of pleasure and pain).

phonemes: The smallest units of sound that make a difference in meaning.

phonology: The sound system of a language; includes rules for arranging the basic sounds or "phonemes" of the language.

physician-assisted suicide: The prescribing of medicine that enables patients to take their own lives.

Piaget's cognitive development theory: Jean Piaget's theory of the development of cognition, which outlines four childhood stages in which the capacity to think logically about both concrete and abstract concepts evolves.

pituitary gland: A tiny structure at the base of the brain that is the source of many hormones, thereby influencing many bodily processes, from growth to responses to stressors.

placebo effect: Occurs when individuals receiving a placebo (a "dummy" version of a treatment) experience improvement in their symptoms and attribute the improvement to the placebo.

placenta: A nourishing barrier that surrounds the developing fetus, allowing nutrients from the mother's blood to pass to the fetus's blood while allowing waste to be removed by the mother's blood. Otherwise, it keeps the two circulatory systems separate.

plaques: In the brain, clumps of insoluble protein that are damaging to neurons and associated with Alzheimer's disease.

pleasure principle: The pursuit of gratification, which motivates the id in Freud's personality theory.

pleiotropy: The same gene contributes to multiple phenotypic traits that appear unrelated.

polygenic: Describes traits that are affected by the products of multiple gene pairs, often located on different chromosomes, so that any one pair of gene alleles has only a limited affect on a given trait.

pons: A brain structure located in the hindbrain that is involved in the regulation of the sleep–wake cycle.

popular: A sociometric category that includes those children who receive many positive nominations and few negative nominations from their peers (have high social preference and high social impact). Popular children are generally well-liked members of the group and have relatively high visibility among their peers.

positive affect: Tendency to express happy mood states by smiling and laughing especially to social stimuli. An aspect of infant temperament.

positive affectivity: The state or trait tendency to experience enthusiasm, alertness, joy, confidence, and determination.

positive correlation: A relationship between variables in which they change in the same direction, either both increasing or both decreasing.

positive reinforcement: A rewarding consequence of a behavior in the presence of a cue. Rewarding consequences increase the likelihood of that behavior in the future when the proper cue is provided. For example, if you give a food treat to your dog when she sits on command, the food treat is a positive reinforcement, and she is likely to repeat the sit in the future when she hears the command.

post-traumatic growth: Positive psychological change experienced as a result of the struggle with highly stressful or traumatic events.

post-traumatic stress disorder (PTSD): A trauma or stress-related disorder that follows a traumatic event. PTSD is characterized by clinically significant symptoms such as re-experience of the traumatic event, general numbing of responsiveness to others, heightened arousal, disturbed sleep, and so forth.

postconventional morality: Kohlberg's third stage of moral reasoning achieved by some adults in whom what is considered right is defined not by specific rules or laws but by general processes such as democratic principles or individual rights.

postformal or fifth-stage thinking: Characteristic of a stage beyond Piaget's sequence of stages that describes the changes in logical thinking that might occur in the adult years. Characterized by the ability of the problem solver to coordinate contradictory formal operational approaches to the same problem. The postformal thinker can understand the logic of each of the contradictory perspectives and integrate the perspectives into a larger whole.

power assertion: One method parents use to enforce control of children's behavior. Can involve physical punishment or the threat of physical punishment, or it can involve withdrawal of privileges. Effective for the immediate control of behavior, but over the long term, children show higher levels of anger, aggressiveness and anxiety.

pragmatics: One of the aspects of language that children must learn that goes beyond learning semantics and syntax and involves using the language effectively to communicate. Includes skills such as crafting a narrative and "code switching," using different language styles in different contexts.

pre-self: An infant's early inklings of the permanence of her body, its separateness from others, and the rhythms of interpersonal connections.

preconventional morality: Kohlberg's first stage of moral reasoning characterizing middle childhood in which what is right is what avoids punishment, what conforms to the dictates of authority, or what serves one's personal interests.

preferential response paradigms: Approaches to studying infant behavior and mental functioning. Multiple stimuli are presented to an infant (e.g., two visual stimuli) and researchers record (e.g., by measuring looking time) which stimulus the baby responds to more (prefers).

prefrontal cortex (PFC): The most anterior part of the frontal lobe, playing a role in planning, decision making, problem solving, and emotion regulation.

premoral stage: In Piaget's theory of moral development, characterizes preschoolers who are unconcerned about established rules or standards.

preoccupied (insecure): An attachment style classifying adults who provide transcripts in the Adult Attachment Interview that are not collaborative and that are characterized by very long, incoherent, egocentric responses that shift from topic to topic. They indicate substantial enmeshment or preoccupation with parents, registered by angry, accusatory language or by conflicted descriptions that connote ambivalence and confusion about early relationships. Their children tend to have anxious-ambivalent attachments. In Bartholomew's typology, these individuals are emotionally demanding, anxious about gaining acceptance, fearful of rejection, and preoccupied with relationships.

preoperational egocentrism: The tendency of preschoolers to be aware only of their own perspective. Demonstrated in their expectations that others will know what they know, believe what they believe, and so on.

preoperational stage: In Piaget's theory of cognitive development, the time period from approximately age 2 to 7 when children are capable of representational thought but appear to be prelogical in their thinking.

pretend play: Play in which children (beginning at about age 2) behave "as if" objects or people were something or someone else, that is, treating them as symbols. In social pretend play, children enact roles "as if" they themselves were other people, simulating the actions or characteristics of others and interacting with other children playing other roles.

prevention science: A new and evolving multidisciplinary mix of human development, psychopathology, epidemiology, education, and criminology that offers us useful guidelines for understanding what constitutes effective prevention.

primary control: Control efforts that are attempts to affect the immediate environment beyond ourselves.

primary prevention: An attempt to forestall the development of problems by promoting health and wellness in the general population through group-oriented interventions.

primary sexual characteristics: The physical traits directly involved in reproduction, such as the genitalia.

principle of equifinality: Many early developmental pathways can produce similar outcomes.

principle of multifinality: The same developmental pathways may result in a wide range of possible outcomes.

procedural knowledge: Describes the often unconscious, nondeclarative knowledge of how to do things that underlies many physical skills.

prodrome: A disorder or set of disorders (e.g., anxiety disorders) that are precursors to another disorder (e.g., depression), predicting the later disorder in a strong, unidirectional fashion.

production deficiency: Failure to use a memory strategy one has knowledge of even in a situation where it is ordinarily helpful.

productive narrowing: A reduction in the variety of babbling sounds that infants make over time, so that by 9 months old they produce primarily sounds that match the phonemes of their native language.

progeria: A fatal genetic disorder that causes rapid aging, so that by late childhood its victims are dying of "old age." Because individuals with progeria do not survive long enough to reproduce, the disease must be caused by a genetic mutation.

progesterone: A hormone involved in the reproductive cycle, especially in females.

projection neuron: One of two main types of neurons in systems of neurons. These have long projections, especially axons that extend far away from the cell body.

prosocial behavior or altruism: Voluntarily acting in ways that seem intended to benefit someone else.

protective factors: Aspects of the organism or the environment that moderate the negative effects of risk.

proteins: The chemical building blocks of the body that are constructed when cells follow the codes provided by genes.

protest: The second phase in the grieving process where bereaved individuals may experience periods of obsessive yearning or searching for the lost loved one as well as bouts of restlessness or irritability.

proximal processes: Reciprocal interactions between a person and her immediate external environment, including other people, the physical environment, or informational sources such as books or movies. In Bronfenbrenner's biological model, all developments are a function of these processes.

proximity maintenance: One of three purposes of the attachment system. Bonds between infant and caregiver encourage and sustain physical closeness.

prudential domain: A category of personal behaviors (such as drinking and smoking) that (unlike other personal behaviors such as hair style choices) can involve safety and health concerns, so that parents may feel obliged to impose restrictions.

psychoanalytic theory: A theory of personality development and its complex functioning in adulthood originated by Sigmund Freud.

psychological control: A kind of parental intrusiveness and interference in children's lives often involving criticizing or derogating children, manipulating their emotional experiences to produce guilt or shame, and/or making love conditional upon children's behavior.

psychoneuroimmunology: The study of the interactions between the central nervous system, the immune system, and behavior.

psychosocial development: Change with age in the psychological processes of interpersonal understanding, skills, and values that affect an individual's capacity for interpersonal relationships, including friendships.

psychotropic drugs: Substances that affect neural functioning, causing cognitive, behavioral, and/or emotional effects.

puberty: A process of sexual maturing in late childhood related to a wide range of emotional, behavioral, and social changes.

qualitative research: Any kind of research that does not use statistical procedures or quantitative methods to arrive at conclusions.

racial group: Groups of people, like Blacks, Whites, and Asians, who have historically been assumed to be genetically different, identifiable by variations in hair, skin color, bone structure, or other physiological markers. Genetic indicators of race have not been found, so that racial groups appear to be a social construction.

reactive attachment disorder (RAD): A lack of ability to form affectional bonds with other people and a pattern of markedly disturbed social relationships. RAD can result when a child receives grossly neglectful or pathological care in the early years.

reality monitoring: The ability to distinguish what is imagined from what is real.

reality principle: A focus on understanding the world and behavioral consequences that leads to sensible and self-protective behavior. In Freud's personality theory, the ego operates on this principle.

recall: Remembering information or events that are not currently available to the senses. Requires the ability to mentally represent the absent information.

recency: A salient characteristic of self-memories. The tendency to remember something that has happened to us recently better than something that happened in the more distant past.

receptor: A chemical located either on the surface of a cell or inside a cell that binds to a transcription factor (coming either from outside or inside the cell) and allowing the transcription factor to then bind with a regulatory portion of DNA to begin the transcription of a gene.

recognition: Remembering in the sense of knowing that information currently available to the senses has been previously experienced.

reflective judgment: In Kitchener's theory of the development of problem solving, the analysis of the elements of a problem and justification of problem solutions.

reflective practice: A method used by counselors that emphasizes careful consideration of theoretical and empirical sources of knowledge, as well as one's own beliefs and assumptions, as a precursor to practice.

refusal of treatment: Patients' refusal of any food, water, or medical treatment that prolongs life.

regulation of loss: In life span developmental theory, a kind of adaptive functioning that involves reorganizing the way we behave by adjusting our expectations and accepting a lower level of functioning.

rehearsal: A strategy for remembering that usually involves continuing to actively process to-be-remembered material, like repeating it to oneself.

reinforcement: An event that an individual experiences as pleasurable or rewarding, which increases the frequency of a behavior that occurred immediately before the pleasurable event.

reintegrative stage: In Schaie's theory, the elder years when individuals do not often need to acquire new domains of knowledge or to figure out new ways of applying what they know. Many are motivated to conserve energy (physical and psychological). Cognitive efforts are aimed at solving immediate, practical problems that seem critically important to daily functioning.

rejected: A sociometric category that includes those children who receive many negative nominations and few positive nominations from their peers. Rejected children are typically disliked (low social preference) but have generally high visibility (high social impact).

rejected-aggressive: Describes children who are rejected because they aggress against their peers.

rejected-withdrawn: Describes children who are rejected because they withdraw from their peers.

relatedness: In self-determination theory, one of three basic needs. Feeling that one is important to others and valued enough to be sensitively and responsively cared for, from infancy onward.

relational aggression: A type of aggression in which relationships are manipulated and/or damaged in order to hurt an individual.

relative subordinate: In Perry's theory, a response to late multiplicity in which students (primarily under the guidance of authority) begin to understand that some opinions are more legitimate than others. The value of a perspective is now understood to be related to the supporting arguments and evidence for the position.

relativistic thought: The essence of postformal thought in which several truth systems exist describing the reality of the same event, and they appear to be logically equivalent.

religious/spiritual struggles: A wide range of problems that clients might grapple with related to spirituality or religion, such as concerns about God's punishment, beliefs that evil spirits might be a source of their troubles, worries about loss of faith, and so on.

reminiscence bump: A salient feature of self-memories, also called the "reminiscence bump." Regardless of age, adults' cue-prompted memories of the self from the young adult period (ages 18–22) are slightly but reliably overproduced.

reorganization: The last phase in the grieving process in which the grieving individual discovers ways to hold on to the memory of the deceased and integrate that memory into their current life and new attachments.

reorganizational stage: In Schaie's theory, a stage of early old age, when responsibilities narrow as children grow up and retirement becomes an option. Flexibility in problem solving is needed to create a satisfying, meaningful environment for the rest of life, but the focus tends to narrow to a changed set of personal goals and needs.

reorientation: The third stage of retirement, which is a time of active trial and error. The retiree seeks solutions to the problems that retirement presents and tries strategies for building a satisfactory life.

representational thought: The capacity to think about things or events that are not currently stimulating one's senses. Utilizes mental images or symbols to "re-present" the absent experience.

representations: According to Craik and Bialystock (2006), the kinds of schemas or systems of schemas one develops over time to interact with the world; the foundation of crystallized intelligence.

resolve: Position 9 in Perry's model that, taken together with initial commitment (Position 7) and multiple commitments (Position 8), suggests a flowering of the commitments anticipated in Positions 5 and 6. Position 9, although placed at the end of the line, does not imply a static resolution of existential conflict; rather, it characterizes a state of courageous resolve to continue the work of reflecting on one's commitments throughout adulthood.

respondent: An automatic response to a stimulus. For example, a rapidly approaching visual stimulus can automatically elicit an eye blink, which is a respondent.

responsible stage: In Schaie's theory, the stage of cognitive development faced during middle adulthood in which ill-defined problems remain the norm, but problem solving must now take into account not only one's own personal needs and goals but also those of others in one's life that have become one's responsibility (spouse, children, coworkers, member of the community).

restoration-focused grief: A type of coping strategy directed toward handling the practical tasks that need to be done to carry on with daily life.

retention: Staying in college long enough to graduate.

reticular activating system: A set of brain structures including the reticular formation located in the brain stem that filters out some of the stimuli we perceive and alerts higher structures to "pay attention" to other stimuli.

reticular formation: A bundle of neural tissue in the brainstem that acts together with other nuclei to form the reticular activating system, which affects attention to incoming stimuli.

retreat: Perry's characterization of the behavior of individuals who move back to dualistic thinking in times of stress to seek the intellectual security of absolute right and wrong.

retrieval: What we usually mean by remembering, that is, getting information out of mental storage so we can use it.

retrieval strategy: An approach to finding and recovering information stored in memory. In math, this refers to solving arithmetic problems by recovering a memorized answer (e.g., remembering that 3 plus 2 equals 5 rather than solving the problem).

reversible relationship: A kind of logical relationship in which one change reverses the effects of another change (and also implies the existence of its reverse). For example, in math, subtraction is the reverse of addition.

rhythmicity: The predictability of an individual's sleep, feeding, elimination, and other biological cycles. An aspect of infant temperament.

risk factors: Aspects of the organism or the environment that compromise healthy development.

risky behaviors: Behaviors that constitute a departure from socially accepted norms or behaviors that pose a threat to the well-being of individuals or groups.

role buffering: For individuals who participate in multiple roles, such as "mother," "wife," "caregiver to ailing parent," and "employee," if one role is a source of psychological stress or failure experiences, success and satisfaction in another role may compensate.

role strain: The stress or strain of meeting obligations that are associated with certain roles (e.g., caregiver).

rough-and-tumble play: Good-natured physical roughness that is an almost exclusive property of boys' play with boys.

rumination: Repeated focusing of attention on negative mood and cognitions. Rumination is sometimes viewed as an ineffective emotion regulation strategy that is related to avoidance of emotional experience.

safe haven: One of the three purposes of the attachment system. Bonds between infant and caregiver make the caregiver a source of comfort when distressed.

sandwich generation: Those who carry the double responsibilities of taking care of both an elderly relative and their own children.

satisficers: Decision makers who are comfortable settling for "good enough"; they have less difficulty making choices than people who assume there is a "best" choice.

scaffolding: The process whereby more advanced thinkers or more capable members of a culture provide novice learners with a supportive temporary prop that enables the novice to learn and to reach higher levels of thinking.

script: A schematic representation of the typical features of an event and the order in which they happen.

secondary control: Control efforts that involve attempts to change ourselves.

secondary prevention: An attempt to reduce the incidence of disorders among those who are at high risk or to provide treatment to forestall the development of more serious psychopathology in cases that are already established.

secondary sexual characteristics: Physical traits not directly involved in reproduction but indicative of sex, such as enlarged breasts in females and deeper voices in males.

secure: In Bartholomew's adult attachment style typology, individuals who have a positive view of themselves and a positive model of others, expecting close others to be supportive and available.

secure base: One of the three purposes of the attachment system. The bond between infant and caregiver provides the infant a protective resource as she develops and learns.

securely attached: An attachment category describing babies who typically show distress on separation from the mother in the strange situation test, but who greet her happily on her return, usually seeking comfort by reaching to be picked up. Once reassured, they tend to return to exploring. In Bartholomew's description of adult attachment categories, describes individuals who expect others to be available and supportive of their needs in close relationships, who are comfortable with emotional closeness, but are also reasonably autonomous.

selection (as an adaptive strategy): A process of narrowing our goals and limiting the domains in which we expend effort that is important for successful development.

selection (as a peer group process): The process by which individuals choose to affiliate with others who share similar behaviors or attributes.

selective attention: Deployment of attention to only a chosen subset of the information available for processing in a situation. Selective attention to information that must be remembered later can be used as a memorization strategy.

selective optimization with compensation: The three combined processes of successful development according to life span development theory (selection, optimization, and compensation).

selective prevention: A category of prevention efforts that target individuals at some epidemiological risk.

selective serotonin reuptake inhibitor: A class of drugs that affect the serotonin system, usually prescribed for depression or anxiety.

self-conscious emotions: Emotions that require self awareness (self-recognition), and are directly relevant to the self, such as pride, shame, embarrassment and guilt. These emotions require more cognitive capacity than basic emotions such as fear, and they do not emerge until the second year of life.

self-determination theory: The theory that three basic psychological needs including autonomy, competence, and relatedness motivate our adaptation efforts at any age.

self-directed coping behaviors: Efforts to deal with stress that appear to be aimed at self comfort. In infants these behaviors include looking away from the source of distress or self-stimulating behavior, such as rocking and sucking.

self-efficacy: Beliefs about our ability to exercise control over events, especially our ability to be successful after failure, criticism, or other challenges.

self-enhancing bias: The motivation to maintain moderately positive beliefs about oneself, which is reflected in a tendency to make comparisons of oneself to people who are similar.

self-esteem: A person's evaluation of his or her attributes or the positive or negative valence associated with those attributes. In William James's opinion, self-esteem depends on the number of successes we enjoy relative to our aspirations.

self-esteem slide: A drop in self-esteem presumably experienced by girls at adolescence.

self-instruction (or self-monitoring): The clinical and educational practices in which the general goal is to affect some behavior change (such as control of impulsivity or improvement in test-taking skills) by attending to, regulating, and sometimes changing cognitions.

self-organizing: Filtering incoming information through one's own existing mental constructs and influencing the environment's inputs with one's actions and reactions.

self-recognition: Awareness of self, usually manifested by the individual's display of self-directed behavior on viewing her own reflection. For example, a child capable of self-recognition will touch a spot of rouge on her nose when she looks in a mirror rather than touching the mirror.

self-regulation: An individual's ability to prevent himself or herself from making a dominant, preferred or automatic response in order to perform a nondominant response, such as when a hungry person is served food at a restaurant but waits to eat until everyone at the table has been served.

self-socialization: Actively seeking to make one's behavior consistent with his or her gender identity without needing social pressure to do so. An intrinsically motivated process that fosters gender role development. Once children have learned their gender label, they attempt to learn what it means to be male or female and then choose to behave in gender consistent ways.

self-system: A term currently used in place of the "self" because "self" seems too unidimensional. Includes multiple aspects of the self, such as self-concept, self-regulation, and self-esteem.

self-transforming: An immature interpersonal style in which an individual gives in so as to reduce the level of tension. He changes his own behaviors or feelings in order to conform to the needs or demands of another.

semantic knowledge: A kind of declarative knowledge that includes factual information ("There are 50 states in the U.S."), rules ("Ride a bicycle on the right-hand side of the street"), and concepts ("*Green* is a color").

semantics (semantic system): An aspect of a language that children must learn, including the words and word parts that express meanings in that language, also called the meaning system of a language.

senescing: The process of declining with age or "growing down."

sensation seeking: The need for varied, novel, and complex sensation and experiences and the willingness to take physical and social risk for the sake of these experiences.

sensitization: Increasing reactivity to a drug or stressor or emotional experience as a result of multiple, intermittent doses, which presumably enhance the chemical memory of the exposure, and lead to progressive illness severity or illness incidence.

sensorimotor stage: In Piaget's theory of cognitive development, the period from birth to about age 2 when infants are not yet capable of representational thought, so they are unable to form mental images or to plan their behavior. Babies have sensory experiences, organize them on the basis of inborn reflexes or patterns of motor responses, and make motor responses to them.

sensory memory: Very brief retention of sensory experiences.

separation anxiety: Distress of an infant or young child when a primary caregiver leaves the child in someone else's care. Usually begins in the second half of the first year, demonstrating the infant's capacity to recall the absent caregiver, and is viewed as a sign of attachment to that caregiver.

septum: A brain structure located in the forebrain that is part of the limbic system or "emotional brain," which produces feelings such as pleasure, pain, anger, sexuality, fear, and affection.

sequential: Describes a kind of study that is like a cross-sectional study in that more than one cohort is included, but is like a longitudinal study in that each cohort is measured at more than one age.

serotonin: A neurotransmitter that is involved in mood, pain perception, and the sleep-wake cycle.

sex chromosomes: The 23rd pair of chromosomes, which play a major role in sex determination. In females these are two relatively large X chromosomes, whereas in males this pair consists of one X chromosome and one much smaller Y chromosome.

sexual debut: The age at which first intercourse occurs.

sexual dimorphism: Both internal and external physical differences between the sexes, which increase during the adolescent growth spurt.

sexual fluidity: Changing one's sexual identification, such as from heterosexual to bisexual or from bisexual to homosexual, and so on.

sexual orientation: A preference for partners of one's own sex (homosexuality), the opposite sex (heterosexuality), or both (bisexuality).

sexually transmitted disease (STD): An infectious disease that is passed from one person to another via sexual activity such as intercourse or oral-genital contact.

shock: The first phase in the grieving process when the loss is met by disbelief and the grieving person may experience blunted emotions, or emotional outbursts.

sickle-cell anemia: A hereditary disease caused by a recessive, defective gene allele affecting the red blood cells. These are abnormally (half-moon) shaped and not as efficient as normal, round red blood cells in carrying oxygen to the tissues. Symptoms can include breathing problems, a variety of organ dysfunctions, and sometimes early death. Most common in individuals of African descent.

slow mapping: After a word has been added to a child's vocabulary, it may take multiple exposures to the word in different situations for a child to work out the word's full meaning, including what features are defining versus characteristic, and the other words to which it is related.

slow-to-warm-up babies: A temperament type described by Thomas and Chess. These babies are like easy babies in most ways, but they are like difficult babies in their fearfulness, showing more wariness in new situations than most other babies.

social capital: Shared norms, values, and understandings within or among groups that fosters cooperation.

social clock: The set of age-related expectations that we all have for the appropriate timing of major life events.

social cognition: A person's mental processing (thoughts, beliefs, and so on) of information about other people and their reasoning about social relationships.

social comparison: The process whereby people observe the performance of others and use it as a basis for evaluating their own abilities and accomplishments.

social dosage effect: The more time children spend in same-gender groups the more gender-typical behaviors they exhibit.

social exchange and behavior theories: Related to marriage, views that assume satisfaction results from negotiated exchange between partners. Problems arise when costs of relationship exceed benefits.

social gradient: Stepwise fashion in which outcomes improve as a function of improvement in social position.

social identity complexity: Describes youth who fit into more than one crowd and/or who change crowd affiliations over time.

social impact: A sociometric measure that is computed by adding the total number of nominations a child receives from her peers, both positive and negative, which indicates the degree to which a child gets noticed within her group.

social information-processing: Model used to explain idiosyncratic ways of processing social information, such as use of a hostile attributional bias to interpret neutral social cues.

social learning theories: Theories that focus specifically on how children acquire personality characteristics and social skills.

social maturity: Referring to the combined personality traits of *agreeableness*, *conscientiousness*, and *neuroticism* (that is, *emotional stablity*).

social preference: A sociometric measure that is computed by adding the total number of positive nominations a child receives from his peers, which indicates the degree to which a child is positively viewed by his social group.

social referencing: A baby's adjustment of its reactions to objects or events based on feedback provided by a caregiver. For example, a baby may look at a caregiver's facial expression before approaching a new toy.

social role theory: The view that the social roles an individual fills, such as parent, spouse, manager, and so on, are important influences on her behavior, and that different individuals will typically behave in similar ways when filling the same role.

social skills: Discrete, observable behaviors such as making eye contact, using appropriate language, asking appropriate questions, and so forth, which promote effective social interaction and which are part of the broader construct of social competence.

socialize: To limit some behaviors of the child while demanding others, so that the child will be safe and she will learn the standards of her culture and behave in ways that are conventionally acceptable.

sociocultural theories: Theories in the tradition of Vygotsky, arguing that important aspects of cognitive development may be qualitatively different in different cultures.

socioeconomic position (SEP): The measure of an individual's or group's position within hierarchically organized society, which determines access to resources and opportunities within the society.

socioeconomic status (SES): Social standing or power characterizing adults in a household. Characteristics defining SES include educational background, income, and occupational type.

sociometry: The classic way of assessing social competence and determining the kinds of categories that describe children's status within peer groups. Usually involves asking members of a social group (e.g., children in a classroom) to indicate which members of the group they prefer to spend time with (sit with, play with, etc.) and which they do not.

specification: In Super's theory, the identification of specific vocational preferences during the middle of the exploratory stage.

spermarche: A boy's first ejaculation.

spiritual transcendence: A proposed "sixth personality trait" defined as the ability to view life from a perspective that transcends space and time and to achieve a sense of unity with nature.

SRY gene: Located on the Y chromosome in males, this gene codes for a transcription factor that binds to regulatory DNA. At about 5 weeks gestation, it turns on genes that start the production of other proteins responsible for the development of gonads into testes.

stability: The fourth stage of retirement, when the retiree settles into a lifestyle that is satisfactory to her.

stabilization: In Super's theory, an individual's settling on a vocational self-concept and job that completes the establishment stage.

stage: A period of time, perhaps several years, during which a person's activities (at least in one broad domain) have certain characteristics in common.

stages of retirement: For many people, adjustment to retirement follows a typical stagelike progression, from honeymoon to disenchantment to reorientation to stability to termination.

stereotype induction: An interview strategy that involves slanting the interviewee's view of an individual, such as implying that an alleged perpetrator is a bad person to encourage children to reveal information.

stereotype threat: The fear that a stereotype might be true of oneself or that one will be judged by that stereotype.

still-face paradigm: A research technique for assessing infant coping strategies. The infant is seated facing the mother who is instructed to interact in normally pleasant and playful ways at first and then is asked to change her behavior and to be completely unresponsive or withdrawn.

strange situation test: A measurement technique designed by Ainsworth to assess the quality of an infant's attachment to a caregiver. Infants (12 months or older) and their caregivers are brought to a room (the strange situation) where the child experiences a series of eight 3-minute episodes, each one introducing changes in the social situation, some of which are likely to be stressful, such as an episode when the mother leaves the baby with a stranger. The infant's willingness to explore the toys and his reactions to his mother and the strangers are observed.

stranger anxiety: The tendency of an infant or young child to be wary of strangers and to seek the comfort and protection of the primary caregiver when a stranger is present. May begin early in infancy but is likely to intensify at about 8 months when separation anxiety begins.

stress: A response to an environmental condition or stimulus that requires adaptation from an organism.

stressor: An event that initiates a bodily adaptation. A stressor can be noxious or positive.

strict dualism: Position 1 in Perry's model that implies a rigid adherence to authoritarian views and a childlike division between in-group and out-group. Individuals in this stage never think to question their belief that authority embodies rightness.

subjective well-being: An individual's experience of overall life satisfaction, including satisfaction with particular domains of life, frequency of positive mood, and relative infrequency of negative mood.

substantia nigra: One structure in the midbrain. It is involved in vision, hearing, and consciousness.

subventricular zone: An area of the brain near the ventricles where new neural stem cells can be generated in adults. These cells migrate to the olfactory bulb and appear to play a role in maintaining its functioning.

superego: In Freud's personality theory, the last of three aspects of personality, which serves as an "internalized parent" that causes one to feel guilty if his behavior deviates from parental and societal restrictions.

superior colliculi: Structures in the midbrain that play a role in vision, hearing, and consciousness.

symbols: Representational indicators or stand-ins for other things, such as words serving as symbols for concepts or drawings serving as symbols of objects.

sympathetic nervous system (SNS): When a threat is perceived, this system releases important chemicals such as epinephrine (adrenaline) and norepinephrine (noradrenalin) that send a burst of energy to those organs necessary for fight or flight (e.g., heart, lungs) while diverting energy from less necessary systems (e.g., growth, reproduction).

sympathy: An emotion related to empathy that involves "feeling for" another; that is, having concern for the other person, but not necessarily sharing the feelings of the other.

synapses: Connections among neurons, usually between the dendrite of one neuron and the axon of another neuron, or between the dendrites of one neuron and the cell body of a second neuron. At the synapse there is a gap between neurons, which can be bridged by chemicals called neurotransmitters.

synaptic gap: The space between neurons where they "connect." In transmission of an electrical impulse from one neuron to the next, the gap is bridged by the release of chemicals called neurotransmitters from the first neuron, which then stimulate or inhibit an electrical impulse in the second neuron.

synaptic overproduction: The generation of more synapses than are needed in the process of brain growth. Those synapses that are not used are later eliminated or "pruned."

synaptogenesis: The generation of synapses or connections between neurons, usually as a result of the growth of axons and dendrites.

synchrony: Infant–adult interactions are often characterized by this repetitive-rhythmic organization. Nonverbal behaviors occur in a patterned, temporally coordinated sequence.

syntax (grammar): The aspect of language that specifies how to link words into meaningful sentences. A system of rules for generating and decoding sentences.

tangles: Twisted filaments of protein, which may interfere with communication between neurons and even cause cell death; they are associated with Alzheimer's disease.

telomere: The ends of the chromosome that are progressively shortened by cell division; telomeres are related to cellular aging and cell death.

temperament: Describes the usual emotional and behavioral characteristics of a given individual. For infants, includes activity level, degree of fearfulness and irritability, attention persistence, typical mood, and so on.

temporal lobe: The part of the cerebrum that is situated on the sides of each hemisphere and is responsible for auditory processing. The left temporal lobe is especially important in language processing.

temporizing: Perry's description of what individuals are doing when they delay movement to the next stage of thought development.

teratogens: Substances or agents that can cross the placental barrier and produce fetal deformities when taken or absorbed by the mother during pregnancy.

terminal drop (terminal decline): A substantial decline in intellectual functioning that adults may show as they approach the end of their lives, between 6 months and 5 years prior to death.

termination: The fifth and final stage of retirement, which is the end-of-life transition when the individual's health declines and he becomes dependent on others for care.

tertiary prevention: An attempt to rehabilitate persons with established disorders; similar to treatment.

testes: Male gonads that primarily produce androgens (such as testosterone), but also produce lesser amounts of estrogen and progesterone. Site of sperm production in males.

testosterone: One of the masculinizing hormones, called androgens, that serve as transcription factors. Testosterone binds with different receptors in cells in several parts of the body (e.g., skin, skeletal muscles, testes, brain) contributing to sexual dimorphism.

thalamus: A part of the forebrain that relays information from sensory organs and other brain structures to appropriate sites on the cerebral cortex.

theory of mind (ToM): Degree of knowledge of the existence of mental (psychological) processes in self and other people. Includes understanding that people have thoughts, beliefs, intentions, desires, feelings, and so on, that these mental experiences may or may not reflect reality accurately, and that they may be different in other people than they are in the self. Makes possible the capacity to take the perspective of another person.

theory theorist: A cognitive developmental theorist who argues that children quite spontaneously construct theories about how the world works: about mind, matter, physical causality, and biology. Such theorists are constructivists, viewing children as re-constructing their understandings of each conceptual domain as they acquire new information. These reconstructions do not occur in a domain general, stage-like fashion but rather are domain specific and depend on the child's experience. Some theorists argue that initial domain theories are innate.

time-out: A disciplinary technique in which for a short span of time a child is required to discontinue his involvement in ongoing activities to quietly sit somewhere apart. This technique involves mild power assertion and is suitable for use with toddlers and preschoolers.

tolerable stress: A chronic bodily response to a stressor, typically initiated by a serious and long-lasting threat, such as loss of a job. The response is considered tolerable if it is turned off eventually as the individual finds ways to cope.

tomboyism: A trait girls exhibit when they prefer to play with boys and prefer boys' toys and activities.

tools or signs: In Vygotsky's theory, anything that people use to help them think and learn, such as numbering or writing systems.

"top-down" processes: Slow, intentional and deliberative information processing that uses working memory space.

toxic stress: A chronic bodily response to a serious and long-lasting threat, which persists because the individual is not able to find ways of coping.

transcription: The complex chain of cellular processes that involves translating the code specified by a gene into the production of a protein. This series of biochemical events ultimately accounts for genetic expression or influence.

transcription factor: Chemicals in cells that bind with the regulatory portions of the DNA, initiating the uncoiling of strands of DNA at a gene location and allowing mRNA production to begin. Transcription factors cannot bind to the regulatory DNA unless they first bind to another chemical called a receptor.

transgender: Describes individuals whose gender identity differs from their sex at birth.

translation: One step in a cell's production of a protein, in which the cell "reads" the code represented in a strand of mRNA and creates a protoprotein based on that code.

translational research: The field of research that translates findings from basic scientific areas into applications like diagnoses, prevention and treatments.

trust versus mistrust: The crisis faced in the first of Erikson's "Eight Stages of Man," in which the responsiveness of an infant's caregiver will determine whether the baby establishes basic trust and a sense of being valuable.

uncharacteristic behavior: A condition that mitigates a criminal defendant's guilt because the crime is not typical of her, such as when it is a first offense or is not consistent with the individual's values.

unipolar disorder: A term used to indicate a clinical course marked by episodes of depression but not of mania.

universal prevention: A category of prevention efforts that are directed to the general population.

unresolved (insecure): An attachment style characterizing adults whose Adult Attachment Interview transcripts show marked lapses in logical thinking, particularly during discussions of loss or other traumatic memories. These individuals may receive a secondary classification of dismissive or preoccupied, and often have children who show more disorganized attachment patterns than other children.

utilization deficiency: A situation in which using a memory strategy does not seem to boost memory.

valence: The degree of pleasantness or unpleasantness of a felt emotion.

verbal responsiveness: Making prompt, contingent, and appropriate (positive and meaningful) verbal responses to children's behaviors or vocalizations.

verification: The third step in the scientific method, when the researcher judges a theory objectively by testing predictions about events and theories to see if they come true.

visual acuity: The level of detail that one can see. Young infants have substantially less visual acuity than adults.

vividness effect: Occurs during decision-making when some salient or vivid facts attract our attention regardless of their actual value as evidence.

vocabulary spurt: Describes the rapid growth of productive vocabulary from 50 to about 500 words in just a few months. Tends to occur between 18 and 24 months in most children.

vocational self-concept: Part of one's total identity that includes ideas about which qualities of the self would or would not provide a match to the requirements of an occupation. Includes person's view of his own characteristics and of his life circumstances, such as the limits or opportunities created by economic conditions and so on.

voicing: In phonology, vibration of the vocal cords in the production of a sound. Some consonant sounds in English are voiced (e.g., the *d* and *v* sounds) and some, which are identical to the voiced consonants in other ways, are not voiced (e.g., *t* and *f*).

warmth dimension (parental responsiveness): One of two major features of parenting style. The degree to which parents create a positive emotional climate for their children by listening to them, being involved and interested in their activities, accepting them, making positive attributions about their behavior, and being sensitive and supportive.

white matter: Brain tissue consisting primarily of myelinated axons, such that the tissue appears white.

wisdom: Expertise in the fundamental pragmatics of life. Superior knowledge and judgment in solving problems or addressing issues that arise in the course of living and that affect the meaning and quality of life.

withdrawal of privileges: A form of parental power assertion that involves withholding resources ("No dessert today") or privileges ("You can't use the car this week").

Wolffian ducts: Prenatal structures in both male and female fetuses. In males, high levels of androgens stimulate these ducts to develop into male reproductive structures, such as seminal vesicles. In females, these ducts deteriorate.

working memory: The part of the cognitive machinery that holds information one is actively thinking about at the moment; also referred to as short-term memory.

working model: In Bowlby's attachment theory, an individual's mental representation of self, other, and relationships, which serves as a prototype of social functioning and affects the individual's expectations and behaviors in future relationships. A cognitive schema that begins in infancy and is refined and elaborated over time; a state of mind about attachment-related issues.

X chromosomes: The female sex chromosomes, a matched pair of elongated chromosomes that determine that one will be a female.

X-linked recessive disorders: A class of genetic disorders that are carried on the X chromosome and are recessive, meaning that they are more likely to affect males, who do not have a matching X chromosome that might have the corresponding (and dominant) normal gene. Examples include hemophilia, baldness, color blindness, night blindness, and Duchenne's muscular dystrophy.

Y chromosome: The male sex chromosome, which pairs with an X chromosome and determines that one will be a male.

young adulthood: The time period from about 18 to 30 years that is often an extended period of transition involving exploration of potential adult identities.

zone of proximal development: In Vygotsky's theory, the range of concepts and skills that a learner is to understand or perform only with support or scaffolding from someone else.

zygote: An ovum that has been fertilized by a sperm and thus contains a full complement of 46 chromosomes, half from the mother and half from the father.

References

AAP Council on Communications and Media. (2016). Media use in school age children and adolescents. *Pediatrics, 138,* e20162592.

Abebe, D., Lien, L., & von Soest, T. (2012). The development of bulimic symptoms from adolescence to young adulthood in females and males: A population-based longitudinal cohort study. *International Journal of Eating Disorders, 45,* 737–745.

Abele, A. E., Hagmaier, T., & Spurk, D. (2016). Does career success make you happy? The mediating role of multiple subjective success evaluations. *Journal of Happiness Studies, 17*(4), 1615–1633.

Aber, J. L., Jones, S., Brown, J. L., Chaudry, N., & Samples, F. (1998). Resolving Conflict Creatively: Evaluating the developmental effects of a school-based violence prevention program in the neighborhood and classroom context. *Development and Psychopathology, 10,* 187–213.

Aboud, F. E., & Yousafzai, A. K. (2015). Global health and development in early childhood. *Annual Review of Psychology, 66,* 433–457.

Aboud-Halabi , Y., & and Shamai, M. (2016). The role of parents in defining collective identity of Arab adolescents in Israel. *Family Relations, 65,* 300–313.

Abrahamson, L., Seligman, M., & Teasdale, J. (1978). Learned helplessness in humans: Critique and reformulation. *Abnormal Psychology, 87,* 49–74.

Abrams, K. Y., Rifkin, A., & Hesse, E. (2006). Examining the role of parental frightened/frightening subtypes in predicting disorganized attachment within a brief observational procedure. *Development and Psychopathology, 18,* 345–361.

Abu-Raiya, H., Pargament, K. I., & Krause, N. (2016). Religion as problem, religion as solution: Religious buffers of the links between religious/spiritual struggles and well-being/mental health. *Quality of Life Research, 25*(5), 1265–1274.

Abu-Raiya, H., Pargament, K. I., & Mahoney, A. (2011). Examining coping methods with stressful interpersonal events experienced by Muslims living in the United States following the 9/11 attacks. *Psychology of Religion and Spirituality, 3,* 1–14.

Achenbach, T., & Edelbrock, C. S. (1983). *Manual for the child behavior checklist and revised child behavior profile.* Burlington, VT: University of Vermont, Department of Psychiatry.

Ackerman, S., Zuroff, D. C., & Moskowitz, D. S. (2000). Generativity in midlife and young adults: Links to agency, communion, and subjective well-being. *International Journal of Aging and Human Development, 50,* 17–41.

Ackil, J. K., & Zaragoza, M. S. (1995). Developmental differences in eyewitness suggestibility and memory for source. *Journal of Experimental Child Psychology, 60,* 57–83.

ACOG. (2006). Committee Opinion No. 343 psychosocial risk factors; perinatal screening, and intervention. *Obstetrics and Gynecology, 108,* 469–477.

Acolet, D., Modi, N., Giannakoulopoulos, X., Bond, C., Clow, A., & Glover, V. (1993). Changes in plasma cortisol and catecholamine concentrations in response to massage in preterm infants. *Archives of Disease in Childhood, 70* (1, Spec. No.), F80.

Adachi, P. J., & Willoughby, T. (2017). The link between playing video games and positive youth outcomes. *Child Development Perspectives, 11,* 202–206.

Addis, D. R., Wong, A. T., & Schacter, D. L. (2008). Age-related changes in the episodic simulation of future events. *Psychological Science, 19,* 33–41.

Addis, M. E. (2008). Gender and depression in men. *Clinical Psychology Science and Practice, 15,* 153–168.

Adelman, R. D., Tmanova, L. L., Delgado, D., Dion, S., & Lachs, M. S. (2014). Caregiver burden: A clinical review. *JAMA, 311,* 1052–1060.

Adler, J. M., Dunlop, W. L., Fivush, R., Lilgendahl, J. P., Lodi-Smith, J., McAdams, D. P., . . . Syed, M. (2017). Research methods for studying narrative identity: A primer. *Social Psychological and Personality Science, 8,* 519–527.

Adolescent Sleep Working Group, Committee on Adolescence & Council on School Health. (2014). Policy statement: School start times for adolescents. *Pediatrics, 34,* 642–649.

Afifi, T. O., Mota, N. P., Dasiewicz, P., MacMillan, H. L., & Sareen, J. (2012). Physical punishment and mental disorders: Results from a nationally representative US Sample. *Pediatrics, 130,* 184–192.

Aguiar, A., & Baillargeon, R. (1999). 2.5-month-old infants' reasoning about when object should and should not be occluded. *Cognitive Psychology, 39,* 116–157.

Aguiar, A., & Baillargeon, R. (2002). Developments in young infants' reasoning about occluded objects. *Cognitive Psychology, 45,* 267–336.

Ahluwalia, M. K., & Pellettiere, L. (2010). Sikh men post-9/11: Misidentification, discrimination, and coping. *Asian American Journal of Psychology, 1,* 303–314.

Ahmad, L., Smetana, J., & Klimstra, T. A. (2015). Maternal monitoring, adolescent disclosure, and adolescent adjustment among Palestinian refugee youth in Jordan. *Journal of Research on Adolescence, 25*(3), 403–411.

Ahnert, L., Gunnar, M. R., Lamb, M. E., & Barthel, M. (2004). Transition to child care: Associations with infant–mother attachment, infant negative emotion, and cortisol elevations. *Child Development, 75,* 639–650.

Ahnert, L., Pinquart, M., & Lamb, M. (2006). Security of children's relationships with nonparental care providers: A meta-analysis. *Child Development, 77,* 664–679.

Ahrens, C. J. C., & Ryff, C. D. (2006). Multiple roles and well-being: Sociodemographic and psychological moderators. *Sex Roles, 55,* 801–815.

Ainsworth, M. D. S. (1967). *Infancy in Uganda: Infant care and the growth of love.* Baltimore, MD: The Johns Hopkins University Press.

Ainsworth, M. D. S., Bell, S. M., & Stayton, D. J. (1972). Individual differences in the development of some attachment behaviors. *Merrill-Palmer Quarterly, 18,* 123–143.

Ainsworth, M. D. S., Blehar, M. C., Waters, E., & Wall, S. (1978). *Patterns of attachment.* Hillsdale, NJ: Erlbaum.

Akhtar, S., & Barlow, J. (2018). *Forgiveness therapy for the promotion of mental well-being: A systematic review and meta-analysis.* Los Angeles, CA: Sage Publications.

Akiskal, H. S., & Benazzi, F. (2007). Continuous distribution of atypical depressive symptoms between major depressive and bipolar II disorders: Dose-response relationship with bipolar family history. *Psychopathology, 41,* 39–42.

Akkermans, J., Brenninkmeijer, V., Schaufeli, W. B., & Blonk, R. W. B. (2015). It's all about CareerSKILLS: Effectiveness of a career development intervention for young employees. *Human Resource Management, 54*(4), 533–551.

Aksan, N., Kochanska, G., & Ortmann, M. R. (2006). Mutually responsive orientation between parents and their young children: Toward methodological advances in the science of relationships. *Developmental Psychology, 42,* 833–848.

Al-Namlah, A. S., Fernyhough, C., & Meins, E. (2006). Sociocultural influences on the development of verbal mediation: Private speech and phonological recoding in Saudi Arabian and British samples. *Developmental Psychology, 42,* 117–131.

Al-Shawaf, L., Conroy-Beam, D., Asao, K., & Buss, D. M. (2016). Human emotions: An evolutionary psychological perspective. *Emotion Review, 8,* 173–186.

Alampay, L. P., Godwin, J., Lansford, J. E., Bombi, A. S., Bornstein, M. H., Chang, L., . . . Bacchini, D. (2017). Severity and justness do not moderate the relation between corporal punishment and negative child outcomes: A multicultural and longitudinal study. *International Journal of Behavioral Development, 41,* 491–502.

Alderson-Day, B., & Fernyhough, C. (2015). Inner speech: Development, cognitive functions, phenomenology, and neurobiology. *Psychological Bulletin, 141,* 931–965.

Aldwin, C. M., & Levenson, M. R. (2004). Posttraumatic growth: A developmental perspective. *Psychological Inquiry, 15,* 19–22.

Alexander, F., & French, T. M. (1946). *Psychoanalytic therapy.* New York, NY: Rolande.

Ali, S., & Alea, N. (2017). Does who I am or how I regulate matter? Consequences of manipulation of emotion regulation strategies. *The International Journal of Aging and Human Development, 85,* 135–163.

Allen, J. W. P., & Bickhard, M. H. (2013). Stepping off the pendulum: Why only an action-based approach can transcend the nativist-empiricist debate. *Cognitive Development, 28,* 96–133.

Allen, T. D., Henderson, T. G., Mancini, V. S., & French, K. A. (2017). Mindfulness and meditation practice as moderators of the relationship between age and subjective wellbeing among working adults. *Mindfulness, 8*(4), 1055–1063.

Alliance for Childhood. (2000). *Fool's gold: A critical look at children and computers.* College Park, MD: Author.

Alpert, A. B., CichoskiKelly, E. M., & Fox, A. D. (2017). What lesbian, gay, bisexual, transgender, queer, and intersex patients say doctors should know and do: A qualitative study. *Journal of Homosexuality, 64,* 1368–1389.

Alzheimer's Association. (2012). Alzheimer's disease facts and figures. *Alzheimer's & Dementia, 8.* Available from https://www.alz.org/downloads/facts_figures_2012.pdfh15

Amato, P. R. (2001). Children of divorce in the 1990s: An update of the Amato and Keith (1991) meta-analysis. *Journal of Family Psychology, 15,* 355–370.

Amato, P. R. (2005). The impact of family formation change on the cognitive, social, and emotional well-being of the next generation. *The Future of Children, 15,* 75–96.

Amato, P. R., & Anthony, C. J. (2014). Estimating the effects of parental divorce and death with fixed effects models. *Journal of Marriage and Family, 76,* 370–386.

Amato, P. R., Booth, A., Johnson, D. R., & Rogers, S. J. (2007). *Alone together: How marriage in America is changing.* Cambridge, MA: Harvard University Press.

Amato, P. R., & Patterson, S. E. (2017). The intergenerational transmission of instability in early adulthood. *Journal of Marriage and Family, 79,* 723–738.

American Academy of Pediatrics [AAP]. (2001). Policy statement: Children, adolescents and television. *Pediatrics, 107,* 423–426.

American Academy of Pediatrics. (2012). Policy statement: Breastfeeding and the use of human milk. *Pediatrics, 129,* e827–e841.

American Academy of Pediatrics, American Public Health Association, and National Resource Center for Health and Safety in Child Care. (2002). *Caring for our children: National health and safety performance standards: Guidelines for out-of-home child care* (2nd ed.). Elk Grove Village, IL: American Academy of Pediatrics.

American Academy of Pediatrics, Committee on Psychosocial Aspects of Child and Family Health. (1998). Guidance for effective discipline. *Pediatrics, 101,* 723–728.

American Nurses Association (ANA). (2015). *Nursing: Scope and standards of practice* (3rd ed.). Silver Springs, MD: Nursesbooks.org.

American Psychiatric Association [APA]. (2000). *Diagnostic and statistical manual of mental disorders* (4th ed.). Washington, DC: Author.

American Psychiatric Association [APA]. (2013). *Diagnostic and statistical manual of mental disorders* (5th ed.). Arlington, VA: American Psychiatric Publishing.

American Psychiatric Association. (2013). Gender dysphoria. *Diagnostic and statistical manual of mental disorders (DSM-5®).* Washington, DC: American Psychiatric Publications.

American Psychological Association. (2003). Guidelines on multicultural education, training, research, practice, and organizational change for psychologists. *American Psychologist, 58,* 377–402.

American Psychological Association, Coalition for Psychology in Schools and Education. (2015). *Top 20 principles from psychology for pre–K–12 teaching and learning.* Available from www.apa.org/ed/schools/cpse/top-twenty-principles.pdf

Ammini, A. C., Somasundaram, S., & Goswami, R. (2017). Andropause. In A. Kumar & M. Sharma (Eds.), *Basics of human andrology* (pp. 283–289). Singapore: Springer Pte Ltd.

Amon, M. J. (2017). Looking through the glass ceiling: A qualitative study of STEM women's career narratives. *Frontiers in Psychology, 8.* doi:10.3389/fpsyg.2017.00236

An, B. P., Loes, C. N., & Trolian, T. L. (2017). The relation between binge drinking and academic performance: Considering the mediating effects of academic involvement. *Journal of College Student Development, 58,* 492–508.

Anda, R. F., Felitti, V. J., Bremner, J. D., Walker, J. D., Whitfield, C., Perry, B. D.,. . . Giles, W. H. (2006). The enduring effects of abuse and related adverse experiences in childhood: A convergence of evidence from neurobiology and epidemiology. *European Archives of Psychiatry and Clinical Neuroscience, 256,* 174–186.

Anderson, C., Kraus, M. W., Galinsky, A. D., & Keltner, D. (2012). The local ladder effect: Social status and subjective well being. *Psychological Science, 23,* 764–771.

Anderson, C. A., Shibuya, A., Ihori, N., Swing, E. L., Bushman, B. J., Sakamoto, . . . Saleem, M. (2010). Violent video game effects on aggression, empathy, and prosocial behavior in Eastern and Western countries: A meta-analytic review. *Psychological Bulletin, 136,* 151–173.

Anderson, D. R., & Kirkorian, H. L. (2015). Media and cognitive development. In R. M. Lerner (Ed. In Chief), & L. S. Liben & U. Miller (Vol. Eds.), *Handbook of child psychology and developmental science: Vol. 2. Cognitive processes* (7th ed., pp. 949–994). Hoboken, NJ: Wiley.

Anderson, E. L., Heron, J., Ben-Shlomo, Y., Kuh, D., Cooper, R., Lawlor, D. A., . . . Howe, L. D. (2017). Adversity in childhood and measures of aging in midlife: Findings from a cohort of British women. *Psychology and Aging, 32,* 521–530.

Anderson, J. R., Van Ryzin, M. J., & Doherty, W. J. (2010). Developmental trajectories of marital happiness in continuously married individuals: A group-based modeling approach. *Journal of Family Psychology, 24,* 587–596.

Anderson, P., Beach, S. R. H., & Kaslow, N. J. (1999). Marital discord and depression: The potential of attachment theory to guide integrative clinical intervention. In T. Joiner & J. C. Coyne (Eds.), *The interactional nature of depression* (pp. 271–297). Washington, DC: American Psychological Association.

Anderson, S. (2015). Disorders of sexual differentiation: Ethical considerations surrounding early cosmetic genital surgery. *Pediatric Nursing, 41,* 176–186.

Anderson, S., & Phillips, D. (2017). Is pre-K classroom quality associated with kindergarten and middle-school academic skills? *Developmental Psychology, 53,* http://dx.doi.org/10.1037/dev0000312

Andrews, N. C., Martin, C. L., Field, R. D., Cook, R. E., & Lee, J. (2016). Development of expectancies about own- and other-gender group interactions and their school-related consequences. *Child Development, 87,* 1423–1435.

Angst, J., & Merikangas, K. R. (2001). Multidimensional criteria for the diagnosis of depression. *Journal of Affective Disorders, 62,* 7–15.

Anthis, K. S., Dunkel, C. S., & Anderson, B. (2004). Gender and identity status differences in late adolescents' possible selves. *Journal of Adolescence, 27,* 147–152.

Anthony, C. J., DiPerna, J. C., & Amato, P. R. (2014). Divorce, approaches to learning, and children's academic achievement: A longitudinal analysis of mediated and moderated effects. *Journal of School Psychology, 52,* 249–261.

Anthonysamy, A., & Zimmer-Gembeck, M. J. (2007). Peer status and behaviors of maltreated children and their classmates in the early years of school. *Child Abuse & Neglect, 31,* 971–991.

Antognini, F. C., & Liptzin, B. (2008). Psychotherapy for late-life mood disorders. In J. M. Ellison, H. Kyomen, & S. Verma (Eds.), *Mood disorders in later life* (2nd ed., pp. 315–337). New York, NY: Informa Healthcare.

António, J. H. C., & Monteiro, M. B. (2015). Minorities' acculturation and social adjustment: The moderator role of meta-perceptions of majority's acculturation attitudes. *International Journal of Psychology, 50,* 422–430.

Antonucci, T. C., Lansford, J. E., & Akiyama, H. (2001). Impact of positive and negative aspects of marital relationships and friendships on well-being of older adults. *Applied Developmental Science, 5,* 68–75.

Antshel, K. M., & Remer, R. (2003). Social skills training in children with attention deficit hyperactivity disorder: A randomized-controlled clinical trial. *Journal of Clinical Child and Adolescent Psychology, 32,* 153–165.

Archer, J. (1999). *The nature of grief: The evolution and psychology of reactions to loss.* London, UK: Routledge.

Archer, M., Steele, M., Lan, J., Jin, X., Herreros, F., & Steele, H. (2015). Attachment between infants and mothers in China: Strange Situation procedure findings to date and a new sample. *International Journal of Behavioral Development, 39,* 485–491.

Archibald, A. B., Linver, M. R., Graber, J. A., & Brooks-Gunn, J. (2002) Parent-adolescent relationships and girls' unhealthy eating: Testing reciprocal effects. *Journal of Research on Adolescence, 12,* 451–461.

Aries, P. (1960). *Centuries of childhood: A social history of family life* (R. Baldick, Trans.). New York, NY: Knopf.

Arım, R. G., Marshall, S. K., & Shapka, J. D. (2010). A domain-specific approach to adolescent reporting of parental control. *Journal of Adolescence, 33*(3), 355–366.

Arlotta, P., & Vanderhaeghen, P. (2017). Editorial overview: Developmental neuroscience 2017. *Current Opinion in Neurobiology, 42,* A1–A4.

Armstrong, B., Gallant, S. N., Li, L., Patel, K., & Wong, B. I. (2017). Stereotype threat effects on older adults' episodic and working memory: A meta-analysis. *The Gerontologist, 57*, S193–S205.

Arnett, J. J. (1992). Reckless behavior in adolescence: A developmental perspective. *Developmental Review, 12*, 339–373.

Arnett, J. J. (1999). Adolescent storm and stress, reconsidered. *American Psychologist, 54*, 317–326.

Arnett, J. J. (2000). Emerging adulthood: A theory of development from the late teens through the twenties. *American Psychologist, 55*, 469–480.

Arnett, J. J. (2002). The psychology of globalization. *American Psychologist, 57*, 774–783.

Arnett, J. J. (2007). Emerging adulthood: What is it, and what is it good for? *Child Development Perspectives, 1*, 68–73.

Arnett, J. J. (2013). *Adolescence and emerging adulthood* (5th ed.). Upper Saddle River, NJ: Pearson Education, Inc.

Arnett, J. J. (2015). Introduction: Emerging adulthood theory and research: Where we are and where we should go. In J. J. Arnett (Ed.), *The Oxford handbook of emerging adulthood* (pp. 1–7). New York, NY: Oxford University Press.

Arnett, J. J., & Brody, G. H. (2008). A fraught passage: The identity challenges of African American emerging adults. *Human Development, 51*, 291–193.

Arnold, J., & Gemma, P. B. (2008). The continuing process of parental grief. *Death Studies, 32*, 658–673.

Aronson, J., & Fried, C. (1998). *Reducing stereotype threat and boosting academic achievement of African Americans: The role of conceptions of intelligence.* Unpublished manuscript.

Aronson, K., & Weiner, M. B. (2007). *Aging parents, aging children.* Lanham, MD: Rowman & Littlefield.

Aronson, P. J., Mortimer, J. T., Zierman, C., & Hacker, M. (1996). Generational differences in early work experiences and evaluations. In J. T. Mortimer & M. D. Finch (Eds.), *Adolescents, work, and family: An intergenerational developmental analysis* (pp. 25–62). Newbury Park, CA: Sage.

Arredondo, P., & Perez, P. (2006). Historical perspectives on the multicultural guidelines and contemporary application. *Professional Psychology: Research and Practice, 37*, 1–5.

Asarnow, J. R., & Miranda, J. (2014). Improving Care for depression & suicide risk in adolescents: Innovative strategies for bringing treatments to community settings. *Annual Review of Clinical Psychology, 10*, 275–303.

Asher, S. R., & Dodge, K. A. (1986). Identifying children who are rejected by their peers. *Developmental Psychology, 22*, 444–449.

Asher, S. R., Markell, R. A., & Hymel, S. (1981). Identifying children at risk in peer relations: A critique of the rate-of-interaction approach to assessment. *Child Development, 52*, 1239–1245.

Asher, S. R., & McDonald, K. L. (2009). The behavioral basis of acceptance, rejection, and perceived popularity. In K. H. Rubin, W. M. Bukowski, & B. Laursen (Eds.), *Handbook of peer interactions, relationships, and groups* (pp. 232–248). New York, NY: The Guilford Press.

Asperger, H. (1991). "Autistic psychopathy" in childhood. In U. Frith (Ed. & Trans.), *Autism and Asperger syndrome* (pp. 37–92). Cambridge,

England: Cambridge University Press. (Original work published 1944)

Assari, S., Lankarani, M. M., & Burgard, S. (2016). Black–white difference in long-term predictive power of self-rated health on all-cause mortality in United States. *Annals of Epidemiology, 26*, 106–114.

Astin, A. W. (1993). *What matters in college? Four critical years revisited.* San Francisco, CA: Jossey-Bass.

Atchley, R. C. (1976). *The sociology of retirement.* New York, NY: Wiley.

Atkins, D. C., Dimidjian, S., & Christensen, A. (2003). Behavioral couple therapy: Past, present, and future. In T. L. Sexton, G. R. Weeks, & M. S. Robbins (Eds.), *Handbook of family therapy: The science and practice of working with families and couples* (pp. 281–302). New York, NY: Brunner-Routledge.

Atzil, S., Hendler, T., & Feldman, R. (2011). Specifying the neurobiological basis of human attachment: Brain, hormones, and behavior in synchronous and intrusive mothers. *Neuropsychopharmacology, 36*, 2603–2615.

Atzil, S., Touroutoglou, A., Rudy, T., Salcedo, S., Feldman, R., Hooker, J. M., . . . Barrett, L. F. (2017). Dopamine in the medial amygdala network mediates human bonding. *Proceedings of the National Academy of Sciences (PNAS), 114*, 2361–2366.

Aucoin, K. J., Frick, P. J., & Bodin, S. D. (2006). Corporal punishment and child adjustment. *Journal of Applied Developmental Psychology, 27*, 527–541.

Augustine, J. M. (2014). Mothers' employment, education, and parenting. *Work and Occupations, 41*, 237–270.

Aupperle, R. L., Melrose, A. J., Stein, M. B., & Paulus, M. P. (2012). Executive function and PTSD: Disengaging from trauma. *Neuropharmacology, 62*, 686–694.

Austin, A. E., & Herrick, H. (2014). *The effect of adverse childhood experiences on adult health: 2012 North Carolina Behavioral Risk Factor Surveillance System Survey.* Raleigh, N.C.: State of North Carolina's Department of Health and Human Services, Division of Public Health's State Center for Health Statistics.

Austin, M., Rhodes, J., & Lewis, D. (1997). Differential distribution of corticotrophin-releasing hormone immunoreactive axons in monoaminergis nuclei of the human brainstem. *Neuropsychopharmacology, 17*, 326–341.

Auyeung, B., Baron-Cohen, S., Ashwin, E., Knickmeyer, R., Taylor, K., Hackett, G., & Hines, M. (2009). Fetal testosterone predicts sexually differentiated childhood behavior in girls and in boys. *Psychological Science, 20*, 144–148.

Avis, N. E., Stellato, R., Crawford, S., Johannes, C., & Longcope, C. (2000). Is there an association between menopause status and sexual functioning? *Menopause, 7*, 297–309.

Azar, B. (1999, February). Consortium of editors pushes for shift in child research methods. *APA Monitor, 30*, 20–21.

Baams, L., Grossman, A. H., & Russell, S. T. (2015). Minority stress and mechanisms of risk for depression and suicidal ideation among lesbian, gay, and bisexual youth. *Developmental Psychology, 51*(5), 688.

Baams, L., Overbeek, G., Dubas, J. S., & van Aken, M. A. G. (2014). On early starters and late bloomers: The development of sexual behavior in adolescence across personality types. *Journal of Sex Research, 5*, 754–764.

Bachman, J. G., Safron, D. J., Sy, S. R., & Schulenberg, J. E. (2003). Wishing to work: New perspectives on how adolescents' part-time work intensity is linked to educational disengagement, substance use, and other problem behaviors. *International Journal of Behavioral Development, 27*, 301–315.

Badanes, L. S., Dmitrieva, J., & Watamura, S. E. (2012). Understanding cortisol reactivity across the day at child care: The potential buffering role of secure attachments to caregivers. *Early Childhood Research Quarterly, 27*, 156–165.

Baer, W. M., & Hanson, L. C. (2000). Families' perceptions of the added value of hospice in the nursing home. *Journal of the American Geriatric Society, 48*, 879–882.

Baez, S., Flichtentrei, D., Prats, M., Mastandueno, R., García, A. M., Cetkovich, M., & Ibáñez, A. (2017). Men, women . . . who cares? A population-based study on sex differences and gender roles in empathy and moral cognition. *PloS one, 12*, e0179336.

Bahrick, L. E., & Pickens, J. N. (1995). Infant memory for object motion across a period of three months: Implications for a four-phase attention function. *Journal of Experimental Child Psychology, 59*, 343–371.

Bailey, E. I. (1998). *Implicit religion: An introduction.* London: Middlesex University Press.

Bailey, J. M., Vasey, P. L., Diamond, L. M., Breedlove, S. M., Vilain, E., & Epprecht, M. (2016). Sexual orientation, controversy, and science. *Psychological Science in the Public Interest, 17*, 45–101.

Bailey, T., Jeong, D. W., & Cho, S-W. (2010). Referral, enrollment, and completion in developmental education sequences in community colleges. *Economics of Education Review, 29*, 255–270.

Baillargeon, R. (2008). Innate ideas revisited: For a principle of persistence in infants' physical reasoning. *Perspectives on Psychological Science, 3*, 2–13.

Baillargeon, R., Scott, R. M., & Bian, L. (2016). Psychological reasoning in infancy. *Annual Review of Psychology, 67*, 159–186.

Bainbridge, K. E., & Wallhagen, M. I. (2014). Hearing loss in an aging American population: Extent, impact, and management. *Annual Review of Public Health, 35*, 139–152.

Baird, A. A., & Fugelsang, J. A. (2004). The emergence of consequential thought: Evidence from neuroscience. *Philosophical Transactions of the Royal Society of London, Series B: Biological Sciences, 359*, 1797–1804.

Baker-Ward, L., Ornstein, P. A., & Holden, D. J. (1984). The expression of memorization in early childhood. *Journal of Experimental Child Psychology, 37*, 555–575.

Bakker, A. B. (2011). An evidence-based model of work engagement. *Current Directions in Psychological Science, 20*, 265–269.

Baldwin, A. L. (1948). Socialization and the parent–child relationship. *Child Development, 19*, 127–136.

Bale, T. L. (2015). Epigenetic and transgenerational reprogramming of brain development. *Nature Reviews Neuroscience, 16*(6), 332.

Balestrino, A., Ciardi, C., & Mammini, C. (2013). On the causes and consequences of divorce. *The Journal of Socio-Economics, 45,* 1–9.

Ballard, C., Gauthier, S., Corbett, A., Brayne, C., Aarsland, D., & Jones, E. (2011). Alzheimer's disease. *The Lancet, 377,* 1019–1031.

Ballard, E., Luckenbaugh, D., Yarrington, J., Lally, N., Lener, M., Machado-Vieira, R., . . . Zarate, C. (2017). A principal components analysis of depression and anhedonia scales: Illustrating the heterogeneity of depression. *Biological Psychiatry, 81*(10), S135.

Balsam, K. F., Beauchaine, T. P., Rothblum, E. D., & Solomon, S. E. (2008). Three-year follow-up of same-sex couples who had civil unions in Vermont, same-sex couples not in civil unions, and heterosexual married couples. *Developmental Psychology, 44,* 102–116.

Baltes, M. M., & Baltes, P. B. (1990). *The psychology of control and aging.* Hillsdale, NJ: Erlbaum.

Baltes, P. B. (1987) Theorical propositions of life–span developmental psychology; On the dynamics between growth and decline. *Developmental Psychology, 23,* 611–626.

Baltes, P. B. (1997). On the incomplete architecture of human ontogeny: Selection, optimization, and compensation as foundation of developmental theory. *American Psychologist, 52,* 366–380.

Baltes, P. B., Lindenberger, U., & Staudinger, U. M. (1998). Life-span theory in developmental psychology. In W. Damon (Series Ed.) & R. M. Lerner (Vol. Ed.), *Handbook of child psychology: Vol. 1. Theoretical models of human development* (5th ed., pp. 1029–1143). New York, NY: Wiley.

Baltes, P. B., Lindenberger, U., & Staudinger, U. M. (2006). Life-span theory in developmental psychology. In W. Damon & R. M. Lerner (Series Eds.) & R. M. Lerner (Vol. Ed.), *Handbook of child psychology: Vol. 1. Theoretical models of human development* (6th ed., pp. 569–664). Hoboken, NJ: Wiley.

Baltes, P. B., & Smith, J. (2008). The fascination of wisdom: Its nature, ontogeny, and function. *Perspectives on Psychological Science, 3,* 56–64.

Baltes, P. B., & Staudinger, U. M. (2000). Wisdom: A metaheuristic (pragmatic) to orchestrate mind and virtue toward excellence. *American Psychologist, 55,* 122–136.

Bancroft, J., Herbenick, D., & Reynolds, M. (2003). Masturbation as a marker of sexual development: Two studies 50 years apart. In J. Bancroft (Ed.), *Sexual development in childhood* (pp. 156–185). Bloomington, IN: Indiana University Press.

Bandura, A. (1974). Behavior theory and the models of man. *American Psychologist, 29,* 859–869.

Bandura, A. (1977). *Social learning theory.* Upper Saddle River, NJ: Prentice Hall.

Bandura, A. (1986). *Social foundations of thought and action: A social cognitive theory.* Upper Saddle River, NJ: Prentice Hall.

Bandura, A. (1989). Human agency in social cognitive theory. *American Psychologist, 44,* 1175–1184.

Bandura, A. (1997). *Self-efficacy: The exercise of control.* New York, NY: Freeman.

Bandura, A. (1999). Social cognitive theory of personality. In L. Pervin & O. John (Eds.), *Handbook of personality* (2nd ed., pp. 154–196). New York, NY: Guilford Press.

Bandura, A., & Bussey, K. (2004). On broadening the cognitive, motivational, and sociocultural scope of theorizing about gender development and functioning: Comment on Martin, Ruble, and Szkerybalo (2002). *Psychological Bulletin, 130,* 691–701.

Barac, R., Moreno, S., & Bialystok, E. (2016). Behavioral and electrophysiological differences in executive control between monolingual and bilingual children. *Child Development, 87,* 1277–1290.

Barakat, S., Maguire, S., Surgenor, L., Donnelly, B., Miceska, B., Fromholtz, K., . . . Touyz, S. (2017). The role of regular eating and self-monitoring in the treatment of bulimia nervosa: A pilot study of an online guided self-help CBT program. *Behavioral Sciences, 7,* 39.

Barber, B. K. (2002). *Intrusive parenting: How psychological control affects children and adolescents.* Washington, DC: American Psychological Association.

Barber, B. K., Stolz, H. E., & Olsen, J. A. (2005). Parental support, psychological control, and behavioral control: Assessing relevance across time, culture, and method. *Monographs of the Society for Research in Child Development, 70* (Serial No. 282), vii–151.

Barber, B. L., Abbott, B. D., Blomfield Neira, C. J., & Eccles, J. S. (2014). Meaningful activity participation and positive youth development. In M. Furlong, R. Gilman, & E. S. Huebner (Eds.), *Handbook of positive psychology in the schools* (2nd ed., pp. 227–244). New York, NY: Routledge.

Barber, B. L., Eccles, J. S., & Stone, M. R. (2001). Whatever happened to the jock, the brain, and the princess? Young adult pathways linked to adolescent activity involvement and social identity. *Journal of Adolescent Research, 16,* 429–455.

Barclay, J. S., Blackhall, L. J., & Tulsky, J. A. (2007). Communication strategies and cultural issues in the delivery of bad news. *Journal of Palliative Medicine, 10,* 958–977.

Bardone-Cone, A. M., Cass, K. M., & Ford, J. A. (2008). Examining body dissatisfaction in young men within a biopsychosocial framework. *Body Image, 5,* 183–194.

Barker, E. D., & Maughan, B. (2009). Differentiating early-onset persistent versus childhood-limited conduct problem youth. *American Journal of Psychiatry, 166,* 900–908.

Barkin, S. L., Gesell, S., Po'e, E. K., Escarfuller, J., & Tempesti, T. (2012). Culturally tailored, family-centered, behavioral obesity intervention for Latino-American preschool-aged children. *Pediatrics.* doi:10.1542/peds.2011-3762.

Barlé, N., Wortman, C. B., & Latack, J. A. (2017). Traumatic bereavement: Basic research and clinical implications. *Journal of Psychotherapy Integration, 27,* 127.

Barnes, G. M., Welte, J. W., & Dintcheff, B. (1992). Alcohol misuse among college students and other young adults: Findings from a general population study in New York State. *International Journal of the Addictions, 27,* 917–934.

Barnes, L. L., de Leon, C. F. Mendes, Wilson, R. S., Bienias, J. L., & Evans, D. A. (2004). Social resources and cognitive decline in a population of older African Americans and whites. *Neurology, 63,* 2322–2326.

Barnett, D., Ganiban, J., & Cicchetti, D. (1997). *Maltreatment, emotional reactivity, and the development of type D attachments from 12 to 24 months of age.* Unpublished manuscript.

Barnett, W., Jung, K., Yarosz, D., Thomas, J., Hornbeck, A., Stechuk, R., & Burns, S. (2008). Educational effects of the Tools of the Mind Curriculum: A randomized trial. *Early Childhood Research Quarterly, 23,* 299–313.

Baron, R. M., & Kenny, D. A. (1986). The moderator-mediator variable distinction in social psychological research: Conceptual, strategic, and statistical considerations. *Journal of Personality and Social Psychology, 51,* 1173–1182.

Barr, D. (1997). Friendship and belonging. In R. L. Selman, C. L. Watts, & L. H. Schultz (Eds.), *Fostering friendship: Pair therapy for treatment and prevention* (pp. 19–30). New York, NY: Aldine de Gruyter.

Barr, R. (2013). Memory constraints on infant learning from picture books, television, and touchscreens. *Child Development Perspectives, 7,* 205–210.

Barrett, J., & Fleming, A. S. (2011). Annual research review: All mothers are not created equal: Neural and psychobiological perspectives on mothering and the importance of individual differences. *Journal of Child Psychology and Psychiatry, 52,* 368–397.

Barrett, L. F., & Satpute, A. B. (2017). Historical pitfalls and new directions in the neuroscience of emotion. *Neuroscience Letters.* Available from http://dx.doi.org/10.1016/j.neulet.2017.07.045

Barry, C. T , Sidoti, C. L., Briggs, S. M., Reiter, S.R., & Lindsey, R. A. (2017). Adolescent social media use and mental health from adolescent and parent perspectives. *Journal of Adolescence, 61,* 1–11.

Bartholomew, K., & Horowitz, L. (1991). Attachment styles among young adults: A test of the four category model. *Journal of Personality and Social Psychology, 61,* 226–244.

Bartholomew, K., & Shaver, P. R. (1998). Methods of assessing adult attachment: Do they converge? In J. A. Simpson & W. S. Rholes (Eds.), *Attachment theory and close relationships* (pp. 25–45). New York, NY: Guilford Press.

Bartolini, S., & Sarracino, F. (2017). Twenty-five years of materialism: Do the US and Europe diverge? *Social Indicators Research, 133*(2), 787–817.

Basseches, M. (1984). *Dialectical thinking and adult development.* Norwood, NJ: Ablex.

Bassok, D., Fitzpatrick, M., Greenberg, E., & Loeb, S. (2016). With- and between-sector quality differences in early childhood education and care. *Child Development, 87,* 1627–1645.

Battle, J., Jarratt, L., Smit, S., & Precht, D. (1988). Relations among self-esteem, depression and anxiety of children. *Psychological Reports, 62,* 999–1005.

Baudson, T. G., Weber, K. E., & Freund, P. A. (2016). More than only skin deep: Appearance self-concept predicts most of secondary school students' self-esteem. *Frontiers in Psychology, 7.* doi:103389/fpsyg.2016.01568

Bauer, P. J., & Larkina, M. (2016). Predicting remembering and forgetting of autobiographical memories in children and adults: A 4-year prospective study. *Memory, 24,* 1345–1368.

Baumeister, D., Akhtar, R., Ciufolini, S., Pariante, C. M., & Mondelli, V. (2016). Childhood trauma and adulthood inflammation: A meta-analysis of peripheral C-reactive protein, interleukin-6 and tumour necrosis factor-α. *Molecular Psychiatry, 21*(5), 642–649. http://doi.org/10.1038/mp.2015.

Baumeister, R. F. (1991). *Meanings of life.* New York, NY: Guilford Press.

Baumeister, R. F., & Bowden, J. M. (1994). Shrinking the self. In T. M. Brinthaupt & R. P. Lipka (Eds.), *Changing the self: Philosophies, techniques, and experiences.* Albany, NY: State University of New York Press.

Baumeister, R. F., Bratslavsky, E., Finkenauer, C., & Vohs, K. D. (2001). Bad is stronger than good. *Review of General Psychology, 5*, 323–370.

Baumeister, R. F., Campbell, J. D., Krueger, J. I., & Vohs, K. D. (2003). Does high self-esteem cause better performance, interpersonal success, happiness, or healthier lifestyles? *Psychological Science in the Public Interest, 4*, 1–44.

Baumrind, D. (1989). Rearing competent children. In W. Damon (Ed.), *Child development today and tomorrow* (pp. 349–378). San Francisco, CA: Jossey-Bass.

Baumrind, D. (1991). Parenting styles and adolescent development. In J. Brooks, R. Lerner, & A. C. Petersen (Eds.), *The encyclopedia of adolescence* (pp. 758–772). New York, NY: Garland.

Baumrind, D. (1993). The average expectable environment is not good enough: A response to Scarr. *Child Development, 64*, 1299–1317.

Baumrind, D. (2001). *Does causally relevant research support a blanket injunction against the use of spanking?* Paper presented at the annual meeting of the American Psychological Association, San Francisco.

Baumrind, D., Larzelere, R. E., & Cowan, P. A. (2002). Ordinary physical punishment: Is it harmful? Comment on Gershoff (2002). *Psychological Bulletin, 128*, 580–589.

Bavelier, D., Green, C. S., & Dye, M. W. G. (2010). Children, wired: For better and for worse. *Neuron, 67*, 692–701.

Bayrampour, H., Ali, E., McNeil, D. A., Benzies, K., MacQueen, G., & Tough, S. (2016). Pregnancy-related anxiety: A concept analysis. *International Journal of Nursing Studies, 55*: 115–130.

Bean, R. A., Bush, K. R., McKenny, P. C., & Wilson, S. M. (2003). The impact of parental support, behavioral control, and psychological control on the academic achievement and self-esteem of African American and European American adolescents. *Journal of Adolescent Research, 18*, 523–541.

Bear, G. G., & Rys, G. S. (1994). Moral reasoning, classroom behavior, and sociometric status among elementary school children. *Developmental Psychology, 30*, 633–638.

Beauchaine, T. (2001). Vagal tone, development, and Gray's motivational theory: Toward an integrated model of autonomic nervous system functioning in psychopathology. *Development and Psychopathology, 13*, 183–214.

Beauchaine, T. P., Neuhaus, E., Brenner, S. L., & Gatzke-Kopp, L. (2008). Ten good reasons to consider biological processes in prevention and intervention research. *Development and Psychopathology, 20*, 745–774.

Beauchaine, T. P., Zisner, A. R, & Sauder, C. L. (2017). Trait impulsivity and the externalizing spectrum. *Annual Review of Clinical Psychology, 13*, 343–368.

Becerra, T. A., Wilhelm, M., Olsen, J., Cockburn, M., & Ritz, B. (2013). Ambient air pollution and autism in Los Angeles County, California. *Environmental Health Perspectives, 121*, 380–386. doi:10.1289/ehp.1205827

Becht, A. L., Nelemans, S. A., Koot, H. M., Branje, S. J. T., Vollebergh, W. A. M., & Meeus, W. H. J. (2017). Identity uncertainty and commitment making across adolescence: Five-year within-person associations using daily identity reports. *Developmental Psychology, 53*, 2103–2112.

Beck, A. T. (1963). *Depression: Causes and treatment.* Philadelphia, PA: University of Pennsylvania Press.

Beebe, D. W., Rose, D., & Amin, R. (2010). Attention, learning, and arousal of experimentally sleep-restricted adolescents in a simulated classroom. *Journal of Adolescent Health, 47*, 523–525.

Beeghly, M., Partridge, T., Tronick, E., Muzik, M., Mashhadi, M. R., Boeve, J. L., & Irwin, J. L. (2017). Associations between early maternal depressive symptom trajectories and toddlers' felt security at 18 months: Are boys and girls at differential risk? *Infant Mental Health Journal, 38*, 53–67.

Beeghly, M., & Tronick, E. (2011). Early resilience in the context of parent-infant relationships: a social developmental perspective. *Current Problems in Pediatric and Adolescent Health Care, 41*, 197–201.

Beekman, C., Neiderhiser, J. M., Buss, K. A., Loken, E., Moore, G. A., Leve, L. D., . . . Reiss, D. (2015). The development of early profiles of temperament: characterization, continuity, and etiology. *Child Development, 86*, 1794–1811.

Beelman, A., Pfingsten, U., & Losel, F. (1994). Effects of training social competence in children: A meta-analysis of recent evaluation studies. *Journal of Clinical Child Psychology, 23*, 260–271.

Beijersbergen, M. D., Juffer, F., Bakersmans-Krananburg, M. J., & van IJzendoorn, M. H. (2012). Remaining or becoming secure: Parental sensitive support predicts attachment continuity from infancy to adolescence in a longitudinal adoption study. *Developmental Psychology, 48*, 1277–1282.

Belfield, C., Bowden, B., Klapp, A., Levin, H., Shand, R., & Zander, S. (2015). *The economic value of social and emotional learning.* New York, NY: Center for Benefit-Cost Studies in Education, Teachers College, Columbia University.

Bell, A. (2014). Life-course and cohort trajectories of mental health in the UK, 1991–2008—A multilevel age-period-cohort analysis. *Social Science and Medicine, 120*, 21–30.

Bell, R. Q., & Chapman, M. (1986). Child effects in studies using experimental or brief longitudinal approaches to socialization. *Developmental Psychology, 22*, 595–603.

Belloc, N. B., & Breslow, L. (1972). Relationships of physical health status and health practices. *Preventive Medicine, 1*, 409–421.

Belsky, J., & Fearon, R. M. (2002). Early attachment security, subsequent maternal sensitivity, and later child development: Does continuity in development depend upon continuity of caregiving? *Attachment and Human Development, 4*, 361–387.

Belsky, J., & Kelly, J. (1994). *The transition to parenthood: How a first child changes a marriage. Why some couples grow closer and some grow apart.* New York, NY: Dell.

Belsky, J., & Pluess, M. (2009). Beyond diathesis-stress: Differential susceptibility to environmental influences. *Psychological Bulletin, 135*, 885–908.

Belsky, J., & Pluess, M. (2013). Beyond risk, resilience, and dysregulation: Phenotypic plasticity and human development. *Development and Psychopathology, 25*, 1243–1261.

Belsky, J., & Volling, B. L. (1987). Mothering, fathering, and marital interaction in the family triad during infancy: Exploring family systems' processes. In P. W. Berman & F. A. Pedersen (Eds.), *Men's transitions to parenthood: Longitudinal studies of early family experience* (pp. 37–63). Hillsdale, NJ: Erlbaum.

Bem, S. L. (1981). Gender schema theory: A cognitive account of sex typing. *Psychological Review, 88*, 354–364.

Bem, S. L. (1989). Genital knowledge and gender constancy in preschool children. *Child Development, 60*, 649–662.

Benady-Chorney, J., Yau, Y., Zeighami, Y., Bohbot, V. D., & West, G. L. (2018). Habitual action video game players display increased cortical thickness in the dorsal anterior cingulate cortex. *NeuroReport: For Rapid Communication of Neurosciene Research, 29*, 393–396.

Benjet, C., Bromet, E., Karam, E. G., Kessler, R. C., McLaughlin, K. A., Ruscio, A. M., . . . Koenen, K. C. (2016). The epidemiology of traumatic event exposure worldwide: results from the World Mental Health Survey Consortium. *Psychological Medicine 46*, 327–343.

Benner, A. (2017). The toll of racial/ethnic discrimination on adolescents' adjustment. *Child Development Perspectives, 11*, 251–256.

Benson, J. E., Sabbagh, M. A., Carlson, S. M., & Zelazo, P. D. (2013). Individual differences in executive functioning predict preshoolers' improvement from theory-of-mind training. *Developmental Psychology, 49*, 1615–1627.

Benson, L. A., McGinn, M. M., & Christensen, A. (2012, 2011). Common principles of couple therapy. *Behavior Therapy, 43*(1), 25–35.

Beraha, E., Eggers, J., Attar, C. H., Gutwinski, S., Schlagenhauf, F., Stoy, M., . . . Bermpohl, F. (2012). Hemispheric asymmetry for affective stimulus processing in healthy subjects—a fMRI study. *PLOS ONE, 7*, 1–9.

Berard, A., Ramos, E., Rey, E., Blais, L., St-Andre, M., & Oraichi, D. (2007). First trimester exposure to paroxotene and risk of cardiac malformations in infants: The importance of dosage. *Birth Defects Research. Part B Devel Reprod. Toxicology, 201*, 1–8.

Berenbaum, S. A. (2004). Androgen and behavior: Implications for the treatment of children with disorders of sexual differentiation. In O. H. Pescovitz & E. A. Eugster (Eds.), *Pediatric endocrinology: Mechanisms, manifestations, and management* (pp. 275–284). Philadelphia, PA: Lippincott, Williams, & Wilkins.

Berg, J. M., Wrzesniewski, A. M., & Dutton, J. E. (2010). Perceiving and responding to challenges in job crafting at different ranks: When proactivity requires adaptivity. *Journal of Organizational Behavior, 31*, 158–186.

Berg, L., Rostila, M., & Hjern, A. (2016). Parental death during childhood and depression in young adults—a national cohort study. *Journal of Child Psychology and Psychiatry, 57*(9), 1092.

Berg, S. (1987). Intelligence and terminal decline. In G. L. Maddox & E. W. Busse (Eds.), *Aging: The universal experience* (pp. 414–415). New York, NY: Springer.

Bergold, S., Wendt, H., Kasper, D., & Steinmayr, R. (2017). Academic competencies: Their interrelatedness and gender differences at their high end. *Journal of Educational Psychology, 109*, 439–449.

Berkman, N. D., Bulik, C. M., Brownley, K. A., Lohr, K. N., Sedway, J. A., Rooks, A., & Gartlehner, G. (February 2006). *Management of Eating Disorders Evidence Report*. Evidence Report/Technology Assessment Number 135. AHRQ Publication No. 06-E010. Prepared by RTI International–University of North Carolina Evidence-Based Practice Center under Contract No. 290-02-0016. Rockville, MD: Agency for Healthcare Research and Quality.

Berkowitz, M. W., & Bier, M. C. (2004). Research based character education. *Annals of the American Academy of Political and Social Science, 591*, 72–85.

Berlin, L. J., Appleyard, K., & Dodge, K. A. (2011). Intergenerational continuity in child maltreatment: Mediating mechanisms and implications for prevention. *Child Development, 82*, 162–176.

Berlin, L. J., Zeanah, C. H., & Lieberman, A. F. (2016). Prevention and intervention programs to support early attachment security: A move to the level of the community. In J. Cassidy & P. R. Shaver (Eds.), *Handbook of attachment: Theory, research, and clinical applications* (3rd ed., pp. 739–758). New York, NY: Guilford Press.

Bernal, M. E., & Knight, G. P. (1993). *Ethnic identity: Formation and transmission among Hispanics and other minorities*. Albany, NY: State University of New York Press.

Bernard, K., Dozier, M., Bick, J., & Gordon, M. K. (2015). Intervening to enhance cortisol regulation among children at risk for neglect: Results of a randomized clinical trial. *Development and Psychopathology, 27*, 829–841.

Bernardy, N. C., & Friedman, M. J. (Eds.). (2015). *A practical guide to PTSD treatment: Pharmacological and psychotherapeutic approaches* (pp. 9–19). Washington, DC: American Psychological Association.

Berndt, T. J., & Keefe, K. (1996). Friends' influence on school adjustment: A motivational analysis. In J. Juvonen & K. R. Wentzel (Eds.), *Social motivation: Understanding children's school adjustment*. New York, NY: Cambridge University Press.

Berndt, T. J., & Murphy, L. M. (2002). Influences of friends and friendships: Myths, truths, and research recommendations. *Advances in Child Development and Behavior, 30*, 275–310.

Bernier, A., Matte-Gagne, C., Belanger, M. E., & Whipple, N. (2014). Taking stock of two decades of attachment transmission gap: Broadening the assessment of maternal behavior. *Child Development, 85*, 1852–1865.

Berninger, V. W., & Hart, T. M. (1992). A developmental neuropsychological perspective for reading and writing acquisition. *Educational Psychologist, 27*, 415–434.

Bernstein, A. C., & Cowan, P. A. (1975). Children's concepts of how people get babies. *Child Development, 46*, 77–91.

Berntsen, D., Johannessen, K. B., Thomsen, Y. D., Bertelsen, M., Hoyle, R. H., & Rubin, D. C. (2012). Peace and war: Trajectories of posttraumatic stress disorder symptoms before, during, and after military deployment in Afghanistan. *Psychological Science, 23*, 1557–1565.

Berntsen, D., & Rubin, D. C. (2002). Emotionally charged autobiography memories across the life span: The recall of happy, sad, traumatic and involuntary memories. *Psychology and Aging, 17*, 636–652.

Berry, K., & Danquah, A. (2016). Attachment-informed therapy for adults: Towards a unifying perspective on practice. *Psychology and Psychotherapy: Theory, Research and Practice, 89*, 15–32.

Berthold, A., & Ruch, W. (2014). Satisfaction with life and character strengths of non-religious and religious people: It's practicing one's religion that makes the difference. *Frontiers in Psychology, 5*, 876.

Bessenoff, G. R., & Del Priore, R. E. (2007). Women, weight, and age: Social comparison to magazine images across the lifespan. *Sex Roles, 56*, 215–222.

Best, D. L. (2010). Gender. In Bornstein, M. H. (Ed.), *Handbook of cultural developmental science* (pp. 209–222). New York, NY: Psychology Press.

Bettleheim, B. (1967). *The empty fortress: Infantile autism and the birth of the self*. New York, NY: Free Press.

Betz, N. E. (2004). Contributions of self-efficacy to career counseling: A personal perspective. *Career Development Quarterly, 52*, 340–353.

Betz, N. E., & Schifano, R. S. (2000). Evaluation of an intervention to increase realistic self-efficacy and interests in college women. *Journal of Vocational Behavior, 56*, 35–52.

Beyers, W., & Luyckx, K. (2016). Ruminative exploration and reconsideration of commitment as risk factors for suboptimal identity development in adolescence and emerging adulthood. *Journal of adolescence, 47*, 169–178.

Bhargava, S., & Witherspoon, D. P. (2015). Parental involvement across middle and high school: Exploring contributions of individual and neighborhood characteristics. *Journal of Youth and Adolescence, 44*(9), 1702–1719.

Bialystok, E. (2017). The bilingual adaptation: How minds accommodate experience. *Psychological Bulletin, 143*, 233–262.

Bialystok, E., & Werker, J. F. (2017). Editorial: The systematic effects of bilingualism on children's development. *Developmental Science, 20*. doi:10.1111/desc.12535

Bidell, T. R., & Fischer, K. W. (1997). Between nature and nurture: The role of human agency in the epigenesis of intelligence. In R. J. Sternberg & E. L. Grigorenko (Eds.), *Intelligence, heredity, and environment* (pp. 193–242). New York, NY: Cambridge University Press.

Bierman, K. (1986). Process of change during social skills training with preadolescents and its relation to treatment outcomes. *Child Development, 55*, 151–162.

Bierman, K. L. (2003). *Peer rejection: Developmental processes and intervention*. New York, NY: Guilford Press.

Bierman, K. L. (2004). *Peer rejection: Developmental processes and intervention strategies*. New York, NY: Guilford Press.

Bierman, K. L., & Furman, W. (1984). The effects of social skills training and peer involvement on the social adjustment of preadolescents. *Child Development, 55*, 151–162.

Bierman, K. L., Greenberg, M. T., Coie, J. D., Dodge, K. A., & Lochman, J. E. (2017). *Social and emotional skills training for children: The fast track friendship group manual*. New York, NY: Guilford Publications.

Bierman, K. L., Morris, P. A., & Abenavoli, R. M. (2017). *Parent engagement practices improve outcomes for preschool children*. Edna Bennett Pierce Prevention Research Center, Pennsylvania State University.

Bijou, S. W., & Baer, D. M. (1966). *Operant behavior: Areas of research and application*. New York, NY: Appleton-Century-Crofts.

Billings, J. A. (1998). What is palliative care? *Journal of Palliative Medicine, 1*, 73–81.

Bilson, S., Yoshida, H., Tran, C. D., Woods, E. A., & Hills, T. T. (2015). Semantic facilitation in bilingual first language acquisition. *Cognition, 140*, 122–134.

Binder, E. B., Bradley, R. G., Liu, W., Epstein, M. P., Deveau, T. C., Mercer, K. B., . . . Ressler, K. J. (2008). Association of *FKBP5* polymorphisms and childhood abuse with risk of posttraumatic stress disorder symptoms in adults. *Journal of the American Medical Association, 299*, 1291–1305.

Binet, A., & Simon, T. (1916). *The development of intelligence in children*. Baltimore, MD: Williams and Wilkins.

Birch, S. A. J., Li, V., Haddock, T., Ghrear, S. E., Brosseau-Liard, P., Baimel, A., & Whyte, M. (2017). Perspectives on perspective taking: How children think about the minds of others. *Advances in Child Development and Behavior, 52*, 185–226.

Birditt, K. S., Fingerman, K. L., & Zarit, S. H. (2010). Adult children's problems and successes: Implications for intergenerational ambivalence. *The Journals of Gerontology Series B: Psychological Sciences and Social Sciences, 65B*, 145–153.

Biringen, Z., Altenhofen, S., Aberle, J., Baker, M., Brosal, A., Bennett, S., . . . Swaim, R. (2012). Emotional availability, attachment, and intervention in center-based child care for infants and toddlers. *Developmental Psychopathology, 24*, 23–34.

Birkeland, M. S., Melkevik, O., Holsen, I., & Wold, B. (2012). Trajectories of global self-esteem development during adolescence. *Journal of Adolescence, 35*, 43–54.

Birmingham, C., Su, J., Hlynsky, J., Goldner, E., & Gao, M. (2005). The mortality rate from anorexia nervosa. *International Journal of Eating Disorders, 38*, 143–146.

Birnbaum, G. E. (2016). Attachment and sexual mating: The joint operation of separate motivational systems. In J. Cassidy & P. R. Shaver (Eds.), *Handbook of attachment: Theory, research, and clinical applications* (3rd ed., pp. 464–483). New York, NY: Guilford Press.

Biro, F. M., Galvez, M. P., Greenspan, L. C., Succop, P., Vangeepuram, N., Pinney, . . . Wolff, M. S. (2010). Pubertal assessment method and baseline characteristics in a mixed longitudinal study of girls. *Pediatrics*. doi:10.1542/peds.2009-3079

Bishop, J. B., Witt, K. L., & Sloane, R. A. (1997). Genetic toxicities of human teratogens. *Mutation Research, 396*, 9–43.

Biswas-Diener, R., Vitterso, J., & Diener, E. (2005). Most people are pretty happy, but there is cultural variation: The Inughuit, the Amish, and the Maasai. *Journal of Happiness Studies, 6*, 205–226.

Biswas-Diener, R., Vitterso, J., & Diener, E. (2010). The Danish effect: Beginning to explore high well-being in Denmark. *Social Indicators Research, 97*, 229–246.

Bjorklund, D. F. (2015). Developing adaptations. *Developmental Review, 38*, 13–35.

Bjørnskov, C. (2010). How comparable are the Gallup World Poll Life Satisfaction Data? *Journal of Happiness Studies 11*(1), 41–60.

Black, B., & Hazen, N. L. (1990). Social status and patterns of communication in acquainted and unacquainted preschool children. *Developmental Psychology, 26*, 379–387.

Black, D. S., & Slavich, G. M. (2016). Mindfulness meditation and the immune system: A systematic review of randomized controlled trials. *Annals of the New York Academy of Sciences, 1373*(1), 13–24.

Blackless, M., Charuvastra, A., Derryck, A., Fausto-Sterling, A., Lauzanne, K., & Lee, E. (2000). How sexually dimorphic are we? Review and synthesis. *American Journal of Human Biology, 12*, 151–166.

Blackmore, E. R., Gustafsson, H., Gilchrist, M., Wyman, C., & O'Connor, T. G. (2016). Pregnancy-related anxiety: Evidence of distinct clinical significance from a prospective longitudinal study. *Journal of Affective Disorders, 197*, 251–258.

Blackwell, D. L., & Lichter, D. T. (2004). Homogamy among dating, cohabiting, and married couples. *The Sociological Quarterly, 45*, 719–737.

Blackwell, L. S., Trzesniewski, K. H., & Dweck, C. S. (2007). Implicit theories of intelligence predict achievement across an adolescent transition: A longitudinal study and an intervention. *Child Development, 78*, 246–263.

Blair, C. (2002). School readiness: Integrating cognition and emotion in a neurobiological conceptualization of children's functioning at school entry. *American Psychologist, 57*, 111–127.

Blair, C. (2016). Developmental science and executive function. *Current Directions in Psychological Science, 25*, 3–7.

Blair, C. (2017). Educating executive function. *WIREs Cogn Sci*, 8:e1403. doi: 10.1002/wcs.1403

Blair, M. M., Glynn, L. M., Sandman, C. A., & Davis, E. P. (2011). Prenatal maternal anxiety and early childhood temperament. *Stress, 14*, 644–651.

Blakemore, J. E. O., Berenbaum, S. A., & Liben, L. S. (2009). *Gender development*. New York, NY: Taylor & Francis Group.

Blakemore, S. J. (2012). Imaging brain development: The adolescent brain. *NeuroImage, 61*, 397–406.

Blanchard, R. (2017). Fraternal birth order, family size, and male homosexuality: Meta-analysis of studies spanning 25 years. *Archives of Sexual Behavior*. doi:10.1007/s10508-017-1007-4

Blanchard-Fields, F. (1986). Reasoning on social dilemmas varying in emotional salience: An adult developmental perspective. *Psychology and Aging, 1*, 325–333.

Blanchard-Fields, F. (2007). Everyday problem solving and emotion: An adult developmental perspective. *Current Directions in Psychological Science, 16*, 26–31.

Blaser, E., & Kaldy, Z. (2010). Infants get five stars on iconic memory tests: A partial-report test of 6-month-old infants' iconic memory capacity. *Psychological Science, 21*, 1643–1645.

Blazer, D. G. (2003). Depression in late life: Review and commentary. *Journal of Gerontology, 58*, 249–265.

Blazer, D. G., Kessler, R. C., McGonagle, K. A., & Schwartz, M. S. (1994). The prevalence and distribution of major depression in a national community sample: The national comorbidity survey. *American Journal of Psychiatry, 151*, 979–986.

Bleidorn, W. (2015). What accounts for personality maturation in early adulthood? *Current Directions in Psychological Science, 24*, 245–252.

Bleidorn, W., Arslan, R. C., Denissen, J. J. A., Rentfrow, P. J., Gebauer, J. E., Potter, J., & Gosling, S. D. (2016). Age and gender differences in self-esteem – A cross-cultural window. *Personality Processes and Individual Differences, 3*, 396–410.

Bleidorn, W., Klimstra, T. A., Denissen, J. J. A., Rentfrow, P. J., Potter, J., & Gosling, S. D. (2013). Personality maturation around the world: A cross-cultural examination of social-investment theory. *Psychological Science, 24*, 2530–2540.

Blewitt, P. (1989). Category hierarchies: Levels of knowledge and skill. *Genetic Epistemologist, 17*, 21–30.

Blewitt, P. (1994). Understanding categorical hierarchies: The earliest levels of skill. *Child Development, 65*, 1279–1298.

Blewitt, P., & Langan, R. (2016). Learning words during shared book reading: The role of extratextual talk designed to increase child engagement. *Journal of Experimental Child Psychology, 150*, 404–410.

Blewitt, P., Rump, K. M., Shealy, S. E., & Cook, S. A. (2009). Shared book reading: When and how questions affect young children's word learning. *Journal of Educational Psychology, 101*, 294–304.

Block, J., & Block, J. H. (2006). Venturing a 30-year longitudinal study. *American Psychologist, 61*, 315–327.

Block, J. H. (1978). Another look at sex differentiation in the socialization behaviors of mothers and fathers. In J. Sherman & F. L. Denmark (Eds.), *The psychology of women: Future directions of research* (pp. 29–87). New York, NY: Psychological Dimensions.

Block, K., Gonzalez, A. M., Schmader, T., & Baron, A. S. (2018). Early gender differences in core values predict anticipated family versus career orientation. *Psychological Science, 29*. doi: 10.1177/0956797618776942

Blos, P. (1975). The second individuation process of adolescence. In A. Esman (Ed.), *The psychology of adolescence* (pp. 156–176). New York, NY: International Universities Press.

Bock, J., Wainstock, T., Braun, K., & Segal, M. (2015). Stress in utero: Prenatal programming of brain plasticity and cognition. *Biological Psychiatry, 78*, 315–326.

Bodhi, B. (Ed.). (1999). *A comprehensive manual of Abhidhamma: The philosophical psychology of Buddhism*. Seattle, WA: BPS Pariyatti Editions.

Bodrova, E., & D. J. Leong. (2007). *Tools of the mind: The Vygotskian approach to early childhood education* (2nd ed.). Upper Saddle River, NJ: Pearson Education/Merrill.

Boduroglu, A., Shah, P., & Nisbett, R. E. (2009). Cultural differences in allocation of attention in visual information processing. *Journal of Cross-Cultural Psychology, 40*, 349–360.

Boelema, S. R., Harakeh, Z., Ormel, J., Hartman, C. A., Vollebergh, W. A. M., & van Zandvoort, M. J. E. (2014). Executive functioning shows differential maturation from early to late adolescence. *Neuropsychology, 28*, 177–187.

Bogaert, A. F. (2006). Biological versus nonbiological older brothers and men's sexual orientation. *Proceedings of the National Academy of Sciences. USA, 103*, 10771–10774.

Bogels, S., & Restifo, K. (2014). *Mindful parenting: A guide for mental health practitioners*. New York, NY: Springer Verlag.

Bogg, T., & Roberts, B. W. (2013). The case for conscientiousness: Evidence and implications for a personality trait marker of health and longevity. *Annals of Behavioral Medicine, 45*(3), 278–288.

Boldt, L. J., Kochanska, G., & Jonas, K. (2017). Infant attachment moderates paths from early negativity to preadolescent outcomes for children and parents. *Child Development, 88*, 584–596.

Bolger, K. E., & Patterson, C. J. (2003). Sequelae of child maltreatment: Vulnerability and resilience. In S. S. Luthar (Ed.), *Resilience and vulnerability: Adaptation in the context of childhood adversities* (pp. 156–181). Cambridge, England: Cambridge University Press.

Bonanno, G. A., & Keltner, D. (1997). Facial expression of emotion and the course of conjugal bereavement. *Journal of Abnormal Psychology, 106*, 126–137.

Bonanno, G. A., Znoj, H., Siddique, H. I., & Horowitz, M. J. (1999). Verbal-autonomic dissociation and adaptation to midlife conjugal loss: A follow-up at 25 months. *Cognitive Therapy and Research, 23*, 605–624.

Bond, J. T., Thompson, C., Galinsky, E., & Prottas, D. (2002). *Highlights of the national study of the changing workforce*. New York, NY: Families and Work Institute.

Bonnesen, J. L., & Hummert, M. L. (2002). Painful self-disclosures of older adults in relation to aging stereotypes and perceived motivations. *Journal of Language and Social Psychology, 21*, 275–301.

Bonomi, A. E., Anderson, M. L., Nemeth, J., Rivara, F. P., & Buettner, C. (2013). History of dating violence and the association with late adolescent health. *BMC Public Health, 13*(1), 821.

Boo, F. P. (2016). Socio-economic status and early childhood cognitive skills: A mediation analysis using the Young Lives panel. *International Journal of Behavioral Development, 40*, 500–508.

Boon, M. Y., & Dain, S. J. (2015). The development of color vision and of the ability to appreciate color in picturebooks. In B. Kummerling-Meibauer, J. Meibauer, K. Nachtigaller, & Rohlfing, K. J. (Eds.), *Learning from picturebooks: Perspectives from child development and literacy studies* (pp. 71–95). London: Routledge.

Booth, C. L., Clarke-Stewart, K. A., Vandell, D. L., McCartney, K., & Owen, M. T. (2002). Child-care usage and mother-infant "quality time." *Journal of Marriage and Family, 64*, 16–26.

Boris, N. W., & Renk, K. (2017). Beyond reactive attachment disorder. *Child and Adolescent Psychiatric Clinics of North America, 26*(3), 455–476.

Bornstein, D. (2011). Hard times for school recess. *New York Times*. Accessed from https://opinionator.blogs.nytimes.com/2011/04/04/hard-times-for-recess/?_r=0

Bornstein, M. H. (2015). Children's parents. In R. M. Lerner (Series Ed.), M. H. Bornstein & T. Leventhal (Vol. Eds.), *Handbook of child psychology and developmental science: Volume 4. Ecological settings and processes* (7th ed., pp. 55–132). Hoboken, NJ: Wiley.

Bornstein, M. H., Hahn, C.-S., & Wolke, D. (2013). Systems and cascades in cognitive development and academic achievement. *Child Development, 84*, 154–162.

Bornstein, M. H., Putnick, D. L., Suwalsky, J. T. D., & Gini, M. (2006). Maternal chronological age, prenatal and perinatal history, social support, and parenting of infants. *Child Development, 77*, 875–892.

Bos, H. M. W., & Sandfort, T. (2010). Childen's gender identity in lesbian and heterosexual two-parent families. *Sex Roles, 62*, 114–126.

Bouchard, G. (2014). How do parents react when their children leave home? An integrative review. *Journal of Adult Development, 21*, 69–79.

Bouza, J., Camacho-Thompson, E. E., Carlo, G., Franco, X., Coll, C. G., Halgunseth, L. C., . . . White, R. M. B. (2018). *SRCD Statement of the Evidence: The science is clear: Separating families has long-term damaging psychological and health consequences for children, families, and communities*. Available at www.srccd.org/policy-media/statmets-evidence.

Bowen, M. (1978). *Family therapy in clinical practice*. New York, NY: Jason Aronson.

Bower, E. M. (1960). *Early identification of emotionally handicapped children in school*. Springfield, IL: Charles C. Thomas.

Bowlby, J. (1969/1982). *Attachment and loss: Vol. 1. Attachment*. New York, NY: Basic Books.

Bowlby, J. (1973). *Attachment and loss: Vol. 2. Separation*. New York, NY: Basic Books.

Bowlby, J. (1980). *Attachment and loss: Vol. 3. Loss: Sadness and depression*. New York, NY: Basic Books.

Bowlby, J. (1988). *A secure base: Parent-child attachment and healthy human development*. New York, NY: Basic Books.

Boyce, C. J., Wood, A. M., Daly, M., & Sedikides, C. (2015). Personality change following unemployment. *Journal of Applied Psychology, 100*, 991–1011.

Boyer, T. W., Levine, S. C., & Huttenlocher, J. (2008). Development of proportional reasoning: Where young children go wrong. *Developmental Psychology, 44*, 1478–1490.

Boykin, A. W., & Toms, F. D. (1985). Black child socialization: A conceptual framework. In H. P. McAdoo & J. L. McAdoo (Eds.), *Black children: Social, educational, and parental environments* (pp. 33–52). Newbury Park, CA: Sage.

Boylan, J. M., & Ryff, C. D. (2013). Varieties of anger and the inverse link between education and inflammation: Toward an integrative framework. *Psychosomatic Medicine, 75*, 566–574.

Boynton-Jarrett, R., Wright, R., Putnam, F., Hibert, E., Michels, K., Forman, M., & Rich-Edwards, J. (2012). Childhood abuse and age at menarche. *Journal of Adolescent Health*. http://dx.doi.org.ezaccess.libraries.psu.edu/10.1016/j.jadohealth.2012.06.006

Braak, H., & Braak, E. (1991). Neuropathological staging of Alzheimer-related changes. *Acta Neuropathologica, 82*, 239–259.

Bracha, H. S., Ralston, T. C., Matsukawa, J. M., Williams, A. E., & Bracha, A. S. (2004). Does "Fight or Flight" need updating? *Psychosomatics, 45*, 448–449.

Bradley, S. J., Oliver, G. D., Chernick, A. B., & Zucker, K. J. (1998). Experiment of nurture: Ablatio penis at 2 months, sex reassignment at 7 months, and psychosexual follow-up in young adulthood. *Pediatrics, 102*, 132–133.

Bradshaw, C. P., Pas, E. T., Debnam, K. J., & Johnson, S. L. (2015). A focus on implementation of positive behavioral interventions and supports in high schools: Associations with bullying and other indicators of school disorder. *School Psychology Review, 44*(4), 480.

Brand, R. J., & Dixon, W. E. (2013). *Difficulty calming predicts infant TV use and mediates the relationship between TV and later attention problems*. Poster presented at the biennial meetings of the Society for Research in Child Development, Seattle, Washington.

Brand, R. J., Hardesty, S., & Dixon, W. E. (2011). *Toddler's difficult temperament predicts television use*. Poster presented at the biennial meetings of the Society for Research in Child Development, Montreal, Canada.

Brandmaier, A. M., Ram, N., Wagner, G. G., & Gerstorf, D. (2017). Terminal decline in well-being: The role of multi-indicator constellations of physical health and psychosocial correlates. *Developmental Psychology, 53*, 996–1012.

Brauner, J., Gordic, B., & Zigler, E. (2004). Putting the child back into child care: Combining care and education for children ages 3–5. *Social Policy Report, 18*, 3–15.

Braungart-Rieker, J. M., Zentall, S., Lickenbrock, D. M., Ekas, N. V., Oshio, T., & Planalp, E. (2014). Attachment in the making: Mother and father sensitivity and infants' responses during the still-face paradigm. *Journal of Experimental Child Psychology, 125*, 63–84.

Braveman, P., & Gottlieb, L. (2014). The social determinants of health: It's time to consider the cause of the causes. *Public Health Reports, 129*, 19–31.

Brazelton, T. B. (1986). Issues for working parents. *American Journal of Orthopsychiatry, 56*, 14–25.

Bremner, J. G., Slater, A. M., & Johnson, S. P. (2015). Perception of object persistence: The origins of object permanence in infancy. *Child Development Perspectives, 9*, 7–13.

Brendgen, M., Girard, A., Vitaro, F., Dionne, G., & Boivin, M. (2016). Personal and familial predictors of peer victimization trajectories from primary to secondary school. *Developmental Psychology, 52*, 1103–1114.

Brennan, K. A., Clark, C. L., & Shaver, P. R. (1998). Self-report measurement of adult attachment: An integrative interview. In J. A. Simpson & W. S. Rholes (Eds.), *Attachment theory and close relationships* (pp. 46–76). New York, NY: Guilford Press.

Brescoll, V. L. (2016). Leading with their hearts? How gender stereotypes of emotion lead to biased evaluations of female leaders. *The Leadership Quarterly, 27*, 415–428.

Brescoll, V. L., & Uhlmann, E. L. (2008). Can an angry woman get ahead? Status conferral, gender, and expression of emotion in the workplace. *Psychological Science, 19*, 268–275.

Brestan, E. V., & Eyberg, S. M. (1998). Effective psychosocial treatment of conduct-disordered children and adolescents: 29 years, 82 studies, and 5275 kids. *Journal of Clinical Child Psychology, 27*, 180–189.

Bretherton, I., & Munholland, K. A. (2016). The internal working model construct in light of contemporary neuroimaging research. In J. Cassidy & P. R. Shaver (Eds.), *Handbook of attachment: Theory, research, and clinical applications* (3rd ed., pp. 63–88). New York, NY: Guilford Press.

Brewer, J. A., Elwafi, H. M., & Davis, J. H. (2013). Craving to quit: Psychological models and neurobiological mechanisms of mindfulness training as treatment for addictions. *Psychology of Addictive Behaviors: Journal of the Society of Psychologists in Addictive Behaviors, 27*(2), 366–379.

Brickman, P. D., & Campbell, D. T. (1971). Hedonic relativism and planning the good society. In M. H. Appley (Ed.). *Adaptation level theory: A symposium* (pp. 287–304). New York, NY: Academic Press.

Briley, D. A., & Tucker-Drob, E. M. (2014). Genetic and environmental continuity in personality development: A meta-analysis. *Psychological Bulletin, 140*, 1303–1331.

Brisch, K. H. (1999). *Treating attachment disorders: From theory to therapy*. New York, NY: Guilford Press.

Brittian, L. A., & Williams, B. V. (2017). The potential for youth programs to promote African American youth's development of ethnic and racial identity. *Child Development Perspectives, 11*(1), 29–38.

Britton, J. R., Britton, H. L., & Gronwaldt, V. (2006). Breastfeeding, sensitivity, and attachment. *Pediatrics, 118*, e1436–e1443.

Broderick, P. C. (1998). Early adolescent differences in the use of ruminative and distracting coping styles. *Journal of Early Adolescence, 18*, 173–191.

Broderick, P. C., & Frank, J. L. (2014). Learning to BREATHE: An intervention to foster mindfulness in adolescence. *New Directions for Youth Development, 2014*(142), 31–44.

Broderick, P. C., & Korteland, C. (2004). A prospective study of rumination and depression in early adolescence. *Clinical Child Psychology and Psychiatry, 9*, 383–394.

Brody, G. H., Ge, X., Conger, R., Gibbons, F. X., Murry, V. M., Gerrard, M., . . . Simons, R. L. (2001). The influence of neighborhood disadvantage, collective socialization, and parenting on African American children's affiliation with deviant peers. *Child Development, 72*, 1231–1246.

Brody, G. H., McBride Murry, V., Gerrard, M., Gibbons, F. X., Molgaard, V., McNair, L., . . . Neubaum-Carlan, E. (2014). Perceived discrimination among African American adolescents and allostatic load: A longitudinal analysis with buffering effects. *Child Development, 85*, 989–1002.

Brody, G. H., Miller, G. E., Yu, T., Beach, S. R. H., & Chen, E. (2016). Supportive family environments ameliorate the link between racial discrimination and epigenetic aging: A replication across two longitudinal cohorts. *Psychological Science, 27*, 530–541.

Brody, G. H., Murry, V. M., Gerrard, M., Gibbons, F. X., Molgaard, V., McNair, L., . . . Neubaum-Carlan, E. (2004). The Strong African American Families Program: Translating research into prevention programming. *Child Development, 75*, 900–917.

Broeren, S., Muris, P., Diamantopoulou, S., & Baker, J. R. (2013). The course of childhood anxiety symptoms: Developmental trajectories and child-related factors in normal children. *Journal of Abnormal Child Psychology, 41*, 81–95.

Broesch, T., Rochat, P., Olah, K., Broesch, J., & Henrich, J. (2016). Similarities and differences in maternal responsiveness in three societies: Evidence from Fiji, Kenya, and the United States. *Child Development, 87*, 700–711.

Bronfenbrenner, U. (1979). *The ecology of human development: Experiments by nature and by design.* Cambridge, MA: Harvard University Press.

Bronfenbrenner, U., & Ceci, S. J. (1994). Nature-nurture reconceptualized in developmental perspective: A bioecological model. *Psychological Review, 101*, 568–586.

Bronfenbrenner, U., & Morris, P. A. (1998). The ecology of developmental processes. In W. Damon (Series Ed.) & R. M. Lerner (Vol. Ed.), *Handbook of child psychology: Vol. 1. Theoretical models of human development* (5th ed., pp. 993–1028). New York, NY: Wiley.

Bronfenbrenner, U., & Morris, P. A. (2006). The bioecological model of human development. In W. Damon & R. M. Lerner (Series Eds.), R. M. Lerner (Vol. Ed.), *Handbook of child psychology: Vol. 1. Theoretical models of human development* (6th ed., pp. 793–828). Hoboken, NJ: Wiley.

Brook, C. A., & Willoughby, T. (2016). Social anxiety and alcohol use across the university years: Adaptive and maladaptive groups. *Developmental Psychology, 52*, 835–845.

Brookes, J. (2015). The effect of overt and covert narcissism on self-esteem and self-efficacy beyond self-esteem. *Personality and Individual Differences, 85*, 172–175.

Brooks-Gunn, J. (1991). Maturational timing variations in adolescent girls, antecedents of. In R. M. Lerner, A. C. Petersen, & J. Brooks-Gunn (Eds.), *Encyclopedia of adolescence* (Vol. 2). New York, NY: Garland.

Brooks-Gunn, J. (2003). Do you believe in magic? What we can expect from early childhood intervention programs. *Social Policy Report, 17*, 3–14.

Brooks-Gunn, J., Han, W., & Waldfogel, J. (2002). Maternal employment and child cognitive outcomes in the first three years of life: The NICHD study of early child care. *Child Development, 73*, 1052–1072.

Brotman, L. M., Calzada, E., Huang, K.-Y., Kingston, S., Dawson-McClure, A., Kamboukos, . . . Petkova, E. (2011). Promoting effective parenting practices and preventing child behavior problems in school among ethnically diverse families from underserved, urban communities. *Child Development, 82*(1), 258–276.

Brown, B. B. (1990). Peer groups and peer cultures. In S. S. Feldman & G. R. Elliott (Eds.), *At the threshold: The developing adolescent* (pp. 171–196). Cambridge, MA: Harvard University Press.

Brown, B. B., & Bakken, J. P. (2011). Parenting and peer relationships: Reinvigorating research on family-peer linkages in adolescence. *Journal of Research on Adolescence, 21*(1), 153–165.

Brown, B. B., Herman M., Hamm, J. V., & Heck, D. J. (2008). Ethnicity and image: Correlates of crowd affiliation among ethnic minority youth. *Child Development, 79*, 529–546.

Brown, C., & Chu, H. (2012). Discrimination, ethnic identity, and academic outcomes of Mexican immigrant children: The importance of school context. *Child Development, 83*, 1477–1485.

Brown, C. S., & Bigler, R. S. (2005). Children's perceptions of discrimination: A developmental model. *Child Development, 76*, 533–553.

Brown, D. A., & Lamb, M. E. (2015). Can children be useful witnesses? It depends how they are questioned. *Child Development Perspectives, 9*, 250–255.

Brown, E., & Blewitt, P. (March, 2014). *Bilingualism and synonym effect.* Poster presented at the annual meeting of the Eastern Psychological Association, Boston, MA.

Brown, E. A., Bekker, H. L., Davison, S. N., Koffman, J., & Schell, J. O. (2016). Supportive care: Communication strategies to improve cultural competence in shared decision making. *Clinical Journal of the American Society of Nephrology*, CJN-13661215.

Brown, G. L., Mangelsdorf, S. C., & Neff, C. (2012). Father involvement, paternal sensitivity and father-child attachment security in the first 3 years. *Journal of Family Psychology, 26*, 421–430.

Brown, J., Steele, J., & Walsh-Childers, K. (2002). *Sexual teens, sexual media: Investigating media's influence on adolescent sexuality.* Hillsdale, NJ: Erlbaum.

Brown, J. L., Roderick, T., Lantiere, L., & Aber, J. L. (2004). The Resolving Conflicts Creatively Program: A school-based social and emotional learning program. In J. E. Zins, R. P. Weissberg, M. C. Wang, & H. J. Walberg (Eds.), *Building academic success on social and emotional learning: What does the research say?* (pp. 151–169). New York, NY: Teachers College Press.

Brown, L., & Gilligan, C. (1992). *Meeting at the crossroads: Women's psychology and girls'*

development. Cambridge, MA: Harvard University Press.

Brown, R., & Hanlon, C. (1970). Derivational complexity and order of acquisition. In J. R. Hayes (Ed.), *Cognition and the development of language* (pp. 11–53). New York, NY: Wiley.

Brown, S. L., Nesse, N. M., Vinokur, A., & Smith, D. M. (2003). Providing social support may be more beneficial than receiving it: Results from a prospective study of mortality. *Psychological Science, 14*, 320–327.

Browning, S. W. (1998). The empathy expansion procedure: A method of assisting couples in healing from traumatic incidents. In L. L. Hecker & S. A. Deacon (Eds.), *The therapist's notebook: Homework, handouts, and activities for use in psychotherapy.* New York, NY: Haworth Press.

Browning, S., & Bray, J. H. (2009). Treating stepfamilies: A subsystems-based approach. In M. Stanton & J. Bray (Eds.), *Blackwell handbook of family psychology.* London: Blackwell Publishing.

Brubaker, R. (2009). Ethnicity, race, and nationalism. *Annual Review of Sociology, 35*, 21–42.

Bruck, M., & Ceci, S. J. (2012). Forensic developmental psychology in the courtroom. In M. Bruck & S. J. Ceci (Eds.), *Coping with psychiatric and psychological testimony: Based on the original work by Jay Ziskin* (6th ed., pp. 723–736). New York, NY: Oxford University Press.

Bruck, M., & Ceci, S. J. (2013). Expert testimony in a child sex abuse case: Translating memory development research. *Memory, 21*, 556–565.

Bruck, M., Ceci, S. J., & Principe, G. F. (2006). The child and the law. In W. Damon & R. M. Lerner (Series Eds.), K. A. Renninger & I. E. Sigel (Vol. Ed.), *Handbook of child psychology: Vol. 4. Child psychology in practice* (6th ed., pp. 776–816). Hoboken, NJ: Wiley.

Bruckner, H., & Bearman, P. (2005). After the promise: The STD consequences of adolescent virginity pledges. *Journal of Adolescent Health, 36*, 271–278.

Brumberg, J. J. (1988). *Fasting girls: The emergence of anorexia nervosa as a modern disease.* Cambridge, MA: Harvard University Press.

Brummelman, E., Crocker, J., & Bushman, B. J. (2016). The praise paradox: When and why praise backfires in children with low self-esteem. *Child Development Perspectives, 10*, 111–115.

Brummelman, E., Thomaes, S., Nelemans, S. A., Orobio de Castro, B., Overbeek, G., Brunwasser, S. M., & Garber, J. (2016). Programs for the prevention of youth depression: Evaluation of efficacy, effectiveness, and readiness for dissemination. *Journal of Clinical Child and Adolescent Psychology, 45*, 763–783. doi:10.1080/15374416.2015.1020541

Brummelman, E., Thomaes, S., & Sedikides, C. (2016). Separating narcissism from self-esteem. *Current Directions in Psychological Science, 25*, 8–13.

Bryant, N. B., & Gómez, R. L. (2015). The teen sleep loss epidemic: What can be done? *Translational Issues in Psychological Science, 1*, 116–125.

Brysbaert, M., Stevens, M., Mandera, P., & Keuleers, E. (2016). How many words do we know? Practical estimates of vocabulary size dependent on word definition, the degree of language input and the participant's age. *Frontiers in Psychology, 7.* doi: 10.3389/psyg.2016.01116

Buchanan, C. M., Eccles, J. S., & Becker, J. B. (1992). Are adolescents the victims of raging hormones? Evidence for activational effects of hormones on moods and behavior at adolescence. *Psychological Bulletin, 111,* 62–107.

Buchtemann, D., Luppa, M., Bramesfeld, A., & Riedel-Heller, S. (2012). Incidence of late-life depression: A systematic review. *Journal of Affective Disorders, 142,* 172–179.

Buckner, J. D., Lopez, C., Dunkel, S., & Joiner, T. E. (2008). Behavior management training for the treatment of Reactive Attachment Disorder. *Child Maltreatment, 13,* 289–297.

Buist, K. L., Deković, M., & Prinzie, P. (2013). Sibling relationship quality and psychopathology of children and adolescents: A meta-analysis. *Clinical Psychology Review, 33,* 97–106.

Bull, R., & Lee, K. (2014). Executive functioning and mathematics achievement. *Child Development Perspectives, 8,* 36-41.

Bullock, M., Sodian, B., & Koerber, S. (2009). Doing experiments and understanding science: Development of scientific reasoning from childhood to adulthood. In W. Scheider & M. Bullock (Eds.), *Human development from early childhood to early adulthood: Findings from a 20 year longitudinal study* (pp. 173–197). New York, NY: Psychology Press.

Bunge, S. A., Dudukovic, N. M., Thomason, M. E., Vaidya, C. J., Chandan, J., & Gabrieli, J. D. E. (2002). Immature frontal lobe contributions to cognitive control in children: evidence from fMRI. *Neuron, 33,* 301–311.

Burchinal, M. (2016). Large-scale evaluations of child care as a context for development: Implications for research and practice. In K. E. Sanders & A. W. Guerra (Eds.), *The culture of child care: Attachment, peers, and quality in diverse communities* (pp. 205–228). New York, NY: Oxford University Press.

Burchinal, M. R., Magnuson, K., Powell, D., & Hong, S. S. (2015). Early childcare and education. In R. M. Lerner (Ed. In Chief) & M. Bornstein & T. Leventhal (Vol. Eds.), *Handbook of child psychology and developmental science: Vol. 4. Ecological settings and processes* (7th ed., pp. 223–267). Hoboken, NJ: Wiley.

Burhan, N. A. S., Yunus, M. Md., Tovar, M. E. L., & Burhan, N. M. G. (2017). Why are cognitive abilities of children so different across countries? The link between major socioeconomic factors and PISA test scores. *Personality and Individual Differences, 195,* 95–106.

Burka, J. B., & Yuen, L. M. (1983). *Procrastination: Why you do it, what to do about it.* Reading, MA: Addison-Wesley.

Burke, H. M., Davis, M. C., Otte, C., & Mohr, D. C. (2005). Depression and cortisol responses to psychological stress: A meta-analysis. *Psychoneuroendocrinology, 30,* 846–856.

Burn, K., & Szoeke, C. (2015). Grandparenting predicts late-life cognition: Results from the Women's Healthy Ageing Project. *Maturitas, 81,* 317–322.

Burns, B. J., Costello, E. J., Angold, A., Erkanli, A., Stangl, D., & Tweed, D. L. (1995). Children's mental health service use across service sectors. *Health Affairs, 14,* 147–159.

Burns, B. J., Hoagwood, K., & Mrazek, P. J. (1999). Effective treatments for mental disorders in children and adolescents. *Clinical Child and Family Psychology Review, 2,* 199–254.

Burr, W. R. (1970). Satisfaction with various aspects of marriage over the life cycle: A random middle class sample. *Journal of Marriage and the Family, 32,* 29–37.

Burri, A., Spector, T., & Rahman, Q. (2015). Common genetic factors among sexual orientation, gender nonconformity, and number of sex partners in female twins: Implications for the evolution of homosexuality. *Journal of Sexual Medicine, 12,* 1004–1011.

Burt, K. B., & Paysnick, A. A. (2012). Resilience in the transition to adulthood. *Development and Psychopathology 24,* 493–505.

Bus, A. G., Takacs, Z. K., & Kegel, C. A. T. (2015). Affordances and limitations of electronic storybooks for young children's emergent literacy. *Developmental Review, 35,* 79–97.

Bushman, B. J. (2015). Origins of narcissism in children. *Proceedings of the National Academy of Sciences of the United States of America, 112,* 3659–3662.

Buss, D. M. (1989). Sex differences in human mate preferences: Evolutionary hypotheses tested in 37 cultures. *Behavioral and Brain Sciences, 12,* 1–49.

Busseri, M. A. (2015). Toward a resolution of the tripartite structure of subjective well-being. *Journal of Personality, 83*(4), 413–428.

Bussey, K., & Bandura, A. (1984). Influence of gender constancy and social power on sex-linked modeling. *Journal of Personality and Social Psychology, 47,* 1292–1302.

Bussey, K., & Bandura, A. (1999). A social cognitive theory of gender development and differentiation. *Psychological Bulletin, 106,* 676–713.

Butler, L. D., & Nolen-Hoeksema, S. (1994). Gender differences in response to depressed mood in a college sample. *Sex Roles, 30,* 331–346.

Butler, R. N. (1963). The life review: An interpretation of reminiscence in the aged. *Psychiatry, 26,* 65–76.

Butler, R. N. (2009). *The longevity revolution: The benefits and challenges of living a long life.* Hachette UK.

Byers, A. L., Levy, B. R., Allore, H. G., Bruce, M. L., & Kasl, S. V. (2008). When parents matter to their adult children: Filial reliance associated with parents' depressive symptoms. *The Journals of Gerontology Series B: Psychological Sciences and Social Sciences, 63,* P33–P40.

Byne, W., Bradley, S. J., Coleman, E., Eyler, A. E., Green R., Menvielle, E., . . . Tompkins, A. (2012). Treatment of gender identity disorder. *American Journal of Psychiatry 169,* 875–876.

Byrne, D. (1964). Repression-sensitization as a dimension of personality. In B. A. Maher (Ed.), *Progress in experimental personality research* (pp. 169–220). New York, NY: Academic Press.

Byrne, M. L., Whittle, S., Vijayakumar, N., Dennison, M., Simmons, J. G., & Allen, N. B. (2017). *Developmental Cognitive Neuroscience, 25,* 12–28.

Cacioppo, J. T., & Berntson, G. G. (1992). Social psychological contributions to the decade of the brain: Doctrine of multilevel analysis. *American Psychologist, 47,* 1019–1028.

Cacioppo, J. T., & Gardner, W. L. (1999). Emotion. *Annual Review of Psychology, 50,* 191–214.

Cagle, J. G., Pek, J., Clifford, M., Guralnik, J., & Zimmerman, S. (2015). Correlates of a good death and the impact of hospice involvement: Findings from the national survey of households affected by cancer. *Supportive Care in Cancer, 23,* 809–818.

Cairns, R. B., & Cairns, B. D. (1994). *Lifelines and risks: Pathways of youth in our time.* New York, NY: Cambridge University Press.

Cairns, R. B., & Cairns, B. D. (2000). The natural history and developmental functions of aggression. In A. J. Sameroff, M. Lewis, & S. M. Miller (Eds.), *Handbook of developmental psychopathology* (2nd ed., pp. 403–429). New York, NY: Kluwer Academic/Plenum Press.

Caldwell, M. F. (2010). Study characteristics and recidivism base rates in juvenile sex offender recidivism. *International Journal of Offender Therapy and Comparative Criminology, 54,* 197–212.

Callanan, M., & Kelley, P. (1992). *Final gifts: Understanding the special awareness, needs and communications of the dying.* New York, NY: Bantam Books.

Calvert, S. L. (2015). Children and digital media. In R. M. Lerner (Ed. In Chief) & M. H. Bornstein & T. Leventhal (Vol. Eds.), *Handbook of child psychology and developmental science: Vol. 4. Ecological settings and processes* (7th ed., pp. 381–424). Hoboken, NJ: Wiley.

Calvert, S. L., Appelbaum, M., Dodge, K. A., Graham, S., Nagayama Hall, G. C., Hamby, S., . . . Hedges, L. V. (2017). The American Psychological Association task force assessment of violent video games: Science in the service of public interest. *American Psychologist, 72*(2), 126–143.

Campbell, A. (2008). The morning after the night before: Affective reactions to one-night stands among mated and unmated women and men. *Human Nature, 19,* 157–173.

Campbell, F. A., Pungello, E. P., Burchinal, M., Kainz, K., Pan, Y., Wasik, B. H., . . . Ramey, C. T. (2012). Adult outcomes as a function of an early childhood educational program: An Abecedarian Project follow-up. *Developmental Psychology, 48,* 1033–1043.

Campbell, J. D. (1990). Self-esteem and clarity of the self-concept. *Journal of Personality and Social Psychology, 59,* 538–549.

Campbell, J. D., & Lavallee, L. F. (1993). Who am I? The role of self-concept confusion in understanding the behavior of people with low self-esteem. In R. F. Baumeister (Ed.), *Self-esteem: The puzzle of low self-regard* (pp. 3–20). New York, NY: Plenum Press.

Campos, B., & Kim, H. S. (2017). Incorporating the cultural diversity of family and close relationships into the study of health. *American Psychologist, 72,* 543-554.

Campos, J., Barrett, K., Lamb, M., Goldsmith, H., & Sternberg, C. (1983). Socioemotional development. In P. H. Mussen (Ed.), *Handbook of child psychology: Vol. 2. Infancy and developmental psychology* (pp. 783–915). New York, NY: Wiley.

Campos, J. J., Frankel, C. B., & Camras, L. (2004). On the nature of emotion regulation. *Child Development, 75,* 377–394.

Cannon, W. B. (1927). The James-Lange theory of emotions: A critical examination and an alternative theory. *American Journal of Psychology, 39,* 106–124.

Cannon, W. B. (1929). *Bodily changes in pain, hunger, fear and rage: An account of recent research into the function of emotional excitement* (2nd ed.) New York, NY: Appleton-Century-Crofts.

Cantor, J., & Wilson, B. J. (1998). Helping children cope with frightening media presentations. *Current Psychology: Research & Reviews, 7,* 58–75.

Cantril, H. (1965). *The pattern of human concerns.* New Brunswick, NJ: Rutgers University Press.

Caplan, M., Vespo, J. E., Pedersen, J., & Hay, D. F. (1991). Conflict over resources in small groups of 1- and 2-year-olds. *Child Development, 62,* 1513–1524.

Capraro, V., & Sippel, J. (2017). Gender differences in moral judgment and the evaluation of gender-specified moral agents. *Cognitive Processing, 18,* 399–405.

Carey, R. M., & Markus, H. R. (2017). Social class shapes the form and function of relationships and selves. *Current Opinion in Psychology, 18,* 123–130.

Carey, R. N., Donaghue, N., & Broderick, P. (2014). Body image concern among Australian adolescent girls: The role of body comparisons with models and peers. *Body Image, 11,* 81–84.

Carey, S. (2000). Science education as conceptual change. *Journal of Applied Developmental Psychology, 21,* 13–19.

Carey, S. (2009). *The origin of concepts.* New York, NY: Oxford University Press.

Carey, S., Zaitchik, D., & Bascandziev, I. (2015). Theories of development: In dialog with Jean Piaget. *Developmental Review, 38,* 35–54.

Carlatt, D. J., Camargo, C. A., & Herzog, D. B. (1997). Eating disorders in males: A report on 135 patients. *American Journal of Psychiatry, 154,* 1127–1132.

Carli, L. L. (1990). Gender, language, and influence. *Journal of Personality and Social Psychology, 59,* 941–951.

Carlson, J., & Lewis, J. (1993). Motivation: Building students' feelings of confidence and self-worth. In J. Carlson & J. Lewis (Eds.), *Counseling the adolescent: Individual, family and school interventions* (2nd ed., pp. 249–270). Denver, CO: Love.

Carlsson, J., Wängqvist, M., & Frisén, A. (2016). Life on hold: Staying in identity diffusion in the late twenties. *Journal of Adolescence, 47,* 220–229.

Carmichael, C. L., Reis, H. T., & Duberstein, P. R. (2015). In your 20s it's quantity, in your 30s it's quality: The prognostic value of social activity across 30 years of adulthood. *Psychology and Aging, 30,* 95–105.

Carnegie Council on Adolescent Development. (1996). *Great transitions: Preparing adolescents for a new century.* New York, NY: Carnegie Corporation of New York.

Carney, A. K. (2014). Wisconsin longitudinal study. *The International Journal of Aging and Human Development, 79*(4), 332–333.

Caro, D. H., Lenkeit, J., & Kyriakides, L. (2016). Teaching strategies and differential effectiveness across learning contexts: Evidence from PISA 2012. *Studies in Educational Evaluation, 49,* 30–41.

Carpendale, J. I. M., & Lewis, C. (2015). The development of social understanding. In R. M. Lerner (Ed. In Chief) & L. S. Liben & U. Miller (Vol. Eds.), *Handbook of child psychology and developmental science: Vol. 2. Cognitive Processes* (7th ed., pp. 381–424). Hoboken, NJ: Wiley.

Carr, D. (2002). The psychological consequences of work-family trade-offs for three cohorts of men and women. *Social Psychology Quarterly, 65,* 103–124.

Carre, J. M., Campbell, J. A., Lozoya, E., Goetz, S. M. M., & Welker, K. M. (2013). Changes in testosterone mediate the effect of winning on subsequent aggressive behavior. *Psychoneuroendocrinology, 38,* 2034–2041.

Carrere, S., Buehlman, K. T., Gottman, J. M., Coan, J. A., & Ruckstuhl, L. (2000). Predicting marital stability in divorced and newlywed couples. *Journal of Family Psychology, 14,* 42–58.

Carrere, S., & Gottman, J. M. (1999). Predicting divorce among newlyweds from the first three minutes of a marital conflict discussion. *Family Process, 38,* 293–301.

Carskadon, M., Vieria, C., & Acebo, C. (1993). Association between puberty and delayed phase preference. *Sleep, 16,* 258–262.

Carstensen, L. L. (1998). A life-span approach to social motivation. In J. Heckhausen & C. S. Dweck (Eds.), *Motivation and self-regulation across the life span* (pp. 341–364). Cambridge, England: Cambridge University Press.

Carstensen, L. L., & Mikels, J. A. (2005). At the intersection of emotion and cognition: Aging and the positivity effect. *Current Directions in Psychological Science, 14,* 117–121.

Carstensen, L. L., & Turk-Charles, S. (1994). The salience of emotion across the adult life span. *Psychology and Aging, 9,* 259–264.

Carter, B., & McGoldrick, M. (Eds.). (1999). *The expanded family life cycle: Individual, family and social perspectives* (3rd ed.). Boston, MA: Allyn & Bacon.

Carver, P. R., Yunger, J. L., & Perry, D. G. (2003). Gender identity and adjustment in middle childhood. *Sex Roles, 49,* 95–109.

Casad, B. J., Salazar, M. M., & Macina, V. (2015). The real versus the ideal: Predicting relationship satisfaction and well-being from endorsement of marriage myths and benevolent sexism. *Psychology of Women Quarterly, 39,* 119–129.

Case, R. (1985). *Intellectual development: Birth to adulthood.* New York, NY: Academic Press.

Case, R. (1991). Stages in the development of the young child's first sense of self. *Developmental Review, 11,* 210–230.

Case, R. (1992). *The mind's staircase: Exploring the conceptual underpinnings of children's thought and knowledge.* Hillsdale, NJ: Erlbaum.

Casey, B. J. (2015). Beyond simple models of self-control to circuit-based accounts of adolescent behavior. *Annual Review of Psychology, 66,* 295–319.

Casper, D. M., & Card, N. A. (2017). Overt and relational victimization: A meta-analytic review of their overlap and associations with social-psychological adjustment. *Child Development, 88,* 466–483.

Casper, R. C. (1990). Personality features of women with good outcome from restricting anorexia nervosa. *Psychosomatic Medicine, 52,* 156–170.

Caspi, A. (2000). The child is father of the man: Personality continuities from childhood to adulthood. *Journal of Personality and Social Psychology, 78,* 158–172.

Caspi, A., Harrington, H., Milne, B., Amell, J. W., Theodore, R. F., & Moffitt, T. E. (2003). Children's behavioral styles at age 3 are linked to their adult personality traits at age 26. *Journal of Personality, 71,* 495–513.

Caspi, A., Houts, R. M., Belsky, D. W., Harrington, H., Hogan, S., Ramrakha, S., . . . Moffitt, T. E. (2016). Childhood forecasting of a small segment of the population with large economic burden. *Nature Human Behaviour, 1,* 1–10.

Caspi, A., McClay, J., Moffitt, T. E., Mill, J., Martin, J., Craig, I. W., . . . Poulton, R. (2002). Role of genotype in the cycle of violence in maltreated children. *Science, 297,* 851–855.

Cass, V. (1979). Homosexual identity formation: A theoretical model. *Journal of Homosexuality, 4,* 143–167.

Cassel, C. K., & Foley, K. M. (1999). *Principles for care of patients at the end of life: An emerging consensus among the specialties of medicine.* New York, NY: Millbank Memorial Fund.

Cassidy, J., & Berlin, L. J. (1994). The insecure/ambivalent pattern of attachment: Theory and research. *Child Development, 65,* 971–991.

Cassidy, J., Woodhouse, S. S., Sherman, L. J., Stupica, B., & Lejuez, C. W. (2011). Enhancing infant attachment security: An examination of treatment efficacy and differential susceptibility. *Development and Psychopathology, 23,* 131–143.

Catalano, R. F., Fagan, A. A., Gavin, L. E., Greenberg, M. T., Irwin, C. E., Ross, D. A., & Shek, D. T. L. (2012). Worldwide application of prevention science in adolescent health. *Lancet, 379*(9826), 1653–1664.

Causadias, J. M. (2013). A roadmap for the integration of culture into developmental psychopathology. *Development and Psychopathology, 25,* 1375–1398.

Cavellini, A., Fazzi, E., & Viviani, V. (2002). Visual acuity in the first two years of life in healthy term newborns: An experience with the Teller Acuity Cards. *Functional Neurology: New Trends in Adaptive & Behavioral Disorders, 17,* 87–92.

Ceci, S. J., & Bruck, M. (1998). Children's testimony: Applied and basic issues. In W. Damon (Series Ed.), I. E. Sigel & K. A. Renninger (Vol. Eds.), *Handbook of child psychology: Vol. 4. Child psychology in practice* (5th ed., pp. 713–774). New York, NY: Wiley.

Ceci, S. J., Hritz, A., & Royer, C. (2016). Understanding suggestibility. In W. T. O'Donohue & M. Fanetti (Eds.), *Forensic interviews regarding child sexual abuse: A guide to evidence-based practice* (pp. 141–153). Cham, Switzerland: Springer International Publishing.

Ceci, S. J., & Liker, J. (1986). A day at the races: A study of IQ, expertise, and cognitive complexity. *Journal of Experimental Psychology: General, 115,* 255–266.

Ceci, S. J., Loftus, E. W., Leichtman, M., & Bruck, M. (1994). The role of source misattributions in the creation of false beliefs among preschoolers. *International Journal of Clinical and Experimental Hypnosis, 62,* 304–320.

Centers for Disease Control and Prevention. *The Adverse Childhood Experiences (ACE) website.* Available from www.cdc.gov/violenceprevention/acestudy/index.html

Centers for Disease Control and Prevention (CDC). (2012). Available from http://www.cdc.gov/chronicdisease/overview/index.htm

Centers for Disease Control and Prevention (CDC). (2015). *Web-based Injury Statistics Query and Reporting System (WISQARS).* Available from www.cdc.gov/injury/wisqars/fatal.html

Centers for Disease Control and Prevention. (2018). *Recommended childhood and adolescent immunization schedule—United States, 2018.* Available from https://www.aap.org/en-us/Documents/immunization_schedule2018.pdf

Centers for Disease Control Autism and Developmental Disabilities Monitoring Network. (2009). Prevalence of Autism Spectrum Disorders. Autism and developmental disabilities monitoring network, United States, 2006. *Morbidity and Mortality Weekly Report, 58,* SS-10. Available from www.cdc.gov/vaccinesafety/concerns/autism.html

Chadha, M. (2017). No-self and the phenomenology of agency. *Phenomenology and the Cognitive Sciences, 16,* 187–205.

Chaffin, M. Hanson, R., Saunders, B. E., Nichols, T., Barnett, D., Zeanah, C., . . . Miller-Perrin, C. (2006). Report of the APSAC Task Force on attachment therapy, reactive attachment disorder, and attachment problems. *Child Maltreatment, 11,* 76–89.

Chaladze, G. (2016). Heterosexual male carriers could explain persistence of homosexuality in men: Individual-based simulations of an X-linked inheritance model. *Archives of Sexual Behavior, 45,* 1705–1711.

Champagne, F. A. (2016). Epigenetic legacy of parental experiences: Dynamic and interactive pathways to inheritance. *Development and Psychopathology, 28,* 1219–1228.

Chan, C. C. Y., Tardif, T., Chen, J., Pulverman, R. B., Zhu, L., & Meng, X. (2011). English- and Chinese-learning infants map novel labels to object and actions differently. *Developmental Psychology, 47,* 1459–1471.

Chan, H., Brown, B. B., & Von Bank, H. (2015). Adolescent disclosure of information about peers: The mediating role of perceptions of parents' right to know. *Journal of Youth and Adolescence, 44*(5), 1048–1065.

Chan, W., McCrae, R. R., De Fruyt, F., Jussim, L., Löckenhoff, C. E., deBolle, M., . . . Terracciano, A. (2012). Stereotypes of age differences in personality traits: Universal and accurate? *Journal of Personality and Social Psychology,* doi:10.1037/a0029712

Chandler, M., & Birch, S. A. J. (2010). The development of knowing. In R. M. Lerner, M. E. Lamb, & A. M. Freund (Eds.), *The handbook of life-span development* (pp. 671–719). Hoboken, NJ: John Wiley and Sons.

Chandler, M. J. (1987). The Othello effect: Essay on the emergence and eclipse of skeptical doubt. *Human Development, 30,* 137–139.

Chandler, M. J., Boyes, M., & Ball, L. (1990). Relativism and stations of epistemic doubt. *Journal of Experimental Child Psychology, 50,* 370–395.

Chandra, A., Mosher, W. D., Copen, C., & Sionean, C. (2011). Sexual behavior, sexual attraction, and sexual identity in the United States: Data from the 2006–2008 National Survey of Family Growth. *National Health Statistics Reports,* March 3, 1–36.

Chandra, V. (2012). Work–life balance: Eastern and western perspectives. *The International Journal of Human Resource Management, 23,* 1040–1056.

Chang, L., Li, K. K., Lei, L., Liu, H., Guo, B., Wang, Y., & Fung, K. Y. (2005). Peer acceptance and self-perceptions of verbal and behavioural aggression and social withdrawal. *International Journal of Behavioral Development, 29,* 48–57.

Chang, R., & Coward, F. L. (2015). More recess time, please! Ensuring that children have multiple breaks from learning each day is a core tenet of education in Shanghai. *Phi Delta Kappan, 97,* 1–17.

Chao, R. K. (1994). Beyond parental control and authoritarian parenting style: Understanding Chinese parenting through the cultural notion of training. *Child Development, 65,* 1111–1119.

Chaplin, T. M., & Aldao, A. (2013). Gender differences in emotion expression in children: A meta-analytic review. *Psychological Bulletin, 139,* 735–765.

Chappell, N. L., & Funk, L. (2012). Filial responsibility: Does it matter for care-giving behaviours? *Ageing and Society, 32,* 1128–1146.

Charles, S. T., & Carstensen, L. L. (2008). Unpleasant situations elicit different emotional responses in younger and older adults. *Psychology and Aging, 23,* 495–504.

Charles, S. T., & Piazza, J. R. (2007). Memories of social interactions: Age differences in emotional intensity. *Psychology and Aging, 22,* 300–309.

Charman, T., & Gotham, K. (2013). Measurement issues: Screening and diagnostic instruments for autism spectrum disorders—lessons from research and practise. *Child and Adolescent Mental Health, 18,* 52–64.

Charness, N., & Bosman, E. A. (1990). Expertise and aging: Life in the lab. In T. H. Hess (Ed.), *Aging and cognition: Knowledge organization and utilization* (pp. 343–385). Amsterdam: Elsevier.

Charney, E. (2012). Behavior genetics and postgenomics. *Behavioral and Brain Sciences, 35,* 331–410.

Charney, E. (2017). Genes, behavior, and behavior genetics. *WIREs Cognitive Science, 8,* e1405. doi:10.1002/wcs.1405

Chater-Diehl, E. J., Laufer, B. I., & Singh, S. M. (2017). Changes to histone modifications following prenatal alcohol exposure: An emerging picture. *Alcohol, 60,* 41–52.

Chatters, L. M. (2000). Religion and health: Public health research and practice. *Annual Review of Public Health, 21,* 335–367.

Chen, E. (2004). Why socioeconomic status affects the health of children: A psychosocial perspective. *Current Directions in Psychological Science, 13,* 112–115.

Chen, E., Miller, G. E., Kobor, M. S., & Cole, S. W. (2011). Maternal warmth buffers the effects of low early-life socioeconomic status on pro-inflammatory signaling in adulthood. *Molecular Psychiatry, 16,* 729–737.

Chen, L. (2000). Understanding the heterogeneity of depression through the triad of symptoms, course and risk factors: A longitudinal, population-based study. *Journal of Affective Disorders, 59,* 1–11.

Chen, L., Eaton, W. W., Gallo, J. J., Nestadt, G., & Crum, R. M. (2000). Empirical examination of current depression categories in a population-based study: Symptoms, course, and risk factors. *American Journal of Psychiatry, 157,* 573–580.

Chen, X., Rubin, K. H., & Li, B. (1995). Social and school adjustment of shy and aggressive children in China. *Development and Psychopathology, 31,* 531–539.

Chen, Y., Yu, T., & Brody, G. H. (2017). Parenting intervention at age 11 and cotinine levels at age 20 among African American youth. *Pediatrics, 140.*

Cheng, M., & Berman, S. L (2012). Globalization and identity development: A Chinese perspective. *New Directions for Child and Adolescent Development, 2012,* 103–121.

Cheng, S., Chow, P. K. M., Song, Y. Q., Yu, E. C., Chan, A. C., Lee, T., & Lam, J. H. (2012). Mental and physical activities delay cognitive decline in older persons with dementia. *American Journal of Geriatric Psychiatry.* doi:10.1097/JGP.0b013e31826d6af1

Cheng, Y., Lee, S., Chen, H., Wang, P., & Decety, J. (2012). Voice and emotion processing in the human neonatal brain. *Journal of Cognitive Neuroscience, 24,* 1411–1419.

Cheng, Y., Newman, I. M., Qu, M., Mbulo, L., Chai, Y., Chen, Y., & Shell, D. F. (2010). Being bullied and psychosocial adjustment among middle school students in China. *Journal of School Health, 80,* 193–199.

Chengappa, K., Kupfer, D. J., Frank, E., Houck, P. R., Grochocinski, V. J., Cluss, P. A., & Stapf, D. A. (2003). Relationship of birth cohort and early age at onset of illness in a bipolar disorder case registry. *American Journal of Psychiatry, 160,* 1636–1642.

Chesley, N., & Flood, S. (2017). Signs of change? At-home and breadwinner parents' housework and child-care time. *Journal of Marriage and Family, 79,* 511–534.

Chess, S., & Hassibi, M. (1978). *Principles and practice of child psychiatry.* New York, NY: Plenum Press.

Chess, S., & Thomas, A. (1987). *Origins and evolution of behavior: From infancy to early adult life.* Cambridge, MA: Harvard University Press.

Chi, M. T. H. (1978). Knowledge structures and memory development. In R. S. Siegler (Ed.), *Children's thinking: What develops?* Hillsdale, NJ: Erlbaum.

Chi, M. T. H., Hutchinson, J. E., & Robin, A. F. (1989). How inferences about novel domain-related concepts can be constrained by structured knowledge. *Merrill-Palmer Quarterly, 35,* 27–62.

Chi, M. T. H., & Koeske, R. D. (1983). Network representation of a child's dinosaur knowledge. *Developmental Psychology, 19,* 29–39.

Chiaburu, D. S., & Harrison, D. A. (2008). Do peers make the place? Conceptual synthesis and meta-analysis of coworker effects on perceptions, attitudes, OCBs, and performance. *Journal of Applied Psychology, 93,* 1082–1103.

Chida, Y., & Steptoe, A. (2009). The association of anger and hostility with future coronary heart disease: A meta-analytic review of prospective evidence. *Journal of the American College of Cardiology, 53*, 936–946.

Child Trends. *Attitudes toward spanking.* Accessed August 9, 2017.

Child Trends Databank. (2016). *Youth employment.* Available at: https://www.childtrends.org/?indicators=youth-employment

Chiriboga, D. A. (1997). Crisis, challenge, and stability in the middle years. In M. E. Lachman & J. B. James (Eds.), *Multiple paths of midlife development* (pp. 293–322). Chicago, IL: University of Chicago Press.

Chiu, L. H. (1972). A cross-cultural comparison of cognitive styles in Chinese and American children. *International Journal of Psychology, 7*, 235–242.

Choi, I., Nisbett, R. E., & Norenzayan, A. (1999). Causal attribution across cultures: Variation and universality. *Psychological Bulletin, 125*, 47–63.

Choi, K., & Kirkorian, H. L. (2016). Touch or watch to learn? Toddlers' object retrieval using contingent and noncontingent video. *Psychological Science, 27*, 726–736.

Chomsky, N. (1968). *Language and mind.* New York, NY: Harcourt Brace World.

Chopik, W. J., Newton, N. J., Ryan, L. H., Kashdan, T. B., & Jarden, A. J. (2017). Gratitude across the life span: Age differences and links to subjective well-being. *The Journal of Positive Psychology,* 1–11.

Chow, S-M., Haltigan, J. D., & Messinger, D. S. (2010). Dynamic infant-parent affect coupling during the face-to-face/still-face. *Emotion, 10*, 101–114.

Christakis, D. A. (2011). The effects of fast-paced cartoons. *Pediatrics, 128*, 772–774.

Christakis, N. (2000). *Death foretold: Prophecy and prognosis in medical care.* Chicago, IL: University of Chicago Press.

Christensen, D. L., Baio, J., Braun, K. V., Bilder, D., Charles, J., Constantino, J. N., . . . Yeargin-Allsopp, M. (2016). *Prevalence and characteristics of Autism Spectrum Disorder among children aged 8 Years — Autism and Developmental Disabilities Monitoring Network, 11 Sites, United States, 2012.* MMWR Surveill Summ 2016;65(No. SS-3)(No. SS-3):1–23. doi:http://dx.doi.org/10.15585/mmwr.ss6503a1

Cicchetti, D. (Ed.). (1984). *Developmental psychopathology.* Chicago, IL: University of Chicago Press.

Cicchetti, D. (1989). How research on child maltreatment has informed the study of child maltreatment: Perspectives from developmental psychopathology. In D. Cicchetti & V. Carlson (Eds.), *Child maltreatment: Theory and research on the causes and consequences of child abuse and neglect* (pp. 377–431). New York, NY: Cambridge University Press.

Cicchetti, D. (2016). Socioemotional, personality, and biological development: Illustrations from a multilevel developmental psychopathology perspective on child maltreatment. *Annual Review of Psychology, 67*, 187–211.

Cicchetti, D., Hetzel, S., Rogosch, F. A., Handley, E. D., & Toth, S. L. (2016). An investigation of child maltreatment and epigenetic mechanisms of mental and physical health risk. *Development and Psychopathology, 28*, 1305–1317.

Cicchetti, D., Hetzel, S., Rogosch, F. A., Handley, E. D., & Toth, S. L. (2016). Genome-wide DNA methylation in 1-year-old infants of mothers with major depressive disorder. *Development and Psychopathology, 28*, 1413–1419.

Cicchetti, D., & Rogosch, F. A. (1996). Equifinality and multifinality in developmental psychopathology. *Development and Psychopathology, 8*, 597–600.

Cicchetti, D., Rogosch, R. A., & Toth, S. L. (2011). The effects of child maltreatment and polymorphisms of the serotonin transporter and dopamine D4 receptor genes on infant attachment and intervention efficacy. *Development and Psychopathology, 23*, 357–372.

Cicchetti, D., & Sroufe, L. A. (2000). The past as prologue to the future: The times, they've been a-changin'. *Development and Psychopathology, 12*, 255–264.

Cicchetti, D., & Toth, S. L. (Eds.). (1994). *Rochester Symposium on Developmental Psychopathology: Vol. 5. Disorders and dysfunctions of the self* (pp. 79–148). Rochester, NY: University of Rochester Press.

Cicchetti, D., & Toth, S. L. (2006). Developmental psychopathology and preventive intervention. In W. Damon & R. M. Lerner (Series Eds.), K. A. Renninger & I. E. Sigel (Vol. Eds.), *Handbook of child psychology: Vol. 4. Child psychology in practice* (6th ed., pp. 497–547). Hoboken, NJ: Wiley.

Cicchetti, D., & Toth, S. L. (2006). Building bridges and crossing them: Translational research in developmental psychopathology. *Development and Psychopathology, 18*, 619–622.

Cicero, E. C., & Wesp, L. M. (2017). Supporting the health and well-being of transgender students. *The Journal of School Nursing, 33*, 95–108.

Cillessen, A. H. N., Schwartz, D., & Mayeaux, L. (2011). *Popularity in the peer system.* New York, NY: Guilford Press.

Cimino, N. M., & McPherson, M. L. (2014). Evaluating the impact of palliative or hospice care provided in nursing homes. *Journal of Gerontological Nursing, 40*, 10–14.

Cimpian, A., Mu, Y., & Erickson, L. C. (2012). Who is good at this game? Linking an activity to a social category undermines children's achievement. *Psychological Science, 23*, 533–541.

Cingel, D. P., Krcmar, M., & Olsen, M. K. (2015). Exploring predictors and consequences of Personal Fable ideation on Facebook. *Computers in Human Behavior, 48*, 28–35.

Clark, C. (2012). *Children's and young people's reading today.* London, England: National Literacy Trust.

Clark, R., Hyde, J. S., Essex, J. J., & Klein, M. H. (1997). Length of maternity leave and quality of mother-infant interactions. *Child Development, 68*, 364–383.

Claxton, S., & Van Dulmen, M. (2015). Casual sexual relationships and experiences in emerging adulthood. In J. J. Arnett (Ed.), *The Oxford handbook of emerging adulthood* (pp. 245–261). New York, NY: Oxford University Press.

Clayton, A. H., & Harsh, V. (2016). Sexual function across aging. *Current Psychiatry Reports, 18.* doi:10.1007/s11920-016-0661-x

Clerc, J., Miller, P. H., & Cosnefroy, L. (2014). Young children's transfer of strategies: Utilization deficiencies, executive function, and metacognition. *Developmental Review, 34*, 378–393.

Cline, F. (1991). *Hope for rage and rage-filled children: Attachment theory and therapy.* Golden, CO: Love and Logic Press.

Coan, J. A. (2016). Toward a neuroscience of attachment. In J. Cassidy & P. R. Shaver (Eds.), *Handbook of attachment: Theory research and clinical applications* (3rd ed., pp. 242–272). New York, NY: Guilford Press.

Cohen, A. O., Breiner, K., Steinberg, L., Bonnie, R. J., Scott, E. S., Taylor-Thompson, K., . . . Casey, B. J. (2016). When is an adolescent an adult? Assessing cognitive control in emotional and nonemotional contexts. *Psychological Science, 27*, 549–562.

Cohen, A. O., & Casey, B. J. (2014). Rewiring juvenile justice: The intersection of developmental neuroscience and legal policy. *Trends in Cognitive Sciences, 18*, 63–65.

Cohen, G. L., & Prinstein, M. J. (2006). Peer contagion of aggression and health risk behavior among adolescent males: An experimental investigation of effects on public conduct and private attitudes. *Child Development, 77*, 967–983.

Cohen, J. M. (1977). Sources of peer group homogeneity. *Sociology of Education, 50*, 227–241.

Cohen, S., Doyle, W. J., Turner, R. B., Alper, C. M., & Skoner, D. P. (2003). Emotional style and susceptibility to the common cold. *Psychosomatic Medicine, 65*, 652–657.

Cohen, S., & Williamson, G. M. (1991). Stress and infectious diseases in humans. *Psychological Bulletin, 109*, 5–24.

Cohen-Mansfield, J., Skornick-Bouchbinder, M., & Brill, S. (2017). Trajectories of end of life: A systematic review. *The Journals of Gerontology: Series B.* doi:10.1093/geronb/gbx093

Coie, J., Terry, R., Lenox, K., & Lochman, J. (1995). Childhood peer rejection and aggression as predictors of stable patterns of adolescent disorder. *Development & Psychopathology, 7*, 697–713.

Coie, J. D., Dodge, K. A., & Coppotelli, H. (1982). Dimensions and types of social status: A cross-age perspective. *Developmental Psychology, 18*, 557–570.

Coie, J. D., & Krehbiehl, G. (1984). Effects of academic tutoring on the social status of low-achieving, socially rejected children. *Child Development, 55*, 1465–1478.

Coie, J. D., & Kupersmidt, J. (1983). A behavioral analysis of emerging social status in boys' groups. *Child Development, 54*, 1400–1416.

Colapinto, J. (2000). *As nature made him: The boy who was raised as a girl.* New York, NY: Harper Perennial.

Colby, A., & Damon, W. (1992). *Some do care: Contemporary lives of moral commitment.* New York, NY: Free Press.

Colby, A., & Kohlberg, L. (1987). *The measurement of moral judgment.* Cambridge, UK: Cambridge University Press.

Cole, D. A., Maxwell, S. E., & Martin, J. M. (1997). Reflected self-appraisals: Strength and structure of the relation of teacher, peer, and parent ratings to children's self-perceived competencies. *Journal of Educational Psychology, 89*, 55–70.

Cole, M. (1998). *Cultural psychology: A once and future discipline.* Cambridge, MA: Belknap.

Cole, M. (2006). Culture and cognitive development in phylogenetic, historical, and ontogenetic perspective. In W. Damon & R. M. Lerner (Series Eds.), D. Kuhn & R. S. Siegler (Vol. Eds.), *Handbook of child psychology: Vol. 2. Cognition, perception and language* (6th ed., pp. 636–683). Hoboken, NJ: Wiley.

Cole, M., & Packer, M. (2011). Culture in development. In M. H. Bornstein & M. E. Lamb (Eds.), *Developmental science: An advanced textbook* (pp. 51–107). New York, NY: Psychology Press.

Cole, M., & Wertsch, J. V. (1996). Beyond the individual-social antinomy in discussions of Piaget and Vygotsky. *Human Development, 39,* 250–256.

Collaer, M. L., & Hines, M. (1995). Human behavioral sex differences: A role for gonadal hormones during early development? *Psychological Bulletin, 118,* 55–107.

Collier, V. P., & Thomas, W. P. (2004). The astounding effectiveness of dual language education for all. *NABE Journal of Research and Practice, 2,* 1–20.

Collins, W. A., & Laursen, B. (2004). Parent-adolescent relationships and influences. In R. Lerner & L. Steinberg (Eds.), *Handbook of adolescent psychology* (2nd ed., pp. 331–361). New York, NY: Wiley.

Collins, W. A., Madsen, S. D., & Susman-Stillman, A. (2002). Parenting during middle childhood. In M. H. Bornstein (Ed.), *Handbook of parenting: Vol. 1. Children and parenting* (2nd ed., pp. 73–101). Mahwah, NJ: Erlbaum.

Collins, W. A., & Steinberg, L. (2006). Adolescent development in interpersonal context. In W. Damon & R. M. Lerner (Series Eds.), N. Eisenberg (Vol. Ed.), *Handbook of child psychology: Vol. 3. Social, emotional, and personality development* (6th ed., pp. 1003–1067). Hoboken, NJ: Wiley.

Comer, J. P. (1988). Educating poor minority children. *Scientific American, 5,* 42–48.

Committee for Economic Development. (2006). *The economic promise of investing in high quality pre-school: Using early education to improve economic growth and the fiscal sustainability of states and the nation.* Washington DC: Committee for Economic Development.

Committee for Economic Development. (2012). *Unfinished business: Continued investment in child care and early education is critical to business and America's future.* Washington DC: Author.

Common Sense Media. (2013). *Zero to eight: Children's media use in America 2013.* Available at www.commonsensemedia.org/research/zero-to-eight-children's-media-use-in-america-2013.

Commons, M. L., & Richards, F. A. (1984). A general model of stage theory. In M. L. Commons, F. A. Richards, & C. Armon (Eds.), *Beyond formal operations: Late adolescent and adult cognitive development* (pp. 120–140). New York, NY: Praeger.

Compas, B. E., Davis, G. E., Forsythe, C. J., & Wagner, B. M. (1987). Assessment of major and daily stressful events during adolescence: The Adolescent Perceived Events Scale. *Journal of Consulting and Clinical Psychology, 55,* 534–541.

Compas, B. E., Howell, D. C., Phares, V., Williams, R. A., & Giunta, C. (1989). Risk factors for emotional/behavioral problems in young adolescents: A prospective analysis of adolescent and parental stress and symptoms. *Journal of Consulting and Clinical Psychology, 57,* 732–740.

Compton, W. C. (2005). *Introduction to positive psychology.* Belmont, CA: Thomson/Wadsworth.

Comstock, G., & Scharrer, E. (1999). *Television: What's on, who's watching, and what it means.* San Diego, CA: Academic Press.

Conduct Problems Prevention Research Group [CPPRG]. (1999). Initial impact of the Fast Track Prevention Trial for conduct problems: II. Classroom effects. *Journal of Consulting and Clinical Psychology, 67,* 648–657.

Conduct Problems Prevention Research Group [CPPRG]. (2007). Fast Track randomized controlled trial to prevent externalizing psychiatric disorders: Findings from grades 3 to 9. *Journal of the American Academy of Child and Adolescent Psychiatry, 46,* 1250–1262.

Conduct Problems Prevention Research Group. (2013). School outcomes of aggressive disruptive children: Prediction from kindergarten risk factors and impact of the Fast Track prevention program. *Aggressive Behavior, 39,* 114–130.

Conduct Problems Prevention Research Group. (2015). Impact of early intervention on psychopathology, crime, and well-being at age 25. *American Journal of Psychiatry, 172,* 59–70.

Conger, R. D., & Elder, G. H., Jr. (in collaboration with Lorenz, F. O., Simons, R. L., & Whitbeck, L. B.). (1994). *Families in troubled times: Adapting to change in rural America.* Hillsdale, NJ: Aldine.

Conger, R. D., Ge, X., Elder, G., Lorenz, F., & Simons, R. (1994). Economic stress, coercive family process, and developmental problems in adolescents. *Child Development, 65,* 541–561.

Conley, D., & Bennett, N. (2002). Comment: Outcomes in young adulthood for very low birth-weight infants. *New England Journal of Medicine, 347,* 141–143.

Connelly, R. (2016). Changes in US mothers' and fathers' time use-causes and consequences. In S. M. McHale, V. King, J. Van Hook, & A. Booth (Eds.), *Gender and couple relationships* (pp. 169–179). Cham, Switzerland: Springer International Publishing.

Conradt, E., Hawes, K., Guerin, D., Armstrong, D. A., Tronick, E., & Marsit, C. J. (2016). The contributions of maternal sensitivity and maternal depressive symptoms to epigenetic processes and neuroendocrine functioning. *Child Development, 87,* 73–85.

Conry-Murray, C., Kim, J. M., & Turiel, E. (2015). Judgments of gender norm violations in children from the United States and Korea. *Cognitive Development, 35,* 122–136.

Conry-Murray, C., & Turiel, E. (2012). Jimmy's baby doll and Jenny's truck: Young children's reasoning about gender norms. *Child Development, 83,* 146–158.

Constantinescu, M., & Hines, M. (2012). Relating prenatal testosterone exposure to postnatal behavior in typically developing children: Methods and findings. *Child Development Perspectives, 6,* 407–413.

Constantino, J. N., & Charman T. (2016). Diagnosis of Autism Spectrum Disorder: Reconciling the syndrome, its diverse origins, and variation-in-expression. *The Lancet Neurology, 15*(3), 279–291.

Constantino, J. N., Kennon-McGill, S., Weichselbaum, C., Marrus, N., Haider, A., Glowinski, A. L., . . . Jones, W. (2017). Infant viewing of social scenes is under genetic control and is atypical in autism. *Nature.* doi:10.1038/nature22999

Constantino, J. N., Todorov, A., Hilton, C., Law, P., Zhang, Y., Molloy, . . . Geshwind, D. (2013). Autism recurrence in half siblings: strong support for genetic mechanisms of transmission in ASD. *Molecular Psychiatry 18,* 137–138.

Cook, C. R., Williams, K. R., Guerra, N. G., Kim, T. E., & Sadek, S. (2010). Predictors of bullying and victimization in childhood and adolescence: A meta-analytic investigation. *School Psychology Quarterly, 25,* 65–83.

Cooley, C. H. (1902). *Human nature and the social order.* New York, NY: Scribner's.

Coontz, S. (2005). *Marriage, a history: From obedience to intimacy or how love conquered marriage.* New York, NY: Viking.

Cooper, M. L., Pioli, M., Levitt, A., Talley, A., Micheas, L., & Collins, N. L. (2006). Attachment styles, sex motives, and sexual behavior: Evidence for gender specific expressions of attachment dynamics. In M. Mikulincer & G. S. Goodman (Eds.), *Dynamics of love: Attachment, caregiving, and sex* (pp. 243–274). New York, NY: Guilford Press.

Copeland, W. E., Brotman, M. A., & Costello, E. J. (2015). Normative irritability in youth: Developmental findings from the Great Smoky Mountain Study. *Journal of the American Academy of Child and Adolescent Psychiatry, 54*(8), 635–642.

Coplan, R. J., Ooi, L. L., & Nocita, G. (2015). When one is company and two is a crowd: Why some children prefer solitude. *Child Development Perspectives, 9,* 133–137.

Coppola, G., Aureli, T., Grazia, A., & Ponzetti, S. (2016). Reunion patterns in the still-face paradigm as predicted by maternal sensitivity and dyadic coordination. *Infancy, 21,* 453–477.

Corbie-Smith, G., Henderson, G., Blumenthal, C., Dorrance, J., & Estroff, S. (2008). Conceptualizing race in research. *Journal of the National Medical Association, 100,* 1235–1243.

Corby, B. C., Hodges, E. V. E., & Perry, D. G. (2007). Gender identity and adjustment in Black, Hispanic, and White preadolescents. *Developmental Psychology, 43,* 261–266.

Cordaro, D. T., Brackett, M., Glass, L., & Anderson, C. L. (2016). Contentment: Perceived completeness across cultures and traditions. *Review of General Psychology, 20*(3), 221–235.

Cornwell, B. (2015). Social disadvantage and network turnover. *The Journals of Gerontology Series B: Psychological Sciences and Social Sciences, 70,* 132–142.

Corr, C. A. (2015). Let's stop "staging" persons who are coping with loss. *Illness, Crisis & Loss, 23*(3), 226–241.

Cortés, M. E., Carrera, B., Rioseco, H., del Río, J. P., & Vigil, P. (2015). The role of kisspeptin in the onset of puberty and in the ovulatory mechanism: A mini-review. *Pediatric and Adolescent Gynecology, 28,* 286–291.

Costanzo, E. Y., Villarreal, M., Drucaroff, L. J., Ortiz-Villafañe, M., Castro, M. N.

. . . Guinjoan, S. M. (2015). Hemispheric specialization in affective responses, cerebral dominance for language, and handedness: Lateralization of emotion, language and dexterity. *Behavioural Brain Research, 288,* 11–19.

Costello, E. J., Foley, D., & Angold, A. (2006). 10-year research update review: The epidemiology of child and adolescent psychiatric disorders: II. Developmental Epidemiology. *Journal of the American Academy of Child & Adolescent Psychiatry, 45,* 8–25.

Côté, S. M., Borge, A. I., Geoffroy, M-C., Rutter, M., & Tremblay, R. E. (2008). Nonmaternal care in infancy and emotional/behavioral difficulties at 4 years old: Moderation by family risk characteristics. *Developmental Psychology, 44,* 155–168.

Cotterill, S. (2017). *Performance psychology: Theory and practice.* New York, NY: Routledge.

Council on Communications and Media. (2016a). *Media and young minds.* American Academy of Pediatrics. doi:10.1542/peds.2016-2591

Council on Communications and Media. (2016b). *Media use in school-aged children and adolescents.* American Academy of Pediatrics. doi:10.1542/peds.2016-2592

Courage, M. L., & Setliff, A. E. (2009). Debating the impact of television and video material on very young children: Attention, learning, and the developing brain. *Child Development Perspectives, 3,* 72–78.

Cowan, C. P., & Cowan, P. A. (1992). *When partners become parents.* New York, NY: Basic Books.

Cowan, N. (2014). Short-term and working memory in childhood. In P. J. Bauer & R. Fivush (Eds.), *The Wiley handbook on the development of children's memory* (pp. 202–249). Hoboken NJ: John Wiley & Sons, Inc.

Cowan, N. (2016). Working memory maturation: Can we get at the essence of cognitive growth? *Perspectives on Psychological Science, 11,* 239–264.

Cowan, N., Ricker, T. J., Clark, K. M., Hinrichs, G. A., & Glass, B. A. (2015). Knowledge cannot explain the developmental growth of working memory capacity. *Developmental Science, 18,* 132–145.

Cowan, P. A. (1978). *Piaget with feeling: Cognitive, social and emotional dimensions.* New York, NY: Holt, Rinehart & Winston.

Cowan, W. M. (1979). The development of the brain. In R. R. Llinas (Ed.), *The workings of the brain: Development, memory, and perception.* New York, NY: Freeman.

Cowen, E. L., Izzo, L. D., Miles, H., Telschow, E. F., Trost, M. A., & Zax, M. A. (1963). A mental health program in the school setting: Description and evaluation. *Journal of Psychology, 56,* 307–356.

Cowen, E. L., Petersen, A., Babigian, H., Izzo, L. D., & Trost, M. A. (1973). Long-term follow-up of early detected vulnerable children. *Journal of Consulting and Clinical Psychology, 41,* 438–446.

Cox, K. S., Wilt, J., Olson, B., & McAdams, D. P. (2012). Generativity, the Big Five, and psychosocial adaptation in midlife adults. *Journal of Personality, 78,* 1185–1208.

Cox, M. J., Paley, B., & Harter, K. (2001). Interparental conflict and parent-child relationships. In J. H. Grych & F. D. Fincham (Eds.), *Interparental conflict and child development:* *Theory, research and application* (pp. 249–272). New York, NY: Cambridge University Press.

Cox, R. C., McIntyre, W. A., & Olatunji, B. O. (2017). Interactive effects of insomnia symptoms and trauma exposure on PTSD: Examination of symptom specificity. *Psychological Trauma: Theory, Research, Practice, and Policy.*doi:10.1037/tra0000336

Cox, R. C., Tuck, B. M., & Olatunji, B. O. (2017). Sleep disturbance in posttraumatic stress disorder: Epiphenomenon or causal factor? *Current Psychiatry Reports, 19*(4), 1–10.

Coy, J. S., & Miller, M. M. (2014). Intimate partners who struggle with formal commitments: Attachment styles, major challenges, and clinical implications. *The American Journal of Family Therapy, 42,* 232–242.

Coyne, J. C. (1976). Depression and the response of others. *Journal of Abnormal Psychology, 85,* 186–193.

Coyne, J. C. (1999). Thinking interactionally about depression: A radical restatement. In T. Joiner & J. C. Coyne (Eds.), *The interactional nature of depression* (pp. 365–392). Washington, DC: American Psychological Association.

Coyne, S. M., Linder, J. R., Rasmussen, E. E., Nelson, D. A., & Collier, K. M. (2014). It's a bird! It's a plane! It's a gender stereotype!: Longitudinal associations between superhero viewing and gender stereotyped play. *Sex Roles, 70,* 416–430.

Craft-Blacksheare, M. G. (2017). Lessons learned from the crisis in Flint, Michigan regarding the effects of contaminated water on maternal and child health. *Journal of Obstetric, Gynecological and Neonatal Nursing, 46,* 258–266.

Craik, F. J. M., & Bialystok, E. (2006). Cognition through the lifespan: Mechanisms of change. *Trends in Cognitive Sciences, 10,* 131–138.

Crain, W. (2005). *Theories of development: Concepts and applications* (5th ed.). Upper Saddle River, NJ: Pearson/Prentice Hall.

Cramer, P. (2017). Childhood precursors of the narcissistic personality. *The Journal of Nervous and Mental Disease, 2015,* 679–684.

Crane, D. A., & Tisak, M. (1995). Mixed-domain events: The influence of moral and conventional components on the development of social reasoning. *Early Education and Development, 6,* 169–180.

Crawford, M. (2003). Sexual double standards: A review and methodological critique of two decades of research. *Journal of Sex Research, 40,* 13–26.

Creswell, J. D. (2017). Mindfulness interventions. *Annual Review of Psychology, 68*(1), 491–516.

Creswell, J. D., & Lindsay, E. K. (2014). How does mindfulness training affect health? A mindfulness stress buffering account. *Current Directions in Psychological Science, 23*(6), 401–407.

Cribb, V. L., & Haase, A. M. (2016). Girls feeling good at school: School gender environment, internalization and awareness of socio-cultural attitudes associations with self-esteem in adolescent girls. *Journal of Adolescence, 46,* 107–114.

Crick, N. R., & Dodge, K. A. (1994). A review and reformation of social information processing mechanisms in children's social adjustment. *Psychological Bulletin, 115,* 74–101.

Crick, N. R., & Grotpeter, J. K. (1995). Relational aggression, gender, and social-psychological adjustment. *Child Development, 66,* 710–722.

Crittendon, P. M. (1994). Peering into the black box: An exploratory treatise on the development of self in young children. In D. Cicchetti & S. L. Toth (Eds.), *Rochester Symposium on Developmental Psychopathology: Vol. 5. Disorders and dysfunctions of the self* (pp. 79–148). Rochester, NY: University of Rochester Press.

Crittendon, P. M. (1997). Patterns of attachment and sexual behavior: Risk of dysfunction versus opportunity for creative integration. In L. Atkinson & K. J. Zucker (Eds.), *Attachment and psychopathology* (pp. 47–93). New York, NY: Guilford Press.

Crittenden, P. M. (2016). *Raising parents: Attachment, representation and treatment.* New York, NY: Routledge.

Crittendon, P. M., & DiLalla, D. L. (1988). Compulsive compliance: The development of an inhibitory coping strategy in infancy. *Journal of Abnormal Child Psychology, 16,* 585–599.

Crocetti, E. (2017). Identity formation in adolescence: The dynamic of forming and consolidating identity commitments. *Child Development Perspectives, 11,* 145–150.

Crocetti, E., Hale, W. W., Dimitrova, R., Abubakar, A., Gao, C. H., Pesigan, I. J. A., . . . Samhällsvetenskapliga fakulteten. (2015). Generalized anxiety symptoms and identity processes in cross-cultural samples of adolescents from the general population. *Child and Youth Care Forum, 44*(2), 159–174.

Crocetti, E., & Meeus, W. (2014) "Family comes first!" Relationships with family and friends in Italian emerging adults. *Journal of Adolescence, 37,* 1463–1473.

Crockenberg, S. C. (2003). Rescuing the baby from the bathwater: How gender and temperament (may) influence how child care affects child development. *Child Development, 74,* 1034–1038.

Crockenberg, S., & Langrock, A. M. (2001). The role of emotion and emotional regulation in children's response to interparental conflict. In J. H. Grych & F. D. Fincham (Eds.), *Child development and interparental conflict: Theory, research and application* (pp. 129–156). New York, NY: Cambridge University Press.

Crockenberg, S., Leerkes, E. M., & Lekka, S. K. (2007). Pathways from marital aggression to infant emotion regulation: The development of withdrawal in infancy. *Infant Behavior & Development, 30,* 97–113.

Crocker, J., & Major, B. (1989). Social stigma and self-esteem: The self-protective properties of stigma. *Psychological Review, 96,* 608–630.

Cronholm, P. F., Forke, C. M., Wade, R., Bair-Merritt, M. H., Davis, M., Harkins-Schwartz, M., . . . Fein, J. A. (2015). Adverse childhood experiences: Expanding the concept of adversity. *American Journal of Preventive Medicine, 49,* 354–361.

Cronin, K. A. (2012). Prosocial behaviour in animals: The influence of social relationships, communication and rewards. *Animal Behaviour, 84,* 1085–1093.

Crosnoe, R. (2006). *Mexican roots, American schools: Helping Mexican immigrant children succeed.* Stanford, CA: Stanford University Press.

Crosnoe, R., & Fuligni, A. J. (2012). Children from immigrant families: Introduction to the special section. *Child Development, 83,* 1471–1476.

Cross, J. R., & Fletcher, K. L. (2009). The challenge of adolescent crowd research: Defining the crowd. *Journal of Youth and Adolescence, 38*(6), 747–764.

Cross, W. E. (1971). The Negro to Black conversion experience. *Black World, 20,* 13–17.

Cross, W. E. (1994). Nigrescence theory: Historical and explanatory notes. *Journal of Vocational Behavior, 44,* 119–123.

Cross, W. E., Jr., & Fhagen-Smith, P. (2001). Patterns of African American identity development: A life span perspective. In B. Jackson & C. Wijeyesinghe (Eds.), *New perspectives on racial identity development: A theoretical and practical anthology* (pp. 243–270). New York, NY: NYU Press.

Cross-National Collaborative Group. (1992). The changing rate of major depression: Cross-national comparisons. *Journal of the American Medical Association, 268,* 3098–3105.

Crow, S. (2013). Eating disorders and risk of death. *American Journal of Psychiatry, 170*(8), 824–825.

Crowder, L. S. (1999). Mortuary practices in San Francisco Chinatown. *Chinese America, History & Perspectives,* pp. 33–47.

Crowell, J. A., Fraley, R. C., & Roisman, G. I. (2016). Measurement of individual differences in adult attachment. In J. Cassidy & P. R. Shaver (Eds.), *Handbook of attachment: Theory, research, and clinical applications* (3rd ed., pp. 598–635). New York, NY: Guilford Press.

Crowell, J. A., Treboux, D., & Waters, E. (2002). Stability of attachment representations: The transition to marriage. *Developmental Psychology, 38,* 467–479.

Crowell, J. A., Waters, E., Treboux, D., O'Connor, E., Colon-Downs, C., Feider, O., et al. (1996). Discriminant validity of the Adult Attachment Interview. *Child Development, 67,* 2584–2599.

Cruz, R. A., King, K. M., Cauce, A. M., Conger, R. D., & Robins, R. W. (2017). Cultural orientation trajectories and substance use: findings from a longitudinal study of Mexican-origin youth. *Child Development, 88,* 555–572.

Csikszentmihalyi, M. (1999). If we are so rich, why aren't we happy? *American Psychologist, 54,* 821–827.

Csikszentmihalyi, M., & Rathunde, K. (1990). The psychology of wisdom: An evolutionary interpretation. In R. J. Sternberg (Ed.), *Wisdom: Its nature, origins and development* (pp. 25–51). Cambridge, UK: Cambridge University Press.

Cuddy, A. J., Fiske, S. T., & Glick, P. (2008). Warmth and competence as universal dimensions of social perception: The stereotype content model and the BIAS map. *Advances in Experimental Social Psychology, 40,* 61–149.

Cuijpers, P., Beekman, A. T. F., & Reynolds, C. F. (2012). Preventing depression: A global priority. *JAMA, 307*(10), 1033–1034.

Cultice, J. C., Somerville, S. C., & Wellman, H. M. (1983). Preschooler's memory monitoring: Feeling-of-knowing judgments. *Child Development, 54,* 1480–1486.

Cumsille, P., Darling, N., & Martínez, M. L. (2009; 2010). Shading the truth: The patterning of adolescents' decisions to avoid issues, disclose, or lie to parents. *Journal of Adolescence, 33*(2), 285–296.

Cunha, F., & Heckman, J. J. (2010). Investing in our young people. In A. J. Reynolds, A. J. Rolnick, M. M. Englund, & J. A. Temple (Eds.), *Childhood programs and practices in the first decade of life: A human capital integration* (pp. 381–414). New York, NY: Cambridge University Press.

Curtis, D. F., Elkins, S. R., Duran, P., & Venta, A. C. (2016). Promoting a climate of reflective practice and clinician self-efficacy in vertical supervision. *Training and Education in Professional Psychology, 10,* 122–140.

Curtis, N. M., & Ronan, K. R. (2004). Multisystemic treatment: A meta-analysis of outcome studies. *Journal of Family Psychology, 18,* 411–419.

Cvencek, D., Meltzoff, A. N., & Greenwald, A. G. (2011). Math-gender stereotypes in elementary school children. *Child Development, 82,* 766–779.

Cynkar, A. (2007). Stay-at-home dads report high job satisfaction. *Monitor on Psychology, 38,* 57.

Cyr, C., Euser, E. M., Bakermans-Kranenburg, M. J., & van IJzendoorn, M. H. (2010). Attachment security and disorganization in maltreating and high-risk families: A series of meta-analyses. *Development and Psychopathology, 22,* 87–108.

D'Souza, D., D'Souza, H., & Karmiloff-Smith, A. (2017). Precursors to language development in typically and atypically developing infants and toddlers: The importance of embracing complexity. *Journal of Child Language, 44,* 591–627.

D'Zurilla, T. J. (1986). *Problem-solving therapy: A social competence approach to clinical intervention.* New York, NY: Springer.

Dalgleish, T. L., Johnson, S. M., Moser, M. B., Lafontaine, M. F., & Wiebe, S. A. (2015). Predicting change in marital satisfaction throughout emotionally focused couple therapy. *Journal of Marital and Family Therapy, 41*(3), 276–291.

Daly, M., & Delaney, L. (2013). The scarring effect of unemployment throughout adulthood on psychological distress at age 50: Estimates controlling for early adulthood distress and childhood psychological factors. *Social Science & Medicine, 80,* 19–23.

Damasio, A., & Carvalho, G. B. (2013). The nature of feelings: Evolutionary and neurobiological origins. *Nature Reviews/Neuroscience, 14,* 143–152.

Damasio, A. R. (1994). *Descartes' error: Emotion, reason, and the human brain.* New York, NY: Grosset/Putnam.

Damon, W. (1988). *The moral child: Nurturing children's natural moral growth.* New York, NY: Free Press.

Damon, W. (1995). *Greater expectations: Overcoming the culture of indulgence in America's homes and schools.* New York, NY: Free Press.

Damon, W., & Hart, D. (1992). Self-understanding and its role in social and moral development. In M. H. Bornstein & M. E. Lamb (Eds.), *Developmental psychology: An advanced textbook* (3rd ed., pp. 421–464). Hillsdale, NJ: Erlbaum.

Danese, A., & Baldwin, J. R. (2017). Hidden wounds? Inflammatory links between childhood trauma and psychopathology. *Annual Review of Psychology, 68,* 517–544.

Danese, A., & McEwen, B. (2012). Adverse childhood experiences, allostasis, allostatic load, and age-related disease. *Physiology and Behavior, 106,* 29–39.

Darling, N., Cumsille, P., & Martinez, M. L. (2007). Adolescents as active agents in the socialization process: Legitimacy of parental authority and obligation to obey as predictors of obedience. *Journal of Adolescence, 30,* 297–311.

Darling, N., Cumsille, P., & Martinez, M. L. (2008). Individual differences in adolescents' beliefs about the legitimacy of parental authority and their own obligation to obey: A longitudinal investigation. *Child Development, 79,* 1103–1118.

Darlow, V., Norvilitis, J. M., & Schuetze, P. (2017). The relationship between helicopter parenting and adjustment to college. *Journal of Child and Family Studies, 26*(8), 2291–2298.

Darwin, C. (1872/1965). *The expression of emotions in man and animals.* Chicago, IL: University of Chicago Press.

Datan, N., & Ginsberg, L. H. (Eds.). (1975). *Life-span developmental psychology: Normative life crises.* New York, NY: Academic Press.

David, E. J. R., Okazaki, S., & Saw, A. (2009). Bicultural self-efficacy among college students: Initial scale development and mental health correlates. *Journal of Counseling Psychology, 56,* 211–226.

Davidson, P., Turiel, E., & Black, A. (1983). The effect of stimulus familiarity on the use of criteria and justifications in children's social reasoning. *British Journal of Developmental Psychology, 1,* 49–65.

Davidson, R. D., O'Hara, K. L., & Beck, C. J. A. (2014). Psychological and biological processes in children associated with high conflict parental divorce. *Juvenile & Family Court Journal, 65,* 29–44.

Davidson, R. J. (2000). Affective style, psychopathology, and resilience: Brain mechanisms and plasticity. *American Psychologist, 55,* 1193–1214.

Davidson, R. J. (2002). Toward a biology of positive affect and compassion. In R. J. Davidson & A. Harrington (Eds.), *Visions of compassion: Western scientists and Tibetan Buddhists examine human nature* (pp. 107–130). New York, NY: Oxford University Press.

Davidson, R. J. (2012). *The emotional life of your brain.* New York, NY: Hudson Street Press.

Davidson, R. J., Coe, C. C., Dolski, I., & Donzella, B. (1999). Individual differences in prefrontal activation asymmetry predicts natural killer cell activity at rest and in response to challenge. *Brain, Behavior, and Immunity, 13,* 93–108.

Davidson, R. J., & Fox, N. A. (1989). Frontal brain asymmetry predicts infants' response to maternal separation. *Journal of Abnormal Psychology, 98,* 127–131.

Davidson, R. J., Kabat-Zinn, J., Schumacher, J., Rosenkranz, M., Muller, D., Santorelli, S. F., ... Sheridan, J. F. (2003). Alterations in brain and immune function produced by mindfulness meditation. *Psychosomatic Medicine, 65,* 564–570.

Davies, J. (2003). Expressions of gender: An analysis of pupils' gendered discourse styles in small group classroom discussions. *Discourse & Society, 14,* 115–132.

Davies, P. T., & Woitach, M. J. (2008). Children's emotional security in the interparental relationship. *Current Directions in Psychological Science, 17,* 269–274.

Davila, J. (2008). Depressive symptoms and adolescent romance: Theory, research, and implications. *Child Development Perspectives, 2,* 26–31.

Davila, J., Capaldi, D. M., & La Greca, A. M. (2015). Adolescent/young adult romantic relationships and psychopathology. In D. Cicchetti (Ed.), *Developmental psychopathology, theory and method* (pp. 631–664). Hoboken NJ: John Wiley & Sons.

Davis, C. (1852). *Lecture on the duties and relations of parents, teachers, and pupils as connected with education.* Delivered at the First Session of the Teachers' Institute at the Normal School at Ypsilanti, MI. Free Press Book and Job Office.

Davis, C. G., Lehman, D. R., & Wortman, C. B. (1997). *Finding meaning in loss and trauma: Making sense of the literature.* Unpublished manuscript, University of Michigan.

Davis, C. G., Wortman, C. B., Lehman, D. R., & Silver, R. C. (2000). Searching for meaning in loss: Are clinical assumptions correct? *Death Studies, 24,* 497–540.

Davis, E. M., Kim, K., & Fingerman, K. L. (2016). Is an empty nest best? Coresidence with adult children and parental marital quality before and after the Great Recession. *Journals of Gerontology: Series B.* Available from https://doi.org/10.1093/geronb/gbw022

Davis, G., & Stevenson, H. (2006). Racial socialization experiences and symptoms of depression among black youth. *Journal of Child and Family Studies, 15,* 293–307.

Davis, J. (1997). *Mapping the mind: The secrets of the human brain and how it works.* Secaucus, NJ: Birch Lane Press.

Davis-Kean, P. E., Jager, J., & Collins, W. A. (2009). The self in action: An emerging link between self-beliefs and behaviors in middle childhood. *Child Development Perspectives, 8,* 184–188.

Davoudzadeh, P., McTernan, M. L., & Grimm, K. J. (2015). Early school readiness predictors of grade retention from kindergarten through eighth grade: A multilevel discrete-time analysis approach. *Early Childhood Research Quarterly, 32,* 183–192.

Dawson, G., Rogers, S., Munson, J., Smith, M., Winter, J., Greenson, J., . . . Varley, J. (2010). Randomized controlled trial of the Early Start Denver Model: A developmental behavioral intervention for toddlers with autism: Effects on IQ, adaptive behavior, and autism diagnosis. *Pediatrics, 125,* 17–23.

Day, F. R., Perry, J. R. B., & Ong, K. K. (2015). Genetic regulation of puberty timing in humans. *Neuroendocrinology, 102,* 247–255.

Deak, G. O. (2014). Development of adaptive tool-use in early childhood: Sensorimotor, social, and conceptual factors. *Advances in Child Development and Behavior, 46,* 149–181.

DeAnda, S., Poulin-Dubois, D., Zesiger, P., & Friend, M. (2016). Lexical processing and organization in bilingual first language acquisition: Guiding future research. *Psychological Bulletin, 142,* 655–667.

Dearing, E., & Zachrisson, H. D. (2017). Concern over internal, external, and incidence validity in studies of childcare quantity and externalizing behavior problems. *Child Development Perspectives, 211,* 133–138.

Dearing, E., Zachrisson, H. D., & Nærde, A. (2015). Age of entry into early childhood education and care as a predictor of aggression: Faint and fading associations for young Norwegian children. *Psychological Science, 26,* 1595–1607.

Deater-Deckard, K., Dodge, K. A., Bates, J. E., & Pettit, G. S. (1996). Physical discipline among African American and European American mothers: Links to children's externalizing behaviors. *Developmental Psychology, 32,* 1065–1072.

DeBolle, M., De Fruyt, F., McCrae, R. R., Löckenhoff, C. E., Costa, P. T., Aguilar-Vafaie, M. E., . . . Terracciano, A. (2015). The emergence of sex differences in personality traits in early adolescence: A cross-sectional, cross-cultural study. *Journal of Personality and Social Psychology, 108,* 171–185.

Decaluwe, V., Braet, C., & Fairburn, C. G. (2003). Binge eating in obese children and adolescents. *International Journal of Eating Disorders, 33,* 78–84.

DeCasper, A. J., & Fifer, W. P. (1980). Of human bonding: Newborns prefer their mothers' voices. *Science, 208,* 1174–1176.

DeCasper, A. J., Lecaneut, J., Busnel, M., Granier-Deferre, C., & Maugeais, R. (1994). Fetal reactions to recurrent maternal speech. *Infant Behavior and Development, 17,* 159–164.

Deci, E. L., Olafsen, A. H., & Ryan, R. M. (2017). Self-determination theory in work organizations: The state of a science. *Annual Review of Organizational Psychology and Organizational Behavior, 4,* 19–43.

Deci, E. L., & Ryan, R. M. (2008). Self-determination theory: A macrotheory of human motivation, development, and health. *Canadian Psychology, 49,* 182–185.

Deci, E. L., Ryan, R. M., Gagne, M., Leone, D. R., Usunov, J., & Kornazheva, B. P. (2001). Need satisfaction, motivation, and well-being in work organizations of a former Eastern Bloc country: A cross-cultural study of self-determination. *Personality and Social Psychology Bulletin, 27,* 930–942.

DeFina, R., & Hannon, L. (2013). The impact of mass incarceration on poverty. *Crime & Delinquency, 59,* 562–586.

DeGarmo, D. S. (2010). Coercive and prosocial fathering, antisocial personality, and growth in children's postdivorce noncompliance. *Child Development, 81,* 503–516.

del Campo, M., & Jones, K. L. (2017). A review of the physical features of the fetal alcohol spectrum disorders. *European Journal of Medical Genetics, 60,* 55–64.

DeLamater, J., & Koepsel, E. (2015). Relationships and sexual expression in later life: A biopsychosocial perspective. *Sexual and Relationship Therapy, 30,* 37–59.

Delehanty, H., & Ginzler, E. (2005). *Caring for your parents: The complete AARP guide.* New York, NY: Sterling.

DeLisi, R., & Gallagher, A. M. (1991). Understanding of gender stability and constancy in Argentinean children. *Merrill-Palmer Quarterly, 37,* 483–502.

Dellas, M., & Jernigan, L. P. (1987). Affective personality characteristics associated with undergraduate ego identity formation. *Journal of Adolescent Research, 3,* 306–324.

DeLoache, J. S., Chiong, C., Sherman, K., Islam, N., Vanderborght, M., Troseth, G. L., . . . O'Doherty, K. (2010). Do babies learn from baby media? *Psychological Science, 21,* 1570–1574.

DeLoss, D. J., Watanabe, T., & Andersen, G. J. (2015). Improving vision among older adults: Behavioral training to improve sight. *Psychological Science, 26,* 456–466.

Delsing, M. J. M. H., Bogt, T. F. M. T., Engels, R. C. M. E., & Meeus, W. H. J. (2007). Adolescents' peer crowd identification in the Netherlands: Structure and associations with problem behaviors. *Journal of Research on Adolescence, 17*(2), 467–467.

Demetriou, A., Spanoudis, G., Shayer, M., van der Ven, S., Brydges, C. R., Kroesbergen, E., . . . Swanson, L. H. (2014). Relations between speed, working memory, and intelligence from preschool to adulthood: Structural equation modeling of 14 studies. *Intelligence, 46,* 107–121.

Deng, W., Cheung, S. T., Tsao, S. W., Wang, X. M., & Tiwari, A. F. Y. (2016). Telomerase activity and its association with psychological stress, mental disorders, lifestyle factors and interventions: A systematic review. *Psychoneuroendocrinology, 64,* 150–163.

Denham, S. A., & Holt, R. W. (1993). Preschoolers' likability as cause or consequence of their social behavior. *Developmental Psychology, 29,* 271–275.

Dennis, C. L., & Dowswell, T. (2013). Psycholosocial and psychological interventions for preventing postpartum depression. *Cochrane Database Systematic Review, 2,* CD001134. doi:10.1002/14651858.CD001134.pub3

Deoni, S. C. L., O'Muircheartaigh, J., Elison, J. T., Walker, L., Doernberg, E., Waskiewicz, N., . . . Jumbe, N. L. (2016). White matter maturation profiles through early childhood predict general cognitive ability. *Brain Structure and Function, 221,* 1189–1203.

Derryberry, D., & Reed, M. A. (1994). Temperament and attention: Orienting toward and away from positive and negative signals. *Journal of Personality and Social Psychology, 66,* 1128–1139.

DeSalvo, K. B., Bloser, N., Reynolds, K., He, J., & Muntner, P. (2006). Mortality prediction with a single general self-rated health question. *Journal of General Internal Medicine, 21,* 267–275.

Despréaux, T., Saint-Lary, O., Danzin, F., & Descatha, A. (2017). Stress at work. *BMJ: British Medical Journal* (Online), 357. doi:10.1136/bmj.j2489

Dessens, A. B., Slijper, F. M. E., & Drop, S. L. S. (2005). Gender dysphoria and gender change in chromosomal females with congenital adrenal hyperplasia. *Archives of Sexual Behavior, 34,* 389–397.

Dettling, A. C., Parker, S., Lane, S. K., Sebanc, A. M., & Gunnar, M. R. (2000). Quality of care and temperament determine whether cortisol levels rise over the day for children in full-day childcare. *Psychoneuroendocrinology, 25,* 819–836.

Deutch, H. (1937). Absence of grief. *Psychoanalytic Quarterly, 6,* 12–22.

Devereux, P. G., Heffner, K. L., Doane, M. J., Gosser, B., & Nolan, M. (2016). Identifying attentional deployment tactics in older adults' written narratives about emotionally upsetting events. *Journal of Health Psychology, 21,* 2247–2258.

Devine, R. T., & Hughes, C. (2014). Relations between false belief understanding and executive function in early childhood: A meta-analysis. *Child Development, 85,* 1777–1794.

Devine, R. T., White, N., Ensor, R., & Hughes, C. (2016). Theory of mind in middle childhood: Longitudinal associations with executive function and social competence. *Developmental Psychology, 52,* 758–771.

Dewey, J. (1911). *Development. The middle works of John Dewey* (Vol. 6). Carbondale, IL: Southern Illinois University Press.

Dewey, J. (1933/1998). *How we think: A restatement of the relation of reflective thinking to the educative process.* Boston, MA: Houghton Mifflin.

Dey, A., Sommers, M. S., & Hasher, L. (2017). An age-related deficit in resolving interference: Evidence from speech perception. *Psychology and Aging, 32,* 572–587.

Dey, E. L., & Hurtado, S. (1999). Students, colleges, and society: Considering the interconnections. In P. G. Altbach, R. O. Berndahl, & P. J. Gumport (Eds.), *American higher education in the twenty-first century: Social, political, and economic challenges* (pp. 298–322). Baltimore, MD: Johns Hopkins University Press.

Diakidoy, I. A., Vosniadou, S., & Hawks, J. D. (1997). Conceptual change in astronomy: Models of the earth and of the day/night cycle in American-Indian children. *European Journal of Education, 12,* 159–184.

Diamond, A. (2005). Attention-deficit disorder (attention-deficit/ hyperactivity disorder without hyperactivity): A neurobiologically and behaviorally distinct disorder from attention-deficit/hyperactivity disorder (with hyperactivity). *Development and Psychopathology, 17,* 807–825.

Diamond, A. (2013). Executive functions. *Annual Review of Psychology, 64,* 135–168.

Diamond, A. (2016). Why improving and assessing executive functions early in life is critical. In J. A. Griffin, P. McCardle, & L. S. Freund (Eds.), *Executive function in preschool-age children* (pp. 11–44). Washington DC: American Psychological Association.

Diamond, A., Barnett, W. S., Thomas, J., & Munro, S. (2007). Preschool program improves cognitive control. *Science, 318,* 1387.

Diamond, A., & Ling, D. S. (2016). Conclusions about interventions, programs, and approaches for improving executive functions that appear justified and those that, despite much hype, do not. *Developmental Cognitive Neuroscience, 18,* 34–48.

Diamond, G., Russon, J., & Levy, S. (2016). Attachment-Based family therapy: A review of the empirical support. *Family Process, 55*(3), 595–610.

Diamond, G., Siqueland, L., & Diamond, G. M. (2003). Attachment-based family therapy for depressed adolescents: Programmatic treatment development. *Clinical Child and Family Psychology Review, 6,* 107–127.

Diamond, G. S. (1998, August). *Anatomy of a family-based model for treating adolescent depression.* Paper presented at the American Psychological Association Convention, San Francisco.

Diamond, L. M. (1998). Development of sexual orientation among adolescent and young adult women. *Developmental Psychology, 34,* 1085–1095.

Diamond, L. M. (2008). Female bisexuality from adolescence to adulthood: Results from a 10-year longitudinal study. *Developmental Psychology, 44,* 5–14.

Diamond, L. M., Bonner, S. B., & Dickenson, J. (2015). The development of sexuality. In R. M. Lerner (Series Ed.) & M. E. Lamb (Vol. Ed.), *Handbook of child psychology and developmental science: Volume 3. Socioemotional processes* (7th ed., pp. 888–931). Hoboken, NJ: Wiley.

Diamond, L. M., & Butterworth, M. (2008). Questioning gender and sexual identity: Dynamic links over time. *Sex Roles, 59,* 365–376.

Diamond, M., & Sigmundson, K. (1997). Sex reassignment at birth: Long-term review and clinical implications. *Archives of Pediatric Adolescent Medicine, 151,* 298–304.

Diazgranados, S., Selman, R. L., & Dionne, M. (2016). Acts of social perspective taking: A functional construct and the validation of a performance measure for early adolescents. *Social Development, 25,* 572–601.

Dick, D. M., & Rose, R. J. (2002). Behavior genetics: What's new? What's next? *Current Directions in Psychological Science, 11,* 70–74.

Diener, E. (2000). Subjective well-being: The science of happiness, and a proposal for a national index. *American Psychologist, 55,* 34–43.

Diener, E., & Diener, M. (2009). Cross-cultural correlates of life satisfaction and self-esteem. In E. Diener (Ed.), *The collective works of Ed Diener* (pp. 71–91). New York, NY: Springer Science and Business Media.

Diener, E., & Emmons, R. A. (1985). The independence of positive and negative affect. *Journal of Personality and Social Psychology, 47,* 71–75.

Diener, E., Emmons, R. A., Larsen, R. J., & Griffin, S. (1985). The Satisfaction with Life Scale. *Journal of Personality Assessment, 49,* 71–75.

Diener, E., Lucas, R. E., & Scollon, C. N. (2006). Beyond the hedonic treadmill: Revising the adaptation theory of well-being. *American Psychologist, 61,* 305–314.

Diener, E., Ng, W., Harter, J., & Arora, R. (2010). Wealth and happiness around the world: Material prosperity predicts life evaluation, whereas psychological prosperity predicts positive feelings. *Journal of Personality and Social Psychology, 99,* 52–61.

Diener, E., Oishi, S., & Lucas, R. E. (2003). Personality, culture, and subjective well-being: Emotional and cognitive evaluations of life. *Annual Review of Psychology, 54,* 403–425.

Diener, E., & Seligman, M. E. P. (2002). Very happy people. *Psychological Science, 13,* 80–83.

Diener, E., & Seligman, M. E. P. (2004). Beyond money: Toward an economy of well-being. *Psychological Science in the Public Interest, 5,* 1–31.

Diener, E., & Tay, L. (2014). Review of the day reconstruction method (DRM). *Social Indicators Research, 116*(1), 255–267.

Diener, E., Tay, L., & Myers, D. (2011). The Religion Paradox: If religion makes people happy, why are so many dropping out?

Journal of Personality and Social Psychology 101, 1278–1290.

Diener, E., Tay, L., & Oishi, S. (2013). Rising income and the subjective well-being of nations. *Journal of Personality and Social Psychology, 104,* 267–276.

Diener, E., Wirtz, D., Tov, W., Kim-Prieto, C., Choi. D., & Oishi, S. (2009). New measures of well-being: Flourishing and positive and negative feelings. *Social Indicators Research, 39,* 247–266.

Dinardo, Q. (1971). *Psychological adjustment to spinal cord injury.* Unpublished doctoral dissertation, University of Houston, TX.

Ding, L., & Mollohan, K. N. (2015). How college-level introductory instruction can impact student epistemological beliefs. *Journal of College Science Teaching, 44*(4), 19–27.

Ding, X. P., Wellman, H. M., Wang, Y., Fu, G., & Lee, K. (2015). Theory-of-mind training causes honest young children to lie. *Psychological Science, 26,* 1812–1821.

Dion, J., Blackburn, M.-E., Auclair, J., Laberge, L., Veillette, S., Gaudreault, M., . . . Touchette, E. (2015). Development and aetiology of body dissatisfaction in adolescent boys and girls. *International Journal of Adolescence and Youth, 20,* 151–166.

DiPietro, J. A. (2004). The role of prenatal maternal stress in child development. *Current Directions in Psychological Science, 13,* 71–74.

Dishion, T. J., Forgatch, M., Chamberlain, P., & Pelham, W. E. (2016). The Oregon Model of Behavior Family Therapy: From intervention design to promoting large-scale system change. *Behavior Therapy, 47*(6), 812–837.

Dishion, T. J., McCord, J., & Poulin, F. (1999). When interventions harm: Peer groups and problem behavior. *American Psychologist, 54,* 755–764.

Dishion, T. J., & McMahon, R. J. (1998). Parental monitoring and the prevention of child and adolescent problem behavior: A conceptual and empirical formulation. *Clinical Child and Family Psychology Review, 1*(1), 61–75.

Dishion, T. J., & Snyder, J. J. (2016). *The Oxford handbook of coercive relationship dynamics.* New York, NY: Oxford University Press.

Dishion, T. J., & Stormshak, E. A. (2007). *Intervening in children's lives: An ecological, family-centered approach to mental health care.* Washington, DC: American Psychological Association.

Dittman, M. (2004). A new face to retirement. *Monitor on Psychology, 35,* 78–79.

Dix, T., Gershoff, E. T., Maunier, L. N., & Miller, P. C. (2004). The affective structure of supportive parenting: Depressive symptoms, immediate emotions, and child-oriented motivation. *Developmental Psychology, 40,* 1212–1227.

Dmiitrova, R., van de Vijver, F. J. R., Tausova, J., Chasiotis, A., Bender, M., Buzea, C., . . . Tair, E. (2017). Ethnic, familial, and religious identity of Roma adolescents in Bulgaria, Czech Republic, Kosovo, and Romania in relation to their level of well-being. *Child Development, 88,* 693–709.

Doan, S. N., Tardif, T., Miller, A., Olson, S., Kessler, D., Felt, B., & Wang, L. (2017). Consequences of 'tiger' parenting: A cross-cultural study of maternal psychological control and children's cortisol stress response. *Developmental Science.* doi:10.1111/desc.12404

Dodge, K. A. (1983). Behavioral antecedents of peer social status. *Child Development, 54,* 1386–1399.

Dodge, K. A., Bai, Y., Ladd, H. F., & Muschkin, C. G. (2017). Impact of North Carolina's early childhood programs and policies on educational outcomes in elementary school. *Child Development, 88,* 996–-1014.

Dodge, K. A., Bates, J. E., & Pettit, G. S. (1990). Mechanisms in the cycle of violence. *Science, 250,* 1678–1683.

Dodge, K. A., Coie, J. D., & Lynam, D. (2006). In W. Damon & R. M. Lerner (Series Eds.), N. Eisenberg (Vol. Ed.), *Handbook of child psychology: Vol. 3. Social, emotional, and personality development* (6th ed., pp. 719–788). Hoboken, NJ: Wiley.

Dodge, K. A., Coie, J. D., Pettit, G. S., & Price, J. M. (1990). Peer status and aggression in boys' groups: Developmental and contextual analyses. *Child Development, 61,* 1289–1309.

Dodge, K. A., Lansford, J. E., Burks, V. S., Bates, J. E., Pettit, G. S., Fontaine, R., & Price, J. M. (2003). Peer rejection and social information-processing factors in the development of aggressive behavior problems in children. *Child Development, 74,* 374–393.

Dodge, K. A., Malone, P. S., Lansford, J. E., Sorbring, E., Skinner, A. T., Tapanya, S., . . . Pastorelli, C. (2015). Hostile attributional bias and aggressive behavior in global context. *Proceedings of the National Academy of Sciences (PNAS), 12,* 9310–9315.

Dodge, K. A., Pettit, J. M., McClaskey, C. L., & Brown, M. M. (1986). Social competence in children. *Monographs of the Society for Research in Child Development, 51,* 1–80.

Doey, L., Coplan, R. J., & Kingsbury, M. (2014). Bashful boys and coy girls: A review of gender differences in childhood shyness. *Sex Roles, 70,* 255–266.

Dohrenwend, B. S., & Dohrenwend, B. P. (1974). Overview and prospects for research on stressful life events. In B. S. Dohrenwend & B. P. Dohrenwend (Eds.), *Stressful life events: Their nature and effects* (pp. 313–331). New York, NY: Wiley.

Dolcos, F., Labar, K. S., & Cabeza, R. (2005). Remembering one year later: Role of the amygdala and the medial temporal lobe memory system in retrieving emotional memories. *Proceedings of the National Academy of Sciences, 102,* 2626–2631.

Dolinoy, D. C. (2008). The agouti mouse model: An epigenetic biosensor for nutritional and environmental alterations on the fetal epigenome. *Nutrition Reviews, 66,* S7–S11.

Dollahite, D. C. (1998). Fathering, faith, and spirituality. *Journal of Men's Studies, 7,* 3–15.

Dolph, D. (2017/2016). Challenges and opportunities for school improvement: Recommendations for urban school principals. *Education and Urban Society, 49*(4), 363–387.

Dozier, M., Cue, K., & Barnett, L. (1994). Clinicians as caregivers: Role of attachment organization in treatment. *Journal of Consulting and Clinical Psychology, 62,* 793–800.

Dozier, M., & Kobak, R. R. (1992). Psychophysiology in attachment interviews: Converging evidence for deactivating strategies. *Child Development, 63,* 1473–1480.

Dozier, M., Peloso, E., Lewis, E., Laurenceau, J. P., & Levine, S. (2008). Effects of an attachment-based intervention on the cortisol production of infants and toddlers in foster care. *Development and Psychopathology, 20*(3), 845–859.

Draper, P. (2005). Patronizing speech to older patients: A literature review. *Reviews in Clinical Gerontology, 15,* 273–279.

Drayton, A. K., Byrd, M. R., Albright, J. J., Nelson, E. M., Andersen, M. N., & Morris, N. K. (2017). Deconstructing the time-out: What do mothers understand about a common disciplinary procedure? *Child & Family Behavior Therapy, 39,* 91–107.

Drizin, S. A. (2003). Research on juvenile competency: A defender's perspective. *Social Policy Report, 17*(4), 8–9.

Dryfoos, J. G. (1990). *Adolescents at risk: Prevalence and prevention.* New York, NY: Oxford University Press.

Dube, S., Felitti, V. J., Dong, M., Giles, W. H., & Anda, R. F. (2003). The impact of adverse childhood experiences on health problems: Evidence from four birth cohorts dating back to 1900. *Preventive Medicine, 37,* 268–277.

Duckworth, A. L., & Seligman, M. E. P. (2006). Self-discipline outdoes IQ in predicting academic performance of adolescents. *Psychological Science, 16,* 939–944.

Duckworth, A. L., & Steinberg, L. (2015). Unpacking self-control. *Child Development Perspectives, 9,* 32–27.

Duggal, S., Carlson, E. A., Sroufe, L. A., & Egeland, B. (2001). Depressive symptomatology in childhood and adolescence. *Development and Psychopathology, 13,* 143–164.

Dunbar, A. S., Leerkes, E. M., Coard, S. I., Supple, A. J., & Calkins, S. (2017). An integrative conceptual model of parental racial/ethnic and emotion socialization and links to children's social-emotional development among African American families. *Child Development Perspectives, 11,* 16–22.

Duncan, G. J., & Brooks-Gunn, J. (Eds.). (1997). *Consequences of growing up poor.* New York, NY: Sage.

Duncan, G. J., & Murnane, R. J. (2014). *Restoring opportunity: The crisis of inequality and the challenge for American education.* Cambridge, MA: Harvard Education Press.

Duncan, L. G., & Bardacke, N. (2010). Mindfulness-based childbirth and parenting education: Promoting family mindfulness during the perinatal period. *Journal of Child and Family Studies, 19,* 190–202.

Duncan, R., & Cheyne, J. A. (2002). Private speech in young adults: Task difficulty, self-regulation, and psychological predication. *Cognitive Development, 16,* 889–906.

Dunkle, M. F., Schraw, G., & Bendixen, L. (1993, April). *The relationship between epistemological beliefs, causal attributions, and reflective judgment.* Paper presented at the Annual Meeting of the American Educational Research Association, Atlanta, GA.

Dunn, J., Bretherton, I., & Munn, P. (1987). Conversations about feeling states between mothers and their young children. *Developmental Psychology, 23,* 132–139.

Dunn, S., & Morgan, V. (1987). Nursery and infant school play patterns: Sex-related

differences. *British Educational Research Journal, 13,* 271–281.

Dunphy, D. C. (1963). The social structure of urban adolescent peer groups. *Sociometry, 26,* 230–246.

Durlak, J. A., Weissberg, R. P., Dymnicki, A. B., Taylor, R. D., & Schellinger, K. B. (2011). The impact of enhancing students' social and emotional learning: a meta-analysis of school-based universal interventions. *Child Development, 82,* 405–432.

Durrant, J., & Ensom, R. (2012). Physical punishment of children: lessons from 20 years of research. *Canadian Medical Association Journal, 184,* 1373–1377.

Durrant, J., Ensom, R., & the Coalition on Physical Punishment of Children and Youth. (2004). *Joint statement on physical punishment of children and youth.* Ottawa (ON): The Coalition; 2004. Available from www.cheo.on.ca/en/physicalpunishment

Durso, L. E., & Gates, G. J. (2012). *Serving our youth: Findings from a national survey of service providers working with lesbian, gay, bisexual, and transgender youth who are homeless or at risk of becoming homeless.* Los Angeles, CA: The Williams Institute with True Colors Fund and The Palette Fund.

Duru, E., & Balkis, M. (2017). Procrastination, self-esteem, academic performance, and well-being: A moderated mediation model. *International Journal of Educational Psychology, 6*(2), 97–119.

Duvall, E. M. (1971). *Family Development* (4th ed.). Philadelphia, PA: J. B. Lippincott.

Dweck, C. S. (1999). *Self-theories: Their role in motivation, personality, and development.* Philadelphia, PA: Taylor & Francis.

Dweck, C. S. (2006). *Mindset: The new psychology of success.* New York, NY: Random House.

Dweck, C. S. (2017). The journey to children's mindsets – and beyond. *Child Development Perspectives, 11,* 139–144.

Dweck, C. S., & Allison, M. (2008). Self-theories motivate self-regulated learning. In D. H. Schunk & B. J. Zimmerman (Eds.), *Motivation and self-regulated learning: Theory, research, and applications* (pp. 31–51). Mahwah, NJ: Erlbaum.

Dykas, M. J., & Cassidy, J. (2011). Attachment and the processing of social information across the life span: Theory and evidence. *Psychological Bulletin, 137,* 19–46.

Dyson, M. W., Olino, T. M., Durbin, C. E., Goldsmith, H. H., Bufferd, S. J., Miller, A. R., & Klein, D. N. (2015). The structural and rank-order stability of temperament in young children based on a laboratory-observational measure. *Psychological Assessment, 27,* 1388–1401.

Eagan, K., Stolzenberg, E. B., Ramirez, J. J., Aragon, M. C., Suchard, M. R., & Rios-Aguilar, C. (2016). *The American freshman: Fifty-year trends 1966–2015.* Los Angeles, CA: Higher Education Research Institute (HERI) University of California, Los Angeles.

Eagan, K., Stolzenberg, E. B., Zimmerman, H. B., Aragon, M. C., Sayson, H. W., & Rios-Aguilar, C. (2017). *The American freshman: National norms Fall 2016.* Los Angeles, CA: Higher Education Research Institute (HERI) of the University of California, Los Angeles.

Eagly, A. H. (2007). Female leadership advantage and disadvantage: Resolving the contradictions. *Psychology of Women Quarterly, 31*, 1–12.

Eagly, A. H. (2013). *Sex differences in social behavior: A social-role interpretation.* Mahwah, NJ: Lawrence Erlbaum.

Eagly, A. H., & Antonakis, J. (2015). Leadership. In M. Mikulincer, P. R. Shaver, E. Borgida, & J. A. Bargh (Eds.), *APA handbooks in psychology. APA handbook of personality and social psychology, Vol. 1. Attitudes and social cognition* (pp. 571–592). Washington, DC: American Psychological Association.

Eagly, A. H., & Heilman, M. E. (2016). Gender and leadership: Introduction to the special issue. *The Leadership Quarterly, 27*, 349–353.

Eagly, A. H., & Johannesen-Schmidt, M. C. (2001). The leadership styles of women and men. *Journal of Social Issues, 57*, 781–797.

Eagly, A. H., Johannesen-Schmidt, M. C., & van Engen, M. L. (2003). Transformational, transactional, and laissez-faire leadership styles: A meta-analysis comparing women and men. *Psychological Bulletin, 129*, 569–591.

Eagly, A. H., & Johnson, B. T. (1990). Gender and leadership style: A meta-analysis. *Psychological Bulletin, 108*, 233–256.

Eagly, A. H., Makhijani, M. G., & Klonsky, B. G. (1992). Gender and the evaluation of leaders: A meta-analysis. *Psychological Bulletin, 117*, 125–145.

Easterlin, R. A. (1974). Does economic growth improve the human lot? Some empirical evidence. In P. David & W. Melvin (Eds.), *Nations and households in economic growth* (pp. 98–125). Stanford, CA: Stanford University Press.

Easterlin, R. A. (1995). Will raising the incomes of all increase the happiness of all? *Journal of Economic Behavior & Organization 27*(1), 35–47.

Eaves, B. S., Jr., Feldman, N. H., Griffiths, T. L., & Shafto, P. (2016). Infant-directed speech is consistent with teaching. *Psychological Review, 123*, 758–771.

Eccles, J. S., Midgley, C., Wigfield, A., Buchanan, C. M., Reuman, D., Flanagan, C., & Iver, D. M. (1993). Development during adolescence: The impact of stage-environment fit on young adolescents' experiences in schools and in families. *American Psychologist, 48*, 90–101.

Eccles, J. S., & Roeser, R. W. (2009). Schools, academic motivation, and stage-environment fit. *Handbook of Adolescent Psychology.* New York, NY: Wiley.

Eccles, J. S., & Roeser, R. W. (2011). Schools as developmental contexts during adolescence. *Journal of Research in Adolescence, 21*, 225–241.

Eckert, P. (1989). *Jocks and burnouts: Social categories and identity in the high school.* New York, NY: Teachers College Press.

Edelstein, B. A., Drozdick, L. W., & Ciliberti, C. M. (2010). Assessment of depression and bereavement in older adults. In P. Lichtenberg (Ed.), *Handbook of assessment in clinical gerontology* (2nd ed., pp. 3–43). San Diego, CA: Elsevier Academic Press.

Edwards, C. P., & Liu, W.-L. (2002). Parenting toddlers. In M. H. Bornstein (Ed.), *Handbook of parenting: Vol. 1. Children and parenting* (2nd ed., pp. 45–71). Mahwah, NJ: Erlbaum.

Egan, G. (1975). *The skilled helper: A model for systemic helping and interpersonal relating.* Monterey, CA: Brooks/Cole.

Egan, S. K., & Perry, D. G. (2001). Gender identity: A multidimensional analysis with implications for psychosocial adjustment. *Developmental Psychology, 37*, 451–463.

Egeland, B., Bosquet, M., & Chung, A. L. (2002). Continuities and discontinuities in the intergenerational transmission of child maltreatment: Implications for breaking the cycle of abuse. In K. D. Browne, H. Hanks, P. Stratton, & C., Hamilton (Eds.), *Early prediction and prevention of child abuse: A handbook* (pp. 217–232). New York, NY: Wiley.

Eggum-Wilkens, N. D., Valiente, C., Swanson, J., & Lemery-Chalfant, K. (2014). Children's shyness, popularity, school liking, cooperative participation, and internalizing problems in the early school years. *Early Childhood Research Quarterly, 29*, 85–94.

Eiland, L., & Romeo, R. D. (2013). Stress and the developing adolescent brain. *Neuroscience, 249*, 162–171.

Eisenberg, N., Cialdini, R., McCreath, H., & Shell, R. (1987). Consistency-based compliance: When and why do children become vulnerable? *Journal of Personality and Social Psychology, 52*, 1174–1181.

Eisenberg, N., & Fabes, R. A. (1992). Emotion, regulation, and the development of social competence. In M. S. Clark (Ed.), *Review of personality and social psychology* (Vol. 12, pp. 34–61). Newbury Park, CA: Sage.

Eisenberg, N., & Fabes, R. A. (1998). Prosocial development. In W. Damon (Ed.) & N. Eisenberg (Vol. Ed.), *Handbook of child psychology: Vol. 3. Social, emotional, and personality development* (5th ed., pp. 701–778). New York, NY: Wiley.

Eisenberg, N., Fabes, R. A., & Spinrad, T. L. (2006). Prosocial development. In W. Damon & R. M. Lerner (Series Eds.), N. Eisenberg (Vol. Ed.), *Handbook of child psychology: Vol. 3. Social, emotional, and personality development* (6th ed., pp. 646–718). Hoboken, NJ: Wiley.

Eisenberg, N., Guthrie, I. K., Cumberland, A., Murphy, B. C., Shepard, S. A., Zhou, Q., & Carlo, G. (2002). Prosocial development in early adulthood: a longitudinal study. *Journal of Personality and Social Psychology, 82*, 993–1006.

Eisenberg, N., & Spinrad, T. L. (2014). Multidimensionality of prosocial behavior: Re-thinking the conceptualization and development of prosocial behavior. In L. Padilla-Walker & G. Carlo (Eds.), *The multidimensionality of prosocial behavior: Biological, socialization, and contextual perspectives* (pp. 17–39). Oxford, England: Oxford University Press.

Eisenberg, N., Spinrad, T. L., & Knafo-Noam, A. (2015). Prosocial development. In R. M. Lerner (Series Ed.) & M. E. Lamb (Vol. Ed.), *Handbook of child psychology and developmental science: Volume 3. Socioemotional processes* (7th ed., pp. 610–656). Hoboken, NJ: Wiley.

Eisenberg, N., Spinrad, T. L., & Sadovsky, A. (2006). Empathy-related responding in children. In N. Eisenberg, T. L. Spinrad, & A. Sadovsky (Eds.), *Handbook of moral development* (pp. 517–549). Mahwah, NJ.: Erlbaum.

Eisma, M. C., & Stroebe, M. S. (2017). Rumination following bereavement: An overview. *Bereavement Care, 36*, 58–64.

Eisner, M. P., & Malti, T. (2015). Aggressive and violent behavior. In R. M. Lerner (Series Ed.) & M. E. Lamb (Vol. Ed.), *Handbook of child psychology and developmental science: Volume 3. Socioemotional processes* (7th ed., pp. 794–841). Hoboken, NJ: Wiley.

Ekman, P. (1992). Are there basic emotions? *Psychological Review, 99*, 550–553.

Ekman, P. (2003). *Emotions revealed: Recognizing faces and feelings to improve communication and emotional life.* New York, NY: Times Books/Henry Holt and Co.

Ekman, P. (2016). What scientists who study emotion agree about. *Perspectives on Psychological Science, 11*, 31–34.

Ekman, P., & Cordaro, D. (2011). What is meant by calling emotions basic. *Emotion Review, 3*, 364–370.

Elder, G. (1974). *Children of the Great Depression.* Chicago, IL: University of Chicago Press.

Elder, G. H., Jr., & Shanahan, M. J. (2006). The life course and human development. In W. Damon & R. M. Lerner (Series Eds.), R. M. Lerner (Vol. Ed.), *Handbook of child psychology: Vol. 1. Theoretical models of human development* (6th ed., pp. 665–715). Hoboken, NJ: Wiley.

Elder, G. H., Shanahan, M. J., & Jennings, J. A. (2015). Human development in time and place. In R. M. Lerner (Series Ed.), M. H. Bornstein, & T. Leventhal (Vol. Eds.), *Handbook of child psychology and developmental science: Volume 4. Ecological settings and processes* (7th ed., pp. 6–54). Hoboken, NJ: Wiley.

Eldridge, K. A., & Christensen, A. (2002). Demand-withdraw communication during couple conflict: A review and analysis. In P. Noller & J. A. Feeney (Eds.), *Understanding marriage: Developments in the study of couple interaction* (pp. 289–322). New York, NY: Cambridge University Press.

Eliason, M. J. (1996). Identity formation for lesbian, bisexual and gay persons: Beyond a "minoritizing" view. *Journal of Homosexuality, 30*, 31–58.

Elkind, D. (1968, May 26). Giant in the nursery—Jean Piaget. *The New York Times Magazine*, 25–80.

Elkind, D. (1984). *All grown up and no place to go: Teenagers in crisis.* Reading, MA: Addison-Wesley.

Elkonin, D. B. (2005). Chapter 1: The subject of our research: The developed form of play. *Journal of Russian and East European Psychology, 45*, 22–48.

Ellefson, M. R., Ng, F. F-Y., Wang, Q., & Hughes, C. (2017). Efficiency of executive function: A two-generation cross-cultural comparison of samples from Hong Kong and the United Kingdom. *Psychological Science.* doi:101177/0956797616687812

Elliott, S. N., Gresham, F., & Witt, J. C. (Eds.). (1988). *Handbook of behavior therapy in education.* New York, NY: Springer-Verlag.

Ellis, L., & Davis, M. (2017). Intimate partner support: A comparison of gay, lesbian, and heterosexual relationships. *Personal Relationships, 24*, 350–369.

Ellis, W. E., & Zarbatany, L. (2017). Understanding processes of peer clique influence in late childhood and early adolescence. *Child Development Perspectives, 11*, 227–232.

Ellis, W., Zarbatany, L., Chen, X., Kinal, M., & Boyko, L. (2017). Peer groups as a context for school misconduct: The moderating role of group interactional style. *Child Development.* Advance Online Publication.

Ellison, C. G. (1991). Religious involvement and subjective well-being. *Journal of Health and Social Behavior, 32,* 80–99.

Ellison, C. G., & Lee, J. (2010). Spiritual struggles and psychological distress: Is there a dark side of religion? *Social Indicators Research, 98*(3), 501–517.

Else-Quest, N. M., Higgins, A., Allison, C., & Morton, L. C. (2012). Gender differences in self-conscious emotional experience: A meta-analysis. *Psychological Bulletin, 138,* 947–981.

Else-Quest, N. M., Hyde, J. S., & Linn, M. C. (2010). Cross-national patterns of gender differences in mathematics: A meta-analysis. *Psychological Bulletin, 136,* 103–127.

Else-Quest, N. M., & Morse, E. (2015). Ethnic variations in parental ethnic socialization and adolescent ethnic identity: A longitudinal study. *Cultural Diversity and Ethnic Minority Psychology, 21,* 54–64.

Emanuel, E., & Emanuel, L. (1998). The promise of a good death. *The Lancet, 251,* 21–29.

Emde, R. N., & Buchsbaum, H. (1990). "Didn't you hear my mommy?" Autonomy with connectedness in moral self-emergence. In D. Cicchetti & M. Beeghly (Eds.), *The self in transition: Infancy to adulthood* (pp. 35–60). Chicago, IL: University of Chicago Press.

Emde, R. N., Johnson, W., & Easterbrooks, M. (1987). The dos and don'ts of early moral development: Psychoanalytic tradition and current research. In J. Kagan & S. Lamb (Eds.), *The emergence of morality in young children* (pp. 245–276). Chicago, IL: University of Chicago Press.

Emmons, R. A., & Paloutzian, R. F. (2003). The psychology of religion. *Annual Review of Psychology, 54,* 377–402.

Endendijk, J. J., Beltz, A. M., McHale, S. M., Bryk, K., & Berenbaum, S. A. (2016). Linking prenatal androgens to gender-related attitudes, identity, and activities: Evidence from girls with congenital adrenal hyperplasia. *Archives of Sexual Behavior, 45,* 1807–1815.

Endendijk, J. J., Groeneveld, M. G., van der Pol, L. D., van Berkel, S. R., Hallers-Haalboom, E. T., Mesman, J., & Bakermans-Kranenburg, M. J. (2014). Boys don't play with dolls: Mothers' and fathers' gender talk during picture book reading. *Parenting, 14,* 141–161.

Ennett, S. T., Bauman, K. E., Hussong, A., Faris, R., Foshee, V. A., Cai, L., & DuRant, R. H. (2006). The peer context of adolescent substance use: Findings from social network analysis. *Journal of Research on Adolescence, 16,* 159–186.

Enright, R. D., & Fitzgibbons, R. P. (2002). *Helping clients forgive: An empirical guide for resolving anger and restoring hope.* Washington, DC: American Psychological Association.

Ensor, R., & Hughes, C. (2008). Content or connectedness? Mother-child talk and early social understanding. *Child Development, 79,* 201–216.

Entringer, S., Buss, C., & Wadhwa, P. D. (2015). Prenatal stress, development, health and disease risk: A psychobiological perspective—2015 Curt Richter Award Paper. *Psychoneuroendocrinology, 62,* 366–375.

Erasmus, V., Daha, T. J., Brug, H., Richardus, J. H., Behrendt, M. D., Vos, M. C., & van Beeck, E. F. (2010). Systematic review of studies on compliance with hand hygiene guidelines in hospital care. *Infection Control and Hospital Epidemiology, 31,* 283–294.

Erdynast, A., Chen, W., & Ikin, A. (2016). Criteria for multidomain research. *Behavioral Development Bulletin, 21,* 74–87.

Erhardt, A. A., & Baker, S. W. (1974). Fetal androgens, human central nervous system, differentiation, and behavior sex differences. In R. C. Friedman, R. M. Richart, & R. L. Van de Wiele (Eds.), *Sex differences in behavior* (pp. 33–51). New York, NY: Wiley.

Erickson, M. F., Sroufe, L. A., & Egeland, B. (1985). The relationship between quality of attachment and behavior problems in preschool in a high-risk sample. In I. Bretherton & E. Waters (Eds.), Growing points of attachment theory and research. *Monographs of the Society for Research in Child Development, 50* (Serial No. 209), 147–166.

Erikson, E. H. (1950/1963). *Childhood and society* (2nd ed.). New York, NY: Norton.

Erikson, E. H. (1968). *Identity, youth, and crisis.* New York, NY: Norton.

Erlich, K. B., Miller, G. E., Jones, J. D., & Cassidy, J. (2016). Attachment and Psychoneuroimmunology. In J. Cassidy & P. R. Shaver (Eds.), *Handbook of attachment: Theory research and clinical applications* (3rd ed., pp.180–201). New York, NY: Guilford Press.

Ernst, M. (2014). The triadic model perspective for the study of adolescent motivated behavior. *Brain and Cognition, 89,* 104–111.

Ernst, M., Pine, D. S., & Hardin, M. (2006). Triadic model of the neurobiology of motivated behavior in adolescence. *Psychological Medicine, 36,* 299–312.

Erwin, P. (1985). Similarity of attitudes and constructs in children's friendships. *Journal of Experimental Child Psychology, 40,* 470–485.

Eti, S. (2011). Palliative care: An evolving field in medicine. *Primary Care: Clinics in Office Practice, 38,* 159–171.

Evans, A. D., Bender, J., & Lee, K. (2016). Can parents detect 8- to 16-year-olds' lies? Parental biases, confidence, and accuracy. *Journal of Experimental Child Psychology, 147,* 152–158.

Evans, A. D., & Lee, K. (2010). Promising to tell the truth makes 8- to 16-year-olds more honest. *Behavioral Sciences and the Law, 28,* 801–811.

Evans, A. D., & Lee, K. (2011). Verbal deception from late childhood to middle adolescence and its relation to executive functioning skills. *Developmental Psychology, 47,* 1108–1116.

Evans, A. D., & Lee, K. (2013). Emergence of lying in very young children. *Developmental Psychology, 49,* 1958–1963.

Evans, A. D., & Lee, K. (2014). The relation between 8- to 17-year-olds' judgments of other's honesty and their own past honest behaviors. *International Journal of Behavioral Development, 38,* 277–281.

Evans, G. W., & Kim, P. (2013). Childhood poverty, chronic stress, self-regulation and coping. *Child Development Perspectives, 7,* 43–48.

Evans, J., St. B. T., & Stanovich, K. E. (2013). Dual-process theories of higher cognition: Advancing the debate. *Perspectives on Psychological Science, 8,* 223–241.

Ewens, J., & Herrington, P. (1983). *Hospice.* Santa Fe, NM: Bear & Co.

Exline, J. J., Pargament, K. I., Grubbs, J. B., & Yali, A. M. (2014). *Psychology of Religion and Spirituality, 6,* 208–222.

Extremera, N., & Rey, L. (2016). Ability emotional intelligence and life satisfaction: Positive and negative affect as mediators. *Personality and Individual Differences, 102,* 98–101.

Fabes, R. A., Martin, C. L., & Hanish, L. D. (2003). Young children's play qualities in same-, other-, and mixed-sex peer groups. *Child Development, 74,* 921–932.

Facio, A., & Micocci, F. (2003). Emerging adulthood in Argentina. In J. J. Arnett & N. Galambos (Eds.), *New directions for child and adolescent development: Cultural conceptions of the transition to adulthood* (pp. 21–31). San Francisco, CA: Jossey-Bass.

Fagot, B. I. (1984). The consequences of problem behavior in toddler children. *Journal of Abnormal Child Psychology, 12,* 385–397.

Fairchild, G., Goozen, S. H., Calder, A. J., & Goodyer, I. M. (2013). Research review: Evaluating and reformulating the developmental taxonomic theory of antisocial behaviour. *Journal of Child Psychology and Psychiatry, 54,* 924–940.

Faraday, M. (2010). The girl-crisis movement: Evaluating the foundation. *Review of General Psychology, 14,* 44–55.

Farah, M. J., Rabinowitz, C., & Quinn, G. E. (2000). Early commitment of neural substrates for face recognition. *Cognitive Neuropsychology, 17,* 117–124.

Farr, R. H., & Patterson, C. J. (2013). Coparenting among lesbian, gay, and heterosexual couples: Associations with adopted children's outcomes. *Child Development, 84,* 1226–1240.

Farr, R. H., Tasker, F., & Goldberg, A. E. (2017). Theory in highly cited studies of sexual minority parent families: Variations and implications. *Journal of Homosexuality, 64,* 1143–1179.

Farver, J. A. M., Narang, S. K., & Bhadha, B. R. (2002). East meets west: Ethnic identity, acculturation, and conflict in Asian Indian families. *Journal of Family Psychology, 16*(3), 338–350.

Fast, A. A., & Olson, K. R. (2018). Gender development in transgender preschool children. *Child Development, 89,* 620–637.

Fausto-Sterling, A., Crews, D., Sung, J., García-Coll, C., & Seifer, R. (2015). Multimodal sex-related differences in infant and in infant-directed maternal behaviors during months three through twelve of development. *Developmental Psychology, 51,* 1351–1366.

Fay-Stammbach, T., Hawes, D. J., & Meredith, P. (2014). Parenting influences on executive function in early childhood: A review. *Child Development Perspectives, 8,* 258-264.

Feagans, L., & Farran, D. C. (1981). How demonstrated comprehension can get muddled in production. *Developmental Psychology, 17,* 718–727.

Fearon, R. M. P., Bakersman-Kranenburg, M. J., van IJzendoorn, M. H., Lapsley, A-M., & Roisman, G. I. (2010). The significance of insecure attachment and disorganization in the development of children's externalizing behavior: A meta-analytic study. *Child Development, 81,* 435–456.

Fearon, R. M. P., & Belsky, J. (2016). Precursors of attachment security. In J. Cassidy & P. R. Shaver (Eds.), *Handbook of attachment: Theory research and clinical applications* (3rd ed., pp. 291–313). New York, NY: Guilford Press.

Feeney, B. C., & Woodhouse, S. S. (2016). Caregiving. In J. Cassidy & P. R. Shaver (Eds.), *Handbook of attachment: Theory, research, and clinical applications* (3rd ed., pp. 827–851). New York, NY: Guilford Press.

Feeney, J. A. (2016). Adult romantic attachment: Developments in the study of couple relationships. In J. Cassidy & P. R. Shaver (Eds.), *Handbook of attachment: Theory, research, and clinical applications* (3rd ed., pp. 435–463). New York, NY: Guilford Press.

Fein, G. (1981). Pretend play in childhood: An integrative review. *Child Development, 52,* 1095–2018.

Feldlaufer, H., Midgley, C., & Eccles, J. S. (1988). Student, teacher, and observer perceptions of the classroom environment before and after the transition to junior high school. *Journal of Early Adolescence, 8,* 133–156.

Feldman, R. (2007). Parent-infant synchrony: Biological foundations and developmental outcomes. *Current Directions in Psychological Science, 16,* 340–345.

Feldman, R. (2012). Oxytocin and social affiliation in humans. *Hormones and Behavior, 61,* 380–391.

Feldman, R. (2015). Sensitive periods in human social development: New insights from research on oxytocin, synchrony, and high-risk parenting. *Development and Psychopathology, 27,* 369–395.

Feldman, R., & Eidelman, A. I. (2007). Maternal postpartum behavior and the emergence of infant-mother and infant-father synchrony in preterm and full-term infants: The role of neonatal vagal tone. *Developmental Psychobiology, 49,* 290–302.

Felitti, V. J., Anda, R. F., Nordenberg, D., Williamson, D. F., Spitz, A. M., Edwards, V., et al. (1998). Relationship of childhood abuse and household dysfunction to many of the leading causes of death in adults: The Adverse Childhood Experiences (ACE) Study. *American Journal of Preventive Medicine, 14,* 245–258.

Fellows, K. J., Chiu, H-Y., Hill, E. J., & Hawkins, A. J. (2016). Work-family conflict and couple relationship quality: A meta-analytic study. *Journal of Family Economics, 37,* 509–518.

Ferguson, C. J., & Donnellan, M. B. (2013). Is the association between children's baby video viewing and poor language development robust? A reanalysis of Zimmerman, Christakis, and Meltzoff (2007). *Developmental Psychology.* Advance online publication. doi:10.1037/a0033628

Ferguson, M. (2016). ESSA opens school door to social-emotional learning. *Phi Delta Kappan, 97,* 74–75.

Ferjan Ramirez, N., & Kuhl, P. (2017). The brain science of bilingualism. *Young Children, 72,* 38–44.

Ferjan Ramirez, N., Ramirez, R. R., Clarke, M., Taulu, S., & Kuhl, P. K. (2017). Speech discrimination in 11-month-old bilingual and monolingual infants: A magnetoencephalography study. *Developmental Science, 20,* doi:10.111/desc.12427

Fernald, A. (2010). Getting beyond the "convenience sample" in research on early cognitive development. *Behavior & Brain Sciences, 33,* 91–92.

Ferreira, A. I., Rodrigues, R. I., & Costa Ferreira, P. (2016). Career interests of students in psychology specialties degrees: Psychometric evidence and correlations with the RIASEC dimensions. *International Journal of Education and Vocational Guidance, 16,* 91–111.

Ferreira, J. F., Basseches, M., & Vasco, A. B. (2017). Guidelines for reflective practice in psychotherapy: A reflection on the benefits of combining moment-by-moment and phase-by-phase mapping in clinical decision making. *Journal of Psychotherapy Integration, 27*(1), 35–46. http://dx.doi.org/10.1037/int0000047

Festinger, L. (1954). A theory of social comparison. *Human Relations, 7,* 117–140.

Ficks, C. A., & Waldman, I. D. (2014). Candidate genes for aggression and antisocial behavior: A meta-analysis of association studies of the 5HTTLPR and MAOA-uVNTR. *Behavior Genetics, 44,* 427–444.

Field, T., & Diego, M. (2008). Vagal activity, early growth and emotional development. *Infant Behavior and Development, 31,* 361–373.

Field, T., Fox, N., Pickens, J., & Nawrocki, T. (1995). Relative right frontal activation in 3- to 6-month-old infants of depressed mothers. *Developmental Psychology, 31,* 358–363.

Field, T., Grizzle, N., Scafidi, F., & Schanberg, S. (1996). Massage and relaxation therapies' effects on depressed adolescent mothers. *Adolescence, 31,* 903–1002.

Field, T., Hernandez-Reif, M., & Diego, M. (2006). Intrusive and withdrawn depressed mothers and their infants. *Developmental Review, 26,* 15–30.

Field, T., Hernandez-Reif, M., Diego, M., Feijo, L., Vera, Y., Gil, K., & Sanders, C. (2007a). Responses to animate and inanimate faces by infants of depressed mothers. *Early Child Development and Care, 177,* 533–539.

Field, T., Hernandez-Reif, M., Diego, M., Feijo, L., Vera, Y., Gil, K., & Sanders, C. (2007b). Still-face and separation effects on depressed mother-infant interactions. *Infant Mental Health Journal, 28,* 314–323.

Field, T., Hernandez-Reif, M., & Freedman, J. (2004). Stimulation programs for preterm infants. *SRCD Social Policy Report, 18,* 1–19.

Field, T., Scafidi, F., & Schanberg, S. (1987). Massage of preterm infants to improve growth and development. *Pediatric Nursing, 13,* 385–387.

Field, T., Schanberg, S. M., Scafidi, F., Bauer, C. R., Vega-Lahr, N., Garcia, R., . . . Kuhn, C. M. (1986). Tactile/kinesthetic stimulation effects on preterm neonates. *Pediatrics, 77,* 654–658.

Fields, R. D. (2016). Don't touch that dial. *Scientific American Mind, 27,* 20–21.

Figueredo, A. J., Vásquez, G., Brumbach, B. H., Schneider, S. M. R., Sefcek, J. A., Tal, I. R., . . . Jacobs, W. J. (2006). Consilience and life history theory: from genes to brain to reproductive strategy. *Developmental Review, 26,* 243–275.

Figueroa, T., Hurtado, S., Cobian, K., Wilkins, A., & Lewis-White, D. (2016). *Cultivating STEM talent: Lessons from STEM pioneers and exemplar institutions.* Los Angeles, CA: Higher Education Research Institute (HERI) of the University of California, Los Angeles.

Fischer, K. W., & Bidell, T. R. (2006). Dynamic development of action and thought. In W. Damon & R. M. Lerner (Series Eds.), R. M.

Lerner (Vol. Ed.), *Handbook of child psychology: Vol. 1. Theoretical models of human development* (6th ed., pp. 313–399). Hoboken, NJ: Wiley.

Fischer, R., & Schwartz, S. (2011). Whence differences in value priorities?: Individual, cultural, or artifactual sources. *Journal of Cross-Cultural Psychology, 42,* 1127–1144.

Fishbein, D. H., Ridenour, T. A., Stahl, M., & Sussman, S. (2016). The full translational spectrum of prevention research: Facilitating the transfer of knowledge to practices and policies that prevent behavioral health problems. *Translational Behavioral Medicine, 6,* 5–16.

Fisher, M. M., & Eugster, E. A. (2014). What is in our environment that effects puberty? *Reproductive Toxicology, 44,* 7–14.

Fiske, A. P., Kitayama, S., Markus, H. R., & Nisbett, R. E. (1998). The cultural matrix of social psychology. In D. T. Gilbert & S. T. Fiske (Eds.), *The handbook of social psychology, Vol. 2* (4th ed., pp. 915–981). New York, NY: McGraw-Hill.

Fiske, S. T. (2009). Cultural processes. In G. G. Berntson & J. T. Cacioppo (Eds.), *Handbook of Neuroscience for the Behavioral Sciences* (pp. 985–1004). New York, NY: Wiley.

Fitzgerald, J. M. (1988). Vivid memories and the reminiscence phenomenon: The role of a self narrative. *Human Development, 31,* 261–273.

Fitzgerald, J. M. (1992). Autobiographical memory and conceptualizations of the self. In M. A. Conway, D. C. Rubin, H. Spinnler, & W. A. Wagenaar (Eds.), *Theoretical perspectives on autobiographical memory* (pp. 99–114). Boston, MA: Kluwer Academic Press.

Fitzgerald, J. M. (1999). Autobiographical memory and social cognition: Development of the remembered self in adulthood. In T. M. Hess & F. Blanchard-Fields (Eds.), *Social cognition and aging* (pp. 145–171). San Diego, CA: Academic Press.

Fivush, R. (2011). The development of autobiographical memory. *Annual Review of Psychology, 62,* 559–582.

Fivush, R., & Haden, C. A. (Eds.) (2003). *Autobiographical memory and the construction of a narrative self: Developmental and cultural perspectives.* Mahwah, NJ: Lawrence Erlbaum.

Flavell, J. H. (1963). *The developmental psychology of Jean Piaget.* New York, NY: Van Nostrand.

Flavell, J. H., Flavell, E. R., & Green, F. L. (1987). Young children's knowledge about the apparent-real and pretend-real distinctions. *Developmental Psychology, 23,* 816–822.

Flavell, J. H., Miller, P. H., & Miller, S. A. (1993). *Cognitive development* (3rd ed.). Upper Saddle River, NJ: Prentice Hall.

Flavell, J. H., Mumme, D. L., Green, F. L., & Flavell, E. R. (1992). Young children's understanding of different types of beliefs. *Child Development, 63,* 960–977.

Flett, G. L., Hewitt, P. L., Davis, R. A., & Sherry, S. B. (2004). Description and counseling of the perfectionistic procrastinator. In H. C. Schouwenburg, C. H. Lay, T. A. Pychyl, & J. R. Ferrari (Eds.), *Counseling the procrastinator in academic settings* (pp. 181–194). Washington, DC: American Psychological Association.

Flynn, J. R. (2012). *Are we getting smarter? Rising IQ in the twenty-first century.* New York, NY: Cambridge University Press.

Folkman, S., Lazarus, R. S., Gruen, R. J., & DeLongis, A. (1986). Appraisal, coping, health status, and psychological symptoms. *Journal of Personality and Social Psychology, 50,* 571–579.

Folstein, S., & Rutter, M. (1977). Infantile autism: A study of 21 twin pairs. *Journal of Child Psychology and Psychiatry, 18,* 297–321.

Fordham, S., & Ogbu, J. U. (1986). Black students' school success: Coping with the burden of "acting white." *Urban Review, 18,* 176–206.

Forgatch, M. S., & Patterson, G. R. (2010). Parent Management Training— Oregon Model: An intervention for antisocial behavior in children and adolescents. In J. R. Weisz & A. E. Kazdin (Eds.), *Evidence-based psychotherapies for children and adolescents* (pp. 159–178). New York, NY: Guilford Press.

Fortenberry, J. D. (2013). Puberty and adolescent sexuality. *Hormones and Behavior, 64,* 280–287.

Fouad, N. A., & Bynner, J. (2008). Work transitions. *American Psychologist, 63,* 241–251.

Fowler, J. W. (1981). *Stages of faith: The psychology of human development and the quest for meaning.* San Francisco, CA: Harper & Row.

Fowler, J. W. (1991). Stages in faith consciousness. *New Directions for Child and Adolescent Development, 1991:* 27-45.

Fox, N. A., Kimmerly, N. L., & Schafer, W. D. (1991). Attachment to mother/attachment to father: A meta-analysis. *Child Development, 62,* 210–225.

Fox, N. A., Snidman, N., Haas, S. A., Degnan, K. A., & Kagan, J. (2015). The relationship between reactivity at 4 months and behavioral inhibition in the second year: Replication across three independent samples. *Infancy, 20,* 98–114.

Foxcroft, L. (2009). *Hot flushes, cold science: A history of the modern menopause.* London: Granta Publishers.

Fraley, R. C., & Roisman, G. I. (2014). The Adult Attachment Interview: Psychometrics, stability and change from infancy, and developmental origins: III. Categories or dimensions? A taxometric analysis of the Adult Attachment Interview. *Monographs of the Society for Research in Child Development, 79*(3), 36–50.

Fraley, R. C., & Shaver, P. R. (1999). Loss and bereavement: Attachment theory and recent controversies concerning "grief work" and the nature of detachment. In J. Cassidy & P. R. Shaver (Eds.), *Handbook of attachment: Theory, research and clinical applications* (pp. 735–759). New York, NY: Guilford Press.

Fraley, R. C., & Shaver, P. R. (2016). Attachment, loss, and grief: Bowlby's views, new developments, and current controversies. In J. Cassidy & P. R. Shaver (Eds.), *Handbook of attachment: Theory research and clinical applications* (3rd ed., pp. 40–62). New York, NY: Guilford Press.

Francis, A. (2010). The medicalization of grief. *Psychiatric Times,* March 16, 2010.

Francis, L. J. (2013). Implicit religion, explicit religion and purpose in life: An empirical enquiry among 13- to 15-year-old adolescents. *Mental Health, Religion and Culture 16,* 969–921.

Francis, L. J., & Penny, G. (2016). Implicit religion and psychological wellbeing: A study among adolescents without formal religious affiliation or practice. *Implicit Religion, 19*(1), 61–78.

Francis, R. C. (2011). *Epigenetics: The ultimate mystery of inheritance.* New York, NY: W.W. Norton.

Franco, A. H. R., Butler, H. A., & Halpern, D. F. (2015). Teaching critical thinking to promote learning. In D. Dunn (Ed.), *The Oxford handbook of undergraduate psychology education* (pp. 65–74). New York, NY: Oxford University Press.

Franklin, J. C., Ribeiro, J., Fox, K., Bentley, K., Kleiman, E., Huang, X., . . . Nock, M. (2016). Risk factors for suicidal thoughts and behaviors: A meta-analysis of 50 years of research. *Psychological Bulletin. 143,* 187–232.

Frede, E. (2008). *Top 10 pre-K questions: What parents need to know about high quality preschool.* Available from http://nieer.org/docs/index.php?DocID=189

Frederick, D. A., Sandhu, G., Morse, P. J., & Swami, V. (2016). Correlates of appearance and weight satisfaction in a U.S. national sample: Personality, attachment style, television viewing, self-esteem, and life satisfaction. *Body Image, 17,* 191–203.

Fredrickson, B. L. (2001). The role of positive emotions in positive psychology: The broaden-and-build theory of positive emotions. *American Psychologist, 56,* 218–226.

Fredrickson, B. L., Boulton, A. J., Firestine, A. M., Van Cappellen, P., Algoe, S. B., Brantley, M. M., . . . Salzberg, S. (2017). Positive emotion correlates of meditation practice: A comparison of mindfulness meditation and loving-kindness meditation. *Mindfulness, 8*(6), 1623–1633.

Fredrickson, B. L., & Carstensen, L. L. (1990). Choosing social partners: How old age and anticipated endings make us more selective. *Psychology and Aging, 5,* 335–347.

Fredrickson, B. L., Cohn, M. A., Coffey, K. A., Pek, J., & Finkel, S. M. (2008). Open hearts build lives: Positive emotions, induced through loving-kindness meditation, build consequential personal resources. *Journal of Personality and Social Psychology, 95,* 1045–1062.

Fredriksson, P., Öckert, B., & Oosterbeek, H. (2013). Long-term effects of class size. *Quarterly Journal of Economics, 128,* 249–285.

Freedman, V. A., & Spillman, B. C. (2014). Disability and care needs among older Americans. *Milbank Quarterly, 92,* 509–541.

Freedy, J. R., Saladin, M. E., Kilpatrick, D. G., Resnick, H. S., & Saunders, B. E. (1994). Understanding acute psychological distress following natural disaster. *Journal of Traumatic Stress, 7,* 257–273.

Freidrich, L. K., & Stein, A. H. (1973). Aggressive and prosocial television programs and the natural behavior of preschool children. *Monographs of Society for Research in Child Development, 38* (Serial No. 3).

Freud, S. (1905/1989). Three essays on the theory of sexuality. In P. Gay (Ed.), *The Freud reader.* New York, NY: Norton.

Freud, S. (1917/1957). Mourning and melancholia. In J. Strachey (Ed.), *Standard edition of the complete works of Sigmund Freud.* London: Hogarth Press.

Freud, S. (1920/1955). Beyond the pleasure principle: In J. Strachey (Ed. and Trans.), *The standard edition of the complete psychological works of Sigmund Freud* (Vol. 18, pp. 7–64). London: Hogarth Press.

Freud, S. (1929/1961). To Ludwig Binswanger [Letter]. In E. L. Freud (Ed.), *Letters of Sigmund Freud 1873–1939* (T. & J. Stern, Trans.). London: Hogarth Press.

Freud, S. (1930/1989). Civilization and its discontents. In P. Gay (Ed.), *The Freud reader* (pp. 722–772). New York, NY: Norton.

Freud, S. (1935/1960). *A general introduction to psychoanalysis.* New York, NY: Washington Square Press.

Freud, S. (1949/1969). *An outline of psychoanalysis.* New York, NY: Norton.

Freund, A. M., & Blanchard-Fields, F. (2014). Age-related differences in altruism across adulthood: Making personal financial gain versus contributing to the public good. *Developmental Psychology, 50,* 1125–1136.

Frey, B. S., & Stutzer, A. (2002). What can economists learn from happiness research? *Journal of Economic Literature 40*(2), 402–435.

Frick, P. J., & Nigg, J. T. (2011). Current issues in the diagnosis of attention deficit hyperactivity disorder, oppositional defiant disorder, and conduct disorder. *Annual Review of Clinical Psychology, 8,* 77–107.

Frick, P. J., & Ray, J. V. (2015). Evaluating callous-unemotional traits as a personality construct. *Journal of Personality, 83,* 710–722.

Friederici, A. D. A., Pannekamp, A., Partsch, C-J., Ulmen, U., Oehler, K., . . . Hesse, V. (2008). Sex hormone testosterone affects language organization in the infant brain. *NeuroReport, 19,* 283–286.

Friedman, E. M., Ruini, C., Foy, R., Jaros, L., Sampson, H., & Ryff, C. D. (2017; 2015). Lighten UP! A community-based group intervention to promote psychological well-being in older adults. *Aging & Mental Health, 21*(2), 199-205.

Friedman, L. A., & Rapoport, J. L. (2015). Brain development in ADHD. *Current Opinion in Neurobiology, 30,* 106–111.

Friedman, S. L., & Boyle, D. E. (2008). Attachment in US children experiencing nonmaternal care in the early 1990s. *Attachment & Human Development, 10,* 225–261.

Friedrich, M. J. (2013). Studies suggest potential approaches for early detection of Alzheimer Disease. *JAMA, 309,* 18–19. doi:10.1001/jama.2012.105106

Frisina, R. D. (2009). Age-related hearing loss: Ear and brain mechanisms. *Annals of the New York Academy of Sciences, 1170,* 708–717.

Fromme, K., Corbin, W. R., & Kruse, M. I. (2008). Behavioral risks during the transition from high school to college. *Developmental Psychology, 44,* 1497–1504.

Fruzzetti, A. E., Shenk, C., & Hoffman, P. D. (2005). Family interaction and the development of borderline personality disorder: A transactional model. *Development and Psychopathology, 17,* 1007–1030.

Fu, J., & Zhou, X. (2014). Influence and mechanism of obesity on the onset of pubertal development in obese children. *Chinese Journal of Applied Clinical Pediatrics, 29,* 574–577.

Fu, X., Padilla-Walker, L. M., & Brown, M. N. (2017). Longitudinal relations between adolescents' self-esteem and prosocial behavior toward strangers, friends and family. *Journal of Adolescence, 57,* 90–98.

Fuhs, M. W., Nesbitt, K. T., Farran, D. C., & Dongm, N. (2014). Longitudinal associations between executive functioning and academic skills across content areas. *Developmental Psychology, 50,* 1698–1709.

Fulcher, M., Sutfin, E. L., Chan, R. W., Scheib, J. E., & Patterson, C. J. (2005). Lesbian mothers and their children: Findings from the contemporary families study. In A. M. Omoto &

H. S. Kurtzman (Eds.), *Sexual orientation and mental health* (pp. 281–299). Washington DC: American Psychological Association.

Fuligni, A. J. (2007). Family obligation, college enrollment, and emerging adulthood in Asian and Latin American families. *Child Development Perspectives, 1*, 96–100.

Fuligni, A. J., & Tsai, K. M. (2015). Developmental flexibility in the age of globalization: Autonomy and identity development among immigrant adolescents. *Annual Review of Psychology, 66*, 411–431.

Fung, H., Carstensen, L. L., & Lutz, A. (1999). The role of time perspective in age differences in social preferences. *Psychology and Aging, 14*, 595–604.

Fung, H., Li, J., & Lam, C. K. (2017). Multifaceted discipline strategies of Chinese parenting. *International Journal of Behavioral Development, 4*, 472–481.

Furman, W., & Rose, A. J. (2015). Friendships, romantic relationships and peer relationships. In R. M. Lerner (Series Ed.) & M. E. Lamb (Vol. Ed.), *Handbook of child psychology and developmental science: Volume 3. Socioemotional processes* (7th ed., pp. 932–974). Hoboken, NJ: Wiley.

Gagne, J. R. (2017). Self-control in childhood: A synthesis of perspectives and focus on early development. *Child Development Perspectives, 11*, 127–132.

Gahler, M., & Palmtag, E-L. (2015). Parental divorce, psychological well-being and educational attainment: Changed experience, unchanged effect among Swedes born 1892–1991. *Social Indicators Research, 123*, 601–623.

Galatzer-Levy, I. R., & Bonanno, G. A. (2012). Beyond normality in the study of bereavement: Heterogeneity in depression outcomes following loss in older adults. *Social Science & Medicine, 74*, 1987–1994.

Galindo, C., & Fuller, B. (2010). The social competence of Latino kindergartners and growth in mathematical understanding. *Developmental Psychology, 40*, 579–592.

Gallagher, S. (2000). Philosophical conceptions of the self: Implications for cognitive science. *Trends in Cognitive Sciences, 4*, 14–21.

Galvao, T. F., Silva, M. T., Zimmermann, I. R., Souza, K. M., Martins, S. S., & Pereira, M. G. (2014). Pubertal timing in girls and depression: A systematic review. *Journal of Affective Disorders, 155*, 13–19.

Gander, M., & Buchheim, A. (2015). Attachment classification, psychophysiology and frontal EEG asymmetry across the lifespan: A review. *Frontiers in Human Neuroscience, 9.* doi:10.3389/fnhum.2015.00079

Garanzini S., Yee, A., Gottman, J., Gottman, J., Cole, Preciado, M., & Jasculca, C. (2017). Results of Gottman method couples therapy with gay and lesbian couples. *Journal of Marital and Family Therapy, 43*, 674–684.

Garbarino, J. (1999). *Lost boys: Why our sons turn violent and how we can save them.* New York, NY: Free Press.

Garber, J., & Flynn, C. A. (2001). Predictors of depressive cognitions in young adolescents. *Cognitive Therapy and Research, 25*, 353–376.

Garcia, J. R., Seibold-Simpson, S. M., Massey, S. G., & Merriwether, A. M. (2015). Casual sex: Integrating social, behavioral, and sexual health research. In J. DeLamater & R. F. Plante

(Eds.), *Handbook of sociology and social research* (pp. 203–222). Cham, Switzerland: Springer International Publishing.

Garcia Coll, C. T. (1990). Developmental outcome of minority infants: A process oriented look into our beginnings. *Child Development 61*, 270–289.

García Coll, C. T., & Marks, A. K. (Eds.). (2012). *The immigrant paradox in children and adolescents: Is becoming American a developmental risk?* Washington, DC: American Psychological Association.

Gardner, M., Roth, J., & Brooks-Gunn, J. (2008). Adolescents' participation in organized activities and developmental success 2 and 8 years after high school: Do sponsorship, duration, and intensity matter? *Developmental Psychology, 44*, 814–830.

Gardner, M., & Steinberg, L. (2005). Peer influence on risk taking, risk preference, and risky decision making in adolescence and adulthood: An experimental study. *Developmental Psychology, 41*(4), 625–635.

Garmezy, N. U. (1993). Vulnerability and resilience. In D. C. Funder, R. D. Parke, & C. Tomlinson-Keasey (Eds.), *Studying lives through time: Personality and development* (pp. 377–398). Washington, DC: American Psychological Association.

Gaster, B., Larson, E. B., & Curtis, J. R. (2017). Advance directives for dementia: Meeting a unique challenge. *JAMA, 318*, 2175–2176.

Gates, G. J. (2015). Marriage and family: LGBT individuals and same-sex couples. *The Future of Children, 25*, 67–87.

Geary, D. C. (2006). Development of mathematical understanding. In W. Damon & R. M. Lerner (Series Eds.), D. Kuhn & R. S. Siegler (Vol. Eds.), *Handbook of child psychology: Vol. 2. Cognition, perception and language* (6th ed., pp. 777–810). Hoboken, NJ: Wiley.

Gee, J. (2007). *What videogames have to teach us about learning and literacy* (2nd ed.). New York, NY: Palgrave Macmillan.

Geist, E. A., & Gibson, M. (2000). The effect of network and public television programs on four- and five-year-olds' ability to attend to educational tasks. *Journal of Instructional Psychology, 27*, 250–261.

Gellis, Z., & Kenaley, B. (2008). Problem-solving therapy for depression in adults: A systematic review. *Social Work Practice, 18*, 117–131.

Gelman, R. (1982). Basic numerical abilities. In R. J. Sternberg (Ed.), *Advances in the psychology of human intelligence* (Vol. 1). Hillsdale, NJ: Erlbaum.

Gelman, R., & Gallistel, C. R. (1978). *The child's understanding of numbers.* Cambridge, MA: Harvard University Press.

Gelman, R., & Williams, E. M. (1998). Enabling constraints for cognitive development and learning: Domain specificity and epigenesis. In W. Damon (Series Ed.), D. Kuhn & R. S. Siegler (Vol. Eds.), *Handbook of child psychology: Vol. 2. Cognition, perception, and language* (5th ed., pp. 575–630). New York, NY: Wiley.

Gelman, S. A., Taylor, M. G., & Nguyen, S. P. (2004). Mother-child conversations about gender. *Monographs of the Society for Research in Child Development, 69* (Serial No. 275), vii–127.

Gelso, C. J., & Bhatia, A. (2012). Crossing theoretical lines: The role and effect of transference

in nonanalytic psychotherapies. *Psychotherapy, 49*(3), 384–390.

Gentile, B., Grabe, S., Dolan-Pascoe, B., Twenge, J. M., Wells, B. E., & Maitino, A. (2009). Gender differences in domain-specific self-esteem: A meta-analysis. *Review of General Psychology, 13*, 34–45.

Germer, C. K., & Siegel, R. D. (Eds.) (2012). *Wisdom and compassion in psychotherapy.* New York, NY: Guilford Press.

Gershoff, E. T. (2008). *Report on physical punishment in the United States: What research tells us about its effects on children.* Columbus, OH: Center for Effective Discipline.

Gershoff, E. T., & Grogan-Kaylor, A. (2016). Spanking and child outcomes: Old controversies and new meta-analyses. *Journal of Family Psychology, 30*, 453–469.

Gershoff, E. T., Grogan-Kaylor, A., Lansford, J. E., Chang, L., Zelli, A., Deater-Deckard, K., & Dodge, K. A. (2010). Parent discipline practices in an international sample: Associations with child behaviors and moderation by perceived normativeness. *Child Development, 81*, 480–495.

Gershoff, E. T., Lansford, J. E., Sexton, H. R., Davis-Kean, P., & Sameroff, A. J. (2012). Longitudinal links between spanking and children's externalizing behaviors in a national sample of White, Black, Hispanic, and Asian American families. *Child Development, 83*, 838–884.

Gerstorf, D., Hoppmann, C. A., Löckenhoff, C. E., Infurna, F. J., Schupp, J., Wagner, G. G., & Ram, N. (2016). Terminal decline in well-being: The role of social orientation. *Psychology and Aging, 31*, 149–165.

Gerstorf, D., Ram, N., Hoppman, C., Willis, S. L., & Schaie, K. W. (2011). Cohort differences in cognitive aging and terminal decline in the Seattle Longitudinal Study. *Developmental Psychology, 47*, 1026–1041.

Gesser, G., Wong, P. T., & Reker, G. T. (1988). Death attitudes across the life span: The development and validation of the Death Attitude Profile (DAP). *Omega: Journal of Death and Dying, 18*, 113–128.

Ghavani, N., Katsiaficas, D., & Rogers, L. O. (2016). Toward an intersectional approach in developmental science: The role of race, gender, sexual orientation, and immigrant status. In S. S. Horn, M. D. Ruck, & L. S. Liben (Eds.), *Equity and justice in developmental science: Theoretical and methodological issues* (Vol. 1, pp. 31–73). San Diego, CA: Elsevier Academic Press.

Gianaros, P. J., & Manuck, S. B. (2010). Neurobiological pathways linking socioeconomic position and health. *Psychosomatic Medicine 72*, 450–461.

Gianotti, G. (2015). Contrasting opinions on the role of the right hemisphere in the recovery of language. A critical survey. *Aphasiology, 29*, 1020–1037.

Gibbons, J. L. (1998). Introduction to adolescents in a changing world: Intracultural diversity in developmental contexts. *Cross Cultural Research, 32*, 211–216.

Gibbons, S. W., Ross, A., & Bevans, M. (2014). Liminality as a conceptual frame for understanding the family caregiving rite of passage: An integrative review. *Research in Nursing and Health 37*, 423–436.

Gibbs, J. (1987). Social processes in delinquency: The need to facilitate empathy as well as sociomoral reasoning. In W. Kurtines & J. Gewirtz (Eds.), *Moral development through social interaction*. New York, NY: Wiley.

Gibbs, J. C., Basinger, K. S., Grime, R. L., & Snarey, J. R. (2007). Moral judgment development across cultures: Revisiting Kohlberg's universality claims. *Developmental Review, 27,* 443–500.

Gibbs, J. C., Potter, G. B., & DiBise, A-M. (2013). Sociomoral development for behaviorally at-risk youth: Mac's group meeting. In C. Proctor & P. A. Linley (Eds.), *Research, applications, and interventions for children and adolescents: A positive psychology perspective* (pp. 225-245). New York, NY: Springer Science & Business Media.

Gibbs, J. J., & Goldbach, J. (2015). Religious conflict, sexual identity, and suicidal behaviors among LGBT young adults. *Archives of Suicide Research, 19*(4), 472–488.

Gibbs, N. (2009, November 30). The growing backlash against overparenting. *Time Magazine.*

Giedd, J. N. (2015). The amazing teen brain. *Scientific American, 312,* 32–37.

Giedd, J. N., & Rapoport, J. L. (2010). Structural MRI of pediatric brain development: What have we learned and where are we going? *Neuron, 67,* 728–734.

Gifford-Smith, M., Dodge, K. A., Dishion, T. J., & McCord, J. (2005). Peer influence in children and adolescents: Crossing the bridge from developmental to intervention science. *Journal of Abnormal Child Psychology, 33,* 255–265.

Gifford-Smith, M. E., & Brownell, C. A. (2003). Childhood peer relationships: Social acceptance, friendships, and peer networks. *Journal of School Psychology, 41*(4), 235–284.

Giles, J. W., & Heyman, G. D. (2004). When to cry over spilled milk: Young children's use of category information to guide inferences about ambiguous behavior. *Journal of Cognition and Development, 5,* 359–386.

Gilligan, C. (1977). In a different voice: Women's conceptions of self and of morality. *Harvard Educational Review, 47,* 481–517.

Gilligan, C. (1982). *In a different voice.* Cambridge, MA: Harvard University Press.

Gilligan, C. (1993). Adolescent development reconsidered. In A. Garrod (Ed.), *Approaches to moral development: New research and emerging themes.* New York, NY: Teachers College Press.

Gilligan, C., & Attanucci, J. (1988). Two moral orientations: Gender differences and similarities. *Merrill-Palmer Quarterly, 23,* 77–104.

Gilstrap, L. L. (2004). A missing link in suggestibility research: What is known about the behavior of field interviewers in unstructured interviews with young children? *Journal of Experimental Psychology: Applied, 10,* 13–24.

Ginsburg, H. P. (1989). *Children's arithmetic: How they learn it and how you teach it* (2nd ed.). Austin, TX: Pro-Ed.

Giri, S., Commons, M. L., & Harrigan, W. J. (2014). There is only one stage domain. *Behavioral Development Bulletin, 19,* 51–61.

Glass, G. (1976). Primary, secondary and meta-analysis of research. *Educational Research, 5,* 3–8.

Gleason, M. M., Fox, N. A., Drury, S., Smyke, A., Egger, H. L., Nelson, C.A., . . . Zeanah, C. H. (2011). Validity of evidence-derived criteria for reactive attachment disorder: Indiscriminately social/disinhibited and emotionally withdrawn/inhibited types. *Journal of the American Academy of Child and Adolescent Psychiatry, 50,* 216–234.

Gleeson, K., & Wise, S. (1993). The do-not-resuscitate order. Still too late. *Archives of Internal Medicine, 153,* 1999–2003.

Glogger, I., Schwonke, R., Holzäpfel, L., Nückles, M., & Renkl, A. (2012). Learning strategies assessed by journal writing: Prediction of learning outcomes by quantity, quality, and combinations of learning strategies. *Journal of Educational Psychology, 104,* 452–468.

Glymour, M. M., Weuve, J., Fay, M. E., Glass, T., & Berkman, L. F. (2008). Social ties and cognitive recovery after stroke: Does social integration promote cognitive resilience? *Neuroepidemiology, 31,* 10–20.

Goetz, T., Bieg, M., Lüdtke, O., Pekrun, R., & Hall, N. C. (2013). Do girls really experience more anxiety in mathematics? *Psychological Science, 24,* 2079–2087.

Goh, J. O., Chee, M. W., Tan, C., Venkatraman, V., Hebrank, A., Leshikar, E. D., . . . Park, D. C. (2007). Age and culture modulate object processing and object-scene binding in the ventral visual area. *Cognitive, Affective, & Behavioral Neuroscience, 7,* 44–52.

Goh, J. O., Hebrank, A. C., Sutton, B. P., Chee, M. W. L., Sim, S. K. Y., & Park, D. C. (2013). Culture-related differences in default network activity during visuo-spatial judgments. *Social, Cognitive and Affective Neuroscience, 8,* 134–142.

Goh, J. O., & Park, D. C. (2009). Culture sculpts the perceptual brain. J. Y. Chiao (Ed.), *Progress in Brain Research, 178,* 95–111.

Goldberg, A. E., & Gartrell, N. K. (2014). LGB-parent families: The current state of the research and directions for the future. *Advances in Child Development and Behavior, 46,* 57–88.

Goldberg, A. E., Kashy, D. A., & Smith, J. Z. (2012). Gender-typed play behavior in early childhood: Adopted children with lesbian, gay and heterosexual parents. *Sex Roles, 67,* 503–515.

Golden, R. L., Furman, W., & Collibee, C. (2016). The risks and rewards of sexual debut. *Developmental Psychology, 52,* 1913–1925.

Goldfried, M. R. (1995). *From cognitive-behavior therapy to psychotherapy integration.* New York, NY: Springer.

Goldman, A. D., & Penner, A. M. (2016). Exploring international gender differences in mathematics self-concept. *International Journal of Adolescence and Youth, 21,* 403–418.

Goldstein, A. P. (1990). *Delinquents on delinquency.* Champaign, IL: Research Press.

Goldston, D. B., Molock, S. D., Whitbeck, L. B., Murakami, J. L., Zayas, L. H., & Nagayama Hall, G. C. (2008). Cultural considerations in adolescent suicide prevention and psychosocial treatment. *American Psychologist, 63,* 14–31.

Goleman, D. (1995). *Emotional intelligence.* New York, NY: Bantam Books.

Goleman, D. (2003). *Destructive emotions: How can we overcome them?* New York, NY: Bantam Books.

Goleman, D., & Davidson, R. J. (2017). *Altered traits: Science reveals how meditation changes your mind, brain, and body.* New York, NY: Avery.

Golinkoff, R. M., Can, D. D., Soderstrom, M., & Hirsh-Pasek, K. (2015). (Baby) talk to me: The social context of infant-directed speech and its effects on early language acquisition. *Current Directions in Psychological Science, 24,* 339–344.

Golombok, S., & Tasker, F. (1996). Do parents influence the sexual orientation of their children? Findings from a longitudinal study of lesbian families. *Developmental Psychology, 32,* 3–11.

Golub, S. (1992). *Periods: From menarche to menopause.* Newbury Park, CA: Sage.

Gong, H., Ni, C., Liu, Y., Zhang, Y., Su, W., Lian, Y., . . . Jiang, C. (2016). Mindfulness meditation for insomnia: A meta-analysis of randomized controlled trials. *Journal of Psychosomatic Research, 89,* 1–6.

Gonzalez, R., Lickel, B., Gupta, M., Tropp, L. R., Valdenegro, D., Miranda, D., . . . Bernardino, M. (2017). Ethnic identity development and acculturation preferences among minority and majority youth: Group norms and contact. *Child Development, 88,* 743–760.

Good, C., Rattan, A., & Dweck, C. S. (2012). Why do women opt out? Sense of belonging and women's representation in mathematics. *Journal of Personality and Social Psychology, 102,* 700–717.

Goode, W. J. (1960). A theory of role strain. *American Sociological Review, 25,* 483–496.

Goodenough, F. L. (1926). Racial differences in the intelligence of school children. *Journal of Experimental Psychology, 9,* 388–397.

Goodman, G. S., & Clarke-Stewart, A. (1991). Suggestibility in children's testimony: Implications for child sexual abuse investigations. In J. L. Doris (Ed.), *The suggestibility of children's recollections* (pp. 92–105). Washington, DC: American Psychological Association.

Goodman, S. H. (2002). Early experiences and depression. In I. H. Gotlib and C. L. Hammen (Eds.), *Handbook of Depression and Its Treatment* (pp. 245–267). New York, NY: Guilford Press.

Goodson, W. D. (1978). Which do college students choose first—their major or their occupation? *Vocational Guidance Quarterly, 30,* 230–235.

Gopnik, A. (2016). *The gardener and the carpenter. What the new science of child development tells us about the relationship between parents and children.* New York, NY: Farrar, Straus, & Giroux.

Gopnik, A., & Wellman, H. M. (2012). Reconstructing constructivism: Causal models, Bayesian learning mechanisms, and the theory. *Psychological Bulletin, 138,* 1085–1108.

Goranson, A., Ritter, R. S., Waytz, A., Norton, M. I., & Gray, K. (2017). Dying is unexpectedly positive. *Psychological Science, 28,* 988–999.

Gordon, B., Ornstein, P. A., Clubb, P. A., Nida, R. E., & Baker-Ward, L. E. (1991). *Visiting the pediatrician: Long-term retention and forgetting.* Paper presented at the annual meeting of the Psychonomic Society, San Francisco.

Gordon, I., Zagoory-Sharon, O., Leckman, J. F., & Feldman, R. (2015). Oxytocin and the development of parenting in humans. *Biological Psychiatry, 68,* 377–382.

Gotink, R. A., Chu, P., Busschbach, J. J. V., Benson, H., Fricchione, G. L., & Hunink, M. G. M. (2015). Standardised mindfulness-based interventions in healthcare: An overview of systematic reviews and meta-analyses of RCTs. *PLoS ONE, 10,* 1–17.

Gottesman, I. I., & Gould, T. D. (2003). The endophenotype concept in psychiatry: Etymology and strategic intentions. *American Journal of Psychiatry, 160*, 636–645.

Gottfredson, G. D., & Holland, J. L. (1990). A longitudinal test of the influence of congruence: Job satisfaction, competency utilization, and counterproductive behavior. *Journal of Counseling Psychology, 37*, 389–398.

Gottlieb, G. (1992). *Individual development and evolution: The genesis of novel behavior.* New York, NY: Oxford University Press.

Gottlieb, G. (2003). Probabilistic epigenesis of development. In J. Valsiner & K. J. Connolly (Eds.), *Handbook of developmental psychology* (pp. 3–17). London: Sage.

Gottman, J. M. (1994a). *What predicts divorce? The relationship between marital processes and marital outcomes.* Hillsdale, NJ: Erlbaum.

Gottman, J. M. (1994b). *Why marriages succeed or fail: And how you can make yours last.* New York, NY: Simon & Schuster.

Gottman, J. M. (1999). *The marriage clinic: A scientifically-based marital therapy.* New York, NY: Norton.

Gottman, J. M., & Gottman, J. S. (2015). Gottman couple therapy. In A. S. Gurman, J. L. Lebow, & D. K. Snyder (Eds.), *Clinical handbook of couple therapy* (5th ed., pp. 129–157). New York, NY: Guilford Press.

Gottman, J. M., & Gottman, J. S. (2017). The natural principles of love. *Journal of Family Theory & Review, 9*(1), 7–26.

Gottman, J. M., & Levenson, R. W. (2000). The timing of divorce: Predicting when a couple will divorce over a 14-year period. *Journal of Marriage and the Family, 62*, 737–745.

Gottman, J., & Silver, N. (1999). *The seven principles for making marriages work.* New York, NY: Three Rivers Press.

Gottman, J. M., & Silver, N. (2015). *The seven principles for making marriage work* (2nd ed.). New York, NY: Harmony Books.

Gould, R. L. (1978). *Transformations: Growth and change in adult life.* New York, NY: Simon & Schuster.

Grabowska, A. (2017). Sex on the brain: Are gender-dependent structural and functional differences associated with behavior? *Journal of Neuroscience Research, 95*, 200–212.

Graham, S., Taylor, A. Z., & Ho, A. (2009). Race and ethnicity in peer relations research. In K. H. Rubin, W. M. Bukowski, & B. Laursen (Eds.), *Handbook of peer interactions, relationships, and groups* (pp. 394–413). New York, NY: Guilford Press.

Graham, Y. P., Hein, C., Goodman, S. H., Miller, A., & Nemeroff, C. B. (1999). The effects of stress on brain development; Implications for psychopathology. *Development and Psychopathology, 11*, 545–565.

Grammer, J. K., Purtell, K. M., Coffman, J. L., & Ornstein, P. A. (2011). Relations between children's metamemory and strategic performance: Time-varying covariates in early elementary school. *Journal of Experimental Child Psychology, 108*, 139–155.

Granqvist, P., & Kirkpatrick, L. A. (2016). Attachment and religious representations and behavior. In J. Cassidy & P. R. Shaver (Eds.), *Handbook of attachment: Theory, research, and clinical applications* (3rd ed., pp. 917–940). New York, NY: Guilford Press.

Grant, H., & Dweck, C. S. (2003). Clarifying achievement goals and their impact. *Journal of Personality and Social Psychology, 85*, 541–553.

Gray, J. A. (1990). Brain systems that mediate both emotion and cognition. *Cognition and Emotion, 4*, 270–288.

Gray, W. M. (1990). Formal operational thought. In W. F. Overton (Ed.), *Reasoning, necessity, and logic: Developmental perspectives* (pp. 227–254). Hillsdale, NJ: Erlbaum.

Gray-Little, B., & Hafdahl, A. R. (2000). Factors influencing racial comparisons of self-esteem: A quantitative review. *Psychological Bulletin, 126*, 26–54.

Green, J., Charman, T., McConachie, H., Aldred, C., Slonims, V., Howlin, P., . . . the PACT Consortium. (2010). Parent-mediated communication-focused treatment in children with autism (PACT): A randomised controlled trial. *Lancet, 375*(9732), 2152–2160. http://doi.org/10.1016/S0140-6736(10)60587-9

Greenberg, M. T., & Kusche, C. (1998). Preventive intervention for school-age deaf children. *Journal of Deaf Studies and Deaf Education, 3*, 49–63.

Greenberg, M. T., & Kusche, C. (2002). Promoting alternative thinking strategies (PATHS). In D. S. Elliot (Series Ed.) & S. F. Mihalic (Contributing Ed.), *Blueprints for violence prevention: Book Ten.* Boulder: University of Colorado, Center for the Study and Prevention of Violence.

Greenberg, M. T., & Speltz, M. L. (1988). Attachment and the ontogeny of conduct problems. In J. Belsky & T. Nezworski (Eds.), *Clinical implications of attachment* (pp. 177–218). Hillsdale, NJ: Erlbaum.

Greenberger, H., & Litwin, H. (2003). Can burdened caregivers be effective facilitators of elder care-recipient health care? *Journal of Advanced Nursing, 41*, 332–341.

Greene, M. L., Way, N., & Pahl, K. (2006). Trajectories of perceived adult and peer discrimination among Black, Latino, and Asian American adolescents: Patterns and psychological correlates. *Developmental Psychology, 42*, 218–238.

Greene, S. M., Anderson, E. R., Forgatch, M. S., DeGarmo, D. S., & Hetherington, E. M. (2012). Risk and resilience after divorce. In F. Walsh (Ed.), *Normal family processes: Growing diversity and complexity* (4th ed., pp. 102–127). New York, NY: Guilford Press.

Greenfield, P. M. (1994). Independence and interdependence as developmental scripts: Implications for theory, research, and practice. In P. M. Greenfield & R. R. Cocking (Eds.), *Cross-cultural roots of minority child development* (pp. 1–40). Hillsdale, NJ: Erlbaum.

Greenfield, P. M., & Suzuki, L. K. (1998). Culture and human development: Implications for parenting, education, pediatrics, and mental health. In W. Damon (Series Ed.), I. E. Sigel & K. A. Renninger (Vol. Eds.), *Handbook of child psychology: Vol. 4. Child psychology in practice* (5th ed., pp. 1059–1109). New York, NY: Wiley.

Greenfield, P. M., Suzuki, L. K., & Rothstein-Fisch, C. (2006). In W. Damon & R. M. Lerner (Series Eds.), K. A. Renninger & I. E. Sigel (Vol. Eds.), *Handbook of child psychology: Vol. 4. Child psychology in practice* (6th ed., pp. 655–699). Hoboken, NJ: Wiley.

Greenough, W. T., & Black, J. E. (1992). Induction of brain structure by experience: Substrates for cognitive development. In M. R. Gunnar & C. A. Nelson (Eds.), *Minnesota Symposium on Child Psychology: Vol. 24. Developmental behavioral neuroscience* (pp. 155–200). Hillsdale, NJ: Erlbaum.

Greenspan, S., & Weider, S. (1999). A functional developmental approach to autism spectrum disorders. *Journal of Association for Persons with Severe Handicaps, 24*, 147–161.

Greenspan, S. I. (2003). Child care research: A clinical perspective. *Child Development, 74*, 1064–1068.

Gregory, A., & Cornell, D. (2009). "Tolerating" adolescent needs: Moving beyond zero tolerance policies in high school. *Theory into Practice, 48*, 106–113.

Gregory, A., & Huang, F. (2013). It takes a village: The effects of 10th grade college-going expectations of students, parents, and teachers four years later. *American Journal of Community Psychology, 52*, 41–55.

Gregory, A., & Weinstein, R. S. (2004). Connection and regulation at home and in school: Predicting growth in achievement for adolescents. *Journal of Adolescent Research, 19*, 405–427.

Gresham, F. M. (1981). Social skills training with handicapped children: A review. *Review of Educational Research, 51*, 139–176.

Grice, P. (1975). Logic and conversation. In P. Cole & J. L. Moran (Eds.), *Syntax and semantics: Vol. 3. Speech acts* (pp. 41–58). New York, NY: Academic Press.

Griffin, K. C., Boldt, L. J., & Kochanska, G. (2017). A secure base from which to cooperate: Security, child and parent willing stance, and adaptive and maladaptive outcomes in longitudinal studies. *Journal of Abnormal Child Psychology.* Available at https://doi.org/10.1007/s10802-017-0352-z

Grigorenko, E. L., Kornilov, S. A., & Naumova, O. Y. (2016). Epigenetic regulation of cognition: A circumscribed review of the field. *Development and Psychopathology, 28*, 1285–1304.

Grigoriadis, S., VonderPorten, E. H., Mamisashvili, L., Roerecke, M., Rehm, J., Dennis, C. L., . . . Ross, E. (2013). Antidepressant exposure during pregnancy and congenital malformations: Is there an association? A systematic review and meta-analysis of the best evidence. *Journal of Clinical Psychiatry, 74*, 293–308.

Grimm, S., Pestke, K., Feeser, M., Aust, S., Weigand, A., Wang, J., et al. (2014). Early life stress modulates oxytocin effects on limbic system during acute psychosocial stress. *Social Cognitive and Affective Neuroscience, 9*, 1828–1835.

Grisso, T., Steinberg, L., Woolard, J., Cauffman, E., Scott, E., Graham, S., . . . Schwartz, R. (2003). Juveniles' competence to stand trial: A comparison of adolescents' and adults' capacities as trial defendants. *Law and Human Behavior, 27*, 333–363.

Groh, A. M., Fearon, M. P., van IJzendoorn, M. H., Bakermans-Kranenburg, M. J., & Roisman, G. I. (2017). Attachment in their early life course: Meta-analytic evidence for its role in socioemotional development. *Child Development Perspectives, 11*, 70–76.

Groh, A. M., Narayan, A. J., Bakermans-Kranenburg, M. J., Roisman, G. I., Vaughn, B.

E., Fearon, R. M. P., & van IJzendoom, M. H. (2017). Attachment and temperament in the early life course: A meta-analytic review. *Child Development, 88,* 770–795.

Gros-Louis, J., West, M. J., & King, A. P. (2014). Maternal responsiveness and the development of directed vocalizing in social interactions. *Infancy, 19,* 385–408.

Gross, J. J., Carstensen, L. L., Pasupathi, M., Tsai, J. L., Gottestam, K., & Hsu, A. Y. C. (1997). Emotion and aging: Changes in experience, expression, and control. *Psychology and Aging, 12,* 590–599.

Grossman, T. (2015). The development of social brain functions in infancy. *Psychological Bulletin, 141,* 1266–1287.

Grossmann, I. (2017). Wisdom in context. *Perspectives on Psychological Science, 12,* 233–257.

Grossmann, I., Gerlach, T. M., & Denissen, J. J. (2016). Wise reasoning in the face of everyday life challenges. *Social Psychological and Personality Science, 7,* 611–622.

Grossmann, I., Karasawa, M., Izumi, S., Na, J., Varnum, M. E., Kitayama, S., & Nisbett, R. E. (2012). Aging and wisdom: Culture matters. *Psychological Science, 23,* 1059–1066.

Grossmann, I., Na, J., Varnum, M. E., Kitayama, S., & Nisbett, R. E. (2013). A route to well-being: Intelligence versus wise reasoning. *Journal of Experimental Psychology: General, 142,* 944–953.

Grossmann, I., Na, J., Varnum, M. E., Park, D. C., Kitayama, S., & Nisbett, R. E. (2010). Reasoning about social conflicts improves into old age. *Proceedings of the National Academy of Sciences, 107,* 7246–7250.

Grossmann, K. E., Grossmann, K., Huber, F., & Wartner, U. (1981). German children's behavior towards their mothers at 12 months and their fathers at 18 months in Ainsworth's strange situation. *International Journal of Behavioral Development, 4,* 157–181.

Grover, S. L., Teo, S. T. T., Pick, D., & Roche, M. (2017). Mindfulness as a personal resource to reduce work stress in the job demands-resources model. *Stress and Health, 33*(4), 426–436.

Gruenenfelder-Steiger, A. E., Harris, M. A., & Fend, H. A. (2016). Subjective and objective peer approval evaluations and self-esteem development: A test of reciprocal, prospective, and long-term effects. *Developmental Psychology, 52,* 1563–1577.

Grusec, J. E., Danyliuk, T., Kil, H., & O'Neill, D. (2017). Perspectives on parent discipline and child outcomes. *International Journal of Behavioral Development, 4,* 465–471.

Gudmundson, J. A., & Leerkes, E. M. (2012). Links between mothers' coping styles, toddler reactivity, and sensitivity to toddler's negative emotions. *Infant Behavior and Development, 35,* 158–166.

Guèvremont, A., Findlay, L., & Kohen, D. (2014). Organized extracurricular activities: Are in-school and out-of-school activities associated with different outcomes for Canadian youth? *Journal of School Health, 84*(5), 317–325.

Guiso, L., Monte, F., Sapienza, P., & Zingales, L. (2008). Culture, gender, and math. *Science, 320,* 1164–1165.

Gunnar, M. R. (2017). Social buffering of stress in development: A career perspective. *Perspectives on Psychological Science, 12,* 355–373.

Gunnar, M. R., Kryzer, E., Van Ryzin, M. J., & Phillips, D. A. (2010). The rise in cortisol in family day care: Associations with aspects of care quality, child behavior, and child sex. *Child Development, 81,* 851–869.

Gunnar, M. R., Kryzer, E., Van Ryzin, M. J., & Phillips, D. A. (2011). The import of the cortisol rise in child care differs as a function of behavioral inhibition. *Developmental Psychology, 47,* 792–803.

Gunnar, M. R., & Sullivan, R. M. (2016). The neurodevelopment of social buffering and fear learning: Integration and crosstalk. *Social Neuroscience 12*(1), 1–7. doi:10.1080/17470919.2016.1151824

Gupta, K. K., Gupta, V. K., & Shirasaka, T. (2016). An update on fetal alcohol syndrome—Pathogenesis, risks, and treatment. *Alcoholism: Clinical and Experimental Research, 40,* 1594–1602.

Gur, R. E., & Gur, R. C. (2016). Sex differences in brain and behavior in adolescence: Findings from the Philadelphia Neurodevelopmental Cohort. *Neuroscience and Biobehavioral Reviews, 70,* 159–170.

Gurwitz, S. B., & Dodge, K. A. (1977). Effects of confirmations and disconfirmations on stereotype-based attributions. *Journal of Personality and Social Psychology, 35,* 495–500.

Gustafsson, H. C., Brown, G. L., Mills-Koonce, W. R., & Cox, M. J. (2017). Intimate partner violence and children's attachment representations during middle childhood. *Journal of Marriage and Family, 79,* 865–878.

Gutman, L. M., Sameroff, A. J., & Cole, R. (2003). Academic growth curve trajectories from 1st grade to 12th grade: Effects of multiple social risk factors and preschool child factors. *Developmental Psychology, 39,* 777–790.

Haas, R. H. (2010). Autism and mitochondrial disease. *Developmental Disabilities Research Reviews, 16,* 144–153.

Hacker, A. (2003). *Mismatch: The growing gulf between women and men.* New York, NY: Scribner.

Haftenberger, M., Mensink, G. B. M., Herzog, B., Kluttig, A., Greiser, K. H., Merz, B., . . . Schienkiewitz, A. (2016). Changes in body weight and obesity status in German adults: Results of seven population-based prospective studies. *European Journal of Clinical Nutrition, 70,* 300–305.

Hagenauer, M. H., Perryman, J. I., Lee, T. M., & Carskadon, M. A. (2009). Adolescent changes in the homeostatic and circadian regulation of sleep. *Developmental Neuroscience, 31,* 276–284.

Haier, R. J., Jung, R. E., Yeo, R. A., Head, K., & Alkire, M. T. (2005). The neuroanatomy of general intelligence: Sex matters. *Neuorimage, 25,* 320–327.

Haigh, E. A., Bogucki, O. E., Sigmon, S. T., & Blazer, D. G. (2018). Depression among older adults: A 20-year update on five common myths and misconceptions. *The American Journal of Geriatric Psychiatry, 26,* 107–122.

Haimovitz, K., & Dweck, C. S. (2017). The origins of children's growth and fixed mindsets: New research and a new proposal. *Child Development, 88,* 1849–1859.

Haith, M. M. (2013). Emergent constructivism has its place—Among other possibilities. Commentary on "Stepping off the pendulum: Why only an action-based approach can transcend the nativist-empiricist debate: by J. Allen and M. Bickhard. *Cognitive Development, 28,* 144–147.

Hakanen, J. J., Peeters, M. C. W., & Schaufeli, W. B. (2017). Different types of employee well-being across time and their relationships with job crafting. *Journal of Occupational Health Psychology.* Available at http://dx.doi.org/10.1037/ocp0000081

Halford, G. S. (2014). *Children's understanding: The development of mental models.* New York, NY: Psychology Press.

Halford, G. S., & Andrews, G. (2006). Reasoning and problem solving. In W. Damon & R. M. Lerner (Series Eds.), D. Kuhn & R. S. Siegler (Vol. Eds.), *Handbook of child psychology: Vol. 2. Cognition, perception and language* (6th ed., pp. 557–608). Hoboken, NJ: Wiley.

Halford, W. K., Markman, H. J., Kline, G. H., & Stanley, S. M. (2003). Best practice in couple relationship education. *Journal of Marital and Family Therapy, 29,* 385–406.

Halim, M. L. D. (2016). Princesses and superheroes: Social-cognitive influences on early gender rigidity. *Child Development Perspectives, 10,* 155–160.

Halim, M. L., Ruble, D. N., Tamis-LeMonda, C. S., Zosuls, K. M., Lurye, L. E., & Greulich, F. K. (2014). Pink frilly dresses and the avoidance of all things "girly": Children's appearance rigidity and cognitive theories of gender development. *Developmental Psychology, 50,* 1091–1101.

Hall, G. S. (1904). *Adolescence: Its psychology and its relation to physiology, anthropology, sociology, sex, crime, religion, and education* (Vols. 1 & 2). New York, NY: Appleton-Century-Crofts.

Halldorsdottir, T., & Binder, E. B. (2017). Gene x Environment interactions: From molecular mechanisms to behavior. *Annual Review of Psychology, 68,* 215–241.

Hallers-Haalboom, E. T., Groeneveld, M. G., van Berkel, S. R., Endendijk, J. J., van der Pol, L. D., Linting, M., . . . Mesman, J. (2017). Mothers' and fathers' sensitivity with their two children: A longitudinal study from infancy to early childhood. *Developmental Psychology, 53,* 860–872.

Halm, M. A., Treat-Jacobson, D., Lindquist, R., & Savik, K. (2006). Correlates of caregiver burden after coronary artery bypass surgery. *Nursing Research, 55,* 426–436.

Halperin, S. (Ed.). (1998a). *The forgotten half revisited: American youth and young families, 1988–2008.* Washington, DC: American Youth Policy Forum.

Halperin, S. (1998b). Today's forgotten half: Still losing ground. In S. Halperin (Ed.), *The forgotten half revisited: American youth and young families, 1988–2008* (pp. 1–26). Washington, DC: American Youth Policy Forum.

Halpern, C. T., Spriggs, A. L., Martin, S. L., & Kupper, L. L. (2009). Patterns of intimate partner violence victimization from adolescence to young adulthood in a nationally representative sample. *Journal of Adolescent Health, 45,* 508–516.

Halpern, D. F. (2014). *Thought and knowledge: An introduction to critical thinking* (5th ed.). New York, NY: Psychology Press.

Halpern, D. F., Benbow, C. P., Gearty, D. C., Gur, R. C., Hyde, J. S., & Gernsbacher, M. A. (2007). The science of sex differences in science and mathematics. *Psychological Science in the Public Interest, 8,* 1–51.

Halpern-Felsher, B., & Cauffman, E. (2001). Costs and benefits of a decision: Decision-making competence in adolescents and adults. *Journal of Applied Developmental Psychology, 22,* 257–273.

Hamilton, B. E., Martin, J. A., Osterman, M. J. K., Curtin, S. C., & Matthews, T. J. (2015). Births: Final data for 2014. *National vital statistics reports, 64*(12). Hyattsville, MD: National Center for Health Statistics.

Hamilton, J. L., Hamlat, E. J., Stange, J. P., Abramson, L. Y., & Alloy, L. B. (2014). Pubertal timing and vulnerabilities to depression in early adolescence: Differential pathways to depressive symptoms by sex. *Journal of Adolescence, 37,* 165–174.

Hamilton, S. F. (2015). Translational research and youth development. *Applied Developmental Science, 19,* 60–73.

Hammen, C. (1996). Stress, families, and the risk for depression. In C. Mundt, M. J. Goldstein, K. Hahlweg, & P. Fiedler (Eds.), *Interpersonal factors in the origin and course of affective disorders* (pp. 101–112). London: Gaskell-Royal College of Psychiatrists.

Hampson, S. E. (2008). Mechanisms by which childhood personality traits influence adult well-being. *Current Directions in Psychological Science, 17,* 264–268.

Hamre, B. K. (2014). Teachers' daily interactions with children: An essential ingredient in effective early childhood programs. *Child Development Perspectives, 8,* 223–230.

Hamre, B. K., & Pianta, R. C. (2007). Learning opportunities in preschool and early elementary classrooms. In R. C. Pianta, M. J. Cox, & K. L. Snow (Eds.), *School readiness and the transition to kindergarten in the era of accountability* (pp. 40–83). Baltimore, MD: Brookes.

Han, W-J. (2012). Bilingualism and academic achievement. *Child Development, 83,* 300–321.

Hane, A. A., & Fox, N. A. (2006). Ordinary variations in maternal caregiving influence human infants' stress reactivity. *Psychological Science, 17,* 550–556.

Hane, A. A., & Fox, N. A. (2016). Studying the biology of human attachment. In J. Cassidy & P. R. Shaver (Eds.), *Handbook of attachment: Theory research and clinical applications* (3rd ed., pp. 223–241). New York, NY: Guilford Press.

Hane, A. A., Henderson, H. A., Reeb-Sutherland, B. C., & Fox, N. A. (2010). Ordinary variations in human maternal caregiving in infancy and biobehavioral development in early childhood: A follow-up study. *Developmental Psychobiology, 52,* 558–567.

Hane, A. A., & Philbrook, L. E. (2012). Beyond licking and grooming: Maternal regulation of infant stress in the context of routine care. *Parenting: Science and Practice, 12,* 144–153.

Hanf, C. (1968). *Modification of mother child controlling behavior during mother-child interactions in a controlled laboratory setting.* Paper presented at the regional meeting of the Association for Advancement of Behavior Therapy, Olympia, WA.

Hanish, L. D., & Guerra, N. G. (2004). Aggressive victims, passive victims, and bullies: Developmental continuity or developmental change. *Merrill-Palmer Quarterly, 50,* 17–38.

Hanke, K., & Fischer, R. (2013). Socioeconomical and sociopolitical correlates of interpersonal forgiveness: A three-level meta-analysis of the Enright forgiveness inventory across 13 societies. *International Journal of Psychology, 48*(4), 514–526.

Harackiewicz, J. M., Canning, E. A., Tibbetts, Y., Priniski, S. J., & Hyde, J. S. (2016). Closing achievement gaps with utility-value interventions: Disentangling race and social class. *Journal of Personality and Social Psychology, 111,* 745–765.

Harakeh, Z., & Vollebergh, W. A. M. (2012). The impact of active and passive peer influence on young adult smoking: An experimental study. *Drug and Alcohol Dependence, 121,* 220–223.

Harden, K. P., Mann, F. D., Grotzinger, A. D., Patterson, M. W., Steinberg, L., Tackett, J. L., & Tucker-Drob, E. M. (2017). Developmental differences in reward sensitivity and sensation seeking in adolescence: Testing sex-specific associations with gonadal hormones and pubertal development. *Journal of Personality and Social Psychology.* Available at http://dx.doi.org/10.1037/pspp0000172

Harmon-Jones, E., Gable, P. A., & Peterson, C. K. (2010). The role of asymmetric frontal cortical activity in emotion-related phenomena: A review and update. *Biological Psychology, 84,* 451–462.

Harrington, R. A., Lee, L. C., Crum, R. M., Zimmerman, A. W., & Hertz-Picciotto, I. (2014). Prenatal SSRI use and offspring with Autism Spectrum Disorder or Developmental Delay. *Pediatrics, 133,* 149–168.

Harris, A. J., Walfield, S. M., Shields, R. T., & Letourneau, E. J. (2016). Collateral consequences of juvenile sex offender registration and notification: Results from a survey of treatment providers. *Sexual Abuse: A Journal of Research and Treatment, 28,* 770–790.

Harris, J. R. (1998). *The nurture assumption: Why children turn out the way they do.* New York, NY: Touchstone.

Harris, M., Brett, C., Starr, J., Deary, I., & Johnson, W. (2016). Personality and other lifelong influences on older-age health and wellbeing: Preliminary findings in two Scottish samples. *European Journal of Personality, 30*(5), 438–455.

Harris-Britt, A., Valrie, C., Kurtz-Costes, B., & Rowley, S. (2007). Perceived racial discrimination and self-esteem in African American youth: Racial socialization as a protective factor. *Journal of Research on Adolescence, 17,* 669–682.

Harris-McKoy, D. (2016). Adolescent delinquency: Is too much or too little parental control a problem? *Journal of Child and Family Studies, 25*(7), 2079–2088. doi:10.1007/s10826-016-0383-z

Harrison, L. J., & Ungerer, J. A. (2002). Maternal employment and infant–mother attachment security at 12 months postpartum. *Developmental Psychology, 38,* 758–773.

Hart, B., & Risley, T. R. (1995). *Meaningful differences in the everyday experience of young American children.* Baltimore, MD: Brookes.

Harter, S. (1985). *The self-perception profile for children.* Unpublished manual, University of Denver, CO.

Harter, S. (1988a). Developmental and dynamic changes in the nature of the self concept: Implications for child psychotherapy. In S. R. Shirk (Ed.), *Cognitive development and child psychotherapy* (pp. 119–160). New York, NY: Plenum Press.

Harter, S. (1988b). *The self-perception profile for adolescents.* Unpublished manual, University of Denver, CO.

Harter, S. (1990). Causes, correlates, and the functional role of global self-worth: A life-span perspective. In R. Sternberg & J. Kolligian, Jr. (Eds.), *Competence considered* (pp. 67–98). New Haven, CT: Yale University Press.

Harter, S. (1999). *The construction of the self: A developmental perspective.* New York, NY: Guilford Press.

Harter, S. (2006). The self. In W. Damon & R. M. Lerner (Series Eds.), N. Eisenberg (Vol. Ed.), *Handbook of child psychology: Vol. 3. Social, emotional, and personality development* (6th ed., pp. 505–570). Hoboken, NJ: Wiley.

Harter, S. (2012). *The construction of the self: Developmental and sociocultural foundations* (2nd ed.). New York, NY: Guilford Press.

Harter, S. (2013). New directions in self development: Resurrecting the I-self. In D. M. McInerney, H. W. Marsh, R. G., Craven, & F. Guay (Eds.), *Theory driving research: New wave perspectives on self-processes and human development* (pp. 1–30). Charlotte, NC: IAP Publishing.

Harter, S. (2016). I-self and me-self processes affecting developmental psychopathology and mental health. In D. Cicchetti (Ed.), *Developmental psychopathology: Theory and method* (Vol. 1, 3rd ed., pp. 470–526). Hoboken, NJ: Wiley and Sons.

Harter, S., Waters, P. L., Whitesell, N. R., & Kastelic, D. (1998). Level of voice among female and male high school students: Relational context, support, and gender orientation. *Developmental Psychology, 34,* 892–901.

Hartshorne, H., & May, M. A. (1928–1930). *Studies in the nature of character* (Vols. 1–3). New York, NY: Macmillan.

Hartshorne, J. K., & Germine, L. T. (2015). When does cognitive functioning peak? The asynchronous rise and fall of different cognitive abilities across the life span. *Psychological Science, 26,* 433–443.

Hartung, P. J., & Vess, L. (2016). Critical moments in career construction counseling. *Journal of Vocational Behavior, 97,* 31–39.

Hartup, W. W. (1983). Peer relations. In P. H. Mussen (Series Ed.) & E. M. Hetherington (Vol. Ed.), *Handbook of child psychology: Vol. 4. Socialization, personality and social development* (pp. 103–196). New York, NY: Wiley.

Hartup, W. W., Glazer, J., & Charlesworth, R. (1967). Peer reinforcement and sociometric status. *Child Development, 38,* 1017–1024.

Haselager, G. J. T., Cillissen, H. N., van Lieshout, D. F. M., Riksen-Walraven, J. M. A., & Hartup, W. W. (2002). Heterogeneity among peer-rejected boys across middle childhood: Developmental pathways of social behavior. *Child Development, 73,* 446–456.

Haslam, C., Cruwys, T., Milne, M., Kan, C. H., & Haslam, S. A. (2016). Group ties protect cognitive health by promoting social identification and social support. *Journal of Aging and Health, 28,* 244–266.

Hastings, P. D., & Grusec, J. E. (1998). Parenting goals as organizers of responses to parent-child disagreement. *Developmental Psychology, 34,* 465–479.

Havighurst, R. J. 1953. *Human development and education.* New York, NY: McKay.

Hawkley, L. C., & Cacioppo, J. T. (2007). Aging and loneliness: Downhill quickly? *Current Directions in Psychological Science, 16,* 187–191.

Hay, D. F. (2017). The early development of human aggression. *Child Development Perspectives, 11,* 102–106.

Hayes, B. K., Goodhew, A., Heit, E., & Gillan, J. (2003). The role of diverse instruction in conceptual change. *Journal of Experimental Child Psychology, 86,* 253–276.

Hayes, D. S., & Birnbaum, D. W. (1980). Preschoolers' retention of televised events: Is a picture worth a thousand words? *Developmental Psychology, 16,* 410–416.

Hayes, S. C. (2002). Acceptance, mindfulness and science. *Clinical Psychology: Science and Practice, 9,* 101–106.

Hayes, S. C. (2004). Acceptance and commitment therapy and the new behavior therapies: Mindfulness, acceptance and relationship. In S. C. Hayes, V. M. Follette, & M. M. Linehan (Eds.), *Mindfulness and acceptance: Expanding the cognitive-behavioral tradition* (pp. 1–29). New York, NY: Guilford Press.

Hayes, S. C. (2016). Acceptance and commitment therapy, relational frame theory, and the third wave of behavioral and cognitive therapies. *Behavior Therapy, 47*(6), 869–885.

Hayes, S. C., Strosahl, K., & Wilson, K. (1999). *Acceptance and commitment therapy: Understanding and treating human suffering.* New York, NY: Guilford Press.

Hazan, C., & Shaver, P. (1987). Romantic love conceptualized as an attachment process. *Journal of Personality and Social Psychology, 52,* 511–524.

Hazan, C., & Shaver, P. R. (1994). Attachment as an organizational framework for research on close relationships. *Psychological Inquiry, 5,* 1–22.

Hazan, C., & Zeifman, D. (1999). Pair bonds as attachments. In J. Cassidy & P. R. Shaver (Eds.), *Handbook of attachment: Theory, research, and clinical applications* (pp. 336–377). New York, NY: Guilford Press.

Hazen, N. L., Allen, S. D., Christopher, C. H., Umemura, T., & Jacobvitz, D. B. (2015). Very extensive nonmaternal care predicts mother-infant attachment disorganization: Convergent evidence from two samples. *Development and Psychopathology, 27,* 649–661.

Healy, J. M. (1998). *Failure to connect: How computers affect our children's minds for better or worse.* New York, NY: Simon & Schuster.

Hecker, L. L., & Sori, C. F. (2016). Helping parents use the time-out procedure. In C. F. Sori, L. Hecker, & M. E. Bachenberg (Eds.), *The therapist's notebook for children and adolescents: Homework, handouts, and activities for use in psychotherapy* (pp. 334–340). New York, NY: Routledge.

Heckhausen, J. (1997). Developmental regulation across adulthood: Primary and secondary control of age-related challenges. *American Psychologist, 33,* 176–187.

Heckhausen, J. (1999). *Developmental regulation in adulthood: Age-normative and sociostructural constraints as adaptive challenges.* New York, NY: Cambridge University Press.

Heckhausen, J., & Wrosch, C. (2016). Challenges to developmental regulation across the life course: What are they and which individual differences matter? *International Journal of Behavioral Development, 40,* 145–150.

Heijmans, B. T., & Mill, J. (2012). Commentary: The seven plagues of epigenetic epidemiology. *International Journal of Epidemiology, 41,* 74–78. doi:10.1093/ije/dyr225

Heijmans, B. T., Tobi, E. W., Stein, A. D., Putter, H., Blauw, G. J., Susser, E. S., . . . Lumey, L. H. (2008). Persistent epigenetic differences associated with prenatal exposure to famine in humans. *Proceedings of the National Academy of Sciences, 105,* 17046–17049.

Heine, S. J., & Hamamura, T. (2007). In search of East Asian self-enhancement. *Personality and Social Psychology Review, 11,* 4–27.

Heine, S. J., Kitayama, S., Lehman, D. R., Takata, T., Ide, E., Leung, C., & Matsumoto, H. (2001). Divergent consequences of success and failure in North America and Japan: An investigation of self-improving motivations and malleable selves. *Journal of Personality and Social Psychology, 81,* 599–615.

Helliwell, J., Layard, R., & Sachs, J. (2017). *World Happiness Report 2017.* New York, NY: Sustainable Development Solutions Network.

Helms, J. E. (1990). An overview of Black racial identity theory. In J. E. Helms (Ed.), *Black and White racial identity: Theory, research and practice* (pp. 9–32). New York, NY: Greenwood Press.

Helson, R., & Roberts, B. W. (1994). Ego development and personality change in adulthood. *Journal of Personality and Social Psychology, 66,* 911–920.

Helwig, N. E., & Ruprecht, M. R. (2017). Age, gender, and self-esteem: A sociocultural look through a nonparametric lens. *Archives of Scientific Psychology, 5,* 19–31.

Hendry, A., Jones, E. J. H., & Charman, T. (2016). Executive function in the first three years of life: Precursors, predictors and patterns. *Developmental Review, 42,* 1–33.

Hendry, L. B., & Kloep, M. (2007). Conceptualizing emerging adulthood: Inspecting the emperor's new clothes? *Child Development Perspectives, 1,* 74–79.

Henggeler, S. W., Schoenwald, S. K., & Pickrel, S. G. (1995). Multisystemic therapy: Bridging the gap between university- and community-based treatments. *Journal of Consulting and Clinical Psychology, 63,* 709–717.

Henggeler, S. W., & Sheidow, A. J. (2012). Empirically supported family-based treatments for conduct disorder and delinquency in adolescents. *Journal of Marital and Family Therapy, 38,* 30–58.

Henrich, J., Heine, S. J., & Norenzayan, A. (2010). The weirdest people in the world? *Behavior & Brain Sciences, 33,* 61–135.

Hepach, R. (2017). Prosocial arousal in children. *Child Development Perspectives, 11,* 50–55.

Herbers, J. E., Cutuli, J. J., Supkoff, L. M., Narayan, A. J., & Masten, A. S. (2014). Parenting and coregulation: Adaptive systems for competence in children experiencing homelessness. *American Journal of Orthopsychiatry, 84,* 420–430.

Herculano-Houzel, S. (2002). Do you know your brain? A survey on public neuroscience literacy at the closing of the decade of the brain. *Neuroscientist, 8,* 98–110.

Herek, G. M. (2006). Legal recognition of same-sex relationships in the United States. *American Psychologist, 61,* 607–621.

Herek, G. M., Norton, A. T., Allen, T. J., & Sims, C. L. (2010). Demographic, psychological and social characteristics of self-identified lesbian, gay, and bisexual adults in US probability sample. *Sexuality Research & Social Policy: A Journal of the NSRC, 7,* 176–200.

Herman, M. (2004). Forced to choose: Some determinants of racial identification in multiracial adolescents. *Child Development, 75,* 730–748.

Herman-Giddens, M. E. (2017). Lessons learned from Australia: Social disadvantage and pubertal timing. *Pediatrics, 139,* e20170837.

Herman-Giddens, M. E., Steffes, J., Harris, D., Slora, E., Hussey, M., Dowshen, S. A., . . . Reiter, E. O. (2012). Secondary sexual characteristics in boys: Data from the Pediatric Research in Office Settings Network. *Pediatrics, 130.* doi:10.1542/peds.2011-3291

Hernández-Arteaga, E., Hernández-González, M., Ramíez-Rentería, M. L., Almanza-Sepúlveda, M. L., Guevara, M. A., Silva, M. A., & Jaime, H. B. (2016). Prenatal stress alters the developmental pattern of behavioral indices of sexual maturation and copulation in male rats. *Physiology & Behavior, 163,* 251–257.

Herr, E. L., Cramer, S. H., & Niles, S. G. (2003). *Career guidance and counseling through the life span: Systematic approaches* (6th ed.). New York, NY: HarperCollins.

Hersch, P. (1998). *A tribe apart: A journey into the heart of American adolescence.* New York, NY: Fawcett Columbine.

Hershenson, D. B. (1996). Work adjustment: A neglected area in career counseling. *Journal of Counseling and Development, 74,* 442–446.

Hertenstein, M. J. (2002). Touch: Its communicative functions in infancy. *Human Development, 45,* 70–94.

Herting, M. M., & Sowell, E. R. (2017). Puberty and structural brain development in humans. *Frontiers in Neuroendocrinology, 44,* 122–137.

Hertz-Picciotto, I., Croen, L., Hansen, R., Jones, C., van de Water, J., & Pessah, I. (2006). The CHARGE study: An epidemiologic investigation of genetic and environmental factors contributing to autism. *Environmental Health Perspectives, 1141,* 1119–1125.

Hesse, E. (2008). The Adult Attachment Interview: Protocol, method of analysis, and empirical studies. In J. Cassidy & P. R. Shaver (Eds.), *Handbook of attachment: Theory, research and clinical applications* (2nd ed., pp. 552–598). New York, NY: Guilford Press.

Hesse, E. (2016). The Adult Attachment Interview. Protocol, method of analysis, and selected empirical studies: 1985–2015. In J. Cassidy & P. R. Shaver (Eds.), *Handbook of attachment: Theory, research, and clinical applications* (3rd ed., pp. 553–597). New York, NY: Guilford Press.

Hesse, E., & Main, M. (1999a). Frightened behavior in traumatizing but non-maltreating parents: Previously unexamined risk factor for offspring. In D. Diamond & S. J. Blatt (Eds.),

Psychoanalytic theory and attachment research I: Theoretical considerations. Psychoanalytic Inquiry, 19, 481–540.

Hesse, E., & Main, M. (1999b). Second generation effects of unresolved trauma in non-maltreating parents: Dissociative, frightened and threatening parental behavior. *Psychoanalytic Inquiry, 19,* 481–540.

Hesse, E., & Main, M. (2006). Frightened, threatening, and dissociative parental behavior in low-risk samples: Description, discussion, and interpretations. *Development and Psychopathology, 18*(2), 309–343.

Hetherington, E. M. (1998). Relevant issues in developmental science. *American Psychologist, 53,* 93–94.

Hetherington, E. M., Bridges, M., & Insabella, G. M. (1998). What matters? What does not? Five perspectives on the association between marital transitions and children's adjustment. *American Psychologist, 53,* 167–184.

Hetherington, E. M., & Kelly, J. (2002). *For better or for worse.* New York, NY: Norton.

Hibel, L. C., Granger, D. A., Blair, C., Cox, M. J., and The Family Life Project Key Investigators. (2011). Maternal sensitivity buffers the adrenocortical implications of intimate partner violence exposure during early childhood. *Development and Psychopathology, 23,* 689–701.

Hill, A. M. (1992). Chinese funerals and Chinese ethnicity in Chiang Mai, Thailand. *Ethnology, 31,* 315–330.

Hill, J. P., & Lynch, M. E. (1983). The intensification of gender-related role expectations during early adolescence. In J. Brooks-Gunn & A. C. Petersen (Eds.), *Girls at puberty: Biological and psychosocial perspectives* (pp. 201–228). New York, NY: Plenum Press.

Hill, M. S., & Yeung, W. J. (1999). How has the changing structure of opportunities affected transitions to adulthood? In A. Booth, A. C. Crouter, & M. J. Shanahan (Eds.), *Transitions to adulthood in a changing economy: No work, no family, no future?* (pp. 3–39). Westport, CT: Praeger.

Hill, P. C., Pargament, K. I., Wood, R. W., Jr., McCullough, M. E., Swyers, J. P., Larson, D., et al. (2000). Conceptualizing religion and spirituality: Points of commonality, points of departure. *Journal of Theory in Social Behavior, 30,* 51–77.

Hill, P. L., & Roberts, B. W. (2010). Propositions for the study of moral personality development. *Current Directions in Psychological Science, 19,* 380–383.

Hill, S. E., & Flom, R. (2007). 18- and 24-month-olds' discrimination of gender-consistent and inconsistent activities. *Infant Behavior & Development, 30,* 168–173.

Hilt, L. M., Armstrong, J. M., & Essex, M. J. (2017). Rumination and moderators of multifinality: Predicting internalizing symptoms and alcohol use during adolescence. *Journal of Clinical Child & Adolescent Psychology, 46,* 746–753.

Hindman, A. H., Miller, A. L., Froyen, L. C., & Skibbe, L. E. (2012). A portrait of family involvement during Head Start: Nature, extent, and predictors. *Early Childhood Research Quarterly, 27,* 654–667. doi:10.1016/j.ecresq.2011.11.002

Hines, K. A., McCarthy Veach, P., & LeRoy, B. S. (2010). Genetic counselors' perceived responsibilities regarding reproductive issues for patients at risk for Huntington disease. *Journal of Genetic Counseling, 19,* 131–147.

Hines, M. (2011). Prenatal endocrine influences on sexual orientation and on sexually differentiated childhood behavior. *Frontiers in Neuroendocrinology, 32,* 170–182.

Hines, M., Constantinescu, M., & Spencer, D. (2015). Early androgen exposure and human gender development. *Biology of Sex Differences, 6,* 3–13. doi:10.1186/s13293-015-0022-1

Hingson, R. W. (2010). Magnitude and prevention of college drinking and related problems. *Alcohol Research & Health, 33,* 45–54.

Hintikka, J., Koskela, T., Kontula, O., Koskela, K., & Viinamaeki, H. (2000). Men, women and friends: Are there differences in relation to mental well-being? *Quality of Life Research, 9,* 841–845.

Hirsh-Pasek, K., Adamson, L. B., Bakeman, R., Owen, M. T., Golinkoff, R. M., Pace, A., . . . Suma, K. (2015). The contribution of early communication quality to low-income children's language success. *Psychological Science, 26,* 1071–1083.

Hirsh-Pasek, K., Golinkoff, R. M., Berk, L. E., & Singer, D. G. (2009). *A mandate for playful learning in preschool: Presenting the evidence.* New York, NY: Oxford University Press.

Hobfoll, S. E. (1989). Conservation of resources: A new attempt at conceptualizing stress. *American Psychologist, 44*(3), 513–524.

Hobfoll, S. E., Canetti-Nisim, D., & Johnson, R. J. (2006). Exposure to terrorism, stress-related mental health symptoms, and defensive coping among Jews and Arabs in Israel. *Journal of Consulting and Clinical Psychology, 74,* 207–218.

Hobfoll, S. E., Stevens, N. R., & Zalta, A. K. (2015). Expanding the science of resilience: Conserving resources in the aid of adaptation. *Psychological Inquiry, 26*(2), 174–180.

Hobfoll, S. E., Watson, P., Bell, C. C., Bryant, R. A., Brymer, M. J., Friedman, et al. (2007). Five essential elements of immediate and mid-term mass trauma intervention: Empirical evidence. *Psychiatry 70,* 283–315.

Hofer, J., Busch, H., Au, A., Solcova, I. P., Tavel, P., & Wong, T. T. (2016). Generativity does not necessarily satisfy all your needs: Associations among cultural demand for generativity, generative concern, generative action, and need satisfaction in the elderly in four cultures. *Developmental Psychology, 52,* 509–519.

Hoffman, M. L. (1982). Development of prosocial motivation: Empathy and guilt. In N. Eisenberg (Ed.), *The development of prosocial behavior* (pp. 281–313). New York, NY: Academic Press.

Hoffman, M. L. (1983). Affective and cognitive processes in moral internalization. In E. T. Higgins, D. Ruble, & W. Hartup (Eds.), *Social cognition and social development: A sociocultural perspective* (pp. 236–274). New York, NY: Cambridge University Press.

Hofmann, A. D. (1997). Adolescent growth and development. In A. D. Hofmann & D. E. Greydanus (Eds.), *Adolescent medicine* (3rd ed.). Stamford, CT: Appleton and Lange.

Holbrook, M., & Schindler, R. M. (1989). Some exploratory findings on the development of musical taste. *Journal of Consumer Research, 16,* 119–124.

Holden, G. W., Brown, A. S., Baldwin, A. S., & Caderao, K. C. (2014). Research findings can change attitudes about corporal punishment. *Child Abuse and Neglect, 38,* 902–908.

Holden, G. W., Williamson, P. A., & Holland, G.W. (2014). Eavesdropping on the family: A pilot investigation of corporal punishment in the home. *Journal of Family Psychology, 28,* 401–406.

Holland, A. S., Fraley, R. C., & Roisman, G. I. (2012). Attachment styles in dating couples: Predicting relationship functioning over time. *Personal Relationships, 19,* 234–246.

Holland, A. S., & Roisman, G. I. (2010). Adult attachment security and young adults' dating relationships over time: Self-reported, observational, and physiological evidence. *Developmental Psychology, 46,* 552–557.

Holland, J. L. (1997). *Making vocational choices: A theory of vocational personalities and work environments* (3rd ed.). Odessa, FL: Psychological Assessment Resources.

Hollifield, M., Gory, A., Siedjak, J., Nguyen, L., Holmgreen, L., & Hobfoll, S. (2016). The benefit of conserving and gaining resources after trauma: A systematic review. *Journal of Clinical Medicine, 5*(11), 104.

Holloway, R. G., Arnold, R. M., Creutzfeldt, C. J., Lewis, E. F., Lutz, B. J., McCann, R. M., . . . Zorowitz, R. D. (2014). Palliative and end-of-life care in stroke. *Stroke, 45,* 1887–1916.

Holmes, B. M., & Johnson, K. R. (2009). Adult attachment and romantic partner preference: A review. *Journal of Social and Personal Relationships, 26,* 833–852.

Holmes, T. H., & Rahe, R. H. (1967). The Social Readjustment Rating Scale. *Journal of Psychosomatic Research, 11,* 213–218.

Holt-Lunstad, J., & Smith, T. B. (2012). Social relationships and mortality. *Social and Personality Psychology Compass, 6,* 41–53.

Holtzman, C. W., Trotman, H. D., Goulding, S. M., Ryan, A. T., MacDonald, A. N., Shapiro, D. I., . . . Walker, E. F. (2013). Stress and neurodevelopmental processes in the emergence of psychosis. *Neuroscience, 249,* 172–191.

Hölzel, B. K., Lazar, S. W., Gard, T., Schuman-Olivier, Z., Vago, D. R., & Ott, U. (2011). How does mindfulness meditation work? Proposing mechanisms of action from a conceptual and neural perspective. *Perspectives on Psychological Science 6,* 537–559.

Hong, S., & Na, J. (2017). How Facebook is perceived and used by people across cultures: The implications of cultural differences in the use of Facebook. *Social Psychological & Personality Science.* doi:10.1177/1948550617711227

Hook, J. N., Davis, D., Owen, J., & DeBlaere, C. (2017). *Cultural humility: Engaging diverse identities in therapy.* Washington, DC: American Psychological Association.

Hooker, S., & Brand, B. (2009). *Success at every step: How 23 programs support youth on the path to college and beyond.* Washington, DC: American Youth Policy Forum.

Hoorn, J., Dijk, E., Meuwese, R., Rieffe, C., & Crone, E. A. (2016). Peer influence on prosocial behavior in adolescence. *Journal of Research on Adolescence, 26,* 90–100.

Hopkins, S. L., & Lawson, M. J. (2002). Explaining the acquisition of a complex skill: Methodological and theoretical considerations uncovered in the study of simple addition and the moving-on process. *Educational Psychology Review, 14*, 121–154.

Hopmeyer, A., & Medovoy, T. (2017). Emerging adults' self-identified peer crowd affiliations, risk behavior, and social–emotional adjustment in college. *Emerging Adulthood, 5*(2), 143–148.

Hopmeyer, A., Troop-Gordon, W., Medovoy, T., & Fischer, J. (2017). Emerging adults' self-identified peer crowd affiliations and college adjustment. *Social Psychology of Education, 20*(3), 643–667.

Hopmeyer, E., & Werk, A. (1994). A comparative study of family bereavement groups. *Death Studies, 18*, 243–256.

Hoppmann, C. A., Gerstorf, D., Willis, S. L., & K. W. Schaie (2011). Spousal interrelations in happiness in the Seattle Longitudinal Study: Considerable similarities in levels and change over time. *Developmental Psychology, 47*, 1–8.

Horn, J. L., & Cattell, R. B. (1966). Refinement and test of the theory of fluid and crystallized intelligence. *Journal of Educational Psychology, 57*, 253–270.

Hornig, M., Briese, T., Buie, T., Bauman, M. L., Lauwers, G., et al. (2008). Lack of association between measles virus vaccine and autism with enteropathy: A case-control study. *PLoS ONE, 3*: e3140.doi:10.1371/journal .pone.0003140

Horowitz, M. J., Siegel, B., Holen, A., Bonanno, G. A., Milbrath, C., & Stinson, C. H. (1997). Diagnostic criteria for complicated grief disorder. *American Journal of Psychiatry, 154*, 904–910.

Horwitz, B. N., Reynolds, C. A., Walum, H., Ganiban, J., Spotts, E. L., Reiss, D., . . . Neiderhiser, J. M. (2016). Understanding the role of mate selection processes in couples' pair-bonding behavior. *Behavior Genetics, 46*, 143–149.

Houck, J. M., Forcehimes, A. A., Davis, M. M. A., & Bogenschutz, M. (2016). Qualitative and quantitative feedback following workshop training in evidence-based practices: A dissemination study. *Professional Psychology: Research and Practice, 47*, 413–417.

Howes, C., & Olenick, M. (1986). Family and child care influences on toddler's compliance. *Child Development, 57*, 202–216.

Hoyme, H. E., Kalberg, W. O., Elliott, A. J., Blandenship, J., Buckley, D., Marais, A.-S., . . . May, P. A. (2016). Updated clinical guidelines for diagnosing fetal alcohol spectrum disorders. *Pediatrics, 138*, e20154256-e20154256 . doi:10.1542/peds.2015-4256

Hsing-Yi, C. H., Chiou, C., & Chen, N. (2010). Impact of mental health and caregiver burden on family caregivers' physical health. *Archives of Gerontology and Geriatrics 50*, 267–271.

Hudson, J. I., Hiripi, E., Pope, H. G., & Kessler, R. C. (2007). The prevalence and correlates of eating disorders in the national comorbidity survey replication. *Biological Psychiatry, 61*(3), 348–358.

Hudson, N. W., Lucas, R. E., Donnellan, M. B., & Kushlev, K. (2016). Income reliably predicts daily sadness, but not happiness: A replication and extension of Kushlev, Dunn, and Lucas (2015). *Social Psychological and Personality Science, 7*(8), 828–836.

Hughes, C., & Devine, R. T. (2015). A social perspective on theory of mind. In R. M. Lerner (Ed. In Chief) & W. Damon (Vol. Ed.), *Handbook of child psychology and developmental science: Vol. 3. Socioemotional processes* (7th ed., pp. 563–609). Hoboken, NJ: Wiley.

Hughes, C., Roman, G., & Ensor, R. (2014). Parenting and executive function: Positive and negative influences. In S. H. Landry & C. L. Cooper (Eds.), *Wellbeing: A complete reference guide. Vol 1. Wellbeing in children and families* (pp. 131–156). Oxford, England: John Wiley & Sons.

Hughes, D., & Chen, L. A. (1999). The nature of parents' race-related communications to children: A developmental perspective. In L. Bolter & C. S. Tamis-LeMonda (Eds.), *Child psychology: A handbook of contemporary issues* (pp. 467–490). Philadelphia, PA: Psychology Press.

Hughes, D., Rodriguez, J., Smith, E. P., Johnson, D. J., Stevenson, H. C., & Spicer, P. (2006). Parents' ethnic-racial socialization practices: A review of research and directions for future study. *Developmental Psychology, 42*, 747–770.

Hughes I. A., Houk, C., Ahmed, S. F., & Lee, P. A. (2006). Consensus statement on management of intersex disorders. *Archives of Diseases in Childhood, 91*, 554–563.

Hulanicka, B. (1999). Acceleration of menarcheal age of girls from dysfunctional families. *Journal of Reproductive and Infant Psychology, 17*, 119–132.

Humes, L. E. (2015). Age-related changes in cognitive and sensory processing: Focus on middle-aged adults. *American Journal of Audiology, 24*, 94–97.

Hummer, D. L., & Lee, T. M. (2016). Daily timing of the adolescent sleep phase: Insights from a cross-species comparison. *Neuroscience and Biobehavioral Reviews, 70*, 171–181.

Hummert, M. L. (1999). A social cognitive perspective on age stereotypes. In T. M. Hess & F. Blanchard-Fields (Eds.), *Social cognition and aging* (pp. 176–196). San Diego, CA: Academic Press.

Hummert, M. L. (2011). Age stereotypes and aging. In K. W. Schaie & S. L. Willis (Eds.), *Handbook of the Psychology of Aging* (7th ed., pp. 249–262).London: Elsevier.

Hummert, M. L., Garstka, T. A., & Shaner, J. L. (1997). Stereotyping of older adults: The role of target facial cues and perceiver characteristics. *Psychology and Aging, 12*, 107–114.

Hummert, M. L., Garstka, T. A., Shaner, J. L., & Strahm, S. (1994). Stereotypes of the elderly held by young, middle-aged, and elderly adults. *Journal of Gerontology: Psychological Sciences, 49*, P240–P249.

Hummert, M. L., Shaner, J. L., Garstka, T. A., & Henry, C. (1998). Communication with older adults: The influence of age stereotypes, context, and communicator age. *Human Communication Research, 25*, 124–151.

Hunter, D. J., McDougall, J. J., & Keefe, F. J. (2008). The symptoms of osteoarthritis and the genesis of pain. *Rheumatic Disease Clinics, 34*, 623–643.

Hurtado, N., Marchman, V. A., & Fernald, A. (2008). Does input influence uptake? Links between maternal talk, processing speed and vocabulary size in Spanish-learning children. *Developmental Science, 11*, F31–F39.

Hurtado, S., Cuellar, M., & Guillermo-Wann, C. (2011). Quantitative measures of students' sense of validation: Advancing the study of diverse learning environments. *Enrollment Management Journal, 5*, 53–71.

Huston, A. C., Bobbit, K. C., & Bentley, A. (2015). Time spent in child care: How and why does it affect social development? *Developmental Psychology, 51*, 621–634.

Huttenlocher, J., & Smiley, P. (1990). Emerging notions of persons. In N. L. Stein, B. Leventhal, & T. Trabasso (Eds.), *Psychological and biological approaches to emotion* (pp. 283–295).

Huurneman, B., & Boonstra, F. N. (2016). Assessment of near visual acuity in 0–13 year olds with normal and low vision: A systematic review. *Ophthalmology, 16*, 215.

Hwang, N., & Domina, T. (2017/2016). The links between youth employment and educational attainment across racial groups. *Journal of Research on Adolescence, 27*(2), 312–327.

Hyde, J. S. (2014). Gender similarities and differences. *Annual Review of Psychology, 65*, 373–398.

Hyde, J. S., & Else-Quest, N. (2012). *Half the human experience: The psychology of women* (8th ed.). Belmont, CA: Wadsworth.

Hyde, J. S., Fennema, E., & Lamon, S. J. (1990). Gender differences in mathematics performance: A meta-analysis. *Psychological Bulletin, 107*, 139–155.

Hyman, I. E., & Faries, J. M. (1992). The function of autobiographical memory. In M. A. Conway, D. C. Rubin, H. Spinnler, & W. A. Wagenaar (Eds.), *Theoretical perspectives on autobiographical memory* (pp. 207–221). Boston, MA: Kluwer Academic Press.

Hyson, M., Copple, C., & Jones, J. (2006). Early childhood development and education. In W. Damon & R. M. Lerner (Series Eds.), K. A. Renninger & I. E. Sigel (Vol. Eds.), *Handbook of child psychology: Vol. 4. Child psychology in practice* (6th ed., pp. 3–47). Hoboken, NJ: Wiley.

Imada, T., Carlson, S. M., & Itakura, S. (2013). East-West cultural differences in context-sensitivity are evident in early childhood. *Developmental Science, 16*, 198–208.

Ingersoll-Dayton, B., Neal, M. B., Ha, J., & Hammer, L. B. (2003). Redressing inequity in parent care among siblings. *Journal of Marriage and Family, 65*, 201–212.

Ingles, J., Spinks, C., Yeates, L., McGeechan, K., Kasparian, N., & Semsarian, C. (2016). Posttraumatic stress and prolonged grief after the sudden cardiac death of a young relative. *JAMA Internal Medicine, 176*, 402–405.

Ingram, R. E., & Price, J. M. (2001). *Vulnerability to psychopathology: Risk across the lifespan*. New York, NY: Guilford Press.

Inhelder, B., & Piaget, J. (1955/1958). *The growth of logical thinking from childhood to adolescence*. New York, NY: Basic Books.

Inhelder, B., & Piaget, P. (1964). *The early growth of logic in the child*. New York, NY: Harper & Row.

Inman, A. G., Yeh, C. J., Madan-Bahel, A., & Nath, S. (2007). Bereavement and coping of South Asian families post 9/11. *Journal of Multicultural Counseling and Development, 35*, 101–115.

Institute of Medicine. (1994). *Reducing risks for mental disorders: Frontiers for preventive intervention research.* Washington, DC: National Academy Press.

Institute of Medicine (IOM). (2012). *Treatment for posttraumatic stress disorder in military and veteran populations: Initial assessment.*

Isen, J. D., McGuie, M. K., & Iacono, W. G. (2015). Aggressive-antisocial boys develop into physically strong young men. *Psychological Science, 26,* 444–455.

Ispas, D., Iliescu, D., Ilie, A., & Johnson, R. E. (2014). Exploring the cross-cultural generalizability of the five-factor model of personality: The Romanian NEO PI-R. *Journal of Cross-Cultural Psychology, 45,* 1074–1088.

Ito, T., Ando, H., & Handa, H. (2011). Teratogenic effects of thalidomide: Molecular mechanisms. *Cellular and Molecular Life Sciences.* doi:10.1007/s00018-010-0619-9

Izard, C. E. (1979). *The maximally discriminative facial movement coding system (Max).* Newark, DE: University of Delaware, Information Technologies and University Media Services.

Izard, C. E. (1991). *The psychology of emotions.* New York, NY: Plenum Press.

Izard, C. E. (1992). Basic emotions, relations among emotions, and emotion-cognition relations. *Psychological Review, 99,* 561–565.

Izard, C. E. (2004). The generality-specificity issue in infants' emotion responses: A comment on Bennett, Bendersky, and Lewis, 2002. *Infancy, 6,* 417–423.

Izard, C. E. (2007). Basic emotions, natural kinds, emotion schemas, and a new paradigm. *Perspectives on Psychological Science, 2,* 260–277.

Izard, C. E. (2009). Emotion theory and research: Highlights, unanswered questions, and emerging issues. *Annual Review of Psychology, 60,* 1–25.

Izard, C. E. (2011). Forms and functions of emotions: Matters of emotion-cognition interactions. *Emotion Review, 3,* 371–378.

Izard, C. E., Dougherty, L. M., & Hembree, E. A. (1983). *A system for identifying affect expression by holistic judgments (Affex).* Newark, DE: University of Delaware, Computer Network Services and University Media Services.

Izard, C. E., & Malatesta, C. Z. (1987). Perspectives on emotional development I: Differential emotions theory of early emotional development. In J. D. Osofsky (Ed.), *Handbook of infant development* (2nd ed., pp. 494–554). New York, NY: Wiley.

Jaccard, J., Lushin, V., & Kaploun, V. (2017). Parental monitoring, adolescent dishonesty and underage drinking: A nationally representative study. *Journal of Adolescence, 57,* 99.

Jackson, L. A., von Eye, A., Biocca, F. A., Barbatsis, G., Zhao, Y., & Fitzgerald, H. E. (2006). Does home Internet use influence the academic performance of low-income children? *Developmental Psychology, 42,* 429–435.

Jackson, M. I., Kiernan, K., & McLanahan, S. (2012). Immigrant-native differences in child health: Does maternal education narrow or widen the gap? *Child Development, 8,* 1501–1509.

Jacobs, J. A., & Stoner-Eby, S. (1998). Adult enrollment in higher education and cumulative educational attainment, 1970–1990. *The Annals of the Academy of Political and Social Science, 559,* 91–108.

Jacobs, J. E., Lanza, S., Osgood, D. W., Eccles, J. A., & Wigfield, A. (2002). Changes in children's self-competence and values: Gender and domain differences across grades one through twelve. *Child Development, 73,* 509–527.

Jacobson, N. C., & Newman. M. G. (2017). Anxiety and depression as bidirectional risk factors for one another: A meta-analysis of longitudinal studies. *Psychological Bulletin, 143*(11), 1155–1200.

Jacobson, N. S., & Christensen, A. (1996). *Integrative couple therapy: Promoting acceptance and change.* New York, NY: Norton.

Jacobvits, D., Leon, K., & Hazen, N. (2006). Does expectant mothers' unresolved trauma predict frightened/frightening maternal behavior? Risk and protective factors. *Development and Psychopathology, 18,* 363–379.

Jaeger, A., Eisenkraemer, R. E., & Stein, L. M. (2015). Test-enhanced learning in third-grade children. *Educational Psychology, 35,* 513–521.

Jäger, D. T., & Rüsseler, J. (2016). Low arousing positive affect broadens visual attention and alters the thought-action repertoire while broadened visual attention does not. *Frontiers in Psychology, 7,* Article 1652.

Jahromi, L. B., Putnam, S. P., & Stifter, C. A. (2004). Maternal regulation of infant reactivity from 2 to 6 months. *Developmental Psychology, 40,* 477–487.

Jahromi, L. B., & Stifter, C. A. (2007). Individual differences in the contribution of maternal soothing to infant distress reduction. *Infancy, 11,* 255–269.

Jakubiak, B. K., & Feeney, B. C. (2016). Daily goal progress is facilitated by spousal support and promotes psychological, physical, and relational well-being throughout adulthood. *Journal of Personality and Social Psychology, 111,* 317–340.

Jambon, M., & Smetana, J. G. (2014). Moral complexity in middle childhood: Children's evaluations of necessary harm. *Developmental Psychology, 50,* 22–33.

James, A., & Brookfield, S. (2014). *Engaging imagination: Helping students become creative and reflective thinkers.* San Francisco, CA: Jossey-Bass.

James, S. L. (2015). Variation in trajectories of women's marital quality. *Social Science Research, 49,* 16–30.

James, W. (1890). *Principles of psychology.* Chicago, IL: Encyclopedia Britannica.

Janoff-Bulman, R. (1993). *Shattered assumptions: Toward a new psychology of trauma.* New York, NY: Free Press.

Jansen, J., de Weerth, C., & Riksen-Walraven, J. M. (2011). Breastfeeding and the mother-infant relationship: A review. *Developmental Review, 28,* 503–521.

Janssen, S. M. J., Chessa, A. G., & Murre, J. M. J. (2007). Temporal distribution of favorite books, movies, and records: Differential encoding and re-sampling. *Memory, 15,* 755–767.

Janssens, A., Goossens, L., Van Den Noortgate, W., Colpin, H., Verschueren, K., & VanLeeuwen, K. (2015). Parents' and adolescents' perspectives on parenting. *Assessment, 22,* 473–489.

Jara-Ettinger, J., Piantadosi, S., Spelke, E. S., Levy, R., & Gibson, E. (2016). Mastery of the logic of natural numbers is not the result of mastery of counting: Evidence from late counters. *Developmental Science, 20*(6). doi:10.1111/desc.12459

Jensen, L. A. (2008). Through two lenses: A cultural-developmental approach to moral psychology. *Developmental Review, 28,* 289–315.

Jensen, L. A. (2012). Bridging universal and cultural perspectives: A vision for developmental psychology in a global world. *Child Development Perspectives, 6,* 98–104.

Jessor, R., Donovan, J. E., & Costa, F. M. (1991). *Beyond adolescence: Problem behavior and young adult development.* New York: Cambridge University Press.

Jewell, J. A., & Brown, C. S. (2014). Relations among gender typicality, peer relations, and mental health during early adolescence. *Social Development, 23,* 137–156.

Ji, L. J., Zhang, Z., & Nisbett, R. E. (2004). Is it culture or is it language? Examination of language effects in cross-cultural research on categorization. *Journal of Personality and Social Psychology, 87,* 57–65.

Jia, Y., Konold, T. R., & Cornell, D. (2016). Authoritative school climate and high school dropout rates. *School Psychology Quarterly, 31*(2), 289–303.

Jin, M. K., Jacobvitz, D., Hazen, N., & Jung, S. H. (2012). Maternal sensitivity and infant attachment security in Korea: Cross-cultural validation of the strange situation. *Attachment & Human Development, 14,* 33–44.

Johns, M., Inzlicht, M., & Schmader, T. (2008). Stereotype threat and executive resource depletion: Examining the influence of emotion regulation. *Journal of Experimental Psychology: General, 137,* 691–705.

Johnson, A., & Ames, E. (1994). The influence of gender labeling on preschoolers' gender constancy judgments. *British Journal of Developmental Psychology, 12,* 241–249.

Johnson, C. L., & Troll, L. (1994). Constraints and facilitators to friendships in late, late life. *The Gerontologist, 34,* 79–87.

Johnson, R. W., & Favreault, M. M. (2004). Economic status in later life among women who raised children outside of marriage. *Journals of Gerontology: Series B: Psychological Sciences & Social Sciences, 59,* 315–323.

Johnson, S. M. (2004). *The practice of emotionally focused couple therapy: Creating connection* (2nd ed.). New York, NY: Brunner-Routledge.

Johnson, S. M., Hunsley, J., Greenberg, L., & Schindler, D. (1999). Emotionally-focused couples therapy: Status and challenges. *Clinical Psychology: Science and Practice, 6,* 67–79.

Johnson, S. M., & Lebow, J. (2000). The "coming of age" of couple therapy: A decade review. *Journal of Marital and Family Therapy, 26,* 23–38.

Johnson, S. P. (2003). The nature of cognitive development. *Trends in Cognitive Science, 7,* 102–104.

Johnston, C., & Ohan, J. L. (1999). Externalizing disorders. In W. K. Silverman & T. H. Ollendick (Eds.), *Developmental issues in the clinical treatment of children* (pp. 279–294). Needham Heights, MA: Allyn & Bacon.

Joliffe, D., & Farrington, D. P. (2006). Examining the relationship between low empathy and bullying. *Aggressive Behavior, 32,* 540–550.

Jones, A. C., Wardlow, L., Pan, S. C., Zepeda, C., Heyman, G. D., Dunlosky, J., & Rickard, T. C. (2016). Beyond the rainbow: Retrieval practice leads to better spelling than does rainbow writing. *Educational Psychology Review, 28,* 385–400.

Jones, D. N. (2016). The 'Chasing Amy' bias in past sexual experiences: Men can change, women cannot. *Sexuality & Culture, 20,* 24–37.

Jones, H. E., & Conrad, H. (1933). The growth and decline of intelligence: A study of a homogeneous group between the ages of ten and sixty. *Genetic Psychological Monographs 13,* 223–298.

Jones, J. D., Cassidy, J., & Shaver, P. R. (2015). Parents' self-reported attachment styles: A review of links with parenting behaviors, emotions, and cognitions. *Personality and Social Psychology Review, 19,* 44–76.

Jones, J. M. (2017). In the U.S., 10.2% of LGBT adults now married to same-sex spouse. *Social & Policy Issues.* Available from http://news.gallup.com/poll/212702/lgbt-adults-married-sex-spouse.aspx?g_source=Social+Issues&g_medium=newsfeed&g_campaign=tiles

Jones, K., Daley, D., Hutchings, J., Bywater, T., & Eames, C. (2008). Efficacy of the Incredible Years Programme as an early intervention for children with conduct problems and ADHD: Long-term follow-up. *Child: Care, Health and Development 33,* 749–756.

Jones, S., Brush, K., Bailey, R., Brion-Meisels, G., McIntyre, J., Kahn, J., . . . Stickle, L. (2017). *Navigating social emotional learning from the inside out: looking inside and across 25 leading SEL programs: A practical resource for schools and OST providers (Elementary School Focus).* Cambridge, MA: Harvard Graduate School of Education.

Jones, W., & Klin, A. (2013). Attention to eyes is present but in decline in 2-6-month-old infants later diagnosed with autism. *Nature, 504,* 427–431.

Josephs, L. (2018). *The dynamics of infidelity: Applying relationship science to psychotherapy practice.* Washington, DC: American Psychological Association.

Josephs, R. A., Sellers, J. G., Newman, M. L., & Mehta, P. H. (2006). The mismatch effect: When testosterone and status are at odds. *Journal of Personality and Social Psychology, 90,* 999–1013.

Josselson, R. L. (1994). The theory of identity development and the question of intervention: An introduction. In S. Archer (Ed.), *Interventions for adolescent identity development* (pp. 12–25). Thousand Oaks, CA: Sage.

Juárez, F., & Gayet, C. (2014). Transitions to adulthood in developing countries. *Annual Review of Sociology, 40,* 521–538.

Judge, T. A., & Livingston, B. A. (2008). Is the gap more than gender? A longitudinal analysis of gender, gender role orientation, and earnings. *Journal of Applied Psychology, 93,* 994–1012.

Juffer, F., Bakermans-Kranenburg, M. J., & van IJzendoorn, M. H. (2007). *Promoting positive parenting: An attachment-based intervention.* Mahwah, NJ: Lawrence Erlbaum.

Jung, C. G. (1963). *Memories, dreams, reflections.* New York, NY: Random House.

Jung, S., Fuller, B., & Galindo, C. (2012). Family functioning and early learning practices in immigrant homes. *Child Development, 83,* 1510–1526.

Juraska, J. M., & Willing, J. (2017). Pubertal onset as a critical transition for neural development and cognition. *Brain Research, 1654,* 87–94.

Jurecic, A. (2015). No protocol for grief. *The Lancet, 386,* 848–849.

Kabat-Zinn, J. (1994). *Wherever you go, there you are.* New York, NY: Hyperion.

Kabat-Zinn, J. (2003). Mindfulness-based interventions in context: Past, present and future. *Clinical Psychology: Science and Practice, 10,* 144–156.

Kabat-Zinn, J. (2005). *Coming to our Senses: Healing ourselves and the world through mindfulness.* New York, N.Y.: Hachette Books.

Kaffman, A., & Meaney, M. J. (2007). Neurodevelopmental sequelae of postnatal maternal care in rodents: Clinical and research implications of molecular insights. *Journal of Child Psychology and Psychiatry, 48,* 224–244.

Kagan, J. (1984). *The nature of the child.* New York, NY: Basic Books.

Kagan, J. (1994). Yesterday's premises: Tomorrow's promises. In R. D. Parke, R. A. Ornstein, J. J. Rieser, & C. Sahn-Waxler (Eds.), *A century of developmental psychology* (pp. 551–568). Washington, DC: American Psychological Association.

Kagan, J., & Fox, N. A. (2006). Biology, culture, and temperamental biases. In W. Damon & R. M. Lerner (Series Eds.), N. Eisenberg (Vol. Ed.), *Handbook of child psychology: Vol. 3. Social, emotional, and personality development* (6th ed., pp. 167–225). Hoboken, NJ: Wiley.

Kagan, J., Snidman, N., Kahn, V., & Towsley, S. (2007). The preservation of two infant temperaments into adolescence. *Monographs of the Society for Research in Child Development, 72,* 1–75.

Kagan, S. L., & Kauerz, K. (2007). Reaching for the whole: Integration and alignment in early education policy. In R. C. Pianta, M. J. Cox, & K. L. Snow (Eds.), *School readiness and the transition to kindergarten in the era of accountability* (pp. 11–30). Baltimore, MD: Brookes.

Kahneman, D. (2011). *Thinking fast and slow.* New York, NY: Farrar, Straus & Giroux.

Kahneman, D., & Deaton, A. (2010). High income improves evaluation of life but not emotional well-being. *Proceedings of the National Academy of Sciences of the United States of America, 107,* 16489–16493.

Kahneman, D., Krueger, A. B., Schkade, D., Schwarz, N., & Stone, A. (2004). A survey method for characterizing daily life experience: The day reconstruction method. *Science, 306,* 1776–1781.

Kahneman, D., & Tversky, A. (1984). Choices, values and frames. *American Psychologist, 39,* 341–350.

Kail, R. B., Lervåg, A., & Hulme, C. (2016). Longitudinal evidence linking processing speed to the development of reasoning. *Developmental Science, 19,* 1067–1074.

Kaiser, R. H., Andrews-Hanna, J. R., Wager, T. D., & Pizzagalli, D. A. (2015). Large-scale network dysfunction in major depressive disorder: A meta-analysis of resting-state functional connectivity. *JAMA Psychiatry, 72,* 603-611.

Kaiser Family Foundation. (2010). *Generation M2: Media in the lives of 8- to 18-year-olds.* Available from www.kff.org/entmedia/upload/8010.pdf

Kalish, R. A. (1985). The social context of death and dying. In R. H. Binstock & E. Shanas (Eds.), *Handbook of aging and the social sciences* (2nd ed., pp. 147–170). New York, NY: Van Nostrand Reinhold.

Kalmijn, M. (2015). Father-child relations after divorce in four European countries: Patterns and determinants. *Comparative Population Studies, 40,* 251–276.

Kamii, C. (1986). Place value: An explanation of its difficulty and educational implications for the primary grades. *Journal of Research in Childhood Education, 1,* 75–86.

Kamii, M. (1990). Why Big Bird can't teach calculus: The case of place value and cognitive development in the middle years. In N. Lauter-Klatell (Ed.), *Readings in child development* (pp. 101–104, 170). Mountain View, CA: Mayfield.

Kaminsky, M. (2014). *The uses of reminiscence: New ways of working with older adults.* New York, NY: Routledge.

Kandel, D. B. (1978). Homophily, selection, and socialization in adolescent friendships. *American Journal of Sociology, 84,* 427–436.

Kane, R. S. (1996). The defeat of aging versus the importance of death. *Journal of the American Geriatric Society, 44,* 321–325.

Kann, L., Kinchen, S., Shanklin, S. L., Flint, K. H., Hawkins, J., Harris, W. A., . . . Wechsler, H. (2014). Youth risk behavior surveillance—United States, 2013. *Morbidity and Mortality Weekly Report, 63*(4), 1–168.

Kann, L., McManus, T., Harris, W. A., Shanklin, S. L., Flint, K. H., Hawkins, J., . . . Wechsler, H. (2016). Youth risk behavior surveillance—United States, 2015. *MMWR Surveillance Summaries, 65*(SS-6), 1–174.

Kann, L., Olsen, E. O., McManus, T., Harris, W. A., Shanklin, S. L., Flint, K. H., . . . Zaza, S. (2016). Sexual identity, sex of sexual contacts, and health-related behavior among students in grades 9-12 – United States and selected sites, 2015. *MMWR Surveillance Summaries, 65*(SS-9), 1–202.

Kanner, L. (1943). Autistic disturbances of affective contact. *The Nervous Child, 2,* 217–250.

Kapan, R. M., Fang, Z., & Kirby, J. (2017). Educational attainment and health outcomes: Data from the medical expenditures panel survey. *Health Psychology, 36,* 598–608.

Karantzas, G. C., McCabe, M. P., Karantzas, K. M., Pizzirani, B., Campbell, H., & Mullins, E. R. (2016). Attachment style and less severe forms of sexual coercion: A systematic review. *Archives of Sexual Behavior, 45,* 1053–1068.

Karbach, J., & Verhaeghen, P. (2014). Making working memory work: A meta-analysis of executive-control and working memory training in older adults. *Psychological Science, 25,* 2027–2037.

Karen, R. (1998). *Becoming attached: First relationships and how they shape our capacity to love.* New York, NY: Oxford University Press.

Karney, B. R. (2015). Why marriages change over time. In M. Mikulincer & P. R. Shaver (Eds.), J. A. Simpson & J. F. Dovidio (Vol. Eds.), *APA handbook of personality and social psychology: Vol. 3. Interpersonal relations* (pp. 557–579). Washington, DC: American Psychological Association.

Karney, B. R., & Bradbury, T. N. (1997). Neuroticism, marital interaction, and the trajectory of marital satisfaction. *Journal of Personality and Social Psychology, 72,* 1075–1092.

Karson, G. L., Kung, T. F., & Hines, M. (2017). Childhood gender-typed behavior and adolescent sexual orientation: A longitudinal population-based study. *Developmental Psychology, 53*, 764–777.

Kashdan, T. B., Barrett, L. D., & McKnight, P. E. (2015). Unpacking emotion differentiation: Transforming unpleasant experience by perceiving distinctions in negativity. *Current Directions in Psychological Science, 24*, 10–16.

Kashdan, T. B., Blalock, D. V., Young, K. C., Machell, K. A., Monfort, S. S., McKnight, P. E., & Ferssizidis, P. (2017). Personality strengths in romantic relationships: Measuring perceptions of benefits and costs and their impact on personal and relational well-being. *Psychological Assessment.* http://dx.doi.org/10.1037/pas0000464

Kasser, T., & Ryan, R. M. (1996). Further examining the American dream: Differential correlates of intrinsic and extrinsic goals. *Personality and Social Psychology Bulletin, 22*, 280–287.

Katz, J., & Schneider, M. E. (2013). Casual hook up sex during the first year of college: Prospective associations with attitudes about sex and love relationships. *Archives of Sexual Behavior, 42*, 1451–1462.

Katz-Wise, S. L., Priess, H. A., & Hyde, J. S. (2010). Gender-role attitudes and behavior across the transition to parenthood. *Developmental Psychology, 46*, 18–28.

Kaufmann, M. C., Krings, F., & Sczesny, S. (2016). Looking too old? How an older age appearance reduces chances of being hired. *British Journal of Management, 27*, 727–739.

Kavalieratos, D., Corbelli, J., Zhang, D., Dionne-Odom, J. N., Ernecoff, N. C., Hanmer, J., . . . & Morton, S. C. (2016). Association between palliative care and patient and caregiver outcomes: A systematic review and meta-analysis. *JAMA, 316*, 2104–2114.

Kaye, W. H., Klump, K. L., Frank, G. K. W., & Strober, M. (2000). Anorexia and Bulimia Nervosa. *Annual Review of Medicine, 51*, 299–313.

Kazdin, A. E. (1991). Effectiveness of psychotherapy with children and adolescents. *Journal of Consulting and Clinical Psychology, 59*(6), 785–798.

Kazdin, A. E. (2003). Psychotherapy for children and adolescents. *Annual Review of Psychology, 54*, 273–276.

Kazdin, A. E. (2010). Problem-solving skills training and parent management training for oppositional defiant disorder and conduct disorder. In J. R. Weisz & A. E. Kazdin (Eds.), *Evidence-based psychotherapies for children and adolescents* (pp. 211–226). New York, NY: Guilford Press.

Keane, L., & Loades, M. (2017). Low self-esteem and internalizing disorders in young people – a systematic review. *Child and Adolescent Mental Health, 22*, 4–15.

Keane, T. M., Marshall, A. D., & Taft, C. T. (2006). Posttraumatic stress disorder: Etiology, epidemiology, and treatment outcome. *Annual review of clinical psychology, 2*, 161–197.

Kebir, O., Chaumette, B., & Krebs, M.-O. (2018). Epigenetic variability in conversion to psychosis: Novel findings from an innovative longitudinal methylomic analysis. *Translational Psychiatry, 8*. doi:10.1038/s41398-018-0138-2

Keel, P. K., Dorer, D. J., Eddy, K. T., Franko, D., Charatan, D. L., & Herzog, D. B. (2003). Predictors of mortality in eating disorders. *Archives of General Psychiatry, 60*, 179–183.

Keen, C. L., Uriu-Adams, J. Y., Skalny, A., Grabeklis, A., Grabeklis, S., Green, K., . . . Chambers, C. D. (2010). The plausibility of maternal nutritional status being a contributing factor to the risk for fetal alcohol spectrum disorders: The potential influence of zinc status as an example. *BioFactors, 36*, 125–135.

Keenan, K., & Shaw, D. (1997). Developmental and social influences on young girls' early problem behavior. *Psychological Bulletin, 121*, 95–113.

Kegan, R. (1982). *The evolving self.* Cambridge, MA: Harvard University Press.

Keijsers, L. G. M. T. (2016). Parental monitoring and adolescent problem behaviors: How much do we really know? *International Journal of Behavioral Development, 40*(3), 271–281.

Keller, H., & Otto, H. (2009). The cultural socialization of emotion regulation during infancy. *Journal of Cross-Cultural Psychology, 40*, 996–1011.

Kellett, J. M. (2000). Older adult sexuality. In L. T. Szuchman & F. Muscarella (Eds.), *Psychological perspectives on human sexuality* (pp. 355–379). New York, NY: Wiley.

Kelley, A. S., & Morrison, R. S. (2015). Palliative care for the seriously ill. *New England Journal of Medicine, 373*, 747–755.

Kelley, P., & Camilli, G. (2007). *The impact of teacher education on outcomes in center-based early childhood education programs: A meta-analysis.* A National Institute for Early Education Research Working Paper. Available from http://nieer.org/resources/research/Teacher_Ed.pdf

Kellman, P. J., & Arterberry, M. E. (2006). Infant visual perception. In W. Damon & R. Lerner (Series Eds.), D. Kuhn & R. Siegler (Vol. Eds.), *Handbook of child psychology: Vol. 2. Cognition, perception, and language* (6th ed., pp. 109–160). New York, NY: Wiley.

Kemeny, M. E. (2003). The psychobiology of stress. *Current Directions in Psychological Science, 12*, 124–129.

Kena, G., Aud, S., Johnson, F., Wang, X., Zhang, J., Rathbun, A., . . . Kristapovich, P. (2014). *Condition of Education 2014.* (NCES 2014-083).

Kendall, P. C. (1991). *Child and adolescent therapy.* New York, NY: Guilford Press.

Kendall, P. C. (1993). Cognitive-behavioral therapies with youth: Guiding theory, current status, and emerging developments. *Journal of Consulting and Clinical Psychology, 61*, 235–247.

Kendall, P. C. (2011). *Child and adolescent therapy: Cognitive-behavioural procedures* (4th ed.). New York, NY: Guilford Press.

Kendall, S., & Tannen, D. (1997). Gender and language in the workplace. In Wodack, R. (Ed.), *Gender and discourse* (pp. 81–105). London: Sage.

Kendler, K. S., Thornton, L. M., & Gardner, C. O. (2001). Genetic risk, number of previous depressive episodes, and stressful life events in predicting onset of major depression. *American Journal of Psychiatry, 158*, 582–586.

Keniston, K. (1971). *Youth in dissent: The rise of a new opposition.* New York, NY: Harcourt Brace Jovanovich.

Kennedy, G. J., & Tanenbaum, S. (2000). Psychotherapy with older adults. *American Journal of Psychotherapy, 54*, 386–407.

Kerig, P. K., Cowan, P. A., & Cowan, C. P. (1993). Marital quality and gender differences in parent–child interaction. *Developmental Psychology, 29*, 931–939.

Kernberg, O. (1976). *Object relations theory and clinical psychoanalysis.* New York, NY: Aronson.

Kerns, K. A., & Brumariu, L. E. (2016). Attachment in middle childhood. In J. Cassidy & P. R. Shaver (Eds.), *Handbook of attachment: Theory, research, and clinical applications* (3rd ed., pp. 349–365). New York, NY: Guilford Press.

Kerr, M., & Stattin, H., Institutionen för beteende-, social- och rättsvetenskap, & Örebro universitet. (2000). What parents know, how they know it, and several forms of adolescent adjustment: Further support for a reinterpretation of monitoring. *Developmental Psychology, 36*(3), 366–380.

Kerr, M., Stattin, H., Burk, W. J., Akademin för juridik, psykologi och socialt arbete, & Örebro universitet. (2010). A reinterpretation of parental monitoring in longitudinal perspective. *Journal of Research on Adolescence, 20*(1), 39–64.

Kessler, R. C., Berglund, P., Demler, O., Jin, R., Koretz, D., Merikangas, K. R., . . . Wang, P. S. (2003). The epidemiology of major depressive disorder: Results from the National Comorbidity Survey Replication (NCS-R). *JAMA, 289*, 3095–3105.

Keup, J. R., & Stolzenberg, E. B. (2004). *The 2003 Your First College Year (YFCY) survey: Exploring the academic and personal experiences of first-year students.* Los Angeles, CA: National Resource Center for The First-Year Experience & Students in Transition & Higher Education Research Institute at UCLA.

Keyes, C. L. M., & Haidt, J. (2003). *Flourishing: Positive psychology and the well-lived life.* Washington, DC: American Psychological Association.

Keyes, K. M., Vo, T., Wall, M. M., Caetano, R., Suglia, S., Martins, S. S., . . . Hasin, D. (2015). Racial/ethnic differences in use of alcohol, tobacco, and marijuana: Is there a cross-over from adolescence to adulthood? *Social Science & Medicine, 124*, 132–141.

Khoury, B., Lecomte, T., Fortin, G., Masse, M., Therien, P., Bouchard, V., . . . Hofmann, S. G. (2013). Mindfulness-based therapy: A comprehensive meta-analysis. *Clinical Psychology Review, 33*(6), 763–771.

Kiang, L., Tseng, V., & Yip, T. (2016). Placing Asian American child development within historical context. *Child Development, 87*, 995–1013.

Kidd, E., & Arciuli, J. (2016). Individual differences in statistical learning predict children's comprehension of syntax. *Child Development, 87*, 184–193.

Kiecolt-Glaser, J. K., Derry, H. M., & Fagundes, C. P. (2015). Inflammation: Depression fans the flames and feasts on the heat. *American Journal of Psychiatry, 172*(11), 1075–1091.

Kiecolt-Glaser, J. K., & Wilson, S. J. (2017). Lovesick: How couples' relationships influence health. *Annual Review of Clinical Psychology, 13*, 421–443.

Kievit, R. A., Davis, S. W., Griffiths, J., Correia, M. M., Cam-CAN, & Henson, R. N. (2016). A watershed model of individual differences in fluid intelligence. *Neuropsychologia, 91,* 186–198.

Kilford, E. J., Garrett, E., & Blakemore, S.-J. (2016). The development of social cognition in adolescence: An integrated perspective. *Neuroscience and Biobehavioral Reviews, 70,* 106–120.

Killen, M., & Rutland, A. (2011). *Children and social exclusion: Morality, prejudice, and group identity.* New York, NY: John Wiley & Sons.

Killen, M., & Smetana, J. (2008). Moral judgment and moral neuroscience: Intersections, definitions, and issues. *Child Development Perspectives, 2,* 1–6.

Killen M., & Smetana, J. G. (2015). Origins and development of morality. In R. M. Lerner (Series Ed.) & M. E. Lamb (Vol. Ed.), *Handbook of child psychology and developmental science: Volume 3. Socioemotional processes* (7th ed., pp. 1–49). Hoboken, NJ: Wiley.

Kilmartin, C. T. (1994). *The masculine self.* New York, NY: Macmillan.

Kim, F-R., Chow, S-M., Bray, B., & Teti, D. M. (2017). Trajectories of mothers' emotional availability: Relations with infant temperament in predicting attachment security. *Attachment & Human Development, 19,* 38–57.

Kim, H. J., Arnold, D. H., Fisher, P. H., & Zeljo, A. (2005). Parenting and preschoolers' symptoms as a function of child gender and SES. *Child & Family Behavior Therapy, 27,* 23–41.

Kim, H. S., Sherman, D. K., & Taylor, S. E. (2008). Culture and social support. *American Psychologist, 63,* 518–526.

Kim, J. J., & Enright, R. D. (2014). A theological and psychological defense of self-forgiveness: Implications for counseling. *Journal of Psychology and Theology, 42*(3), 260.

Kim, S., & Kochanska, G. (2017). Relational antecedents and social implications of the emotion of empathy: Evidence from three studies. *Emotion, 17,* 981–992.

Kim, S., Kochanska, G., Boldt, L. J., Nordling, J. K., & O'Bleness, J. J. (2014). Developmental trajectory from early responses to transgressions to future antisocial behavior: Evidence for the role of the parent-child relationship from two longitudinal studies. *Development and Psychopathology, 26,* 93–109.

Kim, Y., Calzada, E. J., Barajas-Gonzalez, R. G., Huang, K-Y., Brotman, L. M., . . . Pichardo, C. (2018). The role of authoritative and authoritarian parenting in the early academic achievement of Latino students. *Journal of Educational Psychology, 110,* 119–132.

Kim, Y. S., & State, M. W. (2014). Recent challenges to the diagnostic nosology: A focus on the genetics and genomics of neurodevelopmental disorders. *International Journal of Epidemiology, 43,* 465–475.

Kindlon, D., & Thompson, M. (1990). *Raising Cain: Protecting the emotional life of boys.* New York, NY: Ballantine Books.

King, P. E., & Boyatzis, C. J. (2015). Religious and spiritual development. In M. E. Lamb & R. M. Lerner (Eds.), *Handbook of child psychology and developmental science, Vol. 3: Socioemotional processes* (7th ed., pp. 975–1021). Hoboken, NJ: John Wiley & Sons.

King, P. M., & Howard-Hamilton, M. F. (1999). *Becoming a multiculturally competent student affairs professional.* Final report submitted to

the National Association of Student Personnel Administrators, 1999. Available from www.naspa.org

King, P. M., & Kitchener, K. S. (2002). The reflective judgment model: Twenty years of research on epistemic cognition. In B. K. Hofer & P. R. Pintrich (Eds.), *Personal Epistemology* (pp. 37–62). Mahwah, NJ: Erlbaum.

King, P. M., & Kitchener, K. S. (2015). Cognitive development in the emerging adult: The emergence of complex cognitive skills. In J. J. Arnett (Ed.), *The Oxford handbook of emerging adulthood* (pp. 105–125). New York, NY: Oxford University Press.

Kinkaid, C., Jones, D. J., Cuellar, J., & Gonzales, M. (2011). Psychological control associated with youth adjustment and risky behavior in African American single mother families. *Journal of Child and Family Studies, 20,* 102–110.

Kirk, S. A., & Kutchins, H. (1997). *Making us crazy. DSM: The psychiatric bible and the creation of mental disorders.* Hawthorne, NY: Aldine de Gruyter.

Kirkpatrick, L. A., & Davis, K. E. (1994). Attachment style, gender, and relationship stability: A longitudinal analysis. *Journal of Personality and Social Psychology, 66,* 502–512.

Kiselica, M. S. (2003). Transforming psychotherapy in order to succeed with adolescent boys: Male-friendly practices. *Journal of Clinical Psychology, 59,* 1225–1236.

Kisley, M. A., Wood, S., & Burrows, C. L. (2007). Looking at the sunny side of life. *Psychological Science, 18,* 838–843.

Kitayama, S., Duffy, S., Kawamura, T., & Larsen, J. T. (2003). Perceiving an object and its context in different cultures: A cultural look at new look. *Psychological Science, 14,* 201–206.

Kitayama, S., & Park, J. (2010). Cultural neuroscience of the self: Understanding the social grounding of the brain. *Social Cognitive and Affective Neuroscience, 5,* 111–129.

Kitayama, S., Park, J., Boylan, J. M., Miyamoto, Y., Levine, C. S., Markus, H. R., . . . Ryff, C. D. (2015). Expression of anger and ill health in two cultures: An examination of inflammation and cardiovascular risk. *Psychological Science, 26*(2), 211–220.

Kitchener, K. S., & King, P. M. (1981). Reflective judgment: Concepts of justification and their relationship to age and education. *Journal of Applied Developmental Psychology, 2,* 89–116.

Kitchener, K. S., Lynch, C. L., Fischer, K. W., & Wood, P. K. (1993). Developmental range of reflective judgment: The effect of contextual support and practice on developmental stage. *Developmental Psychology, 29,* 893–906.

Kite, M. E., Stockdale, G. D., Whitley, B. E., Jr., & Johnson, B. T. (2005). Attitudes toward younger and older adults: An updated meta-analytic review. *Journal of Social Issues, 61,* 241–266.

Kiuru, N., Aunola, K., Lerkkanen, M.-K., Pakarinen, E., Poskiparta, E., Ahonen, T., . . . Nurmi, J.-E. (2015). Positive teacher and peer relations combine to predict primary school students' academic skill development. *Developmental Psychology, 51,* 434–446.

Klein, M. (1921/1945). *Contributions to psychoanalysis.* London: Hogarth.

Kleinman, A., & Kleinman, J. (1985). Somatization: The interconnections in Chinese

society among culture, depressive experiences, and the meanings of pain. In A. Kleinman & B. Good (Eds.), *Culture and depression: Studies in the anthropology and cross-cultural psychiatry of affect and disorder* (pp. 429–490). Berkeley, CA: University of California Press.

Klerman, G. L., Weissman, M. M., Rounsaville, B. J., & Chevron, E. S. (1984). *Interpersonal psychotherapy for depression.* New York, NY: Basic Books.

Klimstra, T. A., Luyckx, K., Germeijs, V., Meeus, W. H. J., & Goossens, L. (2012). Personality traits and educational identity formation in late adolescents: Longitudinal associations and academic progress. *Journal of Youth Adolescence, 41,* 346–361.

Klimstra, T. A., Luyckx, K., & Meeus, W. H. J. (2012). Personal identity in Belgium and the Netherlands. *New Directions for Child and Adolescent Development, 2012*(138), 19–34.

Kling, K. C., Hyde, J. S., Showers, C. J., & Buswell, B. N. (1999). Gender differences in self-esteem: A meta-analysis. *Psychological Bulletin, 125,* 470–500.

Kling, K. C., Seltzer, M. M., & Ryff, C. D. (1997). Distinctive late-life challenges: Implications for coping and well-being. *Psychology and Aging, 12,* 288–295.

Klingseisen, A., & Lyons, D. A. (2017). Axonal regulation of central nervous system-myelination: Structure and function. *The Neuroscientist, 24,* 7–21.

Kneflekamp, L. L. (1999). Introduction. In W. G. Perry, *Forms of ethical development in the college years: A scheme* (p. xix). San Francisco, CA: Jossey-Bass.

Knežević, M., & Marinković, K. (2017). Neurodynamic correlates of response inhibition from emerging to mid adulthood. *Cognitive Development, 43,* 106–118.

Knifsend, C. A., & Juvonen, J. (2014). Social identity complexity, cross-ethnic friendships, and intergroup attitudes in urban middle schools. *Child Development, 85*(2), 709–721.

Knoke D., & Yang, S. (2008). *Social network analysis* (2nd ed.). Thousand Oaks, CA: Sage.

Knudsen, T. M., Hansen, A. V., Garne, E., & Andersen, A. N. (2014). Increased risk of severe congenital heart defects in offspring exposed to selective serotonin-reuptake inhibitors in early pregnancy—an epidemiological study using validated EUROCAT data. *BMC Pregnancy and Childbirth, 14*:333. doi:10.1186/1471-2393-14-333

Kochanska, G. (1995). Children's temperament, mothers' discipline, and security of attachment: Multiple pathways to emerging internalization. *Child Development, 66,* 597–615.

Kochanska, G. (1998). Mother-child relationship, child fearfulness, and emerging attachment: A short-term longitudinal study. *Developmental Psychology, 34,* 480–490.

Kochanska, G., Aksan, N., & Joy, M. E. (2007). Children's fearfulness as a moderator of parenting in early socialization: Two longitudinal studies. *Developmental Psychology, 43,* 222–237.

Kochanska, G., Aksan, N., & Koenig, A. L. (1995). A longitudinal study of the roots of preschoolers' conscience: Committed compliance and emerging internalization. *Child Development, 66,* 1752–1769.

Kochanska, G., Barry, R. A., Stellern, S. A., & O'Bleness, J. J. (2009). Early attachment organization moderates the parent-child mutually coercive pathway to children's antisocial conduct. *Child Development, 80,* 1288–1300.

Kochanska, G., & Kim, S. (2012). Toward a new understanding of legacy of early attachments for future antisocial trajectories: Evidence from two longitudinal studies. *Development and Psychopathology, 24,* 783–806.

Kochanska, G., & Kim, S. (2013). Early attachment organization with both parents and future behavior problems: From infancy to middle childhood. *Child Development, 84,* 283–296.

Kochanska, G., Koenig, J. L., Barry, R. A., Kim, S., & Yoon, J. E. (2010). Children's conscience during toddler and preschool years, moral self, and a competent, adaptive developmental trajectory. *Developmental Psychology, 46,* 1320–1332.

Kochanska, G., Tjebkes, T. L., & Forman, D. R. (1998). Children's emerging regulation of conduct: Restraint, compliance, and internalization from infancy to the second year. *Child Development, 69,* 1378–1389.

Koenen, K. C., Ratanatharathorn, A., Ng, L., McLaughlin, K. A., Bromet, E. J., Stein, D. J., . . . Kessler, R. C. (2017). Posttraumatic stress disorder in the world mental health surveys. *Psychological Medicine, 47*(13), 2260.

Koenig, A. M., & Eagly, A. H. (2014). Evidence for the social role theory of stereotype content: Observations of groups' roles shape stereotypes. *Journal of Personality and Social Psychology, 107,* 371–392.

Kohlberg, L. (1966). Moral education in the school. *School Review, 74,* 1–30.

Kohlberg, L. (1976). Moral stages and moralization: The cognitive developmental approach. In T. Lickona (Ed.), *Moral development and behavior: Theory, research and social issues* (pp. 31–53). New York, NY: Holt, Rinehart and Winston.

Kohlberg, L. (1984). *Essays on moral development: The psychology of moral development.* San Francisco, CA: Harper & Row.

Kohlberg, L. A. (1966). A cognitive-developmental analysis of children's sex role concepts and attitudes. In E. E. Maccoby (Ed.), *The development of sex differences* (pp. 82–173). Stanford, CA: Stanford University Press.

Kok, B. E., Waugh, C. E., & Fredrickson, B. L. (2013). Meditation and health: The search for mechanisms of action. *Social and Personality Psychology Compass, 7,* 27–39.

Kolb, B., Gibb, R., & Robinson, T. E. (2003). Brain plasticity and behavior. *Current Directions in Psychological Science, 12,* 1–5.

Kolesinska, Z., Ahmed, S. F., Niedziela, M., Bryce, J., Molinska-Glura, M., Rodie, M., . . . Hiort, O. (2014). Changes over time in sex assignment for disorders of sex development. *Pediatrics, 134,* 710–715.

Kong, A., Frigge, M. L., Masson, G., Besenbacher, S., Sulem, P., Magnusson, G., . . . Stefansson, K. (2012). Rate of de novo mutations and the importance of father's age to disease risk. *Nature, 488,* 471–475.

Konner, M. J., & Worthman, C. (1980). Nursing frequency, gonadal function and birth-spacing among !Kung hunters and gatherers. *Science, 207,* 788–791.

Koppel, J., & Rubin, D. C. (2016). Recent advances in understanding the reminiscence bump: The importance of cues in guiding recall from autobiographical memory. *Current Directions in Psychological Science, 25,* 135–140.

Koren-Karie, N., Sagi-Schwartz, A., & Egoz-Mizrachi, N. (2005). The emotional quality of childcare centers in Israel: The Haifa study of early childcare. *Infant Mental Health Journal, 26,* 110–126.

Kornblith, E., Green, R.-J., Casey, S., & Tiet, Q. (2016). Marital stats, social support, and depressive symptoms among lesbian and heterosexual women. *Journal of Lesbian Studies, 20.* Available at https://doi.org/10.1080/1089416 0.2015.1061882

Kornfield, J. (2002). *The art of forgiveness, loving-kindness, and peace.* New York, NY: Bantam Books.

Kosciw, J. G., Greytak, E. A., Giga, N. M., Villenas, C., & Danischewski, D. J. (2016). *The 2015 National School Climate Survey: The experiences of lesbian, gay, bisexual, transgender, and queer youth in our nation's schools.* New York, NY: GLSEN.

Kostelnik, M. J., Soderman, A. K., & Whiren, A. P. (2014). *Developmentally appropriate curriculum: Best practices in early childhood education* (6th ed.). Upper Saddle River, NJ: Pearson.

Kostyrka-Allchorne, K., Cooper, N. R., & Simpson, A. (2017). The relationship between television exposure and children's cognition and behaviour: A systematic review. *Developmental Review, 44,* 19–58.

Koury, A. S., & Votruba-Drzal, E. (2014). School readiness of children from immigrant families: Contributions of region of origin, home, and childcare. *Journal of Educational Psychology, 106,* 268–288.

Kovács, A. M., & Mehler, J. (2009). Cognitive gains in 7-month-old bilingual infants. *Proceedings of the National Academy of Sciences of the United States of America, 106,* 6556–6560.

Kreider, R. M. (2006). *Remarriage in the United States.* Poster presented at the annual meeting of the American Sociological Association, Montreal, Canada. Retrieved from www.census.gov/hhes/socdemo/marriage/data/sipp/us-remarriage-poster.pdf

Krendl, A. C., Richeson, J. A., Kelley, W. M., & Heatherton, T. F. (2008). The negative consequences of threat. *Psychological Science, 19,* 168–175.

Kretschmer, T., Hickman, M., Doerner, R., Emond, A., Lewis, G., Macleod, J., . . . Heron, J. (2014). Outcomes of childhood conduct problem trajectories in early adulthood: Findings from the ALSPAC study. *European Child and Adolescent Psychiatry, 23,* 539–549.

Krettenauer, T., & Victor, R. (2017). Why be moral? Moral identity motivation and age. *Developmental Psychology, 53,* 1589–1596.

Kreutzer, M. A., Leonard, C., & Flavell, J. H. (1975). An interview study of children's knowledge about memory. *Monographs of the Society for Research in Child Development, 40* (Serial No. 159).

Kringelbach, M. L., Stark, E. A., Alexander, C., Bornstein, M. H., & Stein A. (2017). On cuteness: Unlocking the parental brain and beyond. *Trends in Cognitive Sciences, 20,* 545–558.

Kristeller, J. L., & Hallett, C. B. (1999). An exploratory study of meditation-based intervention for binge eating disorder. *Journal of Health Psychology, 4,* 357–363.

Kristeller, J. L., Wolever, R. Q., & Sheets, V. (2014). Mindfulness-Based Eating Awareness Training (MB-EAT) for binge eating: A randomized clinical trial. *Mindfulness, 5,* 282–297.

Kroger, J., & Marcia, J. E. (2011). The identity statuses: Origins, meanings, and interpretations. In S. J. Schwartz, K. Luyckx, & V. L. Vignoles (Eds.), *Handbook of identity theory and research* (pp. 31–53). New York, NY: Springer.

Kroger, J., Martinussen, M., & Marcia, J. E. (2010). Identity status change during adolescence and young adulthood: A meta-analysis. *Journal of Adolescence, 33,* 683–698.

Krohne, H. W., & Rogner, J. (1982). Repression-sensitization as a central construct in coping research. In J. G. Schulterbrandt & A. Raskin (Eds.), *Depression in childhood: Diagnosis, treatment, and conceptual models* (pp. 1–25). New York, NY: Raven.

Kruger, A. C. (1992). The effect of peer and adult-child transductive discussions on moral reasoning. *Merrill-Palmer Quarterly, 38,* 191–211.

Kruger, A. C., & Tomasello, M. (1986). Transactive discussions with peers and adults. *Developmental Psychology, 22,* 681–685.

Krumboltz, J. D. (1966). Behavioral goals for counseling. *Journal of Counseling Psychology, 13,* 153–159.

Krumhansl, C. L., & Zupnick, J. A. (2013). Cascading reminiscence bumps in popular music. *Psychological Science, 24,* 2057–2068.

Kubler-Ross, E. (1969). *On death and dying.* New York, NY: Macmillan.

Kubler-Ross, E. (1974). *Questions and answers on death and dying.* New York, NY: Macmillan.

Kuhl, P. K., Stevens, E., Hayashi, A., Deguchi, T., Kiritani, S., & Iverson, P. (2006). Infants show a facilitation effect for native language phonetic perception between 6 and 12 months. *Developmental Science, 9,* F13–F21.

Kuhn, D. (1991). *The skills of argument.* Cambridge, England: Cambridge University Press.

Kuhn, D. (1992). Thinking as argument. *Harvard Educational Review, 62,* 155–178.

Kuhn, D. (2000a). Does memory development belong on an endangered topic list? *Child Development, 71,* 21–25.

Kuhn, D. (2000b). Metacognitive development. *Current Directions in Psychological Science, 9,* 178–181.

Kuhn, D. (2001). How do people know? *Psychological Science, 12,* 1–8.

Kuhn, D. (2010). What is scientific thinking and how does it develop? In U. Goswami (Ed.), *Handbook of childhood cognitive development* (2nd ed., pp. 371–393). Oxford, England: Blackwell.

Kuhn, D. (2011). What is scientific thinking and how does it develop? In D. Kuhn (Ed.), *The Wiley-Blackwell handbook of childhood cognitive development* (2nd ed., pp. 497–523). Malden, MA: Wiley-Blackwell.

Kuhn, D., & Franklin, S. (2006). The second decade: What develops (and how). In W. Damon & R. M. Lerner (Series Eds.), D. Kuhn & R. S. Siegler (Vol. Eds.), *Handbook of child psychology: Vol. 2. Cognition, perception and language* (6th ed., pp. 953–993). Hoboken, NJ: Wiley.

Kuhn, D., Garcia-Mila, M., Zohar, A., & Andersen, C. (1995). Strategies of knowledge acquisition. *Monographs of the Society for Research in Child Development, 60* (Serial No. 245).

Kuhn, D., Pennington, N., & Leadbeater, B. (1982). Adult thinking in developmental perspective. In P. B. Baltes & O. Brim (Eds.), *Life span development and behavior* (pp. 157–195). New York, NY: Academic Press.

Kuhn, D., Ramsey, S., & Arvidsson, T. S. (2015). Developing multivariable thinkers. *Cognitive Development, 35,* 92–110.

Kuhn, D., Zillmer, N., Crowell, A., & Zavala, J. (2013). Developing norms of argumentation: Metacognitive, epistemological, and social dimensions of developing argumentive competence. *Cognition and Instruction, 31,* 456–496.

Kuiper, J. S., Zuidersma, M., Voshaar, R. C. O., Zuidema, S. U., van den Heuvel, E. R., Stolk, R. P., & Smidt, N. (2015). Social relationships and risk of dementia: A systematic review and meta-analysis of longitudinal cohort studies. *Aging Research Reviews, 22,* 39–57.

Kumar, U., Arya, A., & Agarwal, V. (2017). Neural alterations in ADHD children as indicated by voxel-based cortical thickness and morphometry analysis. *Brain & Development, 39,* 403–410.

Kunzmann, U., & Baltes, P. B. (2003). Wisdom-related knowledge: Affective, motivational, and interpersonal correlates. *Personality and Social Psychology Bulletin, 29,* 1104–1119.

Kunzmann, U., Rohr, M., Wieck, C., Kappes, C., & Wrosch, C. (2017). Speaking about feelings: Further evidence for multidirectional age differences in anger and sadness. *Psychology and Aging, 32,* 93–103.

Kupersmidt, J. B., Burchinal, M., & Patterson, C. J. (1995). Developmental patterns of childhood peer relations as predictors of externalizing problems in adolescence. *Child Development, 61,* 1350–1362.

Kurdek, L. A. (1998). Relationship outcomes and their predictors: Longitudinal evidence from heterosexual married, gay cohabiting, and lesbian cohabiting couples. *Journal of Marriage and the Family, 60,* 553–568.

Kurdek, L. A. (2004). Are gay and lesbian cohabiting couples really different from heterosexual married couples? *Journal of Marriage and Family, 66,* 880–900.

Kushlev, K., Dunn, E. W., & Lucas, R. E. (2015). Higher income is associated with less daily sadness but not more daily happiness. *Social Psychological and Personality Science, 6*(5), 483–489.

Kuwabara, M., Son, J. Y., & Smith, L. B. (2011). Attention to context: U.S. and Japanese children's emotional judgments. *Journal of Cognition and Development, 12,* 502–517.

Kwon, K., Yoo, G., & De Gagne, J. C. (2017). Does culture matter? A qualitative inquiry of helicopter parenting in Korean American college students. *Journal of Child and Family Studies, 26*(7), 1979.

Labouvie-Vief, G. (2015). *Integrating emotions and cognition throughout the lifespan.* Cham, Switzerland: Springer International.

Labouvie-Vief, G., Chiodo, L. M., Goguen, L. A., Diehl, M., & Orwoll, L. (1995). Representations of self across the life span. *Psychology and Aging, 10,* 404–415.

Labouvie-Vief, G., Lumley, M. A., Jain, E., & Heinze, H. (2003). Age and gender differences in cardiac reactivity and subjective emotion responses to emotional autobiographical memories. *Emotion, 3,* 115–126.

Lacaille, H., Duterte-Boucher, D., Liot, D., Vaudry, H., Naassila. M., & Vaudry, D. (2015). Comparison of the deleterious effects of binge drinking-like alcohol exposure in adolescent and adult mice. *Journal of Neurochemistry, 132,* 629–641.

Lace, J. W., Haeberlein, K. A., & Handal, P. J. (2017). Five-factor structure of the spiritual transcendence scale and its relationship with clinical psychological distress in emerging adults. *Religions, 8*(10), 230.

Laceulle, O. M., Nederhof, E., van Aken, M. A. G., & Ormel, J. (2017). Adversity-driven changes in hypothalamic-pituitary-adrenal axis functioning during adolescence. The trails study. *Psychoneuroendocrinology, 85,* 49–55.

Lachman, M. E. (2004). Development in midlife. *Annual Review of Psychology, 55,* 305–331.

Lachman, M. E., Teshale, S., & Agrigoroaei, S. (2015). Midlife as a pivotal period in the life course: Balancing growth and decline at the crossroads of youth and old age. *International Journal of Behavioral Development, 39,* 20–31.

Ladd, G. W., & Burgess, K. B. (1999). Charting the relationship trajectories of aggressive, withdrawn, and aggressive/withdrawn children during early grade school. *Child Development, 70,* 910–929.

Ladd, G. W., Kochenderfer-Ladd, B., Eggum, N. D., Kochel, K. P., & McConnell, E. M. (2011). Characterizing and comparing the friendships of anxious-solitary and unsociable preadolescents. *Child Development, 82,* 1434–1453.

Ladd, G. W., & Ladd, B. K. (1998). Parenting behaviors and parent-child relationships: Correlates of peer victimization in kindergarten? *Developmental Psychology, 34,* 1450–1458.

Ladd, J. M., & Price, J. M. (1987). Predicting children's social and school adjustment following the transition from preschool to kindergarten. *Child Development, 58,* 1168–1189.

LaFreniere, P., & MacDonald, K. (2013). A postgenomic view of behavioral development and adaptation to the environment. *Developmental Review, 33,* 89–103.

LaFromboise, T., Coleman, H. L. K., & Gerton, J. (1993). Psychological impact of biculturalism: Evidence and theory. *Psychological Bulletin, 114,* 395–412.

Lagerveld, S. E., Brenninkmeijer, V., Blonk, R. W. B., Twisk, J. W. R., & Schaufeli, W. B. (2017; 2016). Predictive value of work-related self-efficacy change on RTW for employees with common mental disorders. *Occupational and Environmental Medicine, 74*(5), 381–383.

Laible, D. J., & Thompson, R. A. (2002). Mother-child lessons in emotion, morality, and relationships. *Child Development, 73,* 1187–1203.

Lamb, M. E., & Ahnert, L. (2006). Nonparental child care: Context, concepts, correlates, and consequences. In W. Damon and R. M. Lerner (Series Eds.), K. A. Renninger & I. E. Sigel (Vol. Eds.), *Handbook of child psychology: Vol. 4. Child psychology in practice* (6th ed., pp. 950–1016). Hoboken, NJ: Wiley.

Lamb, M. E., & Lewis, C. (2004). The development and significance of father-child relationships in two-parent families. In M. E. Lamb (Eds.), *The role of the father in child development* (4th ed., pp. 272–306). Hoboken, NJ: Wiley.

Lamb, M. E., & Lewis, C. (2011). The role of parent-child relationships in child development. In M. H. Bornstein & M. E. Lamb (Eds.), *Developmental science: An advanced textbook* (pp. 469–517). New York, NY: Psychology Press.

Lamb, M. E., Malloy, L. C., Hershkowitz, I., & LARooy, D. (2015). Children and the law. In R. M. Lerner (Ed. In Chief) & M. C. Bornstein & T. Leventhal (Vol. Eds.), *Handbook of child psychology and developmental science: Vol. 4. Ecological settings and processes* (7th ed., pp. 464–512). Hoboken, NJ: Wiley.

Lamborn, S. D., Dornbusch, S. M., & Steinberg, L. (1996). Ethnicity and community context as moderators of the relations between family decision making and adolescent adjustment. *Child Development, 67,* 283–301.

Lamborn, S. D., Mounts, N. S., Steinberg, L., & Dornbusch, S. M. (1991). Patterns of competence and adjustment among adolescents from authoritative, authoritarian, indulgent, and neglectful families. *Child Development, 62,* 1049–1065.

The Editors of The Lancet. (2010). Retraction—ileal-lymphoid-nodular hyperplasia, non-specific colitis, and pervasive developmental disorder in children. *The Lancet, 375,* 445.

Lancy, D. F. (2015). *The anthropology of childhood. Cherubs, chattel, changelings.* Cambridge, England: Cambridge University Press.

Landale, N. S., & Fennelly, K. (1992). Informal unions among mainland Puerto Ricans: Cohabitation or an alternative to legal marriage? *Journal of Marriage and the Family, 54,* 269–280.

Lang, F. R., & Carstensen, L. L. (1994). Close emotional relationships in late life: Further support for proactive aging in the social domain. *Psychology and Aging, 9,* 315–324.

Langlois, J. H., & Stephan, C. W. (1981). Beauty and the beast: The role of physical attraction in peer relationships and social behavior. In S. S. Brehm, S. M. Kassin, & S. X. Gibbans (Eds.), *Developmental social psychology: Theory and research* (pp. 152–168). New York, NY: Oxford University Press.

Lansford, J. E. (2009). Parental divorce and children's adjustment. *Perspectives on Psychological Science, 4,* 140–152.

Lansford, J. E., Deater-Deckard, K., Dodge, K. A., Bates, J. E., & Pettit, G. S. (2004). Ethnic differences in the link between physical discipline and later adolescent externalizing behaviors. *Journal of Child Psychology and Psychiatry, 45,* 801–812.

Lansford, J. E., Dodge, K. A., Fontaine, R. G., Bates, J. E., & Pettit, G. S. (2014). Peer rejection, affiliation with deviant peers, delinquency, and risky sexual behavior. *Journal of Youth and Adolescence, 43*(10), 1742–1751.

Lansford, J. E., Wager, L. B., Bates, J. E., Pettit, G. S., & Dodge, K. A. (2012). Forms of spanking and children's externalizing behaviors. *Family Relations, 61,* 224–236.

Lapate, R. C., Rokers, B., Tromp, D. P. M., Orfali, N. S., Oler, J. A., Doran, S. T., . . . Davidson, R. J. (2016). Awareness of emotional stimuli determines the behavioral consequences of amygdala activation and amygdala-prefrontal connectivity. *Scientific Reports*. doi:10.1038/srep25826

Lapsley, D. K. (1993). Toward an integrated theory of adolescent ego development: The "new look" at adolescent egocentrism. *American Journal of Orthopsychiatry, 63*, 562–571.

Lapsley, D. K., FitzGerald, D. P., Rice, K. G., & Jackson, S. (1989). Separation-individuation and the "new look" at the imaginary audience and personal fable: A test of an integrative model. *Journal of Adolescent Research, 4*, 483–505.

Largie, S., Field, T., Hernandez-Reif, M., Sanders, C. E., & Diego, M. (2001). Employment during adolescence is associated with depression, inferior relationships, lower grades, and smoking. *Adolescence, 36*, 395–401.

Larkin, H., Shields, J. J., & Anda, R. F. (2012). The health and social consequences of adverse childhood experiences (ACE) across the lifespan: An introduction to prevention and intervention in the community. *Journal of Prevention and Intervention in the Community, 40*, 263–270.

Larmar, S., & Lodge, J. (2014). Making sense of how I learn: Metacognitive capital and the first year university student. *The International Journal of the First Year in Higher Education, 5*(1), 93–105.

Larsen, S. F. (2000). Memorable books: Recall of reading in its personal context. In M. S. MacNealey & R. Kreuz (Eds.), *Empirical approaches to literature and aesthetics: Advances in discourse processes* (Vol. 52, pp. 583–599). Norwood, NJ: Ablex.

Larson, R., & Richards, M. H. (1994). *Divergent realities: The emotional lives of mothers, fathers, and adolescents*. New York, NY: Basic Books.

Larson, R. W., Hansen, D. M., & Moneta, G. (2006). Differing profiles of developmental experiences across types of organized youth activities. *Developmental Psychology, 42*, 849–863.

Larson, R. W., & Tran, S. P. (2014). Invited commentary: Positive youth development and human complexity. *Journal of Youth and Adolescence, 43*(6), 1012–1017.

Laski, E. V., & Siegler, R. S. (2014). Learning from number board games: You learn what you encode. *Developmental Psychology, 50*, 853–864.

Lathrop, B. L., Cheney, T. B., & Hayman, A. B. (2014). Ethical decision-making in the dilemma of the intersex infant. *Issues in Comprehensive Pediatric Nursing, 37*, 25–38.

Laub, J. H. (1999). Alterations in the opportunity structure: A criminological perspective. In A. Booth, A. C. Crouter, & M. J. Shanahan (Eds.), *Transitions to adulthood in a changing economy: No work, no family, no future?* (pp. 48–55). Westport, CT: Praeger.

Lauche, R., Cramer, H., Dobos, G., Langhorst, J., & Schmidt, S. (2013). A systematic review and meta-analysis of mindfulness-based stress reduction for the fibromyalgia syndrome. *Journal of Psychosomatic Research, 75*(6), 500–510.

Laurent, H. K., Harold, G. T., Leve, L., Shelton, K. H., & van Goozen, S. H. M. (2016). Understanding the unfolding of stress regulation in infants. *Development and Psychopathology, 28*, 1431–1440.

Lavner, J. A., & Bradbury, T. N. (2010). Patterns of change in marital satisfaction over the newlywed years. *Journal of Marriage and Family, 72*, 1171–1187.

Lavner, J. A., & Bradbury, T. N. (2012). Why do even satisfied newlyweds eventually go on to divorce? *Journal of Family Psychology, 26*, 1–10.

Lavoie, J., Nagar, P. M., & Talwar, V. (2017). From Kantian to Machiavellian deceivers: Development of children's reasoning and self-reported use of secrets and lies. *Childhood, 24*, 97–211.

Lazarus, R. S. (1996). The role of coping in the emotions and how coping changes over the life course. In C. Malatesta-Magni & S. H. McFadden (Eds.), *Handbook of emotion, adult development, and aging* (pp. 289–306). New York, NY: Academic Press.

Lazarus, R. S., & Folkman, S. (1984). *Stress, appraisal, and coping*. New York, NY: Springer.

Leaper, C. (1994). Exploring the correlates and consequences of gender segregation: Social relationships in childhood, adolescence, and adulthood. In B. Damon (Series Ed.) & C. Leaper (Vol. Ed.), *New directions for child development: The development of gender relationships*. San Francisco, CA: Jossey-Bass.

Leaper, C. (2002). Parenting girls and boys. In M. H. Bornstein (Ed.), *Handbook of parenting: Children and parenting* (pp. 189–225). Mahwah, NJ: Erlbaum.

Leaper, C. (2015). Gender and social-cognitive development. In R. M. Lerner, L. S. Liben, & U. Muller (Eds.), *Handbook of child psychology and developmental science* (7th ed., Vol. 2, pp. 806–853). New York, NY: Wiley.

Leaper, C., Anderson, K. J., & Sanders, P. (1998). Moderators of gender effects on parents' talk to their children. *Developmental Psychology, 34*, 3–27.

Leaper, C., & Smith, T. E. (2004). A meta-analytic review of gender variations in children's language use: Talkativeness, affiliative speech, and assertive speech. *Developmental Psychology, 40*, 993–1027.

Leavell, A. S., Tamis-LeMonda, C. S., Ruble, D. N., Zosuls, K. M., & Cabrera, N. J. (2012). African American, White and Latino fathers' activities with their sons and daughters in early childhood. *Sex Roles, 66*, 53–65.

Lecce, S., Bianco, F., Devine, R. T., & Hughes, C. (2017). Relations between theory of mind and executive function in middle childhood: A short-term longitudinal study. *Journal of Experimental Child Psychology, 163*, 69–86.

Leckman, J. F., & Fernandez, T. V. (2016). The origins of Tourette syndrome: Prenatal risk factors and the promise of birth cohort studies. *Journal of the American Academy of Child and Adolescent Psychiatry, 55*, 751–753.

LeDoux, J. (2012). Rethinking the emotional brain. *Neuron, 73*, 653–668.

LeDoux, J. E., & Brown, R. (2017). A higher-order theory of emotional consciousness. *Proceedings of the National Academy of Sciences*. Available at www.pnas.org/cgi/doi/10.1073/pnas.1619316114

Lee, C. M., Horvath, C., & Hunsley, J. (2013). Does it work in the real world? The effectiveness of treatments for psychological problems in children and adolescents. *Professional Psychology: Research and Practice, 44*, 81–88.

Lee, D. J., Schnitzlein, C. W., Wolf, J. P., Vythilingam, M., Rasmusson, A. M., & Hoge, C. W. (2016). Psychotherapy versus pharmacotherapy for posttraumatic stress disorder: Systemic review and meta-analyses to determine first-line treatments. *Depression and Anxiety, 33*(9), 792.

Lee, D. M., Nazroo, J., O'Connor, D. B., Blake, M., & Pendleton, N. (2016). Sexual health and well-being among older men and women in England: Findings from the English longitudinal study of ageing. *Archives of Sexual Behavior, 45*, 133–144.

Lee, G. Y., & Kisilevsky, B. S. (2012). Fetuses respond to father's voice but prefer mother's voice after birth. *Developmental Psychobiology, 56*, 1–11.

Lee, J. A. (1973). *The colors of love: An exploration of the ways of loving*. Don Mills, Ontario, Canada: New Press.

Lee, J. L., Steiner, R. J., Yu, Y., Short, S. J., Neale, M. C., Styner, M. A., . . . Gilmore, J. H. (2017). Common and heritable components of white matter microstructure predict cognitive function at 1 and 2 y. *PNAS, 114*, 148–153.

Lee, J. M., Wasserman, R., Kaciroti, N., Gebremariam, A., Steffes, J., Dowshen, S., . . . Herman-Giddens, M. E. (2016). Timing of puberty in overweight versus obese boys. *Pediatrics, 137*. doi: 10.1542/peds.2015-0164

Lee, K. (2013). Little liars: Development of verbal deception in children. *Child Development Perspectives, 7*, 91–96.

Lee, M. R., Boness, C. L., McDowell, Y. E., Vergés, A., Steinley, D. L., & Sher, K. J. (2018). Desistance and severity of alcohol use disorder: A lifespan-developmental investigation. *Clinical Psychological Science, 6*, 90–105.

Lee, P. A., Houk, C. P., Ahmed, S. F., & Hughes I. A. (2006). International consensus conference on intersex organized by the Lawson Wilkins pediatric endocrine society and the European society for paediatric endocrinology: Consensus statement on management of intersex disorders. *Pediatrics, 118*, 488–500.

Lee, P. A., Nordenström, A., Houk, C. P., Ahmed, S. F., Auchus, R., Baratz, A., . . . Mazur, T. (2016). Global disorders of sex development update since 2006: Perceptions, approach and care. *Hormone Research in Paediatrics, 85*, 158–180.

Lee, Y.-C., Lin, Y.-C., Huang, C.-L., & Fredrickson, B. L. (2013). The construct and measurement of peace of mind. *Journal of Happiness Studies, 14*, 571–590.

Lehman, D. R., Lempert, R. O., & Nisbett, R. E. (1988). The effects of graduate training on reasoning. *American Psychologist, 43*, 431–442.

Lehrer, R., & Schauble, L. (2015). The development of scientific thinking. In R. M. Lerner (Series Ed.), L. S. Liben & U. Müller (Vol. Eds.), *Handbook of child psychology and developmental science: Volume 2. Cognitive processes* (7th ed., pp. 671–714). Hoboken, NJ: Wiley.

Leichtman, M. D., Wang, Q., & Pillemer, D. B. (2003). Cultural variations in interdependence and autobiographical memory: Lessons from Korea, China, India, and the United States. In R. Fivush & C. A. Haden (Eds.), *Autobiographical memory and the construction of a narrative self* (pp. 73–97). Mahwah, NJ: Erlbaum.

Leikas, S., & Salmela-Aro, K. (2015). Personality trait changes among young Finns: The role of life events and transitions. *Journal of Personality, 83*, 117–126.

Lemmens, L. H. J. M., Galindo-Garre, F., Arntz, A., Peeters, F., Hollon, S. D., DeRubeis, R. J., & Huibers, M. J. H. (2017). Exploring mechanisms of change in cognitive therapy and interpersonal psychotherapy for adult depression. *Behaviour Research and Therapy, 94*, 81–92. doi:10.1016/j.brat.2017.05.005

LeMoyne, T., & Buchanan, T. (2011). Does "hovering" matter? Helicopter parenting and its effects on wellbeing. *Sociological Spectrum, 31*, 399–418.

Lench, H. C., Flores, S. A., & Bench, S. W. (2011). Discrete emotions predict changes in cognition, judgment, experience, behavior, and physiology: A meta-analysis of experimental emotion elicitations. *Psychological Bulletin, 137*, 834–855.

Lengua, L. J., Honorado, E., & Bush, N. R. (2007). Contextual risk and parenting as predictors of effortful control and social competence in preschool children. *Journal of Applied Developmental Psychology, 28*, 40–55.

Lenhart, A. (2015). *Teen, social media, and technology overview, 2015.* Available from www.pewinternet.org/2015/04/09/teens-social-media-technology-2015/

Lenroot, R. K., & Giedd, J. N. (2011). Annual research review: Developmental consideration of gene by environment interactions. *Journal of Child Psychology and Psychiatry, 52*, 429–441.

Lent, R. W., Brown, S. D., & Hackett, G. (1996). Career development from a social cognitive perspective. In D. Brown, L. Brooks, & Associates (Eds.), *Career choice and development* (3rd ed., pp. 373–421). San Francisco, CA: Jossey-Bass.

Leong, D. J., & Bodrova, E. (2012). Assessing and scaffolding make-believe play. *Young Children,* January, 28–43.

Lerner, R. M. (1998). Theories of human development: Contemporary perspectives. In W. Damon (Series Ed.) & R. M. Lerner (Vol. Ed.), *Handbook of child psychology: Vol. 1. Theoretical models of human development* (5th ed., pp. 1–24). New York, NY: Wiley.

Lerner, R. M., Fisher, C. B., & Weinberg, R. A. (2000). Toward a science for and of the people: Promoting civil society through the application of developmental science. *Child Development, 71*, 11–20.

Lerner, R. M., Lerner, J. V., Bowers, E. P., & Geldof, G. J. (2015). Positive youth development and relational-developmental systems. In W. F. Overton & P. C. M. Molenaar (Eds.), & R. M. Lerner (Series Ed.), *Theory and method: Volume 1: Handbook of child psychology and developmental science* (Chapter 16, 7th ed., pp. 607–651). New York, NY: Wiley.

Letourneau, N., Tryphonopoulos, P., Giesbrecht, G., Dennis, C. L., Bhogal, S., & Watson, B. (2015). Narrative and meta-analytic review of interventions aiming to improve maternal-child attachment security. *Infant Mental Health Journal, 36*, 366–387.

Levenson, R. W., Carstensen, L. L., & Gottman, J. M. (1993). Long-term marriage: Age, gender, and satisfaction. *Psychology and Aging, 8*, 301–313.

Levenson, R. W., & Gottman, J. M. (1985). Physiological and affective predictors of change in relationship satisfaction. *Journal of Personality and Social Psychology, 49*, 85–94.

Leventhal, A. M., & Martell, C. R. (2006). *The myth of depression as disease: Limitations and alternatives to drug treatment.* Westport, CT: Praeger.

Lever, J. (1978). Sex differences in the complexity of children's play and games. *American Sociological Review, 43*, 471–483.

Levine, S. C., Vasilyeva, M., Lourenco, S. F., Newcombe, N. S., & Huttenlocher, J. (2005). Socioeconomic status modifies the sex difference in spatial skill. *Psychological Science, 16*, 841–845.

Levinson, D. J. (1986). A conception of adult development. *American Psychologist, 41*, 3–13.

Levinson, D. J., & Levinson, J. D. (1996). *The seasons of a woman's life.* New York, NY: Knopf.

Levitt, M. Z., & Selman, R. L. (1993). *A manual for the assessment and coding of personal meaning.* Unpublished manuscript, Harvard University, Cambridge, MA.

Levy, B. R., Pilver, C., Chung, P. H., & Slade, M. D. (2014). Subliminal strengthening: Improving older individuals' physical function over time with an implicit-age-stereotype intervention. *Psychological Science, 25*, 2127–2135.

Levy, S. E., Mandell, D. S., & Schultz, R. T. (2009). Autism. *The Lancet, 374*, 1627–1638.

Lewandowsky, S., & Obeauer, K. (2016). Motivated rejection of science. *Current Directions in Psychological Science, 25*, 217–222.

Lewandowsky, S., & Thomas, J. L. (2009). Expertise: Acquisition, limitations, and control. *Reviews of Human Factors and Ergonomics, 5*, 140–165.

Lewin, D. S., Wang, G., Chen, Y. I., Skora, E., Hoehn, J., Baylor, A., & Wang, J. (2017). *Journal of Adolescent Health, 61*, 205–211.

Lewis, J. M., & Kreider, R. M. (2015). Remarriage in the United States. *American Community Survey Reports, U.S. Bureau of the Census.* Available from www.census.gov/content/dam/Census/library/publications/2015/acs/acs-30.pdf

Lewis, M. (1994). Myself and me. In S. T. Parker, R. W. Mitchell, & M. L. Boccia (Eds.), *Self-awareness in animals and humans: Developmental perspectives* (pp. 20–34). New York, NY: Cambridge University Press.

Lewis, M. (2016a). The emergence of human emotions. In L. F. Barrett, M. Lewis, & J. M. Haviland-Jones (Eds.), *Handbook of emotions* (4th ed., pp. 272–292). New York, NY: Guilford Press.

Lewis, M. (2016b). Self-conscious emotions: Embarrassment, pride, shame, guilt, and hubris. In L. F. Barrett, M. Lewis, & J. M. Haviland-Jones (Eds.), *Handbook of emotions* (4th ed., pp. 792–814). New York, NY: Guilford Press.

Lewis, M., & Michalson, L. (1983). *Children's emotions and moods: Developmental theory and measurement.* New York, NY: Plenum Press.

Lewis, M. D., & Ramsay, D. (2004). Development of self-recognition, personal pronoun use, and pretend play during the second year. *Child Development, 75*, 1821–1831.

Lewis, T. T., Cogburn, C. D., & Williams, D. R. (2015). Self-reported experiences of discrimination and health: Scientific advances, ongoing controversies, and emerging issues. *Annual Review of Clinical Psychology, 22*, 407–440.

Lewit, E. M., & Baker, L. S. (1995). School readiness. *Critical issues for children and youths, 5*, 128–139.

Li, J., Holloway, S. D., Bempechat, J., & Loh, E. (2008). Building and using a social network: Nurture for low-income Chinese American adolescents' learning. *New Directions for Child and Adolescent Development, 121*, 9–25.

Li, W., Liu, Q., Deng, X., Chen, Y., Liu, S., & Story, M. (2017). Association between obesity and puberty timing: A systematic review and meta-analysis. *International Journal of Environmental Research and Public Health, 14.* doi:10.3390/ijerph14101266

Li-Korotky, H-S. (2012). Age related hearing loss: Quality of care for quality of life. *The Gerontologist, 52*, 265–271.

Liben, L. S. (2016). We've come a long way, baby (But we're not there yet): Gender past, present, and future. *Child Development, 87*, 5–28.

Liben, L. S., & Bigler, R. S. (2002). The developmental course of gender differentiation. *Monographs of the Society for Research in Child Development, 67*, 1–147.

Liben, L. S., Bigler, R. S., & Hilliard, L. J. (2014). Gender development: From universality to individuality. In E. T. Gershoff, R. Mistry, & D. Crosby (Eds.), *Societal contexts of child development: Pathways of influence and implications for practice and policy* (pp. 2–24). Oxford: Oxford University Press.

Liben, L. S., Bigler, R. S., & Krogh, H. R. (2002). Language at work: Children's gendered interpretations of occupational titles. *Child Development, 73*, 810–828.

Liben, L. S., & Signorella, M. L. (1980). Gender-related schemata and constructive memory in children. *Child Development, 57*, 11–18.

Liben, L. S., & Signorella, M. L. (1993). Gender-schematic processing in children: The role of initial interpretations of stimuli. *Developmental Psychology, 29*, 141–149.

Lieberman, A. F., Chu, A., Van Horn, P., & Harris, W. W. (2011). Trauma in early childhood: Empirical evidence and clinical implications. *Development and Psychopathology, 23*, 397–410.

Lieberman, A. F., & Van Horn, P. (2008). *Psychotherapy with infants and young children: Repairing the effects of stress and trauma on early attachment.* New York, NY: Guilford.

Lien, D., Hu, Y., & Liu, L. (2017). Subjective well-being and income: A re-examination of satiation using the regression kink model with an unknown threshold. *Journal of Applied Econometrics, 32*(2), 463–469.

Lim, C. (2015). Religion and subjective well-being across religious traditions: Evidence from 1.3 million Americans. *Journal for the Scientific Study of Religion, 54*(4), 684–701.

Lin, J., Epel, E., & Blackburn, E. (2011). Telomeres and lifestyle factors: Roles in cellular aging. *Mutation Research, 730*, 85–89.

Lin, P. (2016). Risky behaviors: Integrating adolescent egocentrism with the theory of planned behavior. *Review of General Psychology, 20*, 392–398.

Lin, Y., Worthington, E. L., Griffin, B. J., Greer, C. L., Opare-Henaku, A., Lavelock, C. R., . . . Muller, H. (2014). Efficacy of REACH forgiveness across cultures. *Journal of Clinical Psychology, 70*(9), 781–793.

Lincoln, Y. S., & Guba, E. G. (1985). *Naturalistic inquiry.* Beverly Hills, CA: Sage.

Lind, T., Raby, K. L., Caron, E. B., Roben, C. K., & Dozier, M. (2107). Enhancing executive functioning among toddlers in foster care with an attachment-based intervention. *Development and Psychopathology, 29,* 575–586.

Lindquist, K. A., Siegel, E. H., Quigley, K. S., & Barrett, L. F. (2013). The hundred-year emotion war: Are emotions natural kinds or psychological constructions? Comment on Lench, Flores, and Bench (2011). *Psychological Bulletin, 139,* 255–263.

Lindsey, L. L. (2015). *Gender roles: A sociological perspective.* London: Routledge.

Linehan, M. (1993). *Skills training manual for treating borderline personality disorder.* New York, NY: Guilford Press.

Lionettia, F., Pastore, M., & Barone, L. (2015). Attachment in institutionalized children: A review and meta-analysis. *Child Abuse & Neglect, 42,* 135–145.

Lipsitz, J. D., & Markowitz, J. C. (2013). Mechanisms of change in interpersonal therapy (IPT). *Clinical Psychology Review, 33*(8), 1134–1147.

Liu, H., Li, Y., & Guo, G. (2015). Gene by social-environment interaction for youth delinquency and violence: Thirty-nine aggression-related genes. *Social Forces; a Scientific Medium of Social Study and Interpretation, 93,* 881–903.

Liu, J., Zhao, S., Chen, X., Falk, E., & Albarracín, D. (2017). The influence of peer behavior as a function of social and cultural closeness: A meta-analysis of normative influence on adolescent smoking initiation and continuation. *Psychological Bulletin, 143*(10), 1082.

Livingston, R. W., Rosette, A. S., & Washington, E. F. (2012). Can an agentic black woman get ahead? The impact of race and interpersonal dominance on perceptions of female leaders. *Psychological Science, 23,* 354–358.

Lock, J. (2015). An update on evidence-based psychosocial treatments for eating disorders in children and adolescents. *Journal of Clinical Child & Adolescent Psychology, 44*(5), 707–721.

Lock, J., & LeGrange, D. (2015). *Treatment manual for anorexia nervosa second edition: A family-based approach.* New York, NY: Guilford Press.

Locke, R. L., Lagasse, L. L., Seifer, R., Lester, B. M., Shankaran, S., Bada, H. S., & Bauer, C. R. (2016). Effects of prenatal substance exposure on infant temperament vary by context. *Development and Psychopathology, 28,* 309–326.

Loeber, R., & Farrington, D. P. (2000). Young children who commit crime: Epidemiology, developmental origins, risk factors, early interventions, and policy implications. *Development and Psychopathology, 12,* 737–762.

Loeber, R., & Strouthamer-Loeber, M. (1986). Family factors as correlates and predictors of juvenile conduct problems and delinquency. In M. Tonry & N. Morrys (Eds.), *Crime and justice. An annual review of the research* (pp. 29–149). Chicago, IL: University of Chicago Press.

Loevinger, J. (1976). *Ego development: Conception and theory.* San Francisco, CA: Jossey-Bass.

Loftus, E. F. (1979). *Eyewitness testimony.* Cambridge, MA: Harvard University Press.

Lonnemann, J., Linkersdörfer, J., Hasselhorn, M., & Lindberg, S. (2013). Gender differences in both tails of the distribution of numerical competencies in preschool children. *Educational Studies in Mathematics, 84,* 201–208.

Lopez-Hartmann, M., Wens, J., Verhoeven, V., & Remmen, R. (2012). The effect of caregiver support interventions for informal caregivers of community-dwelling frail elderly: A systematic review. *International Journal of Integrated Care, 12.* doi:10.5334/ijic.845

Lorber, M. F., Erlanger, A. C. E., Heyman, R. E., & O'Leary, K. D. (2015). The honeymoon effect: Does it exist and can it be predicted? *Prevention Science, 16,* 550–559.

Lovaas, O. I. (1987). Behavioral treatment and normal educational and intellectual functioning in young autistic children. *Journal of Consulting and Clinical Psychology, 55,* 3–9.

Love, J. M., Harrison, L., Sagi-Schwartz, A., van Ijzendoorn, M. H., Ross, C., Ungerer, J. A., . . . Chazan-Cohen, R. (2003). Child care quality matters: How conclusions may vary with context. *Child Development, 74,* 1021–1033.

Luan, M., & Li, H. (2017a). Good enough—compromise between desirability and feasibility: An alternative perspective on satisficing. *Journal of Experimental Social Psychology, 70,* 110–116.

Luan, M., & Li, H. (2017b). Maximization paradox: Result of believing in an objective best. *Personality and Social Psychology Bulletin, 43*(5), 652–661.

Lucas, R. E., Clark, A. E., Georgellis, Y., & Diener, E. (2004). Unemployment alters the set point for life satisfaction. *Psychological Science: Research, Theory, and Application in Psychology and Related Sciences, 15,* 8–13.

Lucassen, N., Tharner, A., van IJzendoorn, M. H., Bakersmans-Kranenburg, M. J., Volling, B. L., Verhulst, E. C., . . . Tiemeier, H. (2011). The association between paternal sensitivity and infant-father attachment security: A meta-analysis of three decades of research. *Journal of Family Psychology, 25,* 986–992.

Luedke, C. L. (2017). Person first, student second: Staff and administrators of color supporting students of color authentically in higher education. *Journal of College Student Development, 58,* 37–52.

Lukowski, A. F., & Bauer, P. J. (2014). Long term memory in infancy and early childhood. In P. J. Bauer & R. Fivush (Eds.), *The Wiley handbook on the development of children's memory* (pp. 230–254). Chichester, West Sussex: John Wiley & Sons Inc.

Lumey, L. H., & Van Poppel, F. (2013). The Dutch famine of 1944–1945 as a human laboratory. In L. H. Lumey & A. Vaiserman (Eds.), *Early life nutrition, adult health, and development: Lessons from changing diets, famines, and experimental studies.* Hauppauge, NY: Nova Science Publishers, Inc.

Lund, D. A., Dimond, M. F., Caserta, M. S., Johnson, R. J., Poulton, J. L., & Connelly, J. R. (1985–1986). Identifying elderly with coping difficulties after two years of bereavement. *Omega, 16,* 213–224.

Lundy, B. L. (2016). Preschoolers' mind-related comments during collaborative problem-solving: Parental contributions and developmental outcomes. *Social Development, 25,* 722–741.

Luo, S. (2017). Assortative mating and couple similarity: Patterns, mechanisms, and consequences. *Social and Personality Psychology Compass.* Available at https://doi.org/10.1111/spc3.12337

Luppa, M., Sikorski, C., Luck, T., Weyerer, S., Villringer, A., König, H., & Riedel-Heller, S. G. (2012). Prevalence and risk factors of depressive symptoms in latest life—results of the Leipzig Longitudinal Study of the Aged (LEILA 75+). *International Journal of Geriatric Psychiatry, 27,* 286–295.

Luthar, S. (2003). The culture of affluence: Psychological costs of material wealth. *Child Development, 74,* 1581–1983.

Luthar, S. S., & Ciciolla, L. (2016). What it feels like to be a mother: Variations by children's developmental stages. *Developmental Psychology, 52,* 143–154.

Lutz, A., Greischar, L. L., Rawlings, N. B., Ricard, M., & Davidson, R. J. (2004). Long-term meditators self-induce high-amplitude gamma synchrony during mental practice. *Proceedings of the National Academy of Sciences, 101,* 16369–16373.

Lutz, A., Slagter, H. A., Dunne, J. D., & Davidson, R. J. (2008). Attention regulation and monitoring in meditation. *Trends in Cognitive Sciences, 12,* 163–169.

Lux, V., & van Ommen, C. (2016). The generational brain: Introduction. *Theory & Psychology, 26,* 561–571.

Luyckx, K., Schwartz, S. J., Berzonsky, M. D., Soenens, B., Vansteenkiste, M., Smits, I., & Goossens, L. (2008). Capturing ruminative exploration: Extending the four-dimensional model of identity formation in late adolescence. *Journal of Research in Personality, 42*(1), 58–82.

Luyckx, K., Teppers, E., Klimstra, T. A., & Rassart, J. (2014). Identity processes and personality traits and types in adolescence: Directionality of effects and developmental trajectories. *Developmental Psychology, 50,* 2144–2153.

Lyall, K., Schmidt, R. J., & Hertz-Piciotto, I. (2014). Maternal lifestyle and environmental risk factors for autism spectrum disorders. *International Journal of Epidemiology, 43,* 443–464.

Lyness, J. M. (2004). Treatment of depressive conditions in later life: Real-world light for dark (or dim) tunnels. *Journal of the American Medical Association, 291,* 1626–1628.

Lynn, J. (2000). Learning to care for people with chronic illness facing the end of life. *Journal of the American Medical Association, 284,* 2508–2513.

Lyons, H. A., Manning, W. D., Longmore, M. A., & Giordano, P. C. (2014). Young adult casual sexual behavior: Life-course-specific motivations and consequences. *Sociological Perspectives, 57,* 79–101.

Lyons-Ruth, K., & Jacobvitz, D. (2016). Attachment disorganization from infancy to adulthood: Neurobiological correlates, parenting contexts and pathways to disorder. In J. Cassidy & P. R. Shaver (Eds.), *Handbook of attachment: Theory, research, and clinical applications* (3rd ed., pp. 667–695). New York, NY: Guilford Press.

Lytle, M. C., Clancy, M. E., Foley, P. F., & Cotter, E. W. (2015). Current trends in retirement: Implications for career counseling and vocational psychology. *Journal of Career Development, 42*(3), 170–184.

Lytle, N., London, K., & Bruck, M. (2015). Young children's ability to use two-dimensional and three-dimensional symbols to show placements of body touches and hidden objects. *Journal of Experimental Child Psychology, 134,* 30–42.

Lytton, H., & Romney, D. M. (1991). Parents' differential socialization of boys and girls: A meta-analysis. *Psychological Bulletin, 109*, 267–296.

Lyubomirsky, S. (2001). Why are some people happier than others? The role of cognitive and motivational processes in well-being. *American Psychologist, 56*, 239–249.

Lyubomirsky, S., King, L. A., & Diener, E. (2005). The benefits of frequent positive affect: Does happiness lead to success? *Psychological Bulletin, 131*, 803–855.

Ma, H., & Teasdale, J. (2004). Mindfulness-based cognitive therapy for depression: Replication and exploration of differential relapse prevention effects. *Journal of Consulting and Clinical Psychology, 72*, 31–40.

Maccoby, E. E. (1990). Gender and relationships: A developmental account. *American Psychologist, 45*, 513–520.

Maccoby, E. E. (1998). *The two sexes: Growing up apart, coming together.* Cambridge, MA: Harvard University Press.

Maccoby, E. E., & Jacklin, C. N. (1987). Gender segregation in childhood. In H. W. Reese (Ed.), *Advances in child development* (Vol. 20, pp. 239–288). New York, NY: Academic Press.

Maccoby, E. E., & Martin, J. A. (1983). Socialization in the context of the family: Parent-child interaction. In P. H. Mussen (Series Ed.) & E. M. Hetherington (Vol. Ed.), *Handbook of child psychology: Vol. 4. Socialization, personality and social development* (4th ed., pp. 1–101). New York, NY: Wiley.

MacDonald, K. B., & Parke, R. D. (1986). Parent-child physical play: The effects of sex and age of children and parents. *Sex Roles, 15*, 367–379.

MacDonald, S. W. S., Hultsch, D. F., & Dixon, R. A. (2011). Aging and the shape of cognitive change before death: Terminal decline or terminal drop? *The Journals of Gerontology, Series B: Psychological Sciences and Social Sciences, 66*, 292–301.

Mace, N. L., & Rabins, P. V. (1999). *The 36-hour-day: A family guide to caring for persons with Alzheimer's disease, related dementing illnesses, and memory of later in life* (3rd ed.). Baltimore, MD: Johns Hopkins University Press.

Macfie, J., Brumariu, L. E., & Lyons-Ruth, K. (2015). Parent-child role-confusion: A critical review of an emerging concept. *Developmental Review, 36*, 34–57.

Macfie, J., Cicchetti, D., & Toth, S. L. (2001). Dissociation in maltreated versus nonmaltreated preschool-aged children. *Child Abuse & Neglect, 25*, 1253–1267.

Mackey, A. P., Hill S. S., Stone, S. I., & Bunge, S. A. (2011). Differential effects of reasoning and speed training in children. *Developmental Science, 14*, 582–590.

Mackie, S., Shaw, P., Lenroot, R., Pierson, R., Greenstein, D. K., Nugent, T. F., 3rd, . . . Rapoport, J. L. (2007). Cerebellar development and clinical outcome in attention deficit hyperactivity disorder. *American Journal of Psychiatry, 164*, 647–655.

MacKinnon, S. P., De Pasquale, D., & Pratt, M. W. (2016). Predicting generative concern in young adulthood from narrative intimacy: A 5-year follow-up. *Journal of Adult Development, 23*, 27–35.

MacLean, P. D. (1952). Some psychiatric implications of the physiological studies on the frontotemporal portion of the limbic system. *Electroencephalography and Clinical Neurophysiology, 4*, 407–418.

MacLean, P. D. (1970). The triune brain, emotion, and scientific basis. In F. O. Schmidt (Ed.), *The neurosciences: Second study program* (pp. 336–349). New York, NY: Rockefeller University Press.

Madigan, S., Brumariu, L. E., Villani, V., Atkinson, L., & Lyons-Ruth, K. (2016). Representational and questionnaire measures of attachment: A meta-analysis of relations to child internalizing and externalizing problems. *Psychological Bulletin, 142*, 367–399.

Madkour, A. B., De Looze, M., Ma, P., Halpern, C. T., Farhat, T., ter Bogt, T. F. M., . . . Godeau, E. (2014). Macro-level age norms for the timing of sexual initiation and adolescents early sexual initiation in 17 European countries. *Journal of Adolescent Health, 55*, 114–121.

Madlensky, L., Trepanier, A. M., Cragun, D., Lerner, B., Shannon, K. M., & Zierhut, H. (2017). A rapid systematic review of outcomes studies in genetic counseling. *Journal of Genetic Counseling, 26*, 361–378.

Maercker, A., & Zoellner, T. (2004). The Janus-face of self-perceived growth: Toward a two-component model of posttraumatic growth. *Psychological Inquiry, 15*, 41–48.

Maestripieri, D., Henry, A., & Nickels, N. (2017). Explaining financial and prosocial biases in favor of attractive people: Interdisciplinary perspectives from economics, social psychology, and evolutionary psychology. *Behavioral and Brain Sciences.* doi:10.1017/S0140525X16000340, e19

Maglione, M. A., Das, L., Raaen, L., Smith, A., Chari, R., Newberry, S., . . . Gidengil, C. (2014). Safety of vaccines used for routine immunization of U.S. children: A systematic review. *Pediatrics, 134*, 325–337.

Magnuson, K. A., & Duncan, G. J. (2006). The role of family socioeconomic resources in the black-white test score gap among young children. *Developmental Review, 26*, 365–399.

Magolda, M. B., & Taylor, K. B. (2015). Developing self-authorship in college to navigate emerging adulthood. In J. J. Arnett (Ed.), *The Oxford handbook of emerging adulthood* (pp. 299–315). New York, NY: Oxford University Press.

Maguire-Jack, K., Gromoske, A. N., & Berger, L. M. (2012). Spanking and child development during the first 5 years of life. *Child Development, 83*, 1960–1977.

Mahoney, J. L. (2000). School extracurricular activity participation as a moderator in the development of antisocial patterns. *Child Development, 71*, 502–516.

Mahoney, J. L., Larson, R. W., & Eccles, J. S. (2005). *Organized activities as contexts of development: Extracurricular activities, after-school and community programs.* Mahwah, NJ: Erlbaum.

Mahrer, N. E., Sandler, I. N., Wolchik, S. A., Winslow, E. B., Moran, J. A., & Weinstock, D. (2016). How do parenting time and interparental conflict affect the relations of quality of parenting and child well-being following divorce? In L. Drozd, M. Saini, & N. Olesin (Eds.), *Parenting plan evaluations: Applied research for the family court* (2nd ed., pp. 63–74). New York, NY: Oxford University Press.

Maier, S. F., & Watkins, L. R. (1998). Cytokines for psychologists: Implications of bi-directional immune-to-brain communication for understanding behavior, mood, and cognition. *Psychological Review, 105*, 83–107.

Maier, S. F., Watkins, L. R., & Fleshner, M. (1994). Psychoneuroimmunology: The interface between behavior, brain and immunity. *American Psychologist, 49*, 1004–1017.

Main, M., & George, C. (1985). Responses of abused and disadvantaged toddlers to distress in agemates: A study in the day care setting. *Developmental Psychology, 21*, 407–412.

Main, M., & Goldwyn, R. (1984). Predicting rejection of her infant from mother's representation of her own experience: Implications for the abused-abusing intergenerational cycle. *International Journal of Child Abuse and Neglect, 8*, 203–217.

Main, M., & Goldwyn, R. (1985–1994). *Adult attachment classification system.* Unpublished manuscript, University of California at Berkeley.

Main, M., & Hesse, E. (1992). *Frightening, frightened, timid/deferential, dissociated, or disorganized behavior on the part of the patent: Coding system.* Unpublished manuscript, University of California at Berkeley.

Main, M., Kaplan, N., & Cassidy, J. (1985). Security in infancy, childhood, and adulthood: A move to the level of representation. In I. Bretherton & E. Waters (Eds.), Growing points of attachment theory and research. *Monographs of the Society for Research in Child Development, 50* (Serial No. 209), 55–104.

Main, M., & Solomon, J. (1986) Discovery of a new, insecure-disorganized/disoriented attachment pattern. In T. B. Brazelton & M. Yogman (Eds.), *Affective development in infancy* (pp. 95–124). Norwood, NJ: Ablex.

Main, M., & Solomon, J. (1990). Procedures for identifying infants as disorganized/disoriented during the Ainsworth strange situation. In M. Greenberg, D. Cicchetti, & E. M. Cummings (Eds.), *Attachment in the preschool years: Theory, research, and intervention* (pp. 121–160). Chicago, IL: University of Chicago Press.

Majeed, M. H., Ali, A. A., & Sudak, D. M. (2018). Mindfulness-based interventions for chronic pain: Evidence and applications. *Asian Journal of Psychiatry, 32*, 79–83.

Majidi, N. E., Bouchard, M. H., Gosselin, N., & Carrier, G. (2012). Relationship between prenatal exposure to polychlorinated biphenyls and birth weight: A systematic analysis of published epidemiological studies through a standardization of biomonitoring data. *Regulatory Toxicology and Pharmacology, 64*, 161–176.

Makris, N., Tachmatzidis, D., Demetriou, A., & Spanoudis, G. (2017). Mapping the evolving core of intelligence: Changing relations between executive control, reasoning, language, and awareness. *Intelligence, 62*, 12–30.

Malin, H., Ballard, P. J., & Damon, W. (2015). Civic purpose: An integrated construct for understanding civic development in adolescence. *Human Development, 58*, 103–130.

Malina, R. M. (1990). Physical growth and performance during the transitional years (9–16). In R. Montemayor, G. R. Adams, & T. P. Gullotta (Eds.), *From childhood to adolescence: A transitional period?* (pp. 41–62). Newbury Park, CA: Sage.

Malti, T., Gummerum, M., Keller, M., & Buchmann, M. (2009). Children's moral motivation, sympathy, and prosocial behavior. *Child Development*, *80*, 442–460.

Malti, T., Noam, G. G., Beelmann, A., & Sommer, S. (2016). Good enough? Interventions for child mental health: From adoption to adaptation—From programs to systems. *Journal of Clinical Child & Adolescent Psychology*, *45*, 707–709. doi:10.1080/15374416.2016.1157759

Mansfield, E. D., & McAdams, D. P. (1996). Generativity and themes of agency and communion in adult autobiography. *Personality and Social Psychology Bulletin*, *22*, 721–731.

Marchal, J. P., Maurice-Stam, H., Houtzager, B. A., Rutgers van Rosenburg-Marres, S. L., Oostrom, K. J., Grootenhuis, M. A., & van Trotsenburg, A. S. P. (2016). Growing up with Down syndrome: Development from 6 months to 10.7 years. *Research in Developmental Disabilities*, *59*, 437–450.

Marcia, J. E. (1964). *Determination and construct validity of ego identity status*. Unpublished doctoral dissertation, University of California at Davis.

Marcia, J. E. (1967). Ego identity status: Relationship to change in self-esteem, "general maladjustment," and authoritarianism. *Journal of Personality*, *35*, 118–133.

Marcia, J. E. (1993). The status of the statuses: Research review. In J. E. Marcia, A. S. Waterman, D. R. Matteson, S. L. Archer, & J. L. Orlofsky (Eds.), *Ego identity: A handbook for psychosocial research* (pp. 22–41). New York, NY: Springer-Verlag.

Marcia, J. E., Waterman, A. S., Matteson, D. R., Archer, S. L., & Orlofsky, J. L. (1993). *Ego identity: A handbook for psychosocial research*. New York, NY: Springer-Verlag.

Marcus, R. F. (1975). The child as elicitor of parental sanctions for independent and dependent behavior: A simulation of parent-child interaction. *Developmental Psychology*, *11*, 443–452.

Marcus, R. F. (1976). The effects of children's emotional and instrumental dependent behavior on parental response. *Journal of Psychology*, *92*, 57–63.

Markey, P. M., & Ferguson, C. J. (2017). *Moral combat: Why the war on violent video games is wrong*. Dallas, TX: Banbella Books, Inc.

Markman, H. J., Stanley, S., & Blumberg, S. L. (1994). *Fighting for your marriage: Positive steps for preventing divorce and preserving a lasting love*. San Francisco, CA: Jossey-Bass.

Markovits, H. (2017). In the beginning stages: Conditional reasoning with category based and causal premises in 8- to 10-year olds. *Cognitive Development*, *41*, 1–9.

Markovits, H., Brisson, J., de Chantal, P.-L., & Thompson, V. A. (2017). Interactions between inferential strategies and belief bias. *Memory and Cognition*, *45*, 1182–1192.

Marks, A. K., Ejesi, K., & García Coll, C. (2014). Understanding the U.S. immigrant paradox in childhood and adolescence. *Child Development Perspectives*, *8*, 59–64.

Marks, N. F., Bumpass, L. L., & Jun, H. (2003). Family roles and well-being during the middle life course. In O. G. Brim, C. D. Ryff, & R. Kessler, (Eds.), *How healthy are we: A national study of well-being in midlife* (pp. 514–549). Chicago, IL: University of Chicago Press.

Marks, P. E. L. (2017). Introduction to the special issue: 20th-century origins and 21st-century

developments of peer nomination methodology. In P. E. L. Marks & A. H. N. Cillessen (Eds.), New directions in peer nomination methodology. *New Directions for Child and Adolescent Development*, *157*, 7–19.

Markus, H., Crane, M., Bernstein, S., & Siladi, M. (1982). Self-schemas and gender. *Journal of Personality and Social Psychology*, *42*, 38–50.

Markus, H., & Kitayama, S. (1991). Culture and the self: Implications for cognition, emotion, and motivation. *Psychological Review*, *98*, 224–253.

Markus, H. R. (2017). American = independent? *Perspectives on Psychological Science*, *12*, 855–866.

Marmot, M., & Wilkinson, R. (2009). *Social determinants of health. The life course, the social gradient, and health*. Published to Oxford Scholarship Online: September 2009, doi:10.1093/acprof:oso/9780198565895.001.0001

Marsh, E. J., Cantor, A. D., & Brashier, N. M. (2016). Believing that humans swallow spiders in their sleep: False beliefs as side effects of the processes that support accurate knowledge. *Psychology of Learning and Motivation*, *64*, 93–123.

Marsh, H. W., & Shavelson, R. (1985). Self-concept: Its multifaceted, hierarchical structure. *Educational Psychologist*, *20*, 107–123.

Marshal, M. P., Dietz, L. J., Friedman, M. S., Stall, R., Smith, H. A., McGinley, J., . . . Brent, D. A. (2011). Suicidality and depression disparities between sexual minority and heterosexual youth: A meta-analytic review. *Journal of Adolescent Health*, *49*(2), 115–123.

Marshall, E. A., & Butler, K. (2015). School-to-work transitions in emerging adulthood. In J. J. Arnett (Ed.), *The Oxford handbook of emerging adulthood* (pp. 316–333). New York, NY: Oxford University Press.

Martel, M. M. (2013). Sexual selection and sex differences in the prevalence of childhood externalizing and adolescent internalizing disorders. *Psychological Bulletin*, *139*, 1221–1259.

Martel, M. M., Levinson, C. A., Langer, J. K., & Nigg, J. T. (2016). A network analysis of developmental change in ADHD symptom structure from preschool to adulthood. *Clinical Psychological Science*. doi: 10.1177/2167702615618664

Martin, C. D. (2000). More than the work: Race and gender differences in caregiving burden. *Journal of Family Issues*, *21*, 986–1005.

Martin, C. L., Andrews, N. C., England, D. E., Zosuls, K., & Ruble, D. N. (2017). A dual identity approach for conceptualizing and measuring children's gender identity. *Child Development*, *88*, 167–182.

Martin, C. L., & Fabes, R. A. (2001). The stability and consequences of young children's same-sex peer interactions. *Developmental Psychology*, *37*, 431–446.

Martin, C. L., Fabes, R. A., Hanish, L. D., & Hollenstein, T. (2005). Social dynamics in the preschool. *Developmental Review*, *25*, 299–327.

Martin, C. L., Kornienko, O., Schaefer, D. R., Hanish, L. D., Fabes, R. A., & Goble, P. (2013). The role of sex of peers and gender-typed activities in young children's peer affiliative networks: A longitudinal analysis of selection and influence. *Child Development*, *84*, 921–937.

Martin, C. L., & Ruble, D. N. (2009). Patterns of gender development. *Annual Review of Psychology*, *61*, 353–381.

Martin, C. L., Ruble, D. N., & Szkrybalo, J. (2002). Cognitive theories of early gender development. *Psychological Bulletin*, *128*, 903–933.

Martin-Storey, A. (2016). Gender, sexuality, and gender nonconformity: Understanding variation in functioning. *Child Development Perspectives*, *10*, 257–262.

Marx, K., & Engels, F. (1972). The German ideology. In R. C. Tucker (Ed.), *The Marx-Engels reader*. New York, NY: Norton. (Original work published 1846)

Marzillier, J. (2014). *The trauma therapies*. Oxford, UK: Oxford University Press.

Masangkay, Z. S., McCluskey, K. A., McIntyre, C. W., Sims-Knight, J., Vaughn, B. E., & Flavell, J. H. (1974). The early development of inferences about the visual percepts of others. *Child Development*, *45*, 237–246.

Mascaro, J. S., Rentscher, K. E., Hackett, P. D., Mehl, M. R., & Rilling, J. K. (2017). Child gender influences paternal behavior, language, and brain function. *Behavioral Neuroscience*, *131*, 262–273.

Masche, J. G., Sektionen för lärande och miljö, & Högskolan Kristianstad. (2010). Explanation of normative declines in parents' knowledge about their adolescent children. *Journal of Adolescence*, *33*(2), 271–284.

Mashburn, A. J., Pianta, R. C., Barbarin, O. A., Bryant, D., Hamre, B. K., Downer, J. T., . . . Howes, C. (2008). Measures of classroom quality in prekindergarten and children's development of academic, language, and social skills. *Child Development*, *79*, 732–749.

Maslow, A. H. (1954). *Motivation and personality*. New York, NY: Harper & Row.

Masten, A. (2014). Global perspectives on resilience in children and youth. *Child Development*, *85*, 6–20.

Masters, K. S., & Hooker, S. A. (2013). Religiousness/spirituality, cardiovascular disease, and cancer: Cultural integration for health research and intervention. *Journal of Consulting and Clinical Psychology*, *81*(2), 206–216.

Masuda, T., & Nisbett, R. E. (2001). Attending holistically versus analytically: Comparing the context sensitivity of Japanese and Americans. *Journal of Personality and Social Psychology*, *81*, 922–934.

Masuda, T., & Nisbett, R. E. (2006). Culture and change blindness. *Cognitive Sciences*, *30*, 381–399.

Mather, M. (2016). The affective neuroscience of aging. *Annual Review of Psychology*, *67*, 213–238.

Matosin N., Halldorsdottir, T., & Binder, E. B. (2018). Understanding the molecular mechanisms underpinning gene by environment interactions in psychiatric disorders: The fkbp5 model. *Biological Psychiatry*, *83*, 821–830.

Mattson, M. P., Chan, S. L., & Duan, W. (2002). Modification of brain aging and neurodegenerative disorders by genes, diet, and behavior. *Physiological Review*, *82*, 637–672.

Mau, W. (1995). Educational planning and academic achievement of middle school students: A racial and cultural comparison. *Journal of Counseling and Development*, *73*, 518–526.

Mauss, D., Li, J., & Angerer, P. (2017). Psychometric properties of the work well index: A short questionnaire for Work-Related stress. *Stress and Health*, *33*(1), 80–85.

May, P., & Cotton, S. (2014). *Molecules that amaze us.* Boca Raton, FL: CRC Press.

May, P. A., Baete, A., Russo, J., Elliott, A. J., Blankenship, J., & Kalberg, W. O. (2014). Prevalence and characteristics of fetal alcohol spectrum disorders. *Pediatrics, 134*(5), 855–866.

May, P. A., Blankenship, J., Marais, A. S., Gossage, J. P., Kalberg, W. O., Joubert, B., . . . Seedat, S. (2013). Maternal alcohol consumption producing fetal alcohol spectrum disorders (FASD): Quantity, frequency, and timing of drinking. *Drug and Alcohol Dependence, 133,* 502–512.

May, P. A., Serna, P., Hurt, B. L., & DeBruyn, L. M. (2005). Outcome Evaluation of a Public Health Approach to Suicide Prevention in an American Indian Tribal Nation. *American Journal of Public Health, 95*(7), 1238–1244.

May, R. (1979). *Psychology and the human dilemma.* New York, NY: Norton.

Mayes, S. D., Calhoun, S. L., Waschbusch, D. A., Breaux, R. P., & Baweja, R. (2017). Reactive attachment/disinhibited social engagement disorders: Callous-unemotional traits and comorbid disorders. *Research in Developmental Disabilities, 63,* 28–37.

Mazzio, E., & Soliman, K. F. (2012). Whole genome expression profile in neuroblastoma cells exposed to 1-methyl-4-phenylpyridine. *Neurotoxicology, 33,* 1156–1169.

McAdams, D. P. (2000). Attachment, intimacy, and generativity. *Psychological Inquiry, 11,* 117–120.

McAdams, D. P. (2006). The redemptive self: Generativity and the stories Americans live by. *Research in Human Development, 3,* 81–100.

McAdams, D. P., & Bowman, P. J. (2001). Narrating life's turning points: Redemption and contamination. In D. P. McAdams, R. Josselson, & A. Lieblich (Eds.), *Turns in the road: Narrative studies of lives in transition* (pp. 3–34). Washington, DC: American Psychological Association.

McAdams, D. P., & de St. Aubin, E. (1992). A theory of generativity and its assessment through self-report, behavioral acts, and narrative themes in autobiography. *Journal of Personality and Social Psychology, 62,* 1003–1015.

McAdams, D. P., & Guo, J. (2015). Narrating the generative life. *Psychological Science, 26,* 475–483.

McAdams, D. P., Hart, H. M., & Maruna, S. (1998). The anatomy of generativity. In D. P. McAdams & E. de St. Aubin (Eds.), *Generativity and adult development: How and why we care for the next generation* (pp. 7–44). Washington, DC: American Psychological Association.

McAdams, D. P., & McLean, K. C. (2013). Narrative identity. *Current Directions in Psychological Science, 22,* 233–238.

McAdams, D. P., & Olson, B. D. (2010). Personality development: Continuity and change over the life course. *Annual Review of Psychology, 61,* 517–542.

McAlister, A. R., & Peterson, C. C. (2013). Siblings, theory of mind, and executive functioning in children aged 3-6 years: New longitudinal evidence. *Child Development, 84,* 1442–1458.

McAuliffe, G. J. (1993). Constructive development and career transition: Implications for counseling. *Journal of Counseling and Development, 72,* 23–28.

McAuliffe, G. J., & Emmett, J. (2017). The postmodern impulse and career counselor preparation. In L. A. Busacca & M. C. Rehfuss (Eds.), *Postmodern career counseling: A handbook of culture, context, and cases* (pp. 37–50). Alexandra, VA: American Counseling Association.

McCabe, K. O., Modecki, K. L., & Barber, B. L. (2016). Participation in organized activities protects against adolescents' risky substance use, even beyond development in conscientiousness. *Journal of Youth and Adolescence, 45*(11), 2292–2306.

McCann, I. L., & Pearlman, L. A. (1990). Vicarious traumatization: A framework for understanding the psychological effects of working with victims. *Journal of Traumatic Stress, 3,* 131–149.

McCarthy, J. (2015). Record-high 60% of Americans support same-sex marriage. *Gallup.* Available from www.gallup.com/poll/183272/record-high-americans-support-sex-marriage.aspx?utm_source=Social%20Issues&utm_medium=newsfeed&utm_campaign=tiles.

McCartney, K., Dearing, E., Taylor, B. A., & Bub, K. L. (2007). Quality child care supports the achievement of low-income children: Direct and indirect pathways through caregiving and the home environment. *Journal of Applied Developmental Psychology, 28,* 411–426.

McClelland, M. M., & Cameron, C. E. (2012). Self-regulation in early childhood: Improving conceptual clarity and developing ecologically valid measures. *Child Development Perspectives, 6,* 136–142.

McConnell, S. R., & Odom, S. L. (1986). Sociometrics: Peer-referenced measures and the assessment of social competence. In P. S. Strain, M. J. Guralnick, & H. M. Walker (Eds.), *Children's social behavior: Development, assessment, and modification* (pp. 215–284). New York, NY: Academic Press.

McCrae, R. R., & Costa, P. T. (2008). The five-factor theory of personality. In O. P. John, R. W. Robins, & L. A. Pervin (Eds.), *Handbook of personality: Theory and research* (3rd ed., pp. 159–181). New York, NY: Guilford Press.

McCrae, R. R., Costa, P. T., Ostendorf, F., Angleitner, A., Hrebickova, M., Avia, J., . . . Smith, P. B. (2000). Nature over nurture: Temperament, personality and life span development. *Journal of Personality and Social Psychology, 78,* 173–186.

McCrae, R. R., & John, O. T. (1992). An introduction to the five-factor model and its applications. *Journal of Personality, 60,* 175–215.

McCrae, R. R., & Terracciano, A. (2005). Personality profiles of cultures: Aggregate personality traits. *Journal of Personality and Social Psychology, 89,* 407–425.

McCrory, E., De Brito, S. A., & Viding, E. (2010). Research review: The neurobiology and genetics of maltreatment and adversity. *Journal of Child Psychology and Psychiatry, 51,* 1079–1095.

McCullough, M. E., Pargament, K. I., & Thoresen, C. T. (Eds.). (2002). *Forgiveness: Theory, research and practice.* New York, NY: Guilford Press.

McDonald, P. K. (2018). How 'flexible' are careers in the anticipated life course of young people? *Human Relations, 71,* 23–46.

McEachin, J. J., Smith, T., & Lovaas, O. I. (1993). Long-term outcome for children with autism who received early intensive behavioral treatment. *American Journal of Mental Retardation, 97,* 359–391.

McElwain, A. K., Korabik, K., & Rosin, H. M. (2005). An examination of gender differences in work-family conflict. *Canadian Journal of Behavioral Science, 37,* 283–298.

McElwain, N. L., Booth-LaForce, C., & Wu, X. (2011). Infant-mother attachment and children's friendship quality: Maternal mental-state talk as an intervening mechanism. *Developmental Psychology, 47,* 1295–1311.

McEwen, B. S. (2012). Brain on stress: How the social environment gets under the skin. *Proceedings of the National Academy of Sciences of the United States of America, 109,* 171–180.

McEwen, B. S., Bowles, N. P., Gray, J. D., Hill, M. N., Hunter, R. G., Karatsoreos, I. N., & Nasca, C. (2015). Mechanisms of stress in the brain. *Nature Neuroscience, 18,* 1353–1363.

McEwen, B. S., & Gianaros, P. J. (2010). Central role of the brain in stress and adaptation: Links to socioeconomic status, health, and disease. *Annals of the New York Academy of Sciences, 1186,* 190–222.

McEwen, B. S., & Karatsoreos, I. N. (2015). Sleep deprivation and circadian disruption: Stress, allostasis, and allostatic load. *Sleep Medicine Clinics, 10,* 1–10.

McEwen, B. S., & McEwen, C. A. (2016). Response to Jerome Kagan's essay on stress. *Perspectives on Psychological Science, 22,* 451–455.

McFarland, J., Hussar, B., deBrey, C., Snyder, T., Wang, X., Wilkinson-Flicker, S., . . . Hinz, S. (2017). The condition of education. *National Center for Education Statistics.* Available at https://nces.ed.gov/help/techissues.asp#pdf

McGinnis, D. (2016). Epistemological orientations and evidence evaluation in undergraduates. *Thinking Skills and Creativity, 19,* 279–289.

McGuigan, F., & Salmon, K. (2004). The time to talk: The influence of the timing of adult-child talk on children's event memory. *Child Development, 75,* 669–686.

McHale, S. M., Crouter, A. C., & Whiteman, S. D. (2003). The family contexts of gender development in childhood and adolescence. *Social Development, 12,* 125–148.

McHale, S. M., Kim, J-Y., Dotterer, A. M., Crouter, A. C., & Booth, A. (2009). The development of gendered interests and personality qualities from middle childhood through adolescence: A biosocial analysis. *Child Development, 80,* 482–495.

McHugh, P. (2014, June 12). Transgender surgery isn't the solution. *Wall Street Journal Op-Ed.* Available from http://www.wsj.com/articles/paul-mchugh-transgender-surgery-isnt-the-solution-1402615120.

McKay, R. T., & Dennett, D. C. (2009). The evolution of misbelief. *Behavioral and Brain Sciences, 32,* 493–561.

McKenzie, J. (2016). Happiness vs contentment? A case for a sociology of the good life. *Journal for the Theory of Social Behaviour, 46*(3), 252–267.

McLaughlin, K. A., Sheridan, M. A., & Nelson, C. A. (2017). Neglect as a violation of species-expectant experience: Neurodevelopmental consequences. *Biological Psychiatry, 82,* 462-471.

McLoyd, V. C., & Smith, J. (2002). Physical discipline and behavior problems in African American, European American, and Hispanic children: Emotional support as a moderator. *Journal of Marriage and the Family, 64,* 40–54.

McMahon, J. R., Greenberg, M. T., & the Conduct Problems Prevention Research Group [CPPRG]. (1995). The Fast Track Program: A developmentally focused intervention for children with conduct problems. *Clinician's Research Digest* (Suppl. Bulletin 13), 1–2.

McMahon, R. J., & Forehand, R. L. (2005). *Helping the noncompliant child: Family-based treatment for oppositional behavior.* New York, NY: Guilford Press.

McNeil, N. M., Fyfe, E. R., Petersen, L. A., Dunwiddie, A. E., & Brletic-Shipley, H. (2011). Benefits of practicing 4 = 2 + 2: Nontraditional problem formats facilitate children's understanding of mathematical equivalence. *Child Development, 82,* 1620–1633.

McNulty, J. K., & Karney, B. R. (2004). Positive expectations in the early years of marriage: Should couples expect the best or brace for the worst? *Journal of Personality and Social Psychology, 86,* 729–743.

McWayne, C. M., Melzi, G., Limlingan, M. C., & Schick, A. (2016). Ecocultural patterns of family engagement among low-income Latino families of preschool Children. *Developmental Psychology, 52*(7), 1088–1102. http://doi.org/10.1037/a0040343

Mead, G. H. (1934). *Mind, self, and society.* Chicago, IL: University of Chicago Press.

Meaney M. (2001). Maternal care, gene expression, and the transmission of individual differences in stress reactivity across generations. *Annual Review of Neuroscience, 24,* 1161–1192.

Meaney, M. J. (2010). Epigenetics and the biological definition of gene × environment interactions. *Child Development, 81,* 41–79.

Meeus, W. (2011). The study of adolescent identity formation 2000-2010: A review of longitudinal research. *Journal of Research on Adolescence, 21,* 75–94.

Meeus, W. (2017). Adolescent ethnic identity in social context: A commentary. *Child Development, 88,* 761–766.

Meeus, W., & Dekovic, M. (1995). Identity development, parental and peer support in adolescence: Results of a national Dutch study. *Adolescence, 30,* 931–944.

Meezan, W., & Rauch, J. (2005). Gay marriage, same-sex parenting, and America's children. *The Future of Children, 15,* 97–115.

Mehta, C. M., & Strough, J. (2009). Sex segregation in friendships and normative contexts across the life span. *Developmental Review, 29,* 201–220.

Meichenbaum, D. (1986). Cognitive behavior modification. In F. Kanfer & A. Goldstein (Eds.), *Helping people change: A textbook of methods* (3rd ed., pp. 346–380). New York, NY: Pergamon Press.

Meichenbaum, D. H., & Goodman, J. (1971). Training impulsive children to talk to themselves: A means for self-control. *Journal of Abnormal Psychology, 77,* 115–126.

Meier, E. A., Gallegos, J. V., Thomas, L. P. M., Depp, C. A., Irwin, S. A., & Jeste, D. V. (2016). Defining a good death (successful dying): Literature review and a call for research

and public dialogue. *The American Journal of Geriatric Psychiatry, 24,* 261–271.

Meins, E., Fernyhough, C., de Rosnay, M., Arnott, B., Leekam, S. R., & Turner, M. (2012). Mind-mindedness as a multidimensional construct: Appropriate and nonattuned mind-related comments independently predict infant-mother attachment in a socially diverse sample. *Infancy, 17,* 393–415.

Meir, E. I. (1989). Integrative elaboration of the congruence theory. *Journal of Vocational Behavior, 35,* 219–230.

Melchert, T. P. (2016). Leaving behind our pre-paradigmatic past: Professional psychology as a unified clinical science. *American Psychologist, 71,* 486–496.

Melinder, A., Forbes, D., Tronick, E., Fikke, L. M., & Gredeback, G. (2010). The development of the still-face effect: Mothers do matter. *Infant Behavior and Development, 33,* 472–481.

Mella, N., Fagot, D., Lecerf, T., & de Ribaupierre, A. (2015). Working memory and intraindividual variability in processing speed: A lifespan developmental and individual-differences study. *Memory and Cognition, 43,* 340–356.

Meltzoff, A. N. (1988). Infant imitation and memory: Nine-month-old infants in immediate and deferred tests. *Child Development, 59,* 217–225.

Meltzoff, A. N. (2007). The 'like me' framework for recognizing and becoming an intentional agent. *Acta Psychologica, 124,* 26–43.

Meltzoff, A. N., & Borton, R. W. (1979). Intermodal matching by human neonates. *Nature, 282,* 403–404.

Meltzoff, A. N., & Moore, M. K. (1977). Imitation of facial and manual gestures by human neonates. *Science, 198,* 75–78.

Mendez, J. L. (2010). How can parents get involved in preschool? Barriers and engagement in education by ethnic minority parents of children attending Head Start programs. *Cultural Diversity and Ethnic Minority Psychology, 16*(1), 26–36.

Mendle, J. (2014). Why puberty matters for psychopathology. *Child Development Perspectives, 8,* 218–222.

Mercer, J., Sarner, L., & Rosa, L. (2003). *Attachment therapy on trial: The torture and death of Candace Newmaker.* Westport, CT: Praeger.

Mercer, N., Crocetti, E., Branje, S., van Lier, P., & Meeus, W. (2017). Linking delinquency and personal identity formation across adolescence: Examining between- and within-person associations. *Developmental Psychology, 53,* 2182–2194.

Mermelshtine, R. (2017). Parent-child learning interactions: A review of the literature on scaffolding. *British Journal of Educational Psychology, 87,* 241–254.

Mesman, J., & Groeneveld, M. G. (2017). Gendered parenting in early childhood: Subtle but unmistakable if you know where to look. *Child Development Perspectives.* Advance Online Publication.

Mesman, J., Minter, T., Angnged, A., Cisse, I. A. H., Salali, G. D., & Migliano, A. B. (2017). Universality without uniformity: A culturally inclusive approach to sensitive responsiveness in infant caregiving. *Child Development.* doi:10.1111/cdev.12795

Mesman, J., van IJzendoorn, M. H., & Bakermans-Kranenburg, M. J. (2009). The many faces of

the still-face paradigm: A review and meta-analysis. *Developmental Review, 29,* 120–162.

Mesman, J., van IJzendoorn, M. H., & Sagi-Schwartz, A. (2016). Cross-cultural patterns of attachment: Universal and contextual dimensions. In J. Cassidy & P. R. Shaver (Eds.), *Handbook of attachment: Theory research and clinical applications* (3rd ed., pp. 852–877). New York, NY: Guilford Press.

Metler, S. J., & Busseri, M. A. (2017). Further evaluation of the tripartite structure of subjective wellbeing: Evidence from longitudinal and experimental studies. *Journal of Personality, 85*(2), 192–206.

Meyer, A. (1957). *Psychobiology: A science of man.* Springfield, IL: Charles C. Thomas.

Meyer-Bahlberg, H. F. (2005). Gender identity outcome in female-raised 46, XY persons with penile agenesis, cloacal exstrophy of the bladder, or penile ablation. *Archives of Sexual Behavior, 34,* 423–438.

Meylan, S. C., Frank, M. C., Roy, B. C., & Levy R. (2017). The emergence of an abstract grammatical category in children's early speech. *Psychological Science, 28,* 1–12.

Mickler, C., & Staudinger, U. M. (2008). Personal wisdom: Validation and age-related differences of a performance measure. *Psychology and Aging, 23,* 787–799.

Middleton, W., Raphael, B., Burnett, P., & Martinek, N. (1997). Psychological distress and bereavement. *Journal of Nervous and Mental Diseases, 185,* 447–453.

Midgley, C., Fedlaufer, H., & Eccles, J. S. (1988). The transition to junior high school: Beliefs of pre- and post-transition teachers. *Journal of Youth and Adolescence, 17,* 543–562.

Mihalic, S. W., & Elliot, D. (1997). Short- and long-term consequences of adolescent work. *Youth and Society, 28,* 464–498.

Mikami, A. Y., Lerner, M. D., & Lun, J. (2010). Social context influences on children's rejection by their peers. *Child Development Perspectives, 4,* 123–130.

Mikucka, M., Sarracino, F., & Dubrow, J. K. (2017). When does economic growth improve life satisfaction? Multilevel analysis of the roles of social trust and income inequality in 46 countries, 1981–2012. *World Development, 93,* 447.

Mikulincer, M., & Shaver, P. R. (2016a). Adult attachment and emotion regulation. In J. Cassidy & P. R. Shaver (Eds.), *Handbook of attachment: Theory, research, and clinical applications* (3rd ed., pp. 507–533). New York, NY: Guilford Press.

Mikulincer, M., & Shaver, P. R. (2016b). *Attachment in adulthood: Structure, dynamics, and change* (2nd ed.). New York, NY: Guilford Press.

Miller, A. (1981). *The drama of the gifted child.* New York, NY: Basic Books.

Miller, B. G., Kors, S., & Macfie, J. (2017). No differences? Meta-analytic comparisons of psychological adjustment in children of gay fathers and heterosexual parents. *Psychology of Sexual Orientation and Gender Diversity, 4,* 14–22.

Miller, D. L. (1983). Developmental changes in male/female voice classification by infants. *Infant Behavior and Development, 6,* 313–330.

Miller, G. E., Cohen, S., & Ritchey, A. K. (2002). Chronic psychological stress and the regulation of pro-inflammatory cytokines: A glucocorticoid-resistance model. *Health Psychology, 21,* 531–541.

Miller, J. G. (2006). Insights into moral development from cultural psychology. In M. Killen & J. Smetana (Eds.), *Handbook of moral development.* New York, NY: Erlbaum.

Miller, J. G., Goyal, N., & Wice, M. (2017). A cultural psychology of agency: Morality, motivation and reciprocity. *Perspectives on Psychological Science, 12,* 867–875.

Miller, K. P., Brewer, M. B., & Arbuckle, N. L. (2009). Social identity complexity: Its correlates and antecedents. *Group Processes & Intergroup Relations, 12*(1), 79.

Miller, P. H. (1994). Individual differences in children's strategic behavior: Utilization deficiencies. *Learning and Individual Differences, 6,* 285–307.

Miller, P. J., Fung, H., Lin, S., Chen, E. C-H., & Boldt, B. R. (2012). How socialization happens on the ground: Narrative practices as alternate socializing pathways in Taiwanese and European-American families. *Monographs of the Society for Research in Child Development, 77* (1, Serial No. 302).

Miller, S. A. (2012). *Theory of mind: Beyond the preschool years.* New York, NY: Psychology Press.

Miller, S. M., & Green, M. L. (1984). Coping with stress and frustration: Origins, nature, and development. In M. Lewis & C. Saarni (Eds.), *The socialization of emotions* (pp. 263–314). New York, NY: Plenum Press.

Miller, W. R., & Rollnick, S. (1991). *Motivational interviewing: Preparing people to change addictive behavior.* New York, NY: Guilford Press.

Miller, W. R., & Rollnick, S. (2002). *Motivational interviewing: Preparing people for change.* New York, NY: Guilford Press.

Miller-Heyl, J., MacPhee, D., & Fritz, J. J. (1998). DARE to be you: A family-support early prevention program. *Journal of Primary Prevention, 18,* 257–285.

Mills, K. L., Goddings, A-L., Herting, M. M., Meuwese, R., Blakemore, S-J., Crone, E. A., . . . Tamnes, C. K. (2016). Structural brain development between childhood and adulthood: Convergence across four longitudinal samples. *NeuroImage, 141,* 273–281.

Minges, K. E., & Redeker, N. S. (2016). Delayed school start times and adolescent sleep: A systematic review of the experimental evidence. *Sleep Medicine Reviews, 28,* 86–95.

Minuchin, S. (1974). *Families and family therapy.* Cambridge, MA: Harvard University Press.

Mireault, G. C., Crockenberg, S. C., Sparrow, J. E., Cousineau, K., Pettinato, C., & Woodard, K. (2015). Laughing matters: Infant humor in the context of parental affect. *Journal of Experimental Child Psychology, 136,* 30–41.

Mitka, M. (2000). Suggestions for help when the end is near. *Journal of the American Medical Association, 284,* 2441–2444.

Mix, K. S., Moore, J. A., & Holcomb E. (2011). One-to-one play promotes numerical equivalence concepts. *Journal of Cognition and Development, 12,* 463–480.

Mix, K. S., Smith, L. B., Stockton, J. D., Cheng, Y-L., & Barterian, J. A. (2017). Grounding the symbols for place value: Evidence from training and long-term exposure to base-10

models. *Journal of Cognition and Development, 18,* 129–151.

Miyake, A., Kost-Smith, L. E., Finkelstein, N. D., Pollock, S. J., Cohen, G. L., & Ito, T. A. (2010). Reducing the gender achievement gap in college science: A classroom study of values affirmation. *Science, 330,* 1234–1237.

Moed, A., Gershoff, E. T., & Bringewatt, E. H. (2017). Violence exposure as a mediator between parenting and adolescent mental health. *Child Psychiatry & Human Development, 48*(2), 235–247.

Moffitt, T. E. (1993a). Adolescence-limited and life-course persistent antisocial behavior: A developmental taxonomy. *Psychological Bulletin, 100,* 674–701.

Moffitt, T. E. (1993b). The neuropsychology of conduct disorder. *Development and Psychopathology, 5,* 135–151.

Moffitt, T. E., Arseneault, L., Jaffee, S. R., Kim-Cohen, J., Koenen, K. C., Odgers, C. L., . . . Viding, E. (2008). Research review: DSM-V Conduct Disorder: Research needs for an evidence base. *Journal of Child Psychology and Psychiatry, 49,* 3–33.

Moffitt, T. E., Caspi, A., Belsky, J., & Silva, P. A. (1992). Childhood experience and the onset of menarche. *Child Development, 63,* 47–53.

Moffit, T. E., Caspi, A., Harrington, H., & Milne, B. J. (2002). Males on the life-course-persistent and adolescent-limited antisocial pathways: Follow-up at age 26 years. *Development and Psychopathology, 14,* 179–207.

Moffit, T. E., Caspi, A., Rutter, M., & Silva, P. A. (2001). *Sex differences in antisocial behavior.* New York, NY: Cambridge Press.

Mohades, S. G., Van Schuerbeek, P., Rosseel, Y., Van De Craen, P., Luypaert, R., & Baeken, C. (2015). White matter development is different in bilingual and monolingual children: A longitudinal DTI study. *PLoS ONE, 10.* doi:10.1271/journal.pone.0117968

Mohr, J. J., & Jackson, S. D. (2016). Same-sex romantic attachment. In J. Cassidy & P. R. Shaver (Eds.), *Handbook of attachment: Theory, research, and clinical applications* (3rd ed., pp. 484–506). New York, NY: Guilford Press.

Mojtabai, R., Olfson, M., & Han, B. (2016). National trends in the prevalence and treatment of depression in adolescents and young adults. *Pediatrics, 138,* 1–10.

Molfese, D. (1990). Auditory evoked responses recorded from 16-month-old human infants to words they did and did not know. *Brain and Language, 38,* 345–363.

Moll, H., Meltzoff, A. N., Merzsch, K., & Tomasello, M. (2013). Taking versus confronting visual perspectives in preschool children. *Developmental Psychology, 49,* 646–654.

Moll, H., & Tomasello, M. (2006). Level 1 perspective taking at 24 months of age. *British Journal of Developmental Psychology, 24,* 603–613.

Moll, H., & Tomasello, M. (2007). How 14- and 18-month-olds know what others have experienced. *Developmental Psychology, 43,* 209–317.

Mollborn, S. (2016). Teenage mothers today: What we know and how it matters. *Children Development Perspectives, 11,* 63–69.

Molock, S. D., Matlin, S., Barksdale, C., Puri, R., & Lyles, J. (2008). Developing suicide prevention programs for African American youth

in African American churches. *Suicide & life-threatening behavior, 38,* 323–333.

Monaghan, K., Lee, J. M., & Steinberg, L. (2011). Revisiting the impact of part-time work on adolescent adjustment: Distinguishing between selection and socialization using propensity score matching. *Child Development, 82,* 96–112.

Money, J. (1988). *Gay, straight, and in-between: The sexology of erotic orientation.* New York, NY: Oxford University Press.

Money, J., & Dalery, J. (1977). Hyperadrenocortical 46, XX hermaphroditism with penile urethra: Psychological studies in seven cases, three reared as boys, four as girls. In P. A. Lee, L. P. Plotnick, A. A. Kowarski, & C. J. Migeon (Eds.), *Congenital adrenal hyperplasia* (pp. 433–446). Baltimore, MD: University Park Press.

Money, J., & Ehrhardt, A. (1972). *Man and woman, boy and girl.* Baltimore, MD: Johns Hopkins University Press.

Money, J., & Tucker, P. (1975). *Sexual signatures: On being a man or a woman.* Boston, MA: Little, Brown.

Monk, C., Spicer, J., & Champagne, F. A. (2012). Linking prenatal maternal adversity to developmental outcomes in infants: The role of epigenetic pathways. *Development and Psychopathology, 24,* 1361–1376.

Monroe, S. M., & Simons, A. D. (1991). Diathesis-stress theories in the context of life stress research: Implications for the depressive disorders. *Psychological Bulletin, 110*(3), 406–425.

Montgomery, R. J. V., Borgatta, E. F., & Borgatta, M. L. (2000). Societal and family change in the burden of care. In Liu, W. T. and Kendig, H. (Eds.), *Who should care for the elderly: An East–West value divide* (pp. 27–54). Singapore: Singapore University Press Singapore.

Montirosso, R., Provenzi, L., Fumagalli, M., Sirgiovanni, I., Giorda, R. Possoli, U., . . . Borgatti, R. (2016). Serotonin transporter gene (SLC6A4) methylation associates with neonatal intensive care unit stay and 3-month-old temperament in preterm infants. *Child Development, 87,* 38–48.

Montroy, J. J., Bowles, R. P., Skibbe, L. E., McClelland, M. M., & Morrison, F. J. (2016). The development of self-regulation across early childhood. *Developmental Psychology.* http://dx.doi.org/10.1037/dev0000159

Moore, C., Mealiea, J., Garon, N., & Povinelli, D. (2007). The development of body self-awareness. *Infancy, 11,* 157–174.

Moore, K. J., & Patterson, G. R. (2003). Parent training. In W. O'Donohue, J. E. Fisher, & S. C. Hayes (Eds.), *Cognitive behavior therapy: Applying empirically supported techniques on your practice* (pp. 280–287). Hoboken, NJ: Wiley.

Moore, R. M., Allbright-Campos, M., & Strick, K. (2017). Childlessness in midlife. *The Family Journal, 25*(1), 40.

Moran, M. B., Walker, M. W., Alexander, T. N., Jordan, J. W., & Wagner, D. E. (2017). Why peer crowds matter: Incorporating youth subcultures and values in health education campaigns. *American Journal of Public Health, 107*(3), 389–e7.

Moran, S., & Gardner, H. (2006). Extraordinary achievements: A developmental and systems analysis. In W. Damon & R. M. Lerner (Series

Eds.), D. Kuhn & R. S. Siegler (Vol. Eds.), *Handbook of child psychology: Vol. 2. Cognition, perception and language* (6th ed., pp. 904–952). Hoboken, NJ: Wiley.

Morelli, G. A., Rogoff, B., Oppenheim, D., & Goldsmith, D. (1992). Cultural variations in infants' sleeping arrangements. Questions of independence. *Developmental Psychology, 28,* 604–613.

Moreno, J. L. (1934). *Who shall survive? A new approach to the problem of human interrelations.* Washington, DC: Nervous and Mental Disease Publishing.

Morgan, K., & Hayne, H. (2011). Age-related changes in visual recognition memory during infancy and early childhood. *Developmental Psychobiology, 53,* 157–165.

Morgan, P. L., Farkas, G., Cook, M., Pun, W. H., & Hillemeier, M. M. (2017). Executive functioning deficits increase kindergarten children's risk for reading and mathematics difficulties in first grade. *Contemporary Educational Psychology, 50,* 23–32.

Morita, T., Oyama, Y., Cheng, S. Y., Suh, S. Y., Koh, S. J., Kim, H. S., . . . & Tsuneto, S. (2015). Palliative care physicians' attitudes toward patient autonomy and a good death in East Asian countries. *Journal of Pain and Symptom Management, 50,* 190–199.

Moriuchi, J. M., Klin, A., & Jones, W. (2017). Mechanisms of diminished attention to eyes in autism. *The American Journal of Psychiatry, 174,* 26–35.

Morley, J. E. (2011). Alzheimer's Disease: Future treatments. *Journal of the American Medical Directors Association, 12,* 1–7.

Morris, M. L. (2016). Vocational interests in the United States: Sex, age, ethnicity, and year effects. *Journal of Counseling Psychology, 63,* 604–615.

Morris, M. W., Chiu, C., & Liu, Z. (2015). Polycultural psychology. *Annual Review of Psychology, 66,* 631–659.

Mortimer, J. T., Harley, C., & Aronson, P. J. (1999). How do prior experiences in the workplace set the stage for transitions to adulthood? In A. Booth, A. C. Crouter, & M. J. Shanahan (Eds.), *Transitions to adulthood in a changing economy: No work, no family, no future?* New York, NY: Praeger.

Moser, M. B., Johnson, S. M., Dalgleish, T. L., Lafontaine, M.-F., Wiebe, S. A., & Tasca, G. A. (2015). Changes in relationship-specific attachment in emotionally focused couple therapy. *Journal of Marital and Family Therapy, 42,* 231–245.

Moshman, D. (2015). *Epistemic cognition and development: The psychology of justification and truth.* New York, NY: Psychology Press.

Moskowitz, D. W., Suh, E. J., & Desaulniers, J. (1994). Situational influences on gender differences in agency and communion. *Journal of Personality and Social Psychology, 66,* 753–761.

Mountjoy, K. G. (2015). Pro-opiomelanocortin (POMC) neurons, POMC-derived peptides, melanocortin receptors and obesity: How understanding of this system has changed over the last decade. *Journal of Neuroendocrinology, 27,* 406–418.

Mounts, N. S., & Steinberg, L. (1995). An ecological analysis of peer influence on adolescent grade point average and drug use. *Developmental Psychology, 31,* 915–922.

Movement Advancement Project. (2018). *Foster and adoption laws.* Available from www.lgbtmap.org/equality-maps/foster_and_adoption_laws

Moyer-Mileur, L., Brubstetter, V., McNaught, T., Gill, G., & Chan, G. (2000). Daily physical activity programs increases bone mineralization and growth in very low birth weight infants. *Pediatrics, 106,* 1088–1092.

MTV. (2010). Associated Press: MTV-AP Digital Abuse Study. http://www.athinline.org/MTV-AP_Digital_Abuse_Study_Executive_Summary.pdf

Mufson, L., Moreau, D., Weissman, M. M., & Klerman, G. L. (1993). *Interpersonal psychotherapy for depressed adolescents.* New York, NY: Guilford Press.

Muis, K. (2007). The role of epistemic beliefs in self-regulated learning. *Educational Psychologist, 42,* 173–190.

Müller, U., & Kerns, K. (2015). The development of executive function. In R. M. Lerner (Series Ed.), L. S. Liben & U. Müller (Vol. Eds.), *Handbook of child psychology and developmental science: Volume 2. Cognitive processes* (7th ed., pp. 571–623). Hoboken, NJ: Wiley.

Mulvey, K. L., & Killen, M. (2015). Challenging gender stereotypes: Resistance and exclusion. *Child Development, 86,* 681–694.

Mund, M., Finn, C., Hagemeyer, B., & Neyer, F. J. (2016). Understanding dynamic transactions between personality traits and partner relationships. *Current Directions in Psychological Science, 25,* 411–416.

Murphy, D. M. (1985). Fears in preschool-age children. *Child Care Quarterly, 14,* 171–189.

Murphy, J. A., Sarris, J., & Byrne, G. J. (2017). A review of the conceptualisation and risk factors associated with treatment-resistant depression. *Depression Research and Treatment.* doi:10.1155/2017/4176825

Murphy, M. C., Steele, C. M., & Gross, J. J. (2007). Signaling threat: How situation cues affect women in math, science, and engineering settings. *Psychological Science, 18,* 879–885.

Murray, M. M., Lewkowicz, D. J., Amedi, A., & Wallace, M. T. (2016). Multisensory processes: A balancing act across the lifespan. *Trends in Neurosciences, 39,* 567–579.

Musick, K., & Bumpass, L. (2012). Reexamining the case for marriage: Union formation and changes in well-being. *Journal of Marriage and Family, 74,* 1–18.

Mussen, P. H., Honzik, M., & Eichorn, D. (1982). Early adult antecedents of life satisfaction at age 70. *Journal of Gerontology, 37,* 316–322.

Mustakova-Possardt, E., & Basseches, M. (2014). Processes in the development of individual and collective consciousness and the role of religious and spiritual communities. In M. Basseches & J. Oxenberg (Eds.), *Toward a socially responsible psychology for a global era* (pp. 255–276). New York, NY: Springer.

Mustanski, B. S., Viken, R. J., Kaprio, J., Pulkkinen, L., & Rose, R. J. (2004). Genetic and environmental influences on pubertal development: Longitudinal data from Finnish twins at ages 11 and 14. *Developmental Psychology, 40,* 1188–1198.

Myers, C. A., Vandermosten, M., Farris, E. A., Hancock, R., Gimenez, P., Black, J. M., . . . Hoeft, F. (2014). White matter morphometric changes uniquely predict children's reading acquisition. *Psychological Science, 25,* 1870–1883.

Myers, D. G. (1993). *The pursuit of happiness.* New York, NY: Avon.

Myers, D. G. (2000). The funds, friends, and faith of happy people. *American Psychologist, 55,* 56–57.

Myers, J. E., & Harper, M. C. (2004). Evidence-based effective practices with older adults. *Journal of Counseling and Development, 82,* 207–218.

Myers, S. M., Johnson, C. P., & Council on Children with Disabilities (2007). Management of children with autism spectrum disorders. *Pediatrics, 120,* 1162–1182.

Naiman, R. (2017). Dreamless: The silent epidemic of REM sleep loss. *Annals of the New York Academy of Sciences, 1406*(1), 77–85.

National Academies of Sciences, Engineering, and Medicine. (2016). *Families caring for an aging America.* Washington, DC: National Academies Press.

National Association for the Education of Young Children & Fred Rogers Center for Early Learning and Children's Media. (2012). *Technology and interactive media as tools in early childhood programs serving children from birth through age 8.* Washington, DC: NAEYC.

National Association of Social Workers. (2017). *Standards and indicators for cultural competence in social work practice.* Available from www.socialworkers.org/practice/standards/NASWculturalstandards.pdf

National Center for Education Statistics. (2002). *The condition of education, 2002.* Washington, DC: U.S. Department of Education.

National Center for Education Statistics. (2012). *Digest of Education Statistics: 2011.* Available from http://nces.ed.gov/programs/digest/d11/

National Center for Education Statistics. (2016). *Digest of education statistics: 2015.* Available at https://nces.ed.gov/programs/digest/d15/

National Center for Education Statistics. (2016). *Digest of education statistics: Table 302-60.* Available at https://nces.ed.gov/programs/digest/d16/tables/dt16_302.60.asp

National Center for Education Statistics. (2018). *Post-secondary institutions and cost of attendance 2016–17; Degrees and other awards conferred, 2015–16; and 12-month enrollment, 2015–16.* Available at https://nces.ed.gov/pubs2017/2017075rev.pdf

National Center for Health Statistics. (2017). *Health, United States, 2016: With chartbook on long term trends in health.* Hyattsville, MD: U.S. Department of Health and Human Services, Centers for Disease Control, National Center for Health Statistics.

National Council of Teachers of Mathematics. (2000a). *Principles and standards for school mathematics: Grades 5–8: Standard 9-Algebra.* Available from www.standards.nctm.org/previous/currevstds/5-8s9.htm

National Council of Teachers of Mathematics. (2000b). *Principles and standards for school mathematics: Grades 9–12: Standard 5-Algebra.* Available from www.standards.nctm.org/previous/currevstdsv9-12s5.htm

National Down Syndrome Society. (2018). *What is Down syndrome?* Available from www.ndss.org/about-down-syndrome/down-syndrome/

National Institute of Child Health and Human Development, Early Child Care Research Network. (1997). The effects of infant child care on infant-mother attachment security: Results of the NICHD study of early child care. *Child Development, 68,* 860–879.

National Institute of Child Health and Human Development, Early Child Care Research Network. (2004). Trajectories of physical aggression from toddlerhood to middle childhood. *Monographs of the Society for Research in Child Development, 69*(4, Serial No. 278).

National Institute of Child Health and Human Development, Early Child Care Research Network. (2006). Child-care effect sizes for the NICHD study of early child care and youth development. *American Psychologist, 61,* 99–116.

National Research Council and Institute of Medicine. (2004). *Engaging schools: Fostering high school students' motivation to learn.* Committee on Increasing High School Students' Engagement and Motivation to Learn. Board on Children, Youth, and Families, Division of Behavioral and Social Science and Education. Washington, DC: The National Academy Press.

National Research Council. (2014). *The growth of incarceration in the United States: Causes and consequences.* Committee on Causes and Consequences of High Rates of Incarceration, J. Travis, B. Western, & S. Redburn (Eds.), Committee on Law and Justice, Division of Behavioral and Social Sciences and Education. Washington, DC: The National Academic Press.

National Science Foundation. (2015). *Women, minorities, and persons with disabilities in science and engineering.* Available at www.nsf.gov/statistics/2015/nsf15311/digest/theme5.cfm#trends

National Sleep Foundation. (2017). *How much sleep do we really need?* Available at https://sleepfoundation.org/how-sleep-works/how-much-sleep-do-we-really-need/page/0/2

Neale, B. M., Kou, Y., Liu, L., Ma'ayan, A., Samocha, K. E., Sabo, A., . . . Daly, M. J. (2012). Patterns and rates of exonic de novo mutations in autism spectrum disorders. *Nature, 485,* 242–245.

Neblett, E. W., Shelton, J. N., & Sellers, R. M. (2004). The role of racial identity in managing daily racial hassles. In G. Philogene (Ed.), *Race and identity: The legacy of Kenneth Clark* (pp. 77–90). Washington, DC: APA Press.

Neff, L. A., & Karney, B. R. (2009). Stress and reactivity to daily relationship experiences: How stress hinders adaptive processes in marriage. *Journal of Personality and Social Psychology, 97,* 435–450.

Negru-Subtirica, O., Pop, E. I., Luyckx, K., Dezutter, J., & Steger, M. F. (2016). The meaningful identity: A longitudinal look at the interplay between identity and meaning in life in adolescence. *Developmental Psychology, 52*(11), 1926.

Neimeyer, R. A. (2000). Searching for the meaning of meaning: Grief therapy and the process of reconstruction. *Death Studies, 24,* 541–558.

Neisser, U. (1993). *The perceived self: Ecological and interpersonal sources of self-knowledge.* New York, NY: Cambridge University Press.

Nell, V. (2002). Why young men drive dangerously: Implications for injury prevention.

Current Directions in Psychological Science, 11, 75–79.

Nelson, K. (1993). Events, narratives, memory: What develops? In C. A. Nelson (Ed.), *Minnesota Symposium on Child Psychology: Vol. 26. Memory and affect* (pp. 1–24). Hillsdale, NJ: Erlbaum.

Nelson, L. J., & Luster, S. S. (2015). "Adulthood" by whose definition?: The complexity of emerging adults' conceptions of adulthood. In J. J. Arnett (Ed.), *The Oxford handbook of emerging adulthood* (pp. 421–437). New York, NY: Oxford University Press.

Nelson, M. L., & Neufelt, S. A. (1998). The pedagogy of counseling: A critical examination. *Counselor Education and Supervision, 38,* 70–88.

Nelson, S. K., Kushlev, K., & Lyubomirsky, S. (2014). The pains and pleasures of parenting: When, why, and how is parenthood associated with more or less well-being? *Psychological Bulletin, 140,* 846–895.

Nelson, T. D. (2016). Promoting healthy aging by confronting ageism. *American Psychologist, 71,* 276–282.

Nelson, T. D., Nelson, J. M., James, T. D., Clark, C. A. C., Kidwell, K. M., & Espy, K. A. (2017). Executive control goes to school: Implications of preschool executive performance for observed elementary classroom learning engagement. *Developmental Psychology, 53,* 836–844.

Nenkov, G. Y., Morrin, M., Ward, A., Schwartz, B., & Hulland, J. (2008). A short form of the maximization scale: Factor structure, reliability and validity studies. *Judgment and Decision Making, 3*(5), 371.

Nesbitt, L. T., Farran, D. C., & Fuhs, M. (2015). Executive function skills and academic achievement gains in prekindergarten: Contributions of learning-related behaviors. *Developmental Psychology, 51,* 865–878.

Neumark, D., & Rothstein, D. (2005). Do school-to-work programs help the "forgotten half"? *National Bureau of Economic Research Working Paper Series.* Available from www.nber.org/papers/w11636

Newcomb, A. F., & Bukowski, W. M. (1984). A longitudinal study of the utility of social preference and social impact sociometric classification schemes. *Child Development, 55,* 1434–1447.

Newcomb, A. F., Bukowski, W. M., & Pattee, L. (1993). Children's peer relations: A meta-analytic review of popular, rejected, neglected, and average sociometric status. *Psychological Bulletin, 113,* 99–128.

Newcombe, N. S., Levine, S. C., & Mix, K. S. (2015). Thinking about quantity: The intertwined development of spatial and numerical cognition. *WIREs Cognitive Science, 6,* 491–505.

Newman, P. R., & Newman, B. M. (1999). What does it take to have a positive impact on minority students' college retention? *Adolescence, 34,* 483–492.

Nezu, A. M., Nezu, C. M., & Lombardo, E. (2003). Problem-solving therapy. In W. O'Donohue, J. E. Fisher, & S. C. Hayes (Eds.), *Cognitive behavior therapy: Applying empirically supported techniques in your practice* (pp. 301–307). Hoboken, NJ: Wiley.

Ng, F. F., Pomerantz, E. M., & Deng, C. (2014). Why are Chinese mothers more controlling than American mothers? "My child is my report card." *Child Development, 85*(1), 355.

Ng, F. F.-Y., Sze, I. N.-L., Tamis-LeMonda, C. S., & Ruble, D. N. (2017). Immigrant Chinese mothers' socialization of achievement in children: A strategic adaptation to the host society. *Child Development, 88,* 979–995.

Ng, J. Y., Ntoumanis, N., Thøgersen-Ntoumani, C., Deci, E. L., Ryan, R. M., Duda, J. L., et al. (2012). Self-Determination Theory applied to health contexts: A meta-analysis. *Perspectives on Psychological Science, 7,* 325–340.

NGSS Lead States. (2013). *Next Generation Science Standards: For states, by states.* Washington, DC: National Academics Press.

Nickerson, A. B. (2017). Preventing and intervening with bullying in schools: A framework for evidence-based practice. *School Mental Health.* doi:10.1007/s12310-017-9221-8

Nisbett, R. E., & Masuda, T. (2003). Culture and point of view. *Proceedings of the National Academy of Sciences of the United States of America, 100*(19), 11163–11170.

Nisbett, R. E., Peng, K., Choi, I., & Norenzayan, A. (2001). Culture and systems of thought: Holistic versus analytic cognition. *Psychological Review, 108*(2), 291–310.

Niu, L., Behar-Horenstein, L. S., & Garvan, C. W. (2013). Do instructional interventions influence college students' critical thinking skills? A meta-analysis. *Educational Research Review, 9,* 114.

Nivette, A. E., Eisner, M., Malti, T., & Ribeaud, D. (2014). Sex differences in aggression among children of low and high gender inequality backgrounds: A comparison of gender role and sexual selection theories. *Aggressive Behavior, 40,* 451–464.

Nolen-Hoeksema, S. (1987). Sex differences in unipolar depression: Evidence and theory. *Psychological Bulletin, 101,* 259–282.

Nolen-Hoeksema, S. (1991). Responses to depression and their effects on the duration of depressive episodes. *Journal of Abnormal Psychology, 100,* 569–582.

Nolen-Hoeksema, S. (2002). Gender differences in depression. In I. Gotlib & C. Hammen (Eds.), *Handbook of depression* (pp. 492–509). New York, NY: Guilford Press.

Nolen-Hoeksema, S. (2008). It is not what you have; It is what you do with it: Support for Addis's gendered responding framework. *Clinical Psychology Science and Practice, 15,* 178–181.

Nolen-Hoeksema, S. (2012). Emotion regulation and psychopathology: The role of gender. *Annual Review of Clinical Psychology, 8,* 161–187.

Nolen-Hoeksema, S., Girgus, J. S., & Seligman, M. E. P. (1992). Predictors and consequences of childhood depressive symptoms: A 5-year longitudinal study. *Journal of Abnormal Psychology, 101,* 405–422.

Nolen-Hoeksema, S., & Larson, J. (1999). *Coping with loss.* Mahwah, NJ: Erlbaum.

Nolen-Hoeksema, S., Morrow, J., & Fredrickson, B. L. (1993). Response styles and the duration of episodes of depressed moods. *Journal of Abnormal Psychology, 102,* 20–28.

Nolen-Hoeksema, S., & Watson, E. R. (2011). A heuristic for developing transdiagnostic models of psychopathology: Explaining multifinality and divergent trajectories. *Perspectives on Psychological Science, 6,* 589–609.

Norona, J. C., Preddy, T. M., & Welsh, D. P. (2015). How gender shapes emerging adulthood. In J. J. Arnett (Ed.), *The Oxford handbook of emerging adulthood* (pp. 62–86). New York, NY: Oxford University Press.

North, M. S., & Fiske, S. T. (2015). Modern attitudes toward older adults in the aging world: A cross-cultural meta-analysis. *Psychological Bulletin, 141,* 993–1021.

Nucci, L. P. (2014). The personal and the moral. In M. Killen & J. G. Smetana (Eds.), *Handbook of moral development* (2nd ed., pp. 538–558). Mahwah, NJ: Taylor & Francis.

Nuland, S. B. (2004). *The doctors' plague: Germs, childbed fever, and the strange story of Ignac Semmelweis.* New York, NY: W.W. Norton.

Nurmi, J. (1991). How do adolescents see their future? A review of the development of future orientation and planning. *Developmental Review, 11,* 1–59.

Nyamongo, I. K. (1999). Burying the dead, culture, and economics: An assessment of two Kenyan cases. *International Social Science Journal, 51,* 255–262.

Nye, C. D., Su, R., Rounds, J., & Drasgow, F. (2017). Interest congruence and performance: Revisiting recent meta-analytic findings. *Journal of Vocational Behavior, 98,* 138–151.

Nye, M. D., King, K. E., Darrah, T. H., Maguire, R., Jima, D. D., Huang, Z., . . . Hoyo, C. (2016). Maternal blood lead concentrations, DNA methylation of MEG3 DMR regulating the DLK1/MEG3 imprinted domain and early growth in a multiethnic cohort. *Environmental Epigenetics, 2.* doi:10.1093/eep/dvv009

Oakes, J. (2005). *Keeping track* (2nd ed.). New Haven, CT: Yale University Press.

Oakes, J., Quartz, K. H., Gong, J., Guiton, G., & Lipton, M. (1993). Creating middle schools: Technical, normative, and political considerations. *The Elementary School Journal, 93,* 461–480.

Obradović, J. (2016). Physiological responsivity and executive functioning: Implications for adaptation and resilience in early childhood. *Child Development Perspectives, 10,* 65–70.

O'Brien, L. T., & Hummert, M. L. (2006). Memory performance of late middle-aged adults: Contrasting self-stereotyping and stereotype threat accounts of assimilation to age stereotypes. *Social Cognition, 24,* 338–358.

O'Connell, M. E., Boat, T. F., Warner, K. E., Institute of Medicine (U.S.), Committee on Prevention of Mental Disorders and Substance Abuse Among Children, Youth, and Young Adults: Research Advances and Promising Interventions, & National Research Council (U.S.), Board on Children, Youth, and Families. (2009). *Preventing mental, emotional, and behavioral disorders among young people: Progress and possibilities.* Washington, DC: National Academies Press.

O'Connor, B. P. (1995). Identity development and perceived parental behavior as sources of adolescent egocentrism. *Journal of Youth and Adolescence, 24,* 204–227.

O'Connor, T. G., Monk, C., & Fitelson, E. M. (2014). Practitioner review: Maternal mood in pregnancy and child development—implications for child psychology and psychiatry. *Journal of Child Psychiatry and Psychology, 55,* 99–111.

Odgers, C. L., Moffitt, T. E., Broadbent, J. M., Dickson, N., Hancox, R. J., Harrington, H., . . .

Caspi, A. (2008). Female and male antisocial trajectories: From childhood origins to adult outcomes. *Development and Psychopathology, 20,* 673–716.

Offer, D. (1969). *The psychological world of the teenager.* New York, NY: Basic Books.

Ogbu, J. U. (2003). *Black American students in an affluent suburb: A study of academic disengagement.* Mahwah, NJ: Erlbaum.

Ogden, C. L., Carroll, M. D., Kit, B. K., & Flegal, K. M. (2014). Prevalence of childhood and adult obesity in the United States, 2011–2012. *JAMA, 311,* 806–814.

Oishi, S., & Kesebir, S. (2015). Income inequality explains why economic growth does not always translate to an increase in happiness. *Psychological Science 26,* 1630–1638.

O'Leary, D. D. M., & Stanfield, B. B. (1989). Selective elimination of axons extended by developing cortical neurons is dependent on regional locale: Experiments utilizing fetal cortical transplants. *Journal of Neuroscience, 9,* 2230–2246.

Oldenburg, B., van Duijn, M., Sentse, M., Huitsing, G., van der Ploeg, R., Salmivalli, C., & Veenstra, R. (2015). Teacher characteristics and peer victimization in elementary schools: A classroom-level perspective. *Journal of Abnormal Child Psychology, 43,* 33–44.

Olendzki, A. (2010). *Unlimiting mind: The radical experiential psychology of Buddhism.* Boston: Wisdom Publications.

Olendzki, A. (2014). From early Buddhist traditions to Western psychological science. In A. Ie, C. T. Ngnoumen, & E. J. Langer (Eds.), *The Wiley Blackwell handbook of mindfulness* (Vol. I, pp. 58–73). Hoboken NJ: Wiley Blackwell.

Oliner, S. P., & Oliner, P. M. (1988). *The altruistic personality: Rescuers of Jews in Nazi Europe.* New York, NY: Free Press.

Ollikainen, M., Smith, K. R., Joo, E. J-H., Ng, H. K., Andronikos, R., Novakovic, B., . . . Craig, J. M. (2010). DNA methylation analysis of multiple tissues from newborn twins reveals both genetic and intrauterine components to variation in the human neonatal epigenome. *Human Molecular Genetics, 19,* 4176–4188.

Olson, B. D., & Evans, D. L. (1999). The role of the big five personality dimensions in the direction and affective consequences of everyday social comparison. *Personality and Social Psychology Bulletin, 25,* 1498–1508.

Olson, K. R. (2016). Prepubescent transgender children: What we do and do not know. *Journal of the American Academy of Child & Adolescent Psychiatry, 55,* 155–156.

Olson, K. R., Key, A. C., & Eaton, N. R. (2015). Gender cognition in transgender children. *Psychological Science, 26,* 467–474.

Olweus, D. (1993). Victimization by peers: Antecedents and long-term consequences. In K. H. Rubin & J. B. Asendorf (Eds.), *Social withdrawal, inhibition, and shyness* (pp. 315–341). Hillsdale, NJ: Erlbaum.

Olweus, D., & Limber, S. (2002). *Blueprints for violence prevention: Bullying prevention program.* Boulder: University for the Study and Prevention of Violence, University of Colorado at Boulder.

Olweus, D., & Limber, S. P. (2010). Bullying in school: Evaluation and dissemination of the Olweus Bullying Prevention Program.

American Journal of Orthopsychiatry, 80, 124–134.

Omark, D. R., Omark, M., & Edelman, M. (1973). Formation of dominance hierarchies in young children. In T. R. Williams (Ed.), *Psychological anthropology.* The Hague, Netherlands: Mouton.

O'Muircheartaigh, J., Dean, D. C., Ginestet, C. E., Walker, L., Waskiewicz, N., Lehman, K., . . . Deoni, S. C. (2014). White matter development and early cognition in babies and toddlers. *Human Brain Mapping, 35,* 4475–4487.

Oostenbroek, J., Suddendorf, T., Nielsen, M., Redshaw, J., Kennedy-Constantini, S., Davis, J., . . . Slaughter, V. (2016). Comprehensive longitudinal study challenges the existence of neonatal imitation in humans. *Current Biology, 26,* 1334–1338.

Orcutt, H. (1874). *The parent's manual or home and school training.* Boston, MA: Thompson, Brown.

Orgeta, V., Qazi, A., Spector, A., & Orrell, M. (2015). Psychological treatments for depression and anxiety in dementia and mild cognitive impairment: Systematic review and meta-analysis. *The British Journal of Psychiatry, 207,* 293–298.

Ornstein, P. (1994). *School girls: Young women, self-esteem, and the confidence gap.* New York, NY: Anchor Books, Doubleday.

Orth, U. (2017). The lifespan development of self-esteem. In J. Specht (Ed.), *Personality development across the lifespan* (pp. 181–195). San Diego CA: Elsevier Academic Press.

Orth, U., & Robins, R. W. (2014). The development of self-esteem. *Current Directions in Psychological Science, 23,* 381–387.

Orth, U., Robins, R. W., & Widaman, K. F. (2012). Life-span development of self-esteem and its effects on important life outcomes. *Personality processes and individual differences, 102,* 1271–1288.

Orzack, S. H., Stubblefield, J. W., Akmaev, V. R., Colls, P., Munné, S., Scholl, T., . . . Zuckerman, J. E. (2015). The human sex ratio from conception to birth. *Proceedings of the National Academy of Sciences, 112,* 2102–2111.

Osherson, D. N., & Markman, E. M. (1975). Language and the ability to evaluate contradictions and tautologies. *Cognition, 2,* 213–226.

Ouellet-Morin, I., Cote, S. M., Vitaro, F., Hebert, M., Carbonneau, R., Lacourse, E., . . . Tremblay, R. E. (2016). Effects of the MAOA gene and levels of exposure to violence on antisocial outcomes. *British Journal of Psychiatry, 208,* 42–48.

Overton, W. F. (1990). Competence and procedures: Constraints on the development of logical reasoning. In W. F. Overton (Ed.), *Reasoning, necessity, and logic: Developmental perspectives* (pp. 1–32). Hillsdale, NJ: Erlbaum.

Overton, W. F. (2015). Processes, relations, and relational-developmental-systems. In W. F. Overton & P. C. Molenaar (Eds.), *Handbook of child psychology and developmental science: Theory and method, Vol. 1* (7th ed., pp. 9–62). Hoboken, NJ: Wiley & Sons.

Owen, M. T., & Cox, M. J. (1997). Marital conflict and the development of infant parent attachment relationships. *Journal of Family Psychology, 11,* 152–164.

Owens, J. A., Belon, K., & Moss, P. (2010). Impact of delaying school start time on adolescent sleep, mood, and behavior. *Archives of Pediatrics & Adolescent Medicine, 164,* 608–614.

Owens, M., & McGowan, I. W. (2006). *Madness and the moon: The lunar cycle and psychopathology.* Available from http://www.gjpsy.unigoettingen.de/gjp-article-owens.pdf (Google Scholar)

Owsley, C. (2011). Aging and vision. *Vision Research, 51,* 1610–1622.

Oyserman, D. (2017). Culture three ways: Culture and subcultures within countries. *Annual Review of Psychology, 68,* 435–463.

Oyserman, D., Coon, H. M., & Kemmelmeier, M. (2002). Rethinking individualism and collectivism: Evaluation of theoretical assumptions and meta-analyses. *Psychological Bulletin, 128,* 3–72.

Padilla-Walker, L. M. (2015). Moral development during emerging adulthood. In J. J. Arnett (Ed.), *The Oxford handbook of emerging adulthood* (pp. 449–463). New York, NY: Oxford University Press.

Padilla-Walker, L. M., Barry, C. M., Carroll, J. S., Madsen, S. D., & Nelson, L. J. (2008). Looking on the bright side: The role of identity status and gender on positive orientations during emerging adulthood. *Journal of Adolescence, 31,* 451–467.

Padilla-Walker, L. M., Gustavo, C., Christensen, K. J., & Yorgason, J. B. (2012). Bidirectional relations between authoritative parenting and adolescents' prosocial behaviors. *Journal of Research on Adolescence, 22,* 400–408.

Pak, R., & Stronge, A. (2008). Health maintenance, older adults, and the Internet. *Psychological Science Agenda, 22,* 1–5.

Palmer, N. A., & Greytak, E. A. (2017). LGBTQ student victimization and its relationship to school discipline and justice system involvement. *Criminal Justice Review, 42*(2), 163–187.

Panksepp, J., Lane, R. D., Solms, M., & Smith, R. (2017). Reconciling cognitive and affective neuroscience perspectives on the brain basis of emotional experience. *Neuroscience and Biobehavioral Reviews, 76,* 187–215.

Papastavrou, E., Kalokerinou, A., Papacostas, S. S., Tsangari, H., & Sourtzi, P. (2007). Caring for a relative with dementia: Family caregiver burden. *Journal of Advanced Nursing, 58,* 446–457.

Papathomas, L., & Kuhn, D. (2017). Learning to argue via apprenticeship. *Journal of Experimental Child Psychology, 159,* 129–139.

Papez, J. W. (1937). A proposed mechanism of emotion. *Archives of Neurology and Psychiatry, 79,* 217–224.

Pargament, K. I., Smith, B. W., Koenig, H. G., & Perez, L. M. (1998). Patterns of positive and negative religious coping with major life stressors. *Journal for the Scientific Study of Religion, 37,* 710–724.

Parish-Morris, J., Mahajan, N., Hirsh-Pasek, K., Golinkoff, R. M., & Fuller Collins, M. (2013). Once upon a time: Parent-child dialogue and storybook reading in the electronic era. *Mind, Brain, and Education, 7,* 200–211.

Park, A. (2010). The long-term effects of spanking. New York: *Time Incorporated.*

Park, C. L., & Folkman, S. (1997). Meaning in the context of stress and coping. *Review of General Psychology, 1,* 115–144.

Park, D., Gunderson, E. A., Tsukayama, E., Levine, S. C., & Beilock, S. L. (2016). Young children's motivational frameworks and math achievement: Relation to teacher-reported instructional practices, but not teacher theory of intelligence. *Journal of Educational Psychology, 108,* 300–313.

Park, D. C., & Huang, C. (2010). Culture wires the brain: A cognitive neuroscience perspective. *Perspectives in Psychological Sciences, 5,* 391–400.

Park, H. R., Lee, J. M., Moon, H. E., Lee, D. S., Kim, B.-N., Kim, J., . . . Paek, S. H. (2016). A short review on the current understanding of Autism Spectrum Disorders. *Experimental Neurobiology, 25*(1), 1–13. http://doi.org/10.5607/en.2016.25.1.1

Parke, R. D. (2002). Fathers and families. In M. H. Bornstein (Ed.), *Handbook of parenting: Vol. 3. Being and becoming a parent* (2nd ed., pp. 27–74). Mahwah, NJ: Erlbaum.

Parker, J., Rubin, K., Erath, X., Wojslawowicz, J., & Buskirk, A. (2006). Developmental psychopathology: Risk, disorder, and adaptation. In D. Cicchetti & D. J. Cohen (Eds.), *Developmental psychopathology* (Vol. 1, pp. 419–493). Hoboken, NJ: Wiley.

Parkes, C. M. (1965). Bereavement and mental illness. *British Journal of Medical Psychology, 38,* 388–397.

Parkes, C. M. (2013). Elisabeth Kubler-Ross, on death and dying: A reappraisal. *Mortality, 18,* 94–97.

Parkes, C. M., & Weiss, R. S. (1983). *Recovery from bereavement.* New York, NY: Basic Books.

Parkhurst, J. T., & Asher, S. R. (1992). Peer rejection in middle school: Subgroup differences in behavior, loneliness, and interpersonal concerns. *Developmental Psychology, 28,* 231–241.

Parks, E. E., Carter, R. T., & Gushue, G. V. (1996). At the crossroads: Racial and womanist identity development in Black and White women. *Journal of Counseling and Development, 74,* 624–631.

Parsons, C. E., Young, K. S., Murray, L., Stein, A., & Kringelbach, M. L. (2010). The functional neuroanatomy of the evolving parent–infant relationship. *Progress in Neurobiology, 91,* 220–241.

Parsons, C. E., Young, K. S., Parsons, E., Stein, A., & Kringelbach, M. L. (2012). Listening to infant distress vocalizations enhances effortful motor performance. *Acta Pediatrica, 101,* 189–191.

Parsons, T. (1951). Illness and the role of the physician: A sociological perspective. *American Journal of Orthopsychiatry, 21,* 452–460.

Partee, G. L. (2003). *Preparing youth for employment: Principles and characteristics of five leading United States youth development programs.* Washington, DC: American Youth Policy Forum.

Pascual-Leone, A., & Taylor, M. J. (2011). A developmental framework of brain and cognition from infancy to old age. *Brain Topography, 24,* 183–186.

Pascual-Leone, J., & Johnson, J. (2017). Organismic-causal models "from within" clarify developmental change and stages. In N. Budwig, E. Turiel, & P. D. Zelazo (Eds.), *New perspectives on human development* (pp. 67–87). New York, NY: Cambridge University Press.

Pasterski, V., Zucker, K. J., Hindmarsh, P. C., Hughes, I. A., Acerini, C., Spencer, D., et al. (2015). Increased cross-gender identification independent of gender role behavior in girls with congenital adrenal hyperplasia: Results from a standardized assessment of 4- to 11-year-old children. *Archives of Sexual Behavior, 44,* 1363–1375.

Pasterski, V. L., Geffner, M. E., Brain, C., Hindmarsh, P., Brook, C., & Hines M. (2005). *Child Development, 76,* 264–278.

Pasupathi, M., Staudinger, U. M., & Baltes, P. B. (1999). *The emergence of wisdom-related knowledge and judgment during adolescence.* Berlin: Max Planck Institute for Human Development.

Pasupathi, M., Staudinger, U. M., & Baltes, P. B. (2001). Seeds of wisdom: Adolescents' knowledge and judgment about difficult problems. *Developmental Psychology, 37,* 351–369.

Patrick, M. E., & Schuleberg, J. E. (2011). How trajectories of reasons for alcohol use relate to trajectories of binge drinking: National Panel data spanning late adolescence to early adulthood. *Developmental Psychology, 47,* 311–317.

Patterson, C. J. (2004). Gay fathers. In M. E. Lamb (Ed.), *The role of the father in child development* (pp. 397–416). Hoboken, NJ: Wiley.

Patterson, C. J. (2017). Parents' sexual orientation and children's development. *Child Development Perspectives, 11,* 45–49.

Patterson, G. R. (1982). *Coercive family process.* Eugene, OR: Castalia Press.

Patterson, G. R. (2002). The early development of coercive family process. In J. B. Reid, G. R. Patterson, & J. Snyder (Eds.), *Antisocial behavior in children and adolescents: A developmental analysis and model for intervention* (pp. 25–44). Washington, DC: American Psychological Association.

Patterson, G. R., Chamberlain, P., & Reid, J. B. (1982). A comparative evaluation of parent training procedures. *Behavior Therapy, 13,* 638–651.

Pattwell, S. S., Duhoux, S., Hartley, C. A., Johnson, D. C., Jing, D., . . . Lee, F. S. (2012). Altered fear learning across development in both mouse and human. *Proceedings of the National Academy of Science USA, 108,* 1182–1187.

Paul, K. I., & Moser, K. (2009). Unemployment impairs mental health: Meta-analyses. *Journal of Vocational Behavior, 74,* 264–82.

Pauletti, R. E., Cooper, P. J., & Perry, D. G. (2014). Influences of gender identity on children's maltreatment of gender-nonconforming peers: A person × target analysis of aggression. *Journal of Personality and Social Psychology, 106,* 843.

Pauletti, R. E., Menon, M., Cooper, P. J., Aults, C. D., & Perry, D. G. (2017). Psychological androgyny and children's mental health: A new look with new measures. *Sex Roles, 76,* 705–718.

Paulsen, J. A., Syed, M., Trzesniewski, K., & Donnellan, B. (2016). Generational perspectives on emerging adulthood: A focus on narcissism. In J. J. Arnett (Ed.), *The Oxford handbook of emerging adulthood* (pp. 26–46). New York, NY: Oxford University Press.

Paulus, M. (2017). How to Dax? Preschool children's prosocial behavior, but not their social norm enforcement relates to their peer status. *Frontiers in Psychology, 8.*

Paulus, M., & Sodian, B. (2015). Which way to take? Infants select an efficient path to their goal. *Journal of Experimental Child Psychology, 137,* 111–124.

Paunonen, S. V., & Ashton, M. C. (2001). Big Five predictors of academic achievement. *Journal of Research in Personality, 35,* 78–90.

Pavot, W., Diener, E., & Fujita, F. (1990). Extraversion and happiness. *Personality and Individual Differences, 11,* 1299–1306.

Paxton, S. J., Eisenberg, M. E., & Neumark-Sztainer, D. (2006). Prospective predictors of body dissatisfaction in adolescent girls and boys: A five-year longitudinal study. *Developmental Psychology, 42,* 888–899.

Paxton, S. J., Schutz, H. K., Weitheim, E. H., & Muir, S. L. (1999). Friendship clique and peer influences on body image concerns, dietary restraint, extreme weight-loss behaviors, and binge-eating in adolescent girls. *Journal of Abnormal Psychology, 108,* 255–266.

Pearlman, L. A., Wortman, C. B., Feuer, C. A., Farber, C. H., & Rando, T. A. (2014). *Treating traumatic bereavement: A practitioner's guide.* New York, NY: Guilford Publications.

Pecheux, M. G., & Labrell, F. (1994). Parent-infant interactions and early cognitive development. In A. Vyt, H. Bloch, & M. H. Bornstein (Eds.), *Early child development in the French tradition: Contributions from current research.* Hillsdale, NJ: Erlbaum.

Peets, K., Hodges, E. V. E., Kikas, E., & Salmivalli, C. (2007). Hostile attributions and behavioral strategies in children: Does relationship type matter? *Developmental Psychology, 43,* 889–900.

Pegueroles, J., Vilaplana, E., Montal, V., Sampedro, F., Alcolea, D., Carmona-Iragui, M., . . . & Alzheimer's Disease Neuroimaging Initiative. (2017). Longitudinal brain structural changes in preclinical Alzheimer's disease. *Alzheimer's & Dementia, 13,* 499–509.

Peisner-Feinberg, E. S., Burchinal, M. P., Clifford, R. M., Culkin, M. L., Howes, C., Kagan, S. L., et al. (2001). The relation of preschool child-care quality to children's cognitive and social developmental trajectories through second grade. *Child Development, 72,* 1534–1553.

Penner, A. M., & Saperstein, A. (2008). How social status shapes race. *Proceedings of the National Academy of Sciences, 105,* 19628–19630.

Pennington, H. (2003). Building one system for youth development and opportunity. In A. Lewis (Ed.), *Shaping the future of American youth: Youth policy in the 21st century* (pp. 59–68). Washington, DC: American Youth Policy Forum.

Pentimonti, J. M., Justice, L. M., Yeomans-Maldonado, G., McGinty, A. S., Slocum, L., & O'Connell, A. (2017). Teachers' use of high- and low-support scaffolding strategies to differentiate language instruction in high-risk/economically disadvantaged settings. *Journal of Early Intervention, 39,* 125–146.

Peplau, L. A., & Fingerhut, A. W. (2007). The close relationships of lesbian and gay men. *Annual Review of Psychology, 58,* 405–424.

Pepler, D., Walsh, M., Yuile, A., Levene, K., Jiang, D., Vaughan, A., & Webber, J. (2010). Bridging the gender gap: Interventions with aggressive girls and their parents. *Prevention Science, 11,* 229–238.

Pepping, C. A., Taylor, R., Koh, K., & Halford, W. K. (2017). Attachment, culture and initial romantic attraction: A speed-dating study. *Personality and Individual Differences, 108,* 79–85.

Perelli-Harris, B., & Styrc, M. (2018). Mental well-being differences in cohabitation and marriage: The role of childhood selection. *Journal of Marriage and Family, 80,* 239–255.

Perez, A. D., & Hirschman, C. (2010). The changing racial and ethnic composition of the US population: Emerging American identities. *Population Development Review, 35,* 1–51.

Pergament, E., Todydemir, P. B., & Fiddler, M. (2002). Sex ratio: A biological perspective of "Sex and the City." *Reproductive BioMedicine Online, 5,* 43–46.

Perlman, M., & Ross, H. S. (1997). The benefits of parent intervention in children's disputes: An examination of concurrent changes in children's fighting styles. *Child Development, 68*(4), 690–700.

Perrone, K. M., & Worthington, E. L. (2001). Factors influencing ratings of marital quality by individuals within dual-career marriages: A conceptual model. *Journal of Counseling Psychology, 48,* 3–9.

Perry, W. G. (1970/1999). *Forms of ethical and intellectual development in the college years: A scheme.* San Francisco, CA: Jossey-Bass.

Perry-Jenkins, M. (2016). Women, men, work and family: Action in the interactions. In S. M. McHale, V. King, J. Van Hook, & A. Booth (Eds.), *Gender and couple relationships* (pp. 131–138). Cham, Switzerland: Springer International Publishing.

Pert, C. B. (1997). *Molecules of emotion: The science behind mind-body medicine.* New York, NY: Simon & Schuster.

Petersen, A. C., Compas, B. E., Brooks-Gunn, J., Stemmler, M., Ey, S., & Grant, K. E. (1993). Depression in adolescence. *American Psychologist, 48,* 155–168.

Petersen, A. C., Kennedy, R. E., & Sullivan, P. (1991). Coping with adolescence. In M. E. Colten & S. Gore (Eds.), *Adolescent stress: Causes and consequences* (pp. 93–110). New York, NY: Aldine de Gruyter.

Petersen, A. C., Sarigiani, P. A., & Kennedy, R. E. (1991). Adolescent depression: Why more girls? *Journal of Youth and Adolescence, 10,* 247–271.

Petersen, B. E., & Steward, A. J. (1996). Antecedents and contexts of generativity motivation at midlife. *Psychology and Aging, 11,* 21–33.

Peterson, C., Maier, S., & Seligman, M. (1993). *Learned helplessness.* New York, NY: Oxford University Press.

Peterson, Z. D., & Muehlenhard, C. L. (2007). What is sex and why does it matter? A motivational approach to exploring individuals' definitions of sex. *Journal of Sex Research, 44,* 256–268.

Petrou, P., Bakker, A. B., & den Heuvel, M. (2017). Weekly job crafting and leisure crafting: Implications for meaning-making and work engagement. *Journal of Occupational and Organizational Psychology, 90,* 129–152.

Pettit, F., Fegan, M., & Howie, P. (1990, September). *Interviewer effects on children's testimony.* Paper presented at the International Congress on Child Abuse and Neglect, Hamburg, Germany.

Pettit, G. S., Lansford, J. E., Malone, P. S., Dodge, K. A., & Bates, J. E. (2010). Domain specificity in relationship history, social-information processing, and violent behavior in early adulthood. *Journal of Personality and Social Psychology, 98,* 190–200.

Pew Research Center. (2017). *The share of Americans living without a partner has increased, especially among young adults.* Available from www.pewresearch.org/fact-tank/2017/10/11/the-share-of-americans-living-without-a-partner-has-increased-especially-among-young-adults/

Pfiffner, L. J., & Haack, L. M. (2014). Nonpharmacological treatments for childhood ADHD and their combination with medication. In P. E. Nathan & J. M. Gorman, *A guide to treatments that work* (4th ed., pp. 55–84). New York, NY: Oxford University Press.

Phan, W. M., & Rounds, J. (2018). Examining the duality of Holland's RIASEC types: Implications for measurement and congruence. *Journal of Vocational Behavior, 106,* 22–36.

Phillips, D., Simpson, J. A., Lanigan, L., & Rholes, S. W. (1995). *Providing social support: A study of adult attachment styles.* Paper presented at the joint meeting of the European Association of Social Psychology and the Society of Experimental Social Psychology, Washington, DC.

Phillips, D. A., Fox, N. A., & Gunnar, M. R. (2011). Same place, different experiences: Bringing individual differences to research in child care. *Child Development Perspectives, 5,* 44–49.

Phinney, J. S. (1990). Ethnic identity in adolescents and adults: Review of research. *Psychological Bulletin, 108,* 499–514.

Phinney, J. S. (2000). Identity formation across cultures: The interaction of personal, societal, and historical change. *Human Development, 43,* 27–31.

Phinney, J. S. (2003). Ethnic identity and acculturation. In K. M. Chun, P. B. Organista, & G. Marin (Eds.), *Acculturation: Advances in theory, measurement and applied research* (pp. 63–82). Washington DC: APA Press.

Piaget, J. (1923/1929). *The child's conception of the world.* London: Kegan Paul, Trench & Trubner.

Piaget, J. (1926). *The language and thought of the child.* New York, NY: Harcourt, Brace.

Piaget, J. (1928). *Judgment and reasoning in the child.* New York, NY: Harcourt, Brace.

Piaget, J. (1932/1965). *The moral judgment of the child.* New York, NY: Free Press.

Piaget, J. (1951). *Play, dreams, and imitation in childhood.* London: Kegan Paul, Trench, & Trubner.

Piaget, J. (1952). *The origins of intelligence in children.* New York, NY: International Universities Press.

Piaget, J. (1954). *The construction of reality in the child.* New York, NY: Basic Books.

Piaget, J. (1962). *Play, dreams, and imitation in childhood.* New York, NY: Norton.

Piaget, J. (1964/1968). *Six psychological studies.* New York, NY: Random House.

Piaget, J. (1970). *Science of education and the psychology of the child.* New York, NY: Orion Press.

Piaget, J. (1975/1985). *The equilibration of cognitive structures.* Chicago, IL: University of Chicago Press.

Piaget, J. (1977). *The development of thought. Equilibration of cognitive structures.* New York, NY: Viking Press.

Piaget, J., & Inhelder, B. (1951/1976). *The origin of the idea of chance in children.* New York, NY: Norton.

Piaget, J., & Inhelder, B. (1956). *The child's conception of space.* New York, NY: Norton.

Piaget, J., & Inhelder, B. (1973). *Memory and intelligence.* New York, NY: Basic Books.

Piasta, S. B. (2016). Current understandings of what works to support the development of emergent literacy in early childhood classrooms. *Child Development Perspectives, 20,* 234–239.

Picciolini, O., Porro, M., Meazza, A., Gianni, M. L., Rivoli, C., Lucco, G., . . . Mosca, F, (2014). Early exposure to maternal voice: Effects on preterm infants development. *Early Human Development, 90,* 287–292.

Piccolo, L. R., Merz, E. C., He, X., Sowell, E. R., Noble, K. G., & Pediatric Imaging, Neurocogntion, and Genetics Study. (2016). Age-related differences in cortical thickness vary by socioeconomic status. *PLOS ONE* 11: e0162511. doi:10.1371/journal.pone.0162511.

Piedmont, R. L. (2007). Spirituality as a robust empirical predictor of psycho-social outcomes: A cross-cultural analysis. In R. J. Estes (Ed.), *Advancing quality of life in a turbulent world* (pp. 117–134). New York, NY: Springer.

Piekałkiewicz, M. (2017). Why do economists study happiness? *The Economic and Labour Relations Review, 28*(3), 361–377.

Pietromonaco, P. R., & Beck, L. A. (2015). Attachment processes in adult romantic relationships. In M. Mikulincer, P. R. Shaver, J. A. Simpson, & J. F. Dovidio (Eds.), *APA handbooks in psychology. APA handbook of personality and social psychology, Vol. 3. Interpersonal relations* (pp. 33–64). Washington, DC: American Psychological Association.

Pinker, S. (1994). *The language instinct.* New York, NY: Morrow.

Pinquart, M. (2017). Associations of parenting dimensions and styles with externalizing problems of children and adolescents: An updated meta-analysis. *Developmental Psychology, 53,* 873–932.

Pinquart, M., & Kauser, R. (2017). Do the associations of parenting styles with behavior problems and academic achievement vary by culture? Results from a meta-analysis. *Cultural Diversity and Ethnic Minority Psychology.* Available at http://dx.doi.org/10.1037/cdp0000149

Pintrich, P. R. (2000). Multiple goals, multiple pathways: The role of goal orientation in learning and achievement. *Journal of Educational Psychology, 92,* 544–555.

Pipher, M. (1994). *Reviving Ophelia: Saving the selves of adolescent girls.* New York, NY: Ballantine Books.

Pipher, M. (1999). *Another country: Navigating the emotional terrain of our elders.* New York, NY: Riverhead Books.

Pistole, M. C. (1989). Attachment in adult romantic relationships: Style of conflict resolution and relationship satisfaction. *Journal of Social and Personal Relationships, 6,* 505–510.

Pittman, F. S. (1985). Children of the rich. *Family Process, 24,* 461–472.

Pittman, K. J. (2017). Positive youth development as a strategy for addressing readiness and equity: A commentary. *Child Development, 88,* 1172–1174.

Plante, E., Schmithorst, V. J., Holland, S. K., & Byars, A. W. (2006). Sex differences in the activation of language cortex during childhood. *Neuropsychologia, 44,* 1210–1221.

Pluess, M., & Belsky, J. (2009). Differential susceptibility to rearing experience: The case of childcare. *Journal of Child Psychology and Psychiatry, 50,* 396–404.

Polanin, J. R., & Espelage, d. L. (2015). Using a meta-analytic technique to assess the relationship between treatment intensity and program effects in a cluster-randomized trial. *Journal of Behavioral Education, 24,* 133–151.

Pollack, W. (1998). *Real boys: Rescuing our sons from the myths of boyhood.* New York, NY: Henry Holt.

Pomerantz, E. M., Qin, L., Wang, Q., & Chen, H. (2009). American and Chinese early adolescents' inclusion of their relationships with their parents in their self-construals. *Child Development, 80,* 792–807.

Pomerantz, E. M., Qin, L., Wang, Q., & Chen, H. (2011). Changes in early adolescents' sense of responsibility to their parents in the United States and China: Implications for academic functioning. *Child Development, 82,* 1136–1151.

Pomerantz, E. M., & Wang, Q. (2009). Parents' role in children's personality development. In O. P. John, R. W., Robins, & L. A. Pervin (Eds.), *Handbook of personality, theory and research* (pp. 351–374). New York, NY: Guilford Press.

Pomerantz, E. M., & Wang, Q. (2009). The role of parental control in children's development in Western and East Asian countries. *Current Directions in Psychological Science, 18*(5), 285–289.

Pong, S.-l., & Landale, N. S. (2012). Academic achievement of legal immigrants' children: The roles of parents' pre- and postmigration characteristics in origin-group differences. *Child Development, 83,* 1543–1559.

Ponzo, Z. (1992). Promoting successful aging: Problems, opportunities, and counseling guidelines. *Journal of Counseling and Development, 71,* 210–213.

Popliger, M., Talwar, V., & Crossman, A. (2011). Predictors of children's prosocial lie-telling: Motivation, socialization variables, and moral understanding. *Journal of Experimental Child Psychology, 110,* 373–392.

Porges, S. W., Doussard-Roosevelt, J. A., Portales, A. L., & Greenspan, S. I. (1996). Infant regulation of the vagal "brake" predicts child behavior problems: A psychobiological model of social behavior. *Developmental Psychobiology, 29,* 697–712.

Post, R. M. (1985). Stress sensitization, kindling, and conditioning. *Behavioral and Brain Sciences, 8,* 372–373.

Post, R. M. (2007). Kindling and sensitization as models for affective episode recurrence, cyclicity, and tolerance phenomena. *Neuroscience & Biobehavioral Reviews, 31,* 858–873.

Post, R. M. (2016). Epigenetic basis of sensitization to stress, affective episodes, and stimulants: Implications for illness progression and prevention. *Bipolar Disorders, 18*(4), 315–324.

Pot, A. M., Bohlmeijer, E. T., Onrust, S., Melenhorst, A. S., Veerbeek, M., & De Vries, W. (2010). The impact of life review on depression in older adults: A randomized control trial. *International psychogeriatrics, 22,* 572–581.

Poulin, F., Dishion, T. J., & Burraston, B. (2001). Three year iatrogenic effects associated with aggregating high risk adolescents in cognitive behavioral preventive interventions. *Applied Developmental Science, 5,* 214–224.

Poulin-Dubois, D., & Serbin, L. A. (2006). Infants' knowledge about gender stereotypes and categories. *Enfance, 58,* 283–310.

Powell, L. J., & Carey, S. (2017). Executive function depletion in children and its impact on theory of mind. *Cognition, 164,* 150–162.

Prakash, R. S., Voss, M. W., Erickson, K. I., & Kramer, A. F. (2015). Physical activity and cognitive vitality. *Annual Review of Psychology, 66,* 769–797.

Prasad, S., Sung, B., & Aggarwal, B. B. (2012). Age-associated chronic diseases require age-old medicine: Role of chronic inflammation. *Preventive Medicine, 54,* 29–37.

Prebble, S. C., Addis, D. R., & Tippett, L. J. (2013). Autobiographical memory and sense of self. *Psychological Bulletin, 139,* 815–840.

Pressley, M., & Hilden, K. (2006). Cognitive strategies. In W. Damon & R. M. Lerner (Series Eds.), D. Kuhn & R. S. Siegler (Vol. Eds.), *Handbook of child psychology: Vol. 2. Cognition, perception and language* (6th ed., pp. 511–556). Hoboken, NJ: Wiley.

Price, C. A., & Joo, E. (2005). Exploring the relationship between marital status and women's retirement satisfaction. *International Journal of Aging and Human Development, 61,* 37–55.

Price, R. H. (1992). Psychosocial impact of job loss on individuals and families. *Current Directions in Psychological Science, 1,* 9–11.

Price, R. H., Choi, J. N., & Vinokur, A. D. (2002). Links in the chain of adversity following job loss: How financial strain and loss of personal control lead to depression, impaired functioning, and poor health. *Journal of Occupational Health Psychology, 7,* 302–312.

Price, R. H., & Vinokur, A. D. (1995). Supporting career transitions in time of organizational downsizing: The Michigan JOBS Program. In M. London (Ed.), *Employees, careers, and job creation: Developing growth-oriented human resource strategies and programs* (pp. 191–209). San Francisco, CA: Jossey-Bass.

Price, T. S., Grosser, T., Plomin, R., & Jaffee, S. R. (2010). Fetal genotype for the xenobiotic metabolizing enzyme *NQO1* influences intrauterine growth among infants whose mothers smoked during pregnancy. *Child Development, 81,* 101–114.

Priess, H. A., Lindberg, S. M., & Hyde, J. S. (2009). Adolescent gender-role identity and mental health: Gender intensification revisited. *Child Development, 80,* 1531–1544.

Pringle, J. K., Harris, C., Ravenswood, K., Giddings, L., Ryan, I., & Jaeger, S. (2017). Women's career progression in law firms: Views from the top, views from below. *Gender, Work & Organization, 24.* doi: 10111/gwao.12180

Prinstein, M. J., Rancourt, D., Guerry, J. D., & Browne, C. B. (2009). Peer reputations and psychological adjustment. In K. H. Rubin, M. Bukowski, & B. Laursen (Eds.), *Handbook of peer interactions, relationships, and groups* (pp. 548–567). New York, NY: Guilford Press.

Prinz, W. (2012). *Open minds: The social making of agency and intentionality.* Cambridge, MA: MIT Press.

Prochaska, J. O., & DiClemente, C. C. (1982). Transtheoretical therapy: Toward a more integrated model of change. *Psychotherapy: Theory, Research and Practice, 19,* 276–288.

Provencal, N., & Binder, E. B. (2015). The effects of early life stress on the epigenome: From the womb to adulthood and even before. *Experimental Neurology, 268,* 10–21.

Pruett, M. K., Insabella, G. M., & Gustafson, K. (2005). The Collaborative Divorce Project: A court-based intervention for separating parents with young children. *Family Court Review, 43,* 38–51.

Pryor, R. G. L., & Bright, J. E. H. (2012). The value of failing in career development: A chaos theory perspective. *International Journal of Educational and Vocational Guidance, 12,* 67–79.

Putallaz, M. (1983). Predicting children's sociometric status from their behavior. *Child Development, 54,* 1417–1426.

Putallaz, M., & Wasserman, A. (1990). Children's entry behaviors. In S. P. Asher & J. D. Coie (Eds.), *Peer rejection in childhood.* New York, NY: Cambridge University Press.

Putman, S. P., & Gartstein, M. A. (2017). Aggregate temperament scores from multiple countries: Associations with aggregate personality traits, cultural dimensions and allelic frequency. *Journal of Research in Personality, 67,* 157–170.

Putnam, R. D. (2000). *Bowling alone: The collapse and revival of American community.* New York, NY: Simon & Schuster.

Puzzanchera, C., Adams, B., & Hockenberry, S. 2012 (May). *Juvenile Court Statistics 2009. Report.* Pittsburgh, PA: National Center for Juvenile Justice.

Pyszczynski, T., Greenberg, J., & LaPrelle, J. (1985). Social comparison after success and failure: Biased search for information consistent with a self-servicing conclusion. *Journal of Experimental Social Psychology, 21,* 129–138.

Qiao, Y. J., Xing, Y., Duan, J. L., Bai, C. X., Pan, Y. P., Cui, Y. Q., & Kong, J. H. (2010). Prevalence and associated factors of school physical violence behaviors among middle school students in Beijing. *Chinese Journal of Epidemiology, 31,* 510–512.

Qu, Y., & Pomerantz, E. M. (2015/2014). Divergent school trajectories in early adolescence in the United States and China: An examination of underlying mechanisms. *Journal of Youth and Adolescence, 44*(11), 2095–2109.

Qu, Y., Pomerantz, E. M., Wang, M., Cheung, C., & Cimpian, A. (2016). Conceptions of adolescence: Implications for differences in engagement in school over early adolescence in the United States and China. *Journal of Youth and Adolescence, 45*(7), 1512–1526.

Qualls, S. H. (2016). Caregiving families within the long-term services and support system for older adults. *American Psychologist, 71,* 283–293.

Quattrin, T., Roemmich, J. N., Paluch, R., Yu, J., Epstein, L. H., & Ecker, M. A. (2012). Efficacy of family-based weight control program for preschool children in primary care. *Pediatrics, 130*(4), 660–666. http://doi.org/10.1542/peds.2012-0701

Quigley, K. M., Moore, G. A., Propper, C. B., Goldman, B. D., & Cox, M. J. (2017). Vagal regulation in breastfeeding infants and their mothers. *Child Development, 88,* 919–933.

Quinn, M. M., Kavale, K. A., Mathur, S. R., Rutherford, R. B., Jr., & Forness, S. R. (1999). A meta-analysis of social skill interventions for students with emotional or behavioral disorders. *Journal of Emotional and Behavioral Disorders, 7,* 54–64.

Quintana, E. D. (1999). Racial and ethnic identity development in biracial people. *Dissertation Abstracts International: Section B. The Physical Sciences & Engineering, 60* (3-B), 1313.

Radmacher, K., & Azmitia, M. (2006). Are there gendered pathways to intimacy in early adolescents' and emerging adults' friendships? *Journal of Adolescent Research, 21,* 415–448.

Raeff, C. (2014). Demystifying internalization and socialization: Linking conceptions of how development happens to organismic-developmental theory. *Advances in Child Development and Behavior, 46,* 1–32.

Raikes, H., Pan, B. A., Luze, G., Tamis-LeMonda, C. S., Brooks-Gunn, J., Constantine, J., et al. (2006). Mother-child book reading in low-income families: Correlates and outcomes during the first three years of life. *Child Development, 77,* 924–953.

Raine, A., Fung, A. L. C., Portnoy, J., Choy, O., & Spring, V. L. (2014). Low heart rate as a risk factor for child and adolescent proactive aggressive and impulsive psychopathic behavior. *Aggressive Behavior, 40,* 290–299.

Ramchandani, S., Bhattacharya, S. K., Cervoni, N., & Szyf, M. (1999). DNA methylation is a reversible biological signal. *Proceedings of the National Academy of Sciences, 96,* 6107–6112.

Ramey, C. T., Sparling, J. J., & Ramey, S. L. (2012). *Abecedarian: The ideas, the approach, and the findings.* Los Altos, CA: Sociometrics.

Ramirez, A., Ekselius, L., & Ramklint, M. (2015). Depression in young adult psychiatric outpatients: Delimiting early onset. *Early Intervention in Psychiatry, 9*(2), 108–117.

Ramirez-Esparza, N. A., Garcia-Sierra, A., & Kuhl, P. K. (2017). The impact of early social interactions on later language development in Spanish-English bilingual infants. *Child Development, 88,* 1216–1234.

Rando, T. A. (1993). *Treatment of complicated mourning.* Champaign, IL: Research Press.

Ranzini, G., & Hoek, E. (2017). To you who (I think) are listening: Imaginary audience and impression management on Facebook. *Computers in Human Behavior, 75,* 228–235.

Ratts, M. J., Singh, A. A., Nassar-McMillan, S., Butler, S. K., & McCullough, J. R. (2016). Multicultural and social justice counseling competencies: Guidelines for the counseling profession. *Journal of Multicultural Counseling and Development, 44,* 28–48.

Ravitch, D. (1983). *The troubled crusade: American education,* 1945–1980. New York, NY: Basic Books.

Realo, A. (2016). Disentangling the complex relations among personality, health and well-being. *European Journal of Personality, 30*(5), 423–425.

Reddy, V., Williams, E., Costantini, C., & Lang, B. (2010). Engaging with the self: Mirror behavior in autism, Down syndrome, and typical development. *Autism, 14,* 531–546.

Reed, A. E., Chan, L., & Mikels, J. A. (2014). Meta-analysis of the age-related positivity effect: Age differences in preferences for positive over negative information. *Psychology and Aging, 29,* 1–15.

Reese, E., Haden, C. A., Baker-Ward, L., Bauer, P., Fivush, R., & Ornstein, P. A. (2011). Coherence of personal narratives across the lifespan: A multidimensional model and coding method. *Journal of Cognition and Development, 12,* 424–462.

Reese, E., & Newcombe, R. (2007). Training mothers in elaborative reminiscing enhances children's autobiographical memory and narrative. *Child Development, 78,* 1153–1170.

Regalado, M., Sareen, H., Inkelas, M., Wissow, L. S., & Halfon, N. (2004). Parents' discipline of young children: Results from the National Survey of Early Childhood Health. *Pediatrics, 113,* 1952–1958.

Regier, D. A., Narrow, W. E., Clarke, D. E., Kraemer, H. C., Kuramoto, J., Kuhl, E. A., & Kupfer, D. J. (2013). DSM-5 field trials in the United States and Canada, Part II: Test-retest reliability of selected categorical diagnoses. *American Journal of Psychiatry, 170,* 59–70.

Reifman, A., Oblad, T. & Niehuis, S. (2017). Long-term psychological health among individuals pursuing emerging adulthood-type pathways in the 1950s and 1960s. *Journal of Adult Development, 24,* 119–132.

Reilly, D., & Neumann, D. L. (2013). Gender-role differences in spatial ability: A meta-analytic review. *Sex Roles, 68,* 521–535.

Reilly, D., Neumann, D. L., & Andrews, G. (2015). Sex differences in mathematics and science achievement: A meta-analysis of National Assessment of Educational Progress assessments. *Journal of Educational Psychology, 107,* 645–662.

Reiner, W. G., & Gearhart, J. P. (2004). Discordant sexual identity in some genetic males with cloacal exstrophy assigned to female sex at birth. *New England Journal of Medicine, 350,* 333–341.

Reis, E. (2007). Divergence or disorder? The politics of naming intersex. *Perspectives in Biology and Medicine, 50,* 535–543.

Reis, H. T., & Carothers, B. J. (2014). Black and white or shades of gray: Are gender differences categorical or dimensional? *Current Directions in Psychological Science, 23,* 19–26.

Reisman, J. E. (1987). Touch, motion, and proprioception. In P. Salapatek & L. Cohen (Eds.), *Handbook of infant perception: Vol. 1. From sensation to perception* (pp. 265–304). Orlando, FL: Academic Press.

Reitzes, D. C., & Mutran, E. J. (2004). The transition to retirement: Stages and factors that influence retirement adjustment. *International Journal of Aging and Human Development, 59,* 63–84.

Remes, O., Brayne, C., Linde, R., & Lafortune, L. (2016). A systematic review of reviews on the prevalence of anxiety disorders in adult populations. *Brain and Behavior, 6*(7), e00497-n/a. doi:10.1002/brb3.497

Rentzsch, K., Wenzler, M. P., & Schütz, A. (2016). The structure of multidimensional self-esteem across age and gender. *Personality and individual differences, 88,* 139–147.

Repacholi, B. M., & Gopnik, A. (1997). Early reasoning about desires: Evidence from 14- and 18-month olds. *Developmental Psychology, 33,* 12–21.

Reuter-Lorenz, P. A., & Mikels, J. (2006). The aging mind and brain: Implications of enduring plasticity for behavioral and cultural change. In P. Baltes, P. A. Reuter-Lorenz, & F. Roesler (Eds.), *Lifespan development and the brain: The perspective of bicultural co-constructivism* (pp. 255–276). Cambridge, UK: Cambridge University Press.

Reuter-Lorenz, P. A., & Park, D. C. (2014). How does it STAC up? Revisiting the scaffolding theory of aging and cognition. *Neuropsychology Review, 24,* 355–370.

Reyna, V. F., & Farley, F. (2006). Risk and rationality in adolescent decision making: Implications for theory, practice, and public policy. *Psychological Science in the Public Interest, 7,* 1–44.

Reynolds, A. J., & Ou, S.-R. (2016). Generative mechanisms in early childhood interventions: A confirmatory research framework for prevention. *Prevention Science, 17,* 794–805.

Reynolds, J. E., & Gonzales-Backen, M. A. (2017). Ethnic-racial socialization and the mental health of African Americans: A critical review. *Journal of Family Theory & Review, 9,* 182–200.

Rheingold, H. L. (1956). The modification of social responsiveness in institutional babies. *Monographs of the Society for Research in Child Development, 21*(2, Serial No. 63).

Rhoades, L., & Eisenberger, R. (2002). Perceived organizational support: A review of the literature. *Journal of Applied Psychology, 87,* 698–714.

Rholes, W. S., Kohn, J. L., & Simpson, J. A. (2014). A longitudinal study of conflict in new parents: The role of attachment. *Personal Relationships, 21,* 1–21.

Rholes, W. S., Simpson, J. A., & Stevens, J. G. (1998). Attachment orientations, social support, and conflict resolution in close relationships. In J. A. Simpson & W. S. Rholes (Eds.), *Attachment theory and close relationships* (pp. 166–188). New York, NY: Guilford Press.

Ribeiro, J. D., Pease, J. L., Gutierrez, P. M., Silva, C., Bernert, R. A., Rudd, M. D., & Joiner, T. E. (2012). Sleep problems outperform depression and hopelessness as cross-sectional and longitudinal predictors of suicidal ideation and behavior in young adults in the military. *Journal of Affective Disorders, 136*(3), 743–750.

Ricciardelli, L., & McCabe, M. P. (2004). A biopsychosocial model of disordered eating and the pursuit of muscularity in adolescent boys. *Psychological Bulletin, 130,* 179–205.

Ricco, R. B. (2015). The development of reasoning. In R. M. Lerner (Ed. In Chief) & L. S. Liben & U. Miller (Vol. Eds.), *Handbook of child psychology and developmental science: Vol. 2. Cognitive processes* (7th ed., pp. 519–570). Hoboken, NJ: Wiley.

Rich, J. (2014). What do field experiments of discrimination in markets tell us? A meta-analysis of studies conducted since 2000. *IZA Discussion Paper No. 8584.* Available at SSRN: https://ssrn.com/absract=2517887

Richards, T. A., Wrubel, J., & Folkman, S. (1999–2000). Death rites in the San Francisco gay community: Cultural developments of the AIDS epidemic. *Omega, 40,* 335–350.

Richardson, K. A., Hester, A. K., & McLemore, G. L. (2016). Prenatal cannabis exposure–The "first hit" to the endocannabinoid system. *Neurotoxicology and Teratology, 58,* 5–14.

Richeson, J. A., & Sommers, S. R. (2016). Toward a social psychology of race and race relations for the twenty-first century. *Annual Review of Psychology, 67,* 439–463.

Rickard, I. J., Frankenhuis, W. E., & Nettle, D. (2014). Why are childhood family factors associated with timing of maturation? A role for internal prediction. *Perspectives on Psychological Science, 9,* 3–15.

Rideout, V., Lauricella, A., & Wartella, E. (2011). *Children, media, and race: Media use among White, Black, Hispanic, and Asian American children.* Chicago, IL: Northwestern University Center on Media and Human Development.

Rideout, V. J. (2015). Common sense census: Media use by tween and teens. San Francisco, CA: Common Sense Media.

Rindermann, H., & Ceci, S. J. (2009). Educational policy and country outcomes in international cognitive competence studies. *Perspectives on Psychological Science, 4,* 551–577.

Rindermann, H., & Thompson, J. (2014). The cognitive competences of immigrant and native students across the world: An analysis of gaps, possible causes and impact. *Journal of Biosocial Science, 48,* 66–93.

Rindfuss, R. R. (1991). The young adult years: Diversity, structural change, and fertility. *Demography, 28,* 493–512.

Rittle-Johnson, B. (2017). Developing mathematics knowledge. *Child Development Perspectives, 11,* 184–190.

Rivas-Drake, D., Seaton, E. K., Markstrom, C., Quintana, S., Syed, M., Lee, R. M., & Ethnic and Racial Identity in the 21st Century Study Group. (2014). Ethnic and racial identity in adolescence: Implications for psychosocial, academic, and health outcomes. *Child Development, 85*(1), 40–57.

Rivas-Drake, D., Umaña-Taylor, A., Shaefer, D. R., & Medina, M. (2017). Ethnic-racial identity and friendships in early adolescence. *Child Development, 88,* 710–724.

Rivers, I., Poteat, V. P., & Noret, N. (2008). Victimization, social support, and psychosocial functioning among children of same-sex and opposite-sex couples in the United Kingdom. *Developmental Psychology, 44,* 127–134.

Robben, A. C. (2017). *Death, mourning, and burial: A cross-cultural reader.* Hoboken, NJ: John Wiley & Sons.

Roberto, K. A. (2016). The complexities of elder abuse. *American Psychologist, 71,* 302–311.

Roberts, B. W., Luo, J., Briley, D. A., Chow, P. I., Su, R., & Hill, P. L. (2017). A systematic review of personality trait change through intervention. *Psychological Bulletin, 143,* 117–141.

Roberts, B. W., Walton, K. E., & Viechtbauer, W. (2006). Patterns of mean-level change in personality traits across the life course: A meta-analysis of longitudinal studies. *Psychological Bulletin, 132,* 1–25.

Roberts, B. W., Wood, D., & Caspi, A. (2008). The development of personality traits in adulthood. In O. P. John, R. W. Robins, & L. A. Pervin (Eds.), *Handbook of personality: Theory and research* (3rd ed., pp. 375–398). New York, NY: Guilford Press.

Roberts, C. J., Campbell, I. C., & Troop, N. (2014). Increases in weight during chronic stress are partially associated with a switch in food choice towards increased carbohydrate and saturated fat intake. *European Eating Disorders Review, 22,* 77–82.

Robertson, K. F., Smeets, S., Lubinski, D., & Benbow, C. P. (2010). Beyond the threshold hypothesis: Even among the gifted and top math/science graduate students, cognitive abilities, vocational interests, and lifestyle preferences matter for career choice, performance, and persistence. *Current Directions in Psychological Science, 19,* 346–351.

Robins, R. W., & Pals, J. (1998). *Implicit self-theories of ability in the academic domain: A test of Dweck's model.* Unpublished manuscript.

Robinson, J. P., Espelage, D. L., & Rivers, I. (2013). Developmental trends in peer victimization and emotional distress in LGB and heterosexual youth. *Pediatrics, 131*(3), 423–430.

Robinson, M., Mattes, E., Oddy, W. H., Pennell, C. E., Van Eekelen, A., McLean, N. J., . . . Newnham, J. P. (2011). Prenatal stress and risk of behavioral morbidity from age 2 to 14 years: The influence of the number, type, and timing of stressful life events. *Development and Psychopathology 23,* 507–520.

Robles, T. F. (2014). Marital quality and health: Implications for marriage in the 21st century. *Current Directions in Psychological Science, 23,* 427–432.

Robles, T. F., Glaser, R., & Kiecolt-Glaser, J. K. (2005). Out of balance: A new look at chronic stress, depression, and immunity. *Current Directions in Psychological Science, 14,* 111–115.

Roccas, S., & Brewer, M. B. (2002). Social identity complexity. *Personality and Social Psychology Review, 6*(2), 88–106.

Rodger, H., Vizioli, L., Ouyang, X., & Caldara, R. (2015). Mapping the development of facial expression recognition. *Developmental Science, 18,* 926–929.

Rodkin, P. C., & Roisman, G. I. (2010). Antecedents and correlates of the popular-aggressive phenomenon in elementary school. *Child Development, 81,* 837–850.

Rodriguez, C. I., Magcalas, C. M., Barto, D., Fink, B. C., Rice, J. P., Bird, C. W., . . . Hamilton, D. A. (2016). Effects of sex and housing on social, spatial, and motor behavior in adult rats exposed to moderate levels of alcohol during prenatal development. *Behavioural Brain Research, 313,* 233–243.

Rogers, L. O., & Meltzoff, A. N. (2017). Is gender more important and meaningful than race? An analysis of racial and gender identity among Black, White, and mixed-race children. *Cultural Diversity and Ethnic Minority Psychology, 23,* 323–334.

Rogers, L. O., Scott, M. A., & Way, N. (2015). Racial and gender identity among Black adolescent males: An intersectionality perspective. *Child Development, 86,* 407–424.

Rogers, S., & Lewis, H. (1989). An effective day treatment model for young children with pervasive developmental disorders. *Journal of the American Academy of Child & Adolescent Psychiatry, 28,* 207–214.

Rogers, S. J., Hayden, D., Hepburn, S., Charlifue-Smith, R., Hall, T., & Hayes, A. (2006). Teaching young nonverbal children with autism useful speech: A pilot study of the Denver Model and PROMPT interventions. *Journal of Autism and Developmental Disorders, 36*, 1007–1024.

Rogoff, B. (2003). *The cultural nature of human development*. New York, NY: Oxford University Press.

Roisman, G. I. (2007). The psychophysiology of adult attachment relationships: Autonomic reactivity in marital and premarital interactions. *Developmental Psychology, 43*, 39–53.

Roisman, G. I. (2009). Adult attachment: Toward a rapprochement of methodological cultures. *Current Directions in Psychological Science, 18*, 122–126.

Roisman, G. I., Booth-Laforce, C., Belsky, J., Burt, K. B., & Groh, A. M. (2013). Molecular-genetic correlates of infant attachment: A cautionary tale. *Attachment & Human Development, 15*, 384–406.

Roisman, G. I., & Cicchetti, D. (2017). Special issue editorial: Attachment in the context of atypical caregiving. *Development and Psychopathology, 29*, 331–335.

Roisman, G. I., Fraley, R. C., & Belsky, J. (2007). A taxometric study of the Adult Attachment Interview. *Developmental Psychology, 43*, 675–686.

Roisman, G. I., Susman, E., Barnett-Walker, K., Booth-LaForce, C., Owen, M. T., Belsky, J., . . . Steinberg, L. (2009). Early family and child-care antecedents of awakening cortisol levels in adolescence. *Child Development, 80*, 907–920.

Roisman, G. I., Tsai, J. L., & Chiang K-H. S. (2004). The emotional integration of childhood experience: Physiological, facial expressive, and self-reported emotional response during the adult attachment interview. *Developmental Psychology, 40*, 776–789.

Rollins, B. C., & Feldman, H. (1970). Marital satisfaction over the family life cycle. *Journal of Marriage and the Family, 32*, 20–28.

Rollock, D., & Lui, P. P. (2016). Measurement invariance and the five-factor model of personality: Asian international and Euro American cultural groups. *Assessment, 23*, 571–587.

Rolls, E. T. (2013). *Emotion and decision making explored*. Oxford, U.K.: Oxford University Press.

Roman, G. C. (2013). Nutritional disorders in tropical neurology. *Handbook of Clinical Neurology, 114*, 381–404.

Romeo, R. D. (2010). Adolescence: A central event in shaping stress reactivity. *Developmental Psychobiology, 52*, 244–253.

Romer, D., Reyna, V. F., & Satterthwaite, T. D. (2017). Beyond stereotypes of adolescent risk taking: Placing the adolescent brain in developmental context. *Developmental Cognitive Neuroscience, 27*, 19–34.

Rook, K. S. (2015). Social networks in later life: Weighing positive and negative effects on health and well-being. *Current Directions in Psychological Science, 24*, 45–51.

Rook, K. S., & Charles, S. T. (2017). Close social ties and health in later life: Strengths and vulnerabilities. *American Psychologist, 72*, 567–577.

Roschelle, J. M., Pea, R. D., Hoadley, C. M., Gordin, D. N., & Means, D. N. (2000). Changing how and what children learn in school with computer-based technologies. *Children & Computer Technology, 10*, 76–101.

Rosenbaum, J., Ahearn, C., Becker, K., & Rosenbaum, J. (2015). *The new forgotten half and research directions to support them*. New York, NY: William T. Grant Foundation. Available at http://wtgrantfoundation.org/resource/the-new-forgotten-half-and-research-directions-to-support-them

Rosenberg, M. (1979). *Conceiving the self*. New York, NY: Basic Books.

Rosette, A. S., Koval, C. Z., Ma, A., & Livingston, R. (2016). Race matters for women leaders: Intersectional effects on agentic deficiencies and penalties. *The Leadership Quarterly, 27*, 429–445.

Ross, H., Tesla, C., Kenyon, B., & Lollis, S. (1990). Maternal intervention in toddler peer conflict: The socialization of principles of justice. *Developmental Psychology, 26*, 994–1003.

Ross, J., Yilmaz, M., Dale, R., Cassidy, R., Yildirim, I., & Zeedyk, M. S. (2017). Cultural differences in self-recognition: The early development of autonomous and related selves? *Developmental Science, 20*. doi:10.111/desc.12387

Rosvold, H. E., Mirsky, A. F., Sarason, I., Bransome, E. D., Jr., & Beck, L. H. (1956). A continuous performance test of brain damage. *Journal of Consulting Psychology, 20*, 343–350.

Roth, S., & Cohen, L. J. (1986). Approach, avoidance, and coping with stress. *American Psychologist, 41*, 813–819.

Rothbart, M. K. (2011). *Becoming who we are: Temperament and personality in development*. New York, NY: Guilford Press.

Rothbaum, F., Weisz, J. R., & Snyder, S. (1982). Changing the world and changing the self: A two process model of perceived control. *Journal of Personality and Social Psychology, 42*, 5–37.

Rousseau, D. M., & Gunia, B. C. (2016). Evidence-based practice: The psychology of EBP implementation. *Annual Review of Psychology, 67*, 667–692.

Rousseau, J. J. (1762/1948). *Emile, or education* (B. Foxley, Trans.). New York, NY: Oxford University Press.

Rovee-Collier, C., & Barr, R. (2001). Infant learning and memory. In G. Bremner & A. Fogel (Eds.), *Blackwell handbook of infant development* (pp. 139–168). Malden, MA: Blackwell.

Rovee-Collier, C., & Cuevas, K. (2009). Multiple memory systems are unnecessary to account for infant memory development: An ecological model. *Developmental Psychology, 45*, 160–174.

Rowe, J. W., & Kahn, R. L. (1998). *Successful aging*. New York, NY: Pantheon Books.

Rowe, M. L., Raudenbush, S. W., & Goldin-Meadow, S. (2012). The pace of vocabulary growth helps predict later vocabulary. *Child Development, 83*, 508–525.

Rowe, R., Maughan, B., Worthman, C. M., Costello, E. J., & Angold, A. (2004). Testosterone, antisocial behavior, and social dominance in boys: Pubertal development and biosocial interaction. *Biological Psychiatry, 55*, 546–552.

Rozario, P. A., Morrow-Howell, N., & Hinterlong, J. E. (2004). Role enhancement or role strain? Assessing the impact of multiple productive roles on older caregiver well-being. *Research on Aging, 26*, 413–428.

Rubie-Davies, C. M., & Rosenthal, R. (2016). Intervening in teachers' expectations: A random effects meta-analytic approach to examining the effectiveness of an intervention. *Learning and Individual Differences 50*, 83–92.

Rubin, K. H., Bukowski, W. M., & Bowker, J. C. (2015). Children in peer groups. In M. H. Bornstein, T. Leventhal, & R. M. Lerner (Eds.), *Handbook of child psychology and developmental science, Vol. 4: Ecological settings and processes* (7th ed., pp. 175–222). Hoboken, NJ: Wiley.

Rubin, K. H., Bukowski, W., & Parker, J. G. (1998). Peer interactions, relationships, and groups. In W. Damon (Series Ed.) & N. Eisenberg (Vol. Ed.), *Handbook of child psychology: Vol. 3. Social, emotional, and personality development* (5th ed., pp. 619–700). New York, NY: Wiley.

Rubin, K. H., Bukowski, W. M., & Parker, J. G. (2006). Peer interactions, relationships, and groups. In W. Damon & R. M. Lerner (Series Eds.), & N. Eisenberg (Vol. Ed.), *Handbook of child psychology: Vol. 3. Social, emotional, and personality development* (6th ed., pp. 571–645). Hoboken, NJ: Wiley.

Rubin, K. H., Coplan, R. J., & Bowker, J. C. (2009). Social withdrawal in childhood. *Annual Review of Psychology, 60*, 141–171.

Rubin, K. H., Coplan, R., Chen, X., Bowker, J., & McDonald, K. L. (2011). Peer relationships in childhood. In M. E. Lamb & M. H. Bornstein (Eds.), *Social and personality development: An advanced textbook* (pp. 309–360). New York, NY: Psychology Press.

Rubin, S. S., Witztum, E., & Malkinson, R. (2017). Bereavement and traumatic bereavement: Working with the two-track model of bereavement. *Journal of Rational-Emotive & Cognitive-Behavior Therapy, 35*, 78–87.

Rubio, D. M., Schoenbaum, E. E., Lee, L. S., Schteingart, D. E., Marantz, P. R., Anderson, . . . Esposito, K. (2010). Defining translational research: Implications for training. *Academic Medicine, 85*, 470–475. doi:10.1097/ACM.0b013e3181ccd618

Ruble, D. N., Gruelich, F., Pomerantz, E. M., & Gochberg, G. (1993). The role of gender-related processes in the development of sex differences in self-evaluation and depression. *Journal of Affective Disorders, 29*, 97–128.

Ruble, D. N., Martin, C. L., & Berenbaum, S. A. (2006). Gender development. In W. Damon & R. M. Lerner (Series Eds.), & N. Eisenberg (Vol. Ed.), *Handbook of child psychology: Vol. 3. Social, emotional, and personality development* (6th ed., pp. 789–857). Hoboken, NJ: Wiley.

Ruble, D. N., Taylor, L. J., Cyphers, L., Greulich, F. K., Lurye, L. E., & Shrout, P. E. (2007). The role of gender constancy in early gender development. *Child Development, 78*, 1121–1136.

Rudolph, K. D., & Flynn, M. (2007). Childhood adversity and youth depression: Influence of gender and pubertal status. *Development and Psychopathology, 19*, 497–521.

Ruigrok, A. N., Salimi-Khorshidi, G., Lai, M. C., Baron-Cohen, S., Lombardo, M. V., Tait, R. J., & Suckling, J. (2014). A meta-analysis of sex differences in human brain structure. *Neuroscience & Biobehavioral Reviews, 39*, 34–50.

Ruini, C., Albieri, E., & Vescovelli, F. (2015). Well-being therapy: State of the art and clinical exemplifications. *Journal of Contemporary Psychotherapy, 45*(2), 129–136.

Rush, D., Stein, Z., & Susser, M. (Eds.). (1980). *Diet in pregnancy: A randomized controlled trial of nutritional supplements.* New York, NY: Liss.

Rusk, N., & Rothbaum, F. (2010). From stress to learning: Attachment theory meets goal orientation theory. *Review of General Psychology, 14,* 31–43.

Russell, P., Liebenberg, L., & Ungar, M. (2015). White out: The invisibility of white North American culture and resilience processes. In L. C. Theron, L. Liebenberg, & M. Ungar (Eds.), *Youth resilience and culture: Commonalities and complexities.* New York, NY: Springer Science & Business Media.

Russell, S. T., & Fish, J. N. (2016). Mental health in lesbian, gay, bisexual, and transgender (LGBT) youth. *Annual Review of Clinical Psychology, 12*(1), 465–487.

Russo, F. (2016). Transgender kids. *Scientific American Mind, 27,* 26–35.

Russo, F. B., Jungmann, P., & Beltrão-Braga, P. C. (2017). Zika infection and the development of neurological defects. *Cell Microbiology, 19.* doi:10.111/cmi.12744

Rutland, A., & Killen, M. (2017). Fair resource allocation among children and adolescents: The role of group and developmental processes. *Child Development Perspectives, 11,* 56–62.

Rutter, M. (1986). The developmental pathology of depression: Issues and perspectives. In M. Rutter, C. E. Izard, & P. B. Read (Eds.), *Depression in young people: Developmental and clinical perspectives* (pp. 3–30). New York, NY: Guilford Press.

Rutter, M. (2002). Nature, nurture, and development: From evangelism through science toward policy and practice. *Child Development, 73,* 1–21.

Rutter, M. (2016). Why is the topic of biological embedding of experiences important for translation? *Development and Psychopathology, 28,* 1245–1258.

Rutter, M., Sonuga-Barke, E. J., Colvert, E., Kreppner, J., Beckett, C., . . . Stevens, S. E. (2007). Early adolescent outcomes for institutionally-deprived and non-deprived adoptees. I: Disinhibited attachment. *Journal of Child Psychology and Psychiatry, 48,* 17–30.

Rutter, M., & Sroufe, L. A. (2000). Developmental psychopathology: Concepts and challenges. *Development and Psychopathology, 12,* 265–296.

Rutter, M., Tizard, J., & Whitmore, K. (1970). *Health and behaviour.* London: Longman.

Ryan, M. P. (1984). Monitoring text comprehension: Individual differences in epistemological standards. *Journal of Educational Psychology, 76,* 248–258.

Ryan, R. M., Chirkov, V. I., Little, T. D., Sheldon, K. M., Timoshina, E., & Deci, E. L. (1999). The American Dream in Russia: Extrinsic aspirations and well-being in two cultures. *Personality and Social Psychology Bulletin, 25,* 1509–1524.

Ryan, R. M., & Deci, E. L. (2000). Self-determination theory and the facilitation of intrinsic motivation, social development, and well-being. *American Psychologist, 55,* 68–78.

Ryan, R. M., & Deci, E. L. (2003). On happiness and human potentials: A review of research on hedonic and eudaimonic well-being. *Annual Review of Psychology, 52,* 141–166.

Ryan, R. M., & Deci, E. L. (2017). *Self-determination theory: Basic psychological needs in motivation, development, and wellness.* New York, NY: Guilford Press.

Ryan, R. M., Huta, V., & Deci, E. L. (2008). Living well: A self-determination theory perspective on eudaimonia. *Journal of Happiness Studies, 9,* 139–170.

Ryff, C. D. (2017). Eudaimonic well-being, inequality, and health: Recent findings and future directions. *International Review of Economics, 64*(2), 159.

Ryff, C. D., & Keyes, C. L. M. (1995). The structure of psychological well-being revisited. *Journal of Personality and Social Psychology, 69,* 719–727.

Ryff, C. D., Lee, Y. H., Essex, M. J., & Schmutte, P. S. (1994). My children and me: Mid-life evaluations of grown children and of self. *Psychology and Aging, 9,* 195–205.

Ryff, C. D., & Singer, B. (2000). Interpersonal flourishing: A positive health agenda for the new millennium. *Personality and Social Psychology Review, 4,* 30–44.

Ryff, C. D., & Singer, B. (2003). Flourishing under fire: Resilience as a prototype of challenged thriving. In C. L. M. Keyes & J. Haidt (Eds.), *Flourishing: Positive psychology and the life well-lived* (pp. 15–36). Washington, DC: American Psychological Association.

Ryland, E. B., Riordan, R. J., & Brack, G. (1994). Selected characteristics of high-risk students and their enrollment persistence. *Journal of College Student Development, 35,* 54–58.

Saarento, S., & Salmivalli, C. (2015). The role of classroom peer ecology and bystanders' responses in bullying. *Child Development Perspectives, 9,* 201–205.

Saarni, C., Campos, J. J., Camras, L. A., & Witherington, D. (2006). Emotional development: Action, communication, and understanding. In W. Damon & R. M. Lerner (Series Eds.), N. Eisenberg (Vol. Ed.), *Handbook of child psychology: Vol. 3. Social, emotional, and personality development* (6th ed., pp. 226–299). Hoboken, NJ: Wiley.

Sachdeva, S., Singh, P., & Medin, D. (2011). Culture and the quest for universal principles in moral reasoning. *International Journal of Psychology, 46,* 161–176.

Sadker, M. P., & Sadker, D. M. (1991). *Teachers, schools, and society* (2nd ed.). New York, NY: Random House.

Safer, D. L., Robinson, A. H., & Jo, B. (2010). Outcome from a randomized controlled trial of group therapy for binge eating disorder: Comparing dialectical behavior therapy adapted for binge eating to an active comparison group therapy. *Behavior Therapy, 41*(1), 106–120.

Sagi, A., Koren-Karie, N., Gini, Y. Z., & Tirtsa, J. (2002). Shedding further light on the effects of various types and quality of early child care on infant-mother attachment relationship: The Haifa study of early child care. *Child Development, 73,* 1166–1186.

Sala-Llonch, R., Bartrés-Faz, D., & Junqué, C. (2015). Reorganization of brain networks in aging: A review of functional connectivity studies. *Frontiers in Psychology, 663.*

Salk, R. H., Hyde, J. S., & Abramson, L. Y. (2017). Gender differences in depression in representative national samples: Meta-analyses of diagnoses and symptoms. *Psychological Bulletin, 143*(8), 783–822.

Salmon, D. P., & Bondi, M. W. (2009). Neuropsychological assessment of dementia. *Annual Review of Psychology, 60,* 257–282.

Salmon, K., & Reese, E. (2016). The benefits of reminiscing with young children. *Current Directions in Psychological Science, 25,* 233–238.

Salovey, P., & Mayer, J. D. (1990). Emotional intelligence. *Imagination, Cognition, and Personality, 9,* 185–211.

Salthouse, T. A. (2006). Mental exercise and mental aging: Evaluating the validity of the "Use it or lose it" hypothesis. *Perspectives on Psychological Science, 1,* 68–87.

Salthouse, T. A. (2009). When does age-related cognitive decline begin? *Neurobiology of Aging, 30,* 507–514.

Salthouse, T. A. (2012). Consequences of age-related cognitive declines. *Annual Review of Psychology, 63,* 201–206.

Salvatore, J. E., Kuo, S. I-C., Steele, R. D., Simpson, J. A., & Collins, W. A. (2011). Recovering from conflict in romantic relationships: A developmental perspective. *Psychological Science, 22,* 376–383.

Sameroff, A., & Chandler, M. J. (1975). Reproductive risk and the continuum of caretaking casualty. In F. D. Horowitz, M. Hetherington, S. Scarr-Salapatek, & G. Siegel (Eds.), *Review of child development research* (Vol. 4, pp. 187–244). Chicago, IL: University of Chicago Press.

Sameroff, A. J. (2000). Dialectical processes in developmental psychopathology. In A. J. Sameroff, M. Lewis, & S. M. Miller (Eds.), *Handbook of developmental psychopathology* (2nd ed., pp. 23–40). New York, NY: Kluwer Academic/Plenum Press.

Sameroff, A. J. (2012). Discontinuity: The hallmark of developmental science. *International Journal of Development Science, 6,* 37–39.

Sameroff, A. J., & Mackenzie, M. J. (2003). Research strategies for capturing transactional models of development: The limits of the possible. *Development and Psychopathology, 15,* 613–640.

SAMHSA. (2017). *Behavioral health barometer, United States, Volume 4.* Rockville, MD: Substance Abuse and Mental Health Services Administration. Available at https://store.samhsa.gov/product/Behavioral-Health-Barometer-Volume-4/SMA17-BAROUS-16

Sandberg, D. E., Gardner, M., Callens, N., Mazur, T., & DSD-TRN Psychosocial Workgroup, the DSD-TRN Advocacy Advisory Network, and Accord Alliance. (2017, June). *Interdisciplinary care in disorders/differences of sex development (DSD): The psychosocial component of the DSD—Translational research network.* In *American Journal of Medical Genetics Part C: Seminars in Medical Genetics* (Vol. 175, No. 2, pp. 279–292).

Sandberg, J. G., Brown, A. P., Schade, L. C., Novak, J. R., Denton, W. H., & Holt-Lunstad, J. (2015). Measuring fidelity in emotionally focused couples therapy (EFT): A pilot test of the EFT therapist fidelity scale. *The American Journal of Family Therapy, 43*(3), 251–268.

Sanders, A. R., Martin, E. R., Beecham, G. W., Guo, S., Dawood, K., Riger, G., . . . Bailey, J. M. (2015). Genome-wide scan demonstrates significant linkage for male sexual orientation. *Psychological Medicine, 45,* 1379–1388.

Sanders, M. R., & Murphy-Brennan, M. (2010). The international dissemination of the Triple P–Positive Parenting Program. In J. R. Weisz & A. E. Kazdin (Eds.), *Evidence-based psychotherapies for children and adolescents* (pp. 519–537). New York, NY: Guilford Press.

Sandilos, L. E., Rimm-Kaufman, S. E., & Cohen, J. J. (2017). Warmth and demand: The relation between students' perceptions of the classroom environment and achievement growth. *Child Development, 88,* 1321–1337.

Sandmaier, M. (1996, May/June). More than love. *Family Therapy Networker,* pp. 21–33.

Sandnabba, N. K., & Ahlberg, C. (1999). Parents' attitudes and expectations about children's cross-gender behavior. *Sex Roles, 40,* 249–264.

Sanford, N. (1962). *The American college: A psychological and social interpretation of higher learning.* New York, NY: Wiley.

Saperstein, A., Penner, A. M., & Light, R. (2013). Racial formation in perspective: Connecting individuals, institutions, and power relations. *Annual Review of Sociology, 39,* 359–378.

Sapolsky, R. M. (1992). *Stress: The aging brain and the mechanisms of neuron death.* Cambridge, MA: MIT Press.

Sapolsky, R. M. (2004). *Why zebras don't get ulcers.* New York, NY: Holt.

Saraglou, V. (2002). Religion and the five factors of personality: A meta-analytic review. *Personality and Individual Differences, 32,* 15–25.

Sarason, I. G., & Sarason, B. R. (1985). *Social support: Theory, research, and applications.* Boston, MA: Martinus Nijhoff.

Sarrett, J. C., & Rommelfanger, K. S. (2015). Attention to eyes is present but in decline in 2–6-month-old infants later diagnosed with Autism. *Frontiers in Public Health, 504,* 427–431.

Saudino, K. J., & Micalizzi, L. (2015). Emerging trends in behavioral genetic studies of child temperament. *Child Development Perspectives, 9,* 144–148.

Savickas, M. L. (2009). Career-style counseling. In T. J. Sweeney (Ed.), *Adlerian counseling and psychotherapy: A practitioner's approach* (5th ed., pp. 183–207). New York, NY: Routledge.

Savickas M. L. (2013). Career construction theory. In S. D. Brown & R. W. Lent (Eds.), *Career development and counseling. Putting theory and research to work* (2nd ed., pp. 147–186). Hoboken, NJ: Wiley.

Savickas M. L. (2015). *Life-design counseling manual.* Rootstown, OH. Available at www.vocopher.com

Savin-Williams, R. C. (2016). Sexual orientation: Categories or continuum? Commentary on Bailey et al. (2016). *Psychological Science in the Public Interest, 17,* 37–44.

Savin-Williams, R. C., & Ream, G. L. (2007). Prevalence and stability of sexual orientation components during adolescence and young adulthood. *Archives of Sexual Behavior, 36,* 385–394.

Saxon, S. V., & Etten, M. J. (1987). *Physical change and aging: A guide for the helping professions.* New York, NY: Tiresias Press.

Sayed, S., Iacoviello, B. M., & Charney, D. S. (2015). Risk factors for the development of psychopathology following trauma. *Current Psychiatry Reports, 17*(8), 1–7.

Scafidi, F., Field, T., & Schanberg, S. M. (1993). Factors that predict which preterm infants benefit most from massage therapy. *Journal of Developmental and Behavioral Pediatrics, 14,* 176–180.

Scarr, S. (1993). Biological and cultural diversity: The legacy of Darwin for development. *Child Development, 64,* 1333–1353.

Scarr, S. (1997). Behavior-genetic and socialization theories of intelligence: Truce and reconciliation. In R. J. Sternberg & E. L. Girgorenko (Eds.), *Intelligence, heredity, and environment* (pp. 3–41). Cambridge, England: Cambridge University Press.

Scarr, S., & McCartney, K. (1983). How people make their own environments: A theory of genotype-environment effects. *Child Development, 54,* 424–435.

Schacter, S. (1959). *The psychology of affiliation.* Stanford, CA: Stanford University Press.

Schacter, S., & Singer, J. E. (1962). Cognitive, social, and physiological determinants of emotional state. *Psychological Review, 69,* 379–399.

Schaefer, J. D., Caspi, A., Belsky, D. W., Harrington, H., Houts, R., Horwood, L. J., . . . Moffitt, T. E. (2017). Enduring mental health: Prevalence and prediction. *Journal of Abnormal Psychology, 126,* 212–224.

Schäfer, M., Haun, D. B. M., & Tomasello, M. (2015). Fair is not fair everywhere. *Psychological Science, 26,* 1252–1260.

Schaffer, H. R., & Emerson, P. E. (1964). The development of social attachments in infancy. *Monographs of the Society for Research in Child Development, 29*(3, Serial No. 94).

Schaie, K. W. (1977–1978). Toward a stage theory of adult cognitive development. *Journal of Aging and Human Development, 8,* 129–139.

Schaie, K. W. (1994). The course of adult intellectual development. *American Psychologist, 49,* 304–313.

Schaie, K. W. (1996). *Intellectual development in adulthood: The Seattle Longitudinal Study.* New York, NY: Cambridge University Press.

Schaie, K. W. (2013). *Developmental influences on adult intelligence: The Seattle Longitudinal Study* (2nd ed.). New York: NY: Oxford University Press.

Schaie, K. W., & Willis, S. L. (2000). A stage theory model of adult cognitive development revisited. In R. L. Rubinstein, M. Moss, & M. H. Kleban (Eds.), *The many dimensions of aging* (pp. 175–193). New York, NY: Springer.

Scharf, M., Rousseau, S., & Bsoul, S. (2017). Overparenting and young adults' interpersonal sensitivity: Cultural and parental gender-related diversity. *Journal of Child and Family Studies, 26*(5), 1356.

Scheeringa, M. S., Wright, M. J., Hunt, J. P., & Zeanah, C. H. (2006). Factors affecting the diagnosis and prediction of PTSD symptomatology in children and adolescents. *American Journal of Psychiatry, 163,* 644–651.

Schenck, L. K., Eberle, K. M., & Rings, J. A. (2016). Insecure attachment styles and complicated grief severity: Applying what we know to inform future directions. *OMEGA-Journal of Death and Dying, 73,* 231–249.

Schier, M. F., & Carver, C. S. (1985). Optimism, coping and health: Assessment and implications of generalized outcome expectancies. *Health Psychology, 4,* 219–247.

Schiffrin, H. H., Liss, M., Miles-McLean, H., Geary, K. A., Erchull, M. J., & Tashner, T. (2014). Helping or hovering? The effects of helicopter parenting on college students' well-being. *Journal of Child and Family Studies, 23,* 548–557.

Schindler, R. (1996). Mourning and bereavement among Jewish religious families: A time for reflection and recovery. *Omega, 33,* 121–129.

Schirda, B., Valentine, T. R., Aldao, A., & Prakash, R. S. (2016). Age-related differences in emotion regulation strategies: Examining the role of contextual factors. *Developmental Psychology, 52,* 1370–1380.

Schlossberg, N. K. (2004). *Retire smart, retire happy: Finding your true path in life.* Washington, DC: American Psychological Association.

Schlossberg, N. K. (2009). *Revitalizing retirement: Reshaping your identity, relationships, and purpose.* Washington, DC: American Psychological Association.

Schmidt, L. A., Fox, N. A., & Hamer, D. H. (2007). Evidence for a gene–gene interaction in predicting children's behavior problems: Association of serotonin transporter short and dopamine receptor D4 long genotypes with internalizing and externalizing behaviors in typically developing 7-year-olds. *Development and Psychopathology, 19,* 1105–1116.

Schmidt, M. E., Pempek, T. A., Kirkorian, H. L., Lund, A. F., & Anderson, D. R. (2008). The effects of background television on the toy play behavior of very young children. *Child Development, 79,* 1137–1151.

Schmidt, U., Landau, S., Pombo-Carril, M. G., Bara-Carril, N., Reid, Y., Murray, K., . . . Katzman, M. (2006). Does personalized feedback improve the outcome of cognitive-behavioural guided self-care in bulimia nervosa? A preliminary randomized controlled trial. *The British Journal of Clinical Psychology/The British Psychological Society, 45*(Pt 1), 111–121.

Schmitt, M. T., Branscombe, N. R., Postmes, T., & Garcia, A. (2014). The consequences of perceived discrimination for psychological well-being: A meta-analytic review. *Psychological Bulletin, 140,* 921–948.

Schmitt, S. A., Geldhof, G. J., Purpura, D. J., Duncan, R., & McClelland, M. M. (2017). Examining the relations between executive function, math, and literacy during the transition to kindergarten: A multi-analytic approach. *Journal of Educational Psychology.* http://dx.doi.org/10.1037/edu0000193

Schneider, C., & Brimhall, A. S. (2014). From scared to repaired: Using an Attachment-Based perspective to understand situational couple violence. *Journal of Marital and Family Therapy, 40*(3), 367–379.

Schneider, M., & Preckel, F. (2017). Variables associated with achievement in higher education: A systematic review of meta-analyses. *Psychological Bulletin, 143*(6), 565–600.

Schneider, W., & Bjorklund, B. F. (1998). Memory. In W. Damon (Series Ed.), D. Kuhn & R. S. Siegler (Vol. Eds.), *Handbook of child psychology: Vol. 2. Cognition, perception, and language* (5th ed., pp. 467–522). New York, NY: Wiley.

Schneider, W., & Ornstein, P. A. (2015). The development of children's memory. *Child Development Perspectives, 9*, 190–195.

Schneidman, L., & Woodward, A. L. (2016). Are child-directed interactions the cradle of social learning? *Psychological Bulletin, 142*, 1–17.

Schnurr, P. P., Ford, J. D., Friedman, M. J., Green, B. L., Dain, B. J., & Sengupta, A. (2000). Predictors and outcomes of posttraumatic stress disorder in World War II veterans exposed to mustard gas. *Journal of Consulting and Clinical Psychology, 68*, 258–268.

Schoenthaler, S., Doraz, W., & Wakefield, J. (1986). The impact of a low food additive and sucrose diet on academic performance in 803 New York City public schools. *The International Journal of Biosocial Research, 7*, 189–195.

Schommer, M. A. (1990). Effects of beliefs about the nature of knowledge on comprehension. *Journal of Educational Psychology, 82*, 498–504.

Schommer, M. A. (1993). Epistemological development and academic performance among secondary students. *Journal of Educational Psychology, 85*, 1–6.

Schon, D. (1987). *Educating the reflective practitioner: Toward a new design for teaching and learning in the professions.* San Francisco, CA: Jossey-Bass.

Schoner, G., & Thelen, E. (2006). Using dynamic field theory to rethink infant habituation. *Psychological Review, 113*, 273–299.

Schopp, L. H., Bike, D. H., Clark, M. J., & Minor, M. A. (2015). Act healthy: Promoting health behaviors and self-efficacy in the workplace. *Health Education Research, 30*(4), 542–553.

Schouwenburg, H. C. (2004). Procrastination in academic settings: General introduction. In H. C. Schouwenburg, C. H. Lay, T. A. Pychyl, & J. R. Ferrari (Eds.), *Counseling the procrastinator in academic settings* (pp. 3–17). Washington, DC: American Psychological Association.

Schraw, G., & Moshman, D. (1995). Metacognitive theories. *Educational Psychology Review, 7*, 351–371.

Schroder, L., Tõugu, P., Lenk, M., & De Geer, B. (2011). Cultural expressions of preschoolers' emerging self: Narrative and iconic representations. *Journal of Cognitive Education and Psychology, 10*, 77–95.

Schuengal, C., Bakermans-Kranenburg, M., & van IJzendoorn, M. (1999). Frightening maternal behavior linking unresolved loss and disorganized infant attachment. *Journal of Consulting and Clinical Psychology, 67*, 54–63.

Schug, J., Yuki, M., & Maddux, W. (2010). Relational mobility explains between- and within-culture differences in self-disclosure to close friends. *Psychological Science, 21*(10), 1471–1478.

Schulman, E. P., & Steinberg, L. (2016). Human development and juvenile justice. In K. Heilbrun, D. DeMatteo, & N. E. S. Goldstein (Eds.), *APA handbook of psychology and juvenile justice* (pp. 69–90). Washington, DC: American Psychological Association.

Schulster, J. R. (1996). In my era: Evidence for the perception of a special period of the past. *Memory, 4*, 145–158.

Schultz, L. H. (1993). *Close peer relationship interview scoring manual.* Unpublished manual, Harvard University, Cambridge, MA.

Schultz, L. H., Connolly, J. J., Garrison, S. M., Leveille, M. M., & Jackson, J. J. (2017).

Vocational interests across 20 years of adulthood: Stability, change, and the role of work experiences. *Journal of Research in Personality, 71*, 46–56.

Schultz, R., & Heckhausen, R. (1996). The life span model of successful aging. *American Psychologist, 51*, 702–713.

Schulz, K. M., & Sisk, C. L. (2016). The organizing actions of adolescent gonadal steroid hormones on brain and behavioral development. *Neuroscience and Biobehavioral Reviews, 70*, 148–158.

Schulz, R., & Curnow, C. (1988). Peak performance and age among superathletes: Track and field, swimming, baseball, tennis, and golf. *Journal of Gerontology, 43*, 113–120.

Schwartz, B. (2000). Self-determination: The tyranny of freedom. *American Psychologist, 55*, 79–88.

Schwartz, B. (2004). The tyranny of choice. *Scientific American, 290*, 70–76.

Schwartz, D., Lansford, J. E., Dodge, K. A., Pettit, G. S., & Bates, J. E. (2013). The link between harsh home environments and negative academic trajectories is exacerbated by victimization in the elementary school peer group. *Developmental Psychology, 49*, 305–316. doi: 10.1037/a0028249

Schwartz, R. M., & Garamoni, G. L. (1989). Cognitive balance and psychopathology: Evaluation of an information processing model of positive and negative states of mind. *Clinical Psychology Review, 9*, 271–294.

Schwartz, S. J., & Montgomery, M. J. (2002). Similarities or differences in identity development? The impact of acculturation and gender on identity process and outcome. *Journal of Youth and Adolescence, 31*, 359–372.

Schweinhart, L. J. (2007). Crime prevention by the High/Scope Perry Preschool Program. *Victims & Offenders, 2*, 141–160.

Schweinhart, L. J., Montie, J., Ziang, Z., Barnett, W. S., Belfield, C. R., & Nores, M. (2005). *Lifetime effects: The High/Scope Perry Preschool study through age 40.* (Monographs of the High/Scope Educational Research Foundation, 14.) Ypsilanti, MI: High/Scope Press.

Scott, C. G., Murray, G. C., Mertens, C., & Dustin, E. R. (1996). Student self-esteem and the school system: Perceptions and implications. *Journal of Educational Research, 89*, 286–293.

Scott, R. M., & Baillargeon, R. (2017). Early false belief understanding. *Trends in Cognitive Science, 21*, 237–249.

Scott, S. B., Ram, N., Smyth, J. M., Almeida, D. M., & Sliwinski, M. J. (2017). Age differences in negative emotional responses to daily stressors depend on time since event. *Developmental Psychology, 53*, 177–190.

Seavey, C. A., Katz, P. A., & Zalk, S. R. (1975). Baby X: The effect of gender labels on adult responses to infants. *Sex Roles, 1*, 103–110.

Sebastian, C., Viding, E., Williams, K. D., & Blakemore, S. J. (2010). Social brain development and the affective consequences of ostracism in adolescence. *Brain and Cognition, 72*, 134–145.

Seedall, R. B., & Wampler, K. S. (2012). Emotional congruence within couple

interaction: The role of attachment avoidance. *Journal of Family Psychology, 26*, 948–958.

Segal, Z. V., Williams, J. M. G., & Teasdale, J. D. (2002). *Mindfulness-based cognitive therapy for depression: A new approach to preventing relapse.* New York, NY: Guilford Press.

Segrin, C., & Abramson, L. (1994). Negative reactions to depressed behaviors: A communications theory analysis. *Journal of Abnormal Psychology, 103*, 655–668.

Segrin, C., Givertz, M., Swaitkowski, P., & Montgomery, N. (2015). Overparenting is associated with child problems and a critical family environment. *Journal of Child and Family Studies, 24*(2), 470–479.

Segrin, C., Woszidlo, A., Givertz, M., Bauer, A., & Murphy, M. (2012). The association between overparenting, parent-child communication, and entitlement and adaptive traits in adult children. *Family Relations, 61*, 237–252.

Segrin, C., Woszidlo, A., Givertz, M., & Montgomery, N. (2013). Parent and child traits associated with overparenting. *Journal of Social and Clinical Psychology, 32*(6), 569.

Seitz, D., Purandare, N., & Conn, D. (2010). Prevalence of psychiatric disorders among older adults in long-term care homes: A systematic review. *International Psychogeriatrics, 22*, 1025–1039.

Seligman, M. E. P. (1975). *Helplessness: On depression, development, and death.* San Francisco, CA: Freeman.

Seligman, M. E. P. (1995). *The optimistic child.* Boston, MA: Houghton Mifflin.

Seligman, M. E. P. (2002). *Authentic happiness.* New York, NY: Free Press.

Selman, R. L. (1980). *The growth of interpersonal understanding: Developmental and clinical analysis.* Orlando, FL: Academic Press.

Selman, R. L. (2008). Through thick and thin: Commentary on Martin, Sokol, and Elfers. *Human Development, 51*, 318–325.

Selman, R. L., & Adalbjarnardottir, S. (2000). A developmental method to analyze the personal meaning adolescents make of risk and relationship: The case of "drinking." *Applied Developmental Science, 4*, 47–65.

Selman, R. L., Levitt, M. Z., & Schultz, L. H. (1997). The friendship framework: Tools for the assessment of psychosocial development. In R. L. Selman, C. L. Watts, & L. H. Schultz (Eds.), *Fostering friendship: Pair therapy for treatment and prevention* (pp. 31–52). New York, NY: Aldine de Gruyter.

Selman, R. L., & Schultz, L. H. (1990). *Making a friend in youth: Developmental theory and pair therapy.* Chicago, IL: University of Chicago Press.

Selman, R. L., Watts, C. L., & Schultz, L. H. (Eds.). (1997). *Fostering friendship: Pair therapy for treatment and prevention.* New York, NY: Aldine de Gruyter.

Seltzer, V. C. (1982). *Adolescent social development: Dynamic functional interaction.* Lexington, MA: Heath.

Selye, H. (1950). Forty years of stress research: Principal remaining problems and misconceptions. *CMA Journal, 115*, 53–55.

Selye, H. (1956). *The stress of life.* New York, NY: McGraw Hill.

Selye, H. (1980). The stress concept today. In I. L. Kutash, L. B. Schlesinger, & Associates (Eds.), *Handbook on stress and anxiety* (pp. 127–143). San Francisco, CA: Jossey-Bass.

Semega, J. L., Fontenot, K. R., & Kollar, M. A. (2017). *Income and poverty in the United States: 2016 (Report # P60-259)*. Washington, DC: United States Census Bureau. Available at www.census.gov/library/publications/2017/demo/p60-259.html

Senechal, M., & LeFevre, J. (2002). Parental involvement in the development of children's reading skill: A five-year longitudinal study. *Child Development, 73*, 445–460.

Sentse, M., Kretchmer, T., deHaan, A., & Prinzie, P. (2017). Conduct problem trajectories between age 4 and 17 and their association with behavioral adjustment in emerging adulthood. *Journal of Youth and Adolescence, 46*, 1633–1642.

Sentse, M., Kretschmer, T., & Salmivalli, C. (2015). The longitudinal interplay between bullying, victimization, and social status: Age-related and gender differences. *Social Development, 24*, 659–677.

Shaffer, D. R. (2000). *Social and personality development*. Belmont, CA: Wadsworth/Thomson.

Shahaeian, A., Henry, J. D., Razmjoee, M., Teymoori, A., & Wang, C. (2015). Towards a better understanding of the relationship between executive control and theory of mind: An intra-cultural comparison of three diverse samples. *Developmental Science, 18*, 671–685.

Shahaeian, A., Peterson, C. C., Slaughter, V., & Wellman, H. M. (2011). Culture and the sequence of steps in theory of mind development. *Developmental Psychology, 47*, 1239–1247.

Shallcross, A. J., Ford, B. Q., Floerke, V. A., & Mauss, I. B. (2013). Getting better with age: The relationship between age, acceptance, and negative affect. *Journal of Personality and Social Psychology, 104*, 734–749.

Shapero, B. G., McClung, G., Bangasser, D. A., Abramson, L. Y., & Alloy, L. B. (2017). Interaction of biological stress recovery and cognitive vulnerability for depression in adolescence. *Journal of Youth and Adolescence, 46*(1), 91–103.

Shapiro, A. F., Gottman, J. M., & Carrere, S. (2000). The baby and the marriage: Identifying factors that buffer against decline in marital satisfaction after the first baby arrives. *Journal of Family Psychology, 14*, 59–70.

Shapiro, D., Dundar, A., Huie, F., Wakhungu, P., Yuan, X., Nathan, A., & Hwang, Y. A. (2017). *A national view of student attainment rates by race and ethnicity – Fall 2010 cohort* (Signature Report No. 12b). Herndon, VA: National Student Clearinghouse Research Center.

Shavelson, R. J., Hubner, J. J., & Stanton, G. C. (1976). Validation of construct interpretations. *Review of Educational Research, 46*, 407–441.

Shaver, P. R., & Hazan, C. (1988). A biased overview of the study of love. *Journal of Personal and Social Relationships, 5*, 473–501.

Shaw, A., Choshen-Hillel, S., & Caruso, E. M. (2016). The development of inequity aversion: Understanding when (and why) people give others the bigger piece of the pie. *Psychological Science, 27*, 1352–1359.

Shaw, D. S., & Shelleby, E. C. (2014). Early-starting conduct problems: Intersection of conduct problems and poverty. *Annual Review of Clinical Psychology, 10*, 503–528.

Shaw, P., Eckstrand, K., Sharp, W., Blumenthal, J., Lerch, J. P., Greenstein, D., et al. (2007). Attention-deficit/hyperactivity disorder is characterized by a delay in cortical maturation. *Proceedings of the National Academy of Sciences, 104*, 19649–19654.

Shaw, P., Malek, M., Watson, B., Greenstein, D., de Rossi, P., & Sharp, W. (2013). Trajectories of cerebral cortical development in childhood and adolescence and adult attention-deficit/hyperactivity disorder. *Biological Psychiatry, 74*, 599–606.

Shaw, P., Malek, M., Watson, B., Sharp, W., Evans, A., & Greenstein, D. (2012). Development of cortical surface area and gyrification in attention-deficit/hyperactivity disorder. *Biological Psychiatry, 72*, 191–197.

Shedler, J., & Block, J. (1990). Adolescent drug use and psychological health: A longitudinal inquiry. *American Psychologist, 45*, 612–630.

Shellman, J., Granara, C., & Rosengarten, G. (2011). Barriers to depression care for black older adults. Practice and policy implication. *Journal of Gerontological Nursing, 37*, 13–17.

Sher, K. J., Bartholow, B. D., & Nanda, S. (2001). Short- and long-term effects of fraternity and sorority membership on heavy drinking: A social norms perspective. *Psychology of Addictive Behaviors, 15*, 42–51.

Sheridan, S. M., Knoche, L. L., Kupzyk, K. A., Edwards, C. P., & Marvin, C. A. (2011). A randomized trial examining the effects of parent engagement on early language and literacy: The Getting Ready Intervention. *Journal of School Psychology, 49*, 361–383.

Shin, H., & Ryan, A. M. (2014). Early adolescent friendships and academic adjustment: Examining selection and influence processes with longitudinal social network analysis. *Developmental Psychology, 50*, 2462–2472.

Shiner, R. L. (2015). The development of temperament and personality traits in childhood and adolescence. In M. Mikulincer, P. R. Shaver, M. L. Cooper, & R. J. Larsen (Eds.), *APA handbook of personality and social psychology, Volume 4: Personality processes and individual differences* (pp. 85–105). Washington, DC: American Psychological Association.

Shiner, R. L., Buss, K. A., McClowry, S. G., Putnam, S. P., Saudino, K. J., & Zentner, M. (2012). What is temperament *now*? Assessing progress in temperament research on the twenty-fifth anniversary of Goldsmith et al. (1987). *Child Development Perspectives, 6*, 426–444.

Shiner, R. L., & DeYoung, C. G. (2013). The structure of temperament and personality traits: A developmental perspective. In P. D. Zelazo (Ed.), *The Oxford handbook of developmental psychology, Vol. 2: Self and other* (pp. 113–141). New York, NY: Oxford University Press.

Shiplett, J. L. (1996). *A glass full of tears: Dementia day-by-day*. Aurora, OH: Writers World Press.

Shockley, K. M., & Allen, T. D. (2018). It's not what I expected: The association between dual-earner couples' met expectations for the division of paid and family labor and well-being. *Journal of Vocational Behavior, 104*, 240–260.

Shomaker, L. B., & Furman, W. (2009). Parent-adolescent relationship qualities, internal working models, and attachment styles as predictors of adolescents' interactions with friends. *Journal of Social and Personal Relationships, 26*, 579–603.

Shonkoff, J. P. (2012). Leveraging the biology of adversity to address the roots of disparities in health and development. *Proceedings of the National Academy of Sciences, 109*, 17302–17307.

Shorter, K. R., & Miller, B. H. (2015). Epigenetic mechanisms in schizophrenia. *Progress in Biophysics and Molecular Biology, 118*, 1–7.

Shrum, W., & Cheek, N. H. (1987). Social structure during the school years: Onset of the degrouping process. *American Sociological Review, 52*, 218–223.

Shulman, E. P., Smith, A. R., Silva, K., Icenogle, G., Duell, N., Chein, J., & Steinberg, L. (2016). The dual systems model: Review, reappraisal, and reaffirmation. *Developmental Cognitive Neuroscience, 17*, 103–117.

Shulman, S., & Connolly, J. (2015). The challenge of romantic relationships in emerging adulthood. In J. J. Arnett (Ed.), *The Oxford handbook of emerging adulthood* (pp. 230–244). New York, NY: Oxford University Press.

Sias, P. M., Gallagher, E. B., Kopaneva, I., & Pedersen, H. (2012). Maintaining workplace friendships: Perceived politeness and predictors of maintenance tactic choice. *Communication Research, 39*, 239–268.

Siegel, A. W., & Scovill, L. C. (2000). Problem behavior: The double symptom of adolescence. *Development and Psychopathology, 12*, 763–793.

Siegel, J. M., & Kuykendall, D. H. (1990). Loss, widowhood, and psychological distress among the elderly. *Journal of Consulting and Clinical Psychology, 58*, 519–524.

Siegel, M., & Peterson, C. C. (1998). Preschoolers' understanding of lies and innocent and negligent mistakes. *Developmental Psychology, 34*, 332–341.

Siegler, R. S. (1996). *Emerging minds: The process of change in children's thinking*. New York, NY: Oxford University Press.

Siegler, R. S. (1998). *Children's thinking* (3rd ed.). Upper Saddle River, NJ: Prentice Hall.

Siegler, R. S. (2006). Microgenetic analyses of learning. In W. Damon & R. M. Lerner (Series Eds.), D. Kuhn & R. S. Siegler (Vol. Eds.), *Handbook of child psychology: Vol. 2. Cognition, perception and language* (6th ed., pp. 464–510). Hoboken, NJ: Wiley.

Siegler, R. S. (2007). Cognitive variability. *Developmental Science, 10*, 104–109.

Siegler, R. S., & Braithwaite, D. W. (2017). Numerical development. *Annual Review of Psychology, 68*, 187–213.

Siegler, R. S., & Ramani, G. B. (2009). Playing linear number board games—but not circular ones—improves low-income preschoolers' numerical understanding. *Journal of Educational Psychology, 101*, 545–560.

Siegler, R. S., & Svetina, M. (2006). What leads children to adopt new strategies? A microgenetic/cross-sectional study of class inclusion. *Child Development, 77*, 997–1015.

Siegrist, J. (1996). Adverse health effects of high-effort/low-reward conditions. *Journal of Occupational Health Psychology, 1*, 27–41.

Siegrist, J., & Wahrendorf, M. (2016). *Work stress and health in a globalized economy: The model of* effort-reward imbalance. New York, NY: Springer International Publishing.

Signorella, M. L., Bigler, R. S., & Liben, L. S. (1993). Developmental differences in children's gender schemata about others: A meta-analytic review. *Developmental Review, 13,* 147–183.

Signorella, M. L., & Liben, L. S. (1984). Recall and reconstruction of gender-related pictures: Effects of attitude, task difficulty, and age. *Child Development, 55,* 393–405.

Siguaw, J. A., Sheng, X., & Simpson, P. M. (2017). Biopsychosocial and retirement factors influencing satisfaction with life: New perspectives. *The International Journal of Aging and Human Development, 85,* 332–353.

Silberman, S. (2015). *Neurotribes: The legacy of autism and the future of neurodiversity.* New York, NY: Avery/Penguin Random House.

Silk, J. S., Siegel, G. J., Whalen, D. J., Ostapenko, L. J., Ladoucer, C. D., & Dahl, R. E. (2009). Pubertal changes in emotional information processing: Pupillary, behavioral, and subjective evidence during emotional work identification. *Development and Psychopathology, 21,* 7–26.

Silveira, M., DiPiero, A., Gerrity, M. S., & Feudtner, C. (2000). Patients' knowledge of options at the end of life. *Journal of the American Medical Association, 284,* 2483–2488.

Silverman, P. (2000). Research, clinical practice, and the human experience: Putting the pieces together. *Death Studies, 24,* 469–478.

Sim, T. N., & Koh, S. (2003). A domain conceptualization of adolescent susceptibility to peer pressure. *Journal of Research on Adolescence, 13,* 57–80.

Sim, T. N., & Yeo, G. H. (2012). Peer crowds in Singapore. *Youth and Society, 44,* 201–216.

Simcock, G., Garrity, K., & Barr, R. (2011). The effect of narrative cues on intants' imitation from television and picture books. *Child Development, 82,* 1607–1619.

Simon, H. A. (1955). A behavioral model of rational choice. *Quarterly Journal of Economics, 69*(1), 99–118.

Simon, R. M., Wagner, A., & Killion, B. (2017). Gender and choosing a STEM major in college: Femininity, masculinity, chilly climate, and occupational values. *Journal of Research in Science Teaching, 54,* 299–323.

Simpkins, S. D., Eccles, J. S., & Becnel, J. N. (2008). The mediational role of adolescents' friends in relations between and activity breadth and adjustment. *Developmental Psychology, 44,* 1081–1094.

Simpson, J. A., & Belsky, J. (2016). Attachment theory within a modern evolutionary framework. In J. Cassidy & P. R. Shaver (Eds.), *Handbook of attachment: Theory research and clinical applications* (3rd ed., pp. 91–116). New York, NY: Guilford Press.

Simpson, J. A., Collins, W. A., & Salvatore, J. E. (2011). The impact of early interpersonal experience on adult romantic relationship functioning: Recent findings from the Minnesota Longitudinal Study of Risk and Adaptation. *Current Directions in Psychological Science, 20,* 355–369.

Simpson, J. A., & Rholes, W. S. (1998). *Attachment theory and close relationships.* New York, NY: Guilford Press.

Simpson, J. A., & Rholes, W. S. (2012). Adult attachment orientations, stress, and romantic

relationships. In P. Devine, & A. Plant (Eds.), *Advances in experimental social psychology* (Vol. 45, pp. 279–328). San Diego, CA: Academic Press.

Simpson, J. A., Rholes, W. S., & Phillips, D. (1996). Conflict in close relationships: An attachment perspective. *Journal of Personality and Social Psychology, 71,* 899–914.

Sims, T., Hogan, C. L., & Carstensen, L. L. (2015). Selectivity as an emotion regulation strategy: Lessons from older adults. *Current Opinion in Psychology, 3,* 80–84.

Sinardet, D., & Mortelmans, D. (2009). The feminine side to Santa Claus: Women's work of kinship in contemporary gift-giving relations. *The Social Science Journal, 46,* 124–142.

Singer, B., & Ryff, C. D. (1999). Hierarchies of life stories and associated health risks. In N. E. Adler, B. S. McEwen, & M. Marmot (Eds.), *Socioeconomic status and health in industrialized nations: Social, psychological, and biological pathways* (pp. 96–115). New York, NY: New York Academy of Sciences.

Singer, B., Ryff, C. D., Carr, D., & Magee, W. J. (1998). Life histories and mental health: A person-centered strategy. In A. Raferty (Ed.), *Sociological methodology* (pp. 1–51). Washington, DC: American Sociological Association.

Singer, P., Martin, D., & Merrijoy, K. (1999). Quality of end-of-life care. *Journal of the American Medical Association, 281,* 163–168.

Singer, T., Verhaeghen, P., Ghisletta, P., Lindenberger, U., & Baltes, P. B. (2003). The fate of cognition in very old age: Six-year longitudinal findings in the Berlin Aging Study (BASE). *Psychology and Aging, 18,* 318–331.

Sinnott, J. D. (1984). Postformal reasoning: The relativistic stage. In M. L. Commons, F. A. Richards, & C. Armon (Eds.), *Beyond formal operations: Late adolescent and adult cognitive development* (pp. 298–325). New York, NY: Praeger.

Sinnott, J. D. (1998). *The development of logic in adulthood: Postformal thought and its applications.* New York, NY: Plenum Press.

Sinnott, J., Tobin, E., Chrzanowska, E., & Hilton, S. (2017). The relationship between attachment style and postformal thought. *Journal of Adult Development, 24,* 239–251.

Skinner, B. F. (1938). *The behavior of organisms.* Englewood Cliffs, NJ: Prentice Hall.

Skinner, E. A., Edge, K., Altman, J., & Sherwood, H. (2003). Searching for the structure of coping: A review and critique of category systems for classifying ways of coping. *Psychological Bulletin, 129,* 216–269.

Skoog, T., & Stattin, H. (2014). Why and under what contextual conditions do early-maturing girls develop problem behaviors? *Child Development Perspectives, 8,* 158–162.

Slaby, R. G., & Frey, K. S. (1975). Development of gender constancy and selective attention to same-sex models. *Child Development, 52,* 849–856.

Slade, A. (1999). Attachment theory and research: Implications for the theory and practice of individual psychotherapy with adults. In J. Cassidy & P. R. Shaver (Eds.), *Handbook of attachment: Theory, research, and clinical applications* (pp. 575–594). New York, NY: Guilford Press.

Slade, T., & Andrews, G. (2005). Latent structure of depression in a community sample: A

taxometric analysis. *Psychological Medicine, 35,* 489–497.

Slagt, M., Dubas, J. S., Deković, M., & van Aken, M. A. G. (2016). Differences in sensitivity to parenting depending on child temperament: A meta-analysis. *Psychological Bulletin, 142,* 1068–1110.

Slaughter, V., Imuta, K., Peterson, C. C., & Henry, J. D. (2015). Meta-analysis of theory of mind and peer popularity in the preschool and early school years. *Child Development, 86,* 1159–1174.

Slaughter, V., & Perez-Zapata, D. (2014). Cultural variations in the development of mind reading. *Child Development Perspectives, 8,* 237–241.

Slavin, R. E. (1995). *Cooperative learning: Theory, research, and practice* (2nd ed.). Boston, MA: Allyn & Bacon.

Sloane, S., Baillargeon, R., & Premack, D. (2012). Do infants have a sense of fairness? *Psychological Science, 23,* 196–204.

Slobodskaya, H. R., & Kozlova, E. A. (2016). Early temperament as a predictor of later personality. *Personality and Individual Differences, 99,* 127–132.

Slopen, N., Shonkoff, J. P, Albert, M. A., Yoshikawa, H., Jacobs, A., Stoltz, R., & Williams, D. R. (2016). Racial disparities in child adversity in the US: Interactions with family immigration history and income. *American Journal of Preventive Medicine, 50,* 47–56.

Slutske, W. S., Moffitt, T. E., Poulton, R., & Caspi, A. (2012). Undercontrolled temperament at age 3 predicts disordered gambling at age 32: A longitudinal study of a complete birth cohort. *Psychological Science, 23,* 510–516.

Smetana, J. G. (1989). Toddlers' social interactions in the context of moral and conventional transgressions in the home. *Developmental Psychology, 25,* 499–508.

Smetana, J. G. (1995). Parenting styles and conceptions of parental authority during adolescence. *Child Development, 66,* 299–316.

Smetana, J. G. (1997). Parenting and the development of social knowledge reconceptualized: A social domain analysis. In J. E. Grusec & L. Kuczynski (Eds.), *Parenting and children's internalization of values: A handbook of contemporary theory* (pp. 162–192). New York, NY: Wiley.

Smetana, J. G. (2008). Conflicting views of conflict. *Monographs of the Society for Research in Child Development, 73*(2), 161–168.

Smetana, J. G. (2008). "It's 10 o'clock: Do you know where your children are?" Recent advances in understanding parental monitoring and adolescents' information management. *Child Development Perspectives, 2,* 19–25.

Smetana, J. G. (2011) *Adolescents, families and social development: How teens construct their worlds.* Malden, MA: Wiley, Blackwell.

Smetana, J. G. (2015). Goals, goal pursuit, and adolescent-parent relationships. In P. Gollwitzer & G. Oettingen (Eds.), *Self regulation in adolescence* (pp. 243–265). New York, NY: Cambridge University Press.

Smetana, J. G., & Braeges, J. L. (1990). The development of toddler's moral and conventional judgments. *Merrill-Palmer Quarterly, 36,* 329–346.

Smetana, J. G., Crean, H. F., & Campione-Barr, N. (2005). Adolescents' and parents changing conceptions of parental authority. *New Directions for Child and Adolescent Development, 108*, 31–46.

Smetana, J. G., Metzger, A., Gettman, D. C., & Campione-Barr, N. (2006). Disclosure and secrecy in adolescent-parent relationships. *Child Development, 77*(1), 201–217.

Smetana, J. G., & Rote, W. M. (2015). What do mothers want to know about teens' activities? Levels, trajectories, and correlates. *Journal of Adolescence, 38*, 5–15.

Smetana, J. G., Villalobos, M., Tasopoulos-Chan, M., Gettman, D. C., & Campione-Barr, N. (2009). Early and middle adolescents' disclosure to parents about activities in different domains. *Journal of Adolescence, 32*(3), 693–713.

Smith A. M., Mioduszewski, O., Hatchard, T., Byron-Alhasan, A., Fall, C., & Fried, P. A. (2016). Prenatal marijuana exposure impacts executive functioning into young adulthood: An fMRI study. *Neurotoxicology and Teratology, 58*, 53–59.

Smith, C. E., & Rizzo, M. T. (2017). Children's confession- and lying-related emotion expectancies: Developmental differences and connections to parent-reported confession behavior. *Journal of Experimental Child Psychology, 156*, 113–128.

Smith, C. L. (1979). Children's understanding of natural language hierarchies. *Journal of Experimental Child Psychology, 27*, 437–458.

Smith, D. K., & Chamberlain, P. (2010). Multidimensional treatment foster care for adolescents: Processes and outcomes. In J. R. Weisz & A. E. Kazdin (Eds.), *Evidence-based psychotherapies for children and adolescents* (pp. 243–258). New York, NY: Guilford Press.

Smith, D. S., & Juvonen, J. (2017). Do I fit in? Psychosocial ramifications of low gender typicality in early adolescence. *Journal of Adolescence, 60*, 161–170.

Smith, G. E. (2016). Healthy cognitive aging and dementia prevention. *American Psychologist, 71*, 268–275.

Smith, J., Staudinger, U. M., & Baltes, P. B. (1994). Occupational settings facilitating wisdom-related knowledge: The sample case of clinical psychologists. *Journal of Counseling and Clinical Psychology, 62*, 989–999.

Smith, L. A., Geller, N. L., Kellams, A. L., Colson, E. R., Rybin, D. V., Heeren, T., & Corwin, M. J. (2016). Infant sleep location and breastfeeding practices in the United States, 2011–2014. *Academic Pediatrics, 16*(6), 540–549.

Smith, M., Rogers, S., & Dawson, G. (2008). The Early Start Denver Model: A comprehensive early intervention approach for toddlers with autism. In J. S. Handleman & S. L. Harris (Eds.), *Preschool education programs for children with autism* (3rd ed.). Austin, TX: Pro-Ed.

Smith, R. E., & Smoll, F. L. (1990). Self-esteem and children's enhancement to youth coaching behaviors: A field study of self-enhancement processes. *Developmental Psychology, 26*, 987–993.

Smith, T. M., Cannata, M., Cohen-Vogel, L., & Rutledge, S. A. (2016). Design and implementation of high school reform: Perspectives from research and practice. *Teachers College Record, 118*(13), 1.

Smyke, A. T., Dumitrescu, A., & Zeanah, C. (2002). Attachment disturbances in young children. I: The continuum of caretaking casualty. *Journal of the American Academy of Child and Adolescent Psychiatry, 41*, 972–982.

Snapp, S. D., Watson, R. J., Russell, S. T., Diaz, R. M., & Ryan, C. (2015). Social support networks for LGBT young adults: Low cost strategies for positive adjustment. *Family Relations, 64*(3), 420–430.

Snarey, J. (1985). The cross-cultural universality of social-moral development: A critical review of Kohlbergian research. *Psychological Bulletin, 97*, 202–232.

Sneed, J. R., Johnson, J. G., Cohen, P., Gilligan, C., Chen, H., Crawford, T. N., & Kasen, S. (2006). Gender differences in the age-changing relationship between instrumentality and family contact in emerging adulthood. *Developmental Psychology, 42*, 787–797.

Sneed, R. S., & Schulz, R. (2017). Grandparent caregiving, race, and cognitive functioning in a population-based sample of older adults. *Journal of Aging and Health.* Advance Online Publication.

Snowdon, D. A. (1997). Aging and Alzheimer's disease: Lessons from the Nun Study. *Gerontologist, 37*, 150–156.

Snowling, M. J., & Melby-Lervag, M. (2016). Oral language deficits in familial dyslexia: A meta-analysis and review. *Psychological Bulletin, 142*, 498–545.

Snyder, H. N., & Sickmund, M. (2006). *Juvenile offenders and victims: 2006 national report.* Washington, DC: U.S. Department of Justice, Office of Justice Programs, Office of Juvenile Justice and Delinquency Prevention.

Snyder, J. J., & Patterson, G. R. (1995). Individual differences in social aggression: A test of a reinforcement model of socialization in information-processing mechanisms in children's social adjustment. *Behavior Therapy, 26*, 371–391.

Sobral, M. P., Teixeira, C. P., & Costa, M. E. (2015). Who can give me satisfaction? Partner matching in fear of intimacy and relationship satisfaction. *The Family Journal: Counseling and Therapy for Couples and Families, 23*, 247–253.

Solomon-Krakus, S., Sabiston, C. M., Brunet, J., Castonguay, A. L., Maximova, K., & Henderson, M. (2017). Body image self-discrepancy and depressive symptoms among early adolescents. *Journal of Adolescent Health, 60*, 38–43.

Song, J., Volling, B. L., Lane, J. D., & Wellman, H. M. (2016). Aggression, sibling antagonism, and theory of mind during the first year of siblinghood: A developmental cascade model. *Child Development, 87*(4), 1250–1263.

Sorich, L., & Dweck, C. S. (1996). Mastery-oriented thinking. In C. R. Snyder (Ed.), *Coping.* New York, NY: Oxford University Press.

Sorkhabi, N., & Middaugh, E. (2014). How variations in parents' use of confrontive and coercive control relate to variations in parent–adolescent conflict, adolescent disclosure, and parental knowledge: Adolescents' perspective. *Journal of Child and Family Studies, 23*(7), 1227–1241.

Soto, C. J. (2015). Is happiness good for your personality? Concurrent and prospective relations of the big five with subjective well-being. *Journal of Personality, 83*(1), 45–55.

Soto, C. J., & Luhmann, M. (2013). Who can buy happiness? Personality traits moderate the effects of stable income differences and income fluctuations on life satisfaction. *Social Psychological and Personality Science, 4*, 46–53.

Sowell, E. R., Thompson, P. M., Welcome, S. E., Henkenius, A. L., Toga, A. W., & Peterson, B. S. (2003). Cortical abnormalities in children and adolescents with attention-deficit hyperactivity disorder. *The Lancet, 362*, 1699–1707.

Spack, N. P., Edwards-Leeper, L., Feldman, H. A., Leibowitz, S., Mandel, F., Diamond, D. A., & Vance, S. R. (2012). Children and adolescents with gender identity disorder referred to a pediatric medical center. *Pediatrics*, peds-2011.

Spanoudis, G., Demetriou, A., Kazi, S., Giorgala, K., & Zenonos, V. (2015). Embedding cognizance in intellectual development. *Journal of Experimental Child Psychology, 132*, 32–50.

Sparzo, F. J. (2011). Functional behavioral assessment. In A. S. Davis (Ed.), *Handbook of pediatric psychology* (pp. 1017–1025). New York, NY: Springer.

Spear, L. P. (2010). *The behavioral neuroscience of adolescence.* New York, NY: W.W. Norton.

Spencer, R. L., & Deak, T. (2016). A users guide to HPA axis research. *Physiology & Behavior, 178*, 43–65.

Spencer, S. J., Logel, C., & Davies, P. G. (2016). Stereotype threat. *Annual Review of Psychology, 67*, 415–437.

Sperry, R. W. (1964). The great cerebral commissure. *Scientific American, 201*, 42–52.

Spieker, S. J., Campbell, S. B., Vandergrift, N., Pierce, K. M., Cauffman, E., et al. (2012). Relational aggression in middle childhood: Predictors and adolescent outcomes. *Social Development, 21*, 354–375.

Spielberger, C. D. (1996). *State-Trait Anger Expression Inventory: Professional manual.* Odessa, FL: John Wiley & Sons.

Sprecher, S., & Hatfield, E. (2017). The importance of love as a basis of marriage: Revisiting Kephart (1967). *Journal of Family Issues, 38*, 312–335.

Springer, K. W., Pudrovska, T., & Hauser, R. M. (2011). Does psychological well-being change with age? Longitudinal tests of age variations and further exploration of the multidimensionality of Ryff's model of psychological well-being. *Social Science Research, 40*, 392–398.

Srivastava, S., McGonigal, K. M., Richards, J. M., Butler, E. A., & Gross, J. J. (2006). Optimism in close relationships: How seeing things in a positive light makes them so. *Journal of Personality and Social Psychology, 91*, 143–153.

Sroufe, L. A. (1989). Pathways to adaptation and maladaptation: Psychopathology as developmental deviation: The roots of maladaptation and competence. In D. Cicchetti (Ed.), *Rochester Symposium on Developmental Psychopathology: Vol. 1. The emergence of a discipline* (pp. 13–40). Hillsdale, NJ: Erlbaum.

Sroufe, L. A. (1996). *Emotional development: The organization of emotional life in the early years.* New York, NY: Cambridge University Press.

Sroufe, L. A. (2016). The place of attachment in development. In J. Cassidy & P. R. Shaver (Eds.), *Handbook of attachment: Theory research and clinical applications* (3rd ed., pp. 997–1011). New York, NY: Guilford Press.

Sroufe, L. A., Bennett, C., Englund, M., Urban, J., & Shulman, S. (1993). The significance of gender boundaries in preadolescence: Contemporary correlates and antecedents of boundary violation and maintenance. *Child Development, 64*, 455–466.

Sroufe, L. A., Egeland, B., Carlson, E., & Collins, W. (2005). *Minnesota Study of Risk and Adaptation from birth to maturity: The development of the person.* New York, NY: Guilford Press.

Sroufe, L. A., Fox, N. E., & Pancake, V. R. (1983). Attachment and dependency in developmental perspective. *Child Development, 54*, 1615–1627.

St. Lawrence, J. S., Brasfield, T. L., Jefferson, K. W., Alleyne, E., O'Bannon, R. E., & Shirley, A. (1995). Cognitive behavioral interventions to reduce African-American adolescents risk for HIV infection. *Journal of Consulting and Clinical Psychology, 63*, 154–157.

Staff, J., & Schulenberg, J. E. (2010). Millennials and the world of work: Experiences in paid work during adolescence. *Journal of Business and Psychology, 25*, 247–255.

Stanovich, K. E. (1998). *How to think straight about psychology.* New York, NY: Addison-Wesley/Longman.

Stanovich, K. E. (2016). The comprehensive assessment of rational thinking. *Educational Psychologist, 51*, 23–34.

Stanovich, K. E., & West, R. F. (2014). The assessment of rational thinking: IQ ‡ Q. *Teaching of Psychology, 41*, 265–271.

Stattin, H., Kerr, M., Institutionen för beteende-, social- och rättsvetenskap, & Örebro universitet. (2000). Parental monitoring: A reinterpretation. *Child Development, 71*(4), 1072–1085.

Staudinger, U. M. (1999). Social cognition and a psychological approach to an art of life. In Blanchard-Fields, F. & Hess, T. (Eds.), *Social cognition, adult development, and aging* (pp. 343–375). New York, NY: Academic Press.

Staudinger, U. M., & Baltes, P. B. (1996). Interactive minds: A facilitative setting for wisdom-related performance? *Journal of Personality and Social Psychology, 71*, 746–762.

Staudinger, U. M., & Gluck, J. (2011). Psychological wisdom research: Commonalities and differences in a growing field. *Annual Review of Psychology, 62*, 215–241.

Staudinger, U. M., Maciel, A. G., Smith, J., & Baltes, P. B. (1998). What predicts wisdom-related performance? A first look at personality, intelligence, and facilitative experiential contexts. *European Journal of Personality, 12*, 1–17.

Steensma, T. D., McGuire, J. K., Kreukels, B. P., Beekman, A. J., & Cohen-Kettenis, P. T. (2013). Factors associated with desistence and persistence of childhood gender dysphoria: A quantitative follow-up study. *Journal of the American Academy of Child & Adolescent Psychiatry, 52*, 582–590.

Stein, D. J., Naudé, P. J., & Berk, M. (2018). Stress, depression, and inflammation: Molecular and microglial mechanisms. *Biological Psychiatry, 83*(1), 5–6.

Steinberg, L. (1994). *Crossing paths: How your child's adolescence triggers your own crisis.* New York, NY: Simon & Schuster.

Steinberg, L. (1996). *Beyond the classroom: Why school reform has failed and what parents need to do.* New York, NY: Simon & Schuster.

Steinberg, L. (2007). Risk taking in adolescence: New perspectives from brain and behavioral science. *Current Directions in Psychological Science, 16*, 55–59.

Steinberg, L. (2008). A social neuroscience perspective on adolescent risk-taking. *Developmental Review, 28*, 78–106.

Steinberg, L. (2017). Adolescent brain science and juvenile justice policymaking. *Psychology, Public Policy, and Law, 23*, 410–420.

Steinberg, L., & Belsky, J. (1991). *Infancy, childhood, and adolescence: Development in context.* New York, NY: McGraw-Hill.

Steinberg, L., Dornbusch, S. M., & Brown, B. B. (1992). Ethnic differences in adolescent achievement: An ecological perspective. *American Psychologist, 47*, 723–729.

Steinberg, L., Fegley, S., & Dornbusch, S. M. (1993). The negative impact of part-time work on adolescent adjustment: Evidence from a longitudinal study. *Developmental Psychology, 29*, 171–180.

Steinberg, L., Lamborn, S. D., Darling, N., Mounts, N. S., & Dornbusch, S. M. (1994). Overtime changes in adjustment and competence among adolescents from authoritative, authoritarian, indulgent and neglectful families. *Child Development, 65*, 754–770.

Steinberg, L., Lamborn, S. D., Dornbusch, S. M., & Darling, N. (1992). Impact of parenting practices on adolescent achievement: Authoritative parenting, school involvement and encouragement to succeed. *Child Development, 63*, 1266–1281.

Steinberg, L., & Monahan, K. C. (2007). Age differences in resistance to peer influence. *Developmental Psychology, 43*, 1531–1543.

Steinberg, L., & Scott, E. S. (2003). Less guilty by reason of adolescence: Developmental immaturity, diminished responsibility, and the juvenile death penalty. *American Psychologist, 58*, 1009–1018.

Steinberg, L., & Silk, J. S. (2002). Parenting adolescents. In M. H. Bornstein (Ed.), *Handbook of parenting: Vol. 1. Children and parenting* (2nd ed., pp. 103–133). Mahwah, NJ: Erlbaum.

Steinberg, L., & Silverberg, S. B. (1986). The vicissitudes of autonomy in early adolescence. *Child Development, 57*, 841–851.

Steinberg, S. J., & Davila, J. (2008). Romantic functioning and depressive symptoms among early adolescent girls: The moderating role of parental emotional availability. *Journal of Clinical Child and Adolescent Psychology, 37*, 350–362.

Steinhauser, K. E., Christakis, N. A., Clipp, E. C., McNeilly, M., McIntyre, L., & Tulsky, J. A. (2000). Factors considered important at the end of life by patients, family, physicians, and other care providers. *Journal of the American Medical Association, 284*, 2476–2482.

Stenberg, C., & Campos, J. (1990). The development of anger expressions in infancy. In N. Stein, T. Trabasso, & B. Leventhal (Eds.), *Concepts in emotion* (pp. 75–99). Hillsdale, NJ: Erlbaum.

Stenberg, G. (2017). Does contingency in adults' responding influence 12-month-old infants' social referencing? *Infant Behavior and Development, 46*, 67–79.

Stephen, J., Fraser, E., & Marcia, J. E. (1992). Moratorium-achievement (MAMA) cycles in life span identity development: Value orientations and reasoning system. *Journal of Adolescence, 15*, 283–300.

Stephens, N. M., Hamedani, M. G., & Destin, M. (2014). Closing the social-class achievement gap: A difference-education intervention improves first-generation students' academic performance and all students' college transition. *Psychological Science, 25*, 943–953.

Steptoe, A., Willemsen, G., Owen, N., Flower, L., & Mohamed-Ali, V. (2001). Acute mental stress elicits delayed increases in circulating inflammatory cytokine levels. *Clinical Science, 101*, 185–192.

Sterling, C. M., & Van Horn, K. R. (1989). Identity and death anxiety. *Adolescence, 24*, 321–326.

Sternberg, R. J. (1985). *Beyond IQ: A triarchic theory of human intelligence.* New York, NY: Cambridge University Press.

Sternberg, R. J. (1986). A triangular theory of love. *Psychological Review, 93*, 119–135.

Sternberg, R. J. (2001). What is the common thread of creativity: Its dialectical relation to intelligence and wisdom. *American Psychologist, 56*, 360–362.

Sternberg, R. J. (2006). A duplex theory of love. In R. J. Sternberg (Ed.), *The new psychology of love* (pp. 184–199). New Haven, CT: Yale University Press.

Sternberg, R. J. (2014). The development of adaptive competence: Why cultural psychology is necessary and not just nice. *Developmental Review, 34*, 208–224.

Stevens, R. L. (2014). Affect regulation styles in avoidant and anxious attachment. *Individual Differences Research, 12*, 123–130.

Stevens, T., & Muslow, M. (2006). There is no meaningful relationship between television exposure and symptoms of attention-deficit/ hyperactivity disorder. *Pediatrics, 117*, 665–672.

Stevens-Long, J. (1973). The effect of behavioral context on some aspects of adult disciplinary practice and affect. *Child Development, 44*, 476–484.

Stevenson, B., & Wolfers, J. (2013). Subjective well-being and income: Is there any evidence of satiation? *American Economic Review, Papers and Proceedings 103*(3), 598–604.

Stevenson, H. W., Chen, C., & Lee, S. (1993). Mathematics achievement of Chinese, Japanese, and American children: Ten years later. *Science, 159*, 53–59.

Stevenson, H. W., & Stigler, J. W. (1992). *The learning gap: Why our schools are failing and what we can learn from Chinese and Japanese education.* New York, NY: Simon & Schuster.

Stewart, A. J., & Vandewater, E. A. (1998). The course of generativity. In D. P. McAdams & E. de St. Aubin (Eds.), *Generativity and adult development: How and why we care for the next generation* (pp. 45–74). Washington, DC: American Psychological Association.

Stewart, E. B. (2008). School structural characteristics, student effort, peer associations, and parental involvement: The influence of school- and individual-level factors on academic achievement. *Education and Urban Society, 40*(2), 179–204.

Stewart, N., Winborn, B., Johnson, R., Burks, H., & Engelkes, J. (1978). *Systematic counseling.* Upper Saddle River, NJ: Prentice Hall.

Stice, E. (2016). Interactive and mediational etiologic models of eating disorder onset: Evidence from prospective studies. *Annual Review of Clinical Psychology, 12*(1), 359–381.

Stice, E., Gau, J. M., Rohde, P., & Shaw, H. (2017). Risk factors that predict future onset of each DSM-5 eating disorder: Predictive specificity in high-risk adolescent females. *Journal of Abnormal Psychology, 126*(1), 38–51.

Stice, E., & Shaw, H. (2004). Eating disorder prevention programs: A meta-analytic review. *Psychological Bulletin, 130*, 206–227.

Stiles, J. (2001). Neural plasticity and cognitive development. *Developmental Neuropsychology, 18*, 237–272.

Stiles, J. (2009). On genes, brains, and behavior: Why should developmental psychologists care about brain development? *Child Development Perspectives, 3*, 196–202.

Stiles, J., Brown, T. T., Haist, F., & Jernigan, T. L. (2015). In R. M. Lerner (Ed. In Chief) & L. S. Liben & U. Miller (Vol. Eds.), *Handbook of child psychology and developmental science: Vol. 2. Cognitive processes* (7th ed., pp. 9–62). Hoboken, NJ: Wiley.

Stillmaker, J., & Kasser, T. (2013). Instruction in problem-solving skills increases the hedonic balance of highly neurotic individuals. *Cognitive Therapy and Research, 37*(2), 380–382.

Stith, S. M., McCollum, E. E., Amanor-Boadu, Y., & Smith, D. (2012). Systemic perspectives on intimate partner violence treatment. *Journal of Marital and Family Therapy, 38*(1), 220–240.

Stoet, G., & Geary, D. C. (2013). Sex differences in mathematics and reading achievement are inversely related: Within- and across-nation assessment of 10 years of PISA data. *PloS One, 8*, e57988.

Stoet, G., & Geary, D. C. (2015). Sex differences in academic achievement are not related to political, economic, or social equality. *Intelligence, 48*, 137–151.

Stoll, G., Rieger, S., Lüdtke, O., Nagengast, B., Trautwein, U., & Roberts, B. W. (2017). Vocational interests assessed at the end of high school predict life outcomes assessed 10 years later over and above IQ and big five personality traits. *Journal of Personality and Social Psychology, 113*, 167–184.

Stoltenberg, C. D., & Delworth, U. (1987). *Supervising counselors and therapists: A developmental approach.* San Francisco, CA: Jossey-Bass.

Stoltenborgh, M., Bakermans-Kranenburg, M. J., & van Ijzendoorn, M. H. (2013). The neglect of child neglect: A meta-analytic review of the prevalence of neglect. *Social Psychiatry and Psychiatric Epidemiology, 48* (55), 345–343.

Stone, D. M., Simon, T. R., Fowler, K. A. (2018). Vital signs: Trends in state suicide rates—United States, 1999–2016 and circumstances contributing to suicide—27 States, 2015. *Morb Mortal Wkly Rep, 67*, 617–624.

Stonewater, B. B., & Stonewater, J. K. (1984). Teaching problem-solving: Implications from cognitive development research. *AAHE Bulletin, 36*, 7–10. Washington, DC: American Association for Higher Education.

Stoppa, T. M., & Lefkowitz, E. S. (2010). Longitudinal changes in religiosity among emerging adult college students. *Journal of Research on Adolescence, 20*, 23–38.

Storli, R., & Sandseter, E. B. H. (2015). Preschool teachers' perceptions of children's rough-and-tumble play (R&T) in indoor and outdoor environments. *Early Child Development and Care, 185*, 838–853.

Stovall-McClough, K. C., & Dozier, M. (2016). Attachment states of mind and psychopathology in adulthood. In J. Cassidy & P. R. Shaver (Eds.), *Handbook of attachment: Theory, research, and clinical applications* (3rd ed., pp. 715–738). New York, NY: Guilford Press.

Strachan, T., & Read, A. P. (2000). *Human molecular genetics* (2nd ed.). New York, NY: Wiley.

Straus, M. A. (1994). *Beating the devil out of them: Corporal punishment in American families.* New York, NY: Lexington Books.

Straus, M. A., Sugarman, D. B., & Giles-Sims, J. (1997). Spanking by parents and subsequent antisocial behavior of children. *Archives of Pediatric and Adolescent Medicine, 151*, 761–767.

Strauss, A., & Corbin, J. (1990). *Basics of qualitative research: Grounded theory, procedures, and techniques.* Newbury Park, CA: Sage.

Streit, C., Carlo, G., Ispa, J. M., & Palermo, F. (2017). Negative emotionality and discipline as long-term predictors of behavioral outcomes in African American and European American Children. *Developmental Psychology.* http://dx.doi.org/10.1037/dev0000306

Stroebe, M. (1992). Coping with bereavement: A review of the grief work hypothesis. *Omega, 26*, 19–42.

Stroebe, M., & Schut, H. (1999). The dual process model of coping with bereavement: Rationale and description. *Death Studies, 23*, 197–224.

Stroebe, M., & Schut, H. (2010). The dual process model: A decade on. *Omega: Journal of Death and Dying, 61*, 273–291.

Stroebe, M., Schut, H., & Boerner, K. (2017). Cautioning health-care professionals: Bereaved persons are misguided through the stages of grief. *OMEGA-Journal of Death and Dying, 74*, 455–473.

Stroebe, M., & Stroebe, W. (1993). Determinants of adjustment to bereavement among younger widows and widowers. In M. Stroebe, W. Stroebe, & R. O. Hansson (Eds.), *Handbook of bereavement: Theory, research, and intervention* (pp. 208–226). New York, NY: Cambridge University Press.

Strohminger, N., & Nichols, S. (2015). Neurodegeneration and identity. *Psychological Science, 26*, 1469–1479.

Stroope, S., McFarland, M. J., & Uecker, J. E. (2015). Marital characteristics and the sexual relationships of U.S. older adults: An analysis of national social life, health, and aging project data. *Archives of Sexual Behavior, 44*, 233–247.

Stroud, C. B., Davila, J., Hammen, C., & Vrshek-Schallhorn, S. (2011). Severe and nonsevere events in first onsets versus recurrences of depression: Evidence for stress sensitization. *Journal of Abnormal Psychology, 120*(1), 142–154.

Stroud, L., Foster, E., Handwerger, K., Papandonatos, G. D., Granger, D., Kivilighan, K. T., & Niaura, R. (2009). Stress response and the adolescent transition: Performance versus peer rejection stress. *Development and Psychopathology, 21*, 47–68.

Strouse, J., Goodwin, M. P., & Roscoe, B. (1994). Correlates of attitudes toward sexual harassment among early adolescents. *Sex Roles, 31*, 559–577.

Strube, M. J. (1981). Meta-analysis and cross-cultural comparison: Sex differences in child competitiveness. *Journal of Cross-Cultural Psychology, 12*, 3–20.

Stuart, S., & Koleva, H. (2014). Psychological treatments for perinatal depression. *Best Practice and Research in Clinical Obstetrics and Gynaecology, 28*, 61–70.

Styron, W. (1990). *Darkness visible: A memoir of madness.* New York, NY: Random House.

Substance Abuse and Mental Health Services Administration. (2017). *Behavioral health barometer. United States, Volume 4: Indicators as measured through the 2015 National Survey on Drug Use and Health and National Survey of Substance Abuse Treatment Services.* HHS Publication No. SMA-17-BaroUS-16. Rockville, MD: Substance Abuse and Mental Health Services Administration.

Sue, D., Mack, W. S., & Sue, D. W. (1998). Ethnic identity. In L. C. Lee & N. W. S. Zane (Eds.), *Handbook of Asian American psychology* (pp. 289–323). Thousand Oaks, CA: Sage.

Sue, D. W., Arredondo, P., & McDavis, R. J. (1992). Multicultural counseling competencies and standards: A call to the profession. *Journal of Counseling and Development, 70*, 477–486.

Sugimura, N., Berry, D., Troop-Gordon, W., & Rudolph, K. D. (2017). Early social behaviors and the trajectory of peer victimization across the school years. *Developmental Psychology, 53*, 1447–1461.

Sullivan, H. S. (1953a). *Conceptions of modern psychiatry.* New York, NY: Norton.

Sullivan, H. S. (1953b). *The interpersonal theory of psychiatry.* New York, NY: Norton.

Sullivan, M. W., & Lewis, M. (2003). Contextual determinants of anger and other negative expressions in young infants. *Developmental Psychology, 39*, 693–705.

Sumontha, J., Farr, R. H., & Patterson, C. J. (2016). Social support and coparenting among lesbian, gay, and heterosexual adoptive parents. *Journal of Family Psychology, 30*, 987–996.

Sun, W., Cheng, K., Wu, F., Chou, T., Su, I., Liang, K., & Hsieh, S. (2016). Pain perception can be modulated by mindfulness training: A resting-state fMRI study. *Frontiers in Human Neuroscience, 10.* doi:10.3389/fnhum.2016.00570

Sun, Y., Mensah, F. K., Azzopardi, P., Patton, G. C., & Wake, M. (2017). Childhood social disadvantage and pubertal timing: A national birth cohort from Australia. *Pediatrics, 139.* doi:10.1542/peds.2016-4099

Sundqvist, A., Nordqvist, E., Koch, F.-S., & Heimann, M. (2016). Early declarative memory predicts productive language: A longitudinal study of deferred imitation and communication at 9 and 16 months. *Journal of Experimental Child Psychology, 151*, 109–119.

Sung, S., Simpson, J. A., Griskevicius, V., Kuo, S. I.-C. Schlomer, G. L., & Belsky, J. (2016). Secure infant-mother attachment buffers the effect of early-life stress on age of menarche. *Psychological Science, 27*, 667–674.

Super, C. M., Guldan, G. S., Ahmed, N., & Zeitlin, M. (2012). The emergence of separation protest is robust under conditions of severe developmental stress in rural Bangladesh. *Infant Behavior and Development, 35*, 393–396.

Super, D. E. (1990). A life-span, life-space approach to career development. In D. Brown & I. Brooks (Eds.), *Career choice and development: Applying contemporary theories to practice* (pp. 197–261). San Francisco, CA: Jossey-Bass.

Super, D. E., & Overstreet, P. L. (1960). *The vocational maturity of ninth-grade boys*. New York, NY: Teachers College, Columbia University.

Supple, A. J., Ghazarian, S. R., Frabutt, J. M., Plunkett, S. W., & Sands, T. (2006). Contextual influences on Latino adolescent ethnic identity and academic outcomes. *Child Development, 77*, 1427–1433.

Susman, E. J., Dockray, S., Schiefelbein, V. L., Werwehe, S., Heaton, J., & Dorn, L. D. (2007). Morningness/eveningness, morning-to-afternoon cortisol ratio, and antisocial behavior problems during puberty. *Developmental Psychology, 43*, 811–822.

Susman, E. J., Peckins, M. K., Bowes, J. L., & Dorn, L. D. (2017). Longitudinal synergies between cortisol reactivity and diurnal testosterone and antisocial behavior in young adolescents. *Development and Psychopathology, 29*, 1–17.

Swaab, D. F. (2008). Sexual orientation and its basis in brain structure and function. *Proceedings of the National Academy of Sciences of the United States of America, 105*, 10273–10274.

Swain, J. E., Kim, P., Spicer, J., Ho, S. S., Dayton, C. J., Elmadih, A., & Abel, K. M. (2014). *Brain Research, 1580*, 78–101.

Swanson, S. A., Crow, S. J., Le Grange, D., Swendsen, J., & Merikangas, K. R. (2011). Prevalence and correlates of eating disorders in adolescents: Results from the national comorbidity survey replication adolescent supplement. *Archives of General Psychiatry, 68*, 714–723.

Syed, M. (2015). Emerging adulthood: Developmental stage, theory, or nonsense? In J. J. Arnett (Ed.), *The Oxford handbook of emerging adulthood* (pp. 11–25). New York, NY: Oxford University Press.

Syed, M., & Mitchell, L. L. (2015). How race and ethnicity shape emerging adulthood. In J. J. Arnett (Ed.), *The Oxford handbook of emerging adulthood* (pp. 87–101). New York, NY: Oxford University Press.

Symons, D. K. (2010). A review of the practice and science of child custody and access assessment in the United States and Canada. *Professional Psychology: Research and Practice, 41*, 267–273.

Szinovacz, M. E., & Davey, A. (2005). Retirement and marital decision making: Effects on retirement satisfaction. *Journal of Marriage and Family, 67*, 387–398.

Taber-Thomas, B., & Pérez-Edgar, K. (2015). Emerging adulthood brain development. In J. J. Arnett (Ed.), *The Oxford handbook of emerging adulthood* (pp. 126–141). New York, NY: Oxford University Press.

Takahashi, M., & Overton, W. F. (2005). Cultural foundations of wisdom: An integrated developmental approach. In R. J. Sternberg & J. Jordan (Eds.), *A handbook of wisdom: Psychological perspectives* (pp. 32–60). New York, NY: Cambridge University Press.

Talamantes, M. A., Lawler, W. R., & Espino, D. V. (1995). Hispanic American elders. Care giving norms surrounding dying and the use of hospice services. *Hospital Journal, 10*, 35–49.

Tamis-LeMonda, C. S., Kuchirko, Y., & Song, L. (2014). Why is infant language learning facilitated by parental responsiveness? *Current Directions in Psychological Science, 23*, 121–126.

Tanaka, H., & Seals, D. R. (2003). Dynamic exercise performance in master athletes: Insight into effects of primary human aging on physiological functional capacity. *Journal of Applied Physiology, 95*, 2152–2162.

Tang, A. C., Reeb-Sutherland, B. C., Romeo, R. D., & McEwen, B. S. (2014). On the causes of early life experience effects: Evaluating the role of mom. *Frontiers in Neuroendocrinology, 35*, 245–251.

Tang, Y. Y. (2017). The neuroscience of mindfulness meditation: How the body and mind work together to change our behaviour. Palgrave Macmillan, Cham.

Tang, Y. Y., Hölzel, B. K., & Posner, M. I. (2015). The neuroscience of mindfulness meditation. *Nature Reviews Neuroscience, 16*(4), 213–225.

Tang, Y. Y., & Tang, R. (2015). Mindfulness: Mechanism and application. In Arthur W. Toga (Ed.), *Brain mapping: An encyclopedic reference* (Vol. 3, pp. 59–64). Amsterdam: Elsevier.

Tangney, J. P., Stuewig, J., & Mashek, D. J. (2007). Moral emotions and moral behavior. *Annual Review of Psychology, 58*, 344–372.

Tanguay, P. E. (2000). Pervasive developmental disorders: A 10-year review. *Journal of the American Academy of Child and Adolescent Psychiatry, 39*, 1079–1095.

Tanner, J. M. (1990). *Fetus into man: Physical growth from conception to maturity* (2nd ed.). Cambridge, MA: Harvard University Press.

Tao, Y., Oliver, M., & Venville, G. (2013). Chinese and Australian children's understandings of the earth: A cross cultural study of conceptual development. *Cultural Studies of Science Education, 8*, 253–283.

Tarampi, M. R., Heydari, N., & Hegarty, M. (2016). A tale of two types of perspective taking: Sex differences in spatial ability. *Psychological Science, 27*, 1507–1516.

Tardif, T., Shatz, M., & Naigles, L. (1997). Caregiver speech and children's use of nouns versus verbs: A comparison of English, Italian, and Mandarin. *Journal of Child Language, 24*, 535–565.

Tarokh, L., Saletin, J. M., & Carskadon, M. A. (2016). Sleep in adolescence: Physiology, cognition and mental health. *Neuroscience and Biobehavioral Reviews, 70*, 182–188.

Tatlow-Golden, M., & Guerin, S. (2017). Who I am: The meaning of early adolescents' most valued activities and relationships, and implications for self-concept research. *Journal of Early Adolescence, 37*, 236–266.

Tatum, B. D. (1997). *"Why are all the Black kids sitting together in the cafeteria?" and other conversations about race*. New York, NY: Basic Books.

Tay, L., Chan, D., & Diener, E. (2014). The metrics of societal happiness. *Social Indicators Research, 117*(2), 577–600.

Taylor, C. A., Al-Hiyari, R., Lee, S. J., Priebe, A., Guerrero, L. W., & Bales, A. (2016). Beliefs and ideologies linked with approval of corporal punishment: A content analysis of online comments. *Health Education Research, 31*, 563–575.

Taylor, J. S. H., Duff, F. J., Woollams, A. M., Monaghan, P., & Ricketts, J. (2015). How word meaning influences word reading. *Current Directions in Psychological Science, 24*, 322–328.

Taylor, P. J., Rietzschel, J., Danquah, A., & Berry, K. (2015). The role of attachment style, attachment to therapist, and working alliance in response to psychological therapy. *Psychology and Psychotherapy: Theory, Research and Practice, 88*(3), 240–253.

Taylor, R. D., Oberle, E., Durlak, J. A., & Weissberg, R. P. (2017). Promoting positive youth development through school-based social and emotional learning interventions: A meta-analysis of follow-up effects. *Child Development, 88*, 1156–1171.

Taylor, S. E. (1983). Adjustment to threatening events: A theory of cognitive adaptation. *American Psychologist, 38*, 1161–1173.

Taylor, S. E., & Brown, J. D. (1988). Illusion and well-being: A social-psychological perspective on mental health. *Psychological Bulletin, 103*, 193–210.

Tedeschi, R. G., & Calhoun, L. G. (1996). The posttraumatic growth inventory: Measuring the positive legacy of trauma. *Journal of Traumatic Stress, 9*, 455–471.

Tedeschi, R. G., & Calhoun, L. G. (2004). Posttraumatic growth: Conceptual foundations and empirical evidence. *Psychological Inquiry, 15*, 1–18.

Telch, C. F., Agras, W. S., Linehan, M. M. (2001). Dialectical behavior therapy for binge eating disorder. *Journal of Consulting and Clinical Psychology, 69*, 1061–1065.

Telingator, C. J., & Woyewodzic, K. T. (2011). Sexual minority identity development. *Psychiatric Times, 28*, 39–42.

Telzer, E. H., Fuligni, A. J., Lieberman, M. D., & Gálvan, A. (2013). The effects of poor quality sleep on brain function and risk taking in adolescence. *NeuroImage, 71*, 275–283.

Telzer, E. H., Goldenberg, D., Fuligni, A. J., Lieberman, M. D., & Gálvan, A. (2015). Sleep variability in adolescence is associated with altered brain development. *Developmental Cognitive Neuroscience, 14*, 16–22.

Tempel, T., Frings, C., & Mecklenbräuker, S. (2015). Dual processes of false recognition in kindergarten children and elementary school pupils. *Journal of Experimental Child Psychology, 138*, 125–142.

ten Brummelhuis, L. L., & Bakker, A. B. (2012). A resource perspective on the work-home interface: The work-home resources model. *American Psychologist, 67*, 545–556.

Terplan, M., & Wright, T. (2011). The effects of cocaine and amphetamine use during pregnancy on the newborn: Myth versus reality. *Journal of Addictive Diseases, 30*, 1–5.

Tessler, M., & Nelson, K. (1994). Making memories: The influence of joint encoding on later recall by young children. *Consciousness and Cognition, 3*, 307–326.

Teti, D. M., & Gelfand, D. M. (1991). Behavioral competence among mothers of infants in the first year: The mediational role of maternal self-efficacy. *Child Development, 62*, 918–929.

Thapar, A., Collishaw, S., Pine, D. S., & Thapar, A. K. (2012). Depression in adolescence. *The Lancet, 379*, 1056–1067.

The Pew Center. (2008). *One in 100: Behind Bars in America 2008*. Washington DC: The Pew Charitable Trusts. Available from www.pewstates.org/uploadedFiles/PCS_Assets/2008/one%20in%20100.pdf

Thelen, E., & Smith, L. B. (1998). Dynamic systems theories. In W. Damon (Series Ed.) & R. M. Lerner (Vol. Ed.), *Handbook of child psychology: Vol. 1. Theoretical models of human development* (5th ed., pp. 563–634). New York, NY: Wiley.

Thew, G. R., Gregory, J. D., Roberts, K., & Rimes, K. A. (2017). The phenomenology of self-critical thinking in people with depression, eating disorders, and in healthy individuals. *Psychology and Psychotherapy: Theory, Research and Practice, 90*, 751–769.

Thijssen, S., Muetzel, R. L., Bakermans-Kranenburg, M. J., Jaddoe, V. W., Tiemeier, H., Verhulst, F. C., . . . Van Ijzendoorn, M. H. (2017). Insensitive parenting may accelerate the development of the amygdala–medial prefrontal cortex circuit. *Development and Psychopathology, 29*, 505–518.

Thomaes, S., Brummelman, E., Bushman, B. J., Reijntjes, A., & Orobio de Castro, B. (2015). *Is it time to rethink the pervasiveness and nature of low self-esteem in children?* Unpublished manuscript.

Thomaes, S., Reijntjes, A., Orobio de Castro, B., Bushman, B. J., Poorthuis, A., & Telch, M. J. (2010). I like me if you like me: On the interpersonal modulation and regulation of preadolescents' state self-esteem. *Child Development, 81*, 811–825.

Thomas, A., & Chess, S. (1977). *Temperament and development*. New York, NY: Brunner/Mazel.

Thomas, K. M., Drevets, W. C., Whalen, P. J., Eccard, C. H., Dahl, R. E., Ryan, N. D., & Casey, B. J. (2001). Amygdala response to facial expressions in children and adults. *Biological Psychiatry, 49*, 309–316.

Thomas, S., & Kunzmann, U. (2013). Age differences in wisdom-related knowledge: Does the age relevance of the task matter? *Journals of Gerontology Series B: Psychological Sciences and Social Sciences, 69*, 897–905.

Thompson, R. (2015). Social support and child protection: Lessons learned and learning. *Child Abuse and Neglect, 41*, 19–29.

Thompson, R. A. (1998). Early sociopersonality development. In W. Damon (Series Ed.) & N. Eisenberg (Vol. Ed.), *Handbook of child psychology: Vol. 3. Social, emotional, and personality development* (5th ed., pp. 25–104). New York, NY: Wiley.

Thompson, R. A. (2012). Whither the preconventional child? Toward a life-span moral development theory. *Child Development Perspectives, 6*, 423–429.

Thompson, R. A. (2014). Conscience development in early childhood. In M. Killen & J. G. Smetana (Eds.), *Handbook of moral development* (2nd ed., pp. 73–92). New York, NY: Psychology Press.

Thompson, R. A. (2015). Relationships, regulation, and early development. In R. M. Lerner (Series Ed.) & M. E. Lamb (Vol. Ed.), *Handbook of child psychology and developmental science: Volume 3. Socioemotional processes* (7th ed., pp. 201–246). Hoboken, NJ: Wiley.

Thompson, R. A. (2016). Early attachment and later development: Reframing the questions. In J. Cassidy & P. R. Shaver (Eds.), *Handbook of attachment: Theory research and clinical applications* (3rd ed., pp. 330–348). New York, NY: Guilford Press.

Thompson, R. A., & Leger, D. W. (1999). From squalls to calls: The cry as a developing socio-emotional signal. In B. Lester, J. Newman, & F. Pedersen (Eds.), *Biological and social aspects of infant crying*. New York, NY: Plenum Press.

Thompson, R. A., Winer, A. C., & Goodvin, R. (2011). The individual child: Temperament, emotion, self, and personality. In M. H. Bornstein & M. E. Lamb (Eds.). *Developmental science: An advanced textbook* (pp. 427–468). New York, NY: Psychology Press.

Thompson, W. W., Price, C., Goodson, B., Shay, D. K., Benson, P., Hinrichsen, V. L., . . . DeStefano, F. (2007). Early thimerosal exposure and neuropsychological outcomes at 7 to 10 years. *New England Journal of Medicine, 357*, 1281–1292.

Thomsen, D. K., Pillemer, D. B., & Ivcevic, Z. (2011). Life story chapters, specific memories and the reminiscence bump. *Memory, 19*, 267–279.

Thorne, B. (1986). Girls and boys together, but mostly apart: Gender arrangements in elementary schools. In W. W. Jartup & Z. Rubin (Ed.), *Relationships and development*. Hillsdale, NJ: Erlbaum.

Thorne, B. (1994). *Gender play: Girls and boys in school*. New Brunswick, NJ: Rutgers University Press.

Tienda, M., & Mitchell, F. (Eds.). (2006). *Hispanics and the future of America*. Washington, DC: National Academy Press.

Tims, M., Bakker, A. B., & Derks, D. (2012). Development and validation of the job crafting scale. *Journal of Vocational Behavior, 80*, 173–186.

Tither, J. M., & Ellis, B. J. (2008). Impact of fathers on daughters' age at menarche: A genetically and environmentally controlled sibling study. *Developmental Psychology, 44*, 1409–1420.

Tobi, E. W., Lumey, L. H., Talens, R. P., Kremer, D., Putter, H., Stein, A. D., . . . Heijmans, B. T. (2009). DNA methylation differences after exposure to prenatal famine are common and timing- and sex-specific. *Human Molecular Genetics, 18*, 4046–4053.

Tobin, J., Wu, D., & Davidson, D. (1989). *Preschool in three cultures: Japan, China, and the United States*. New Haven, CT: Yale University Press.

Todd, A. R., Forstmann, M., Burgmer, P., Brooks, A. W., & Galinsky, A. D. (2015). Anxious and egocentric: How specific emotions influence perspective taking. *Journal of Experimental Psychology General, 144*, 374–391.

Todd, B. K., Fischer, R. A., Di Costa, S., Roestorf, A., Harbour, K., Hardiman, P., & Barry, J. A. (2017). Sex differences in children's toy preferences: A systematic review, meta-regression, and meta-analysis. *Infant and Child Development*. Advance Online Publication.

Toga, A. W., Thompson, P. M., & Sowell, E. R. (2006). Mapping brain maturation. *Trends in Neurosciences, 29*, 148–159.

Tomarken, A. J., Davidson, R. J., & Henriques, J. B. (1990). Resting frontal activation asymmetry predicts emotional reactivity to film clips. *Journal of Personality and Social Psychology, 59*, 791–801.

Tomlin, A. M., & Viehweg, S. A. (2003). Infant mental health: Making a difference. *Professional Psychology: Research and Practice, 34*, 617–625.

Tong, V. T., Dietz, P. M., Morrow, B., D'Angelo, D. V., Farr, S. L., Rockhill, K. M., & England, L. J. (2013). Trends in smoking before, during, and after pregnancy—Pregnancy Risk Assessment Monitoring System, United States, 40 sites, 2000–2010. *Morbidity and Mortality Weekly Report Surveillance Summaries, 62*, 1–19.

Toth, S. L., Gravener-Davis, J. A., Guild, D. J., & Cicchetti, D. (2013). Relational interventions for child maltreatment: Past, present, future perspectives. *Developmental Psychopathology, 25*, 1601–1617.

Tout, K., de Haan, M., Campbell, E. K., & Gunnar, M. R. (1998). Social behavior correlates of cortisol activity in child care: Gender differences and time-of-day effects. *Child Development, 69*, 1247–1262.

Trace, S. E., Baker, J. H., Peñas-Lledó, E., & Bulik, C. M. (2013). The genetics of eating disorders. *Annual Review of Clinical Psychology, 9*(1), 589–620.

Treadway, M. T., Waskom, M. L., Dillon, D. G., Holmes, A. J., Park, M. T. M., Chakravarty, M. M., . . . Pizzagalli, D. A. (2015). Illness progression, recent stress, and morphometry of hippocampal subfields and medial prefrontal cortex in major depression. *Biological Psychiatry, 77*(3), 285–294.

Trillingsgaard, T., & Sommer, D. (2016). Associations between older maternal age, use of sanctions, and children's socio-emotional development through 7, 11, and 15 years. *European Journal of Developmental Psychology*. doi:10.1080/17405629.2016.1266248

Trivits, L. C., & Repucci, N. D. (2002). Application of Megan's law to juveniles. *American Psychologist, 57*, 690–704.

Tronick, E. (1989). Emotions and emotional communication in infants. *American Psychologist, 44*, 112–119.

Tronick, E., Als, H., Adamson, L., Wise, S., & Brazelton, T. B. (1978). Infants' response to entrapment between contradictory messages in face-to-face interaction. *Journal of the American Academy of Child and Adolescent Psychiatry, 17*, 1–13.

Tronick, E., & Beeghly, M. (2011). Infants' meaning-making and the development of mental health problems. *American Psychologist, 66*, 107–119.

Troop-Gordon, W. (2015). The role of the classroom teacher in the lives of children victimized by peers. *Child Development Perspectives, 9*, 55–60.

Troop-Gordon, W., & Ladd, G. W. (2015). Teachers' victimization-related beliefs and strategies: Associations with students' aggressive behavior and peer victimization. *Journal of Abnormal Child Psychology, 43*, 45–60.

Troop-Gordon, W., Sugimura, N., & Rudolph, K. D. (2017). Responses to interpersonal stress: Normative changes across childhood and the impact of peer victimization. *Child Development, 88*, 640–657.

Trotman, H. D., Holtzman, C. W., Ryan, A. T., Shapiro, D. I., Macdonald, A. N., Goulding, S. M., . . . Walker, E. F. (2013). The development of psychotic disorders in adolescence: A potential role for hormones. *Hormones and Behavior, 64*, 411–419.

Trzesniewski, K. H., & Donnellan, M. B. (2010). Rethinking "generation me": A study of cohort effects from 1976–2006. *Perspectives on Psychological Science, 5*, 58–75.

Tu, W., Wagner, E. K., Eckert, G. J., Yu, Z., Hannon, T., Pratt, H., et al. (2015). Associations between menarche-related genetic variants and pubertal growth in male and female adolescents. *Journal of Adolescent Health, 56*, 66–72.

Tucker-Drob, E. M. (2011). Global and domain-specific changes in cognition throughout adulthood. *Developmental Psychology, 47*, 331–343.

Tuckman, B. W., Abry, D. A., & Smith, D. R. (2002). *Learning and motivational strategies: Your guide to success.* Upper Saddle River, NJ: Prentice Hall.

Tudge, J. R. H., Doucet, F., Odero, D., Sperb, T. M., Piccinini, C. A., & Lopes, R. S. (2006). A window into different cultural worlds: Young children's everyday activities in the United States, Brazil, and Kenya. *Child Development, 77*, 1446–1469.

Turiel, E. (1978). Social regulation and domains of social concepts. In W. Damon (Ed.), *Social cognition: New directions for child development* (pp. 45–74). San Francisco, CA: Jossey-Bass.

Turiel, E. (2006). The development of morality. In W. Damon & R. M. Lerner (Series Eds.), N. Eisenberg (Vol. Ed.), *Handbook of child psychology: Vol. 3. Social, emotional, and personality development* (6th ed., pp. 789–857). Hoboken, NJ: Wiley.

Turiel, E. (2015). Moral development. In R. M. Lerner (Series Ed.), W. F. Overton, & P. C. M. Molenaar (Vol. Eds.), *Handbook of child psychology and developmental science: Volume 1. Theory and Method* (7th ed., pp. 484–522). Hoboken, NJ: Wiley.

Turner, F. J. (1986). *Social work treatment: Interlocking theoretical approaches* (3rd ed.). New York, NY: Free Press.

Turner, R. J., & Lloyd, D. A. (1995). Lifetime traumas and mental health: The significance of cumulative adversity. *Journal of Health and Social Behavior, 36*, 360–376.

Tversky, A., & Kahneman, D. (1974). Judgment under uncertainty: Heuristics and biases. *Science, 185*, 1124–1131.

Twenge, J. M. (2000). The age of anxiety? The birth cohort change in anxiety and neuroticism, 1952–1993. *Journal of Personality & Social Psychology, 79*, 1007–1021.

Twenge, J. M. (2013). The evidence for generation me and against generation we. *Emerging Adulthood, 1*, 11–16.

Twenge, J. M., Campbell, W. K., & Carter, N. T. (2014). Declines in trust in others and confidence in institutions among American adults and late adolescents, 1972–2012. *Psychological Science, 25*, 1914–1923.

Twenge, J. M., & Crocker, J. (2002). Race and self-esteem: Meta-analyses comparing Whites, Blacks, Hispanics, Asians, and American Indians and comment on Gray-Little and Hafdahl (2000). *Psychological Bulletin, 128*, 371–408.

Twenge, J. M., Joiner, T. E., Rogers, M. L., & Martin, G. N. (2017). Increases in depressive symptoms, suicide-related outcomes, and suicide rates among U.S. adolescents after 2010 and links to new media screen time. *Clinical Psychological Science.* https://doi.org/10.1177/2167702617723376

Twenge, J. M., & Park, H. (2017). The decline in adult activities among U.S. adolescents, 1976–2016. *Child Development.* doi:10.1111/cdev.12930

Tyrka, A. R., Ridout, K. K., & Parade, S. H. (2016). Childhood adversity and epigenetic regulation of glucocorticoid signaling genes: Associations in children and adults. *Development and Psychopathology, 28*, 1219–1331.

Uba, L., & Huang, K. (1999). *Psychology.* New York, NY: Longman.

Uccelli, P., Hemphill, L., Pan, B. A., & Snow, C. E. (1999). Telling two kinds of stories: Sources of narrative skill. In L. Batter & C. S. Tamis-LeMonda (Eds.), *Child psychology: A handbook of contemporary issues* (pp. 215–233). Philadelphia, PA: Psychology Press.

Umana-Taylor, A., & Fine, M. A. (2001). Methodological implications of grouping Latino adolescents into one collective ethnic group. *Hispanic Journal of Behavioral Sciences, 23*, 347–362.

Umaña-Taylor, A. J., Quintana, S. M., Lee, R. M., Cross, W. E., Rivas-Drake, D., Schwartz, S. J., . . . Ethnic and Racial Identity in the 21st Century Study Group. (2014). Ethnic and racial identity during adolescence and into young adulthood: An integrated conceptualization. *Child Development, 85*(1), 21–39.

Underwood, M. K., & Ehrenreich, S. E. (2017). The power and the pain of adolescents' digital communication: Cyber victimization and the perils of lurking. *American Psychologist, 72*(2), 144–158.

Unger, D., Sonnentag, S., Niessen, C., & Kuonath, A. (2015). The longer your work hours, the worse your relationship? The role of selective optimization with compensation in the associations of working time with relationship satisfaction and self-disclosure in dual-career couples. *Human Relations, 68*, 1889–1912.

United Nations. (1989). *United Nations Convention on the Rights of the Child.* Geneva. Washington, DC: Office of the United Nations High Commissioner for Human Rights. Available from http://www2.ohchr.org/english/law/crc.htm

U.S. Bureau of Justice Statistics. (2000). *Violent crime rate trends.* Washington, DC: Author.

U.S. Bureau of Labor Statistics. (2011). *Women at work.* Available from www.bls.gov/spotlight/2011/women/pdf/women_bls_spotlight.pdf

U.S. Bureau of Labor Statistics. (2014). *Women in the labor force: A databook.* Available at www.bls.gov/opub/reports/womens-databook/archive/women-in-the-labor-force-a-databook-2014.pdf

U.S. Bureau of Labor Statistics. (2017, April 27). *College enrollment and work activity of 2016 high school graduates.* News Release, Bureau of Labor Statistics, U.S. Department of Labor. Available at www.bls.gov/news.release/pdf/hsgec.pdf

U.S. Bureau of Labor Statistics. (2017). *Women in the labor force: A databook.* Retrieved from www.bls.gov/opub/reports/womens-databook/2016/home.htm

U.S. Bureau of Labor Statistics. (2018). *Current employment statistics highlights, December 2017.* Available at www.bls.gov/web/empsit/ceshighlights.pdf

U.S. Bureau of the Census. (2012). *Licensed Drivers and Number in Accidents by Age: 2009.* Available from www.census.gov/compendia/statab/2012/tables/12s1114.pdf

U.S. Bureau of the Census. (2017). *The changing economics and demographics of young adulthood: 1975–2016.* Available from www.census.gov/content/dam/Census/library/publications/2017/demo/p20-579.pdf

U.S. Bureau of the Census. (2018). *America's families and living arrangements: 2016, Table A1.* Available from www.census.gov/data/tables/2016/demo/families/cps-2016.htm

U.S. Department of Education. (1990). *National goals for education.* Washington, DC: U.S. Government Printing Office.

U.S. Department of Education. (2014). *Guiding principles: A resource guide for improving school climate and discipline.* Available from http://www2.ed.gov/policy/gen/guid/school-discipline/guiding-principles.pdf

U.S. Department of Health & Human Services, Administration for Children and Families, Administration on Children, Youth and Families, Children's Bureau. (2017). *Child maltreatment 2015.* Available from www.acf.hhs.gov/programs/cb/research-data-technology/statistics-research/child-maltreatment

U.S. Department of Health and Human Services and U.S. Department of Agriculture. (2015). *2015–2020 dietary guidelines for Americans* (8th ed.). Washington DC: Author. Available at https://health.gov/dietaryguidelines/2015/guidelines.

U.S. Department of Transportation. (1996). Traffic Safety CD-ROM, 1975–1994 (BTS-CD-10). Washington, DC: Bureau of Transportation Statistics.

U.S. National Center for Health Statistics, Health, United States. (2017). https://www.cdc.gov/nchs/products/nvsr.htm and National Vital Statistics Report (NVSR), *Deaths: Final Data for 2015,* Vol. 66, No. 6, November 2017.

Urry, H. L., Nitschke, J. B., Dolski, I., Jackson, D. C., Dalton, K. M., Mueller, C. J., et al. (2004). Making a life worth living: Neural correlates of well-being. *Psychological Science, 15*, 367–372.

Ursache, A., Blair, C., Stifter, C., & Voegtline, K. (2013). Emotional reactivity and regulation in infancy interact to predict executive functioning in early childhood. *Developmental Psychology, 49*, 127–137.

Uttal, D. H., Meadow, N. G., Tipton, E., Hand, L. L., Alden, A. R., Warren, C., & Newcombe, N. S. (2013). The malleability of spatial skills: A meta-analysis of training studies. *Psychological Bulletin, 139*, 352–402.

Vachon, M. L., Rogers, J., Lyall, W. A., Lancee, W. J., Sheldon, A. R., & Freeman, S. J. J. (1982). Predictors and correlates of adaptation to conjugal bereavement. *American Journal of Psychiatry, 139*, 998–1002.

Vago, D. R., & Silbersweig, D. A. (2012). Self-awareness, self-regulation, and self-transcendence (S-ART): A framework for understanding the neurobiological mechanisms of mindfulness. *Frontiers in Human Neuroscience, 6*, 1–30.

Vaillancourt, T., deCatanzaro, D., Duku, E., & Muir, C. (2009). Androgen dynamics in the context of children's peer relations: An examination of the links between testosterone and peer victimization. *Aggressive Behavior, 35*, 103–113.

Vaillant, C. O., & Vaillant, G. E. (1993). Is the U-curve of marital satisfaction an illusion? A

40-year study of marriage. *Journal of Marriage and the Family, 55,* 230–239.

Vaillant, G. E. (1977). *Adaptation to life.* Boston, MA: Little, Brown.

Vaillant, G. E. (1993). *The wisdom of the ego.* Cambridge, MA: Harvard University Press.

Vaillant, G. E. (2012). *Triumphs of experience: The men of the Harvard Grant study.* Cambridge, MA: Harvard University Press.

Vaish, A. (2016). Flexible concern: The development of multideterrmined and context-dependent empathic responding. *Child Development Perspectives, 10,* 149–154.

Valenzuela, M. (1990). Attachment in chronically underweight young children. *Child Development, 61,* 1984–1996.

Valiante, A. G., Barr, R. G., Zelazo, P. R., Brant, R., & Young, S. N. (2013). Effects of familiarity and feeding on newborn speech-voice recognition. *Infancy, 18,* 443–461.

Valiente, D., Eisenberg, N., Fabes, R. A., Shepard, S. A., Cumberland, A., & Losoya, S. H. (2004). Prediction of children's empathy-related responding from their effortful control and parents' expressivity. *Developmental Psychology, 40,* 911–926.

Vallejos, M., Cesoni, O. M., Farinola, R., Bertoni, M. S., & Prokopez, C.R. (2016). Adverse childhood experiences among men with schizophrenia. *Psychiatric Quarterly, 87,* 1–9. doi:10.1007/s11126-016-9487-2

Van de Bongardt, D., Reitz, E., Sandfort, T., & Dkovic, M. (2015). A meta-analysis of the relations between three types of peer norms and adolescent sexual behavior. *Personality and Social Psychology Review, 19,* 203–234.

van den Boom, D. C. (1994). The influence of temperament and mothering on attachment and exploration: An experimental manipulation of sensitive responsiveness among lower-class mothers with irritable infants. *Child Development, 65,* 1457–1477.

Van der Kolk, B. (2014) The body keeps the score: Brain, mind, and body in the healing of trauma. New York, NY: Penguin.

van der Lee, J., Bakker, T. J., Duivenvoorden, H. J., & Dröes, R. M. (2014). Multivariate models of subjective caregiver burden in dementia: A systematic review. *Aging Research Reviews, 15,* 76–93.

van der Noordt, M., Ijzelenberg, H., Droomers, M., & Proper, K. I. (2014). Health effects of employment: A systematic review of prospective studies. *Occup Environ Med,* 71:730–6.

van der Pol, L. D., Groeneveld, M. G., van Berkel, S. R., Endendijk, J. J., Hallers-Haalboom, E. T., Bakermans-Kranenburg, M. J., & Mesman, J. (2015). Fathers' and mothers' emotion talk with their girls and boys from toddlerhood to preschool age. *Emotion, 15,* 854–864.

van der Steen, J. T., Radbruch, L., Hertogh, C. M., de Boer, M. E., Hughes, J. C., Larkin, P., . . . & Koopmans, R. T. (2014). White paper defining optimal palliative care in older people with dementia: A Delphi study and recommendations from the European Association for Palliative Care. *Palliative Medicine, 28,* 197–209.

van der Veer, R., & Valsiner, J. (1994). *The Vygotsky reader.* Cambridge, MA: Blackwell.

van der Waal, J. (1989–1990). The aftermath of suicide: A review of empirical evidence. *Omega, 20,* 149–171.

van Doorninck, W. J., Caldwell, B. M., Wright, C., & Frankenberg, W. K. (1981). The relationship between twelve-month home stimulation and school achievement. *Child Development, 52,* 1080–1083.

van Emmerik, A. P., Kamphuis, J. H., Hulsbosch, A. M., & Emmelkamp, P. M. (2002). Single session debriefing after psychological trauma: A meta-analysis. *The Lancet, 360,* 766–771.

van Essen, T., van den Heuvell, S., & Ossebaard, M. (2004). A student course on self-management for procrastinators. In H. C. Schouwenburg, C. Lay, T. Pychyl, & J. R. Ferrari (Eds.), *Counseling the procrastinator in academic settings* (pp. 59–73). Washington, DC: American Psychological Association.

van Geert, P. (1998). A dynamic systems model of basic developmental mechanisms: Piaget, Vygotsky and beyond. *Psychological Review, 105,* 634–677.

Van Hesteren, F., & Ivey, A. E. (1990). Counseling and development: Toward a new identity for a profession in transition. *Journal of Counseling and Development, 68,* 524–528.

van IJzendoorn, M. H. (1995). Adult attachment representations, parental responsiveness, and infant attachment: A meta-analysis on the predictive validity of the Adult Attachment Interview. *Psychological Bulletin, 117,* 387–403.

Van IJzendoorn, M. H., Schuengel, C., & Bakermans-Kranenburg, M. J. (1999). Disorganized attachment in early childhood: Meta-analysis of precursors, concomitants, and sequelae. *Development and Psychopathology, 11*(2), 225–250.

van Rooij, E. C. M., Jansen, E. P. W. A, & van de Grift, Wim J. C. M. (2017). Secondary school students' engagement profiles and their relationship with academic adjustment and achievement in university. *Learning and Individual Differences, 54,* 9–19.

van Scheppingen, M. A., Denissen, J. J. A., Tambs, K., Chung, J. M., & Bleidorn, W. (2017). Self-esteem and relationship satisfaction during the transition to motherhood. *Journal of Personality and Social Psychology.* Available from http://dx.doi.org/10.1037/pspp0000156

Vandell, D. L., Burchinal, M., & Pierce, K. M. (2016). Early child care and adolescent functioning at the end of high school: Results from the NICHD study of early child care and youth development. *Developmental Psychology, 52,* 1634–1645.

Vara, A. S., Pang, E. W., Vidal, J., Anagnostou, E., & Taylor, M. J. (2014). Neural mechanisms of inhibitory control continue to mature in adolescence. *Developmental Cognitive Neuroscience, 10,* 129–139.

Varela, F. J., Thompson, E., & Rosch, E. (1991). *The embodied mind: Cognitive science and human experience.* Cambridge, MA: MIT Press.

Vargas, J. S. (2009). *Behavior analysis for effective teaching.* New York, NY: Routledge.

Västfjäll, D., Peters, E., & Bjälkebring, P. (2011). The experience and regulation of regret across the adult life span. In *Emotion regulation and well-being* (pp. 165–180). New York, NY: Springer.

Vaughn, B. E., & Bost, K. K. (2016). Attachment and temperament as intersecting developmental products and interacting developmental contexts throughout infancy and childhood. In J. Cassidy & P. R. Shaver (Eds.), *Handbook of*

attachment: Theory research and clinical applications (3rd ed., pp. 202–222). New York, NY: Guilford Press.

Vaughn, B. E., Egeland, B., Sroufe, L. A., & Waters, E. (1979). Individual differences in infant-mother attachment at twelve and eighteen months: Stability and change in families under stress. *Child Development, 50,* 971–975.

Veenhoven, R. (1984). *Conditions of happiness.* Dordrecht, The Netherlands: Kluwer Academic.

Veenstra, R., Lindenberg, S., Munniksma, A., & Dijkstra, J. K. (2010). The complex relation between bullying, victimization, acceptance, and rejection; Giving special attention to status, affection, and sex differences. *Child Development, 81,* 480–486.

Venkat, P., Chopp, M., & Chen, J. (2015). Models and mechanisms of vascular dementia. *Experimental Neurology, 272,* 97–108.

Verhage, M. L., Schuengel, C., Fearon, R. M. P., Madigan, S., Oosterman, M., Cassibba, R., . . . van IJzendoom, M. H. (2017). Failing the duck test: Reply to Barbaro, Boutwell, Barnes, and Shackleford (2017). *Psychological Bulletin, 143,* 114–116.

Verhage, M. L., Schuengel, C., Madigan, S., Fearon, R. M. P., Oosterman, M., Cassibba, R., . . . van IJzendoom, M. H. (2016). Narrowing the transmission gap: A synthesis of three decades of research on intergenerational transmission of attachment. *Psychological Bulletin, 142,* 337–366.

Verschoor, S. A., & Hommel, B. (2017). Self-by-doing: The role of action for self-acquisition. *Social Cognition, 35,* 127–145.

Victor, E. C., & Hariri, A. R. (2016/2015). A neuroscience perspective on sexual risk behavior in adolescence and emerging adulthood. *Development and Psychopathology, 28*(2), 471–417.

Vidal-Piñeiro, D., Sneve, M. H., Storsve, A. B., Roe, J. M., Walhovd, K. B., & Fjell, A. M. (2017). Neural correlates of durable memories across the adult lifespan: Brain activity at encoding and retrieval. *Neurobiology of Aging, 60,* 20–33.

Vidoni, E. D., Johnson, D. K., Morris, J. K., Van Sciver, A., Greer, C. S., Billinger, S. A., . . . & Burns, J. M. (2015). Dose-response of aerobic exercise on cognition: A community-based, pilot randomized controlled trial. *PLoS One, 10,* e0131647.

Vinokur, A. D., Schul, Y., Vuori, J., & Price, R. H. (2000). Two years after a job loss: Long-term impact of the JOBS program on reemployment and mental health. *Journal of Occupational Health Psychology, 5,* 32–47.

Volk, H. E., Hertz-Picciotto, I., Delwiche, L., Lurmann, F., & McConnell, R. (2011). Residential proximity to freeways and Autism in the CHARGE Study. *Environmental Health Perspectives, 119,* 873–877.

Volkmar, F. R., Paul, R., & Pelphrey, K. A. (2014). Assessment, interventions, and policy. In *Handbook of autism and pervasive developmental disorders, assessment, interventions, policy, the future, Volume 2.* Somerset, US: John Wiley & Sons, Incorporated.

Volling, B. L., Kennedy D. E., & Jackey L. M. H. (2010). The development of sibling jealousy. In S. Hart, & M. Legerstee (Eds.), *Handbook of jealousy: Theory, research, and multidisciplinary approaches* (pp. 387–417). New York, NY: Wiley-Blackwell.

Volodina, A., Nagy, G., & Köller, O. (2015). Success in the first phase of the vocational career: The role of cognitive and scholastic abilities, personality factors, and vocational interests. *Journal of Vocational Behavior, 91,* 11–22.

von Bertalanffy, L. (1968). *General systems theory: Foundations, development, applications.* New York, NY: Braziller.

von Bonsdorff, M. B., Kuh, D., von Bonsdorff, M. E., & Cooper, R. (2016). Mid-career work patterns and physical and mental functioning at age 60–64: Evidence from the 1946 British birth cohort. *European Journal of Public Health, 26,* 486–491.

Vosniadou, S., & Brewer, W. F. (1992). Mental models of the earth: A study of conceptual change in childhood. *Cognitive Psychology, 24,* 535–585.

Vosniadou, S., & Mason, L. (2012). Conceptual change induced by instruction: A complex interplay of multiple factors. In S.Vosniadou & L. Mason (Eds.), *APA educational psychology handbook, Vol 2: Individual differences and cultural and contextual factors* (pp. 221–246). Washington, DC: American Psychological Association.

Voyer, D., & Voyer, S. D. (2014). Gender differences in scholastic achievement: A meta-analysis. *Psychological Bulletin, 140,* 1174.

Vrangalova, Z. (2015). Does casual sex harm college students' well-being? A longitudinal investigation of the role of motivation. *Archives of Sexual Behavior, 44,* 945–959.

Vukasović, T., & Bratko, D. (2015). Heritability of personality: A meta-analysis of behavior genetic studies. *Psychological Bulletin, 141,* 769–785.

Vygotsky, L. S. (1934). *Thought and language.* Cambridge, MA: MIT Press.

Vygotsky, L. S. (1978). *Mind and society.* Cambridge, MA: MIT Press.

Vygotsky, L. S. (1981). Development of higher mental functions. In J. V. Wertsch (Ed.), *The concept of activity in Soviet psychology* (pp. 144–188). Armonk, NY: Sharpe. (Originally published in 1931)

Vygotsky, L. S., & Luria, A. R. (1930). The function and fate of egocentric speech. In J. M. Cattell (Ed.), *Ninth International Congress of Psychology. Proceedings and papers* (pp. 464–465). Princeton, NJ: Psychological Review Company.

Wade, N. G., Hoyt, W. T., Kidwell, J. E. M., & Worthington, E. L. (2014; 2013). Efficacy of psychotherapeutic interventions to promote forgiveness: A meta-analysis. *Journal of Consulting and Clinical Psychology, 82*(1), 154–170.

Wadsworth, T. (2016). Marriage and subjective well-being: How and why context matters. *Social Indicators Research, 126*(3), 1025–1048.

Wahler, R. G., Winkel, G. H., Peterson, R. F., & Morrison, D. C. (1965). Mothers as behavior therapists for their own children. *Behaviour Research and Therapy, 3,* 113–124.

Wahlstrom, K. L., Berger, A. T., & Widome, R. (2017). Relationships between school start time, sleep duration, and adolescent behaviors. *Sleep Health, 3,* 216–221.

Wahlstrom, K. L., Dretzke, B., Gordon, M., Peterson, K., Edwards, K., & Gdula, J. (2014).

Examining the impact of later school start times on the health and academic performance of high school students: A multi-site study. St. Paul, MN: University of Minnesota, Center for Applied Research and Educational Improvement.

Waite, L. J., & Joyner, K. (2001). Emotional satisfaction and physical pleasure in sexual unions: Time horizon, sexual behavior, and sexual exclusivity. *Journal of Marriage and the Family, 63,* 247–264.

Waite, L. J., Laumann, E. O., Das, A., & Schumm, L. P. (2009). Sexuality: Measures of partnerships, practices, attitudes, and problems in National Social Life, Health, and Aging Study. *The Journals of Gerontology: Series B: Psychological Sciences and Social Sciences, 64,* I56–I66.

Walhovd, K. B., Fjell, A. M., Giedd, J., Dale, A. M., & Brown, T. T. (2017). Through thick and thin: A need to reconcile contradictory results on trajectories in human cortical development. *Cerebral Cortex, 17,* 1472–1481.

Walker, L. J., & Pitts, R. C. (1998). Naturalistic conceptions of moral maturity. *Developmental Psychology, 34,* 403–419.

Walker, L. J., & Taylor, J. H. (1991). Family interactions and the development of moral reasoning. *Child Development, 62,* 264–283.

Walker-Barnes, C. J., & Mason, C. A. (2001). Ethnic differences in the effect of parenting on gang involvement and gang delinquency: A longitudinal, hierarchical linear modeling perspective. *Child Development, 72,* 1814–1831.

Wallace, I., & McCarton, C. (1997). Neurodevelopmental outcomes of the premature, small-for-gestational infant through age 6. *Clinical Obstetrics and Gynecology, 40,* 843–852.

Walle, E. A., Reschke, P. J., Camras, L. A., & Campos, J. J. (2017). Infant differential behavioral responding to discrete emotions. *Emotion.* Available at http://dx.doi.org//10.1037/emo0000307

Waller, J. (2004). *Discovery of the germ.* London: Icon Books.

Waller, R., Gardner, F., Viding, E., Shaw, D. S., Dishion, T. J., Wilson, M. N., & Hyde, L. W. (2014). Bidirectional associations between parental warmth, callous unemotional behavior, and behavior problems in high-risk preschoolers. *Journal of Abnormal Child Psychology, 42,* 1275–1285.

Waller, R., & Hyde, L. W. (2017). Callous-unemotional behaviors in early childhood: Measurement, meaning, and the influence of parenting. *Child Development Perspectives, 11,* 120–126.

Wallis, A., Alford, C., Hanson, A., Titterton, J., Madden, S., & Kohn, M. (2013). Innovations in Maudsley family-based treatment for anorexia nervosa at the children's hospital at Westmead: A family admission programme. *Journal of Family Therapy, 35,* 68–81.

Wang, A-C., Chiang, J. T-J., Tsai, C-Y., Lin, T-T., & Cheng, B-S. (2013). Gender makes the difference: The moderating role of leader gender on the relationship between leadership styles and subordinate performance. *Organizational Behavior and Human Decision Processes, 122,* 101–113.

Wang, D. (2004). Ritualistic coresidence and the weakening of filial practice in rural China. In Ikels, C. (Ed.), *Filial Piety: Practice and discourse*

in contemporary East Asia (pp. 16–33). Stanford, CA: Stanford University Press.

Wang, M., & Huguley, J. P. (2012). Parental racial socialization as a moderator of the effects of racial discrimination on educational success among African American adolescents. *Child Development, 83,* 1716–1731.

Wang, M., & Shi, J. (2014). Psychological research on retirement. *Annual Review of Psychology, 65,* 209–233.

Wang, M-T., Eccles, J. S., & Kenny, S. (2013). Not lack of ability but more choice: Individual and gender differences in choice of careers in science, technology, engineering, and mathematics. *Psychological Science, 24,* 770–775.

Wang, Q. (2016). Why should we all be cultural psychologists? Lessons from the study of social cognition. *Perspectives on Psychological Science, 11,* 583–596.

Wang, Q., & Pomerantz, E. M. (2009). The motivational landscape of early adolescence in the United States and China: A longitudinal investigation. *Child Development, 80*(4), 1272–1287.

Wang, Q., Pomerantz, E. M., & Chen, H. (2007). The role of parents' control in early adolescents' psychological functioning: A longitudinal investigation in the United States and China. *Child Development, 78,* 1592–1610.

Wang, Y. C. (2014). In search of the Confucian family: Interviews with parents and their middle school children in Guangzhou, China. *Journal of Adolescent Research, 29*(6), 765-782. doi:10.1177/0743558414538318

Ward, B. A., Mergendoller, J. R., Tikunoff, W. J., Rounds, T. S., Dadey, G. J., & Mitman, A. L. (1982). *Junior high school transition study: Executive summary.* San Francisco, CA: Far West Laboratory.

Ward, I. L. (1992). Sexual behavior: The product of perinatal hormonal and prepuberal social factors. In A. A. Gerall, H. Moltz, & I. L. Ward (Eds.), *Handbook of behavioral neurobiology: Vol. 11. Sexual differentiation* (pp. 157–180). New York, NY: Plenum Press.

Ward, I. L., & Stehm, K. E. (1991). Prenatal stress feminizes juvenile play patterns in male rats. *Physiology and Behavior, 50,* 601–605.

Ward, L. M. (2002). Does television exposure affect emerging adults' attitudes and assumptions about sexual relationships? Correlational and experimental confirmation. *Journal of Youth and Adolescence, 31,* 1–15.

Warner, C. W., Santelli, J. S., Everett, S. A., Kann, L., Collins, J. L., Cassell, C., et al. (1998). Sexual behavior among U.S. high school students, 1990–1995. *Family Planning Perspectives, 30,* 170–172, 200.

Warr, P. (1999). Well-being and the workplace. In D. Kahneman, E. Diener, & N. Schwarz (Eds.), *Well-being: The foundations of hedonic psychology* (pp. 392–412). New York, NY: Russell Sage Foundation.

Warren, K. R. (2016). A review of the history of attitudes toward drinking in pregnancy. *Alcoholism: Clinical and Experimental Research, 39*(7), 1110–1117.

Warren, K. R., & Murray, M. M. (2013). Alcohol and pregnancy: Fetal alcohol spectrum disorders and the fetal alcohol syndrome. In P. Boyle, P. Boffetta, A. B. Lowenfels, H. Burns, & O. Brawley (Eds.), *Alcohol: Science, policy, and public health* (pp. 307–314). Oxford, UK: Oxford U. Press.

Watamura, S. E., Coe, C. L., Laudenslager, M. L., & Robertson, S. S. (2010). Child care setting affects salivary cortisol and antibody secretion in young children. *Psychoneuroendocrinology*, *35*, 1156–1166.

Watamura, S. E., Donzella, B., Alwin, J., & Gunnar, M. R. (2003). Morning-to-afternoon increases in cortisol concentrations for infants and toddlers at child care: Age differences and behavioral correlates. *Child Development*, *74*, 1006–1020.

Waterman, A. S. (1993a). Developmental perspectives on identity formation. In J. E. Marcia, A. S. Waterman, D. R. Matteson, S. L. Archer, & J. L. Orlofsky (Eds.), *Ego identity: A handbook for psychosocial research* (pp. 42–68). New York, NY: Springer-Verlag.

Waterman, A. S. (1993b). Two conceptions of happiness: Contrasts of personal expressiveness (eudaimonia) and hedonic enjoyment. *Journal of Personality and Social Psychology*, *64*, 678–691.

Watson, D., & Pennebaker, J. W. (1989). Health complaints, stress, and distress: Exploring the central role of negative affectivity. *Psychological Review*, *96*, 234–254.

Watson, D., Wiese, D., Vaidya, J., & Tellegen, A. (1999). The two general activation systems of affect: Structural findings, evolutionary considerations, and psychobiological evidence. *Journal of Personality and Social Psychology*, *76*, 820–838.

Watson, J. B. (1913). Psychology as the behaviorist views it. *Psychological Review*, *20*, 158–177.

Waxman, S. (Ed.). (2005). *From neuroscience to neurology: Neuroscience, molecular medicine, and the therapeutic transformation of neurology*. New York, NY: Elsevier/Academic Press.

Way, N. (2011). *Deep secrets: Boys' friendships and the crisis of connection*. Cambridge MA: Harvard University Press.

Weaver, J. M., & Schofield, T. J. (2015). Mediation and moderation of divorce effects on children's behavior problems. *Journal of Family Psychology*, *29*, 39–48.

Webb, H. J., & Zimmer-Gembeck, M. J. (2014). The role of friends and peers in adolescent body dissatisfaction: A review and critique of 15 years of research. *Journal of Research on Adolescence*, *24*, 564–590.

Webster, J. D., Westerhof, G. J., & Bohlmeijer, E. T. (2014). Wisdom and mental health across the lifespan. *Journals of Gerontology Series B: Psychological Sciences and Social Sciences*, *69*, 209–218.

Webster-Stratton, C., & Hammond, M. (1997). Treating children with early-onset conduct problems: A comparison of child and parent training interventions. *Journal of Consulting and Clinical Psychology*, *65*, 93–109.

Webster-Stratton, C., Mihalic, S., Fagan, A., Arnold, D., Taylor, T., & Tingley, C. (2001). *The Incredible Years: Parent, Teacher And Child Training Series: Blueprints for Violence Prevention, Book Eleven*. Blueprints for Violence Prevention Series (D. S. Elliott, Series Editor). Boulder, CO: Center for the Study and Prevention of Violence, Institute of Behavioral Science, University of Colorado.

Webster-Stratton, C., & Reid, M. J. (2003). Treating conduct problems and strengthening social emotional competence in young children (ages 4 to 8 years): The Dina Dinosaur treatment program. *Journal of Emotional and Behavioral Disorders*, *11*, 130–143.

Webster-Stratton, C., & Reid, M. J. (2004). Strengthening social and emotional competence in young children: The foundation for early school readiness and success: Incredible years classroom social skills and problem-solving curriculum. *Infants & Young Children*, *17*, 96–113.

Webster-Stratton, C. H, & Reid, M. J. (2010). The Incredible Years parents, teachers, and children training series: A multifaceted treatment approach for young children with conduct disorders. In J. R. Weisz & A. E. Kazdin (Eds.), *Evidence-based psychotherapies for children and adolescents* (pp. 194–210). New York, NY: Guilford Press.

Webster-Stratton, C., Reid, M. J., & Stoolmiller, M. (2008). Preventing conduct problems and improving school readiness: Evaluation of the Incredible Years Teacher and Child Training Programs in high-risk schools. *Journal of Child Psychology and Psychiatry*, *49*, 471–488.

Wege, N., Angerer, P., & Li, J. (2017). Effects of lifetime unemployment experience and job insecurity on two-year risk of physician-diagnosed incident depression in the German working population. *International Journal of Environmental Research and Public Health*, *14*(8), 904.

Wei, M., Liao, K. Y-H., Chao, R. C-L., Mallinckrodt, B., Tsai, P-C., & Botello-Zamarron, R. (2010). Minority stress perceived bicultural competence, and depressive symptoms among ethnic minority college students. *Journal of Counseling Psychology*, *57*, 411–422.

Weimer, A. A., Parault Dowds, S. J., Fabricius, W. V., Schwanenflugel, P. J., & Suh, G. W. (2017). Development of constructivist theory of mind from middle childhood to early adulthood and its relation to social cognition and behavior. *Journal of Experimental Child Psychology*, *154*, 28–45.

Weiner, B. (1974). *Achievement motivation and attribution theory*. Morristown, NJ: General Learning Press.

Weinraub, M., Clemens, L. P., Sockloff, A., Ethridge, R., Gracely, E., & Myers, B. (1984). The development of sex role stereotypes in the third year: Relationships to gender labeling, gender identity, sex-typed toy preferences, and family characteristics. *Child Development*, *55*, 1493–1503.

Weisberg, D. S. (2015). Pretend play. *WIREs Cognitive Science*, *6*, 249–261.

Weisleder, A., & Fernald, A. (2013). Talking to children matters: Early language experience strengthens processing and builds vocabulary. *Psychological Science*, *24*, 2143–2152.

Weisman, O., Zagoory-Sharon, O., & Feldman, R. (2012). Oxytocin administration to parent enhances infant physiological and behavioral readiness for social engagement. *Biological Psychiatry*, *72*, 982–989.

Weisner, T. S. (2015). The socialization of trust: Plural caregiving and diverse pathways in human development across cultures. In H. Otto & H. Keller (Eds.), *Different faces of attachment* (pp. 263–277). Cambridge, UK: Cambridge University Press.

Weiss, B., & Garber, J. (2003). Developmental differences in the phenomenology of depression. *Development and Psychopathology*, *15*, 403–430.

Weissman, J. R., Kelley, R. I., Bauman, M. L., Cohen, B. H., Murray, K.F., Mitchell, R. L., et al. (2008). Mitochondrial disease in autism spectrum disorder patients: A cohort analysis. *PLos One*, *3*, 1–6.

Weissman, M. M., Markowitz, J. C., & Klerman, G. L. (2000). *Comprehensive guide to interpersonal psychotherapy*. New York, NY: Basic Books.

Welch-Ross, M. K., & Schmidt, E. R. (1996). Gender-schema development and children's constructive story memory: Evidence for a developmental model. *Child Development*, *67*, 820–835.

Wellman, H. M., Fang, F., & Peterson, C. C. (2011). Sequential progressions in a theory-of-mind scale: Longitudinal perspectives. *Child Development*, *82*, 780–792.

Wellman, H. M., & Lagattuta, K. H. (2004). Theory of mind for learning and teaching: The nature and role of explanation. *Cognitive Development*, *19*, 479–497.

Wentzel, K. (2002). Are effective teachers like good parents? Teaching styles and student adjustment in early adolescence. *Child Development*, *73*, 287–301.

Wentzel, K. R., Baker, S. A., & Russell, S. L. (2012). Young adolescents' perceptions of teachers' and peers' goals as predictors of social and academic goal pursuit. *Applied Psychology*, *61*, 605–633.

Westling, E., Andrews, J. A., & Peterson, M. (2012). Gender differences in pubertal timing, social competence, and cigarette use: A test of the early maturation hypothesis. *Journal of Adolescent Health*, *51*, 150–155.

Westrick, P. A., Le, H., Robbins, S. B., Radunzel, J. M. R., & Schmidt, F. L. (2015). College performance and retentions: A meta-analysis of the predictive validities of ACT scores, high school grades, and SES. *Educational Assessment*, *20*, 23–45.

Weststrate, N. M., & Glück, J. (2017). Hard-earned wisdom: Exploratory processing of difficult life experience is positively associated with wisdom. *Developmental Psychology*, *53*, 800–814.

Wheedon, A., Scafidi, F., Field, T., Ironson, G., Valdeon, C., & Bandstra, E. (1993). Massage effects on cocaine-exposed preterm neonates. *Journal of Developmental and Behavioral Pediatrics*, *14*, 318–322.

Whillans, A. V., Dunn, E., Smeets, P. M., Bekkers, R. H. F. P., & Norton, M. I. (2017). Buying time promotes happiness. *Proceedings of the National Academy of Sciences of the United States of America*, *114*(32), 8523–8527.

Whillans, A. V., Weidman, A. C., & Dunn, E. W. (2016). Valuing time over money is associated with greater happiness. *Social Psychological and Personality Science*, *7*(3), 213–222.

Whiston, S. C., & Cinamon, R. G. (2015). The Work–Family interface: Integrating research and career counseling practice. *The Career Development Quarterly*, *63*(1), 44–56.

Whitaker, D., & Miller, K. (2000). Parent-adolescent discussions about sex and condoms: Impact on peer influences of sexual risk behavior. *Journal of Adolescent Research*, *15*, 251–273.

Whitbourne, S. K. (1989). Psychological treatment of the aging individual. *Journal of Integrative and Eclectic Psychotherapy*, *8*, 161–173.

Whitbourne, S. K. (2002). The aging individual: Physical and psychological perspectives (2nd ed). New York, NY: Springer.

Whitbourne, S. K., Sneed, J. R., & Sayer, A. (2009). Psychosocial development from college through midlife: A 34-year sequential study. *Developmental Psychology, 45*, 1328–1340.

Whitbourne, S. K., & Whitbourne, S. B. (2016). *Adult development and aging: Biopsychosocial perspectives* (6th ed.). Hoboken, NJ: John Wiley & Sons.

White, L. J., & Greenfield, D. B. (2017). Executive functioning in Spanish- and English-speaking Head Start preschoolers. *Developmental Science, 20*. doi:10.1111/desc.12502

Whiting, B. B., & Edwards, C. P. (1988). *Children of different worlds: The formation of social behavior*. Cambridge, MA: Harvard University Press.

Whitton, S. W., Weitbrecht, E. M., & Kuryluk, A. D. (2015). Monogamy agreements in male same-sex couples: Associations with relationship quality and individual well-being. *Journal of Couple & Relationship Therapy: Innovations in Clinical and Educational Interventions, 14*, 39–63.

Whyte, D. (2001). *Crossing the unknown sea: Work as a pilgrimage of identity*. New York, NY: Riverhead Books.

Wicher, C. P., & Meeker, M. A. (2012). What influences African American end-of-life preferences? *Journal of Health Care for the Poor and Underserved, 23*, 28–58.

Wichstrom, L. (1999). The emergence of gender differences in depressed mood during adolescence: The role of intensified gender socialization. *Developmental Psychology, 35*, 232–245.

Wichstrøm, L., & von Soest, T. (2016). Reciprocal relations between body satisfaction and self-esteem: A large 13-year prospective study of adolescents. *Journal of Adolescence, 47*, 16–27.

Wickrama, K. A. S., Lorenz, F. O., Wallace, L. E., Peiris, L., Conger, R. D., & Elder, G. H. (2001). Family influence on physical health during the middle years: The case of onset of hypertension. *Journal of Marriage and the Family, 63*, 527–539.

Wiebe, S. A., & Johnson, S. M. (2016). A review of the research in emotionally focused therapy for couples. *Family Process, 55*(3), 390–407.

Wiesel, T. N., & Hubel, D. H. (1965). Comparison of the effects of unilateral and bilateral eye closure on cortical response in kittens. *Journal of Neurophysiology, 26*, 1029–1040.

Wilcox, B. L. (2003). Developmental research and the formulation and evaluation of legal policy. *Social Policy Report, 17*, 12.

Wilhoit, L. F., Scott, D. A., & Simecka, B. A. (2017). Fetal alcohol spectrum disorders: Characteristics, complications, and treatment. *Community Mental Health Journal, 53*, 711–718.

Wilkinson, W. K., & Maxwell, S. (1991). The influence of college students' epistemological style on selected problem-solving processes. *Research in Higher Education, 32*, 333–350.

Willatts, P. (1989). Development of problem-solving in infancy. In A. Slater & G. Bremner (Eds.), *Infant development*. Hove, England: Erlbaum.

Wille, B., Tracey, T. J. G., Feys, M., & De Fruyt, F. (2014). A longitudinal and multi-method examination of interest-occupation congruence within and across time. *Journal of Vocational Behavior, 84*, 59–73.

Willey, J. Z., Gardener, H., Caunca, M. R., Moon, Y. P., Dong, C., Cheung, Y. K., . . . Wright, C. B. (2016). Leisure-time physical activity associates with cognitive decline: The Northern Manhattan Study. *Neurology, 86*, 1897–1903.

William T. Grant Foundation Commission on Work, Family, and Citizenship. (1988). *The forgotten half: Noncollege-bound youth in America*. New York, NY: William T. Grant Foundation.

Williams, J. C., Berdahl, J. L., & Vandello, J. A. (2016). Beyond work-life "integration." *Annual Review of Psychology, 67*, 515–519.

Williams, J. F., & Smith, V. C., Committee on Substance Abuse. (2015). Fetal alcohol spectrum disorders. *Pediatrics, 136*, e1395–1406.

Williams, J. L., & Rheingold, A. A. (2015). Barriers to care and service satisfaction following homicide loss: Associations with mental health outcomes. *Death Studies, 39*, 12–18.

Williams, S., Moore, K., Crossman, A. M., & Talwar, V. (2016). The role of executive functions and theory of mind in children's prosocial lie-telling. *Journal of Experimental Child Psychology, 141*, 256–266.

Willingham, D. T. (Winter 2009/10). Is it true that some people just can't do math? *American Educator, 33*, 14–19, 39.

Willingham, D. T. (2015). Moving educational psychology into the home: The case of reading. *Mind, Brain, and Education, 9*, 107–111.

Willingham, D. T., Hughes, E. M., & Dobolyi, D. G. (2015). The scientific status of learning styles theories. *Teaching of Psychology, 42*, 266–271.

Willoughby, M. T., & Blair, C. B. (2016). Longitudinal measurement of executive function in preschoolers. In J. A. Griffin, P. McCardle, & L. S. Freund (Eds.), *Executive function in preschool-age children* (pp. 91–114). Washington DC: American Psychological Association.

Willoughby, T. (2008). A short-term longitudinal study of Internet and computer game use by adolescent boys and girls: Prevalence, frequency of use, and psychosocial predictors. *Developmental Psychology, 44*, 195–204.

Willoughby, T., Adachi, P. J. C., & Good, M. (2012). A longitudinal study of the association between violent video game play and aggression among adolescents. *Developmental Psychology, 48*, 1044–1057.

Wilson, R. S., Barnes, L. L., Aggarwal, N. T., Boyle, P. A., Hebert, L. E., de Leon, C. M., & Evans, D. A. (2010). Cognitive activity and the cognitive morbidity of Alzheimer disease. *Neurology, 75*, 990–996.

Wilson, R. S., Beck, T. L., Bienias, J. L., & Bennet, D. A. (2007). Terminal cognitive decline: Accelerated loss of cognition in the last years of life. *Psychosomatic Medicine, 69*, 131–137.

Wilson, T. D., & Brekke, N. (1994). Mental contamination and mental correction: Unwanted influences on judgments and evaluations. *Psychological Bulletin, 116*, 117–142.

Wilson, W. J. (1996). *When work disappears: The world of the new urban poor*. New York, NY: Random House.

Wilt, J. A., Grubbs, J. B., Exline, J. J., & Pargament, K. I. (2016). Personality, religious and spiritual struggles, and well-being. *Psychology of Religion and Spirituality, 8*(4), 341–351.

Wilt, J. A., Grubbs, J. B., Pargament, K. I., & Exline, J. J. (2017). Religious and spiritual struggles, past and present: Relations to the big five and well-being. *The International Journal for the Psychology of Religion, 27*(1), 51–64.

Wink, P., & Staudinger, U. M. (2016). Wisdom and psychosocial functioning in later life. *Journal of Personality, 84*, 306–318.

Winnicott, D. W. (1965). *The maturational processes and the facilitating environment*. New York, NY: International Universities Press.

Winsler, A. (2009). Still talking to ourselves after all these years: A review of current research on private speech. In A. Winsler, C. Fernyhough, & I. Montero (Eds.), *Private speech, executive functioning and the development of verbal self-regulation* (pp. 3–41). New York, NY: Cambridge University Press.

Winsler, A., Diaz, R. M., & Montero, I. (1997). The role of private speech in the transition from collaborative to independent task performance in young children. *Early Childhood Research Quarterly, 12*, 59–79.

Wisniewski, S. R., Gaynes, B. N., Rush, A. J., Fava, M., Trivedi, M. H., & Warden, D. (2009). What did STARD teach us? Results from a large-scale, practical, clinical trial for patients with depression. *Psychiatric Services, 60*(11), 1439–1445.

Wittayanukorn, S., Qian, J., & Hansen, R. A. (2014). Prevalence of depressive symptoms and predictors of treatment among US adults from 2005 to 2010. *General Hospital Psychiatry, 36*, 330–336.

Wittling, W., & Pflüger, M. (1990). Neuroendocrine hemisphere asymmetries: Salivary cortisol secretion during lateralized viewing of emotion-related and neutral films. *Brain and Cognition, 14*, 243–265.

Witvliet, C. V., Ludwig, T. E., & Vander Laan, K. L. (2001). Granting forgiveness or harboring grudges: Implications for emotion, physiology, and health. *Psychological Science, 12*, 117–123.

Witvliet, M., Van Lier, P. A., Cuijpers, P., & Koot, H. M. (2009). Change and stability in childhood clique membership, isolation from cliques, and associated child characteristics. *Journal of Clinical Child & Adolescent Psychology, 39*, 12–24.

Wolfe, J. L., & Fodor, I. G. (1996). The poverty of privilege: Therapy with women of the "upper classes." *Women and Therapy, 18*, 73–89.

Wolfle, J., Hopffner, W., Sippell, W. G., Bramswig, J. H., Heidemann, P., Deib, D., et al. (2002). Complete virilization in congenital adrenal hyperplasia: Clinical course, medical management and disorder-related complications. *Clinical Endocrinology, 56*, 231–238.

Wolke, D., Copeland, W. E., Angold, A., & Costello, E. J. (2013). Impact of bullying in childhood on adult health, wealth, crime, and social outcomes. *Psychological Science, 24*, 1958–1970.

Wong, A. H. C., Caspi, A., Williams, B., Craig, I. W., Houts, R., Ambler, A., et al. (2010). A longitudinal study of epigenetic variation in twins. *Epigenetics, 5*, 516–526.

Wood, D., & Middleton, D. (1975). A study of assisted problem solving. *British Journal of Educational Psychology, 66*, 181–191.

Woodward, A. L. (1998). Infants selectively encode the goal object of an actor's reach. *Cognition, 69*, 1–34.

Woolf, S. H. (2008). The meaning of translational research and why it matters. *JAMA, 299,* 211–213.

Woolley, M. E., & Grogan-Kaylor, A. (2006). Protective family factors in the context of neighborhood: Promoting positive school outcomes. *Family Relations, 55,* 93–104.

Worden, J. W. (1982). *Grief counseling and grief therapy: A handbook for the mental health practitioner.* New York, NY: Springer.

World Alzheimer Report. (2009). Alzheimer's disease international. Available from www.alz. co.uk/research/files/WorldAlzheimerReport. pdf

World Alzheimer Report. (2015). *The global impact of dementia: An analysis of prevalence, incidence, cost and trends.* London, England: Alzheimer's Disease International (ADI).

World Health Organization (WHO). (2017). *Depression and other common mental disorders: Global health estimates.* Geneva, Switzerland: World Health Organization. License: CC BY-NC-SA 3.0 IGO.

World Health Organization. (2017). Depression: Leading cause of disability. *WHO Drug Information, 31*(2), 198.

Worrell, F. C. (2007). Ethnic identity, academic achievement, and global self-concept in four groups of academically talented adolescents. *Gifted Child Quarterly, 51*(1), 23–38.

Worthington, E. L., Jr. (2006). *Forgiveness and reconciliation: Theory and application.* New York, NY: Routledge.

Wortman, C. B., & Silver, R. C. (1987). Coping with irrevocable loss. In G. R. Vanden Bos & B. K. Bryant (Eds.), *Cataclysms, crises, and catastrophes: Psychology in action* (pp. 189–235). Washington, DC: American Psychological Association.

Wortman, C. B., & Silver, R. C. (1989). The myths of coping with loss. *Journal of Consulting and Clinical Psychology, 57,* 349–357.

Wortman, C. B., & Silver, R. C. (2001). The myths of coping with loss revisited. In M. S. Stroebe, R. O. Hansson, W. Stroebe, & H. Schut (Eds.), *Handbook of bereavement research: Consequences, coping, and care* (pp. 405–429). Washington, DC: American Psychological Association.

Wright, B. A. (1983). *Physical disability: A psychosocial approach.* New York, NY: Harper & Row.

Wright, M. O., Fopma-Loy, J., & Oberle, K. (2012). In their own words: The experience of mothering as a survivor of childhood sexual abuse. *Development and Psychopathology, 24,* 537–552.

Wrosch, C., Heckhausen, J., & Lachman, M. E. (2006). Goal management across adulthood and old age: The adaptive value of primary and secondary control. In D. K. Mroczek & T. D. Little (Eds.), *Handbook of personality development* (pp. 399–421). Mahwah, NJ: Erlbaum.

Wrosch, C., & Schulz, R. (2008). Health-engagement control strategies and 2-year changes in older adults' physical health. *Psychological Science, 19,* 537–541.

Wrzesniewski, A., & Dutton, J. E. (2001). Crafting a job: Revisoning employees as active crafters of their work. *Academy of Management Review, 26,* 179–201.

Wrzis, C., Hänel, M., Wagner, J., & Neyer, F. J. (2013). Social network changes and life events across the life span: A meta-analysis. *Psychological Bulletin, 139,* 53–80.

Wyciszkiewicz, A., Pawlak, M. A., & Krawiec, K. (2017). Cerebellar volume in children with attention-deficit hyperactivity disorder (ADHD): Replication study. *Journal of Child Neurology, 32,* 215–221.

Wyden, R. (2000). Steps to improve the quality of life for people who are dying. *Psychology, Public Policy, and Law, 6,* 575–581.

Xiang, S., Liu, Y., & Bai, L. (2017). Parenting styles and adolescents' school adjustment: Investigating the mediating role of achievement goals within the 2 × 2 framework. *Frontiers in Psychology, 8.* doi:10.3389/fpsyg.2017.01809

Yang, C., Bear, G. G., Chen, F. F., Zhang, W., Blank, J. C., & Huang, X. (2013). Students' perceptions of school climate in the U.S. and China. *School Psychology Quarterly, 28*(1), 7–24.

Yang, F., Chen, X., & Wang, L. (2015). Shyness-sensitivity and social, school, and psychological adjustment in urban Chinese children: A four-wave longitudinal study. *Child Development, 86*(6), 1848–1864.

Yang, S. Y. (2014). Wisdom and learning from important and meaningful life experiences. *Journal of Adult Development, 21,* 129–146.

Yarger, H. A., Hoye, J. R., & Dozier, M. (2016). Trajectories of change in attachment and biobehavioral catch-up among high-risk mothers: A randomized clinical trial. *Infant Mental Health Journal, 5,* 525–536.

Yasui, M., & Dishion, T. J. (2007). The ethnic context of child and adolescent problem behavior: Implications for child and family interventions. *Clinical Child and Family Review, 10,* 137–179.

Yatkin, U. S., & McClaren, D. S. (1970). The behavioral development of infants recovering from severe malnutrition. *Journal of Mental Deficiency Research, 14,* 25–32.

Yazigi, A., De Pecoulas, A. E., Vauloup-Fellous, C., Grangeot-Keros, L., Ayoubi, J-M., & Picone, O. (2016). Fetal and neonatal abnormalities due to congenital rubella syndrome: A review of the literature. *The Journal of Maternal-Fetal & Neonatal Medicine, 30,* 274–278.

Ybarra, M. L., Strasburger, V. C., & Mitchell, K. J. (2014). Sexual media exposure, sexual behavior, and sexual violence victimization in adolescence. *Clinical Pediatrics, 53*(13), 1239–1247.

Yeager, D. S., Purdie-Vaughns, V., Hooper, S. Y., & Cohen, G. L. (2017). Loss of institutional trust among racial and ethnic minority adolescents: A consequence of procedural injustice and a cause of life-span outcomes. *Child Development, 88,* 658–676.

Yeh, C. J., Inman, A. G., Kim, A. B., & Okubo, Y. (2006). Asian American families' collectivistic coping strategies in response to 9/11. *Cultural Diversity and Ethnic Minority Psychology, 12,* 134–148.

Yin, T., Zhou, Q., & Bashford, C. (2002). Burden on family members. Caring for frail elderly: A meta-analysis of interventions. *Nursing Research, 51,* 199–208.

Yip, T., & Douglass, S. (2013). The application of experience sampling approaches to the study of ethnic identity: New developmental insights and directions. *Child Development Perspectives, 7,* 211–214.

Yip, T., Seaton, E. K., & Sellers, R. M. (2006). African American racial identity across the lifespan: Identity status, identity content, and depressive symptoms. *Child Development, 77,* 1504–1517.

Yoder, C. Y., Mancha, R., & Smith, P. (2014). Differences in belief-consistent and belief-inconsistent learning in traditional college students. *Behavioral Development Bulletin, 19,* 119–127.

Yonkers, K. A., Blackwell, K. A., Glover, J., & Forray, A. (2014). Antidepressant use in pregnant and postpartum women. *Annual Review of Clinical Psychology, 10,* 369–392.

Yoshikawa, H., & Kalil, A. (2011). The effects of parental undocumented status on the developmental contexts of young children in immigrant families. *Child Development Perspectives, 5,* 291–297.

Young, D., & Borland, R. (2011). Conceptual challenges in the translation of research into practice: It's just not a matter of communication. *Translational Behavioral Medicine.* doi: 10.1007/s13142-011-0035-1

Young, K. S., Parsons, C. E., Stein, A., Vuust, P., Craske, M. G., & Kringelbach, M. L. (2017). The neural basis of responsive caregiving behavior: Investigating the temporal dynamics within the parental brain. *Behavioural Brain Research, 325,* 105–116.

Yu, R., Branje, S., Meeus, W., Koot, H. M., van Lier, P., & Fazel, S. (2017). Victimization mediates the longitudinal association between depressive symptoms and violent behaviors in adolescence. *Journal of Abnormal Child Psychology, 46,* 839–848.

Yunger, J. L., Carver, P. R., & Perry, D. G. (2004). Does gender identity influence children's psychological well-being? *Developmental Psychology, 40,* 572–582.

Zabin, L. S., Hirsch, M. B., Smith, E. A., Streett, R., & Hardy, J. B. (1986). Evaluation of a pregnancy prevention program for urban teenagers. *Family Planning Perspectives, 18,* 119–126.

Zachar, P., First, M. B., & Kendler, K. S. (2017). The bereavement exclusion debate in the DSM-5: A history. *Clinical Psychological Science, 5,* 890–906.

Zacks, R. T., Hasher, L., & Li, K. Z. H. (2000). Human memory. In F. I. M. Craik & T. A. Salthouse (Eds.), *The handbook of aging and cognition* (2nd ed., pp. 293–357). Mahwah, NJ: Erlbaum.

Zagar, R., Arbit, J., Sylvies, R., & Busch, K. G. (1991). Homicidal adolescents: A replication. *Psychological Reports, 67,* 1235–1242.

Zaporozhets, A. V. (1986). *Izbrannye psychologicheskie trudy* [Selected Works in Psychology]. Moscow: Pedagogika.

Zarbatany, L., Hartmann, D. P., & Rankin, D. B. (1990). The psychological functions of preadolescent peer activities. *Child Development, 61,* 1067–1080.

Zarit, S. H., Bangerter, L. R., Liu, Y., & Rovine, M. J. (2017). Exploring the benefits of respite services to family caregivers: Methodological issues and current findings. *Aging & Mental Health, 21,* 224–231.

Zaslow, M., Anderson, R., Redd, Z., Wessel, J., Daneri, P., Green, K., . . . Martinez-Beck, I. (2016). Quality thresholds, features, and dosage in early care and education: Introduction and literature review. In M. Burchinal, M. Zaslow, & L. Tarullo (Issue Eds.), Quality thresholds, features, and dosage in early care and education: Secondary data analyses of child outcomes. *Monographs of the Society for Research in Child Development, 81* (Serial No. 321), 7–26.

Zeanah, C. H. (1996). Beyond insecurity: A reconceptualization of attachment disorders of infancy. *Journal of Consulting and Clinical Psychology, 64,* 42–52.

Zeanah, C. H., & Gleason, M. M. (2015). Annual research review: Attachment disorders in early childhood—clinical presentation, causes, correlates and treatment. *Journal of Child Psychology and Psychiatry, and Allied Disciplines, 56*(3), 207–222.

Zeanah C. H., & Smyke, A. T. (2008). Attachment disorders in family and social context. *Infant Mental Health Journal, 29,* 219–233.

Zeanah, C. H., Smyke, A. T., Koga, S. F., & Carlson, E. A. (2005). Attachment in institutionalized and community children in Romania. *Child Development, 76,* 1015–1028.

Zeanah, C. H., & Zeanah, P. D. (2001). Towards a definition of infant mental health. *Zero to three, 22,* 13–20.

Zeidan, F., & Vago, D. R. (2016). Mindfulness meditation-based pain relief: A mechanistic account: Mechanisms supporting mindfulness-based analgesia. *Annals of the New York Academy of Sciences, 1373*(1), 114–127.

Zeifman, D. M., & Hazan, C. (2016). Pair bonds as attachments: Mounting evidence in support of Bowlby's hypothesis. In J. Cassidy & P. R. Shaver (Eds.), *Handbook of attachment: Theory, research, and clinical applications* (3rd ed., pp. 416–434). New York, NY: Guilford Press.

Zelazo, P. D. (2015). Executive function: Reflection, iterative reprocessing, complexity, and the developing brain. *Developmental Review, 38,* 55–68.

Zelazo, P. D., Anderson, J. E., Richler, J., Wallner-Allen, K., Beaumont, J. L., & Weintraub, S. (2013). NIH Toolbox Cognition Battery (CB): Measuring executive function and attention. In P. D. Zelazo & P. J. Bauer (Eds.), National Institutes of Health Toolbox-Cognition Battery (NIH Toolbox CB): Validation for children between 3 and 15 years. *Monographs of the Society for Research in Child Development, 78,* 16–33.

Zelazo, P. D., Blair, C. B., & Willoughby, M. T. (2017). *Executive function: Implications for education.* Washington, DC: National Center for Education Research, Institute of Education

Sciences, U.S. Department of Education. Available at http://ies.ed.gov/.

Zelazo, P. D., & Carlson, S. M. (2012). Hot and cool executive function in childhood and adolescence: Development and plasticity. *Child Development Perspectives, 6,* 354–360.

Zelazo, P. D., Hevlwig, C. C., & Lau, A. (1996). Intention, act, and outcome in behavioral prediction and moral judgment. *Child Development, 67,* 2478–2492.

Zelazo, P. D., & Lyons, K. E. (2012). The potential benefits of mindfulness training in early childhood: A developmental social cognitive neuroscience perspective. *Child Development Perspectives, 6*(2), 154–160.

Zhao, L., Heyman, G. D., Chen, L., & Lee, K. (2017). Praising young children for being smart promotes cheating. *Psychological Science.* doi:10.1177/0956797617721529

Zhao, Y., & Encinosa, W. Update on hospitalizations for eating disorders, 1999 to 2009. *HCUP Statistical Brief #120. September, 2011.* Agency for Healthcare Research and Quality, Rockville, MD. Available from http://www.hcupus.ahrq.gov/reports/statbriefs/sb120.pdf

Zhong, J., & Arnett, J. J. (2014). Conceptions of adulthood among migrant women workers in China. *International Journal of Behavioral Development, 38,* 255–265.

Zhou, N., Cao, H., & Leerkes, E. M. (2017). Interparental conflict and infants' behavior problems: The mediating role of maternal sensitivity. *Journal of Family Psychology, 31,* 464–474.

Zhu, Y., Zhang, L., Fan, J., & Han, S. (2007). Neural basis of cultural influence on self-representation. *NeuroImage, 34,* 1310–1326.

Ziegler, G., Ridgway, G. R., Blakemore, S.-J., Ashburner, J., & Penny, W. (2017). Multivariate dynamical modelling of structural change during development. *NeuroImage, 147,* 746–762.

Zigler, E., Gilliam, W. S., & Barnett, W. S. (Eds.) (2011). *The pre-k debates: Current controversies and issues.* Baltimore, MD: Paul H. Brookes Publishing.

Zimmerman, C. (2007). The development of scientific thinking skills in elementary and middle school. *Developmental Review, 27,* 172–223.

Zimmerman, F. J., & Christakis, D. A. (2007). Associations between content types of early media exposure and subsequent attentional problems. *Pediatrics, 120,* 986–992.

Zimmerman, F. J., Christakis, D. A., & Meltzoff, A. N. (2007). Associations between media viewing and language development in

children under age 2 years. *Journal of Pediatrics, 151,* 364–368.

Zinnbauer, B. J., Pargament, K. I., & Scott, A. B. (1999). The emerging meanings of religiousness and spirituality: Problems and prospects. *Journal of Personality, 67,* 889–920.

Ziol-Guest, K. M., & Kalil, A. (2012). Health and medical care among the children of immigrants. *Child Development, 83,* 1486–1493.

Zisser, A., & Eyberg, S. M. (2010). Parent-child interaction therapy and the treatment of disruptive behavior disorders. In J. R. Weisz & A. E. Kazdin (Eds.), *Evidence-based psychotherapies for children and adolescents* (pp. 170–193). New York, NY: Guilford Press.

Zoellner, L. A., Rothbaum, B. O., & Feeny, N. C. (2011). PTSD not an anxiety disorder? DSM committee proposal turns back the hands of time. *Depression and Anxiety, 28,* 853–856.

Zolotor, A. J., & Carlough, M. C. (2014). Update on prenatal care. *American Family Physician, 89,* 199–208.

Zonderman, A. B., Mode, N. A., Ejiogu, N., & Evans, M. K. (2016). Race and poverty status as a risk for overall mortality in community-dwelling middle-aged adults. *JAMA Internal Medicine, 176,* 1394–1395.

Zoogman, S., Goldberg, S. B., Hoyt, W. T., & Miller, L. (2014). Mindfulness interventions with youth: A meta-analysis. *Mindfulness.* doi:10.1007/s12671-013-0260-4

Zosuls, K. M., Field, R. D., Martin, C. L., Andrews, N. C., & England, D. E. (2014). Gender-based relationship efficacy: Children's self-perceptions in intergroup contexts. *Child Development, 85,* 1663–1676.

Zosuls, K. M., Ruble, D. N., Bornstein, M. H., & Greulich, F. K. (2009). The acquisition of gender labels in infancy: Implications for gender-typed play. *Developmental Psychology, 45,* 688–701.

Zovkic, I. B., & Sweatt, J. D. (2015). Memory-associated dynamic regulation of the "stable" core of the chromatin particle. *Neuron, 87*(1).

Zucker, K. J. (1999). Intersexuality and gender identity differentiation. *Annual Review of Sex Research, 10,* 1–69.

Zuckerman, M. (1979). *Sensation seeking: Beyond the optimal level of arousal.* Hillsdale, NJ: Erlbaum.

Zuckerman, M. (1999). *Vulnerability to psychopathology: A biosocial model.* Washington, DC: American Psychological Association.

Zuckerman, M., Li, C., & Hall, J. A. (2016). When men and women differ in self-esteem and when they don't: A meta-analysis. *Journal of Research in Personality, 64,* 34–51.

Author Index

Subject Index

Bicultural competence, 456
Bidirectional processes, 16
Big 5 model, 508
Bilingual children, 101–103, 105
Binge drinking, 402
Bioecological theory, 17–19
Biology
    of infant attachment, 140–141
    in middle adulthood, 505–506
    role in gender identity, 305–306
    role in generating gender differences,
        312–313
    of sex, 297–300
Bio-social-ecological theory, 17
Bipolar disorder, 453
Bisexuality, 357
Body image, 354
Body-mind
    meditation for, 580–583
    stressors and, 575–577
Borderwork, 310, 311
"Bottom up" processes, 218
Bowlby, John, 136
Bowlby's attachment theory, 135, 136
Boy and Girl Scouts, 413
Boys
    meeting special needs of, 336–337
    susceptibility to depression, 351,
        354–355
Brain
    and behavior, 208–209
    change
        in adolescence, 345–348
        in late adulthood, 593–594
    development
        early prenatal, 55–59
        lateral, 61
        neurons, structure and function of,
            59–60
        postnatal, 61–63
        stages of, 56
        structures of brain, 57–59
    mindfulness practice and, 580–583
    and sex/gender differences, 313
    in young adulthood, 431–432
Breadth and depth of knowledge, 222,
    224–225
Broad socialization practices, 412
Bronfenbrenner, Urie
    bioecological theory, 17–19
Bulimia nervosa, 381–382
Bullies and victims, 281–282, 307
"Bump, the," 601

C
Callous-unemotional (CE) traits, 165
Campfire Girls, 413
Cannon, Walter, 128

Cannot classify individuals, 466–467
Cantril's Ladder of Life Scale, 555
Care burden, 599–600
Career consolidation (*vs.* self-
    absorption), 516
Career development. *See also* Work
    theories
        Holland's theory of personality–
            environment types, 478–480
        Super's developmental approach,
            480–481
    in young adulthood, realities of,
        481–490
Carrier, 46
Cell, as scene of action, 41–43
Central sulcus, 58
Centration, 91
Cerebellum, 57
Cerebral cortex, 56, 59
Cerebrovascular accidents (strokes), 597
Cerebrum, 57
Character education (CE), 286–287
Child centered attitude, 183
Childhood-limited (CL) model, 288
Child outcomes, parenting style and,
    186, 189–194
Child psychotherapy, 114–115
Child rearing, experience of, 535–538
Children
    antisocial behavior, 277–282
    average, 325, 328
    cognitively competent children,
        educating, 229
    controversial, 325
    elementary-school-aged,
        244–247
    of gay and lesbian parents, 525–526
    gender stereotypes, knowledge of,
        315–316
    of immigrant families, 230–232
    impact of divorce on, 529–530
    information processing of, 213
    neglected, 325, 328
    popular, 325–327
    prosocial behavior, 273–277
    rejected, 325, 327–328, 334–335
Chromosomes, 39
Chunking of information, 224
Cingulate cortex, 57
Circuits, 60
Classical (respondent) conditioning,
    14–15
Classic stage theories, 7–13
Client conceptualizations, at counselor
    development stages, 452
Climacteric, 512
Cliques, 324, 331
Closed identity domains, 378

Coaction, 41
Cocaine, effects on fetus, 52, 54
Code switching, 101
Codominance, 46
Coercive family interaction, 290
Coercive parent–child interaction, 290
Cognition
    role in gender identity, 304–305
    role in generating gender differences,
        313–316
Cognitive Behavior Therapy (CBT), 69,
    383
Cognitive change
    in late adulthood, 593–602
    in middle adulthood, 514–516
Cognitive development, 77–123,
    210–236
    adjusting to environmental
        pressures, 436–437
    in adolescents, 359–365
    breadth and depth of knowledge,
        222, 224
    case study, 123
    constructing ideals, 363–364
    construction of knowledge, 210–211
    constructivist theory of, 78–81
    electronic media and, 214–216
    emergence of concrete operations,
        210–216
    eyewitness testimony, case
        illustration, 223–224
    formal operational thought,
        360–361
    and formal schooling, 229–236
    infants' cognitive functioning, 81–90
    information processing, 361
    information processing approach,
        213, 217–219, 504
    language skills, 226
    logical thinking, 211–213, 225–226,
        435–436
    memory, 219–222
    memory strategies, 226–227
    memory terminology, 220–221
    metacognition skills, 227–228
    metacognitive skills, 364–365
    postformal thought, 437–446
    preschoolers' cognitive functioning,
        90–109
    problem solving, 211–213
    processing speed, 222
    scientific problem solving, 361–363
    sociocultural theory of, 109–113
    theory, 12–13
    in young adulthood, 434–448
Cognitive-developmental theories, of
    sex differences, 313–314
Cognitive flexibility, 91, 92, 115, 218

Hemophilia, 49
Heroin, effects on fetus, 54
Heteronomous stage, 268
Heterosexuality, 357
Hidden object test, 84
Hierarchical integration, 13
High/Scope Perry Preschool Program, 106
Hindbrain, 56
Hippocampus, 57
Histones, 41
History-graded changes, in middle adulthood, 518–521
Holland's theory of personality–environment types, 478–480
Homeostatic steady state, 533
Homogamy, 527
Homophily group, 332
Homosexuality, 357
Honeymoon, 606
Hook-up culture, 476–477
Hospice movement, 616–617
Hostile attributional bias (HAB), 280, 284–285, 290
Human development, 1–36
  Bronfenbrenner's bioecological theory, 17–19
  case study, 35–36
  classic stage theories, 7–13
  critical (sensitive) periods, 9, 22
  developmental research applications, guidelines for, 27–31
  Erikson's personality theory, 10–12
  expert–novice differences, 4
  Freud's personality theory, 8–10
  gap between science and practice, 3–5
  incremental change, 13–16
  information processing theories, 15
  issues in, 15–16, 21–26
  learning theories, 13–15
  life span developmental theories, 19
  multidimensional or systems theories, 16–21
  nature *versus* nurture, 21–22
  Piaget's cognitive development theory, 12–13
  specificity and, 22–26
  theoretical orientations to development, 19–21
  universality and, 22–26
Huntington's disease, 49
Hypertension, 597
Hypothalamic-pituitary-adrenal (HPA) axis, 65
Hypothalamus, 57

I
Id, 8
Ideals, constructing, 363–364
Identification, 265
Identity
  achievement, 367
  choosing, 376
  commitment, 366–367
  development, in adolescents, 365–381
    basic considerations for, 365–366
    case of multiracial youth, 376
    developmental sequence, 370
    and diverse groups, 370–375
    domains assessment, 369–370
    identity crisis, 366
    identity status, 366–368
    influence of culture and context on, 377
  diffusion, 367
  exploration, 366
  narrative, 369
Ill-defined or ill-structured problems, 436
Imaginary audience, 364
"I–Me" distinction, 174, 176–179
Imitation, 87
Immanent justice, 269
Immigrant families, children of, 230–232
Immigrant paradox model, 230
Immigrant risk model, 230
Immunosuppression, 576
Implantation, 41
Implementation, 480
Incredible Years (IY), 291
Incremental change, 13–16
Incremental models, 13
Incremental theorists, 493
Indicated prevention, 30
Induction, 186
Indulgent parenting, 397
Industry, 491–493
Industry, sense of, 259
Infant-directed speech (IDS), 104
Infantile amnesia, 109
Infants
  attachment
    biology of, 140–141
    bond with caregiver, 138–139
    cultural influences on, 152–153
    with father, 149, 152
    with mother, 149–152
  cognitive functioning, 81–90
  day care risk to, 150–152, 161–162
  of depressed mothers, 143
  development, parenting practices *versus* relationship quality in, 156–157

mental health, 160–161
temperament, 144–149
  origin of, 145–146
  relationship with parents' caregiving, 146, 147
  role in relationship development, 147–149
  traits, activity level of, 145
Inferior colliculi, 57
Inferring others' intentions, 89–90
Inflammation, 576–577
Influence, 332
Information processing
  in adolescence, 361
  approach, 217–219, 504
  of children, 213
  middle age, 504
  theories, 15
Initial commitment, 443
Inner speech, 113
Insecure parents, 156
Insensitive parenting, 143–144
Instrumental aggression, 279
Integrative Behavioral Couple therapy (ICBT), 543
Integrative health, 547
Integrity, 628–629
Intention, 89
Intergenerational transmission, 159
Intermodal perception, 84
Internalization, 188, 195
Internalizing problems, 186
Interneurons, 60
Interpersonal orientation, 243
Interpersonal Therapy (IP), 69, 383
Intersensory integration (intermodal perception), 84
Intersex children, 303, 306
Intersubjectivity, 112
Intervention programs, choosing, 30–31
Intimacy
  definition of families, 522–523
  middle adulthood, 522–534
  young adulthood, 462, 473
Intrapersonal models, 532
Invincibility fable, 364–365
Irritability or negative emotionality, 145
"I-Self" or self-as-subject, 174, 176–179

J
James, William, 128
Job crafting, 479–480
JOBS project, 547
John D. and Catherine T. MacArthur Foundation, 627
Junior Achievement, 413
Just world, 441